MODELS OF COMPUTATION AND FORMAL LANGUAGES

MODELS OF COMPUTATION AND FORMAL LANGUAGES

R. Gregory Taylor

New York   Oxford
OXFORD UNIVERSITY PRESS
1998

Oxford University Press

Oxford   New York
Athens   Auckland   Bangkok   Bogota   Bombay   Buenos Aires
Calcutta   Cape Town   Dar es Salaam   Delhi   Florence   Hong Kong
Istanbul   Karachi   Kuala Lumpur   Madras   Madrid   Melbourne
Mexico City   Nairobi   Paris   Singapore   Taipei   Tokyo   Toronto   Warsaw

and associated companies in
Berlin   Ibadan

Published by Oxford University Press, Inc.,
198 Madison Avenue, New York, New York, 10016
http://www.oup-usa.org

Library of Congress Cataloging-in-Publication Data
Taylor, Ralph Gregory.
    Models of computation and formal languages / R. Gregory Taylor.
        p.   cm.
    Includes bibliographical references and index.
    ISBN 0-19-510983-X (cloth)
    1. Computable functions.   2. Formal languages.   I. Title.
QA9.59.T39   1997
004 ' .01 ' 5113--dc21   96-37454
                                                                   CIP

Printing (last digit): 9 8 7 6 5 4 3 2 1

Printed in the United States of America
on acid-free paper

Von fernher kommen wir gezogen
Und flehen um ein wirtlich Dach.
Sei uns der Gastliche gewogen,
Der von dem Fremdling wehrt die Schmach!

About the cover

The pictographs forming the substance of the Japanese writing system were introduced into Japan, from China, during the fifth and sixth centuries A.D. at a time when Chinese books on philosophy and Chinese translations of Sanskrit works on Buddhism were eagerly being studied within the Japanese court. One such pictograph is the character reproduced on the cover of this book. It is pronounced san *in Japanese and carries the general sense of "computation" or "calculation." The two three-stroke figures at its top denote bamboo, while the lower part may indicate some tool in the role of a calculating device. In modern Japanese, this character figures in literally dozens of combinations signifying terms for calculating and counting. We mention* sanjutsu *for "arithmetic,"* keisanki *for "computer,"* keisangakari *for "accountant," as well as the important concept of* kawasan'yō—*counting one's pelts before actually having caught the raccoons.*

CONTENTS

Chapter 4   Markov Algorithms

Chapter 5   Register Machines

Chapter 6   Post Systems (Optional)

Chapter 7   The Vector Machine Model of Parallel Computation (Optional)

Chapter 8   The Bounds of Computability

Chapter 11

Context-Sensitive Languages and Linear-Bounded Automata

Chapter 12

Generative Grammars and the Chomsky Hierarchy

PREFACE

Audience

This book is an attempt to write an introductory, comprehensive, and yet rigorous textbook covering computability theory and complexity theory that will be appropriate for those—whether undergraduate or graduate students—who are approaching the theory of computability for the first time. At many institutions this will mean undergraduate computer science and mathematics students planning graduate study in computer science. In other contexts, the book might be used to advantage by beginning-level graduate students. Given the accompanying software and the extent to which solutions to virtually all the exercises are available, it is hoped that some readers will find it useful for self-study as well.

Overview of the Book

We attempt a brief summary of the contents of this text.

- At the very beginning of Chapter 1, we introduce three computational paradigms, namely, the function computation paradigm, the language recognition paradigm, and the transduction paradigm. We show that the three paradigms are interreducible in the sense that any instance of one paradigm may be redescribed so as to become an instance of either of the other two.

- The function computation paradigm may be implemented in a variety of ways. Implementations include the notions of a Turing-computable function (Chapter 1), a partial recursive function (Chapter 3), a Markov-computable function (Chapter 4), a register-machine-computable function (Chapter 5), a Post-computable function (Chapter 6), and, finally, a vector-machine-computable function (Chapter 7). Moreover, we show that these notions characterize one and the same family of number-theoretic functions. This collection of equivalence results lends support to the Church–Turing Thesis, introduced in §8.1, and suggests that our characterization of an intuitive notion of effectively computable function is model-independent and, in that sense, robust.

- Nonetheless, certain well-defined number-theoretic functions are shown to be uncomputable—at least if Church–Turing is assumed. These functions are not computable even "in principle"—that is, even assuming that no restrictions are placed upon the resources available for computation.

- We concern ourselves with the concept of feasible computation and mean, thereby, computations whose resource requirements do not exceed what is likely to be available, given the usual assumptions about the world and the place of human beings in it. We argue for construing feasible computation as polynomially (time-)bounded computation. Demonstrations of the so-called Invariance Principle (Chapter 5) suggest that this notion of feasible computation is robust—again, in the sense of being model-independent.

- Worst-case time and space analyses of various language-acceptance problems lead to the definition of several important complexity classes, namely, P, NP, $LOGSPACE$, and NC. The relations holding between these classes are explored and culminate in the presentation of the open questions $P =? NP$ and $NC =? P$.

- The class of NP-complete problems is defined in §8.5. Intuitively, an NP-complete problem is one that is at least as hard as a wide class of well-known problems—such as the Traveling Salesman Problem—none of which has yet been shown to be feasible. We demonstrate the existence of NP-complete problems by first proving the Cook–Levin Theorem. Afterward, we show that a number of easily described problems from graph theory are NP-complete.

- Suppose that a given problem is solvable using a sequential algorithm. Typically, the development of a faster parallel algorithm involves identifying subproblem(s) of the given problem that are amenable to parallelization with concomitant improvement in performance. If such is possible, then the given problem is said to be *feasible and highly parallel*. On the other hand, some (feasible) problems appear to resist parallel treatment and are termed *inherently sequential*. In this connection, we introduce the notion of P-completeness. Intuitively, each P-complete problem is at least as hard as a number of well-known problems that, although feasible, have not been shown to be highly parallel. In other words, for all we know now, the P-complete problems are all inherently sequential. We develop the theory of P-completeness in a manner that emphasizes analogies with the theory of NP-completeness. A full proof of Ladner's result showing the existence of a P-complete problem is presented in §8.9. Afterward, a restricted version of the Traveling Salesman Problem is shown to be P-complete.

- The language recognition paradigm of §1.1 may be implemented in terms of each of the models of Chapters 1 through 7. Once again, the resulting implementations are shown to characterize one and the same family of languages. These equivalence results suggest that our characterization of an intuitive notion of solvability or decidability is robust.

- In Part II we introduce three new types of automata. These are finite-state automata (Chapter 9), pushdown-stack automata (Chapter 10), and linear-bounded automata (Chapter 11). Each of the new models is shown to be weaker than the models introduced in Part I. Furthermore, each of the new models may be associated with a family of generative grammars. Consequently, we have, for each family of languages within the so-called Chomsky hierarchy, both an automata-theoretic characterization and a grammar-theoretic characterization of that language family.

- Several decidability results regarding the family of context-free languages and the family of context-sensitive languages are obtained in Chapters 10 and 11. Then, in Chapter 12, the Post Correspondence Problem is used to obtain a succession of undecidability results both for phrase-structure languages generally and for context-free languages in particular.

- The implications of computability theory for the philosophy of mind, artificial intelligence, and cognitive science are the topic in later sections of Chapters 1, 7, and 8. The application of generative grammars to work in theoretical linguistics is recognized in §10.1 and §11.1. Elsewhere (e.g., §2.10, §4.7, and §6.6), the relation of computation theory to certain general themes within mathematics and science is considered. Our goal has been to give the text an interdisciplinary aspect, however modest.

Approach

Part I of the text, entitled "Models of Computation," implements a models approach to the theory of computability. We introduce a number of distinct models of computation, as well as variants of them. In particular, one model of parallel computation—that of bit-vector machines—is introduced (Chapter 7). Most likely, few instructors will attempt to cover all of these models in a single-semester course. Consequently, the text has been organized so as to make it possible to proceed to Chapter 8, entitled "The Bounds of Computability," having covered only the Turing machine model and some other (sequential) model—it makes no difference which one. (Omitting Chapter 7 on parallel computation would require passing over §8.8 through §8.10, however.) This has been made possible by considering alternative equivalence proofs in some cases, either in the text itself or in full solutions available both on-line and in the Instructor's Manual. (See the accompanying Chapter Dependency Chart.)

It is hoped that many instructors will be able to cover several of the described models; and the companion software implementing the Turing machine model, the Markov algorithm model, the register machine model, and the vector machine model should make this at least easier than it would otherwise be. The Church–Turing Thesis is first mentioned, in Chapter 8, only after each of these "universal" models has been investigated. This may seem to be very late by some lights. On the other hand, if introduced too early, there is the definite risk that students will view the thesis as essentially tautologous. Our delaying tactic is intended to make that less likely.

Considerations of the resource requirements of computation are promptly introduced. As early as §1.7, the concepts of time and space are introduced with respect to the single-tape Turing machine model, and big-O notation is used to express worst-case analyses of individual machines. We acknowledge that this integrated approach to complexity theory is not without incumbent risks. However, we have endeavored to ensure that our discussion aids the reader in clearly distinguishing issues of computability-in-principle, on the one hand, from complexity-theoretic concerns, on the other. The goal has been to make it possible for the beginner to truly comprehend the theory of NP-completeness by the time this essential material is presented in Chapter 8. It is our view that a result as difficult as the Cook–Levin Theorem is entirely inappropriate as an *introduction* to complexity theory. Consequently, it has been our intention that, by the time Cook–Levin is presented in Chapter 8, the reader will have acquired considerable experience in reasoning about complexity. Taken alone, Chapters 0, 1, 2, 5, 7, and 8 should serve reasonably well as the basis for a course in complexity theory.

Given that there is more material in this text than could likely be covered in any single-semester course, a number of sections (or parts of sections) have been marked as either optional or advanced. In addition, Chapter 6 (Post Systems) and Chapter 7 (Vector Machines) have been marked optional in their entirety. A reader who skips over optional sections or chapters will have no difficulty reading later parts of the book. Similarly, omitting sections marked advanced will not impede the reader's understanding of later sections (that are not themselves marked as advanced).

This is a large book in part just because it attempts to address a diverse audience. Although the book will not serve all readers equally well, it is nonetheless our intention that readers with widely varying mathematical experience should all be able to benefit from reading this book. For some mathematically more sophisticated readers, our example-driven exposition will be unnecessarily slow. (There is not even one theorem in all of Chapter 1, for instance.) On the other hand, the majority, who will benefit from the slower-paced introductory material, are unlikely to gain much from our development of the theory of P-completeness at the end of Chapter 8, say—surely advanced material for undergraduates anywhere.

Many instructors may wish to read our guide "To the Instructor/Suggestions for Using This Textbook," which is included in the Instructor's Manual. Therein we map out, in some detail, three distinct paths through the book. Each path is designed with a particular type of reader/student in mind.

Finally, we have endeavored at key points to emphasize applications of theoretical ideas within the rest of computer science. In this connection, we mention Example 4.5.4 (Perl), Example 8.1.1 (C language), and Example 8.3.1 (ML). Comprehensive discussions of Rice's Theorem (§8.4), the theory of NP-completeness, and the theory of P-completeness were motivated by a desire to communicate the contributions, on the part of theory, to the lives of working computer scientists—and, by implication, the potential for outstanding future contributions (see [Aho et al. 1996]).

Software

Windows-based software designed by Nicolae O. Savoiu accompanies this text and is available on the Internet. To download the software via HTTP, point your WWW browser to `http://www.ics.uci.edu/~savoiu/dem` and follow the on-line instructions. If, for any reason, this method is unavailable, other delivery options can be worked out. (Address e-mail to the author of the software at `savoiu@ics.uci.edu`.)

Many examples from the text have been implemented using this software and will be among these downloaded files. With three exceptions, these examples have been created by the author of the textbook. In all cases, an explicit reference to the relevant example on disk is given, for instance, "Open the icon labeled **Reverse Word** within the Markov folder." This software has shown itself to be a highly effective means of giving tangible form to abstract concepts and of reinforcing those concepts among students. Occasional lab sessions have served as a welcome break—for students and instructor—from the routine of lectures.

Exercises

Many exercises have been included together with solutions. These exercises range from very easy to very difficult and, in addition, serve a variety of purposes.

- A great many exercises are intended to check the reader's understanding of the discussion in the text. These exercises are usually relatively easy—in some cases trivial. Solutions to virtually all such exercises are provided within the instructor's manual as well as on-line at `www.jcstate.edu/thcomp/`. Those whose solutions are not on-line, and thus not in general available to the student reader, are marked **hwk** for the benefit of those instructors who may wish to use them for written **homework**.

- Another sort of exercise is intended to deepen the reader's understanding of the discussion in the text. These exercises range from the moderately difficult to the extremely difficult. Solutions to these exercises are invariably provided both on-line and in the instructor's manual.

- Some exercises fill a gap in the text at a point where it is felt that a lengthy digression would break the flow. In such a case, the reader is referred to an exercise as a way of facilitating the discussion without sacrificing rigor. Solutions to such exercises appear both on-line and in the manual, since it is deemed especially important that every reader have access to these solutions in particular.

- Some—typically rather difficult—exercises are truly extensions of the text. In a few cases, the level of difficulty of these exercises even exceeds that of the discussion within the text itself.

- Exercises for the final section of each chapter function as end-of-chapter exercises. The earlier ones typically review the work of the entire chapter whereas the later ones usually extend it.

Additional Materials On-Line

A variety of supplementary materials are available on-line at `www.jcstate.edu/thcomp/`. These include the following: (1) a complete proof that Ackermann's function is not primitive recursive, which will be of interest to the reader of Chapter 3; (2) an 11-page discussion of the application of finite-state automata to lexical analysis, which might be used in conjunction with Chapter 9; and (3) a 110-page document detailing the application of pushdown-stack automata to compiler design theory.

Communication

A list of errata is being maintained at `www.jcstate.edu/thcomp/`. The author would greatly appreciate learning from readers of any mistakes, however trivial, within the text, within solutions to exercises, or within the examples included with the various machine simulations. E-mail regarding such errors may be sent to `taylor@jcs1.jcstate.edu`. Suggestions from readers regarding improvements are always welcome, and the author will attempt to respond to each such communication.

Acknowledgments

This book—at least in its present form—would not have been possible without the involvement of several individuals. First and foremost is the author's debt to Nick Savoiu for having written the software, "Deus ex Machina," that accompanies the text. His fine programming skills, his excellent knowledge of the personal computing environment, and his boundless energy were essential to this large project. The superb debugging features that he has incorporated made possible the creation of examples larger than would have been thinkable otherwise. Work with this software has deepened the author's understanding of the simulated models. No doubt many readers will have a similar experience.

Phillip Aikey, Randall Dipert, and May Hamdan read earlier drafts of portions of the text and made valuable suggestions. In addition, the generous comments of reviewers have led to numerous improvements, both major and minor. In this connection, the author wishes to thank Mark Clement (Brigham Young University), James Foster (University of Idaho), Robert S. Roos (Allegheny College), and Benjamin Wells (University of San Francisco).

The author wishes to thank the many students at Jersey City State College who have helped him over the past four years in testing the material for this book. Their patience when presented with preliminary versions has been much appreciated. The following persons deserve special mention: Waddah Alimam, Naranjan Hira, Daniel Klein, Hany Nagib, Nick Savoiu, Ronald Singh, and Wan Tin Wong.

The author is deeply grateful to his former student Alexandra Nichifor, who has seen this project through from beginning to end. Her reactions and suggestions have proved invaluable, and the author has learned much about the theory of computability from her. She has uncovered countless errors and oversights, and, consequently, the author is much in her debt—as is the reader. Any remaining errors are due to the author himself, of course.

The author wishes to thank several people at Oxford University Press: editor Bill Zobrist, for his encouragement and belief in this project, and Krysia Bebick and Terri O'Prey, for their coordination of the numerous activities that ultimately resulted in this book.

Mona Morgan helped with graphics at an early stage. Mohammed Khan set up the author's website. Thanks are extended to Julio Velasco for regular, and essential, technical advice.

The author wishes to thank his good friend Jane Stanton for painstaking editorial assistance and, more generally, for her long-term involvement with, and commitment to, this project. Last, but not least, the author expresses gratitude to his friend Hisami for significant contributions of the nonintellectual variety.

Final work on the book was undertaken during 1995–1996 while on sabbatical leave from the Department of Computer Science at Jersey City State College. Earlier, the college's Office of Separately Budgeted Research was generous in providing financial assistance and release-time from teaching.

In the dedication of his book, the author seeks to commemorate the exceptional generosity that made possible for him an important yearlong stay in Göttingen some 25 years ago.

Chapter Dependency Chart

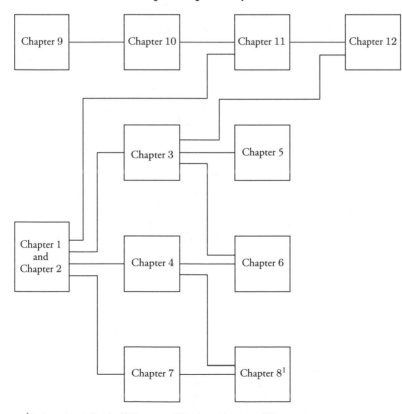

[1]In fact, the reader should have no difficulty with most of Chapter 8
provided he or she has studied at least one of Chapters 3 or 4. Only the
final sections concerning the theory of P-completeness presuppose Chapter 7.

MODELS OF COMPUTATION AND FORMAL LANGUAGES

Chapter <u>0</u>

Mathematical Preliminaries

The theory of computability is one of the newer branches of mathematics. Almost none of the ideas contained in this text predate 1930, and one of the results concerning parallel computation that we describe later is less than 10 years old. As such, computability theory presupposes some background in what is usually known as *discrete mathematics*—roughly, the mathematics of finite structures and operations on them. Most readers will already be familiar with everything that is needed to comprehend Chapters 1 through 12. Still, for the sake of completeness, we include in the present chapter a quick review of all the mathematical ideas that will be used later.

From a sufficiently abstract point of view, the theory of computability constitutes a part of abstract set theory. Consequently, we shall begin with a quick review of set-theoretic concepts. This leads naturally to a consideration of formal languages, which are nothing but sets of a certain sort and which provide an important vehicle in the study of computability. Several sections are devoted to functions since functions of a certain restricted variety—the ones that we shall call *number-theoretic*—provide a second important vehicle. The big-O notation discussed in §0.5 will provide a way in which to talk about and compare the growth of such functions.

This leaves two topics. The first of these is graph theory and is covered in §0.7. Graph-theoretic concepts will play two rather different roles in our study. First, many of the machine models of computation that we shall consider will be represented as directed graphs. Second, specific problems from graph theory itself will be used in Chapter 8 in order to advance our investigations of *feasible computation* and *highly parallel computation*. The remaining topic is logic—so-called *propositional logic* in particular. Here again, inclusion of this material is motivated by our eventual use of a certain problem concerning propositional logic in order to gain an important insight into the bounds of feasibility. Having said this little bit by way of an introduction, we proceed with the following section.

§0.1 Sets and Set-Forming Operations

Although the *elements* or *members* of a set may be physical objects, the set itself is not a physical object. In this sense, the concept of set is *abstract*. We write $a \in S$ to mean that a is a member of set S. As such, the membership relation is undefined. Members of sets may themselves be sets. Thus if $S = \{0, 1, \{0, 1\}\}$, then S has three members and $\{0, 1\} \in A$. In general, we write $card(S)$ for the *cardinality* of any finite set S, by which we mean the number of elements in set S. So where $S = \{0, 1, \{0, 1\}\}$, we have

$card(S) = 3$. The set $S = \{a\}$, which contains element a only, is referred to as the *singleton* of a. We note in passing that sets differ from lists in that (1) sets are unordered objects and (2) there is no sense in which an element can be repeated within a set.

There are several basic ways of specifying or naming sets.

(i) If a set is finite, then its elements may be listed or *enumerated*. The finite set {Reuben, Simeon, Levi, Judah, Issachar, Zebulun, Joseph, Benjamin, Dan, Naphtali, Gad, Asher} comprises the sons of Jacob as listed in Genesis 35.

(ii) In the case of a certain sort of infinite set, it is possible to list or enumerate the elements of the set in an extended sense. Since the physical universe, as presently understood, provides examples of finite sets only, examples of such infinite sets by necessity come from mathematics. Thus we have the set of natural numbers $\mathcal{N} = \{0, 1, 2, \ldots\}$ and the set of integers $\mathcal{Z} = \{\ldots -2, -1, 0, 1, 2, \ldots\}$ or perhaps $\{0, -1, 1, -2, 2, \ldots\}$. Here the ellipsis $(\ldots)$ is intended to suggest continuation in accordance with an established pattern.

(iii) One also uses *set abstraction* in order to specify a set. So we write $\{n | n \text{ is prime}\}$, or sometimes $\{n : n \text{ is prime}\}$, to name the set of all primes. The symbols $\{n | \ldots n \ldots\}$ (or $\{n : \ldots n \ldots\}$) are collectively known as the *set abstraction operator* and are read as "the set of all n such that $\ldots n \ldots$". To give another example, writing $2|n$ to mean that 2 divides n without remainder, we can use $\{n | n \in \mathcal{N} \,\&\, 2|n\}$ to denote the set of even natural numbers. (We shall also vary our notation and write either $\{n \in \mathcal{N} | 2|n\}$ or $\{n \in \mathcal{N} : 2|n\}$ for this set.)

By convention, one uses variables n, m, k, j, and so on, when the current topic or *domain of discourse* is either the natural numbers or the integers. Variables x, y, z, and so on, are frequently used to "range over" the rational numbers or the real numbers. These same variables are also used when the domain of discourse has been left unspecified. Set variables are commonly uppercase letters $A, B, C, \ldots$.

We use the symbol **U** to denote the *universal set*—the set of all elements of the current domain of discourse. We define **U** by set abstraction as $\{x | x = x\}$, making use of the fact that all objects are self-identical. We use the symbol $\emptyset$ to denote the *null set* or *empty set*, the unique set having no members, and we define it using set abstraction as $\emptyset =_{\text{def.}} \{x | x \neq x\}$.[1]

If A is $\{0, 1, 2, 3, 4\}$, then A is a *subset* of $\mathcal{N}$; in symbols, $A \subseteq \mathcal{N}$. We can define the subset relation in terms of the membership relation in that, for any sets A and B, $A \subseteq B$ if and only if, for any x, $x \in A$ implies $x \in B$. One consequence of this definition of the subset relation, however, is that every set is a subset of itself: in symbols, $A \subseteq A$, for all sets A. Also, $\emptyset \subseteq A$, for any set A. We introduce the term "proper subset" for those subsets of set B that are not identical with B; in symbols, $\{1, 2, 3\} \subset \{1, 2, 3, 4\}$.

We define the power set of set S to be the set of all subsets of S. We write $\mathcal{P}(S)$ for the power set of S as defined by $\mathcal{P}(S) =_{\text{def.}} \{A | A \subseteq S\}$. Thus, where $S = \{1, 2, 3\}$, we have $\mathcal{P}(S) = \{\emptyset, \{1\}, \{2\}, \{3\}, \{1, 2\}, \{1, 3\}, \{2, 3\}, \{1, 2, 3\}\}$. The power set operation is a unary set-forming operation; that is, given arbitrary set S, one forms a new set $\mathcal{P}(S)$ by applying the power set operation to S. A simple combinatorial (or counting) argument can be given showing that, for any finite set S, we have $card(\mathcal{P}(S)) = 2^{card(S)}$.

---

[1] We shall regularly use $=_{\text{def.}}$ in defining mathematical objects such as sets and functions when we wish to emphasize that the object in question is being characterized for the very first time. In other contexts, we shall write merely $=$.

We introduce certain binary set-forming operations as well. We write $A \cup B$, and speak of the *union* of sets A and B, for the set defined as $\{x | x \in A$ or $x \in B\}$. We write $A \cap B$—read as "A intersection B"—for the set defined as $\{x | x \in A$ and $x \in B\}$. The *complement of B relative to A* is denoted $A \backslash B$ and is defined as $\{x | x \in A$ and $x \notin B\}$. We write B^c, and speak of the *complement* of B, for the set $\mathbf{U} \backslash B$. (Note that complementation is a unary operation.) Finally, the *symmetric difference* of sets A and B is denoted $A \oplus B$ and defined as $\{x | (x \in A$ and $x \notin B)$ or $(x \in B$ and $x \notin A)\}$. The usual Venn diagrams are presented in Figure 0.1.1.

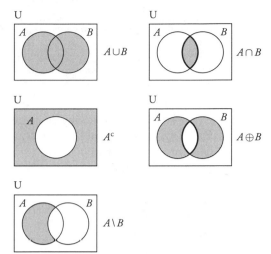

Figure 0.1.1 Five Set-Forming Operations.

Certain *laws of set algebra* follow immediately from these definitions of the various set-forming operations. We mention just a few that will be useful later. For any set S, we have $S \cup S^c = \mathbf{U}$, $S \cap S^c = \varnothing$, and $(S^c)^c = S$. For any sets A, B, and C, we have that $A \cup B = B \cup A$ and $A \cap B = B \cap A$; furthermore, $(A \cup B) \cup C = A \cup (B \cup C)$ and $(A \cap B) \cap C = A \cap (B \cap C)$. Finally, $A \cup (B \cap C) = (A \cup B) \cap (A \cup C)$ and $A \cap (B \cup C) = (A \cap B) \cup (A \cap C)$. We shall frequently need DeMorgan's laws. Namely, for any sets A and B, $(A \cap B)^c = A^c \cup B^c$. Similarly, $(A \cup B)^c = A^c \cap B^c$.

We write $\langle a, b \rangle$ for the *ordered pair* whose first element is a and whose second element is b and stipulate that $\langle a, b \rangle = \langle c, d \rangle$ if and only if $a = c$ and $b = d$. We write $A \times B$—and speak of the *Cartesian product* of sets A and B or just "A cross B"—for the set of all ordered pairs whose first element comes from A and whose second element comes from B. In symbols, we have $A \times B = \{\langle a, b \rangle | a \in A$ and $b \in B\}$. Similarly, we write $\langle a, b, c \rangle$ for the *ordered triple* whose first element is a, whose second element is b, and whose third element is c. Set $A \times B \times C$ is defined as the set of ordered triples $\{\langle a, b, c \rangle | a \in A$ and $b \in B$ and $c \in C\}$. In full generality, we write $A_1 \times A_2 \times \cdots \times A_k$ for the set of *ordered k-tuples* $\{\langle a_1, a_2, \ldots, a_k \rangle | a_1 \in A_1$ and $a_2 \in A_2$ and $\ldots$ and $a_k \in A_k\}$ for fixed $k \geq 2$. We let A^k, for fixed $k \geq 2$, be

$$\overbrace{A \times A \times \cdots \times A}^{k \text{ times}}.$$

That is, A^k is $\{\langle a_1, a_2, \ldots, a_k \rangle | a_1, a_2, \ldots, a_k \in A\}$. As a special limiting case, we write $\langle \ \rangle$ for the unique 0-tuple of elements of set A and we set $A^0 = \{\langle \ \rangle\}$. On the other hand, it is convenient to identify 1-tuple $\langle a \rangle$ with a itself, from which it follows that $A^1 = A$.

With regard to ordered k-tuples, a special use of subscripts is helpful on occasion. Namely, given k-tuple $\langle a_1, a_2, \ldots, a_k \rangle$, we write $\langle a_{i_1}, a_{i_2}, \ldots, a_{i_k} \rangle$ for an arbitrary *permutation* of k-tuple $\langle a_1, a_2, \ldots, a_k \rangle$. In other words, it is understood that the subscripts $i_1, i_2, \ldots, i_k$ are mutually distinct and that each lies between 1 and k, respectively. For example, if $\langle a_1, a_2, a_3, a_4 \rangle$ is $\langle 10, 15, 20, 25 \rangle$, then writing $\langle a_{i_1}, a_{i_2}, a_{i_3}, a_{i_4} \rangle$ for $\langle 20, 10, 25, 15 \rangle$ amounts to setting $i_1 = 3, i_2 = 1, i_3 = 4$, and $i_4 = 2$.

We note that sets are *extensional* in that if two sets A and B possess the very same elements, then $A = B$. We may formulate this most usefully as a technique for giving proofs.

> **THE PRINCIPLE OF EXTENSIONALITY:** Let A and B be sets. In order to demonstrate that $A = B$, it is sufficient to show that (i) every element of A is an element of B—that is, $A \subseteq B$; and (ii) every element of B is an element of A—that is, $B \subseteq A$.

We shall use the terms *class* and *family* as synonyms for *set* in certain contexts. In dozens of places throughout this text we shall be concerned to show that one set (class, family) A is identical with another set (class, family) B. In such a case, we will invariably show that both (i) and (ii) hold and then invoke the Principle of Extensionality.

Two sets A and B are said to be *disjoint* if $A \cap B = \varnothing$. By a "finite family of mutually disjoint sets" we shall mean a family of sets $A_1, A_2, \ldots, A_n$ with $n \geq 0$ such that, for any $i, j \leq n$ with $i \neq j$, we have $A_i \cap A_j = \varnothing$.

In general, for finite sets A and B, we have that $card(A \cup B) \leq card(A) + card(B)$. Furthermore, $card(A \cup B) = card(A) + card(B)$ only if $A \cap B = \varnothing$. We can generalize this result to an arbitrary finite family of finite sets $A_1, A_2, \ldots, A_n$. We write $\cup_i A_i$ for the union or *sumset* of family $A_1, A_2, \ldots, A_n$. Then $card(\cup_i A_i) \leq card(A_1) + card(A_2) + \cdots + card(A_n)$. Also, $card(\cup_i A_i) = card(A_1) + card(A_2) + \cdots + card(A_n)$ only if, for any $i, j \leq n$ with $i \neq j$, $A_i \cap A_j = \varnothing$.

Certain sets of numbers have special names.

- We designate by $\mathcal{N}$ the set of all natural numbers $0, 1, 2, \ldots$. We say that $\mathcal{N}$ is *closed under addition* since the sum of any two members of $\mathcal{N}$ is a member of $\mathcal{N}$. Similarly, $\mathcal{N}$ is closed under multiplication but is closed under neither subtraction nor division.

- The set $\{\ldots, -2, -1, 0, 1, 2, \ldots\}$ of all integers is $\mathcal{Z}$. The set $\mathcal{Z}$ is closed under addition, subtraction, and multiplication but not under division.

- We write $\mathcal{Q}$ for the set of all rational numbers. That is, $\mathcal{Q} = \{x | x = p/q \text{ for some } p, q \in \mathcal{Z} \text{ with } q \neq 0\}$. Set $\mathcal{Q}$ is closed under addition, subtraction, and multiplication, and $\mathcal{Q} \backslash \{0\}$ is closed under division as well.

- Finally, $\mathcal{R}$ is the set of all real numbers. Set $\mathcal{R}$ is closed under addition, subtraction, and multiplication, and $\mathcal{R} \backslash \{0\}$ is closed under division.

We define a *partition of a set* A to be a family of mutually disjoint subsets $A_1, A_2, \ldots, A_n$ such that $A = A_1 \cup A_2 \cup \cdots \cup A_n$. Thus $\mathcal{N} = \{n \in \mathcal{N} | n \text{ is even}\} \cup \{n \in \mathcal{N} | n \text{ is odd}\}$ represents a partition of $\mathcal{N}$. Similarly, $\mathcal{Z} = \{\ldots, -2, -1\} \cup \{0\} \cup \{1, 2, \ldots\}$ represents a partition of $\mathcal{Z}$.

Finally, we close this section by presenting one of several possible formulations of the set-theoretic principle known as the Axiom of Choice.

> **THE AXIOM OF CHOICE:** Let $\mathcal{F}$ be any family of mutually disjoint, nonempty sets. Then there exists a set $C_{\mathcal{F}}$ containing exactly one member of each set within $\mathcal{F}$. Set $C_{\mathcal{F}}$ is said to be a *choice set* of the family $\mathcal{F}$.

We shall not be interested in *proving* the Axiom of Choice since, as its name implies, it is itself a fundamental proposition within axiomatic set theory and hence is not provable from anything more basic within that theory. (The same can be said of the Principle of Extensionality introduced above.)

§0.2 Introduction to Formal Language Theory

We shall now give a set-theoretic concept of language; that is, formal languages will be certain sorts of sets. The term "formal" is introduced in order to distinguish such languages from natural languages, programming languages, and so on. It is, in fact, possible to regard natural languages such as Spanish and programming languages such as PROLOG as formal languages, provided that one ignores their semantic aspects. Thus formal language theory is a general study that has impressive applications in linguistics, compiler design theory, and artificial intelligence as well as in computability theory.

Several important concepts are central to our study. By an *alphabet* Σ, we shall mean any finite set of symbols. The standard example will be the two-symbol alphabet $\Sigma = \{a, b\}$. Next, a *word over alphabet* Σ will be any finite string of elements of Σ allowing repetitions. The *length* of such a word w, denoted $|w|$, is the number of symbol occurrences in w. Thus for $\Sigma = \{a, b\}$, we have two words of length 1, four of length 2, eight of length 3, and so on, as enumerated in Table 0.2.1. For $\Sigma = \{a, b\}$, we have 2^n distinct words over Σ of length n. More generally, for $card(\Sigma) = m$, there exist m^n distinct words over Σ of length n.

In the last line of Table 0.2.1, we introduce a standard superscript notation for specifying words over Σ. Namely, $a^n b^m$ denotes the word consisting of n occurrences of a followed by m occurrences of b. Thus $a^3 b^2$ names the word $aaabb$ and $a^2 b^3 a^1 = a^2 b^3 a$ denotes word $aabbba$. (Superscript 1 is normally suppressed.) We write $n_s(w)$ for the number of distinct occurrences of symbol s within word w. For example, $n_a(aba) = 2$ and $n_b(aba) = 1$.

One important word has been omitted from Table 0.2.1, namely, the unique word of length 0 consisting of zero occurrences of a and zero occurrences of b. We obviously require some special way in which to name this word. We shall use ε and refer to the *null word* or *empty word*. We note in particular that a^0 denotes ε. Also, we have $n_a(\varepsilon) = 0$ and $n_b(\varepsilon) = 0$.

Given alphabet Σ, we write Σ^* for the set of all words over Σ and define a *language over* Σ to be any subset of Σ^*. Thus, at the two extremes we have the empty language $\varnothing$ containing no words and the universal language Σ^* containing every word over Σ. In between we have the following languages, where, once again, alphabet $\Sigma = \{a, b\}$.

$$\{w \in \Sigma^* : |w| = 3\} = \{aaa, aab, aba, abb, baa, bab, bba, bbb\}$$

$$\{w \in \Sigma^* : |w| \text{ is even}\} = \{\varepsilon, aa, ab, ba, bb, aaaa, aaab, \ldots\}$$

The first of these languages has finite cardinality, whereas the second is infinite. Any language $L = \{w\}$, containing word w only, is referred to as the *unit language* of w.

We introduce certain operations on words. If w and w' are two words, then we write $\widehat{w}w'$ or just ww' for the *catenation* or *concatenation* of w and w', in that order; that is, w' is appended to the end of w. Thus if w is aba and w' is bba, then ww' is $ababba$. If w is a word, then w^{R} is the *reverse* of w.

Thus abb^{R} is bba and aba^{R} is aba. The set of *palindromes* over Σ is the language $\{w \in \Sigma^* | w = w^{\mathrm{R}}\}$. A word w' is an *initial segment* or *prefix* of word w if w can be written $w'w''$ for some (possibly empty) word w''. Thus ε, a, ab, aba, and $abaa$ are prefixes of word $abaa$. The first four are said to be *proper*

Table 0.2.1 Words over $\Sigma = \{a, b\}$.	
Words of length 1 over Σ:	a, b
Words of length 2 over Σ:	aa, ab, ba, bb
Words of length 3 over Σ:	aaa, aab, aba, abb, baa, bab, bba, bbb
$\cdots$	$\cdots$
Words of length n over Σ:	a^n, $a^{n-1}b, \cdots, ab^{n-1}$, b^n

prefixes of *abaa*. Similarly, a word w'' is a *suffix* of word w if w can be written $w'w''$ for some (possibly empty) word w'. Thus ε, a, aa, baa, and $abaa$ are suffixes of word $abaa$. The first four are said to be *proper suffixes* of *abaa*. A word w'' is a *substring* of word w if w can be written $w'w''w'''$ for some (possibly) null words w' and w'''. Thus all of the following are substrings of $abaa$: aba, ba, baa.

Since formal languages are just sets, set-forming operations $\cup, \cap, \setminus$, and $\oplus$ can be used to specify languages. Assume $\Sigma = \{a, b\}$ and let

$$L = \{w \in \Sigma^* \mid |w| \leq 3\}$$
$$L' = \{w \mid w \text{ is of the form } a^n b^n \text{ for some } n \geq 0\}$$
$$L'' = \{aba, abba, abbba, abbababb\}$$
$$L''' = \{aw \mid w \in \Sigma^*\} = \{w \mid w \text{ begins with symbol } a\}$$

Then $L \cap L'''$ is $\{a, aa, ab, aaa, aab, aba, abb\}$. $L \cup L''$ is the language that results when the three words $abba, abbba$, and $abbababb$ are added to language L. $L \setminus L'''$ is $\{\varepsilon, b, ba, bb, baa, bab, bba, bbb\}$.

We define additional language-forming operations. The first is the binary *concatenation operation* denoted by symbol . and defined, for languages L_1 and L_2, by

$$L_1.L_2 =_{\text{def.}} \{w_1 w_2 \mid w_1 \in L_1 \,\&\, w_2 \in L_2\} \qquad (0.2.1)$$

In other words, $L_1.L_2$ is the language consisting of all and only the words formed by taking a word of L_1 and appending to it a word of L_2. Thus if $L = \{a^n b^n \mid n > 0\}$ and $L' = \{(ab)^m \mid m > 0\}$, then each of the following words belongs to $L.L'$: $abab, aabbab, aabbb, abababab$, and $aabbababab$. (Note the analogy between this new language-forming operation . and the set-forming operation $\times$.) Clearly, $L_1 \subseteq L_1.L_2$ if and only if $\varepsilon \in L_2$. Also, $L_2 \subseteq L_1.L_2$ if and only if $\varepsilon \in L_1$. For the record, we point out that . is associative but not commutative. In general, we have $L_1.(L_2 \cup L_3) = (L_1.L_2) \cup (L_1.L_3)$. In other words, . distributes over $\cup$. On the other hand, language $L_1 \cup (L_2.L_3)$ is not, in general, identical to language $(L_1 \cup L_2).(L_1 \cup L_3)$; in other words, $\cup$ does not distribute over catenation. Note also that, as a consequence of our definition at (0.2.1), we have both that $L.\emptyset = \emptyset$ and that $L.\{\varepsilon\} = L$ for arbitrary language L.

We introduce symbol *, called the *Kleene-closure operator*, to denote a certain unary operation on languages. Thus, given language L, we have

$$L^* =_{\text{def.}} \{w \mid \text{ for some } n \geq 0, w \text{ is the concatenation of } n \text{ words of } L\}$$

In other words, L^* is the result of concatenating 0 or more words of L. Where $L = \{a^n b^n \mid n > 0\}$, each of $\varepsilon, abaabb$, and $aabbababbaaabbb$ belongs to L^*. Note that ε is a member of L^* for any language L—even if ε is not in L itself. Also, $L \subseteq L^*$, for any language L. In fact, unless L is either Σ^* or $\{\varepsilon\}$, we have $L \subset L^*$.

It will sometimes be convenient to have

$$L^+ =_{\text{def.}} \{w \mid \text{ for some } n > 0, w \text{ is the concatenation of } n \text{ words of } L\}$$

Thus we can see that $L^+ \subseteq L^*$ and that $L^+ \subset L^*$ as long as $\varepsilon \notin L$.

§0.3 Mappings and Functions

By a *mapping* between two sets we shall mean any association of members of one set with members of another (not necessarily different) set. The first of these two sets is commonly referred to as the *domain* of the mapping, while the second is known as its *codomain* or *range*. Members of the domain serve as *arguments* of the mapping, whereas members of the codomain serve as *values* of the mapping for members of its domain. We shall frequently write $Dom(f)$ and $Cod(f)$ for the domain and codomain, respectively, of a given mapping f. We shall write $f: A \rightarrow B$ to indicate that $Dom(f) = A$ and $Cod(f) = B$.

Many, but not all, of the mappings that will concern us in this book will be functions in the sense of the following definition. After presenting the definition, we shall consider some simple examples.

DEFINITION 0.1: A mapping f is a *function* if each member of $Dom(f)$ is mapped to one and only one member of $Cod(f)$. One says that a function is *single-valued* or that it is a *single-valued mapping*.

EXAMPLE 0.3.1 The complete description of any mapping f consists of (1) the specification of $Dom(f)$ and $Cod(f)$ and (2) a description of the value of f for any member of $Dom(f)$ taken as argument. Thus the complete description of the *successor function* is

$$f: \mathcal{N} \rightarrow \mathcal{N}$$

$$f(n) = n + 1$$

In other words, f maps natural numbers onto natural numbers, and the value of f for any given argument n is the successor of n.

We mention several other mappings that will play a major role in this book.

EXAMPLE 0.3.2 We shall use C_7^1 for the unary constant-7 function defined by

$$C_7^1: \mathcal{N} \rightarrow \mathcal{N}$$

$$C_7^1(n) = 7$$

In general, the (unary) constant-j function C_j^1, for arbitrary natural number j, is defined by

$$C_j^1: \mathcal{N} \rightarrow \mathcal{N}$$

$$C_j^1(n) = j$$

Thus $C_5^1(n) = 5$ for all n, and $C_6^1(n) = 6$ for all n.

EXAMPLE 0.3.3 The so-called "floor" function will already be familiar to many readers. It is fully defined by

$$f : \mathcal{R} \to \mathcal{Z}$$

$$f(x) = \lfloor x \rfloor = \text{ the greatest integer } \leq x$$

We mention the related "ceiling" function, which may be defined by writing

$$f : \mathcal{R} \to \mathcal{Z}$$

$$f(x) = \lceil x \rceil = \text{ the least integer } \geq x$$

EXAMPLE 0.3.4 Finally, where Σ is an alphabet, the word-reversal function relative to Σ may be defined by writing

$$f : \Sigma^* \to \Sigma^*$$

$$f(w) = w^R$$

EXAMPLE 0.3.5 Of course not every mapping is a function. Thus consider the mapping defined by

$$f : \mathcal{Z} \to \mathcal{Z}$$

$$f(n) = n \pm 3$$

which maps argument 2 onto both -1 *and* 5. In this book we shall usually be concerned with mappings that happen to be functions. On those occasions where mappings that are not functions are the topic, we shall emphasize that fact by speaking of *multivalued mappings*.

We write $Image(f)$ for the *image* of function f and define the image of f to be that subset of $Cod(f)$ consisting precisely of the values of f for members of $Dom(f)$. In symbols, we have $Image(f) =_{\text{def.}} \{y \in Cod(f) | y = f(x) \text{ for some } x \in Dom(f)\}$. It is possible that $Image(f)$ does not equal $Cod(f)$, as in the case of any of the constant functions of Example 0.3.2.

It is customary to refer to functions such as 0.3.1 and 0.3.2, which map natural numbers onto natural numbers, as *number-theoretic functions*. These functions will play a central role in this text. So far, only functions of a single argument—so-called *unary* number-theoretic functions—have been considered. We wish to generalize this so as to work with number-theoretic functions of two or more arguments. For example, the usual addition function on the natural numbers is *binary*, taking two arguments. Thus we might write $f(n, m) = n + m$. We can think of f as taking ordered pairs $\langle n, m \rangle$ as arguments. Accordingly, we write

$$f : \mathcal{N}^2 \to \mathcal{N}$$

$$f(n, m) = n + m$$

as a complete characterization of our binary addition. More generally, a number-theoretic function f of k arguments for fixed $k \geq 1$ will be a function whose arguments are k-tuples $\langle n_1, n_2, \ldots, n_k \rangle$ of natural numbers. We shall write $f : \mathcal{N}^k \to \mathcal{N}$ in characterizing $Dom(f)$ and $Cod(f)$, and we shall also write $f(n_1, n_2, \ldots, n_k)$ for $f(\langle n_1, n_2, \ldots, n_k \rangle)$. We say that f is *k-ary*. As a special limiting case of the foregoing, we describe a collection of 0-ary number-theoretic functions—functions of no arguments. Clearly, any such function must be a constant function that invariably maps onto some one natural number j (why?). We shall use $C_0^0, C_1^0, C_2^0, \ldots$ to denote them. Apparently, 0-ary function C_2^0 is fully described by writing

$$C_2^0 : \mathcal{N}^0 \to \mathcal{N}$$

$$C_2^0(\ ) = 2$$

and in general the 0-ary constant-j function C_j^0 for fixed $j \geq 0$ is describable as

$$C_j^0 : \mathcal{N}^0 \to \mathcal{N}$$

$$C_j^0(\ ) = j$$

There are various ways of classifying functions. Note that the floor function maps numerous elements of its domain onto integer 1. On the other hand, the successor function never maps two distinct arguments onto one and the same member of its codomain. Functions such as the successor function are termed *1-to-1* or *injective* in the sense of the following definition.

DEFINITION 0.2: A function f is *1-to-1* or *injective* if no two distinct elements of $Dom(f)$ are mapped onto one and the same member of $Cod(f)$.

It is easy to see that, in addition, the word-reversal function is injective, whereas the ceiling function and the constant-7 function are not.

We note further that the floor function is such that every element of codomain $\mathcal{Z}$ is the "image" of at least one element of its domain. Such a function is termed *onto* or *surjective* in accordance with the following definition.

DEFINITION 0.3: A function f is said to be *onto* or *surjective* provided that every element of $Cod(f)$ is the value of f for at least one element of $Dom(f)$. Equivalently, a function f is *onto* or *surjective* if $Cod(f) = Image(f)$.

We see that the ceiling and word-reversal functions are surjective functions. In contrast, the successor function is not surjective since 0 is not the successor of any natural number. Finally, we have the following definition.

DEFINITION 0.4: A function that is both injective and surjective is termed a *1–1 correspondence* or a *bijective function.*

Among the functions considered thus far, only word-reversal is bijective.

We go on now to mention certain special number-theoretic functions. We have already cited, for fixed natural number j, the (unary) constant-j function C_j^1 defined by

$$C_j^1 : \mathcal{N} \to \mathcal{N}$$

$$C_j^1(n) = j$$

As was seen earlier, C_7^1 is that function that takes every natural number to 7. Evidently, such a constant function is neither injective nor surjective. The class of 0-ary constant functions was discussed above. Such functions are seen to be injective (why?) but not surjective. We go on to describe k-ary constant functions for $k \geq 2$. For example, the binary constant-7 function C_7^2 maps arbitrary ordered pairs of natural numbers onto 7.

$$C_7^2 : \mathcal{N}^2 \to \mathcal{N}$$

$$C_7^2(n, m) = 7$$

We have $C_7^2(3, 5) = 7$ and $C_7^2(2, 9) = 7$. (The superscript reflects the number of arguments of function C_7^2.) In general, for arbitrary fixed $k, j \geq 0$, k-ary constant-j function C_j^k is defined as

$$C_j^k : \mathcal{N}^k \to \mathcal{N}$$

$$C_j^k(n_1, n_2, \ldots, n_k) = j$$

We define the class of *projection functions*. One of these is unary, two are binary, three are ternary, and in general k are k-ary. For the case $k = 3$, we have the three functions $p_1^3(n_1, n_2, n_3) =_{\text{def.}} n_1$, $p_2^3(n_1, n_2, n_3) =_{\text{def.}} n_2$, and $p_3^3(n_1, n_2, n_3) =_{\text{def.}} n_3$. In each case we have domain $\mathcal{N}^3 = \mathcal{N} \times \mathcal{N} \times \mathcal{N}$ and codomain $\mathcal{N}$. For the case $k = 7$, we have $p_4^7(34, 45, 244, 9, 347, 939, 8) = 9$. Note that the function p_1^1 is just the identity function on $\mathcal{N}$—sometimes written $1_{\mathcal{N}}$. Note also that in writing p_j^k, we assume that subscript j does not exceed superscript k.

Given a set S of natural numbers, the function $\chi_S : \mathcal{N} \to \mathcal{N}$ defined by

$$\chi_S(n) = \begin{cases} 1 & \text{if } n \in S \\ 0 & \text{otherwise} \end{cases}$$

is called the *characteristic function of set S.*

Certain function-forming operations will interest us in later chapters. Earlier, certain set-forming operations were introduced. Thus, given two sets A and B, we formed $A \backslash B$ (the complement of B relative to A). Here $\backslash$ was a binary set-forming operation. Other binary set-forming operations were intersection, union, symmetric difference, and Cartesian product. We mentioned two unary set-forming operations: taking the complement and forming the power set. Now we introduce comparable operations for functions.

Let $g: \Sigma^* \to \mathcal{N}$, where $\Sigma = \{a, b\}$, be the function defined by $g(w) =_{\text{def.}} n_a(w)$. Furthermore, let $f: \mathcal{N} \to \mathcal{N}$ be the number-theoretic function defined by $f(n) =_{\text{def.}} 3n + 2$. We next define function $h: \Sigma^* \to \mathcal{N}$ as $h(w) =_{\text{def.}} g(f(w))$. That is, $h(abbbababa) = 14$. Function h here is referred to as the *composition of g and f*. One sometimes writes $h = g \circ f$. On the other hand, no sense can be made of $h' =_{\text{def.}} f(g(w))$. Composing g and f, in that order, is possible because $Cod(f)$ is a subset of $Dom(g)$. Under other circumstances, such composition is not defined.

Next, consider the "doubling" function defined by

$$f: \mathcal{N} \to \mathcal{N}$$

$$f(n) = 2n$$

as well as the function defined by

$$g: \mathcal{N} \to \mathcal{N}$$

$$g(n) = n/2$$

where / indicates so-called integer division. Note that $f(3) = 6$, whereas $g(6) = 3$. We will say that g is the *inverse* of f and write $g = f^{-1}$. Thus the inverse operation $^{-1}$ is a unary function-forming operation. In fact, however, f^{-1} is not always defined. For example, problems arise if we try to make sense of f^{-1} for the case where f is the ceiling function $f(x) = \lceil x \rceil$. In general, inverse f^{-1} will be defined just in case f is injective. Thus f^{-1} is defined in the case of Example 0.3.1 and Example 0.3.4 but not in the case of Example 0.3.2 or Example 0.3.3.

We pause momentarily to consider the binary function g defined by

$$g: \mathcal{N}^2 \to \mathcal{N}$$

$$g(n, m) = n - m$$

where $-$ denotes the usual subtraction operator on the natural numbers. Note that, given that $Cod(g) = \mathcal{N}$, we can make no sense of $g(n, m)$ when $n < m$. For such pairs $\langle n, m \rangle$, we shall say that $g(n, m) = g(\langle n, m \rangle)$ is undefined. Number-theoretic functions that are undefined for some $n \in \mathcal{N}$ are termed *partial functions*. Such functions will concern us extensively in later chapters. (We shall even have occasion to speak of the *everywhere undefined function of k arguments* for each fixed k.) When a k-ary number-theoretic function f just happens to be defined for every k-tuple $\langle n_1, n_2, \ldots, n_k \rangle \subset \mathcal{N}^k$, then we shall say that f is *total*. When k-ary partial number-theoretic functions are generally the issue, then we shall use $Dom_p(f)$ to denote that subset of $\mathcal{N}^k$ on which function f is actually defined. In this context, if f should be a total function, then $Dom_p(f) = Dom(f) = \mathcal{N}$.

Finally, for number-theoretic functions f and g defined by $f(n) = 2n$ and $g(n) = n/2$, we saw that f^{-1} is none other than function g. Consequently, we see that, for example, $f(f^{-1}(10)) = f \circ g(10) = f(g(10)) = 10$, which shows that $f \circ f^{-1}$ is just the identity function on $Cod(f)$.

REMARK 0.3.1: If function f is injective, then f^{-1} is defined and $f \circ f^{-1}$ is none other than $1_{Cod(f)}$.

Similar reasoning justifies a companion remark.

> **REMARK 0.3.2:** If function f is injective, then f^{-1} is defined and $f^{-1} \circ f$ is none other than $1_{Dom(f)}$.

Let us briefly consider the real-valued function defined by $f_2(x) =_{\text{def.}} 2^x$. Since it passes the well-known *horizontal line test*, we see from its graph that function $f_2(x)$ is injective. Consequently, it has an inverse. We could denote this inverse by writing $f_2^{-1}(x)$. However, it is customary to refer to this function as $\log_2 x$. A related number-theoretic function—specifically, function $f(n) = \lceil \log_2 n \rceil$—will figure prominently in our investigations.

> **REMARK 0.3.3** For any real $x > 0$, we have that $2^{\log_2 x} = x$.

> **REMARK 0.3.4** For any real $x \geq 0$, we have that $\log_2 2^x = x$.

We want to see that these propositions turn out to be special instances of Remarks 0.3.1 and 0.3.2 above. Start with the left-hand side of Remark 0.3.3:

$$
\begin{aligned}
2^{\log_2 x} &= f_2(\log_2 x) \\
&= f_2(f_2^{-1}(x)) \\
&= f_2 \circ f_2^{-1}(x) \\
&= 1_{Cod(f)}(x) \quad \text{by Remark 0.3.1} \\
&= x
\end{aligned}
$$

The justification of Remark 0.3.4 is similar and is left as an easy exercise.

Several other binary function-forming operations will concern us later. Although these operations are perfectly general, we specialize them to number-theoretic functions.

EXAMPLE 0.3.6 Let partial number-theoretic functions $f(n)$ and $g(n)$ be given. Then we can define a new partial number-theoretic function $h(n)$ as $h(n) =_{\text{def.}} f(n) + g(n)$ and understand this to mean that (1) $h(n)$ is defined just in case both $f(n)$ and $g(n)$ are defined and (2) for any $n \in Dom(h) = Dom(f) \cap Dom(g)$, we have that $h(n)$ is the sum of $f(n)$ and $g(n)$. For example, where $f(n)$ and $g(n)$ are the successor and doubling functions, respectively, then $h(10) = f(10) + g(10) = 11 + 20 = 31$. Similarly, $h(15) = 46$ and $h(20) = 61$.

EXAMPLE 0.3.7 Let partial number-theoretic functions $f(n)$ and $g(n)$ be given. Then we can define a new partial number-theoretic function $h(n)$ as

$$
h(n) = max\{f(n), g(n)\}
$$

and construe this to mean that (1) $h(n)$ is defined just in case both $f(n)$ and $g(n)$ are defined and (2) for any $n \in Dom(h) = Dom(f) \cap Dom(g)$, we have that $h(n)$ is the maximum of $f(n)$ and $g(n)$.

For example, where $f(n)$ and $g(n)$ are defined as $f(n) = n \bmod 10$ and $g(n) = n \bmod 14$, we obtain $h(17) = max\{f(17), g(17)\} = max\{7, 3\} = 7$, whereas $h(20) = max\{f(20), g(20)\} = max\{0, 6\} = 6$.

We shall find so-called *polynomial functions* especially useful in this book. We shall restrict our attention to unary polynomial functions. First, by a *polynomial in n of degree k* we shall mean any expression of the form $a_k n^k + a_{k-1} n^{k-1} + a_{k-2} n^{k-2} + \cdots + a_1 n^1 + a_0 n^0$, where k is any natural number constant and where *coefficients* $a_k, a_{k-1}, a_{k-2}, \ldots, a_1, a_0$ are integer constants with $a_k \neq 0$. So, for example, $2n^5 + 2n^3 + 4n^2 - 16n + 7$ is a polynomial in n of degree 5 with coefficients $a_5 = 2, a_4 = 0, a_3 = 2, a_2 = 4, a_1 = -16$, and $a_0 = 7$. In this case, $2n^5$ is the *term of highest degree*. Note that polynomials of degree 0 are numerals; thus, letting $a_0 = 3$, we have $a_0 n^0 = 3 \cdot 1 = 3$. It is worth emphasizing that polynomials in n are not themselves natural numbers or integers, say. Rather, as was just said, they are *expressions*. However, when a natural number is substituted for n in such a polynomial, the result is a number. For example, letting $n = 2$ in polynomial $2n^5 + 2n^3 + 4n^2 - 16n + 7$ yields value $2 \cdot 2^5 + 2 \cdot 2^3 + 4 \cdot 2^2 - 16 \cdot 2 + 7 = 64 + 16 + 16 - 32 + 7 = 71$. Finally, the unary *polynomial function* defined by

$$f: \mathcal{N} \to \mathcal{N}$$

$$f(n) = 2n^5 + 2n^3 + 4n^2 - 16n + 7$$

maps arguments $n \in Dom(f) = \mathcal{N}$ onto the corresponding values of polynomial $2n^5 + 2n^3 + 4n^2 - 16n + 7$. Thus we have seen that $f(2) = 71$. Note that polynomial functions involving negative coefficients may be partial. For example, $f(n) = 2n^5 + 2n^3 + 4n^2 - 16n + 7$ is undefined for argument 1—note that $Cod(f)$ is $\mathcal{N}$. Also, note that polynomials of degree 0 correspond to constant functions. One sometimes writes $p(n)$ for a unary polynomial function of n.

Finally, suppose that $p_1(n)$ and $p_2(n)$ are both polynomials in n. Let $p_2[p_1(n)]$ be the result of replacing every occurrence of n in polynomial $p_2(n)$ with polynomial $p_1(n)$. We note that $p_2[p_1(n)]$ may itself be rewritten as a polynomial in n.

§0.4 Defining Functions Recursively

Number-theoretic functions may be defined in a variety of ways. We have already considered straightforward function definitions such as that which can be given for any polynomial function—for example, $f(n) =_{\text{def.}} n^2 + 3n - 5$. (Note that this number-theoretic function will be undefined for some small arguments.) We have also seen how functions and, in particular, number-theoretic functions may be defined by cases. So, for example,

$$f(n) = \begin{cases} n + 3 & \text{if } n \text{ is even} \\ n - 1 & \text{if } n \text{ is odd} \end{cases}$$

is seen to be a bijection of $\mathcal{N}$ onto $\mathcal{N} \setminus \{1\}$. In this section we shall consider yet another way in which number-theoretic functions may be defined, namely, by *recursion*.

Preliminary to presenting our first definition by recursion, we shall make some general remarks concerning the unary factorial function. Of course, in general, we have

$$n! = n \cdot (n - 1) \cdot (n - 2) \cdots 2 \cdot 1 \tag{0.4.1}$$

where the ellipsis ... has to be understood in the usual way. In particular, 5! turns out to be $5 \cdot 4 \cdot 3 \cdot 2 \cdot 1 = 120$; and if 50! is k, then 51! is seen to be $51 \cdot k$. For the case $n = 0$, we supplement equation (0.4.1) by stipulating outright that $0! = 1$. Now this sort of characterization of the factorial function is adequate to the extent that it does express our intentions well enough. Programming this sort of definition would involve checking for $n = 0$ and otherwise executing a for-loop, say. However, that is usually not how most programmers would do it. Rather, one tends to program the factorial function *recursively*, meaning thereby that a certain subroutine will call itself. This way of proceeding corresponds to the following pair of *recursion equations* for the factorial function, where, for the purpose of standardization only, we begin writing $n!$ using the prefix notation $fact(n)$:

$$fact(0) = 1 \qquad\qquad\qquad \text{(i)}$$
$$fact(n + 1) = (n + 1) \cdot fact(n) \qquad \text{(ii)}$$

These equations, taken together, are *recursive* in that the right-hand side of the second one contains a reference to $fact$ itself. This might at first appear circular but is not. To see this, consider how one can use these two equations and our knowledge of multiplication to compute the value of $fact(5)$:

$$
\begin{aligned}
fact(5) &= 5 \cdot fact(4) & \text{by (ii)} \\
&= 5 \cdot (4 \cdot fact(3)) & \text{by (ii)} \\
&= 5 \cdot (4 \cdot (3 \cdot fact(2))) & \text{by (ii)} \\
&= 5 \cdot (4 \cdot (3 \cdot (2 \cdot fact(1)))) & \text{by (ii)} \\
&= 5 \cdot (4 \cdot (3 \cdot (2 \cdot (1 \cdot fact(0))))) & \text{by (ii)} \\
&= 5 \cdot (4 \cdot (3 \cdot (2 \cdot (1 \cdot 1)))) & \text{by (i)} \\
&= 120
\end{aligned}
$$

Ultimately, an appeal to equation (i) is made, and, since (i) involves no self-reference, there was no real threat of circularity after all.

Recursion equations for both addition and multiplication can also be given. Again, let us use prefix notation rather than the more usual infix. So we shall write $sum(n, m)$ for $n + m$ and $mult(n, m)$ for $n \cdot m$. For addition, note that if the $sum(50^7, 75^8)$ is k, then $sum(50^7, 75^8 + 1)$ is $k + 1$. Then we have

$$sum(n, 0) = n$$
$$sum(n, m + 1) = succ(sum(n, m))$$

As for multiplication, note that if $mult(50^\prime, 75^8)$ is k, then $mult(50^7, 75^8 + 1)$ is $50^7 + k$. Then we have

$$mult(n, 0) = 0$$
$$mult(n, m + 1) = n + mult(n, m) = sum(n, mult(n, m))$$

EXAMPLE 0.4.1 Another easy example is provided by the following famous sequence of natural numbers:

$$1, 1, 2, 3, 5, 8, 13, 21, 34, 55, 89, 144, \ldots \qquad (0.4.2)$$

Let us define a unary number-theoretic function

$fib(n) =_{\text{def.}}$ the nth number in the sequence (0.4.2), where we start counting from the 0th position

So $fib(0) = 1$ and $fib(1) = 1$. Moreover, for $n \geq 2$, $fib(n)$ is the sum of $fib(n - 2)$ and $fib(n - 1)$. Equivalently, for $n \geq 0$, $fib(n + 2)$ is the sum of $fib(n)$ and $fib(n + 1)$. These facts provide the basis for the following triple of recursion equations:

$$fib(0) = 1$$

$$fib(1) = 1$$

$$fib(n + 2) = fib(n) + fib(n + 1)$$

$$= sum(fib(n), \ fib(n + 1))$$

§0.5 The Mathematics of Big-O Notation

One important part of theoretical computer science involves analyzing the time and space requirements of particular algorithms. Already in Chapter 1 we shall see our first such analysis. Certain unary number-theoretic functions will play an important role there as a formal means of expressing the time and space requirements of algorithms. We shall be especially interested in the *growth* of such functions as argument n goes to infinity. So-called *big-O(micron) notation* provides the standard means of comparing the growth of one number-theoretic function with that of another such function. Consequently, it is an essential tool of the theoretical computer scientist.

Preliminary to introducing this new notation, we shall review several important concepts. A unary number-theoretic function $f(n)$ will be said to be *monotone increasing (growing)* if for all $n_1, n_2 \in \mathcal{N}$, we have $n_1 < n_2$ implies $f(n_1) \leq f(n_2)$. Similarly, number-theoretic function $f(n)$ is said to be *strictly monotone increasing* if for all n_1, n_2, we have $n_1 < n_2$ implies $f(n_1) < f(n_2)$. Clearly, strict monotonicity implies monotonicity.

Consider, first, the four (partial) number-theoretic functions

$$k(n) =_{\text{def.}} 2^n$$

$$h(n) =_{\text{def.}} n^2 + 1$$

$$g(n) =_{\text{def.}} 3n$$

$$f(n) =_{\text{def.}} 7\lfloor \log_2 n \rfloor$$

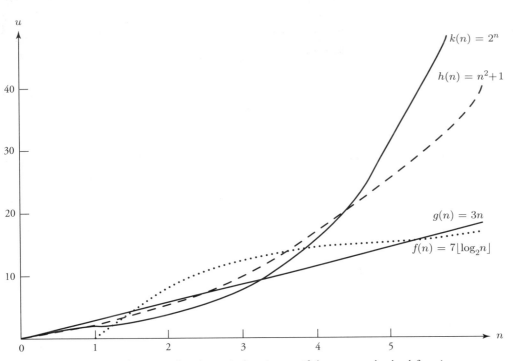

Figure 0.5.1 We graph our number-theoretic functions as if they were real-valued functions.

The first three functions here are strictly monotone increasing, and function f is monotone increasing although not strictly (see Figure 0.5.1). Big-O notation will provide us with a way of comparing the rates of growth of these four functions. First, note that for $n = 2$, we have the values $k(2) = 4$, $h(2) = 5$, $g(2) = 6$, and $f(2) = 7$. That is, $k(2) < h(2) < g(2) < f(2)$. Nonetheless, one sees that, despite this, it is function k that is growing fastest as argument n goes to infinity. Next in terms of the rate of growth is function h. Then comes g and, finally, f growing most slowly of all. We seek some mathematical means of expressing the fact that function g is growing faster than function f is, despite the fact that f exceeds g for some small arguments. This is exactly what big-O notation will afford us. Once big-O notation has been defined, we will be able to say that *function $f(n)$ is* $O(g(n))$ and take this to mean that $g(n)$ is at least as great as $f(n)$ ultimately—that is, for all sufficiently large n. Similarly, we will say that function $g(n)$ is $O(h(n))$ and that function $h(n)$ is $O(k(n))$. Also, it will be a consequence of our definition that transitivity holds. Namely, from the fact that $f(n)$ is $O(g(n))$ and that $g(n)$ is $O(h(n))$, it will follow that $f(n)$ is $O(h(n))$, and so on. Without further delay we present the central definition. Its slightly peculiar form will be explained afterward.

DEFINITION 0.5: Let $f(n)$ and $g(n)$ be partial number-theoretic functions. Then function $f(n)$ is $O(g(n))$ [read: "f of n is O of g of n"] if there exist natural number constants C and n_0 such that for any $n \geq n_0$ we have $f(n) \leq C \cdot g(n)$ whenever both $f(n)$ and $g(n)$ are defined. As usual, by a *constant* we mean a number that does not depend upon n.

We immediately show that this definition coincides with our earlier comparison of the growth rates of functions f, g, h, and k.

Table 0.5.1   Function $f(n)$ is $O(g(n))$.

Argument n	$f(n) = 7\lfloor \log_2(n) \rfloor$	$C \cdot g(n) = 1 \cdot 3n$
4	14	12
$5 = n_0$	**14**	**15**
...	...	...
7	14	21
8	21	24
9	21	27
...	...	...
15	21	45
16	28	48
...	...	...

Table 0.5.2   Function $g(n)$ is $O(h(n))$.

Argument n	$g(n) = 3n$	$C \cdot h(n) = 1 \cdot (n^2 + 1)$
2	6	5
$3 = n_0$	**9**	**10**
4	12	17
5	15	26
...	...	...

EXAMPLE 0.5.1 Function $f(n)$ is $O(g(n))$: letting $C = 1$ and $n_0 = 5$ in Definition 0.5, we see that $C \cdot g(n)$ always exceeds $f(n)$ when $n \geq n_0$ (see Table 0.5.1).

EXAMPLE 0.5.2 Function $g(n)$ is $O(h(n))$. This time we let $C = 1$ and $n_0 = 3$ (see Table 0.5.2).

EXAMPLE 0.5.3 Function $h(n)$ is $O(k(n))$. Letting $C = 1$ and $n_0 = 5$, consider Table 0.5.3. Since in all of our examples so far we have chosen $C = 1$, we note that in the case of Example 0.5.3 we could just as well have chosen $C = 2$ and $n_0 = 0$. These choices are reflected in Table 0.5.4. Note that either choice for the pair C and n_0 will suffice since Definition 0.5 requires only that *some* such pair be found. After first choosing $C = 1$ and $n_0 = 5$, we saw that n_0 can be decreased provided that C is increased. We will regularly observe such tradeoffs between choices for C and n_0 in Definition 0.5.

In analyzing algorithms later on, we will be especially interested in the unary number-theoretic functions in the following sequence.

Table 0.5.3   Function $h(n)$ is $O(k(n))$.

Argument n	$h(n) = n^2 + 1$	$C \cdot k(n) = 1 \cdot 2^n$
2	5	4
3	10	8
4	17	16
$5 = n_0$	**26**	**32**
6	37	64
...	...	...

Table 0.5.4   Function $h(n)$ is $O(k(n))$.

Argument n	$h(n) = n^2 + 1$	$C \cdot k(n) = 2 \cdot 2^n$
$0 = n_0$	1	2
1	2	4
2	5	8
3	10	16
4	17	32
5	26	64
...	...	...

$$f_0(n) = C_0^1(n) = 0$$

$$f_1(n) = C_1^1(n) = 1$$

$$f_2(n) = \lfloor \log_2 n \rfloor$$

$$f_3(n) = \lfloor \sqrt{n} \rfloor$$

$$f_4(n) = 1_{\mathcal{N}}(n) = n$$

$$f_5(n) = n \cdot \lfloor \log_2 n \rfloor$$

$$f_6(n) = n \lfloor \sqrt{n} \rfloor$$

$$f_{7.2}(n) = n^2$$

$$f_{7.3}(n) = n^3$$

$$\vdots$$

$$f_{7.k}(n) = n^k \text{ for constant } k$$

$$\vdots$$

$$f_8(n) = 2^n$$

$$f_9(n) = n!$$

$$f_{10}(n) = n^n$$

In fact, we can show the following:

THEOREM 0.1: Any function f_i in this sequence is $O(f_j)$ for all $j \geq i$.

For example, $f_3(n)$ is $O(f_4(n))$ as well as $O(f_5(n))$, and so on.

As mentioned earlier, we will be concerned later with unary number-theoretic functions that express the time or space requirements of various algorithms under consideration. We will frequently want to compare the growth rates of some function f_{time} or f_{space} with members of the sequence above. More specifically, we will want to say that such a function f_{time}, say, is $O(f_i)$ for one of the f_i in this sequence. In such a case, we will simply say that f_{time} is $O(1)$ or $O(n)$ or $O(n \cdot \lfloor \log_2 n \rfloor)$ and so forth. We shall begin to speak in this manner immediately. In other words, instead of stating that function $f_4(n)$ is $O(f_{7.2}(n))$, we shall say that *function n* is $O(n^2)$.

Several members of our sequence of functions deserve special comment.

- As for function f_0, functions that take no values except 0 are obviously $O(0)$. But so is a function such as

$$f(n) = \begin{cases} n & \text{if } n < 100 \\ 0 & \text{otherwise} \end{cases}$$

since for $n \geq n_0 = 100$, we have $f(n) \leq C \cdot 0$ for $C = 1$, say.

- We can see that a function $f(n)$ is $O(1)$ if and only if $f(n)$ is bounded above by a constant for sufficiently large arguments n—that is, if and only if there exist some constants L and n_0 such that $n \geq n_0$ implies $f(n) \leq L$ (see Exercise 0.5.3).

- A function f that is $O(n)$ will be said to *exhibit linear growth.*

- If f is $O(n^2)$ or $O(n^3)$ or, more generally, $O(n^k)$ for any fixed $k \geq 2$, then f is said to *exhibit polynomial growth.*

- Finally, if f is $O(2^n)$ or $O(3^n)$ or, more generally, $O(k^n)$ for any fixed $k \geq 2$, then f is said to *exhibit exponential growth.*[2]

Some Mathematical Details

We wish to prove Theorem 0.1. We justify only the more challenging cases and leave the others as exercises (see Exercise 0.5.7). We start at the bottom of our sequence of functions.

(a) *Claim:* 2^n is $O(n!)$.

  Justification: It appears from Table 0.5.5 that for $n \geq 4$ we might have $2^n < n!$. Indeed, for $n = 4$, this is apparent from the table itself. For $n > 4$, we can write

$$n! - (4!) \cdot 5 \cdot 6 \cdots (n - 1) \cdot n$$

> There are $n-4$ factors, each of which is > 2.

$$> 2^4 \cdot 5 \cdot 6 \cdots (n-1) \cdot n$$

$$> 2^4 \cdot 2^{n-4}$$

$$= 2^n$$

So, letting $C = 1$ and $n_0 = 4$, we have $2^n \leq C \cdot n!$ for all $n \geq n_0$.

(b) *Claim:* n^2 is $O(2^n)$.

  Justification: For $n \geq 5$, we can write

> All numerators and denominators cancel except for this last numerator.

$$n^2 = 4^2 \cdot \underbrace{\left(\frac{5}{4}\right)^2 \cdot \left(\frac{6}{5}\right)^2 \cdots \left(\frac{n-1}{n-2}\right)^2 \cdot \left(\frac{n}{n-1}\right)^2}_{n-4 \text{ factors}}$$

But, except for 4^2, each of the square factors on the right is < 2. (To see this, note that $(5/4)^2$ is the largest of them and equals $25/16$, which is strictly less than 2.) So for $n \geq 5$, we obtain

Table 0.5.5 2^n is $O(n!)$.

Argument n	2^n	$n!$
0	1	1
1	2	1
2	4	2
3	8	6
$4 = n_0$	16	24
...	...	...

---

[2]One must be a little careful here. Strictly speaking, it is the functions that are $O(a^n)$ for constant $a > 1$ but that are not $O(n^k)$ for any constant k that are said to exhibit exponential growth. Similarly, it is the functions that are $O(n^k)$ for some fixed $k \geq 2$ but not $O(n)$ that are said to exhibit polynomial growth. The functions exhibiting linear growth are those that are $O(n)$ but not $O(\log_2 n)$.

$$n^2 < 4^2 \cdot 2^{n-4}$$

There were $n - 4$ factors, each of which was < 2.

$$= 2^4 \cdot 2^{n-4}$$

$$= 2^n$$

Thus, letting $C = 1$ and $n_0 = 5$, we have $n^2 \leq C \cdot 2^n$ for $n \geq n_0$.

(c) *Claim:* n^3 and n^4 are also $O(2^n)$. More generally, for any constant $m \in \mathcal{N}$, we have that n^m is $O(2^n)$.

Justification: One can show that

$$(i) \qquad \log_2 x < x \quad \text{for all real } x > 0$$

(see Exercise 0.5.6). Then for $n \in \mathcal{N}$ with $n > 0$, we obtain

$$(ii) \qquad \frac{1}{2} \log_2 n = \log_2 n^{1/2} = \log_2 \sqrt{n} < \sqrt{n} \quad \text{by (i)}$$

This is not a natural number in general.

So

$$\log_2 n^m = m \, \log_2 n$$

$$= 2m \left(\frac{1}{2} \, \log_2 n \right)$$

$$< 2m \cdot \sqrt{n} \qquad \text{by (ii)}$$

$$= \frac{2m}{\sqrt{n}} \cdot n$$

But for $n \geq 4m^2$ we have $2m/\sqrt{n} \leq 1$, so $\log_2 n^m < n$ for $n \geq 4m^2$. Hence $n^m < 2^n$ for $n \geq 4m^2$ by Remark 0.3.3. (For example, $n^3 < 2^n$ for $n \geq 36$, and $n^4 < 2^n$ for $n \geq 64$.) So for fixed m and letting $C = 1$ and $n_0 = 4m^2$, we have that $n^m < C \cdot 2^n$ for $n \geq n_0$.

(d) *Claim:* $\log_2 n$ is $O(\sqrt{n})$.
Justification: This will be a special case of (e) below.

(e) *Claim:* $\log_2 n$ is $O(\sqrt[2]{n})$, $O(\sqrt[3]{n})$, $O(\sqrt[4]{n})$, and, more generally, $O(\sqrt[m]{n})$ for any fixed $m \in \mathcal{N}$.
Justification: By (c) we have $\log_2 n^m < n$ for $n \geq 4m^2$, where m is any fixed natural number. Since the proof of (c) holds for any real n, we can substitute $\sqrt[m]{n}$ for n to obtain $\log_2 (\sqrt[m]{n})^m < \sqrt[m]{n}$ for $\sqrt[m]{n} \geq 4m^2$. But since $(\sqrt[m]{n})^m = n$, it follows that $\log_2 n < \sqrt[m]{n}$ for $n = (\sqrt[m]{n})^m \geq (4m^2)^m$. That is, for sufficiently large n, we have $\log_2 n < \sqrt[m]{n}$ and hence $\log_2 n$ is $O(\sqrt[m]{n})$.
Q.E.D.

EXAMPLE 0.5.4 Consider function $f(n) = 3n^2 + 2n + 5$. It is easy to see that $f(n)$ is $O(n^2)$, as reflected in Table 0.5.6, where $C = 4$ and $n_0 = 5$.

Concerning $f(n) = 3n^2 + 2n + 9$, note that as n goes to infinity, the term $3n^2$ grows much faster than do the two lower-degree terms (l.d.t.). We say that the term of highest degree *dominates* in that, for sufficiently large n, terms $2n$ and 9 are making a negligible contribution to $f(n)$ relative to the contribution of term $3n^2$. Consequently, the value of $f(n)$ as n goes to infinity will be bounded above by $C \cdot n^2$ for any $C > 3$. It is convenient to let $C = 4$ and then do a few calculations to find n_0.

Table 0.5.6 Function $f(n) = 3n^2 + 2n + 5$ is $O(n^2)$.

Argument n	$f(n) = 3n^2 + 2n + 9$	$C \cdot g(n) = 4 \cdot n^2$
0	9	0
1	14	4
2	25	16
3	42	36
4	65	64
$5 = n_0$	94	100
6	129	144
$\ldots$	$\ldots$	$\ldots$

Example 0.5.4 should enable the reader to see that function $g(n) = 6n^3 + 4n^2 + 2n - 7$, say, is $O(n^3)$ and that function $h(n) = 2n^4 + 6n^3 + 4n^2 + 2n - 7$ is $O(n^4)$. More generally, in the case of any *polynomial function*

$$f(n) = a_k n^k + \text{l.d.t.}$$

of degree k, we have that $f(n)$ is $O(n^k)$ (see also Exercise 0.5.10(a)).

THEOREM 0.2(a): Suppose that number-theoretic functions $f(n)$ and $g(n)$ are $O(s(n))$ and $O(t(n))$, respectively. Then the function defined by $h(n) = f(n) + g(n)$ is $O(s(n) + t(n))$.

PROOF By hypothesis, there exist natural number constants n_f and C_f such that for $n \geq n_f$ we have $f(n) \leq C_f \cdot s(n)$. Similarly, there exist natural number constants n_g and C_g such that for $n \geq n_g$ we have $g(n) < C_g \cdot t(n)$. Now, letting $n_0 = max(n_f, n_g)$ and $C = max(C_f, C_g)$, we can write $h(n) = f(n) + g(n) \leq C \cdot s(n) + C \cdot t(n) = C \cdot [s(n) + t(n)]$ for all $n \geq n_0$. By Definition 0.5, we have that $h(n)$ is $O(s(n) + t(n))$.   Q.E.D.

THEOREM 0.2(b): Suppose that number-theoretic functions $f(n)$ and $g(n)$ are $O(s(n))$ and $O(t(n))$, respectively. Then the function defined by $h(n) = f(n) \cdot g(n)$ is $O(s(n) \cdot t(n))$.

PROOF The proof is strictly analogous to that of Theorem 0.2(a). By hypothesis, $f(n)$ and $g(n)$ are bounded above by $C_f \cdot s(n)$ and $C_g \cdot t(n)$, respectively, for sufficiently large n. But then, letting $C = max(C_f, C_g)$, we have $h(n) = f(n) \cdot g(n) \leq C \cdot s(n) \cdot C \cdot t(n) = C^2 \cdot [s(n) \cdot t(n)]$ for sufficiently large n. By Definition 0.5, this in turn means that $h(n)$ is $O(s(n) \cdot t(n))$.   Q.E.D.

In concluding, we address a common misunderstanding. It is true that big-O notation concerns functions. We will be using it to characterize the rates of growth of number-theoretic functions in particular. That said, the symbol string $O(\cdot)$ does not denote the application of some function to its argument. Rather, to say that function $f(n)$ is $O(g(n))$ is to assert that functions f and g stand to one another in a certain relation: Roughly, $f(n)$ is bounded above by $g(n)$ for sufficiently large values of n, where what is meant by "sufficiently large" depends upon f and g.

§0.6 Mathematical Induction

We introduce a new proof technique that is useful within mathematics generally and within the theory of computability in particular. This new proof technique is called *proof by mathematical induction.*

Suppose that one wishes to prove that every natural number has a certain property P. Then one might proceed as follows.

  (i) First prove that 0 has the property. That is, prove that $P(0)$ holds.

 (ii) Next prove that, for arbitrary $k \in \mathcal{N}$, if k has the property, then so does $k + 1$. That is, we prove that if $P(k)$ holds, then $P(k + 1)$ holds as well.

Having carried out (i) and (ii), we can see that every natural number has property P. For 0 has property P by (i). And since 0 has it, then 1 has it by (ii). And since 1 has it, then 2 has it by (ii) again. And because $P(2)$ holds, $P(3)$ holds, and so on.

Part (i) of our proof is termed the *base case*. Part (ii), called the *inductive case*, consists of showing that, if $P(k)$ is assumed as a temporary hypothesis, then it follows that $P(k + 1)$. In the context of proving (ii), statement "$P(k)$" is known as the *induction hypothesis* of the proof.

Preliminary to the presentation of a first proof by mathematical induction, note that $k \cdot (k + 1)$ is even for arbitrary $k \in \mathcal{N}$. As noted earlier, we write $a|b$, for a, $b \in \mathcal{N}$, to mean that a divides b without remainder. (Note that $a|b$ is not the name of a number but is rather a proposition—something that is either true or false for a particular a and b.) Given that $6|36$ and $6|24$, it comes as no surprise then that $6|60$. More generally, we have that $a|b$ and $a|c$ together imply that $a|b + c$. As a first example of a proposition to be proved by mathematical induction, consider the following proposition.

THEOREM 0.3: For all n in $\mathcal{N}$, $6|n^3 - n$.

PROOF (by mathematical induction)

> **Base case.** $n = 0$. We have $6|0^3 - 0$.
> **Inductive case.** $n = k + 1$. We assume as induction hypothesis that $6|k^3 - k$. We can write
>
> $$(k + 1)^3 - (k + 1) = [k^3 + 3k^2 + 3k + 1] - k - 1$$
> $$= [k^3 - k] + [3k^2 + 3k]$$
> $$= [k^3 - k] + 3(k \cdot (k + 1))$$
>
> But $6|[k^3 - k]$ by the induction hypothesis. And the second term here is divisible by 6 because $k \cdot (k + 1)$ is even. So both terms are divisible by 6, which means that 6 divides their sum as well.
> Q.E.D.

We may interpret the foregoing proof as follows. Let us say that a natural number n has the "nice" property if the result of cubing n and then subtracting n is divisible by 6. Using this terminology, our theorem says that all natural numbers have the nice property. How did we prove this proposition? First, our base case established that 0 in particular has the nice property. Then, in our inductive step, we showed that if k has the nice property, for an arbitrary $k \in \mathcal{N}$—we called that the induction hypothesis of the proof—then it follows that $k + 1$ must also have the nice property. Since k here was an arbitrary member of $\mathcal{N}$, we have, in fact, shown that every member of $\mathcal{N}$ has the nice property in accordance with (i)–(ii) above.

Another example will be useful. The following proposition is worth reviewing since it will figure indirectly in our work in later chapters.

THEOREM 0.4: For all $n \in \mathcal{N}$, $2^0 + 2^1 + \cdots + 2^n = 2^{n+1} - 1$.

PROOF (by mathematical induction)

Base case. Suppose that $n = 0$. We see that 2^0 does equal $2^{0+1} - 1$.

Inductive case. Suppose $n = k + 1$. Then

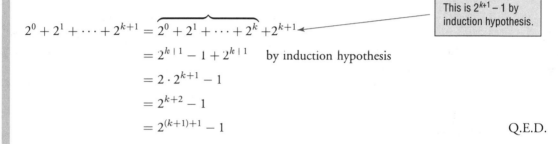

$$2^0 + 2^1 + \cdots + 2^{k+1} = \overbrace{2^0 + 2^1 + \cdots + 2^k} + 2^{k+1}$$

This is $2^{k+1} - 1$ by induction hypothesis.

$$= 2^{k+1} - 1 + 2^{k+1} \quad \text{by induction hypothesis}$$

$$= 2 \cdot 2^{k+1} - 1$$

$$= 2^{k+2} - 1$$

$$= 2^{(k+1)+1} - 1$$

Q.E.D.

Theorem 0.4 has immediate bearing upon base-2 or binary notation. For instance, given the positional character of binary notation, we have that

$$\underbrace{1111\ldots1111}_{n+1 \text{ digits}}{}_2 = 2^0 + 2^1 + \cdots + 2^n = 2^{n+1} - 1$$

For example, binary numeral 11111_2, consisting of $5 = 4 + 1$ digits, has decimal equivalent $2^5 - 1 = 31$.

§0.7 Graphs

We shall define a *graph* $G = (V, E)$ to be a pair consisting of a *vertex set* V and an *edge set* E. So the graph of Figure 0.7.1(a) is fully described by giving its vertex set as $V = \{a, b, c, d, e\}$ and its edge set as $E = \{\langle a, c \rangle, \langle c, d \rangle, \langle d, e \rangle, \langle e, c \rangle, \langle c, b \rangle, \langle b, a \rangle\}$, where we are writing $\langle v, v' \rangle$ for the edge from vertex

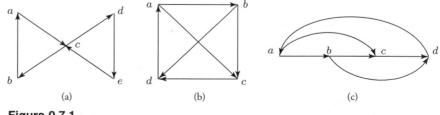

(a)   (b)   (c)

Figure 0.7.1

v to vertex v'. The vertex set V and edge set E of graph G are also referred to as the *node set* of G and the *arc set* of G, respectively.

The set-theoretic character of graphs is illustrated by Figures 0.7.1(b) and 0.7.1(c). Note that the vertex set of the graph of Figure 0.7.1(b) is identical with the vertex set of the graph of Figure 0.7.1(c). Both may be given as $V = \{a, b, c, d\}$. Also, the reader should verify that the edge set of Figure 0.7.1(b) is identical with the edge set of Figure 0.7.1(c). For example, both contain edge $\langle c, d \rangle$ but do not contain edge $\langle d, c \rangle$. Since, by definition, a graph is just a vertex set together with an edge set, we have no choice but to conclude that the graph of Figure 0.7.1(b) is identical with the graph of Figure 0.7.1(c), despite their very different pictures. In other words, graphs are set-theoretic objects that are not to be identified with their representations.

The graphs of Figures 0.7.1(a)–(c) are so-called *directed graphs*, or *digraphs* for short. We review several important concepts concerning digraphs. An edge $\langle v, w \rangle$ from vertex v to vertex w in digraph G is *incident upon* both v and w. Vertex v is the *tail* of such an edge, and vertex w is its *head*. If there exists an edge from v to w, then we also say that vertex w is a *successor* of vertex v. (In this sense, vertex v may have multiple successors.) A *self-loop* is an edge whose head and tail are one and the same vertex—for example, the edge from vertex c to vertex c in the graph of Figure 0.7.2.

A *finite path within a digraph* is a sequence of edges $e_1 e_2 e_3 \ldots e_n$ such that, for any two consecutive edges e_k and e_{k+1} with $1 \leq k < n$, the head of e_k is the tail of e_{k+1}. The *length of a path* $e_1 e_2 \ldots e_n$ is the number of edges in that path, in other words, n. (Infinite paths are also possible.) If $P = e_1 e_2 \ldots e_n$ is a path and $e = \langle v, w \rangle$ is an edge within P, then P is said to *traverse* e and to *visit* both v and w. For example, the edge sequence $\langle a, c \rangle \langle c, d \rangle \langle d, e \rangle \langle e, c \rangle$ describes a path of length 4 within the digraph of Figure 0.7.1(a). This path traverses edge $\langle d, e \rangle$, among others, and visits all vertices of the graph except b. Equivalently, we may specify the same path as the vertex sequence $a\,c\,d\,e\,c$.

By a *closed path within a digraph* we shall mean a finite path $e_1 e_2 \ldots e_n$ such that the tail of e_1 is identical with the head of e_n. Edge sequence $\langle a, c \rangle \langle c, d \rangle \langle d, e \rangle \langle e, c \rangle \langle c, b \rangle \langle b, a \rangle$ constitutes a closed path within the digraph of Figure 0.7.1(a). A *cycle* within a digraph is a special sort of closed path whereby we require that (1) no edge is retraversed, (2) no vertex except the initial vertex is visited more than once, and (3) the initial vertex is visited exactly twice. The closed path

$$\langle a, c \rangle \langle c, d \rangle \langle d, e \rangle \langle e, c \rangle \langle c, b \rangle \langle b, a \rangle$$

within the digraph of Figure 0.7.1(a) is not a cycle since vertex c is revisited. On the other hand, the closed path

$$\langle a, c \rangle \langle c, b \rangle \langle b, a \rangle$$

within the same digraph is a cycle. A path $P = e_1 e_2 \ldots e_n$ is said to be *cyclic* if some subsequence of edges within P is a cycle. An *acyclic path* $P = e_1 e_2 \ldots e_n$ is a path that is not cyclic. Equivalently, an acyclic path $P = e_1 e_2 \ldots e_n$ is one in which no node is revisited. Thus, the digraph of Figure 0.7.1(a) has four acyclic paths of length 3 but only two of length 4. Finally, a digraph is said to be *acyclic* if it contains no paths that are cycles.

We define the *indegree of a vertex* v within a digraph to be the number of distinct edges e such that v is the head of e. We define the *outdegree of a vertex* v to be the number of distinct edges e such that v is the tail of e. The *degree of vertex* v is then the sum of its indegree and its outdegree. Note that, as a consequence of this definition, a self-loop incident upon vertex v contributes twice to the degree

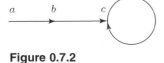

Figure 0.7.2

of v. A *sink* is a vertex of outdegree 0; equivalently, a vertex is a sink if it has no successors. A *source* is a vertex with indegree 0. For example, in the digraph of Figure 0.7.3, nodes a and f are sources, and nodes b, c, and e are sinks. Node d, on the other hand, is neither a source nor a sink since indegree$(d) = 2$ and outdegree$(d) = 2$.

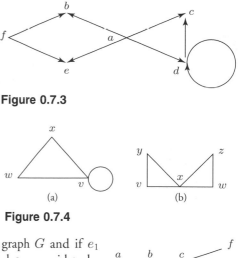

Figure 0.7.3

In addition to directed graphs, we shall need to consider so-called *undirected graphs*. An undirected graph $G = (V, E)$ consists of a vertex set V and an edge set E, where E now consists of unordered pairs of members of V. If $v, w \in V$, then we write both (v, w) and (w, v) to designate one and the same edge between v and w. Most of the definitions given above for digraphs now require only slight modification. Edge $(v, w) = (w, v)$ is *incident upon* both vertices v and w. *Self-loops* are edges of the form (v, v). If v and w are vertices of an undirected graph G and if e_1 and e_2 are two distinct edges between v and w, then e_1 and e_2 are said to be *parallel*. A *path* P *within an undirected graph* $G = (V, E)$ is a sequence of edges $e_1 \, e_2 \, e_3 \ldots$ in E, finite or infinite, such that it is possible to simultaneously assign directions to all of the edges in P so that, for any two consecutive edges e_k and e_{k+1} in P, the head of e_k is the tail of e_{k+1}. If such a simultaneous assignment of directions to the edges of a finite path P results in the tail of the first edge of P being identical with the head of the last edge in P, then P is said to be a *closed path*. The *length of a path* within an undirected graph is again the number of edges in the path. An undirected graph is said to be *connected* if there exists a path between any two distinct vertices. The *degree* of a vertex v within an undirected graph G is the number of edges of G that are incident upon v, where self-loops are counted twice. For example, where v is the indicated vertex in the undirected graph of Figure 0.7.4(a), $degree(v) = 4$.

A *cycle* within an undirected graph is a closed path retraversing no edges and revisiting no vertex except the first, which it visits exactly twice. A path within an undirected graph is *acyclic* if it contains no subpath that is a cycle, and an undirected graph G is *acyclic* provided that all paths within G are acyclic. We define a *tree* to be an undirected graph that is both connected and acyclic. Hence neither of the graphs in Figures 0.7.4(a) and 0.7.4(b) is a tree since, although connected, both contain cycles. On the other hand, the undirected graph of Figure 0.7.5 is a tree. We shall use the term *forest* for a collection of trees.

Figure 0.7.4 area:

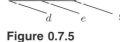

(a)   (b)

Figure 0.7.4

Figure 0.7.5

§0.8 Introduction to Propositional Logic

By a *proposition* we shall mean any statement that possesses a *truth value*—that is, any statement that is either true or false. Thus the following mathematical statements, expressed in English, are propositions.

(1) For all n in P, $n^3 - n$ is divisible by 6. (In symbols, $6 | n^3 - n$.)

(2) The complement of the complement of A is A, where A is any set. (In symbols, $(A^c)^c = A$)

(3) n^2 is $O(n^3)$.

(4) 6 is a prime number.

Propositions (1), (2), and (3) happen to be true. In fact, we proved each of them in earlier sections of this chapter. On the other hand, (4) is false, but it is nonetheless a proposition.

Of course, propositions need not have mathematical content. An example of a nonmathematical proposition is (5), which happens to be true.

(5) Momotombo is located in Nicaragua.

Statement (6), which is known as *Goldbach's Conjecture*, remains unproven. However, since it is the sort of statement that must be either true or false, it qualifies as a proposition.

(6) Every even integer strictly greater than 4 is the sum of two primes.

Lest one get the impression that every grammatical sentence of English expresses a proposition, consider (7)–(9), none of which can be said to have a truth value.

(7) Don't forget to vote.

(8) Is Yellowstone still burning?

(9) We define the *degree* of a vertex v within an undirected graph G to be the number of edges in G that are incident upon v.

A definition such as (9) amounts to a stipulation[3]—the expression of an intention to use a certain term in a certain way in future discourse. One thereby *does* something in uttering (9) without *asserting* anything to be true or false.

We shall use Σ_{PL} to denote the infinite symbol set consisting of (i) lowercase letters of the Roman alphabet $p, q, r, p', q', r', p'', q'', r'', \ldots$, which are used to stand for propositions and which we shall refer to as *sentence letters*, (ii) the five *propositional connectives* $\neg$, $\vee$, $\&$, $\rightarrow$, and $\leftrightarrow$, and (iii) three signs of aggregation, (), [], and {}. (Later on, we shall define the *language of propositional (sentential) logic* as a certain set of strings over alphabet Σ_{PL}.)

The unary connective $\neg$ is used to express *negation*. In other words, letting sentence letter p stand for "John is tall," we shall write $\neg p$ for the following proposition:

(10) John is not tall.

We define connective $\neg$ using the truth table of Table 0.8.1, which shows the way in which the truth value of $\neg p$ depends upon the truth value of component sentence letter p.

The binary connective $\&$ is used to express propositional conjunction. (An alternative is symbol $\wedge$.) Letting p and q stand for "John is tall" and "Andrew is short," respectively, we shall write $p \& q$ (or $p \wedge q$) for their *conjunction*:

(11) John is tall and Andrew is short.

---

[3] We are to imagine that (9) occurs at a place within some text such that, previously, there has been no mention whatever of any notion of degree as applied to vertices within graphs.

Table 0.8.1 Definition of ¬.		**Table 0.8.2** Definition of &.			**Table 0.8.3** Definition of ∨.			**Table 0.8.4** Definition of →.			**Table 0.8.5** Definition of ↔.		
p	$\neg p$	p	q	$p \& q$	p	q	$p \vee q$	p	q	$p \to q$	p	q	$p \leftrightarrow q$
T	F	T	T	T	T	T	T	T	T	T	T	T	T
F	T	T	F	F	T	F	T	T	F	F	T	F	F
		F	T	F	F	T	T	F	T	T	F	T	F
		F	F	F	F	F	F	F	F	T	F	F	T

We define connective & using the truth table of Table 0.8.2, which shows the way in which the truth value of the whole depends upon the truth value of component sentence letters or *conjuncts* p and q. We summarize this dependence as follows: a conjunction is true if both its conjuncts are true and is otherwise false.

The binary connective ∨ is used to express *disjunction*. Letting p and q stand for "John is tall" and "Andrew is short," respectively, we write $p \vee q$ for their disjunction:

(12) Either John is tall or Andrew is short.

Again, a truth table defines connective ∨ by indicating the way in which the truth value of the disjunction depends upon the truth value of *disjuncts* p and q (see Table 0.8.3). A disjunction is false if both its disjuncts are false and is otherwise true. Thus our use of ∨ corresponds to so-called *inclusive or*.

The binary connective → is used to express *conditional statements*. We shall write $p \to \neg q$ for the following conditional:

(13) If World War III begins tomorrow, then CS405 (Theory of Computability) will not be offered during the Spring Semester.

Here p and q stand for propositions "World War III begins tomorrow" and "CS405 (Theory of Computability) will be offered during the Spring Semester," respectively. We define connective → using Table 0.8.4, which indicates the way in which the truth value of the conditional depends upon the truth value of *antecedent* p and *consequent* q. A conditional is false just in case its antecedent is true and its consequent false; otherwise the conditional is true. We note without further comment that the semantics for → are not fully in accordance with our usual understanding of if-then statements in English to the extent that we shall be regarding the following conditional uttered in 1997 as true since its antecedent is false:

(14) If Palme is Prime Minister of Sweden, then $2 + 2 = 5$.

(Many English speakers would tend to regard (14) either as false or as lacking any truth value whatever—and hence not a genuine proposition in our sense.)

Finally, the binary connective ↔ figures in so-called *biconditional statements*. Letting p and q stand for "John is tall" and "Andrew is short," respectively, we write $p \leftrightarrow q$ for the following biconditional:

(15) John is tall if and only if Andrew is short.

A biconditional is true if its component sentence letters have the same truth value and is otherwise false (see Table 0.8.5).

It will be useful to make a few additional remarks regarding conditionals in particular. Consider the following statements:

(16) Output will be sent to the monitor if FLAG = TRUE.

(17) Output will be sent to the monitor only if FLAG = TRUE.

Students frequently have trouble distinguishing between (16) and (17). To help with this, consider the following program segment.

```
. . .

if FLAG then

    if FOUND then

        write(monitor, num)

    else write(printer_1, num)

else write(printer_2, num);

. . .
```

In this setting, (17) is true: If output has managed to find its way to the monitor, then variable FLAG must have been true. On the other hand, (16) is false: It does not follow merely from the fact that FLAG is true that output will be sent to the monitor. But that is what (16) says. So (16) is false. Apparently, (16) and (17) say very different things. (If they really had the same meaning, then it would be impossible to present a script in which they have differing truth values.)

Statement (16) expresses a purported *sufficient condition* for output being sent to the monitor: Statement (16) says that it is enough that FLAG be true. Since, in the described setting, this condition is in fact *not* sufficient, we see that (16) is false in that setting. Statement (17), on the other hand, expresses a *necessary condition* for output being sent to the monitor. Since, in the described context, this condition is truly necessary for output being sent to the monitor, we conclude that (17) is true in that context.

We next move on to a consideration of additional semantic issues concerning propositional logic. Sentences of propositional logic may be classified as either *tautologous, contradictory*, or *contingent*. A sentence such as $p \vee \neg p$, which is true under all assignments of truth values to component sentence letters, is said to be *tautologous* (see Table 0.8.6). Furthermore, a sentence such as $p \& \neg p$, which is false for all assignments of truth values to component sentence letters, is said to be *contradictory* (see Table 0.8.7). Finally, sentences that are neither tautologous nor contradictory are sometimes termed *contingent*. Sentence $p \vee q$ is an example.

The notion of *satisfiability* will concern us extensively in Chapter 8: A *satisfiable* sentence of propositional logic is one that is true for at least one assignment of truth values to component sentence letters. That is, a satisfiable sentence is one that is not contradictory. In fact, truth tables afford an algorithm or *decision procedure* for satisfiability. That is, given any sentence S of propositional logic, one can determine whether S is satisfiable by creating the usual truth table for S and then examining the column for S itself—typically the rightmost column. If there is at least one T

Table 0.8.6 $p \vee \neg p$ is a tautology.

p	$\neg p$	$p \vee \neg p$
T	F	T
F	T	T

Table 0.8.7 $p \& \neg p$ is a contradiction.

p	$\neg p$	$p \& \neg p$
T	F	F
F	T	F

in this column, then S is satisfiable. Otherwise, S is *unsatisfiable*. Given this decision procedure, we say that the Satisfiability Problem for Propositional Logic is *decidable*.

We review the important concept of logical equivalence. Let-

Table 0.8.8 $\neg p$ & $\neg q$ and $\neg(p \vee q)$ are logically equivalent.

(a)					(b)			
p	**q**	**¬p**	**¬q**	**¬p & ¬q**	**p**	**q**	**p ∨ q**	**¬(p ∨ q)**
T	T	F	F	F	T	T	T	F
T	F	F	T	F	T	F	T	F
F	T	T	F	F	F	T	T	F
F	F	T	T	T	F	F	F	T

ting p be "Side A agreed to the proposed terms of the cease-fire" and letting q be "Side B agreed to the proposed terms of the cease-fire," we note that there are two distinct ways to translate the following sentence (18) into the language of propositional logic.

(18) Neither Side A nor Side B agreed to the proposed terms of the cease-fire.

Either sentence $\neg p$ & $\neg q$ or sentence $\neg(p \vee q)$ is an acceptable translation. We must conclude that the two sentences $\neg p$ & $\neg q$ and $\neg(p \vee q)$ are in some sense the same. But, clearly, the sameness that is involved here is not a matter of the formal properties of these symbol strings, since they look very different indeed. Rather, sameness here must be a matter of their meaning or *semantic content*. It is this semantic concept of sameness, as applied to two sentences of propositional logic, that we now wish to characterize rigorously.

If we make a truth table for each of $\neg p$ & $\neg q$ and $\neg(p \vee q)$, we notice that the last columns of the two truth tables are identical (see Tables 0.8.8(a) and 0.8.8(b)). This reflects the fact that, given any assignment of truth values to components p and q, propositions $\neg p$ & $\neg q$ and $\neg(p \vee q)$ always have one and the same truth value—they are either both true or both false. This, in turn, leads us to formulate the following important definition.

DEFINITION 0.7: Two sentences S_1 and S_2 of propositional logic are (*logically*) *equivalent* if, for any given assignment of truth values to component sentence letters, the resulting truth value of S_1 is identical with the resulting truth value of S_2.

The logical equivalence of the two sentences $\neg p$ & $\neg q$ and $\neg(p \vee q)$ is one of DeMorgan's Laws, named for English logician Augustus DeMorgan (1806–1871). As an exercise, the reader should verify that the sentences $p \rightarrow q$ and $\neg p \vee q$ are logically equivalent by creating a truth table for each. This equivalence is sometimes called *Implication* and appears in the table of important equivalences in Table 0.8.9, where we are using $S_1, S_2, S_3, \ldots$ as *syntactic variables* over sentences of propositional logic. As is standard, we write $S_1 \Leftrightarrow S_2$ to mean that sentences S_1 and S_2 are logically equivalent in the sense of Definition 0.7.

Let S_1 be the sentence $(p \rightarrow q)$ & $(q \rightarrow r)$ and let S_2 be the sentence $p \rightarrow r$. Table 0.8.10 shows that S_1 is not equivalent to S_2. We do notice, however, that there is a T in the S_2 column whenever there is a T in the S_1 column. Accordingly, we say that S_1 (*logically*) *implies* S_2 and write $S_1 \Rightarrow S_2$.

DEFINITION 0.8: Let S_1 and S_2 be two sentences of propositional logic. We shall say that S_1 (*logically*) *implies* S_2 if any truth-value assignment making S_1 true makes S_2 true also.

The logical implication $(p \rightarrow q)$ & $(q \rightarrow r) \Rightarrow p \rightarrow r$ bears the name *Hypothetical Syllogism* and appears in Table 0.8.11 together with several other important logical implications.

Table 0.8.9   Some Important Logical Equivalences.

Name of Logical Equivalence	In Symbols
Idempotence	$S_1 \Leftrightarrow S_1$
Commutativity	$S_1 \vee S_2 \Leftrightarrow S_2 \vee S_1$
	$S_1 \,\&\, S_2 \Leftrightarrow S_2 \,\&\, S_1$
Associativity	$S_1 \vee (S_2 \vee S_3) \Leftrightarrow (S_1 \vee S_2) \vee S_3$
	$S_1 \,\&\, (S_2 \,\&\, S_3) \Leftrightarrow (S_1 \,\&\, S_2) \,\&\, S_3$
Distributivity	$S_1 \vee (S_2 \,\&\, S_3) \Leftrightarrow (S_1 \vee S_2) \,\&\, (S_1 \vee S_3)$
	$S_1 \,\&\, (S_2 \vee S_3) \Leftrightarrow (S_1 \,\&\, S_2) \vee (S_1 \,\&\, S_3)$
DeMorgan's Laws	$\neg S_1 \,\&\, \neg S_2 \Leftrightarrow \neg(S_1 \vee S_2)$
	$\neg S_1 \vee \neg S_2 \Leftrightarrow \neg(S_1 \,\&\, S_2)$
Double Negation	$S_1 \Leftrightarrow \neg\neg S_1$
Implication	$S_1 \rightarrow S_2 \Leftrightarrow \neg S_1 \vee S_2$
Contraposition	$S_1 \rightarrow S_2 \Leftrightarrow \neg S_2 \rightarrow \neg S_1$
Equivalence	$S_1 \leftrightarrow S_2 \Leftrightarrow (S_1 \,\&\, S_2) \vee (\neg S_1 \,\&\, \neg S_2)$
	$S_1 \leftrightarrow S_2 \Leftrightarrow (S_1 \rightarrow S_2) \,\&\, (S_2 \rightarrow S_1)$

Table 0.8.10 $(p \rightarrow q) \,\&\, (q \rightarrow r)$ logically implies $p \rightarrow r$.

p	q	r	$p \rightarrow q$	$q \rightarrow r$	$S_1 = (p \rightarrow q) \,\&\, (q \rightarrow r)$	$S_2 = p \rightarrow r$
T	T	T	T	T	T	T
T	T	F	T	F	F	F
T	F	T	F	T	F	T
T	F	F	F	T	F	F
F	T	T	T	T	T	T
F	T	F	T	F	F	T
F	F	T	T	T	T	T
F	F	F	T	T	T	T

Table 0.8.11   Some Important Logical Implications.

Name of Logical Implication	In Symbols
Hypothetical Syllogism	$(S_1 \rightarrow S_2) \,\&\, (S_2 \rightarrow S_3) \Rightarrow S_1 \rightarrow S_3$
Modus Ponens	$(S_1 \rightarrow S_2) \,\&\, S_1 \Rightarrow S_2$
Modus Tollens	$(S_1 \rightarrow S_2) \,\&\, \neg S_2 \Rightarrow \neg S_1$
Disjunctive Syllogism	$(S_1 \vee S_2) \,\&\, \neg S_1 \Rightarrow S_2$

Some additional terminology regarding conditionals will also be useful later. Consider the following conditional:

(19) If I have the day completely free, then I accomplish absolutely nothing.

Now consider these two related conditionals:

(20) If I accomplish absolutely nothing, then I must have had the day completely free.

(21) If I do not accomplish absolutely nothing, then I must not have had the day completely free.

We call conditional (20) the *converse* of conditional (19). A pair of truth tables can be used to show that a conditional $p \rightarrow q$ is not logically equivalent to its converse $q \rightarrow p$. Conditional (21), on the other hand, is the *contrapositive* of conditional (19). The reader should verify, by creating a pair of tables, that conditional $p \rightarrow q$ is logically equivalent to its contrapositive $\neg q \rightarrow \neg p$ (see Table 0.8.9).

§0.9 Two Important Proof Techniques

In this section we consider two important ways in proofs can be structured. The first of these is sometimes known as *conditional proof.*

Conditional Proof

Suppose that I want to convince you that if Jones is elected, then the treasury will be bankrupted. You may imagine me arguing as follows.

> Well, suppose for the moment that Jones is elected. Given his penchant for partying, it follows that he will spend vast amounts on the annual banquet. Besides, given his slackness in supervising his subordinates, you know there will be widespread corruption. Furthermore, ... (I go on to list additional undesirable certainties that will be the result of Jones' prodigal character and spendthrift ways.) It follows that the treasury will be depleted. Therefore, I conclude, if Jones is elected, then the treasury will be depleted.

We reason this way in mathematics whenever our goal is to demonstrate or prove a proposition whose form is that of a conditional—that is, something of the form $p \rightarrow q$. In such a case, we begin, as in the example above concerning Jones, by assuming the truth of antecedent p. Our goal is then to reason to the truth of consequent q. That is, we show that if p is true, then q is also true, which amounts to showing that conditional $p \rightarrow q$ is true.

To illustrate this proof technique, we prove two propositions concerning directed graphs that will be of use later.

THEOREM 0.5: Let u and v be distinct vertices of digraph G. If there is a path from u to v in G, then there is an acyclic path from u to v in G.

PROOF If there are paths from u to v, then there must be some shortest such paths—that is, paths such that no other path from u to v is shorter. Suppose that the shortest paths from u to v are of length n and that $x_1 x_2 \ldots x_n x_{n+1}$, where $x_1 = u$ and $x_{n+1} = v$, is one such path. Let us call this path P. Suppose that, for some distinct i and j with $1 \leq i, j \leq n+1$, $x_i = x_j$. Then that portion of P from x_i to x_j inclusive, namely, $x_i x_{i+1} \ldots x_j$, is a closed path. The path $x_1 \ldots x_i x_{j+1} \ldots x_{n+1}$, formed from P by omitting this closed portion, is yet a path from u to v (see Figure 0.9.1). However, its length is strictly less than n, which contradicts P's being a shortest path. We conclude that every node in $x_1 x_2 \ldots x_n x_{n+1}$ must be distinct, which means that $x_1 x_2 \ldots x_n x_{n+1}$ is acyclic. Q.E.D.

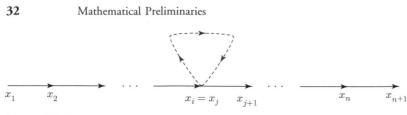

Figure 0.9.1

COROLLARY 0.1: If there is a closed path from vertex v to v in digraph G, then there is a cycle from v to v.

PROOF If G has an edge from v to v, then that edge itself constitutes a cycle and we are done. Otherwise, there is a closed path of the form $x_1 x_2 \ldots x_n x_{n+1}$ in G with $v = x_1 = x_{n+1}$ and $x_n \neq v = x_1 = x_{n+1}$ (why?). But then, since $x_1 x_2 \ldots x_n$ describes a path from x_1 to x_n with $x_1 \neq x_n$, by Theorem 0.5 there exists an acyclic path P from $v = x_1$ to x_n. Since P is acyclic, no vertex occurs twice within P. In particular, vertex $v = x_1 = x_{n+1}$ occurs only once within P. Appending the edge $\langle x_n, v \rangle$ to P produces the desired cycle.   Q.E.D.

The second technique that we consider is called *indirect proof.*

Indirect Proof

Suppose that I wish to convince you that 11 is a prime number. I might reason as follows:

> Well, suppose that 11 is *not* prime. Then it must have a nontrivial factor. But it is not 2, it is not 3, it is not 4, . . . , and it is not 10. But that is a contradiction, since factors of a number must in general be smaller than n. Thus, you see 11 must be prime after all.

This proof technique is also called *reductio ad absurdum* or *proof by contradiction* and is widely used within mathematics. Indirect proofs are especially appropriate when the proposition p that one wishes to prove is relatively unstructured—for example, a simple existence claim to the effect that some number having a certain property exists. One proceeds, as in the preceding example concerning 11, by assuming the truth of the negation of the proposition to be proved—that is, by assuming that $\neg p$ is true. The goal is then to derive any contradiction—that is, any sentence of the form $q \ \& \ \neg q$. In other words, having assumed that p is true, we have been led to conclude that contradiction $q \ \& \ \neg q$ is true as well, which is patently absurd. We conclude that $\neg p$ cannot be true, which is to say that p must itself be true. (One says that $\neg p$ is true "upon pain of contradiction.") As a first illustration of indirect proof, we prove the so-called Pigeonhole Principle.

THEOREM 0.6 (The Pigeonhole Principle): If a finite set S is partitioned into n sets, then at least one of the sets has at least $\lceil card(S)/n \rceil$ elements.

PROOF (indirect). Suppose for the sake of proving a contradiction that S is partitioned into $S_1, S_2, \ldots, S_n$, each of which has strictly fewer than $\lceil card(S)/n \rceil$ elements. It then follows that

$$card(S_i) \leq \lfloor card(S)/n \rfloor \tag{0.9.1}$$

for $1 \leq i \leq n$. There are two cases to consider.

First, suppose that $card(S) \, mod \, n$ is equal to 0 so that $\lfloor card(S)/n \rfloor = card(S)/n = \lceil card(S)/n \rceil$. Then, since $S_1, S_2, \ldots, S_n$ are mutually disjoint, we can write

$$card(S) = card(S_1) + card(S_2) + \cdots + card(S_n)$$
$$< \underbrace{\lceil card(S)/n \rceil + \lceil card(S)/n \rceil + \cdots + \lceil card(S)/n \rceil}_{n \text{ times}} \quad \text{by hypothesis}$$
$$= card(S)/n + card(S)/n + \cdots + card(S)/n$$
$$= n \cdot (card(S)/n)$$
$$= card(S)$$

which is an obvious contradiction.[4]

The other case arises when $card(S) \, mod \, n$ is not equal to 0. In that case, we have

$$\lfloor card(S)/n \rfloor < card(S)/n < \lceil card(S)/n \rceil \tag{0.9.2}$$

and we can write

$$card(S) = card(S_1) + card(S_2) + \cdots + card(S_n)$$
$$\leq \underbrace{\lfloor card(S)/n \rfloor + \lfloor card(S)/n \rfloor + \cdots + \lfloor card(S)/n \rfloor}_{n \text{ times}} \quad \text{by (0.9.1)}$$
$$= n \cdot \lfloor card(S)/n \rfloor$$
$$< n \cdot card(S)/n \quad\quad\quad\quad\quad\quad\quad\quad \text{by (0.9.2)}$$
$$= card(S)$$

which, once again, is a clear contradiction. We conclude that if S is partitioned into $S_1, S_2, \ldots, S_n$, then at least one of $S_1, S_2, \ldots, S_n$ has $\lceil card(S)/n \rceil$ or more elements. Q.E.D.

We mention an alternative, more suggestive, specialization of the Pigeonhole Principle: If $n + 1$ objects are each to receive one of a possible n colors, then at least two objects must receive one and the same color.

As additional examples of indirect proofs, we present proofs of two propositions from number theory.

THEOREM 0.7: There exists no upper bound on the difference between consecutive perfect squares. That is, there exists no natural number K such that, for all $n \in \mathcal{N}$, $(n + 1)^2 - n^2 \leq K$.

PROOF (indirect). Suppose that there exists a fixed K such that $(n + 1)^2 - n^2 \leq K$ for all n. We may assume without loss of generality that K is even. (If K happens to be odd, then we can use

---

[4]To see that a contradiction of the form $q \, \& \, \neg q$ is hereby derivable, we have only to put $card(S) < card(S)$ together with formula $card(S) \geq card(S)$, which is obviously true. Clearly, the latter is the negation of the former so that their conjunction is of the form $q \, \& \, \neg q$.

$K + 1$ here, since $K + 1$ will be even and will also be an upper bound.) But now, for all n, $2n + 1 = (n + 1)^2 - n^2 \leq K$. Substituting $n = K/2$, we have that $K + 1 = 2[K/2] + 1 \leq K$, which is surely a contradiction. We conclude that such a K cannot exist.   Q.E.D.

We note the following equivalent formulation of the preceding theorem.

> **THEOREM 0.7 (Alternative Formulation):** Given any natural number m, there exists natural number k such that $(k + 1)^2 - k^2 > m$.

We can use this result in proving the following proposition.

> **THEOREM 0.8:** There can exist no natural numbers n and m such that $n + im$ is a perfect square for all $i \in \mathcal{N}$. That is, there exist no natural numbers n and m such that all of $n, n + m, n + 2m, n + 3m, \ldots$ are perfect squares.

PROOF (indirect). Suppose that there do exist natural numbers n and m such that all of

$$n, n + m, n + 2m, n + 3m, \ldots \tag{0.9.3}$$

are perfect squares. Note that the difference between successive terms in this sequence is invariably m. By Theorem 0.7 (alternative formulation), there exists a k such that $(k + 1)^2 - k^2 > m$. That is, the difference between this k^2 and the *very next* perfect square exceeds m. For some i, we have $n + im \leq k^2 < n + (i + 1) \cdot m$. We then see that $[n + (i + 1) \cdot m] - k^2 \leq m$. (This follows from the fact that the difference between the member on the left and the member on the right in this inequality is m.) But this contradicts what was just stated, namely, that the difference between this k^2 and the very next perfect square exceeds m. We conclude that there can be no natural numbers n and m such that every term at (0.9.3) is a perfect square.   Q.E.D.

§0.10 Defining Sets Recursively

In a previous section of this chapter, we considered several ways in which a set might be defined. These included enumeration, quasi-enumeration, and the use of the set abstraction operator. In the present section we shall introduce one more very important technique for defining sets, namely, *definition by recursion*.

We call the reader's attention once again to our earlier characterization of the symbol set Σ_{PL}—an infinite alphabet consisting of (i) sentence letters $p, q, r, p', q', r', \ldots$, (ii) the five propositional connectives $\neg$, $\vee$, &, $\rightarrow$, and $\Leftrightarrow$, and (iii) signs of aggregation (), [], and {}. A notion of *well-formedness* for words over Σ_{PL} is embodied in our informal understanding of the five connectives. For example, the strings $((p \vee q) \leftrightarrow \neg r)$ and $((p \rightarrow (q \rightarrow r)) \& s)$ are intuitively well-formed—they make sense—whereas the strings $(p \& (q \rightarrow r)$ and $pq \leftrightarrow$ are not. We should like to define the set of all *well-formed formulas* (wffs) of propositional logic. First, we need a *base clause* or *initial clause* so as to introduce all the simplest wffs.

(i) Any sentence letter $p, q, r, p', q', r', \ldots$ by itself is a wff.

Now we present an *inductive* or *recursive clause* that enables us to start with simple wffs and construct more complex wffs from them. There are five ways of constructing more complex wffs—one for each of the five propositional connectives.

(ii) If S_1 and S_2 are wffs, then so is each of $\neg S_1, (S_1 \vee S_2), (S_1 \,\&\, S_2), (S_1 \rightarrow S_2)$, and $(S_1 \leftrightarrow S_2)$.

Finally, clause (iii) below is the *terminal* or *extremal clause* of the definition. It says that nothing more is a member of the set of wffs.

(iii) No string of symbols is a wff unless this can be seen from clauses (i) and (ii).

A set definition such as (i)–(iii) is called a *recursive* (or *inductive*) *definition*. Symbols S_1 and S_2 as they occur in clause (ii), range over Σ_{PL}^*—that is, the set of all words over alphabet Σ_{PL}. In other words, they are variables whose values can be not numbers but, rather, words (or, really, word types). By virtue of this fact, we shall refer to S_1 and S_2 as *syntactic variables*. We illustrate their function by showing how clauses (i)–(iii) imply that $((p \vee q) \leftrightarrow \neg r)$ is a wff. First, by clause (i), each of p, q, and r are wffs. Next, by (ii), $\neg r$ is a wff. Also, by (ii) again, $(p \vee q)$ is a wff. Finally, since both $(p \vee q)$ and $\neg r$ are wffs, so is $((p \vee q) \leftrightarrow \neg r)$, letting S_1 be $(p \vee q)$ and S_2 be $\neg r$ in (ii).[5]

In this application of (ii) we are letting S_1 be r.

This time S_1 is p and S_2 is q.

§0.11 Infinite Sets

In general, we have no difficulty in classifying sets as either finite or infinite. Thus the set of nations currently represented in the United Nations is a finite set, whereas the set $\mathcal{N}$ of natural numbers, the set of prime numbers, or the set of real numbers is an infinite set. But how might we define *infinite set*? We might give an operational definition of *finite set* in terms of our ability in principle to reach the end of an enumeration process and then define the infinite sets as those that are not finite. But this sort of definition would not be useful mathematically; in fact, it would not be a *mathematical* definition at all, referring as it does to human abilities. So what sort of mathematical definition of infinity is available to us? The one that we shall present below appeals to our concepts of proper subset and bijective function. As a motivating example, note that the set $\mathcal{E} = \{n \in \mathcal{N} | n \text{ is even}\}$ is a proper subset of $\mathcal{N}$ and that the function

$$f: \mathcal{N} \rightarrow \mathcal{E}$$
$$f(n) = 2n$$

is a bijection of $\mathcal{N}$ onto $\mathcal{E}$—that is, a bijection of $\mathcal{N}$ onto a proper subset of itself. This possibility of mapping a set onto a proper subset of itself is a distinguishing feature of the sets that we describe as infinite

---

[5]The reader will have noted that clause (iii) was not used in our demonstration that $((p \vee q) \leftrightarrow \neg r)$ is a wff. In fact, (iii) comes into play only when we wish to show that some word over Σ_{PL} is *not* a wff. See Exercise 0.10.2.

sets; no such possibility exists for any finite set. Thus we shall say that a set S is (*Dedekind-*)*infinite*[6] if and only if there exists a proper subset S' of S and a bijection f from S onto S'. More symbolically,

$$inf(S) \Leftrightarrow_{\text{def.}} \text{ there exists an } f \text{ and an } S' \text{ such that } S' \subset S \text{ \& } f\colon S \overset{1-1}{\rightarrow} S'$$

A set that is not (Dedekind-)infinite will be termed (*Dedekind-*)*finite*.

In the late nineteenth century, mathematicians began to distinguish among different "orders" of infinity. The lowest such order of infinity is provided by the so-called *countable sets*. If there exists a bijection between $\mathcal{N}$ and some set S, then S is said to be *countably infinite*. A set S that is either finite or countably infinite is said to be *countable*.

DEFINITION 0.9: Let S be a set. Then S is said to be *countably infinite* if there exists a bijection that maps $\mathcal{N}$ onto S.

DEFINITION 0.10: Let S be a set. Then S is *countable* or *enumerable* if it is either finite or countably infinite.

Clearly, $\mathcal{N}$ is itself countable since the identity function $1_{\mathcal{N}}\colon \mathcal{N} \rightarrow \mathcal{N}$ with $1_{\mathcal{N}}(n) = n$ is a bijection from $\mathcal{N}$ onto $\mathcal{N}$. $\mathcal{Z}$ is shown countable by the diagram of a bijection f from $\mathcal{N}$ to $\mathcal{Z}$ (see Figure 0.11.1). We shall now use the fact that $\mathcal{Z}$ is countable to show that $\mathcal{Q}$ is countable as well. Consider Figure 0.11.2, where the rows are labeled by members of $\mathcal{Z}$ and columns are labeled by $\mathcal{Z}\backslash\{0\}$. The entry in row -3 and column 2 is the fraction whose numerator is -3 and whose denominator is 2—that is, the rational number $-3/2$. Note that every member of $\mathcal{Q}$ will appear as an entry of this chart—in fact, infinitely many times. So, for example, rational $-3/2$ also occurs in row -6 and column 4, in row -12 and column 8, and so on. The entries in the chart may be enumerated by listing them in the order suggested by the path indicated in Figure 0.11.2. Next, imagine that this enumeration is revised so as to eliminate duplication: Only the first occurrence of a given rational is retained. The revised list corresponds to a bijection f of $\mathcal{N}$ onto $\mathcal{Q}$: Let $f(0)$ be the first rational on the list, let $f(1)$ be the second, and so on. The existence of this bijection, in turn, implies the countability of $\mathcal{Q}$.

The foregoing might suggest that all infinite sets are countably infinite. But that is not the case. The great nineteenth-century mathematician Georg Cantor showed that in fact $\mathcal{R}$, although infinite, is not countably infinite. In other words, $\mathcal{R}$ is an *uncountable* set. We present Cantor's celebrated "diagonal" proof below. In fact, we shall show only that $[0, 1]$—the closed interval from 0 to 1 on the real number line—is uncountable, from which it follows immediately that $\mathcal{R}$ itself is uncountable as well. Our

Figure 0.11.1 $\mathcal{Z}$ is countable.

---

[6]German mathematician Richard Dedekind (1831–1916) completed his doctoral dissertation at Göttingen under Carl Friedrich Gauss (1777–1855). He was among the first to give a rigorous characterization of the real number system and did important work in number theory and algebra.

	1	-1	2	-2	3	-3	4	-4	5	. . .
0	0/1	0/-1	0/2	0/-2	0/3	0/-3	0/4	0/-4	0/5	. . .
1	1/1	1/-1	1/2	1/-2	1/3	1/-3	1/4	1/-4	1/5	. . .
-1	-1/1	-1/-1	-1/2	-1/-2	-1/3	-1/-3	-1/4	-1/-4	-1/5	. . .
2	2/1	2/-1	2/2	2/-2	2/3	2/-3	2/4	2/-4	2/5	. . .
-2	-2/1	-2/-1	-2/2	-2/-2	-2/3	-2/-3	-2/4	-2/-4	-2/5	. . .
3	3/1	3/-1	3/2	3/-2	3/3	3/-3	3/4	3/-4	3/5	. . .
-3	-3/1	-3/-1	-3/2	-3/-2	-3/3	-3/-3	-3/4	-3/-4	-3/5	. . .
4	4/1	4/-1	4/2	4/ 2	4/3	4/ 3	4/4	4/ 4	4/5	. . .
-4	-4/1	-4/-1	-4/2	-4/-2	-4/3	-4/-3	-4/4	-4/-4	-4/5	. . .
5	5/1	5/-1	5/2	5/-2	5/3	5/-3	5/4	5/-4	5/5	. . .

Figure 0.11.2 $\mathcal{Q}$ is countable.

proof is indirect. As a preliminary, we recall that each number in $[0, 1]$ has a decimal expansion (either repeating or not repeating) $d_1 d_2 d_3 d_4 \ldots$, where each d_j here is a decimal digit—that is, a member of $\{0, 1, 2, 3, 4, 5, 6, 7, 8, 9\}$. Thus the decimal expansion of $\pi/4$ commences $0.7853\ldots$. In order to facilitate the proof that follows, we introduce some new notation. Let us write $(\pi/4)^n$ for the nth digit in the decimal expansion of $\pi/4$, where we begin counting with the 0th digit. Thus we see that $(\pi/4)^0$ is 7, $(\pi/4)^1$ is 8, $(\pi/4)^2$ is 5, $(\pi/4)^3$ is 3, and so on. Since $1.0 = .999\ldots$, we see that $(1.0)^n$ is 9 for all $n \geq 0$.

THEOREM 0.9: $[0, 1]$ is uncountable. That is, it is infinite but not countably infinite.

PROOF (indirect). Suppose, for the sake of deriving a contradiction, that $[0, 1]$ were countably infinite. By definition, this means that there exists a 1–1 correspondence f between $\mathcal{N}$ and $[0, 1]$. That is, f maps each natural number n onto some real number in $[0, 1]$ in such a way that (1) no two distinct natural numbers n and m are mapped onto one and the same real and (2) every real in $[0,1]$ is the image under f of some member of $\mathcal{N}$. Let $r_0 = f(0)$ be the real number in $[0, 1]$ associated with natural number 0, let $r_1 = f(1)$ be the real in $[0, 1]$ associated with natural number 1, and so on. Thus we can enumerate $[0, 1]$ as

$$r_0, r_1, r_2, r_3, r_4, r_5, r_6, \ldots \tag{0.11.1}$$

Also, the decimal expansion of each member of $[0, 1]$ appears as one row of the chart in Figure 0.11.3.

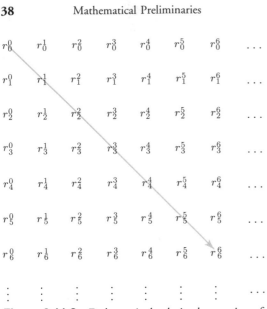

r_0^0 r_0^1 r_0^2 r_0^3 r_0^4 r_0^5 r_0^6 . . .

r_1^0 r_1^1 r_1^2 r_1^3 r_1^4 r_1^5 r_1^6 . . .

r_2^0 r_2^1 r_2^2 r_2^3 r_2^4 r_2^5 r_2^6 . . .

r_3^0 r_3^1 r_3^2 r_3^3 r_3^4 r_3^5 r_3^6 . . .

r_4^0 r_4^1 r_4^2 r_4^3 r_4^4 r_4^5 r_4^6 . . .

r_5^0 r_5^1 r_5^2 r_5^3 r_5^4 r_5^5 r_5^6 . . .

r_6^0 r_6^1 r_6^2 r_6^3 r_6^4 r_6^5 r_6^6 . . .

$\vdots$ $\vdots$ $\vdots$ $\vdots$ $\vdots$ $\vdots$ $\vdots$ . . .

Figure 0.11.3   Each row is the decimal expansion of one member of $[0, 1]$.

Next, let us denote by δ the infinite decimal defined in terms of our enumeration (0.11.1) as

$$\delta^n = \begin{cases} 7 & \text{if } r_n^n \text{ is } 3 \quad \text{(i)} \\ 3 & \text{otherwise} \quad \text{(ii)} \end{cases} \qquad (0.11.2)$$

What we shall show is that δ, although a real in $[0, 1]$, will not be in the enumeration (0.11.1). For suppose that δ were in (0.11.1). That is, suppose that δ were r_k for some particular k. This would mean that the decimal expansion of $\delta = r_k$ would appear in the kth row of Figure 0.11.3. A problem arises with regard to the kth digit δ^k of δ. Supposing that r_k^k is 0, say, then δ^k must also be 0 also since δ just *is* r_k. But by clause (ii) of (0.11.2), δ^k must be 3 in this case. Evidently this is a contradiction since δ^k cannot be *both* 0 and 3. Similarly, if we suppose that r_k^k is 3, then clause (i) of (0.11.2) gives rise to a contradiction, and so on. In short, the decimal expansion of δ can appear as a row of Figure 0.11.3 only upon pain of contradiction, as one says. And that is just to say that δ does not appear at (0.11.1). But since δ is a well-defined real number as soon as we assume the existence of enumeration (0.11.1), we are forced to conclude that no such enumeration of $[0, 1]$ can, in fact, exist. In other words, $[0, 1]$ is not countable after all.   Q.E.D.

§0.12 Conjunctive Normal Form

By the equivalences called Associativity we have that $(p \vee q) \vee r \Leftrightarrow p \vee (q \vee r)$ and $(p \& q) \& r \Leftrightarrow p \& (q \& r)$. This means that we can write $p \vee q \vee r$ and $p \& q \& r$ with impunity. For, whereas both connectives here are binary, which means that, strictly speaking, one or the other grouping must be chosen, it really makes no difference which grouping we choose. The result of grouping one way is equivalent to the result of grouping the other way. So in the future we can replace $(p \vee (q \vee (r \vee (s \vee (t \vee u)))))$ and $(p \& (q \& (r \& (s \& (t \& u)))))$ with the simpler $p \vee q \vee r \vee s \vee t \vee u$ and $p \& q \& r \& s \& t \& u$.

Incidentally, this indifference with regard to grouping disjuncts makes possible an alternative notation for disjunctions of indexed families of literals. Thus we shall write $\bigvee_{1 \le i \le r}\{p_i\}$ for the disjunction $p_1 \vee p_2 \vee \cdots \vee p_{r-1} \vee p_r$. Similarly, given the associativity of &, we shall write $\bigwedge_{1 \le i \le r}\{p_i\}$ for the conjunction $p_1 \& p_2 \& \cdots \& p_{r-1} \& p_r$.

Next, consider the following sentences of the language of propositional logic:

(1) $(p \vee q) \& (r \vee s)$

(2) $(p \vee \neg q) \& (r \vee s) \& (\neg p \vee q \vee r)$

Note that (1) and (2) may both be described as conjunctions of disjunctions of (possibly negated) sentence letters. We are going to say that such sentences are in *conjunctive normal form* (*CNF*) or, more simply, are *CNFs*. Note that the definition is purely syntactic or *formal*, speaking only of what such sentences *look like* and making no reference whatever to truth, which is a semantic concept.

While we are at it, it will prove useful to have the dual notion of *disjunctive normal form* (*DNF*). These sentences may be described informally as disjunctions of conjunctions of (possibly negated) sentence letters (see Exercise 0.12.4).

The foregoing definition of conjunctive normal form is basically correct. However, we wish to enlarge the class of CNFs so as to include, in addition, sentences such as p, $\neg p$, $p \& \neg q$, and $p \vee \neg r$ as degenerate cases—"honorary" CNFs, if you will.

DEFINITION 0.11: A *literal* is either a sentence letter or a negated sentence letter. Thus the following are literals: p, $\neg p$, q, $\neg q$, and so on.

DEFINITION 0.12:

   (i) A literal by itself is a *clause*.
   (ii) If $A_1, A_2, \ldots, A_n$ are all *clauses*, then so is $(A_1 \vee A_2 \vee \cdots \vee A_n)$.
   (iii) Nothing else is a *clause* except what can be obtained from (i) and (ii).

Finally, here is the new, formal definition of conjunctive normal form.

DEFINITION 0.13:

   (i) A clause by itself is a CNF.
   (ii) If $A_1, A_2, \ldots, A_n$ are all CNFs, then so is $(A_1 \& A_2 \& \cdots \& A_n)$.
   (iii) Nothing else is a CNF except what can be obtained from (i) and (ii).

We shall regularly drop outermost parentheses and write $A_1 \& A_2 \& \cdots \& A_n$ for $(A_1 \& A_2 \& \cdots \& A_n)$. We shall also introduce additional signs of aggregation to enhance readability.

Evidently, each of p, $\neg p$, $p \& \neg q$, and $p \vee \neg r$ is a CNF in accordance with Definition 0.13. It is equally obvious that the sentence

(3) $(p \rightarrow q) \& [\neg p \& \neg(\neg r \& q)]$

is not a CNF. Nonetheless, sentence (3) is equivalent to a sentence that is a CNF since we have

$$(p \to q) \ \& \ [\neg p \ \& \ \neg(\neg r \ \& \ q)]$$

$$\Leftrightarrow (\neg p \vee q) \ \& \ [\neg p \ \& \ \neg(\neg r \ \& \ q)] \qquad \text{by Implication}$$

$$\Leftrightarrow (\neg p \vee q) \ \& \ [\neg p \ \& \ (\neg\neg r \vee \neg q)] \qquad \text{by DeMorgan}$$

$$\Leftrightarrow (\neg p \vee q) \ \& \ \neg p \ \& \ (r \vee \neg q)] \qquad \text{by Double Negation}$$

Note that the final line here is in CNF. In fact, given a sentence S, it is always possible to obtain an equivalent CNF S'. That is, we can prove the following proposition.

THEOREM 0.10: Let S be a sentence of propositional logic. Then there is a sentence S' of propositional logic that is in CNF and such that $S \Leftrightarrow S'$.

Before proving Theorem 0.10, let us consider one more example so as to familiarize ourselves with the class of CNFs. Finding an equivalent CNF, in harder cases, invariably involves applying the equivalence Distributivity.

We illustrate Theorem 0.10 for the case of sentence $(p \leftrightarrow \neg q) \to r$ by writing

$$(p \leftrightarrow \neg q) \to r \Leftrightarrow [(p \ \& \ \neg q) \vee (\neg p \ \& \ \neg\neg q)] \to r \qquad \text{by Equivalence}$$

$$\Leftrightarrow [(p \ \& \ \neg q) \vee (\neg p \ \& \ q)] \to r \qquad \text{by Double Negation}$$

$$\Leftrightarrow \neg[(p \ \& \ \neg q) \vee (\neg p \ \& \ q)] \vee r \qquad \text{by Implication}$$

$$\Leftrightarrow [\neg(p \ \& \ \neg q) \ \& \ \neg(\neg p \ \& \ q)] \vee r \qquad \text{by DeMorgan}$$

$$\Leftrightarrow [(\neg p \vee \neg\neg q) \ \& \ (\neg\neg p \vee \neg q)] \vee r \qquad \text{by DeMorgan twice}$$

$$\Leftrightarrow [(\neg p \vee q) \ \& \ (p \vee \neg q)] \vee r \qquad \text{by Double Negation twice}$$

$$\Leftrightarrow r \vee [(\neg p \vee q) \ \& \ (p \vee \neg q)] \qquad \text{by Commutativity}$$

$$\Leftrightarrow (r \vee \neg p \vee q) \ \& \ (r \vee p \vee \neg q)] \qquad \text{by Distributivity}$$

Our work above suggests the following technique for transforming a sentence into an equivalent CNF.

TECHNIQUE FOR TRANSFORMING A SENTENCE S OF PROPOSITIONAL LOGIC INTO AN EQUIVALENT CNF:

- Eliminate $\to$ and $\leftrightarrow$ using Implication and Equivalence, respectively.
- Use DeMorgan to move $\neg$ inward past parentheses.
- Eliminate consecutive occurrences of $\neg$ using Double Negation.
- If the result of the preceding steps is still not a sentence in CNF, then try applying Distributivity.

We are now ready to prove our central theorem. But first the reader would do well to review the inductive definition of *sentence* (*wff*) *of propositional logic* given as clauses (i)–(iii) of §0.10.

PROOF OF THEOREM 0.10 (by induction on the number of connectives occurring in S).

Base case. Suppose that S is a sentence letter. Then S is itself already in CNF and of course $S \Leftrightarrow S$ trivially.

Inductive case. We divide the inductive case up into five subcases—one for each of our propositional connectives.

Subcase (1). Suppose that S is a conjunction. That is, suppose that S is of the form $A \mathbin{\&} B$. Of course, each of A and B must be of strictly lower complexity than S, of which they are proper subexpressions. Hence, by induction hypothesis, we may assume that A and B are each equivalent to CNFs A' and B', respectively. That is, $A \Leftrightarrow A'$ as well as $B \Leftrightarrow B'$. So $S(= A \mathbin{\&} B) \Leftrightarrow A \mathbin{\&} B \Leftrightarrow A' \mathbin{\&} B'$. Letting S' be $A' \mathbin{\&} B'$, we have our desired equivalent CNF, given that a conjunction of CNFs is itself a CNF.

Subcase (2). Suppose that S is a disjunction. That is, suppose that S is of the form $A \vee B$. Again, each of A and B must be of strictly lower complexity than S, of which they are proper subexpressions. Hence, by induction hypothesis, we may assume that A and B are each equivalent to CNFs A' and B', respectively. That is, $A \Leftrightarrow A'$ as well as $B \Leftrightarrow B'$. For simplicity, let us assume that A' is $(p \vee q) \mathbin{\&} (r \vee s)$ and that B' is $(t \vee u) \mathbin{\&} (w \vee y)$. So

$$S(= A \vee B) \Leftrightarrow A' \vee B'$$
$$\Leftrightarrow [(p \vee q) \mathbin{\&} (r \vee s)] \vee [(t \vee u) \mathbin{\&} (w \vee y)]$$
$$\Leftrightarrow \{[(p \vee q) \mathbin{\&} (r \vee s)] \vee (t \vee u)\}$$
$$\mathbin{\&} \{[(p \vee q) \mathbin{\&} (r \vee s)] \vee (w \vee y)\} \qquad \text{by Distributivity}$$
$$\Leftrightarrow \{(t \vee u) \vee [(p \vee q) \mathbin{\&} (r \vee s)]\}$$
$$\mathbin{\&} \{(w \vee y) \vee [(p \vee q) \mathbin{\&} (r \vee s)]\} \qquad \text{by Commutativity}$$
$$\Leftrightarrow (t \vee u \vee p \vee q) \mathbin{\&} (t \vee u \vee r \vee s)$$
$$\mathbin{\&} (w \vee y \vee p \vee q) \mathbin{\&} (w \vee y \vee r \vee s)] \qquad \text{by Distributivity}$$

The other three subcases are left as exercises (see Exercise 0.12.5).   Q.E.D.

We next present the dual of Theorem 0.10.

THEOREM 0.11: Let S be a sentence of propositional logic. Then there is a sentence S' of propositional logic that is in DNF and such that $S \Leftrightarrow S'$.

Theorem 0.11 could be proved by induction on the number of sentential connectives occurring in S. On the other hand, an alternative proof is forthcoming from the following considerations.

It is not hard to see that a few applications of Distributivity can be used to transform a DNF $\mathcal{A}$ into an equivalent CNF $\mathcal{A}'$. In general, the length of $\mathcal{A}'$ may well exceed that of $\mathcal{A}$. We shall be especially interested in the relation between the length of DNF $\mathcal{A}$ and the length of equivalent CNF $\mathcal{A}'$. Consider the result of transforming the DNF $(p \mathbin{\&} q) \vee (r \mathbin{\&} s)$ into an equivalent CNF.

$$(p \,\&\, q) \vee (r \,\&\, s) \Leftrightarrow ((p \,\&\, q) \vee r) \,\&\, ((p \,\&\, q) \vee s) \qquad \text{by Distributivity}$$

$$\Leftrightarrow (r \vee (p \,\&\, q)) \,\&\, (s \vee (p \,\&\, q)) \qquad \text{by Commutativity}$$

$$\Leftrightarrow ((r \vee p) \,\&\, (r \vee q)) \,\&\, ((s \vee p) \,\&\, (s \vee q)) \quad \text{by Distributivity}$$

Note that DNF $(p \,\&\, q) \vee (r \,\&\, s)$, containing four occurrences of sentence letters, turns out to be equivalent to a CNF containing eight occurrences of sentence letters. These eight occurrences result from each of p and q being paired with each of r and s for a total of four pairings and, hence, $4 \cdot 2$ occurrences of sentence letters. Without loss of generality, we may refer to the number of occurring sentence letters in a sentence $\mathcal{A}$ of propositional logic as the *length* of $\mathcal{A}$. The reader can verify that the DNF $(p \,\&\, q) \vee (r \,\&\, s) \vee (t \,\&\, u)$ of length 6 is equivalent to the CNF

$$(p \vee r \vee t) \,\&\, (p \vee q \vee u) \,\&\, (q \vee r \vee t) \,\&\, (q \vee r \vee u) \,\&\, (p \vee s \vee t) \,\&\, (p \vee s \vee u) \,\&\, (q \vee s \vee t) \,\&\, (q \vee s \vee u)$$

of length 24. The combinatorial principle at work here is readily discernible. A DNF of length n whose $n/2$ disjuncts are each of length 2 is equivalent to a CNF of length $2^{n/2} \cdot n/2$.

REMARK 0.12.1: A DNF $\mathcal{A}$ of length n, for sufficiently large n, is equivalent to a CNF of length $O(2^n \cdot n)$.

We cite the following dual:

REMARK 0.12.2: A CNF $\mathcal{A}$ of length n, for sufficiently large n, is equivalent to a DNF of length $O(2^n \cdot n)$.

---

§0.13 Number-Theoretic Predicates

Generally, one uses *predicates* to express properties of objects, relations holding between pairs of objects, relations holding among triples of objects, and so on. When the objects in question are members of $\mathcal{N}$ (i.e., the natural numbers), then one speaks of *number-theoretic predicates*.

- For example, *prime*(n) is a unary number-theoretic predicate that is *satisfied* by both 2 and 3, say, but that is not satisfied by 4 or 6.

- The binary number-theoretic predicate $n|m$ holds just in case m is a multiple of n so that $2|6$ and even $2|0$. On the other hand, $4|6$ is false. Note that $n|m$ is not the name of a number. If anything, $n|m$ denotes a truth value.

- As another example, we might define a binary number-theoretic predicate $cube\_of\,(n, m)$ by writing

$$cube\_of\,(n, m) \Leftrightarrow_{\text{def.}} n = m^3$$

so that $cube\_of\,(n, m)$ is satisfied by the ordered pairs $\langle 27, 3 \rangle$ and $\langle 64, 4 \rangle$ but not by the ordered pairs $\langle 8, 3 \rangle$ or $\langle 4, 64 \rangle$, say.

We shall write $C(n_1, n_2, \ldots, n_k)$, or the like, for an arbitrary k-ary number-theoretic predicate, where the notation is intended to suggest a condition that may or may not be satisfied by k-tuple $\langle n_1, n_2, \ldots, n_k \rangle$.

The *extension of a unary number-theoretic predicate* is the set of all and only those natural numbers satisfying that predicate. For example, the extension of the predicate $prime(n)$ is the set $\{n \in \mathcal{N} | prime(n)\}$. More generally, the extension of a k-ary predicate $C(n_1, n_2, \ldots, n_k)$ is the set of all and only those k-tuples $\langle n_1, n_2, \ldots, n_k \rangle$ of natural numbers such that $C(n_1, n_2, \ldots, n_k)$ holds. In symbols, this extension is just $\{\langle n_1, n_2, \ldots, n_k \rangle \in \mathcal{N}^k | C(n_1, n_2, \ldots, n_k)\}$. We see that the extension of $cube\_of(n, m)$ is none other than the infinite set of ordered pairs $\{\langle 0, 0 \rangle, \langle 1, 1 \rangle, \langle 8, 2 \rangle, \langle 27, 3 \rangle, \langle 64, 4 \rangle, \ldots\}$.

Given k-ary number-theoretic predicates $C_1(n_1, n_2, \ldots, n_k)$ and $C_2(n_1, n_2, \ldots, n_k)$, we can form new k-ary number-theoretic predicates using the five propositional connectives $\neg$, &, $\vee$, $\rightarrow$, and $\leftrightarrow$. For example, k-ary predicate $C_1(n_1, n_2, \ldots, n_k)$ & $C_2(n_1, n_2, \ldots, n_k)$ will be satisfied by k-tuple $\langle n_1, n_2, \ldots, n_k \rangle$ just in case $\langle n_1, n_2, \ldots, n_k \rangle$ satisfies both $C_1(n_1, n_2, \ldots, n_k)$ and $C_2(n_1, n_2, \ldots, n_k)$. Similarly, k-ary predicate $C_1(n_1, n_2, \ldots, n_k) \rightarrow C_2(n_1, n_2, \ldots, n_k)$ will be satisfied by k-tuple $\langle n_1, n_2, \ldots, n_k \rangle$ just in case either $\langle n_1, n_2, \ldots, n_k \rangle$ does not satisfy predicate $C_1(n_1, n_2, \ldots, n_k)$ or $\langle n_1, n_2, \ldots, n_k \rangle$ does satisfy predicate $C_2(n_1, n_2, \ldots, n_k)$. The reader can see that this is strictly in accordance with the truth-table definitions of connectives & and $\rightarrow$. Predicates

$$C_1(n_1, n_2, \ldots, n_k) \vee C_2(n_1, n_2, \ldots, n_k)$$

$$C_1(n_1, n_2, \ldots, n_k) \leftrightarrow C_2(n_1, n_2, \ldots, n_k)$$

$$\neg C_1(n_1, n_2, \ldots, n_k)$$

are defined similarly.

A binary predicate $C(n_1, n_2)$ is said to be *reflexive* if, for any and all $n \in \mathcal{N}$, we have $C(n, n)$. A binary predicate $C(n_1, n_2)$ is said to be *symmetric* if, for any $n, m \in \mathcal{N}$, we have that $C(n, m)$ implies $C(m, n)$. Finally, if, for all $n, m, k \in \mathcal{N}$, we have that $C(n, m)$ and $C(m, k)$ together imply $C(n, k)$, then predicate $C(n_1, n_2)$ is said to be *transitive*. If $C(n_1, n_2)$ is reflexive, symmetric, and transitive, then it is said to express an *equivalence relation*.

Quantifiers may play a role in the specification of predicates. For our purposes, the *universal quantifier* consists of symbol $\forall$ followed by a variable from among $n, m, \ldots$ taken to range over the set $\mathcal{N}$. For example, if $C_1(n)$ is interpreted to mean that n is prime, then the statement

$$(\forall n)(C_1(n) \vee \neg C_1(n)) \longleftarrow$$

"Given any natural number n, either n is prime or n is not prime."

asserts that every natural number is either prime or not prime. Similarly, letting $C_2(n)$ mean that n is odd, the statement

$$(\forall n)((C_1(n) \text{ \& } n > 2) \rightarrow C_2(n)) \longleftarrow$$

"Given any natural number n, if n is prime and $n > 2$, then n is odd."

asserts that every prime greater than 2 is odd. The *existential quantifier* consists of symbol $\exists$ followed by a variable from among $n, m, \ldots$ again taken to range over $\mathcal{N}$. The statement

$$(\exists n)(C_1(n)\ \&\ \neg C_2(n)) \longleftarrow$$

> "There exists an n such that n is prime and n is not odd."

asserts the existence of an even prime, whereas

$$\neg(\exists n)(C_1(n)\ \&\ n > 2\ \&\ \neg C_2(n)) \longleftarrow$$

> "It is not the case that there exists an n such that n is prime and $n > 2$ and n is not odd."

says that no prime greater than 2 is even.

In general, if $C_1(n_1, n_2, \ldots, n_k)$ is a k-ary predicate with $k \geq 1$, then both $(\forall n_1)C_1(n_1, n_2, \ldots, n_k)$ and $(\exists n_1)C_1(n_1, n_2, \ldots, n_k)$ are $(k-1)$-ary predicates. For example, letting $k = 2$, we have binary predicate[7] $n < m$ and unary predicate $(\exists n)n < m$, the latter being satisfied by natural numbers $m = 1$, 2, 3, ... but not by $m = 0$. On the other hand, binary predicate $m \leq n$ gives rise to unary predicate $(\forall n)m \leq n$, the latter being true of $m = 0$ and nothing else. Combinations of two or more quantifiers may figure in predicates. For example, in 1742, Goldbach conjectured that the following unary predicate is satisfied by every natural number n:

$$[n \geq 4\ \&\ \neg C_2(n)] \rightarrow (\exists k)(\exists m)[C_1(k)\ \&\ C_1(m)\ \&\ n = k + m]$$

(As before, we are interpreting predicates $C_1(n_1)$ and $C_2(n_1)$ to mean that n_1 is prime and that n_1 is odd, respectively.)

We shall write $(\forall k \leq n)C(k)$ as an abbreviation of the universally quantified conditional $(\forall k)(k \leq n \rightarrow C(k))$. It is also standard to write $(\exists k \leq n)C(k)$ as an abbreviation of the existentially quantified conjunction $(\exists k)(k \leq n\ \&\ C(k))$.

We turn again to binary predicate $n|m$ in order to bring out one final point. Namely, whereas $n|0$ is true for all natural numbers n, we shall take $0|m$ to be false for all natural numbers m just because division by 0 is undefined. We do recognize an inclination to view predicate $n|m$ as itself undefined when $n = 0$—as neither true nor false. But we shall not adopt such an approach in this text. Rather, $0|m$ will be false just in the sense that it is *not true* that 0 divides m. In other words, we do not introduce any notion of partiality for number-theoretic predicates—in stark contrast to what was done in the case of number-theoretic functions. A k-ary number-theoretic predicate $C(n_1, n_2, \ldots, n_k)$ is either true of $\langle n_1, n_2, \ldots, n_k \rangle$ or it is false of $\langle n_1, n_2, \ldots, n_k \rangle$, and there is nothing more to be said.

§0.14 Further Reading

Much of the material contained in this preliminary chapter is covered in [Velleman 1994]. Many readers will no doubt benefit from Velleman's unique and careful presentation. His Chapter 6 on mathematical induction is especially good. Generally speaking, readers can expect to come away with a deepened understanding of the nature of mathematical proof.

Big-O, big-Omega, and big-Theta notation go back 100 years or so (see [Knuth 1976] or [Graham, Knuth, and Patashnik 1989]). Just for the sake of completeness, we mention so-called *little-o notation*. Thus function $f(n)$ is said to be $o(g(n))$ [read as "little o of g of n"] if, for *every* natural number $C \geq 1$,

---

[7] In the case of binary predicates $n \leq m$ and $n \geq m$, we opt for the usual infix notation, writing the symbol for the relation between the two variables. This option is available for binary predicates only.

there exists natural number n_0 with $f(n) \leq (1/C) \cdot g(n)$ for $n \geq n_0$. In other words, $f(n)$ grows more slowly than any small constant multiple of $g(n)$. As such, this is a stronger relation than that expressed by saying that $f(n)$ is said to be $O(g(n))$ (see Exercise 0.14.1). On the other hand, we have that $\log_2(n)$ is $o(n)$, that n is $o(n^2)$, that n^2 is $o(n^3)$, and so forth. So, in important cases, the relations expressed by big-O and little-o notation hold simultaneously. Unfortunately, there is no complete agreement among mathematicians regarding these notations. In fact, some writers (e.g., [Sommerhalder and van Westrhenen 1988]) define big-O notation using the definition we have just given for little-o notation.

EXERCISES FOR §0.1

0.1.1. (DeMorgan's laws).
 (a) Use the Principle of Extensionality to prove that, for any sets A and B, $(A \cap B)^c = A^c \cup B^c$.
 (b) Use the Principle of Extensionality to prove that, for any sets A and B, $(A \cup B)^c = A^c \cap B^c$.

0.1.2. (a) Use the Principle of Extensionality to prove that, for any sets A and B, $A \backslash B = (A \oplus B) \cap A$.
 (b) Use the Principle of Extensionality to prove that, for any sets A and B, $A \oplus B = (A \cup B) \backslash (A \cap B)$.
 (c) Use the Principle of Extensionality to prove that, for any set A, $(A^c)^c = A$.

0.1.3. Prove that, for any finite set S, $card(\mathcal{P}(S)) = 2^{card(S)}$.

0.1.4. **hwk** Prove that, for any finite sets A and B, $card(A \times B) = card(A) \cdot card(B)$.

0.1.5. Suppose that $\langle a_1, a_2, a_3, a_4, a_5 \rangle$ is $\langle 8, 12, 16, 20, 24 \rangle$ and that permutation $\langle a_{i_1}, a_{i_2}, a_{i_3}, a_{i_4}, a_{i_5} \rangle$ is $\langle 16, 24, 8, 12, 20 \rangle$. Identify i_1, i_2, i_3, i_4, and i_5.

EXERCISES FOR §0.2

0.2.1. List five elements in each of the following languages.
 (a) Σ^*, where $\Sigma = \{a, b, c\}$
 (b) $\{w \in \Sigma^* | length(w) \leq 2\}$, where $\Sigma = \{a, b\}$
 (c) $\{w \in \Sigma^* | length(w) = 4\}$, where $\Sigma = \{a, b\}$
 (d) $\{w \in \Sigma^* | length(w) = 4\}$, where $\Sigma = \{\alpha, \beta\}$
 (e) $\{a^n b | n \text{ is prime}\}$
   (The primes are 2, 3, 5, 7, 11, 13, ...)
 (f) Which sets in (a) through (e) above contain ε?

0.2.2. What is the cardinality of each of the following languages? Write ∞ if the language is infinite.
 (a) Σ^*, where $\Sigma = \{a, b, c\}$
 (b) $\{w \in \Sigma^* | length(w) = 4\}$, where $\Sigma = \{a, b, c\}$
 (c) $\{a^n b | n \geq 1\}$
 (d) $\{w \in \Sigma^* | length(w) = 2\}$, where $\Sigma = \{a, b, c, \ldots, z\}$

Remark. In Exercises 0.2.3 and 0.2.5, it is suggested that we regard the inscription ca, for example, as a *single* alphabet symbol. This may seem strange to you, since the a and the c are not connected. But consider that the letters i and j of the Roman alphabet each consist of two unconnected parts, and we have no difficulty in regarding *them* as single symbols.

0.2.3. Consider the following three alphabets: $\Sigma_1 = \{a, b, c\}$, $\Sigma_2 = \{a, b, ca\}$, and $\Sigma_3 = \{a, b, Ab\}$. Determine to which of Σ_1^*, Σ_2^*, Σ_3^* each word below belongs, and give its length as a member of each language to which it belongs.
 (a) aba
 (b) bAb
 (c) cba
 (d) cab
 (e) $caab$
 (f) $baAb$

0.2.4. Let $\Sigma = \{a, b, c, d\}$. List as many words as you can that are words in the language

$$\{w \in \Sigma^* | length(w) = 3 \text{ and } w \text{ happens to be a word of the English language}\}$$

For example, word $w = bad$ belongs to this language.

0.2.5. Let alphabet $\Sigma = \{ab, aa, baa\}$. Which of the following strings (words) are in Σ^*: *abaabaaabaa, aaaabaaaa, baaaaabaaaab*, and *baaaaabaa*?

0.2.6. Suppose w is a word of length n. How many prefixes does w have? How many suffixes? How many proper suffixes?

0.2.7. How many distinct substrings of length 4 are there in the case of the word *ababababababababababa*?

0.2.8. Suppose that w is ab and that w' is bab. Now identify each of the following words.
  (a) ww'
  (b) w^R
  (c) $(ww')^R$
  (d) ww'^R

0.2.9. ^hwk Which of the following are palindromes?
  (a) ww^R for any $w \in \Sigma^*$
  (b) w^R for any palindrome $w \in \Sigma^*$
  (c) ww for any palindrome $w \in \Sigma^*$
  (d) waw^R for any $w \in \Sigma^*$
  (e) $ww'w^R$ for any $w \in \Sigma^*$ and any palindrome $w' \in \Sigma^*$
  (f) ε

EXERCISES FOR §0.3

0.3.1. **(a)** Justify Remark 0.3.4.
  (b) Use Remarks 0.3.3 and 0.3.4 to show that, for positive reals x and y, we have $\log_2 xy = \log_2 x + \log_2 y$.

0.3.2. Let number-theoretic functions $f_1(n)$ and $f_2(n)$ be defined as $f_1(n) = n \bmod 12$ and $f_2(n) = n \bmod 14$.
  (a) Define $g(n) = max\{f_1(n), f_2(n)\}$. Evaluate $g(100)$ and $g(109)$.
  (b) What is the maximum value ever attained by g? Give an example of an argument n such that $g(n)$ will be maximal.
  (c) Define $h(n) = f_1(n) + f_2(n)$. Evaluate $h(100)$ and $h(109)$.
  (d) What is the maximum value ever attained by h? Give an example of an argument n such that $h(n)$ will be maximal.

0.3.3. Classify each of the following functions as injective or not injective, as surjective or not surjective, and also as bijective or not bijective.
  (a) $f: \mathcal{N} \to \mathcal{N}$

  $$f(n) = n \ div \ 3$$
  (b) $g: \mathcal{N} \to \mathcal{N}$

  $$g(n) = n^2 + 2n + 1$$
  (c) $h: \Sigma^* \to \Sigma^*$, where $\Sigma = \{a, b\}$

  $$h(w) = a^{n_a(w)}$$

  (d) $f: \mathcal{N} \to \mathcal{N}$

  $$f(n) = \begin{cases} n - 1 & \text{if } n \text{ is odd} \\ n + 1 & \text{otherwise} \end{cases}$$

0.3.4. ^hwk For what values of n are each of the following unary partial number-theoretic functions defined?
  (a) $f(n) = \sqrt[3]{n}$
  (b) $f(n) = n/3$
  (c) $f(n) = \log_2 n$
  (d) $f(n) = n - 1$

0.3.5. Consider the polynomial $4n^3 - 8n^2 + 3$.
  (a) What is the degree of this polynomial?
  (b) What is the coefficient of the highest-degree term—that is, the so-called *leading coefficient*?
  (c) What is the coefficient of the term of degree 1? That is, what is coefficient a_1?
  (d) What is the coefficient of the term of degree 0? That is, what is coefficient a_0?
  (e) Evaluate polynomial $4n^3 - 8n^2 + 3$ for $n = 2$.
  (f) Is polynomial function $p: \mathcal{N} \to \mathcal{N}$ with $p(n) = 4n^3 - 8n^2 + 3$ a total number-theoretic function?

EXERCISE FOR §0.4

0.4.1. **(a)** Write a recursive subroutine in Pascal or C language that computes the unary function fib of Example 0.4.1.

(b) Write an iterative, nonrecursive subroutine in Pascal or C language for computing fib.

EXERCISES FOR §0.5

0.5.1. Characterize each of the functions whose graphs appear in Figure 0.5.2 as monotone increasing, strictly monotone increasing, or neither.

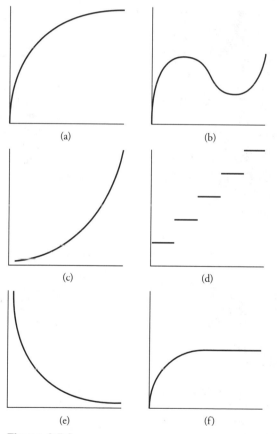

(a)

(b)

(c)

(d)

(e)

(f)

Figure 0.5.2

0.5.2. A binary number-theoretic function $f(n, m)$ is *strictly monotone in its first argument* if $n < k$ implies $f(n, m) < f(k, m)$. Similarly, binary number-theoretic function $f(n, m)$ is *monotone in its second argument* if $m < k$ implies $f(n, m) \leq f(n, k)$. Using the new terminol-

ogy, characterize completely each of the following binary functions. Unless otherwise indicated, the function's domain is taken to be $\mathcal{N}^2$.

(a) $f(n, m) = n + m$
(b) $g(n, m) = n \cdot m$
(c) $h(n, m) = n - m$ with $h\colon \mathcal{Z}^2 \to \mathcal{Z}$
(d) $j(n, m) = n\ div\ m$ with $j\colon \mathcal{N} \times (\mathcal{N}\backslash\{0\}) \to \mathcal{N}$
(e) $k(n, m) = n\ mod\ m$ with $j\colon \mathcal{N} \times (\mathcal{N}\backslash\{0\}) \to \mathcal{N}$
(f) $f(n, m) = n^m$

0.5.3. Which of the following functions are $O(1)$?
(a) $f(n) = \lceil \log_2 n \rceil$
(b) $g(n) = \lfloor \log_{10} n \rfloor$
(c) $h(n) = min(n, 100)$
(d) $j(n) = 4n^2 + 7n + 3$
(e) $k(n) = 5n^5 + n^3 + n + 68$

0.5.4. Find a necessary and sufficient condition for a number-theoretic function f being $O(0)$. In other words, what sort of function is going to be $O(0)$?

0.5.5. **(a)** Prove that the relation that holds between function f and g such that $f(n)$ if $O(g(n))$ is a transitive relation. That is, show that if $f(n)$ is $O(g(n))$ and $g(n)$ is $O(h(n))$, then $f(n)$ is $O(h(n))$.

(b) Prove that if $f(n)$ is $O(g(n))$, then, for any constant c, we have $c \cdot f(n)$ is $O(g(n))$ as well.

(c) Prove that if $f(n)$ and $g(n)$ are both $O(h(n))$, then function $f(n) + g(n)$ is $O(h(n))$ as well.

0.5.6. **(a)** Show that for all $n \in \mathcal{N}$ with $n > 0$, we have $n \leq 2^{n-1}$. (*Hint:* Verify the inequality for small values of n. For $n \geq 4$, n may be written as the product $2 \cdot \frac{3}{2} \cdot \frac{4}{3} \cdot \cdots \cdot \frac{n-1}{n-2} \cdot \frac{n}{n-1}$.)

(b) Use (a) to prove that $\log_2 x < x$ for all real $x > 0$. (*Hint:* Apply (a) to $\lceil x \rceil$.)

0.5.7. (a) Show that $n!$ is $O(n^n)$. (*Hint:* Write out $n!$ as the product of n factors.)

   (b) Show that $n \cdot \log_2 n$ is $O(n \cdot \sqrt{n})$.

0.5.8. **hwk** For each number-theoretic function $f(n)$ listed below, find the smallest natural number k such that $f(n)$ is $O(n^k)$.

   (a) $f(n) = 5n^2 + 7n - 6$

   (b) $f(n) = (n + 4)(n + 3)(n^2 + 4n - 2)$

   (c) $f(n) = (5n^2 + 7n - 6)^4$

   (d) $f(n) = \lfloor \sqrt[3]{n + 2} \rfloor$

   (e) $f(n) = \lfloor \sqrt[3]{4n^5 + 1} \rfloor$

0.5.9. Consider the sequence of number-theoretic functions given by

$$0, 1, \lfloor \log_2 n \rfloor, \ldots, \sqrt[4]{n}, \sqrt[3]{n}, \sqrt[2]{n}, n,$$

$$n \cdot \lfloor \log_2 n \rfloor, n \cdot \lfloor \sqrt[2]{n} \rfloor, n^2, n^3, n^4, \ldots, 2^n, n!, n^n$$

For each number-theoretic function $f(n)$ listed below, give the leftmost member $g(n)$ of the above sequence such that $f(n)$ is $O(g(n))$. Justify your answer with reference to Theorems 0.1, 0.2(a), and 0.2(b) and Exercises 0.5.5 and 0.5.7 when possible.

   (a) $f(n) = 3^n$

   (b) $f(n) = n^3 \cdot \log_2 n$

   (c) $f(n) = (n + 1)!$

   (d) $f(n, m) = \begin{cases} n^4 & \text{if } n < 100 \\ 0 & \text{otherwise} \end{cases}$

   (e) $f(n) = 4n^2 + \log_2 n$

   (f) $f(n) = \sqrt{\log_2 n}$

   (g) $f(n) = (n \cdot \log_2 n + 2)^3$

   (h) $f(n) = n^2 \bmod 100$

0.5.10. (**Big-Omega Notation and Big-Theta Notation**). In Definition 0.5 we introduced big-O notation, which concerns the upper bounds of number-theoretic functions. Roughly, function $f(n)$ is $O(g(n))$ if $f(n)$ is bounded above by $g(n)$ for sufficiently large n. We define so-called *big-Omega notation*, which concerns lower bounds, as follows.

DEFINITION 0.6: Partial number-theoretic function $f(n)$ is $\Omega(g(n))$ [read as "Omega of g of n"] if there exist natural number constants C and n_0 such that for any $n \geq n_0$ we have $f(n) \geq \frac{1}{C} \cdot g(n)$ whenever both $f(n)$ and $g(n)$ are defined.

The reader will note that function $f(n)$ is $\Omega(g(n))$ just in case $g(n)$ is $O(f(n))$.

Furthermore, function $f(n)$ will be said to be $\Theta(g(n))$ [read as "big-Theta of g of n"] provided that $f(n)$ is $O(g(n))$ *and* $\Omega(g(n))$. In other words, $f(n)$ is $\Theta(g(n))$ if $f(n)$ has the same rate of growth as $g(n)$.

   (a) Let $p(n)$ be a polynomial function of degree k whose leading coefficient $a_k \geq 1$. Show that $p(n)$ is $\Theta(n^k)$.

   (b) Let $p(n)$ be a polynomial function of degree k whose leading coefficient $a_k \geq 1$. Show that $p(n)$ is $O(n^{k+1})$ but not $\Omega(n^{k+1})$ and hence not $\Theta(n^{k+1})$.

   (c) Let $p(n)$ be a polynomial function of degree k whose leading coefficient $a_k \geq 1$. Show that $p(n)$ is $O(2^n)$ but $f(n) = 2^n$ is not $O(p(n))$. In other words, $f(n) = 2^n$ grows strictly faster than any polynomial function.

0.5.11. Show that function $f(n) = \lceil \log_{10} n \rceil$ is $\Theta(\lceil \log_2 n \rceil)$. (*Hint:* Use Remark 0.3.3 to show that $\log_{10} x = \log_{10} 2 \cdot \log_2 x$ for all real $x > 0$.)

0.5.12. Show that (i) and (ii) below are equivalent.

   (i) For arbitrary function h, if $f(n)$ is $O(h(n))$, then $g(n)$ is $O(h(n))$.

   (ii) Function $g(n)$ is $O(f(n))$.

0.5.13. Suppose that function $f(n)$ is $O(g(n))$ for some polynomial $g(n)$. Show that there then exists polynomial $g'(n)$ with $f(n) \leq g'(n)$ for sufficiently large n. (*Remark:* This exercise is truly trivial, which is the whole point of its inclusion.)

EXERCISES FOR §0.6

0.6.1. Show that $4 + 10 + 16 + \cdots + (6n - 2) = n(3n + 1)$ for all n in $\mathcal{N} \setminus \{0\}$. (*Hint:* We have base case $n = 1$.)

0.6.2. Prove by mathematical induction that $|\sin nx| \le n \cdot |\sin x|$ for all $x \in \mathcal{R}$ and all $n \in \mathcal{N}$. You will need to appeal to the following general propositions.

   (i) For $a, b \in \mathcal{R}$, $|\sin(a + b)| \le |\sin a + \sin b|$.

   (ii) For $a, b \in \mathcal{R}$, $|a + b| \le |a| + |b|$ (the so-called Triangle Inequality).

   (iii) For $a, b, c \in \mathcal{R}$ with $c \ge 0$, if $a \le b$ then $a + c \le b + c$.

0.6.3. (Gauss' Formula).[hwk] Prove by mathematical induction that, for all $n \in \mathcal{N}$, $0 + 1 + 2 + \cdots + n = n(n+1)/2$.

0.6.4. Prove by mathematical induction that, for all $n \in \mathcal{N}$, $0^2 + 1^2 + 2^2 + \cdots + n^2 = n(n+1)(2n+1)/6$.

0.6.5. Prove by mathematical induction that, for all $n \in \mathcal{N}$, $0^3 + 1^3 + 2^3 + \ldots + n^3 = [n(n+1)/2]^2$.

EXERCISES FOR §0.7

0.7.1. (a) Give a path of length 8 from vertex a to vertex b in the directed graph of Figure 0.7.1(a).

   (b) Give a closed path of length 3 starting at vertex a in the directed graph of Figure 0.7.1(c).

   (c) Give a closed path of length 4 starting at vertex y in the undirected graph of Figure 0.7.4(b).

0.7.2. By a *rooted tree*, one means some tree together with some one distinguished vertex v designated as the *root*. The *level* of vertex y within such a tree is the length of the unique path from root v to y. For instance, in the tree of Figure 0.7.5, designating vertex a as root entails that vertices f and g will occur at level 3. Furthermore, if vertex x is of level k and vertex y is of level $k + 1$ and there is an edge (x, y), then x is said to be the *parent* of y, and y is said to be the *child* of x. Childless vertices are referred to as *leaves*. For example, in the tree of Figure 0.7.5, vertices b and d are both children of root a, and e—but not c—is a leaf. The *height* of a rooted tree is the maximum level of any vertex within it. Thus, the height of the rooted tree of Figure 0.7.5 is 3, where we assume a to be the root.

   A rooted tree is a *binary tree*, provided that every vertex has at most two children. (Thus the tree of Figure 0.7.5, with a chosen as root, is a binary tree.) Finally, a binary tree is said to be *full* provided that (1) every nonleaf has exactly two children and (2) all leaves are at one and the same level of the tree. For example, of the two binary trees of Figure 0.7.6, only the one on the right is full.

Figure 0.7.6

   (a) Prove by mathematical induction that any full binary tree of height $h \ge 0$ possesses 2^h leaves. (Note that a tree of height 0 consists of a root only.)

   (b) Prove by mathematical induction that any full binary tree of height $h \ge 0$ possesses $2^{h+1} - 1$ vertices.

0.7.3. A *weighted undirected graph* is an undirected graph $G = (V, E)$ such that integer *weights* have been assigned to each and every member of E. Intuitively, one might think of the weight associated with a given edge (v_1, v_2) as the cost of traversing the edge in either direction. (In applications involving transportation networks, weights commonly represent distances between destinations.) The *cost of a path* within a weighted undirected graph is then the sum of the weights assigned to the edges within that path. A *least-cost path from vertex v to vertex w* is a path from v to w whose cost does not exceed that of any other path from v to w.

   (a) What is the cost of path $v_1\ v_4\ v_5\ v_3\ v_4\ v_6$ within the weighted undirected graph of Figure 0.7.7?

   (b) Find a least-cost path from v_1 to v_6 within the weighted undirected graph of Figure 0.7.7. Is your least-cost path unique?

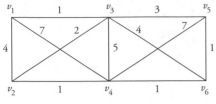

Figure 0.7.7

0.7.4. (Hamiltonian circuits).^{hwk} A *Hamiltonian circuit* within an undirected graph $G = (V, E)$ is a closed path within G that involves visiting every member of V exactly once with the sole exception of the first, and last, vertex in the path, which is visited just twice.

(a) Find a Hamiltonian circuit, if any exists, within the undirected graph of Figure 0.7.4(a).

(b) Find a Hamiltonian circuit, if any exists, within the undirected graph of Figure 0.7.4(b).

(c) Find a Hamiltonian circuit, if any exists, within the weighted undirected graph of Figure 0.7.7. (Simply ignore the weights.)

0.7.5. (The Traveling Salesman Problem).^{hwk} The *Traveling Salesman Problem for Undirected Graphs* is that of finding a shortest Hamiltonian circuit for a given undirected graph $G = (V, E)$ starting at a given vertex $v \in V$. The *Traveling Salesman Problem for Weighted Undirected Graphs* is that of finding a least-cost Hamiltonian circuit for a given weighted undirected graph $G = (V, E)$ starting at a given vertex $v \in V$.

(a) Find a least-cost Hamiltonian circuit within the weighted undirected graph of Figure 0.7.7. Is your least-cost circuit unique?

(b) We claim that the Traveling Salesman Problem for Undirected Graphs is a special case of the Traveling Salesman Problem for Weighted Undirected Graphs. What is the justification for this claim?

EXERCISES FOR §0.8

0.8.1. Determine whether each of the following sentences is satisfiable. (*Suggestion:* Either construct a truth table or simply present a single truth-value assignment that makes the given sentence true.)

(a) $(p \lor \neg r) \,\&\, (p \to (\neg q \,\&\, r))$
(b) $(\neg p \lor q) \lor (p \,\&\, \neg q) \lor (p \leftrightarrow q)$
(c) $(p \to r) \to ((q \to s) \to ((p \lor q) \to r))$
(d) $(\neg p \lor \neg q) \,\&\, (\neg p \lor q) \,\&\, (p \lor \neg q) \,\&\, (p \lor q)$

0.8.2. Use truth tables to verify the logical equivalences of Table 0.8.9.

0.8.3. Use truth tables to verify the logical implications of Table 0.8.11.

0.8.4. Use mathematical induction to prove that the following generalizations of the Distributivity Laws hold.

$$R \lor (S_1 \,\&\, S_2 \,\&\, \cdots \,\&\, S_n) \Leftrightarrow$$
$$(R \lor S_1) \,\&\, (R \lor S_2) \,\&\, \cdots \,\&\, (R \lor S_n)$$
$$R \,\&\, (S_1 \lor S_2 \lor \cdots \lor S_n) \Leftrightarrow$$
$$(R \,\&\, S_1) \lor (R \,\&\, S_2) \lor \cdots \lor (R \,\&\, S_n)$$

0.8.5. Show that $S_1 \Leftrightarrow S_2$ holds if and only if $S_1 \leftrightarrow S_2$ is a tautology, where S_1 and S_2 are sentences of the language of propositional logic.

0.8.6. Show that $S_1 \Rightarrow S_2$ holds if and only if $S_1 \to S_2$ is a tautology, where S_1 and S_2 are sentences of the language of propositional logic.

0.8.7. ^{hwk} The binary propositional connective $\downarrow$ is known as the *Sheffer stroke*. Proposition $p \downarrow q$ will be true just in case p and q are not both true.

(a) Give a truth-table definition of the Sheffer stroke.

(b) Show that each of the five connectives $\neg$, $\lor$, $\&$, $\to$, and $\leftrightarrow$ is definable in terms of $\downarrow$. (This is pretty much what one means by saying that the Sheffer stroke is *complete* or, more strictly, that $\{\downarrow\}$ is a *complete set of connectives*.)

EXERCISE FOR §0.9

0.9.1. Use the Pigeonhole Principle to show that the decimal expansion of an arbitrary rational number eventually repeats. (*Hint:* It is familiar that $1/3 = .3333333333\ldots$ and $2/9 = .2222222222\ldots$. Also, $1/7 =$ .142857142857142857.... To see that repetition is inevitable, consider the rational number 7/13. Compute the decimal expansion by performing the usual long division.)

EXERCISES FOR §0.10

0.10.1. Use clauses (i)–(iii) of the definition of wff to show that $((p \to (q \to r)) \mathbin{\&} s)$ is a wff.

0.10.2. Use clauses (i)–(iii) of the definition of wff to show that $(p \mathbin{\&} (q \to r)$ is not a wff. (*Hint:* Proceed indirectly. That is, start by assuming that $(p \mathbin{\&} (q \to r)$ is a wff. Then use clause (iii).)

EXERCISES FOR §0.11

0.11.1. (**a**) Show that the union (sumset) of a countable set of finite sets is itself countable.
(**b**) Show that the union (sumset) of a countable set of countable sets is itself countable.

0.11.2. Define the bijection from $\mathcal{N}$ onto $\mathcal{Z}$ shown in Figure 0.11.1. Use definition by cases. That is, fill in the blanks below so as to give the required definition of f.

$$f : \mathcal{N} \to \mathcal{Z}$$

$$f(n) = \begin{cases} \underline{} & \text{if } n \text{ is even} \\ \underline{} & \text{if } n \text{ is odd} \end{cases}$$

0.11.3. Let L be a language over finite alphabet Σ. Show that if language L is infinite, then there is no upper bound on the length of words within L. (*Hint:* Proceed indirectly by assuming that L is infinite but that no word of L exceeds length n_0, say. Derive a contradiction.)

0.11.4. hwk
(**a**) Let $\{0, 1, 2, \ldots, n\}$ and $\{0, 1, 2, \ldots, m\}$ be proper initial segments of $\mathcal{N}$ with $m < n$. Show that there is no bijection from $\{0, 1, 2, \ldots, n\}$ onto $\{0, 1, 2, \ldots, m\}$.
(**b**) Let $\{0, 1, 2, \ldots, n\}$ be a proper initial segment of $\mathcal{N}$. Show that there can be no bijection from $\{0, 1, 2, \ldots, n\}$ onto a proper subset of itself.

0.11.5. hwk Show that set S is finite if and only if there exists a bijection from S onto some proper initial segment $\{0, 1, 2, \ldots, n\}$ of $\mathcal{N}$. (*Hint:* For the forward direction, the Axiom of Choice is needed.)

0.11.6. hwk Show that set S is countable in the sense of Definition 0.10 if and only if there exists a bijection from S onto some subset of $\mathcal{N}$.

EXERCISES FOR §0.12

0.12.1. Which of the following sentences are in CNF according to Definition 0.13?
(**a**) $(p \vee q) \mathbin{\&} (r \vee q \vee p)$
(**b**) $p \mathbin{\&} (\neg r \vee q)$
(**c**) $p \to (q \mathbin{\&} r)$
(**d**) $(p \vee (r \mathbin{\&} q)) \mathbin{\&} (r \vee q \vee p)$
(**e**) $(p \vee \neg\neg q) \mathbin{\&} (r \vee q \vee p)$
(**f**) r

0.12.2. Using Definitions 0.11 through 0.13, show that $(p \vee q) \mathbin{\&} (r \vee \neg q) \mathbin{\&} p$ is a CNF.

0.12.3. hwk Find an equivalent CNF for each of the following sentences.
(**a**) $[p \to (q \vee r)] \mathbin{\&} [\neg(\neg r \mathbin{\&} q)]$
(**b**) $(p \mathbin{\&} \neg q) \vee (r \mathbin{\&} q \mathbin{\&} p)$
(**c**) $(p \mathbin{\&} q) \leftrightarrow \neg(r \vee \neg q)$

0.12.4. Give a formal definition of disjunctive normal form (DNF) parallel to that given in Definitions 0.11 through 0.13 for conjunctive normal form. (*Hint:* No change in Definition 0.11 is necessary.)

0.12.5. Complete the proof of Theorem 0.10 by establishing the remaining three subcases within the inductive case.

EXERCISES FOR §0.13

0.13.1. ^{hwk} Assume the following interpretations of predicates $C_1(n)$, $C_2(n, m, k)$, and $C_2(n, m, k)$. Namely, for all $n, m, k \in \mathcal{N}$

$$C_1(n_1) \Leftrightarrow_{\text{def.}} n_1 \text{ is prime}$$

$$C_2(n_1, n_2, n_3) \Leftrightarrow_{\text{def.}} n_1 = n_2 + n_3$$

$$C_3(n_1, n_2, n_3) \Leftrightarrow_{\text{def.}} n_1 = n_2 \cdot n_3$$

For each of the binary predicates below, say whether it is satisfied by the pair $\langle 4, 12 \rangle$—that is, $n = 4$ and $m = 12$.
- **(a)** $C_1(n) \rightarrow C_1(m)$
- **(b)** $(\exists k) C_2(n, m, k)$
- **(c)** $(\exists k)[C_2(k, n, m,) \,\&\, C_1(k)]$
- **(d)** $(\forall k) \neg C_3(n, m, k)$
- **(e)** $(\exists k) C_3(k, n, m)$
- **(f)** $(\exists k)[C_3(k, n, m) \,\&\, C_1(k)]$
- **(g)** $(\exists k \leq n)[C_3(m, k, n) \,\&\, C_1(k)]$

0.13.2. Show that the relation $f(n)$ is $\Theta(g(n))$ as defined in Exercise 0.5.10 is an equivalence relation. Note that this is not a number-theoretic relation but, rather, a binary relation holding between number-theoretic functions. Showing it to be an equivalence relation amounts to showing that it is reflexive, symmetric, and transitive.

- (Reflexivity). Any number-theoretic function $f(n)$ is $\Theta(f(n))$.
- (Symmetry). Given functions $f(n)$ and $g(n)$, if $f(n)$ is $\Theta(g(n))$, then $g(n)$ is $\Theta(f(n))$.
- (Transitivity). Given functions $f(n)$, $g(n)$, and $h(n)$, if $f(n)$ is $\Theta(g(n))$ and $g(n)$ is $\Theta(h(n))$, then $f(n)$ is $\Theta(h(n))$.

0.13.3. **(a)** Evaluate binary function $f(m, n) =_{\text{def.}} m \ div \ n$ in the case where $m = 10$ and $n = 4$. What if $m = 10$ and $n = 5$? What if $m = 0$ and $n = 5$? What if $m = 5$ and $n = 0$?
   (b) Evaluate binary function $f(m, n) =_{\text{def.}} m \ mod \ n$ in the case where $m = 10$ and $n = 4$. What if $m = 10$ and $n = 5$? What if $m = 0$ and $n = 5$? What if $m = 5$ and $n = 0$?
   (c) Finally, evaluate binary predicate $n|m$ in the case where $m = 10$ and $n = 4$. What if $m = 10$ and $n = 5$? What if $m = 0$ and $n = 5$? What if $m = 5$ and $n = 0$?

EXERCISES FOR §0.14

0.14.1. **(a)** Show that if function $f(n)$ is $o(g(n))$, then $f(n)$ is $O(g(n))$.
   (b) Show that $f(n)$'s being $O(g(n))$ does not imply that $f(n)$ is $o(g(n))$ by presenting a pair of unary functions.

0.14.2. ^{hwk} Show that the class of total, unary number-theoretic functions is uncountable. (*Hint:* Give a diagonal argument.)

MODELS OF COMPUTATION

## Chapter 1

Turing Machines

§1.1 What Is Computation?

For the contemporary reader, the term *computation* most likely conjures up images of computing *machines*, namely, computers and related devices such as calculators. But of course the concept of computation predates modern digital processing. Recall that, in earlier times, calculation of the positions of heavenly bodies, of navigational direction, and of actuarial statistics was performed without the aid of electronic calculating devices. Up until the 1930s, it was human beings alone who computed. As such, the concept of computation belongs to virtually all human cultures past and present. Although computation is no longer the exclusive domain of human beings, it remains an essentially human activity to this day.

Talk of computation suggests numbers, of course. Clear examples of *numerical computation* are binary arithmetic operations such as addition and subtraction as well as unary operations such as finding the square root of a number—without looking it up in some table of course. However, computation need not involve numbers at all. Operations on strings of symbols provide many examples of *non-numeric computation*—for example, searching for an occurrence of one string within another longer one or sorting a collection of strings lexicographically.

The concept of computation is related to that of an algorithm. For the moment, let us say only that by *algorithm* we mean a certain sort of general method for solving a family of related questions. Examples of familiar algorithms are the truth-table algorithm for argument validity in the propositional calculus (cf. Exercise 1.1.1), the column method for conversion of decimal to binary numerals (cf. Exercise 1.1.2), and the Euclidean algorithm for determining the greatest common divisor of two integers (cf. Exercise 1.1.3). Such algorithms are the end result of the mathematician's quest for a general method or procedure for answering any one of some infinite family of questions. To take the easiest sort of example, the *question-template*

$$\text{Is natural number } n \text{ a prime number?} \tag{1.1.1}$$

corresponds to such an infinite family of yes/no questions, one for each substitution of a numeral for variable n. Thus:

$$\text{Is natural number 1 a prime number?} \qquad (1.1.2)$$
$$\text{Is natural number 2 a prime number?}$$
$$\text{Is natural number 3 a prime number?}$$

. . .

A yes/no question-template such as (1.1.1) corresponds to a *decision problem*, and each question at (1.1.2) corresponds to one *instance* of that general problem. In the case of the particular decision problem cited at (1.1.1), a general method for solving the problem will be well known to the reader. Namely, we make a special case of 1, giving the answer "No" outright to the question, Is natural number 1 a prime number? We might as well think of the next two questions in the family as special cases as well, although this is not strictly necessary. Namely, without performing any calculations whatever, we shall give affirmative answers to both, Is natural number 2 a prime number? and Is natural number 3 a prime number? So far we have

$$\text{Is natural number 1 a prime number? No}$$
$$\text{Is natural number 2 a prime number? Yes}$$
$$\text{Is natural number 3 a prime number? Yes}$$

. . .

For cases of $n > 3$—for $n = 807$, say—what shall we do? Obviously, we shall attempt successive division by divisors $k = 2, 3, 4, \ldots$, at least up to a certain point. If any such division is successful—if k is seen to divide n without remainder—then we stop immediately and answer the question, Is n prime? negatively. (In the case of $n = 807$, division by 2 is unsuccessful. Division by 3, however, is successful, and we have effectively determined that 807 is composite.) Otherwise, we continue dividing by larger and larger divisors k and checking to see whether such division is successful. When can we safely stop dividing and give a negative answer to the question, Is n prime? Plainly, there is no point in division by $k > n/2$. (Even better: We can stop as soon as k exceeds $\sqrt{n}$. Why?) So in a case such as $n = 907$, which happens to be prime, we can stop once divisor k reaches 31. The important point here is that we do possess a general procedure or algorithm for primality testing. We schematize this general procedure below.

Euclidean Algorithm for Primality Testing
Input: natural number $n > 0$
Output: **yes** if n is prime
         no otherwise
begin
       if $n = 1$ then return **no**
       else if $n = 2$ then return **yes**
       else if $n = 3$ then return **yes**
       else begin $\{n \geq 4\}$
            $dvs := 2;$
            while $dvs \leq \sqrt{n}$ do
               if $n \bmod dvs = 0$ then return **no**
               else $dvs := dvs + 1;$
            return **yes**
       end
end.

For large values of n, answering the question, Is n prime? will involve many steps. Still, there is no possibility that the procedure will be indeterminate in the case of a particular n: Given sufficient time and resources (paper, ink, and so forth), we can always give a definite answer to the question, Is n prime? By virtue of our possessing such a general method, we shall say that the decision problem expressed by question-template (1.1.1) is a *decidable problem*.

In addition to yes/no questions, mathematicians regularly consider questions such as What is the nth prime number? For a given n, the required procedure, whatever it is, must return a particular value—that is, a particular prime number. For example, the answer to the question, What is the eighth prime number? is 19. We might call such questions *what-questions*. Again, we seek a general method or procedure that is capable in principle of yielding the correct answer for any one of an infinite family of questions.

What is the first prime number?

What is the second prime number?

What is the third prime number?

What is the fourth prime number?

. . .

Of course, we do possess such a procedure for this particular family of questions—one derived from our Euclidean algorithm for primality testing. Namely, finding the kth prime amounts to finding the kth yes/no question in the list at (1.1.2) to which an affirmative answer can be given. Thus a general procedure for answering one sort of question—a what-question, say—may depend upon a general procedure for answering some other sort question—a yes/no question perhaps. The following schematization of our procedure for answering the question, What is the nth prime? makes this dependence explicit.

Algorithm for Finding the nth Prime Number
Input: natural number $n \geq 1$
Output: the nth prime number
begin
        $i := 1$;
        $k := 1$;
        while $i \leq n$ do begin
          $k := k + 1$;
          if $\boxed{k \text{ is prime}}$ then $i := i + 1$
        end;
        return k
end.

This is a call to the Euclidean algorithm.

We have suggested defining an algorithm to be a general method or procedure for answering any one of an infinite family of questions. On the other hand, an algorithm must itself be finitely describable; otherwise it could not be communicated from one person to another.

- In addition, an algorithm must be *definite* in the sense that, at each point in carrying it out, there is a *determinate next step*. In this sense, algorithms are frequently said to be "mechanical" in character: No ingenuity is required in executing them. More to the point, we shall take the notion of algorithm to be inherently *deterministic*.

- Typically, application of an algorithm to a given input will be a *finite* process in that, after a finite number of steps, algorithm execution comes to an end. (This is not to deny, however, that nonterminating executions are possible, for some inputs, even in the case of otherwise very useful algorithms.)

- Finally, any terminating application of an algorithm must be *conclusive* in that, when the algorithm terminates, an unambiguous result or "output" is generated.

We must grant that the algorithm concept is somewhat vague to the extent that notions like "next step," "carrying out," and "output," although clear enough for most purposes, are not themselves characterized in any way and are hence subject to varying interpretations. As such, the algorithm concept belongs to the philosophy of mathematics.

Three Computational Paradigms

In what follows, we shall take the computation of a given k-ary number-theoretic function f as paradigmatic of numerical computation. By this we shall mean the computation of the unique value $f(n_1, n_2, \ldots, n_k)$ of f for given arguments $n_1, n_2, \ldots, n_k$. We thereby give special prominence to the notion *computable function*. Since this notion of computable function is intuitive and hence a somewhat vague concept, we shall be content in this introductory discussion to give a couple of examples and to discuss them in a very general way. No real characterization of *computable function* will be possible in the few pages that we are committing to this introductory discussion. This is not to say that no characterizations are possible in general, however, or that we shall be uninterested in such characterizations. On the contrary, much of Part I of this book may be regarded as the record of various attempts to say just what it is for a number-theoretic function to be computable.

As an easy example of a computable function, consider the unary number-theoretic function f defined by writing

$$f(n) =_{\text{def.}} \text{ the } n\text{th prime number}$$

Thus $f(1) = 2$, that $f(2) = 3$, that $f(3) = 5$, and so on. Obtaining the value of f for such small arguments may not seem to involve genuine computation. But no one could doubt that determining the value of $f(100)$, say, would require computation. And the reason why f belongs to the class of *computable* functions is that, given any natural number n, one can in principle find the value of f for argument n using something like the algorithm presented earlier.

Although we shall usually restrict our attention to number-theoretic functions (i.e., functions from $\mathcal{N}$ to $\mathcal{N}$) the notion of computable function is more general than this. Here is an example of a computable, binary function on the integers[1]:

$$g(n, m) =_{\text{def.}} \left\lceil \frac{n}{m} \right\rceil$$

Again, function g is computable because it is *effectively calculable*. We possess an algorithm that invariably

---

[1] Throughout this book, the term *binary*, as applied to functions, will always mean *taking two arguments*. On those few occasions when we use it to refer to base-2 notation or the like, the context can be relied upon to make this meaning clear.

produces, after some finite number of steps, the correct value of g for any argument pair $\langle n, m \rangle$—provided that $g(n, m)$ is defined. Accordingly, one speaks of g's *effectiveness*. Note that g is a partial function, being undefined for pairs of the form $\langle n, 0 \rangle$. *We shall not regard g's partiality as in any way compromising its effectiveness.* If $g(n, m)$ is defined, then our algorithm enables us to find out what it is. If $g(n, m)$ is *not* defined, however, then our algorithm does not mislead us by returning some purported value, and we cannot ask for more than this.

The class of computable functions provides us with one way of thinking about computation in general to the extent that computing the value of a numeric function is a paradigmatic instance of the phenomenon that we call computation. We shall henceforth speak of the *function computation paradigm* when we wish to approach computability from this point of view. On the other hand, it is easy to give examples of computations that, on the face of it, do not involve anything like function computation. Thus consider the following example.

Suppose that one is presented with a finite symbol string w consisting of occurrences of symbols a and b only and then asked to determine whether w is a palindrome. Just to make things definite, suppose that w is the string

$$abbbababbbabbbababbbba$$

How might one approach this problem? There are of course a number of possibilities. Perhaps the easiest to describe would involve comparing the leftmost and rightmost symbols of w and, if they are identical, removing them. This process of comparing and then removing could be iterated until (1) the leftmost remaining symbol is not identical with the rightmost remaining symbol, (2) just one symbol remains, or (3) no symbol remains. In cases (2) and (3), it is plain that the original w is a palindrome. On the other hand, if (1) is ever true, then w is not a palindrome.

The palindrome example is instructive in that it permits us to point out once again that many instances of computation do not involve computing the values of numeric functions. In particular, the palindrome example does not concern numbers in any way. Rather, the algorithm used to determine whether input string w is a palindrome is explicable in terms of symbol comparisons and of deletions of symbols from strings in order to obtain shorter strings. One uses the generic term *symbol manipulation* to describe such operations on strings. As another example of a computation based upon symbol manipulation, imagine being asked to determine whether a given string of as and bs, in any order, contains the same number of as as bs. This might mean iterating the removal of the leftmost occurrence of a within w together with the leftmost occurrence of b until either (1) no symbols remain or (2) just as remain or (3) just bs remain. Apparently, in case (1), we have $n_a(w) = n_b(w)$—that is, the number of as in w equals the number of bs in w. In either case (2) or case (3), we have $n_a(w) \neq n_b(w)$.

The class of computations, like those just described, that are based upon symbol manipulation, provides us with a second computational paradigm. In each case, symbol strings are being manipulated—transformed in various ways—in order to classify the original string as belonging either to the class of strings possessing a certain property or to its complement—for example, to the class of strings that are palindromes or to the complement of that class. In virtue of the centrality of symbol manipulation to many instances of computation, we shall occasionally speak of the *string classification paradigm* when we wish to think about computation in this manner. More often, however, we shall refer to this paradigm as the *language recognition paradigm*. The latter usage reflects the standard use of the term *language* to denote any class of strings or *words* over some given alphabet. Thus, instances of the language recognition paradigm involve determining whether or not an arbitrary word w belongs to some language L, where

L is assumed to be given—that is, defined—in advance. An algorithm that successfully does this in the case of language L will be said to *recognize L*.

In connection with the language recognition paradigm in particular, we mention the possibility of construing any decision problem as a case of language recognition. For example, let L_{Prime} be that language over alphabet $\{1\}$ consisting of all and only those strings having the form

$$I^n = \underbrace{1111\ldots1111}_{n \text{ times}}$$

where n happens to be prime. Thus we have

$$L_{Prime} = \{11, 111, 11111, 1111111, 11111111111, \ldots\}$$

Consequently, asking whether natural number n is prime is tantamount to asking whether string I^n is in language L_{Prime}. This association of problems with languages will be very important in our study. (Eventually we shall use the terms "problem" and "language" as virtually synonymous based on this association.) Language recognition will provide us with a way of thinking about problem solving as well as a way of formulating the problems themselves.

There is yet one more paradigm that we wish to introduce. The *transduction paradigm* is operant whenever one considers instances of computation that involve some well-defined transformation—or *transduction*—of symbol strings. For example, consider the computation involved in reversing a given word w consisting of as and bs. We might regard the string w itself—*aabaabb*, say—as the input to the computation and the result $w^R = bbaabaa$ of reversal as its output. As a second example of transduction, consider being asked to rearrange input string w so that all of the as occur before any of the bs. In other words, input word w would be transformed into output word $a^{n_a(w)}b^{n_b(w)}$.

It is our view that the three paradigms introduced above—function computation, language recognition, and transduction—must have equal standing within any investigation of computability. Sometimes it is function computation that will be emphasized as, for example, when we are investigating "in-principle" computability—that is, computability without any consideration of the resource requirements (time and space) of computation. On the other hand, when such resource requirements are the issue, it will be convenient to view computability in terms of language recognition or transduction. No one of the three paradigms appears to us to be more important than the others. This catholic approach to the theory of computability is only reinforced by reflection upon the *interreducibility* of our three paradigms. By this we mean the possibility of regarding any instance of *one* of our three paradigms, with equal justification, as an instance of *either of the other two*. For example, it is easy to see how any case of function computation may be construed as an instance of the language recognition paradigm. Using binary numerals to represent natural numbers, we can redescribe computation of function

$$f(n) =_{\text{def.}} m, \quad \text{where } m \text{ is the } n\text{th prime number}$$

in terms of the symbol string classification paradigm. Namely, computing the value of f for argument 3 amounts to determining which *one* of the symbol strings

$$11\#0$$

$$11\#1$$

$$11\#10$$

$$11\#11$$

$$11\#100$$

$$11\#101$$

$$11\#110$$

$$11\#111$$

$$\cdots$$

is in that class of symbol strings of the general form

$$Binary\_repr(n)\#Binary\_repr(m)$$

with m equal to the nth prime. (By the way, which one of the words above *is* in that language?) Generalizing this example shows that function computation may be viewed as a special case of symbol string classification or language recognition.

Conversely, how can a computation of the symbol-string-classification variety be reconstrued as a case of function computation? Well, first, imagine that the input symbols figuring in the computation have been assigned *symbol codes* of some sort. (One might utilize an ASCII-like encoding scheme for this purpose.) In any case, each symbol will be associated with some unique natural number that is its code. This assignment of symbol codes to individual symbols induces an encoding of symbol *strings* as natural numbers. (For example, if symbols a and b have been assigned codes $01_2 = 1$ and $10_2 = 2$, respectively, then string $aaba$ "inherits" natural number code $01011001_2 = 89$.) Now it becomes possible to regard the problem of determining whether an arbitrary word w over alphabet $\{a, b\}$ is a palindrome as a function computation problem. Namely, it amounts to computing a value of characteristic function χ_{Pal} of the set Pal of codes of palindromes over alphabet $\{a, b\}$. In other words, where χ_{Pal} is defined, as usual, by

$$\chi_{Pal}(n) = \begin{cases} 1 & \text{if } n \text{ is the code of a palindrome} \\ 0 & \text{otherwise} \end{cases}$$

it follows that classifying string $w = aaba$ correctly as a nonpalindrome amounts to determining that $\chi_{Pal}(89) = 0$. Our point is that we have successfully reinterpreted string classification in terms of function computation. We leave it to the reader to verify that instances of the transduction paradigm are interpretable in terms of both function computation and symbol string classification, and vice versa (see Exercise 1.1.5). We shall, on occasion, speak of *Paradigm Interreducibility* in referring to the possibility of redescribing any given instance of computation—however presented initially—in alternative terms.

Models of Computation

In Chapters 1 through 7 we shall consider no fewer than six technical proposals for characterizing or *analyzing* the intuitive notion of computable function. That is, each proposal considered will put forth some mathematical definition of a class of number-theoretic functions that, if one accepts the proposed analysis, *is* precisely the class of computable number-theoretic functions. Focusing exclusively for the moment upon the function computation paradigm, each of the six proposals constitutes a *model of computation.*

We shall also investigate the bounds or limits of the notion of computable function. Ultimately, we shall present several examples of number-theoretic functions that, regarded from a certain point of view, are not computable in an intuitive sense despite being well-defined. Unfortunately, it is not possible at this early point to cite an example of such a well-defined, but noncomputable, function since such functions tend to be of a somewhat arcane and theoretical character. (Any reader who cannot wait might glance at the functions defined within the proofs of Theorems 2.10 and 8.1 in order to get an idea of what we have in mind.)

A final word of caution is in order with respect to our usage of the term *computable function* and the synonymous *effectively calculable function*. Throughout this text we shall always use these terms to describe an intuitive, informal, nontechnical notion that we all share—that is part of our intellectual and cultural heritage, if you will. We are all in possession of this notion—even those among us who do not yet know much of anything about the so-called theory of computability. This is because the notion of computable function is *pretheoretic* in the sense that we are in possession of it *before we begin to theorize.* Indeed, this notion of computable function is one of the principal data that we shall be attempting to account for in theorizing about computation. If anything, the notion *computable function* is an intuitive and *philosophical* concept and, as such, is *nonmathematical.* If the latter assertion appears surprising, consider that there is a difference between (1) rigorously defined, mathematical concepts such as those of prime number or perfect cube and (2) philosophical, somewhat imprecise, concepts such as those of proof and mathematical truth that are nonetheless *about mathematics.* We wish to emphasize that the concept *computable function* is of the latter variety—a nonmathematical, philosophical notion that concerns mathematics—and we shall never depart from this point of view. Over the course of the next several chapters, a number of technical, truly mathematical concepts will be introduced as proposed analyses or models of the intuitive concept *computable function.* But we shall always refer to these technical concepts by their designated names—for example, *Turing-computable function, partial recursive function,* or *Markov-computable function.* We shall never use the terms *computable function* or *effectively calculable function* in referring to these technical concepts. The reader who fully grasps this at the outset will be spared much confusion later.

As reflected in its title, this book will have as one goal the investigation of a number of *models of computation.* In particular, in the present chapter we introduce what is surely the most well known and probably the most important such model. Machines of the sort to be considered were first described by Turing in his seminal paper, "On Computable Numbers, with an Application to the *Entscheidungsproblem.*"[2] Consequently, these machines have come to be called *Turing machines.* (Of course Turing, being a modest man, did not himself call them this.)

It is our point of view that *all* of the models of computation that we shall consider in this book are of interest, not merely to theoretical computer scientists but to mathematicians, cognitive scientists, and

---

[2] This paper is listed as [Turing 1936–1937] in the bibliography at the end of this text. Incidentally, the term *Entscheidungsproblem* is German for "decision problem."

philosophers of mind as well. Still, it is only Turing machines that have been considered by these other groups with any frequency. This is not unrelated to the fact that Turing machines have come to be seen as the standard model of (sequential) computation.

In the present chapter, Turing machines will be seen to play two different roles, each reflecting one of our computation paradigms. Some Turing machines will serve as language acceptors (language recognizers). Other Turing machines will compute number-theoretic functions. We shall consider each role in turn. First, however, it is necessary to characterize Turing machines—to say what just they are. We start with a few easy examples and a very informal description in §1.2. Afterward, in §1.3, we turn to a more rigorous, mathematical definition. Before considering Turing machines, there is another important intuitive notion that must be introduced.

Feasible Computation

So far we have considered only what we might call "computability-in-principle," by which we mean computation in the absence of any restrictions on either time or space. But our study will encompass *computational feasibility* as well. An envisioned computation is said to be *feasible* if it would consume only a quantity of resources that does not exceed what is likely to be available to the computational process. By extension, a general problem will be said to be *feasible* or *tractable* if solving any individual instance of it consumes only a reasonable quantity of resources. For example, the problem of deciding whether natural numbers are prime is certainly feasible or tractable since we possess an algorithm for primality testing that, applied to any natural number n, requires something on the order of n division steps, each involving only a reasonable number of computation steps. Note that feasibility of a problem is quite compatible with our usual expectation that the quantity of resources consumed will increase with the "size" of the problem instances considered. Thus, deciding whether a six-digit number is prime will in general require more time and more space than deciding whether a two-digit number is prime.

We proceed on the assumption that all readers—even those who have never studied the theory of computability previously—possess certain shared intuitive concepts that will concern us in our investigations. Important among them is a concept of feasibility. And all that is meant by "possession" of this concept is that the reader has some beliefs concerning it. Just to fix ideas, we present a brief example that is intended to convince the reader that he or she does indeed have certain beliefs regarding feasibility. So consider a case that arose recently at a small college on the eastern coast of North America. Students would for the first time be permitted to repeat a course in an effort to supplant an earlier, presumably low, grade with something higher. But how would the registrar's grade point computation program come to recognize that a single course was listed twice on a student transcript? Routine checking of all transcripts for duplicated course listings would be *feasible* to the extent that the necessary resources—essentially time—could be made available. However, as determined by the registrar, such routine checking would not be *cost-effective*, given the number of comparisons involved and the relative rarity of duplications. Consequently, it was decided that there would be no routine checking. Instead, students who had repeated a course would be expected to submit a written request for grade point recomputation.

Well, if the situation just related was comprehensible to the reader, then he or she does indeed possess certain beliefs regarding feasible computation. In particular, the reader believes that feasibility is something distinct from cost-effectiveness—that the feasibility of a certain sort of computation does not entail its being economical to actually do the computation. (If the reader did not already believe this, then presumably our little story would have appeared baffling in the relevant respect.) This is all we mean by saying that the reader possesses an intuitive concept of feasible computation: He or she has certain beliefs about it.[3] On the other hand, having such beliefs is quite consistent with never having articulated those beliefs in the past. To this extent, an individual's concept of feasible computability and the like may be tacit. (In Exercise 1.1.4 the reader will have an opportunity to elicit his or her own, possibly tacit, beliefs concerning computability-in-principle.)

Despite its being a branch of mathematics, the theory of computation does make frequent appeals to intuitive concepts of feasible computability and of computability-in-principle. More accurately, such appeals will occur at the interface between the theory of computation and the philosophy of mathematics. To this extent, any successful student of computation theory is necessarily a philosopher as well. He or she must be willing on occasion to contemplate, in highly self-conscious fashion, our everyday use of terms such as "computation," "algorithm," "effective procedure," "feasible," and the like, in an effort to extract some core of meaning. Using concrete instances of such usage as a vehicle, the student of computation theory must become adept at reflection upon the corresponding intuitive concepts of computability, effectiveness, and feasibility. These *intuitive* concepts can then be compared with the various *technical* notions that we shall introduce in an effort to characterize them mathematically.

§1.2 An Informal Description of Turing Machines

Our first few examples of Turing machines are deliberately quite simple. As a direct consequence of their extreme simplicity, these first machines will do very little.

EXAMPLE 1.2.1 Consider the diagram in Figure 1.2.1. Here we have the so-called *state diagram* or *transition diagram* of a Turing machine M. M's *read/write tape* is divided into *tape squares* and is infinite in both directions (see Figure 1.2.2).

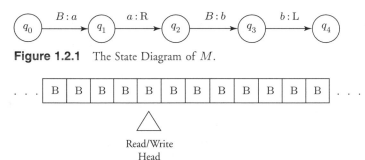

Figure 1.2.1   The State Diagram of M.

Figure 1.2.2 M's tape contains nothing but blanks initially.

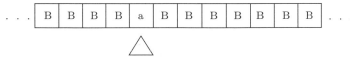

Figure 1.2.3 M writes an a.

We assume M's tape to be entirely blank initially and use symbol B to denote a blank tape square. M's *read/write head* or *tape head* is shown reading, or *scanning,* one of these blanks. The state diagram of M is essentially a digraph whose arcs have been labeled in a certain way. When interpreted in the appropriate manner, this state diagram amounts to a full description of M's behavior, as we shall see. First, nodes of the diagram represent *states* of M, and labeled arcs represent M's *instructions*. By convention, we assume that M is initially in state q_0, the node for which appears at the far left of Figure 1.2.1. Let us also continue to assume that M's tape is completely blank. From state q_0 there is just one arc—that is, one instruction. That instruction—see the arc from q_0 to q_1—stipulates that M must overwrite the *B*lank it is currently

---

[3]One of these beliefs would be that a computation's being infeasible *does* imply that it is cost-prohibitive. That fact, after all, explains why we are interested in feasibility in the first place.

scanning with symbol **a** and afterward enter state q_1 (see Figure 1.2.3).

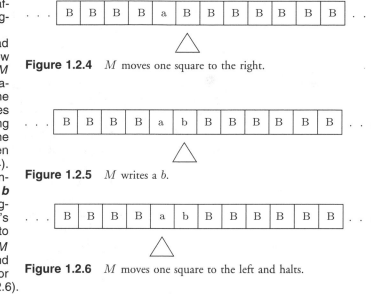

Figure 1.2.4 M moves one square to the right.

Note that M's read/write head has not moved and that M is now scanning symbol **a**. In addition, M is now in state q_1. The single labeled arc extending from the node for state q_1 now specifies that if M happens to be reading an **a**, then M should move one tape square to the **R**ight and then enter state q_2 (see Figure 1.2.4). Next, from state q_2 while scanning a **B**lank, M writes symbol **b** and enters state q_3 (see Figure 1.2.5). Once in state q_3, M's tape head moves one square to the **L**eft[4] and enters state q_4. M has no instruction for state q_4 and hence ceases execution or *halts* in state q_4 (see Figure 1.2.6).

Figure 1.2.5 M writes a b.

Figure 1.2.6 M moves one square to the left and halts.

We might summarize M's behavior as follows, where M is the Turing machine whose state diagram appears in Figure 1.2.1:

> When started scanning a square on a completely blank tape, M writes word *ab* and halts scanning symbol *a*   (1.2.1)

We shall use the term *tape configuration*, relativized to a particular Turing machine M, to refer to the contents of M's tape together with the location of M's read/write head on it at any given step in M's "computation." Thus (1.2.1) says in effect that, where M is the machine whose state diagram appears in Figure 1.2.1, if M's initial tape configuration is the one depicted in Figure 1.2.2, then M's final tape configuration is shown in Figure 1.2.6. We shall use the term *machine configuration*, relativized to a particular Turing machine M, to refer to M's tape configuration together with M's current state at a given step. Thus, where M is once again the Turing machine of Figure 1.2.1, the *final machine configuration* of M may be described by saying that M is in state q_4 with its tape configured as shown in Figure 1.2.6.

Note that description (1.2.1), although adequate, is in a certain sense incomplete, since (1.2.1) says nothing about what happens if the Turing machine is initially *not* scanning a square on a completely blank tape. For example, suppose that the initial contents of M's tape is as in Figure 1.2.7,

---

[4]This move to the **L**eft on the tape is dictated by arc label **b**:**L**. The reader must not be misled by the fact that the node for state q_4 occurs to the *right* of the node for state q_3 in the diagram of Figure 1.2.1. In fact, the relative positioning of state nodes within state diagrams has nothing whatever to do with the directional movement of read/write heads on machine tapes.

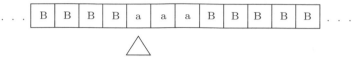

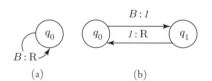

Figure 1.2.7 *M* starts scanning the leftmost of three *a*s.

with read/write head scanning the leftmost of an unbroken sequence of three *a*s on an otherwise blank tape. As usual, *M* would initially be in state q_0. But since there is no instruction that stipulates what *M* should do when in state q_0 reading symbol *a*, in this case *M* halts immediately in state q_0 without having executed even a single instruction. Description (1.2.1) speaks neither to this case nor to countless others that we might consider. This situation is not unusual, however. Typically, we shall design a Turing machine with a particular initial tape configuration in mind. In the case of *M* of Figure 1.2.1, we had in mind a tape that is completely blank initially. Most often we shall not be interested in the behavior of such an *M* when its initial tape configuration is other than what was intended.

Our next two examples, although still extremely simple, illustrate the iterative capability of Turing machines.

EXAMPLE 1.2.2 Consider the state diagram of Figure 1.2.8(a). Here we have a description of a Turing machine *M* with but a single state q_0 and a single instruction. This one instruction is represented by a self-loop labeled **B:R** on state node q_0. Unlike instructions considered up to this point, this new sort of instruction causes no change of state: If in state q_0 scanning a **B**lank, *M*'s read/write head moves one square to the **R**ight and proceeds into—remains in—state q_0. It should be clear enough that, assuming a completely blank tape to start with, *M*'s read/write head will move off to the right one square at a time without ever writing anything and without ever halting.

At this point, the reader may be wondering how Turing's idea—on the face of it, so unpromising—could be of any real interest. In fact, the Turing machine concept will turn out to be an extremely powerful one at the very center of theoretical computer science. Making the case for Turing machines will require a little work, however. In the meantime, we continue laying the necessary groundwork.

Figure 1.2.8 These Turing machines never halt when started scanning a square on a completely blank tape.

EXAMPLE 1.2.3 Consider the state diagram of Figure 1.2.8(b) describing Turing machine *M*. Note, in particular, the presence of a cycle of length 2 beginning at state node q_0. Suppose that *M* starts scanning a square on a completely blank tape. First, *M* writes symbol *1* and enters state q_1. Now *M* finds itself in state q_1 scanning symbol *1*. The instruction represented by the arc from state node q_1 to state node q_0 requires that *M* move its tape head one square to the **R**ight and reenter state q_0. Thus *M* has traversed the cycle from q_0 to q_1 and back exactly once and, in the course of doing so, has written a single *1* and moved one square to its **R**ight. But since *M* is again in state q_0 reading a blank, it will retraverse this cycle, writing another *1* and again moving one square to its **R**ight. Given our assumption that *M*'s tape is infinite and completely blank initially, we see that *M* will continue to write *1*s off to the right without ever halting. (For another example of a Turing machine that computes forever, see **God** within the Turing Machine folder of the accompanying software.)

Despite our talk of tapes and read/write heads, Turing machines are, in fact, *abstract mathematical objects*. To begin to appreciate the *abstractness* of the Turing machine concept, notice that the tape of a Turing machine may be regarded as the counterpart of memory or storage within the modern digital computer: It is on this tape that the Turing machine stores the results—both intermediate and final—of its computations. But since we have assumed Turing machine tapes to be infinite in both directions and since no physically realizable machine can have more than a finite amount of storage, it follows that Turing machines are inherently *abstract*. As a first step toward understanding just what sort of *mathematical objects* Turing machines might be, we next introduce the concept of a *Turing machine transition function* δ.

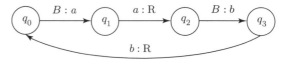

EXAMPLE 1.2.4 Let *M* be the Turing machine whose transition diagram appears in Figure 1.2.9. Suppose that *M*'s tape contains nothing but blanks initially. One traversal of the cycle from state node q_0 and back puts symbol pair *ab* on the tape, with *M* scanning the blank immediately to the right of *b* (see Figure 1.2.10). Evidently, *M* continues writing *ab* pairs off to the right without ever halting. Seeing this is a matter of interpreting *M*'s state diagram in the appropriate way since, as noted earlier, a state diagram amounts to a graphic *description* of *M*'s computational behavior. Our present interest lies in presenting an alternative descrip-

Figure 1.2.9 Another Turing machine that never halts when started scanning a square on a completely blank tape.

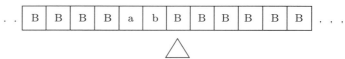

Figure 1.2.10

tion of *M*. This alternative description consists in the presentation of a transition function δ_M for *M*:

$$\delta_M(q_0, B) = (a, q_1)$$
$$\delta_M(q_1, a) = (R, q_2)$$
$$\delta_M(q_2, B) = (b, q_3)$$
$$\delta_M(q_3, b) = (R, q_0)$$

Each of the four equations or *clauses* in the definition of δ_M represents one instruction and hence corresponds to one labeled arc in the transition diagram of Figure 1.2.9. Thus the first clause says, in effect, that if *M* is currently in state q_0 scanning a blank, then it will write symbol *a* and enter state q_1. The second clause states in effect that if *M* is currently in state q_1 reading symbol *a*, then *M*'s read/write head moves one square to the right and *M* enters state q_2. Each of the four clauses has the general form

$$\delta_M(q_i, \sigma) = (action, q_j)$$

and indicates the (unique) value of binary transition function δ_M for an argument pair consisting of a state q_i and a symbol σ. Note that δ_M is *undefined* for certain state/symbol pairs. Thus $\delta_M(q_0, a)$ has no value, which causes *M* to halt immediately if *M* is started scanning symbol *a*.

Generally, we shall write δ_M for the transition function of Turing machine M. The subscript will be omitted, however, when it is plain from the context which Turing machine is under discussion. As already noted, the presentation of a transition function δ_M for a Turing machine M is an alternative to the presentation of a transition or state diagram for M. We shall see later that transition functions will figure prominently in our formal, mathematical characterization of Turing machines. Transition diagrams such as those of Figures 1.2.1, 1.2.8, and 1.2.9 will continue to be useful, however, as graphical representations. In fact, predicting the behavior of a machine M is usually easier if one is given a state diagram for M. On the other hand, transition functions will sometimes be useful in formal proofs concerning Turing machines.

Before continuing with additional examples, let us adopt the following convention to facilitate our presentation of tape configurations. We shall on occasion find it convenient to write

$$\ldots Baa\mathbf{H}baaB \ldots \tag{i}$$

or, omitting the ellipses, just

$$Baa\mathbf{H}baaB \tag{ii}$$

to indicate that M's read/write head is currently scanning symbol b on a tape that contains the string $aabaa$ and that is otherwise blank. In other words, we place $\mathbf{H}$ immediately to the left of the tape square currently being scanned. Any tape square that is not represented in (i) or (ii) is assumed to be blank. It will sometimes be convenient to indicate the state of the Turing machine as well. In that case we may write

$$aa\mathbf{q_3}baa \tag{iii}$$

to indicate that the Turing machine in question is in state q_3 scanning symbol b on a tape that contains the string $aabaa$ and that is blank everywhere else. Thus a string such as (iii) represents what we are calling a machine configuration for some Turing machine M at some step during its computation. We shall refer to strings such as (iii) as *instantaneous (Turing machine) descriptions*, given that they provide tape contents, read/write head location, and current state at a particular "instant" during M's computation. Instantaneous descriptions will occasionally be of use in formal proofs. Note that neither symbol $\mathbf{H}$ in (i) and (ii) nor symbol $\mathbf{q_3}$ in (iii) indicates the presence of a tape square between symbol b and the occurrence of symbol a to its left. Finally, we shall simplify our presentation of Turing machine state diagrams by labeling a node corresponding to state q_k with numeral k only. This is done in Figures 1.2.11(a)–(e) of Exercise 1.2.1, which the reader should complete immediately.

§1.3 The Formal Definition of Turing Machines

We proceed toward a more formal description of Turing machines. We assume some finite input alphabet $\Sigma = \{a_1, \ldots, a_k\}$. In Example 1.2.1, this alphabet was the two-member alphabet $\Sigma = \{a, b\}$. In other words, $k = 2$, where a_1 is a and a_2 is b. Any given Turing machine is associated with a nonempty finite set $Q = \{q_0, q_1, \ldots, q_n\}$ of *states*, among which is a distinguished *initial state* q_{init}. We shall in general assume that q_{init} is state q_0. In the earlier Example 1.2.1, we have $Q = \{q_0, q_1, q_2, q_3, q_4\}$. Finally,

Table 1.3.1 Possible Turing Machine Actions.

Action	Informal Description
L	Move one tape square to the left
R	Move one tape square to the right
B	Erase whatever is on the square currently being scanned
a_1	Erase whatever is on the square currently being scanned and write symbol a_1
a_2	Erase whatever is on the square currently being scanned and write symbol a_2
...	...
a_k	Erase whatever is on the square currently being scanned and write symbol a_k

assuming $\Sigma = \{a_1, a_2, \ldots, a_k\}$, we identify $k + 3$ *read/write head actions* or, more simply, *machine actions* (see Table 1.3.1). By an *instruction* we shall mean a quadruple of the form

$$\langle q_i, \sigma; action, q_j \rangle$$

where q_i and q_j are machine states, σ is any alphabet symbol or the blank, and *action* is any one of $k + 3$ possible machine actions. Such instructions are understood conditionally: If currently in state q_i scanning σ, then perform *action* and enter state q_j. As an example of such an instruction, we have

$$\langle q_1, a; \mathrm{R}, q_2 \rangle$$

which is interpreted from left to right as, "If currently in state q_1 scanning symbol a, then move one square to the right and enter state q_2." Incidentally, we do not require that the current state q_i and the successor state q_j of an instruction be distinct. Thus we shall find ample use for instructions such as

$$\langle q_2, B; \mathrm{R}, q_2 \rangle$$

This instruction is to be interpreted as, "If currently in state q_2 reading a blank, then move one square to the right while remaining in state q_2." We emphasize that all Turing machine instructions have the conditional form: "**If** the situation is such and such, **then** do this."

The instruction set of M is embodied in M's transition function δ_M. Each instruction

$$\langle q_i, s; action, q_j \rangle$$

corresponds to one clause $\delta_M(q_i, s) = (action, q_j)$ in the definition of δ_M. Note that δ_M is in no sense a number-theoretic function. Since the arguments of δ_M are state/symbol pairs, we can see that $Dom(\delta_M)$ is $Q \times (\Sigma \cup \{B\})$.

As described so far, a Turing machine consists of

(i) a finite, nonempty set Q of states, among which is initial state q_{init}, and

(ii) a set of instructions over $Q \times \Sigma \cup \{B\}$ as embodied in a transition function δ_M.

In fact, this characterization is not yet general enough for several reasons. Most importantly, we want to allow for the introduction of auxiliary tape symbols that do not actually belong to input alphabet Σ. A

Turing machine will typically use such auxiliary symbols as temporary "markers" that it will usually erase before halting. In order to illustrate the use of such auxiliary symbols, we now consider a new example. Afterward, we shall give a final definition of Turing machines.

EXAMPLE 1.3.1 (Same Number of as and bs) We are about to describe a Turing machine M that behaves as follows. Suppose that M's tape initially contains a finite, unbroken string of as and bs and is otherwise blank. We designate this string of as and bs as w. We do not assume that the as and bs that make up w appear in any particular order within w. As usual, M will start scanning the leftmost symbol of w. M will perform in accordance with the following specification:

> When starting scanning the leftmost symbol of word w consisting of an unbroken string of as and bs in any order, Turing machine M halts scanning a single 1 on an otherwise blank tape if and only if the number of as in w is equal to the number of bs in w—that is, if and only if $n_a(w) = n_b(w)$.   (1.3.1)

Thus for initial tape configuration

$$BHabbbaaB$$

we require that M halt in configuration

$$BH1B$$

Our task is now to design such an M. One rather straightforward solution is the following. M will eliminate as and bs *in pairs* until either

(1) every symbol has been eliminated, in which case the number of as was equal to the number of bs or

(2) some symbol is eliminated for which no companion can be found, in which case the number of as was initially *not* equal to the number of bs.

Implementing this idea has M first replacing the leftmost symbol of w by some marker—the asterisk, say:

$$BH*bbbaaB$$

Since the replaced symbol was an a, the read/write head of M moves off to the right searching for the nearest b, which is also replaced by an asterisk:

$$B*H*bbaaB$$

M then repositions its read/write head over the leftmost remaining occurrence of either a or b:

$$B**HbbaaB$$

For our sample input tape, this cycle is repeated twice more. The first of these two cycles involves eliminating a b and then a companion a and then "resetting":

$$B***Hb*aB$$

The second cycle eliminates a *b* and then a companion *a*, at which point there occurs another attempt at resetting. This time, however, all input symbols have already been replaced by asterisks:

$$B*****\mathbf{H}*B$$

In order to determine this, however, *M* must first pass to the left over all asterisks until it encounters the first blank on the left:

$$\mathbf{H}B******B$$

Then it will pass to the right over all asterisks until it encounters the first blank on the right:

$$B******\mathbf{H}B$$

Since it now "sees" that there is nothing on the tape but asterisks and blanks and that, consequently, resetting is not possible, *M* erases all the asterisks from right to left and then writes a single *1* and halts, as required:

$$B\mathbf{H}1B$$

    The state diagram of a machine *M* that behaves as just described appears as Figure 1.3.1. The reader should now verify *M*'s behavior for initial tape configuration *BHabbbaaB*. The first cycle takes *M* along the "high road" of the diagram from state q_0 through state q_1 to state q_5 and then back to q_0. The next two cycles proceed along the "low road" from state q_0 through state q_2 to state q_5 and then back to q_0. Erasure of asterisks is accomplished by the loop between states q_6 and q_7. The reader is invited to view the simulation of this Turing machine using the software accompanying this text.[5]

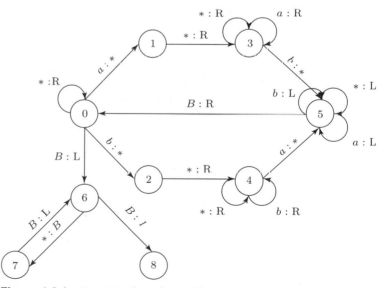

Figure 1.3.1   Same Number of *a*s and *b*s.

---

[5]A brief word concerning the software is in order. We have spoken of read/write heads moving to the right or left along machine tapes. However, those readers who try the companion software will immediately notice that it is the *tapes* that do the actual

Within the Turing Machine folder, open the icon labeled **Same Number of a's and b's—single-tape machine**. Then load either tape `4a4b.tt` or `5a4b.tt`.

We make one more important point with regard to Example 1.3.1 and the state diagram of Figure 1.3.1. Although rather more complex than the trivial state diagrams of §1.2, one feature of those simple diagrams has been retained. Namely, from no state node i in Figure 1.3.1 do we find two distinct arcs both emanating from i and such that both arcs involve one and the same member of input alphabet Σ. Similarly, from no state node i in Figure 1.3.1 do we find two distinct arcs both emanating from i and such that both arcs are for B. Disallowing multiple instructions for a single state and for a single member of $\Sigma \cup \{B\}$ amounts to a requirement that any Turing machine M be *deterministic* (cf. also Figure 1.3.2). That is, whenever M is in state q_i scanning $\sigma \in \Sigma \cup \{B\}$, there is at most one instruction that dictates M's behavior in thissituation. Consequently, M's behavior is strictly determined at every point:

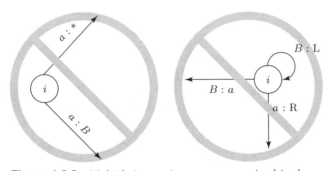

Figure 1.3.2 Multiple instructions are not permitted in the case of deterministic Turing machines.

- If in state q_i scanning $\sigma \in \Sigma \cup \{B\}$ such that there is a (unique) instruction for q_i and σ, then M must proceed in accordance with that instruction.

- If in state q_i scanning $\sigma \in \Sigma \cup \{B\}$ such that there is no instruction for q_i and σ, then M must halt.

For the present, all Turing machines that we consider will be deterministic in this sense. Only much later—in §2.6—will we relax this requirement in order to consider *nondeterministic* Turing machines. In fact, as we shall see, the dichotomy determinism/nondeterminism constitutes one of the principal themes of the theory of computability.

EXAMPLE 1.3.2 (Copying Machine) As another example of the use of markers, let us design a Turing machine M that starts scanning the leftmost *1* of an unbroken string of *n* *1*s and halts scanning the leftmost *1* of an unbroken string of *n* *1*s, followed by a blank followed by another *n* *1*s. That is, for the case $n = 4$, machine M would start in configuration

BH1111B

---

moving while read/write heads remain stationary at the center of the display. This change has been made for reasons that have nothing to do with Turing machines themselves. It just happens that such an arrangement greatly facilitates the implementation of multitape Turing machines, which are introduced in §2.3. We have chosen to treat single-tape Turing machines in a like manner. If anything, this feature of our implementation makes Turing machines rather more like actual digital computers. (Try to imagine a digital computer reading from and writing to a paper tape, say. Surely it is the tape that would move and not the computer itself or any of its components.)

and halt in configuration

$$BH\mathit{1111B1111B}$$

In other words, M makes a single copy of its initial tape contents over at the right. One simple way to do this is to permit M to use the initially given *1*s as a "master": It reads a *1* on the left, replaces it with an asterisk, then copies that *1* on the far right, and returns to the left. This is done until all *1*s on the left have been replaced by asterisks, at which point all of these asterisks are themselves replaced by *1*s. M has only to position its read/write head at the leftmost tape square containing a *1* before halting. The state diagram of M appears as Figure 1.3.3. (Open the icon that is labeled **Copying Machine** and afterward load tape `8.tt`.)

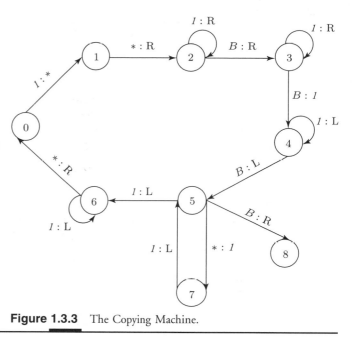

Figure 1.3.3 The Copying Machine.

The previous two examples involve tape symbols that do not appear within input strings: Both Examples 1.3.1 and 1.3.2 use symbol $*$ as a marker, and Example 1.3.1 uses symbol *1* to indicate a particular response to its input string. The use of such auxiliary symbols motivates a distinction between an *input alphabet* Σ and a *tape alphabet* Γ. In general, we shall have $\Sigma \subseteq \Gamma$; that is, any symbol that may occur within an input string is obviously a permissible tape symbol. In Example 1.3.1 we have input alphabet $\Sigma - \{a, b\}$ and tape alphabet $\Gamma = \Sigma \cup \{*, \mathit{1}\}$. In Example 1.3.2 we have input alphabet $\Sigma = \{\mathit{1}\}$ and tape alphabet $\Gamma - \Sigma \cup \{*\}$. Moreover, machine instructions are not restricted to Σ but rather extend over $\Gamma \cup \{B\}$. Thus in Example 1.3.1 we have the instruction

$$\langle q_6, *; B, q_7 \rangle$$

corresponding to an arc at the bottom left in Figure 1.3.1. We mention in passing that B is a member of neither Σ nor Γ. After all, the blank, which we are representing by B, is not a symbol but, rather, the *absence* of symbol. (This having been said, we shall sometimes speak as if B were a symbol.)

Our examples motivate the following set-theoretic definition of Turing machines.

DEFINITION 1.1: A *deterministic Turing machine M* is anything of the form

$$\langle Q, \Sigma, \Gamma, q_{init}, \delta \rangle$$

where Q is a nonempty finite set, Σ and Γ are nonempty finite alphabets with $\Sigma \subseteq \Gamma$, $q_{init} \in Q$, and δ is a (partial) function with domain and codomain given by

$$\delta: \quad Q \times (\Gamma \cup \{B\}) \rightarrow (\Gamma \cup \{B\} \cup \{L, R\}) \times Q$$

Set Q is the set of *states* of M, q_{init} is the *initial state* of M, Σ is M's *input alphabet*, and Γ is its *tape alphabet*. Finally, δ is the *transition function* of M.

We noted earlier that we shall normally write q_0 for initial state q_{init}. As was done in §1.2, we shall on occasion write δ_M for the transition function of Turing machine M. Similarly, Q_M, Σ_M, Γ_M, and q_0^M (or the like) will be used, when necessary, to distinguish the components of machine M.

We mention the following regarding Definition 1.1.

- A transition function δ is permitted to be partial; that is, δ may be undefined for certain state/symbol pairs. Thus, we see that the transition function of the Turing machine of Example 1.3.2 is undefined for argument $\langle q_0, B \rangle$. It should be clear that a Turing machine M with δ_M total will in fact never halt. (Why?)

- Transition function δ is a *function*—that is, a single-valued mapping. This means that any given state/symbol pair $\langle q_i, \sigma \rangle$, for which δ happens to be defined, is mapped by δ onto a unique action/state pair $\langle action, q_j \rangle$. This feature of transition functions is reflected in the requirement, mentioned earlier, that no two arcs emanating from one and the same state node q_i within a state diagram may involve one and the same σ. Again, until further notice, only deterministic Turing machines will be considered.

- Describing δ, without further restriction, as a (partial) function from $Q \times (\Gamma \cup \{B\})$ to $(\Gamma \cup \{B\} \cup \{L, R\}) \times Q$ amounts to permitting instructions of the form $\langle q_i, s; s, q_j \rangle$, which effect state transitions without altering a machine's tape configuration: The same symbol s is read and then written without movement either to the right or the left on the tape. We shall occasionally find such instructions useful. Our description of δ also permits *useless instructions* of the form $\langle q_i, s; s, q_i \rangle$, each of which corresponds to a self-loop on state q_i causing scanned symbol s to be written without any movement of the tape head. We could explicitly disallow useless instructions if we wished and, in §8.6, we shall assume ourselves to have done just that.

- By Definition 1.1, a Turing machine M turns out to be a certain sort of ordered quintuple. This quintuple consists of three sets Q, Σ, and Γ, together with a special element q_{init} belonging to set Q, and, finally, a partial function δ from set $Q \times (\Gamma \cup \{B\})$ to set $(\Gamma \cup \{B\} \cup \{L, R\}) \times Q$. Thus, whereas our informal description involved talk of a read/write head moving along a machine tape, in giving a mathematical definition of Turing machines, we drop such talk and instead speak only of sets, their elements, and functions on these sets. Indeed, as a quintuple, a Turing machine is itself just a set and Definition 1.1 thus richly deserves the "set-theoretic" label. In future chapters we shall have cause to define new sorts of abstract machines. At such times, we shall move rather more quickly to the set-theoretic definition of the abstract machines in question, foregoing, at least in some measure, the lengthy informal description that preceded our mathematical definition in the case of the Turing machine concept.

§1.4 Turing Machines as Language Acceptors and as Language Recognizers

As indicated in its title, this textbook will focus on formal languages, where by *formal language* we mean only some set of *words* or *strings* over some (finite) alphabet Σ. We shall be interested in the ability of various types of abstract machines—for example, Turing machines—to process words over Σ in certain well-defined ways. Turing machines, in particular, will be seen to *accept* formal languages, on the one hand, and to *recognize* languages, on the other. We shall give a technical meaning to each of these terms. *Language acceptance* and *language recognition* will designate two different, albeit related, roles for Turing machines. In this book we focus on language acceptance. At key points, however, the distinction between language acceptance and language recognition will become very important. Consequently, it is essential that the reader be able to differentiate these two roles from the outset. Incidentally, as will already be apparent, it is Turing machines in the second of these two roles that implement the language recognition paradigm introduced in §1.1.

Let L be a language (over alphabet Σ) that we consider to be given in advance. In other words, we are in no sense constructing L. Rather, L's character or identity has already been fixed: Which words belong to L and which do not is not a matter of debate. For example, L might be the language $\{w \in \Sigma^* | n_a(w) = n_b(w)\}$, where $\Sigma = \{a, b\}$. (Of course, this is just the language, considered in Example 1.3.1, consisting of all and only those words over $\Sigma - \{a, b\}$ containing the same number of as as bs.) In that case, it follows from the definition of L that words $aabb$, $ababba$, and ε each belong to L whereas words aba and $aaab$ do not. Now, what is going to count as acceptance of such a language L on the part of some Turing machine M? Essentially, M will be said to accept language L provided that, given an arbitrary word w as input, where w consists solely of symbols of Σ, machine M processes w—*reads w, if you will*—and ultimately identifies w as a member of L if and only if indeed $w \in L$.

- In other words, given an arbitrary word w over Σ as input, if it just happens to be the case that $w \in L$, then M will respond in an affirmative manner so as to indicate this.

- On the other hand, if it just happens that $w \notin L$, then M will *not* respond affirmatively. In the latter case, the issue of what M *does* do is left quite open; we require only that M not respond affirmatively.

Thus, we shall say that Turing machine M accepts language $\{w \in \Sigma^* | n_a(w) = n_b(w)\}$ with $\Sigma = \{a, b\}$ provided that

- M gives its affirmative response—whatever that is—when presented in turn with input words such as $aabb$, $ababba$, and ε

- but M does not respond affirmatively when presented with input words such as aba and $aaab$.

Of course, it is necessary to specify in advance what will count as an affirmative response on M's part. There are many possibilities here—all of them equally good. So we proceed in Definition 1.2 below to lay down certain conventions regarding "affirmative response" to input words on the part of Turing machines. Some such conventions are indispensable. But it really makes little difference *which* conventions are actually adopted in that a decision to do things this way rather than that way will turn out to have no important theoretical consequences. (More on this later.) We begin with a technical definition of *word acceptance* on the part of Turing machines. Afterward, the notion of *language acceptance* will be defined in terms of the notion of word acceptance.

DEFINITION 1.2: *Deterministic Turing machine M accepts nonempty word w if*, when started scanning the leftmost symbol of w on an input tape that contains w and is otherwise blank, M ultimately halts scanning a *1* on an otherwise blank tape. (We shall speak of M's halting in an *accepting configuration*.) *Turing machine M accepts empty word ε if*, when started scanning a blank on a completely blank tape, M ultimately halts scanning a *1* on an otherwise blank tape. (Again, M halts in an accepting configuration.)[6]

---

[6]Our definition gives a special role to the symbol *1*. Complications arise if *1* happens to be a member of input alphabet Σ. We shall henceforth assume that this is not the case whenever language acceptance is the issue.

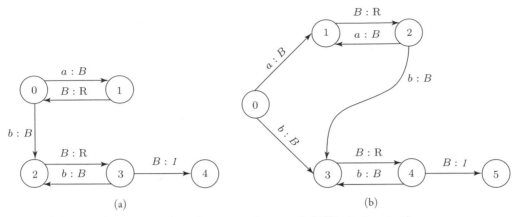

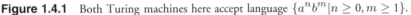

Figure 1.4.1   Both Turing machines here accept language $\{a^n b^m | n \geq 0, m \geq 1\}$.

Definition 1.2 should be understood to stipulate that if Turing machine M halts in any other configuration (e.g., reading a *0* or reading a *1* on a tape that contains other symbols) or never halts at all, then word w is not accepted by M.

EXAMPLE 1.4.1 Next, consider the Turing machines of Figures 1.4.1(a) and 1.4.1(b). Both machines can be seen to accept the word *ab* since, if either is started scanning the first symbol of this word, then a is erased, b is erased, a single *1* is written, and the machine halts. The reader should verify that the word *aaba* is not accepted, in the sense of Definition 1.2, by either machine here. The reader should further verify that each word in the left column of Table 1.4.1 is accepted by both machines and each word in the right column is not accepted.

Plainly, the set of words accepted will be infinite and is none other than the formal language $\{a^n b^m | n \geq 0, m \geq 1\}$. In accordance with Definition 1.3 below, we shall proceed to say that the Turing machines of Figures 1.4.1(a) and 1.4.1(b) accept the language $\{a^n b^m | n \geq 0, m \geq 1\}$.

Table 1.4.1

Accepted Words	Words That Are Not Accepted
b	a
ab	aa
bb	ba
aab	aaa
abb	aba
bbb	bba
aaab	bab
. . .	. . .

Two machines have been given here, both of which accept the language $\{a^n b^m | n \geq 0, m \geq 1\}$ in accordance with Definition 1.3, merely in order to emphasize the fact that alternative, equivalent designs are always possible. The machine of Figure 1.4.1(a) is perhaps more elegant, involving fewer states. Both machines exhibit a certain desirable symmetry—to the extent that this is possible, given that $n \geq 0$ while $m \geq 1$. In general, we shall not be overly concerned with such issues. Sometimes we shall opt for designs involving a greater number of states if doing so enhances the clarity of a state diagram.

DEFINITION 1.3: *Deterministic Turing machine M accepts language L if M accepts all and only the words w in L.* Furthermore, we shall write $L(M)$ for the language accepted by Turing machine M. So if Turing machine M accepts language L, then $L(M) = L$. A language L is said to be *Turing-acceptable* if there exists some deterministic Turing machine M that accepts L.

Finally, we note that, in accordance with Definitions 1.2 and 1.3, the Turing machine M of Example 1.3.1 and Figure 1.3.1 accepts the language $L = \{w \in \Sigma^* | n_a(w) = n_b(w)\}$, where $\Sigma = \{a, b\}$. After all, it was seen that M, when started scanning the leftmost symbol of input word w, halts scanning a 1 on an otherwise blank tape just in case w contains an equal number of as and bs. By Definitions 1.2 and 1.3, this is precisely what it means for M to accept L. Exercising our new terminology, we shall say that $L = \{w \in \Sigma^* | n_a(w) = n_b(w)\}$ is Turing-acceptable.

As mentioned earlier, the notion of language acceptance will be central to our investigations in what follows. It is easy to read too much into it, however. In order to gain a better understanding of what language acceptance on the part of a Turing machine really is—*and also what it isn't*—we consider another example of a Turing machine in the role of language acceptor.

EXAMPLE 1.4.2 The simple Turing machine M whose state diagram appears in Figure 1.4.2(a) is seen to accept the language $L = \{a^n | n \geq 0\}$ over alphabet $\Sigma = \{a, b\}$.

- In accordance with Definition 1.2, any input word $w \in L$ causes M to halt in state q_2 scanning a single 1 on an otherwise blank tape. That is, if M's input is some $w \in L$, then M responds affirmatively.

- On the other hand, if it happens that input word $w \notin L$ because $n_b(w) \neq 0$, then M never halts execution: M's read/write head moves off to the right without ever stopping. This is the result of the self-loop at state q_4. (The reader should take a moment to verify this now.)

It is tempting, but ultimately misleading, to view M as responding "negatively" in the latter case: If $w = ab$, say, so that $w \notin L$, then, according to this view, M responds "negatively" by computing forever. It is hoped that the reader can see the problem here. Namely, in what sense are we to view an infinite computation as a "response" on M's part? We wish to convince the reader that an infinite computation cannot count as a bona fide "negative response" on M's part.

So suppose that the activity of M's read/write head is observable but that no knowledge of M's state diagram itself is available, where M is again the Turing machine of Figure 1.4.2(a). Furthermore, suppose that one has been informed only that M accepts some language L over alphabet $\Sigma = \{a, b\}$ but that one does not know which language L is. Could one now use M's observed behavior in order to determine whether a given input word w is in fact a member of L? The answer to this question is no, and to see why, suppose that $w = ab$. M's read/write head will be observed proceeding off to the right, of course. But at what point in M's computation is one entitled to conclude that M is never going to write a 1 and halt, thereby accepting $w = ab$ after all? It should be plain that one will never be justified in doing so. (Recall that neither M's state diagram nor the identity of the language $L(M)$ is available.) This is because human beings are not capable of determining in general whether or not a computation, currently in process, will ever halt. However long a given computation has continued so far, it is always just possible that it will terminate if permitted to go on only a bit longer. Consequently, a Turing machine such as that of Figure 1.4.2(a), which does accept the language $L = \{a^n | n \geq 0\}$, cannot be said to provide a *decision procedure* for L. Generally speaking, a Turing machine M that merely *accepts* some language L in the sense of Definition 1.3 cannot be used to *decide* whether an arbitrary word w is, in fact, a member of L.

Example 1.4.2 leads us to consider Turing machines in a new role with respect to formal languages. Given a language L over Σ, can some Turing machine be found that *can* decide whether an arbitrary word w over Σ is in L? It turns out that for a wide class of languages this is possible. Each such language L can be associated with a Turing machine M_L that, for an arbitrary word w over Σ taken as input, responds affirmatively if $w \in L$ and responds negatively if $w \notin L$. Machine M_L will be said to *recognize*

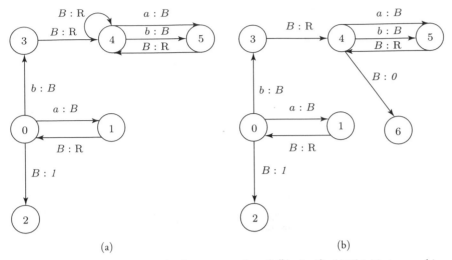

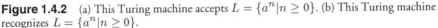

Figure 1.4.2   (a) This Turing machine accepts $L = \{a^n | n \geq 0\}$. (b) This Turing machine recognizes $L = \{a^n | n \geq 0\}$.

language L. It is again open to us to adopt any reasonable conventions with regard to "affirmative" and "negative" responses. What is essential is only that the two responses be plainly distinguishable: Whatever counts as the affirmative response to the effect that input word w *is* a member of L must differ in some clear way from what is to count as the negative response to the effect that input word w *is not* a member. Given Definition 1.2, it is natural to take a single *1* as affirmative response and a single *0* as negative response. This convention is incorporated into Definition 1.4.

DEFINITION 1.4: Let L be a language over alphabet Σ.[7] *Deterministic Turing machine M recognizes language L* if both (i) and (ii) hold:

(i) If w is an arbitrary nonempty word over Σ and M is started scanning the leftmost symbol of w on a tape that contains w and that is otherwise blank, then M ultimately halts scanning a *1* on an otherwise blank tape if $w \in L$ but halts scanning a *0* on an otherwise blank tape if $w \notin L$.

(ii) If M is started scanning a square on a completely blank tape, then M ultimately halts scanning a *1* on an otherwise blank tape if $\varepsilon \in L$ but halts scanning a *0* on an otherwise blank tape if $\varepsilon \notin L$.

A language L is termed *Turing-recognizable* if there exists a Turing machine M that recognizes L.

In the case of a Turing machine functioning as a language recognizer, we shall speak of an "*accepting 1*" and a "*rejecting 0*."

EXAMPLE 1.4.3 Note that we can easily turn the Turing machine *M* of Figure 1.4.2(a), which *accepts* the language $L = \{a^n | n \geq 0\}$, into a new machine *M′* that recognizes *L*. Namely, we remove the self-loop at state q_4 and add a single instruction *B:0* from state q_4 to a new state q_6. This new instruction

---

[7]For reasons already mentioned in conjunction with Definition 1.2, we assume that Σ contains neither symbol *1* nor symbol *0*.

will ultimately be executed just in case input word *w* contains an occurrence of symbol *b*. The state diagram of *M'* appears in Figure 1.4.2(b).

EXAMPLE 1.4.4 The Turing machine *M* of Figure 1.4.3 recognizes the language of palindromes over alphabet $\Sigma = \{a, b\}$. *M* erases a symbol from the very front of input word *w* and then attempts to find and erase an occurrence of the same symbol at the very end of *w*. So long as such attempts are successful, this cycle is repeated until either (1) no symbols remain, in which case $|w|$ was even, or (2) just one letter remains, in which case $|w|$ was odd. In either case, *M* halts in an accepting configuration at state q_{11}. Otherwise, *M* manages to erase its tape contents completely and to write a rejecting *0* before halting in state q_{14}. Note that merely deleting state nodes q_{12}, q_{13}, and q_{14} and all incident arcs results in a Turing machine that merely accepts $\{w \in \Sigma^* | w = w^R\}$.

Open the icon **Recognizer** within the Turing Machine folder and load tapes `evenpali.tt` and `oddpalin.tt` in order to observe the operation of this machine.

We make a few final remarks regarding Definition 1.4.

- Any Turing machine that recognizes a given language L in the sense of Definition 1.4 accepts language L in the sense of Definition 1.3. In other words, language recognition implies language acceptance.

- All of the language acceptors that we have considered up to this point can in fact be modified so as to yield language recognizers. That is, if a Turing machine M accepts language $L = L(M)$, then it

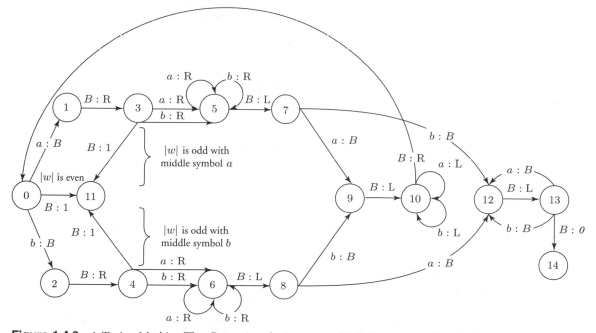

Figure 1.4.3   A Turing Machine That Recognizes the Language of Palindromes over $\Sigma = \{a, b\}$.

is often enough the case that M can be modified so as to yield a new machine M' that recognizes L (see Exercises 1.4.2 and 1.4.6).

- Turing-acceptability and Turing-recognizability are not equivalent notions, however, since, as will be shown later, there exist languages that are Turing-acceptable but not Turing-recognizable.

- A simple construction can be used to show that if language L is Turing-recognizable, then so is L^c, and vice versa. Also, language L is Turing-recognizable if and only both L and L^c are Turing-acceptable languages (see Exercises 1.4.7 and 2.10.11).

Finally, a simple analogy may help to fix in the mind of the reader the distinction between language acceptance and language recognition on the part of Turing machines. (The reader is warned in advance, however, that the analogy that we are about to describe is hardly perfect in every respect.) Consider two computer science graduate departments, say, one at University A and one at University R. Let us describe University R's department first—a responsible department with adequate support staff. Any applicant for graduate study within the Department of Computer Science at University R receives from that department—by April 15, say—either a letter offering admission or a letter denying admission to the department. Of course, this is the way the world should be, as the reader will no doubt agree. But the world is not always as it should be. As evidence of this, consider the Department of Computer Science at University A now. This time it is only students who are being offered admission who receive any letter—by April 15, say, from the department at University A. For whatever reasons, it turns out that all the remaining applicants receive no notification—*ever*. These students make repeated inquiries to the department at University A and are told, for example, that they have been placed on a waiting list, that final decisions have not been made, or that the persons responsible for these decisions are not available. The point of the analogy is perhaps obvious. University R's behavior with respect to applicants for graduate study resembles that of any Turing machine that recognizes some formal language L: After a finite period of time a determinate answer is rendered—a definite yes or no. University A's behavior, on the other hand, is analogous to that of a Turing machine that merely accepts language L.

§1.5 Turing Machines as Computers of Number-Theoretic Functions

In the previous section we considered how Turing machines may serve as language acceptors. We now turn to a consideration of Turing machines in a very different role, namely, that of computers of number-theoretic functions. (The reader will recall that a number-theoretic function is one whose arguments and values are all members of $\mathcal{N}$.) The reader will thereby see how the Turing machine model may be used to implement the function computation paradigm introduced in §1.1.

Surely the most natural representation of number n on a Turing machine tape would be an unbroken string of n *1*s. This would be to use so-called unary notation: Positive integer n is represented or denoted by a string of n *1*s. However, since, in general, number-theoretic functions are permitted to take argument 0, we need to do something slightly different: We will represent natural number n by an unbroken string of $n + 1$ *1*s. Thus the number 2 will be represented by three *1*s. We shall refer to the third or extra *1* here, necessitated by our convention, as the *representational 1*. (It won't make any real difference, however, whether we regard the leftmost or the rightmost occurrence of *1* as the representational *1*.)

Also, since a function may have multiple arguments—for example, the addition function is binary—we need another convention: We shall let the two arguments n and m of binary function f be represented on a Turing machine tape as an unbroken string of $n + 1$ *1*s followed by a single blank followed by an unbroken string of $m + 1$ *1*s. Thus tape contents

$$\ldots B111111B111B\ldots$$

will be taken to represent the argument pair $\langle 5, 2 \rangle$.

We are now almost ready to say what it is for Turing machine M to compute a number-theoretic function f. But before we give the definition, consider a very simple example.

EXAMPLE 1.5.1 Suppose that the Turing machine of Figure 1.5.1 is started scanning the leftmost of three *1*s, say, representing natural number 2. Plainly it will write a single additional *1* to the left and halt scanning four *1*s representing natural number 3. On the other hand, if started scanning a representation of 3, it will halt scanning a representation of 4. More generally, if started scanning an unbroken string of $n + 1$ *1*s **representing natural number *n***, for any $n \geq 0$, it will halt scanning an unbroken string of $n + 2$ *1*s **representing natural number n + 1**. This leads us to say that this Turing machine *computes* the number-theoretic function defined by

$$f(n) = n + 1$$

Function f is just the unary successor function.

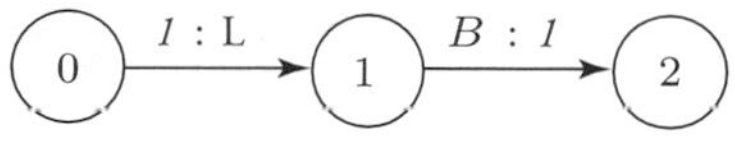

Figure 1.5.1 A Turing machine that computes the successor function.

The successor function is, of course, a total number-theoretic function. We should like Turing machines to be able to compute partial number-theoretic functions as well—that is, functions whose domains are proper subsets of $\mathcal{N}$.

EXAMPLE 1.5.2 Consider the partial number-theoretic function defined by

$$f : \mathcal{N} \to \mathcal{N}$$

$$f(n) = \sqrt{n}$$

As a number-theoretic function, f is defined only for those natural numbers that happen to be 0 or perfect squares. Accordingly, we shall require that a Turing machine M that computes $f(n) = \sqrt{n}$ behave as follows. If started scanning the leftmost *1* of an unbroken string of $n + 1$ *1*s on an otherwise blank tape, where n is a perfect square, then M will halt scanning the leftmost *1* in an unbroken string of $\sqrt{n} + 1$ *1*s on an otherwise blank tape. For example, if started scanning the leftmost of 17 *1*s, representing argument 16, then M should halt scanning the leftmost of 5 *1*s, representing value $\sqrt{16} = 4$. On the other hand, if M is started scanning a representation of some n that is not a perfect square (e.g., $n = 20$), then we require only that M not halt in a *value-representing configuration*—that is, scanning the leftmost *1* of an unbroken sequence of *1*s on an otherwise blank tape. The point here is that, having started scanning a representation of $n = 20$, M is required to behave in a way that reflects the behavior of function f. Since f is not defined for argument $n = 20$, machine M, which computes f, is not permitted to halt in a value-representing configuration. But otherwise, we will not much care what M does do when started scanning a representation of $n = 20$—just so long as it *does not* halt in a value-representing configuration: So M might halt scanning a blank, or halt scanning a *1* on a tape that contains occurrences of symbol $*$, or fail to halt altogether.

Definitions 1.5 and 1.6 below are intended to reflect the nature of Examples 1.5.1 and 1.5.2 above. We recall that, as defined in Chapter 0, a total number-theoretic function is a special sort of partial number-theoretic function. We have taken advantage of this fact in formulating Definitions 1.5 and 1.6. Namely, our definitions explicitly mention only partial number-theoretic functions. But since the total number-theoretic functions are among the partial number-theoretic functions, our definitions apply to them as well.

> **DEFINITION 1.5:** *Deterministic Turing machine M computes (unary) partial number-theoretic function f* provided that:
> (i) If M is started scanning the leftmost *1* of an unbroken string of $n + 1$ *1*s on an otherwise blank tape, where function f is defined for argument n, then M halts scanning the leftmost *1* of an unbroken string of $f(n) + 1$ *1*s on an otherwise blank tape.
> (ii) If M is started scanning the leftmost *1* of an unbroken string of $n + 1$ *1*s on an otherwise blank tape, where function f is undefined for argument n, then M does not halt in a value-representing configuration; that is, either M does not halt at all or, if M does halt, it does not halt scanning the leftmost *1* of an unbroken string of *1*s on an otherwise blank tape.

Note that Definition 1.5 speaks only to the case where Turing machine M, computing number-theoretic function f, starts scanning the leftmost *1* in an unbroken string of $n + 1$ *1*s on a tape that is otherwise blank. In other words, we care only what happens when M starts scanning the leftmost *1* in a representation of a possible argument of f. We do not care what M does if the initial tape configuration cannot be construed as the representation of a single natural number.

EXAMPLE 1.5.3 As a third example, let us describe a Turing machine that computes

$$f(n) = 2n$$

We could adapt the Copying Machine of Example 1.3.2 and Figure 1.3.3 for this purpose. However, a more straightforward design is desirable. To begin, we might first design a Turing machine that, when started scanning the leftmost of an unbroken sequence of n *1*s with $n > 0$, halts scanning the leftmost of $2n$ *1*s. The basic idea is to repeatedly erase *1*s and, for each *1* erased, write exactly two *1*s. Thus, if started scanning the leftmost of three *1*s, say, such a machine would halt scanning the leftmost of six *1*s. This would be very close to what is needed but is not quite right since it is not in accordance with our convention regarding representation of natural numbers: Three *1*s is a representation of 2, while six *1*s is a representation of 5. Plainly, we can accommodate our convention by eliminating exactly one of the *1*s on the tape at the end. The state diagram of something that works is shown in Figure 1.5.2.

The preceding Definition 1.5 covers only the case of unary function computation. But we should like Turing machines to be able to compute k-ary number-theoretic functions for arbitrary $k \geq 0$. As an instance of a Turing machine computing a binary number-theoretic function, consider Example 1.5.4.

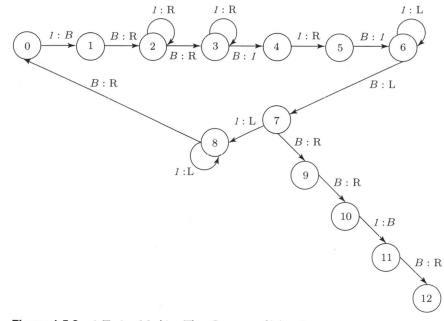

Figure 1.5.2   A Turing Machine That Computes $f(n) = 2n$.

EXAMPLE 1.5.4 Our goal is a Turing machine M that computes the addition function

$$f(n, m) = n + m$$

in the following sense. Suppose that M is initially scanning the leftmost *1* of a string representing its first argument n, which is followed by a single blank, to the right of which blank is a string representing its second argument m. Suppose further that M's tape contains nothing but blanks otherwise. Then M should ultimately halt scanning the leftmost *1* of a string representing natural number $n + m$ on a tape that is otherwise blank. For example, assuming that M starts in the configuration representing arguments $n = 5$ and $m = 3$:

$$\ldots BH111111B1111B \ldots$$

we shall require that it halt in the configuration representing value $f(n, m) = n + m = 8$:

$$\ldots BH111111111B \ldots$$

The design of such a machine is quite simple. Since initially there is a total of $n + m + 2$ *1*s on the tape and since we desire just $n + m + 1$ of them to remain in the end, one solution is to merely erase both the leftmost *1* and the rightmost *1* on the tape and then write a *1* in the blank separating the argument representations before returning to the left. The machine of Figure 1.5.3 computes the binary addition function in the sense of Definition 1.6 below, which is a generalization of Definition 1.5.

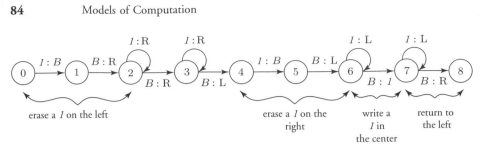

Figure 1.5.3 A Turing Machine That Computes the Binary Addition Function.

DEFINITION 1.6: *Deterministic Turing machine M computes k-ary partial number-theoretic function f* with $k \geq 1$ provided that:

(i) If M is started scanning the leftmost *1* of an unbroken string of $n_1 + 1$ *1*s followed by a single blank followed by an unbroken string of $n_2 + 1$ *1*s followed by a single blank ... followed by an unbroken string of $n_k + 1$ *1*s on an otherwise blank tape, where function f happens to be defined for arguments $n_1, n_2, \ldots, n_k$, then M halts scanning the leftmost *1* of an unbroken string of $f(n_1, n_2, \ldots, n_k) + 1$ *1*s on an otherwise blank tape.

(ii) If M is started scanning the leftmost *1* of an unbroken string of $n_1 + 1$ *1*s followed by a single blank followed by an unbroken string of $n_2 + 1$ *1*s followed by a single blank ... followed by an unbroken string of $n_k + 1$ *1*s on an otherwise blank tape, where function f is undefined for arguments $n_1, n_2, \ldots, n_k$, then M does not halt scanning the leftmost *1* of an unbroken string of *1*s on an otherwise blank tape.

It should be plain that Example 1.5.4 is strictly in accordance with this definition where $k = 2$ and $f(n, m) = n + m$.

EXAMPLE 1.5.5 (Multiplication Machine) As a more complicated example of a Turing machine computing a binary number-theoretic function, let us design a Turing machine that computes the multiplication function $f(n, m) = n \cdot m$. There are of course many ways to do this. Although not absolutely necessary, let us use the asterisk as a marker. To see how the Turing machine will work, suppose that we have $n = 3$ and $m = 2$, so that initially the tape configuration is **H***1111B111BB*. The basic idea will be to reproduce, starting at the blank tape square in boldface, n copies of m *1*s. Thus we shall use the *1*s representing n as a "counter" and the *1*s representing m as our "master" for copying. Lest our convention regarding natural-number representations get in the way, we should first delete a single *1* from the left of the *1*s representing n and another *1* from the right of the 1s representing m. This might also be a good time to write a representational *1* for the product. This much is accomplished by states q_0 through q_{10} of the Turing machine transition diagram found by opening the icon labeled **Multiplication Machine**. We can now suppose that the tape is configured as *B***H***111B11B1*. A single "counter" *1* is now erased—our counter is decremented—and the copying routine of Example 1.3.2 is used to copy m *1*s at the far right, afterward returning to the far left. One such cycle takes us from state q_{14} to state q_{25} and back. For the case $n = 3$, two more such cycles are necessary, after which all *1*s on the tape except those representing the product must be erased (states q_{28} and q_{29}). States q_{31} through q_{38} are required to accommodate the possibility that either n or m is 0. Load the tape contained in file `3and5.tt` and observe the operation of this machine.

We point out that any of the 0-ary constant functions $C_0^0, C_1^0, C_2^0, \ldots$ may be associated with a Turing machine, although Definition 1.6, as it stands, does not cover such a case. (As pointed out in

§0.3, any 0-ary function is of the form C_m^0 for some fixed $m \geq 0$.) Since it will be technically useful in Chapter 3, we now extend Definition 1.6 so as to describe how 0-ary functions $C_0^0, C_1^0, C_2^0, \ldots$ can be computed by Turing machines.

DEFINITION 1.6 (extension): *Deterministic Turing machine M computes 0-ary function C_m^0 for fixed $m \geq 0$ if M*, started scanning a blank on a completely blank tape, halts scanning the leftmost of $m + 1$ *1s* on an otherwise blank tape.

The reader should verify that machine M_1 of Exercise 1.2.1 and Figure 1.2.11 computes function C_2^0. We are now ready to define a very important class of number-theoretic functions.

DEFINITION 1.7: A partial number-theoretic function f is said to be *Turing-computable* if there exists a Turing machine M that computes f in the sense of Definition 1.6.

EXAMPLE 1.5.6 In Examples 1.5.4 and 1.5.5 we saw that the usual addition and multiplication functions are Turing-computable functions. The reader may open the icon **Factorial Machine** in order to test a 45-state Turing machine, created by Alexandra Nichifor, that computes factorial function $f(n) = n!$, thereby showing that function to be Turing-computable.

EXAMPLE 1.5.7 Open the icon labeled **Square Root** in order to test a Turing machine, due to Wade Alimam, that computes the total, unary number-theoretic function defined as

$$t(n) = \lfloor \sqrt{n} \rfloor$$

Load tape file `50.tt` in order to observe the operation of this machine for argument $n = 50$.

In fact, we shall be concerned with the class of Turing-computable functions throughout Part I of this book. Later discussions will show that this class of functions is in a certain sense a very "natural" class: Philosophical arguments will be presented to the effect that this class comprises precisely those functions that are "effective" or "algorithmic" in the usual sense—that is, those functions f such that we can, for any given argument(s), arrive at the value of f for such argument(s) by carrying out some finite, mechanical procedure involving symbol manipulation or the like. This more-or-less philosophical discussion will occur at the beginning of Chapter 8. Further investigation of the class of Turing-computable functions in Chapters 2 through 7 will provide the technical background for that discussion.

Before concluding this section, we note an important consequence of Definitions 1.5 and 1.6. Let us begin by considering the partial number-theoretic function

$$f : \mathcal{N} \to \mathcal{N}$$
$$f(n) = \sqrt{n}$$

We are regarding f as partial in that it is defined for perfect squares only and is undefined everywhere else. Similarly,

$$g: \mathcal{N} \times \mathcal{N} \to \mathcal{N}$$

$$g(n, m) = n - m$$

is a partial number-theoretic function that is undefined for pairs such as $\langle 4, 7 \rangle$. Even

$$f: \mathcal{N} \to \mathcal{N}$$

$$f(n) \text{ is undefined}$$

can now be construed as a partial number-theoretic function: It is that unique, unary, partial number-theoretic function that is *undefined everywhere*. Similarly, there is just one everywhere undefined number-theoretic function of two arguments

$$f: \mathcal{N} \times \mathcal{N} \to \mathcal{N}$$

$$f(n, m) \text{ is undefined}$$

Given this very general notion of partial number-theoretic function, we can see the truth of

---

REMARK 1.5.1: Every Turing machine with input alphabet $\Sigma = \{1\}$ computes some unary partial number-theoretic function.

This follows immediately from Definitions 1.5 and 1.6. After all, according to those definitions, what function, or functions, are computed by the single-state Turing machine M whose transition function δ_M is defined by the two clauses below?

$$\delta_M(q, 1) = (\text{R}, q)$$

$$\delta_M(q, B) = (\text{R}, q)$$

It is not hard to see that, in accordance with Definition 1.5, M computes the unary partial number-theoretic function that is undefined everywhere: When started scanning the leftmost 1 of an unbroken string of $n+1$ 1s on an otherwise blank tape, representing argument n, machine M moves off to the right without ever halting—no matter what n is. But this is exactly what is required by Definition 1.5(ii): If f is undefined for argument n, then M, which computes it, should do something like compute forever. A little reflection should convince the reader that the very same Turing machine computes the everywhere undefined partial number-theoretic function of k arguments for any fixed $k \geq 2$. (What happens if M starts scanning the leftmost 1 of an unbroken string of $n_1 + 1$ 1s followed by a single blank followed by an unbroken string of $n_2 + 1$ 1s followed by a single blank ... followed by an unbroken string of $n_k + 1$ 1s on an otherwise blank tape?) Finally, we note that, by Definition 1.7, the everywhere undefined function of k arguments, for fixed $k \geq 1$, is Turing-computable.

Turing Machines as Transducers

So far we have considered Turing machines in three distinct roles. In §1.4 we saw how Turing machines may serve either as language acceptors or as language recognizers. The latter role was seen to subsume the former in the sense that any deterministic Turing machine that recognizes language L thereby accepts it as well. In the present section we described how Turing machines may also play a third role, namely, as computers of number-theoretic functions. We have hereby accounted for two of the three computational paradigms of §1.1. Only the transduction paradigm remains, and we turn to this issue now.

Happily, the matter is handled easily since some Turing machines, by design, are not language acceptors, language recognizers, or computers of number-theoretic functions. We have in mind a Turing machine that reverses its input word, say, or one that merely makes a second copy of its input word. As mentioned earlier, a transducer merely transforms its input word w so as to produce some output word w'. (In the case of a Turing machine implementing word reversal, say, w' will be w^R.) As already suggested in §1.1, transduction is the most general of the various roles in which a Turing machine may serve, in the sense that any language acceptor, language recognizer, or function computer may be regarded as a special sort of transducer.[8]

EXAMPLE 1.5.8 (Word Reversal) The Turing machine of Figure 1.5.4 reverses any input word w over alphabet $\Sigma = \{a, b\}$, writing w^R one character at a time from left to right while erasing w one character

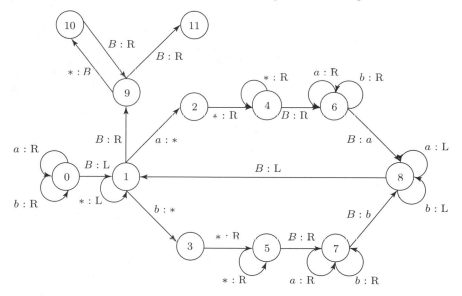

Figure 1.5.4   A Turing Machine That Reverses Any Input Word over $\Sigma = \{a, b\}$.

---

[8]A truly rigorous notion of transduction would require that we adopt some technical conventions with regard to (i) the possible occurrence of blanks within an output word and (ii) the position of the read/write head with respect to that output word. For example, concerning (ii), we might require that, when the machine halts, the read/write head be scanning the leftmost nonblank on the tape. This might mean regarding a machine as undefined for a given input word if, upon halting, the machine's read/write head is not scanning the leftmost nonblank on the tape.

at a time from right to left. Open the icon **Reverse Word** and load tape `abbab.tt` in order to observe the operation of this Turing machine. We note once again that this machine neither computes a function nor accepts (recognizes) any language. Rather, the most that can be said is that it transforms its input in a certain way and thereby plays the role of transducer.

§1.6 Modular Construction of Turing Machines

Our use of the Copying Machine of Example 1.3.2 as one component or *module* within the Multiplication Machine of Example 1.5.5 is a fairly typical example of a valuable design tool: It is frequently useful to design more complex Turing machines by first designing several smaller Turing machines and then combining them in appropriate ways. Such *modularity* is especially useful when designing Turing machines that compute number-theoretic functions. In the present section, we shall illustrate the general principle with a couple more examples. This topic will be continued later in §2.6, where nondeterministic Turing machines are introduced.

EXAMPLE 1.6.1 As a first, relatively simple example of modular construction, suppose that we wish to design a Turing machine M^* that computes the binary number-theoretic function $h(n, m) = 2 \cdot (n + m)$. This can be done by combining the Turing machine M of Figure 1.5.3, which computes the binary function $f(n, m) = n + m$, with the Turing machine M' of Figure 1.5.2, which computes function $g(n) = 2n$. Creating a new state diagram for machine M^* from these two modules is easy. Given a representation of arguments n and m as input, M^* will first simulate M so as to obtain a representation of $n + m$ and afterward simulate M' so as to obtain a representation of $2 \cdot (n + m)$. Figure 1.6.1 shows the state diagram of such an M^*, where we have identified M's state q_8 (see Figure 1.5.3) with M''s initial state q_0 (see Figure 1.5.2); that is, the arc from q_7 to q_8 in Figure 1.5.3 now leads from q_7 into what is, in essence, state q_0 of Figure 1.5.2. So imagine that M^* is started scanning the leftmost *1* of an unbroken string of *1*s representing first argument n followed on the right by an unbroken string of *1*s representing second argument m.

$$B\,q_0 \underbrace{1111\ldots11111}_{n+1\,1s}\,B\,\underbrace{11111\ldots1111}_{m+1\,1s}\,B$$

M^* will eventually enter its state q_8, scanning the leftmost *1* of an unbroken string of *1*s representing $n + m$

$$B\,q_8 \underbrace{11111111111\ldots1111111111}_{n+m+1\,1s}\,B$$

Now the behavior of M' is simulated; that is, M^* will eventually halt in its state q_{20} scanning the leftmost *1* in a representation of $h(n, m) = 2 \cdot (n + m)$.

$$B\,q_{20} \underbrace{11111111111\ldots1111111111}_{2\cdot(n+m)+1\,1s}\,B$$

This example illustrates a general design principle that we might express roughly as follows: If a new Turing machine is to consist of module M followed by module M', then simply identify any state(s)

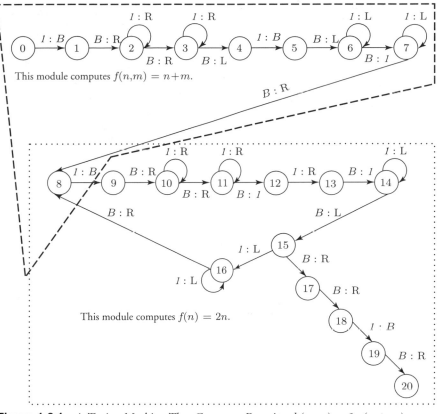

Figure 1.6.1   A Turing Machine That Computes Function $h(n, m) = 2 \cdot (n + m)$.

q_{halt} of M in which M is expected to halt (function computers tend to have one or two such states) with the initial state q'_{init} of M' and renumber the states of M'. In other words, we redirect all arcs that before led into q_{halt} so that they now lead into q'_{init}.[9]

EXAMPLE 1.6.2 As a second example of modular design of Turing machines, consider the Turing machine M found at icon **n to the nth Power** within the Turing Machine folder. M will be seen to

---

[9]This "general" principle does not, in fact, always work. Namely, if q_{halt} possesses a self-loop for symbol s, say, and if q'_{init} just happens to possess an arc (but not a self-loop) for that same s, then applying the general principle will result in a machine M^* that is nondeterministic. That is, the state corresponding to q_{halt} and q'_{init} in M^* will possess two instruction arcs for one and the same symbol s. Our work in §2.6 will show that this is not an insuperable problem, since any such nondeterministic Turing machine is equivalent to one that is deterministic in the sense of Definition 1.1.

compute the unary function defined as

$$f: \mathcal{N} \to \mathcal{N}$$

$$f(n) = n^n$$

Try loading the tape file `3.tt` and verifying that M halts scanning the leftmost of $3^3 + 1 = 28$ *1s* on an otherwise blank tape. Incidentally, the software will count strings of *1s*—right-click once on the square in the center of the tape. M's state diagram involves upwards of 80 states. It was not so very difficult to create, however, since (modifications of) both the Copying Machine and the Multiplication Machine were incorporated as submachines. The former is found at submachine nodes 5 and 7, while the latter appears at node 18.

§1.7 Introduction to Complexity Theory

In §1.4 we saw how the language recognition paradigm may be implemented on the Turing machine model of computation, and we then introduced notions of *Turing-acceptable language* and *Turing-recognizable language*. Then in §1.5 we turned to an implementation of the function computation paradigm and introduced a notion of *Turing-computable function*. Both discussions concern what we might now call *computability-in-principle*. In other words, our focus in §1.4 and §1.5 was the computational capacities of Turing machines in the absence of any proscribed limits on the length of computations or on the number of tape squares that may be visited over the course of such computations. We shall continue to be interested in computability-in-principle, and, when computability-in-principle is the issue, we will not concern ourselves with the quantity of resources—time and space—consumed by the Turing machines in question.

At other points, however, more pragmatic interests will motivate us to ask about the capabilities of Turing machines given some prior resource limitation(s). Often enough, we shall be investigating the notion of *computational feasibility*—roughly, just which problems are going to be solvable by Turing machines given the quantities of resources that are likely to be available to us in the real world. On rarer occasions, we shall be interested in determining which among the feasible problems also happen to be *highly parallel* in the sense that a parallel algorithm for solving the problem really does result in an appreciable reduction in the time required for computation as compared with sequential algorithms for solving the same problem. The investigation of these and other related questions belongs to that part of the theory of computability known as *complexity theory*. We might define complexity theory to be the study of *resource-bounded computability*.

In this text we shall be studying both computability-in-principle and various notions of resource-bounded computability. Moreover, we shall be pursuing both interests simultaneously. Frankly, this is not the way it is usually done. But there are some decided advantages to our integrated approach—in particular, the greater coverage of complexity-theoretic issues that will become possible. Confusion can be avoided provided only that the reader bear in mind the important distinction between computability-in-principle, on the one hand, and resource-bounded computability, on the other. Since big-O notation will be an essential tool in our investigation of the latter notion, we turn to it now.

We recall what it is for number-theoretic function $f(n)$ to be $O(g(n))$, where g here is some number-theoretic function. (We restrict our attention to total functions for the moment.) Very roughly, it is for

$f(n)$ to be bounded above by $g(n)$ for sufficiently large values of n. Thus in the graphs of Figure 1.7.1 we have functions f and g such that, for values of n greater than a certain n_0, $g(n)$ is always greater that $f(n)$.[10] We direct the reader's attention to Definition 0.5 in §0.5 in order to emphasize just how rough our suggestion here really is. (Our earlier remark to the effect that $f(n)$ is $O(g(n))$ if $f(n)$ is bounded above by $g(n)$ for

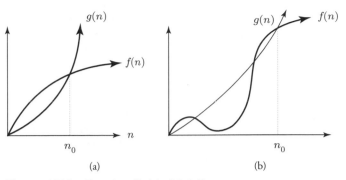

Figure 1.7.1 Function $f(n)$ is $O(g(n))$.

sufficiently large values of n involves the assumption that the constant C in Definition 0.5 may be assumed to be 1.)

We shall use big-O notation to provide a so-called (*worst-case*) *time analysis* of the Turing machine M of Example 1.3.1. The reader will recall that M accepts the language $\{w \in \Sigma^* | n_a(w) = n_b(w)\}$. We are interested in the maximum number of "steps" in M's computations for input words of some given length n. We define a number-theoretic function that is the subject of much of the study of complexity theory and algorithm analysis.

DEFINITION 1.8: Let M be a Turing machine and let n be an arbitrary natural number. The unary number-theoretic function $time_M$ is defined by

$time_M(n) = $ the maximum number of "steps" in any

terminating computation of M for an input

of size n

Of course, Definition 1.8 is not very useful so long as we have not specified what is meant by a "step" within a Turing machine computation nor what we mean by size of input. As for the latter, we shall usually, but not always, take "size of input" to mean the length of a given input word. And as for the former, there is a very natural construal of "step" in the case of Turing machines: By a step, we shall mean the execution of a single instruction. Thus each move along an arc within M's state diagram will count as one step. If we assume that each such instruction is executed in one time unit, then the maximum number of steps is a measure of time in the worst case. Letting M be the Turing machine of Example 1.3.1 and Figure 1.3.1 and simply by counting, let us evaluate $time_M(0)$. There is but one possible input word of length 0, namely, ε. Referring to Figure 1.3.1, we see that M halts in state q_8 after executing two instructions. Thus we have

$$time_M(0) = 2$$

---

[10]Although functions $f(n)$ and $g(n)$ are number-theoretic functions rather than real-valued functions, we follow the convenient practice of graphing these functions as unbroken curves.

As for $time_M(1)$, we have two cases to consider, corresponding to the two possible input words of length 1. Input word a causes M to halt in state q_3 after two steps; input word b causes M to halt in state q_4 after two steps. Thus

$$time_M(1) = 2$$

also. There are four possible input words of length 2: aa, ab, ba and bb. The reader should verify that accepted inputs ab and ba both cause M to halt in state q_8 after 14 steps whereas inputs aa and bb cause M to halt in states q_3 and q_4, respectively, after three steps. Thus, since the maximum of 14 and 3 is 14, we have

$$time_M(2) = 14$$

It should be plain that, for any fixed n, accepted inputs of length n involve a greater number of computation steps than do nonaccepted inputs of length n. Also, the symmetry of M's design means that inputs aba and bab, say, will involve the same number of steps. The reader should verify the following values. (The companion software may be used to accomplish this.)

$$time_M(3) = 12$$
$$time_M(4) = 32$$
$$time_M(5) = 28$$
$$time_M(6) = 56$$
$$time_M(7) = 50$$
$$time_M(8) = 86$$
$$time_M(9) = 78$$
$$time_M(10) = 122$$

$$\cdots$$

Of course no input word of odd length has any chance of acceptance by M, which, given our earlier remark, explains why $time_M$ is not strictly increasing. Focusing on even-length inputs only, we notice that the longer the input string, the greater the number of steps in the computation of the machine worst case. More specifically, we notice that for $n \geq 4$ the value of $time_M(n)$ is bounded above by $2n^2$ certainly. That is, the function $time_M(n)$ is $O(n^2)$. Or, as we will sometimes say, M has time complexity $O(n^2)$. Of course, counting steps, as we have done, is tedious. Fortunately there is an easier way to see matters if we refer to the state diagram of Figure 1.3.1.

To see why the exponent here is 2, consider the following questions. In each case we assume input of length n, where n is even.

- Referring to Figure 1.3.1, what is a good upper bound on the number of times M will traverse one of the two possible cycles—either the "high road" or the "low road"— leading from state q_0 through state q_5 and back to state q_0? Well, since accepted inputs (i.e., words containing an equal number of as and bs) will result in the greatest number of such traversals, it is obvious that the maximum number here will be precisely $n/2$.

- What is an upper bound on the number of computation steps involved in any traversal of one of these two cycles from q_0 to q_5 and back? It is hoped that the reader can see that the most costly such traversal occurs when M is scanning the leftmost symbol of a word such as

$$\underbrace{****\cdots*****}_{(n-1)/2 \text{ times}} a \underbrace{*****\cdots****}_{(n-1)/2 \text{ times}} b$$

The reader should verify that, in such a case, one traversal of either of the two cycles will involve $2n + 2$ steps.

- Assuming that the maximum $n/2$ traversals have been completed, how many times will M execute the instruction corresponding to the self-loop at state q_0, thereby verifying that only asterisks now appear on its tape? Well, at this point we are supposing that the tape contains n asterisks and nothing else and that M is currently in state q_0 scanning the leftmost of these asterisks.

$$B\, \boldsymbol{q_0} \underbrace{***********\cdots**********}_{n \text{ times}} B$$

Thus M will execute the instruction "$*$:R" precisely n times.

$$B \underbrace{***********\cdots**********}_{n \text{ times}} \boldsymbol{q_0} B$$

- How many times will the machine go from state q_0 into state q_6 maximum? The answer is easy: once, of course.

$$B***********\cdots********\boldsymbol{q_0}*B$$

- What is the maximum number of times M will traverse the cycle from state q_6 and back, each time erasing an asterisk and moving one square to the left? Plainly it will do this n times maximum. This makes for a total of $2n$ steps maximum between exiting state q_6 for the first time and entering state q_6 for the last time.

- How many more computation steps are required before M halts? Plainly just the one step that causes an accepting *1* to appear on the tape.

Summing up, we have

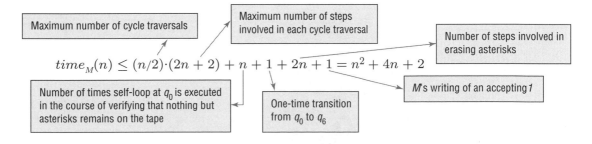

$$time_M(n) \le (n/2)\cdot(2n + 2) + n + 1 + 2n + 1 = n^2 + 4n + 2$$

Since for $n \geq 5$ we have $n^2 + 4n + 2 \leq 2n^2$, we can see that $time_M(n)$ is $O(n^2)$ and hence that M *computes in polynomial time.*

It is worth making a few additional remarks concerning function $time_M$.

- Function $time_M$ is number-theoretic in the sense that both its domain and its range are natural numbers. First of all, since the length of a Turing machine input can be neither negative nor fractional, it makes sense that $Dom(time_M)$ is $\mathcal{N}$. Also, since the number of steps in a computation that halts can be neither negative nor fractional, it follows that $Cod(time_M)$ is $\mathcal{N}$ as well.

- Turing machine computations, as we have seen, need not terminate. In fact, it may just happen that a given machine M halts for *no* input word of length n. In that case, there will be no natural number that is the maximum number of steps in any terminating computation for input word of length n. In such a case, we will say that $time_M(n)$ is undefined. Thus, in general, $time_M$ will not be a total function.

- That function $time_M$ measures worst-case performance on the part of Turing machine M is a matter of its definition in terms of the maximum of some class of natural numbers—that is, of some class of running times.

Let us use this opportunity to introduce a notion of *space* for Turing machines and to give a *worst-case space analysis* of the Turing machine of Example 1.3.1.

DEFINITION 1.9: Let M be a Turing machine and let n be an arbitrary natural number. The number-theoretic function $space_M$ is defined by

$$space_M(n) = \text{the maximum number of tape squares scanned}$$

$$\text{over the course of any terminating computation}$$

$$\text{of } M \text{ for arbitrary input of size } n$$

- As mentioned earlier, size of input will usually be taken to mean length of input word.

- Also, if a tape square is visited six times in the course of a computation, it will be counted only once.

- Finally, even if input word w is empty, any machine M nonetheless visits at least one tape square so that, in general, we have $space_M(n) \geq 1$.

Letting M be the Turing machine of Example 1.3.1 and Figure 1.3.1, we see that

$$space_M(0) = 2$$
$$space_M(1) = 2$$

$$space_M(2) = 4$$

$$space_M(3) = 5$$

$$space_M(4) = 6$$

$$space_M(5) = 7$$

$$space_M(6) = 8$$

. . .

(Again, the accompanying software can be of use here.) Of course, the number of squares visited (i.e., required storage) increases with length of input. More specifically, we note that for $n \geq 0$, where n is the length of input, the value of $space_M(n)$ is bounded above by $n + 2$. So the function $space_M(n)$ is $O(n)$ and we shall say that M *computes in linear space*.

Henceforth we shall regularly speak not merely of what a particular Turing machine does but also of how fast it does it, worst case, and using how much memory or space. Worst-case analyses of Turing machines of every variety are possible. However, for reasons that will become plain later, we shall be primarily interested in providing such analyses for Turing machines functioning as language acceptors or as language recognizers. (The common form of Definitions 1.8 and 1.9 already reflect this interest.) We shall say that the Turing machine of Example 1.3.1 accepts language $\{w \in \Sigma^* | n_a(w) = n_a(w)\}$, with $\Sigma = \{a, b\}$, in time $O(n^2)$ and space $O(n)$—that is, in polynomial time and linear space.

Incidentally, polynomial-time Turing-acceptable languages will play an important role in our study due to the generally accepted identification of feasibility with polynomial time. We define the *complexity class P* to be the class of all languages accepted in polynomial time by some Turing machine of the sort that we have been considering. Thus our time analysis of the machine of Example 1.3.1 establishes that language $\{w \in \Sigma^* | n_a(w) = n_a(w)\}$ is a member of complexity class P by virtue of its being accepted by a (deterministic) Turing machine that computes in polynomial time. (Again, we still owe the reader a fuller explanation of why our Turing machines are being labeled *deterministic*. That will come later.)

DEFINITION 1.10: A language L over alphabet Σ is said to be *polynomial-time Turing-acceptable* if there exist both a deterministic Turing machine M and a polynomial $p(n)$ such that, for any $w \in \Sigma^*$, we have $w \in L$ if and only if M accepts w in $O(p(|w|))$ steps. Equivalently, language L over alphabet Σ is polynomial-time Turing-acceptable if there exists a deterministic Turing machine M such that M accepts L and M computes in $O(n^k)$ steps for some constant $k \in N$, where $n = |w|$. (As usual, we are writing $|w|$ for the length of word w.)

DEFINITION 1.11: The class of all languages that are accepted in polynomially bounded time by some (deterministic, single-tape) Turing machine is known as P.

We should like to say something to motivate our identification of computational feasibility with polynomially bounded time. To this end, consider Table 1.7.1 and note the explosive growth of function $time_M(n) = 2^n$ for larger n. Again, we expect that as the size of a problem increases, more time will be consumed in obtaining a solution. However, the sort of increases observed in Table 1.7.1 for

Table 1.7.1 Comparison of the Growth Rates of Several Functions, Where We Are Assuming That Each Computation Step Requires One Microsecond[a]

	$n = 10$	$n = 20$	$n = 30$
$time_M(n) = n$	0.00001 seconds	0.00002 seconds	0.00003 seconds
$time_M(n) = n^2$	0.0001 seconds	0.0004 seconds	0.0009 seconds
$time_M(n) = n^3$	0.001 seconds	0.008 seconds	0.027 seconds
$time_M(n) = n^4$	0.01 seconds	0.16 seconds	0.81 seconds
$time_M(n) = 2^n$	0.001024 seconds	1.048576 seconds	17.8957 minutes
	$n = 40$	$n = 50$	$n = 60$
$time_M(n) = n^2$	0.00004 seconds	0.00005 seconds	0.00006 seconds
$time_M(n) = n^3$	0.0016 seconds	0.0025 seconds	0.0036 seconds
$time_M(n) = n^3$	0.064 seconds	0.125 seconds	0.216 seconds
$time_M(n) = n^4$	2.56 seconds	6.25 seconds	12.96 seconds
$time_M(n) = 2^n$	12.72583 days	35.67843 years	365.34711 centuries

[a] One microsecond equals 0.000001 second.

$time_M(n) = 2^n$ indicate plainly that an algorithm that requires $O(2^n)$ steps worst case cannot be of any real use in obtaining a solution at least in the case of some inputs. Consequently, to be on the safe side, one should avoid machines M where $time_M$ exhibits exponential growth (or worse).

This leads us to formulate the following

> **COBHAM–EDMONDS THESIS REGARDING COMPUTATIONAL FEASIBILITY:** The problem of determining whether a given string is a member of a given language L is feasible (or tractable) if and only if L is in P.

Turing Machines and Big-Omega Notation

The use of big-O notation to express upper bounds on the resource requirements of Turing machines is essential to that part of the theory of computability known as complexity theory. Similarly, so-called *big-Omega notation*, introduced in Exercise 0.5.10, is useful in expressing *lower bounds* on the resources required, worst case, by Turing machines. Having said this, we are forced to admit that big-Omega notation will play the smallest of roles in this text whereas big-O notation will loom large. Why the difference? Rather than leave this as a mystery, we shall explain this now.

Recall that, in general, function $f(n)$ is $\Omega(g(n))$ just in case $g(n)$ is $O(f(n))$—that is, just in case $f(n)$ is bounded below by (some constant multiple of) $g(n)$. For instance, the Turing machine M of Example 1.3.1 can be seen to compute in time $\Omega(n)$ and space $\Omega(n)$ in that both $time_M(n)$ and $space_M(n)$ are bounded below by function $g(n) = n$. To see this quickly, consider nonaccepted input words of the form a^n or b^n. We have M halting either in state q^3 or q^4 after precisely $n + 1$ steps. Moreover, all other input words of length n will require strictly more steps. Incidentally, note that we are yet engaged here in giving a *worst-case analysis* of M's performance since we are saying something about the lower bounds of functions $time_M(n)$ and $space_M(n)$—both defined in terms of some maximum.

So far it may appear that big-O notation and big-Omega would be on a par with respect to our future investigations of machine models. However, there is an important disanalogy between big-O notation and big-Omega notation as used to express a worst-case analysis of the resource requirements of an individual language acceptor M. This difference concerns the information conveyed concerning accepted language $L(M)$ itself.

First, suppose that some Turing machine M accepts language L in time $O(n)$, say. Of course, learning of this analysis, we acquire important information concerning machine M. But, *in addition*, we learn something important about language L itself; namely, if it is a matter of accepting L with optimal efficiency, then we need not consider running any machine M' that accepts L in time $O(n^2)$, say. This is because, in general, we will do better with the faster M. In other words, knowing that M accepts language L in time $O(n)$ amounts to knowing an upper bound on the complexity of language L itself, at least with respect to Turing machines: We have learned that it can be accepted in linear time. This information in turn permits us to henceforth disregard an entire class of equivalent, but less efficient, machines. And although it may turn out later that we can do better than $O(n)$—someone could always find a machine that is strictly faster than M—there is probably no reason at this point to spend time considering machines that are slower than M, given our general interest in efficiency. In short, we have learned something about M, and we have also learned something important about L.

Contrast this now with the situation in which we learn that some Turing machine M accepts language L in time $\Omega(n)$. This new knowledge is informative enough regarding M itself: We learn that M's computation requires on the order of n steps for some input words of length n for n sufficiently large. On the other hand, this knowledge *by itself* tells us nothing very useful about the computational complexity of accepting language L itself.[11] We know now only that, *for a particular Turing machine M*, function $time_M(n)$ is bounded below by n. But obviously it cannot be concluded on this basis alone that *no* Turing machine accepts L in time $\Omega(\log_2 n)$, say. It may be only that we have not been clever enough to discover the more efficient design.

---

[11] This has much more to do with us than with Turing machines. Given our own limited duration, we are generally interested in getting to a result as fast as possible. ("To save time is to lengthen life," to quote Woodrow Wilson.) But try to imagine another species of intelligent beings—perhaps of infinite duration—whose peculiar interests lie in consuming as much time as possible while yet attaining the desired result ultimately. For such beings, learning that a particular Turing machine M accepts L in time $\Omega(n^2)$, say, would, by itself, be of tremendous interest. In their quest for inefficiency, they would have learned that it would be irrational, from their unusual point of view, to ever bother running a Turing machine M' that accepts L in time $\Omega(n)$, say. And this would be because they could instead run the equivalent but more costly M, being assured of ultimately getting the right results but killing more time in the process.

In fact, we are overstating the case. This is because a time waster who knows a little theory will also know that one can insert arbitrarily slow do-nothing loops into *any* Turing machine, thereby achieving an arbitrary degree of inefficiency in the case of any Turing-acceptable language. So this more knowledgeable individual will not be so interested, after all, in learning that a particular Turing machine accepts in $\Omega(n^2)$ steps. Given arbitrary function $f(n)$ with n the length of input, he or she already knows how to waste $f(n)$ or more steps in accepting, or not accepting, any word of any Turing-acceptable language.

To put matters another way, to learn that machine M accepts language L in time $O(n)$, say, is to learn something important about the difficulty or the *complexity* of language L itself. It is to learn that we possess a Turing machine whose computation involves at most something on the order of n steps for input words of length n. Although some more efficient machine may nonetheless be possible, there will be no point in running a Turing machine M' that accepts L in $O(n^2)$ time, given our general interest in conserving resources. At some point in our quest for a faster machine accepting L, it would be nice to know that we had arrived at an optimal design so that we could go on to other projects. That is, it would be nice to know that *any* machine accepting L requires at least n steps for some input words of length n—that is, that *any* machine accepting L computes in time $\Omega(n)$. So, already having one such machine, we would know that there would be no point in continuing to look for something better. But this sort of general information obviously cannot be obtained from examining a single language acceptor M, since it amounts to information regarding an entire *class* of acceptors—that is, all those accepting language L. There is no denying that this general sort of information would be useful, but how is it to be had? Perhaps a divine being could arrive at it through examination of all of the infinitely many machines accepting L. (If L is, in fact, Turing-acceptable, then there are infinitely many machines that accept it.) Human beings, on the other hand, must resort to some sort of *argument* or *proof* regarding the resource requirements of the entire class of Turing machines accepting L. Typically, such proofs are technical, involving advanced analytic techniques. Consequently, we shall not concern ourselves with such lower-bound arguments in this text. Rather, we shall focus exclusively on using big-O notation to express upper bounds on the resource requirements of language acceptors. And, happily, upper-bound arguments are easy: To show that language L can be accepted by some Turing machine in time $O(f(n))$, one merely presents some one Turing machine M that does just that.

§1.8 Suggestions for Further Reading

Our informal introduction of Turing machines was much influenced by the presentation in [Boolos and Jeffrey 1989]. That text can be highly recommended as a general introduction to mathematical logic and is ideal for self-study. There are any number of more advanced texts that discuss Turing computability. We mention [Davis, Sigal, and Weyuker 1994]. [Hopcroft and Ullman 1979] includes a valuable study of complexity theory using the Turing machine model, as does [Lewis and Papadimitriou 1981]. Readers will surely enjoy Martin Davis' popular essay "What is a Computation?," where Turing machines are discussed in historical context (see [Davis 1980]).

The importance of complexity class P was first pointed out in [Cobham 1964] and [Edmonds 1965].

EXERCISES FOR §1.1

1.1.1. Consider the algorithm below for determining whether a given argument expressed in the language of propositional logic is valid. (Recall that, by definition, an argument A is valid pro- vided that every truth-value assignment that makes all of A's premises true makes A's conclusion true as well.)

Algorithm for Determining Whether an Argument Expressed in the Language of Propositional Logic Is Valid
Input: argument A consisting of premises $\pi_1, \pi_2, \ldots, \pi_k$ for $k \geq 0$ and conclusion γ,
  j = number of distinct sentence letters occurring in $\pi_1, \pi_2, \ldots, \pi_k, \gamma$
Output: 1 if A is a valid argument
    0 if A is not a valid argument
begin
  $Truth\_table := create\_truth\_table\ (\pi_1, \pi_2, \ldots, \pi_k, \gamma)$;   {$Truth\_table$ will contain 2^j rows}
  $i := 0$;
  while $i < 2^j$ do begin
    $i := i + 1$;
    if $Truth_table\ [i, \pi_1] = $ T & $Truth_table\ [i, \pi_2] = $ T & $\cdots$ & $Truth_table\ [i, \pi_k] = $ T
      then if $Truth_table[i, \gamma] = $ F
        then return 0
  end;
  return 1
end.

(a) Use the algorithm above to determine whether the argument below is valid.

$$(p \vee q) \rightarrow r$$

$$\neg r\ \&\ \neg q$$

$$\therefore p$$

(b) Use the algorithm to determine whether the argument below is valid.

$$p \rightarrow (q \vee r)$$

$$\neg r$$

$$\therefore \neg p$$

(c) Describe the several senses in which the algorithm is *determinate*.

1.1.2. [hwk] Consider the following algorithm for finding the binary equivalent of a given decimal numeral.

Algorithm for Determining the Binary Equivalent of a Decimal Numeral
Input: natural number n
Output: bit array $b[\ ]$ containing a string of binary digits $b_k b_{k-1} \ldots b_1 b_0$ whose value is n
begin
  $quot := n$;
  $i := 0$;
  while $quot \neq 0$ do begin
    $b[i](= b_i) := quot\ mod\ 2$;
    $quot := quot\ div\ 2$;
    $i := i + 1$
  end;
  return b
end.

(a) Use the algorithm above to find the binary equivalent of decimal numeral 783.
(b) Describe the several senses in which the algorithm is *determinate*.

1.1.3. Consider the algorithm below for finding the greatest common divisor (GCD) of a pair of natural numbers.

Algorithm for Determining the GCD of a Pair of Natural Numbers

Input: natural numbers n and m
Output: $gcd(n, m)$—that is, the greatest common
        divisor of n and m

begin
    $a_0 := n$;
    $a_1 := m$;
    while $a_1 \neq 0$ do begin
        $temp := a_0$;
        $a_0 := a_1$;
        $a_1 := temp \bmod a_1$;
    end;
    return a_0
end.

(a) Use the algorithm above to find $gcd(612, 224)$.

(b) Describe the several senses in which the algorithm is *determinate*.

1.1.4. In his essay entitled "The Twins," psychiatrist Oliver Sacks describes the intriguing case of mentally defective brothers who, by all appearances, are capable of directly apprehending numbers and their properties. Read Sacks' account in [Sacks 1970] and discuss whether this, as well as other similar cases mentioned by him, pose a challenge to our usual way of thinking about computation. In particular, to what extent do such cases suggest the possibility of "quasi-algorithmic" computation? Or, rather, is it best not to regard the brothers' activity as genuine computation at all?

1.1.5. (a) Explain how any instance of our function computation paradigm may be reconstrued in terms of the transduction paradigm. Similarly, explain how any instance of language recognition may be redescribed as an instance of transduction.

(b) Explain how any instance of the transduction paradigm may be reinterpreted as an instance of either the function computation paradigm or the language recognition paradigm. (*Hint:* For the former, use natural-number codes for alphabet symbols.)

EXERCISES FOR §1.2

1.2.1. [hwk] As is now familiar, we can represent a Turing machine either by a state diagram—a certain sort of labeled digraph—or by a transition function δ. As additional examples of Turing machines, consider M_0 through M_4 appearing in Figures 1.2.11(a)–(e). Recall, also, that a Turing machine may or may not halt. Again, a Turing machine M halts in state q_i reading symbol σ if and only if M finds itself in state q_i reading symbol σ and $\delta_M(q_i, \sigma)$ is undefined; that is, there is no instruction for state q_i and symbol σ.

(a) Describe in a single sentence the computation of each of the Turing machines M_0 through M_4 of Figures 1.2.11(a)–(e), assuming that each starts scanning a square on a completely blank tape. Your description should indicate clearly whether the given machine ever halts and, if so, where it halts on the tape. (*Suggestion:* In each case, complete the following sentence: "If this machine is started scanning a blank on a completely blank tape, then ... ")

(b) Give the transition function δ_{M_1} of Turing machine M_1.

1.2.2. (a) Design a Turing machine that, when started scanning a square on a completely blank tape, writes the string *abab* on the tape and halts scanning the leftmost symbol of this string. Try to design a machine that has no more than four states, q_0 through q_3. (*Hint:* Consider machine M_2 of Figure 1.2.11(c).)

(b) Suppose that you were asked to design a Turing machine that, when started scanning a square on a completely blank tape, writes the string *ababbaab* on the tape and halts scanning the leftmost symbol of this string. What is the minimal number of states required in order to accomplish this?

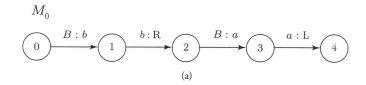

M_0

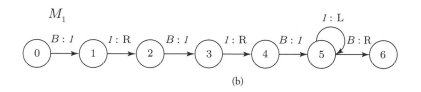

M_1

(a)

(b)

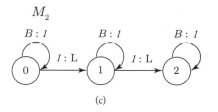

M_2

(c)

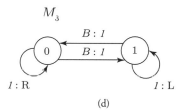

M_3

(d)

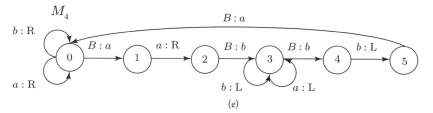

M_4

(e)

Figure 1.2.11

EXERCISES FOR §1.3

1.3.1. ^{hwk} **(a)** Suppose that the Turing machine of Example 1.3.1 is started scanning the leftmost symbol of the input string *abaaab*. In what state will the Turing machine halt? What will be the final tape configuration of M? Given that $n_a(abaaab) \neq n_b(abaaab)$, is this the answer required by (1.3.1)?

(b) Suppose that this Turing machine is started scanning the leftmost symbol of the input string *abbbb*. In what state will the Turing machine halt? What will be the final tape configuration?

1.3.2. Design a Turing machine that starts scanning the leftmost symbol of an unbroken (possibly null) string of *1*s on an otherwise blank tape.

If there was initially an even number of *1*s on the tape, then the Turing machine should halt scanning a *1* on an otherwise blank tape. On the other hand, if there was initially an odd number of *1*s on the tape, then the Turing machine should halt scanning the leftmost of two *1*s on an otherwise blank tape. (*Note:* In general, the reader need not worry about what the machine does if the input conditions are *not* as described.)

1.3.3. (Convert-to-Unary). Design a Turing machine M that, when started scanning the leftmost digit of a binary digit string on an otherwise blank tape, ultimately halts scanning the leftmost *1* of the equivalent unary digit string. Thus, if the tape contains *101* initially, then ultimately the tape contains *11111*. Similarly, binary digit string *1000* will be converted to unary digit string *11111111*. If the input string is binary digit string *0* representing 0, then M should halt scanning a blank on a completely blank tape, thereby reflecting the fact that there is no unary representation of 0. (*Hint:* A solution should make use of the following two facts regarding binary representations:

(1) If binary representation $B(n)$ represents natural number n, then binary representation $B(n)⌢0$—that is, the result of appending a single *0* to $B(n)$—represents natural number $2n$.

(2) If binary representation $B(n)$ represents natural number n, then binary representation $B(n)⌢1$—that is, the result of appending a single *1* to $B(n)$—represents natural number $2n + 1$.

1.3.4. (Balanced Parentheses). Design a Turing machine M that, when started scanning the leftmost symbol of an arbitrary word w over al-

phabet $\Sigma = \{(,)\}$ on an otherwise blank tape, ultimately halts scanning a single *1* on an otherwise blank tape if and only if w is a string of balanced parentheses. Thus, if M's tape contains *( )((( )( )))* initially, then ultimately M will halt scanning *1*. In contrast, if M's tape contains *(( )))* initially, then M may do anything *except* halt scanning a single *1* on an otherwise blank tape.

1.3.5. Design a Turing machine M that, when started scanning the leftmost symbol of nonempty word w over $\Sigma = \{a, b\}$, halts scanning the leftmost symbol of word $a^{n_a(w)}b^{n_b(w)}$. That is, M will rearrange the symbols occurring within w so that as come before bs.

1.3.6. Design a Turing machine M that, when started scanning the leftmost symbol of nonempty word w over $\Sigma = \{a, b\}$, halts scanning the leftmost symbol of word $(ab)^{min[n_a(w),n_b(w)]}$. That is, M will rearrange the symbols occurring within w so as to produce as many ab pairings as possible and merely erase any remaining symbols. For example, words $aabaabbb$ and $aabaaaababb$ will both be transformed into $abababab$.

1.3.7. (Sequences). Design a Turing machine M that generates all finite sequences of *0*s and *1*s without ever halting. M might first generate all sequences of length 1, then all sequences of length 2, and so on. Among sequences of a fixed length n, sequences might be ordered according to increasing value as binary numerals. Thus the order of generation might be

0 1 00 01 10 11 000 001 010
011 100 101 110 111 0000 . . .

EXERCISES FOR §1.4

1.4.1. ^{hwk} Consider the Turing machine M whose state diagram appears in Figure 1.4.4.

(a) What is the shortest word accepted by M?

(b) Is word *aba* accepted by M? What about *abab*?

(c) What language over $\Sigma = \{a, b\}$ is accepted by M?

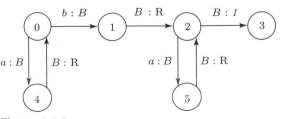

Figure 1.4.4

1.4.2. ^{hwk} We saw in Exercise 1.4.1 that the Turing machine M whose state diagram appears in Figure 1.4.4 accepts a certain language L over $\Sigma = \{a, b\}$. Add states and instructions to the state diagram of M so as to obtain a new machine M' that recognizes L in the sense of Definition 1.4.

1.4.3. Design Turing machines that accept the following languages over $\Sigma = \{a, b\}$. The reader should present a state diagram as well as one or two sentences describing the activity of the machine.
 (a) $L = \{b^n a b^m | n, m \geq 0\}$
 (b) $L = \{a^n b^n | n \geq 0\}$
 (c) $L = \{a^n b a^n | n \geq 0\}$

1.4.4. For each of the languages below, give one or two sentences describing a Turing machine that would accept it.
 (a) $L = \{a^n b a^{2n} | n \geq 0\}$
 (b) $L = \{a^n b (ab)^n | n \geq 0\}$

1.4.5. ^{hwk} For each of the languages below, use the accompanying software to design and test a Turing machine that accepts that language. (There are enough languages here so that each member of the class might do one or two of them.) Assume alphabet $\Sigma = \{a, b\}$ or $\Sigma = \{a, b, c\}$ as appropriate. Add documentation by choosing Set Description from the Machine menu, and then print out the result. Alternatively, for each of the languages below, simply describe, in a few English sentences, the operation of a Turing machine that accepts the language.
 (a) $\{a^2 b^n | n \geq 0\}$

EXERCISES FOR §1.5

1.5.1 ^{hwk} (a) Suppose that Turing machine M, when started scanning the leftmost *1* of an unbroken string of 4 *1*s on an otherwise blank tape, ultimately halts scanning the leftmost of 10 *1*s on an otherwise blank tape. Also, M, when started scanning the leftmost *1* of any unbroken string of 5 *1*s on an otherwise blank tape, ultimately halts scanning the leftmost of 13 *1*s on an otherwise blank tape. Other input/output pairs are indicated in Table 1.5.1.

 (b) $\{a^2 b^n | n \geq 1\}$
 (c) $\{a^3 b^n | n \geq 2\}$
 (d) $\{a^n b^2 | n \geq 0\}$
 (e) $\{a^n b^3 | n \geq 1\}$
 (f) $\{a^2 b^n a^3 | n \geq 0\}$
 (g) $\{b a^2 b^n | n \geq 0\}$
 (h) $\{b^2 a^2 b^n a | n \geq 0\}$
 (i) $\{b^2 a^2 b^n | n \geq 1\}$
 (j) $\{a^2 b^n | n \geq 2\}$
 (k) $\{a^n b^m | n, m \geq 0\}$
 (l) $\{a^2 b^n | n \geq 4\}$
 (m) $\{a^2 b^n c^n | n \geq 0\}$
 (n) $\{(ab)^n | n \geq 0\}$
 (o) $\{a^{2n} | n \geq 0\}$
 (p) $\{a^n b^m a^n | n, m \geq 0\}$
 (q) $L = \{a^{n^2} | n \geq 0\} = \{\varepsilon, a, aaaa, a^9, \ldots\}$
 (r) $L = \{a^{2^n} | n \geq 0\} = \{a, aa, aaaa, a^8, \ldots\}$
 (s) $L = \{a^n | n \text{ prime}\} = \{aa, aaa, a^5, a^7, \ldots\}$

1.4.6. Modify the Turing machine M of Example 1.3.1 and Figure 1.3.1, which accepts the language $L = \{w \in \Sigma^* | n_a(w) = n_b(w)\}$ with $\Sigma = \{a, b\}$, so as to obtain a new Turing machine M' that recognizes L. (*Hint:* Add instructions at states q_3 and q_4 leading to a routine that causes the entire tape contents to be erased and a single *0* to be written.)

1.4.7. (a) Show that if language L is Turing-recognizable, then so is L^c, and vice versa. (*Hint:* Start with a Turing machine M that recognizes L. Modify it so as to obtain a new machine M' that accepts L^c.)
 (b) Prove that if language L is Turing-recognizable, then both L and L^c are Turing-acceptable languages.

Table 1.5.1

Number of *1*s on Tape Initially	Number of *1*s on Tape Ultimately
1	1
2	4
3	7
4	10
5	13
6	16
...	...

What unary number-theoretic function is computed by M in accordance with our conventions?

(b) Suppose that Turing machine M, when started scanning the leftmost *1* of an unbroken string of 9 *1*s on an otherwise blank tape, ultimately halts scanning the leftmost of 4 *1*s on an otherwise blank tape. Also, M, when started scanning the leftmost *1* of any unbroken string of 17 *1*s on an otherwise blank tape, ultimately halts scanning the leftmost of 5 *1*s on an otherwise blank tape. Other input/output pairs are indicated in Table 1.5.2. Furthermore, all omitted first-column entries cause M to not halt in a value-representing configuration. What number-theoretic function is computed by M in accordance with our conventions?

Table 1.5.2

Number of *1*s on Tape Initially[a]	Number of *1*s on Tape Ultimately
2	1
3	2
5	3
9	4
17	5
33	6
...	...

[a] Note that all entries in the first column are of the form $2^n + 1$ for $n \geq 0$.

1.5.2. What trivial modification is required to turn the solution for Exercise 1.3.2 into a Turing machine that computes $f(n) = n \bmod 2$?

1.5.3. Show that each of the unary partial number-theoretic functions below is Turing-computable by designing a Turing machine that computes it. Use the accompanying software to test your design.
(a) $f(n) = 2n + 3$
(b) $f(n) = 3n$

(c) $f(n) = 3n + 4$
(d) $f(n) = n \operatorname{div} 2$
(e) $f(n) = n \operatorname{div} 3$
(g) $f(n) = n \bmod 3$
(h) $f(n) = \sqrt[3]{n}$ (Note that, as a number-theoretic function, f is not total since it is defined for perfect cubes only.)
(i) $f(n) = \log_2 n$ (Note that, as a number-theoretic function, f is not total since it is defined for powers of 2 only. (*Hint:* $2^{k+1} - 1 = 2^0 + 2^1 + 2^2 + \cdots + 2^k$)

1.5.4. Show that each of the binary number-theoretic functions below is Turing-computable by designing a Turing machine that computes it. Use the accompanying software to test your design. Some of these functions are only partial.
(a) $f(n, m) = n^m$
(b) $f(n, m) = max(n, m)$
(c) $f(n, m) = n \operatorname{div} m$ (Note that f is not total.)
(d) $f(n, m) = n \bmod m$ (Note that f is not total.)
(e) $f(n, m) = n - m$ (Note that, as a number-theoretic function, f is not total.)
(f)

$$f(n, m) = \begin{cases} n - m & \text{if } n \geq m \\ 0 & \text{otherwise} \end{cases}$$

(This function is sometimes called the *monus* function and written $n \mathbin{\dot-} m$. We shall see it again in Chapter 3. Note that this function, unlike that of (e), is total.)

1.5.5. (a) Suppose Turing machine M computes 0-ary function C_5^0. What is the minimal number of states that M may have?
(b) Suppose Turing machine M computes 0-ary function C_m^0, for some fixed $m \geq 0$. What is the minimal number of states that M may have?

EXERCISES FOR §1.6

1.6.1. Design a Turing machine that computes the number-theoretic function $f(n) = n^2$. (*Hint:* First use the Copying Machine of Example 1.3.2, which, when started scanning the leftmost of $n + 1$ *1*s representing n, halts scanning the leftmost of $n + 1$ *1*s followed by a single blank followed by another $n + 1$ *1*s. Now incorporate as a second module the Multiplication Machine of Example 1.5.5. Note that the software permits the user to paste existing machines into submachine diagrams. Consequently, this exercise should not take long to complete: The two needed submachines already exist in files `copying.tm` and `multiply.tm`.)

1.6.2. Use modular techniques to show that each of the unary number-theoretic functions below

is Turing-computable. Use the accompanying software to test your design. Some of the functions shown to be Turing-computable in the exercises for §1.5 may prove helpful.
  (a) $f(n) = n^2 + 2n + 5$
  (b) $f(n) = n^3 + 4n^2 + 6n + 1$
  (c) $f(n) = 2^n + 3^n$
  (d) $f(n) = 3n^2 + n + 3$
  (e) $f(n) = \lfloor \log_2 n \rfloor$
  (f) $f(n) = (n^2)!$

EXERCISES FOR §1.7

1.7.1. (a) Give a worst-case time analysis of the Turing machine M of Example 1.3.2. That is, find a number-theoretic function $g(n)$ such that $time_M(n)$ is $O(g(n))$ worst case. You may find the accompanying software useful for counting steps.
  (b) Give a worst-case space analysis of the Turing machine of Example 1.3.2.

1.7.2. (a) Using big-O notation, give a worst-case time analysis of the Turing machine of Example 1.5.8 (Word Reversal) and Figure 1.5.4.
  (b) Give a worst-case space analysis of the Turing machine of Example 1.5.8.

1.7.3. Give an argument to show that if Turing machine M computes in time $O(f(n))$ worst case, where $f(n) \geq 1$ at least for sufficiently large n, then M computes in space $O(f(n))$ worst case as well. (*Note:* In referring to this result in the future, we shall not always bother to make explicit our assumption that $f(n) \geq 1$.) Alternative formulation: Show that function $space_M(n)$ is $O(time_M(n))$ provided $time_M(n) \geq 1$ for sufficiently large n.

1.7.4. One says that the Turing machine M of Example 1.5.1 computes in time $O(1)$. Explain.

1.7.5. Show that if language L is Turing-acceptable, then there are infinitely many Turing machines that accept it.

EXERCISES FOR §1.8 (END-OF-CHAPTER REVIEW EXERCISES)

1.8.1. ^{hwk} Use set abstraction to describe the language accepted by each Turing machine whose state diagram appears in Figures 1.8.1(a)–(f).

1.8.2. Consider the Turing machine M_1 whose state diagram appears in Figure 1.8.2(a).
  (a) What happens if M_1 is started scanning the leftmost of three *1*s on an otherwise blank tape. That is, what is M_1's halting configuration?
  (b) What happens if M_1 is started scanning the leftmost of four 1s on an otherwise blank tape. That is, what is M_1's halting configuration?
  (c) Using your answers to (a) and (b) and observing our adopted conventions regarding representation of numerical input/output, fill in the four blanks below, where f is

the number-theoretic function computed by M_1.

$$f(\underline{\quad}) = \underline{\quad} \text{ (corresponding to } (a))$$
$$f(\underline{\quad}) = \underline{\quad} \text{ (corresponding to } (b))$$

  (d) Finally, using your answers to (c), fill in the blank below so as to characterize the unary function f computed by M_1.

$$f(n) = \underline{\quad\quad}$$

  (e) Answer each of parts (a) through (d) with respect to the machine M_2 whose state diagram appears in Figure 1.8.2(b).

M_1

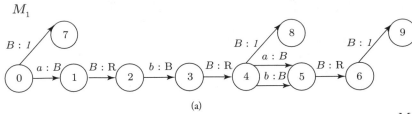

(a)

M_2

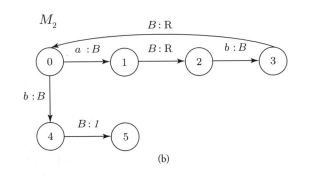

(b)

M_3

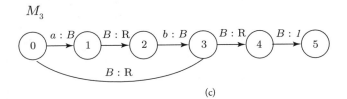

(c)

M_4

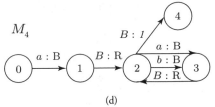

(d)

M_5

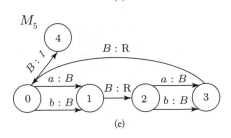

(e)

M_6

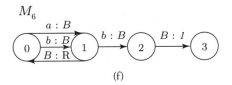

(f)

Figure 1.8.1

M_1

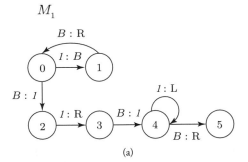

(a)

M_2

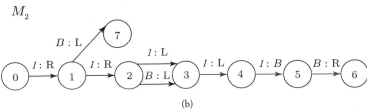

(b)

Figure 1.8.2

1.8.3. Present the state diagram of a Turing machine that, in accordance with Definitions 1.2 and 1.3, accepts the language whose only member is the empty word.

1.8.4. Show that the unary number-theoretic function defined by

$$f(n) = 2n + 3$$

is Turing-computable by designing a single-tape Turing machine that computes it. Use the companion software to test your design. The machine of Example 1.5.3 will prove helpful.

1.8.5. **hwk** **(a)** Describe in a few English sentences a Turing machine that accepts the language

$$\{a^n b^{3n} c^{2n} | n \geq 1\}$$

Explain the use of any needed auxiliary symbols.

(b) Implement your design using the companion software and test it on words *abbbcc*, *aabbbbbbcccc*, and *aabbbcccc*.

1.8.6. **hwk** **(a)** Suppose that Turing machine M computes the unary number-theoretic function f defined by

$$f(n) = n^2 + 6n + 3$$

and suppose, further, that M is started scanning the leftmost *1* in an unbroken string of six *1*s on an otherwise blank tape. Then M will halt scanning the leftmost *1* in an unbroken string of how many *1*s?

(b) Suppose that Turing machine M computes the binary number-theoretic function f defined by

$$f(n, m) = n^2 + m^2$$

and suppose further that M is started scanning the leftmost *1* in an unbroken string of six *1*s followed by a blank fol-

lowed by an unbroken string of ten *1*s on an otherwise blank tape. Then M will halt scanning the leftmost *1* in an unbroken string of how many *1*s?

(c) Suppose that Turing machine M computes the unary number-theoretic function f defined by

$$f(n) = \lceil \log_2 n \rceil + 1$$

and suppose, further, that M is started scanning the leftmost *1* in an unbroken string of 60 *1*s on an otherwise blank tape. Then M will halt scanning the leftmost *1* in an unbroken string of how many *1*s?

(d) Suppose that Turing machine M computes the unary number-theoretic function f defined by

$$f(n) = \lceil \log_2 n + 1 \rceil = \lceil (\log_2 n) + 1 \rceil$$

and suppose, further, that M is started scanning the leftmost *1* in an unbroken string of 60 *1*s on an otherwise blank tape. Then M will halt scanning the leftmost *1* in an unbroken string of how many *1*s?

1.8.7. Present the state diagram of a Turing machine that accepts the language of all words over alphabet $\Sigma = \{a, b\}$ that are of the form *ww*.

1.8.8. **hwk** Present the state diagram of a Turing machine that accepts the language of words over $\{a, b\}$ whose length is 3 or more.

1.8.9. **hwk** Present the state diagram of a Turing machine that accepts the language of words over $\{a, b\}$ that begin with symbol a and end with symbol b.

1.8.10. Suppose that f and g are two unary, total number-theoretic functions that are Turing-computable. Moreover, suppose that each is computed by some Turing machine that computes in polynomial time. Show that function $f \circ g$ is computed by a machine that likewise computes in polynomial time.

Chapter $\underline{2}$

Additional Varieties of Turing Machines

§2.1 Turing Machines with One-Way-Infinite Tape

Turing machines, as described in §1.2, possess a single read/write head and a tape that is infinite in both directions. In fact, Alan Turing in his original paper of 1936 described machines whose tapes are infinite only to the right, having a first, or leftmost, tape square. We shall consider such machines in this section. It would be natural to suppose that this restriction would limit the computational capacity of the new machines when compared with standard, two-way-infinite machines. But, as it will turn out, the new restriction makes no difference ultimately with respect to computational power. It is possible to formulate this sameness of computational power in any number of ways—most generally in terms of transduction. For our purposes, it will be enough to formulate this sameness in terms of the concept of Turing-computable function: In other words, we shall show that the class of Turing-computable functions remains constant over changes in the character of Turing-machine tapes. First, we need to formally define the new variety of Turing machines.

Essentially, the difference will come to this. Since there is now a leftmost tape square, we require that any Turing machine M of the new variety be capable of recognizing when it is scanning this leftmost square so as to always return to the right. One way to do this is to include within M's tape alphabet Γ a special symbol λ to mark this square. Upon encountering λ, M will invariably move one square to the right. This involves placing a new restriction upon M's transition function δ_M to the effect that δ_M will map any pair of the form (q_i, λ) onto a pair of the form (R, q_j), where q_i and q_j are members of M's state set Q. In other words, M is not permitted to move past λ, to erase λ, or to write λ. This is the only change to our earlier set-theoretic definition of Turing machines as presented in Definition 1.1. The new sort of Turing machine will be called a *Turing machine with one-way-infinite tape*. In this section only, we shall refer to Turing machines, as originally defined in Definition 1.1, as *Turing machines with two-way-infinite tape*.

Our notion of Turing computability for machines with two-way-infinite tape is easily modified so as to yield a corresponding notion for machines with one-way-infinite tape. We recall that Turing machine M with two-way-infinite tape computes number-theoretic function $f(n_1, \ldots, n_k)$ if, for arbitrary natural numbers $n_1, \ldots, n_k$, when M is started scanning the leftmost 1 in a representation of $n_1, \ldots, n_k$, M ultimately halts scanning the leftmost 1 of a representation of $f(n_1, \ldots, n_k)$. Modifying this idea for machines of the new variety means only that we must allow for the presence of left endmarker λ. In particular, λ must be assumed to already be on the tape when execution commences and to remain on the tape when execution halts.

DEFINITION 2.1: Let M be a Turing machine with one-way-infinite tape. Then M *one-way computes k-ary number-theoretic function* f if, whenever M starts scanning the leftmost 1 of an unbroken string of $n_1 + 1$ 1s followed by a single blank followed by an unbroken string of $n_2 + 1$ 1s followed by a single blank ... followed by an unbroken string of $n_k + 1$ 1s on a tape that is otherwise blank except for left endmarker λ (which occurs immediately to the left of the leftmost 1 on the tape),

$$\lambda q_0 \underbrace{1111\ldots11111}_{n_1+1\,1s}B\underbrace{11111\ldots1111}_{n_2+1\,1s}B\ldots\ldots\underbrace{1111\ldots11111}_{n_k+1\,1s}B$$

then M halts scanning the leftmost 1 in an unbroken string of $f(n_1, n_2, \ldots, n_k) + 1$ 1s on a tape that is otherwise blank except for left endmarker λ (which, again, occurs immediately to the left of the leftmost 1 on the tape),

$$\lambda q_{\text{halt}} \underbrace{11111111111\ldots1111111111}_{f(n_1,n_2,\ldots,n_k)+1\,1s}B$$

In this section only, we shall describe the behavior of a Turing machine M with two-way-infinite tape that computes f in the original sense of Definition 1.6 by saying that M *two-way computes* f.

EXAMPLE 2.1.1 The Turing machine of Figure 2.1.1 one-way computes the unary number-theoretic *predecessor function* defined by

$$pred(n) = \begin{cases} n - 1 & \text{if} \quad n \geq 1 \\ 0 & \text{if} \quad n = 0 \end{cases}$$

The reader is invited to create this machine using the accompanying software. Open icon **Turing Machine** and choose *Machine* and then *New* from the File menu. Check the option **One-way-infinite tape(s)**. Left endmarker λ will automatically appear on any machine tape.

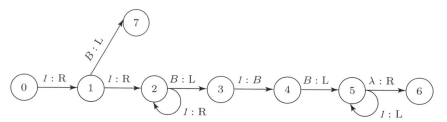

Figure 2.1.1   The State Diagram of a Turing Machine with One-Way-Infinite Tape That Computes the Predecessor Function.

EXAMPLE 2.1.2 We have described in Definition 2.1 how Turing machines with one-way-infinite tape can compute number-theoretic functions. An analogous notion of language acceptance for Turing machines with one-way-infinite tape can be given. We leave this to the reader. Basically, one might require only that an accepting *1* appear immediately to the right of left endmarker λ. (See Exercise 2.1.3.) Opening the icon labeled **Palindromes** within the Turing Machine folder brings to the screen the state diagram of a Turing machine *M* with one-way-infinite tape that one-way accepts the language $\{w \in \Sigma^* | w = w^R\}$ with $\Sigma = (a, b)$. Load tapes `oddpalin.tt` or `evenpali.tt`.

Assuming the notions of time and space adopted in the case of two-way-infinite machines, one sees without difficulty that *M* computes in time $O(n^2)$ and space $O(n)$. (See Exercise 2.1.4.)

We are now ready to formulate the first of the many *equivalence results* that are central to the theory of computability.

THEOREM 2.1: Let f be a k-ary number-theoretic function. Then there exists a Turing machine with two-way-infinite tape that two-way computes f if and only if there exists a Turing machine with one-way-infinite tape that one-way computes f.

PROOF The **reverse direction** here is, of course, trivial. Since, as a mathematically defined object, any Turing machine M with one-way-infinite tape simply involves an additional restriction upon its transition function δ_M, it should be sufficiently clear that any Turing machine M with one-way-infinite tape is automatically a Turing machine with two-way-infinite tape as well. This, in turn, implies that if M is a Turing machine with one-way-infinite tape that one-way computes function f, then M can easily be transformed into a Turing machine M' that two-way computes f: M' must simply add λ to the left initially, erase it ultimately, and, in the interim, behave just as M behaves.

The **forward direction** is more work and will have us splitting a one-way-infinite tape into two "tracks" so as to represent both "halves" of a two-way-infinite tape. (See Figure 2.1.2.) At any given time during execution, just one of the two tracks will be *active*. Suppose that M^2 is a Turing machine with two-way-infinite tape and that M^2 two-way computes number-theoretic function f, which for definiteness we assume to be binary. We show how to construct a Turing machine M^1 with one-way-infinite tape that one-way computes f. Our construction will consist in effect of transforming—rather radically—M^2's transition diagram so as to obtain the transition diagram of the equivalent M^1.

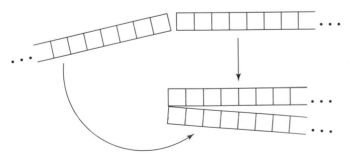

Figure 2.1.2

Step 1. The first step in the construction involves introducing instructions and states so as to create the two-track setup. Let us assume for definiteness that M^2's tape alphabet Γ is $\Sigma \cup \{B\}$ with $\Sigma = \{1\}$. In that case, M^1's tape alphabet will contain the two symbols 1, B, left endmarker λ, as well as the symbols $U^1_1, U^1_B, U^B_1, U^B_B, L^1_1, L^1_B, L^B_1,$ and L^B_B. We interpret U^1_B, say, to indicate both that the upper track is active and that there is a 1 on the upper track and a blank on the lower track of the tape square in which symbol U^1_B appears. Similarly, we interpret L^B_1, say, to indicate both that the lower track is active and that there is a blank on the upper track and a 1 on the lower track of the tape square in which symbol L^B_1 appears. The portion of M^1's state diagram pictured in Figure 2.1.3(a) causes each of the 1s as well as one of the blanks that M^1 finds on its tape initially to be replaced by symbols U^1_1 and U^B_B, respectively. (Thus M^1's lower track is initially inactive and blank.) Having made these substitutions, M^1 returns to the left and enters M^2's initial state q^2_0. Figure 2.1.3(b) shows the effect of this transformation of the initial contents of M^1's tape.

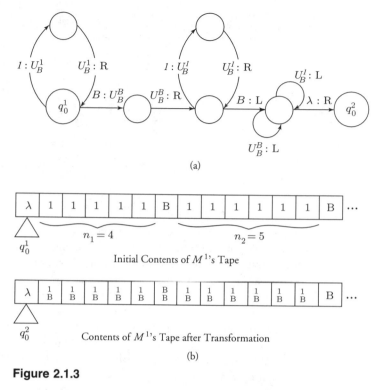

(a)

Initial Contents of M^1's Tape

Contents of M^1's Tape after Transformation

(b)

Figure 2.1.3

Step 2. The second step of our construction of M^1 involves replacing each write instruction of the form $\langle q, 1; B, q' \rangle$, say, in M^2's state diagram with the following four instructions:

$$\langle q, U^1_1; U^B_1, q' \rangle \qquad \langle q, U^1_B; U^B_B, q' \rangle \qquad \langle q, L^1_1; L^1_B, q' \rangle \qquad \langle q, L^B_1, L^B_B, q' \rangle$$

Also, each instruction of the form $\langle q, 1; R, q' \rangle$, say, in M^2's state diagram is replaced by four instructions:

$$\langle q, U^1_1; R, q' \rangle \qquad \langle q, U^1_B; R, q' \rangle \qquad \langle q, L^1_1; L, q' \rangle \qquad \langle q, L^B_1; L, q' \rangle$$

reflecting the fact that a move right by M^2 working on the "left half" of its two-way-infinite tape will be simulated by a move *left* on M^1's lower track. Similarly, each instruction of the form $\langle q, 1; L, q' \rangle$, say, in M^2's state diagram is replaced by four instructions:

$$\langle q, U^1_1; L, q' \rangle \qquad \langle q, U^1_B; L, q' \rangle \qquad \langle q, L^1_1; R, q' \rangle \qquad \langle q, L^B_1; R, q' \rangle$$

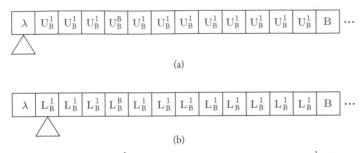

Figure 2.1.4   (a) M^1's upper track has been active. (b) M^1's lower track has become active.

Step 3. The third step in the construction of M^1 consists, first, of adding instructions and states to simulate M^2's moves from the right half to the left half of its two-way-infinite tape: such moves will correspond to transitions from M^1's upper track being the active track to M^1's lower track being the active track. Since M^2's moves from the right half onto the left half of its two-way-infinite tape must be the result of a move left, we focus now on instructions of the form $\langle q, \sigma; L, q' \rangle$, which cause M^2, when in state q scanning symbol σ, to move one square to the left and enter state q' . Let us assume for definiteness that σ is 1 so that we are talking about instruction $\langle q, 1; L, q' \rangle$. We have already introduced four instructions in order to simulate such a move left by a move left on the upper track or a move right on the lower track. Our concern is for the possibility that the simulated move left takes M^2 from the right half onto the left half of its two-way-infinite tape. If so, then, after simulating this move left, M^1 finds itself in state q', scanning left endmarker λ, with its upper tape track active (see Figure 2.1.4(a)). Before continuing from state q' in its simulation of M^2, simulator M^1 must now make its lower tape track active and move one square to the *right* of left endmarker λ, thereby simulating M^2's move *left* onto the first square of the left half of its two-way-infinite tape. Making its lower track active has M^1 passing over its entire work area, replacing every occurrence of U_1^1 by L_1^1, every occurrence of U_B^1 by L_B^1, and so on (see Figure 2.1.4(b)). Figure 2.1.5 shows the states and instructions that must be added to every pair of states q and q' in the state diagram of M^2 such that there is a move-left instruction from q to q'. Analogous instructions and states must be added in order to simulate M^2's move from the left half to the right half of its two-way-infinite tape.

Step 4. We must allow M^1 to extend its work space by converting blanks off to the right on its one-way tape to either U_B^B or L_B^B, as appropriate. As a result of Step 2, M^1 currently has no instructions of the form $\langle q, B; \_\_\_, q' \rangle$, where q and q' are states of M^2. So now, to each state q of M^2 that is the target state of a move-right instruction of M^2, we add a routine whose effect is to replace any encountered blank by either U_B^B or L_B^B, as determined by the square to its immediate left. (This square can never be left endmarker λ, given our assumption that M^2 computes a number-theoretic function.) Figure 2.1.6 shows the states and instructions that must be added to every state q of M^2 that is the target state of a move-right instruction.

Step 5. When M^1's simulation of M^2 terminates, its read/write head will, by assumption, be scanning what corresponds to the leftmost 1 in the representation of $f(n_1, n_2)$. Two possible cases must be considered. First, this leftmost 1 may be on M^1's upper track, which means only that a certain number of occurrences of symbols U_B^1 and U_B^B must be replaced by 1s and Bs, respectively, before the read/write head returns to the left. The other possible case is that this leftmost one is found on M^1's lower track. This means that any occurrence of either L_1^B or L_B^1 must be replaced by a 1

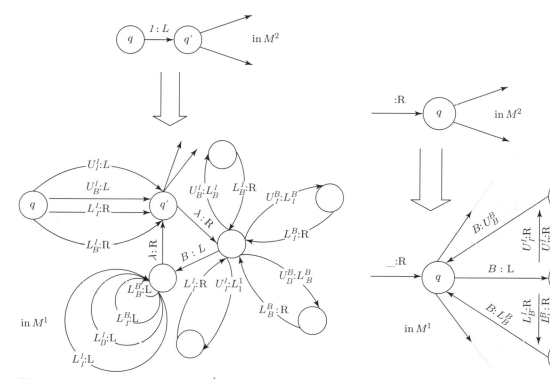

Figure 2.1.5 Instructions Causing M^1's Lower Track to Become Active.

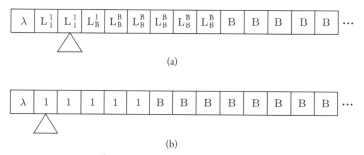

Figure 2.1.6 Routine Enabling M^1 to Extend its Workspace to the Right.

and that occurrences of L_B^B must be replaced by Bs. On the other hand, any occurrence of L_1^1 must be replaced in effect by *two 1s*. For example, if at the end of its simulation of M^2, machine M^1's configuration is as shown in Figure 2.1.7(a), then M^1 will transform its tape so as to halt in the configuration shown in Figure 2.1.7(b). Some routine

λ	L_1^1	L_1^1	L_B^1	L_B^B	L_B^B	L_B^B	L_B^B	L_B^B	B	B	B	B	B	...

(a)

λ	1	1	1	1	1	B	B	B	B	B	B	B	B	...

(b)

Figure 2.1.7 M^1's Final Transformation of Its Tape.

that effects this transformation must be added to every state of M^2 that lacks an instruction for symbol *1*. (See Exercise 2.1.1.)

This completes the description of M^1. It should be plain enough that M^1 one-way computes function f.   Q.E.D.

We refer to Theorem 2.1 as an *equivalence result* because it has the form of a (universally quantified) biconditional ... if and only if ..., where each side here is replaced by some proposition. Typically, the two sides express alternative characterizations of some sort of mathematical object—some set or function, say. In the present case, we may take Theorem 2.1 to say that any number-theoretic function f has the property of one-way Turing computability if and only if f has the property of two-way Turing computability as well. In symbols, we have

$$(\forall f\colon \mathcal{N} \to \mathcal{N})(f \text{ is one-way Turing-computable} \leftrightarrow f \text{is two-way Turing-computable})$$

As mentioned in Example 2.1.2, we could give a notion of word acceptance for Turing machines with one-way-infinite tape. This new notion of word acceptance would have only to make the obvious allowances for left endmarker λ occurring immediately to the left of input word w and immediately to the left of any accepting 1. It should be plain that only trivial changes would then be required in order to transform the proof of Theorem 2.1 into proofs of the following propositions.

THEOREM 2.2: Let L be a language over alphabet Σ. Then L is accepted (recognized) by a Turing machine with two-way-infinite tape if and only if L is accepted (recognized) by a Turing machine with one-way-infinite tape.

In symbols we may write both

$$(\forall L \subseteq \Sigma^*)(L \text{ is one-way Turing-acceptable} \leftrightarrow L \text{ is two-way Turing-acceptable})$$

and

$$(\forall L \subseteq \Sigma^*)(L \text{ is one-way Turing-recognizable} \leftrightarrow L \text{ is two-way Turing-recognizable})$$

In later sections, unless stated otherwise, we shall continue to use the term *Turing machine* to mean a Turing machine with two-way-infinite tape.

§2.2 Turing Machines That Accept by Terminal State

Earlier we adopted certain conventions regarding word acceptance on the part of Turing machines. Namely, we said that Turing machine M accepts word w if, when started scanning the leftmost symbol of w on a tape that contains w and is otherwise blank, M ultimately halts scanning a single 1 on an otherwise blank tape. In what follows, let us refer to this notion of word acceptance as *acceptance by 1*. It will be useful for technical reasons to introduce another, equivalent notion of word acceptance on the part of Turing machines.

To this end, let us change our notion of Turing machine slightly so as to allow a Turing machine to have a single *terminal state*. If q_t is the unique terminal state of M, then M will be permitted no instructions whatever for q_t and hence will halt immediately whenever in state q_t. Aside from this change, Turing machines will be just what they were before. That is, a *Turing machine M with terminal state q_t* will be a sextuple $\langle Q, \Sigma, \Gamma, q_{init}, q_t, \delta_M \rangle$ where Q, Σ, Γ, and q_{init} are all as in Definition 1.1 and where, in addition, we have that $q_t \in Q$ and that δ_M is undefined for all pairs of the form (q_t, σ). Note that it will still be possible in principle for M to halt in a state other than q_t, since halting will still mean arriving at a state q such that there is no instruction for q and the currently scanned symbol. Also, we do not assume that q_{init} and q_t are distinct.

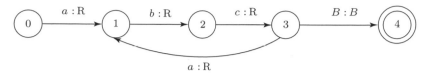

Figure 2.2.1 The State Diagram of a Turing Machine That Accepts Language $\{(abc)^n | n \geq 1\}$ by Terminal State.

We shall be interested in Turing machines with terminal state as language acceptors only. For such a Turing machine, we now give a new notion of word acceptance, which we call *acceptance by terminal state*.

> **DEFINITION 2.2:** Let $M = \langle Q, \Sigma, \Gamma, q_{init}, q_t, \delta_M \rangle$ be a Turing machine with terminal state. Then M *accepts nonempty word w by terminal state* if, when started scanning the first symbol of w on a tape that contains w and nothing else, M ultimately arrives at, and hence halts in, terminal state q_t. Similarly, M *accepts the empty word by terminal state* if, when started scanning a square on a completely blank tape, M ultimately arrives at, and hence halts in, terminal state q_t.

Note that we do not require that the tape contents upon halting in state q_t be anything in particular. Nor do we even require that M have read w completely. Incidentally, what is true of M if it happens that $q_{init} = q_t$?

Our new notion of language acceptance is analogous to that given earlier in Definition 1.3.

> **DEFINITION 2.3:** Let $M = \langle Q, \Sigma, \Gamma, q_{init}, q_t, \delta_M \rangle$ be a Turing machine with terminal state and let L be a language over alphabet Σ. Then M *accepts language L by terminal state* provided that M accepts, by terminal state, all and only the words of L.

EXAMPLE 2.2.1 As a simple example of a Turing machine with terminal state, consider the machine $M = \langle Q, \Sigma, \Gamma, q_0, q_4, \delta_M \rangle$, with $\Sigma = \Gamma = \{a, b, c\}$, whose state diagram appears in Figure 2.2.1. We place a double circle around q_4 to mark it as terminal state. The reader should verify that M accepts by terminal state the language $\{(abc)^n | n \geq 1\}$. Notice that M erases nothing and manages to enter terminal state q_4 just in case input word w is of the required form.

EXAMPLE 2.2.2 As another example, consider the Turing machine M whose state diagram appears in Figure 2.2.2. M accepts the language of balanced parentheses $\{\varepsilon, ( ), (( )), ( )( ), ((( ))), \ldots\}$ defined inductively by clauses (i)–(iii) below.

(i) ε is a balanced string of parentheses.

(ii) If S_1 and S_2 are balanced strings of parentheses, then so are both $S_1 \frown S_2$ and (S_1).

(iii) Nothing else is a balanced string of parentheses except that which can be obtained from clauses (i) and (ii).

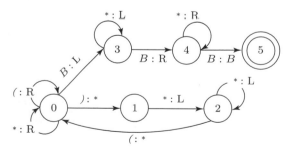

Figure 2.2.2 The State Diagram of a Turing Machine That Accepts the Language of Balanced Parentheses by Terminal State.

Open icon **Balanced Parentheses** within the Turing Machine folder in order to test this machine. Try loading tapes `balstr.tt` and `unbalstr.tt`.

EXAMPLE 2.2.3 Open icon **Example 2.2.3** to observe the operation of a 12-state Turing machine that accepts language $\{w \in \Sigma^* | w = w^R\}$ by terminal state, where $\Sigma = \{a, b\}$. Load tapes `oddpalin.tt` and `evenpali.tt` from the File menu. (Incidentally, the state diagram of this machine appears as Figure 12.1.1.)

We shall now prove that the two notions of language acceptance—acceptance by *1* and acceptance by terminal state—are equivalent in the sense that any language that is accepted by some Turing machine in the one way is accepted by some Turing machine in the other way, and conversely.

THEOREM 2.3: Let L be a language over alphabet Σ. Then there exists a Turing machine that accepts L by *1* if and only if there exists a Turing machine that accepts L by terminal state.

PROOF As usual, we split the proof into two parts—the forward direction and the reverse direction. For the **reverse direction**, we start by assuming that L is accepted by terminal state by some given machine M_t. We then transform M_t into a new machine M_1 that accepts L by *1*. The basic idea is simple enough: We would let M_1 be just like M_t except that we add instructions for M_t's terminal state q_t that cause M_1, upon entering q_t, to erase the contents of its entire tape before writing a single *1* and halting. The difficulty here lies in M_1's knowing when it has succeeded in erasing every symbol on its tape. To this end, we add two new tape symbols λ and ρ to the input alphabet Γ of M_1 as left and right endmarkers, respectively. This means adding a new initial state q_0' and a routine for adding λ and ρ immediately to the left and right ends of any input word w. (See Figure 2.2.3, where we assume for the sake of simplicity that $\Sigma = \{a, b\}$.) Using λ and ρ as endmarkers means adding instructions so as to cause λ and ρ, whenever encountered during execution, to be moved outward to the left or to the right, respectively, so as to mark the new limits of M_1's work area. This involves erasing λ, moving to the left, writing λ anew, and returning one square to the right. Endmarker ρ is treated similarly. Consequently, we add two routines—one for λ and one for ρ—to absolutely every state of M_t except q_t (see Figure 2.2.4). In general, this will make for a certain amount of overkill, but this need not concern us. Finally, in Figure 2.2.5 we see how M_1, upon entering state q_t, will erase the entire contents of its tape and write a single *1* before halting. Endmarkers λ and ρ are used

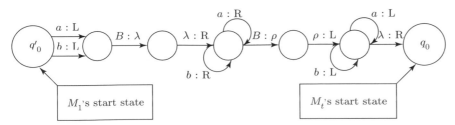

Figure 2.2.3 Routine for Adding Endmarkers λ and ρ.

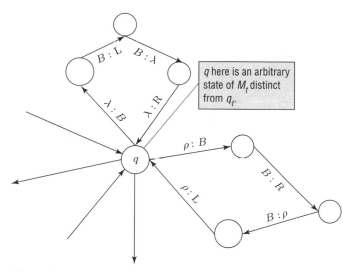

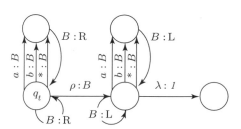

Figure 2.2.4 Routine Whereby M_1 Extends its Workspace.

Figure 2.2.5 Routine Whereby M_1 Erases the Entire Contents of Its Tape and Writes an Accepting *1*.

to enable M_1 to recognize the limits of its work space. They must themselves be erased, of course. (In Figure 2.2.5 we assume for simplicity that M_1's tape alphabet Γ is $\Sigma \cup \{*\}$.) Note that, in the context of M_1, state q_t is in no sense terminal.

We now take the **forward direction**. Let us begin by reflecting on the situation whereby some machine M_1, say, accepts word w by *1*. Whatever else the accepting computation may be like, M_1 is certain to halt in some state q such that q has no instruction for tape alphabet symbol *1*—otherwise M_1 would not halt in state q reading a *1* (on an otherwise blank tape). So all that we need to do in order to transform M_1 into a machine M_t that accepts w by terminal state is to add, to each such state q, a routine that (1) checks to see whether M is currently scanning a *1* on an otherwise blank tape and, if so, (2) enters a new terminal state q_t for which M_t necessarily will have no instructions and hence will halt. Once again, M_t needs to know how far to check in looking for nonblanks in its attempt to verify that the *1* currently being scanned does indeed represent acceptance of w. We can again use endmarkers λ and ρ precisely as they were used in the reverse direction. This means adding a new start state and a routine for establishing λ and ρ immediately to the left and right, respectively, of input word w before entering M_1's q_0 (see again Figure 2.2.3). Also, as before, we add, to *every* state this time, a three-state routine for moving λ to the left and ρ to the right whenever encountered (see again Figure 2.2.4). This leaves only the verification routine mentioned a moment ago: Figure 2.2.6 shows the new instructions and states that must be linked to every state q of M_1 possessing no instruction for tape symbol *1*.

This routine enters the new terminal state q_t immediately upon ascertaining that the scanned *1* is that of acceptance. Note that there is no need to erase anything even in the case of acceptance since tape content is no longer the issue.   Q.E.D.

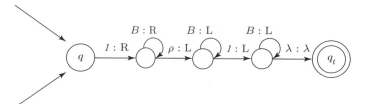

Figure 2.2.6 Routine Enabling M_t to Determine That the *1* Currently Being Scanned Indicates Acceptance on the Part of M_1.

§2.3 Multitape Turing Machines

The standard Turing machine, as described in §1.2 and §1.3, has a single read/write head moving along a single tape that is infinite in both directions. In §2.1 we considered one useful variation on the Turing machine concept, namely, Turing machines with one-way-infinite tape. It is possible to define Turing machines so as to vary their resources in other ways as well. In the present section, we consider one such variation—that of *multitape Turing machine*. Thus we shall describe Turing machines that, instead of having a single tape, have n tapes and n read/write heads, one for each tape. The details of the formal definition are left until later. For the moment, we proceed with an informal characterization. Multitape Turing machines will serve variously as language acceptors, language recognizers, and computers of number-theoretic functions. Of course, we will need to modify somewhat our conventions regarding word acceptance and function computation.

Multitape Turing machines will have a minimum of two tapes: Any given multitape Turing machine will be assumed to have $k + 2$ tapes for some fixed $k \geq 0$. We shall further assume some ordering of these $k + 2$ tapes. We shall speak of the first tape of M as the *input tape* of M and of the last tape of M as the *output tape* of M. Furthermore, we shall usually assume that the input tape is read-only and that the output tape is write-only,[1] in which case the machine is said to be *off-line*. All other tapes are *worktapes*. Definition 2.4 below says, in effect, that if Turing machine M begins execution with its $k + 2$ tapes as shown here:

input tape:	**H**abab*B*
worktape$_1$:	**H***BBBBB*
worktape$_2$:	**H***BBBBB*
...	
worktape$_k$:	**H***BBBBB*
output tape:	**H***BBBBB*

and ultimately halts with its $k + 2$ tapes as shown here:

input tape:	**Habab***B*
worktape$_1$:	...

---

[1] It is perhaps obvious enough what it means for the input tape to be read-only: If anything—symbol or blank—is written to the input tape, then it must be the very thing currently being scanned on that tape—in other words, no *real* write at all. On the other hand, the "write-only" requirement for output tapes may appear puzzling. In an effort to avoid needless formalism, let us say only that the machine's behavior will in no way be determined by the contents of its output tape. While the accompanying software does not enforce this requirement, it will be met in effect by any two-tape machine M, say, for which $\delta_M(q, \alpha_1, \beta_1) \neq \delta_M(q, \alpha_2, \beta_2)$ invariably implies $\alpha_1 \neq \alpha_2$. Since most of our multitape machines will be language acceptors that at most write a single *1* to their output tapes and then halt immediately, we need not be too concerned about the write-only requirement. But the curious reader might consider Exercise 2.3.17(b) and its solution.

worktape$_2$:   . . .

. . .

worktape$_k$:   . . .

output tape: **H1**$BBBB$

then we shall say that M accepts word **abab**.

DEFINITION 2.4: Suppose that $(k + 2)$-tape Turing machine M is started scanning the leftmost symbol of nonempty input word w on its input tape, which is otherwise blank initially. Suppose further that all of M's other tapes are totally blank. Then if M halts with its first read-head scanning the leftmost symbol of w on its input tape, which is otherwise blank, and scanning a single 1 on its output tape, which is otherwise blank, then we shall say that M *accepts word* w.

On the other hand, suppose that $(k + 2)$-tape Turing machine M is started scanning a blank on a completely blank tape. Suppose further that all of M's other tapes are totally blank as well initially. Then if M halts with its first read-head scanning a blank on a completely blank input tape and scanning a single 1 on its output tape, which is otherwise blank, then we shall say that M *accepts the empty word* ε.

Note that in the definition of word acceptance for multitape Turing machines we do not care about the final contents of worktapes. Finally, given the new definition of *word* acceptance, our earlier definition of *language* acceptance requires no changes. Namely, a multitape Turing machine will accept a language L provided that it accepts all and only the words of L. We leave it to the reader to formulate the corresponding—and obvious—notion of language recognition for multitape Turing machines.

EXAMPLE 2.3.1 Opening icon **Same Number of a's and b's - multitape machine** brings to the screen the state diagram of a four-tape Turing machine M that accepts the language $\{w \in \Sigma^* | n_a(w) = n_b(w)\}$ with $\Sigma = \{a, b\}$. Either of the tape sets `6a4bmult.tt` or `9a9bmult.tt` may be used with this machine. Since we have four read/write heads and four tapes, the arcs of M's state diagram are labeled so as to give a current symbol/action pair for *each* of the four tapes. Since frequently only one of the four read/write heads will be moving or writing during a given time unit, it is convenient to introduce instructions such as B:B or a:a for the inactive heads. M reads its input word w from left to right and, as it does so, copies any occurrence of a onto worktape$_1$ and any occurrence of b onto worktape$_2$. Afterward, M ascertains whether the number of as on worktape$_1$ is equal to the number of bs on worktape$_2$. A single 1 is written to the output tape just in case equality holds.

The reader will recall that we earlier considered a single-tape machine that accepts $\{w \in \Sigma^* | n_a(w) = n_b(w)\}$ in $O(n^2)$ steps worst case, where $n = |w|$ for input word w (see Example 1.3.1 and its time analysis in §1.7). Our multitape machine does better, accepting $\{w \in \Sigma^* | n_a(w) = n_b(w)\}$ in $O(n)$ steps worst case (see Exercise 2.3.5). We avail ourselves of an opportunity to emphasize the *model-dependent character* of all such complexity measures. (More on this later.)

We next turn to function computation. The new definition of what it is for a multitape Turing machine to compute a number-theoretic function is analogous to the new definition of word acceptance. For simplicity, we assume in Definition 2.5 below that function f is unary and total. (Talk of $m + 2$

tapes is just one way of saying that M has at least two tapes—one for input and one for output—where m then represents the number of worktapes proper.)

DEFINITION 2.5: *Turing machine M with $m + 2$ tapes computes unary number-theoretic function f* provided the following is true of M for any $n \geq 0$. Namely, if M is started with its input tape head scanning the leftmost *1* of an unbroken string of $n + 1$ *1*s and with all other tapes completely blank, then M eventually halts and

(1) upon halting, M's input tape head is scanning the leftmost *1* of an unbroken string of $n + 1$ *1*s— in other words, M's input tape is unchanged—and
(2) upon halting, M's output tape head is scanning the leftmost *1* of an unbroken string of $f(n) + 1$ *1*s on an output tape that is otherwise blank.

Again, we do not care about the final configurations of worktapes, which can be expected, upon termination, to contain the residue of M's computation for argument n (see Figure 2.3.1). Definition 2.5 is easily emended so as to accommodate partial functions f that take several arguments:

DEFINITION 2.5 (k-ary version): *Turing machine M with $m + 2$ tapes computes partial k-ary number-theoretic function f* provided that the following is true of M for any $n_1, n_2, \ldots, n_k \geq 0$.

First, assume that function f happens to be defined for arguments $n_1, n_2, \ldots, n_k$ and that M is started with its input tape head scanning the leftmost *1* of an unbroken string of $n_1 + 1$ *1*s followed by a single blank, followed by an unbroken string of $n_2 + 1$ *1*s, followed by a single blank, $\ldots$, followed by an unbroken string of $n_k + 1$ *1*s and with all other tapes completely blank. Then M eventually halts and

(1) upon halting, M's input tape head is scanning the leftmost *1* of an unbroken string of $n_1 + 1$ *1*s followed by a single blank, followed by an unbroken string of $n_2 + 1$ *1*s, followed by a single blank, $\ldots$, followed by an unbroken string of $n_k + 1$ *1*s—in other words, M's input tape is unchanged–and
(2) upon halting, M's output tape head is scanning the leftmost *1* of an unbroken string of $f(n_1, n_2, \ldots, n_k) + 1$ *1*s on an output tape that is otherwise blank.

On the other hand, suppose that function f is not defined for arguments $n_1, n_2, \ldots, n_k$ and that M is started with its input tape read-head scanning the leftmost *1* of an unbroken string of $n_1 + 1$ *1*s followed by a single blank, followed by an unbroken string of $n_2 + 1$ *1*s, followed by a single blank, $\ldots$, followed by an unbroken string of $n_k + 1$ *1*s and with all other tapes completely blank. Then M may or may not halt. But if it does halt, then it is not the case that both (1) and (2) above hold.

Consider the single-tape Turing machine M whose state diagram appears in Figure 2.3.2. The reader should verify that M computes the number-theoretic function $f(n) =_{\text{def.}} n \, div \, 2$ in the sense of Definition 1.5. (Open the icon labeled **n div 2 - single-tape machine** and load either tape 8.tt or 9.tt.) Basically, M removes *1*s in pairs from the input string, each time writing a single *1* off to the right. When the input string has been completely erased, the *1*s on the right represent the quotient under integer division by 2.

Initially:

Input tape contains
representation of
argument n.

Worktapes
are completely
blank.

Output tape is
blank as well.

Upon termination:

Input tape contains
representation of
argument n.

Worktapes are not
assumed to be
configured in any
particular way.

Output tape contains
representation of $f(n)$.

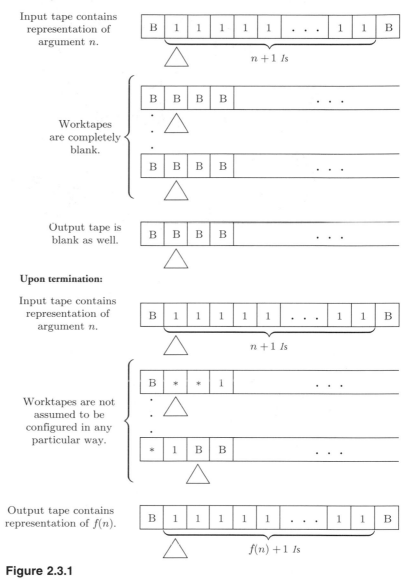

Figure 2.3.1

EXAMPLE 2.3.2 Integer division by 2 suggests another simple example of a multitape Turing machine—this time in the role of function computer. Consider a two-tape Turing machine that computes function $f(n) = n$ *div* 2 in accordance with Definition 2.5. We have an input tape and an output tape but no worktapes. Since we have two read/write heads and two tapes, we must label the arcs of M's state diagram so as to give a current symbol/action pair for *each* of our two tapes. Again, since frequently only one of the two read/write heads will be moving or writing during a given time unit, it is convenient to introduce null instructions such as *B:B* or *1:1* for the inactive head.

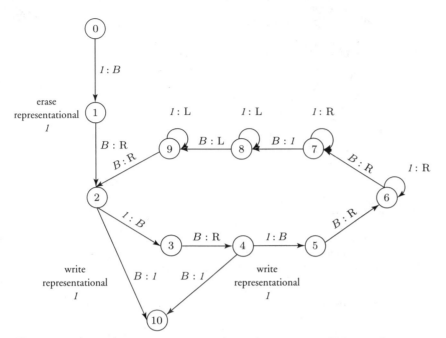

Figure 2.3.2 A Single-Tape Turing Machine That Computes $f(n) = n \ div \ 2$.

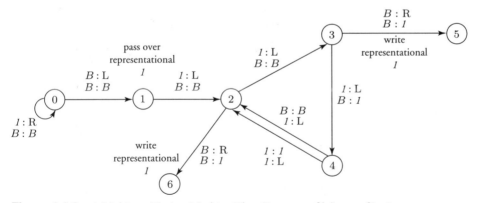

Figure 2.3.3 A Multitape Turing Machine That Computes $f(n) = n \ div \ 2$.

A multitape solution appears in Figure 2.3.3. Basically, the Turing machine works by writing a single 1 on the output tape for each pair of 1s read on the input tape. As required by Definition 2.5, if the two tapes of the machine of Figure 2.3.3 are initially as follows:

input tape :   **H**11111111

output tape :   **H**B

then M ultimately halts in the configuration

input tape :   **H**11111111 (unchanged)

output tape :   **H**1111

reflecting the fact that 7 *div* 2 = 3. Open icon **n div 2 - multitape machine** in the Turing Machine folder to observe the operation of this machine. (Load either tape set `mult7.tt` or `mult8.tt`.)

Corresponding to our state diagrams for multitape Turing machines, we must alter slightly our notion of transition function so as to accommodate each of our several read/write heads. Thus, in the case of the single instruction that takes us from state q_3 to state q_4 in Figure 2.3.3, we have that

$$\delta(q_3, 1, B) = (L, 1, q_4)$$

with the interpretation "if in state q_3 reading a 1 on the first tape and a blank on the second tape, then move to the left on the first tape, write a 1 on the second tape, and go into state q_4." Otherwise, no change in our original definition of Turing machines (Definition 1.1) is required. Having said this, we omit any formal definition of multitape Turing machines.

We make the following important remark regarding multitape Turing machines using the state diagram fragment of Figure 2.3.4, for some hypothetical M, as reference. Notice that if M is in state q_2, then it may or may not write a 1 on its output tape. In particular, if the currently scanned symbol on the input tape is 1, then a 1 will be written on the output tape. On the other hand, if the currently scanned symbol on the input tape is a blank, then a 1 will not be written on the output tape. The important point here is that whether a 1 is written on the output tape will depend not on the contents of the output tape itself but, rather, on the contents of the input tape square currently being scanned. This leads us to formulate the following general remark.

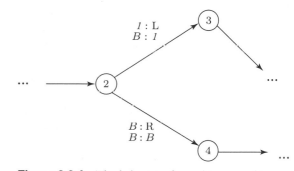

Figure 2.3.4   The behavior of a multitape machine, on any one of its tapes, depends in general upon the current contents of all of its tapes.

> **REMARK 2.3.1:** Let M be a multitape Turing machine. Suppose that tape t is one of M's $k + 2$ tapes. In general, determination of which action is to be taken by the read/write head on tape t will depend on the symbols currently being scanned on tapes *other* than t and not merely on the symbol currently being scanned on tape t itself.

This fact about multitape Turing machines shows why they really have nothing to do with so-called *parallel computation*. Parallel computation, after all, involves multiple processors operating independently of one another. But nothing like that is going on in the case of multitape Turing machines since no one

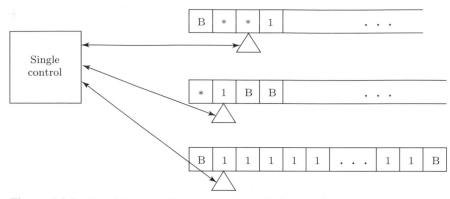

Figure 2.3.5 A multitape machine involves but a single control.

of the read/write heads is truly independent of the others. Rather, a multitape Turing machine M is best regarded as a single processor controlling multiple tape heads, and, as we just saw, these tape heads hardly operate independently: The action of any given head depends in general upon the symbols being scanned on all $k + 2$ tapes (see Figure 2.3.5).

One might have expected that increasing the number of tapes and read/write heads would have been accompanied by increased processing capacity. In fact, however, we shall see that the addition of extra tapes affords no additional computational capacity in the sense that (1) any language accepted by a multitape Turing machine is accepted by some single-tape Turing machine as well, and (2) any function computed by a multitape Turing machine can be computed by some single-tape Turing machine as well. This is not to deny, however, that adding tapes *does* enable us to speed things up. Surely one reason for the interest in multitape Turing machines stems from the time savings afforded by algorithms for multitape machines over corresponding algorithms for single-tape machines. It can be seen without much difficulty that the single-tape machine of Figure 2.3.2 computes in $O(n^2)$ steps, whereas the two-tape machine of Figure 2.3.3 computes in $O(n)$ steps—that is, in linear time (see Exercise 2.3.4). One can count on such improved performance quite generally: Namely, if one is willing to give oneself the extra resources of additional tapes and read/write heads, then an improvement in computation time will frequently follow. Thus we note, only for the first time, a certain time/space trade-off: If one allocates additional tapes, then computation time may be significantly reduced.[2] (A related phenomenon was at least implicit in our discussion of one-way-infinite machines, which, in general, are less efficient—that is, require more time—than their two-way-infinite counterparts.)

Another reason for the interest in multitape Turing machines lies in the greater ease with which algorithms for multitape Turing machines may be described informally. As an example of a nontrivial language acceptance algorithm, consider the example below. Notice that it would be rather awkward, although hardly impossible, to describe a single-tape Turing machine that accepts the language that will concern us in this example.

---

[2]There is a law of diminishing returns at work here, however. Going from one tape to two tapes is one of the *rare* instances where the speedup is truly dramatic. In general, allocation of additional resources—going from two to three tapes or from three to four—produces only minor improvements in performance times and is probably not worth the trouble.

EXAMPLE 2.3.3 As preparation for our description of a rather complicated multitape machine, we consider again the following algorithm for deciding primality.

Input: $n > 1$
Output: 1 if n is prime and 0 if n is composite.
Algorithm:
        begin
           dvs := 2;
           while dvs $< n$
               if n mod dvs $\neq 0$ then
                   dvs := dvs $+ 1$
               else return 0;
           return 1
        end.

We wish to describe a multitape Turing machine M that accepts the language

$$L = \{a^n \mid n \text{ is prime}\} = \{aa, aaa, aaaaa, aaaaaaa, \ldots\}$$

Let us assume four tapes: the input tape, two worktapes, and the output tape. The initialization phase of the algorithm will involve reading through the as on the input tape, checking that there are at least two of them, and copying a 1 onto worktape$_1$ for each a read. Read/write heads are reset on both tapes, two 1s are written on worktape$_2$, and processing of the 1s on worktape$_1$ may begin. (If fewer than two as are found on the input tape, then M halts immediately in a nonaccepting configuration.) If we assume input word a^7, then M is now configured as shown below.

Input tape :   **H**$aaaaaaa$

Worktape$_1$:   **H**1111111

Worktape$_2$:   **H**11

Output tape :   **H**BB

We shall use worktape$_1$ as dividend tape and worktape$_2$ as divisor tape. There are currently two 1s on the divisor tape: hence we read 1s in pairs on the dividend tape until none are left, in which case n is divisible by 2 and hence composite, causing M to halt immediately in a nonaccepting configuration. Or else there is a 1 left over, which means that n is not divisible by 2. In the latter case, n may be prime—but we cannot be certain yet: We must go on to divide by 3. So worktape$_2$ is incremented and used to divide the dividend by 3. If the division is successful, the machine again halts in a nonaccepting configuration. Otherwise, we increment worktape$_2$ and use it to divide by 4. After each incrementation of worktape$_2$, M will compare it with worktape$_1$. If the contents of the two worktapes are identical, then execution ceases, reflecting the fact that $dvs = n$. Since every division has been unsuccessful, n has been shown to be prime, so M writes an accepting 1 on the output tape and halts. Summarizing, we have

---

Step 1. If $w = a^0$ or $w = a^1$, then halt. Otherwise go on to Step 2.
Step 2. Write $1^{|w|}$ to worktape$_1$ and then reset read/write heads.
Step 3. Write exactly two 1s on worktape$_2$.

Step 4. If the number of *1*s on worktape$_1$ is equal to the number of *1*s on worktape$_2$, then write an accepting *1* and halt. Otherwise, go on to Step 5.

Step 5. Divide the contents of worktape$_1$ by the contents of worktape$_2$. If remainder is 0, then halt; otherwise, increment worktape$_2$ and go to Step 4.

Our next example provides an opportunity to compare the performance of a multitape machine with a single-tape machine performing the same task—in the present instance, word reversal. Just as in case of a single-tape Turing machine, giving a time analysis for a multitape machine means counting the number of instructions executed. As for space analysis, we take the total number of squares visited on all tapes over the course of a computation. In the case of an off-line machine, space means the total number of squares visited on all *worktapes*—squares visited on input and output tapes are not counted.

EXAMPLE 2.3.4 (Multitape Word Reversal) Open icon **Multitape Reverse Word** and load the tape set `abbab2.tt` to observe the operation of a two-tape Turing machine M that reverses any input word w over alphabet $\Sigma = \{a, b\}$. M first positions its input tape read-head at the right end of w in O(n) steps. Then, proceeding from right to left, M reads the characters of w in reverse, copying each character onto the output tape, proceeding from left to right. This copying routine requires another O(n) steps. Thus M computes in O(n) steps overall. (The software can be used to verify that $time_M(n) = 4n + 3$.) It is easy to see that M computes in O(n) space as well.

Earlier, in Example 1.5.4, we presented a single-tape Turing machine that reverses its input word. As it turns out, that single-tape machine computes in O(n^2) time worst case (see Exercise 1.7.2). Thus, comparing the single- and multitape machines, we see that the multitape machine is much more efficient for long input words. On the other hand, both machines require O(n) space.

We now turn to the main result of this section. Theorem 2.4 below is important because it shows that, whereas we might choose for the sake of convenience to describe an algorithm for a Turing machine with five tapes, say, we can always know that it is possible to design an equivalent machine with but a single tape. This will greatly simplify proofs in this and later chapters.

THEOREM 2.4(a): A language L is accepted by some multitape Turing machine in accordance with Definition 2.4 if and only if L is accepted by some single-tape Turing machine in accordance with Definition 1.3.

THEOREM 2.4(b): A language L is recognized by some multitape Turing machine if and only if L is recognized by some single-tape Turing machine in accordance with Definition 1.4.

THEOREM 2.4(c): Similarly, a function f is computed by some multitape Turing machine in accordance with Definition 2.5 (k-ary version) if and only if it is computed by some single-tape Turing machine in accordance with Definition 1.6.

PROOF The reverse direction of all three propositions (a), (b), and (c) here is trivial, because it should be clear that whatever can be done using a single tape can surely be done using $k + 2$ tapes for some $k \geq 0$. (To take a rough analogy, surely whatever can be done using 1 megabyte of memory can be done using $k + 2$ megabytes of memory for some $k \geq 0$.) For example, suppose that single-tape Turing machine M_1 computes function f so that, given a representation of n as input, M_1 ultimately halts with a representation of value $f(n)$ on its single tape. We can easily describe a three-tape Turing machine M_2 that computes f in accordance with our new conventions regarding multitape machines. M_2 first copies its input—a representation of argument n—from input tape to its (single) worktape, simulates M_1's computation on this worktape, and afterward copies the representation of value $f(n)$ from worktape to output tape before halting.

The **forward direction** requires considerably more work, as one might expect. As an illustration of our completely general construction technique, we consider the two-tape machine M of Figure 2.3.3 and describe an algorithm for turning it into an equivalent single-tape machine M_1—that is, one that computes the function $f(n) = n\ div\ 2$. The construction described below will not in general produce the simplest equivalent machine. Rather, our purpose is to describe a general method of construction that can be mechanically applied to *any* multitape Turing machine so as to produce an equivalent single-tape Turing machine.

The central idea of the construction is to let each of M's two tapes be represented by two tracks on M_1's single tape. The result will be a total of four tracks—all four represented on a single tape. We will use the second and fourth of these tracks to indicate read/write head locations (**H**). Thus, assuming argument $n = 5$, we imagine M_1's single tape to initially contain

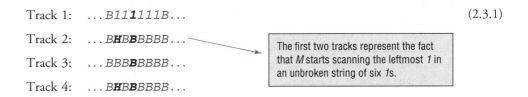

Track 1:	$...B111\mathbf{1}111B...$	(2.3.1)
Track 2:	$...B\mathbf{H}B\mathbf{B}BBBB...$	
Track 3:	$...BBB\mathbf{B}BBBB...$	
Track 4:	$...B\mathbf{H}B\mathbf{B}BBBB...$	

The first two tracks represent the fact that *M* starts scanning the leftmost *1* in an unbroken string of six *1*s.

(Keep in mind that each column here represents a single tape square.) Two symbols, namely, B and *1*, are possible on Track 1. The same is true of Track 3. Two symbols, namely, B and **H**, are possible on Track 2. The same is true of Track 4. This means that there are $2^4 = 16$ possibilities for any tape square of M_1. It is convenient, although not absolutely necessary, to use the 16 hexadecimal digits as auxiliary tape symbols representing these 16 possibilities.[3] Table 2.3.1 presents the 16 possibilities and, in the last column, the hexadecimal digits representing them. Thus the initial tape configuration of M_1 corresponding to argument $n = 5$ is

$$...F277\mathbf{7}777F...\qquad(2.3.1)$$

To reiterate, what we actually have on M_1's tape initially is (2.3.2); but, by means of Table 2.3.1, what this represents is (2.3.1). As another arbitrarily chosen example, the reader should verify that

---

[3]The context in which these new auxiliary symbols can occur on M_1's tape will make it possible for M_1 to distinguish those occurrences of auxiliary symbols *0* and *1* representing four tracks within a single tape square from other occurrences of digits *0* and *1* in their more usual roles—for example, occurrences of *1* within an input word representing a natural number argument. Also, there is no possibility that M_1 could confuse auxiliary symbol B, representing a certain configuration of the four tracks, with the blank. The latter is, after all, not a symbol but, rather, the absence of symbol.

M's being configured as

Input tape: $\ldots B\mathbf{H111111B}\ldots$

Output tape: $\ldots B\mathbf{H111BBB}\ldots$

will be reflected on M_1's single tape as

$$\ldots F0555777F\ldots$$

where $\ldots$ stands for F's to the left and to the right forever. (Note the deliberate omission of any indication of M_1's read/write head position. That issue is quite independent of the manner in which a configuration of M_1's single tape must reflect a configuration of M's two tapes.)

Reflection upon the relation between (2.3.1) and (2.3.2) shows that before beginning the simulation of M's computation as described below, M_1 must replace a leftmost 1 by auxiliary symbol 2 and all other occurrences of 1 by auxiliary symbol 7. M_1 then repositions its single read/write head over the 2 on the left and is ready to begin its simulation of M's computation. Before describing that simulation, we make a few important preliminary remarks.

With reference to Table 2.3.1, we note the following:

- Changing an **H** to a B on the second track, while making no further change, amounts to replacement of a 0 by a 4, a 1 by a 5, a 2 by a 6, a 3 by a 7, or an 8 by a C, and so on. In other words, changing an **H** to a B on the second track amounts to adding 4.

- Changing a B to an **H** on the second track, while making no further change, amounts to replacement of a 4 by a 0, a 5 by a 1, a 6 by a 2, a 7 by a 3, or a C by an 8, and so on. In other words, changing a B to an **H** on the second track amounts to subtracting 4.

- Changing an **H** to a B on the fourth track, while making no further change, amounts to replacement of a 0 by a 1, a 2 by a $3, \ldots$, or an E by an F. In other words, changing an **H** to a B on the fourth track amounts to adding 1.

- Changing a B to an **H** on the fourth track, while making no further change, amounts to replacement of a 1 by a 0, a 3 by a $2, \ldots$, or an F by an E. In other words, changing a B to an **H** on the fourth track amounts to subtracting 1.

We might assume that M_1 initially writes out some representation of M's state diagram on its single tape. This could be something like a sequence of sextuples separated by blanks or some special character, each sextuple being one of M's instructions. That part of M_1's tape on which these sextuples would be located would not be divided into tracks; that is, it would not contain occurrences of auxiliary symbols $0, 1, 2, \ldots, A, B, C, D, \ldots$, say. It is of course possible that that part of M_1's tape on which it carries out its simulation of M's behavior could threaten to interfere with these sextuples. In such a case, M_1 would need to shift these sextuples outward on the tape so as to create more space for the simulation proper. We shall speak below of M_1's "knowledge of M" and thereby mean this sequence of sextuples. (The alternative would be to assume that M_1's own state diagram—or transition function—incorporates that of M. Either way, M_1 has knowledge of M, and this knowledge is built into δ_{M_1} one way or another.)

We are now ready to describe M_1's simulation of the execution of one of M's instructions. To begin, assume that M_1 is currently scanning the leftmost tape square containing one of M's two

Table 2.3.1   The 16 Auxiliary Tape Symbols of M_1.

Track 1	Track 2	Track 3	Track 4	New Symbol
1	H	1	H	0
1	H	1	B	1
1	H	B	H	2
1	H	B	B	3
1	B	1	H	4
1	B	1	B	5
1	B	B	H	6
1	B	B	B	7
B	H	1	H	8
B	H	1	B	9
B	H	B	H	A
B	H	B	B	B
B	B	1	H	C
B	B	1	B	D
B	B	B	H	E
B	B	B	B	F

tape heads. M_1 records the symbol currently being scanned by this head and then searches to the right for the other tape head. When it is found, the symbol being read is recorded. Only now does M_1 have enough information to determine, based upon its knowledge of M, which action is to be performed by each of the two heads (recall Remark 2.3.1 above). M_1 now performs these actions on the appropriate tracks, proceeding from right to left. As an example, suppose that the first tape head of M is to be moved to the right. This will have M_1 changing an **H** to a B on the second track, moving one square to the right on its tape, and changing a B to an **H** on the second track. That is, M_1 will add 4, move one square to the right, and then subtract 4. In other words, three instructions will be required for M_1's simulation of a move to the right by M's first tape head (see Figure 2.3.6).

Summarizing, the simulation of M by M_1 takes the form of M_1's sweeping to the right, recording the symbols currently scanned by each of M's tape heads, followed by a sweep back to the right during which the action of each tape head is carried out on the appropriate track. If, after a fact-finding sweep to the right, M_1 determines that no action whatever is to be carried out by either tape head, then M_1 itself halts. The result of M_1's computation is found on track 3.

The above argument is fully generalizable to machines with n tapes for $n > 2$. M_1 must know how many tape heads there are and will sweep to the right until all of them have been seen and the scanned symbols recorded. On the return sweep to the left, M_1 must keep track of how many tape

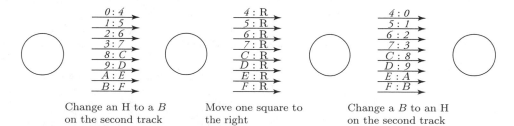

Figure 2.3.6 M_1's Simulation of M's Moving One Square to the Right on Its First Tape.

head actions have been carried out. The cycle sweep left/sweep right is completed once the action of the leftmost tape head has been carried out. Only then is M_1 ready to simulate the next of M's multipart instructions.

Once M_1's simulation of M's computation is complete, all that is necessary is to replace the auxiliary symbols representing the four-tracks with 1s or Bs corresponding to the third of these tracks, which is M's output tape. This will mean replacing the eight auxiliary symbols $0, 1, 4, 5, 8, 9, C$, and D with 1s and the other eight auxiliary symbols with Bs. M_1 then positions itself on the leftmost of these 1s and halts.   Q.E.D.

The moral here is that if one wishes to get along with no more than a single tape, this is, in fact, always possible. In general, however, this will mean giving oneself additional alphabet symbols. Thus, there is a certain tradeoff between number of tapes and size of tape alphabet.

We have said that, in general, a multitape language acceptor $M_{multitape}$ will be faster than its single-tape counterpart M_1. But we are able to be a little more specific than this. Namely, examination of the proof of Theorem 2.4 reveals that, worst case, if multitape M computes in m steps, then M_1 will compute in something on the order of m^2 steps. For instance, the four-tape machine of Example 2.3.1 accepts language $L = \{w \in \Sigma^* | n_a(w) = n_b(w)\}$, with $\Sigma = \{a, b\}$, in $\mathrm{O}(n)$ steps whereas the single-tape machine of Example 1.3.1 was seen to accept L in $\mathrm{O}(n^2)$ steps. We formulate

> **COROLLARY 2.1:** Suppose that language L is accepted by k-tape Turing machine M. Then L is accepted by a single-tape Turing machine M_1 such that $time_{M_1}(n)$ is $\mathrm{O}([time_M(n)]^2)$.

We leave the proof of Corollary 2.1 as an exercise (see Exercise 2.3.7(a) and its solution). Furthermore, reflection upon our construction in the proof of Theorem 2.4—in particular, (2.3.1) and (2.3.2)—reveals the truth of

> **COROLLARY 2.2:** Suppose that language L is accepted by k-tape Turing machine M. Then L is accepted by a single-tape Turing machine M_1 such that $space_{M_1}(n)$ is $\mathrm{O}(space_M(n))$.

Note that Theorem 2.4 concerns what we have been calling "computability-in-principle," whereas its corollaries belong to complexity theory, wherein the resource requirements of computation are the issue. Throughout the remainder of this section we pursue the complexity theme.

Off-Line Turing Machines and Memory

We have spoken of the greater ease with which multitape Turing machines may be described and of improved time analyses. There is another, perhaps more important, reason for preferring multitape to single-tape machines, however. Namely, the multitape model affords us a more flexible measure of the *memory* required by a computation, whereby one frequently means the quantity of storage required to hold the *intermediate* data leading to the ultimate result of that computation. The notion of space that was introduced with respect to single-tape machines—number of tape squares visited over the course of a computation—is somewhat inflexible: Space consumed by the input itself will most likely be counted in reckoning the machine's memory needs—at least if this input is read from end to end. This, in turn, means that no interesting single-tape machines will compute in less than $\mathrm{O}(n)$ space. The advantage of the multitape, off-line concept of space which we introduce now is that what happens on input and output tapes will not affect space: As mentioned earlier, space will now concern the number of tape squares visited *on worktapes only*. Consequently, an off-line machine might consume only $O(\log_2 n)$ space worst case, as our next example illustrates.

Before turning to that example, however, we present our formal definition of space for multitape, off-line machines. Our formulations of later complexity results can be made most perspicuous if we give our definition the following form.

DEFINITION 2.6: Let M be a $(k+2)$-tape, off-line Turing machine and let n be an arbitrary natural number. The unary, number-theoretic function $space_M$ is then defined by

$$space_M(n) = \text{the maximum number of tape squares visited } on$$
$$\textit{any one of } M\text{'s } k \text{ worktapes over the course}$$
$$\text{of any terminating computation of } M \text{ for}$$
$$\text{input of size } n$$

If M is a multitape machine having at least one worktape, then, analogously to what was done in conjunction with Definition 1.9, we shall assume that $space_M(n) \geq 1$ for all n. After all, even if no worktape action is taken throughout M's computation, a worktape read/write head must be positioned on some square of the given worktape. On the other hand, if M is a two-tape, off-line machine, then it has just an input tape and an output tape and no worktapes whatever. In that case alone we shall take $space_M(n)$ to be 0 for all n.

EXAMPLE 2.3.5 (LOGSPACE) If asked to design a three-tape, off-line Turing machine for converting the unary representation 1^{n+1} of natural number n to the corresponding binary representation, it would be most reasonable to implement the familiar two-column method of Exercise 1.1.2 (see Exercise 2.3.8). This would entail first copying the input string to the worktape and then iterating division by 2 in the usual way—that is, writing one *1* for each two *1*s read. So each division would require $O(n)$ steps. Moreover, since there would be $\lceil \log_2 n \rceil$ divisions, total run time would certainly be $O(n \cdot \lceil \log_2 n \rceil)$. As for space, one can arrange things so that no more that $2n$ squares would be visited on the worktape, which means that $space_M(n)$ would be $O(n)$. And it is space that we wish to focus on momentarily. Suppose that, for some reason, conservation of space is paramount—even if efficiency with respect to time must be sacrificed. Is there some way to produce the binary equivalent of input n while consuming only $O(\lceil \log_2 n \rceil)$ space, say? Well, as it turns out, this *is* possible, although the two-column method can be of no further use to us here. Think about it, keep in mind Exercise 1.3.7, and, when ready, open icon **LOGSPACE** in order to observe the operation of a three-tape conversion machine that visits only $\lceil \log_2 n \rceil + 3$ squares[4] on its middle tape. Accordingly, this busy little machine will be said to compute in *logarithmic space*.

---

[4] Strictly for the sake of clarification, we mention a small technical issue. In this example, we are taking n to be not the *length* of an input string but, rather, the *value* of that string. (This is the first case we have considered in which *size* of input does not mean *length* of input word.) Given this understanding of variable n, it follows that writing $\lceil \log_2 n \rceil + 3$ makes no sense for input of size $n = 0$ so that, strictly speaking, it is necessary to make a special case of 0 in this and similar circumstances. Usually we shall not bother to do that. The reader should be aware of this situation, however, and be prepared to emend our assertions slightly for the zero case. For example, in the case of machine M of Example 2.3.5, we have $space_M(0) = 3$. (The reader can readily verify this fact by running the machine at icon **LOGSPACE** on input word *1*—that is, on input word 1^{0+1}.) Similar remarks would be in order regarding the claim that M computes in $O(\lceil \log_2 n \rceil)$ space, where n is the value of the unary representation taken as input.

The preceding example is the first involving function $f(n) = \lceil \log_2 n \rceil$ that we have considered. Consequently, our discussion is deliberately quite explicit in bringing out the role of this function. We shall be less fastidious in the future. Following customary usage, we shall usually write $O(\log_2 n)$ for $O(\lceil \log_2 n \rceil)$ and $O(n \log_2 n)$ instead of $O(n \cdot \lceil \log_2 n \rceil)$, say. This practice is justified by the fact that function $\lceil \log_2 n \rceil$ and function $\log_2 n$ exhibit the same rate of growth. (Function $\lceil \log_2 n \rceil$ is $\Theta(\log_2 n)$ in the terminology of Exercise 0.5.10.) By extension, complexity theorists frequently write "there will be $\log_2 n$ divisions," say, when what is really meant is "there will be $\lceil \log_2 n \rceil$ divisions." We shall endeavor to avoid the latter slip—but make no promises. (Of course, talk of $\log_2 n$ divisions makes no real sense in general since $f(n) = \log_2 n$ is not a number-theoretic function.)

Earlier we introduced the complexity class P, defined as the class of all and only those languages accepted in polynomially bounded time by some single-tape Turing machine of the sort that we have been considering. We shall designate the class of languages accepted by Turing machines in logarithmically bounded space as *LOGSPACE*.[5] (For reasons already given, the Turing machines in question here must be of the multitape, off-line variety.) In Exercise 2.3.10, the reader is asked to demonstrate that a number of languages that we have considered previously are, in fact, members of *LOGSPACE*. In each case, the ideas needed have their source in Example 2.3.5. Moreover, Exercise 2.3.13 asserts that $LOGSPACE \subseteq P$; that is, any language accepted by a multitape, off-line Turing machine in logarithmically bounded space is accepted by a single-tape Turing machine in polynomially bounded time.

> **DEFINITION 2.7:** The class of all languages that are accepted in logarithmically bounded space by some (multitape, off-line) Turing machine is known as *LOGSPACE*.

While on the topic of off-line machines and space, we take advantage of an opportunity to introduce the general phenomenon of *compression*. Namely, by augmenting the tape alphabet of a given off-line machine M, we can reduce space consumption by a constant factor. We illustrate the point with a small example. Suppose, for the sake of simplicity only, that M's tape alphabet is just $\{a, b\}$. We now imagine constructing, on the basis of M, a new off-line machine M' having nine new tape alphabet symbols— each one representing or "encoding" one possible pair of adjacent worktape squares. For instance, we might use the encodings of Table 2.3.2. To appreciate how space consumption can be reduced, consider

Table 2.3.2 Encodings of Adjacent Worktape Squares.

New Tape Alphabet Symbol	Encoded Pair
α	aa
β	ab
γ	aB
δ	ba
ε	bb
ζ	bB
η	Ba
θ	Bb
ι	BB

---

[5] In the literature, this complexity class is usually known as $DSPACE(\log_2 n)$.

how M might copy input string $abaa$, say, to four adjacent squares on some worktape. Normally, this would involve eight steps—a write followed by a move right for each of four symbols. The new machine M' will achieve the same effect by first writing symbol γ, then overwriting it with symbol β, then moving to the right, writing symbol γ again, and immediately overwriting it with symbol α. Moreover, M' will have visited only two worktape squares in the process. In short, assuming the off-line concept of space, machine M' consumes just half the space used by M. Moreover, there is no upper limit to the compression obtainable using this technique. For example, encoding *triples* by new alphabet symbols results in a new machine M' consuming only one-third of the space required by M.[6] We prove the following general proposition regarding compression.

THEOREM 2.5: Suppose language L is accepted by some $(k+2)$-tape, off-line Turing machine M. Then, for arbitrary natural number $r \geq 1$, there exists a $(k+2)$-tape, off-line Turing machine M' accepting L with $space_{M'}(n)$ equal to $1/r \cdot space_M(n)$ essentially.

PROOF By assumption, M accepts language L using at most $space_M(n)$ squares on any single worktape, worst case, for input words of length n. We augment M's tape alphabet Γ_M by adding new symbols for arbitrary r-tuples of members of $\Gamma_M \cup \{B\}$ in the manner described earlier. Then, a new machine M' may be constructed whose behavior for the new symbols, as they occur on its k worktapes, simulates the behavior of M on *its* k worktapes with the result that M' accepts L. Moreover, since M visits at most $space_M(n)$ worktape squares on any one worktape, the resultant compression by factor r means that M' will visit at most $1 + \lfloor (1/r) \cdot space_M(n) \rfloor + 1$ tape squares on any one of its worktapes. (Maximal compression can be achieved only if the number of squares visited by M on a maximal worktape is an exact multiple of r. Any surplus—either on the left or on the right—means an extra worktape square must be consumed incompletely by M'.) We may conclude that

$$\lfloor (1/r) \cdot space_M(n) \rfloor \leq space_{M'}(n) \leq \lfloor (1/r) \cdot space_M(n) \rfloor + 2$$

Q.E.D

§2.4 Encoding of Turing Machines

Later on, we should like to be able to represent or *encode* individual Turing machines as either symbol strings or natural numbers. This will make it possible for one Turing machine to take another Turing machine—in encoded form—as (part of) its input. We postpone until the next section any explanation of why that is of any real interest to us. Instead, in this section, we focus our attention to schemes

---

[6] We have deliberately overstated the case. To see this, imagine how M' would get the effect of M's writing string $w = abaab$ from left to right on five adjacent squares of its worktape. Most naturally, M' would first write symbol γ, overwrite it with α, and then move to the right. Next, M' would write symbol γ, overwrite it with α, and again move to the right. Finally, symbol ζ would be written. The resulting string $\beta\alpha\zeta$ would consume $3 = \lfloor (1/2) \cdot |w| \rfloor + 1$ worktape squares, the rightmost square being incompletely consumed by M' due to the fact that $abaab$ cannot be partitioned into blocks of two symbols each. Other situations give rise to an extra square on the left as well. So imagine an encoding of *triples* of symbols this time and off-line machines M and M' as described above. How will M' get the effect of M's first writing string $aabaaca$ in seven adjacent squares on its worktape and *afterward* prefixing the string by symbol d, say, so as to have $w = daabaaca$ on eight adjacent worktape squares? Briefly, blocks aab and aac will each be represented ultimately by a single symbol on M''s worktape. On the right, block aBB will require another square, and afterward, on the left, block BBd will require another, for a total of $4 = 1 + \lfloor (1/3) \cdot |w| \rfloor + 1$ squares.

for encoding Turing machines. There are many such schemes, all equally good from a theoretical point of view. In this section we shall consider only two of them. (A third encoding scheme is discussed in Example 2.5.1 in the next section.) The first will, in all probability, already be familiar to the reader in its essentials. It is based on the manner in which character data are represented numerically using the encoding scheme known as ASCII. Hence we shall use the term *ASCII style* when referring to this particular scheme and, by extension, we shall speak of the *ASCII codes* of Turing machines.

EXAMPLE 2.4.1 (ASCII Codes for Turing Machines) Consider the Turing machine M of Figure 2.4.1(a), having tape alphabet $\Gamma = \{a, 1\}$ and consisting of just three states and three instructions. The reader can easily verify that M accepts the language $\{a^n \mid n \geq 0\}$, although that in itself is not the issue in what follows. To facilitate matters, we make the slightest change by renaming M's states: q_0 becomes simply q, q_1 becomes q', and q_2 becomes q''. Similarly, we redesignate tape symbols a and 1 as s' and s'', respectively, and use s itself for the blank (see Figure 2.4.1(b)). Transition function δ_M is now completely defined as

$$\delta_M(q, s') = (s, q') \qquad \delta_M(q', s) = (R, q) \qquad \delta_M(q, s) = (s'', q'')$$

The reader will see in a moment why we have chosen to keep our example very simple.

   The principal idea here is this. If we adopt the convention that q will always be start state, then any Turing machine is just a finite set of quadruples. In particular, the three-instruction Turing machine M of Figure 2.4.1(b) will be the set S consisting of the three quadruples

$$\langle q, s', s, q' \rangle \qquad \langle q', s, R, q \rangle \qquad \langle q, s, s'', q'' \rangle$$

Set S is an unordered object, as it were. We shall want to represent S by a symbol string, which implies imposing some order on S. Clearly, there are $3 \cdot 2 = 6$ different ways in which this might be done. Dropping brackets and separating quadruples by semicolons, we have the six alternative strings.

$$q, s', s, q'; q', s, R, q; q, s, s'', q'' \tag{2.4.1}$$

$$q, s', s, q'; q, s, s'', q''; q', s, R, q \tag{2.4.2}$$

$$q', s, R, q; q, s', s, q'; q, s, s'', q'' \tag{2.4.3}$$

$$q', s, R, q; q, s, s'', q''; q, s', s, q' \tag{2.4.4}$$

$$q, s, s'', q''; q, s', s, q'; q', s, R, q \tag{2.4.5}$$

$$q, s, s'', q''; q', s, R, q; q, s', s, q' \tag{2.4.6}$$

Each of (2.4.1) through (2.4.6) is a string over *Turing machine description alphabet* Ψ containing the seven symbols

$$q \qquad ' \qquad s \qquad L \qquad R \qquad , \qquad ;$$

In other words, we have six alternative descriptions of one and the same machine M. We next establish that any one of the strings (2.4.1) through (2.4.6)—any string over alphabet Ψ, for that matter—may be encoded as a binary-digit string, provided that we first associate the symbols of alphabet Ψ with binary-digit strings of length 3, say. We shall use the *symbol codes* listed in Table 2.4.1. First alternative (2.4.1) among our

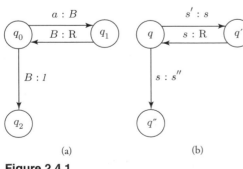

(a)   (b)

Figure 2.4.1

descriptions of M is now encoded by the binary-digit string obtained by concatenating the three-digit symbol codes of each of the 30 characters within (2.4.1). In other words, M is encoded as a binary-digit string of length $30 \cdot 3 = 90$ as follows:

Table 2.4.1

Member of Ψ	Symbol Code	Member of Ψ	Symbol Code
,	000	L	100
q	001	;	101
s	010	/	110
R	011		

001 000 010 110 000 010 000 001 110 101 001 110 000 010 000 011 000 ⌐

    q   ,   s   /   ,   s   ,   q   /   ;   q   /   ,   s   ,   R   ,

⌐001 101 001 000 010 000 010 110 110 000 001 110 110   (2.4.7)

    q   ;   q   ,   s   ,   s   /   /   ,   q   /   /   (2.4.1)

By extension, we shall speak of the *symbol code of machine M* in referring to the likes of (2.4.7). Most frequently, we shall want to encode M as a natural number. At such times, we shall speak of the *ASCII code* of M and mean thereby that natural number denoted by the 90-digit string at (2.4.7) interpreted as a binary numeral. We shall not bother to determine the decimal equivalent of (2.4.7). Suffice it to say that ASCII codes of even the simplest machines will be very large numbers by any standard.

We make several important remarks regarding our ASCII-style encoding scheme:

- Turing machines will not have unique ASCII codes in general. Thus we see that the machine M of Figure 2.4.1(b) will have no fewer than six distinct codes, each one corresponding to one of the alternative descriptions (2.4.1) to (2.4.6).

- On the other hand, no natural number that is the ASCII code of a Turing machine will be the ASCII code of more than one Turing machine. Most commonly, a given natural number will not be the ASCII code of even one Turing machine. (Why not?)

- Most important of all is the fact that, given an arbitrary natural number n, there is a simple algorithm for determining if n is the ASCII code of some Turing machine and, if so, which Turing machine it is the code of. It is this "retrievability" property that makes possible our adoption of the ASCII-style encoding scheme. Retrievably is part of what we mean when we say that the ASCII-style encoding scheme is *effective*.

An Alternative Encoding Scheme (the Euler–Gödel Encoding Scheme)

As an alternative to the ASCII-style encoding schema already introduced, we consider another, older encoding scheme of a somewhat more mathematical character. The reader will need to be familiar with this second scheme in order to follow certain equivalence proofs presented in Chapters 3 and 4. Otherwise, the reader should feel free to omit the remainder of this section. On the other hand, consideration of another alternative will enable us to bring home an important, general point regarding encoding schemes. Namely, what is truly essential, from both a theoretical and a practical point of view, is that such a scheme be *effective* in the following sense:

(1) We possess an algorithm such that, given arbitrary Turing machine M, we can, in a finite number of steps, find some (not necessarily unique) natural number encoding M in accordance with the encoding scheme.

(2) We possess an algorithm such that, given arbitrary natural number n, we can, in a finite number of steps, determine whether n is the code of some Turing machine and, if so, which Turing machine is encoded by n.

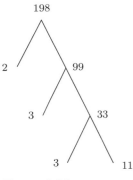

198

2   99

3   33

3   11

Figure 2.4.2

The ASCII-style encoding scheme considered above is effective in the sense of (1) and (2). Similarly, both (1) and (2) hold for the alternative scheme to be introduced next.

Preliminary to introducing our second encoding scheme, we review some ideas concerning prime numbers that go back to Euler. First of all, the reader will remember that every natural number n with $n \geq 2$ has a unique prime decomposition. Thus 18720 happens to equal $2^5 \cdot 3^2 \cdot 5^1 \cdot 13^1$. To take a second example, what is the prime decomposition of 198? Instinctively, the reader will begin by dividing by 2 as many times as possible, then by 3, and so on. The result of applying this simple algorithm is usually represented as a rooted binary tree whose root is labeled by 198 (see Figure 2.4.2). The prime decomposition of 198 can be read off the leaves of this tree from left to right. What is known as the Euclidean algorithm may be implemented in a Pascal-like pseudocode as follows:

```
Input: n
Output: The prime decomposition of n—that is, the prime factors of
        n including repetitions and in ascending order
Algorithm:
        begin
          dividend := n;
          divisor := 2;
          while dividend ≠ 1 do begin
              if dividend mod divisor = 0 then begin
                    print divisor;
                    dividend := dividend div divisor
              end
              else divisor := divisor + 1
          end
        end.
```

Prime numbers have proven to be highly useful in cryptography, as the reader is no doubt aware, and we shall use them as the basis for our second encoding scheme. In honor of logician Kurt Gödel (1903–1978), who used this particular encoding scheme to great effect in a rather different context, we shall refer to our new codes for Turing machines as *gödel numbers*.

Again, we begin by remarking that, in each of (2.4.1) through (2.4.6) above, we have a string over alphabet

$$q \quad ' \quad s \quad \mathbf{L} \quad \mathbf{R} \quad , \quad ;$$

describing the machine M of Figure 2.4.1(b). Again, we associate the symbols of alphabet Ψ with natural numbers. This time we shall use the symbol codes given in Table 2.4.2.

Next, let us write $\ulcorner \urcorner$ for the function defined by

$$\ulcorner \urcorner : \Psi \rightarrow \{1, 2, 3, 4, 5, 6, 7\}$$

$\ulcorner \sigma \urcorner =$ the code of symbol σ as given in Table 2.4.2

Thus $\ulcorner , \urcorner = 1$, $\ulcorner q \urcorner = 2$, and so forth. (Function $\ulcorner \quad \urcorner$ is of course not to be confused with ceiling function $\lceil \quad \rceil$.)

The final step in obtaining an encoding of M involves using function $\ulcorner \quad \urcorner$ and the primes in ascending order. Namely, we shall encode string (2.4.1), say, as

Table 2.4.2 Symbol Codes for Members of Ψ.

Member of Ψ	Symbol Code	Member of Ψ	Symbol Code
,	1	L	5
q	2	;	6
s	3	'	7
R	4		

$$2^{\ulcorner q \urcorner} \cdot 3^{\ulcorner , \urcorner} \cdot 5^{\ulcorner s \urcorner} \cdot 7^{\ulcorner ' \urcorner} \cdot 11^{\ulcorner , \urcorner} \cdot 13^{\ulcorner s \urcorner} \cdot 17^{\ulcorner , \urcorner} \cdot 19^{\ulcorner q \urcorner} \cdot 23^{\ulcorner ' \urcorner} \cdot 29^{\ulcorner ; \urcorner} \cdot 31^{\ulcorner q \urcorner} \cdot 37^{\ulcorner ' \urcorner} \cdot 41^{\ulcorner , \urcorner} \cdot 43^{\ulcorner s \urcorner} \cdot 47^{\ulcorner , \urcorner} \cdot 53^{\ulcorner R \urcorner} \cdot$$
$$59^{\ulcorner , \urcorner} \cdot 61^{\ulcorner q \urcorner} \cdot 67^{\ulcorner ; \urcorner} \cdot 71^{\ulcorner q \urcorner} \cdot 73^{\ulcorner , \urcorner} \cdot 79^{\ulcorner s \urcorner} \cdot 83^{\ulcorner , \urcorner} \cdot 89^{\ulcorner s \urcorner} \cdot 97^{\ulcorner ' \urcorner} \cdot 101^{\ulcorner ' \urcorner} \cdot 103^{\ulcorner , \urcorner} \cdot 107^{\ulcorner q \urcorner} \cdot 109^{\ulcorner ' \urcorner} \cdot 113^{\ulcorner ' \urcorner}$$
$$= 2^2 \cdot 3^1 \cdot 5^3 \cdot 7^7 \cdot 11^1 \cdot 13^3 \cdot 17^1 \cdot 19^2 \cdot 23^7 \cdot 29^6 \cdot 31^2 \cdot 37^7 \cdot 41^1 \cdot 43^3 \cdot 47^1 \cdot 53^4 \cdot$$
$$59^1 \cdot 61^2 \cdot 67^6 \cdot 71^2 \cdot 73^1 \cdot 79^3 \cdot 83^1 \cdot 89^3 \cdot 97^7 \cdot 101^7 \cdot 103^1 \cdot 107^2 \cdot 109^7 \cdot 113^7$$

The reader will note the occurrence of the symbols of string (2.4.1) in the exponents here. We shall take $2^2 \cdot 3^1 \cdot 5^3 \cdot 7^7 \cdot 11^1 \cdot \ldots \cdot 107^2 \cdot 109^7 \cdot 113^7$ as M's gödel number—that is, as an encoding of machine M in accordance with the Euler–Gödel encoding scheme.

Of course, there is nothing privileged about string (2.4.1), as was noted earlier during our discussion of the ASCII-style encoding scheme. Namely, each of the strings (2.4.2) through (2.4.6) could be used to obtain a new, different gödel number for M. Again, our encodings are extremely large numbers. (Extending our software so as to enable computation of a Turing machine's gödel number is out of the question. But see Exercise 2.10.17.) But, happily, we shall not have to spend any time working with actual gödel numbers. Rather, their interest for us lies in their existence in principle and in the fact that, presented with any one of its several gödel numbers, one could in principle retrieve machine M from that number alone.

We shall refer to the scheme just described as the *Euler–Gödel scheme for encoding Turing machines.* We make several important remarks regarding the Euler–Gödel scheme—each one quite analogous to an earlier remark regarding the ASCII-style scheme.

- Turing machines do not have unique gödel numbers: in general, each Turing machine can be encoded in several ways in accordance with the Euler–Gödel scheme. Thus the machine M of Figure 2.4.1(b) has no fewer than six distinct gödel numbers.

- On the other hand, no natural number that is the gödel number of a Turing machine will be the gödel number of more than one Turing machine. Again, most natural numbers will not be the gödel number of even one Turing machine.

- Most important of all is the fact that, given a natural number, there is a simple algorithm for determining if it is the gödel number of a Turing machine and, if so, which Turing machine it is the gödel number of. In Example 2.4.2 below, we show how a natural number that *is* the gödel number of a Turing machine M may undergo decryption so as to yield M.

EXAMPLE 2.4.2 (Decoding Gödel Numbers) Consider the 12-digit number 577565488500. We wish to see whether this is the gödel number of a Turing machine and, if so, we wish to identify that machine.

B : R

q

Figure 2.4.3

We first use the Euclidean algorithm to determine the prime decomposition of 577565488500. We begin by dividing by 2.

$$577565488500 = 2 \cdot 188782755250$$

$$= 2^2 \cdot 144391372125$$

Further attempts to divide by 2 are unsuccessful. So we attempt to divide the second factor on the right by the next prime, which is 3.

$$577565488500 = 2^2 \cdot 3 \cdot 48130457375$$

But further attempts to divide by 3 are unsuccessful. Moving on to 5, we find that we can divide three times but no more.

$$577565488500 = 2^2 \cdot 3^1 \cdot 5^3 \cdot 38043659$$

Similarly, we can divide by 7 once, 11 four times, 13 once and 17 twice, yielding

$$577565488500 = 2^2 \cdot 3^1 \cdot 5^3 \cdot 7^1 \cdot 11^4 \cdot 13^1 \cdot 17^2$$

Now, having obtained our prime decomposition, we check the *exponents* against the symbol codes given in Table 2.4.2. Thus we have that $2 = \ulcorner q \urcorner$, that $1 = \ulcorner , \urcorner$, that $3 = \ulcorner s \urcorner = \ulcorner B \urcorner$, and so on. This gives string

$$q, B, R, q$$

which is a description of the simple machine of Figure 2.4.3.

As mentioned several times now, it is the possibility of effectively decoding ASCII codes or gödel numbers so as to retrieve the encoded machines that renders either scheme acceptable. If it seems to the reader that any encoding scheme whatever would enjoy this algorithmic, or effective, retrievability property, then consider a natural, but ultimately unacceptable, encoding scheme. This alternative scheme involves encoding a machine M by simply adding the symbol codes of the symbols in some string over Ψ that represents M. (We use Table 2.4.2 again.) Thus, the single-state, single-instruction machine shown in Figure 2.4.4 will correspond to the unit set of quadruples $\{\langle q, s', s'', q \rangle\}$. Its encoding under the new "addition" scheme will be

$$\ulcorner q \urcorner + \ulcorner , \urcorner + \ulcorner s \urcorner + \ulcorner \prime \urcorner + \ulcorner , \urcorner + \ulcorner s \urcorner + \ulcorner \prime \urcorner + \ulcorner \prime \urcorner + \ulcorner , \urcorner + \ulcorner q \urcorner$$

$$= 2 + 1 + 3 + 7 + 1 + 3 + 7 + 7 + 1 + 2$$

$$= 34$$

a : 1

q

Figure 2.4.4

To see why this is unsatisfactory, suppose that the reader were presented with number 34 and wished to retrieve the machine of which it is the code in accordance with the addition scheme. After messing around a little bit, the reader would no doubt figure out that it is the code of the simple machine presented in Figure 2.4.4. But is this the only machine whose code is 34 under the addition scheme? Clearly not, because it is also the code of the machine describable as $\{\langle q, 1, a, q \rangle\} = \{\langle q, s'', s', q \rangle\}$. In other words, according to our addition scheme, natural number 34 encodes two distinct Turing machines. Apparently, in our eagerness to supplant the ASCII-style scheme or the Euler–Gödel scheme with something simpler, we have sacrificed effective retrievability. This example should make clear why we are going to use these relatively complicated schemes. The uniqueness of its prime decomposition ensures that any natural number will be the encoding of at most one Turing machine in accordance with Euler–Gödel. We can express much the same thing by noting that the Euler–Gödel scheme corresponds to a mapping of Turing machines onto natural numbers that, although neither single-valued nor surjective, *is injective*.

In Example 2.4.2 we considered a Turing machine M whose tape alphabet Γ contained just the two symbols a and 1. In general, of course, the tape alphabet of Turing machines will contain additional symbols—for example, additional input symbols or markers such as $*$. Moreover, there is no upper bound on the number of such symbols that may be used by Turing machines. On the other hand, any *given* Turing machine will make use of only finitely many tape symbols. Since there are only countably many Turing machines, it follows that we can, without loss of generality, assume that the set of all tape symbols used by the collection of all Turing machines is a countable set given by

$$s, s', s'', s''', \ldots$$

say (see Exercises 2.4.8 and 0.11.1(a)). In other words, we might take s to be the blank, a to be s', 1 to be s'', and so on. Letting $\ulcorner s \urcorner = 3$, we can now use this, together with the fact that $\ulcorner ' \urcorner = 7$, to encode any occurrence of an auxiliary tape symbol from among $s, s', s'', s''', \ldots$.[7] The same holds true of machine states from among $q, q', q'', q''', \ldots$.[8] (This point applies equally to the ASCII-style encoding scheme that we introduced first.)

We make one final general remark regarding encoding schemes. It concerns the fact that, under either the ASCII-style scheme or the Euler–Gödel scheme, most natural numbers do not encode any Turing machine whatever. (This feature of encoding schemes is quite general.) On the other hand, later formulations of definitions and theorems can be rendered more perspicuous if absolutely every natural number is somehow the code of some Turing machine under whichever scheme is being used. Happily, we are able to arrange things so that this will be the case. Namely, suppose that

$$C_0, C_1, C_2, \ldots \tag{2.4.8}$$

is an enumeration, in ascending order, of just those natural numbers that happen to encode Turing machines according to the Euler–Gödel scheme, say. (Of course, $C_0 = 5,775,654,885,000$ is already large.) We next assign to each Turing machine M a new sort of gödel number. Namely, if Turing machine M is encoded by C_0, then the new gödel number of M will be 0. If Turing machine M is encoded by C_1, then the new gödel number of M will be 1. In other words, the new gödel number of

---

[7] Incidentally, the reader may wonder at our assignment of a "symbol" code to the blank. As noted several times now, the blank is not a symbol at all but, rather, the absence of symbol. Nonetheless, the misuse of language involved in talk of the blank's symbol code is highly convenient and, assuming the reader's understanding, we shall indulge in it again later.

[8] The point with respect to machine states is one of some subtlety—one that is not implicit already in our standard use of $q_0, q_1, \ldots$ to designate machine states. On the one hand, any given Turing machine is a finite-state machine, having states $q_0, q_1, \ldots, q_n$ for some fixed n. Nonetheless, if the class of all Turing machines had turned out to be uncountable, then the set of all states of all Turing machines would likewise be uncountable and, consequently, not enumerable as $q, q', q'', \ldots$.

any Turing machine M will be the position of its *old* gödel number in the enumeration at (2.4.8). We leave it to the reader to verify that this revision of the Euler–Gödel encoding scheme remains effective in the sense of (1) and (2) above. Moreover, since all of the foregoing remains true when (2.4.8) is taken to be an enumeration of ASCII codes, we have justified the following general

> **REMARK 2.4.1:** We may assume without loss of generality that every natural number is the encoding of some unique Turing machine in accordance with any effective encoding scheme.

In this section we have seen how Turing machines may be encoded as natural numbers in two distinct ways. Our stated motivation for doing this is our intention that Turing machines be capable of taking other Turing machines—albeit in encoded form—as input. The reader is no doubt wondering why one would be interested in doing such a thing in the first place. Why should it be desirable that one Turing machine operate on another in this sense? We will answer this question in the next section, where the important concept of *universal Turing machine* is introduced.

§2.5 Universal Turing Machines

All Turing machines considered so far have been machines in a peculiar sense: They run only under a single program or set of instructions. Change the program and you have changed the machine. This use of "machine" is at odds with current usage, of course, and no doubt reflects the fact that the beginnings of automata theory predate the advent of modern digital computers. The more usual sense in which computer scientists use the term "machine" allows that a machine (hardware) be capable of running under a variety of programs (software). To put this another way, the modern digital computer might be described as a *universal computing device* in the sense that, suitably programmed and ignoring resource limits, it is capable of computing any number-theoretic function that is, in principle, computable. The Turing machines that we have considered up to this point lack this property of universality, as noted above. Our interest now is in describing a notion of universality for Turing machines. This is Definition 2.8, which we formulate twice and which is due to Alan Turing himself. Our first formulation is rather rough and is intended merely to convey Turing's general idea that a *universal Turing machine* can be programmed so as to simulate the behavior of any Turing machine whatever.

> **DEFINITION 2.8 (preliminary version):** Turing machine M^* is *universal* if, for any Turing machine M with input alphabet Σ, when M^* is started scanning the leftmost *1* in an unbroken string of $n_0 + 1$ *1*s (where n_0 is the gödel number of machine M) followed by a single blank followed by word w over Σ, then M^* transforms w exactly as machine M would transform it.

In other words, if M^* starts reading $n_0 + 1$ *1*s followed by a blank followed by the word $w = abbaa$, where n_0 is the gödel number of a Turing machine that reverses its input, then M^* will itself turn *abbaa* into $w^R = aabba$. Intuitively, M^* will first decode n_0 in the manner of Example 2.4.2 so as to retrieve M. Afterward, M^* will simulate M on input word $w = aabba$ so as to obtain $w^R = abbaa$. Thus, M^* may be described as "running under program n_0" on input $w = aabba$ so as to produce output $w^R = abbaa$ (see Figure 2.5.1).

Since we view computation of a number-theoretic function as a paradigm instance of computation, it will be interesting to reformulate Definition 2.8 to reflect this orientation (see also Figure 2.5.2).

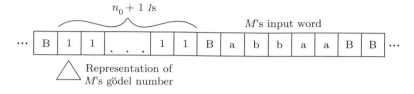

This is the starting configuration for universal Turing machine M^*. We suppose that n_0 is the encoding of a Turing machine M that reverses words over alphabet $\Sigma = \{a,b\}$.

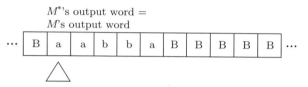

Figure 2.5.1

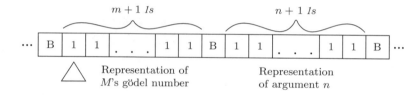

This is the starting configuration for universal Turing machine M^*. We suppose that m is the encoding of a Turing machine M that computes unary number-theoretic function f.

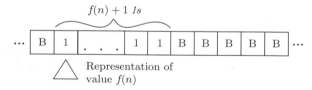

Final configuration for universal Turing machine M^*

Figure 2.5.2

DEFINITION 2.8 (reformulation): Turing machine M^* is *universal with respect to unary function computation* if, whenever M^* is started scanning the leftmost *1* of $m + 1$ *1*s followed by a blank, followed by an unbroken string of $n + 1$ *1*s on an otherwise blank tape, where m is the gödel number of a Turing machine M computing (partial) number-theoretic function f, then M^* halts scanning the leftmost *1* of an unbroken string of $f(n) + 1$ *1*s on an otherwise blank tape.[9]

---

[9] If $f(n)$ happens to be undefined, then, as usual, we do not particularly care what M^* does—just so long as it does not halt in a value-representing configuration (cf. Definitions 1.5 and 1.6).

Of course formulating a concept of universality for Turing machines is one thing. It is quite another thing to show that there actually are any such universal machines. Recognizing this, Turing in his original 1936 paper went on to prove that such machines do indeed exist.

THEOREM 2.6: There exists a universal Turing machine.

PROOF (sketch). We describe the construction of a Turing machine M^* that is universal with respect to unary function computation. Although the notion of a universal Turing machine as presented in Definition 2.8 is that of a single-tape machine, we shall find it easier to describe M^* as a multitape machine. By Theorem 2.4(c) essentially, there then exists a *single*-tape machine that is universal.

To begin, let us suppose that M^*'s input tape contains an unbroken string of $m + 1$ *1*s followed by an unbroken string of $n + 1$ *1*s. Also, we assume that the language of M^* is our Turing machine description alphabet Ψ—no doubt augmented by various symbols to be used as markers. We also assume that something like the chart of symbolic equivalences given as Table 2.5.1 has been "hardwired" into M^*.

M^*'s operation may now be sketched in terms of three macrosteps.

(1) M^* must first decode its first argument m, which is the gödel number of a machine that we may consider to be M^*'s current "program." This decoding will require displaying the exponents in the prime decomposition of m. As was shown in Example 2.3.2, integer division by 2 is easy using two tapes. Clearly, that algorithm can be generalized to larger divisors. M^* can thereby generate all the divisors in sequence up to m (or $m/2$ or $\sqrt{m}$). As each divisor k is generated, M^* divides m by k as many times as possible, recording on some worktape the number of successful divisions by k. This number will, of course, be the exponent of k in the prime decomposition of m. (In fact, any successful divisor will be prime.)

(2) Next, M^* converts these exponents into their symbolic equivalents in accordance with Table 2.5.1. For example, exponents 3 and 4 produce symbols *1* and R, respectively. In this manner, M^* comes to have a copy of its program on one or more of its worktapes. This program is in essence the state diagram of the unique single-tape machine M_m encoded by m.

(3) M^* copies the representation I^{n+1} of its second argument n onto some worktape$_i$. Afterward, M^*'s ith read/write head positions itself on the square containing the first of these $n + 1$ *1*s. M^* now checks its program to see whether there is an instruction of the form, "If in state q reading a *1*, then ...." (Recall that we are using $q, q', q'', \ldots$ to designate encoded machine states $q_0, q_1, q_2, \ldots$ so that symbol q by itself represents the start state of the encoded machine M_m.) If such an instruction exists, M^* executes that instruction on worktape$_i$, afterward continuing with its simulation of M_m's behavior for input I^{n+1} as dictated by its program, that is, by its stored copy of M_m's state diagram. (For this purpose, M^* will maintain a record of M_m's current state on one of its worktapes.) On the other hand, if there is no such instruction so that the simulation of M_m halts, then M^* checks to see whether its ith tape head has halted in a value-representing configuration—that is, reading the leftmost *1* of an unbroken string of *1*s on an otherwise blank tape. If this is the case, then M^* copies these *1*s from

Table 2.5.1 Symbol Codes for Members of Ψ.

Symbol	Code	Symbol	Code
,	1	*L*	5
q	2	'	6
1	3	;	7
R	4		

worktape$_i$ to its output tape and itself halts. Otherwise, M^* halts without writing anything to its output tape. As for how M^* can determine whether its ith tape head has halted in a value-representing configuration, the endmarker technique introduced previously in §2.2 will be useful. That is, M^* will introduce and then maintain tape symbols λ and ρ as left and right endmarkers, respectively, of M^*'s workspace on worktape$_i$. Q.E.D.

Of course, the concept of universality entails that a Turing machine that is truly universal with regard to function computation be able to compute an arbitrary k-ary Turing-computable function. With this in mind, we give the final, most general, formulation of Definition 2.8.

> **DEFINITION 2.8 (most general formulation):** Turing machine M^* is *universal with respect to function computation* if, whenever M^* is started scanning the leftmost *1* of $m + 1$ *1*s followed by a blank, followed by an unbroken string of $n_1 + 1$ *1*s, followed by a blank, followed by an unbroken string of $n_2 + 1$ *1*s, followed by a blank, . . . , followed by an unbroken string of $n_k + 1$ *1*s on an otherwise blank tape, where m is the gödel number of a Turing machine M that computes (partial) k-ary number-theoretic function f for some $k \geq 0$, then M^* halts scanning the leftmost *1* of an unbroken string of $f(n_1, n_2, \ldots, n_k) + 1$ *1*s on an otherwise blank tape.[10]

With appropriate changes to macrostep (3) only, our proof of Theorem 2.6 can be turned into the construction of a Turing machine that is universal with regard to k-ary function computation for arbitrary $k \geq 0$. Furthermore, given Paradigm Interreducibility, it is apparent that Turing machines universal with respect to language acceptance/recognition are also possible.

EXAMPLE 2.5.1 A three-tape universal Turing machine M_{Univ} has been included in the accompanying software. Open icon **Universal Turing Machine** and load any one of tapes `utm1.tm` through `utm3.tm` to observe M_{Univ}'s simulations of various single-tape function computers. The encoded descriptions of Turing machines used by M_{Univ} make use of a nonnumeric encoding scheme distinct from either the Euler–Gödel or the ASCII-style schemes of §2.4. For details regarding this and other aspects of M_{Univ}, see the documentation accompanying the example. (Select *Set Description* from within the Machine menu.)

Our progress to this point mirrors the history of computer design over the past 50 years in a very real sense. Initially, computers like the ENIAC (1943) were programmed by manually setting flip-flops and plugging wires into circuit boards, following pencil-and-paper instructions. Somewhat later, von Neumann realized that these instructions could themselves be stored in the manner of input data. The result was the EDVAC (1946), one of the world's first *stored-program computers*. (In addition, we mention Turing's own stored-program machine, the ACE, developed near London at about the same time.) The immediate practical benefit of the new technology lay in the rapidity with which new programs could now be loaded and executed, thereby replacing old programs. But the long-term advantage lay in the eventual appearance of general-purpose, executive programs known as *operating systems* that could accept

---

[10]See previous footnote.

other programs as input data in effect and see to it that such programs were executed. It is not hard to see that a universal Turing machine is the automata-theoretic analog of the modern operating system. (The analogy is perhaps clearest if one thinks of the situation whereby the user submits an object language program for execution, where this program in turn reads in data contained in a data file.[11]) This foreshadowing of later developments on Turing's part is all the more remarkable in that his 1936 paper appeared 10 years before the advent of the stored-program computer. The influence of Turing's paper upon von Neumann is beyond question.

There is yet another sense in which Turing's notion of universal Turing machine prefigured later developments in the history of computer science. Namely, the manner in which a universal Turing machine, given inputs m and n, simulates the operation of an arbitrary Turing machine M_m on input n, is suggestive of our notion of *hardware plasticity*, whereby one refers to the ability of one general-purpose machine architecture (hardware) to mimic other, diverse machine architectures by means of dedicated software.

§2.6 Nondeterministic Turing Machines

In defining complexity classes P and *LOGSPACE*, we mentioned in passing that the sorts of Turing machines that we have considered so far are all deterministic in some sense. Although this term was never explained, our use of it certainly would imply the existence of machines that are somehow nondeterministic. In this section we introduce nondeterministic Turing machines and begin to investigate their properties as language acceptors in particular. As it turns out, nondeterminism is an extremely important concept within the theory of computability. In general, the adjective "nondeterministic," applied to a computation, signifies the existence of alternative execution paths within that computation. We proceed immediately to an example.

EXAMPLE 2.6.1 Consider the transition diagram of Figure 2.6.1, which is intended as the representation of a single-tape Turing machine M in the role of language acceptor. The reader will notice immediately a striking difference between this diagram and all those presented previously. Namely, at state q_0,

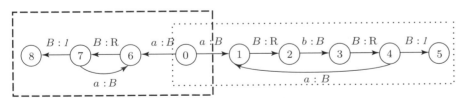

Figure 2.6.1   A Nondeterministic Turing Machine That Accepts Language $\{(ab)^n \mid n \geq 1\}$ $\cup \{a^n \mid n \geq 1\}$.

---

[11] The analogy is not perfect, however, since operating systems need not engage in anything like decoding of input as described in macrosteps (1) and (2) of the proof of Theorem 2.6. On the other hand, any object language file is the product of compilation, which is, after all, a sort of decoding process. Since that process is set in motion by the operating system as well, the universal Turing machine/operating system analogy appears to hold up rather well.

two distinct arcs are labeled by alphabet symbol *a*. In other words, there are two distinct instructions corresponding to the situation whereby *M* finds itself in state q_0 scanning symbol *a*. We shall think of *M* as having a choice as to which of the two instructions it executes when in state q_0 scanning an *a*. Such talk of choices introduces a certain nondeterminism, and, consequently, such a Turing machine is termed nondeterministic. All of the Turing machines that have been considered previously lack any such element of choice and hence are said to be deterministic.

The transition diagram of Figure 2.6.1 is divisible into two deterministic components, each of which has been enclosed in a box. The component on the right is recognizable as a deterministic Turing machine that accepts the language $L = \{(ab)^n | n \geq 1\}$. The component on the left is a deterministic Turing machine that accepts the language $L' = \{a^n | n \geq 1\}$. Our intention is that the nondeterministic machine of Figure 2.6.1, which combines these two deterministic machines, should accept the language $L \cup L'$ in the sense that for each word *w* in $L \cup L'$ there is *some* computation that produces an accepting *1*. For instance, if input word *w* is *ababab*, then *M* will accept *w* by first entering state q_1, passing from state q_1 to state q_4 three times, and then terminating in state q_5. On the other hand, if *w* is *aaa*, then acceptance will be the result of ultimately entering state q_8 by way of q_6.

Before continuing, we pause for a moment to clarify the sense in which we shall speak of nondeterministic machines having *choices*. For example, consider the case of a machine *M* that finds itself in state *q* scanning symbol *a* such that there are two instructions for just this situation—one a move-left and the other a move-right, say. In saying that *M* has a choice here, we mean only that there are two distinct ways in which *M*'s computation may be continued. We do not mean to suggest that *M* may "choose" to execute *neither* of the two instructions at state *q*. *M* has no such "choice." There are two ways to continue *M*'s computation from state *q*, and one of them must be chosen.

The notion of word acceptance implicit in Example 2.6.1 is presented as Definition 2.9 below. As in Definition 1.2, we must make a special case of input word ε.

DEFINITION 2.9: A *nondeterministic Turing machine M accepts nonempty word w* if and only if there exists some computation of *M* (i.e., some instruction sequence) such that *M* starts scanning the leftmost symbol of *w* on an otherwise blank tape and ultimately halts scanning a single *1* on an otherwise blank tape. *Nondeterministic Turing machine M accepts word* ε if and only if there exists some computation of *M* such that *M* starts scanning a blank on a completely blank tape and ultimately halts scanning a single *1* on an otherwise blank tape.

Our definition of word acceptance for nondeterministic Turing machines is in one sense not different from the one given earlier for deterministic machines: Word acceptance still means the existence of an accepting computation. On the other hand, the context of that accepting computation has changed to the extent that nondeterminism allows for the possibility of both accepting and nonaccepting computations for given input word *w*. For example, in the case of the machine of Figure 2.6.1 and input word *ababab*, one choice at state q_0 causes termination in state q_5—an accepting computation. At the same time, a different choice at state q_0 results in a nonaccepting computation terminating in state q_7. The important point here is that word *ababab* is accepted, in accordance with Definition 2.9, because of the existence of this first accepting computation—*despite the existence of the second, nonaccepting computation*. Contrast the case of input word *aba*, which is not accepted according to Definition 2.9 because there is *no* accepting computation whatever in this case: Whichever choice is made at q_0, no accepting *1* is produced.

The notion of language acceptance for nondeterministic Turing machines is precisely that given for deterministic machines.

DEFINITION 2.10: *Nondeterministic Turing machine M accepts language L if M* accepts all and only the words of *L*. Furthermore, we shall write *L(M)* for the language accepted by nondeterministic Turing machine *M*. So if Turing machine *M* accepts language *L*, then $L(M) = L$.

EXAMPLE 2.6.2 Open icon **Example 2.6.2** in order to observe the operation of a nondeterministic machine that accepts the language consisting of all and only words of the form a^{2n} or of the form a^{3n} with $n \geq 0$. Load tapes `8a.tt` and `9a.tt` in succession.

EXAMPLE 2.6.3 The nondeterministic machine *M* associated with icon **Example 2.6.3** accepts language $\{a^{n^2} | n \geq 0\}$. Try running it on stored tape `9a.tt`. Given input word *w*, machine *M* nondeterministically selects some natural number *m* that it then multiplies by itself, in effect, so as to obtain m^2. This quantity is next compared with *w* and, if the comparison is positive, an accepting *1* is written. If the comparison is negative, then *M* either halts without writing an accepting *1* or, in some cases, computes forever.

So far we have described the role of nondeterministic Turing machines as language acceptors without having given any formal definition of such machines. The needed mathematical definition requires only one change in the mathematical characterization of (deterministic) Turing machines given in Definition 1.1. This change concerns the nature of transition function δ_M. In Definition 1.1 we defined such a δ_M as a *function* from $Q \times (\Gamma \cup \{B\})$ to $(\Gamma \cup \{B\} \cup \{L, R\}) \times Q$:

> This is the set of possible actions.

$$\delta_M : Q \times (\Gamma \cup \{B\}) \to (\Gamma \cup \{B\} \cup \{L, R\}) \times Q$$

The difference now is that, in the case of a nondeterministic Turing machine *M* with choices, δ_M will be multivalued. For instance, where *M* is again the nondeterministic machine of Figure 2.6.1, we have both that $\delta_M(q_0, a) = (B, q_6)$ and $\delta_M(q_0, a) = (B, q_1)$. Since any function is, by definition, single-valued, it is evident that δ_M for nondeterministic *M* will not be a transition *function*. For this reason we shall speak of *transition mappings* in the case of nondeterministic Turing machines.

It is customary to arrange matters so that deterministic Turing machines are a special kind of nondeterministic Turing machine. One does this by (1) permitting—but not requiring—mappings of nondeterministic Turing machines to be multiple-valued and (2) defining deterministic Turing machines as those nondeterministic Turing machines whose transition mappings just happen to be single-valued.

REMARK 2.6.1: Any deterministic Turing machine qualifies as a nondeterministic Turing machine. In other words, determinism amounts to a special case of nondeterminism (see Figure 2.6.2).

Those nondeterministic machines that are not also deterministic will, on occasion, be termed *properly* nondeterministic. In most instances, we shall label a machine as nondeterministic just in case it is properly nondeterministic. Still, Remark 2.6.1 will come into play in a number of our proofs.

EXAMPLE 2.6.4 (Select-a-String) Without further comment we introduce a new type of example of a nondeterministic (multitape) Turing machine. Machines of this type, which are not language acceptors but, rather, nondeterministic implementations of the transduction paradigm of §1.1, will figure prominently in the discussions and proofs of Chapter 8. Consequently, it is quite essential that, early on, the reader gain a grasp of the way in which we shall talk about such machines later.

Try opening the icon **Select-a-String** within the Turing Machine folder and then, from the File menu, load tape `stringsq.tt` containing five nonempty strings over alphabet $\{a, b\}$ separated by single blanks. (The reader should feel free to add additional strings or to change those that appear on the stored tape. The strings must be separated by single blanks, however.) The two-tape Turing machine entitled Select-a-String may choose a single string from among those appearing on its input tape and then copy that string to its output tape. After

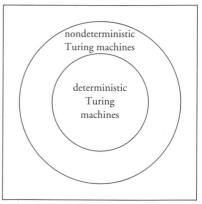

$U = \{M \mid M \text{ is an automaton}\}$

nondeterministic Turing machines

deterministic Turing machines

Figure 2.6.2

copying, both tape heads return to the far left and the machine halts in state q_7. We note that Select-a-String may also choose to copy no string whatever, in which case it halts in state q_0 with input tape read head at the far right.

The reader is encouraged to spend some time with Select-a-String so as to gain an understanding of just what is meant by saying that it nondeterministically selects or chooses one string from the input tape for copying to the output tape. In running Select-a-String, the user must make a sequence of choices at state q_0. In each case, one must decide whether the currently scanned string is to be copied, which means entering state q_1, or merely passed over from left to right, which means entering state q_8. Note that the user is free to choose any one of the strings appearing on the input tape—or to choose none of them. The same thing is true of machine Select-a-String in the sense that, for any given string w occurring on the input tape initially, there is a computation of Select-a-String that involves copying w to the output tape before returning to the left. And this is all that we shall mean in the future when we say that some Turing machine nondeterministically selects a string and copies it.

Finally, note that, as is often the case, the nondeterminism of machine Select-a-String is highly localized. Namely, there is a choice to be made at state q_0—*but nowhere else*. In other words, Select-a-String, when in state q_0, chooses either to copy or to pass over the currently scanned string—call it w—on the input tape. But once having made that choice, its subsequent processing of w is completely deterministic, involving no further choices. Thus, passing over w means reading it from left to right and copying w means copying it, one symbol at a time, from left to right. It is not Select-a-String's option to copy from right to left, say. Similarly, after copying, the tape heads return to the far left—first the input-tape read head and then the output-tape write head. It is not Select-a-String's option to reverse the return order.

The role of nondeterminism relative to computability-in-principle, as opposed to feasible computability, is quite well understood. We turn to the former issue now. We shall demonstrate a certain equivalence result with respect to language acceptance. This result will probably be surprising: It might naturally have been supposed that there should exist some language L accepted by (properly) nondeterministic machines but accepted by no deterministic machine.[12] This turns out to not be the case, however, as the following

---

[12]The source of this supposition—this prejudice, one might say—seems to be extramathematical. In human affairs, having choices is generally felt to be a good thing; having and making choices is empowering, as one says. The various liberation movements— that of women, of ethnic and racial groups, and of gays and lesbians—all share this assumption: to have choices is to have power. But however true this may be in the realm of human affairs, it does not hold for computability-in-principle, as our theoretical

Theorem 2.7 shows. In other words, from the point of view of computability-in-principle, nondeterminism is not the powerful idea it might at first appear to be. Preliminary to presenting our proof of Theorem 2.7, we first seek to establish the truth of the following proposition.

REMARK 2.6.2: Suppose that M is a nondeterministic Turing machine accepting language $L = L(M)$. It is possible to effectively enumerate all possible finite instruction sequences of M for given input word w.

Any finite instruction sequence of M, relative to input word w, corresponds to some finite path starting at state node q_0 within M's state diagram. The length of the instruction sequence is then the length of the corresponding path within M's state diagram. For some machines and some input words, this enumeration will be infinite, of course, since some machines never halt for some inputs.

We illustrate Remark 2.6.2 using the nondeterministic Turing machine $M = \langle Q, \Sigma, \Gamma, q_0, \delta \rangle$ of Figure 2.6.1. Suppose that M is started scanning input word $w = ab$ on an otherwise blank tape. We assume the following ordering of tape actions $\Gamma \cup \{B\} \cup \{L, R\}$:

$$a < b < 1 < B < L < R \tag{2.6.1}$$

as well as the most natural ordering of state set Q:

$$q_0 < q_1 < \cdots < q_7 < q_8 \tag{2.6.2}$$

Our enumeration of all finite instruction sequences of M for input word ab will consist of a list of all instruction sequences of length 1, ordered lexicographically, and then all computations of length 2, ordered lexicographically, and so on. (We have no interest in the instruction sequence of length 0.) We use square brackets to enclose instruction sequences, separating instructions themselves by commas. Thus, we first list both instruction sequences of length 1, relative to input word ab, in lexicographic order in accordance with (2.6.1) and (2.6.2):

$$[\langle q_0, a, B, q_1 \rangle]$$
$$[\langle q_0, a, B, q_6 \rangle]$$

Next, we have two sequences of length 2:

$$[\langle q_0, a, B, q_1 \rangle, \langle q_1, B, R, q_2 \rangle]$$
$$[\langle q_0, a, B, q_6 \rangle, \langle q_6, B, R, q_7 \rangle]$$

The reader should verify that the second sequence of length 2 shown above cannot be extended. (Recall that input word ab is being assumed.) Consequently, there is but one sequence of length 3, one of length 4, and one of length 5:

---

results will show. On the other hand, the analogy may have a certain aptness with regard to feasible computability. But that is another (long) story, which we postpone until Chapter 8.

$$[\langle q_0, a, B, q_1 \rangle, \langle q_1, B, R, q_2 \rangle, \langle q_2, b, B, q_3 \rangle]$$

$$[\langle q_0, a, B, q_1, q_1 \rangle, \langle q_1, B, R, q_2 \rangle, \langle q_2, b, B, q_3 \rangle, \langle q_3, B, R, q_4 \rangle]$$

$$[\langle q_0, a, B, q_1 \rangle, \langle q_1, B, R, q_2 \rangle, \langle q_2, b, B, q_3 \rangle, \langle q_3, B, R, q_4 \rangle, \langle q_4, B, 1, q_5 \rangle]$$

Note that both of the terminating computations of nondeterministic Turing machine M for input ab appear on this list—one nonaccepting of length 2 and one accepting of length 5. (Which ones are they above?) Obviously, sequences of length $n + 1$ are the result of extending the collection of sequences of length n in all possible ways. In the case of the nondeterministic machine of Figure 2.6.1, the enumeration of finite instruction sequences is itself finite and even rather short. However, in general, for some machines M and some input words w, such an enumeration could be infinite since, as noted earlier, M may never terminate for input w.

In the proof of Theorem 2.7, we shall ask the reader to imagine a deterministic Turing machine capable of enumerating all finite instruction sequences of a given nondeterministic M relative to some given input word w.

THEOREM 2.7: For any language L over alphabet Σ, there exists some nondeterministic Turing machine M_{nd} that accepts L if and only if there exists some deterministic Turing machine M_d that accepts L.

PROOF (sketch). The **reverse direction** here is trivial since, by Remark 2.6.1, deterministic machine M_d is nondeterministic as well. As for the **forward direction**, we shall assume the existence of nondeterministic M_{nd} accepting L and then sketch the behavior of deterministic M_d, based upon M_{nd}, that also accepts L. We shall describe M_d as a four-tape, off-line machine. Suppose M_d's input tape initially contains input word w over Σ. First, M_d copies w to worktape$_2$, say. On worktape$_1$, M_d will generate, one at a time and in lexicographic order, all finite instruction sequences of M_{nd} for input word w, simultaneously simulating each such sequence on worktape$_2$ (cf. Remark 2.6.2). Obviously, each such simulation comes to an end after a finite number of steps. At that point, if an accepting 1 has been written, then M_d itself writes an accepting 1 to its output tape. If not, input word w is recopied from input tape to worktape$_2$ and the next finite sequence is generated on worktape$_1$ and simulated on worktape$_2$. More concisely perhaps:

Step 1. Copy input word w from the input tape to worktape$_2$.
Step 2. Generate, on worktape$_1$, the next finite instruction sequence of M_{nd} relative to input word w, afterward simulating it on worktape$_2$.
Step 3. Determine whether an accepting 1 appeared on worktape$_2$. If so, then write a 1 to the output tape. Otherwise, proceed to Step 1.

If M_{nd} does not accept w, then, depending upon w, M_d may simply halt or it may continue forever generating instruction sequences on worktape$_1$ and simulating them on worktape$_2$. This is not a problem: All we care about is that, for such input w, no accepting 1 be written by M_d. On the other hand, if M_{nd} *does* accept w, then, by the definition of word acceptance, there must exist some computation $\mathcal{C}$ of M_{nd}, consisting of n steps, say, that results in an accepting 1. This means that, at some point during M_d's computation, an instruction sequence S corresponding to $\mathcal{C}$ will be generated and simulated. When the accepting 1 appears, M_d will itself write an accepting 1 and halt.

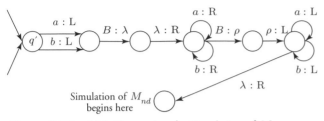

Figure 2.6.3 M_d's Preparation for Simulation of M_{nd}.

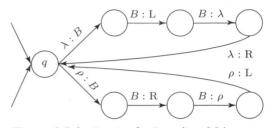

Figure 2.6.4   Routine for Extending M_d's Simulation of M_{nd}'s Workspace.

The astute reader may be wondering how M_d is going to recognize that its simulation of sequence S has resulted in the production of an accepting 1 on worktape$_2$. After all, an accepting 1 is a 1 such that (1) M_{nd} has in fact *halted* scanning that 1 and (2) no other symbol appears on worktape$_2$. As for (1), M_d must ascertain that at the end of S, machine M_{nd} finds itself in a state having no instruction for symbol 1, which is easy enough to do. As for (2), we shall assume the following endmarker technique, already familiar from the proof of Theorem 2.3. Namely, rather than merely copying input word w onto worktape$_2$, as described above, M_d will copy it and then add symbol λ immediately to its left and symbol ρ immediately to its right. This is easily accomplished by adding the routine of Figure 2.6.3 at an appropriate place in M_d's state diagram. (In Figure 2.6.3, which is essentially the same as Figure 2.2.3, we have assumed alphabet $\Sigma = \{a, b\}$ and that, upon entering state q', machine M_d is scanning the leftmost symbol of w on worktape$_2$. Also, for the sake of simplicity, we have shown only that part of each of M_d's four-part instructions that directs its behavior on worktape$_2$.) Endmarkers λ and ρ are maintained throughout M_d's simulation of S on worktape$_2$: Whenever M_{nd}'s simulated workspace on worktape$_2$ must be extended, then either λ is moved to the left or ρ is moved to the right. This can be accomplished effectively by adding something like the routine of Figure 2.6.4 to *every* state of M_d except those involved in introducing the endmarkers. (Again, we show only those parts of M_d's multipart instructions that concern worktape$_2$, so that Figure 2.6.4 is identical with Figure 2.2.4 seen earlier.) Consequently, endmarkers λ and ρ will indicate the extent of M_{nd}'s workspace at any point during its simulated computation. This, in turn, means that a 1 on worktape$_2$ can now be recognized as an accepting 1 by determining that no other symbol occurs between endmarkers λ and ρ on worktape$_2$.   Q.E.D.

A fuller discussion of nondeterminism must consider nondeterministic Turing machines as language recognizers and as computers of number-theoretic functions. We present—largely for the purposes of comparison—a formal definition of language recognition. (Note clause (v) in particular.)

DEFINITION 2.11: A *nondeterministic Turing machine M recognizes language L* over alphabet Σ provided that:

(i) For any nonempty word w over Σ with $w \in L$, there exists some accepting computation of M—that is, some instruction sequence such that M starts scanning the leftmost symbol of w on an otherwise blank tape and ultimately halts scanning a single 1 on an otherwise blank tape.

(ii) If $\varepsilon \in L$, there exists some accepting computation of M such that M starts scanning a blank on a completely blank tape and ultimately halts scanning a single 1 on an otherwise blank tape.

(iii) For any nonempty word w over Σ with $w \notin L$, there exists some rejecting computation of M—that is, some instruction sequence such that M starts scanning the leftmost symbol of w on an otherwise blank tape and ultimately halts scanning a single 0 on an otherwise blank tape.

(iv) If $\varepsilon \notin L$, there exists some rejecting computation of M such that M starts scanning a blank on a completely blank tape and ultimately halts scanning a single *0* on an otherwise blank tape.

(v) For no word w over Σ does there exist both an accepting and a rejecting computation on the part of M.

Given our earlier work, it is easily shown that any language recognized by a nondeterministic Turing machine is recognized by some deterministic machine as well (see Exercise 2.10.11(b)).

Nondeterministic Turing machines provide an important nondeterministic implementation of the function computation paradigm of §1.1. (Another such model is provided by so-called Post systems, which are introduced in §6.1.) In other words, we shall allow for the possibility that a Turing machine with choices computes a function. Just as in the case of language recognition, we must exercise a little care so as to avoid conflicts between alternative computations for one and the same input string. To get right to the point, suppose that unary number-theoretic function f is given, and consider the following hypothetical case. Suppose that M is a properly nondeterministic Turing machine that exhibits two different sorts of behavior for argument n_0:

- Started scanning the leftmost *1* in an unbroken string of *1*s representing argument n_0, machine M may make choices that cause it to halt scanning the leftmost *1* in a representation of value $f(n_0)$.

- Started scanning the leftmost *1* in an unbroken string of *1*s representing argument n_0, machine M may make *other* choices that cause it to halt scanning the leftmost *1* in a representation of some $m \neq f(n_0)$.

Even if M behaves well for all other arguments $n \neq n_0$, we obviously cannot count M as computing function f—at least if we wish to retain the principle that a given Turing machine computes a *unique* number-theoretic function.

The formal definition of function computation follows. For simplicity, our formulation concerns unary number-theoretic functions only. The generalization to k-ary f is straightforward.

> **DEFINITION 2.12:** Let f be a unary number-theoretic function and let M be a properly nondeterministic Turing machine. We shall say that M *computes* f if, for any n, we have that (i) there exists a computation of M such that M starts scanning the leftmost *1* in an unbroken sequence of $n + 1$ *1*s on an otherwise blank tape and halts scanning the leftmost *1* in an unbroken sequence of $f(n) + 1$ *1*s on an otherwise blank tape and (ii) there exists no computation of M such that M starts scanning the leftmost *1* in an unbroken sequence of $n + 1$ *1*s on an otherwise blank tape and halts scanning the leftmost *1* in an unbroken sequence of $m + 1$ *1*s on an otherwise blank tape for any $m \neq f(n)$.

We have been careful to avoid making Definition 2.12 unnecessarily restrictive. Namely, M will count as computing f provided that any computation of M for argument n leading to a value-representing configuration is such that the value represented by that configuration is none other than $f(n)$. We are thus allowing that some of M's computations for argument n never terminate; still others may terminate but not in value-representing configurations.

Given Theorem 2.7 and the phenomenon of Paradigm Interreducibility, the reader will have come to expect

---

> **THEOREM 2.8:** Let f be a number-theoretic function. Then f is computed by some nondeterministic Turing machine M_{nd} if and only if f is computed by some deterministic Turing machine M_d.

We leave its proof as an exercise for the reader since it is not very different than that of Theorem 2.7 above (see Exercise 2.6.5).

EXAMPLE 2.6.5 As an example of a nondeterministic machine computing a number-theoretic function, consider the machine M at icon **Example 2.6.5**. This machine computes the partial unary function $f(n)$ defined by

$$f(n) = \begin{cases} \sqrt[3]{n} & \text{if } n \text{ is a perfect cube} \\ \text{undefined} & \text{otherwise} \end{cases}$$

Given a representation of argument $n \geq 2$ on its tape, M nondeterministically selects some natural number m and then, quite deterministically, cubes m to obtain m^3. Afterward, M compares n with m^3. If identity holds, then M halts scanning the leftmost 1 in a representation of m itself. Otherwise, M halts in what is not a value-representing configuration. The reader should study this example in order to verify that this machine does compute $f(n)$ in the sense of Definition 2.12. Note the sense in which nondeterministic M, given argument n, may be said first to guess value $f(n) = \sqrt[3]{n}$ and then to confirm that guess by cubing it and comparing with n.

We leave it to the reader to devise examples of nondeterministic language recognizers. (Try Exercise 2.6.9.)

Resource Requirements of Nondeterministic Turing Machines (Advanced)

We shall be interested in analyzing the resource requirements—time and space—of nondeterministic Turing machines just as this was done for deterministic Turing machines. However, this requires some care. In order to see why, let us contrast the case of a nondeterministic language acceptor, say, with a deterministic language acceptor. We take the deterministic case first. Suppose that M is a deterministic machine accepting language L in accordance with Definition 1.3. Given input word w, the course of M's computation is completely determined, and the *cost* of that computation is, by an earlier assumption, the number of instructions executed—at least if M's computation for w terminates. The worst-case time analysis of M, as defined by $time_M(n)$, is then the maximum, taken over all input words of length n, of these computation costs.

The case of nondeterministic language acceptor M must be handled somewhat differently. After all, given input word w, there will in general be several distinct computation sequences on the part of M involving varying numbers of computation steps. Which of these numbers should be taken to represent the cost of M's computation for input word w? There are two cases to consider.

- In the case of an accepted word w, nondeterministic M will in general exhibit both accepting behavior (computation sequences leading up to the writing of an accepting 1) and nonaccepting behavior (basically, anything other than an accepting 1). In such a case, it seems reasonable to ignore the nonaccepting behavior. In other words, the cost of M's computation for input word w will be the minimum number of steps involved in any computation sequence leading to acceptance. (Nonaccepting computation sequences for w could conceivably fall below this minimum but, nonetheless, it seems reasonable not to count them.)

- The case of a nonaccepted word w is more straightforward. In this case, M exhibits nonaccepting behavior only, although, again, M may fail to accept in a variety of ways. So this time we can simply take the minimum number of steps, over all computation sequences, to be the cost of M's computation for input word w. (Practically speaking, it is frequently the case that M's behavior for nonaccepted input words may not need to be considered in providing a worst-case time analysis.)

In determining the cost of M's computation for input word w, we ignore computation sequences that fail to terminate, as usual. In consequence of this, we can see that the cost of M's computation for input word w will be undefined only if every computation sequence for w is nonterminating.

Assuming this notion of the cost of nondeterministic M's computation for input word w, we can now give a worst-case analysis of M's time requirements in the guise of number-theoretic function $time_M(n)$ defined essentially as in Definition 1.8.

DEFINITION 2.13: Let M be a nondeterministic, single-tape Turing machine and let n be an arbitrary natural number. Then unary number-theoretic function $time_M$ is defined by

$$time_M(n) =_{\text{def.}} \text{the maximum cost of } M\text{'s computation for any input}$$

$$\text{word } w \text{ with } |w| = n \text{ and such that } M \text{ has some computation}$$

$$\text{sequence for } w \text{ that does terminate}$$

We remark the "maxmin" character of $time_M(n)$: Since our notion of cost was defined as a certain minimum value, quantity $time_M(n)$ is being defined as the *max*imum of certain *min*imums.

We should also like to be able to provide worst-case space analyses of nondeterministic Turing machines. This means that we need some definition of function $space_M(n)$ for nondeterministic M. First, we define the *space consumption* of nondeterministic Turing machine M, relative to input word w, to be a certain minimum value. Again, there are two cases to consider.

- In the case of accepted word w, nondeterministic M will in general exhibit both accepting behavior and nonaccepting behavior. We ignore the nonaccepting behavior. In other words, the space consumption of M for input word w will be the minimum number of tape squares visited over the course of any computation sequence that results in acceptance.

- In the case of nonaccepted input word w, M exhibits nonaccepting behavior only, although, again, M may fail to accept in a variety of ways. We take the minimum number of squares visited, over all computation sequences, to be the space consumption of M's computation for input word w.

In determining the space consumption of M's computation for input word w, we ignore computation sequences that fail to terminate, as usual. In consequence of this, we can see that the space consumption of M's computation for input word w will be undefined only if every computation sequence for w is nonterminating.

In that space consumption is defined as a certain minimum, we see that Definition 2.14 exhibits the maxmin character already observed in Definition 2.13.

DEFINITION 2.14: Let M be a nondeterministic, single-tape Turing machine and let n be an arbitrary natural number. Then unary number-theoretic function $space_M$ is defined by

$$space_M(n) =_{\text{def.}} \text{the maximum space consumption of } M\text{'s computation for any input}$$

$$\text{word } w \text{ with } |w| = n \text{ and such that } M \text{ has some computation}$$

$$\text{sequence for } w \text{ that does terminate}$$

We recall from the preceding discussion that a given nondeterministic Turing machine M may accept a given word in a variety of ways. That is, there may be multiple accepting computations of word w on the part of M. Moreover, if at least one of these accepting computations involves $O(p(|w|))$ steps, for polynomial $p(n)$, then we say that M accepts w in time $O(p(|w|))$. (We are not saying anything new here but are, rather, merely reiterating our conception of time for nondeterministic machines.) This leads us to formulate an important definition.

DEFINITION 2.15: A language L is said to be *polynomial-time nondeterministically Turing-acceptable* if there exist both a nondeterministic Turing machine M and a polynomial $p(n)$ such that M accepts L and, for any $w \in L$, M accepts w in $O(p(|w|))$ steps.

Corresponding to Definition 1.11, we have the following definition of a new complexity class.

DEFINITION 2.16: We define NP to be the class of polynomial-time nondeterministically Turing-acceptable languages.

Questions naturally arise regarding the relation of complexity class P to the new complexity class NP.

(1) Suppose that language L is polynomial-time Turing-acceptable and hence in complexity class P. Does it follow that L is polynomial-time nondeterministically Turing-acceptable and hence in complexity class NP? The answer is yes. In other words, we have that P is a subset of NP. But seeing this does not require any argument really. Rather, it is an artifact of our conception of determinism as a special case of nondeterminism (cf. Remark 2.6.1).

(2) In Example 2.6.3, language $\{a^{n^2} | n \geq 0\}$ was shown in effect to be in NP (see Exercise 2.6.10(a)). Now it just happens that this language is in P as well (see Exercise 2.6.10(c)). Does this situation hold in general? In other words, if language L is accepted in polynomially bounded time by some nondeterministic Turing machine M_{nd}, does it invariably follow that L is accepted by some deterministic Turing machine M_d *in polynomially bounded time*? To ask the same question using different terminology, if language L is polynomial-time nondeterministically Turing-acceptable and hence in complexity class NP, does it follow that L is polynomial-time Turing-acceptable and hence in complexity class P? At present, no one knows the answer to these questions. For the moment, let us say only that there exists a large class of languages all of which are known to be in NP but none of which are known to be in P. In other words, although each language L in this class is accepted in polynomially bounded time by some nondeterministic machine, nonetheless, the only known *deterministic* machines accepting L compute in exponential time.

This may suggest that P is indeed a proper subset of NP. We will have much more to say about this in Chapter 8.

Obviously, every language in either P or NP is Turing-acceptable.

REMARK 2.6.3: We have $P \subseteq NP$. Also, every language in either P or NP is Turing-acceptable.

It is natural to ask whether there exist Turing-acceptable languages that are not in NP, say. These would be languages that, although Turing-acceptable, are accepted by no machines that compute in polynomial time.

- One can give an informal argument suggesting that there must be such languages. For example, the language $\{a^{2^n} | n \geq 0\}$ is accepted by a nondeterministic machine M that accepts input word w by guessing exponent n and then verifying that w is a^{2^n} by iterating, n times, multiplication by 2. Ultimately, a representation of 2^n will appear on some tape. Note, however, that such a string of $1s$ cannot be generated in polynomial time (cf. Exercise 0.5.10(c)).

- The foregoing argument proves nothing, of course, since nowhere has it been shown that there might not exist a more clever algorithm that does *not* involve producing unary 2^n. Hence, if one is to show that there exist Turing-acceptable languages not in NP, then a more rigorous argument is needed.

- To this end, let us assume an effective enumeration

$$L_0, L_1, L_2, \ldots \tag{2.6.3}$$

of the languages over $\Sigma = \{a, b\}$ that happen to be members of NP. (Imagine an ordering of all nondeterministic Turing machines with input alphabet Σ from which all those that do not compute in polynomially bounded time have been eliminated.) Similarly, assume an effective enumeration w_0, $w_1, w_2, \ldots$ of all words over Σ. Next, we define language L_{diag} by writing

$$w_n \in L_{diag} \Leftrightarrow w_n \notin L_n$$

Clearly, L_{diag} cannot be among the members of NP as listed at (2.7.3). (Why not?) Moreover, it is not hard to see that L_{diag} is, nonetheless, Turing-acceptable. We leave the details to the reader and proceed to formulate

---

REMARK 2.6.4: The class NP, and hence P, is a proper subset of the class of Turing-acceptable languages.

The time requirements of deterministic language acceptors are often seen to exceed those of their nondeterministic counterparts. For example, a deterministic machine that accepts language $\{a^{n^2} | n \geq 0\}$ might do so by enumerating the perfect squares $0, 1, 4, 9, \ldots, m^2, \ldots$ until the length of input word w has been attained or exceeded. The nondeterministic machine of Example 2.6.3, on the other hand, merely guesses m and then verifies that accepted word w has length m^2. Given Definitions 1.8 and 2.13 of $time_M(n)$ for deterministic and nondeterministic M, respectively, we see that the nondeterministic machine requires less time. Of course, one can conclude nothing regarding two entire complexity classes based only upon comparison of two representative machines. So our comparison is intended as no more than a suggestion: Nondeterminism appears to be more efficient than determinism. And as we shall see in Chapter 8, not much more can be said, at present, with any real certainty.

In one sense, the situation with respect to space is quite analogous: Deterministic machines seem to need more of it. But is this all that can be said this time? Or can we place some bound on the amount of additional space needed? It turns out that the answer to the latter question is yes. Our first important complexity-theoretic result will be presented as Theorem 2.9 below and is usually known as Savitch's Theorem. This proposition relates the space requirements of nondeterministic Turing machines to the space requirements of corresponding deterministic machines. Roughly, Theorem 2.9 will state that if a given language L is accepted by a nondeterministic machine in $f(n)$ space, for $f(n)$ sufficiently large, then some deterministic machine accepts L in $O([f(n)]^2)$ space. In brief, deterministic space is, worst-case, on the order of nondeterministic space squared. So, for example, if L is accepted by nondeterministic M_{nd} with $space_{M_{nd}}(n) = n^2$, say, then some deterministic M_d accepts L, where $space_{M_d}(n)$ is $O(n^4)$. Before we can state and prove Savitch's Theorem rigorously, we must introduce and motivate a certain technical notion that is not uninteresting in its own right.

The power of the Turing machine model of computation is reflected in its capacity for "self-conscious" activity. We have already seen an example of this in the way in which a Turing machine may use endmarkers λ and ρ to mark the boundaries of its own workspace. Later on, we shall make use of the fact that a Turing machine may be designed so as to count its own computation steps in a certain sense and then to enter a new computational phase if and when some limit, fixed in advance, has been exceeded (see Exercise 2.10.14). These are just two ways in which particular Turing machines may be self-conscious. What is needed for Savitch's Theorem is a type of self-consciousness resembling both these examples. Namely, we need Turing machines capable of (1) counting, in effect, how many tape squares have been visited so far in their own computations and (2) entering some new mode of operation when some fixed limit on the size of workspace has been reached. To this end, we introduce the notion of a *fully space-constructible (number-theoretic) function*.

DEFINITION 2.17: Let $f(n)$ be a total, unary number-theoretic function and let Σ be any nonempty alphabet. Then $f(n)$ is said to be *fully space-constructible* provided that there exists a deterministic multitape Turing machine M with input alphabet Σ such that, given arbitrary input word w over Σ with $|w| = n$, machine M visits exactly $f(n)$ tape squares on some one of its tapes over the course of its entire computation for w.

The concept of full space-constructibility is straightforward enough. (The reader is not expected to see in advance why we need it in the first place, however. So he or she should not be worrying about whether the machine M of Definition 2.17 is functioning as a language acceptor or as the computer of some number-theoretic function and so forth; in the end, given the way in which the notion of full space-constructibility will be used, it will make no difference which sort of machine M is.) In the meantime, we present

---

EXAMPLE 2.6.6 As an illustration of Definition 2.17, consider the deterministic, four-tape machine M associated with icon **Fully Space-Constructible** in the accompanying software. The input alphabet of M is $\{a,b\}$ so that, in general, there will be 2^n input words of length n. For any one of them, M manages to mark off exactly n^2 squares on its fourth tape. Run M on input *abab* or *aaab*, say, and observe that M visits exactly 16 squares on its fourth tape. The very existence of machine M establishes that function $f(n) = n^2$ is fully space-constructible, which is the whole point of this example.

In fact, every total, unary number-theoretic function $f(n)$ that is likely to occur to the reader turns out to be fully space-constructible (see Exercise 2.6.11). On the other hand, as the reader will have guessed, there do exist total, unary functions that are not fully space-constructible (see Exercise 2.6.12). We are now ready to state and prove

> **THEOREM 2.9 (Savitch's Theorem):** Suppose that language L is accepted by some nondeterministic, multitape, off-line Turing machine M_{nd} such that function $space_{M_{nd}}(n)$ is a fully space-constructible function and $space_{M_{nd}}(n) \geq \log_2 n$ for $n \geq 1$. Then there exists a deterministic, single-tape Turing machine M_d^1 that accepts L using $\mathrm{O}([space_{M_{nd}}(n)]^2)$ space.

PROOF To start, we make a number of remarks regarding nondeterministic, multitape, off-line M_{nd}. It is suggested that the reader merely accept these assertions regarding M_{nd} upon first reading and afterward return to verify them. We also make a number of simplifying assumptions (see Exercise 2.6.15 for the more general case).

(i) If M_{nd} accepts nonempty input word w with $|w| = n$, then it does so in $C^{Space_{M_{nd}}(n)}$ or fewer steps, where C is a constant determined by M_{nd}. (In particular, constant C will depend upon the number of M_{nd}'s states, the number of its tapes, and the size of its tape alphabet. For the details, we direct the reader's attention to the solution to Exercise 2.6.13, where our assumption that $space_{M_{nd}}(n) \geq \log_2 n$ comes into play.) In what follows, it will be convenient to assume that $C^{Space_{M_{nd}}(n)}$ is a power of 2—that is, 2^r for some fixed natural number r.

(ii) Recall that a machine configuration of M_{nd} consists of a complete description of M_{nd} at some point during its computation. This description will include the contents of M_{nd}'s several tapes and read/write head positions on those tapes, as well as M_{nd}'s current state. (Tape contents plus tape-head positions are what we are calling a tape(-set) configuration. So a machine configuration is a tape configuration together with information concerning M_{nd}'s state.) Any machine configuration of M_{nd} for input word w may be completely represented by a string of multitrack symbols over some alphabet Γ, as in the proof of Theorem 2.4. By Exercise 2.6.14, we may assume that any such string has length $space_{M_{nd}}(n) + 1$. (Again, this exercise makes use of our assumption that $space_{M_{nd}}(n) \geq \log_2 n$.)

(iii) Also, given two strings α_1 and α_2 over alphabet Γ purporting to describe machine configurations $conf_1$ and $conf_2$ of M_{nd}, it is easy to determine whether, in fact, M_{nd} can get from $conf_1$ to $conf_2$ in a single computation step, a situation that we shall denote by writing $\alpha_1 \xrightarrow{1} \alpha_2$. (Of course, we here assume access to some representation of M_{nd}'s state diagram.)

(iv) Putting (i) and (ii) together, one sees that M_{nd} accepts w just in case M_{nd} can get from initial machine configuration $conf_{init}$ to some accepting configuration $conf_{accept}$ in $C^{Space_{M_{nd}}(n)}$ or fewer steps, a situation that we represent by writing $Yields(conf_{init}, conf_{accept}, C^{Space_{M_{nd}}(n)})$. In general, there will be many possible accepting configurations since we do not care where on its output tape M_{nd} writes an accepting *1* nor how worktapes are ultimately configured. However, we shall ignore this complication and speak as if $conf_{accept}$ were unique (see Exercise 2.6.15).

We next proceed to describe a deterministic, multitape, off-line Turing machine M_d that accepts L in $\mathrm{O}([space_{M_{nd}}(n)]^2)$ space. The tape alphabet of M_d includes all symbols of alphabet Γ as in (ii). Given any two strings α_1 and α_2 over alphabet Γ purporting to describe machine configurations $conf_1$ and $conf_2$ of M_{nd}, machine M_d is capable of determining whether, in fact, M_{nd} can make the transition from $conf_1$ to $conf_2$ in a single computation step—that is, whether $\alpha_1 \xrightarrow{1} \alpha_2$ holds (see Exercise 2.6.16). Moreover, as we shall show, M_d can use this capacity in order to determine whether $Yields(conf_{init}, conf_{accept}, C^{Space_{M_{nd}}(n)})$ holds, where $conf_{init}$ is the initial machine configuration of M_{nd} corresponding to input word w and $conf_{accept}$ is the accepting configuration of M_{nd} for input word w. Note, once again, that in determining whether $Yields(conf_{init}, conf_{accept}, C^{Space_{M_{nd}}(n)})$ holds, M_d will be determining, in effect, whether M_{nd} accepts w. The reader is surely wondering how M_d will determine, using $\mathrm{O}([space_{M_{nd}}(n)]^2)$ space, whether $Yields(conf_{init}, conf_{accept}, C^{Space_{M_{nd}}(n)})$ is true. We explain this next.

Consider the following recursive routine for determining whether two strings α_1 and α_2 over alphabet Γ describing machine configurations $conf_1$ and $conf_2$ of M_{nd} are such that M_{nd} can get from $conf_1$ to $conf_2$ in k or fewer computation steps. (We assume that k is a power of 2.)

```
    subroutine Yields(α₁, α₂: machine_configuration_description_type;
                      k: natural_number): boolean;
        var α: machine_configuration_description_type;
(1)     begin
(2)         if α₁ = α₂ then return true
(3)         else if k = 1 and α₁ ──¹──→ α₂ then return true
(4)         else if k ≥ 2 then
(5)             for each α do /* very roughly, for each α over Γ with |α| = space_Mₙd(n) + 1 */
(6)                 if Yields(α₁, α, k/2) and Yields(α, α₂, k/2) then return true;
(7)         return false
(8)     end;
```

M_d implements the recursion at line (6) by reserving one worktape as a recursion stack to be used in a manner that will be familiar to most readers. Initially, M_d calls $Yields(conf_{init}, conf_{accept}, C^{Space_{M_{nd}}(n)})$ by pushing the three parameters here onto its stack. By (ii), the first two parameters may be assumed to have length $space_{M_{nd}}(n) + 1$. Moreover, since

$$\boxed{\text{By (i).}} \quad r = \log_2 2^r = \log_2 C^{Space_{M_{nd}}(n)} = space_{M_{nd}}(n) \cdot \log_2 C \qquad \boxed{\text{Factor } \log_2 C \text{ is a constant.}} \tag{2.6.4}$$

one can see that parameter 2^r may be represented in binary using $\mathrm{O}(space_{M_{nd}}(n))$ worktape squares on the stack worktape. Similarly, each pair of subsequent calls to $Yields$ at line (6) causes a fixed number of parameters, each representable by $\mathrm{O}(space_{M_{nd}}(n))$ symbols, to be pushed onto the stack worktape, that is, written to the right end of that worktape. In other words,

(v) Each pair of calls to $Yields$ involves writing $\mathrm{O}(space_{M_{nd}}(n))$ additional symbols to the stack worktape.

Moreover, since each successive pair of calls halves the third parameter, we can see that

(vi) The number of pairs of calls to *Yields* reflected on the stack at any given point will not exceed r itself and hence is $\mathrm{O}(space_{M_{nd}}(n))$ by (2.6.4) again.

From (v) and (vi) together, it follows that the number of symbols appearing on the stack worktape at any point during M_d's computation will be $\mathrm{O}([space_{M_{nd}}(n)]^2)$. Of course, there will be many strings to consider at line (5). But since $space_{M_{nd}}(n)$ is fully space-constructible by hypothesis, M_d can mark off precisely $space_{M_{nd}}(n)$ squares on one of its worktapes for the purpose of deterministically constructing, in sequence, M_{nd}'s various machine configurations.

   That M_d accepts language L follows from the fact that M_d will be designed so as to accept word w just in case $Yields(conf_{init}, conf_{accept}, 2^r)$ returns value true, where $conf_{init}$ is the machine configuration of M_{nd} corresponding to input word w and $conf_{accept}$ is the accepting configuration of M_{nd} for input word w. Moreover, since M_d may be designed so that all other worktapes will hold relatively little information, use of $\mathrm{O}([space_{M_{nd}}(n)]^2)$ squares on the stack worktape itself determines $space_{M_d}(n)$. Finally, by Corollary 2.2, some deterministic, single-tape machine M_d^1 likewise accepts L in $\mathrm{O}([space_{M_{nd}}(n)]^2)$ space.   Q.E.D.

We bring the reader's attention, once again, to the fact that Savitch's Theorem applies only when $space_{M_{nd}}(n) \geq \log_2 n$. Indeed, it is an open question whether $LOGSPACE = NLOGSPACE$, where the latter is the class of languages accepted in logarithmic space by some nondeterministic Turing machine. (That $LOGSPACE \subseteq NLOGSPACE$ is immediate from Remark 2.6.1, however.)
   As an immediate consequence of Savitch's Theorem and Remark 2.6.1, we have the following:

> **COROLLARY 2.3:** Language L is polynomial-space nondeterministically Turing-acceptable if and only if L is polynomial-space deterministically Turing-acceptable. More succinctly, $NPSPACE = PSPACE$.

(We assume the new terminology here to be transparent.)

§2.7 A Number-Theoretic Function That Is Not Turing-Computable

So far, we have presented one proposal for implementing the function computation paradigm of §1.1, namely, the mathematical notion of Turing-computable function, given in Definition 1.7. In later chapters we shall consider other, similar proposals—all of them intended to capture the most important features of the phenomenon that we call computation.
   Our interest in computability, as a property of number-theoretic functions, necessitates our being interested in the complementary notion of noncomputability or, as it is usually expressed, *uncomputability*. After all, if there exist well-defined number-theoretic functions that are uncomputable in an intuitive sense, we would be well-advised to learn which ones they are so as to avoid wasting time in attempts to compute them. We postpone any general discussion of uncomputability until Chapter 8. At this point we shall be content to raise—and answer—a question that is closely related to the general issue of uncomputability. Namely, we are already in a position now to ask whether there exist well-defined

number-theoretic functions—partial or total—that are *not Turing-computable*. Having raised the question, we go on to answer it in the affirmative. Specifically, we shall define a total number-theoretic function Θ that is Turing-computable only upon pain of contradiction. With this end in mind, we make the following remarks.

- For any $n \geq 0$, let $\mathcal{TM}_n$ be the class of all deterministic, single-tape, $(n + 1)$-state Turing machines with input alphabet $\varnothing$ and tape alphabet $\{1\}$. Of course, the requirement that M's input alphabet be empty entails that M start scanning a blank on a completely blank tape. We have rarely considered such machines up till now. However, the five machines of Exercise 1.2.1 and Figures 1.2.11(a)–(e) can be seen to be members of $\mathcal{TM}_4$, $\mathcal{TM}_6$, $\mathcal{TM}_2$, $\mathcal{TM}_1$, and $\mathcal{TM}_5$, respectively.

- Two Turing machines, which both have $n + 1$ states and which differ only with regard to the names chosen for those states, might as well be regarded as one and the same machine. For example, from a certain point of view, there is little to be gained by regarding the two machines of Figure 2.7.1 as genuinely distinct. We are not denying that these two machines differ as set-theoretic objects. Rather, we are suggesting that they might be identified from a certain point of view, given their structural similarity or *isomorphism*, as mathematicians are wont to describe it.

- Assuming such an identification, the reader should be able to see that, for any $n \geq 0$, the class $\mathcal{TM}_n$ has only finitely many members. After all, within any state diagram with $n + 1$ nodes there are only $2 \cdot 4 = 8$ possible arc labels and, from any given state, only $n + 1$ states to which such an arc may be directed.

- We are going to be interested in a certain sort of behavior on the part of Turing machines with input alphabet $\varnothing$ and tape alphabet $\{1\}$. Namely, we shall want to know what happens when such a Turing machine M is started scanning a square on a completely blank tape. From our present point of view, there is just one important question: If started scanning a square on a completely blank tape, does M halt and, if so, how many *1s* are on the tape when M halts? The machine of Figure 2.7.1 never halts, of course. On the other hand, the machine whose state diagram appears in Figure 2.7.2 will halt with exactly three *1s* on its tape.

- Next, we define a notion of *productivity* for Turing machines with input alphabet $\varnothing$ and tape alphabet $\{1\}$. Namely, if, started scanning a square on a completely blank tape, M halts, then the productivity of M will be the total number of *1s* on its tape at that point. (Note that we do not require that these be consecutive *1s*.) On the other hand, if M never halts, then it will be said to have productivity

Figure 2.7.1 We shall regard these two Turing machines as identical.

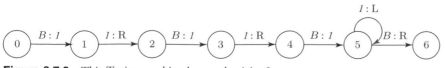

Figure 2.7.2 This Turing machine has productivity 3.

0—even if it manages to write some *1*s along the way. To take a couple of examples, the seven-state Turing machine of Figure 2.7.2 has productivity 3, while the two-state machine of Figure 2.7.1 has productivity 0. Note that the productivity of a Turing machine is a natural number.

- Armed with our notion of productivity for (a restricted class of) Turing machines, we go on to define a certain total number-theoretic function

$$\Theta(n) =_{\text{def.}} \text{ the maximum productivity of any member of } \mathcal{TM}_n$$

Function $\Theta(n)$ is clearly a unary number-theoretic function. That $\Theta(n)$ is a total function follows from the fact that $\mathcal{TM}_n$ may be regarded as a finite class of Turing machines. In other words, for any n, $\Theta(n)$ will simply be the largest member of a finite set of natural numbers, namely, the set of productivities of members of $\mathcal{TM}_n$. It is worth making a few additional remarks regarding function $\Theta(n)$.

- First of all, reflection on the Turing machine of Figure 2.7.3 should convince the reader that $\Theta(2) > 2$. Extrapolating, one sees that $\Theta(n) > n$ for all n. For arbitrary $n \geq 0$, we shall refer to the use of $n + 1$ states, each with a single self-loop, in order to generate $n + 1$ consecutive *1*s as *canonical generation* of those $n + 1$ *1*s.[13]

- Also, Θ is a monotone increasing function. Namely, if $n \leq m$, then $\Theta(n) \leq \Theta(m)$ (see Exercise 2.7.3).

We next show that function Θ is not Turing-computable. To this end, let f be an arbitrary unary, total, Turing-computable function—computed by single-tape machine M_f, say. It then follows that the unary function g defined by $g(n) =_{\text{def.}} f(2n)$ is Turing-computable as well. (To see this, let M^* be a three-tape machine that, given a representation of argument n on its input tape, produces a representation of $2n$ on worktape$_1$ and then simulates M_f on worktape$_1$. When M^*'s simulation of M_f halts, a representation of $f(n)$ will be found on worktape$_1$ and now need only be copied onto M^*'s output tape.) Let M_g be a single-tape machine computing g and suppose that M_g has $k + 1$ states, say. Now, for each $n \geq 0$, we let M_n be a single-tape machine that, when started scanning a square on a blank tape, generates, in the canonical manner, exactly $n + 1$ *1*s, positions its read/write head over the leftmost of these *1*s, and then behaves like M_g. One can see that M_n is a member of $\mathcal{TM}_{n+k+1}$ (see Figure 2.7.4.) Also, since M_g computes g, it halts scanning the leftmost of $g(n) + 1 = f(2n) + 1$ *1*s. It follows, by the definition of Θ, that $g(n) + 1 \leq \Theta(n + k + 1)$ so that $f(2n) = g(n) < \Theta(n + k + 1)$. But $k + 1 \leq n$ implies

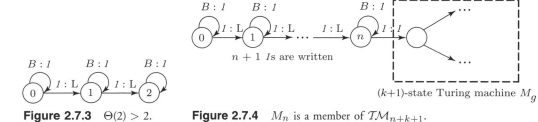

Figure 2.7.3 $\Theta(2) > 2$.   **Figure 2.7.4** M_n is a member of $\mathcal{TM}_{n+k+1}$.

---

[13]The reader will have noticed that in all other contexts, for the purpose of good machine design, we have avoided introducing self-loops that are never executed more than once.

$\Theta(n + k + 1) \leq \Theta(n + n) = \Theta(2n)$ by monotonicity. So for sufficiently large n, $f(2n) < \Theta(2n)$. But this is enough to see that Θ is distinct from f. Since f was an arbitrary Turing-computable function and since Θ has been shown to differ from f for sufficiently large arguments, we may take ourselves to have proved

---

THEOREM 2.10: There exists a unary, total number-theoretic function that is not Turing-computable.

The function Θ is commonly known as the Busy Beaver function. Its discovery was announced in [Rado 1962].

EXAMPLE 2.7.1 Open icon **Busy Beaver** in order to observe the operation of a six-state machine, discovered by Chris Nielsen, showing that $\Theta(5) \geq 21$.

Finally, Rado's Busy Beaver function affords us a welcomed opportunity to introduce an important clarification with respect to our use of the term *universal*. Namely, in §2.5 we saw how a universal Turing machine, interpreting part of its input as encoded instructions, can achieve a maximal functional plasticity. We are purposely varying our terminology here and avoiding talk of any *universal* functional plasticity. This is because all that can truly be said of a universal Turing machine is that it is capable of computing any function that happens to be Turing-computable in the sense of Definitions 1.5 and 1.6. It remains true that there are, indeed, infinitely many number-theoretic functions that cannot be computed by any Turing machine and therefore cannot be computed by a universal Turing machine, either—Busy Beaver being just one of them. To this degree, the term *universal Turing machine* is potentially misleading. It must not be interpreted to suggest an ability to compute arbitrary number-theoretic functions. Rather, properly construed, it implies only an ability to compute arbitrary *Turing-computable* functions.

§2.8 Turing Machines and Artificial Intelligence

Turing is sometimes credited as the founder of the research field known as artificial intelligence. This attribution is not the result of any particular work on Turing's part in the research areas that make up that field but has more to do with his early and passionate advocacy of machine intelligence as a sustainable goal for the scientific community. In this section we seek to relate the Turing machine model of computation to Turing's own criterion for machine intelligence. Before doing that, however, we must first describe that criterion. Obviously some explicit criterion for machine intelligence is needed, given that the English adjective "intelligent" has generally been applied, up to the present, only to human beings and other higher mammals. What will now count as intelligent behavior on the part of an artifact such as a digital computer? We shall consider several reform proposals—that is, proposals to the effect that, under certain circumstances to be specified, it would in the future be reasonable to attribute intelligence to machines despite our never having used the term "intelligent" in such a manner previously.

The Descartes Test

The first proposal for a criterion of machine intelligence was put forth by philosopher and polymath René Descartes (1596–1650), who suggested that machine intelligence would rest in a machine's ability to use language. Even this proposal appeared unattainable to Descartes, no doubt due to the limited capacities of seventeenth-century computing devices such as those designed by Descartes' contemporary Blaise Pascal (1623–1662).

> For we can certainly conceive of a machine so constructed that it utters words, and even utters words which correspond to bodily actions causing a change in its organs (e.g. if you touch it in one spot it asks what you want of it, if you touch it in another it cries out that you are hurting it, and so on). But it is inconceivable that such a machine should produce different arrangements of words so as to give an appropriately meaningful answer to whatever is said in its presence, as the dullest of men can do. (*Discourse on Method* (1637))[14]

It will be useful to consider Descartes' proposal, implicit in the quoted passage, as a starting point in our search for a useful characterization of the important concept of machine intelligence. If we can succeed in sharpening Descartes' ideas even somewhat, we might be able to gain some understanding of what machine intelligence would be.

First, what would count as successful use of language on the part of a machine? Obviously, something more than a mere ability to distinguish grammatical from ungrammatical input strings—what we have called *language recognition*—must be involved, although some such ability may well be a necessary condition for successful language use. Rather, use of language surely means use of language for the purposes of communication with other language users—something like an ability to converse in English with a human being. One might envision such an interaction proceeding as follows with a **H**uman **B**eing seated at a terminal keyboard, before a monitor screen, both of which are connected to a microcomputer. The user enters his or her own remarks and questions, which are echo printed on the screen. Those of the computer appear on the same screen followed by the **HB**> prompt.

HB>   Hello. How are you today?

MACHINE> Fine, thank you. How are you?

HB>   Good. I confess that my enjoyment of this unseasonably warm weather is not unmixed, however. With such warm temperatures coming already in February, what will the summer be like?

MACHINE> Intolerable no doubt. By the way, how did your calculus midterm go? I recall that you were worried about it . . . .

What types of knowledge must the machine possess in order to play its role in such a conversation? Obviously, it must be capable of natural language processing. That is, it must be capable of taking one English sentence as input, analyzing that sentence syntactically and semantically, and then generating some appropriate English sentence in response. Moreover, this capacity for natural language processing must go well beyond the pattern-matching techniques that characterized the early successes of natural-language-processing programs such as Weizenbaum's ELIZA (see Exercise 2.8.3). Rather, stored representations of the syntax and semantics of English must be involved. In addition, tremendous amounts of background information must be readily available to the machine. For example, the machine must know that February in northern, temperate climates is generally characterized by very cold temperatures, that summer temperatures are much higher, that human beings are physically uncomfortable once a certain

---

[14]See [Cottingham et al. 1988], p. 44.

temperature is exceeded, and so on. Such knowledge constitutes the assumed background information of any discussion of weather. Artificial intelligence researchers have developed a number of techniques for knowledge representation that would enable a machine to draw upon such knowledge. Unfortunately, to date, no knowledge representation scheme has proven adequate for the herculean task of storing such vast amounts of information in usable format. For our purposes, however, it is enough to note that such information, or "knowledge," is a necessary condition for full participation in conversation and hence for machine intelligence, according to the Descartes Test.

On the other hand, we should not require too much of the machine. In particular, truly universal knowledge is not necessary for attribution of intelligence. For example, we cannot require of a machine that it know that Millard Fillmore was the thirteenth president of the United States, that he was born in western New York State in 1800, that his sister was living in Toledo, and so on. After all, few human beings possess this knowledge, and we nonetheless want to count them as intelligent. Still, if informed that Millard Fillmore was the thirteenth president, we would expect that the machine be able to store this new information at least briefly. In other words, we should be disappointed if, upon "hearing" Fillmore mentioned a second time a few minutes later, the machine must once again ask for the identity of Fillmore. We might not want to count such a machine as intelligent. This suggests that low-level intellectual improvement (i.e., learning) is yet another necessary condition of successful language use.

The Turing Test

The so-called *Turing Test* was Alan Turing's own proposal for a criterion of machine intelligence. Although in his day—unlike our own—no candidate machines could even come close to satisfying the criterion that we are about to describe, Turing could, nonetheless, be more sanguine than Descartes about future prospects for such machines. This, as much as anything else, has ensured his place in the artificial intelligence pantheon. His own description of what we now call the Turing Test is found in a semipopular article entitled "Computing Machinery and Intelligence," which appeared in the philosophical journal *Mind* (see [Turing 1950]).

As described in his 1950 paper, the test situation is essentially as follows. To begin, there are three human participants—two men and one woman. They are engaged in playing what Turing calls the *Imitation Game*. One of the men is located in Room 1 and plays the role of *Interrogator*. The woman and the other man are together in Room 2. The man and woman in Room 2 can neither see nor hear the Interrogator in Room 1 (see Figure 2.8.1). Similarly, he can neither see nor hear them. All communication between the two rooms proceeds by way of networked microcomputers, one per room. The Interrogator knows that one of the participants in Room 2 is female and one is male. It is the Interrogator's goal to correctly identify the male in Room 2 based upon his responses to the Interrogator's questions.

The Interrogator proceeds by asking questions of the players in Room 2, directing some of his questions to "player X" and some questions to "player Y." Prior to beginning, the man and woman in Room 2 together decide that one of them will answer all and only those questions directed to X and that the other will answer all and only those questions directed to Y. They are required to abide by this decision throughout the game. The Interrogator does not know what decision they have made. It is his goal to determine whether the man is player X or player Y.

In playing the game, the man and woman in Room 2 have access to no reference works or databases of any sort. (Readers are likely to ask whether this requirement is truly essential, and the answer is no.) Their responses are based solely on their own knowledge. Similarly, the Interrogator has no access to such additional sources of information. After 15 minutes, say, based solely on communication over the network, the Interrogator must identify one of X and Y as the male and one as the female. Throughout the game, the woman in Room 2 will attempt to help the Interrogator to ultimately make the correct

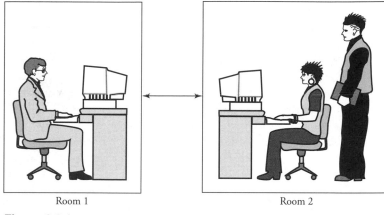

Room 1   Room 2

Figure 2.8.1

identifications. If she succeeds in this, then she and the Interrogator together win the game. So, if asked about her shoe size, it will probably be in her interest to respond truthfully, perhaps adding that, as a woman who happens to be rather short, she occasionally wears low heels so as to increase her stature in the office environment in which she works, although she finds high heels unthinkable. It is the goal of the man in Room 2 to confuse the Interrogator so as to cause him to make an incorrect identification at the end of play. Correspondingly, if asked about *his* shoe size, he will probably want to lie, responding as he thinks a woman would most likely respond. For example, he might report a shoe size of $7\frac{1}{2}$, adding that he greatly prefers one particular manufacturer/designer over all others.

The Interrogator may direct a question to player X, wait for a response, then direct the very same question to Y, wait for the response, and, finally, compare the two responses. As described by Turing, the male and female in Room 2 are aware of one another's answers to the Interrogator's questions. Given the nature and goal of the Imitation Game and assuming that each question is asked of both players, what sort of questions will the Interrogator want to ask? Well, the most interesting questions from his point of view will be those that force the male in Room 2 to inadvertently reveal that he is the male. For example, the Interrogator might ask X to name a single women's shoe manufacturer or designer. Suppose that X responds with the name of a shoe designer for women that the Interrogator recognizes. The Interrogator might next ask Y to name a women's shoe manufacturer other than the one just given by X. If Y is unable to come up with such, then this *might* suggest that Y is the male and that X is the female. Here we are assuming that the male and female in Room 2 are a *typical* contemporary male and female. If they are at least somewhat atypical, on the other hand, then the described response pattern is likely to mislead the Interrogator into making an incorrect identification.

We should imagine that the three participants play the Imitation Game 20 times in quick succession, each time recording who wins. If the three participants are of roughly equal intelligence and experience, we might expect that the Interrogator will usually end up merely guessing which of X and Y is the male and which is the female. This in turn suggests that at the end of the 20 games, the Interrogator–woman team will have won about half the games and the man in Room 2 will have won about half.

So far no computer has played any truly essential role in the proceedings. That comes next. For we now imagine that *another* 20 games are played with the same Interrogator and the same woman but with role of the man in Room 2 now played by the microcomputer that the man and woman were using. The woman and the computer agree upon who will be X and who will be Y. Now the Interrogator's goal is to correctly identify which of X and Y is the computer and which is the woman, and again the woman seeks to help the Interrogator. The computer, on the other hand, will attempt to trick the Interrogator into making a false identification. At the end of 20 games, perhaps the Interrogator–woman team will have won 12 games, say, and the computer eight games. Or perhaps both sides will have won 10 games apiece. In any case, the tallies for the two sets of 20 games are now compared. If the number of games won by the computer in the second series of games is at least as great as the number of games won by the male in the first series, then we pronounce the computer intelligent. Otherwise, the computer will be said to be unintelligent.

What sort of database will a machine require in order to play the Imitation Game well? Well, in addition to general knowledge about the real world and its own place in it, the computer will need to have a substantial knowledge of human affairs and human abilities (and their limits), as well as all aspects of human psychology. We can bring this point home by considering one way in which a poorly prepared machine is certain to reveal its identity and thereby lose the game. Imagine that the Interrogator asks each of the players to add 10 five-digit numbers. Any machine than responds in less than one second real time with the true sum will obviously reveal itself as the machine. A more clever machine will compute the sum—almost instantaneously, of course—but then wait several minutes, during which time it might complain vehemently to the Interrogator about having been required to do something so unpleasant as this. When it does finally respond, the machine might cleverly choose to return a sum that is off just slightly.

Our point here is that the computer's knowledge of human limitations will be as important as any truly computational skills in playing the Imitation Game well. This in itself should give rise to reservations regarding the Turing Test. After all, why should its knowledge of *human beings* be decisive in determining whether a machine deserves the label *intelligent*? If, in the twenty-first century, higher forms of life are discovered in distant galaxies, is their knowledge of Earth's inhabitants going to figure in our assessment of the intelligence of *those* creatures? And if not, then why should such knowledge be playing so large a role in our criterion of machine intelligence? Without dwelling further on this point, it is reasonable to question whether the Turing Test, as a criterion of machine intelligence, is not more than a little anthropocentric. Who, after all, would propose anything like the Turing Test as a criterion of extraterrestrial intelligence?

Behaviorism and the Turing Test

We digress momentarily in order to describe the *behaviorism* associated principally with philosopher W. V. O. Quine (born 1908) by way of psychologist B. F. Skinner (1904–1990). According to the psychological theory, the only possible objective criteria for the attribution of beliefs, intentions, emotions, and the like, to human subjects is the overt, public behavior of those subjects. In its philosophical manifestation, behaviorism becomes a theory concerning the meaning of belief attributions—statements to the effect that so-and-so believes such-and-such. So, for example, a sentence such as

$$\text{Jones believes that pitbulls are dangerous.} \tag{2.8.1}$$

has the following meaning: If Jones is in the presence of a pitbull, then (i) his blood pressure and heart rate tend to increase, (ii) there is increased sweat production on his part, and (iii) . . . . All manner of other physical changes to Jones' body are imaginable. The point is that all such changes are overt to the extent that they are measurable by appropriate clinical apparatus. A behaviorist has no interest in giving the meaning of (2.8.1) in terms of talk of Jones' mental life, as a traditional "mentalist" could be expected to do. This is because the behaviorist typically does not believe that human beings have anything that counts as a mental life. According to the behaviorist, minds and their contents—beliefs, intentions, hopes, and so on—are merely convenient fictions for describing human behavioral tendencies. For the behaviorist, talk of minds no more describes an aspect of reality than did talk of souls in an earlier era.

The point that we wish to make here is that Turing's criterion for machine intelligence—an ability to play the Imitation Game well—amounts to a *behaviorist criterion* in the sense that it refers to only the overt, public behavior of any candidate machine. Earlier, we saw that a universal Turing machine, interpreting part of its input as encoded instructions, achieves a maximal functional plasticity. The existence of such machines—recall Example 2.5.1—would probably have suggested to Turing the possibility of an artificial intelligence, whereby a machine becomes capable of the myriad, diverse functionings characteristic of human and nonhuman cognition. We can readily grant that any machine that passes the Turing Test successfully does *simulate* intelligent behavior. Turing's point—the one for which he is arguing in 1950—is that, solely by virtue of its *behavior*, such a machine *is* intelligent. Rejecting traditional mentalist criteria of intelligence, Turing is claiming that, by virtue of the machine's successful playing of the Imitation Game, we ought to count it as having beliefs and ideas in the same sense—whatever that is—in which human beings have beliefs and ideas. Similarly, appropriate responses in the case of the Millard Fillmore script mean, according to Turing, that we must count the machine as learning in the very same sense in which human beings learn. Again, this is because Turing assumes that the only possible objective criteria for attributing learning—either to human beings or to machines—concern their overt, public behavior. In both cases, this behavior is just observable output.

We are not claiming that a universal Turing machine could pass the Turing Test. We do claim, however, that the functional plasticity of such a universal Turing machine provides the prototype for any machine that *could* pass the test. Finally, we make a second, purely historical claim. Namely, it was the demonstrated existence of universal Turing machines in the sense of Definition 2.8 that motivated Turing's confident promotion of machine intelligence, thereby preparing the way for the emergence of a burgeoning research field in our own time.

Block's Critique of the Turing Test

We turn now to a recent, highly influential critique of Turing's criterion for machine intelligence. This critique is due to philosopher of mind Ned Block (see [Block 1990]). Block's starting point is the description of a hypothetical computer that, it is claimed, would play the Imitation Game well and hence would pass the Turing Test. We describe that machine now. We shall follow Block in describing a physical machine[15] but place greater emphasis on the program under which it runs. With appropriate changes, the program to be described could be simulated by something much like the software accompanying this text. (This fact provides the [tenuous] link between this section and the rest of this book.)

Block begins by making the following reasonable assumptions.

(1) There is an upper limit on the speed with which any human being can type. This applies in particular to persons engaged in playing Turing's Imitation Game.

(2) There are only finitely many characters—88, say—available on the microcomputer keyboard used to play the Imitation Game.

---

[15]The machine that we describe is different in many inessential ways from Block's own version. This difference is largely due to Block's having made different assumptions regarding Turing's Imitation Game.

From (1) and (2) together, it follows that:

(3) There is an upper bound N_0 on the total number of characters, including blanks and punctuation, that can occur in any Imitation Game conversation lasting precisely one hour, say, between human players. This, in turn, enables one to see that there can be no more than $88^{N_0} = \underbrace{88 \cdot 88 \cdot \cdots \cdot 88 \cdot 88}_{N_0 \text{ times}}$ distinct hour-long Imitation Game conversations. Taking into account the fact that conversations need not be of maximal length, we have

$$88^1 + 88^2 + 88^3 + \cdots + 88^{N_0 - 1} + 88^{N_0} \tag{2.8.2}$$

as an upper bound on the number of possible hour-long Imitation Game conversations between human players. And, though (2.8.2) is an extremely large number, it is unquestionably finite, so that

(4) The class of all hour-long Imitation Game conversations between human players is finite and hence enumerable as

$$C_0, C_1, C_2, \ldots, C_{N^*} \tag{2.8.3}$$

where N^* is the sum at (2.8.2).

Of course, many of the conversations in the list at (2.8.3) are nonsensical. For example, a "conversation" consisting only of numerals or punctuation would not be interpretable as a genuine conversation, given standard assumptions regarding meaningful English dialogue. Furthermore, most otherwise meaningful conversations will make no sense in the specialized context of the Imitation Game. For instance, assuming only the statements of the Interrogator ever take the form of a question, then all questions in a meaningful conversation will have to be preceded by directives such as "This one is for player X" or "I want to ask Y whether ...."

So imagine now that a computer program has been written that is capable of generating the conversations enumerated at (2.8.3) but with all the nonsense removed. Suppose, similarly, that the program also eliminates exchanges in which a machine player does an unsatisfactory job of concealing its identity according to some reasonable performance standard.[16] Of course, there will be many different ways of programming this pruning of the enumeration at (2.8.3)—many different standards of conversational meaningfulness. But let us simply assume, for the sake of argument, that some one way of doing it has been chosen so that the revised enumeration contains only conversations that everyone agrees to be meaningful in the context of the Imitation Game. (If our design team leaves in too many losing sequences at (2.8.3), then subsequent revisions can be assumed to eventually get them all out.) Further, let *Aunt Bubbles* be the "loquacious" program generating the revised enumeration of strictly meaningful conversations.

---

[16]As a trivial example, any conversation containing the string "I am a machine" can be eliminated. After all, it is in no player's interest to type in such a string. It would be pointless on the part of either the Interrogator or the woman. (Recall that her role is to help the Interrogator to make the proper identification and that the Interrogator knows this and trusts her never to lie.) Similarly, a successful machine can never respond with "I am a machine," since any reasonably intelligent Interrogator will realize that such a response could not come from his female collaborator and hence could issue only from a (stupid) machine. Many other examples of overly revealing responses needing elimination are less trivial but still interesting to ponder (see Exercise 2.8.4).

We next describe Block's hypothetical machine M that, he claims, plays the Imitation Game well and hence satisfies Turing's criterion for machine intelligence. We make the simplifying assumption that the Interrogator starts things off by typing in a first question Q addressed to player X and that M is answering all questions addressed to X. Confronted with question Q, machine M uses *Aunt Bubbles* to find the first conversation in the revised enumeration at (2.8.3) that just happens to begin with Q. Having found this conversation—suppose that it is C_i—machine M next responds with the sentence or two—let us speak of R—that follow question Q in conversation C_i. M then awaits the Interrogator's next question. Suppose the Interrogator now directs some question Q' to Y. In this case, M need not do anything except record Q' and the woman player's response R' to it. If the next question Q'' is again directed to X, then M will use Aunt Bubbles to find the first conversation C_j that starts with Q, followed by R, followed by Q', then R', and finally Q''. Whatever follows sequence Q, R, Q', R', Q'' in conversation C_j will be M's response to the Interrogator. We suppose that play continues in this manner for precisely one hour.

Block makes the following claim.

BLOCK'S CLAIM: The construction of M—in particular its use of Aunt Bubbles—makes it highly plausible that the Interrogator will ultimately be forced to merely guess the identity of the machine at the end of one hour. In other words, M will almost surely win the Imitation Game according to Block. By Turing's criterion, M is an intelligent machine.

Perhaps the reader is thinking that the execution time of Aunt Bubbles, under current assumptions and given the number of strings to be examined, will mean that such an M cannot be realized physically at present. After all, if Aunt Bubbles' search algorithm takes 60 minutes real time, so that the Interrogator spends the entire hour waiting for M's first response, then M will surely have revealed its machine nature. (Most likely, the Interrogator would not wait for a response that is so long in coming but, rather, would begin addressing questions to the woman player only. In any case, all would be lost from M's point of view.) But this objection is easily dealt with. After all, even if M cannot be realized now, it is certainly conceivable that M will be realizable at some point in the future. And this is all that Block needs to support the argument that we present next.

Block's argument takes the form of a critique of the Turing Test as a criterion for machine intelligence. Block does not deny that the described M plays the Imitation Game well and hence passes the Turing Test. However, he concludes from this not that M deserves to be considered intelligent. Rather, he takes M to show that Turing was just wrong to claim that playing the Imitation Game well is a sufficient condition for machine intelligence. After all, Block continues, M plays well despite being little more than a glorified search algorithm. In playing the Imitation Game, M uses none of the advanced AI techniques for knowledge representation, theorem proving, and so forth, that Turing would surely have expected on the part of any successful machine. As Block puts it, M "has the intelligence of a jukebox."

The reader may be thinking that Block's argument is quite decisive as a critique of the Turing Test. We point out, however, that Block is in a certain sense highly optimistic regarding future extensions of currently available search algorithms. Namely, he assumes without argument that it is at least conceivable that a future Aunt Bubbles program would achieve the performance times required for successful play of the Imitation Game by making access to memory using extensions of currently available techniques— exhaustive search, hash tables, 2–3 trees, and the like. But it just may be that no such program will ever be possible. It may turn out that the only way for Aunt Bubbles to achieve the required speed will be to make use of search techniques such as those that human brains apparently use—those involving something analogous to so-called associative content-addressable memory. And if this should turn out to be the case, then Block's jukebox comparison will surely be unfair.

§2.9 Turing Machines and Cognitive Science

Although cognition is popularly used as a synonym for thinking, we shall use the term in a less restricted sense to encompass everything that makes up the life of the mind: sensory perception, natural language processing, reasoning, judgment, memory, and so on. By cognitive science we mean the study of human cognition—including perception and all the rest. Roughly, the cognitive scientist seeks to discover the general principles according to which our mental lives unfold.

Modeling of natural phenomena is one of the most basic techniques of the natural sciences. One could reasonably assert that aggregate scientific knowledge is nothing but a collection of models of natural phenomena, where a typical model consists of a set of equations whose mathematical characteristics mirror those of the natural systems being modeled. Computation, as noted earlier, is one sort of human cognitive activity and, as such, is a naturally occurring phenomenon. Hence, cognitive scientists, who seek an understanding of the nature of human cognitive activity, seek plausible models of human computation just as they seek plausible models of human vision and human memory. Consequently, it is undeniable that the theory of computability can make a contribution to cognitive science. After all, it is within the theory of computability that models of computation such as the Turing machine model have been developed. Our first point, then, is that the theory of computability is of undisputed relevance to cognitive science.

One of the deep features of cognitive activity is its dependence upon knowledge or, more generally, belief. A natural approach to explaining this dependence upon belief is to assume that any system (e.g., mind/brain) engaged in cognition must incorporate certain internal structures that represent that belief—certain belief structures, if you will. Certainly the most well-understood way of doing that is to introduce symbolic representations—meaningful symbol strings essentially—and to manipulate them computationally. In this way, cognition is conceived as a sort of computation. The current tape contents of a Turing machine M—more generally, its overall machine configuration—is *representational* if, by virtue of some general representational scheme, it stands in for some other state of affairs, thereby enabling us to view M as behaving appropriately with regard to that state of affairs. For example, input string I^{n+1} occurring on M's tape *represents* argument n, and M's subsequent manipulation of that symbolic representation comprises its computation of the value function f, say, for argument n. The hypothesis under consideration amounts to supposing that mental contents are symbolic representations in just this sense and that cognition amounts to manipulation of them in accordance with certain syntactic rules analogous to the instruction set of M. According to this hypothesis, descriptions of cognitive activity must refer to entities that are symbolic in two senses. First, these entities are symbolic in the semantic sense that they refer to objects external to the mind—objects out in the world. Second, they are symbolic in the syntactic sense that cognitive processing is describable as formal manipulation of these entities in a manner familiar to computer scientists.

Our principal purpose in this section is to present a view according to which the theory of computability has a yet greater role to play within cognitive science. According to the view that we present next, the theory of computability serves as one of the cognitive scientist's two primary sources of explanatory models—the other source being psychology—and, consequently, is not merely relevant to cognitive science but central to it. The view we wish to expound is known by several names, but we shall refer to it as the *Computer Model of Mind*. Roughly, the Computer Model of Mind holds that cognition itself is nothing but computation. Of course, if this is true, it would have obvious implications for the status of the Turing machine model, say, within cognitive science: As a model of computation, the Turing machine would simultaneously be an analysis of cognition. To put matters most succinctly, if the Computer Model of Mind is true, then the theory of computability is not merely relevant to cognitive science as the mathematical study of one special sort of cognitive activity. Rather, the theory of computability becomes central to cognitive science in that one of its primary artifacts—the Turing machine model of computation and its variants—simultaneously provides the basis for a plausible model of cognition as a whole.

The Computer Model of Mind has been prominent within the philosophy of mind for nearly 50 years now. In one popular formulation, it starts from a certain conception of the computational activity of digital computers and goes on to claim that the cognitive activity of human minds/brains may be described in much the same terms. Hence human minds/brains are essentially computers, according to this view. As for digital computers, they are assumed to be, at bottom, symbol manipulators—a view that we earlier associated with our string classification paradigm (see §1.1). A program is then a sequence of rules that, when executed, causes a computer to manipulate structured data objects—arrays, strings, records—in accordance with precise syntactic rules reflecting the structure of the symbolic objects in question. For example, if A is a two-dimensional array of characters, then an assignment statement that makes access to elements of A must do so in accordance with the structure of A as in

$$ch := A[n, m]$$

say, but not either

$$ch := A[n] \quad \text{or} \quad ch := A[n, m, k]$$

To the extent that such instructions correspond to executable machine operations, they have semantic content (meaning) and hence are *representational*. In any case, according to the Computer Model of Mind, our minds/brains are not essentially different: Cognitive activity amounts to manipulation of structured representations in accordance with syntax rules reflecting the structure of those representations. According to the computational conception of cognition, our brains are intrinsically information processing systems. Moreover, on this view, the computational methods used by the brain to process information are not essentially different from those used by digital computers to process the same information.

We shall consider two different proposals regarding the bearing of Turing's work upon the Computer Model of Mind—one stronger, specific proposal and another weaker, more general proposal. To take the stronger, specific proposal first, recall that a universal Turing machine has the capability of interpreting a natural number as the encoding of a sequence of instructions that it then proceeds to execute. We mentioned earlier the analogy between universal Turing machines and modern operating systems. In the present context, this analogy suggests regarding a universal Turing machine as a model of the human mind in its entirety—encompassing all its activities. To make the suggestion plausible, we would need to say what in the human mind corresponds to the universal Turing machine's input—an issue that could presumably be handled by reference to sensory input. What makes this stronger modeling proposal questionable in the end is its high-focus bias. By this we mean the implication that, at any point in time, our mental lives are focused and goal-oriented in the manner in which the activity of a universal Turing machine is focused upon computation of a certain function or upon acceptance of a certain language, say. To the extent that our mental lives generally lack such goal-directedness and appear, instead, quite unfocused and chaotic, the stronger, specific proposal that the human mind is modeled by a universal

Turing machine is subject to question. It is one thing to propose that a DEC Alpha machine is modeled by a universal Turing machine. It is quite another to suggest that the human mind is so modeled.[17] In the latter case, it is the very richness of our mental lives—ranging from high-focus to low-focus activity—that renders the stronger, specific proposal implausible. (But see Exercise 2.9.1.)

It is obvious that human beings compute in the narrow sense: Surely, part of our mental life is taken up with arithmetic calculations, string matching, and other tasks whose computational nature is beyond doubt. The really controversial issue is whether the remainder of our mental lives amounts to computation. The safest approach is to agree that at least certain of our cognitive activities are individually modeled by Turing machines. Indeed, if some such computational model does not model cognition in the way the physicist's field equations model gravity, then it is unclear whether we could understand cognition in the traditional scientific sense at all.

This leads us to emphasize a more general, weaker proposal. Namely, our claim is now only that all aspects of human cognition—each individual type of genuine cognitive activity—can be modeled by a Turing machine operating on some symbolic representation(s) presented on its tape(s). This permits us to regard some of the random chaos that characterizes our mental lives as noncognitive noise or as health maintenance (dreaming) and hence in no need of modeling. This is the best approach on other grounds as well. After all, no one would claim that an equation *is* gravity. Rather, an equation models gravity in the way that a Turing machine may model some aspect of the mind. And just as natural science should not immediately aim for a model of all of reality, cognitive science should not attempt to model all of the mind. To reiterate, we shall not emphasize the specific, stronger proposal whereby the human mind is, in its essentials, modeled by a universal Turing machine. Rather, we concern ourselves with the weaker, general proposal according to which much of our cognitive functioning is modeled by Turing machines. The latter proposal is what we shall henceforth call the Computer Model of Mind.

The reader must resist any temptation to regard our weaker, general proposal as mere metaphor. We stress that in putting forth this weaker version of the Computer Model of Mind, we are presenting an empirical hypothesis that is either true or false. After all, the claim is not that the human mind is essentially a DEC Alpha machine, say. Surely the only way to understand *that* claim would be as metaphor since, as an empirical claim, it is plainly false: minds necessarily lack the physical components making up DEC Alpha machines. (For that matter, assuming that minds are distinct from brains, the former lack any physical components whatever.) We are claiming only that the human mind qua adder, say, is modeled by a Turing machine. But there is no need to regard this weaker claim as merely metaphorical. Again, we are making an empirical claim that is either true or false. And showing it to be false will involve demonstrating that a particular cognitive activity of the right sort is not modeled in a convincing manner by any Turing machine.

Finally, it is standard to distinguish between *competence models* of cognition and *performance models* of cognition. We are proposing the Turing machine as a competence model of cognition only. By this we mean to suggest that the class of Turing machines provides a formal analysis of the overall input/output relations of human computational/cognitive proficiency. Performance models of cognition, on the other hand, are the domain not of theoretical computer science but, rather, of psychology. There one attempts to account for the ways in which cognition is actually achieved. For instance, a performance model would concern itself with issues of cognitive efficiency, with comparisons of cognitive tasks with respect

---

[17]Strictly speaking, it is an Alpha machine running under some operating system or other that would be, in essence, a universal Turing machine. Similarly, a human mind running under the executive "program" known as the "self" would perhaps be, in essence, a universal Turing machine.

to difficulty, and with the question of how information is represented within minds/brains. We do not mean to suggest that the Turing machine model has anything to teach us regarding these aspects of cognition. To put matters more succinctly, the Turing machine model is one proposal regarding *what* cognitive "functions" can be computed by minds. It does not speak to the question of *how* those functions are computed.

§2.10 Regarding Theoretical Computer Science and Number-Theoretic Functions

In Chapter 1 we introduced the concept of a Turing machine, which we then characterized informally in terms of tapes, read/write heads, and state diagrams as well as formally in terms of transition functions δ_M. The "standard" Turing machine of Definition 1.1 is deterministic and involves a single tape, infinite in both directions; equivalently, δ_M is a single-valued, binary function taking state/symbol pairs (q, σ) as arguments. Furthermore, in §1.4 we described a sense in which such Turing machines either accept or recognize formal languages, thereby implementing the language recognition paradigm of §1.1. In §1.5 we described a sense in which such Turing machines compute number-theoretic functions, thereby implementing the function computation paradigm. In early sections of the present chapter, variations on the standard Turing machine were considered. Thus, there are Turing machines with one-way-infinite tape, multitape Turing machines, and nondeterministic Turing machines. For each of these variations, we introduced notions of language acceptance/recognition and function computation. Moreover, our several equivalence proofs demonstrated that, both as language acceptors and as function computers, the new sorts of Turing machines have the same power as does the standard, single-tape, deterministic machine. This is not to deny, however, that there are important differences in the resource requirements of the several varieties of Turing machines, as reflected in Corollary 2.1 and Theorem 2.9.

Specifically with regard to Turing machines in the role of language acceptor, we described an alternative notion of language acceptance by terminal state and showed that this new notion is equivalent to the original of Definition 1.3. Specifically with regard to Turing machines in the role of function computer, we can show that one can assume without loss of generality that a Turing machine that computes k-ary partial function f never halts for inputs $n_1, n_2, \ldots, n_k$ for which $f(n_1, n_2, \ldots, n_k)$ is undefined (see the solution to Exercise 2.10.8(b)). The real interest of these equivalence results, as well as those mentioned earlier, will become apparent only in later chapters where proofs will become easier by virtue of our being able to make a simplifying assumption justified by one or another of these equivalence results.

In Definition 1.7 we stipulated that a number-theoretic function f is Turing-computable provided that some Turing machine computes f in the sense of Definition 1.6. The reader may well be questioning our exclusive focus upon number-theoretic functions. Could Turing machines not compute functions from $\mathcal{Z}$ to $\mathcal{Z}$ or from $\mathcal{Q}$ to $\mathcal{Q}$? The answer to this question is a resounding yes. Although it is convenient to assume that function arguments and values are members of $\mathcal{N}$, there is, in fact, no great obstacle to our describing a sense in which integer-valued functions might be computed by Turing machines. We describe very briefly just one way in which this might be accomplished. First, integers can be modeled as pairs $\langle n, m \rangle$, where $n \in \{0, 1\}$ and $m \in \mathcal{N}$. For example, $+5$ becomes $\langle 0, 5 \rangle$ whereas -7 becomes $\langle 1, 7 \rangle$. Intuitively, any member of $\mathcal{Z}$ is modeled by a pair $\langle n, m \rangle$, where n gives its sign and m gives its magnitude. Following a convention well known to computer scientists, we are letting 0 and 1 represent positive and negative signs, respectively. Such a pair might be represented on a Turing machine tape as

$$I^{n+1} * I^{m+1}$$

where, once again, $n \in \{0, 1\}$ and $m \in \mathcal{N}$. Function computation would be precisely what it was before. A Turing machine M that computes the binary addition function

$$f: \mathcal{Z} \to \mathcal{Z}$$
$$f(n, m) = n + m$$

would behave as follows. Started scanning the leftmost I on a tape configured as

$$\dots BB1 * 11111B11 * 111BB\dots$$

$$\uparrow$$

and hence representing arguments $n = +4$ and $m = -2$, machine M computing f will halt scanning the leftmost I of

$$\dots BB1 * 111BB\dots$$

representing value $+2$. (Try Exercise 2.10.9.) This should be enough to convince the reader that a notion of Turing-computable integer-valued function is possible. Similarly, Turing machines can compute functions on the rational numbers, given that a rational number p/q for $p, q \in \mathcal{Z}$ with $q \neq 0$ can be modeled as the pair $\langle p, q \rangle$. (Try Exercise 2.10.10.)

So, given these additional possibilities, why have we restricted our attention to functions f with $f: \mathcal{N} \to \mathcal{N}$? The answer is simplicity. After all, consideration of functions from $\mathcal{Q}$ to $\mathcal{Q}$ would have complicated our description of algorithms considerably. Of course, complicating matters in this way could be justified if there were some significant gains at the theoretical level. However, the fact of the matter is that there would be no such gain. Since the reader who has read only Chapters 1 and 2 is most likely not in a good position to assess this last assertion, we will say a few words here to set the stage for what is to come in Chapters 3 through 7.

As reflected in its title, Part I of this text primarily concerns the modeling of an intuitive notion of computation. The first model considered is that of Turing-computable function as presented in Definition 1.1, where we have deliberately restricted our view to functions on the natural numbers. In later chapters we go on to consider other, alternative models of computation, in each case observing the same restriction to number-theoretic functions. Thus Chapter 3 introduces the so-called *partial recursive functions*; Chapter 4, the notion *Markov-computable function*; Chapter 5, the notion *register-machine computable function*; Chapter 6, the notion *Post-computable function*, and, finally, Chapter 7, the notion *vector-machine-computable function*. Moreover, at the theoretical level, it will turn out that these alternative notions or models are equivalent in a sense to be described later, and the fact that they are equivalent is without question the most important theoretical result of Part I. Now, as to the assertion at the end of the last paragraph, one can show that our decision to restrict attention to number-theoretic functions has absolutely no bearing on these equivalence results. In other words, the various models of computation would all still be equivalent to each other if we had instead opted for a discussion that considered functions from integers to integers or functions from rationals to rationals. This is what was meant by the assertion that there would be no theoretical advantage to considering a more inclusive class of functions: We would have ended up with the very same equivalence results but only after much added effort due to the complications inherent in dealing with the new sorts of functions. (For a notion of Turing-computable real-valued function, see [Minsky 1967].)

§2.11 Further Reading

Cognitive science and the philosophy of mind are broad disciplines that address many fundamental questions—such as the nature of consciousness—that we have not considered. Our interest in §2.8 and §2.9 was to relate these fields to the theory of computation. For a fuller perspective, see [Goldman 1993] and [Osherson et al. 1990].

The computational conception of cognition—that is, what we have called the Computer Model of Mind—represents a certain orthodoxy within current cognitive science. It receives its classic expression in Newell and Simon's *Physical Symbol System Hypothesis*: "A physical symbol system has the necessary and sufficient means for general intelligent action," where by *physical symbol system* they mean "a machine that produces through time an evolving collection of symbol structures." (See [Newell and Simon 1976].) Thus a Turing machine is the abstract model of such a physical symbol system, and any computer is a concrete realization of it. The alternative presentation of the computational conception of cognition found in [Haugeland 1985] is highly recommended. An influential critique of the computational conception is found in [Searle 1980].

EXERCISES FOR §2.1

2.1.1. Design a routine that fulfills the requirements of Step 5 in the proof of Theorem 2.1. Your routine should transform symbols U_B^1 and U_B^B into 1 and B, respectively, and do something appropriate with the other two-track symbols.

2.1.2. Design a Turing machine M with one-way-infinite tape that reverses any input word w over input alphabet $\Sigma = \{a, b\}$. When M halts, its read/write head should be scanning the tape square immediately to the right of left

endmarker λ, on which square should appear the leftmost symbol of w^R.

2.1.3. Formulate a definition of word acceptance for Turing machines with one-way-infinite tape analogous to Definition 1.2.

2.1.4. Justify the stated time and space analyses of the one-way-infinite machine M of Example 2.1.2. Namely, show that M computes in time $O(n^2)$ and space $O(n)$.

EXERCISES FOR §2.2

2.2.1. **(a)** Design a Turing machine that accepts by terminal state the language $\{a^n ba^m \mid n, m \geq 0, \}$.

(b) Apply the construction of the forward direction of Theorem 2.3 to the Turing machine of Figure 1.4.1(a) so as to obtain a Turing machine that accepts by terminal state the language $\{a^n ba^m \mid n, m \geq 0, \}$.

(c) Now compare the machines of (a) and (b). What conclusion can one draw here with respect to the construction of the proof? Does it ensure that the machine constructed is optimally designed?

(d) Apply the construction of the reverse direction of Theorem 2.3 to your solution to part (a) so as to obtain yet another

Turing machine that accepts by *1* the language $\{a^n ba^m | n, m \geq 0, \}$. Compare this with the machine of Figure 1.4.1(a). What conclusion can one draw here?

2.2.2. Our characterization of Turing machines with terminal state was very restrictive in two distinct ways. First, we assumed that any Turing machine has at most one terminal state as opposed to have several such states. Second, we assumed that a Turing machine with terminal state q_t has no instructions whatever for q_t. In fact, relaxing either or both of these restrictions has no important theoretical consequences. We take the second of the restrictions first.

(a) Show that we might have permitted instructions for terminal states, in which case acceptance by terminal state would mean actually halting in a terminal state as opposed to merely entering it. You are asked to show that any language that is accepted by some machine M with terminal state in the original sense is accepted by some machine M' with terminal state in this new, less restrictive sense, and conversely. (*Hint:* The forward direction here is trivial. As for the reverse direction, present a construction transforming a machine with instructions for its terminal state into an equivalent ma-

chine with a terminal state for which there are no instructions.)

(b) Show that we could have permitted a finite *set* of terminal states. Namely, you are asked to show that any language that is accepted by some machine M with exactly one terminal state is accepted by some machine M' with a set of terminal states, and vice versa. (*Hint:* The forward direction is again trivial. As for the reverse direction, present a construction that transforms a machine with two terminal states, say, into an equivalent machine with but a single terminal state.)

(c) Show that both requirements may be relaxed simultaneously without loss of generality. That is, you are asked to show that any language that is accepted by some machine M with exactly one terminal state, for which no instructions are permitted, is accepted by some machine M' with a set of terminal states for which instructions *are* permitted, and vice versa. (*Hint:* Combine the arguments of (a) and (b).)

2.2.3. ᵸᵂᵏ Show that language L is Turing-recognizable in the sense of Definition 1.4 if and only if there exists a Turing machine accepting L by terminal state that halts for every input word.

EXERCISES FOR §2.3

2.3.1. Using the accompanying software, design a three-tape Turing machine—an input tape, one worktape, and an output tape—that accepts the language $\{w \in \Sigma^* | w = w^R\}$ with $\Sigma = \{a, b\}$. Be sure to include a couple of sentences documenting what your machine does. Using big-O notation, give both a time and space analysis of your machine. (*Hint:* Consider starting with the machine of Example 2.3.4 (**Multitape Word Reversal**).)

2.3.2. ᵸᵂᵏ Design and test a multitape Turing machine that recognizes language $\{ww | w \in \Sigma^*\}$ with $\Sigma = \{a, b\}$.

2.3.3. We saw in the sketch of the proof of Theorem 2.4 that simulating a move right by M's

first tape head meant "adding 4," moving one square to the right, and then "subtracting 4." Assuming Table 2.3.1, similarly describe each of the tape head actions below.

(a) M's first tape head erasing a *1*
(b) M's second tape head erasing a *1*
(c) M's first tape head overwriting a blank by a *1*
(d) M's second tape head overwriting a blank by a *1*

2.3.4. (a) Let M be the single-tape Turing machine of Figure 2.3.2 computing function $f(n) = n \ div \ 2$. We wish to see that M computes $f(n)$ in $O(n^2)$ steps. Refer to Figure 2.3.2 in answering the questions below.

(i) How many steps must be executed before state q_2 is reached for the first time?

(ii) For given argument n, what is the maximum number of times that the cycle $q_2, q_3, \ldots, q_9, q_2$ will be traversed completely?

(iii) What is the maximum number of steps involved in completing one such cycle?

(iv) If n is even, how many steps remain after the last of these traversals of the cycle from state q_2 and back?

(v) If n is odd, how many steps remain after the last of these traversals of the cycle from state q_2 and back?

(vi) Putting your answers to (iv) and (v) together, what is the maximum number of steps generally after state q_2 is left for the last time?

(vii) Using your answers to (i), (ii), (iii), and (vi) above, give an expression for $time_M(n)$ that shows that $time_M(n)$ is $O(n^2)$.

(b) Now let M be the two-tape Turing machine of Figure 2.3.3 computing function $f(n) = n \; div \; 2$. We wish to see that M computes $f(n)$ in $O(n)$ steps. Refer to Figure 2.3.3 in answering the following questions.

(i) How many steps must be executed before state q_2 is reached for the first time?

(ii) For given argument n, what is the maximum number of times that the cycle q_2, q_3, q_4, q_2 will be traversed completely?

(iii) What is the maximum number of steps involved in completing one such cycle?

(iv) If n is even, how many steps remain after the last of these complete traversals of the cycle from state q_2 and back?

(v) If n is odd, how many steps remain after the last of these complete traversals of the cycle from state q_2 and back?

(vi) Putting your answers to (iv) and (v) together, what is the maximum num-

ber of steps generally after state q_2 is left for the last time?

(vii) Using your answers to (i), (ii), (iii), and (vi) above, give an expression for $time_M(n)$ that shows that M computes $f(n)$ in linear time.

2.3.5. The single-tape Turing machine of Example 1.3.1 accepts language $L = \{w \in \Sigma^* \mid n_a(w) = n_b(w)\}$, where $\Sigma = \{a, b\}$. Moreover, we saw in §1.7 that that machine computes in $O(n^2)$ time worst case, where n is the length of input word w. In Example 2.3.1 we presented a four-tape Turing machine M that accepts language L. Show that M accepts L in linear time worst case—that is, in $O(n)$ steps for $n = |w|$.

2.3.6. Use Theorem 2.4 to show that the class of Turing-acceptable languages is closed under intersection. In other words, show that if L_1 and L_2 are two Turing-acceptable languages over alphabet Σ, then so is $L_1 \cap L_2$. (*Hint:* Assume that single-tape Turing machines M_1 and M_2 accepting languages L_1 and L_2, respectively, are given. Describe a multitape machine M^* that simulates the behavior of M_1 on one worktape and afterward simulates the behavior of M_2 on another worktape.)

2.3.7. (a) Prove Corollary 2.1. (*Hint:* Review the proof of Theorem 2.4 (forward direction) and recall Exercise 1.7.3.)

(b) **hwk** Complexity class P was defined with respect to single-tape Turing machines only (cf. Definition 1.11). But suppose that language L is accepted in polynomially bounded time by some *multitape* Turing machine. Why are we nonetheless justified in concluding that L is in P?

2.3.8. (a) Design a multitape Turing machine M that implements the column-method algorithm for finding the binary equivalent of a given natural number input. For example, if given input 1^{13+1}, M would produce output *1101*, reflecting the fact that $13_{10} = 1101_2$. (See Exercise 1.1.2 for a description of the column method.)

(b) Give both a time and space analysis of M and compare these with the corresponding results for the machine of Example 2.3.5 (**LOGSPACE**).

2.3.9. Design a multitape Turing machine that implements the Euclidean algorithm for finding the greatest common divisor (GCD) of two natural numbers. For example, given input $1^{12+1}B1^{20+1}$, M would produce output 1^{4+1}, reflecting the fact that $gcd(12, 20) = 4$. (See Exercise 1.1.3 for a description of this algorithm.)

2.3.10. ^{hwk} Each of the languages below was earlier seen to be Turing-acceptable (see Exercise 1.4.5). You are now asked to show that each of these languages is a member of complexity class *LOGSPACE* by showing, for each language L, that there exists a multitape, off-line Turing machine that accepts L in $\mathrm{O}(\log_2 n)$ space. (*Hint*: The ideas embodied in Example 2.3.5 are primarily what is needed here as well.)

(a) $L = \{a^{n^2} | n \geq 0\}$
$= \{\varepsilon, a, aaaa, a^9, \dots\}$

(b) $L = \{a^{2^n} | n \geq 0\}$
$= \{a, aa, aaaa, a^8, \dots\}$

(c) $L = \{a^n | n \text{ prime}\}$
$= \{aa, aaa, a^5, a^7, \dots\}$

2.3.11. Each of the languages below was seen to be Turing-acceptable in Exercise 1.4.5. The single-tape Turing machines that you are likely to have designed would all have computed in linear space—that is, $\mathrm{O}(n)$ space—presumably. Now, however, we have introduced a more flexible notion of space—that for multitape, off-line Turing machines—such that some of the languages below will be accepted by machines computing in *less* than linear space. So which of the languages below are accepted by multitape, off-line machines requiring less than linear space (e.g., $\mathrm{O}(1)$ space or even $\mathrm{O}(0)$ space), and which are accepted only by machines yet requiring linear space? You should be able to answer this question, in the case of each language below, without designing any actual machine. Recall that the determining factor here will be just what intermediate data, if any, would have to be written to worktapes by a multitape, off-line machine

that accepts the language in question.

(a) $\{a^2 b^n | n \geq 2\}$
(b) $\{a^n b^m | n, m \geq 0\}$
(c) $\{a^2 b^n c^n | n \geq 0\}$
(d) $\{(ab)^n | n \geq 0\}$
(e) $\{a^{2n} | n \geq 0\}$
(f) $\{a^n b^m a^n | n, m \geq 0\}$

2.3.12. ^{hwk} Use the idea implemented in Example 2.3.5 (**LOGSPACE**) in order to design a three-tape, off-line Turing machine M that computes unary function $f(n) = \lceil \log_2 n \rceil$ using only logarithmic space. In other words, if started scanning the leftmost 1 in a representation of natural number 126 on its input tape, machine M will visit only seven squares or so on its worktape. (How many 1s will M write to its output tape in that case?)

2.3.13. Show that if language L is accepted by some multitape, off-line Turing machine in logarithmic space (i.e., in space $\mathrm{O}(\log_2 n)$), then L is accepted by some single-tape Turing machine in polynomial time—that is, in time $\mathrm{O}(n^k)$ for some constant k. In other words, you are being asked to show that $LOGSPACE \subseteq P$.

2.3.14. Show that if L is accepted by a $(k + 2)$-tape, off-line Turing machine M, then there exists a three-tape Turing machine M' accepting L that satisfies $space_{M'}(n) = space_M(n)$ for arbitrary $n \geq 0$.

2.3.15. ^{hwk} **(Call Me).** Design a two-tape Turing machine M that takes three arguments i, n, and m, where i is assumed to be either 0 or 1. If i is 0, then on its second tape M should compute $n + m$. If i is 1, then on its second tape M should compute $|n - m|$.

2.3.16. ^{hwk} Show that language $\{wcw^{\mathrm{R}} | w \in \Sigma^*\}$ with $\Sigma = \{a, b\}$ is in *LOGSPACE* by designing a multitape, off-line Turing machine that accepts it using only logarithmic space. (*Hint*: Your machine might use two worktapes to hold binary counters. It will need to determine whether the 101_2th symbol in the front half of the input word is identical with the 101_2th symbol in its back half.)

2.3.17 (a) Give a formal definition of *(deterministic) multitape Turing machine* analogous to that given for single-tape machines in Definition 1.1.

(b) Modify the definition at (a) so as to define *(deterministic) multitape, off-line Turing machine.* In other words, the modification will ensure that any input tape is read-only and that any output tape is write-only.

2.3.18. Suppose that language L is accepted by a multitape, off-line Turing machine M with input alphabet Σ. Show that we may assume without loss of generality that, for nonempty input word $w \in \Sigma^*$, any square on its input tape that is visited by machine M is either (1) a square that is occupied by a symbol of w itself or (2) one of the two blank squares to the immediate left and right, respectively, of

w. Furthermore, given input word ε, machine M may be assumed to visit but a single (blank) square on its input tape.

2.3.19. Suppose that M is a multitape machine that accepts language L in O(1) space. Show that there exists some Turing machine that accepts L in O(0) space—that is, an off-line Turing machine that consists of input and output tapes only.

2.3.20. Design a multitape Turing machine that, when started scanning the leftmost 1 in representation 1^{n+1} of natural number n, halts after producing on its output tape the first n rows of Pascal's triangle. You might use an extra blank to separate successive rows. Alternatively, feel free to introduce some special separation character.

EXERCISES FOR §2.4

2.4.1. Describe an algorithm that may be applied to any natural number n in order to determine whether n is the ASCII code of a Turing machine in accordance with Table 2.4.1 and, if so, what Turing machine is encoded by n.

2.4.2. ^{hwk} **hwk** Use Table 2.4.1 to find the ASCII code of the Turing machine whose state diagram appears in Figure 2.4.5. Assume that a is s'. (You may express your answer as a binary numeral.)

$a : \text{R}$

q

Figure 2.4.5

2.4.3. Give the prime decomposition of 906 by constructing a tree.

2.4.4. Suppose that the Euler–Gödel representation scheme is to be used to encode the message: **HELP!** Assuming the codes of Table 2.4.3, give the encoding of this string of length 5. (The answer may be given as a product of powers of primes.)

Table 2.4.3

Symbol	Symbol Code
A	1
B	2
C	3
D	4
E	5
...	...
H	8
...	...
L	12
...	...
P	15
...	...
Z	26
!	27

2.4.5. Assuming the Euler–Gödel encoding scheme and Table 2.4.3, what message is encoded by 5038848?

2.4.6. (a) Use the Euler–Gödel scheme and Table 2.4.2 to find an encoding of the Turing machine M whose transition function is defined as

$$\delta_M(q, B) = (1, q')$$
$$\delta_M(q', 1) = (\text{R}, q)$$

Of course, you may leave your answer as a product of powers of primes.

(b) Is your answer to (a) the only possible encoding of M that is in accordance with the Euler–Gödel scheme and Table 2.4.2? If not, what is another one?

2.4.7. [hwk] Natural number 1,312,648,837,500 is the encoding of a Turing machine in accordance with the Euler–Gödel scheme and Table 2.4.4. Use the algorithm of Example 2.4.2 to decrypt 1,312,648,837,500 so as to obtain the transition function δ_M of encoded machine M. Draw M's state diagram. Assume that B is s, that a is s', and so forth.

Table 2.4.4

Member of Ψ	Symbol Code
,	1
q	2
L	3
R	4
s	5
;	6
'	7

2.4.8. Justify our assertion that the class of all Turing machines is countable. (*Hint:* Consider again the enumeration at (2.4.8).)

EXERCISES FOR §2.5

2.5.1. Suppose that Turing machine M_1 computes the function $f(n) =_{\text{def.}} 2n + 7$ and has gödel number n_1. Suppose that Turing machine M_2 computes the function $f(n) =_{\text{def.}} n \, div \, 4$ and has gödel number n_2. Now suppose M^* is a universal Turing machine. Suppose further that M^* is a multitape machine so that it makes sense to speak of M^*'s input and output tapes.

(a) What will be the final contents of M^*'s output tape if M^*'s input tape initially contains $n_1 + 1$ *1*s followed by a single blank, followed by seven *1*s?

(b) What will be the final contents of M^*'s output tape if M^*'s input tape initially contains $n_2 + 1$ *1*s followed by a single blank, followed by seven *1*s?

2.5.2. [hwk] Formulate a notion of *universality with respect to language acceptance* on the part of Turing machines. Use Definition 2.8 as your guide.

EXERCISES FOR §2.6

2.6.1. [hwk] Design a Turing machine M that takes as input some representation of natural number n and nondeterministically transforms it into a representation of some multiple of n—that is, either 0 or n itself or $2n$ or $3n$, and so on. Describe the sense in which it can be said that M chooses some value m by which to multiply input n. (*Suggestion:* Implement your design using the accompanying software and use the Multiplication Machine of Example 1.5.5 as a submachine.)

2.6.2. Use the companion software to design a nondeterministic Turing machine that accepts language $\{ww|w \in \Sigma^*\}$ with $\Sigma = \{a, b\}$. (*Hint:* design a machine that nondeterministically selects a candidate midpoint within its input word and then proceeds to compare its

front half with its back half, one character at a time.)

2.6.3. [hwk] Characterize each of the following Turing machines as either deterministic or properly nondeterministic based upon its transition function. In the case of a properly nondeterministic machine M, say why it is nondeterministic with specific reference to transition function δ_M.

(a) $\delta_M(q_0, a) = (B, q_1)$
$\delta_M(q_0, a) = (R, q_1)$
$\delta_M(q_0, b) = (R, q_2)$
$\delta_M(q_0, B) = (L, q_0)$

(b) $\delta_M(q_0, a) = (B, q_1)$
$\delta_M(q_0, a) = (B, q_2)$
$\delta_M(q_0, b) = (R, q_3)$
$\delta_M(q_0, B) = (L, q_0)$

(c) $\delta_M(q_0, a) = (B, q_1)$
$\delta_M(q_0, a) = (b, q_2)$
$\delta_M(q_0, b) = (R, q_3)$
$\delta_M(q_0, B) = (L, q_0)$
(d) $\delta_M(q_0, a) = (B, q_0)$
$\delta_M(q_0, b) = (R, q_1)$
$\delta_M(q_0, B) = (L, q_2)$

2.6.4. Show that the class of Turing-acceptable languages is closed under union. That is, show that if L_1 and L_2 are two Turing-acceptable languages over alphabets Σ_1 and Σ_2, respectively, then language $L_1 \cup L_2$ is also Turing-acceptable. (*Hint:* Assume that deterministic Turing machines M_1 and M_2 accepting L_1 and L_2 are given. Consider Example 2.6.1 but be careful since, in general, nothing so simple as this will work. Namely, if the indegree of $q_0 \neq 0$, then merely identifying the initial state of M_1 and M_2 will not work. In general, you will need instructions of the form $\langle q_i, s; s, q_j \rangle$ for $s \in \Sigma_1 \cup \Sigma_2$.)

2.6.5. Prove Theorem 2.8.

2.6.6. Use the companion software to design a nondeterministic Turing machine that accepts language $\{a^n | n$ is composite, i.e., not prime$\}$. (*Hint:* Reconsider Example 2.6.3 and recall that n is composite provided that it is the product of two natural numbers m_1 and m_2 with $m_1, m_2 > 1$. Use the Multiplication Machine of Example 1.5.5 as a submachine.)

2.6.7. Use the companion software to design a nondeterministic Turing machine that accepts language $\{a^{2^n} | n \geq 0\}$.

2.6.8 [hwk] **(a)** What trivial change in Definition 1.1 yields a formal definition of *nondeterministic single-tape Turing machine*?
(b) What trivial change in the solution to Exercise 2.3.17(a) yields a formal definition of *nondeterministic multitape Turing machine*?
(c) What trivial change in the solution to Exercise 2.3.17(b) yields a formal definition of *nondeterministic multitape off-line Turing machine*?

2.6.9. Describe a nondeterministic Turing machine that recognizes language $\{a^n | n$ is composite$\}$.

(*Remark:* Your machine will behave nondeterministically only in the case of accepted input words—not in the case of rejected words.)

2.6.10 [hwk] **(a)** Provide a worst-case time analysis of the nondeterministic machine of Example 2.6.3 so as to show that language $\{a^{n^2} | n \geq 0\}$ is in *NP*.
(b) Does it follow from Theorem 2.7 that language $\{a^{n^2} | n \geq 0\}$ is in P as well? If not, why not?
(c) How can one see that language $\{a^{n^2} | n \geq 0\}$ is, in fact, in P?

2.6.11 **(a)** Show that function $f(n) = 2^n$ is fully space-constructible by describing a Turing machine.
(b) Show that function $f(n) = \lfloor \log_2 n \rfloor$ is fully space-constructible by describing a Turing machine. (*Hint:* Base your design on that of the machine of Example 2.3.5.)
(c) Show that if functions $f(n)$ and $g(n)$ are both fully space-constructible, then so is $h(n) =_{\text{def.}} f(n) + g(n)$.
(d) Show that if functions $f(n)$ and $g(n)$ are both fully space-constructible, then so is $h(n) =_{\text{def.}} f(n) \cdot g(n)$.
(e) Show that if functions $f(n)$ and $g(n)$ are both fully space-constructible, then so is $h(n) =_{\text{def.}} f(n)^{g(n)}$.
(f) Show that if function $f(n)$ is fully space-constructible, then so is $g(n) =_{\text{def.}} 2^{f(n)}$.

2.6.12. We saw in §2.4 that single-tape Turing machines may be associated with gödel numbers by way of the Euler–Gödel encoding scheme. It is easy to see that the same holds true of multitape, off-line machines. Essentially by Remark 2.4.1, we may assume without loss of generality that every natural number is the gödel number of some deterministic, $(k + 2)$-tape, off-line Turing machine with input alphabet $\{1\}$, where $k \geq 1$ is fixed. Let us write M_n for the deterministic, $(k + 2)$-tape, off-line Turing machine with gödel number n. Of course, machine M_n may or may not halt when started scanning the representation of its own gödel number. Moreover, since I^n is the only input string of length n, we have that $space_{M_n}(n)$ is defined if and only if M_n halts for input 1^n. We next define unary number-theoretic function f_d as

$$f_d(n) = \begin{cases} space_{M_n}(n) + 1 & \text{if } M_n \text{ halts when started scanning the leftmost } 1 \text{ in an unbroken string of } n \text{ } 1s \text{ on an (otherwise blank) input tape} \\ 5 & \text{otherwise} \end{cases}$$

Show that function f_d is total but not fully space-constructible.

2.6.13. Justify assertion (i) at the beginning of the proof of Theorem 2.9. That is, show that if nondeterministic, multitape, off-line M_{nd} accepts language L with $space_{M_{nd}}(n) \geq \log_2 n$, then it accepts any nonempty word $w \in L$ with $|w| = n$ in $C^{Space_{M_{nd}}(n)}$ or fewer steps, where C is a constant determined by M_{nd}.

2.6.14. Justify assertion (ii) at the beginning of the proof of Theorem 2.9. That is, where M_{nd} is a nondeterministic, multitape, off-line Turing machine with $space_{M_{nd}}(n) \geq \log_2 n$, show that any machine configuration of M_{nd} for input word w may be completely represented by a string of precisely $space_{M_{nd}}(n) + 1$ symbols. (*Hint*: Use the multitrack technique of the proof of Theorem 2.4.)

2.6.15 **(a)** What change in the proof of Theorem 2.9 is needed if we wish to account for the unquestionable fact that $conf_{accept}$ is not unique?

(b) Suppose, contrary to our assumption at (i) in the proof of Theorem 2.9, that $C^{Space_{M_{nd}}(n)}$ is not a power of 2. What change is required in subroutine *Yields*?

2.6.16. In the proof of Theorem 2.9 (Savitch's Theorem), we have asserted that, given any two strings α_1 and α_2 over alphabet Γ purporting to describe machine configurations $conf_1$ and $conf_2$ of M_{nd}, machine M_d is capable of determining whether in fact M_{nd} can make the transition from $conf_1$ to $conf_2$ in a single computation step—that is, whether $\alpha_1 \overset{1}{\longrightarrow} \alpha_2$ holds. You are asked to justify this assertion by informally describing an appropriate subroutine.

EXERCISES FOR §2.7

2.7.1. ^{hwk} Find the productivity of each of the machines of Exercise 1.2.1 and Figures 1.2.14(a)–(e).

2.7.2 **(a)** Show that $\Theta(28) \geq 40$. (*Hint*: Amalgamate (i) a 20-state machine that, in canonical fashion, writes 20 $1s$ with (ii) a modification of the machine of Figure 1.5.2, which computes the doubling function. Specifically, modify the machine of Figure 1.5.2 by eliminating states q_9 through q_{12}.)

(b) Use the argument of (a) to find a lower bound for $\Theta(58)$.

2.7.3. Show that function Θ is monotone increasing. That is, show that if $n \leq m$, then $\Theta(n) \leq \Theta(m)$.

2.7.4. We again define $\mathcal{TM}_n$ to be the class of all $(n + 1)$-state Turing machines with input alphabet $\varnothing$ and tape alphabet $\{1\}$. Started scanning a square on a completely blank tape, a given member M of $\mathcal{TM}_n$ may or may not halt, of course. If M does halt after executing k instructions, then let us say that M's *time* is k. On the other hand, is M never halts, then we shall say that M's *time* is 0. Let $S(n)$ be defined as the maximum value of *time* for members of $\mathcal{TM}_n$. Show that function $S(n)$ is not Turing-computable. (*Hint*: Show that if it were Turing-computable, then Busy Beaver function Θ would be Turing-computable as well.)

EXERCISES FOR §2.8

2.8.1. [hwk] List five or more necessary conditions for successful language use on the part of a machine. (Reconsider our discussion of the Descartes Test for machine intelligence.)

2.8.2. [hwk] We noted in the text that any ability required in order for a machine to pass Descartes' test will be required by Turing's test as well. List any additional necessary conditions for a machine's passing the Turing Test. (Reconsider our discussion of Turing's Imitation Game.)

2.8.3 (Weizenbaum's ELIZA).[hwk] The programming technique known as *pattern matching* was the basis for Joseph Weizenbaum's natural-language-processing program ELIZA (see [Weizenbaum 1976]). That program was designed to simulate the psychiatrist's role within psychiatrist–patient interactions. (We shall see that, as a psychiatrist, ELIZA falls squarely within the noninterventionist school.)

- ELIZA has an ordered list of keywords, including words like "father," "mother," "brother," "everybody," and so forth. A match to one of its keywords elicits one of several standard responses on ELIZA's part.

- ELIZA is able to carry out simple grammatical transformations, substituting "I" or "me" for "you," and vice versa, and altering word order. The user/patient's statement may thereby be transformed into a related question.

- ELIZA is able to store each of the user's responses for use at a later point when no keyword has occurred recently and no statement-to-question transformation is possible.

- ELIZA has a standard response to input containing words that are not contained in its lexicon.

A sample ELIZA–user interaction might run roughly as follows.

USER> My father is afraid of everyone.

ELIZA> What else comes to mind when you think of your father?

. . .

USER> Everybody laughed at me.

ELIZA> Whom in particular are you thinking of?

. . .

USER> You don't agree with me.

ELIZA> Why do you think that I don't agree with you?

. . .

USER> You never really suggest anything very useful.

ELIZA> Why do you think that I never really suggest anything very useful?

. . .

USER> My girlfriend made me come here.

. . .

USER> (remark containing no keywords)

ELIZA> Does that have anything to do with the fact that your girlfriend made you come here?

. . .

USER> My mother says that makes no difference.

ELIZA> What else comes to mind when you think of your mother?

. . .

USER> (another remark containing no keywords)

ELIZA> Who is the psychiatrist here, you or me?

. . .

USER> ¿Habla español?

ELIZA> I speak only English.

. . .

Suppose that, after much effort, an extremely sophisticated version of ELIZA was created that was yet based upon pattern-matching techniques, albeit advanced ones. Suppose, further, that a machine running under this enhanced version of ELIZA played the Imitation Game very well and hence passed the Turing Test. You are asked to discuss any implications for Turing's criterion of machine intelligence.

2.8.4. ^{hwk} We have described Block's machine M, which uses the Aunt Bubbles program to successfully play Turing's Imitation Game and thus passes the Turing Test for machine intelligence. Explain why the enumeration of conversational sequences generated by Aunt Bubbles should probably not contain any conversation sequences of the following sorts:

(a) Any conversational sequence containing a true arithmetic identity asserting that the sum of 25 specified natural numbers, each of 3 or more digits, is equal to 274,290,144,433

(b) Any conversational sequence containing, as one of its utterances, what appears to be a complete memory dump of a machine with 32-bit fullword

(c) Any conversational sequence in which one party appears to be successfully tracking the number of times that the letter e has occurred so far within the conversation.

EXERCISE FOR §2.9

2.9.1 We rejected the proposal that minds are modeled by universal Turing machines on the grounds that such machines model only the high-focus end of the cognitive spectrum. But perhaps this was hasty. Can you describe ways in which universal Turing machines could indeed model the chaotic stream of consciousness that constitutes the bulk of our mental lives?

EXERCISES FOR §2.10 (END-OF-CHAPTER REVIEW EXERCISES)

2.10.1. Design and test a Turing machine that accepts, by terminal state, the language of Exercise 1.8.1 and Figure 1.8.1(a).

2.10.2 Assume some encoding of Turing machines. Thus each Turing machine has (at least one) code. Assume, further, that every natural number is the code of some (unique) Turing machine. Now consider the following description of Turing machine M^*. Imagine that M^* starts scanning the leftmost 1 of $n+1$ 1s followed by a blank followed by $m+1$ 1s on an otherwise blank tape, where n and m are arbitrary natural numbers. In such a case, M^* can be counted on to halt scanning the leftmost 1 of $f_n(m)+1$ 1s on an otherwise blank tape, where f_n is that partial number-theoretic function computed by the Turing machine with code n. Such a machine M^* is known as a(n) _____.

2.10.3. Describe in English a multitape Turing machine that computes the number-theoretic function $f(n) =_{\text{def.}} 4n + 3$. To make your description simpler, you may assume that argument n is represented on the tape by n 1s rather than by $n+1$ 1s.

2.10.4. Consider the following suggestion for encoding Turing machines as natural numbers. First, we assign a symbol code to each symbol within Turing machine description language $\Psi = \{q, ', \mathbf{L}, \mathbf{R}, a, b, B, ,, ;\}$ and then encode Turing machines by the *product* of the codes of the symbols occurring in the string representing the machine as a set of quadruples. Thus, as an example, if transition function δ_M is represented by the string

$$q, a, R, q'; q', b, L, q$$

then M's gödel number will be the product

$$\ulcorner q \urcorner \cdot \ulcorner , \urcorner \cdot \ulcorner a \urcorner \cdot \ulcorner , \urcorner \cdot \ulcorner R \urcorner \cdot \ulcorner , \urcorner \cdot \ulcorner q \urcorner \cdot$$
$$\cdot \ulcorner ' \urcorner \cdot \ulcorner ; \urcorner \cdot \ulcorner q \urcorner \cdots .$$

Briefly explain why such an encoding scheme not viable.

2.10.5. ^{hwk} Consider the nondeterministic Turing machine M whose state diagram appears in Figure 2.10.1. M is intended as a language acceptor over alphabet $\Sigma = \{a, b\}$.

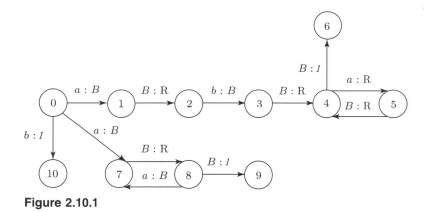

Figure 2.10.1

(a) Does M accept the word aba^3?
(b) Does M accept the word aba^4?
(c) The word a^3?
(d) The word a^3b?
(e) The word b?
(f) What language over alphabet $\Sigma = \{a, b\}$ is accepted by M? (It might be easiest to describe the language as the union of several easily describable languages.)

2.10.6. ^{hwk} The state diagram of Figure 2.10.2 is an unfortunate attempt to present a deterministic Turing machine M that accepts all and only words over alphabet $\Sigma = \{a, b\}$ containing at least two consecutive occurrences of a. In fact, M does not accept this language.

(a) Present a word of length 6 that contains two consecutive as and hence should have been accepted but that is not accepted by this machine in fact.

(b) Design a Turing machine—either deterministic or nondeterministic—which does accept the language $L = \{waaw' | w, w' \in \Sigma^*\}$ The reader should be able to do this using just 10 states.

(c) Supposing that the reader was able to come up with a nondeterministic machine that accepts language L, what conclusion can be drawn regarding the possibility of a deterministic Turing machine accepting L? Explain briefly.

2.10.7. ^{hwk} What language is accepted by the nondeterministic Turing machine of Figure 2.10.3? (The reader may either characterize this language set-theoretically or describe it in a couple of sentences.)

2.10.8. (a) Show that any unary partial number-theoretic f that is Turing-computable is

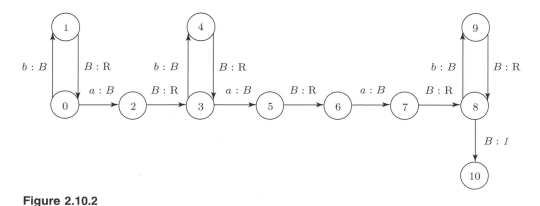

Figure 2.10.2

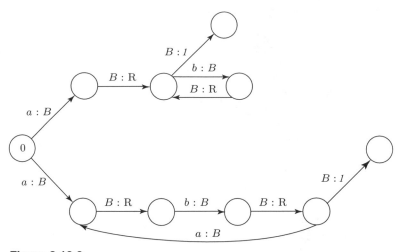

Figure 2.10.3

computed by some deterministic, single-tape Turing machine that never halts when started scanning the leftmost *1* in the representation of an argument for which f is undefined. (*Hint*: Introduce endmarkers λ and ρ as in the proof of Theorem 2.3 in §2.2.)

(b) Generalize this result to k-ary partial number-theoretic functions f.

(c) Show that any Turing-acceptable language L over Σ is accepted by some deterministic, single-tape Turing machine that never halts if started scanning the leftmost symbol of any word w over Σ with $w \notin L$.

2.10.9. (a) Suppose that M is a deterministic, single-tape Turing machine that computes the binary multiplication function defined as

$$f: \mathcal{Z} \to \mathcal{Z}$$
$$f(n, m) = n \cdot m$$

Let us assume the convention mentioned in §2.10 for representing integers on Turing machine tapes.

Suppose, further, that M is started scanning the leftmost *1* on a tape configured as

$$\ldots BB1 * 111111B11 * 1111BB \ldots$$

What would M's final tape configuration be in that case?

(b) Design a multitape Turing machine that computes the binary addition function on the integers. Use the convention mentioned in §2.10 for representing integers on Turing machine tapes.

2.10.10. (a) Design a Turing machine that takes as input the representation of a single natural number $n \geq 2$ and generates, as output, the prime decomposition of n. The machine might generate just the exponents of successive primes. For example, input $n = 198 = 2^1 \cdot 3^2 \cdot 5^0 \cdot 7^0 \cdot 11^1$ would produce output $1^{1+1}B1^{2+1}B1^{0+1}B1^{0+1}B1^{1+1}$.

(b) Design a Turing machine that computes the binary number-theoretic function

$$f: \mathcal{N} \times \mathcal{N} \to \mathcal{N}$$

$$f(n, m) = \text{the least common multiple}$$

$$\text{of } n \text{ and } m$$

Thus, $f(25, 20) = 100$. (*Hint*: Incorporate your solution to (a) within your machine.)

(c) Design a multitape Turing machine that computes the binary addition function on the rationals. We extend the convention mentioned in §2.10 for representing integers on Turing machine tapes so as to obtain a representation of rational numbers. (Recall that a rational number is merely a pair of integers.) For example, input tape configuration

$$\dots BB1*111/1*1111B11$$

$$\uparrow \qquad *11/1*111BB\dots$$

would yield output

$$\dots BB1*11/1*1111111BB\dots$$

reflecting the fact that $\left(\frac{2}{3}\right) + \left(\frac{-1}{2}\right) = \left(\frac{1}{6}\right)$. (*Hint:* Incorporate your solution to (b) within your design.)

2.10.11. **(a)** Let L be a language over alphabet Σ. Show that if both L and L^c are Turing-acceptable languages, then L and L^c are both Turing-recognizable as well. (*Hint:* Describe the behavior of a multitape machine that alternately simulates the behavior of language acceptors for L and L^c on worktape$_1$ and worktape$_2$, respectively.)

(b) Use (a) to show that language L is Turing recognizable by a deterministic Turing machine in the sense of Definition 1.4 if and only if L is Turing-recognizable by a nondeterministic Turing machine in the sense of Definition 2.11.

2.10.12. **(a)** Suppose that f is a unary number-theoretic function that is total, bijective, and Turing-computable. Show that inverse f^{-1} is Turing-computable as well.

(b) What if f is total and injective but not onto?

(c) What if f is partial, injective, and not onto?

2.10.13. Give an argument to show that the unary function $f(n) = n!$, although Turing-computable, is computable by no machine—either single-tape or multitape—which computes in polynomial time.

2.10.14. Show that language L is polynomial-time Turing-acceptable if and only if there exists a deterministic Turing machine that recognizes L in polynomially bounded time. Incidentally, this result explains why other authors define complexity class P as the class of all polynomial-time Turing-*recognizable* languages.

2.10.15. In Exercise 2.3.6, it was shown that the family of Turing-acceptable languages is closed under intersection. That is, it was shown that, if L_1 and L_2 are both Turing-acceptable, then so is $L_1 \cap L_2$. In the present exercise, we consider additional closure properties of the family of Turing-acceptable languages.

(a) Show that the family of Turing-acceptable languages is closed under union. That is, if L_1 and L_2 are both Turing-acceptable, then so is $L_1 \cup L_2$.

(b) Show that the family of Turing-acceptable languages is closed under concatenation. That is, if L_1 and L_2 are both Turing-acceptable, then so is $L_1.L_2$.

(c) Show that the family of Turing-acceptable languages is closed under Kleene closure. That is, if L is Turing-acceptable, then so is L^*.

(d) Show that the family of Turing-acceptable languages is closed under reversal. That is, if language L over alphabet Σ is Turing-acceptable, then so is the language $L^R = \{w^R | w \in L\}$.

2.10.16. Show that the family of Turing-recognizable languages is closed under complementation. That is, show that, if L is Turing-recognizable, then so is L^c.

2.10.17. Write a program that calculates the encoding, in accordance with the Euler–Gödel scheme, of an arbitrary Turing machine, given as a set of quadruples. Professor James Foster has suggested writing Perl code that makes use of arbitrary precision arithmetic.

2.10.18. Write your own program to simulate single-tape Turing machines. Input might consist of a data file containing (1) a representation of a set of quadruples defining some machine M together with (2) a representation of an initial tape configuration.

Chapter 3

An Introduction to Recursion Theory

In this chapter we introduce three important classes of number-theoretic functions and investigate their properties—in particular, their relation to the class of Turing-computable functions introduced in Chapter 1. Ultimately, we propose a general analysis of computation that gives prominence to the function computation paradigm. A related analysis featuring the language recognition paradigm is postponed until Chapter 12.

§3.1 The Primitive Recursive Functions

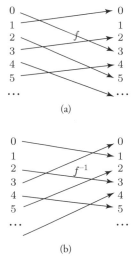

(a)

(b)

Figure 3.1.1 The unary function f is injective so that f^{-1} is defined.

The reader will be familiar with several *function-forming operations*—operations that may be applied to functions generally and to number-theoretic functions in particular, so as to yield new functions. Thus, consider the unary function

$$f(n) = \begin{cases} n + 3 & \text{if } n \text{ is even} \\ n - 1 & \text{if } n \text{ is odd} \end{cases}$$

which maps 0 to 3, 1 to 0, 2 to 5, 3 to 2, and so on (see Figure 3.1.1(a)). Since f is injective or 1-to-1, we can speak of its inverse f^{-1} mapping 0 to 1, 2 to 3, 3 to 0, and so on. Hence, f^{-1} is the result of merely reversing the arrows in Figure 3.1.1(a) (see Figure 3.1.1(b)). Note that f^{-1} is undefined for argument 1.

We can think of f^{-1} as the result of applying a unary inversion operation, denoted by operator $^{-1}$, to function f. As another example of a function-forming operation, consider function composition. Thus if f and g are unary functions defined by $f(n) = 3n + 2$ and $g(n) = n + 1$, respectively, then we define $f \circ g(n) = f(g(n))$. In that case, we have $f \circ g(4) = f(g(4)) = 17$. Here $\circ$ names a binary function-forming operation that, applied to two functions f and g, yields a third function $h = f \circ g$. In this section we shall have occasion to consider two other very important function-forming operations, one of which is merely a generalization of function composition as just described.

Let us now define a new class of number-theoretic functions.

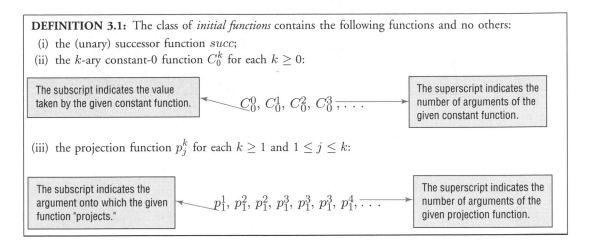

DEFINITION 3.1: The class of *initial functions* contains the following functions and no others:

(i) the (unary) successor function $succ$;

(ii) the k-ary constant-0 function C_0^k for each $k \geq 0$:

> The subscript indicates the value taken by the given constant function. $\longleftarrow$ $C_0^0, C_0^1, C_0^2, C_0^3, \ldots$ $\longrightarrow$ The superscript indicates the number of arguments of the given constant function.

(iii) the projection function p_j^k for each $k \geq 1$ and $1 \leq j \leq k$:

> The subscript indicates the argument onto which the given function "projects." $\longleftarrow$ $p_1^1, p_1^2, p_1^2, p_1^3, p_1^3, p_1^3, p_1^4, \ldots$ $\longrightarrow$ The superscript indicates the number of arguments of the given projection function.

Clearly, the initial functions form an infinite class of number-theoretic functions.

We next introduce two new function-forming operations. The first is called *function composition* and, as mentioned above, is merely a more general version of the function-forming operation ∘ considered earlier.

DEFINITION 3.2 (Function Composition): Suppose we are given function $\boldsymbol{f}\colon \mathcal{N}^m \to \mathcal{N}$ with $m \geq 1$ and functions $\boldsymbol{g_1}, \boldsymbol{g_2}, \ldots, \boldsymbol{g_m}$, each of which is $\mathcal{N}^k \to \mathcal{N}$ with $k \geq 0$. Then applying function composition to the $m + 1$ functions $\boldsymbol{f}, \boldsymbol{g_1}, \boldsymbol{g_2}, \ldots, \boldsymbol{g_m}$ yields a new function $\boldsymbol{h}\colon \mathcal{N}^k \to \mathcal{N}$ defined by

(Schema A) $\quad \boldsymbol{h}(n_1, \ldots, n_k) = \boldsymbol{f}(\boldsymbol{g_1}(n_1, \ldots, n_k), \boldsymbol{g_2}(n_1, \ldots, n_k), \ldots, \boldsymbol{g_m}(n_1, \ldots, n_k))$

We shall write $\mathbf{Comp}[\boldsymbol{f}, \boldsymbol{g_1}, \boldsymbol{g_2}, \ldots, \boldsymbol{g_m}]$ for function $\boldsymbol{h}$ here, where $\mathbf{Comp}$ indicates the function composition operator.

Note that applying $\mathbf{Comp}$ to an m-ary function f and m k-ary functions $g_1, g_2, \ldots, g_m$ is another k-ary function. As an additional notational simplification we shall in the future write $\vec{n}$ for the parameter list $n_1, \ldots, n_k$. Assuming these simplifications, Schema A can now be rewritten as

$$\mathbf{Comp}[f, g_1, g_2, \ldots, g_m](\vec{n}) = f(g_1(\vec{n}), g_2(\vec{n}), \ldots, g_m(\vec{n}))$$

In an effort to achieve a certain concreteness, we describe a classroom scenario that models Schema A. There are exactly $m + 1$ students in the class, each of whom is equipped with pencil and paper and each of whom is able to compute the value of a particular number-theoretic function. Expressed differently, each student knows how to calculate the value of his or her personal number-theoretic function for any given tuple consisting of an appropriate number of arguments. For convenience, we assume that the students are seated in two rows. In the front row there are m students, computing k-ary functions that we designate $g_1, g_2, \ldots, g_m$, respectively. Immediately behind them is a single student who knows how to calculate an m-ary function that we designate f (see Figure 3.1.2(a)). We describe a scenario

(a)

(b)

Figure 3.1.2 The class collectively computes function $h = \mathbf{Comp}[f, g_1, g_2, \ldots, g_m]$.

whereby the class as a whole computes k-ary function $h = \textbf{Comp}[f, g_1, g_2, \ldots, g_m]$. The computation of h begins when the instructor enters the classroom with m distinct copies of k-tuple $\langle n_1, \ldots, n_k \rangle$—written on pieces of paper, say—and gives one copy to each and every one of the m students in the *front* row only, who now proceed to calculate. After a brief time, when the calculations are completed, each student in the front row will be in possession of a single natural number that is the value of his or her personal function for arguments $\langle n_1, \ldots, n_k \rangle$ as provided by the instructor. In other words, the first student in the front row will now be in possession of a natural number that is none other than $g_1(n_1, \ldots, n_k)$, the second student will be in possession of $g_2(n_1, \ldots, n_k)$, and so on. Next, at one and the same time, the students in the front row communicate—on slips of paper, say—the values of their personal functions for arguments $\langle n_1, \ldots, n_k \rangle$ to the single student seated behind them. That student now proceeds to compute the value of his or her personal function f for arguments $g_1(n_1, \ldots, n_k)$ through $g_m(n_1, \ldots, n_k)$, in that order, as provided by the students in the front row. After a brief time, when these calculations are completed, this student is in possession of a single natural number that is none other than $f(g_1(n_1, \ldots, n_k), g_2(n_1, \ldots, n_k), \ldots, g_m(n_1, \ldots, n_k))$. It is convenient to assume that the student writes this number on the chalkboard, at which point the computation terminates (see Figure 3.1.2(b)).

Schema A invites us to regard the entire class as a single, multipart computer of a k-ary number-theoretic function that we might designate h. The arguments $\langle n_1, \ldots, n_k \rangle$ of h are provided by the instructor upon entering the classroom. The value of h for these k arguments—that is, $h(n_1, \ldots, n_k)$—is found on the chalkboard at the end of the class' calculations. Of course, calculating $h(n_1, \ldots, n_k)$ involves calculating values of functions $f, g_1, g_2, \ldots, g_m$, of which h is "composed." This is reflected in an alternate name for h, namely, $\textbf{Comp}[f, g_1, g_2, \ldots, g_m]$. Summarizing, we note that if both

(1) individual members of the class variously compute k-ary functions $g_1, g_2, \ldots, g_m$ as well as m-ary function f and

(2) the activities of the instructor and the students are coordinated as described earlier, then

(3) the class *collectively* computes a well-defined k-ary function $\textbf{Comp}[f, g_1, g_2, \ldots, g_m]$ whose value for arguments $\langle n_1, \ldots, n_k \rangle$ is $f(g_1(n_1, \ldots, n_k), g_2(n_1, \ldots, n_k), \ldots, g_m(n_1, \ldots, n_k))$.

EXAMPLE 3.1.1 As a first example of function composition in the sense of Definition 3.2, suppose that j is the binary function defined as $j(n, m) = n^3 + m^2 + 7$. Thus we have $j(8, 6) = 512 + 36 + 7 = 555$. Let us evaluate

$$\textbf{Comp}[j, p_3^3, p_2^3](57849, 6, 8)$$

By the definition of function composition, this is just

$$j(p_3^3(57849, 6, 8), p_2^3(57849, 6, 8))$$

But $p_3^3(57849, 6, 8)$ and $p_2^3(57849, 6, 8)$ are 8 and 6, respectively. So $\textbf{Comp}[j, p_3^3, p_2^3](57849, 6, 8)$ has value 555. The reader should verify that $\textbf{Comp}[p_1^2, p_2^2, j](8, 6) = 6$ and that $\textbf{Comp}[p_2^3, p_1^2, j, p_2^2](8, 6) = 555$.

Note that our preliminary example $h =_{\text{def.}} f \circ g$ is **Comp**$[f, g]$ in the sense of Definition 3.2, and thus the general definition $f \circ g(n) = (f \circ g)(n) = f(g(n))$ is a special instance of Schema A where we set $m = 1$ and $k = 1$.

To motivate our second function-forming operation, which is called *primitive recursion*, consider the recursion equations for the binary addition function on the natural numbers, where we are writing $succ$ for the successor function:

$$\text{(i)} \qquad plus(n, 0) = n$$

$$\text{(ii)} \quad plus(n, m + 1) = succ(plus(n, m))$$

Using (i) and (ii) we can evaluate $plus(5, 2)$. First, note that we cannot apply (i) to the pair $(5, 2)$ since (i) requires that the second argument be 0. On the other hand we *can* apply (ii) to the pair $(5, 2)$ if we let n be 5 and construe 2 as $m + 1$, which means that m is 1. Thus

$$
\begin{aligned}
plus(5, 2) &= plus(5, 1 + 1) & &\text{by } 2 = 1 + 1 \\
&= succ(plus(5, 1)) & &\text{from (ii)} \\
&= succ(plus(5, 0 + 1)) & &\text{by } 1 = 0 + 1 \\
&= succ(succ(plus(5, 0))) & &\text{from (ii)} \\
&= succ(succ(5)) & &\text{from (i)} \\
&= succ(6) & &\text{by definition of } succ \\
&= 7 & &\text{by definition of } succ
\end{aligned}
$$

Note that our definition of $plus$ is recursive in the sense that $plus(5, 2)$ involves applying $plus$ to smaller operands—that is, to $(5, 1)$ and to $(5, 0)$—in turn. What we seek now is a function-forming operation that enables us to construct $plus$ from the function $succ$ and perhaps some other function(s) so as to achieve this effect of building up from smaller arguments. ($succ$ is pronounced "successor," of course.) One way in which we can do this is to use the function-forming operation defined as follows.

DEFINITION 3.3 (Primitive Recursion): Given function $\boldsymbol{f}: \mathcal{N}^k \to \mathcal{N}$ with $k \geq 0$ and function $\boldsymbol{g}: \mathcal{N}^{k+2} \to \mathcal{N}$, we can form a new function $\boldsymbol{h}: \mathcal{N}^{k+1} \to \mathcal{N}$ defined by

(Schema B)   (i) $\boldsymbol{h}(n_1, \ldots, n_k, 0) = \boldsymbol{f}(n_1, \ldots, n_k)$

     (ii) $\boldsymbol{h}(n_1, \ldots, n_k, m + 1) = \boldsymbol{g}(n_1, \ldots, n_k, m, h(n_1, \ldots, n_k, m))$

Now we shall write **Pr**$[\boldsymbol{f}, \boldsymbol{g}]$ for the function h formed by applying primitive recursion to given functions $\boldsymbol{f}$ and $\boldsymbol{g}$.

As before, we can abbreviate Schema B as

$$\text{(i)} \qquad h(\vec{n}, 0) = f(\vec{n})$$

$$\text{(ii)} \quad h(\vec{n}, m + 1) = g(\vec{n}, m, h(\vec{n}, m))$$

One should think of **Pr** as the name of a new function-forming operator that, applied to f and g, in that order, yields the new number-theoretic function h defined in Schema B. Also, note that if f is a k-ary function and g is a $(k + 2)$-ary function, then h is a $(k + 1)$-ary function.

We again take a moment to describe a classroom scenario that may help the reader to better comprehend Schema B. This time there are only two students in the classroom. Both are equipped with pencils and an unlimited quantity of paper. One of the students is adept at computing a certain k-ary number-theoretic function f: Given any k-tuple of arguments $\langle n_1, \ldots, n_k \rangle$, this student calculates value $f(n_1, \ldots, n_k)$. The second student knows how to calculate the value of a certain $(k + 2)$-ary function g for any given $(k + 2)$-tuple $\langle n_1, \ldots, n_{k+2} \rangle$. We show how the two students, through coordination of their calculating activities, can together compute the value of the new $(k + 1)$-ary function $h = \mathbf{Pr}[f, g]$ for any given $(k + 1)$-tuple $\langle n_1, \ldots, n_{k+1} \rangle$.

The instructor enters the classroom and writes $(k + 1)$-tuple $\langle n_1, \ldots, n_k, m \rangle$ on the chalkboard. This $(k + 1)$-tuple remains on the chalkboard throughout the collective computation of the two students. There are two cases to consider.

- If $m = 0$, then, in accordance with Schema B(i), all that is required is that the first student report the value of f for k-tuple $\langle n_1, \ldots, n_k \rangle$.

- If $m \neq 0$, then the collective computation of the two students is more extended, but it still must start with the first student. Namely, to begin, this first student must compute the value of f for k-tuple $\langle n_1, \ldots, n_k \rangle$. By Schema B(i), this value is just $h(n_1, \ldots, n_k, 0)$ and will now be used by the second student, who computes the value of function g for $(k + 2)$-tuple

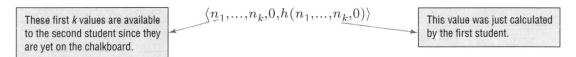

By (B)(ii), this value $g(n_1, \ldots, n_k, 0, h(n_1, \ldots, n_k, 0))$ is $h(n_1, \ldots, n_k, 1)$, which will now be used by the second student who computes the value of function g for $(k + 2)$-tuple

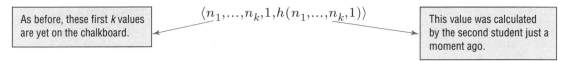

This process is iterated by the second student exactly m times, eventually resulting in the computation of $\mathbf{Pr}[f, g](n_1, \ldots, n_k, m + 1) = h(n_1, \ldots, n_k, m + 1) = g(n_1, \ldots, n_k, m, h(n_1, \ldots, n_k, m))$.

We note that neither student alone computes $h = \mathbf{Pr}[f, g]$. It is rather the two students *together* who, through coordination of their computational activities as directed by Schema B(i) and (ii), compute $h = \mathbf{Pr}[f, g]$. (Obviously, the division of labor is not optimal: If $m \neq 0$, then the second student does most of the work.)

EXAMPLE 3.1.2 (Addition is primitive recursive) As an application of these ideas, we show that the binary addition function is the result of applying the primitive recursion operator to other functions.

Consider again the recursion equations for addition, which we write as

$$\text{(i)} \qquad plus(n, 0) = n$$

$$\text{(ii)} \quad plus(n, m + 1) = succ(plus(n, m))$$

Note that n in the right-hand side of (i) is just $p_1^1(n)$. (Why?) So (i) may be rewritten

$$\text{(i)} \quad plus(n, 0) = \boldsymbol{p_1^1}(n)$$

Also $plus(n, m) = p_3^3(n, m, plus(n, m))$ so that (ii) is

$$\text{(ii)} \quad plus(n, m + 1) = succ(p_3^3(n, m, plus(n, m)))$$

$$= \textbf{Comp}[\boldsymbol{succ}, \boldsymbol{p_3^3}](n, m, plus(n, m))$$

Finally, these rewritings of (i) and (ii) show that $plus$ is none other than

$$\textbf{Pr}[\boldsymbol{p_1^1}, \textbf{Comp}[\boldsymbol{succ}, \boldsymbol{p_3^3}]] \qquad\qquad (3.1.1)$$

Apparently the addition function results from applying **Pr** to p_1^1 and **Comp**$[succ, p_3^3]$.[1]

We now define a very important class of number-theoretic functions called the class of *primitive recursive functions*. We define this class by recursion.

DEFINITION 3.4: We define the class of *primitive recursive functions* as follows:
  (i) Any initial function is a primitive recursive function.
  (ii) If $g_1, \ldots, g_m$ are each k-ary primitive recursive functions for some $k \geq 0$ and f is an m-ary primitive recursive function for some $m \geq 1$, then **Comp**$[f, g_1, \ldots, g_m]$ is a k-ary primitive recursive function.
  (iii) If f is an k-ary primitive recursive function and g is an $(k + 2)$-ary primitive function for some $k \geq 0$, then **Pr**$[f, g]$ is a $(k + 1)$-ary primitive recursive function.
  (iv) No other number-theoretic functions are primitive recursive except those obtained from clauses (i)–(iii).

The definition tells us, in effect, that a function is primitive recursive if and only if either (1) it is among the initial functions or (2) it can be constructed from initial functions using **Comp** and **Pr**. We often express this by saying that the class of primitive recursive functions is the smallest class that contains all initial functions and that is closed under the function-forming operations **Comp** and **Pr**.

---

[1] We have defined addition in terms of $succ$. The usual characterization of $succ$ as $succ(n) =_{\text{def.}} n + 1$ might then appear to have defined $succ$ in terms of addition—an apparent circularity. This would be to misunderstand our intention in writing $succ(n) =_{\text{def.}} n + 1$. In fact, our purpose here is only to appeal to the reader's understanding of what the successor function *is*—namely, that unary function that takes 0 to 1, 1 to 2, 2 to 3, and so on. That is all we mean by writing $succ(n) =_{\text{def.}} n + 1$: Given any natural number n, $succ(n)$ is that unique natural number immediately following n in the progression $0, 1, 2, 3, \ldots$.

EXAMPLE 3.1.2 (continued) (Addition is primitive recursive) Our definition of addition at (3.1.1) shows that addition is primitive recursive. For p_1^1, *succ* and p_3^3 are initial functions and hence primitive recursive by clause (i) of Definition 3.4. By clause (ii) of that definition, **Comp**[*succ*, p_3^3] is primitive recursive. Finally, **Pr**[p_1^1, **Comp**[*succ*, p_3^3]] is itself primitive recursive by clause (iii).

Summarizing, function *plus* is primitive recursive by virtue of the fact that (1) p_1^1, *succ*, and p_3^3 are initial functions and (2) the primitive recursive functions are closed under **Comp** and **Pr**.

EXAMPLE 3.1.3 (Any constant function C_j^k is primitive recursive) As a further application of Definition 3.4, we now show that all constant functions are primitive recursive. Take as an example the unary constant-1 function defined by $C_1^1(n) = 1$ for all n. Apparently, $C_1^1(n) = succ(C_0^1(n))$ for all n. So C_1^1 is **Comp**[*succ*, C_0^1]. Similarly, the unary constant-2 function C_2^1 is **Comp**[*succ*, **Comp**[*succ*, C_0^1]]. It is easy enough to see that all other constant functions are primitive recursive as well (see Exercise 3.7.3).

We emphasize that it is only the constant-0 functions that are primitive recursive by virtue of being among the initial functions. That all other constant functions are primitive recursive follows only by clause (ii) of Definition 3.4 (closure under **Comp**).

We claim that every primitive recursive function is a total function. We prove this by induction on the complexity of primitive recursive functions, by which we mean the number of times we have applied operations **Comp** and **Pr**. First of all, it is obvious that all of our initial functions are total. So we need only verify that the property of being a total function is preserved under the operations **Comp** and **Pr**. Take **Comp** first and suppose that functions $f, g_1, \ldots, g_m$ in Schema A are all total. (This is our induction hypothesis.) But if $f, g_1, \ldots, g_m$ are all total, then the right-hand side of schema (A) is defined for all $n_1, \ldots, n_k$. That is, $h = \textbf{Comp}[f, g_1, \ldots, g_m]$ is defined for all $n_1, \ldots, n_k$, which means that $h = \textbf{Comp}[f, g_1, \ldots, g_m]$ is total. Next, we show that if functions f and g are both total, then so is $\textbf{Pr}[f, g]$. This requires induction on the natural numbers *within* our induction on the complexity of primitive recursive functions. First, since f is total, we have, by (i) of Schema B, that $h(\vec{n}, 0)$ is defined for all $\vec{n}$. Next, assuming that $h(\vec{n}, m)$ is total (for fixed m), the right-hand side of (ii) of Schema B is total, given that g is total. So $h(\vec{n}, m+1)$ is total. We have proved, by so-called *double induction*, the following proposition.

THEOREM 3.1 Every primitive recursive function is total.

In fact, every total number-theoretic function that is likely to occur to you is primitive recursive. We now show that the binary multiplication function and the binary exponentiation function are both primitive recursive. In each case, we first write a pair of recursion equations, on the model of those for addition given above, for the given function. In doing so, we are free to refer to functions previously shown to be primitive recursive—for example, addition. We then begin rewriting these recursion equations so that they eventually conform to the definitions of function-forming operations **Comp** and **Pr** as given in Definitions 3.2 and 3.3, respectively.

EXAMPLE 3.1.4 (Multiplication is primitive recursive) We use the recursion equations

$$\text{(i)} \qquad mult(n, 0) = 0$$

$$\text{(ii)} \quad mult(n, m + 1) = mult(n, m) + n$$

$$= n + mult(n, m)$$

Let us use prefix notation for the addition function, which gives

$$\text{(i)} \qquad mult(n, 0) = 0$$

$$\text{(ii)} \quad mult(n, m + 1) = plus(n, mult(n, m))$$

But now notice that the right-hand side of (i) is just $C_0^1(n)$ so that (i) may be written

$$\text{(i)} \quad mult(n, 0) = C_0^1(n)$$

Also, note that $n = \boldsymbol{p_1^3(n, m, mult(n, m))}$ and that $mult(n, m) = \boldsymbol{p_3^3(n, m, mult(n, m))}$, so that (ii) may be rewritten as

$$\text{(ii)} \quad mult(n, m + 1) = plus(\boldsymbol{p_1^3(n, m, mult(n, m))}, \boldsymbol{p_3^3(n, m, mult(n, m))})$$

$$= \textbf{Comp}[plus, p_1^3, p_3^3](n, m, mult(n, m))$$

This means that *mult* is none other than $\textbf{Pr}[C_0^1, \textbf{Comp}[plus, p_1^3, p_3^3]]$. We are permitted to name *plus* here since that function was previously shown to be primitive recursive: It is just $\textbf{Pr}[p_1^1, \textbf{Comp}[succ, p_3^3]]$. Substituting, we have that *mult* is $\textbf{Pr}[C_0^1, \textbf{Comp}[\textbf{Pr}[p_1^1, \textbf{Comp}[succ, p_3^3]], p_1^3, p_3^3]]$.

EXAMPLE 3.1.5 (Exponentiation is primitive recursive) Let us write $exp(n, m)$ for n^m. We then have recursion equations

$$\text{(i)} \qquad exp(n, 0) = 1$$

$$\text{(ii)} \quad exp(n, m + 1) = exp(n, m) \cdot n$$

$$= n \cdot exp(n, m)$$

Again, introducing prefix notation, we rewrite (i) and (ii) as

$$\text{(i)} \qquad exp(n, 0) = 1$$

$$\text{(ii)} \quad exp(n, m + 1) = mult(n, exp(n, m))$$

We saw in Example 3.1.3 that $1 = C_1^1(n) = \textbf{Comp}[succ, C_0^1](n)$ so that (i) becomes

$$\text{(i)} \quad exp(n, 0) = \textbf{Comp}[succ, C_0^1](n)$$

Also, $n = p_1^3(n, m, exp(n, m))$ and $exp(n, m) = p_3^3(n, m, exp(n, m))$ so (ii) becomes

(ii) $exp(n, m + 1) = mult(p_1^3(n, m, exp(n, m)), p_3^3(n, m, exp(n, m)))$

$$= \text{\textbf{Comp}}[mult, p_1^3, p_3^3](n, m, exp(n, m))$$

This means that exp is none other than $\textbf{Pr}[\textbf{Comp}[succ, C_0^1], \textbf{Comp}[mult, p_1^3, p_3^3]]$. Again, we are permitted to use $mult$ here since it was previously shown to be primitive recursive. Substituting that definition and pretty printing, we have that exp is

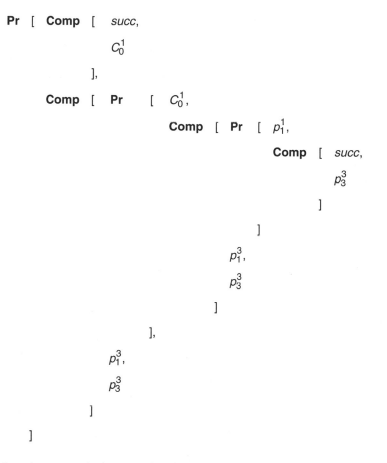

The availability of such a *canonical expression*, involving operators **Comp** and **Pr** applied ultimately to initial functions in accordance with Definitions 3.2 and 3.3, respectively, shows that binary number-theoretic function exp is primitive recursive.

In various exercises the reader is led through demonstrations that other well-known number-theoretic functions are primitive recursive. For example, in Exercise 3.7.1 we lead the reader through a demonstration that the unary factorial function is primitive recursive.

In later sections of this chapter, we will need to know that several other functions, some of which are not so well known, are primitive recursive. For example, let us define the function $\overline{sg}$ as follows:

$$\overline{sg}(n) = \begin{cases} 1 & \text{if } n = 0 \\ 0 & \text{otherwise} \end{cases}$$

Then $\overline{sg}$ is seen to be primitive recursive since $\overline{sg}(n) = monus(1, sg(n))$, where both $monus$ and sg are themselves shown to be primitive recursive in Exercise 3.1.8. (Try that exercise immediately.)

EXAMPLE 3.1.6 (Generalized sums and products) It will also be useful in the next section to have shown that several functions involving sums and products of series are primitive recursive. The peculiar character of Schema B of Definition 3.3 requires that our approach be carefully chosen. First, it will prove convenient to assume that $\sum_{0 \leq i < 0} a_i = 0$ and that $\prod_{0 \leq i < 0} a_i = 1$, where the a_i are arbitrary natural numbers. Next, we show that, if f is any $(k+1)$-ary primitive recursive function, then the $(k+1)$-ary function $\eta(n_1, n_2, \ldots, n_k, m) = \sum_{0 \leq i < m} f(n_1, n_2, \ldots, n_k, i)$ is primitive recursive. First, by convention we have that

$$\eta(n_1, n_2, \ldots, n_k, 0) = \sum_{0 \leq i < 0} f(n_1, n_2, \ldots, n_k, i) = 0 = C_0^k(n_1, n_2, \ldots, n_k) \tag{i}$$

Also,

$$\eta(n_1, n_2, \ldots, n_k, j+1) = \sum_{0 \leq i < j+1} f(n_1, n_2, \ldots, n_k, i) = \left[\sum_{0 \leq i < j} f(n_1, n_2, \ldots, n_k, i) \right] + f(n_1, n_2, \ldots, n_k, j)$$

$$= \eta(n_1, n_2, \ldots, n_k, j) + f(n_1, n_2, \ldots, n_k, j)$$

$$= plus(\eta(n_1, n_2, \ldots, n_k, j), f(n_1, n_2, \ldots, n_k, j))$$

$$= \xi(n_1, n_2, \ldots, n_k, j, \eta(n_1, n_2, \ldots, n_k, j)) \tag{ii}$$

where $\xi(n_1, n_2, \ldots, n_k, j, m) = plus(m, f(n_1, n_2, \ldots, n_k, j))$. So ξ is seen to be a primitive recursive $(k+2)$-ary function and, given (i) and (ii), η is seen to be none other than $\mathbf{Pr}[C_0^k, \xi]$ and hence itself primitive recursive.

Having seen that $\sum_{0 \leq i < m} f(n_1, n_2, \ldots, n_k, i)$ is primitive recursive provided f is primitive recursive, it is easily shown that $\sum_{0 \leq i \leq m} f(n_1, n_2, \ldots, n_k, i) = \sum_{i=0}^{m} f(n_1, n_2, \ldots, n_k, i)$ is primitive recursive provided f is (see Exercise 3.1.16). It can also be shown that both $\prod_{0 \leq i < m} f(n_1, n_2, \ldots, n_k, i)$ and $\prod_{0 \leq i \leq m} f(n_1, n_2, \ldots, n_k, i) = \prod_{i=0}^{m} f(n_1, n_2, \ldots, n_k, i)$ are primitive recursive provided that f is primitive recursive (see Exercises 3.1.17 and 3.1.18).

---

§3.2 Primitive Recursive Predicates

In §3.1 our focus was the association of primitive recursive functions with canonical expressions. We will return to that issue below. However, in the meantime we turn to a consideration of k-ary number-theoretic predicates for $k \geq 1$, whereby we mean any relation holding of k natural numbers. In general, we shall write $C(n_1, n_2, \ldots, n_k)$, or sometimes $C(\vec{n})$, to mean that natural numbers $n_1, n_2, \ldots, n_k$ *satisfy* predicate C or that predicate C *holds of* natural numbers $n_1, n_2, \ldots, n_k$. We write χ_C for the *characteristic function of predicate* C defined as

$$\chi_C(n_1, n_2, \ldots, n_k) = \begin{cases} 1 & \text{if } C(n_1, n_2, \ldots, n_k) \\ 0 & \text{otherwise} \end{cases}$$

In other words, χ_C takes on value 1 for any k-tuple of arguments $n_1, n_2, \ldots, n_k$ such that $n_1, n_2, \ldots, n_k$ satisfy predicate C, and χ_C takes on value 0 for any k-tuple of arguments $n_1, n_2, \ldots, n_k$ that do not satisfy predicate C. Only values 1 and 0 are possible. Note that characteristic function $\chi_C(n_1, n_2, \ldots, n_k)$ is a total function. (See also our discussion at the very end of §0.13.)

EXAMPLE 3.2.1 As an easy example, consider the binary predicate $gr\_eq(n, m)$ that holds of natural numbers n and m just in case $n \geq m$. We associate with predicate $gr\_eq(n, m)$ a characteristic function $\chi_{gr\_eq}(n, m)$ defined by

$$\chi_{gr\_eq}(n, m) = \begin{cases} 1 & \text{if } n \geq m \\ 0 & \text{otherwise} \end{cases}$$

Now function $\chi_{gr\_eq}(n, m)$ is primitive recursive since we have $\chi_{gr\_eq}(n, m) = \overline{sg}(monus(m, n))$. We shall in turn refer to $gr\_eq(n, m)$ as a *primitive recursive predicate* in accordance with Definition 3.5, which follows.

DEFINITION 3.5: Let $C(n_1, n_2, \ldots, n_k)$ be a number-theoretic predicate with $k \geq 0$ and let $\chi_C(n_1, n_2, \ldots, n_k)$, the characteristic function of $C(n_1, n_2, \ldots, n_k)$, be defined as usual by

$$\chi_C(n_1, n_2, \ldots, n_k) = \begin{cases} 1 & \text{if } C(n_1, n_2, \ldots, n_k) \\ 0 & \text{otherwise} \end{cases}$$

Then if $\chi_C(n_1, n_2, \ldots, n_k)$ happens to be a primitive recursive function, we shall say that $C(n_1, n_2, \ldots, n_k)$ is a *primitive recursive predicate*.

EXAMPLE 3.2.2 As another example of a primitive recursive predicate, consider the binary equality predicate $eq(n, m)$ holding of natural numbers n and m just in case $n = m$. The characteristic function of $eq(n, m)$ is of course just

$$\chi_{eq}(n, m) = \begin{cases} 1 & \text{if } n = m \\ 0 & \text{otherwise} \end{cases}$$

We establish that $eq(n, m)$ is a primitive recursive predicate by showing that $\chi_{eq}(n, m)$ is primitive recursive. To this end, we can write

$$\chi_{eq}(n, m) = \overline{sg}(plus(monus(n, m), monus(m, n)))$$

$$= \overline{sg}(plus(monus(n, m), monus(p_2^2(n, m), p_1^2(n, m))))$$

$$= \overline{sg}(plus(monus(n, m), \mathbf{Comp}[monus, p_2^2, p_1^2](n, m)))$$

$$= \overline{sg}(\mathbf{Comp}[plus, monus, \mathbf{Comp}[monus, p_2^2, p_1^2]](n, m))$$

$$= \mathbf{Comp}[\overline{sg}, \mathbf{Comp}[plus, monus, \mathbf{Comp}[monus, p_2^2, p_1^2]]](n, m)$$

If we were to substitute definitions of functions $\overline{sg}$ and $monus$, we would obtain a canonical expression for function χ_{eq}, thereby showing that χ_{eq} is primitive recursive. In the future, we shall forego the display of canonical expressions for primitive recursive functions. Instead, we will be satisfied to display an equation such that the definiens (the right-hand side) mentions only functions previously shown to be primitive recursive. We shall also permit natural number constants in light of our having shown that all of the constant functions C_j^k are primitive recursive. In such a case, we shall point out merely that the definiens is *visually* or *prima facie* primitive recursive.

EXAMPLE 3.2.3 (Definition by cases) The characteristic function $\chi_C(n_1, n_2, \ldots, n_k)$ of any number-theoretic predicate $C(n_1, n_2, \ldots, n_k)$ is definable as

$$\chi_C(n_1, n_2, \ldots, n_k) = \begin{cases} 1 & \text{if } C(n_1, n_2, \ldots, n_k) \\ 0 & \text{otherwise} \end{cases}$$

and, as such, can be said to be *defined by cases*. Of course, in the case of any characteristic function $\chi_C(n_1, n_2, \ldots, n_k)$ there are precisely two cases to consider for any given k-tuple $n_1, n_2, \ldots, n_k$: either $C(n_1, n_2, \ldots, n_k)$ or $\neg C(n_1, n_2, \ldots, n_k)$. We wish now to generalize this so as to consider definitions by cases where the number of cases exceeds two. In fact, under certain special circumstances, which we are about to describe, number-theoretic functions defined by cases are invariably primitive recursive.

Suppose that the k-ary function f is defined by cases as

$$f(n_1, n_2, \ldots, n_k) = \begin{cases} g_1(n_1, n_2, \ldots, n_k) & \text{if } C_1(n_1, n_2, \ldots, n_k) \\ g_2(n_1, n_2, \ldots, n_k) & \text{if } C_2(n_1, n_2, \ldots, n_k) \\ \cdots \\ g_m(n_1, n_2, \ldots, n_k) & \text{if } C_m(n_1, n_2, \ldots, n_k) \end{cases}$$

where (1) $g_1, g_2, \ldots, g_m$ are each primitive recursive k-ary functions; (2) $C_1, C_2, \ldots, C_m$ are each primitive recursive k-ary predicates; and (3) given any $n_1, n_2, \ldots, n_k$, exactly one of $C_1(n_1, n_2, \ldots, n_k)$, $C_2(n_1, n_2, \ldots, n_k), \ldots, C_m(n_1, n_2, \ldots, n_k)$ holds. In such a case, it can be seen that $f(n_1, n_2, \ldots, n_k)$ is itself a primitive recursive function. For, letting $\chi_{C_1}, \chi_{C_2}, \ldots,$ and χ_{C_m} be the (primitive recursive) characteristic functions of $C_1, C_2, \ldots, C_m$, respectively, we can write

$$f(\vec{n}) = g_1(\vec{n}) \cdot \chi_{C_1}(\vec{n}) + g_2(\vec{n}) \cdot \chi_{C_2}(\vec{n}) + \cdots + g_m(\vec{n}) \cdot \chi_{C_m}(\vec{n})$$

First, we note that the right-hand side here mentions only primitive recursive functions. Next, we note that by (3), for any $n_1, n_2, \ldots, n_k$, exactly one of the $\chi_{C_i}(\vec{n})$s is 1 and all of the others are 0. Let us suppose that it is $\chi_{C_4}(\vec{n})$ that is 1. This means that $C_4(\vec{n})$ holds, whereas $C_1(\vec{n}), C_2(\vec{n}), C_3(\vec{n}), C_5(\vec{n}), \ldots,$ $C_m(\vec{n})$ do not. It also means that $f(\vec{n}) = g_4(\vec{n}) \cdot \chi_{C_4}(\vec{n}) = g_4(\vec{n}) \cdot 1 = g_4(\vec{n})$, as required. (Why?) We note in passing that the g_i need not be distinct.

As a specific example of definition by cases, consider the following definition:

$$\alpha(n, m) =_{\text{def.}} \begin{cases} 0 & \text{if } m = 0 \\ 1 & \text{if } m = 1 \\ n & \text{otherwise} \end{cases}$$

We see that $\alpha(10, 0) = 0$, $\alpha(10, 1) = 1$, and that $\alpha(10, 2) = 10$. By the foregoing discussion, $\alpha(n, m)$ is a binary primitive recursive function. (We can also see this by noting that $\alpha(n, m) = \overline{sg}(\chi_{eq}(m, 1)) \cdot \overline{sg}(\chi_{eq}(m, 0)) \cdot n + \chi_{eq}(m, 1)$.)

Incidentally, the requirement at (3) that, given any k-tuple of natural numbers $n_1, n_2, \ldots, n_k$, exactly one of predicates $C_1(n_1, n_2, \ldots, n_k), C_2(n_1, n_2, \ldots, n_k), \ldots, C_m(n_1, n_2, \ldots, n_k)$ holds is usually described by saying that predicates $C_1(n_1, n_2, \ldots, n_k), C_2(n_1, n_2, \ldots, n_k), \ldots, C_m(n_1, n_2, \ldots, n_k)$ must be both *mutually exclusive* and *exhaustive*.

EXAMPLE 3.2.4 (The logical connectives) We next show that, given a fund of primitive recursive predicates, it is easy to obtain more primitive recursive predicates by applying logical operations. To begin, suppose that k-ary primitive recursive predicates $C_1(n_1, n_2, \ldots, n_k)$ and $C_2(n_1, n_2, \ldots, n_k)$ are given. We shall see that their logical conjunction $C_1(n_1, n_2, \ldots, n_k) \& C_2(n_1, n_2, \ldots, n_k)$ is primitive recursive as well. For suppose that χ_{C_1} and χ_{C_2} are the characteristic functions of C_1 and C_2, respectively. Then, where $\chi_{C_1 \& C_2}(n_1, n_2, \ldots, n_k)$ is the characteristic function of their conjunction, we can write

$$\chi_{C_1 \& C_2}(n) = \chi_{C_1}(n_1, n_2, \ldots, n_k) \cdot \chi_{C_2}(n_1, n_2, \ldots, n_k)$$

noting that the definiens—that is, the right-hand side here—is visually primitive recursive. But this means that predicate $C_1(n_1, n_2, \ldots, n_k) \& C_2(n_1, n_2, \ldots, n_k)$ is primitive recursive as well.

Continuing in this vein, suppose that predicate $C(n_1, n_2, \ldots, n_k)$ is primitive recursive, and let χ_C be its characteristic function. Then it is easy to see that $\neg C(n_1, n_2, \ldots, n_k)$ is primitive recursive as well. For, where $\chi_{\neg C}(n_1, n_2, \ldots, n_k)$ is the characteristic function of predicate $\neg C(n_1, n_2, \ldots, n_k)$, we can write

$$\chi_{\neg C}(n_1, n_2, \ldots, n_k) = \overline{sg}(\chi_C(n_1, n_2, \ldots, n_k))$$

which shows that $\neg C(n_1, n_2, \ldots, n_k)$ is primitive recursive as well. Moreover, the other logical operations may be defined ultimately in terms of conjunction and negation using

$$C_1(n_1, n_2, \ldots, n_k) \vee C_2(n_1, n_2, \ldots, n_k) \Leftrightarrow \neg(\neg C_1(n_1, n_2, \ldots, n_k) \& \neg C_1(n_1, n_2, \ldots, n_k))$$

$$C_1(n_1, n_2, \ldots, n_k) \to C_2(n_1, n_2, \ldots, n_k) \Leftrightarrow \neg C_1(n_1, n_2, \ldots, n_k) \vee C_2(n_1, n_2, \ldots, n_k)$$

$$C_1(n_1, n_2, \ldots, n_k) \leftrightarrow C_2(n_1, n_2, \ldots, n_k) \Leftrightarrow (C_1(n_1, n_2, \ldots, n_k) \& C_2(n_1, n_2, \ldots, n_k)) \vee (\neg C_1(n_1, n_2, \ldots, n_k)$$
$$\& \neg C_2(n_1, n_2, \ldots, n_k))$$

It follows that the logical operations corresponding to connectives $\vee$, $\to$, and $\leftrightarrow$, when applied to primitive recursive predicates, yield primitive recursive predicates (see Exercise 3.2.1). We conclude that the class of primitive recursive predicates is closed under the five logical operations corresponding to propositional connectives $\&$, $\neg$, $\vee$, $\to$, and $\leftrightarrow$.

EXAMPLE 3.2.5 (Bounded existential quantification) We next show that the class of primitive recursive predicates is closed under so-called *bounded existential quantification*. We write

$$(\exists i)_{\leq j} C(n_1, n_2, \ldots, n_k, i) \quad \text{or} \quad \exists i_{\leq j} C(n_1, n_2, \ldots, n_k, i) \quad \text{or} \quad \exists i \leq j[C(n_1, n_2, \ldots, n_k, i)]$$

as an abbreviation for $(\exists i)(i \leq j \,\&\, C(n_1, n_2, \ldots, n_k, i))$. Let us for the moment think of j as any constant—any fixed natural number. Thus letting $j = 2$, we have

$$(\exists i)_{\leq 2} C(n_1, n_2, \ldots, n_k, i) \quad \text{or} \quad (\exists i)(i \leq 2 \,\&\, C(n_1, n_2, \ldots, n_k, i)$$

We can show that if $C(n_1, n_2, \ldots, n_k, i)$ is a $(k + 1)$-ary primitive recursive predicate, then

$$(\exists i)_{\leq 2} C(n_1, n_2, \ldots, n_k, i)$$

is a k-ary primitive recursive predicate. To see this, note that we have

$$(\exists i)_{\leq 2} C(n_1, n_2, \ldots, n_k, i) \Leftrightarrow C(n_1, n_2, \ldots, n_k, 0) \vee C(n_1, n_2, \ldots, n_k, 1) \vee C(n_1, n_2, \ldots, n_k, 2)$$

But then the characteristic function of predicate $(\exists i)_{\leq 2} C(n_1, n_2, \ldots, n_k, i)$ may be written

$$sg(\chi_C(n_1, n_2, \ldots, n_k, 0) + \chi_C(n_1, n_2, \ldots, n_k, 1) + \chi_C(n_1, n_2, \ldots, n_k, 2))$$

and is visually primitive recursive. (See Exercise 3.1.8(c) for the definition of sg.) More generally, we may write

$$sg\left(\sum_{i=0}^{j} \chi_C(n_1, n_2, \ldots, n_k, i)\right) \tag{3.2.1}$$

for the characteristic function of k-ary predicate $(\exists i)_{\leq j} C(n_1, n_2, \ldots, n_k, i)$, where j is held fixed. We have shown in effect that, for any fixed j, (3.2.1) is a primitive recursive function of arguments $n_1, n_2, \ldots, n_k$. From this it follows that, for fixed j, $(\exists i)_{\leq j} C(n_1, n_2, \ldots, n_k, i)$ is a primitive recursive predicate in $n_1, n_2, \ldots, n_k$. But we can go farther. Namely, suppose that $(\exists i)_{\leq j} C(n_1, n_2, \ldots, n_k, i)$ is now taken to be a $(k + 1)$-ary predicate in $n_1, n_2, \ldots, n_k, j$. In that case also, it is a primitive recursive predicate provided that $C(n_1, n_2, \ldots, n_k, i)$ is primitive recursive. This is because, by Exercise 3.1.16, $\sum_{i=0}^{j} \chi_C(n_1, n_2, \ldots, n_k, i)$, and hence (3.2.1), is a primitive recursive function of arguments $n_1, n_2, \ldots, n_k, j$.

EXAMPLE 3.2.6 (Bounded universal quantification) We next show that the class of primitive recursive predicates is closed under *bounded universal quantification*. We write

$$(\forall i)_{\leq j} C(n_1, n_2, \ldots, n_k, i) \quad \text{or} \quad \forall i_{\leq j} C(n_1, n_2, \ldots, n_k, i) \quad \text{or} \quad \forall i \leq j[C(n_1, n_2, \ldots, n_k, i)]$$

as an abbreviation for $(\forall i)(i \leq j \rightarrow C(n_1, n_2, \ldots, n_k, i))$. Let us again think of j as any constant—any fixed natural number. Thus letting $j = 4$, we have

$$(\forall i)_{\leq 4} C(n_1, n_2, \ldots, n_k, i) \quad \text{or} \quad (\forall i)(i \leq 4 \rightarrow C(n_1, n_2, \ldots, n_k, i))$$

We can show that if $C(n_1, n_2, \ldots, n_k, i)$ is a $(k + 1)$-ary primitive recursive predicate, then

$$(\forall i)_{\leq 4} C(n_1, n_2, \ldots, n_k, i)$$

is a k-ary primitive recursive predicate. On analogy with Example 3.2.5, note that

$$(\forall i)_{\leq 4} C(n_1, n_2, \ldots, n_k, i) \Leftrightarrow C(n_1, n_2, \ldots, n_k, 0) \ \& \ C(n_1, n_2, \ldots, n_k, 1) \ \& \ C(n_1, n_2, \ldots, n_k, 2)$$
$$\& \ C(n_1, n_2, \ldots, n_k, 3) \ \& \ C(n_1, n_2, \ldots, n_k, 4)$$

It follows that the characteristic function of predicate $(\forall i)_{\leq 4} C(n_1, n_2, \ldots, n_k, i)$ may be written

$$\chi_C(n_1, n_2, \ldots, n_k, 0) \cdot \chi_C(n_1, n_2, \ldots, n_k, 1)$$
$$\cdot \chi_C(n_1, n_2, \ldots, n_k, 2) \cdot \chi_C(n_1, n_2, \ldots, n_k, 3) \cdot \chi_C(n_1, n_2, \ldots, n_k, 4)$$

and is hence visually primitive recursive. More generally, we may write

$$sg \left(\prod_{i=0}^{j} \chi_C(n_1, n_2, \ldots, n_k, i) \right) \tag{3.2.2}$$

for the characteristic function of k-ary predicate $(\forall i)_{\leq j} C(n_1, n_2, \ldots, n_k, i)$, where j is fixed. Apparently, for any fixed j, (3.2.2) is primitive recursive. We have shown that if $C(n_1, n_2, \ldots, n_k, i)$ is primitive recursive, then so is $(\forall i)_{\leq j} C(n_1, n_2, \ldots, n_k, i)$ for fixed j. In addition, however, $(\forall i)_{\leq j} C(n_1, n_2, \ldots, n_k, i)$ is a primitive recursive $(k+1)$-ary predicate in $n_1, n_2, \ldots, n_k, j$. (This time, see Exercise 3.1.18.)

EXAMPLE 3.2.7 The unary predicate $prime(n)$ is primitive recursive. To this end, we write

$$prime(n) \leftrightarrow (\forall i)_{\leq n} (\forall j)_{\leq n} [(i = 1 \ \& \ j = n) \vee (j = 1 \ \& \ i = n) \vee i \cdot j \neq n]$$

which says that for no $i, j \leq n$ is n the product of i and j unless one of i, j is equal to 1 and the other is n itself. By our earlier work, predicate $prime(n)$ is primitive recursive.

---

§3.3 The Partial Recursive Functions

We saw in Chapter 1 that one computational paradigm is that of function computation. Thus, the Turing machine model of computation proposes the identification of the class of computable functions with the class of Turing-computable functions. In this section we shall consider another proposal regarding the computable functions. This new proposal takes the form of a characterization of the so-called *partial recursive functions*. This characterization consists of defining the class of partial recursive functions to be the smallest class of number-theoretic functions containing certain basic (or "initial") functions and then closing under certain function-forming operations preserving effectiveness. If this approach sounds familiar, it is because it is the sort of thing that we did in §3.1 in defining the class of primitive recursive functions. This is not to say that the class of partial recursive functions coincides with the class of primitive recursive functions. Our point is only that the two classes are defined in a similar manner. We shall see that the class of primitive recursive functions fails to capture the notion of computable function.

Afterward, we shall go on to consider how the new notion of partial recursive function represents an attempt to overcome the deficiencies that lead to that failure.

We defined the primitive recursive functions to be the smallest class of number-theoretic functions that is closed under **Comp** and **Pr**. We also saw that all primitive recursive functions are total. It may also seem, given the plethora of examples, that every number-theoretic function must be primitive recursive. But, in fact, that is not the case, as is shown by the next theorem. In preparation for this theorem we digress briefly. By definition, every primitive recursive function can be described in the canonical way using the following symbols: $C_0^1, \ldots, succ, p_1^1, \ldots,$ **Comp**, **Pr**, (,), „, [,]. Thus we saw that the unary constant-1 function is **Comp**$[succ, C_0^1]$. (In fact, all functions that are primitive recursive will have many such descriptions [see Exercise 3.3.5]. But this multiplicity does not affect the point we are about to make.) Although absolutely all primitive recursive functions can be described using these symbols, let us focus for the moment on unary primitive recursive functions. First, it should be clear that the set of all well-formed strings (over our canonical alphabet) that denote unary functions is infinite. Let us imagine ordering this set of strings in some way—perhaps the shortest strings first and then the longer. For strings of equal length, let us order them lexicographically. The result is an enumeration $E_0, E_1, E_2,$ ... of canonical expressions for unary primitive recursive functions. This enumeration, in turn, induces an enumeration $f_0, f_1, f_2, \ldots$ of unary primitive recursive functions: Every primitive recursive function occurs in this enumeration—indeed, infinitely many times due to multiplicity. In short, we can agree that *the primitive recursive functions are effectively enumerable.*

With our next result we establish the inadequacy of the class of primitive recursive functions as an analysis of computability. We do so by presenting a unary function that is unquestionably computable but that is definitely not primitive recursive.

THEOREM 3.2: There exists a computable function that is total but not primitive recursive.[2]

PROOF (indirect). Let $f_0, f_1, f_2, \ldots$ be our enumeration of unary primitive recursive functions. Consider the function f^* defined by

$$f^*(n) =_{\text{def.}} f_n(n) + 1 \tag{3.3.1}$$

Note, first, that f^* is unary and total, since, for any n, f_n is primitive recursive and hence total. Suppose, now, f^* were itself primitive recursive. That implies that f^* occurs somewhere within our enumeration $f_0, f_1, f_2, \ldots$. Let us suppose that f^* is f_k for some particular k. Perversely, we ask for the value of f^* at argument k. Well, because f^* is just f_k by assumption, we have that $f^*(k)$ is just $f_k(k)$. But then, substituting k for n at (3.3.1), we have that $f^*(k)$ is $f_k(k) + 1$ as well, which is a contradiction. We conclude that f^* cannot be primitive recursive. Note further that f^* is intuitively computable in the sense that, given any argument n, one can in principle find the value of function f^* for argument n by doing the following: (1) find the nth function in the enumeration of primitive

---

[2]Our formulation of Theorem 3.2, although defensible from the point of view of perspicuity, can be criticized on other grounds. Namely, as it stands, Theorem 3.2 is not, strictly speaking, a mathematical proposition at all since it involves the informal, nonmathematical concept of *computable function*. A more rigorous formulation might run as follows: Given enumeration $f_0, f_1,$ $f_2, \ldots$ of unary primitive recursive functions, the unary and total function defined by $f^*(n) =_{\text{def.}} f_n(n) + 1$ is not primitive recursive. One would then go on to argue, extramathematically, that function $f^*(n)$ is nonetheless computable in an intuitive sense.

recursive functions f_0, f_1, f_2, ...; (2) determine the value of f_n for argument n; and (3) add 1 to that value. Incidentally, it is not hard to see that f^* is Turing-computable (see Exercise 3.3.10).

Q.E.D.

EXAMPLE 3.3.1 (Ackermann's Function) The unary function f^* of the proof of Theorem 3.2 is an example of a computable function that is not primitive recursive. However, that example assumes some enumeration of the primitive recursive functions that, although available in principle, is not feasible in practice. Consequently, example f^*, however well-defined, retains a certain necessary abstractness—a remoteness from experience. Before working out the details of some enumeration of the primitive recursive functions, one cannot say what the value of f^* is even for very small arguments. We now present yet another example of a computable number-theoretic function that is not primitive recursive. This time, though, our function, which happens to be binary, will be explicitly defined by a triple of recursion equations so that, with a little work, we can calculate its value at least for certain small argument pairs. This is not to say that the new example is transparent. In fact, the peculiar character of its definition will bring home once again just how difficult it is to describe (total) functions that are not primitive recursive. (However, once one has a single such function, it is a trivial matter to obtain others (see Exercise 3.3.4).)

What is referred to as Ackermann's function is defined by *double recursion* using recursion equations

$$\text{(i)} \quad H(0, m) \quad\quad = m + 1$$

$$\text{(ii)} \quad H(n + 1, 0) \quad = H(n, 1)$$

$$\text{(iii)} \quad H(n + 1, m + 1) = H(n, H(n + 1, m))$$

Just to see what Ackermann's function is like, let us evaluate $H(1,1)$.

$$H(1, 1) = H(0, H(1, 0)) \quad \text{by (iii)}$$

$$= H(0, H(0, 1)) \quad \text{by (ii)}$$

$$= H(0, 2) \quad\quad\quad \text{by (i)}$$

$$= 3 \quad\quad\quad\quad\quad \text{by (i)}$$

It is easy enough to see that this function is intuitively computable: Given a pair of arguments n and m, equations (i)–(iii) provide the necessary means of computing $H(n, m)$. It is also not hard to see that $H(n, m)$ is a total function (see Exercise 3.3.3). The interest of Ackermann's function stems from the fact that $H(n, m)$ is demonstrably not primitive recursive. (As to the proof, see preface.) On the other hand, it can be shown that Ackermann's function does belong to the more inclusive class of so-called *partial recursive functions*. Our goal in the remainder of this section is to define and investigate that larger class of functions.

To begin our study of the partial recursive functions, we introduce some new notation. In the future we shall write

$$\mu m[C(n_1, n_2, \ldots, n_k, m)]$$

to mean the least natural number m such that $C(n_1, n_2, \ldots, n_k, m)$ holds, where $C(n_1, n_2, \ldots, n_k, m)$

is any $(k+1)$-ary predicate. (Think of $n_1, n_2, \ldots, n_k$ as fixed.) In particular, we write

$$\mu m[f(n_1, n_2, \ldots, n_k, m) = 0]$$

to mean the least natural number m such that $f(\vec{n}, m)$ is equal to 0, where $f(\vec{n}, m)$ is any $(k+1)$-ary number-theoretic function. The Greek letter μ followed by a number variable is referred to as the *least-number operator*. We see that the semantics of the least-number operator itself are very simple.

We now introduce a new function-forming operation, which we denote **Mn**.

DEFINITION 3.6 (Minimization): Suppose that function $f: \mathcal{N}^{k+1} \to \mathcal{N}$ with $k \geq 0$ is given. We write **Mn**$[f]$ for the function $g: \mathcal{N}^k \to \mathcal{N}$ defined as

(Schema C) $g(n_1, n_2, \ldots, n_k) = \mu m[f(n_1, n_2, \ldots, n_k, m) = 0$ and such that,

for all $j < m$, $f(n_1, n_2, \ldots, n_k, j)$ is defined and $\neq 0]$

A couple of examples will be useful. First, suppose that k is 1, and that we have

$$f(3, 0) = 7 \qquad f(3, 4) = 9 \qquad f(3, 8) = 4$$
$$f(3, 1) = 4 \qquad f(3, 5) = 0 \qquad f(3, 9) = 4$$
$$f(3, 2) = 4 \qquad f(3, 6) = 4 \qquad f(3, 10) = 4$$
$$f(3, 3) = 2 \qquad f(3, 7) = 4 \qquad \cdots$$

Then $g(3) = $ **Mn**$[f](3) = \mu m[f(3, m) = 0$ and such that, for all $j < m$, $f(3, j)$ is defined and $\neq 0] = 5$.

On other hand, if we have that

$$f(3, 0) = 7 \qquad\qquad f(3, 3) = 2 \qquad f(3, 6) = 4$$
$$f(3, 1) \text{ is undefined} \qquad f(3, 4) = 9 \qquad f(3, 7) = 4$$
$$f(3, 2) = 4 \qquad\qquad f(3, 5) = 0 \qquad f(3, 8) = 4$$
$$\cdots$$

then, in this case, $\mu m[f(3, m) = 0] = 5$ but $g(3) = $ **Mn**$[f](3)$ is undefined.

Finally, if

$$f(3, 0) = 7 \qquad f(3, 3) = 5 \qquad f(3, 6) = 7$$
$$f(3, 1) = 5 \qquad f(3, 4) = 7 \qquad f(3, 7) = 5$$
$$f(3, 2) = 7 \qquad f(3, 5) = 5 \qquad f(3, 8) = 7$$
$$\cdots$$

so that $f(3, m)$ is always either 7 or 5 and thus never equal to 0, then, in this case, $g(3) = $ **Mn**$[f](3)$ is again undefined.

Note that the semantics of the minimization operator **Mn** are related to, but do not coincide with, the semantics of the least-number operator. If function $f(\vec{n}, m)$ just happens to be total, then $\mathbf{Mn}[f](\vec{n})$ is just the function described by "the least number m such that $f(\vec{n}, m) = 0$." However, only in these special circumstances does $\mathbf{Mn}[f]$ mean anything quite so simple as that. In the general case, its semantics are a bit more complicated. We give one more example and make an important remark.

EXAMPLE 3.3.2 Suppose that $f: \mathcal{N}^2 \to \mathcal{N}$ has the following values:

$f(0,0) = 6$	$f(1,0) = 8$	$f(2,0) = 3$	$f(3,0) = 9$	$f(4,0) = 6$
$f(0,1) = 4$	$f(1,1) = 8$	$f(2,1) = 1$	$f(3,1) = 6$	$f(4,1) = 6$
$f(0,2) = 6$	$f(1,2) = 6$	$f(2,2) = 6$	$f(3,2) = 4$	$f(4,2) = 6$
$f(0,3) = 0$	$f(1,3) = 6$	$f(2,3)$ is undefined	$f(3,3) = 6$	$f(4,3) = 6$
$f(0,4) = 6$	$f(1,4) = 5$	$f(2,4) = 6$	$f(3,4) = 0$	$f(4,4) = 6$
$f(0,5) = 6$	$f(1,5) = 0$	$f(2,5) = 0$	$f(3,5) = 6$	$f(4,5) = 6$
$\cdots$	$\cdots$	$\cdots$	$\cdots$	with $f(4, m) = 6$ for all m

Hence, we have $g(0) = \mathbf{Mn}[f](0) = 3$, $g(1) = \mathbf{Mn}[f](1) = 5$, $g(2) = \mathbf{Mn}[f](2)$ is undefined, $g(3) = \mathbf{Mn}[f](3) = 4$, and $g(4) = \mathbf{Mn}[f](4)$ is again undefined. Even if we amend f so that $f(2,3) = 37$ and assume that $f(n, m)$ is defined for all n and m, $\mathbf{Mn}[f](n) = g(n)$ will nonetheless be *partial* since it will be undefined for argument 4.

The preceding example illustrates clearly our

REMARK 3.3.1: The result of applying minimization operator **Mn** to a total function may be a partial function. That is, $\mathbf{Mn}[f]$ may be undefined for certain arguments even if f itself is total.

In §3.1 we illustrated function-forming operations **Comp** and **Pr** by describing two classroom scenarios. It is easy to do this for **Mn** as well. Only a single student is required. Assuming that the student has the resources and knowledge necessary to compute $(k + 1)$-ary function f, we go on to show how he can now be trained to compute k-ary function $g = \mathbf{Mn}[f]$. Provided by the instructor with k-tuple $n_1, n_2, \ldots, n_k$ as input, he proceeds to compute $f(n_1, n_2, \ldots, n_k, 0)$ and, assuming that the computation terminates, then compares that value with 0. If the value is 0, then he reports $g(n_1, n_2, \ldots, n_k) = 0$. Otherwise, he computes $f(n_1, n_2, \ldots, n_k, 1)$. Again, if and when that computation terminates, value $f(n_1, n_2, \ldots, n_k, 1)$ is compared with 0 and, if equality holds, then $g(n_1, n_2, \ldots, n_k) = 1$ is reported. Otherwise, he goes on to compute $f(n_1, n_2, \ldots, n_k, 2)$, compare that value with 0, and, if equality holds, report the value $g(n_1, n_2, \ldots, n_k) = 2$. If, for some m, the computation of $f(n_1, n_2, \ldots, n_k, m)$ fails to terminate, then the student will spend the rest of time engaged in computing $f(n_1, n_2, \ldots, n_k, m)$ without every reporting value $g(n_1, n_2, \ldots, n_k)$. Similarly, if each of the computations $f(n_1, n_2, \ldots, n_k, 0)$, $f(n_1, n_2, \ldots, n_k, 1)$, $f(n_1, n_2, \ldots, n_k, 2)$, $\ldots$, terminates but none ever equals 0, then, in this case also, our student continues computing forever without ever reporting a value for $g(n_1, n_2, \ldots, n_k)$.

Now we continue our excursion into the elements of recursion theory by defining the important class of functions mentioned in Example 3.3.1. This class of functions is absolutely central to the theory of computability.

DEFINITION 3.7: The class of *partial recursive functions* is the smallest class containing all initial functions and closed under the operations **Comp**, **Pr**, and **Mn**.

The following equivalent recursive definition of the class of partial recursive functions will prove useful in the next section.

DEFINITION 3.7 (alternative formulation): We define the class of *partial recursive functions* as follows:

(i) Every initial function is partial recursive. That is, the successor function *succ*, the k-ary constant-0 functions C_0^k for arbitrary $k \geq 0$, as well as all projection functions p_j^k for $k \geq 1$, $1 \leq j \leq k$, are all partial recursive.

   function with $m \geq 1$, then **Comp**$[f, g_1, \ldots, g_m]$ is partial recursive.

(iii) If f is a k-ary partial recursive function and g is a $(k+2)$-ary partial recursive function with $k \geq 0$, then **Pr**$[f, g]$ is partial recursive.

(iv) If f is a $(k+1)$-ary partial recursive function with $k \geq 0$, then **Mn**$[f]$ is partial recursive.

(v) Nothing else is a partial recursive function.

The foregoing discussion explains why this class is so-named. Also, it is obvious from our definition that every primitive recursive function is partial recursive. We introduce the term *recursive* for those partial recursive functions that happen to be total.

DEFINITION 3.8(a): Any partial recursive function that is total is referred to simply as a *recursive function*.

Note, in connection with Definition 3.8a, that since any characteristic function $\chi_C(n)$ is of necessity total, $\chi_C(n)$'s being partial recursive implies that $\chi_C(n)$ is recursive. This reflection motivates the following terminology.

DEFINITION 3.8(b): A number-theoretic predicate whose characteristic function is partial recursive (and hence recursive) will be referred to as a *recursive predicate*.

We note immediately that any primitive recursive predicate, as defined in Definition 3.5, is recursive since, by Theorem 3.1, every primitive recursive function is recursive. On the other hand, Ackermann's function is an example of a recursive function that is not primitive recursive. (Again, we have not presented the required proofs.) The world of number-theoretic functions can now be pictured as in the Venn diagram of Figure 3.3.1.

EXAMPLE 3.3.3 It was mentioned earlier that Ackermann's function is (partial) recursive, although this is hardly easy to see. For a simpler example of a partial recursive function that is not primitive recursive, consider *div*(n, m), whereby integer division is intended. We note that this function is not defined for all pairs—m cannot be 0—and hence is not primitive recursive. But it is partial recursive since we can write

$$div(n, m) = \mu t[succ(n) \dot{-} (t \cdot m + m) = 0] \tag{3.3.2}$$

That the right-hand side here behaves as required can be seen, for the case $n = 19$ and $m = 7$, by consulting Table 3.3.1. Apparently $\mu t[succ(n) \dot{-} (t \cdot m + m) = 0]$ is 2 for the case $n = 19$ and $m = 7$, so that (3.3.2) appears to hold, given that 19 *div* 7 is indeed 2.

It is instructive to show that (3.3.2) can be made to conform to Schema C. Let us write $f(n, m, t)$ for the ternary

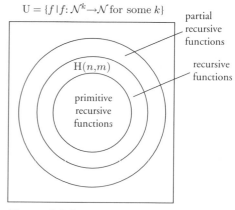

$U = \{f \mid f : \mathcal{N}^k \to \mathcal{N} \text{ for some } k\}$

partial recursive functions

recursive functions

$H(n,m)$

primitive recursive functions

Table 3.3.1

Value of t	Value of $succ(n) \dot{-} (t \cdot m + m))$
0	$20 \dot{-} (0 \cdot 7 + 7) = 13$
1	$20 \dot{-} (1 \cdot 7 + 7) = 6$
2	$20 \dot{-} (2 \cdot 7 + 7) = 0$
3	$20 \dot{-} (3 \cdot 7 + 7) = 0$
4	$20 \dot{-} (4 \cdot 7 + 7) = 0$
...	...

Figure 3.3.1

primitive recursive, and hence partial recursive, function $succ(n) \dot{-} (t \cdot m + m)$. Then (3.3.2) may be rewritten as $div(n, m) = \mu t[f(n, m, t) = 0]$, so that $div(n, m)$ is none other than **Mn**$[f]$ and hence partial recursive by Definition 3.7(iv). Finally, we remind the reader that we shall frequently write infix n *div* m, as was already done in Exercise 3.2.4(a) and elsewhere.

In what follows, we shall not take such pains to demonstrate that a function is partial recursive but shall be satisfied to merely present an expression such as (3.3.2), whose right-hand side mentions only functions previously shown to be partial recursive as well as the μ-operator. By analogy with our method of proceeding in the case of primitive recursive functions, we shall speak of such expressions, as well as the functions defined by them, as *visually* or *prima facie partial recursive*. Again, this is a matter of convenience. As in the case of Example 3.3.3, with a little work we can invariably show that such function definitions are strictly in accordance with Schemata A, B, and C and are thereby partial recursive by Definition 3.7. In particular, we note that many of our arguments with respect to the primitive recursive functions and predicates carry over to the partial recursive functions and predicates.

- By analogy with Example 3.2.3, if a function f is definable by cases from partial recursive functions together with mutually exclusive and exhaustive recursive predicates, then f is itself partial recursive (see Exercise 3.7.9).

- By analogy with Examples 3.2.4 through 3.2.6, the class of recursive predicates is closed under the five logical connectives as well as bounded universal and existential quantification (see Exercises 3.7.10 and 3.7.11).

EXAMPLE 3.3.4 Having seen that $div(n, m)$ is partial recursive, it is easy to show that binary function

$$mod(n, m) =_{\text{def.}} \text{the remainder that results when } n \text{ is divided by } m$$

is also partial recursive, since we have $mod(n, m) = n \dot{-} [div(n, m) \cdot m]$. So $mod(n, m)$ is visually partial recursive. (Again, we frequently use infix $n \bmod m$.)

With regard to the manner in which partial recursive functions will be introduced informally in the following pages, we comment specifically upon our use of the least-number operator. Let $C(n_1, n_2, \ldots, n_k, j)$ be any $(k + 1)$-ary recursive predicate. We claim that

$$\mu j[C(n_1, n_2, \ldots, n_k, j)] \tag{3.3.3}$$

is then a k-ary partial recursive function. Note, however, that (3.3.3) will not in general be of the special form required by Schema C of Definition 3.6. So how is our claim to be justified? Well, consider that the denotation of (3.3.3) is identical to that of

$$\mu j[\overline{sg}(\chi_C(n_1, n_2, \ldots, n_k, j)) = 0] \tag{3.3.4}$$

and (3.3.4) is of the form required. So, in what follows, we shall feel free to write the likes of (3.3.3) and assert on that basis that the function so-defined is (prima facie) partial recursive.

EXAMPLE 3.3.5 For any constant j, the (unary) number-theoretic function

$$\mu i_{\leq j}[\textbf{\textit{C}}(\textbf{\textit{n}}, \textbf{\textit{i}})] = \begin{cases} \text{the least } i \leq j \text{ such that } C(n, i) \text{ holds if there exists such an } i \\ 0 \quad \text{otherwise} \end{cases}$$

is (primitive) recursive whenever predicate $C(n, i)$ is a (primitive) recursive predicate. To see this, note that

$$\mu i_{\leq j}[\textbf{\textit{C}}(\textbf{\textit{n}}, \textbf{\textit{i}})] = \left[\sum_{m=0}^{j} \left[\prod_{k=0}^{m} (\chi_{\neg C}(n, k)) \right] \right] \bmod (j + 1)$$

Our earlier work and Example 3.3.4 shows that the right-hand side here, and hence $\mu i_{\leq j}[C(n,i)]$, is partial recursive. Moreover, since $\mu i_{\leq j}[C(n,i)]$ is total, we may conclude that it is (primitive) recursive (see also Exercise 3.2.4).

$$\begin{aligned} = \big[&\chi_{\neg C}(n, 0) \\ &+ [\chi_{\neg C}(n, 0) \cdot \chi_{\neg C}(n, 1)] \\ &+ [\chi_{\neg C}(n, 0) \cdot \chi_{\neg C}(n, 1) \cdot \chi_{\neg C}(n, 2)] \\ &+ [\chi_{\neg C}(n, 0) \cdot \chi_{\neg C}(n, 1) \cdot \chi_{\neg C}(n, 2) \cdot \chi_{\neg C}(n, 3)] \\ &+ \cdots \\ &+ [\chi_{\neg C}(n, 0) \cdot \chi_{\neg C}(n, 1) \cdot \cdots \cdot (\chi_{\neg C}(n, j)] \big] \bmod (j + 1) \end{aligned} \tag{3.3.5}$$

Note that if the least $i \leq j$ such that $C(n, i)$ holds happens to be 3, then the first three products at (3.3.5) will each be equal to 1 while all later products will be 0. On the other hand, if there exists no

$i \leq j$ such that $C(n, i)$, then all $j + 1$ products at (3.3.5) will be 1. Their sum will then be $j + 1$, and $(j + 1) \bmod (j + 1)$ is 0 as required.

Moreover, if we replace the constant bound j by any partial recursive function f in n, then the result is yet partial recursive. To see this, note that the only change within (3.3.5) will be in the last line, which now becomes

$$+[\chi_{\neg C}(n, 0) \cdot \chi_{\neg C}(n, 1) \cdots (\chi_{\neg C}(n, f(n)))]\} \bmod (f(n) + 1)$$

which is again, prima facie, partial recursive.

The next two examples introduce functions—both primitive recursive—that will be needed in §3.4.

EXAMPLE 3.3.6 Let us define $\pi(n)$ to be the nth prime, where 2 is the 0th prime, 3 is the 1st prime, and so on. In other words, by definition $\pi(0) = 2$, $\pi(1) = 3$, and so on. We show that $\pi(n)$ is primitive recursive by writing

$$\pi(0) = 2$$

$$\pi(m + 1) = \mu i_{\leq \pi(m)! + 1}[\pi(m) < i \ \& \ prime(i)]$$

The factorial function simply supplies the needed bound on the μ-operator—many other (primitive recursive) functions could serve here. Essentially, the second clause here says only that the $(m + 1)$th prime is the least prime number that exceeds the mth prime. It will be convenient in what follows to sometimes write π_n for $\pi(n)$. That is, $\pi_0 = 2$, $\pi_1 = 3$, $\pi_2 = 5$, and so on.

EXAMPLE 3.3.7 Let binary number-theoretic function $(n)_i$ be defined as follows.

$$(n)_i = \begin{cases} \text{the exponent of the } i\text{th prime in the prime decomposition of } n \text{ if } n > 0 \\ 0 \quad \text{for all } i \geq 0 \text{ if } n = 0 \end{cases}$$

As an example, we have $(3402)_1 = 5$, $(3402)_0 = 1$, and $(3402)_j = 0$ for all $j \geq 4$, since $3402 = 2^1 \cdot 3^5 \cdot 5^0 \cdot 7^1$. (Recall that 2 is the 0th prime.) We shall sometimes write $extr_i(n)$ for $(n)_i$. This *extraction* function can be shown to be partial recursive using Examples 3.3.5 and 3.3.6 since

$$(n)_m = \mu i_{\leq n}[\pi_m^i | n \ \& \ \neg \pi_m^{i+1} | n]$$

where ternary predicate $\pi_m^i | n$ is (primitive) recursive (see Exercise 3.2.3). In conjunction with this example, we note that if j is of the form $2^n \cdot 3^m \cdot 5^k$, then we have

$$2^{(j)_0} \cdot 3^{(j)_1} \cdot 5^{(j)_2} = j \tag{3.3.6}$$

In Definition 1.7 of §1.5 we defined the class of Turing-computable number-theoretic functions. It is natural to ask where the class of Turing-computable functions is to be situated within the Venn diagram of Figure 3.3.1. We take up this important question in the next section.

§3.4 The Class of Partial Recursive Functions Is Identical to the Class of Turing-Computable Functions

We now present what is certainly the central result of this chapter—indeed, arguably the central result of the entire theory of computability. For we shall be able to prove a very surprising result: The class of Turing-computable functions coincides with the class of partial recursive functions.

THEOREM 3.3: A number-theoretic function is partial recursive if and only if it is Turing-computable.

We first prove Theorem 3.3 in the forward direction. This is not really too difficult.

THEOREM 3.3(a): If number-theoretic function h is partial recursive, then h is Turing-computable.

PROOF Our proof is by induction on the complexity of h—that is, by induction on the complexity of some canonical expression for h. Hence we consider four cases, one for each of the clauses (i)–(iv) in Definition 3.7. In Cases (ii)–(iv) we shall assume that a Turing-machine that computes a number-theoretic function f never halts when started scanning the representation of a k-tuple of arguments $n_1, \ldots, n_k$ for which f is undefined. We are justified in making this assumption by the solution to Exercise 2.10.8(b). We shall refer to the Nonhalting Assumption in the discussion that follows.

    Case (i) We suppose that h is an initial function. This case is in turn subdivided into three subcases.

        Subcase (i)(a) Suppose that h is the successor function. Then the Turing machine of Figure 3.4.1(a) is easily seen to compute h. Hence h is Turing-computable.

        Subcase (i)(b) We need to see that C_0^k is Turing-computable for arbitrary $k \geq 0$. First, suppose that $k = 0$—that is, that h is the 0-ary constant-0 function C_0^0. Then the Turing machine of Figure 3.4.1(b) shows this function to be Turing-computable. On the other hand, suppose that h is the unary constant-0 function C_0^1. Then the Turing machine of Figure 3.4.1(c) shows h to be Turing-computable. Moreover, it is easy enough to see that all of the other constant-0 functions are Turing-computable: C_0^k is computed by a machine that erases exactly k groups of *1*s off to the right, writes a single *1*, and then halts.

        Subcase (i)(c) Suppose that h is a projection functions p_j^k for some $k \geq 1$ and $1 \leq j \leq k$. The schematic transition diagram of Figure 3.4.1(d) shows that h is Turing-computable in this case as well. Thus we see that every projection function is Turing-computable.

    Case (ii) Suppose that h is **Comp**$[f, g_1, \ldots, g_m]$, where f is an m-ary partial recursive function and $g_1, \ldots, g_m$ are k-ary partial recursive functions. We assume as induction hypothesis that f and $g_1, \ldots, g_m$ are all Turing-computable functions. In particular, we shall further assume the

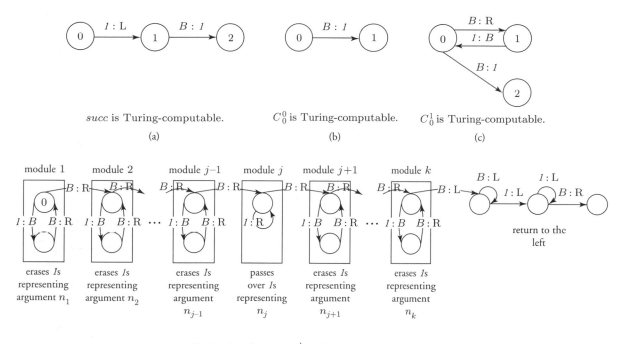

$succ$ is Turing-computable.

(a)

C_0^0 is Turing-computable.

(b)

C_0^1 is Turing-computable.

(c)

Projection function p_j^k is Turing-computable.

(d)

Figure 3.4.1

availability of single-tape Turing machines $M_f, M_{g_1}, \ldots, M_{g_m}$, computing $f, g_1, \ldots, g_m$, respectively. What follows is a rough sketch of an $(m + 2)$-tape Turing machine $M_{\textbf{Comp}}$ that computes $h = \textbf{Comp}[f, g_1, \ldots, g_m]$. We assume that, initially, h's arguments $n_1, \ldots, n_k$ appear on its input tape with all other tapes blank. Of course, h may or may not be defined for arguments $n_1, \ldots, n_k$. Let us assume first that $h(n_1, \ldots, n_k)$ is defined. In that case, $M_{\textbf{Comp}}$ starts by copying all k arguments onto each of worktape$_1$ through worktape$_m$ (see Figure 3.4.2(a)). $M_{\textbf{Comp}}$ now simulates, in sequence, the operations of $M_{g_1}, \ldots, M_{g_m}$ on worktape$_1, \ldots,$worktape$_m$, respectively. By assumption, each of these m simulations eventually comes to a halt with the corresponding worktape in a value-representing configuration. So $M_{\textbf{Comp}}$ finds itself with values $g_1(n_1, \ldots, n_k), \ldots, g_m(n_1, \ldots, n_k)$ on worktape$_1, \ldots,$ worktape$_m$, respectively (see Figure 3.4.2(b)). $M_{\textbf{Comp}}$ next arranges all m values, in order and separated by single blanks, on worktape$_1$ (see Figure 3.4.2(c)). Finally, $M_{\textbf{Comp}}$ simulates M_f on worktape$_1$. By assumption, this simulation also terminates with worktape$_1$ in a value-representing configuration: worktape$_1$'s read/write head will be scanning the leftmost 1 in a representation of $f(g_1(n_1, \ldots, n_k), g_2(n_1, \ldots, n_k), \ldots, g_m(n_1, \ldots, n_k)) = h(n_1, \ldots, n_k)$. That is, $M_{\textbf{Comp}}$ will have computed the value of h for arguments $n_1, \ldots, n_k$. It has only to copy this value from worktape$_1$ to its output tape.

We must yet consider the possibility that $h(n_1, \ldots, n_k) = f(g_1(n_1, \ldots, n_k), g_2(n_1, \ldots, n_k), \ldots, g_m(n_1, \ldots, n_k))$ is undefined. If so, then this is because either (1) one of $g_1, \ldots, g_m$ is undefined for arguments $n_1, \ldots, n_k$ or (2) f is undefined for arguments $g_1(n_1, \ldots, n_k), g_2(n_1, \ldots, n_k), \ldots, g_m(n_1, \ldots, n_k)$. If (1), then by the Nonhalting Assumption at least one of the mentioned simulations

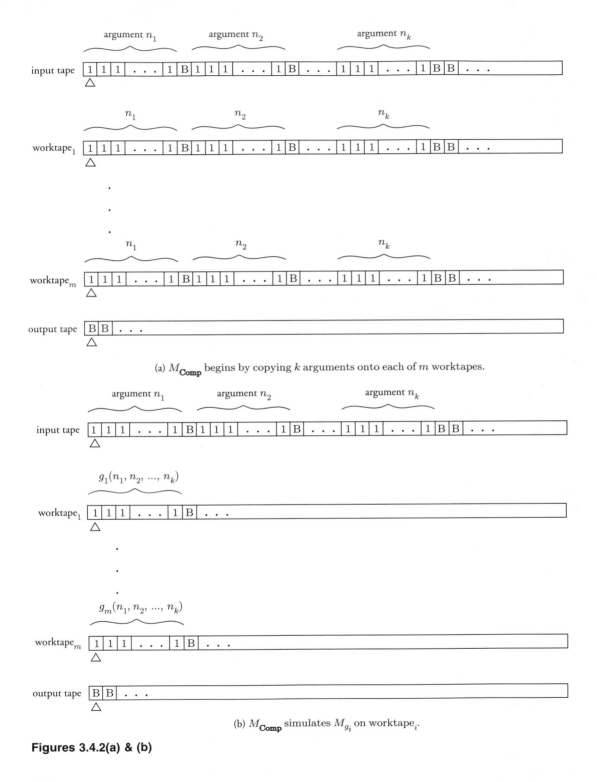

(a) $M_{\mathbf{Comp}}$ begins by copying k arguments onto each of m worktapes.

(b) $M_{\mathbf{Comp}}$ simulates M_{g_i} on worktape$_i$.

Figures 3.4.2(a) & (b)

(c) $M_{\textbf{Comp}}$ simulates M_f on worktape$_1$.

Figure 3.4.2(c)

of $M_{g_1}, \ldots, M_{g_m}$ fails to halt. If (2), then we can similarly assume that the simulation of M_f fails to halt. Whichever is the case, it should be clear enough that $M_{\textbf{Comp}}$ will likewise fail to halt so that $M_{\textbf{Comp}}$ behaves as required when h is undefined for arguments $n_1, \ldots, n_k$.

   Case (iii) Suppose that h is $\textbf{Pr}[f, g]$, where f is a k-ary partial recursive function and g is a $(k+2)$-ary partial recursive function. By induction hypothesis, we may assume that both f and g are Turing-computable. Let M_f and M_g be single-tape Turing machines that compute f and g, respectively. We sketch the operation of a five-tape Turing machine $M_{\textbf{Pr}}$ that computes h by a process of iteration. First, suppose that, initially, the $k + 1$ arguments $n_1, \ldots, n_k, 0$ are represented on $M_{\textbf{Pr}}$'s input tape, and assume that h is defined for these $k + 1$ arguments. In that case, $M_{\textbf{Pr}}$ will copy arguments $n_1, \ldots, n_k$ only onto worktape$_1$ and then simulate the operation of M_f on worktape$_1$. By assumption, $M_{\textbf{Pr}}$'s simulation of M_f will eventually halt in a value-representing configuration, at which point $M_{\textbf{Pr}}$ has only to copy the contents of worktape$_1$ representing $h(n_1, \ldots, n_k, 0) = f(n_1, \ldots, n_k)$ onto its output tape before halting. Suppose, on the other hand, that arguments $n_1, \ldots, n_k, m + 1$ are represented on $M_{\textbf{Pr}}$'s input tape, and assume that h happens to be defined for these $k + 1$ arguments. In that case, $M_{\textbf{Pr}}$ will copy arguments $n_1, \ldots, n_k$ only onto worktape$_1$ and then simulate the operation of M_f on worktape$_1$. Again, this simulation of M_f will eventually halt in a value-representing configuration, at which point $M_{\textbf{Pr}}$ writes a single *1* on worktape$_3$—indicating that iteration 0 has been completed—and copies several items onto worktape$_2$ in the following order:

(1) Arguments $n_1, \ldots, n_k$ only are copied from the input tape.

(2) The entire contents of worktape$_3$—in the present case a single *1*—are copied.

(3) The contents of worktape$_1$, currently representing $h(n_1, \ldots, n_k, 0) = f(n_1, \ldots, n_k)$, are copied (see Figure 3.4.3(a)).

$M_{\mathbf{Pr}}$ now simulates the operation of M_g on its worktape$_2$, thereby obtaining a representation of $h(n_1, \ldots, n_k, 1)$ on that tape. This value is now copied onto worktape$_1$ and the representation on worktape$_3$ is incremented by 1. The current contents of worktape$_2$ are now overwritten as follows:

(i) Arguments $n_1, \ldots, n_k$ only are copied from the input tape.

(ii) The entire contents of worktape$_3$—in the present case a representation of 1—are copied.

(iii) The contents of worktape$_1$, currently representing $h(n_1, \ldots, n_k, 1) = f(g(n_1, \ldots, n_k, 0, h(n_1, \ldots, n_k, 0))$, are copied (see Figure 3.4.3(b)).

$M_{\mathbf{Pr}}$ now simulates the operation of M_g on worktape$_2$, thereby obtaining a representation of $h(n_1, \ldots, n_k, 2)$ on that tape. This process of copying from input tape, worktape$_3$, and worktape$_1$ onto worktape$_2$ and then simulating M_g on the latter is iterated until the representation on worktape$_3$ exceeds the rightmost argument on the input tape. ($M_{\mathbf{Pr}}$ must make a comparison after each iteration.) At that point, the representation on worktape$_2$ is none other than $h(n_1, \ldots, n_k, m + 1)$.

It is easy enough to see that, by the Nonhalting Assumption again, $M_{\mathbf{Pr}}$ will behave appropriately if h happens to be undefined for the arguments appearing on its input tape.

Case (iv) Suppose that h is $\mathbf{Mn}[f]$, where f is a $(k+1)$-ary partial recursive function. By induction hypothesis, f is Turing-computable. Let M_f be a single-tape Turing machine that computes f. We sketch the operation of a four-tape Turing machine $M_{\mathbf{Mn}}$ that computes h. Suppose that, initially, representations of arguments $n_1, \ldots, n_k$ appear on $M_{\mathbf{Mn}}$'s input tape, and suppose that $h(n_1, \ldots, n_k)$ is defined. Then $M_{\mathbf{Mn}}$ first writes a single *1* representing 0 onto worktape$_1$ and copies arguments $n_1, \ldots, n_k$ followed by the single *1* from worktape$_1$ onto worktape$_2$ (see Figure 3.4.4). $M_{\mathbf{Mn}}$ next simulates the operation of M_f on the contents of worktape$_2$. By assumption, this simulation will eventually terminate, at which point $M_{\mathbf{Mn}}$ compares the value represented on worktape$_2$, which is $f(n_1, \ldots, n_k, 0)$, with 0. If equality obtains, then the contents of worktape$_1$ are copied onto the output tape and $M_{\mathbf{Mn}}$ halts. Otherwise, the representation on worktape$_1$ is incremented and the argument representations on the input tape are recopied onto worktape$_2$ followed by the representation of 1 on worktape$_1$. The operation of M_f is again simulated on worktape$_2$ and the result, which is just $f(n_1, \ldots, n_k, 1)$, is compared with 0. If equality holds, the two *1*s from worktape$_1$ are copied onto the output tape and $M_{\mathbf{Mn}}$ halts. Otherwise, the described incrementing/copying/simulating/comparing procedure is repeated. Ultimately, $M_{\mathbf{Mn}}$ will terminate with a representation of $h(n_1, \ldots, n_k)$ on its output tape.

On the other hand, if h happens to be undefined for the arguments $n_1, \ldots, n_k$ initially represented on its input tape, then this must be because $\mu m[f(n_1, \ldots, n_k, m) = 0$ and such that . . .] is undefined. But then, by the Nonhalting Assumption, that means that either (1) one of the simulations of M_f fails to halt or (2) the simulations all halt with nonzero result. In either case, $M_{\mathbf{Mn}}$ will also fail to halt. This is to say that $M_{\mathbf{Mn}}$ behaves appropriately when $h(n_1, \ldots, n_k)$ is undefined.   Q.E.D.

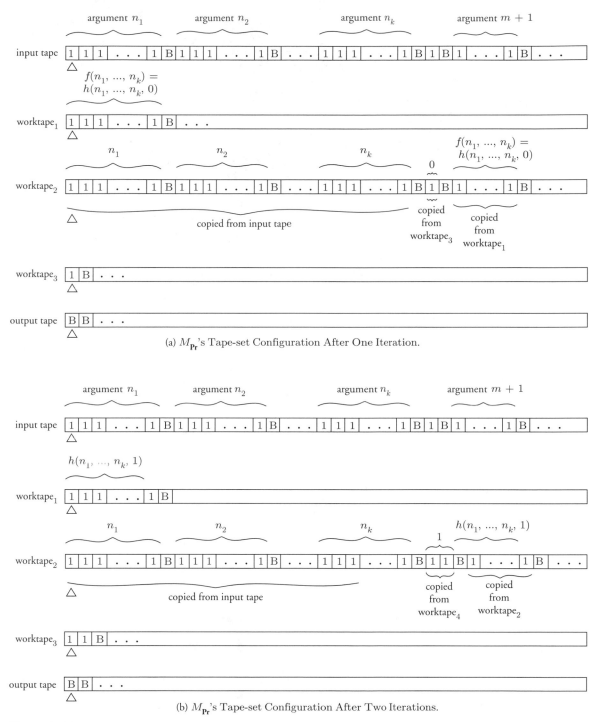

(a) $M_{\mathbf{Pr}}$'s Tape-set Configuration After One Iteration.

(b) $M_{\mathbf{Pr}}$'s Tape-set Configuration After Two Iterations.

Figure 3.4.3

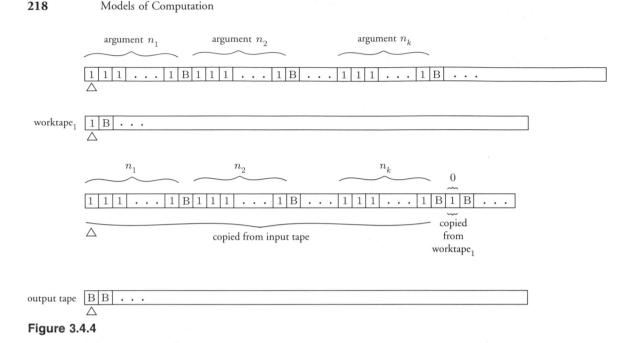

Figure 3.4.4

We now show that the reverse direction in Theorem 3.3 holds as well. That is, we must show that any Turing-computable function is partial recursive. This is a greater challenge. Our proof will consist of showing that a number of functions and predicates are either primitive recursive or partial recursive. (Of course, any function or predicate that is primitive recursive is also partial recursive.)

THEOREM 3.3(b): Every Turing-computable function is partial recursive.

PROOF Let f be a Turing-computable function. For the sake of simplicity, we shall assume that f is a unary function. We saw in §2.1 that we may assume without loss of generality that f is computed by a Turing machine M with one-way-infinite tape. As usual, we assume the presence of left endmarker λ.

(1) We adopt the following standard encoding of $\Gamma_M \cup \{B\} = \{a_0, a_1, \ldots, a_{k-1}\}$, where Γ_M is M's tape alphabet. We associate a natural number with each member of $\Gamma_M \cup \{B\}$. This number might as well be its index in the enumeration $a_0, a_1, \ldots, a_{k-1}$. As before, we let a_0 be B so that the blank is encoded as **0**. It will also prove convenient to assume that symbol λ is a_{k-2} and that symbol 1 is a_{k-1} so that symbols λ and 1 are encoded as $k-2$ and $k-1$, respectively.

(2) Next, we encode the contents of M's entire tape—but excluding left endmarker λ—as the (value of) a certain base-k numeral. As an example, suppose that Γ_M is just $\{*, \lambda, 1\}$ so that $B, *, \lambda,$ and 1 are associated with codes 0, 1, 2, and 3, respectively, as described in (1). Tape contents $\lambda \mathbf{\textit{111}} * B\mathbf{\textit{11}}BBBBBBBBBBBBBBB \ldots$ are now encoded as the base-4 numeral $\ldots 000000000003301333$. Note that the *rightmost* digits of this numeral correspond to the contents of the *leftmost* squares on the tape. In any case, this base-4 numeral denotes the natural number.

$$\underbrace{\cdots + (0 \cdot 4^8) + (0 \cdot 4^7)}_{\text{All these terms vanish.}} + (\mathbf{3} \cdot 4^6) + (\mathbf{3} \cdot 4^5) + (\mathbf{0} \cdot 4^4) + (\mathbf{1} \cdot 4^3) + (\mathbf{3} \cdot 4^2) + (\mathbf{3} \cdot 4^1) + (\mathbf{3} \cdot 4^0)$$

which happens to be equal to 15487_{10}. We have thus managed to represent, as a natural number, the contents of M's tape at any point during execution. (The reader should now be able to see why we chose to assume a one-way-infinite tape.)

(3) Next we wish to see that the unary predicate *unbr1* is primitive recursive, where

$$unbr\,1(n) \Leftrightarrow_{\text{def.}} n \text{ is the encoding of a finite, nonempty, unbroken}$$
$$\text{string of } 1\text{s, starting at the ``leftmost'' tape square,}$$
$$\text{on an otherwise blank tape}$$

To this end, suppose once again that $\Gamma_M = \{*, \lambda, 1\}$ so that B, $*$, λ, and 1 continue to be associated with codes 0, 1, 2 and 3, respectively. Our encoding of tape contents—and in particular our choice of 3 as the symbol code of tape symbol 1—entails that an unbroken string of seven 1s, say, starting at the far left on a tape that is otherwise blank will be encoded as $4^7 - 1$. Specifically, $\lambda 1111111BB\ldots$ will be encoded as the value of base-4 numeral

$$\underbrace{\cdots + (0\cdot 4^8) + (0\cdot 4^7)}_{\text{All these terms vanish.}} + (3\cdot 4^6) + (3\cdot 4^5) + (3\cdot 4^4) + (3\cdot 4^3) + (3\cdot 4^2) + (3\cdot 4^1) + (3\cdot 4^0) = 4^7 - 1 = 16383$$

Thus, in the general case whereby $\Gamma_M \cup \{B\} = \{a_0, a_1, \ldots, a_{k-1}\}$ and a_{k-1} is 1, we can see that n is the encoding of a tape that is blank except for a nonempty, unbroken string of 1s starting at the far left if and only if n is of the form $k^j - 1$ for some $j \geq 1$. We conclude that the unary predicate *unbr1* is primitive recursive since our discussion has shown that

> The bound on the existential quantifier here is a primitive recursive function of n, namely, $p_1^1(n)$.

$$unbr\,1(n) \Leftrightarrow \exists j_{\leq n}[j > 1\ \&\ n = \boldsymbol{k}^j - 1]))$$

> k here is a constant given by $|\Gamma_M|$.

where the right-hand side here is primitive recursive.

(4) We associate tape squares with natural numbers—0 with the leftmost tape square, 1 with the next square, 2 with the next one, and so on (see Figure 3.4.5). The reader must not confuse this with what was done in **(2)**. There it was tape *contents* that were encoded

(5) We associate machine states with natural numbers in the most natural way—in fact, we have been doing this all along—0 with initial state q_0, 1 with state q_1, and so on. In what follows, we assume that M has r states associated with natural numbers $0, 1, \ldots, r - 1$. In particular, no state is associated with r itself, although we shall sometimes speak as if r were a state. Note that, relative to a given Turing machine M, quantity r is a fixed constant.

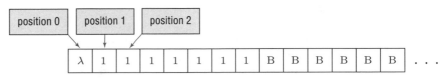

Figure 3.4.5

(6) We associate natural numbers with machine actions as well: **0** with **L** and **1** with **R**. This, together with **(1)** and **(5)**, enables us to express M's instructions in terms of three number-theoretic functions that we describe below. In what follows, talk of state q or symbol s is, strictly speaking, an abbreviation: What is meant strictly is "that (unique) state encoded as natural number q" and "that (unique) tape symbol encoded as natural number s."

$$action(q, s) = \begin{cases} \mathbf{0} & \text{if, when in state } q \text{ scanning symbol } s, \\ & \text{machine } M \text{ moves one square to the } \textbf{left} \\ \mathbf{1} & \text{if, when in state } q \text{ scanning symbol } s, \\ & \text{machine } M \text{ moves one square to the } \textbf{right} \\ 2 & \text{otherwise} \end{cases}$$

$$next\_symbol(q, s) = \begin{cases} s' & \text{if, when in state } q \text{ scanning symbol } s, \text{ machine } M \text{ writes symbol } s' \\ s & \text{otherwise} \end{cases}$$

A word of caution here is in order. The foregoing function concerns the "next symbol in the square currently being scanned." One must be careful not to interpret it as "next symbol scanned."

$$next\_state(q, s) = \begin{cases} q' & \text{if, when in state } q \text{ scanning symbol } s, \text{ machine } M \text{ enters state } q' \\ r & \text{if machine } M \text{ has no instruction for the state/symbol pair } \langle q, s \rangle \end{cases}$$

For a given machine M, all three functions are primitive recursive since they can be defined by cases from primitive recursive functions and predicates (see Figure 3.4.6 for details). We note at this time the following:

- If M has halted in state q scanning symbol s, then $next\_state(q, s)$ is r. Also, $next\_state(r, s)$ is r for any symbol s.

- If M has halted in state q scanning symbol s, then $next\_symbol(q, s)$ is s. Also, $next\_symbol(r, s)$ is s for any symbol s.

- If M has halted in state q scanning symbol s, then $action(q, s)$ is 2.

(7) The machine configuration of M at any point during computation can be represented as a triple $\langle w, q, p \rangle$ of natural numbers, where w is a natural number encoding the current tape contents as described in **(2)**, q is a natural number associated with M's current state as described in **(5)**, and p is a natural number giving the tape square currently being scanned by M's read/write head as described in **(4)**. Thus, if M is in state q_5, say, scanning the single asterisk on a tape whose current contents are

$$\lambda 111*B11BBB\ldots$$

then the corresponding configuration triple is $\langle 15487, \mathbf{5}, 4 \rangle$ (see **(2)** for clarification).

(8) Given configuration triple $\langle w, q, p \rangle$, it is possible to ascertain the symbol currently being scanned using the following line of reasoning. First of all, let us note at the outset that middle element q will not figure in our calculations. On the other hand, element p gives the position of the read/write head, while element w encodes the contents of M's entire tape. Moreover, the nature of this encoding permits one to determine the current contents of square p. To take an example, suppose that

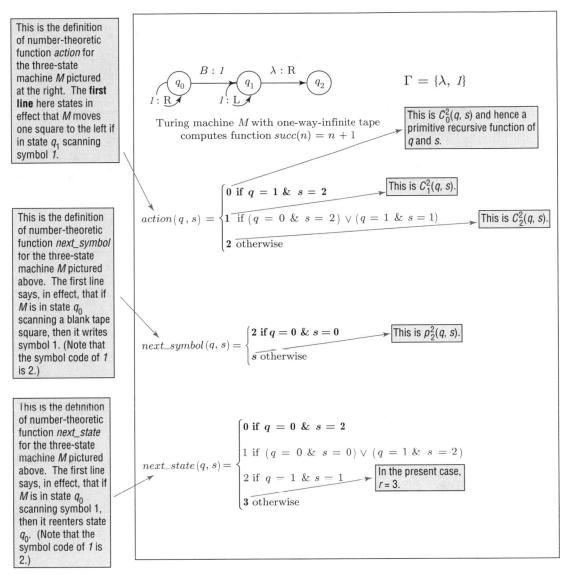

This is the definition of number-theoretic function *action* for the three-state machine *M* pictured at the right. The **first line** here states in effect that *M* moves one square to the left if in state q_1 scanning symbol *1*.

This is $C_0^2(q, s)$ and hence a primitive recursive function of *q* and *s*.

This is $C_1^2(q, s)$.

This is $C_2^2(q, s)$.

This is the definition of number-theoretic function *next_symbol* for the three-state machine *M* pictured above. The first line says, in effect, that if *M* is in state q_0 scanning a blank tape square, then it writes symbol 1. (Note that the symbol code of *1* is 2.)

This is $p_2^2(q, s)$.

This is the definition of number-theoretic function *next_state* for the three-state machine *M* pictured above. The first line says, in effect, that if *M* is in state q_0 scanning symbol 1, then it reenters state q_0. (Note that the symbol code of *1* is 2.)

In the present case, *r* = 3.

Turing machine *M* with one-way-infinite tape computes function $succ(n) = n + 1$

$\Gamma = \{\lambda, 1\}$

$$action(q, s) = \begin{cases} 0 \text{ if } q = 1 \ \& \ s = 2 \\ 1 \text{ if } (q = 0 \ \& \ s = 2) \vee (q = 1 \ \& \ s = 1) \\ 2 \text{ otherwise} \end{cases}$$

$$next\_symbol(q, s) = \begin{cases} 2 \text{ if } q = 0 \ \& \ s = 0 \\ s \text{ otherwise} \end{cases}$$

$$next\_state(q, s) = \begin{cases} 0 \text{ if } q = 0 \ \& \ s = 2 \\ 1 \text{ if } (q = 0 \ \& \ s = 0) \vee (q = 1 \ \& \ s = 2) \\ 2 \text{ if } q = 1 \ \& \ s = 1 \\ 3 \text{ otherwise} \end{cases}$$

Figure 3.4.6

- $\Gamma_M = \{*, \lambda, 1\}$ so that $|\Gamma_M \cup \{B\}|$ is still 4,

- *p* is 4, and

- *w* is $15487_{10} = 3301333_4$.

It is clear that the symbol currently being scanned has code **1** and hence is symbol *. But how can this information be obtained from $w = 15487$ and $p = 4$?

We shall approach this problem by first showing how this information can first be obtained from 3301333_4 itself. Recall that dividing 3301333_4 by $4^3 = 1000_4$ yields quotient 3301_4 and remainder

333_4. Note that the desired **1** is now the rightmost digit in the quotient. We can divide 3301_4 by $4^1 = 10_4$ and take the remainder, which is **1**. Returning to 15487_{10}, we see that the analogous steps involve first dividing by $4^3 = 64$ to obtain quotient 241 and remainder 23. Next we divide 241 by 4^1 to obtain the desired remainder **1**. That is, we have $1 = (15487 \, div \, 64) \, mod \, 4$. In the general case where $\Gamma_M \cup \{B\} = \{a_0, a_1, \ldots, a_{k-1}\}$, we have

$$current\_symbol(w, p) = (w \, div \, k^{p \dot{-} 1}) \, mod \, k$$

It is true that div and mod, as defined earlier, are both merely partial recursive functions. However, since k is a nonzero constant, divisors k and $k^{p \dot{-} 1}$ are both nonzero. It follows that function $current\_symbol$ is a primitive recursive function of arguments w and p (see Exercise 3.2.4).

(9) The following function is seen to be partial recursive.

$next\_square: \mathcal{N}^3 \to \mathcal{N}$

$next\_square(w, q, p) = p \dot{-} \chi_{eq}(action(q, current\_symbol(w, p)), \mathbf{0})$

> If action is L, then p is decremented. (Recall that action L is represented by natural number 0).

$+ \chi_{eq}(action(q, current\_symbol(w, p)), \mathbf{1})$

> If action is R, then p is incremented. (Recall that action R is represented by natural number 1).

Given configuration triple $\langle w, q, p \rangle$, function $next\_square(w, q, p)$ returns the position of M's read/write head after the current instruction is executed. There are four distinct cases to consider.

- If the instruction to be executed is a write action, then $action(q, current\_symbol(w, p))$ is 2 by **(6)**. Consequently, $\chi_{eq}(action(q, current\_symbol(w, p)), 0)$ and $\chi_{eq}(action(q, current\_symbol(w, p)), 1)$ are both 0, so that $next\_square(w, q, p)$ is just $p \dot{-} 0 + 0 = p$, as required. That is, if the current action is a write action, the next square is identical to the currently scanned square.

- If M has halted in state q scanning position p on tape w, then, since $action(q, current\_symbol(w, p))$ is 2 by **(6)**, we have $next\_square(w, q, p)$ equal to $p \dot{-} 0 + 0 = p$ in this case as well. Similarly, $next\_square(w, r, p) = p$.

- If the instruction to be executed is a move left, then $action(q, current\_symbol(w, p))$ is 0 by **(6)**. Consequently, $\chi_{eq}(action(q, current\__symbol(w, p)), 0)$ is 1 whereas $\chi_{eq}(action(q, current\_symbol(w, p)), 1)$ is 0. This means that $next\_square(w, q, p)$ is $p \dot{-} 1 + 0 = p \dot{-} 1$, as required. In other words, if the current action is a move left, then the next square is the one immediately to the left of the currently scanned square (see Figure 3.4.5).

- If the instruction to be executed is a move-right instruction, then $action(q, current\_symbol(w, p))$ is 1 by **(6)**. Consequently, $\chi_{eq}(action(q, current\_symbol(w, p)), 0)$ is 0, whereas $\chi_{eq}(action(q, current\_symbol(w, p)), 1)$ is 1. This means that $next\_square(w, q, p)$ is $p \dot{-} 0 + 1 = p + 1$, as required. In other words, if the current action is a move right, then the next square is the one immediately to the right of the currently scanned square.

It is easy to see that function *next_square* is primitive recursive since it is defined in terms of function *current_symbol*, which was seen to be primitive recursive at **(8)**.

(10) Given configuration triple $\langle w, q, p \rangle$ representing the configuration of M at some point during its computation, ternary function *next_tape_contents* returns the (encoding of) the configuration of M's tape after its next instruction has been executed.

$$next\_tape\_contents: \mathcal{N}^3 \to \mathcal{N}$$

$$next\_tape\_contents(w, q, p) = w \mathbin{\dot{-}} (k^{p \dot{-} 1} \cdot current\_symbol(w, p))$$

$$+ (k^{p \dot{-} 1} \cdot next\_symbol(q, current\_symbol(w, p)))$$

- Function *next_tape_contents* should be interpreted in terms of the substitution of one digit for another digit at the $k^{p \dot{-} 1}$ position within the base-k numeral corresponding to w. Specifically, the digit encoded by $next\_symbol(q, current\_symbol(w, p))$ is substituted for the digit encoded by $current\_symbol(w, p)$.

- Function *next_tape_contents* is seen to be primitive recursive, having been defined in terms of functions previously seen to be primitive recursive.

- Finally, note that if M has halted in state q scanning position p on tape w, then, by **(6)**, $next\_symbol(q, current\_symbol(w, p))$ is equal to $current\_symbol(w, p)$. So it follows that $next\_tape\_contents(w, q, p) = w$. Similarly, $next\_tape\_contents(w, r, p) = w$.

(11) We define ternary function *next_configuration*, which, given current configuration triple $\langle w, q, p \rangle$ as argument, returns an encoding of the machine configuration triple after the next instruction is executed.

$$next\_configuration: \mathcal{N}^3 \to \mathcal{N}$$

$$next\_configuration(w, q, p) = 2^{next\_tape\_contents(w,q,p)} \cdot 3^{next\_state(q, current\_symbol(w,p))}$$

$$\cdot 5^{next\_square(w,q,p)}$$

Evidently, function *next_configuration* is primitive recursive. Note that if M has halted in state q scanning position p on tape w, then it follows from our earlier discussion that $next\_configuration(w, q, p)$ will be $2^w \cdot 3^r \cdot 5^p$.

(12) As defined below, function *execute*(w, t) returns the encoding of that unique configuration triple that is the result of starting M in state q_0 scanning position 1 on tape w and allowing M to run for exactly t steps—that is, to execute exactly t instructions.

$$execute: \mathcal{N}^2 \to \mathcal{N}$$

$$execute(w, 0) = 2^w \cdot 3^0 \cdot 5^1 \quad /* \text{ By convention, } M \text{ starts in state } q_0 \text{ scanning position 1. } */$$

$$execute(w, t + 1) = next\_configuration([execute(w, t)]_0, [execute(w, t)]_1, [execute(w, t)]_2)$$

The subscripts here are references to the extraction function shown to be primitive recursive in Example 3.3.7. Since function *execute* is being defined by what is essentially **Pr** starting from primitive recursive functions, it is itself primitive recursive. (In fact, what has been used is not quite Schema C of course, but our definition could be recast so as to conform to that schema.)

If M halts after t_{halt} steps, then function *execute* returns a constant value thereafter:

$$execute(w, t_{halt} + 1) = execute(w, t_{halt} + 2) = execute(w, t_{halt} + 3) = \cdots$$

To begin to see this, note that if M, started in state q_0 scanning position p on tape w, has halted after step t_{halt}, then by definition

$$execute(w, t_{halt} + 2)$$

$$=_{\text{def.}} next\_configuration([execute(w, t_{halt} + 1)]_0,$$

$$[execute(w, t_{halt} + 1)]_1, [execute(w, t_{halt} + 1)]_2)$$

$$= next\_configuration([execute(w, t_{halt} + 1)]_0, r, [execute(w, t_{halt} + 1)]_2)$$

$$= 2^{next\_tape\_contents([execute(w, t_{halt}+1)]_0, r, [execute(w, t_{halt}+1)]_2)} \cdot$$

$$3^{next\_state(r, current\_symbol([execute(w, t_{halt}+1)]0, [execute(w, t_{halt}+1)]_2)} \cdot$$

$$5^{next\_square([execute(w, t_{halt}+1)]_0, r, [execute(w, t_{halt}+1)]_2)}$$

$$= 2^{[execute(w, t_{halt}+1)]_0} \cdot 3^r \cdot 5^{[execute(w, t_{halt}+1)]_2} \qquad \text{by hypothesis and remarks}$$
$$\text{at } \textbf{(6)}, \textbf{(9)}, \text{ and } \textbf{(10)}$$

$$= 2^{[execute(w, t_{halt}+1)]_0} \cdot 3^{[execute(w, t_{halt}+1)]_1}$$

$$5^{[execute(w, t_{halt}+1)]_2}$$

$$= execute(w, t_{halt} + 1) \qquad \text{(See (3.3.6) in Example 3.3.7.)}$$

(13) Finally, the value of function f computed by M is a matter of the number of *1*s on the tape when M finds itself in a state q scanning a symbol s such that $next\_state(q, s) = r$ (see **(6)**). If M is started in state q_0 scanning the square at position 1 of a tape whose configuration is given by w, then the number of steps required for M to halt in a value-representing configuration is given by $num\_steps(w)$ as defined below.

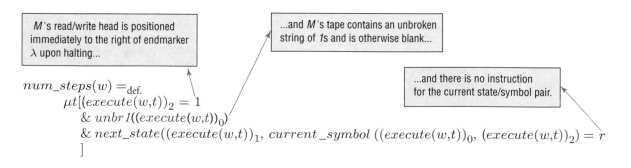

M's read/write head is positioned immediately to the right of endmarker λ upon halting...

...and M's tape contains an unbroken string of *1*s and is otherwise blank...

...and there is no instruction for the current state/symbol pair.

$$num\_steps(w) =_{\text{def.}}$$
$$\mu t[(execute(w,t))_2 = 1$$
$$\& \; unbr1((execute(w,t))_0)$$
$$\& \; next\_state((execute(w,t))_1, \; current\_symbol \; ((execute(w,t))_0, \; (execute(w,t))_2) = r$$
$$]$$

Function $num\_steps(w)$ is seen to be partial recursive since it is of the form $\mu t[C(w, t)]$ for (primitive) recursive predicate $C(w, t)$ (see Exercise 3.7.8).

Finally, if $f: \mathcal{N} \to \mathcal{N}$ is the function computed by M, then we can write

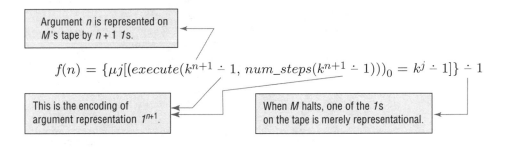

which shows that f is partial recursive. (Exercise 3.7.8 is being used again here.)   Q.E.D.

We have now seen that Turing computability and partial recursiveness are two distinct characterizations of one and the same class of number-theoretic functions. The immediate payoff for the reader will probably be a better understanding of the more elusive, but nonetheless important, notion of partial recursive function. Generally speaking, one tends to have a better intuitive grasp of what it is for a function to be Turing-computable. This will be especially true of those readers who have experience with companion software for simulating Turing machines. Given the equivalence of Theorems 3.3(a) and 3.3(b), this experience is now brought to bear upon the notion of partial recursive function. A second, more long-range, consequence for the reader who pursues the study of recursion theory will be the possibility of applying the large body of results concerning the class of partial recursive functions to the class of Turing-computable functions.

§3.5 Recursive Sets

We know what it is for a number-theoretic function to be (partial) recursive. We next employ our notion of *recursive function* to obtain a derivative notion of *recursive set*.

DEFINITION 3.9: A set S of natural numbers is *recursive* if its characteristic function χ_S is (partial) recursive, where χ_S is defined, as usual, by

$$\chi_S(n) = \begin{cases} 1 & \text{if } n \in S \\ 0 & \text{if } n \notin S \end{cases}$$

Once again, any partial recursive characteristic function χ_S is total and hence recursive.

EXAMPLE 3.5.1 As a first example, the set $\mathcal{E} = \{n \in \mathcal{N} \mid n \text{ is even}\}$ can be seen to be a recursive set since the unary function defined by

$$\overline{sg}(n \bmod 2)$$

(which is clearly recursive) is seen to be the characteristic function $\chi_{\mathcal{E}}$ of set $\mathcal{E}$. First, note that, if n is even so that $n \in \mathcal{E}$, then $n \bmod 2$ is 0 so that $\chi_{\mathcal{E}}(n) = \overline{sg}(n \bmod 2) = 1$. On the other hand, if n is odd so that $n \notin \mathcal{E}$, then $n \bmod 2$ is 1 so that $\chi_{\mathcal{E}}(n) = \overline{sg}(n \bmod 2) = 0$.

If the argument of Example 3.5.1 has a familiar ring, this is because, with only trivial changes, this reasoning is exactly how we would have shown that the unary predicate "n is even" is a recursive predicate. And this is no accident: The recursive sets are precisely those that are the extensions of recursive predicates as defined in Definition 3.8(b). (Recall that the *extension of a (unary) number-theoretic predicate* C is the set of natural numbers n such that $C(n)$ holds true. Thus the extension of predicate "n is even" is $\mathcal{E} = \{n \in \mathcal{N} | n \text{ is even}\}$.)

> **DEFINITION 3.9 (alternative formulation):** A set S of natural numbers is *recursive* if it is the extension of a recursive predicate in the sense of Definition 3.8(b).

Suppose that S is a recursive set of natural numbers. By Definition 3.9, this means that characteristic function

$$\chi_S(n) = \begin{cases} 1 & \text{if } n \in S \\ 0 & \text{if } n \notin S \end{cases}$$

is recursive. Next, consider unary function $\overline{sg}(\chi_S(n))$, which, as the composition of two (partial) recursive functions, is itself (partial) recursive. Function $\overline{sg}(\chi_S(n))$ takes value 0 if $n \in S$ and value 1 if $n \notin S$. Consequently, $\overline{sg}(\chi_S(n))$ is seen to be the characteristic function χ_{S^c} of $S^c = \mathcal{N} \backslash S$. We have hereby justified

> **REMARK 3.5.1:** The family of recursive sets of natural numbers is closed under complementation. That is, if S is a recursive set, then so is $S^c = \mathcal{N} \backslash S$.

We shall think of a recursive set S as *effectively decidable* or just *decidable* in the following sense: The question whether a given natural number n is in S can be answered by applying recursive χ_S to n so as to yield either value 1 or value 0. One says that *membership in S is decidable*.

§3.6 Recursively Enumerable Sets

One can effectively list or *enumerate* the primes by applying a certain algorithm to each of the natural numbers starting with 2 and reporting just those numbers for which said algorithm responds affirmatively. By virtue of this, we say that the set of primes is *effectively enumerable*. (Recall that we use the term "effective" as a synonym for "algorithmic.") In the present section, we attempt to capture this intuitive notion of effective enumerability with a new mathematical notion of *recursively enumerable set of natural numbers*. First, we present an example.

EXAMPLE 3.6.1 Consider again the unary number-theoretic function defined by $f(n) = 2n$. This function maps the natural numbers onto the even natural numbers (see Figure 3.6.1). It is natural to think of f as enumerating the set of even natural numbers, which is what our diagram is intended to suggest. Moreover, since this particular f has earlier been shown to be a recursive function, we shall say that $\{n \in \mathcal{N} \mid n \text{ is even}\}$ is *recursively enumerable*.

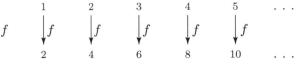

Figure 3.6.1   Set $\{n \in \mathcal{N} \mid n \text{ is even}\}$ is recursively enumerable.

DEFINITION 3.10: Let S be a set of natural numbers. Then S is *recursively enumerable*—or, more simply, *r.e.*—if S is either the empty set $\varnothing$ or S is $Image(f)$ for some unary recursive function f.

Another example will enable us to relate Definition 3.10 to a previous remark.

EXAMPLE 3.6.2 In Example 3.3.6 we showed that the number-theoretic function defined by

$$\pi(n) =_{\text{def.}} \text{ the } n\text{th prime number where 2 is the 0th prime}$$

is primitive recursive and hence recursive (see Figure 3.6.2). By Definition 3.10, this means that the set $\{n \mid n \text{ is prime}\}$ is r.e.

Both Examples 3.6.1 and 3.6.2 involve infinite sets. But it is easy to see that an r.e. set may be finite as well. In point of fact, we can show the following.

THEOREM 3.4 Any finite set of natural numbers is r.e.

PROOF A finite set S is either empty or nonempty. If empty, then S is r.e. already by Definition 3.10. If nonempty, then there are two subcases to consider.

- S may be a singleton; that is, $S = \{m\}$ for some m. Then S is the image of C_m^1 and hence r.e. by Definition 3.10.

- Otherwise, suppose that S is of the form $\{m_0, m_1, \ldots, m_k\}$ for some fixed $k \geq 1$. We define unary function f by cases as

$$f(n) = \begin{cases} m_0 & \text{if } n = 0 \\ m_1 & \text{if } n = 1 \\ \ldots & \\ m_{k-1} & \text{if } n = k - 1 \\ m_k & \text{otherwise} \end{cases}$$

Thus f is (primitive) recursive with $Image(f) = S$. Again, by Definition 3.10, S is r.e.   Q.E.D.

Figure 3.6.2   Set $\{n \mid n \text{ is prime}\}$ is recursively enumerable.

We have seen that the class of partial recursive functions is identical to the class of Turing-computable functions. Consequently, we can at any point show that a set is recursively enumerable by showing that it is $Image(f)$ for some total, Turing-computable function f. This may be easier than giving an explicit expression for f, and we avail ourselves of this option in the proof of the very next proposition. This new proposition states in effect that, although, by Definition 3.10, a set S is r.e. just in case it is $Image(f)$ for some unary *recursive* function f, in point of fact a partial recursive f will do just as well.

THEOREM 3.5: A nonempty set S of natural numbers is recursively enumerable if and only if $S = Image(f)$ for some unary partial recursive function f.

PROOF The "only if" or forward direction here is trivial. As for the "if" or reverse direction, suppose that S is $Image(f)$ for some unary partial recursive function f. If S happens to be empty, then it is r.e. by definition. If S is finite, then it is r.e. by Theorem 3.4, and we are done. So assume that S is infinite. By Theorem 3.3(a), there exists a single-tape Turing machine M that computes f. Since f is partial, however, M may not halt in a value-representing configuration for certain arguments. This possibility leads us to describe a special sort of multitape Turing machine M', the existence of which will establish that S is an r.e. set. Given a representation of natural number n on its input tape, machine M' proceeds to simulate M for arguments $0, 1, 2, \ldots$, in succession, on worktape$_1$, say. Moreover, M' will do this in "dovetailing" fashion, as we now describe.

Again, M' is assumed to have argument n on its input tape initially. First, M' will simulate M's behavior for argument 0 *for one step only*, after which it will check to see whether M halted in a value-representing configuration. Assuming it did not, M' will next go on to simulate M for arguments 0 and 1, in succession, *for exactly two steps each*, checking once again to see whether either simulation halted in a value-representing configuration. Assuming neither did, M' will then go on to simulate M for arguments 0, 1, and 2, in succession, *for three steps each*, and so forth. (M' may be assumed to use the familiar endmarker technique in order to recognize when one of these simulations halts in a value-representing configuration.) Using a counter on worktape$_2$, M' keeps track of the number of simulations that have halted in value-representing configurations so far. Finally, immediately after the $(n + 1)$th such simulation halts on worktape$_1$, M' will copy the contents of that tape to its own output tape and then itself halt. (Since S is infinite, there will be such a simulation, no matter how large argument n is.) We claim the following:

(1) M' computes a unary function—call it f'—that is Turing-computable and hence partial recursive.

(2) Function f' is total and hence, by (1), recursive.

(3) By the construction of M', we have that $Image(f')$ is none other than S.

It follows, by Definition 3.10, that S is r.e.   Q.E.D.

And while we are at it, it turns out that the requirements on function f in Definition 3.10 can be relaxed even further. Namely, a binary or, in general, a k-ary f will serve.

THEOREM 3.6: A nonempty set S of natural numbers is recursively enumerable if and only if $S = Image(f)$ for some k-ary partial recursive function f with $k \geq 1$.

PROOF The proof is left as an exercise (see Exercise 3.6.3 and its solution).

In Theorems 3.5 and 3.6, we have succeeded in characterizing the r.e. sets as the *images* of partial recursive functions. But it can be shown that *domains* could be used with similar effect: that is, the family of r.e. sets comprises the domains of partial recursive functions.

THEOREM 3.7: A nonempty set S of natural numbers is recursively enumerable if and only if S is $Dom(f)$ for some unary partial recursive function f.

PROOF See Exercise 3.6.4 and its solution.

It follows immediately from Theorem 3.7 that any enumeration $f_0, f_1, f_2, \ldots, f_n, \ldots$ of the family of partial recursive functions induces an enumeration $Dom(f_0), Dom(f_1), Dom(f_2), \ldots, Dom(f_n), \ldots$ of the family of r.e. sets.

We have introduced notions of recursive set and recursively enumerable set. In Theorems 3.8–3.11 below, we explore the relation between these two important notions.

THEOREM 3.8: Every recursive set of natural numbers is recursively enumerable.

PROOF Let S be a recursive set of natural numbers.

- If S happens to be empty, then S is recursively enumerable by definition, and we are done.

- Similarly, if S is nonempty but finite, then S is recursively enumerable by Theorem 3.4.

- Suppose, on the other hand, that S is recursive and infinite. Let M_S be a single-tape Turing machine that computes the characteristic function χ_S of S. In other words, if M_S is started scanning a representation of natural number n, then M_S ultimately halts either scanning the leftmost of exactly two *1*s on an otherwise blank tape, representing $\chi_S(n) = 1$, or scanning a single *1* on an otherwise blank tape, representing $\chi_S(n) = 0$. Given M_S, we construct a new, multitape Turing machine M^* that computes a unary, total function f^* with $Image(f^*) = S$. (As usual, we describe M^*'s behavior for various input values and take the nature of its construction to be implicit in that description.)

Suppose that M^* is given a representation of argument 0 on its input tape. M^* then simulates M_S on arguments 0, 1, 2, and so on, in succession on worktape₁, say, until one of these arguments—call it n_0—results in (the simulation of) M_S halting scanning a representation of 1, reflecting the fact that $n_0 \in S$. (There must be such an n_0, since S is assumed to be infinite.) M^* now copies argument n_0 to its output tape and halts. Thus $f^*(0) = n_0$ is the smallest member of S. Given a representation of argument $k > 1$ on its input tape, M^* carries out successive simulations of M_S on worktape₁, say, using worktape₂ to keep track of the arguments to the simulations and worktape₃ to record the number of elements of S found so far. By comparison of input tape and worktape₃, M^* can identify the $(k + 1)$th smallest element of S—call it n_k—which it copies to its output tape before halting. Summarizing, we see that

$$f^*(0) = n_0 = \text{ the smallest element of } S$$

$$f^*(1) = n_1 = \text{ the second smallest element of } S$$

$$f^*(2) = n_2 = \text{ the third smallest element of } S$$

$$\cdots$$

$$f^*(k) = n_k = \text{ the } (k+1)\text{th smallest element of } S$$

$$\cdots$$

Clearly, $Image(f^*) = \{n_0, n_1, \ldots, n_k, \ldots\}$ is none other than S, so that, by Definition 3.10, set S is recursively enumerable.   Q.E.D.

THEOREM 3.9: Let S be a set of natural numbers. If S is recursive, then both S and S^c are recursively enumerable.

PROOF Suppose that S is recursive. Then, by Theorem 3.8, S is r.e. As for S^c, we have by Remark 3.5.1 that the recursive sets are closed under complementation. So S^c is recursive. But then, by Theorem 3.8 again, S^c is r.e.   Q.E.D.

We show next that the converse of Theorem 3.8 does not hold.

THEOREM 3.10: There exists an r.e. set that is not recursive.

PROOF We can assume without loss of generality that every natural number is the gödel number of some (unique) Turing machine. (See the discussion leading up to Remark 2.4.1.) Also, we recall that it is possible to think of absolutely every Turing machine as computing some unary number-theoretic function. We write M_k for the Turing machine with gödel number k; we write f_k for the unary function that M_k computes. Thus

$$f_0, f_1, f_2, \cdots \tag{3.6.1}$$

is an enumeration of the class of unary Turing-computable, and hence partial recursive, functions. We next define

$D^* =_{\text{def.}} \{k|$ if Turing machine M_k is started scanning the leftmost 1 in a representation

of natural number k, then M_k halts scanning a single 1 on an otherwise blank tape$\}$

Given our adopted conventions regarding function computation, we have

$$D^* = \{k|f_k(k) \text{ is defined and equals } 0\} \tag{3.6.2}$$

First, we show that D^* is r.e. If D^* happens to be empty or finite, then it is r.e. by Definition 3.10 or Theorem 3.4. But D^* might be infinite. In that case, our goal is the description of a Turing machine M^* that, in effect, maps natural numbers onto members of D^* in such a way that $Image(f^*) = D^*$, where f^* is the unary partial recursive function computed by M^*. By Theorem 3.5, we will have shown that D^* is r.e.

We recall that the state diagram of a Turing machine is effectively retrievable, given its gödel number. As a first shot, consider a multitape machine M^* that starts scanning the leftmost 1 in a representation of argument n. M^* first recovers Turing machine M_0 and then simulates M_0 on a representation of argument 0. Afterward, M^* recovers M_1 and then simulates it on a representation of argument 1. M^* continues in this way and tallies the number of simulations that halt with the simulated read/write head scanning a single *1* on an otherwise blank tape. The gödel number of the nth machine to return 0 in this manner will be written to M^*'s output tape. Unfortunately, such an M^* does not work, in general. This is because, should any one of M^*'s simulations fail to halt because the corresponding $f_i(i)$ is undefined, then M^* will itself never halt. In any case, our construction of M^* cannot be so straightforward.

Dovetailing provides the solution. To begin, we suppose that M^* starts scanning the leftmost *1* in a representation of argument n. To begin, M^* recovers Turing machine M_0 and then simulates M_0, for argument 0, for only one instruction and then checks to see whether the simulation halted scanning a single *1* on an otherwise blank tape. Next, both M_0 and M_1 are simulated for arguments 0 and 1, respectively, for only two instructions each. After each partial simulation, M^* checks to see whether the simulated machine halted scanning a single *1* on an otherwise blank tape. Afterward, M_0, M_1, and M_2 are successively simulated for arguments 0, 1, and 2, respectively, for three instructions each. Again, after each simulation, M^* checks to see whether the simulated machine halted scanning a single *1* on an otherwise blank tape. Eventually, some simulated machine will return 0, then a second machine will return 0, and so on. M^* should return the gödel number of the nth machine to halt reading a representation of 0. (How is it that we can be certain that there will, in fact, be such an nth machine, for arbitrary n?) It should be clear that every member of D^* will be the value returned by M^* for some argument n. That is, where f^* is defined as the function computed by M^*, we have $Image(f^*) = D^*$ (see Figure 3.6.3). So D^* is r.e. by Theorem 3.5.

We next show that D^* is not recursive. Our argument is indirect. We suppose, for the sake of producing a contradiction, that D^* is recursive. By definition, this means that characteristic function

$$\chi_{D^*}(n) = \begin{cases} 1 & \text{if } n \in D^* \\ 0 & \text{if } n \notin D^* \end{cases}$$

is recursive. By (3.6.2), we can rewrite this as

$$\chi_{D^*}(n) = \begin{cases} 1 & \text{if } f_n(n) \text{ is defined and equals 0} \\ 0 & \text{if } f_n(n) \text{ is either defined and nonzero or undefined} \end{cases} \tag{3.6.3}$$

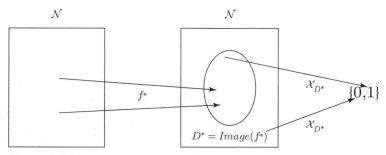

Figure 3.6.3

Now, since χ_{D^*} is unary and recursive, it must be identical to f_d, for a particular d, at (3.6.1). In other words, we are supposing that d is fixed and that χ_{D^*} and f_d are one and the same function. Substituting d for n at (3.6.3), we have

$$f_d(d) = \chi_{D^*}(d) = \begin{cases} 1 & \text{if } f_d(d) \text{ is defined and equals } 0 \\ 0 & \text{if } f_d(d) \text{ is either defined and nonzero or undefined} \end{cases}$$

Evidently, whether $f_d(d)$ is 1 or 0, we are confronted with a patent contradiction. We conclude that D^* cannot be recursive, after all.   Q.E.D.

Our diagonal argument to the effect that D^* is not a recursive set will reemerge at the beginning of Chapter 8 in a somewhat different context. We may summarize the preceding Theorems 3.6 and 3.8 by remarking that the recursive sets form a proper subfamily of the r.e. sets (see Figure 3.6.4).

We can prove the converse of Theorem 3.9.

THEOREM 3.11: Let $S \subseteq \mathcal{N}$. Then if both S and its complement S^c are r.e. sets, then S is a recursive set.

PROOF If either S or S^c are empty, then S is trivially recursive. (Why?) So let us suppose that both S and its complement S^c are nonempty r.e. sets. By Theorem 3.7, there exist partial recursive functions f_S and f_{S^c} with $Dom(f_S) = S$ and $Dom(f_{S^c}) = S^c$. It follows that there exist Turing machines M_S and M_{S^c} that compute f_S and f_{S^c}, respectively. We now describe a new multitape Turing machine M^* that computes the characteristic function χ_S of set S:

$$\chi_S(n) = \begin{cases} 1 & \text{if } n \in S \\ 0 & \text{if } n \notin S \end{cases}$$

U = {$S|S$ is a subset of $\mathcal{N}$}

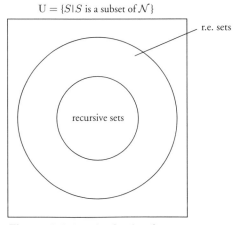

r.e. sets

recursive sets

Figure 3.6.4 The family of recursive sets is properly contained within the family of recursive sets.

Given representation I^{n+1} of n on M^*'s input tape, M^* must determine whether $n \in S = Dom(f_S)$ or whether $n \notin S^c = Dom(f_{S^c})$. M^* simulates M_S and M_{S^c} on I^{n+1} for one step each, then for two steps each, then for three steps each, and so on. We can assume without loss of generality that exactly one of M_S and M_{S^c} will eventually halt for input I^{n+1}. If M^* halts in its simulation of M_S, then M^* will write 11, representing 1, on its output tape and halt. On the other hand, if M^* halts in its simulation of M_{S^c}, then M^* will write 1, representing 0, on its output tape and halt. It follows that the function computed by M^* is none other than χ_S. Consequently, χ_S is Turing-computable and hence recursive so that, by Definition 3.9, set S is recursive.   Q.E.D.

Finally, as an easy consequence of the previous two theorems, we have

---

COROLLARY 3.1: There exist r.e. sets whose complements are not r.e. Alternative formulation: The family of r.e. sets is not closed under complementation.

The simple argument here is left to the reader as an exercise.

§3.7 Historical Remarks and Suggestions for Further Reading

The primitive recursive functions were introduced in [Gödel 1931], where our Schemata A and B were first presented. (Gödel himself referred to "recursive" functions.) The key ideas, however, are due to Norwegian logician Thoralf Skolem (1887–1963) and French logician Jacques Herbrand (1903–1931).

The class of primitive recursive functions has been important in foundations of mathematics to the extent that this class of functions has been thought of as delineating a subsystem of number theory or arithmetic whose statements are true in some unimpeachable sense. The class of primitive recursive functions is thus of great importance historically and philosophically. It does also correspond to a certain natural notion of computability, however, because Gödel showed that the primitive recursive functions are precisely the class of number-theoretic functions that includes the ordinary addition and multiplication functions and is closed under **Comp** and **Pr**. To the extent that we tend to think of the addition and multiplication operations as paradigmatic of computation, the primitive recursive functions may be regarded as the embodiment of a natural, albeit *limited*, notion of computability. For, as Theorem 3.2 and the existence of Ackermann's function show, the class of primitive recursive functions is inadequate as an analysis of computability in the fullest sense: There turn out to be computable functions that are not primitive recursive. Hence, as a general analysis of computability, primitive recursiveness must be deemed a failure. (Just for the sake of the historical record, we point out that most likely no one ever seriously considered proposing the class of primitive recursive functions as a fully general analysis of *computable function*.) Incidentally, Ackermann's function first appeared in [Ackermann 1928], where it is proved, in effect, that this function is recursive but not primitive recursive. We mention the so-called *Ackermann benchmark*, a use of Ackermann's function to measure computer performance. Typically, in excess of 10^5 recursive calls to the function are effected, and the number of completed calls per second is tallied. One thereby obtains a reliable estimate of the overhead associated with subroutine calls on the machine in question.

Of truly central importance to computability theory is the class of partial recursive functions. Given the equivalence of the notions *partial recursive function* and *Turing-computable function*, as established in

Theorem 3.3, we may regard Definition 3.7 as an alternative characterization, or mathematical model of, our intuitive notion of *effectively computable function*. This equivalence result appeared in [Kleene 1943], although Turing's own proof of the equivalence of *Turing-computable function* and Church's notion of *lambda-definable function* provided an important prototype (see [Turing 1937]).

Our discussion of the rudiments of recursion theory would certainly be incomplete without mention of yet another important class of number-theoretic functions. This is the class of so-called *general recursive* or *μ-recursive functions*. This is the smallest class of functions containing all the initial functions and closed under **Comp**, **Pr**, and **Mn**, where, in addition, we restrict the application of **Mn** to $(k+1)$-ary functions f such that (1) for any k-tuple $n_1, n_2, \ldots, n_k$, there exists an m with $f(n_1, n_2, \ldots, n_k, m) = 0$ and (2) for all $j < m$, $f(n_1, n_2, \ldots, n_k, j)$ is defined. Recalling the classroom scenario used to illustrate minimization, we are now to assume that the single student computer knows how calculate the values of a *special sort* of $(k + 1)$-ary function f, namely, one such that, for any input k-tuple $n_1, n_2, \ldots, n_k$ introduced by the instructor, the student's calculations are certain to terminate. The new concept merits a formal definition, if only for perspicuity. The reader will want to compare it with Definition 3.7.

DEFINITION 3.11: The class of *general recursive functions* is defined as follows.

(i) Every initial function is general recursive. That is, all of the following are general recursive:
   - the successor function $succ$
   - the k-ary constant-0 functions C_0^k for all $k \geq 0$
   - the projection functions p_j^k for all $k \geq 1$, $1 \leq j \leq k$

(ii) If $g_1, \ldots, g_m$ are k-ary general recursive functions with $k \geq 0$ and f is an m-ary general recursive function with $m \geq 1$, then **Comp**$[f, g_1, \ldots, g_m]$ is also general recursive.

(iii) If f is a k-ary general recursive function and g is a $(k + 2)$-ary general recursive function with $k \geq 0$, then **Pr**$[f, g]$ is also general recursive.

(iv) If f is a $(k + 1)$-ary general recursive function with $k \geq 0$ such that, **for any k-tuple $n_1, n_2, \ldots, n_k$, there exists an m with $f(n_1, n_2, \ldots, n_k, m) = 0$ and, for all $j < m$, $f(n_1, n_2, \ldots, n_k, j)$ is defined**, then **Mn**$[f]$ is also general recursive.

(v) Nothing else is a general recursive function.

It should be easy to convince oneself that that every general recursive function is total. Moreover, it is obvious that every general recursive function is partial recursive in the sense of Definition 3.7, since any function obtainable from the restricted Definition 3.11(iv) is likewise obtainable from unrestricted Definition 3.7(iv). In fact, one can prove the following proposition relating the two classes of functions.

THEOREM 3.12: Let f be a k-ary number-theoretic function. Then f is general recursive if and only if f is partial recursive and total. That is, f is general recursive if and only if f is recursive in the sense of Definition 3.8(a).

We leave the proof of Theorem 3.12 as an exercise (see Exercise 3.7.13).

Our discussion of recursion theory provides the reader with only the fundamentals of a science that has flourished in the period since [Kleene 1936a]. Incidentally, the forms of schemata (A), (B), and (C) of Definitions 3.2, 3.3, and 3.6 may be varied in numerous ways with no change at the theoretical level (see [Mendelson 1987]). That is, we have numerous equivalent characterizations of one and the same class of partial recursive functions. Given the equivalence of Theorem 3.3, this phenomenon may be viewed as the analog of the several equivalent variations on the standard Turing machine considered in Chapter 2.

The study of the class of r.e. sets was initiated in [Post 1944]. The reader will find more advanced material in [Davis, Sigal, and Weyuker 1994].

EXERCISES FOR §3.1

3.1.1. [hwk] **(a)** Letting $j(n, m) = n^2 + 2m + 3$, what is $j(3, 5)$?

(b) We wish to compute the value of function $h = \textbf{Comp}[j, p_1^3, p_2^3]$ for certain arguments. Referring to Schema A of Definition 3.2, what is the value of m in the case of this particular function h? What is the value of k in this case? So how many arguments will h have?

(c) What is the value of $h(3, 5, 38) = \textbf{Comp}[j, p_1^3, p_2^3](3, 5, 38)$?

3.1.2. [hwk] **(a)** We wish to compute the value of function $h = \textbf{Comp}[plus, p_3^4, p_4^4]$ for certain arguments. Referring to Schema A of Definition 3.2, what is the value of m in the case of this particular h? What is the value of k in this case? So how many arguments will h have?

(b) What is the value of $h(3, 5, 0, 22) = \textbf{Comp}[plus, p_3^4, p_4^4](3, 5, 0, 22)$?

(c) Let $j(n, m) = n^2 + 2m + 3$. We wish to compute the value of function $h = \textbf{Pr}[j, \textbf{Comp}[plus, p_3^4, p_4^4]]$. Referring to Schema B of Definition 3.3, what function serves as f in that schema in the present case? What function is serving as g? What is the value of k in the case of this h? (*Hint:* Note that k is the "-arity" of f.)

(d) What is $h(3, 5, 0)$? What is $h(3, 5, 1)$? What is $h(3, 5, 2)$? What is $h(3, 5, 3)$?

3.1.3. **(a)** If $j(n_1, n_2, n_3) = n_1 \cdot n_2 + n_3$, what is $j(6, 0, 7)$?

(b) We wish to be able to compute $\textbf{Comp}[plus, j, p_3^3]$ for various arguments. Referring to Schema A of Definition 3.2, what is the value of m in the particular case of $h = \textbf{Comp}[plus, j, p_3^3]$? What is the value of k in the particular case of $h = \textbf{Comp}[plus, j, p_3^3]$? So how many

arguments will $h = \textbf{Comp}[plus, j, p_3^3]$ have?

(c) What is f in Schema A? What is g_1 in Schema A? What is g_2 in Schema A?

(d) Finally, again referring to Schema A, what is $h(6, 0, 7) = \textbf{Comp}[plus, j, p_3^3](6, 0, 7)$? What is $h(6, 1, 14) = \textbf{Comp}[plus, j, p_3^3](6, 1, 14)$? (These particular values will be useful in Exercise 3.1.4 below.)

3.1.4. **(a)** Again, let $j(n_1, n_2, n_3) = n_1 \cdot n_2 + n_3$ as before. We wish to compute $\textbf{Pr}[succ, \textbf{Comp}[plus, j, p_3^3]]$ applied to certain small arguments. Referring to Schema B of Definition 3.3 and letting $h = \textbf{Pr}[succ, \textbf{Comp}[plus, j, p_3^3]]$, what is f in the schema? What is the value of k in the particular case of $h = \textbf{Pr}[succ, \textbf{Comp}[plus, j, p_3^3]]$? What is g in the schema?

(b) What is $h(6, 0) = \textbf{Pr}[succ, \textbf{Comp}[plus, j, p_3^3]](6, 0)$?

(c) What is $h(6, 1) = \textbf{Pr}[succ, \textbf{Comp}[plus, j, p_3^3]](6, 1)$?

(d) What is $h(6, 2) = \textbf{Pr}[succ, \textbf{Comp}[plus, j, p_3^3]](6, 2)$?

3.1.5. Evaluate each of the following expressions. In each case your answer should be a natural number.

(a) $\textbf{Comp}[p_2^2, C_0^1, succ](9)$.

(b) $p_2^6(8, 45, 23, 79, 1, 1)$

(c) $\textbf{Comp}[succ, \textbf{Comp}[succ, \textbf{Comp}[succ, C_0^1]]](9)$

(d) $\textbf{Pr}[p_2^2, \textbf{Comp}[succ, p_4^4]](6, 35, 2)$

3.1.6. Explain why $\textbf{Comp}[p_2^3, C_0^1, succ]$ in fact names no function.

3.1.7. [hwk] Evaluate each of the following expressions given in canonical notation. In each case, your answer should be a natural number. Assume that *mult* is the usual binary multiplication function defined by $mult(n, m) = n \cdot m$. Also, assume that sum_3 is the ternary addition function on the natural numbers, that is, $sum_3(n, m, k) = n + m + k$.

(a) **Comp**$[succ, p_1^3](7, 14, 8)$

(b) **Comp**$[mult, p_2^3, p_2^3](7, 14, 8)$

(c) **Comp**$[succ,$ **Comp**$[mult, p_2^3, p_2^3]]$ $(7, 14, 8)$

(d) **Pr**$[succ, sum_3](7, 2)$

3.1.8. We wish to see that several other useful functions are primitive recursive. Fill in the blanks below so as to complete the following demonstrations that the functions in question are primitive recursive. Of course, we freely appeal to functions that have been shown previously to be primitive recursive.

(a) **Proposition.** The function *pred* defined by

$$pred(n) = \begin{cases} 0 & \text{if } n = 0 \\ n - 1 & \text{otherwise} \end{cases}$$

is primitive recursive. Note that *pred* is just the ordinary (unary) predecessor function except that the predecessor of 0 is now not -1 but, rather, 0 itself.

Proof. Function *pred* can be defined by

(i) $pred(0) = 0$

(ii) $pred(m + 1) = p_1^2(m, pred(m))$

But this shows that *pred* is primitive recursive, since in the first equation 0 can be written $C_0^0()$. Letting k be 0 in Schema B in Definition 3.3, we have that *pred* is **Pr**$[\underline{\hspace{1cm}}, \underline{\hspace{1cm}}]$.

(b) **Proposition.** The function defined by

$$monus(n, m) = \begin{cases} n - m & \text{if } n \geq m \\ 0 & \text{otherwise} \end{cases}$$

is primitive recursive. Note that *monus* is just like ordinary subtraction except that negative values are blocked: $monus(4, 7)$ equals 0. It will sometimes be convenient to write $n \overset{.}{-} m$ for $monus(n, m)$.

Proof. We have the following recursion equations:

(i) $monus(n, 0) = n$

(ii) $monus(n, m + 1) =$
$$pred(monus(n, m))$$

These can, of course, be recast as

(i) $monus(n, 0) = \underline{\hspace{1cm}} (n)$

(ii) $monus(n, m + 1) = pred(p_3^3(n, m,$
$$monus(n, m)))$$
$$= \textbf{Comp}[pred, p_3^3](n, m,$$
$$monus(n, m))$$

which shows that *monus* is **Pr**$[\underline{\hspace{1cm}},$ $\underline{\hspace{1cm}}]$. Thus *monus* is primitive recursive.

(c) **Proposition.** The (unary) *signum* function defined by

$$sg(n) = \begin{cases} 0 & \text{if } n = 0 \\ 1 & \text{otherwise} \end{cases}$$

is primitive recursive.

Proof. Note that $sg(n) = monus(1,$ $monus(1, n))$. (Verify this for $n = 0$ and $n = 3$, say.) But everything on the right here is primitive recursive. For 1 is just $C_1^1(n)$, giving

$$sg(n) = monus(C_1^1(n), monus(\underline{\hspace{1cm}}, n))$$
$$= monus(p_\square^2(C_1^1(n), n), monus(\underline{\hspace{1cm}}, n))$$
$$= \textbf{Comp}[\underline{\hspace{1cm}}, \underline{\hspace{1cm}}, \underline{\hspace{1cm}}](C_1^1(n), n)$$
$$= \textbf{Comp}[\underline{\hspace{1cm}}, \underline{\hspace{1cm}}, \underline{\hspace{1cm}}](C_1^1(n), p_1^1(n))$$
$$= \textbf{Comp}[\textbf{Comp}[\underline{\hspace{1cm}}, \underline{\hspace{1cm}}, \underline{\hspace{1cm}}],$$
$$C_1^1, p_1^1](n)$$

3.1.9. Show that the unary function $f(n) = n^2$ is primitive recursive.

3.1.10. (a) Show that binary function $max(n, m)$ is primitive recursive. (*Hint:* Define $max(n, m)$ by cases: $max(n, m) = n$ if $n \geq m$ and $max(n, m) = m$ otherwise.)

(b) Show that binary function $min(n, m)$ is primitive recursive using definition by cases.

3.1.11. Show that the binary number-theoretic function $f(n, m) =_{\text{def.}} |n - m|$ is primitive recursive. (*Hint:* Use definition by cases.)

3.1.12. (a) (**Permutation of Variables**). Show that if f is a binary primitive recursive function, then the binary function g that results from f by permuting variables (i.e., $g(m, n) =_{\text{def.}} f(n, m)$) is also primitive recursive.

    (b) Use (a) and Exercise 3.1.11 to show that function $g(m, n) =_{\text{def.}} |n - m|$ is primitive recursive.

3.1.13. (a) (**Substitution of Constants**). Show that if f is a binary primitive recursive function, then the unary function g that results from f by substitution of a constant n_0 (e.g., $g(n) =_{\text{def.}} f(n_0, n)$) is also primitive recursive.

    (b) Use (a) and our earlier demonstration that multiplication is primitive recursive to show that function $g(n) =_{\text{def.}} 7n$ is primitive recursive.

3.1.14. (a) (**Identification of Variables**). Show that if f is a binary primitive recursive function, then the unary function g that results from f by identifying variables (i.e., $g(n) =_{\text{def.}} f(n, n)$) is also primitive recursive.

    (b) Use (a) and Example 3.1.5 to show that function $g(n) =_{\text{def.}} n^n$ is primitive recursive.

3.1.15. (a) (**Adjunction of Variables**). Show that if f is a unary primitive recursive function,

then the binary function g that results from f by adjoining a new variable (i.e., $g(n, m) =_{\text{def.}} f(n)$) is also primitive recursive.

    (b) Use (a) and our earlier demonstration that the predecessor function *pred* is primitive recursive to show that function $g(n, m) =_{\text{def.}} pred(n)$ is primitive recursive.

3.1.16. Show that if f is a $(k + 1)$-ary primitive recursive function, then $(k + 1)$-ary function $\sum_{0 \leq i \leq m} f(n_1, n_2, \ldots, n_k, i) = \sum_{i=0}^{m} f(n_1, n_2, \ldots, n_k, i)$ is also primitive recursive. (*Hint*: Use the fact that function $\sum_{0 \leq i < m} f(n_1, n_2, \ldots, n_k, i)$ is primitive recursive.)

3.1.17. Show that if f is a $(k + 1)$-ary primitive recursive function, then $(k + 1)$-ary function $\Pi_{0 \leq i < m} f(n_1, n_2, \ldots, n_k, i)$ is also primitive recursive. (*Hint*: Model your proof on our demonstration that $\sum_{0 \leq i < m} f(n_1, n_2, \ldots, n_k, i)$ is primitive recursive provided f is primitive recursive. You will need to use the adopted convention whereby $\Pi_{0 \leq i < 0} a_i = 1$.)

3.1.18. Show that if f is a $(k + 1)$-ary primitive recursive function, then $(k + 1)$-ary function $\Pi_{0 \leq i \leq m} f(n_1, n_2, \ldots, n_k, i) = \Pi_{i=0}^{m} f(n_1, n_2, \ldots, n_k, i)$ is primitive recursive also. (*Hint*: Use 3.1.17.)

EXERCISES FOR §3.2

3.2.1. [hwk] Use the definitions of logical operations $\vee$, $\rightarrow$, and $\leftrightarrow$ given in the text to show that, if $C_1(n)$ and $C_2(n)$ are primitive recursive predicates, then so are

$$C_1(n) \vee C_2(n)$$

$$C_1(n) \rightarrow C_2(n)$$

$$C_1(n) \leftrightarrow C_1(n)$$

3.2.2. Recall that the binary predicate $n|m$ holds just in case m is a multiple of n. Show that the $n|m$ is primitive recursive, where $0|m$ is taken to be false for all $m \geq 0$. (*Hint*: Write out a

symbolic characterization of this predicate of the form $n|m \Leftrightarrow \ldots$, where $\ldots$ is replaced by an expression that involves only propositional connectives, bounded quantifiers, and predicates and functions previously shown to be primitive recursive.)

3.2.3. Show that the ternary predicate $\pi_m^i | n$ is primitive recursive.

3.2.4 (a) Show that the integer division function $f(n, m) =_{\text{def.}} n \, div \, (m + 1)$ is primitive recursive.

    (b) Show that the remainder function $g(n, m) =_{\text{def.}} n \, mod \, (m+1)$ is primitive recursive.

EXERCISES FOR §3.3

3.3.1. **(a)** Verify that the value of Ackermann's function for arguments 3 and 1 is 13. We begin the computation:

$$H(3, 1) = H(2, H(3, 0)) \qquad \text{by (iii)}$$
$$= H(2, H(2, 1)) \qquad \text{by (ii)}$$
$$= H(2, H(1, H(2, 0))) \qquad \text{by (iii)}$$
$$= H(2, H(1, H(1, 1))) \qquad \text{by (ii)}$$
$$= H(2, H(1, H(0, H(1, 0)))) \quad \text{by (iii)}$$
$$= H(2, H(1, H(0, H(0, 1)))) \quad \text{by (ii)}$$
$$= H(2, H(1, H(0, 2))) \qquad \text{by (i)}$$
$$= H(2, H(1, 3)) \qquad \text{by (i)}$$
$$= \cdots$$

(b) ^{hwk} Evaluate $H(2, 2)$.

(c) Write a program that computes Ackermann's function and test it using $\langle 3, 1 \rangle$ and $\langle 2, 2 \rangle$. (This is quite easy in Prolog, for example.) Try other very small argument pairs; unfortunately arguments of even moderate size quickly produce stack overflow.

3.3.2. **(a)** Give an inductive argument that shows that, for all $m \in N$, we have $H(1, m) = m + 2$.

(b) Similarly, show that, for all $m \in N$, we have $H(2, m) = 2m + 3$.

3.3.3. Present an argument showing that Ackermann's function is a total function. (*Hint*: Give an inductive argument.)

3.3.4. **(a)** Show by an indirect argument that binary function $f(n, m) =_{\text{def.}} H(n, m) + 1$ is recursive but not primitive recursive, where $H(n, m)$ is Ackermann's function as defined in Example 3.3.1. (*Hint*: Feel free to assume that $H(n, m)$ has itself been shown to be recursive but not primitive recursive.)

(b) Show that there exist infinitely many recursive functions that are not primitive recursive.

3.3.5. **(a)** Consider the unary constant-1 function, the standard canonical expression for which is C_1^1. Given that $C_1^1(n) = 1 + 1 - 1$ holds for all n, find an alternate canonical expression for C_1^1.

(b) Present an informal argument to the effect that C_1^1 has infinitely many canonical descriptions.

(c) Present an informal argument to the effect that any primitive recursive function has infinitely many canonical descriptions.

3.3.6. We defined $div(n, m)$ as $div(n, m) =_{\text{def.}} \mu t[(succ(n) \dot- (t \cdot m + m)) = 0]$. Letting n be 71 and m be 10, verify that the right-hand side here is equal to 7. Why is the successor function needed here?

3.3.7. ^{hwk} **(a)** Suppose that f is a ternary function whose values for certain argument pairs are presented in the chart below.

$f(3, 7, 0) = 4$	$f(2, 6, 0) = 84$	$f(4, 2, 0) = 56$	$f(30, 22, 0) = 4$
$f(3, 7, 1) = 24$	$f(2, 6, 1) = 84$	$f(4, 2, 1) = 6$	$f(30, 22, 1) = 4$
$f(3, 7, 2) = 4$	$f(2, 6, 2) = 0$	$f(4, 2, 2) = 563$	$f(30, 22, 2) = 4$
$f(3, 7, 3) = 42$	$f(2, 6, 3) = 34$	$f(4, 2, 3) = 26$	$f(30, 22, 3) = 4$
$f(3, 7, 4) = 0$	$f(2, 6, 4) = 0$	$f(4, 2, 4) = 39$	$f(30, 22, 4) = 4$
$f(3, 7, 5) = 4$	$f(2, 6, 5) = 444$	$f(4, 2, 5)$ is undefined	$f(30, 22, 5) = 4$
$f(3, 7, 6) = 4$	$f(2, 6, 6) = 84$	$f(4, 2, 6) = 0$	$f(30, 22, 6) = 4$
$f(3, 7, 7) = 4$	$f(2, 6, 7) = 84$	$f(4, 2, 7) = 56$	$f(30, 22, 7) = 4$
$\cdots$	$\cdots$	$\cdots$	and, for all $n > 7$, $f(30, 22, n) = 4$

Now let g be the binary function defined as $\mathbf{Mn}[f]$. What is the value of each of the following expressions? (If g is undefined for a particular pair of arguments, simply indicate this.)

(i) $g(3,7) \quad = \mathbf{Mn}[f](3,7)$
(ii) $g(2,6) \quad = \mathbf{Mn}[f](2,6)$
(iii) $g(4,2) \quad = \mathbf{Mn}[f](4,2)$
(iv) $g(30,22) = \mathbf{Mn}[f](30,22)$

(b) Is function f a total function or a partial function?

(c) Is function g a total function or a partial function?

(d) Critique—say what is wrong with it—the following proposition: For any number-theoretic function f, we have that $\mathbf{Mn}[f]$ is total if and only if f is total.

3.3.8. **(a)** Suppose that f is a binary function whose values are presented in the chart below.

$$f(n,0) = 4 \text{ for all } n \in \mathcal{N}$$

$$f(n,1) = 5 \text{ for all } n \in \mathcal{N}$$

$$f(n,2) = 7 \text{ for all } n \in \mathcal{N}$$

$$f(n,3) = 9 \text{ for all } n \in \mathcal{N}$$

$$f(n,4) = 0 \text{ for all } n \in \mathcal{N}$$

$$f(n,5) = 4 \text{ for all } n \in \mathcal{N}$$

$$f(n,6) = 1 \text{ for all } n \in \mathcal{N}$$

$$f(n,m) \text{ is undefined for all } m \geq 7$$

Now let g be the binary function defined as $\mathbf{Mn}[f]$. What is the value of each of the following expressions? (If g is undefined for a particular pair of arguments, simply indicate this.)

(i) $g(0) = \mathbf{Mn}[f](0)$
(ii) $g(1) = \mathbf{Mn}[f](1)$
(iii) $g(2) = \mathbf{Mn}[f](2)$
(iv) $g(3) = \mathbf{Mn}[f](3)$

(b) What is the more usual name for $\mathbf{Mn}[f]$?

(c) Is function f a total function or a partial function?

(d) Is function g a total function or a partial function?

(e) What conclusion can be drawn from this example? (Does it follow from the fact that f is partial that $\mathbf{Mn}[f]$ is also partial?)

3.3.9. [hwk] Explain why every primitive recursive predicate is a recursive predicate.

3.3.10. Show that the unary function defined at (3.3.1) in the proof of Theorem 3.2 is a Turing-computable function. (*Hint*: Describe a deterministic, multitape Turing machine.)

3.3.11. Number-theoretic functions are said to be *primitive recursive* or *partial recursive* or just *recursive*. On the other hand, number-theoretic predicates may be *primitive recursive* or *recursive*—end of story. Explain why we have introduced no notion of *partial recursive predicate*.

EXERCISES FOR §3.4

The 13 exercises below are intended to help the reader to better grasp the rather difficult proof of Theorem 3.3(b). Each exercise corresponds to one of items **(1)** through **(13)** in that proof.

3.4.1. Suppose that $\Gamma_M = \{\&, *, \lambda, 1\}$. Give a standard encoding of $\Gamma_M \cup \{B\}$ in accordance with **(1)**. (There are two possible answers here.)

3.4.2. Suppose that $\Gamma_M = \{\&, *, \lambda, 1\}$ and that symbols $\&$, $*$, and λ correspond to codes 1, 2, and 3, respectively. Give the encoding of tape

contents $\lambda 111 * 1 \& 1 * BBBBBBBBBB \ldots$ following the example of **(2)**. Your answer will be a natural number.

3.4.3. We continue to assume that $\Gamma_M = \{\&, *, \lambda, 1\}$ and that symbols $\&$, $*$, and λ correspond to codes 1, 2, and 3, respectively. The unary primitive recursive predicate $unbr1(n)$ of **(3)** will be false for most n. Find the first seven values of n for which $unbr1(n)$ is true. (*Hint*: What is the value of constant k at the end of **(3)** in the present case?)

| λ | 1 | 1 | 1 | * | 1 | 1 | & | B | B | B | B | B | B |

. . .

Figure 3.4.7

3.4.4. In which position on the tape in Figure 3.4.7 is symbol * located? Symbol &?

3.4.5. Consider the Turing machine with one-way-infinite tape of Figure 2.1.1. What is the value of constant r in this case?

3.4.6. **(a)** Define by cases the binary function $action(q, s)$ for the Turing machine M of Figure 2.1.1. Note that, since $\Gamma_M = \{\lambda, 1\}$, the code of the blank is 0 as usual, the code of λ is 1, and the code of symbol 1 happens to be 2.

    (b) Define by cases the binary function $next\_symbol(q, s)$ for the Turing machine of Figure 2.1.1.

    (c) Define by cases the binary function $next\_state(q, s)$ for the Turing machine of Figure 2.1.1.

3.4.7. Suppose that $\Gamma_M = \{\&, *, \lambda, 1\}$ again and that symbols &, *, and λ correspond to codes 1, 2, and 3, respectively. Suppose that, at some point during its computation, machine M is in its state q_9 scanning symbol * on a tape configured as

$$\lambda 111*1\&1*BBBBBBBBB \ldots$$
$$\uparrow$$

Find the corresponding configuration triple $\langle w, q, p \rangle$ as described in **(7)**. Refer to your answer to Exercise 3.4.2.

3.4.8. Suppose that $\Gamma_M = \{\&, *, \lambda, 1\}$ again and that symbols &, *, and λ correspond to codes 1, 2, and 3, respectively. Suppose further that, at some point during its computation, the machine configuration of M is given by the triple $\langle 224749, 14, 6 \rangle$. Use the definition of binary function $current\_symbol(w, p)$ given at the end of **(8)** in order to determine which symbol, if any, is currently being scanned by M's read/write head. As noted in the text, this computation will make no use of the current value of q, which happens to be 14.

3.4.9. Let M once again be the Turing machine of Figure 2.1.1 so that $\Gamma_M = \{\lambda, 1\}$. Refer to your answer in Exercise 3.4.6(a) in order to evaluate each of the following.
    (a) $next\_square(80, 0, 1)$
    (b) $next\_square(80, 1, 2)$
    (c) $next\_square(80, 2, 3)$
    (d) $next\_square(80, 2, 4)$
    (e) $next\_square(80, 2, 5)$
    (f) $next\_square(80, 3, 4)$

3.4.10. We continue to let M be the seven-state Turing machine of Figure 2.1.1 so that $\Gamma_M = \{\lambda, 1\}$ and $k = 3$. Use your answers to Exercise 3.4.6 to evaluate $next\_tape\_contents(80, 3, 4)$.

3.4.11. For the same M, what is $next\_configuration(80, 3, 4)$? Express your answer as a product of powers of primes.

3.4.12. Calculate each of the following—again for the machine of Figure 2.1.1. Express any answer as a product of powers of primes.
    (a) $execute(80, 0)$
    (b) $execute(80, 1)$
    (c) $execute(80, 2)$
    (d) $execute(80, 3)$
    (e) $execute(80, 4)$
    (f) $execute(80, 5)$
    (g) $execute(80, 6)$

3.4.13. Calculate $num\_steps(80)$ for the machine of Figure 2.1.1.

EXERCISES FOR §3.5

3.5.1. In Example 3.2.7 the unary predicate $prime(n)$ was shown to be primitive recursive and hence recursive. What set of natural numbers has thereby been shown to be a recursive set?

3.5.2. Show that the family of recursive sets of natural numbers is closed under union. That is, show that if S_1 and S_2 are both recursive sets, then so is $S_1 \cup S_2$.

3.5.3. Show that the family of recursive sets of natural numbers is closed under intersection. That is, show that if S_1 and S_2 are both recursive sets, then so is $S_1 \cap S_2$.

3.5.4. Show that the family of recursive sets of natural numbers is closed under relative complementation. That is, show that if S_1 and S_2 are both recursive sets, then so is $S_1 \backslash S_2$.

3.5.5. Show that the family of recursive sets of natural numbers is closed under symmetric difference. That is, show that if S_1 and S_2 are both recursive sets, then so is $S_1 \oplus S_2$.

EXERCISES FOR §3.6

3.6.1. Each of the number-theoretic functions below has been shown to be recursive. In the case of each function, say what set of natural numbers has thereby been shown to be recursively enumerable.
  (a) $f(n) = n^2$
  (b) $f(n) = n$

3.6.2. ^{hwk} In the proof of Theorem 3.4 we showed that any finite set S of natural numbers is recursively enumerable. Show that such a set is in fact recursive.

3.6.3. (a) (**Proof of Theorem 3.6**). Let S be a nonempty set of natural numbers. Show that S is r.e. if and only if S is $Image(f)$ for some k-ary partial recursive function f with $k \geq 1$. (*Hint*: The forward direction is trivial. As for the reverse direction, use the Euler–Gödel scheme to encode k-tuple $\langle n_1, n_2, n_3, \ldots, n_k \rangle$ as a natural number. Then use the extraction function of Example 3.3.7.)
  (b) How can (reasoning about) Turing machines be used to show that if S is $Image(f)$ for some k-ary partial recursive function f with $k \geq 1$, then S is r.e.?

3.6.4. (**Proof of Theorem 3.7**). Prove that a set S of natural numbers is recursively enumerable if and only if S is the domain of a unary partial recursive function. (Recall that in Theorem 3.5 we showed that the r.e. sets are the *images* of unary partial recursive functions.) In other words, prove both of the following statements:
  (a) If S is a nonempty r.e. set, then there exists a unary partial recursive f with $Dom(f) = S$.
  (b) If f is a unary partial recursive function,

then $Dom(f)$ is r.e. (*Hint for both (a) and (b)*: Use Theorem 3.3 and dovetailing.)

3.6.5. Suppose that f is partial recursive. What do we know about both $Dom(f)$ and $Image(f)$?

3.6.6. (a) Prove that a nonempty set S of natural numbers is recursively enumerable if and only if S is $Image(f)$ for some injective partial recursive function f. (*Hint*: One direction is, of course, trivial. For the other direction, describe the construction of a Turing machine.)
  (b) Prove that a nonempty set S of natural numbers is r.e. if and only if there exists a bijective partial recursive function f that maps some subset of $\mathcal{N}$ onto S.

3.6.7. (a) Let f be a unary partial recursive function and let $S \subseteq Dom(f)$ be an r.e. set. Show that $Image_f(S) = \{n \in \mathcal{N} | n = f(m)$ for some $m \in S\}$ is r.e. (*Hint*: Show that $Image_f(S)$ is $Image(h)$ for some partial recursive h. Use the closure of the class of partial recursive functions under composition.)
  (b) Show that the assumption in (a) that S is r.e. is essential by showing that there exist partial recursive f and $S \subseteq Dom(f)$ such that $Image_f(S) = \{n \in \mathcal{N} | n = f(m)$ for some $m \in S\}$ is not r.e. (*Hint*: Give an indirect argument that appeals to Theorem 3.10.)

3.6.8. Show how Corollary 3.1 follows from Theorems 3.10 and 3.11. (*Hint*: Give an indirect argument.)

3.6.9. ^{hwk} (a) Show that the class of r.e. sets is closed under union. (*Hint*: Use Theorem 3.7.)

(b) Show that the class of r.e. sets is closed under intersection. (*Hint*: Use Theorem 3.7 again.)

(c) Show that the class of r.e. sets is closed under neither relative complementation nor symmetric difference.

EXERCISES FOR §3.7 (END-OF-CHAPTER REVIEW EXERCISES)

3.7.1. ^hwk Fill in the blanks and boxes below thereby demonstrating that the factorial function is primitive recursive. Note that the factorial function is unary. We write $fac(n)$ for $n!$ Our recursion equations are

(i) $fac(0) = 1$

(ii) $fac(n+1) = succ(n) \cdot fac(n)$

We can write $1 =$ _____ . Also, since $n = p_\square^1(n, fac(n))$, (ii) can be written as

(ii) $fac(n+1)$

$= \underline{\quad}(\underline{\quad}(p_\square^2(n, fac(n))),$
$\qquad\qquad p_2^2(n, fac(n)))$

$= \underline{\quad}(\mathbf{Comp}[\underline{\quad}, p_\square^2]$
$\qquad (n, fac(n)), p_2^2(n, fac(n)))$

$= \mathbf{Comp}[\underline{\quad}, \mathbf{Comp}[\underline{\quad},$
$\qquad\qquad p_\square^2], p_2^2](n, fac(n))$

So fac is just

$\mathbf{Pr}[\underline{\qquad\qquad}, \mathbf{Comp}[\underline{\quad},$

$\qquad\quad \mathbf{Comp}[\underline{\quad}, p_\square^2], p_2^2]]$

3.7.2. Show that the function f defined by $f(n, m) = n \bmod m$ is partial recursive by either (1) presenting an explicit definition of f or (2) describing a Turing machine and then appealing to Theorem 3.3(b).

3.7.3. ^hwk Give a general argument to the effect that the k-ary constant function C_j^k is primitive recursive for arbitrary $k, j \geq 0$.

3.7.4. ^hwk Consider the Venn diagram of Figure 3.7.1.

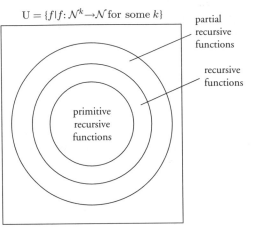

$U = \{f \mid f: \mathcal{N}^k \to \mathcal{N} \text{ for some } k\}$

partial recursive functions

recursive functions

primitive recursive functions

Figure 3.7.1

For each of the number-theoretic functions listed below, indicate where the function is located within the diagram by writing the Roman numeral associated with the function directly on the diagram in the appropriate place.

(I) the addition function *plus*
(II) the multiplication function *mult*
(III) the integer division function *div*
(IV) Ackermann's function
(V) the function f^* defined by

$$f^*(n) = \begin{cases} n & \text{if } f_n(n) \text{ is undefined} \\ \text{undefined} & \text{otherwise} \end{cases}$$

where an enumeration $f_0, f_1, f_2, \ldots$ of the class of (unary) partial recursive functions is assumed.

3.7.5. We wish to evaluate $\mathbf{Comp}[plus, p_1^2, \mathbf{Comp}[exp, p_2^2, p_2^2]](3, 4)$, where *plus* and *exp* denote the binary addition function and binary exponentiation function, respectively, as defined earlier. In particular, $exp(4, 4) = 4^4 = 256$. As usual, we start from the inside, so to speak, focusing first on $\mathbf{Comp}[exp, p_2^2, p_2^2]$.
(a) Referring to Schema A, what is the value of m in the case of $\mathbf{Comp}[exp, p_2^2, p_2^2]$?
(b) What is the value of k in this case?

(c) What then is the value of **Comp**$[exp, p_2^2, p_2^2](3, 4)$?

(d) Let us take h in Schema A to be **Comp**$[plus, p_1^2, $**Comp**$[exp, p_2^2, p_2^2]]$ next. What function serves in the role of f in this case?

(e) Hence, what is the value of m in Schema A in this case? What function serves as g_1? As g_2? What is the value of k in this case?

(f) Finally, referring to Schema A and using the established identifications, what is the value of **Comp**$[plus, p_1^2, $**Comp**$[exp, p_2^2, p_2^2]](3, 4)$?

3.7.6. Show that there exists a recursive function $\eta(n)$ such that, for any n, $\eta(n)$ is the gödel number of a Turing machine computing function

$$\nu(m) = \begin{cases} 0 & \text{if } f_n(m) \text{ is defined} \\ \text{undefined} & \text{otherwise} \end{cases}$$

where f_n is the number-theoretic function computed by Turing machine M_n. (We are writing M_n for the Turing machine with gödel number n.)

3.7.7. We assume an enumeration $f_0, f_1, f_2, \ldots, f_n$, ... of all unary partial recursive functions.

(a) Let binary predicate $R_1(n, m)$ hold just in case n is a member of $Image(f_m)$. Show that $R_1(n, m)$ is not a recursive predicate. (*Hint*: Use Exercise 3.1.13 and Theorem 3.10.)

(b) Let binary predicate $R_2(n, m)$ hold just in case n is a member of $Dom(f_m)$. Show that $R_2(n, m)$ is not a recursive predicate. (*Hint*: Use Exercise 3.1.13, Theorem 3.7, and Theorem 3.10.)

3.7.8. Suppose that $C(n, m)$ is a binary recursive predicate. Show that $\mu m[C(n, m)]$ is then a unary partial recursive function (see remarks in §3.3).

3.7.9. Show that the class of partial recursive functions is closed under definition by cases. That is, show that any function that is definable by cases from partial recursive functions, and from mutually exclusive and mutually exhaus-

tive recursive predicates, is itself partial recursive. (*Hint*: Use the argument of Example 3.2.3.)

3.7.10. Show that the class of recursive predicates is closed under logical connectives &, ¬, ∨, → and ↔. That is, show that if $C_1(n_1, n_2, \ldots, n_k)$ and $C_2(n_1, n_2, \ldots, n_k)$ are both k-ary recursive predicates, then so are all of

$$C_1(n_1, n_2, \ldots, n_k) \,\&\, C_2(n_1, n_2, \ldots, n_k)$$

$$\neg C_1(n_1, n_2, \ldots, n_k)$$

$$C_1(n_1, n_2, \ldots, n_k) \lor C_2(n_1, n_2, \ldots, n_k)$$

$$C_1(n_1, n_2, \ldots, n_k) \to C_2(n_1, n_2, \ldots, n_k)$$

$$C_1(n_1, n_2, \ldots, n_k) \leftrightarrow C_2(n_1, n_2, \ldots, n_k)$$

(*Hint*: Use the arguments of Example 3.2.4.)

3.7.11 (a) Show that the class of recursive predicates is closed under bounded existential quantification. That is, show that if $C(n_1, n_2, \ldots, n_k, i)$ is a $(k + 1)$-ary recursive predicate, then so is $\exists i_{\leq j} C(n_1, n_2, \ldots, n_k, i)$. (*Hint*: Use the argument of Example 3.2.5.)

(b) Show that the class of recursive predicates is closed under bounded universal quantification. That is, show that if $C(n_1, n_2, \ldots, n_k, i)$ is a $(k + 1)$-ary recursive predicate, then so is $\forall i_{\leq j} C(n_1, n_2, \ldots, n_k, i)$. (*Hint*: Use the argument of Example 3.2.6.)

3.7.12. Show that, given an arbitrary single-tape, deterministic Turing machine M, the unary number-theoretic functions $time_M(n)$ and $space_M(n)$, as defined in Definitions 1.8 and 1.9, are both partial recursive. (*Hint*: In each case, describe a multitape Turing machine M^* that simulates M for each input word of length n—there are, of course, finitely many such input words. Then use Theorem 3.3(b).)

3.7.13. Prove Theorem 3.12. (*Hint*: To show that any partial recursive and total function f is general recursive, use Theorem 3.3(a) and then reconsider the proof of Theorem 3.3(b). Let Turing machine M compute f. One then needs to see that, since every computation of M for appropriate input string can be assumed to halt in a value-representing configuration, the sequence of functions defined in **(1)–(13)** of that proof are all general recursive in the sense of Definition 3.11. You will want to focus on the unary function num_steps defined at **(13)**.)

3.7.14. Show that if $f \colon \mathcal{N} \to \mathcal{N}$ is a strictly monotone increasing and recursive function, then $\chi_{Cod(f)}$ is a recursive set of natural numbers. (*Hint*: Describe a Turing machine that computes function $\chi_{Cod(f)}$ and use the fact that f is total.)

3.7.15. Show that every infinite r.e. set has an r.e. subset that is not recursive. (*Hint*: Show that, were this not the case, then every r.e. set would be recursive.)

3.7.16. In Exercise 3.6.9(a), we showed that the class of r.e. sets is closed under finite union. That is, for arbitrary $k \in \mathcal{N}$, if $S_1, S_2, \dots, S_k$ are r.e., then so is $S_1 \cup S_2 \cup \dots \cup S_k$. You are now asked to show that the class of r.e. sets is not closed under *countable* union. Namely, there exist countable families $\{S_i\}_{i \in \mathcal{N}}$ of r.e. sets

such that $\bigcup_i S_i$ is not r.e. (*Hint*: Use Theorem 3.10.)

3.7.17. In Exercise 3.6.9(b), we showed that the class of r.e. sets is closed under finite intersection. That is, for arbitrary $k \in \mathcal{N}$, if $S_1, S_2, \dots, S_k$ are r.e., then so is $S_1 \cap S_2 \cap \dots \cap S_k$. You are now asked to show that the class of r.e. sets is not closed under *countable* intersection. Namely, there exist countable families $\{S_i\}_{i \in \mathcal{N}}$ of r.e. sets such that $\bigcap_i S_i$ is not r.e. (*Hint*: Use Theorem 3.10.)

3.7.18. Write a program that evaluates the application of any k-ary primitive recursive function, canonically presented, to an arbitrary k-tuple of natural number arguments. For example, your program would evaluate the likes of $\mathbf{Pr}[C_0^1, \mathbf{Comp}[\mathbf{Pr}[p_1^1, \mathbf{Comp}[succ, p_3^3]], p_1^3, p_3^3]](8, 5)$ as 40 (see Example 3.1.4). (*Suggestion*: Use LISP.)

3.7.19. Write a C language program implementing Ackermann's function. Display the run-time stack at its deepest point when evaluating $H(2, 6) = 15$.

## Chapter 4

Markov Algorithms

Historically, the first attempts at giving a precise account of the notion of algorithm took our function computation paradigm as basic. In contrast, the *string-rewriting systems* that were first described in the 1950s by Russian mathematician A. A. Markov (1903–1979) are an attempt to give an analysis of sequential computation in its fullest generality. In this sense, Markov took our transduction paradigm as his starting point and stressed symbol manipulation. We shall see how each of the three computational paradigms introduced in §1.1 can be implemented using Markov's model. Moreover, that model will turn out to be formally equivalent to Turing's.

§4.1 An Alternative Model of Sequential Computation

Before presenting a formal definition, we first consider some simple examples of so-called *Markov algorithms*. The reader is encouraged to use the companion software in order to enter and test Examples 4.1.1 through 4.1.3, which follow.

EXAMPLE 4.1.1 Let Σ be alphabet $\{a, b, c, d\}$. By a *Markov algorithm scheme* or *schema* we shall mean a finite sequence of *productions* or *rewrite rules*. As a first example, consider the following two-member sequence of productions.

$$\text{(i)} \quad a \to c$$

$$\text{(ii)} \quad b \to \varepsilon$$

We now apply this production sequence to words over Σ. Let *input word w* be *baba*. We must first attempt to apply production (i), which means substituting its right-hand side for the leftmost occurrence of its left-hand side. Since the left-hand side of (i) does occur in w, rule (i) transforms input word w into *computation word* $w_1 = bcba$.

$$ba\underline{ba} \Rightarrow bc\underline{ba} \quad \text{by (i)}$$

Production (i) is now applied again—we are not permitted to apply (ii) unless we find that (i) can no longer be applied. This second application of (i) transforms w_1 into computation word $w_2 = bcbc$.

$$bcb\underline{a} \Rightarrow bcb\underline{c} \quad \text{by (i)}$$

At this point (i) cannot be applied again—there are no more *a*s. So (ii) is applied, causing the right-hand side of (ii), which is the empty word, to be substituted for the leftmost *b* in w_2. This gives $w_3 = cbc$.

$$\underline{b}cbc \Rightarrow \varepsilon cbc = cbc \quad \text{by (ii)}$$

Continuing, production (i) is still not applicable—we are required to attempt to apply it—but production (ii) may be applied once more to give $w_4 = cc$.

$$c\underline{b}c \Rightarrow c\varepsilon c = cc \quad \text{by (ii)}$$

Since neither production can be applied to w_4, the substitution process ceases: The Markov algorithm scheme consisting of productions (i) and (ii) has transformed input word *abab* into output word *cc*. We summarize by writing

$$baba \Rightarrow^* cc$$

The general effect of applying this particular Markov algorithm scheme to a given input word *w* is to replace any and all occurrences of symbol *a* by symbol *c* and to eliminate occurrences of symbol *b* altogether. Thus, this Markov algorithm scheme transforms input words *abcd*, *bbbb*, *cdcd*, and ε into words *ccd*, ε, *cdcd*, and ε, respectively. In symbols:

$$abcd \Rightarrow^* ccd$$

$$bbbb \Rightarrow^* \varepsilon$$

$$cdcd \Rightarrow^* cdcd$$

$$\varepsilon \Rightarrow^* \varepsilon$$

In each case, the substitution process implicit in the given Markov algorithm scheme ceases when no production is applicable. Equivalently, this substitution process terminates if an attempt to apply the physically last production is unsuccessful. (In the case of input words ε and *cdcd*, no production can be applied, which means that the substitution process halts immediately.) Example 4.1.2, which follows, shows that there is yet another way in which the substitution process may terminate.

Before proceeding, we pause to make an important distinction. The described substitution process that results when the Markov algorithm schema of Example 4.1.1 is applied to some input word will be referred to as the *Markov algorithm* corresponding to, or implicit in, that Markov algorithm scheme. Thus, one makes a distinction between the production sequence (i)–(ii) on the one hand, which we call the Markov algorithm scheme, and, on the other hand, the substitution process that results when the Markov algorithm scheme (i)–(ii) is applied. We shall sometimes use italic symbol *S* to designate an arbitrary Markov algorithm scheme and A_S for the corresponding Markov algorithm.

EXAMPLE 4.1.2 Let Σ be alphabet $\{a, b, c, d\}$. Next, consider the following three-member sequence of productions.

(i) $a \rightarrow c$

(ii) $bc \rightarrow cb$

(iii) $b \rightarrow .cd$

Consider input word $w = baba$. Again, we must first attempt to apply (i), which means substituting its right-hand side for the leftmost occurrence of its left-hand side. Since the left-hand side of (i) does occur in w, applying rule (i) transforms w into $w_1 = bcba$.

$$b\underline{a}ba \Rightarrow b\underline{c}ba \quad \text{by (i)}$$

Production (i) is now applied again—after application of any production, we are required to return to the very first production in our sequence. This second application of (i) gives $w_2 = bcbc$.

$$bcb\underline{a} \Rightarrow bcb\underline{c} \quad \text{by (i)}$$

At this point (i) cannot be applied again, so (ii) is applied, causing the right-hand side of (ii) to be substituted for the leftmost occurrence of substring bc in w_2. This yields $w_3 = cbbc$.

$$\underline{bc}bc \Rightarrow \underline{cb}bc \quad \text{by (ii)}$$

Production (ii) is applied once more to give $w_4 = cbcb$.

$$cb\underline{bc} \Rightarrow cb\underline{cb} \quad \text{by (ii)}$$

Finally, productions (ii) and (iii) are applied in sequence to give output word $cccdb$.

$$c\underline{bc}b \Rightarrow c\underline{cb}b \quad \text{by (ii)}$$

$$cc\underline{b}b \Rightarrow cc\underline{cd}b \quad \text{by (iii)}$$

The dot occurring on the right side of (iii) indicates a so-called *terminal production*: The substitution process ceases *immediately* upon successful application of such a production even if this production or others could yet be applied to the resulting computation word. So the result of applying the productions (i)–(iii) to input word *baba* is output word *cccdb*, which we summarize by writing

$$baba \Rightarrow^* cccdb$$

The reader should verify that applying (i)–(iii) to words *aaab*, *baaa*, *abcd*, and ε yields *ccccd*, *ccccd*, *cccdd*, and ε, respectively. That is:

$$aaab \Rightarrow^* ccccd$$

$$baaa \Rightarrow^* ccccd$$

$$abcd \Rightarrow^* cccdd$$

$$\varepsilon \Rightarrow^* \varepsilon$$

More interesting examples require that we permit temporary "markers"—symbols not in alphabet Σ—to appear in the course of the substitution process. We shall use special symbols #, \$, %, *, and the like, as markers and distinguish *input alphabet* Σ from *work alphabet* Γ, where Γ is Σ plus, possibly, one or more of these special markers. Typically, such markers will not appear in the output word of the Markov algorithm in question, having been eliminated earlier on.

Our next example exploits the fact that empty word ε is a (proper) prefix of any (nonempty) word w.

EXAMPLE 4.1.3 Let input alphabet $\Sigma = \{a, b\}$. Let work alphabet Γ be $\Sigma \cup \{\#\}$. We see that the Markov algorithm scheme consisting of the four-member production sequence

$$\text{(i)} \quad \#a \rightarrow a\#$$

$$\text{(ii)} \quad \#b \rightarrow b\#$$

$$\text{(iii)} \quad \# \rightarrow .ab$$

$$\text{(iv)} \quad \varepsilon \rightarrow \#$$

has the effect of appending string ab to any word over Σ. As an example, consider input word $w = abbaba = \varepsilon abbaba$. Neither (i) nor (ii) nor (iii) apply initially since w contains no occurrence of #. But (iv) may be applied to $w = \varepsilon abbaba$ to obtain $w_1 = \#abbaba$:

$$abbaba \Rightarrow \#abbaba \quad \text{by (iv)}$$

Now, productions (i) and (ii) are each applied several times so as to position auxiliary symbol # to the right of all the as and bs.

$$\#abbaba \Rightarrow^* abbaba\# \quad \text{by repeated applications of (i) and (ii)}$$

Finally, production (iii) is used to replace symbol # by string ab.

$$abbaba\underline{\#} \Rightarrow abbaba\underline{ab} \quad \text{by (iii)}$$

Thus $abbabaab$ is the *output word* in this case and we write

$$abbaba \Rightarrow^* abbabaab$$

(What would happen if (iii) were not a terminal production? Would the algorithm ever halt?)

Designating $\Sigma = \{a, b\}$ as input alphabet of an algorithm schema means that we will not consider input words containing symbols other that a and b. With regard to the preceding Example 4.1.3 in particular, note that, for any input word over Σ, auxiliary symbol # will not appear in the resulting output word. Despite this, one sees that # plays an essential role in the algorithm—a role that neither a nor b could play. Thus temporary markers such as # are sometimes indispensable in the design of Markov algorithm schemata.

In Example 4.1.3 we saw how to use an auxiliary symbol so as to append a string to any given input word. In the next example we see an interesting application of this highly useful device.

EXAMPLE 4.1.4 (Reverse Word) Consider the algorithm schema S whose productions appear below.

$$
\begin{array}{rl}
\text{(i)} & \#@a \rightarrow a\#@ \\[4pt]
\text{(ii)} & \#@b \rightarrow b\#@ \\[4pt]
\text{(iii)} & \$aa \rightarrow a\$a \\[4pt]
\text{(iv)} & \$ab \rightarrow b\$a \\[4pt]
\text{(v)} & \$ba \rightarrow a\$b \\[4pt]
\text{(vi)} & \$bb \rightarrow b\$b \\[4pt]
\text{(vii)} & \$a@ \rightarrow a@ \\[4pt]
\text{(viii)} & \$b@ \rightarrow b@ \\[4pt]
\text{(ix)} & a\# \rightarrow \#\$a \\[4pt]
\text{(x)} & b\# \rightarrow \#\$b \\[4pt]
\text{(xi)} & \# \rightarrow \varepsilon \\[4pt]
\text{(xii)} & @ \rightarrow .\varepsilon \\[4pt]
\text{(xiii)} & \varepsilon \rightarrow \#@
\end{array}
$$

We let $\Sigma = \{a, b\}$ and $\Gamma = \Sigma \cup \{\#, @, \$\}$. Let us apply it to input word $w = aab$. Initially, only production (xiii) is applicable:

$$aab \Rightarrow \#@aab$$

Productions (i) and (ii) are now used to move the string $\#@$ past all as and bs.

$$\#@aab \Rightarrow^{+} aab\#@$$

(The use of symbol $^{+}$ here will be explained in a moment.) At this point, the physically highest applicable production is (x) followed by (viii).

$$aab\#@ \Rightarrow aa\#\$b@$$
$$\Rightarrow aa\#b@$$

Continuing, we have

$$aa\#b@ \Rightarrow a\#\$ab@ \quad \text{by (ix)}$$
$$\Rightarrow a\#b\$a@ \quad \text{by (iv)}$$
$$\Rightarrow a\#ba@ \quad \text{by (vii)}$$
$$\Rightarrow \#\$aba@ \quad \text{by (ix) again}$$
$$\Rightarrow \#b\$aa@ \quad \text{by (iv)}$$
$$\Rightarrow \#ba\$a@ \quad \text{by (iii)}$$
$$\Rightarrow \#baa@ \quad \text{by (vii)}$$
$$\Rightarrow baa@ \quad \text{by (xi)}$$
$$\Rightarrow baa \quad \text{by (xii)}$$

In the case of each line above, the reader should verify that the applied production is the first production in the production sequence (i)–(xiii) that is applicable to the current computation word. Also, it should be noted that applying a production to a computation word always means replacing the leftmost occurrence of its left-hand side. In the preceding example, it just happens that in most cases the leftmost occurrence of a production left-hand side is its unique occurrence. However, in the case of one of the production applications above, there are, at the point of application, multiple occurrences of its left-hand side within the current computation word. Which production is this? (*Hint:* Where in word *aab* are occurrences of ε to be found?)

Open the icon labeled **Reverse Word** within the Markov Algorithm folder in order to verify that the Markov algorithm A_S corresponding to schema S has the general effect of reversing its input word; that is, input word w over $\Sigma = \{a, b\}$ is transformed by A_S into output word w^R.

An ordered sequence of productions such as those of Examples 4.1.1 through 4.1.4 is the central component of what will henceforth be called a *Markov algorithm scheme* or *schema* (plural, *schemata*). Assuming work alphabet Γ, each production is of the form

$$\alpha \rightarrow \beta \quad \text{or} \quad \alpha \rightarrow .\beta$$

where both α and β are (possibly empty) words over Γ. Productions of the form $\alpha \rightarrow \beta$ are called *nonterminal productions,* whereas those of the form $\alpha \rightarrow .\beta$ are called *terminal productions.* (Incidentally, a Markov algorithm schema may contain several terminal productions. But see Exercise 4.1.3 below.) Application of such a scheme S to computation word w is thoroughly deterministic in the sense that at every point within that computation there is a definite next step. One applies that production π such that (1) there is an occurrence of the left-hand side of π in w and (2) π is the first such production in the sequence of productions making up S. Suppose π to be of the form

$$\alpha \rightarrow \beta$$

Then applying π to w means replacing the leftmost occurrence of α within w by β.

By a Markov algorithm we shall mean a certain *process type*. Any instance of that process type consists in applying the productions of the corresponding Markov algorithm scheme in the prescribed order and in the prescribed manner until either (1) no production is applicable or (2) a terminal production has been applied. The distinction here is subtle but important: (The production sequence of) a Markov algorithm scheme is a physical inscription[1]—something consisting of ink on paper or chalk on a chalkboard—whereas the Markov algorithm corresponding to it is probably best thought of as a (type of) process occurring in time. Thus Markov algorithm schemata *determine* Markov algorithms but are distinct from them. In practice, however, we shall tend to identify an algorithm schema with the Markov algorithm that it determines. In any case, it is time to give a formal, set-theoretic definition of Markov algorithm schema.

DEFINITION 4.1: A Markov algorithm schema S is any triple $\langle \Sigma, \Gamma, \Pi \rangle$, where Σ is a nonempty *input alphabet*, Γ is a finite *work alphabet* with $\Sigma \subseteq \Gamma$, and Π is a finite, ordered sequence of productions either of the form $\alpha \rightarrow \beta$ or of the form $\alpha \rightarrow .\beta$, where both α and β are (possibly empty) words over Γ.

Some new terminology was introduced in the course of discussing Example 4.1.4. We shall write $w \Rightarrow_S w'$ to describe one step in the application of a Markov algorithm schema S. Thus if the current computation word is w, then writing $w \Rightarrow_S w'$ will mean that w' is obtained from w by applying whichever production is applied next in accordance with schema S. When the context is clear, we will frequently drop the subscript and write simply $w \Rightarrow w'$. Extending this, we shall write $w \Rightarrow_S^* w'$, or just $w \Rightarrow^* w'$, to mean that w' is obtained from w in zero or more steps. Thus the application of the algorithm scheme of Example 4.1.4 to input word aab may be described by writing

$$aab \Rightarrow^* baa$$

as was seen. Occasionally we shall write $w \Rightarrow^+ w'$ to mean that w' is obtained from w in one or more steps.

EXAMPLE 4.1.5 Let $\Sigma = \{a, b\}$ and consider the algorithm schema

$$a \rightarrow .\varepsilon$$

$$b \rightarrow b$$

Let us consider input word $w = aba$ first. The first production turns w into $w_1 = \varepsilon ba = ba$ and the substitution process terminates. Evidently, if the productions here are applied to word w containing one or more *a*s, then output word w' is obtained from w by eliminating the leftmost a. If w is ε, then

---

[1]Strictly speaking, a Markov algorithm schema is what philosophers refer to as a physical inscription *type*. To see why, consider the following situation. The instructor has copied production sequence (i)–(xiii) of Example 4.1.4 on the chalkboard, while a student has copied it into his notes. This makes for two distinct physical inscriptions, one of chalk and one of ink, say. If Markov algorithm schemata are really *physical inscriptions*, then what the instructor has written on the chalkboard is one Markov algorithm schema while what appears in the student's notes is a second, distinct Markov algorithm schema. But clearly we do not want to have to speak in this manner. We want to be able to say that it is one and the same Markov algorithm schema that appears on the chalkboard and in the student's notes. This can be accomplished by (i) agreeing that the two inscriptions in question are of the same inscription type and then (ii) stipulating that Markov algorithm schemata are not inscriptions but, rather, inscription types. (Saying what it means for an inscription to be of this or that type is not so easy, as it turns out, but that need not concern us here.)

the result of the substitution process is also ε, since neither production can be applied. What if, on the other hand, w is not ε but contains no occurrences of a? In that case, w must be b^n for some $n \geq 1$. Now the second production does apply. The problem is that the substitution process never terminates. In such a case we say that the algorithm schema is undefined for word w. In other words, an algorithm schema is defined for a given input word only if the corresponding substitution process—an instance of the corresponding Markov algorithm—eventually terminates.

As described in this section, a Markov algorithm schema S halts for a given input word if either (i) in the course of S's computation, some terminal production is applied or (ii) in the course of S's computation, the situation arises whereby no production of S is applicable to the current computation word. In fact, we can without loss of generality assume that a Markov algorithm halts by virtue of (i). To see this, suppose that Markov algorithm schema S does halt by virtue of (ii) in the case of some input words. Then, by merely adding the single production

$$\varepsilon \rightarrow .\varepsilon$$

at the very end of S's production sequence, we obtain a new Markov algorithm schema S' that halts only by applying a terminal production and whose output word, for a given input word, will not be different from that of S. To see this, note first that S cannot itself have any productions of the form

$$\varepsilon \rightarrow \alpha$$

nor any of the form

$$\varepsilon \rightarrow .\alpha$$

since otherwise it could never have halted by virtue of (ii), as we are supposing it to do. So the production $\varepsilon \rightarrow .\varepsilon$ that we added at the very end will be S''s only production with left-hand side ε and will be applied just in case no production above it can be applied.

A notational simplification will be helpful in presenting later schemata. In Example 4.1.3, we note that productions (i) and (ii) were used together to move # to the end of input word w. Productions (i) and (ii) share a common form. We shall combine such productions into a single production schema *template*, using the Greek letters α, β, and so on, as syntactic variables ranging over $\Sigma = \{a, b\}$. Thus we abbreviate the algorithm schema of Example 4.1.3 as

(i) $\#\alpha \rightarrow \alpha\#$ (for $\alpha \in \Sigma = \{a, b\}$)

(ii) $\# \rightarrow .ab$

(iii) $\varepsilon \rightarrow \#$

§4.2 Markov Algorithms as Language Acceptors and as Language Recognizers

We saw in Chapter 1 that a Turing machine M can accept a formal language L in the sense that, given any word $w \in L$, M is in effect able to identify w as belonging to L and respond appropriately, where "appropriately" here means in accordance with a stipulated convention. We now wish to describe a notion of language acceptance for Markov algorithm schemata as well. Again, this is a matter of adopting certain conventions. We opt for conventions rather similar to those used for Turing machines.

EXAMPLE 4.2.1 Consider the following algorithm schema with input alphabet $\Sigma = \{a, b\}$ and work alphabet $\Gamma = \Sigma \cup \{@, \%, \$, 1\}$.

$$@\alpha \rightarrow \alpha@ \quad \text{for } \alpha \text{ in } \Sigma$$
$$\%a \rightarrow \%$$
$$\%b \rightarrow \$$$
$$\$b \rightarrow \$$$
$$\$@ \rightarrow .1$$
$$\varepsilon \rightarrow \%@$$

Note that

$$aabbb \Rightarrow \%@aabbb \Rightarrow^+ \%aabbb@ \Rightarrow^+ \%bbb@ \Rightarrow \$bb@ \Rightarrow^+ \$@ \Rightarrow 1$$

Note further that

$$aabab \rightarrow^* \%aabab@ \rightarrow^* \%bab@ \rightarrow \$ab@$$

It is not too hard to see that the schema transforms any word consisting of a (possibly empty) string of as followed by a string of at least one b into a single 1. Auxiliary alphabet symbol $\%$ is used to eliminate all of the as and the leftmost occurrence of b, at which point auxiliary symbol $\$$ is used to eliminate the remaining bs (if any). Thus, this schema transforms all and only words in language $\{a^n b^m | n \geq 0, m \geq 1\}$ to word 1. We shall say that each of these words is *accepted* by the Markov algorithm schema (and by the corresponding Markov algorithm) in accordance with Definition 4.2 below.

Open icon **Example 4.2.1** of the Markov Algorithm folder and try running this algorithm on the three input words that have been saved in the Input Words clickbox. Two of the three will be accepted.

DEFINITION 4.2: Let S be a Markov algorithm schema with input alphabet Σ and work alphabet Γ with $1 \in \Gamma$. Then S *accepts word* w if $w \Rightarrow^* 1$. That is, S accepts w if S transforms input word w into word 1. (We shall refer to this 1 as an *accepting 1*. Also, we assume that symbol 1 is not a member of input alphabet Σ.) If Markov algorithm schema S accepts word w, then we shall say that the Markov algorithm A_S corresponding to S accepts w as well.

Note that schema S accepts language L provided only that it produces the appropriate affirmative response just in case input word w happens to belong to L. If input word w is not in L, then, so long as S does not respond affirmatively, we do not care what S does do. For example, S may transform w into something other than 1. It is equally permissible that, for input word $w \notin L$, the substitution process corresponding to S never terminates. Of course, this is perfectly analogous to what was done in

§1.4 with regard to Turing machines and word acceptance. As before, we define language acceptance in terms of word acceptance.

DEFINITION 4.3: A Markov algorithm schema S (as well as the corresponding Markov algorithm A_S) accepts language L if S accepts all and only the words in L. A language that is accepted by some Markov algorithm is said to be a *Markov-acceptable language*.

EXAMPLE 4.2.1 (continued) The reader can now see that, in accordance with Definition 4.3, the Markov algorithm schema considered above accepts language $\{a^n b^m | n \geq 0, m \geq 1\}$. What happens if this schema is applied to input word *aabbba*, say? (*Hint:* Use the software to apply the algorithm of **Example 4.2.1** to this word. Be ready to click *Stop Algorithm* under the Run menu.)

Markov algorithm schemata may also recognize languages. Again, we adopt conventions analogous to those introduced in §1.4 for Turing machines. Without further comment, we present the needed definition.

DEFINITION 4.4: Let S be a Markov algorithm schema with input alphabet Σ and work alphabet Γ such that $0, 1 \in \Gamma \backslash \Sigma$. Then S *recognizes language L over Σ* provided that:

(i) S transforms input word w with $w \in L$ into *1*; that is, $w \Rightarrow^* 1$. (Again, we shall refer to this *1* as an *accepting 1*.

(ii) S transforms input word w with $w \notin L$ into *0*; that is, $w \Rightarrow^* 0$. (We shall refer to this *0* as a *rejecting 0*.)

If Markov algorithm schema S recognizes language L, then we shall say that the Markov algorithm A_S corresponding to S recognizes language L as well. A language that is recognized by some Markov algorithm is said to be a *Markov-recognizable language*.

EXAMPLE 4.2.2 The three-production sequence below represents a Markov algorithm S that accepts the language $L = \{(ab)^n | n \geq 0\}$.

$$\$ab \rightarrow \$$$

$$\$ \rightarrow .1$$

$$\varepsilon \rightarrow \$$$

If we want language L to be recognized rather than merely being accepted, then some additional productions are needed. The eight-production schema given below will do the trick.

$$\$ab \rightarrow \$$$

$$\$a \rightarrow \#$$

$$\$b \rightarrow \#$$

$$\#a \rightarrow \#$$

$$\#b \rightarrow \#$$

$$\$ \rightarrow .1$$

$$\# \rightarrow .0$$

$$\varepsilon \rightarrow \$$$

Open icon **Example 4.2.2** in order to run this language recognizer on the several words stored in the Input Words clickbox.

Exercise 4.2.4 further illustrates the concept of language recognition on the part of Markov algorithms and its relation to language acceptance.

We use our next example as an opportunity to introduce considerations of time and space in relation to Markov algorithm computations. It is reasonable to regard each production application as one step within a computation.[2] Analogous to Definition 1.8, we have the following

---

DEFINITION 4.5: Let S be a Markov algorithm schema and let n be an arbitrary natural number. The unary number-theoretic function $time_S$ is defined by

$$time_S(n) = \text{the maximum number of steps in any} \\ \text{terminating computation of } S \text{ for input} \\ \text{word of length } n$$

Computation word length suggests itself immediately as a plausible measure of the space requirements of Markov algorithms. Thus, analogous to Definition 1.9, we have

---

[2]In general, before a given production π of schema S is actually applied to computation word w, a number of productions—namely, those preceding π in the production sequence constituting S—will have been considered and rejected as inapplicable to w because there is no occurrence within w of their left-hand sides. Some readers will be wondering, quite reasonably, whether it might not be more appropriate to regard the mere *consideration* of a production, whether or not it is then applied, as one step in the computation of S. Happily, this alternative approach turns out to yield precisely the same time analyses, when expressed in big-O notation, as does the adopted approach. To begin to see why, recall that any production sequence consists of a fixed, constant number of productions. This in turn means that the number of productions considered and rejected before production π is applied is O(1) worst case.

DEFINITION 4.6: Let S be a Markov algorithm schema and let n be an arbitrary natural number. The number-theoretic function $space_S$ is defined by

$$space_S(n) = \text{the maximum length of any computation word in any terminating computation of } S \text{ for input word of length } n$$

We apply both of these definitions in giving worst-case time and space analyses of our next example.

EXAMPLE 4.2.3 The Markov algorithm schema S associated with the icon labeled **Example 4.2.3** accepts the language $\{w \in \Sigma^* | n_a(w) = n_b(w)\}$ with $\Sigma = \{a, b\}$, as the reader should now verify. The computation of S is operationally quite like that of the Turing machine M of Example 1.3.1 (**Same Number of as and bs**). Briefly, as and bs are erased in pairs from input word w until either nothing remains, in which case an accepting 1 is written, or just as or just bs remain, in which case no accepting 1 is written. (See the on-line documentation accompanying S.)

As for a time analysis of S, considerations come into play that are perfectly analogous to those that arose in §1.7 with regard to M.

- In general, longer input words correspond to longer computations. Also, all else being equal, accepted words involve a greater number of computation steps than do nonaccepted words. In particular, input words of odd length may be disregarded altogether in giving a time analysis of S.

- Among accepted words of length n, the most costly will be $a^{n/2}b^{n/2}$ and $b^{n/2}a^{n/2}$. Moreover, the reader can use the software to verify that these words are accepted after $(n/2)^2 + n + 2$ computation steps (see Exercise 4.2.5 below). In other words, according to Definition 4.5 we have that $time_S(n) = (n/2)^2 + n + 2$ for even n so that $time_S(n)$ is $O(n^2)$.

The space analysis of S is easy enough. Examination of the productions of S—see the software—reveals that, with one exception, none are length-increasing: Applied to a given computation word w, they each yield a new word w' whose length is less than or equal to that of w. The single exception is the physically last production $\varepsilon \to @$, which is applied precisely once to any input word. Moreover, since it is invariably applied first, it follows that $space_S(n) = n + 1$ so that $space_S(n)$ is $O(n)$.

We note that one feature of our characterization of space in Definition 4.6 is that no Markov algorithm A_S computes in sublinear space. That is, $space_{A_S}(n) \geq n$ for all n. This situation is certainly no worse than the one that resulted from our adoption of Definition 1.9 as the definition of space for single-tape Turing machines. However, the reader will recall that the later characterization of space for the multitape case afforded greater flexibility. Thus, in accordance with Definition 2.6, a multitape Turing machine such as Example 2.3.5 computes in $O(\lceil \log_2 n \rceil)$ space. Nothing analogous is possible for Markov algorithms—at least using Definition 4.6.

§4.3 Markov Algorithms as Computers of Number-Theoretic Functions

We intend Markov algorithms as a model of sequential computation. So, in particular, we require some convention in accordance with which a number-theoretic function can be computed by a Markov algorithm, thereby implementing the function computation paradigm of §1.1. We shall use the familiar representation scheme for natural numbers: the natural number n will be represented by a string or word consisting of $n + 1$ 1s. Any such string over $\Sigma = \{1\}$ will be termed a *numeral*. The pair of natural numbers $\langle 2, 3 \rangle$ will be represented by the corresponding numerals separated by a single asterisk.

$$111*1111$$

Similarly the triple $\langle 2, 3, 1 \rangle$ will be represented by the word

$$111*1111*11$$

EXAMPLE 4.3.1 Let schema S consist of the single terminal production

$$1 \rightarrow .11$$

Apparently, schema S applied to 1 yields 11. When applied to 11, S yields 111. Generally for $n \geq 1$, S applied to 1^n yields 1^{n+1}. Expressed differently, S applied to the representation of an arbitrary natural number n yields a representation of natural number $n + 1$. Quite reasonably, we shall say that the schema S computes the successor function in accordance with the following definition.

> **DEFINITION 4.7:** *Markov algorithm schema S computes unary partial number-theoretic function f* provided that
> (i) if S is applied to input word 1^{n+1}, where function f is defined for argument n, then S yields output word $1^{f(n)+1}$; and
> (ii) if S is applied to input word 1^{n+1}, where function f is not defined for argument n, then either S is undefined or, if S is defined, then its output word is not of the form 1^m for $m \geq 1$.

If Markov algorithm schema S computes unary partial number-theoretic function f in the sense of Definition 4.7, then we shall also say that the corresponding Markov algorithm A_S computes f.

EXAMPLE 4.3.2 Next consider the algorithm schema over $\Gamma = \Sigma = \{1\}$ having a single production

$$11 \rightarrow 1$$

It should be clear that the result of applying this algorithm to the numerals *1, 11, 111, 1111*, and so on is, invariably, numeral *1* representing 0. We can see that schema S computes the number-theoretic function

$$C_0^1(n) = 0 \quad \text{for all } n$$

in accordance with the foregoing definition. Thus, the unary constant-zero function C_0^1 is Markov-computable.

EXAMPLE 4.3.3 The next example of a Markov algorithm computing a unary function is only slightly more difficult. Let f be defined as

$$f(n) = \begin{cases} 2n - 1 & \text{if } n \geq 1 \\ 0 & \text{if } n = 0 \end{cases}$$

The three-member production sequence

$$\$1 \rightarrow 11\$$$

$$\$ \rightarrow .\varepsilon$$

$$\varepsilon \rightarrow \$$$

will double the number of 1s in any input numeral. This is a good start but is plainly not what is needed ultimately: As things stand, input word 1^5, representing argument $n = 4$, will be transformed into 1^{10}, whereas what is desired is 1^8, representing value $f(n) = 2 \cdot 4 - 1 = 7$. This suggests changing the middle production above so as to eliminate exactly two of the final 1s.

$$\$1 \rightarrow 11\$$$

$$11\$ \rightarrow .\varepsilon$$

$$\varepsilon \rightarrow \$$$

This schema now works correctly for $n \geq 1$ but not yet for the special case $n = 0$: A single 1 representing 0 is transformed into ε, whereas the output word should be 1 representing $f(0) = 0$. One way in which this can be handled is to require that, if after doubling there are at least three 1s, then two of them should be erased. On the other hand, if after doubling there are only two 1s, then only one of them should be erased. This gives the four-member production sequence

$$\$1 \rightarrow 11\$$$

$$111\$ \rightarrow .1$$

$$11\$ \rightarrow .1$$

$$\varepsilon \rightarrow \$$$

We want Markov algorithms to also be able to compute number-theoretic functions that are not unary. Conventions are needed. We shall use the following definition.

DEFINITION 4.8: *Markov algorithm S computes k-ary partial number-theoretic function f provided that*
(i) if S is applied to input word

$$1^{n_1+1} * 1^{n_2+1} * \cdots * 1^{n_k+1}$$

where function f is defined for arguments $n_1, n_2, \ldots, n_k$, then S yields output word

$$1^{f(n_1,n_2,\ldots,n_k)+1}$$

(ii) if S is applied to input word

$$1^{n_1+1} * 1^{n_2+1} * \cdots * 1^{n_k+1}$$

where function f is not defined for arguments $n_1, n_2, \ldots, n_k$, then either S never halts at all or, if S does halt, then its output word is not of the form 1^m for $m \geq 1$.

Again, if Markov algorithm schema S computes k-ary partial number-theoretic function f in the sense of Definition 4.8, then we shall also say that the corresponding Markov algorithm A_S computes f. Furthermore, number-theoretic function f will be said to be *Markov-computable* provided that there is a Markov algorithm that computes f.

EXAMPLE 4.3.4 (All constant functions and projection functions are Markov-computable) We saw earlier that the unary constant-zero function C_0^1 is Markov-computable. In fact, all of the other constant-zero functions $C_0^2, C_0^3, C_0^4, \ldots$ are Markov-computable as well. Thus the following production rule sequence over $\Gamma = \{1, *\}$ computes the binary constant-zero function C_0^2.

$$\$1 \to \$$$
$$\$*1 \to \$$$
$$\$ \to .1$$
$$\varepsilon \to \$$$

We now give a production rule sequence that computes the projection function p_1^2.

$$\$1 \to 1\$$$
$$\$* \to \%$$
$$\%1 \to \%$$
$$\% \to .\varepsilon$$
$$\varepsilon \to \$$$

As an exercise, the reader should use special markers #, £, %, and & to present a production sequence that computes p_2^2. By adding another pair of markers—@ and +, say—one could similarly show that each of p_1^3, p_2^3, and p_3^3 is Markov-computable.

In conjunction with Markov algorithms such as Example 4.3.4, we shall refer to words of the form

$$111\ldots111 * 111\ldots111 * 111\ldots111 * 111\ldots111$$

as k-tuples of numerals. (Here k happens to equal 4.)

EXAMPLE 4.3.5 The total, unary number-theoretic function defined as

$$f(n) = \begin{cases} \lfloor \log_2 n \rfloor & \text{if } n > 0 \\ 0 & \text{otherwise} \end{cases}$$

is Markov-computable. Open icon **log n** to observe the operation of a Markov algorithm that computes this function.

EXAMPLE 4.3.6 Open icon **Example 4.3.6** in order to observe the operation of a seven-production schema that computes the binary function $f(n, m) =_{\text{def.}} |n - m| \bmod 3$. (We shall use this example as an illustration in Example 4.5.1 below.)

Markov Algorithms and the Transduction Paradigm

We have now considered Markov algorithms in three roles. In §4.2, we saw how Markov algorithms may serve either as language acceptors or as language recognizers. In the present section, we have described how Markov algorithms may compute k-ary number-theoretic functions. Just like Turing machines, however, many Markov algorithms are not by design language acceptors, language recognizers, or computers of number-theoretic functions. As an example, consider again the Markov algorithm of Example 4.1.4 that transforms input word w into w^{R}. As before, we shall use the term "transducer" here. A Markov algorithm functioning as a transducer merely transforms input word w into output word w'—that is, $w \Rightarrow^* w'$. What was noted at the end of §1.5 is applicable in the context of Markov algorithms as well: Namely, any language acceptor, language recognizer, or function computer may be regarded as a special sort of transducer. (Again, this is an instance of what we have called Paradigm Interreducibility.)

§4.4 Labeled Markov Algorithms

Having introduced the Markov algorithm concept and considered Markov algorithms both as language acceptors and as computers of number-theoretic functions, we now describe a variation of the Markov algorithm concept. Namely, we shall permit *production labels* as well as *branching* and speak of *labeled Markov algorithms*. The advantage of doing so is that Markov algorithm schemata with "gotos" are much easier to design and to comprehend. Moreover, it will be shown that the new concept of Markov algorithm is equivalent to the concept of Markov algorithm introduced in Definition 4.1.

Production labels will be among $\mathcal{L}_1, \mathcal{L}_2, \mathcal{L}_3, \ldots$, or sometimes $\mathcal{L}, \mathcal{L}', \mathcal{L}'', \ldots$. The semantics of Markov algorithm schemata involving such labels may be described as follows. As before, an algorithm A_S begins with the application of the first applicable production within production sequence Π—that is, the physically highest production π such that the left-hand side of π occurs within input word w. Suppose that π is either of the form

$$\mathcal{L}_i: \; \alpha \rightarrow \beta; \; \mathcal{L}_j$$

or of the form

$$\alpha \rightarrow \beta; \; \mathcal{L}_j$$

Then the leftmost occurrence within w of left-hand side α is replaced by right-hand side β. Afterward, execution *branches* to the production labeled $\mathcal{L}_j$. We refer to $\mathcal{L}_j$ as the *goto* of production π. Should π have no goto, that is, should π be either of the form

$$\mathcal{L}_i: \quad \alpha \rightarrow \beta$$

or of the form

$$\alpha \rightarrow \beta$$

then, after replacement of the leftmost occurrence of α by β, execution returns, as usual, to the very top of production sequence Π.

EXAMPLE 4.4.1 Consider the following labeled Markov algorithm schema S with input alphabet $\Sigma = \{a, b, c\}$ and work alphabet $\Gamma = \Sigma \cup \{1\}$. We wish to see that S accepts language $\{w \mid n_a(w) = n_b(w) = n_c(w)\}$.

$$\mathcal{L}_1: \quad a \rightarrow \varepsilon; \; \mathcal{L}_2$$
$$\varepsilon \rightarrow \varepsilon; \; \mathcal{L}_4$$
$$\mathcal{L}_2: \quad b \rightarrow \varepsilon; \; \mathcal{L}_3$$
$$\varepsilon \rightarrow \varepsilon; \; \mathcal{L}_5$$
$$\mathcal{L}_3: \quad c \rightarrow \varepsilon; \; \mathcal{L}_1$$
$$\varepsilon \rightarrow \varepsilon; \; \mathcal{L}_5$$
$$\mathcal{L}_4: \quad b \rightarrow \varepsilon; \; \mathcal{L}_5$$
$$c \rightarrow \varepsilon; \; \mathcal{L}_5$$
$$\varepsilon \rightarrow 1; \; \mathcal{L}_5$$
$$\mathcal{L}_5: \quad \varepsilon \rightarrow .\varepsilon$$

Production sequence Π consists of ten productions, five of which are labeled. The production labeled $\mathcal{L}_5$ is the sole production without a goto. Moreover, because it is a terminal production, execution will halt immediately after any application of this production.

Let us see that input word *bccbaa* is accepted by algorithm schema *S*.

- Starting at the top of production sequence Π, execution proceeds to the first applicable production— that is, to the first production π such that the left-hand side of π occurs within input word *bccbaa*. Evidently, the very first production, which is labeled $\mathcal{L}_1$, is applicable. Applying this production causes the leftmost occurrence of symbol *a* to be erased, yielding computation word *bccba*. Afterward, rather than returning to the beginning of the production sequence, execution branches to the production labeled $\mathcal{L}_2$.

- Applying the production labeled $\mathcal{L}_2$ causes the leftmost occurrence of symbol *b* to be erased and then effects a branch to production $\mathcal{L}_3$.

- Production $\mathcal{L}_3$, in its turn, causes the leftmost occurrence of symbol *c* to be erased and then effects a branch to $\mathcal{L}_1$.

- At this point, a single occurrence of each of the symbols *a*, *b*, and *c* has been erased, leaving computation word *cba*.

- Another application of productions $\mathcal{L}_1, \mathcal{L}_2$, and $\mathcal{L}_3$, in that order, produces computation word ε, followed by a branch to $\mathcal{L}_1$.

- Since no occurrence of symbol *a* remains, production $\mathcal{L}_1$ cannot itself be applied. Consequently, execution proceeds to the physically next production in production sequence Π—that is, to the second production. This production can be applied and a branch to production $\mathcal{L}_4$ is effected.

- At $\mathcal{L}_4$ neither production $b \to \varepsilon$ nor production $c \to \varepsilon$ can be applied. Finally, production $\varepsilon \to 1$ is applied, followed by a branch to production $\mathcal{L}_5$.

- The algorithm halts immediately after application of terminal production $\mathcal{L}_5$, as mentioned earlier. Output word *1* is interpreted as acceptance of input word *bccbaa*, in accordance with the convention adopted earlier.

The reader should verify that input words *ab*, *abcc*, and *aa* cause *S* to terminate without accepting, given that production $\varepsilon \to 1$; $\mathcal{L}_5$ is never applied.

Our solution to Exercise 4.2.4 presents a standard Markov algorithm schema that accepts language $\{w \mid n_a(w) = n_b(w) = n_c(w)\}$, albeit one of considerably greater complexity than that of Example 4.4.1 above. One might then ask whether, given an arbitrary labeled Markov algorithm, it is always possible to construct a Markov algorithm, in the sense of Definition 4.1, that exhibits the same input/output behavior. This turns out to be the case, as we shall see in the proof of Theorem 4.1 below. Before turning to that proof, however, we introduce some additional terminology regarding labeled Markov algorithm schemata and describe their semantics a bit more fully.

As usual, we let Σ and Γ be the input and work alphabets, respectively, of a given Markov algorithm schema *S*, with $\Sigma \subseteq \Gamma$. A *production with goto* is either of the form

$$\mathcal{L}: \quad \alpha \to \beta; \ \mathcal{L}'$$

or of the form

$$\alpha \to \beta; \ \mathcal{L}'$$

where $\alpha, \beta \in (\Sigma \cup \Gamma)^*$. The first sort of production is a *labeled production with goto*, whereas the second is an *unlabeled production with goto*. Applying either sort of production will mean replacing the leftmost occurrence of string α in the current computation word with string β and next attempting to apply the production with label $\mathcal{L}'$. (If no such production exists, then let us agree that computation will halt. However, we can assume without loss of generality that no such *meaningless gotos* occur. See Exercise 4.4.2). In addition, we shall permit productions—with or without labels—that have no goto. These productions may be either terminal productions or nonterminal productions. Terminal productions (without goto[3]) will be of the forms

$$\mathcal{L}: \quad \alpha \to .\beta \qquad \text{or} \qquad \alpha \to .\beta$$

As before, applying such a production causes the leftmost occurrence of string α in the current computation word to be replaced by string β, after which computation halts. Nonterminal productions without gotos will be of the forms

$$\mathcal{L}: \quad \alpha \to \beta \qquad \text{or} \qquad \alpha \to \beta$$

As before, applying such a production causes the leftmost occurrence of string α in the current computation word to be replaced by string β, at which point execution returns to the first production in the sequence of productions constituting Markov algorithm schema S.

A final point bears emphasizing. As Example 4.4.1 makes clear, if in the current computation word there is no occurrence of string α, then consideration of production with goto

$$\mathcal{L}_1: \quad \alpha \to \beta; \ \mathcal{L}'$$

causes no branch to the production labeled $\mathcal{L}'$. Rather, execution continues to the next production in the production sequence—that is, the physically next production.

We now define a labeled Markov algorithm to be a Markov algorithm whose productions are of any of the forms mentioned above. Note that we do not require that a labeled Markov algorithm involve even a single labeled production. Nor do we require that its productions involve gotos. This has as consequence that any Markov algorithm in the earlier sense of Definition 4.1 is a labeled Markov algorithm. It will be instructive to observe the newly adopted conventions in three additional examples.

---

[3] Terminal productions with goto might be given some sense. However, we shall not permit them; after all, given that execution of a terminal production causes computation to cease, the goto will never be effected.

EXAMPLE 4.4.2 The labeled Markov algorithm below accepts the language of palindromes over alphabet $\Sigma = \{a, b\}$.

$$@\alpha \rightarrow \alpha @ \qquad \text{for } \alpha \in \Sigma$$

$$\mathcal{L}_1: \quad \$\alpha @ \rightarrow .1 \qquad \text{for } \alpha \in \Sigma \qquad /* \text{ See footnote 4. } */$$

$$\$\alpha \rightarrow \$; \quad \mathcal{L}_2$$

$$\$b \rightarrow \$; \quad \mathcal{L}_3$$

$$\$@ \rightarrow .1$$

$$\varepsilon \rightarrow \$@$$

$$\mathcal{L}_2: \quad a@ \rightarrow @; \quad \mathcal{L}_1$$

$$\varepsilon \rightarrow .\varepsilon$$

$$\mathcal{L}_3: \quad b@ \rightarrow @; \quad \mathcal{L}_1$$

$$\varepsilon \rightarrow .\varepsilon$$

To observe the result of applying this algorithm, look for the icon **Palindromes**. Run the Markov algorithm found there on the several input words stored in the Input Words clickbox.

EXAMPLE 4.4.3 The following labeled Markov algorithm computes the function

$$f(n, m) = \begin{cases} 1 & \text{if } m|n \\ 0 & \text{otherwise} \end{cases}$$

where we note that $f(n, 0) = 0$ for all n.

---

[4]We may take this labeled production template to be an abbreviation of

$$\mathcal{L}_1: \quad \$a@ \rightarrow .1$$

$$\$b@ \rightarrow .1$$

$$1 * 1 \rightarrow *; \quad \mathcal{L}_0 \quad /* \text{ eliminate representational } 1s \ */$$

$\mathcal{L}_0$: $\quad @1 \rightarrow 1@; \quad \mathcal{L}_0$

$$1 * 1 \rightarrow *@; \quad \mathcal{L}_0$$

$$1 * @ \rightarrow 1 * @; \quad \mathcal{L}_1$$

$$* @ \rightarrow * @; \quad \mathcal{L}_2 \quad /* \ n \text{ is a multiple of } m \neq 0 \ */$$

$$* 1 \rightarrow * 1; \quad \mathcal{L}_3 \quad /* \ n \text{ is not a multiple of } m \neq 0 \ */$$

$$* \rightarrow *; \quad \mathcal{L}_3 \quad /* \ m = 0 \ */$$

$\mathcal{L}_1$: $\quad @ \rightarrow 1; \quad \mathcal{L}_1$

$$\varepsilon \rightarrow \varepsilon; \quad \mathcal{L}_0$$

$\mathcal{L}_2$: $\quad 1 \rightarrow \varepsilon; \quad \mathcal{L}_2$

$$@ \rightarrow \varepsilon; \quad \mathcal{L}_2$$

$$* \rightarrow .11$$

$\mathcal{L}_3$: $\quad 1 \rightarrow \varepsilon; \quad \mathcal{L}_3$

$$@ \rightarrow \varepsilon; \quad \mathcal{L}_3$$

$$* \rightarrow .1$$

To observe the result of applying the algorithm of Example 4.4.3, look for the icon **m divides n**.

EXAMPLE 4.4.4 Open icon **log n - labeled algorithm** to observe the operation of a labeled Markov algorithm that computes the unary function

$$f(n) = \begin{cases} \lfloor \log_2 n \rfloor & \text{if } n > 0 \\ 0 & \text{otherwise} \end{cases}$$

THEOREM 4.1: Let S be a labeled Markov algorithm schema with input alphabet Σ. Then there exists a standard Markov algorithm schema S' with input alphabet Σ that is computationally equivalent to S. That is, for any $w, w' \in \Sigma^*$, we have

$$w \Rightarrow_S^* w' \text{ if and only if } w \Rightarrow_{S'}^* w'$$

For instance, S accepts language L if and only if S' does, and S computes number-theoretic function f if and only if S' does.

PROOF We can assume without loss of generality that S has but a single production without goto, that this production is $\varepsilon \rightarrow .\varepsilon$, and that this production occurs last physically (see Exercise 4.4.1(b)).

Otherwise, as remarked earlier, we may assume that every production of S is labeled. Let Σ and Γ be the input and work alphabets of S, respectively. Suppose that S is the production sequence

$$\mathcal{L}_1: \quad \alpha_1 \to \beta_1; \ \mathcal{L}_{i_1}$$

$$\mathcal{L}_2: \quad \alpha_2 \to \beta_2; \ \mathcal{L}_{i_2} \longleftarrow$$

$$\cdots$$

$$\mathcal{L}_n: \quad \alpha_n \to \beta_n; \ \mathcal{L}_{i_n}$$

$$\mathcal{L}_{n+1}: \quad \varepsilon \ \to .\varepsilon$$

> $1 \le i_k \le n+1$ for all k. In other words, the $\mathcal{L}_{i_k}$ are among $\mathcal{L}_1, \mathcal{L}_2, \dots, \mathcal{L}_{n+1}$ (see Exercise 4.4.2).

We note that S's computation terminates if and when production $\mathcal{L}_{n+1}$ is applied. An equivalent Markov algorithm schema S' can now be constructed. The input alphabet of S' is Σ. The work alphabet of S' is Γ plus new symbols $\equiv_1, \equiv_2, \dots, \equiv_n, \equiv_{n+1}$ and $\square_1, \square_2, \dots, \square_n, \square_{n+1}$. The production sequence of S' is

$$\alpha \equiv_1 \to \equiv_1 \alpha \quad \text{for all } \alpha \in \Sigma \cup \Gamma$$

$$\equiv_1 \to \square_1$$

$$\square_1 \alpha_1 \to \equiv_{i_1} \beta_1$$

$$\square_1 \alpha \to \alpha \square_1 \quad \text{for all } \alpha \in \Sigma \cup \Gamma$$

$$\square_1 \to \equiv_2$$

$$\alpha \equiv_2 \to \equiv_2 \alpha \quad \text{for all } \alpha \in \Sigma \cup \Gamma$$

$$\equiv_2 \to \square_2$$

$$\square_2 \alpha_2 \to \equiv_{i_2} \beta_2$$

$$\square_2 \alpha \to \alpha \square_2 \quad \text{for all } \alpha \in \Sigma \cup \Gamma$$

$$\square_2 \to \equiv_3$$

$$\cdots$$

$$\alpha \equiv_n \to \equiv_n \alpha \quad \text{for all } \alpha \in \Sigma \cup \Gamma$$

$$\equiv_n \to \square_n$$

$$\square_n \alpha_n \to \equiv_{i_n} \beta_n$$

$$\square_n \alpha \to \alpha \square_n \quad \text{for all } \alpha \in \Sigma \cup \Gamma$$

$$\square_n \to \equiv_{n+1}$$

$$\equiv_{n+1} \to .\varepsilon$$

$$\varepsilon \to \square_1$$

When S' begins computation, symbol $\square_1$ is introduced and the production $\square_1 \alpha_1 \to \equiv_{i_1} \beta_1$ is applied so as to replace the leftmost occurrence of the left-hand side α_1 of S's first production, if such occurrence exists, with the right-hand side β_1 of that production. Doing so introduces symbol $\equiv_{i_1}$

which migrates to the far left and is then replaced by symbol $\square_{i_1}$ as the result of productions

$$\alpha \equiv_{i_1} \rightarrow \equiv_{i_1} \alpha \quad \text{and} \quad \equiv_{i_1} \rightarrow \square_{i_1}$$

This process is iterated and, in the case of an input word to which S's production $\mathcal{L}_{n+1}$ is eventually applied, symbol $\equiv_{n+1}$ will be introduced and then immediately erased by an application of terminal production

$$\equiv_{n+1} \rightarrow .\varepsilon \qquad\qquad \text{Q.E.D.}$$

A final word of clarification is in order regarding one way in which labeled Markov algorithms may terminate execution. We noted already in Example 4.1.1 that a standard Markov algorithm schema S terminates execution if an attempt to apply its final production to the current computation word is unsuccessful. This continues to be true of labeled Markov algorithms. However, there is a difference. In the case of a standard Markov algorithm, this failure carries the implication that no production whatever is applicable to the current computation word. In the case of a labeled Markov algorithm, this may no longer be true. To take a simple example, consider the labeled Markov algorithm schema S whose production sequence appears below.

$$\mathcal{L}: \quad a \rightarrow \varepsilon; \ \mathcal{L}'$$
$$\mathcal{L}': \quad b \rightarrow \varepsilon; \ \mathcal{L}$$

Applied to input word $baaaaaaaa$, schema S deletes the leftmost a, then the leftmost b, and then the leftmost remaining a, leaving computation word $aaaaaa$. An unsuccessful attempt is now made to apply the second production here so that, in accordance with our convention, execution ceases. In other words, execution terminates despite the fact that the first production of S is applicable to computation word $aaaaaa$.

The programming language SNOBOL4 is a character-string-processing language designed for natural-language applications. SNOBOL4 programs involve pattern-matching commands that may be regarded as extensions of Markov algorithm productions. In this connection, we mention the possibility of permitting, within labeled Markov algorithms, productions of the form

$$\mathcal{L}: \quad \alpha \Psi \beta \rightarrow \gamma; \ \mathcal{L}'$$

where Ψ is a wildcard standing for any (possibly empty) string. In other words, such a production can be applied whenever the current computation word contains a substring $\alpha \delta \beta$ with $\delta \in (\Sigma \ \cup \ \Gamma)^*$, in which case the leftmost occurrence of substring $\alpha \delta \beta$ is replaced by γ. We show that this extension of the concept of a labeled Markov algorithm is equivalent to our earlier concept. We do this by constructing a sequence of labeled productions that effect this new sort of "wildcard" production. The reader should ponder why the production sequence below is computationally equivalent to the wildcard production presented above, where $\mathcal{L}_{next}$ is assumed to be the label of the instruction following the wildcard production as in

$$\mathcal{L}: \quad \alpha \Psi \beta \to \gamma; \; \mathcal{L}'$$
$$\mathcal{L}_{next}: \qquad \cdots$$

For simplicity we assume that $\Sigma = \Gamma = \{a, b\}$ in the case of the Markov algorithm schema containing the wildcard production. We will need to add the three markers $*$, @, and # to work alphabet Γ.

$\mathcal{L}:$ $\alpha \to \alpha *; \; \mathcal{L}_1$ {Is there a leftmost occurrence of α?}

     $\varepsilon \to \varepsilon; \; \mathcal{L}_{next}$ {If not, then no substitution takes place.}

$\mathcal{L}_1:$ $*\beta \to \beta *; \; \mathcal{L}_2$ {If so, is there an occurrence of β to the right of that occurrence of α?}

     $*a \to a*; \; \mathcal{L}_1$

     $*b \to b*; \; \mathcal{L}_1$

     $* \to \varepsilon; \; \mathcal{L}_{next}$ {If not, then no substitution takes place.}

$\mathcal{L}_2:$ $\alpha \to \#; \; \mathcal{L}_3$ {If so, then replace α, β, and everything in between with γ.}

$\mathcal{L}_3:$ $\beta \to @\gamma; \; \mathcal{L}_4$

$\mathcal{L}_4:$ $\#a \to \#; \; \mathcal{L}_4$

     $\#b \to \#; \; \mathcal{L}_4$

     $\#@ \to \varepsilon; \; L'$ {Afterward, branch to $\mathcal{L}'$.}

§4.5 The Class of Markov-Computable Functions Is Identical to the Class of Partial Recursive Functions

Now that a new class of number-theoretic functions has been defined—that of the Markov-computable functions—it is natural to ask how this class is related to classes of functions characterized in earlier chapters. Once again, having raised the question, a striking result is obtainable without too much trouble. Namely, we shall show that the class of Markov-computable functions coincides with both the class of partial recursive functions and the class of Turing-computable functions. The following proposition, together with its proof, is the central result of the present chapter.

> **THEOREM 4.2:** Let f be a number-theoretic function. Then f is Markov-computable if and only if f is partial recursive.[5]

The theorem has two parts. We take the easier one first.

---

[5] The reader who has skipped over Chapter 3 should mentally substitute "Turing-computable" for the term "partial recursive" wherever it occurs.

THEOREM 4.2(a): Let f be a number-theoretic function. If f is partial recursive, then f is Markov-computable.

PROOF By Theorem 3.3(a), it suffices to show that if f is Turing-computable, then f is Markov-computable. So suppose that f is Turing-computable and let M be a deterministic Turing machine that computes f. We describe the construction of a Markov algorithm schema S that simulates Turing machine M. For the sake of simplicity, let us suppose that M's tape alphabet Γ is $\{B, 1, \&\}$ and that M has k states q_0 through q_{k-1}, where q_0 is M's initial state. We let the work alphabet of S consist of $B, 1, \&$, and $*$ as well as "state" symbols $\boldsymbol{q}_0$ through $\boldsymbol{q}_{k-1}$ and a few other auxiliary markers. The productions of schema S fall naturally into three groups.

   Group 1 consists of a sequence of productions that, at the beginning of S's computation, causes the symbol pair $\#\boldsymbol{q}_0$ and symbol @ to be positioned at the beginning and at the end, respectively, of S's input string. Symbols # and @ will serve as left and right endmarkers of S's modeling of M's workspace. Symbol $\boldsymbol{q}_0$, representing M's start state, enables S's simulation of M's computation to begin. Thus, adapting an earlier example and recalling that S's input string will contain symbols 1 and $*$ only, we have

$$@1 \to 1@$$
$$@* \to *@$$
$$\$ \to \boldsymbol{q}_0$$
$$* \to B$$
$$\varepsilon \to \#\$@$$

As a result, S's input word

$$1111 * 111111$$

representing argument pair $\langle 3, 5 \rangle$ will be transformed by the productions of Group 1 into computation word

$$\ldots \#\boldsymbol{q}_0 1111B111111@ \ldots$$

modeling M's initial machine configuration

$$\ldots B\boldsymbol{q}_0 1111B111111B \ldots$$

Of course, it is essential that the final production of Group 1 be applied only once. This means that the productions of Group 1 must be positioned carefully relative to the productions of the other groups (see below). Incidentally, the second and fourth of the five productions of Group 1 will play no role if f happens to be unary, and they could just as well be omitted in that case.

Group 2 consists of productions corresponding to M's various instructions.

- Thus, for each instruction of the form $\langle q_i, \mathbf{1}; \mathrm{R}, q_j \rangle$, say, which dictates that M, when in state q_i scanning a $\mathbf{1}$, moves one square to the right and enters state q_j, we have in Group 2 the two productions

$$q_j \mathbf{1} @ \rightarrow \mathbf{1} q_j B @$$
$$q_i \mathbf{1} \rightarrow \mathbf{1} q_j \tag{i}$$

Simulating a move to the right might mean that the simulation has reached the right end of S's representation of M's workspace. Thus the first of these two productions in effect extends S's modeling of M's tape by adding a single "blank" immediately preceding S's right endmarker.

- Similarly, for each move-left instruction of the form $\langle q_i, \mathbf{1}; \mathrm{L}, q_j \rangle$, say, which dictates that M, when in state q_i scanning a $\mathbf{1}$, moves one square to the left and enters state q_j, we introduce into Group 2 the four productions

$$B q_i \mathbf{1} \rightarrow q_j B \mathbf{1}$$
$$1 q_i \mathbf{1} \rightarrow q_j 1 \mathbf{1}$$
$$\& q_i \mathbf{1} \rightarrow q_j \& \mathbf{1} \tag{ii}$$
$$\# q_i \mathbf{1} \rightarrow \# q_j B \mathbf{1}$$

The last of these four productions effects the extension to the left of S's modeling of M's workspace.

- For each write instruction of the form $\langle q_i, \mathbf{B}; \mathbf{1}, q_j \rangle$, say, which requires that, when in state q_i scanning a blank, M should write a 1, we add the single production

$$q_i \mathbf{B} \rightarrow q_j \mathbf{1} \tag{iii}$$

Two final remarks regarding the productions of Group 2 are in order. First, note that, since M is deterministic, we will be adding, for any given state q_i and each member of $\Gamma \cup \{B\}$, at most one of the three described production sequences. Also, the relative order of these production sequences is immaterial since, at any point during S's simulation of M's computation, exactly one of the $\boldsymbol{q}_i$s appears in the current computation word.

Finally, the productions of **Group 3** effect (1) the removal of endmarkers # and @, (2) the removal of any blanks off to the left or to the right, and (3) the removal of whichever symbol from among the $\boldsymbol{q}_i$s yet occurs within S's computation word when its simulation of M's computation terminates. We require a total of $k + 3$ productions in Group 3. The last in the sequence must be a terminal production so as to prevent the reintroduction of $\#\boldsymbol{q}_0$ and @ by the Group 1 productions. The placement of the Group 3 productions relative to the productions of Groups 1 and 2 is not arbitrary: The productions of Group 2 must precede those of Group 3, bracketed by those of Group 1.

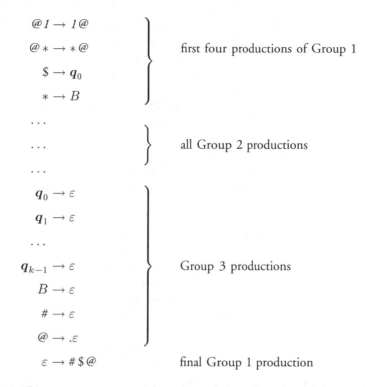

$$@1 \to 1@$$
$$@* \to *@$$
$$\$ \to q_0$$
$$* \to B$$

first four productions of Group 1

. . .

. . .

. . .

all Group 2 productions

$$q_0 \to \varepsilon$$
$$q_1 \to \varepsilon$$

. . .

$$q_{k-1} \to \varepsilon$$
$$B \to \varepsilon$$
$$\# \to \varepsilon$$
$$@ \to .\varepsilon$$

Group 3 productions

$$\varepsilon \to \#\$@$$

final Group 1 production

By Exercise 2.10.8(b), we can assume without loss of generality that if f is undefined for given arguments, then M never halts. In such a case, S's simulation of M's computation will never halt either. We leave it to the reader to verify that S does indeed compute function f in the sense of Definition 4.8.   Q.E.D.

As for the remaining half of Theorem 4.2, we have

THEOREM 4.2(b) If f is Markov-computable, then f is partial recursive.

PROOF For simplicity and definiteness, let us assume that f is a binary Markov-computable function. (A more general proof whereby f is taken to be k-ary for some $k \geq 0$ is not essentially different from the one we shall present.) By Theorem 3.3(b), it suffices to show that f is Turing-computable.

Suppose that Markov algorithm schema S with work alphabet Γ computes f. We describe a six-tape, off-line Turing machine M that simulates the application of S to arguments n and m. We assume, as usual, that representations of n and m appear initially on M's input tape, separated by a single blank. To begin, M uses this input string to create initial computation word

$$1^{n+1}*1^{m+1}$$

on its worktape₁—essentially just a matter of copying, of course. Then, assuming that S's first production is

$$\alpha_1 \to \beta_1$$

machine M, proceeding from the left, attempts to locate an occurrence of α_1 on worktape$_1$. If successful, then M uses the contents of worktape$_1$ to produce, on worktape$_2$, the result of replacing this leftmost occurrence of α_1 by β_1 (cf. Exercise 4.5.14). Afterward, the contents of worktape$_1$ are overwritten by the contents of worktape$_2$, and M repeats the process of attempting to find a leftmost occurrence of α_1. If unsuccessful, M will look for a leftmost occurrence of α_2, the left-hand side of S's second production, and so on (cf. Exercise 4.5.15). After any substitution resulting from a nonterminal production, the result of that substitution is copied onto worktape$_1$ in preparation for M's search for leftmost occurrences of α_1, α_2, and so on. On the other hand, if an accomplished substitution is the result of applying a terminal production, then the contents of worktape$_2$ are copied onto M's output tape and M's computation ceases. Similarly, if no occurrences of α_1, α_2, ... can be located, then the result of the most recent substitution is copied from worktape$_1$ onto the output tape (cf. Exercise 4.5.16).

Returning now to the issue of how M will know to look for the leftmost occurrence of α_2 only after it has failed to find occurrences of α_1, consider the following. At the very outset, M writes on worktape$_4$ the sequence of all j productions of S separated by blanks, perhaps introducing a new symbol not in Γ to represent ε. Now, using worktape$_4$, M searches for α_1 on worktape$_1$ and, if unsuccessful, moves on to α_2. Terminal production right-hand sides on worktape$_4$ must be marked by some special symbol, which is used in an appropriate manner by M. Worktape$_3$ will play a role in the substitution step at line (9) in the pseudocode below (see Example 4.5.1).

```
         procedure simulate_Markov_algorithm_schema_M(n, m: integer);
         /* n and m are assumed to be represented as I^(n+1) and I^(m+1) on input tape */
         const j: integer;   /* number of M's productions */
         var i: integer;      /* index of production being considered on worktape₄ */
(1)      begin
(2)          set worktape₁ contents to I^(n+1)*I^(m+1);
(3)          write M's productions in sequence on worktape₄ and mark the right-hand sides of those
                 that correspond to terminal productions;
(4)          i := 1;
(5)          while i ≥ j do begin
(6)              if αᵢ as it appears on worktape₄ occurs within the string on worktape₁ then
(7)                  begin
(8)                      find βᵢ on worktape₄;
(9)                      write to worktape₂ the result of substituting βᵢ for the leftmost
                             occurrence of αᵢ within the string on worktape₁;
(10)                     if βᵢ is marked as a terminal production right-hand side then
(11)                         begin
(12)                             output_tape := worktape₂;
(13)                             halt
(14)                         end
(15)                     else begin
(16)                             worktape₁ := worktape₂;
(17)                             erase contents of worktape₂;
(18)                             i := 1;     /* return to the far left on worktape₄ */
(19)                         end
(20)              end
```

(21)   else $i := i + 1$ /* consider the next production on worktape$_4$ */
(22)   end;   /* while */
(23)   output_tape := worktape$_1$;
(24)   halt
(25)   end.

Q.E.D.

We illustrate the algorithm of the proof of Theorem 4.2(b) with the following

---

EXAMPLE 4.5.1 (A Turing Machine That Simulates a Markov Algorithm) Open the icon **Example 4.5.1** within the Turing Machine folder in order to observe the operation of a four-tape Turing machine M that implements the algorithm of Theorem 4.2(b) for the Markov algorithm schema S having the seven productions

$$1*1 \rightarrow *$$
$$* \rightarrow \varepsilon$$
$$@111 \rightarrow @$$
$$@11 \rightarrow .111$$
$$@1 \rightarrow .11$$
$$@ \rightarrow .1$$
$$\varepsilon \rightarrow @$$

Schema S is already familiar to the reader, having been used in Example 4.3.6 to compute the binary function $f(n, m) =_{def.} |n - m| \bmod 3$. The reader should load tape set `ex4-5-1.tt` and witness M's simulation of S's computation for $n = 2$ and $m = 10$.

The accompanying software limits us to five tapes, so there is no possibility of implementing the off-line machine having four worktapes described in the proof of Theorem 4.2(b). Instead, we have designed a machine whose input tape serves in the role of worktape$_1$. Similarly, the output tape might as well double as worktape$_4$. Otherwise, M works just as described in the pseudocode of the proof of Theorem 4.2(b). We use tape symbol % to denote the empty word, and symbol # appearing at the *end* of a string on worktape$_4$ marks the right-hand side of a terminal production. We separate production left-hand sides from corresponding right-hand sides by symbol $+$.

When running the software, note the following.

- When the breakpoint preceding submachine node 10 is reached, it is easy to verify that M has completed writing a list of seven productions on worktape$_4$.

- By the time the breakpoint preceding submachine node 11 has been reached, M is ready to enter the while-loop of lines (5)–(22).

- Counter variable i within the pseudocode above gives the relative position of M's read/write head on worktape$_4$.

- After M has established that a leftmost occurrence of α_i within the string on worktape$_1$ does exist, its read/write head on worktape$_1$ will already have moved to the right past that occurrence. An unbroken string of *1*s on worktape$_3$ is used to relocate the beginning of that occurrence of α_i (cf. submachine 11.3).

- Breakpoints within submachine 11.4 enable the user to observe M's simulation of the application of S's final production $\varepsilon \rightarrow @$.

- In this particular case, nothing corresponds to lines (23) and (24) since S can halt only as the result of applying one of its three terminal productions. (Why?) Lines (23) and (24) do have a place within the most general sort of construction, however.

And, as long as we are on this topic, we might as well give an example illustrating the proof of Theorem 4.2(a) as well.

EXAMPLE 4.5.2 One may apply the construction of the proof of Theorem 4.2(a) to any deterministic Turing machine M computing k-ary number-theoretic function f and thereby obtain a Markov algorithm schema S that computes f. As an illustration, we do this using the 13-state Turing machine M of Example 1.5.3 and Figure 1.5.2. The result is the Markov algorithm schema S found under icon **Example 4.5.2** within the Markov folder. Since M computes the unary function $f(n) = 2n$, so does S.

It would be interesting—although tedious—to apply the same construction to the 45-state Turing machine of our earlier Example 1.5.6, say, so as to obtain a Markov algorithm schema computing the factorial function. In any case, this suggests a method of designing Markov algorithms: Design a Turing machine first, assuming that is somewhat easier, and then apply said construction to it.

We next present an alternative proof of Theorem 4.2(b). That is, instead of proving that any Markov-computable function is Turing-computable and then appealing to Theorem 3.3(b), we show directly that any Markov-computable f is partial recursive. Some readers may choose to omit this alternative proof. However, it is recommended for those who wish to attain additional fluency with recursion-theoretic techniques introduced in Chapter 3. Also, to the extent that our earlier proof appealed extensively to the reader's informal understanding of the capabilities of multitape Turing machines, the proof that we give next would generally be considered more rigorous. To those readers who choose to skip over this alternative proof, we strongly suggest reading immediately the short §4.6, which follows. Our discussion there presupposes some of the details of our earlier proofs of Theorems 4.2(a) and 4.2(b). So it will be an advantage to have those proofs fresh in mind.

In the meantime, we turn to our alternative, more rigorous proof of

THEOREM 4.2(b): If number-theoretic function f is Markov-computable, then f is partial recursive as well.

ALTERNATIVE PROOF Again, for simplicity, let us suppose that f is binary. Also, suppose that f is computed by Markov algorithm schema S with production sequence Π consisting of $|\Pi|$ productions. Furthermore, suppose that S's work alphabet Γ is the minimal $\{*, 1\}$.

(1) As will be reminiscent of our representation of Turing machine tape configurations in the proof of Theorem 3.3(b), we first represent any computation word of S as a base-3 numeral. (In general, if $|\Gamma| = k$, then base-$(k+1)$ numerals will be used.) To this end, we represent alphabet symbol $*$ by base-3 digit 1 and alphabet symbol 1 by base-3 digit 2. (In general, it will be convenient to avoid using base-3 digit 0 to represent any symbol and to represent symbol 1 as base-$(k+1)$ digit k.) An initial computation word

$$111 * 1111$$

will be represented as the base-3 numeral 22221222, obtained by proceeding *from right to left* and replacing each alphabet symbol by the corresponding base-3 digit. The encoding of computation word *111∗1111* is then the natural number denoted by base-3 numeral 22221222:

$$22221222_3 = (2 \cdot 3^0) + (2 \cdot 3^1) + (2 \cdot 3^2) + (1 \cdot 3^3) + (2 \cdot 3^4) + (2 \cdot 3^5) + (2 \cdot 3^6) + (2 \cdot 3^7)$$

$$= 2 + 6 + 18 + 27 + 162 + 486 + 1458 + 4374$$

$$= 6533_{10}$$

Let us write $\ulcorner w \urcorner$ for the natural number that encodes computation word w. Thus we have $\ulcorner 111 * 1111 \urcorner = 6533$ and $\ulcorner 11 \urcorner = 8$. Finally, let us encode ε as 0—that is, $\ulcorner \varepsilon \urcorner = 0$. As in the proof of Theorem 3.3(b), we shall frequently speak of word n when what is actually intended is the word w encoded by n—that is, the word w such that $\ulcorner w \urcorner = n$. (Try Exercise 4.5.1 now.)

(2) We start by showing that the binary encoding function

$$encode\_arg(n, m) =_{\text{def}} \ulcorner 1^{n+1} * 1^{m+1} \urcorner$$

as a function of arguments n and m is primitive recursive. (Note that the previous paragraph shows that $encode\_arg(2, 3) = 6533$.) To this end, we can write

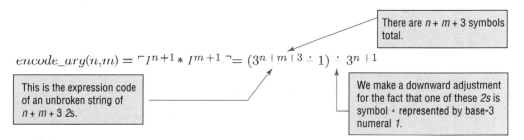

There are $n + m + 3$ symbols total.

$$encode\_arg(n,m) = \ulcorner 1^{n+1} * 1^{m+1} \urcorner = (3^{n\,|\,m\,|\,3} \doteq 1) \doteq 3^{n\,|\,1}$$

This is the expression code of an unbroken string of $n + m + 3$ *2*s.

We make a downward adjustment for the fact that one of these *2s* is symbol ∗ represented by base-3 numeral *1*.

The right-hand side here is prima facie primitive recursive and, hence, partial recursive.

(3) Next, let the productions of Π be indexed from 1 to $|\Pi|$, starting with the first production in the sequence and working downward. Every production in Π is either of the form

$$\alpha \to \beta$$

or of the form

$$\alpha \to . \beta$$

and can hence be associated with a pair of natural numbers $\ulcorner \alpha \urcorner$ and $\ulcorner \beta \urcorner$. Thus, a production

$$\mathbf{11* \to 1*}$$

comes to be associated with the pair $\ulcorner \mathbf{11*} \urcorner = 122_3 = 2 + 6 + 9 = 17$ and $\ulcorner \mathbf{1*} \urcorner = 12_3 = 2 + 3 = 5$. We are now ready to define, by cases, two unary functions *prod_lhs* and *prod_rhs* as follows. We write α_i and β_i for the left-hand side and right-hand side, respectively, of production i, where $1 \leq i \leq |\Pi|$.

$$prod\_lhs(i) = \begin{cases} \ulcorner \alpha_1 \urcorner & \text{if } i = 1 \\ \ulcorner \alpha_2 \urcorner & \text{if } i = 2 \\ \ldots \\ \ulcorner \alpha_{|\Pi|} \urcorner & \text{if } i = |\Pi| \\ 3 & \text{otherwise} \end{cases}$$

Note that 3 cannot encode any production left- or right-hand side. (Why not?)

$$prod\_rhs(i) = \begin{cases} \ulcorner \beta_1 \urcorner & \text{if } i = 1 \\ \ulcorner \beta_2 \urcorner & \text{if } i = 2 \\ \ldots \\ \ulcorner \beta_{|\Pi|} \urcorner & \text{if } i = |\Pi| \\ 3 & \text{otherwise} \end{cases}$$

Example 3.2.3 (Definition by cases) makes clear that both functions are primitive recursive and, hence, partial recursive.

(4) We write $length(n)$ for the length of the unique string encoded by n. Since $length(n) = \mu l[n < 3^l]$, we see that $length$ is a partial recursive function by Exercise 3.7.8. As an example, we have $length(6533) = 8$ since $3^7 < 6533 < 3^8$ and $length(0) = 0$ since $0 < 3^0$.

(5) Positions within a computation word begin with position 1 on the left. Thus computation word $111*1111$ contains an occurrence of $*$ in position 4. We define

$$segment(k, l, m) = \begin{cases} \text{the (expression code of the) string extending from position } k \text{ to position} \\ l \text{ inclusive in the word encoded by } m \text{ if } 1 \leq k \leq l \leq length(m) \\ 0 \quad \text{otherwise} \end{cases}$$

As an example, the reader should verify that $segment(3, 5, 6533) = \ulcorner 1*1 \urcorner = 2 + 3 + 18 = 23$. As a first step toward establishing that function $segment$ is partial recursive, we consider

$$segment(k, l, m) = (m \; div \; 3^{k \dot- 1}) \; mod \; 3^{l \dot- k + 1} \tag{4.4.1}$$

In fact, as it stands, equation (4.4.1) does not hold, since $segment(k, l, m)$ does not equal 0 if $1 \leq k \leq l \leq length(m)$ fails. However, this can be corrected through a trick involving the application of appropriate characteristic functions. Thus, letting $h(k, l, m)$ be the characteristic function of the ternary recursive relation

$$1 \leq k \quad \text{and} \quad k \leq l \quad \text{and} \quad l \leq length(m)$$

we can write

$$segment(k, l, m) = [(m \; div \; 3^{k \dot- 1}) \; mod \; 3^{l \dot- k + 1}] \cdot h(k, l, m)$$

and now $segment(k, l, m)$ does indeed equal 0 if $1 \leq k \leq l \leq length(m)$ fails. (And it is still partial recursive.)

(6) The following predicate, is recursive—essentially by Exercise 3.7.11(a).

$$occurs\_in(n, m) \Leftrightarrow \exists k, j \leq length(m)[segment(k, j, m) = n]$$

(7) Next, we introduce binary function $leftmost\_occur\_start\_pos(n, m)$ to denote the leftmost position at which an occurrence of string n begins within word m, if there is such an occurrence, and 0 otherwise. As examples, we have $leftmost\_occur\_start\_pos(23, 6533) = 3$ and $leftmost\_occur\_start\_pos(8, 6533) = 1$. We can begin to see that this function is partial recursive by noting that, if an occurrence of n within m exists, then we have

$$leftmost\_occur\_start\_pos(n, m) = \mu k \underbrace{[\exists l \leq length(m)(segment(k, l, m) = n)]}_{\substack{\text{a recursive predicate by closure of the recursive} \\ \text{predicates under bounded quantification}}} \quad (4.4.2)$$

$$\underbrace{}_{\text{a partial recursive function by Exercise 3.7.8}}$$

As already stated, however, we wish $leftmost\_occur\_start\_pos(n, m)$ to be 0 if there exists no occurrence of n within m. As things stand in (4.4.2), $leftmost\_occur\_start\_pos(n, m)$ is merely undefined in that case. So we use (4.4.2) to define $leftmost\_occur\_start\_pos(n, m)$ by cases.

$leftmost\_occur\_start\_pos(n, m)$

$$= \begin{cases} \mu k[\exists l \leq length(m)(segment(k, l, m) = n)] & \text{if } occurs\_in(n, m) \\ 0 & \text{otherwise} \end{cases}$$

By closure of the partial recursive functions under definition by cases (Exercise 3.7.9), $leftmost\_occur\_start\_pos(n, m)$ is seen to be partial recursive.

(8) Let us define a four-place number-theoretic function $subst(n, k, l, m)$ whose value for n, k, l, and m is the result of inserting string n in place of that substring of string m beginning at position k and ending at position l, if $1 \leq k \leq l \leq length(m)$, and 0 otherwise. As an example, consider that

$$subst(17, 3, 6, 6533) = subst(\ulcorner 11* \urcorner, 3, 6, \ulcorner 111*1111 \urcorner)$$

$$= \ulcorner 1111*11 \urcorner$$

$$= 2 + 6 + 18 + 54 + 81 + 486 + 1458$$

$$= 2105$$

To see that $subst$ is partial recursive, consider first the equation

$$subst(n, k, l, m) = (m \bmod 3^{k \dot{-} 1}) + (n \cdot 3^{k \dot{-} 1}) + (m \operatorname{div} 3^l) \cdot 3^{k + length(n) \dot{-} 1} \quad (4.4.3)$$

Leave positions preceding the *k*th position unaltered.	Position *k* to position *k* + *length*(*n*) will consist of an occurrence of string *n*.	Leave unchanged the symbols occurring to the right of the *l*th position in *m*.

As an example, consider that:

$$subst(17, 3, 6, 6533) = (6533 \bmod 9) + (17 \cdot 9) + (6533 \ div \ 729) \cdot 243$$
$$= 8 + 153 + 8 \cdot 243$$
$$= 8 + 153 + 1944$$
$$= 2105$$

Again, at (4.4.3) we do not have $subst$ equal to 0 when $1 \leq k \leq l \leq length(m)$ fails, so definition by cases may be used and we write

$$subst(n, k, l, m)$$
$$= \begin{cases} (m \bmod 3^{k \dot- 1}) + (n \cdot 3^{k \dot- 1}) + (m \ div \ 3^l) \cdot 3^{k+length(n) \dot- 1} & \text{if } 1 \leq k \leq l \leq \text{length}(m) \\ 0 & \text{otherwise} \end{cases}$$

(Alternatively, use characteristic function $h(k, l, m)$, as at (5). The effect is quite the same.)

(9) The following function is seen to be partial recursive.

$$first\_applicable\_rule(m)$$
$$= \begin{cases} \mu r[occurs\_in(prod\_lhs(r), m)] & \text{if } \exists r \leq |\Pi| \ [occurs\_in(prod\_lhs(r), m)] \\ 0 & \text{otherwise} \end{cases}$$

(10) The next function is binary. Assume that m is a word over work alphabet Γ and that r is a production of Π. Then $apply\_rule(r, m)$ will be that word over Γ that is the result of applying production r to word m. Our choice of function names is intended to afford a certain self-documentation.

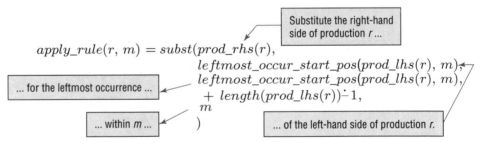

This function is prima facie partial recursive. As it stands, this is not yet what we will need since, if r is not applicable to m, we will want $apply\_rule(r, m)$ to be m. But this is easy to arrange using definition by cases and simply setting $apply\_rule(r, m)$ equal to m if $leftmost\_occur\_start\_pos$ $(prod\_lhs(r), m)$ happens to be 0 (see (7)).

(11) Unary predicate $terminal\_rule(r)$, whose interpretation is quite obvious, is recursive since we can write

$$terminal\_rule(r) \Leftrightarrow r = t_1 \lor r = t_2 \lor \cdots$$

where $t_1, t_2, \ldots$ are the (indices of) the terminal productions of S. Similarly, the predicate $not\_terminal\_rule(r)$ defined by

$$not\_terminal\_rule(r) \Leftrightarrow \neg(terminal\_rule(r))$$

is primitive recursive. We shall write $\chi_{term\_rule}(r)$ and $\chi_{not\_term\_rule}(r)$ for the characteristic functions of these two predicates. Incidentally, we can assume without loss of generality that, if Markov algorithm schema S halts, then it does so by virtue of the application of some terminal production (see Exercise 4.3.6).

Also, let us write $\langle n, m \rangle$ for natural number $2^n 3^m$ so that $\langle n, m \rangle$ is a primitive recursive function of n and m. Also, by Example 3.3.7, both of the binary functions

$$\langle n, m \rangle_1 = n \quad \text{and} \quad \langle n, m \rangle_2 = m$$

are then primitive recursive.

(12) The binary function $step(m, t)$ is defined next. Intuitively, its value always represents the current computation word at step t together with the production to be applied at step t, where the very first production application occurs at step 0 and input word m is assumed. Typically, its value for arguments m and t will be of the form

$\langle$code of the current computation word at step t, index of the production to be applied at step $t\rangle$

In particular, function $step(m, t)$ will be defined so that

- $step(m, 0)$ will be $\langle m, first\_applicable\_rule(m) \rangle$
- $step(m, t+1)$ will be equal to $\langle apply\_rule((step(m, t))_2, (step(m, t))_1), 0 \rangle$ if a terminal rule was applied at step t;
- otherwise, $step(m, t + 1)$ will be equal to

$\langle apply\_rule((step(m, t))_2, (step(m, t))_1),$

$$first\_applicable\_rule(apply\_rule((step(m, t))_2, (step(m, t))_1))\rangle$$

Function $step(m, t)$ is not a total function since it will be defined only for those arguments m that happen to encode words over Σ. However, for any such m, we shall have $step(m, t)$ defined for all $t \geq 0$. In any case, the definition of $step(m, t)$ by primitive recursion is the following:

$$step(m, 0) = \langle m, first\_applicable\_rule(m) \rangle$$

$$step(m, t + 1) = \langle apply\_rule((step(m, t))_2, (step(m, t)_1)),$$

$$first\_applicable\_rule(apply\_rule((step(m, t))_2, (step(m, t)_1))$$

$$\cdot \chi_{not\_term\_rule}(step(m, t)_2)\rangle$$

(13) Finally, if function $length\_comp(m)$ is defined as

$$length\_comp(m) = \mu t[step(m, t + 1))_2 = 0] + 1$$

we see that $length\_comp(m)$ is a unary partial recursive function. Also, it should be clear that if S never halts for input word m, then $length\_comp(m)$ is undefined. Finally, where f is the binary function computed by Markov algorithm schema S, then the value of f for arguments n_1 and n_2 is none other than

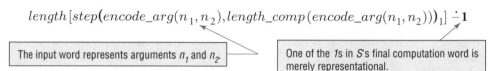

$$length\,[step\big(encode\_arg(n_1, n_2), length\_comp\,(encode\_arg(n_1, n_2)))_1] \mathbin{\dot-} 1$$

The input word represents arguments n_1 and n_2

One of the 1s in S's final computation word is merely representational.

and hence f is a partial recursive function. Recall that, by **(11)**, $step(encode\_arg(n_1, n_2),$ $length\_comp(encode\_arg(n_1, n_2)))_1$ is the code of the output word when S halts. Function $length$, as in **(4)**, then returns the number of occurrences of symbol 1 in this output word. Note that we are assuming that S never terminates if f is undefined for n_1 and n_2 (see Exercise 4.5.17 regarding this issue). Q.E.D.

The preceding theoretical results have the following practical application.

EXAMPLE 4.5.3 (Implementing Markov Algorithms in Perl) The programming language Perl was designed for text and file manipulation and has become standard on many UNIX platforms. (Perl is an acronym for **P**ractical **E**xtraction and **R**eport **L**anguage.) We describe several Perl functions that are together reminiscent of the way in which a Markov algorithm production is applied to a given computation word.

So-called *scalar variables* begin with character $. Their values may be character strings or numbers. Positions within character strings are numbered starting from 0 on the left. A call to function `index( )` returns the position within its first argument of (the leftmost character of) its second argument. Thus assignment statement

```
$where = index('hello','e');
```

causes variable `$where` to take value 1. On the other hand, execution of

```
$where = index('hello','j');
```

causes `$where` to become −1. If the second parameter, which may itself be a string, has more than one occurrence, then the position of the leftmost occurrence is returned. Thus

```
$leftmost = index('bbbababa','aba');
```

sets `$leftmost` to 3. A call to function

```
substr($string,$start,$length)
```

returns that substring consisting of $length characters starting at position $start within $string. Thus

$$\text{\$suffix = substr('greeting',5,3);}$$

sets $suffix to 'ing'. Finally, if the first argument of substr() happens to be a variable, then the call to substr() may occur to the left of the assignment operator as in

$$\text{\$hw = 'Hello, World!';}$$

$$\text{substr(\$hw,0,5) = 'Howdy';}$$

which returns Howdy, World! in $hw.

The availability of functions index() and substr() means that the application of any Markov algorithm production is easily implemented in Perl. For instance, the assignment statement

$$\text{substr(\$w,index(\$w,'bc'),2) = 'cb';}$$

implements the application of production

$$bc \rightarrow cb$$

to the current value of $w—assumed to contain an occurrence of bc. Furthermore, the computation of Markov algorithm schema

$$\left.\begin{array}{l} a \rightarrow c \\ \\ bc \rightarrow cb \\ \\ b \rightarrow .cd \end{array}\right\} \quad \text{our earlier Example 4.1.2}$$

for input word *w* is implemented in Perl by the block

```
MARKOV:   {
          if (index($w,'a') != -1)
          {
             substr($w,index($w,'a'),1) = 'c';
             redo MARKOV;
          }
          if (index($w,'bc') != -1)
          {
             substr($w,index($w,'bc'),2) = 'cb';
             redo MARKOV;
          }
          if (index($w,'b') != -1)
          {
             substr($w,index($w,'b'),1) = 'cd';
             last MARKOV;        # exits block
          }
       }
       print $w,"\n";
```

Our construction is perfectly general. Namely, given any Markov algorithm schema S, we introduce one if-statement within the block labeled MARKOV for each production within S. These if-statements preserve the order of their counterparts in S, of course, and any terminal production of S will correspond to a last statement. This should be enough to see that any Markov algorithm whatever can be emulated by a Perl program. In other words, *Perl can do anything that a Markov algorithm can do*. In particular, any Markov-computable function may be programmed in Perl, as can the problem of deciding membership in any Markov-recognizable language.

A greater challenge would be to demonstrate that, conversely, any number-theoretic function, say, which may be programmed in Perl is Markov-computable as well. We shall not show this—directly, anyway. However, eventually our ambitious Example 8.1.1 (**C Interpreter**) will show, in effect, that Turing machines can do anything that C language programs can do. It will then follow by Theorem 4.2(a) that Markov algorithms can do anything that C language programs can do. Finally, since Perl compilers can be and have been written in C, it is reasonable to suppose that anything that can be programmed in Perl can be programmed in C.

We will have shown that the concept *Markov algorithm* and the concept *Perl program* are "computationally equivalent," to put matters very roughly. By virtue of this and related results, we shall occasionally speak of Markov algorithms as a *universal computational model*. (Turing machines and partial recursive functions provide other universal models, for the same sorts of reasons.) We emphasize that, in saying this, we do not wish to imply that the Markov-computable functions encompass all number-theoretic functions. That would be false, and the reader is already familiar with a function that is not Turing-computable and, hence, not Markov-computable either. (Recall Busy Beaver and our remarks at the end of §2.7.) Rather, the term *universal computational model* is meant to suggest only that every function that *is* computable, in an intuitive sense, turns out to be Markov-computable as well.

§4.6 Considerations of Efficiency

In §4.5 we demonstrated, in effect, that the class of Turing-computable functions is identical to the class of Markov-computable functions. This was Theorem 4.2. Given Paradigm Interreducibility as outlined in §1.1, it will then come as no particular surprise that the class of Turing-acceptable languages coincides with the class of Markov-acceptable languages. We shall include this result within Theorem 4.3 below. Like Theorem 4.2, this second equivalence belongs to that part of the theory of computability that concerns computability-in-principle—classical computability theory, if you will. Our primary goal in this section, however, is to move beyond the classical theory to introduce complexity-theoretic issues. In particular, our proof of Theorem 4.3 will involve (1) the construction of a Turing machine that simulates a Markov algorithm as well as (2) the construction of a Markov algorithm that simulates a Turing machine—just as in the case of Theorem 4.2. This time, however, we shall show that the simulations at (1) and (2) are both *efficient*.

- In particular, suppose that Markov algorithm schema S accepts language L. Then we shall show that there exists a single-tape Turing machine M that simulates Markov algorithm A_S, thereby accepting L. Moreover, this M will be such that $time_M(n)$ is $O(p(time_{A_S}(n)))$ for some polynomial function p. In other words, M simulates A_S "with polynomially bounded overhead," as one says. This is Theorem 4.3(b) actually, and, as our proof will show, $p(n)$ may be taken to be n^4. So if A_S accepts L in $O(n^2)$ steps, say, then M will accept L in $O((n^2)^4)$ steps—that is, $O(n^8)$ steps.

- The simulation of a Turing machine by a Markov algorithm can also be efficient, although this time polynomial function $p(n)$ may be taken to be identity function $1_{\mathcal{N}}$. That is, if Turing machine M

accepts L, then we are able to construct a Markov algorithm schema S that simulates M and thereby accepts L in $O(time_M(n))$ steps.

We turn now to the statement and proof of

THEOREM 4.3: Any language that is Markov-acceptable is Turing-acceptable, and, conversely, any Turing-acceptable language is Markov-acceptable. Moreover, where L is any arbitrary language,

(a) Given any Turing machine M accepting L, there exists a Markov algorithm A_S that accepts L in $O(time_M(n))$ steps, provided that $time_M(n) \geq n$ for sufficiently large n.
(b) Given any Markov algorithm A_S accepting L, there exists a Turing machine M that accepts L in $O([time_{A_S}(n)]^4)$ steps, provided that $time_{A_S}(n) \geq n$ for sufficiently large n.

PROOF As for (b), consider again the deterministic, six-tape, off-line Turing machine M described in the proof of Theorem 4.2(b).

- In point of fact, the only change required in the pseudocode given in that proof occurs at line (2): To begin, M merely copies input word w to worktape$_1$ in $O(n)$ steps, where $n = |w|$.

- Next, we may imagine that the productions of A_S are written in sequence to worktape$_4$. This requires $O(1)$ steps. (After all, do the number and properties of A_S's productions depend upon n in any way?)

- Having found an occurrence of some production left-hand side α_i within the current computation word w' on worktape$_1$, simulator M substitutes the corresponding right-hand side β_i at line (9). The substitution of β_i for α_i itself requires $O(1)$ steps. Otherwise, line (9) requires copying what precedes α_i and what follows it within w' from worktape$_1$ to worktape$_2$. The number of computation steps involved in this copying will depend upon the length of w', of course, and this length will itself be bounded above by $space_{A_S}(n)$. (Why?) Moreover, since $space_{A_S}(n)$ is $O(time_{A_S}(n))$—see Exercise 4.6.1—provided only that $time_{A_S}(n) \geq n$ for sufficiently large n, we have that line (9) by itself requires $O(time_{A_S}(n))$ steps.

- Similar reasoning shows that finding an occurrence of α_i in the first place requires $O(time_{A_S}(n))$ steps. The same is true of the copying/erasing at lines (10)–(17). In short, each execution of the body of the while-loop of lines (6)–(21) requires $O(time_{A_S}(n))$ steps.

- Moreover, for given input word w, the while-loop will be executed no more than $time_{A_S}(n)$ times total since each execution implements one production application—that is, one step in A_S's computation.

- The copying of the contents of worktape$_1$ to the output tape at line (23) requires $O(time_{A_S}(n))$ steps for reasons already given.

- Summarizing, M's computation for input word w consumes $O(n)$ steps at lines (2)–(4), $O([time_{A_S}(n)]^2)$ steps in lines (5)–(22), and then another $O(time_{A_S}(n))$ steps at lines (23)–(24). Consequently, the total running time of multitape M is $O([time_{A_S}(n)]^2)$ steps provided $time_{A_S}(n) \geq n$. By Corollary 2.1, there exists a single-tape Turing machine M that accepts L in $O(([time_{A_S}(n)]^2)^2)$—that is, $O([time_{A_S}(n)]^4)$—steps worst case.

As for Theorem 4.3(a), suppose that Turing machine M accepts language L. This time the very same argument given for Theorem 4.2(a) enables us to construct a Markov algorithm schema S that simulates M and thereby accepts L. (Appropriate changes in the productions of Groups 1 through 3 must be assumed, however.) As for the time analysis of this simulation for an arbitrary input word w with $|w| = n$, recall, first, that the productions of the constructed schema S are divided into Groups 1 through 3. The reader can easily verify each of the following items.

(1) Total running time in applying the initialization productions of Group 1 will be O(n). (Typically, $n + 2$ production applications will be involved.)

(2) One production of Group 2 will be applied for each of M's moves-right, one for each of M's moves-left, and one for each of M's writes. Thus the total number of applications of Group 2 productions is bounded above by $time_M(n)$.

(3) The applications of the productions of Group 3 require O($space_M(n)$) and, hence, O($time_M(n)$) computation steps, assuming that $time_M(n) \geq 1$ (see Exercise 1.7.3).

Thus, assuming only that $time_M(n) \geq n$ for sufficiently large n, we may conclude that the total number of steps in S's simulation of M is O($time_M(n)$), and we are done. (Incidentally, why is it reasonable to assume that $time_M(n) \geq n$?)   Q.E.D.

The interest of Theorem 4.3 lies in its implications for an earlier proposal regarding feasible computation whereby it was suggested that feasibility of a problem concerning language acceptance be taken to mean polynomial-time Turing-acceptability. This was the so-called Cobham–Edmonds Thesis introduced in §1.7. In other words, it was suggested there that the problem of accepting language L is feasible if there exists a deterministic single-tape Turing machine M that accepts L in polynomial time—that is, in O($p(n)$) steps for some polynomial function $p(n)$. Theorem 4.3 shows that we might have couched Cobham–Edmonds in terms of Markov algorithms. For, by (a), if L is polynomial-time Turing-acceptable, then it is polynomial-time Markov-acceptable as well. Similarly, by (b), if language L is polynomial-time Markov-acceptable, then it is also polynomial-time Turing-acceptable—essentially because the composition of two polynomial functions is another polynomial function. In short, we might have proposed, with equal effect, that feasibility of a problem concerning language acceptance amounts to polynomial-time *Markov* acceptability.

Although we shall continue this discussion in §5.4, we point out now that Theorem 4.3 has positive implications for the Cobham–Edmonds Thesis. Namely, it suggests a certain limited *invariance* of that proposal with respect to choice of computational model. It turns out that it could have formulated either in terms of (deterministic) Turing machines or in terms of Markov algorithms; the same class of problems turns out to be feasible either way. And as long as we are on this topic, note that Corollary 2.1 demonstrates that the Cobham–Edmonds Thesis could just as well have been formulated in terms of (deterministic) *multitape* Turing machines. Furthermore, Exercise 4.6.2 shows that it might have been formulated in terms of *labeled* Markov algorithms. In short, it is beginning to look as if the invariance of the proposal is not really so limited after all but, rather, quite broad in scope. And this invariance casts the proposal itself in a favorable light. Apparently, small, or even rather large, qualitative changes in the computational model used to formulate the Cobham–Edmonds Thesis have no effect at the theoretical level: The same class of languages is involved no matter which formulation we choose. This, in turn, suggests that, in all likelihood, we are truly onto something with the proposal. Just possibly, we really have managed to rigorously characterize our intuitive notion of computational feasibility.

§4.7 Computation Theory and the Foundations of Mathematics

We have described Turing and Markov as intending *analyses* or *models* of some intuitive concept of computability. Talk of computability is sure to conjure up images of motherboards, disk drives, and the like, in the mind of the contemporary reader. In the interest of historical accuracy, however, it must be said that, especially in the case of Turing, the original purpose of the analysis had little to do with computing devices themselves. Rather, Turing was motivated by a desire to provide a secure foundation for mathematics—that is, some way of establishing, once and for all, that provable mathematical propositions are indubitable. (Philosophers and logicians would themselves more likely describe this project as an attempt to show that the theorems of mathematics are *logically necessary* or *analytic*.)

Most likely, the reader will be puzzled by the suggestion that Turing machines could be used to justify mathematics. After all, how could anyone think that an analysis of mere computability—recall the computation involved in determining whether n is prime—would provide an epistemic foundation for the entire edifice of mathematics, including both number theory and analysis? Implausible as this may seem initially, the reader should remember that epistemic foundations are not concerned with the act of *mathematical discovery*, whose study properly belongs to cognitive science and psychology. Rather, epistemic foundations focus on the process of *verifying mathematical proofs*—verifying that what purports to be a proof truly is a proof. Logicians and philosophers of mathematics working during the 1930s had come to think of this verification process as being essentially computational—they themselves would have described it as *formal*—a matter of mere symbol manipulation involving no consideration of the meanings of those symbols. Seeing how such a view had arisen in the first place requires a historical digression. We start with a brief description of the state of mathematics in Europe toward the end of the nineteenth century.

Certainly in the eighteenth century, say, the various areas of mathematics were relatively disorganized. Typically, a branch of mathematics consisted of some constellation of "true propositions," expressed in a wide variety of notations, whose truth had been certified on the basis of some other propositions that, in turn, had some claim to truth. The propositions serving as basis here varied from author to author. Moreover, the means by which one brought about this certification of truth—the permissible methods of proof—were left largely unspecified and, again, varied from author to author. By the end of the nineteenth century, mathematicians—particularly those in Germany—had come to regard the chaotic state of mathematics as intolerable. As they saw it, stability and progress in mathematical science would necessitate some communitywide agreement with regard to both (1) the propositions taken as basic within a given area of mathematics and (2) the methods of argument that would be permitted within mathematical demonstrations.

It is now standard for historians to view late nineteenth-century mathematics in terms of just such a quest for secure foundations in the form of *axiomatizations* of the principal areas of mathematics—that is, arithmetic (number theory), analysis, algebra, and geometry. An axiomatization of arithmetic, say, would involve some collection—finite or infinite—of basic arithmetic propositions called *axioms*, which are assumed without demonstration. One might be inclined to insist that these axioms be *self-evident* in the sense that their truth is so obvious that no proof is required. In this connection, we mention Dedekind's axioms for arithmetic (1888), Hilbert's axioms for Euclidean geometry (1899), Hilbert's axioms for real analysis (1900), and Zermelo's axioms for set theory (1908). See [van Heijenoort 1967] for relevant bibliography.

On another front, what we now call mathematical logic was brought into being with the 1879 publication of Gottlob Frege's monograph entitled *Begriffschrift*—German for something like "conceptual notation." The modern notion of a *formal system* traces its origins to Frege's work. By a formal system, we mean the presentation of some set of axioms, as described above, as well as some finite number of *rules of inference* for deriving new propositions from propositions already established. Examples of such rules are the logical implications Modus Ponens and Modus Tollens. Early in this century, theoreticians identified a requirement of anything that is to count as a formal system; namely, it should be effectively decidable whether any given sequence of formulas constitutes a proof within that system.[6]

These two intellectual currents—the quest for axiomatizations and the logic of formal systems—converged within the research area loosely known as *foundations of mathematics*. Axiom systems in the sense of Dedekind and Hilbert were reconceived as formal systems in Frege's sense so that verifying a proof came to mean verifying that the proof starts with axioms and proceeds strictly in accordance with logical rules of inference. In other words, effectively determining whether a given sequence of formulas is, in fact, a deduction within a given formal system should be possible by applying some algorithm or effective procedure so as to determine whether every formula in said sequence is either (1) an axiom or (2) the result of applying a rule of inference to formulas occurring earlier in the sequence. But just what does it mean to *apply a rule of inference?* For instance, what does it mean to say that the application of Modus Ponens to propositions

$$n \text{ is prime } \rightarrow (n = 2 \lor n \text{ is odd})$$

and

$$n \text{ is prime}$$

yields the further proposition

$$n = 2 \lor n \text{ is odd}$$

as result? We are inclined to answer this question by saying that the logical implication

$$[n \text{ is prime} \rightarrow (n = 2 \lor n \text{ is odd})] \ \& \ n \text{ is prime} \Rightarrow n = 2 \lor n \text{ is odd} \qquad (4.7.1)$$

is an *instance* of the schema

This is just Modus Ponens.

$$[S_1 \rightarrow S_2] \ \& \ S_1 \Rightarrow S_2 \qquad (4.7.2)$$

Operationally, we may think of this in terms of making uniform substitutions for S_1 and S_2 or in terms of pattern matching. In any case, we can agree that the recognition that (4.7.1) is an instance of (4.7.2) is by nature "mechanical," requiring no ingenuity. Expressed another way, this recognition, so typical of proof verification, is merely "algorithmic" or "computational," which brings us to the point of this historical digression. One could have been satisfied with a rough characterization of proof verification within formal systems as "involving purely computational processes." Since the validity of mathematical science hung in the balance, however, mathematicians such as Turing were not satisfied with anything

---

[6]This is not to require that theoremhood itself be effective or decidable. In other words, we do not require that the general problem of determining whether an individual proposition is deducible within the system be solvable. In fact, it can be shown that the usual systems of quantificational logic are not decidable in this sense.

so rough. Instead, one felt a need to press for some rigorous characterization of *computational process*. This need gave birth to what we now know as the theory of computability. We close by noting that the passage from (4.7.2) to (4.7.1) can readily be construed in terms of the iterated application of two Markov algorithm productions—one for S_1 and one for S_2.

§4.8 Bibliography

Additional material regarding Markov algorithms may be found in [Mendelson 1987]. The original source of these ideas is [Markov 1954]. Theorem 4.2 was first proved in [Detlovs 1958]. Our treatment of labeled Markov algorithms—in particular, the proof of Theorem 4.1—is based upon [Kurki-Suonio 1971]. [Pratt 1984] contains a good overview of the programming language SNOBOL4. [Wall and Schwartz 1991] provide a full description of Perl.

EXERCISES FOR §4.1

4.1.1. ^{hwk} Show the steps in the application of the Markov algorithm of Example 4.1.4 (**Reverse Word**) to input word *abb*. In other words, complete the computation record whose first two steps are

$$abb \Rightarrow \#@abb \quad \text{by (xiii)}$$
$$\Rightarrow a\#@bb \quad \text{by (i)}$$

4.1.2. Evaluate the statements below as either true or false.
  (a) Given any Markov algorithm schema S, if $w \Rightarrow_S w'$, then $w \Rightarrow_S^* w'$.
  (b) Given any Markov algorithm schema S, if $w \Rightarrow_S^+ w'$, then $w \Rightarrow_S^* w'$.
  (c) Given any Markov algorithm schema S, if $w \Rightarrow_S^* w'$, then $w \Rightarrow_S^+ w'$.

4.1.3. Show that, in designing a Markov algorithm scheme, one need include no more than one terminal production. (*Hint:* Suppose that schema S possesses two terminal productions

$$\cdots$$
$$\alpha_1 \rightarrow .\beta_1$$
$$\cdots$$
$$\alpha_2 \rightarrow .\beta_2$$
$$\cdots$$

Design an equivalent schema with just one terminal production. You will need to introduce a new nonterminal symbol &, say, which we assume is not in Γ. A new production for & will be needed and the two displayed productions must be altered slightly. Be careful in positioning the new production.)

EXERCISES FOR §4.2

4.2.1. ^{hwk} (a) Modify the Markov algorithm schema of Example 4.2.1 so as to obtain a schema that accepts language $\{a^n b^m | n \geq 0, m \geq 0\}$.
  (b) Modify the Markov algorithm schema of Example 4.2.1 so as to obtain a schema that recognizes language $\{a^n b^m | n \geq 0, m \geq 1\}$. (*Hint:* Use the technique introduced in Example 4.2.2.)

4.2.2. For each of the languages below, give a Markov algorithm schema that accepts the language. Note that in every case, input alphabet Σ is $\{a, b\}$. On the other hand, symbol *1* and perhaps some other auxiliary symbols will be members of work alphabet Γ.
  (a) $\{a^n b^m a | n \geq 0, m \geq 0\}$
  (b) ^{hwk} $\{a^n (ab)^m | n \geq 0, m \geq 0\}$
  (c) $\{a^n (ab)^m | n > 0, m > 0\}$

(d) $\{a^n ba^n | n \geq 0\}$
(e) $\{w \in \Sigma^* | w = w^R\}$, where $\Sigma = \{a, b\}$

4.2.3. Consider the Markov algorithm schema below:

$$\$a \rightarrow a\$$$

$$\$b \rightarrow b\$$$

$$@ab \rightarrow @$$

$$@b \rightarrow \#$$

$$\#b \rightarrow \#$$

$$@\$ \rightarrow .1$$

$$\#\$ \rightarrow .1$$

$$\varepsilon \rightarrow @\$$$

What language is accepted by this Markov algorithm schema? Test it using the accompanying software.

4.2.4. (a) Present a Markov algorithm schema that accepts the language $\{w \in \Sigma^* | n_a(w) = n_b(w) = n_c(w)\}$, where $\Sigma = \{a, b, c\}$.

EXERCISES FOR §4.3

4.3.1. We adopted certain conventions (i) regarding representation of natural numbers by strings of 1s and (ii) regarding representation of k-tuples of natural numbers by words over $\{1, *\}$. Under our conventions, what number is represented by 11111? What triple of numbers is represented by word $11111*11111111*11$?

4.3.2. ^{hwk} Consider the Markov algorithm schema below.

$$\varepsilon \rightarrow .1111$$

(a) What string will result from applying this schema to input 111?
(b) What string will result from applying this schema to input 1111?
(c) A moment's reflection concerning the numbers represented by these strings should reveal that this schema computes a certain unary number-theoretic function. Which one?

(b) Modify your solution to (a) so as to obtain a Markov algorithm schema that recognizes the language $\{w \in \Sigma^* | n_a(w) = n_b(w) = n_c(w)\}$.

4.2.5. (a) Where S is the Markov algorithm schema of Example 4.2.3, use the accompanying software to determine the value of $time_S(6)$. (Select input word $aaabbb$ from the Input Words clickbox, run the algorithm, and let the software count the number of productions applied.)
(b) Similarly, determine the value of $time_S(8)$.
(c) What is $time_S(10)$?
(d) What is $time_S(12)$?
(e) Based on (a) through (d), find an expression in n for $time_S(n)$.

4.2.6. Find an expression in n for function $time_S(n)$, where S is the Markov algorithm schema of Example 4.1.4 (**Reverse Word**). Again, use the accompanying software to count computation steps.

4.3.3. Consider the Markov algorithm schema below.

$$1* \rightarrow *$$

$$* \rightarrow .\varepsilon$$

(a) What string will result from applying this schema to input word $111 * 1111$?
(b) What string will result from applying this schema to input word $1111 * 1$?
(c) A moment's reflection concerning the k-tuples of numbers represented by these strings should reveal that this schema computes a well-known binary number-theoretic function. What is it?

4.3.4. ^{hwk} (a) Design an algorithm schema that computes the identity function.
(b) Design an algorithm schema that computes the doubling function defined by

$$f(n) = 2n$$

(c) Design an algorithm schema that computes the function

$$f(n) = f \ div \ 2$$

(d) Design an algorithm schema that computes the function

$$f(n) = f \ mod \ 2$$

(e) Design an algorithm schema that computes the binary function

$$monus(n, m) = n \dot{-} m$$
$$= \begin{cases} n - m & \text{if } n \geq m \\ 0 & \text{otherwise} \end{cases}$$

(This is the definition given earlier in Exercise 3.1.8(b).)

(f) Design an algorithm schema that computes the binary function

$$f(n, m) = max(n, m)$$

(g) Design an algorithm schema that computes the binary function

$$f(n, m) = n \cdot m$$

4.3.5. Show that each of the following number-theoretic functions is Markov-computable.
   (a) $f(n) = sg(n)$
   (b) $f(n) = \overline{sg}(n)$
   (c) $f(n, m) = |n - m|$

4.3.6. Show that we may assume without loss of generality that if a Markov algorithm halts, then it does so by virtue of applying a terminal production.

EXERCISES FOR §4.4

4.4.1. (a) Show that any labeled Markov algorithm schema S is equivalent to one in which all productions have gotos.
   (b) Show that any labeled Markov algorithm schema S with production sequence Π is equivalent to one in which the only production without a goto is a terminal production of the form

$$\mathcal{L}: \quad \varepsilon \to .\varepsilon$$

that is the final production in production sequence Π. (*Hint:* Use (a).)

4.4.2. Show that any labeled Markov algorithm schema S is equivalent to one in which there are no meaningless gotos—that is, no labels that fail to correspond to some production within S.

EXERCISES FOR §4.5

Exercises 4.5.1 through 4.5.13 correspond to items (1) through (13) of the second, alternative proof of Theorem 4.2(b).

4.5.1. Let alphabet symbol $*$ be represented by base-3 digit *1* and alphabet symbol *1* by base-3 digit *2*. Determine $\ulcorner 11 * 111 \urcorner$ in accordance with (1) of the proof of Theorem 4.2(b)

4.5.2. What is $encode\_arg(1, 2)$?

4.5.3. Let S be the Markov algorithm schema

$$*1 \to *$$

$$* \to .\varepsilon$$

(Note that S computes the binary projection function p_1^2.) Define unary functions *prod_lhs* and *prod_rhs* relative to S in accordance with (3).

4.5.4. Find $length(719)$.

4.5.5. Find $segment(3, 4, 719)$.

4.5.6. Find two distinct values of n such that $occurs\_in(n, 719)$ holds.

4.5.7. Use (4.4.2) to determine the value of $leftmost\_occur\_start\_position(5, 719)$.

4.5.8. Use (4.4.3) to find $subst(1, 3, 4, 719)$.

4.5.9. Let S be the Markov algorithm schema of Exercise 4.5.3. Relative to S, evaluate $first\_applicable\_rule(53)$.

4.5.10. Evaluate $apply\_rule(2, 53)$ relative to the schema of Exercise 4.5.3.

4.5.11. Evaluate $\chi_{term\_rule}(1)$ and $\chi_{term\_rule}(2)$ relative to the schema of Exercise 4.5.3.

4.5.12. Let S be the Markov algorithm schema of Exercise 4.5.3. Evaluate each of the following relative to S.
  (a) $step(6533, 0)$
  (b) $step(6533, 1)$
  (c) $step(6533, 2)$
  (d) $step(6533, 3)$
  (e) $step(6533, 4)$
  (f) $step(6533, 5)$
  (g) $step(6533, 6)$

4.5.13. Evaluate $length[step(encode\_arg(n, m),$ $length\_comp(encode\_arg(n, m)))_1] \dotminus 1$ for $n = 2$ and $m = 3$.

4.5.14. Design a Turing machine with input alphabet $\Sigma = \{a, b\}$ that, given input word w, transforms w into w', where w' is the result of replacing the leftmost occurrence of string aba within w by string $bbab$. M should halt scanning the leftmost symbol of w'.

4.5.15. Design a Turing machine M that is like that of Exercise 4.5.14 except that now M makes as many substitutions as possible. That is, M makes a first substitution of $bbab$ for the leftmost occurrence of aba in w so as to obtain w', if such an occurrence exists. Then M makes a substitution of $bbab$ for the leftmost occurrence of aba in w' so as to obtain w'', if such an occurrence exists, and so on, until no further substitutions are possible. M should halt scanning the leftmost symbol of its output string.

4.5.16. Design a Turing machine M that simulates the application of the Markov algorithm scheme that appears below, following something like the suggestion contained in our first proof of Theorem 4.2(b).

$$ba \rightarrow ab$$

$$\varepsilon \rightarrow .\varepsilon$$

4.5.17. Suppose that Markov algorithm schema S computes k-ary number-theoretic function f. Show that we can assume without loss of generality that Markov algorithm A_S never halts when started on an input word representing a k-tuple of arguments for which f is undefined.

EXERCISES FOR §4.6

4.6.1. Use Definitions 4.5 and 4.6 to show that if Markov algorithm schema S computes in time $O(f(n))$ worst case with $f(n) \geq n$ for sufficiently large n, then S computes in space $O(f(n))$ worst case as well. In other words, show that $space_S(n)$ is $O(time_S(n))$ provided $time_S(n) \geq n$ for sufficiently large n. Readers who are having difficulty appreciating the equivalence of our two formulations of this exercise are encouraged to review Exercise 0.5.12 and its solution. (Note that in referring to this result in the future, we shall not always make explicit our assumption that $f(n) \geq n$ for sufficiently large n.)

4.6.2. In Definition 4.5 we defined time for Markov algorithms as maximum number of computation steps, where each production application constitutes one computation step. We may use the same definition, without alteration, for labeled Markov algorithms as presented in §4.4.
  (a) Show that if language L is accepted by Markov algorithm schema S, then there exists a labeled Markov algorithm schema S_{Lab} such that function $time_{S_{Lab}}$ is $O(time_S)$.
  (b) Show that if language L is accepted by a labeled Markov algorithm schema S_{Lab}, then there exists a Markov algorithm schema S without labels such that function $time_S$ is $O([time_{S_{Lab}}(n)]^2)$ provided only that $time_{S_{Lab}}(n) \geq n$ for sufficiently large n. (*Hint:* Review the proof of Theorem 4.1.)
  (c) Use (a) and (b) to show that, given any language L, there exists a Markov algorithm schema with labels that accepts L

in polynomially bounded time if and only if there exists a Markov algorithm schema without labels that accepts L in polynomially bounded time.

4.6.3. At (2) in the proof of Theorem 4.3, it was stated that the total number of applications of Group 2 productions is *bounded above* by $time_M(n)$. Some readers may have wanted to say, instead, that the total number of applications of Group 2 productions is *precisely* $time_M(n)$. Explain why one cannot, in general, say this.

EXERCISES FOR §4.7 (END-OF-CHAPTER REVIEW EXERCISES)

4.7.1. ^{hwk} We adopted a certain convention regarding representation of natural numbers by strings of 1s. Under this convention, what number is represented by 11111? How is the pair $\langle 4, 7 \rangle$ going to be represented? The triple $\langle 4, 0, 7 \rangle$?

4.7.2. ^{hwk} Consider the Markov algorithm schema below.

$$111111 \to .1$$

(a) What string will result from applying this schema to input 1111111?

(b) What string will result from applying this schema to input 111111?

(c) A moment's reflection concerning the numbers represented by these strings should reveal that this schema computes a certain number-theoretic function. What is it?

4.7.3. ^{hwk} Consider the Markov algorithm schema below.

$$1* \to .\varepsilon$$

(a) What string will result from applying this schema to input $111*1111$?

(b) What string will result from applying this schema to input $1111*1$?

(c) A moment's reflection concerning the numbers represented by these strings should reveal that this schema computes a well-known number-theoretic function. What is it?

4.7.4. Consider the Markov algorithm schema below.

$$*\$a \to a*\$$$

$$*\$b \to b*\$$$

$$\&a \to \varepsilon$$

$$b* \to \varepsilon$$

$$@a \to @$$

$$@b \to @$$

$$@\$ \to .1$$

$$\varepsilon \to @\&*\$$$

(a) Considered as a language acceptor, does the corresponding Markov algorithm accept the word ε?

(b) the word ab?

(c) the words aa or ba or bb?

(d) the word $aababab$?

(e) the word $bababaa$?

(f) What language over $\{a, b\}$ is accepted by this Markov algorithm?

4.7.5. ^{hwk} Let $\Sigma = \{a, b\}$.

(a) Present a Markov algorithm schema that converts any word w over Σ^* to the result of simultaneously substituting as for bs and bs for as.

(b) Present a Markov algorithm schema that converts any word w over Σ^* to $1^{|w|+1}$.

(c) Let w be a fixed word over Σ. (In other words, suppose that w is $aabb$, say.) Present a Markov algorithm schema that converts any word $w' \neq w$ to ε while leaving w itself unchanged.

(d) Present a Markov algorithm schema that converts any word w to ww.

4.7.6. The *Fibonacci strings* are defined by setting

$$w_1 = b, \qquad w_2 = a, \qquad \text{and}$$

$$w_n = w_{n-1}w_{n-2} \quad \text{for } n > 2$$

(The reader might verify that w_7 is *abaababaabaab*.) Design a (labeled) Markov algorithm schema that, for arbitrary $n \geq 1$, transforms n into w_n.

4.7.7. **(a)** Show that the family of Markov algorithms with input alphabet $\Sigma = \{1\}$ is countable by sketching a scheme for encoding Markov algorithm schemata as natural numbers. (*Hint:* Review the Euler–Gödel scheme used in §2.4 to encode Turing machines.)

      (b) Describe a notion of *universal Markov algorithm* analogous to that of universal Turing machine given in Definition 2.8 and sketch a proof to the effect that such a universal Markov algorithm exists.

4.7.8. Suppose that Markov algorithm scheme S computes k-ary number-theoretic function f. Show that we may assume without loss of generality that S never halts for input words w representing k-tuples for which f is undefined. (*Hint:* Use Exercise 4.3.6 and then describe a labeled Markov algorithm schema.)

4.7.9. Design a labeled Markov algorithm schema S that recognizes the language $\{a^i b^j c^k \mid i \cdot j = k$ and $i, j, k \geq 1\}$. For example, S will accept input words *abc* and *aabbbccccc* but reject input word *aabbbcc*. Use the companion software to test your design.

4.7.10. Design a labeled Markov algorithm schema S that recognizes the language $\{a^i b^j c^k \mid i \neq j$ or $j \neq k\}$. For example, S will accept input words *aabc* and *aabbb* but reject input word *aabbcc*. Use the companion software to test your design.

4.7.11. Let alphabet $\Sigma = \{a, b, c\}$. Design a labeled Markov algorithm schema S that recognizes the language $\{w_1 c w_2 \mid w_1, w_2$ contain *a*s and *b*s only and $w_1 \neq w_2\}$. For example, S will accept input words *aabcba* and *aacbbb* but reject input words *aabcaab* and *acbcacb*. Use the companion software to test your design.

4.7.12. Let alphabet $\Sigma = \{a, b, \$\}$. Design a labeled Markov algorithm schema S that accepts the language consisting of all and only words over Σ of the form $\$w_1 \$w_2 \$ \ldots \$w_k$ for $k \geq 1$ such that (1) each of the w_i is nonempty, consisting of *a*s and *b*s only and (2) $i \neq j$ implies $w_i \neq w_j$ for all i, j with $1 \leq i, j \leq k$. In other words, S should accept only words $\$w_1 \$w_2 \$ \ldots \$w_k$ with all of the w_i distinct, nonempty, and containing no occurrences of $\$$. Use the companion software to test your design.

4.7.13. Show that the class of Markov-acceptable languages is closed under union. In other words, show that if languages L_1 and L_2 are both Markov-acceptable, then so is $L_1 \cup L_2$. (*Hint:* Assume that Markov algorithm schemata S_1 and S_2 accepting L_1 and L_2, respectively, are given. Describe the construction of a new schema S^* accepting $L_1 \cup L_2$.)

4.7.14. Show that the class of Markov-acceptable languages is closed under intersection. In other words, show that if languages L_1 and L_2 are both Markov-acceptable, then so is $L_1 \cap L_2$.

4.7.15. Show that the class of Markov-acceptable languages is closed under concatenation. In other words, show that if languages L_1 and L_2 are both Markov-acceptable, then so is $L_1 . L_2$.

4.7.16. Give an argument to the effect that the class of Turing-recognizable languages is closed under complementation. (*Hint:* Describe a labeled Markov algorithm and refer to Exercise 4.3.6.)

Chapter 5

Register Machines

§5.1 Register Machines

Whereas most of the models that we consider in this text—for example, Turing machines, Post systems—predate the advent of the modern digital computer, the register machine model, which we introduce next, is of later vintage. It will come as no surprise, then, that this model reflects modern computer design to a degree. As a consequence, the reader will probably find register machines natural to work with.

EXAMPLE 5.1.1 Figure 5.1.1 shows the flow diagram for a register machine M with two *registers* R_1 and R_2, where a register in this context is merely variable storage—that is, storage whose contents are permitted to vary during M's computation. Let us assume that register R_1 initially contains natural number n. Starting at the top of the diagram, execution of instruction $R_2 := 0$ causes the contents of register R_2 to be initialized to 0. M then checks to see whether the contents of registers R_1 and R_2 are currently identical. If not, then the contents of register R_2 are incremented by 1. This incrementation is repeated until the condition $R_1 = R_2$? has become true, at which point the program causes the machine to halt. Summarizing, it can be seen that M copies the contents of register R_1 into register R_2 so that, when computation ceases, both R_1 and R_2 contain n.

The flow diagram of Figure 5.1.1 is a graphical representation of the labeled program

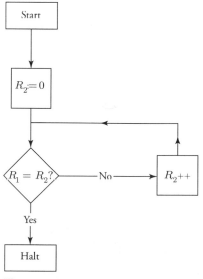

Figure 5.1.1. This register machine causes the contents of register R_2 to become equal to those of register R_1.

293

Input: $R_1 = n$
Output: $R_2 = n$
Algorithm
        Start;
        $R_2 := 0;$ /∗ initialize R_2 to 0 ∗/
loop: $R_1 = R_2$? goto *end*;   /∗ if $R_1 = R_2$, then branch to instruction *end*;
                                          otherwise continue to next instruction ∗/

        R_2++;   /∗ $R_2 := R_2 + 1$ ∗/
        goto *loop*;   /∗ branch to instruction *loop* ∗/
end: Halt.

The instruction "goto *loop*" here is an example of an *unconditional branch instruction*.

Open the icon **Set R2 Equal to R1** within the Register Machine folder to observe the operation of this machine. Try running this machine on register set `r1_eq_10.rs`.

Any register machine M is assumed to have some nonempty collection of registers R_1, R_2, R_3, ... The contents of any given register R_i will always be a natural number. Consequently, register incrementation will always make sense. Usually it will be sufficient to assume that the collection of M's registers is finite, although occasionally it will be convenient to assume that the number of registers is unbounded. In other words, we shall permit a register machine M to have either a finite or an infinite collection of registers. To this extent, register machines represent an idealization of modern computers. On the other hand, even in the case where M has access to infinitely many registers, it will still be true that, up to any given point in M's computation for a given input, only finitely many registers will have been used.

Any register machine M will be associated with a finite, labeled sequence of instructions, each of which is of one of the five types listed below.

(i) The **Start** instruction causes machine execution to begin. Within flowcharts it will be represented as indicated in Figure 5.1.2(a). This instruction is invariably the first instruction within any register machine program. Of course, any program will contain only one **Start** instruction.

(ii) The **Halt** instruction causes program execution to cease (see Figure 5.1.2(b)). Halt instructions need not be unique (but see Exercise 5.5.12).

(iii) Instructions of the form $\boldsymbol{R_m}$++, where $m \geq 1$, cause the contents of register R_m to be incremented by 1 (see Figure 5.1.2(c)).

(iv) Instructions of the form $\boldsymbol{R_m} := \mathbf{0}$, where $m \geq 1$, cause the contents of register R_m to be set to 0 (see Figure 5.1.2(d)).

(v) Instructions of the form $\boldsymbol{R_i} = \boldsymbol{R_j}$? **goto** $\mathcal{L}$, where $i, j \geq 1$, are *branch instructions*. They are interpreted as follows: If the current contents of registers R_i and R_j are identical, then execution proceeds to the instruction with label $\mathcal{L}$; otherwise the physically next instruction is executed. (We can take labels to be (short) alphanumeric strings over $\{a, b, c, \ldots, z\} \cup \{0, 1, 2, \ldots, 9\}$ that begin with

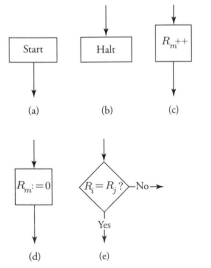

Figure 5.1.2 Five types of register machine instructions.

a letter.) Branch instructions will be represented within flow diagrams as in Figure 5.1.2(e). Should there be no instruction with label $\mathcal{L}$, then execution of instruction $R_i = R_j?$ **goto** $\mathcal{L}$ will cause termination in the case where the current contents of registers R_i and R_j happen to be identical. (So this is a second way that a register machine computation may terminate.)

For the time being, this completes our informal presentation of the syntax and semantics of register machine programs. Later on, we shall be adding to our instruction set, but we prefer to consider a couple more examples before doing so. In any case, we shall keep our instruction set small; this will be an advantage later in presenting proofs about register machines. What we shall mean by a *register machine computation* is implicit in the flowcharts and pseudocode used to define particular machines. Consequently, no formal definition will be presented. We shall formally define the notion *register machine*, however (see Definition 5.1 below).

Since we are interested in register machines as a model of sequential computation, we shall first focus on register machines that compute number-theoretic functions. Afterward, a concept of language acceptance (recognition) for register machines will be developed (see §5.3 below). At that later point, we shall also add instructions that enable a register machine to read from an input tape and write to an output tape.

EXAMPLE 5.1.2 As another simple example, consider the register machine *M* whose flow diagram appears in Figure 5.1.3.

- If register R_1 initially contains natural number 2, then, upon termination, register R_1 will contain 2 and R_2 will contain 3.

- Similarly, if register R_1 initially contains natural number 3, then, upon termination, register R_1 will contain 3 and R_2 will contain 4.

- In general, if register R_1 initially contains natural number n, then, upon termination, R_1 will contain n and R_2 will contain $n + 1$.

By virtue of this general state of affairs, we are going to say that *M* computes the successor function (see Definition 5.2 below).

EXAMPLE 5.1.3 (Addition Machine) As a third example, consider the register machine *M* of Figure 5.1.4.

- If registers R_1 and R_2 initially contain natural numbers 2 and 3, respectively, then what are the final contents of registers R_1, R_2, and R_3? A little work will reveal that register R_1 will contain 2, R_2 will contain 3, and R_3 will contain 5.

- Similarly, if registers R_1 and R_2 initially contain natural numbers 4 and 1, respectively, then ultimately register R_1 will contain 4, R_2 will contain 1, and R_3 will contain 5.

Reasonably, we are going to say that *M* computes the binary addition function (again, see Definition 5.2 below).

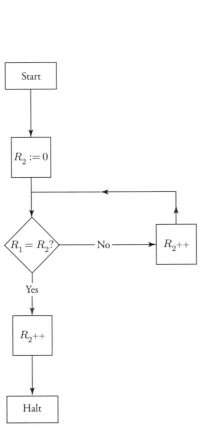

Figure 5.1.3 This register machine computes the successor function.

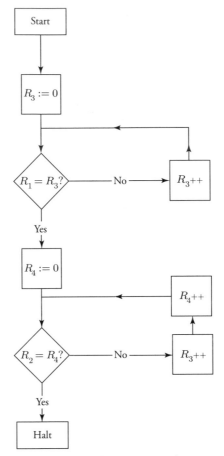

Figure 5.1.4 This register machine computes the binary addition function.

The program of this register machine is as follows.

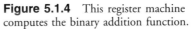

Input: $R_1 = n$
             $R_2 = m$
Output: $R_3 = n + m$
Algorithm
            Start;
            $R_3 := 0$;   /∗ initialize R_3 to 0 ∗/
loop1: $R_1 = R_3$? goto *end1*;   /∗ if $R_1 = R_3$, then branch to instruction *end1*;
                                     otherwise continue to next instruction ∗/

            R_3++;   /∗ increment R_3 ∗/
            goto *loop1*;   /∗ (unconditional) branch to *loop1* ∗/
end1: $R_4 := 0$;   /∗ initialize R_4 to 0 ∗/
loop2: $R_2 = R_4$? goto *end2*;   /∗ if $R_2 = R_4$, then branch to instruction *end2* ∗/
            R_3++;   /∗ increment R_3 ∗/
            R_4++;   /∗ increment R_4 ∗/
            goto *loop2*;   /∗ (unconditional) branch to *loop2* ∗/
end2: Halt.

Open icon **Addition Machine** within the Register Machine folder to observe the operation of this machine. Try running this machine on register set `addends.rs`.

EXAMPLE 5.1.4 Click twice on icon **Multiplication Machine** within the Register Machine folder to observe the operation of a register machine that computes the binary multiplication function. Use register set `factors.rs`.

EXAMPLE 5.1.5 Open icon **Factorial Machine** within the Register Machine folder to observe the operation of a register machine that computes the factorial function. The operation of this machine is fully described by the following program. (We cease to always make Start and Halt instructions explicit and begin using pseudocode to abbreviate sequences of primitive instructions.)

Input: $R_1 = n$
Output: $R_2 = n!$
Algorithm
begin
    if $R_1 = 0$ or $R_1 = 1$, then $R_2 = 1$ /* register R_2 will hold output. */
    else begin
        $R_2 := 2$;   /* $R_2 := 0$; R_2++; R_2++ */
        $R_3 := 3$;
        $R_4 := R_1 + 1$;
        while $R_3 \neq R_4$ do begin
            $R_2 := R_2 * R_3$;   /* Multiplication Machine of Example 5.1.4 */
            R_3++
        end
    end
end.

Consideration of more interesting examples—and implementation of them using the companion software—will be greatly facilitated if we augment our instruction set somewhat. Namely, we shall begin to permit a new type of instruction operand, which will be indicated through the use of a preceding asterisk. For example, whereas an instruction of the form R_i++ effects the incrementation of register R_i, execution of an instruction $*R_i$++ will cause incrementation of register R_j, where j is the natural number currently stored in register R_i. Similarly, executing an instruction of the form $R_i = *R_j$? **goto** $\mathcal{L}$ causes a branch to the instruction labeled $\mathcal{L}$ just in case the contents of register R_i are identical to the contents of register R_k, where k is the current contents of register R_j. We leave it to the reader to discern the semantics of instructions of the form $*R_i = R_j$? **goto** $\mathcal{L}$ or $*R_i = *R_j$? **goto** $\mathcal{L}$ or $*R_i := 0$.

Note that the contents of register operands preceded by an asterisk are being interpreted as register addresses. For this reason, one speaks of *indirect addressing*, a term that will be familiar to many readers from assembler language programming. Since there is no register R_0, an instruction such as $*R_2$++ makes no sense if register R_2 happens to contain 0. So let us agree that execution of any such instruction in such circumstances will cause execution to halt. Our next example illustrates the usefulness of indirect addressing in register machine programs.

EXAMPLE 5.1.6 (Ackermann's Function) Open up the icon labeled **Ackermann's Function** to observe the operation of a register machine *M* that computes the binary number-theoretic function defined in Example 3.3.1. Register machine *M* is our first example of a machine that requires an unbounded number of registers. So, for instance, if *M*'s two arguments are 2 and 3, respectively, then 16 registers are required, as the reader can easily verify. On the other hand, if arguments 4 and 3 are supplied, then *M* makes access to 20 registers. In general, given input values *n* and *m*, a total of $2n + 12$ registers are needed. In other words, the larger the input, the more registers will be involved. This aspect of our notion of register machine—specifically, the fact that an unbounded number of registers is permitted—makes for a highly natural implementation of Ackermann's function. (Again, see the software and documentation.) In fact, however, we could in principle manage with a fixed number of registers—*fixed* in the sense that the number of registers would not depend upon the size of input. We do not go into this matter now but merely remind the reader of the manner in which any finite sequence of natural numbers (read: finite sequence of register contents) can be encoded as a single natural number (read: single register contents) using the Euler–Gödel scheme of §2.4. (The impatient reader is invited to skip now to the discussion following Example 5.3.2 below.)

Since register machine *M* is considerably more complex than earlier examples, a few words of explanation will be useful. Ackermann's function was defined in Example 3.3.1 by recursion equations

$$\text{(i)} \qquad H(0, m) = m + 1$$

$$\text{(ii)} \qquad H(n + 1, 0) = H(n, 1)$$

$$\text{(iii)} \qquad H(n + 1, m + 1) = H(n, H(n + 1, m))$$

We remind the reader that the theoretical significance of Ackermann's function resides in the fact that it is a recursive function that is demonstrably not primitive recursive.

Our preliminary goal is an iterative algorithm for computing Ackermann's function—an algorithm consisting solely of the equivalents of while-loops and the like. To this end, we present the reader with the infinite Table 5.1.1, which we hope to be self-explanatory. Roughly, the first row of the table reflects equation (i) whereas the first column reflects equation (ii). All remaining entries "descend" from above right in accordance with equation (iii). To calculate $H(n, m)$—the *m*th entry in the *n*th row with *n* and *m* both nonzero, we need something that has been passed down from each preceding row: In particular, we shall need to know the $[H(n, m - 1)]$th entry in the $(n - 1)$th row.

The register machine *M* at icon **Ackermann's Function** implements the following iterative algorithm.

```
function ackermann (n, m : integer) : integer;
    var
            col_ptr_array : array[0 ... n] of integer; {rightmost column entries in rows 0 through n}
            rightmost_entry_in_row_array : array[0 ... n] of integer; {values of those entries}
    begin
(1)         col_ptr_array[0] := 0;
(2)         rightmost_entry_in_row_array[0] := 1; /* H(0,0) = 1 */
(3)         while (col_ptr_array[n] ≠ m or
                rightmost_entry_in_row_array[n] = 0) do begin
                {while mth entry in nth row not yet calculated}
(4)             col_ptr_array[0] := col_ptr_array[0] + 1; /* calculate farther in the 0th row */
(5)             rightmost_entry_in_row_array[0] :=
                    rightmost_entry_in_row_array[0] + 1; /* H(0, k) = k + 1 */
(6)             if col_ptr_array[0] = 1 then begin
(7)                 col_ptr_array[1] := 0;
(8)                 rightmost_entry_in_row[1] := rightmost_entry_in_row[0]
(9)             end;
```

Table 5.1.1 Ackermann's Function. (Can you extend this table of values?)

$H(n,m)$	$m=0$	$m=1$	$m=2$	$m=3$	$m=4$	$m=5$	$m=6$	$m=7$	$m=8$	$m=9$	$m=10$	...
$n=0$	$H(0,0)$ 1	$H(0,1)$ 2	$H(0,2)$ 3	$H(0,3)$ 4	$H(0,4)$ 5	$H(0,5)$ 6	$H(0,6)$ 7	$H(0,7)$ 8	$H(0,8)$ 9	$H(0,9)$ 10	$H(0,10)$ 11	...
$n=1$	$H(1,0)$ 2	$H(1,1)$ 3	$H(1,2)$ 4	$H(1,3)$ 5	$H(1,4)$ 6	$H(1,5)$ 7	$H(1,6)$ 8	$H(1,7)$ 9	$H(1,8)$ 10	$H(1,9)$ 11	$H(1,10)$ 12	...
$n=2$	$H(2,0)$ 3	$H(2,1)$ 5	$H(2,2)$ 7	$H(2,3)$ 9	$H(2,4)$ 11	$H(2,5)$ 13	$H(2,6)$ 15	$H(2,7)$ 17	$H(2,8)$ 19	$H(2,9)$ 21	$H(2,10)$ 23	...
$n=3$	$H(3,0)$ 5	$H(3,1)$ 13	$H(3,2)$ 29	$H(3,3)$ 61	$H(3,4)$ 125	$H(3,5)$ 253	$H(3,6)$ 509	$H(3,7)$ 1021	$H(3,8)$ 2045	$H(3,9)$ 4093	$H(3,10)$ 8189	...
$n=4$	$H(4,0)$ 13	...	...	...	...	...	...	...	...	...	...	...

```
(10)            i := 0;
(11)            while col_ptr_array[i] > 1 and
                   col_ptr_array[i] = rightmost_entry_in_row_array[i + 1] do begin
(12)               col_ptr_array[i + 1] := col_ptr_array[i + 1] + 1;
(13)               rightmost_entry_in_row_array[i + 1] :=
                        rightmost_entry_in_row_array[i];
(14)               if col_ptr_array[i + 1] = 1 then begin
(15)                  col_ptr_array[i + 2] := 0;
(16)                  rightmost_entry_in_row[i + 2] := rightmost_entry_in_row[i + 1]
(17)               end;
(18)               i := i + 1
(19)            end {while}
(21)         end; {while}
(22)         ackermann:=rightmost_entry_in_row array[n]
(23)   end.
```

M's use of registers is hardly transparent. The reader should consult the software documentation for help with this issue. Again, the total number of registers used by M depends upon first argument n but not upon second argument m. On the other hand, computation time will depend upon both n and m. (Even on a reasonably fast microcomputer, M runs for over an hour for arguments $n = 3$ and $m = 5$.)

Having considered a sufficient number of examples, a formal definition of register machines is now in order, followed by the definition of function computation on the part of register machines.

DEFINITION 5.1: A *register machine* M is any pair $\langle \Re, \Im \rangle$, where $\Re = \{R_1, R_2, \ldots, R_m, \ldots\}$ with $m \geq 1$ is a possibly infinite set of *registers* and $\Im = \langle \iota_1, \iota_2, \ldots, \iota_t \rangle$ with $t \geq 2$ is a finite, nonempty sequence of *instructions* such that

(i) Instruction ι_1 is the Start instruction

(ii) Each of $\iota_2, \ldots, \iota_{t-1}$ is either the Halt instruction or an instruction of one of the forms

      (a) $R_i := 0$ or $*R_i := 0$

      (b) $R_i{+}{+}$ or $*R_i{+}{+}$

(c) $R_i = R_j$? **goto** $\mathcal{L}$ or $*R_i = R_j$? **goto** $\mathcal{L}$ or

$R_i = *R_j$? **goto** $\mathcal{L}$ or $*R_i = *R_j$? **goto** $\mathcal{L}$

where R_i and R_j are members of set $\Re$ while $\mathcal{L}$ is an identifier associated with exactly one of instructions $\iota_1, \iota_2, \ldots, \iota_t$

(iii) Instruction ι_t is the Halt instruction.

We shall regularly refer to instruction sequence $\Im = \langle \iota_1, \iota_2, \ldots, \iota_t \rangle$ as the program of register machine $M = \langle \Re, \Im \rangle$. Our requirement that every such instruction sequence end in the Halt instruction should not be misconstrued to mean that every register machine ceases execution after some finite number of steps. Here is an instruction sequence for a register machine that in fact never halts:

$$\begin{aligned} & \text{Start;} \\ loop: \quad & R_1 = R_1\text{? goto } loop; \\ & \text{Halt.} \end{aligned}$$

In general, we shall assume that register machine M computing k-ary number-theoretic function f will use registers R_1 through R_k for f's arguments and will use register R_{k+1} for f's value for those arguments, assuming that f is defined for those arguments.

DEFINITION 5.2: Let $M = \langle \Re, \Im \rangle$ be a register machine, and suppose that f is a k-ary partial number-theoretic function. Then we shall say that M *computes f* provided that:

(i) If M's registers $R_1, R_2, \ldots, R_k$ initially contain natural numbers $n_1, n_2, \ldots, n_k$, all other registers contain 0; and if $f(n_1, n_2, \ldots, n_k)$ is defined, then, upon termination, registers $R_1, R_2, \ldots, R_k$ contain natural numbers $n_1, n_2, \ldots, n_k$, as before, and register R_{k+1} contains $f(n_1, n_2, \ldots, n_k)$.

(ii) If M's registers $R_1, R_2, \ldots, R_k$ initially contain natural numbers $n_1, n_2, \ldots, n_k$, all other registers contain 0; and if $f(n_1, n_2, \ldots, n_k)$ is undefined, then M never terminates.

DEFINITION 5.3: Let f be a k-ary partial number-theoretic function. Then f is said to be *register-machine-computable* if there exists a register machine that computes f.

The reader should verify that the register machines of Examples 5.1.2 through 5.1.6 compute their respective functions in precisely the sense of Definition 5.2. Incidentally, what unary number-theoretic function is computed by Example 5.1.1?

Although not required by Definition 5.2, it should be apparent that we may assume that a register machine $M = \langle \Re, \langle \iota_1, \iota_2, \ldots, \iota_t \rangle \rangle$, where $\Re$ is finite and where M computes k-ary number-theoretic function f, halts only after having reset all registers other than $R_1, \ldots, R_k, R_{k+1}$ to 0. After all, if $\Re = \{R_1, R_2, \ldots, R_s\}$, then we have only to insert, immediately before each and every Halt instruction in M's program, the $(s–k–1)$-instruction sequence

$$R_{k+2} := 0;$$

$$R_{k+3} := 0;$$

$$\cdots$$

$$R_{s-1} := 0;$$

$$R_s := 0;$$

and possibly make some other minor changes involving labels and branching.

Consider again the flowchart of Figure 5.1.4 and Example 5.1.3. Since the purpose of the loop consisting of instructions

$loop1:$ $R_1 = R_3$? goto $end1$;
               R_3++;
               goto $loop1$;

$end1:$

is to set register R_3 equal to register R_1, it will be convenient to introduce the *macro instruction* $\boldsymbol{R_3 := R_1}$ as an abbreviation of this instruction sequence. Thus, although such an instruction is not one of our basic instructions, it can be implemented as a finite sequence of basic instructions. Hence there is no harm in permitting an instruction such as that of Figure 5.1.5 to appear within register machine flow diagrams, and we shall do so in the future. Similarly, in the interest of producing instruction sequences and flowcharts that are to a degree self-documenting, we shall permit the macro instruction $\boldsymbol{R_i = k}$? **goto** $\boldsymbol{\mathcal{L}}$ (where $k \geq 0$ is any fixed constant) as an abbreviation of the instruction sequence

$$R_j := 0;$$
$$R_j++;$$
$$R_j++;$$
$$R_j++;$$
$$\left.\vphantom{\begin{array}{c}a\\a\\a\\a\end{array}}\right\} k \text{ times}$$
$$\cdots$$
$$R_j++;$$
$$R_i = R_j? \text{ goto } \mathcal{L};$$

The macro instruction R_i-- will prove useful later whenever the contents of register R_i, assumed to be nonzero, are to be decremented by 1 (see Exercise 5.1.8).

A final note of clarification may be helpful. In Definition 5.1 we described a register machine as a pair $\langle \mathfrak{R}, \mathfrak{I} \rangle$, where $\mathfrak{I}$ is an instruction sequence each member of which is of one of the forms (i)–(iii), as described there. On the other hand, we shall permit ourselves to describe register machine programs in a Pascal-like language involving unconditional branching as well as while-loops and if-then-else statements (cf. Example 5.1.5). But (i)–(v) say nothing about unconditional branches or iteration of any sort. The reader

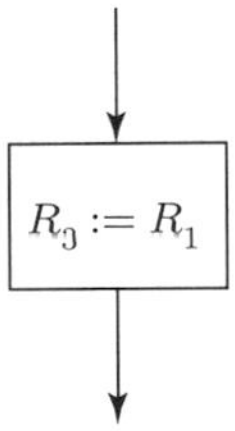

Figure 5.1.5
Macro Instruction Causing Register R_3 to Become Equal to Register R_1.

may have been troubled by this apparent discrepancy between the formal definition and our actual practice in describing machine programs. In fact, there is no cause for concern since it is an elementary result from programming language theory that both unconditional branching and iteration can be contextually defined in terms of conditional branching. Thus, the unconditional branch **goto** $\mathcal{L}$ may be defined by the conditional branch $R_i = R_i?$ **goto** $\mathcal{L}$. Furthermore, the while-loop

$$\text{while } R_i \neq R_j \text{ do begin}$$
$$\text{statement}_1;$$
$$\text{statement}_2;$$
$$\ldots$$
$$\text{statement}_n$$
$$\text{end};$$
$$\text{following\_statement};$$

may be defined as

$$loop: \quad R_i = R_j? \text{ goto } end;$$
$$\text{statement}_1;$$
$$\text{statement}_2;$$
$$\ldots$$
$$\text{statement}_n;$$
$$R_i = R_i? \text{ goto } loop;$$
$$end: \quad \text{following\_statement};$$

We leave it to the reader to show that if-then-else statements as well can be implemented in terms of our primitive instructions.

§5.2 The Class of Register-Machine-Computable Functions Is Identical to the Class of Partial Recursive Functions

We now show that the register machine model of sequential computation is equivalent to the several models considered in Chapters 1 through 4 in the sense that any function that is register-machine-computable is partial recursive, and vice versa. As usual, our proof of this equivalence falls into two demonstrations—one for each direction.

THEOREM 5.1(a): Let h be a partial number-theoretic function. If h is partial recursive, then h is register-machine-computable.

PROOF Our proof proceeds by induction on the canonical definition of h, assumed to be a k-ary partial recursive function with $k \geq 0$.

(i) As base case, we consider the possibility that h is an initial function. This, in turn, leads us to consider three subcases.

(i)(a) If h is the unary successor function, then h is computed by the register machine whose flowchart appeared in Figure 5.1.3.

(i)(b) If h is the unary constant-0 function C_0^1, then h is computed by the register machine M with register set $\Re = \{R_1, R_2\}$ whose flowchart appears in Figure 5.2.1(a). The 0-ary constant-0 function C_0^0 is computed by the register machine M with register set $\Re = \{R_1\}$ and the flowchart as in Figure 5.2.1(b). In general, the k-ary constant-zero function C_0^k is computed by the register machine M with register set $\Re = \{R_1, \ldots, R_{k+1}\}$ and instruction sequence

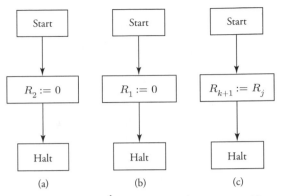

Figure 5.2.1 (a)C_0^1 is register-machine-computable; (b) C_0^0 is register-machine-computable; (c) p_j^k is register-machine-computable.

> Start;
>
> $R_{k+1} := 0$;
>
> Halt.

(i)(c) Any projection function p_j^k with $1 \leq j \leq k$ is register-machine-computable (see Figure 5.2.1(c)). We now address the three inductive cases.

(ii) Suppose that h is of the form **Comp**$[f, g_1, g_2, \ldots, g_m]$, where each of $f, g_1, g_2, \ldots, g_m$ is partial recursive and, by induction hypothesis, register-machine-computable. Let register machines $M_f = \langle \Re_f, \Im_f \rangle$, $M_{g_1} = \langle \Re_{g_1}, \Im_{g_1} \rangle$, $M_{g_2} = \langle \Re_{g_2}, \Im_{g_2} \rangle$, $\ldots$, $M_{g_m} = \langle \Re_{g_m}, \Im_{g_m} \rangle$ compute $f, g_1, g_2, \ldots, g_m$, respectively. As noted earlier, we can assume without loss of generality that, before halting, each of $M_{g_1}, M_{g_2}, \ldots, M_{g_m}$ resets all its registers other than $R_1, R_2, \ldots, R_k, R_{k+1}$ to 0. Similarly, we assume that before halting, M_f resets all its registers other than $R_1, R_2, \ldots, R_m, R_{m+1}$ to 0. We construct a new register machine M_h, which computes $h = $ **Comp**$[f, g_1, g_2, \ldots, g_m]$, by composing $M_f, M_{g_1}, M_{g_2}, \ldots, M_{g_m}$. We write $R_{maxreg(f)}$ for the machine register with highest index used by register machine M_f.[1] Similarly, $R_{maxreg(g_i)}$ will be the machine register with highest index used by register machine M_{g_i}. Finally, we let $p = max[maxreg(f), maxreg(g_1), \ldots, maxreg(g_m)] + 1$, so that R_p is the register with lowest index such that none of $M_f, M_{g_1}, M_{g_2}, \ldots, M_{g_m}$ ever uses it. This means that M_h can use registers $R_p, R_{p+1}, \ldots, R_{p+k-1}$ to store h's arguments $n_1, n_2, \ldots, n_k$. Each of $M_{g_1}, M_{g_2}, \ldots, M_{g_m}$ must be simulated on arguments $n_1, n_2, \ldots, n_k$. We introduce the macro instruction of Figure 5.2.2 to indicate the result of eliminating the single Start instruction and single Halt instruction of M_{g_i}'s flow diagram and directing flowchart arrows in the obvious way—similarly for M_f. The values $g_1(n_1, n_2, \ldots, n_k), g_2(n_1, n_2, \ldots, n_k), \ldots,$ $g_m(n_1, n_2, \ldots, n_k)$ are stored in registers $R_{p+k}, R_{p+k+1}, \ldots, R_{p+k+m-1}$, respectively. The flow diagram for M_h appears in Figure 5.2.3.

(iii) Suppose that h is of the form **Pr**$[f, g]$, where f and g are both partial recursive and, by induction hypothesis, register-machine-computable. For simplicity, let us assume

Figure 5.2.2 Function g_i, for $1 \leq i \leq m$, is assumed to be register-machine-computable.

---

[1] The registers used by any register machine $M = \langle \Re, \Im \rangle$ are, of course, just the members of register set $\Re$.

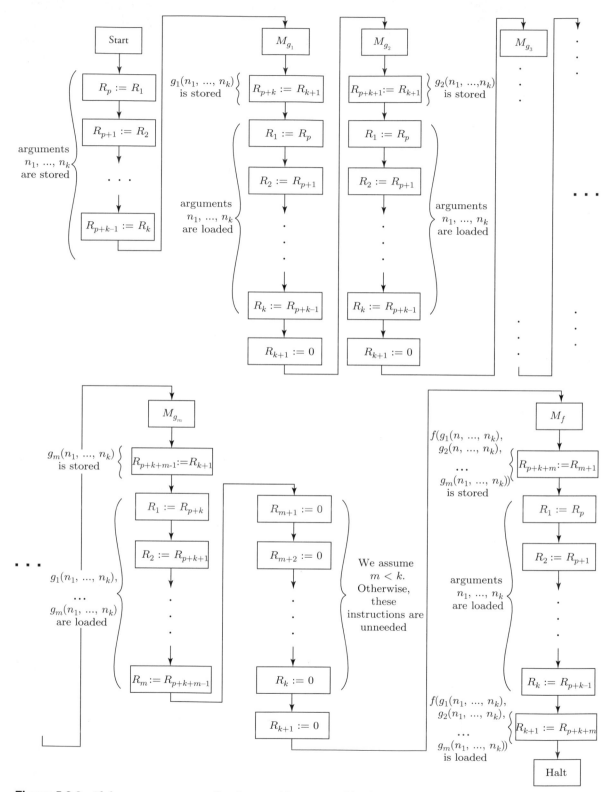

Figure 5.2.3 If $f, g_1, g_2, \ldots, g_m$ are all register-machine-computable, then so is **Comp**$[f, g_1, g_2, \ldots, g_m]$.

that f is unary and that g is ternary, which means that h is binary and that h is defined by

$$h(n, 0) = f(n)$$

$$h(n, m+1) = g(n, m, h(n, m))$$

Let register machines $M_f = \langle \Re_f, \Im_f \rangle$ and $M_g = \langle \Re_g, \Im_g \rangle$ compute f and g, respectively. As noted earlier, we can assume without loss of generality that, before halting, M_f resets all its registers other than R_1 and R_2 to 0. Similarly, we assume that, before halting, M_g resets all its registers other than R_1, R_2, R_3, and R_4 to 0. We construct a new register machine M_h, which computes $h = \mathbf{Pr}[f, g]$, by combining M_f and M_g. As in case (ii), we assume that R_p is a register that is not in either $\Re_f$ or $\Re_g$. The flow diagram of register machine M_h appears in Figure 5.2.4.

(iv) Finally, suppose that h is of the form $\mathbf{Mn}[f]$, where f is partial recursive and, by induction hypothesis, register-machine-computable. For the sake of simplicity, let us assume that f is binary so that h is unary and given by

$$h(n) = \mu m [f(n, m) = 0 \text{ and such that, for all } k < m, f(n, k) \text{ is defined and nonzero}]$$

Let register machine $M_f = \langle \Re_f, \Im_f \rangle$ compute f. The flowchart of a register machine M_h computing h is shown in Figure 5.2.5. (The reader should recall that if f is undefined for arguments n and m, then, by Definition 5.2, M_f never terminates for inputs n and m.)   Q.E.D.

> **THEOREM 5.1(b):** Let f be a number-theoretic function. If f is register-machine-computable, then f is partial recursive.

PROOF Suppose that f is a k-ary register-machine-computable function. We show that f is Turing-computable, from which it follows by Theorem 3.3(b) that f is partial recursive. Since, by assumption, f is register-machine-computable, there exists a register machine $M_{RM} = \langle \Re_{RM}, \Im_{RM} \rangle$ that computes f in the sense of Definition 5.2. We may assume without loss of generality that $\Im_{RM}$ contains but a single Halt instruction (see Exercise 5.5.12). Suppose further that $\Re_{RM}$ is $\{R_1, \ldots, R_j\}$ for some $j \geq k+1$. (As suggested at the beginning of Example 5.1.6, we may assume without loss of generality that any register machine makes use of some fixed *finite* collection of registers.)

We describe a multitape Turing machine M_{TM} having $j + 2$ tapes: an input tape, worktape$_1$, ..., worktape$_j$, and an output tape. Suppose that M_{TM}'s input tape is initially configured as

$$\ldots B I^{n_1+1} B I^{n_2+1} B \ldots I^{n_k+1} B \ldots$$

with M_{TM}'s read/write head scanning the leftmost of these Is. M_{TM} first copies I^{n_1+1} onto worktape$_1$, I^{n_2+1} onto worktape$_2$, ..., and I^{n_k+1} onto worktape$_k$. Throughout M_{TM}'s computation, the contents of worktape$_1$, ..., worktape$_j$ will correspond to the contents of M_{RM}'s registers R_1, ..., R_j. To each instruction of $\Im_{RM}$ other than Start there will correspond a routine to be executed by M_{TM}. Thus each instruction of the form $R_i := 0$ will correspond to a routine that will involve M_{TM} in effect erasing all but a single I from worktape$_i$ and leaving all other tapes unchanged. Similarly, an instruction in $\Im_{RM}$ of the form R_i++ will correspond to a routine that will involve M_{TM} in effect introducing a single additional I on worktape$_i$. On the other hand, an instruction in $\Im_{RM}$ of the form $*R_i$++ will correspond to a routine that involves M_{TM} in effect introducing a single additional I

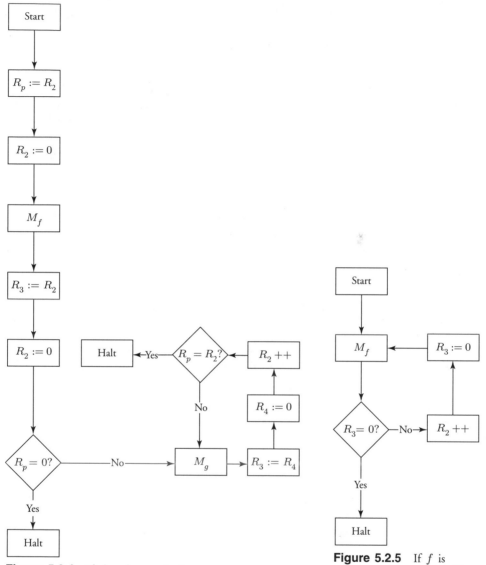

Figure 5.2.4 If f and g are both register-machine-computable, then so is **Pr**$[f, g]$.

Figure 5.2.5 If f is register-machine-computable, then so is **Mn**$[f]$.

on worktape$_j$, where j is the number represented on worktape$_i$. An instruction of the form

$$R_i = R_j? \text{ goto } \mathcal{L} \tag{5.2.1}$$

will correspond to a routine that will involve M_{TM} first checking whether worktape$_i$ and worktape$_j$ currently hold the same unbroken string of 1s and, if so, entering (the first state of) the routine of M_{TM} corresponding to the instruction at $\mathcal{L}$ in $\Im_{\text{RM}}$. If not, then M_{TM} enters (the first state of) the routine corresponding to the instruction that physically follows (5.2.1) in $\Im_{\text{RM}}$. Corresponding to

M_{RM}'s Halt instruction, M_{TM} must have a routine that copies the contents of worktape$_{k+1}$ to M_{TM}'s output tape. We conclude that M_{RM} computes f.   Q.E.D.

The central equivalence results of this and the preceding chapters may now be summarized as follows.

REMARK 5.2.1: Let f be a partial k-ary number-theoretic function. Then we have

f is Turing-computable $\Leftrightarrow$ f is partial recursive

$\Leftrightarrow$ f is Markov-computable $\Leftrightarrow$ f is register-machine-computable

---

§5.3 Register Machines and Formal Languages

In this section we briefly describe a sense in which register machines may accept and recognize formal languages. There are a number of ways in which this might be done. Probably the most natural way is to change our informal description of a register machine so as to add a read-only input tape and a write-only output tape, equipped with a read-head and write-head, respectively. We shall think of both tapes as divided into squares, the contents of any nonblank square being a natural number, and infinite in one direction only. The heads on both these tapes move to the right only. (Incidentally, it would have been possible to describe function computation on the part of register machines in such a way that machine M computing ternary function f would read its three arguments n_1, n_2, n_3 from an input tape, one argument per tape square, and write value $f(n_1, n_2, n_3)$ to an output tape. As usual, there are no important theoretical consequences of making the switch.)

To handle input and output, two new primitive instructions will be necessary. First, executing an instruction of the form **Read(R_i)** will cause the contents, assumed to be a natural number, of the currently scanned square on the input tape to be copied into register R_i, overwriting the previous contents of that register. Afterward, the input-tape read-head will move one square to the right. Second, executing an instruction of the form **Write(R_i)** will cause the current natural-number contents of register R_i to be copied to the currently scanned square on the output tape, after which the output-tape write-head is advanced one square to the right. We shall also permit so-called *immediate operands*. For example, the instruction **Write(1)** causes natural number 1 to be written to the output tape. We shall also find it useful to permit indirect addressing. So an instruction of the form **Read($*R_i$)** causes the contents of the currently scanned input tape square to be copied to register R_j, where j is the natural number currently stored in register R_i. Similarly, an instruction of the form **Write($*R_i$)** causes the contents of register R_j to be copied to the currently scanned output tape square, where j is the natural number currently stored in register R_i.

The reader is to imagine that the formal definition of register machines as given in Definition 5.1 has been emended so as to accommodate both read and write instructions, as just described. The change is less substantial than it might at first appear to be. After all, any register machine in the original sense may be regarded as a register machine with input and output tapes—one that just happens to involve neither read nor write instructions and hence never makes access to either tape.

Our goal is a notion of language acceptance, and yet, as we have described them, input tape squares and registers contain natural numbers exclusively. Hence some means of representing character data will be essential. It will prove convenient to use natural numbers 1 and 2 as representatives of symbols a and b, respectively, extending this for larger alphabets. We shall reserve 0 as an end-of-input sentinel.

The empty word will then be represented on the input tape by 0 occurring in the leftmost tape square. A formal definition of language acceptance for register machines will follow the next two examples.

EXAMPLE 5.3.1 Our first example is very easy. Let $\Sigma = \{a, b\}$. The flowchart of Figure 5.3.1 is that of a register machine M that accepts the language $L = \{w \in \Sigma^* | n_a(w) = n_b(w)\}$ in the following sense. We recall, first, our plan to represent an input word w over Σ as a sequence of 1s and 2s, one per tape square, terminated by end-of-input sentinel 0. If started scanning the leftmost square of its input tape, on which w is represented, M reads until sentinel 0 is encountered. Whenever a 1 is read, M increments register R_2. Whenever 2 is read, M increments register R_3. Afterward, M writes a 1 to the output tape just in case the contents of R_2 equals the contents of R_3—that is, just in case $w \in L$. By virtue of this, we shall say that M accepts language L.

Generally speaking, we shall not much care what a register machine does in response to an input word that is not in the accepted language—so long as it does not write an accepting 1. In fact, however, M does something very nice in that case as well; namely, M writes 0 to the output tape just in case the contents of R_2 do *not* equal the contents of R_3—that is, just in case input word $w \notin L$. And by virtue of this, we shall say that, in addition, M *recognizes language* L. As usual, our notion of language recognition amounts to computation of characteristic function χ_L defined as

$$\chi_L(w) = \begin{cases} 1 & \text{if } w \in L \\ 0 & \text{if } w \notin L \end{cases}$$

Open the icon labeled **Same Number of a's as b's** in the Register Machine folder and load tapes `4a4b.rt` and `5a3b.rt` in succession in order to observe the operation of this machine.

Finally, a word regarding M's time analysis will set the stage for what comes later. Let us agree to count each primitive operation, *regardless of the size of its natural number operand(s)*, as one step in M's computation. In this context, this is called the *uniform cost assumption*. (We omit a formal definition of $time_M(n)$ for register machines. Something analogous to Definitions 1.8 and 4.5 is what we have in mind.) It is not hard to see that, for each symbol in input word w, M carries out exactly four steps as it traverses the loop at the top of Figure 5.3.1. Before entering that loop for the first time, there are two steps. Finally, after end-of-input sentinel 0 is encountered, exactly five steps are executed. In summary, where n is the length of input word w, register mine M executes $4n + 7$ computation steps. Consequently, we shall say that M computes in linear time—that is, in $O(n)$ steps worst case.

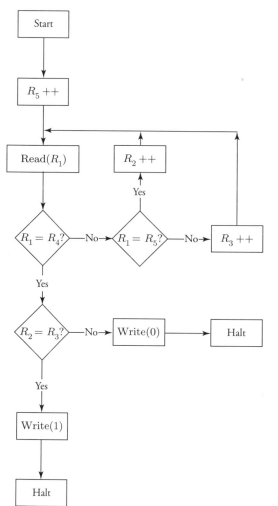

Figure 5.3.1   This register machine accepts the language $\{w \in \Sigma^* | n_a(w) = n_b(w)\}$, where $\Sigma = \{a, b\}$.

Our next example illustrates the usefulness of indirect addressing in the present context.

EXAMPLE 5.3.2 The register machine M of Figure 5.3.2 accepts—in fact, recognizes—the language of palindromes over alphabet $\Sigma = \{a, b\}$. (Again, we have not yet said what language acceptance on the part of register machines is really. But what we have in mind should be plain enough from this and the preceding example.) Machine M uses indirect addressing to store one character (code) in registers R_3, R_4, ... until end-of-input sentinel 0 is encountered. Afterward, these codes are compared, starting from the two ends and proceeding inward. If the comparison is always positive, then ultimately an accepting 1 is written to the output tape. Otherwise, a rejecting 0 is written. Open the icon labeled **Palindromes** within the Register Machine folder in order to observe the operation of this machine. A number of tapes have been created for use with this machine. Try loading abbbbbba.rt and any others with similar filenames.

Note that the number of registers utilized by M depends upon the length of input word w. For instance, if w is aba, then a total of six registers is used: Codes 1, 2, 1, and 0 are read into registers R_3 through R_6, respectively. In general, if w is of length n, then $n + 3$ registers will be used, which makes this our second example of a machine that uses an unbounded number of registers. (The first was Example 5.1.6.) Consequently, we write $M = \langle \Re, \Im \rangle$ with the understanding that $\Re = \{R_1, R_2, \ldots\}$ is an infinite set.

Finally, we note that M accepts palindrome w over $\Sigma = \{a, b\}$ in $O(n^2)$ steps, where n is the length of w. This is comparable apparently to the time analysis of the (one-way-infinite) single-tape Turing machine of Example 2.1.2. Roughly, the loop at the bottom of Figure 5.3.2 is executed $n/2$ times, and the decrementation macro $R_1 --$, when converted to primitive operations, itself requires $O(n)$ steps. We make this explicit in the software where, in the case of this particular example, only primitive operations have been introduced.

Incidentally, in the preceding example one can circumvent indirect addressing by using the Euler–Gödel scheme of §2.4 in order to store the entire contents of the input tape in a single register R. Thus, having read symbol codes 1, 2, and then 1 so far, the value $2^1 \cdot 3^2 \cdot 5^1$ will be stored in R. If the next symbol is b, encoded by 2, then the current contents of R will be multiplied by 7^2. In this manner, a fixed number of registers can be used regardless of the input word. This little trick gives us a sort of compression result with respect to register machines, which we formulate as

> **REMARK 5.3.1:** Suppose that language L is accepted by some register machine. Then there exists some register machine $M = \langle \Re, \Im \rangle$ that accepts L and such that $\Re = \{R_1, R_2, \ldots, R_k\}$ for some fixed k.

On the other hand, the time requirements of a machine M whose input is compressed in the manner described would be greater due to the cost of primality testing. (Function $time_M(n)$ would yet be polynomially bounded, however.) We have introduced indirect addressing essentially because it is highly convenient. Without it, interesting examples of language acceptance would be very awkward to describe either on paper or using the accompanying software.

We now present the formal definitions presupposed by our two examples. The reader will find no surprises here.

> **DEFINITION 5.4:** Let $M = \langle \Re, \Im \rangle$ be a register machine with input and output tapes. Let Σ be a finite alphabet, and let the symbols of Σ be represented by codes 1, 2, 3, ... as described earlier. Then M *accepts word w over alphabet Σ* provided that:
>
> (1) Initially, M's input tape contains word w in encoded form, one symbol code per tape square, starting at the left and followed by end-of-input sentinel 0.

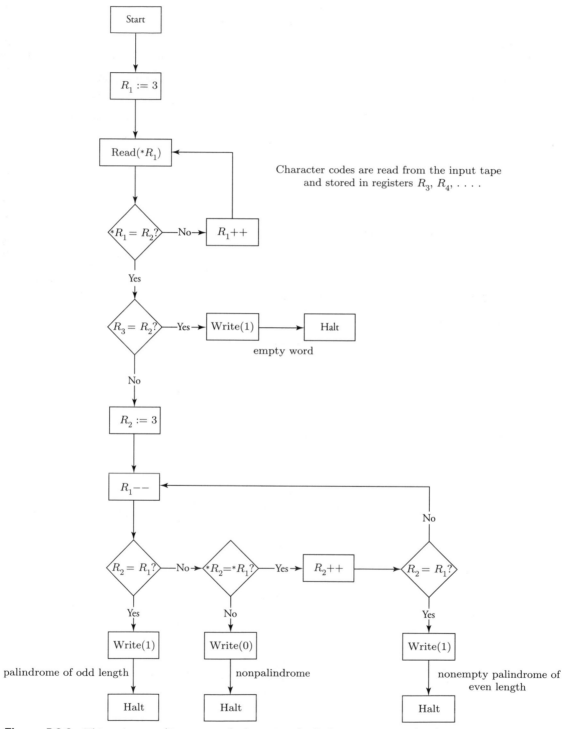

Figure 5.3.2 This register machine accepts the language of palindromes over $\Sigma = \{a, b\}$.

> (2) M proceeds to read (the encoding of) w from its input tape from left to right until 0 is encountered.
>
> (3) Ultimately, M halts having written a 1 to the leftmost square on its output tape.[1]

As usual, we do not much care what M does in the case of an input word w that it does not accept. Language acceptance is next defined in terms of word acceptance in the usual way.

> **DEFINITION 5.5:** Let $M = \langle \Re, \Im \rangle$ be a register machine with input and output tapes. Then M accepts language L provided M accepts all and only the words of L.

We leave it to the reader to formulate the definition of language recognition implicit in Examples 5.3.1 and 5.3.2.

> **DEFINITION 5.6:** A language L is said to be *register-machine-acceptable* (*recognizable*) if there exists a register machine that accepts (recognizes) L.

Finally, the equivalence result, which the reader has no doubt come to expect, is formulated as Theorem 5.2.

> **THEOREM 5.2:** Let L be a language over alphabet Σ. Then L is register-machine-acceptable (recognizable) if and only if it is Turing-acceptable (recognizable).

PROOF That every Turing-acceptable language is register-machine-acceptable follows from Theorem 5.3(a) in the next section. Similarly, for the converse, see Theorem 5.3(b).   Q.E.D.

§5.4 A Model-Independent Characterization of Computational Feasibility

In §1.7 we contrasted algorithms that compute in polynomially bounded time, worst case, with those that may require exponential time. Working computer scientists consider the latter, in particular, to be beyond the limits of what is computationally feasible. Our identification of problems having polynomially bounded solutions as the class of tractable problems can serve as a starting point in considering the relations between the several models of computation that we have introduced. We formulate

> **EDMONDS' THESIS REGARDING COMPUTATIONAL FEASIBILITY:** A problem is computationally feasible provided that it has a polynomial-time solution.

---

[1] Upon halting, M's write-head will be scanning the second square on the output tape, which happens to be a blank square. We do not require that M's write-head somehow return to the left before halting, as was done in the case of Turing machines. Indeed, according to our description of register machines with input and output tapes, this is not even possible.

In keeping with our practice throughout this book, we restrict our attention to language-acceptance problems. (This is not nearly so limiting as one might initially imagine—but more on that later.) This leads us to

> **EDMONDS' THESIS REGARDING COMPUTATIONAL FEASIBILITY (reformulation):** A language-acceptance problem is computationally feasible provided that the language in question is accepted in polynomially bounded time.

But now wait. Is there not something important missing from our reformulation? As it stands, it asserts that computational feasibility means acceptance in polynomial time. *But acceptance by what?* As we have described things heretofore, it is (particular instances of) machine models that accept languages. And whereas we have a variety of notions of language acceptance—Turing-acceptable, Markov-acceptable, register-machine-acceptable—we have no notion of language acceptance *simpliciter*. So we must ask whether Edmonds' Thesis makes any sense at all without some supplementation. Is there some *model-independent* notion of computational feasibility that redeems Edmonds' Thesis, as we have formulated it?

We can start by considering again a proposition already presented in Chapter 1 that we now reformulate in terms of language acceptance.

> **COBHAM–EDMONDS THESIS REGARDING COMPUTATIONAL FEASIBILITY (restatement):** With respect to formal languages, computational feasibility means acceptance in polynomially bounded time by a (single-tape) deterministic Turing machine.

Note, first, that Cobham–Edmonds is quite definite as to the model of computation being assumed. So, quite apart from the issue of truth or falsity, Cobham–Edmonds at least makes sense. Still, important questions remain.

(i) By virtue of what does the single-tape Turing machine merit the special status conferred by Cobham–Edmonds? Why not multitape Turing machines? What about the Markov algorithm model? The register machine model? Why should any one of them be given priority over the others?

(ii) Consider the following hypothetical situation. Suppose that we have shown that a given language L is accepted in polynomial time by some single-tape Turing machine. This much would suggest that L is computationally feasible, given Cobham–Edmonds. Suppose further that, as it turns out, the only register machines that accept L require *exponential time*. Does this not suggest that L is not feasible after all according to a reasonable alternative formulation of Cobham–Edmonds giving priority to polynomial-time register-machine-acceptability? Can such a situation actually arise? That is, can there exist a language L accepted in polynomial time by a single-tape Turing machine but accepted by register machines only in exponential time?

We can approach (i) and (ii) together by reviewing our earlier work.

(a) In presenting the register machine M of Example 5.3.1, we noted that M accepts language $L = \{w \in \Sigma^* | n_a(w) = n_b(w)\}$ in $O(n)$ steps, where n is the length of input word w.

(b) Of course, that was hardly the first time that we had considered L. Namely, much earlier on, in Example 1.3.1, we presented a single-tape Turing machine that turned out to accept L in $O(n^2)$ steps worst case. (See our discussion of this example in §1.7.)

(c) Later, in Example 2.3.1, we considered a four-tape Turing machine that accepts the same L in linear time.

(d) Finally, Example 4.2.3 described a Markov algorithm schema that was seen to accept L in $O(n^2)$ steps.

This is enough to see that, in the case of $L = \{w \in \Sigma^* | n_a(w) = n_b(w)\}$, register machine M performs as well as the multitape Turing machine and somewhat better than the single-tape Turing machine or the Markov algorithm schema. In fact, from the present point of view, which is that of computational feasibility in general, all of the above performance times are essentially the same: After all, both $O(n)$ time and $O(n^2)$ time are special cases of polynomially bounded time, and we are entertaining the general proposal that acceptance in polynomially bounded time amounts to computational feasibility.

Items (c) and (a), taken in that order, suggest a certain general correlation between multitape Turing machines and register machines; that is, if multitape Turing machine M accepts some language L in $O(n)$ steps, then some register machine can be found that does the same. And, in fact, it can be shown that essentially this relationship does hold quite generally between the multitape Turing machine and register machine models. In particular, we have the following theorem.

THEOREM 5.3(a): Suppose that some multitape Turing machine M_{TM} accepts language L in $O(f(n))$ steps. Then there exists a register machine M_{RM} that accepts L in time $O([f(n)]^2)$ under the uniform cost assumption.

The proof of Theorem 5.3(a) is not hard really but is somewhat lengthy. For this reason, we delay presenting it so as not to impede the flow of our discussion. While we are on this topic, it is natural to ask whether the converse relation holds between the two machine models. Namely, if some register machine (with input and output tapes) accepts some language L in time $O(f(n))$ under uniform cost, is there a multitape Turing machine that does essentially the same? Here again the answer turns out to be yes, and again we delay presentation of our proof of

---

THEOREM 5.3(b): Suppose that some register machine M_{RM} accepts language L in $O(g(n))$ steps under the assumption of uniform cost. Then there exists a multitape Turing machine M_{TM} that accepts L in time $O([g(n)]^3)$.

We take this opportunity to formulate a general principle relating distinct machine models.

DEFINITION 5.7: Let $Model_1$ and $Model_2$ be machine models of sequential computation. Then $Model_1$ and $Model_2$ are said to be *polynomially related* if there exist natural numbers k and j such that, given an arbitrary language L,

(1) L's being accepted by (some instance of) $Model_1$ in $O(f(n))$ steps implies that L is accepted by (some instance of) $Model_2$ in $O([f(n)]^k)$ steps and

> (2) L's being accepted by (some instance of) $Model_2$ in $O(g(n))$ steps implies that L is accepted by (some instance of) $Model_1$ in $O([g(n)]^j)$ steps.

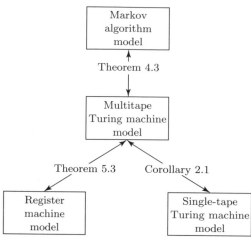

Figure 5.4.1 Polynomial Relatedness of Machine Models.

We note that polynomial relatedness is an equivalence relation on the class of machine models (see Exercise 5.4.1). Furthermore, we call the reader's attention to Corollary 2.1, wherein it was shown that the single-tape Turing machine model and the multitape Turing machine model are polynomially related in the sense of Definition 5.7, although no such terminology was introduced in Chapter 2. Similarly, the proof of Theorem 4.3 showed in effect that the multitape Turing machine model and the Markov algorithm model are polynomially related (see Figure 5.4.1). Indeed, our present remarks should be regarded as a continuation of the discussion initiated in §4.6.

We are finally in a position to formulate

> **AN INVARIANCE PRINCIPLE FOR MODELS OF SEQUENTIAL COMPUTATION:** Let $Model$ be some machine model of sequential computation. Then $Model$ will be said to be a *reasonable model* of sequential computation if it is polynomially related to the multitape Turing machine model.

The Invariance Principle is not itself a mathematical proposition and hence cannot be demonstrated. It is a proposal regarding what "reasonableness" on the part of machine models should mean and, in this sense, is normative in character: It stipulates how a certain term might or should be used. In short, like Cobham–Edmonds, the Invariance Principle can be argued for but cannot be proved.

It should be easy to see that Theorems 5.3(a) and 5.3(b) together with the Invariance Principle justify

> **REMARK 5.4.1:** The register machine model is polynomially related to the multitape Turing machine model. In other words, the register machine model is a *reasonable model of sequential computation* in the sense of the Invariance Principle.

Perhaps more important is the fact that our notion of polynomially bounded time is invariant with respect to an entire class of reasonable models of computation: It is quite enough to demonstrate the existence of some language acceptor that computes in polynomially bounded time using some reasonable model—it makes no difference which one. As for Edmonds' Thesis, we can now see that, in a very real sense, it is quite defensible as it stands. In other words, although Cobham–Edmonds, say, cites the single-tape Turing machine model, the class of languages thereby characterized as feasible does not change if we substitute a reference to multitape Turing machines or a reference to register machines. On a related point, note that Remark 5.4.1, together with related results, establishes that our definition of the complexity class P, as given in Definition 1.11, is *robust* in the same sense: Although Definition 1.11 gives priority to the single-tape Turing machine, the class of languages defined does not change if we substitute one of our other models.

We close this section with the two promised demonstrations, restating Theorems 5.3(a) and 5.3(b) for the reader's convenience. Note that proving Theorem 5.3(a) amounts to proving that (1) of Definition 5.7 holds for the multitape Turing machine and register machine models (under uniform cost) with $k = 2$.

THEOREM 5.3(a): Suppose that some multitape Turing machine M_{TM} accepts language L in $O(f(n))$ steps. Then there exists a register machine M_{RM} that accepts L in time $O([f(n)]^2)$ under the uniform cost assumption.

PROOF Suppose that multitape Turing machine M_{TM} accepts language L in $O(f(n))$ steps and that M_{TM} has a total of j one-way-infinite tapes. We describe a register machine M_{RM} that simulates M_{TM} and thereby accepts any word $w \in L$ in time $O([f(n)]^2)$ with $n = |w|$. Our proof takes advantage of the potentially infinite number of registers available to M_{RM}. Namely, in addition to some auxiliary registers needed for workspace and j pointer registers $R_1^{ptr}, R_2^{ptr}, \ldots, R_J^{ptr}$ recording

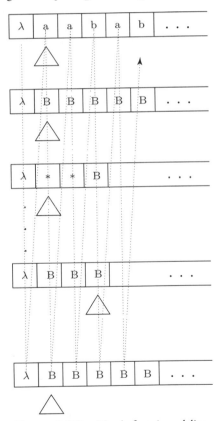

the current position of each tape head, M_{RM} uses one register to model one tape square on any one of M_{TM}'s j tapes. Figure 5.4.2 indicates the order of these modeling registers. The first j modeling registers model the leftmost tape squares of M_{TM}'s j tapes, the next j modeling registers model the next tape square from the left on each of M_{TM}'s j tapes, and so on.

It will prove convenient to have the pointer registers store not the absolute positions of the tape heads on their respective tapes but, rather, the indices of the registers modeling those positions. For example, if M_{TM}'s input tape head is currently scanning its leftmost square, then R_1^{ptr} will be 1. On the other hand, if it is currently scanning the square just one position to the right, then R_1^{ptr} will be $j + 1$. If M_{TM}'s second tape head is scanning the leftmost tape square on worktape$_1$, then R_2^{ptr} will have value 2. If it is currently scanning the next square to the right, then R_2^{ptr} will have value $j + 2$ (see Figure 5.4.2).

During its initialization phase, M_{RM} reads input word w from its input tape, one (encoded) symbol at a time, and stores symbol codes for each of the symbols of w in the registers modeling M_{TM}'s input tape. Pointer register R_1^{ptr} is set to $j + 1$, reflecting the initial position of the read head on M_{TM}'s input tape. Otherwise, the contents of each of the registers corresponding to leftmost tape squares on M_{TM}'s j tapes are set to $\ulcorner \lambda \urcorner$, and pointer registers $R_2^{ptr}, \ldots, R_J^{ptr}$ are set to $j+2, \ldots, 2j$, respectively. The entire initialization phase is completed in $O(n)$ steps.

During its simulation phase, M_{RM} must simulate each multitape instruction executed by M_{TM} by executing a sequence of register machine instructions.

Figure 5.4.2 M_{RM}'s first j modeling registers model the leftmost tape squares on M_{TM}'s j tapes, M_{RM}'s next j modeling registers model the next square from the left on each of M_{TM}'s j tapes, and so on.

- For example, a move right on M_{TM}'s ith tape will mean incrementing the ith pointer register R_i^{ptr} by j. This incrementation requires O(1) steps only.

- Similarly, a move left means, in effect, decrementing a pointer register by j. Since the current contents of any pointer register are O($f(n)$), by Exercise 1.7.3, this decrementation routine requires O($f(n)$) steps worst case. (Why?)

- A write action—the writing of symbol #, say—on M_{TM}'s ith tape is simulated by the assignment $*R_i^{ptr} := \ulcorner \# \urcorner$. Note that register R_i^{ptr} is not itself changed by this assignment. Also, this assignment, although not a primitive register machine instruction, can be accomplished in O(1) steps.

If and when its simulation phase terminates, M_{RM} must copy to its output tape the contents of that register modeling the tape square immediately to the right of endmarker λ on M_{TM}'s output tape, after having first ascertained, using a technique well-known to the reader, that all other output tape squares are blank. This requires O($f(n)$) steps worst case—essentially by Exercise 1.7.3 again.

This completes our proof. Since M_{TM} itself computes in O($f(n)$) steps worst case, and since simulation of moves left are the most costly part of M_{RM}'s simulation, it can be seen that M_{RM}'s simulation phase requires no more than O($[f(n)]^2$) steps. Moreover, since the simulation phase dominates, we have that M_{RM} accepts word $w \in L$ in time O($[f(n)]^2$) as well.   Q.E.D.

Thus, we see that register machines are not only capable of simulating Turing machines. Theorem 5.3(a) shows that they are capable of doing so *efficiently*. Finally, we prove

---

THEOREM 5.3(b): Suppose that some register machine M_{RM} accepts language L in O($g(n)$) steps under the assumption of uniform cost. Then there exists a multitape Turing machine M_{TM} that accepts L in time O($[g(n)]^3$).

Note that proving Theorem 5.3(b) amounts to proving that (2) of Definition 5.7 holds for the multitape Turing machine and register machine models (under uniform cost) with $j = 3$. We shall actually prove the stronger

---

THEOREM 5.4: Suppose that language L is accepted by register machine M_{RM} in $time_{M_{RM}}(n)$ steps under the uniform cost assumption, where n gives the length of an arbitrary input word and where we assume that $time_{M_{RM}}(n) \geq n$. Then there exists a multitape Turing machine M_{TM} that accepts L in O($[time_{M_{RM}}(n)]^3$) steps.

It is easy to see that Theorem 5.3(b) follows from Theorem 5.4. For suppose that L is accepted by some register machine M in O($g(n)$) steps assuming uniform cost. This is just to say that $time_{M_{RM}}(n)$ is O($g(n)$). Theorem 5.4 now states that L is accepted by a multitape Turing machine in O($[time_{M_{RM}}(n)]^3$) steps, which is also O($[g(n)]^3$) steps.

PROOF OF THEOREM 5.4   Let M_{RM} be a register machine with input and output tapes that accepts L in $time_{M_{RM}}(n)$ steps under the uniform cost assumption. We describe a six-tape Turing machine M_{TM}—input and output tapes and four worktapes—that simulates M_{RM}, thereby accepting L. Moreover, M_{TM}'s simulation will involve O($[time_{M_{RM}}(n)]^3$) steps.

Those registers of M_{RM} whose current contents are not 0 will be represented on M_{TM}'s worktape$_2$ as follows: Any register R_i containing natural number $n_i \neq 0$ will be represented by the string

$I^{i+1}\#I^{n_i+1}$ on worktape$_2$. These representations will themselves be separated by symbol $, say. The registers of M_{RM} will not, in general, be represented in sequential order from left to right, say, on worktape$_2$. For example, if M_{RM}'s four registers R_1, R_2, R_3, and R_4 currently contain natural numbers 3, 2, 0, and 2, respectively, then this might be represented on worktape$_2$ by the unbroken string *111#111$11#1111$11111#111*.

M_{TM}'s worktape$_1$, on the other hand, will model M_{RM}'s input tape. At the inception of execution, M_{TM}'s own input tape will contain input word $w \in \Sigma^*$. Recall that M_{TM}'s input consists of actual symbols a, b, ... or the like, whereas the squares on M_{RM}'s input tape will contain (small) integers and hence must be modeled by (short) strings of *1*s on M_{TM}'s worktape$_1$. Input word w is read from left to right. After reading any symbol s, M_{TM} writes string $I^{\ulcorner s \urcorner +1}$ to worktape$_1$, separating these representations by a single blank, say. (We may suppose that a table of symbol codes has been written to worktape$_4$ and is consulted during this process.) Afterward, a single *1* representing end-of-input sentinel 0 is added at the far right on worktape$_1$. The read/write head on worktape$_1$ now returns to the far left. Note that, if we assume the usual symbol codes $1, 2, 3, \ldots$, then the process of creating this model of M_{RM}'s input tape requires no more than $|\Sigma| \cdot n$, which is O(n), steps, where $n = |w|$. By assumption, this is O($time_{M_{RM}}(n)$) steps as well.

We next describe Turing machine subroutines simulating various register machine instructions. First, an instruction of the form Read(R_i) involves M_{TM}'s first locating the representation of R_i, if it exists, on worktape$_2$.

- If it does not exist, then M_{TM} adds the string $\$I^{i+1}\#$ at the far right of worktape$_2$ and then scans worktape$_1$ until a separating blank is encountered and, for each *1* read, writes a *1* at the far right of worktape$_2$.

- On the other hand, if R_i is represented on worktape$_2$, then M_{TM} moves everything to the right of that representation onto worktape$_3$, overwrites the old contents of R_i by the new as found on worktape$_1$, and then moves the contents of worktape$_3$ back to the right end of worktape$_2$.

Consider next an instruction of the form $*R_i$++. Simulation means first searching for a representation of R_i on worktape$_2$. If none is found, then the simulation automatically halts, we can suppose, since there is no register with index 0. Otherwise, the contents of R_i are copied to worktape$_3$. Suppose that these contents are n_i. M_{TM} now searches for a representation of R_{n_i} on worktape$_2$.

- If none is found, then a new representation is added at the far right: symbol $, followed by representation I^{n_i+1}, followed by #, followed by *11* representing the new content 1.

- Otherwise, in accordance with the routine described earlier, a single *1* is appended to the string representing the content of register R_{n_i}.

The other instructions of M_{RM} are simulated in a similar manner. The most costly aspect of each such simulation is the search on worktape$_2$ for the representation of a register operand, the moving of tape contents to worktape$_3$, and then the restoration of that data to worktape$_2$. Consequently, the length of the nonblank portion of worktape$_2$ is crucial. First, how many registers might be represented, worst case, on worktape$_2$? Well, by Exercise 5.4.2, the number of registers used by M_{RM} is O($time_{M_{RM}}(n)$). So there will be O($time_{M_{RM}}(n)$) register representations on worktape$_2$, worst case.

Within any one such representation, the various symbols fall into the three categories

(1) separators $ and #

(2) 1s occurring within the representation of the register index, and

(3) 1s occurring within the representation of the register's current contents.

First, within one representation, the number of separators is evidently $O(1)$. As for (2), we have, by Exercise 5.4.4, that the length of the index representation is $O(time_{M_{RM}}(n))$. Similarly, the length of the representation of the register's contents is also $O(time_{M_{RM}}(n))$, by Exercise 5.4.3. It follows that the length of the entire nonblank portion of worktape$_2$ is $O([time_{M_{RM}}(n)]^2)$. And, by an earlier remark, this means that the simulation of each of M_{RM}'s instructions requires $O([time_{M_{RM}}(n)]^2)$ steps worst case.

The length of the nonblank portion of worktape$_4$, used in simulating M_{RM}'s output tape, is always $O([time_{M_{RM}}(n)]^2)$. Hence M_{TM}'s termination phase will involve transferring the contents of worktape$_4$ to its own output tape in $O([time_{M_{RM}}(n)]^2)$ steps. (Alternatively, M_{TM} might simulate M_{RM}'s write actions by writing directly to its own output tape.)

By definition, M_{RM} itself computes in $time_{M_{RM}}(n)$ steps. Since simulating each of these steps involves $O([time_{M_{RM}}(n)]^2)$ steps on M_{TM}'s part, it follows that M_{TM}'s entire simulation phase involves $O([time_{M_{RM}}(n)]^3)$ steps. Moreover, we saw that M_{TM}'s initialization phase is completed in $O(time_{M_{RM}}(n))$ steps, and its termination phase in $O([time_{M_{RM}}(n)]^2)$ steps. So we conclude that, overall, M_{TM} accepts L in $O([time_{M_{RM}}(n)]^3)$ steps worst case, which is what we set out to prove.

Q.E.D.

We have now seen that Turing machines can simulate register machines. Moreover, Theorem 5.3(b) shows, in addition, that they can do so with polynomial overhead.

§5.5 Final Remarks and Suggestions for Further Reading

The register machine model of sequential computation was first presented in [Shepherdson and Sturgis 1963]. Register machines serve as the basis for the development of the theory of computability in [Fisher 1982]. A register machine with input and output tapes is closely related to what is usually referred to in the literature as a *random access machine* (*RAM*). Essentially, a RAM is a register machine where the incrementation instruction has been supplanted by both addition and multiplication instructions. The relation between the RAM model and the Turing machine model is addressed in [Aho, Hopcroft, and Ullman 1974].

We have considered only deterministic register machines. Nondeterminism may be introduced by permitting two or more instructions to occur on one and the same line of a register machine program presented canonically. In other words, a nondeterministic register machine program would be a sequence of pairs or triples of instructions where the machine chooses one of these instructions for execution at each step. Given the possibility of enumerating all finite computations of any nondeterministic register machine M, one can then prove the equivalence of nondeterministic and deterministic register machines as language acceptors (cf. Theorem 2.7).

The reader will have noticed the absence of any mention of *space* with respect to register machine computations. One very coarse notion of the space requirements of a computation would be the number of registers used. This notion of space is not affected by the actual magnitude of register contents to the extent that we never considered how those contents are represented within registers. (One says that the register machine model "abstracts" from such representations.) Consequently, number of registers is not a very realistic measure of space. (This may be overstating the case with respect to register machines that accept languages; see, for instance, our Example 5.3.1.) Something better is suggested by the usual binary representations of numeric data in the modern digital computer. Namely, where $c \neq 0$ is the contents of register R_i, we can use

$$sp(R_i) =_{\text{def.}} \lceil \log_2(c+1) \rceil$$

as a measure of the space required by the contents of that register. (If $c = 0$, then set $sp(R_i) = 1$.) Thus if R_1 contains 4, then $sp(R_1) = 3$; and if R_2 contains 5000, then $sp(R_2)$ is 13. The space requirements of a register machine M for a given input word w would then be defined in terms of the sums over all registers R_i of $sp(R_i)$. We forego the details.

This brings up another important issue. All of our time analyses of individual register machines have involved uniform cost assumption. But how realistic is it really to suppose that the incrementation of a single-digit number and the incrementation of a 13-digit number both require one time unit? (Consider the possibility that a carry must be propagated throughout the length of the latter.) Here, too, the base-2 logarithm of its operand(s) is commonly used to give a more realistic measure of the time of an instruction. The idea would be that incrementing a number such as 4 would require three time units, whereas incrementing 5000 would require 13 time units, worst case. One speaks of the *logarithmic cost assumption* (again, see [Aho, Hopcroft, and Ullman 1974]). Our description of register machines has been chosen so as to make the assumption of uniform cost at least admissible. In other contexts (e.g., that of the RAM model mentioned above), the assumption of uniform cost yields time estimates that are far better than those of the multitape Turing machine or of any other reasonable model that we have considered. But that is not a good thing, to the degree that such overly optimistic analyses are perceived to bear no relation to what real machines can do. For this reason, logarithmic cost, rather than uniform cost, is standard in the case of the RAM model.

What we have called Edmonds' Thesis first appeared in [Edmonds 1965]. Our formulation of the Invariance Principle differs in two important respects from what is usually referred to as the Invariance Thesis (see, e.g., [van Emde Boas 1990]). First of all, as usually formulated, the latter involves a reference to space as well as time: "Reasonable" machines simulate one another with polynomially bounded overhead in time *and constant-factor overhead in space.* We have felt justified in omitting the reference to space, given the difficulty of this material for an introductory text. However, it is an omission worth noting. After all, is feasibility preserved by a machine model that simulates a multitape Turing machine with no real change in time but with an exponential increase in space? In any case, the interested reader can return to the solution of Exercise 2.3.7 and to the proofs of Theorems 4.3, 5.3(a), and 5.3(b) in order to verify that our simulations involve at most a constant-factor increase in space usage.

The second difference between our Invariance Principle and the Invariance Thesis of the recent literature is the special prominence that we have given to the multitape Turing machine. This major change was made for personal reasons: As usually formulated, the Invariance Thesis does not make a whole lot of sense to one author anyway.

EXERCISES FOR §5.1

5.1.1. [hwk] In this exercise we consider the case of a register machine that computes a number-theoretic function that is not total. So consider the register machine whose flow diagram appears in Figure 5.1.6.
  (a) If register R_1 initially contains natural number 0, characterize the behavior of M.
  (b) If register R_1 initially contains natural number 3, what are the final contents of registers R_1 and R_2?
  (c) If register R_1 initially contains natural number 102, what are the final contents of registers R_1 and R_2?
  (d) The register machine defined by this flow diagram computes what number-theoretic function?

5.1.2. [hwk] Consider the register machine whose flow diagram appears in Figure 5.1.7.
  (a) If registers R_1 and R_2 initially contain natural numbers 2 and 3, respectively, what are the final contents of registers R_1, R_2, and R_3?
  (b) If registers R_1 and R_2 initially contain natural numbers 4 and 1, respectively, what are the final contents of registers R_1, R_2, and R_3?
  (c) If registers R_1 and R_2 initially contain natural numbers 12 and 37, respectively, what are the final contents of registers R_1, R_2, and R_3?
  (d) What number-theoretic function is computed by this register machine?

5.1.3. Design a register machine that computes the unary number-theoretic function

$$sg(n) = \begin{cases} 0 & \text{if } n = 0 \\ 1 & \text{otherwise} \end{cases}$$

5.1.4. (a) Design a register machine that computes the binary function $f(n, m) = |n - m|$.

  (b) Present a flow diagram for a register machine that computes the monus function defined by

$$n \mathbin{\dot{-}} m = \begin{cases} n - m & \text{if } n \geq m \\ 0 & \text{otherwise} \end{cases}$$

5.1.5. Design a register machine that computes the binary function $f(n, m) =_{\text{def.}} n^m$.

5.1.6. Design a register machine that computes the binary number-theoretic function $f(n, m) =_{\text{def.}} n \, div \, m$. (*Hint*: Use your solution to Exercise 5.1.4 and count the number of successful subtractions of m from n.)

5.1.7. Design a register machine that computes the binary number-theoretic function $f(n, m) =_{\text{def.}} n \, mod \, m$. (*Hint*: What remains after the last successful subtraction of m from n?)

5.1.8. Present a flowchart representing an instruction sequence effecting the decrementation macro R_i−− where R_i is known to be nonzero. (*Hint*: Introduce two additional work registers R_j and R_k.)

5.1.9. The accompanying software enables the user to define macros and thereby introduce a certain modularity into the design of register machines. (See Example 5.1.5 for an example of how the Multiplication Machine of Example 5.1.4 may figure as a macro within another register machine.) Use macros to design register machines computing each of the following unary number-theoretic functions.
  (a) $f(n) = n^2 + 3n + 5$
  (b) $f(n) = n^3 + 2n^2 + n + 3$
  (c) $f(n) = 2^n + 3^n$
  (d) $f(n) = 3n^2 + n + 3$
  (e) $f(n) = \lfloor \log_2 n \rfloor$
  (f) $f(n) = \lceil \log_3 n \rceil$

EXERCISE FOR §5.2

5.2.1. [hwk] Explain how the results of §5.1 and §5.2 establish that Ackermann's function is in fact a recursive function.

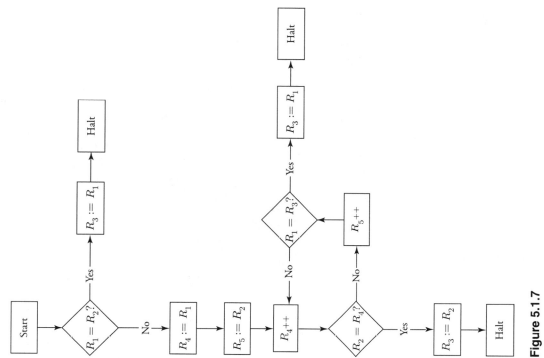

Figure 5.1.7

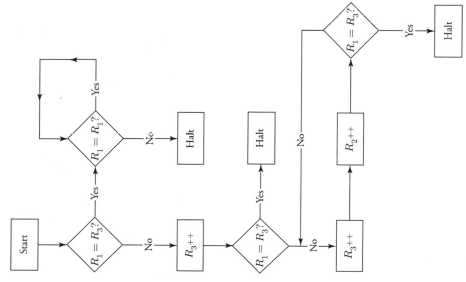

Figure 5.1.6

EXERCISES FOR §5.3

5.3.1. For each language over alphabet $\Sigma = \{a, b\}$ given below, design a register machine that accepts it.
   (a) $\{a^n b^n | n \geq 0\}$
   (b) $\{(ab)^n | n \geq 0\}$
   (c) $\{a^n | n$ is a multiple of $5\}$
   (d) $\{a^n | n$ is prime$\}$

5.3.2. For each of the languages of Exercise 5.3.1(a)–(d), design a register machine that recognizes it.

5.3.3. What is the relation between the family of Markov-acceptable languages and the family of register-machine-acceptable languages? Explain.

5.3.4. We have not explicitly formulated how the register machine model implements the transduction paradigm of §1.1. However, it is rather obvious how this might be done. Design a register machine M with input and output tapes that reverses its input word in $O(n)$ steps, where n is the length of input. Machine M should read word w, appearing on its input tape, completely and ultimately produce word w^R on its output tape.

EXERCISES FOR §5.4

5.4.1. [hwk] Show that polynomial relatedness is an equivalence relation on the class of machine models of sequential computation.

5.4.2. Suppose that M is a register machine with input and output tapes and suppose that M computes in $O(f(n))$ steps worst case under uniform cost, where n is the length of an arbitrary input word w. Show that the number of registers used by M in the case of input word w is then $O(f(n))$.

5.4.3. Suppose that M is a register machine with input and output tapes and suppose that M computes in $O(f(n))$ steps worst case under uniform cost, where n is the length of an arbitrary input word w. Show that the contents of any register used by M in the case of input word w is then $O(f(n))$.

5.4.4. Suppose that M is a register machine with input and output tapes and suppose that M computes in $O(f(n))$ steps worst case under uniform cost, where n is the length of an arbitrary input word w. Show that the index of any register used by M in the case of input word w is then $O(f(n))$.

EXERCISES FOR §5.5 (END-OF-CHAPTER REVIEW EXERCISES)

5.5.1. Design a register machine that computes the unary number-theoretic function defined by $f(n) =_{\text{def.}} n + 2$.

5.5.2. [hwk] Design a register machine that computes the ternary number-theoretic function defined by

$$f(n, m, k) = \begin{cases} m & \text{if } n > 0 \\ k & \text{otherwise} \end{cases}$$

5.5.3. [hwk] Present a flow diagram for a register machine that computes the number-theoretic function

$$f(n) = \begin{cases} 1 & \text{if } 5 | n \\ \text{undefined} & \text{otherwise} \end{cases}$$

(cf. Exercise 5.1.7.)

5.5.4. Show that the unary, everywhere undefined function is register-machine-computable.

5.5.5. Show that the unary number-theoretic function fib defined in Example 0.4.1 is register-machine-computable. (*Hint*: Reconsider Exercise 0.4.1(b) and its solution.)

5.5.6. (a) Show that the multitape Turing machine model and the Markov algorithm model are polynomially related.
   (b) What can be concluded concerning the Markov algorithm model and the regis-

ter machine model (under uniform cost) based on (a)?

5.5.7. **(a)** Show that the family of register machines is countable by sketching a scheme for encoding register machines as natural numbers. (*Hint:* Review the Euler–Gödel scheme used in §2.4 to encode Turing machines.)

(b) Describe a notion of *universal register machine* analogous to that of *universal Turing machine* given in Definition 2.8, and sketch a proof to the effect that such a universal register machine exists.

5.5.8. Design a register machine with input and output tapes that accepts the language of balanced parentheses. (*Hint:* On the input tape, let natural numbers 1 and 2 represent the left and right parentheses, respectively. Furthermore, the following algorithm, suitably adapted for register machines, will be useful. A counter is initialized to 0. Then, as each parenthesis within the input string is read starting from the left, this counter is either incremented or decremented depending upon whether the symbol read was a left or a right parenthesis, respectively. If the counter ever becomes negative or if it is nonzero when the end of input is encountered, then the input string is unbalanced. Otherwise, it is balanced.)

5.5.9. Design a register machine that computes the binary number-theoretic function $f(n, m) = gcd(n, m)$. (See Exercise 1.1.3, where we have presented the Euler algorithm for computing the greatest common divisor of two natural numbers.)

5.5.10. In Chapter 1 we introduced the concept of a *machine configuration* of a (single tape) Turing machine M and meant, thereby, a full description of M at any point during computation, i.e., its current state, tape contents, and read/write head position on its tape. Describe an analogous concept of machine configuration for register machines.

5.5.11. Show that the labeled Markov algorithm model is polynomially related to the Markov algorithm model, thereby extending the diagram of Figure 5.4.1.

5.5.12. **hwk** Show that we may assume without loss of generality that any register machine program has a unique Halt instruction.

5.5.13. Let alphabet $\Sigma = \{a, b\}$. Design a register machine that transforms any input word by replacing every occurrence of an a by a b, and vice versa.

5.5.14. Let alphabet $\Sigma = \{a, b\}$. Design a register machine that transforms any input word w into output word $a^{n_a(w)} b^{n_b(w)}$. In other words, all the as will now precede all of the bs.

5.5.15. Write a register machine that reads, from its input tape, an arbitrary input string representing an English sentence and writes, to its output tape, the result of translating that sentence into Pig Latin. Words might be separated by # with code 27, and the 26 letters of the Roman alphabet may be encoded as 1 through 26, respectively. The (encoded) string

a#screaming#comes#across#the#sky

will emerge as

a#creamings#omesc#crossa#het#kys

5.5.16. Show that the family of register-machine-acceptable languages is closed under union. (*Hint:* Given register machines M_1 and M_2 accepting languages L_1 and L_2, respectively, construct a new machine accepting language $L_1 \cup L_2$.)

5.5.17. Show that the family of register-machine-acceptable languages is closed under intersection.

5.5.18. Show that the family of register-machine-acceptable languages is closed under concatenation.

5.5.19. Write a Pascal or C language program that simulates any register machine program provided as input, using reasonable conventions for representing such programs as character data.

Chapter 6

Post Systems (Optional)

§6.1 Post Systems and Formal Languages

Let alphabet $\Sigma = \{a, b\}$ be given. In addition, suppose that V_1 and V_2 are *variables* in the sense that one is interested in replacing their occurrences within symbol strings by words over Σ.

- So, for example, replacing V_1 as it occurs in aaV_1a by bb produces word $aabba$. Accordingly, we say that word $aabba$ is a *substitution instance* of aaV_1a. The other substitution instances of aaV_1a of length 5 are $aaaaa$, $aaaba$, and $aabaa$. String aaV_1a has a single substitution instance of length 3, on the other hand—namely, aaa, obtained by substituting ε for variable V_1.

- Next, consider the string abV_1abV_2b. Replacing V_1 with ba and V_2 with aa, one obtains substitution instance $abbaabaab$.

- There is no requirement that simultaneous replacements for V_1 and V_2 be distinct. So, for example, $abaaabaab$ is a substitution instance of abV_1abV_2b—we substitute aa for both V_1 and V_2.

- Finally, consider the two strings abV_1a and V_1bb. Suppose that we substitute aa for variable V_1 in both strings so as to obtain words $abaaa$ and $aabb$, respectively. In such a case, we shall speak of *corresponding substitution instances*. In other words, given two strings S_1 and S_2 over $\Sigma \cup \{V_1, V_2, V_3, \ldots\}$ and substitution instances w_1 and w_2 of S_1 and S_2, respectively, we shall say that w_1 and w_2 are *corresponding substitution instances* if they can be obtained from S_1 and S_2 by making one and the same substitution for all occurrences of variable V_1 as well as one and the same substitution for variable V_2 and so on for all variables occurring in either S_1 or S_2 or both.

- As one final example, consider strings

$$aV_1abV_2aa \quad \text{and} \quad bV_1aV_2baaa$$

Substituting ab for V_1 and aaa for both V_2 and V_3, we obtain corresponding substitution instances

$$aababaaaaaaaa \quad \text{and} \quad babaaaabaaa$$

Since the notion of corresponding substitution instances will be important in what follows, the reader is urged to immediately complete Exercise 6.1.1.

A model of sequential computation that is based upon this notion of substitution instance will be the focus of the present chapter. Like the Markov algorithm model of Chapter 4, this new model—that of so-called *Post systems*—takes as its starting point a view of computation as symbol manipulation.

EXAMPLE 6.1.1 As a first example of a Post system, consider letting

$$\Sigma = \{a, b\} \qquad \text{\{a finite set of \textit{terminal symbols}\}}$$

$$\Gamma = \varnothing \qquad \text{\{a finite set of \textit{nonterminal symbols}\}}$$

$$\Theta = \{V_1\} \qquad \text{\{a finite set of \textit{variables}\}}$$

$$\Delta = \{\varepsilon\} \qquad \text{\{a finite set of \textit{axioms}\}}$$

$$\Pi = \{V_1 \rightarrow aV_1b\} \qquad \text{\{a finite set of \textit{productions}\}}$$

In this case, we have the following *derivation* of word *aabb* from our unique axiom.

(i) $\varepsilon \Rightarrow ab$ | our only axiom |

(ii) $ab \Rightarrow aabb$

Here (i) is the result of substituting ε for variable V_1 in production $V_1 \rightarrow aV_1b$. That is, the left- and right-hand sides of (i) are corresponding substitution instances of the left- and right-hand sides, respectively, of production $V_1 \rightarrow aV_1b$. Similarly, (ii) is the result of substituting ab for V_1 in production $V_1 \rightarrow aV_1b$. Again, the left- and right-hand sides of (ii) are corresponding substitution instances of the left- and right-hand sides of our one production. Apparently, each step in a derivation consists of the application of some production $\alpha \rightarrow \beta$ so as to transform a substitution instance of left-hand side α into the corresponding substitution instance of right-hand side β.

In the future we shall present a derivation such as (i)–(ii) in abbreviated form as

(i) $\varepsilon \Rightarrow ab$

(ii) $\Rightarrow aabb$

We have seen that words *ab* and *aabb* are both derivable within this simple Post system. Furthermore, we may take axiom ε to be derivable in zero steps. It should be clear that any word of the form $a^n b^n$ with $n \geq 0$ is derivable within this Post system.

EXAMPLE 6.1.2 A second example will illustrate the role of nonterminal symbols, for which we shall use uppercase letters of the Roman alphabet other than V. (It is essential that the terminal alphabet and the nonterminal alphabet be disjoint.) So consider the Post system defined by setting

$$\Sigma = \{a, b\}$$

$$\Gamma = \{A, B\} \qquad\qquad \text{\{our \textit{nonterminal alphabet}\}}$$

$$\Theta = \{V_1\}$$

$$\Delta = \{AbB\}$$

$$\Pi = \{AV_1 \rightarrow AaaV_1, \qquad \text{(i)}$$

$$V_1 B \rightarrow V_1 bbB, \qquad \text{(ii)}$$

$$AV_1 \rightarrow V_1, \qquad\qquad \text{(iii)}$$

$$V_1 B \rightarrow V_1\} \qquad\qquad \text{(iv)}$$

The following is a derivation of word *aabbb* from this Post system:

$$AbB \Rightarrow AaabB \qquad \text{by (i)}$$

$$\Rightarrow aabB \qquad \text{by (iii)}$$

$$\Rightarrow aabbbB \qquad \text{by (ii)}$$

$$\Rightarrow aabbb \qquad \text{by (iv)}$$

Note that this is not the only derivation of *aabbb* within this Post system. The reader should verify that this Post system can be used to derive any word over $\Sigma = \{a, b\}$ consisting of an even number of *a*s followed by an odd number of *b*s.

- First, any derivation begins with axiom *AbB*, which has the effect of introducing a single *b* into any derived word.
- Second, productions (i) and (ii) alone introduce new terminals. Moreover, they each introduce two—that is, an even number of—identical terminal symbols: either two *a*s or two *b*s.
- Productions (iii) and (iv) serve only to eliminate nonterminals.
- Finally, the peculiar form of productions (i) and (ii) ensures that any occurrences of *a* are to the left of all occurrences of *b*.

It is worth pointing out that variables $V_1, V_2, V_3, \ldots, V_k$ do not themselves occur within derivations of S. (A fortiori, variables do not occur within axioms.) Rather, the lines of derivations are substitution instances of strings containing variables. Having seen two examples, we are now ready for some formal definitions.

DEFINITION 6.1: A *Post system* $S = \langle \Sigma, \Gamma, \Theta, \Delta, \Pi \rangle$ consists of (1) a finite, nonempty set Σ of *terminal symbols*, (2) a finite set Γ of *nonterminal symbols* with $\Sigma \cap \Gamma = \emptyset$, (3) a finite set $\Theta = \{V_1, V_2, V_3, \ldots, V_k\}$ of *variables*, (4) a finite (possibly empty) set Δ of *axioms*, where an axiom is any (possibly empty) word over $\Sigma \cup \Gamma$, and, finally, (5) a finite set Π of *productions* of the form

$$\alpha \to \beta$$

where $\alpha, \beta \in (\Sigma \cup \Gamma \cup \Theta)^*$ subject to the restrictions that (i) no member of Θ occurs more than once in either α or β and (ii) each member of Θ occurring in β occurs in α as well.

In fact, restriction (i) can be relaxed, and it will occasionally be convenient to do so (see Exercise 6.1.14).

DEFINITION 6.2: Let $S = \langle \Sigma, \Gamma, \Theta, \Delta, \Pi \rangle$ be a Post system. By a *derivation in S* we shall mean any finite, nonempty sequence $w_0, w_1, w_2, \ldots, w_n$ of words over $\Sigma \cup \Gamma$ such that (1) w_0 is an axiom of S (i.e., $w_0 \in \Delta$), and (2) for $0 \le i < n$, w_{i+1} and w_i are corresponding substitution instances of the left- and right-hand sides, respectively, of some production of S (i.e., of some production π in Π). We shall say that such a sequence $w_0, w_1, \ldots, w_n$ is a *derivation of w_n of length n*.

Apparently a derivation of length n within Post system S will consist of n applications of productions of S. Each such application will be counted as one *step* in the derivation. Letting $n = 0$ in Definition 6.2, we have that any axiom of S can itself be derived within S in zero steps.

Post Systems and Formal Languages

Given the notion of a derivation in a Post system, we can associate individual Post systems with particular formal languages.

DEFINITION 6.3: Let $S = \langle \Sigma, \Gamma, \Theta, \Delta, \Pi \rangle$ be a Post system. The *language generated by Post system S* will be that set of words over terminal alphabet Σ that are derivable in S—that is, derivable in zero or more steps from axioms in set Δ. We write $L(S)$ for the language generated by S.

Note that, in accordance with this definition, any member of Δ consisting of terminals only is a member of the language generated by Post system $\langle \Sigma, \Gamma, \Theta, \Delta, \Pi \rangle$. We have seen that the Post system of Example 6.1.1 generates language $\{a^n b^n | n \ge 0\}$ and that the Post system of Example 6.1.2 generates language $\{a^n b^m | n \text{ is even and } m \text{ is odd}\}$. We emphasize that the language generated by S is the set of all derivable strings consisting of terminal alphabet symbols only.

Our next example illustrates again an essential use of nonterminal symbols—that is, members of set Γ.

EXAMPLE 6.1.3 Consider the Post system S defined by

$$\Sigma = \{a, b, c\}$$

$$\Gamma = \{B, C\}$$

$$\Theta = \{V_1, V_2\}$$

$$\Delta = \{\varepsilon\}$$

$$\Pi = \{V_1 \rightarrow aV_1 BC, \qquad \text{(i)}$$

$$V_1 CBV_2 \rightarrow V_1 BCV_2, \qquad \text{(ii)}$$

$$V_1 aBV_2 \rightarrow V_1 abV_2, \qquad \text{(iii)}$$

$$V_1 bBV_2 \rightarrow V_1 bbV_2, \qquad \text{(iv)}$$

$$V_1 bCV_2 \rightarrow V_1 bcV_2, \qquad \text{(v)}$$

$$V_1 cCV_2 \rightarrow V_1 ccV_2\} \qquad \text{(vi)}$$

We number the productions of S for ease of reference.

Referring to the members of Π as productions (i) through (vi), we present a derivation in S of word *aabbcc*.

$$\varepsilon \Rightarrow aBC \qquad \text{by (i)}$$
$$\Rightarrow aaBCBC \qquad \text{by (i)}$$
$$\Rightarrow aaBBCC \qquad \text{by (ii)}$$
$$\Rightarrow aabBCC \qquad \text{by (iii)}$$
$$\Rightarrow aabbCC \qquad \text{by (iv)}$$
$$\Rightarrow aabbcC \qquad \text{by (v)}$$
$$\Rightarrow aabbcc \qquad \text{by (vi)}$$

We shall summarize this derivation by writing

$$\varepsilon \Rightarrow_S^* aabbcc$$

or just

$$\varepsilon \Rightarrow^* aabbcc$$

following our practice in Chapter 4. It should be easy to see that S generates the language $\{a^n b^n c^n | n \geq 0\}$. A derivation in S of word $a^m b^m c^m$, for fixed m, will begin with m successive applications of production (i) so as to generate computation word $a^m (BC)^m$. Afterward, successive applications of (ii) yield $a^m B^m C^m$. Finally, (iii)–(vi) are applied so as to replace nonterminal symbols B and C by terminal symbols b and c, respectively, starting from the left.

On the other hand, word *aabcbc* cannot be generated. To see this, note that

$$\varepsilon \Rightarrow_S^* aaBCBC \qquad \text{by two applications of (i)}$$

$$\Rightarrow_S aabCBC \qquad \text{by (iii)}$$

$$\Rightarrow_S aabcBC \qquad \text{by (v)}$$

At this point, no production is applicable. (For more on this example, see Exercise 6.1.11.)

With respect to formal languages, Post systems are rather different in character from the other models of computation that we have considered. We can make this point by digressing momentarily to consider our own capacities as natural language processors. Presented with the English string "All Patagonians wear Armani suits," any English speaker is able to recognize it as a grammatically correct English sentence—quite apart from the issue of its truth or falsity. Similarly, analysis of "Patagonians suits Armani wear all" reveals its ungrammaticality. In either case, our language processing amounts to *language recognition* in precisely the sense in which we have been using that term throughout this textbook. Contrast this now with a situation in which one is required to express one's view on some topic, say. In the latter case, one is expected to produce or *generate* an English sentence. In so doing, one functions not as a language recognizer but, rather, as a *language generator*.

The point of our digression is perhaps already obvious. With respect to formal languages, the other models that we have considered—Turing machines, Markov algorithms, and register machines—all implement our language recognition paradigm and hence suggest our own capacities as language recognizers. The operation of a Turing machine M qua language recognizer, say, constitutes an analysis of an input word w, which is then either accepted or rejected. But M must be presented with w initially. The language accepted by M is the language of all and only those words w that, having been presented, are accepted. The operation of a Post system S is quite different. No word is presented initially. Rather, S starts with some one of its axioms and selects a sequence of rule applications in order to *generate* some word w. The language generated by S is the set of all words so generated. Thus Post systems more nearly approximate our capacities as language generators. (But Post systems do model our language recognition paradigm at one remove [see Theorem 6.4 and §6.5 below].)

A word of caution with respect to the generation of formal languages by Post systems is in order. We say that the Post system S of Example 6.1.3 with productions (i)–(vi) generates language $L = \{a^n b^n c^n | n \geq 0\}$ by virtue of the fact that

- every word in L is derivable in S and

- no word in $L^c = \Sigma^* \backslash L$ is derivable in S.

For example, whereas each of ε, *abc*, *aabbcc*, ... is derivable in S, a word such as *aabbbcccc* is not derivable in S. (Why not?) Nor is word *abcabc* derivable. (Why not?) This leads us to formulate

---

REMARK 6.1.1: Suppose that language L is given and that one is required to find a Post system S that generates L, that is, a Post system S such that $L(S) = L$. Then it is not enough to ensure merely that the productions of S permit all words of L to be derived. One must also be satisfied that any word that is not in L is not derivable within S.

Post Systems and Function Computation

Since Post systems are being proposed as an analysis of computation, it is essential that we describe some sense in which they model the function computation paradigm. For this purpose, we introduce

---

EXAMPLE 6.1.4 (Addition) Consider the Post system $S = \langle \Sigma, \Gamma, \Theta, \Delta, \Pi \rangle$ defined by

$$\Sigma = \{1, \Psi, (,), =, , \}$$

$$\Gamma = \varnothing$$

$$\Theta = \{V_1, V_2, V_3\}$$

$$\Delta = \{\Psi(1, 1) = 1\}$$

$$\Pi = \{\Psi(V_1, V_2) = V_3 \rightarrow \Psi(V_1 1, V_2) = V_3 1, \quad \text{(i)}$$

$$\Psi(V_1, V_2) = V_3 \rightarrow \Psi(V_1, V_2 1) = V_0 1 \quad \text{(ii)}$$

The idea here is that axioms and productions involving Ψ should collectively define some number-theoretic function f. Given the familiar representation of natural numbers whereby natural number n is given by an unbroken sequence of $n + 1$ 1s, we suggest that the single axiom of S be interpreted as asserting that the value of f for argument pair $\langle 0, 0 \rangle$ is 0. Similarly, production (i) says that f applied to the successor of n and to m is identical to the successor of the value of f applied to n and m. Production (ii) tells us that f applied to n and the successor of m is identical to the successor of $f(n, m)$. This should sound familiar. Indeed, comparing this with recursion equations[1]

$$f(0, 0) = 0 \qquad \{\text{cf. axiom } \Psi(1, 1) = 1\}$$

$$f(succ(n), m) = succ(f(n, m)) \qquad \{\text{cf. production (i)}\}$$

$$f(n, succ(m)) = succ(f(n, m)) \qquad \{\text{cf. production (ii)}\}$$

we can see that the described f is the binary addition function.

We present a derivation of equation $f(11, 111) = 1111$ within S.

> Of necessity we begin with S' single axiom.

$$\Psi(1, 1) = 1 \Rightarrow \Psi(11, 1) = 11 \qquad \text{by (i), letting } V_1 \text{ be } 1, V_2 \text{ be } 1, \text{ and } V_3 \text{ be } 1$$

$$\Rightarrow \Psi(11, 11) = 111 \qquad \text{by (ii), letting } V_1 \text{ be } 11, V_2 \text{ be } 1, \text{ and } V_3 \text{ be } 11$$

$$\Rightarrow \Psi(11, 111) = 1111 \qquad \text{by (ii), letting } V_1 \text{ be } 11, V_2 \text{ be } 11, \text{ and } V_3 \text{ be } 111$$

Let us interpret the derived equation as an assertion that $f(1, 2) = 3$, where f is the binary number-theoretic function characterized by Post system S. It should not be too hard to see that all truths of the form

$$f(n_1, n_2) = n_1 + n_2$$

---

[1] These three equations are equivalent to those presented in Example 3.1.2.

similarly correspond to equations derivable in S. By virtue of this fact, we shall want to say that Post system S *computes* the binary addition function. This example gives the essentials of Definition 6.4 below. However, full generality requires that we accommodate k-ary functions f for arbitrary $k \geq 0$.

DEFINITION 6.4: Let f be a k-ary number-theoretic function. Let $S = \langle \Sigma, \Gamma, \Theta, \Delta, \Pi \rangle$ be a Post system such that $\Sigma = \{ I, \Psi, (,), =, , \}$. Then S *computes* f if, for all $n_1, n_2, \ldots, n_k$ and m, S derives equation

$$\Psi(I^{n_1+1}, I^{n_2+1}, \ldots, I^{n_k+1}) = I^{m+1}$$

just in case $f(n_1, n_2, \ldots, n_k) = m$. We shall say that k-ary number-theoretic function f is *Post-computable* provided there is some Post system S that computes f.

As another illustration of Definition 6.4, consider the following example.

EXAMPLE 6.1.5 (Multiplication) Reflection upon the recursion equations

$$f(0, 0) = 0$$

$$f(succ(n), m) = f(n, m) + m$$

$$f(n, succ(m)) = f(n, m) + n$$

for the binary multiplication function, suggests the Post system S defined as

$$\Sigma = \{ 1, \Psi, (,), =, , \}$$

$$\Gamma = \varnothing$$

$$\Theta = \{ V_1, V_2, V_3 \}$$

$$\Delta = \{ \Psi(1, 1) = 1 \}$$

$$\Pi = \{ \Psi(1 V_1, 1 V_2) = V_3 \rightarrow \Psi(1 V_1 1, 1 V_2) = V_3 V_2, \qquad \text{(i)}$$

$$\Psi(1 V_1, 1 V_2) = V_3 \rightarrow \Psi(1 V_1, 1 V_2 1) = V_3 V_1 \} \qquad \text{(ii)}$$

(The *1*s occurring in production left-hand sides are needed in order to prevent the proliferation of representational *1*s in products.) We show that equation $\Psi(11, 11) = 11$ is derivable in S, referring to productions (i) and (ii).

$$\Psi(1, 1) = 1 \Rightarrow \Psi(11, 1) = 1 \qquad \text{by (i), letting } V_1 \text{ and } V_2 \text{ be } \varepsilon \text{ and } V_3 \text{ be } 1$$

$$\Rightarrow \Psi(11, 11) = 11 \qquad \text{by (ii), letting } V_1 \text{ be } 1, V_2 \text{ be } \varepsilon, \text{ and } V_3 \text{ be } 1$$

Our plan for the remainder of this chapter is as follows. We shall first show that Post systems are computationally equivalent to Turing machines and hence to Markov algorithms in the sense that a number-theoretic function is Post-computable if and only if it is both Turing-computable and Markov-computable. This is Theorems 6.1(a) and 6.1(b). In addition, it will be shown that the class of languages generated by Post systems coincides with the class of Turing-acceptable languages—which coincides with the class of Markov-acceptable languages. Of course, the latter result consists of two parts.

> - If L is Turing-acceptable, then L is generated by some Post system.
> - If L is generated by some Post system, then L is Turing-acceptable.

This important result is Theorem 6.4 in §6.4.

§6.2 The Class of Post-Computable Functions Is Identical to the Class of Partial Recursive Functions

We pursue and extend our survey of equivalent computational models by demonstrating

> **THEOREM 6.1(a):** Every partial recursive function is Post-computable.

PROOF Let h be a k-ary partial recursive function with $k \geq 0$. We show that $h(n_1, n_2, \ldots, n_k)$ is computed by some Post system. Our proof proceeds by induction on the canonical form of h. To begin, we have base cases (i)–(iii).

(i) Suppose that h is the successor function, which is to suppose that h is unary. Then h is computed by the Post system with axiom set

$$\Delta = \{\Psi(1) = 11\} \qquad /\text{*The successor of 0 is 1.}$$

and production set

$$\Pi = \{\Psi(V_1) = V_2 \rightarrow \Psi(V_1 1) = V_2 1\} \qquad \begin{array}{l} /\text{*If } n \text{ is the successor of } m, \text{ then } n+1 \\ \text{is the successor of } m+1. \end{array}$$

(ii) If h is the 0-ary constant-zero function C_0^0, then h is computed by Post system

$$\Delta = \{\Psi( ) = 1\} \qquad /\text{*Any 0-tuple of natural numbers is mapped onto 0.}$$

with $\Pi = \varnothing$. On the other hand, if h is the unary constant-zero function C_0^1, then h is computed by the Post system with

$$\Delta = \{\Psi(1) = 1\} \qquad /\text{*Natural number 0 is mapped onto 0.}$$

and with

$$\Pi = \{\Psi(V_1) = V_2 \to \Psi(V_1\,I) = V_2\} \qquad \text{/*If natural number } n \text{ is mapped onto } m,$$
$$\text{then so is } n+1.$$

Similarly, each remaining k-ary constant-zero function C_0^k for $k \geq 2$ is seen to be Post-computable.

(iii) Any projection function p_j^k, for $0 < j \leq k$, is Post-computable. To take an example, p_2^3 is computed by the Post system with

$$\Delta = \{\Psi(I,\,I,\,I) = I\} \qquad \text{/* Triple } \langle 0,0,0 \rangle \text{ is mapped onto } 0.$$

and with

$$\Pi = \{\Psi(V_1, V_2, V_3) = V_4 \to \Psi(V_1\,I, V_2, V_3) = V_4 \qquad \text{/*If } \langle n_1, n_2, n_3 \rangle \text{ is mapped onto } m,$$
$$\text{then so is } \langle n_1+1, n_2, n_3 \rangle.$$

$$\Psi(V_1, V_2, V_3) = V_4 \to \Psi(V_1, V_2\,I, V_3) = V_4\,I, \qquad \text{/*If } \langle n_1, n_2, n_3 \rangle \text{ is mapped onto } m,$$
$$\text{then } \langle n_1, n_2+1, n_3 \rangle \text{ is mapped onto } m+1.$$

$$\Psi(V_1, V_2, V_3) = V_4 \to \Psi(V_1, V_2, V_3\,I) = V_4\} \qquad \text{/*If } \langle n_1, n_2, n_3 \rangle \text{ is mapped onto } m,$$
$$\text{then so is } \langle n_1, n_2, n_3+1 \rangle.$$

Inductive cases (iv)–(vi) correspond to composition, primitive recursion, and minimization—the three function-forming operations under which the class of partial recursive functions is closed (see Definition 3.7).

(iv) Suppose, for the sake of simplicity, that h is of the form $\mathbf{Comp}[f, g]$, where f and g are both partial recursive and g, and hence h, are both binary functions. This is to suppose that h is defined as

$$h(n_1, n_2) =_{\text{def.}} f(g(n_1, n_2)) \tag{6.2.1}$$

Of course, (6.2.1) is just an instance of Schema A of Definition 3.2, letting $k = 2$ and $m = 1$. The more general case, where h is of the form $\mathbf{Comp}[f, g_1, g_2, \ldots, g_m]$ and the g_i are k-ary for arbitrary k, is not essentially different although a little more complicated. It should be easy enough for the reader to make out the more general argument based on our discussion.

As induction hypothesis we assume that both f and g, since partial recursive, are Post-computable as well. In particular, let f be computed by Post system $S_f = (\Sigma_f, \Gamma_f, \Theta_f, \Delta_f, \Pi_f)$ and let g be computed by Post system $S_g = (\Sigma_g, \Gamma_g, \Theta_g, \Delta_g, \Pi_g)$. As is standard for Post systems computing number-theoretic functions, we can assume that $\Sigma_f = \Sigma_g = \{I, \Psi, (,), =, ,\}$.

The construction of Post system $S_h = (\Sigma_h, \Gamma_h, \Theta_h, \Delta_h, \Pi_h)$ computing $h = \mathbf{Comp}[f, g]$ is described below. We let

$$\Sigma_h = \{I, \Psi, (,), =, ,\} \longleftarrow$$

> This is the terminal alphabet of the Post system S_h under construction...

as usual. Furthermore, we set

... and this is its nonterminal alphabet.

Nonterminals Ψ_f and Ψ_g will track computations within Post systems S_f and S_g, respectively.

$$\Gamma_h = \Gamma_f \cup \Gamma_g \cup \{\Psi_f, \Psi_g, @\}$$

where Ψ_f, Ψ_g, and $@$ are three new nonterminal symbols not occurring in $\Gamma_f \cup \Gamma_g$. We can usually set $\Theta_h = \Theta_f \cup \Theta_g$ but must sometimes add just a few more variables in forming Θ_h. As for axioms, the members of Δ_h will be the results of replacing symbol Ψ with nonterminal symbol Ψ_g throughout each of the axioms in Δ_g. (Compare (6.2.1) above, which makes it apparent that computing the value of h for arguments $\langle n_1, n_2 \rangle$ must begin by computing the value of g for arguments $\langle n_1, n_2 \rangle$. Hence the axioms of system S_g serve as starting points.) The productions of Π_h will consist of all of the productions of Groups (a) through (d) and nothing more.

- **Group (a)** will consist of the results of transforming each production $\alpha \to \beta$ of Π_g into a new production $\alpha' \to \beta'$, where α' and β' are the results of replacing symbol Ψ with nonterminal symbol Ψ_g in α and β, respectively. The productions of Group (a) have the effect of simulating the application of function g to given arguments.

- **Group (b)** will consist of the results of transforming each axiom γ in Δ_f into a production $V_1 \to \gamma'@V_1$, where γ' is the result of replacing symbol Ψ with nonterminal symbol Ψ_f throughout γ. Applying any one of these productions will effect the transition to S_h's simulation of the application of function f.

- **Group (c)** comprises the results of transforming each production $\alpha \to \beta$ in Π_f into $\alpha'@V \to \beta'@V$, where (i) α' and β' are the results of replacing symbol Ψ with nonterminal symbol Ψ_f in α and β, respectively, and (ii) V is some new variable that does not occur in either α or β. (We can require that V be that variable with least index from among those variables in Θ_h not occurring in either α or β.) The productions of Group (c) have the effect of simulating the application of function f on the left while retaining, on the right, the results of an earlier simulation of the application of function g.

- Finally, **Group (d)** contains the two productions

$$\Psi_f(V_1 1) = V_2 @ \Psi_g(V_3, V_4) = V_5 1 \to \Psi_f(V_1) = V_2 @ \Psi_g(V_3, V_4) = V_5$$

and

$$\Psi_f(1) = V_2 @ \Psi_g(V_3, V_4) = 1 \to \Psi(V_3, V_4) = V_2$$

which can be used, under appropriate circumstances, to eliminate marker $@$ and to reduce the current computation word to a representation of the application of $h = \mathbf{Comp}[f, g]$ (see Example 6.2.1).

Note that since every member of Δ_h contains nonterminal symbol Ψ_g, the productions of Group (a), which correspond to g, must be applied first. Moreover, once an axiom of Δ_f has been introduced, in effect, by a production of Group (b), no production of Group (a) can ever be applied again. Rather, only productions of Group (c)—corresponding to f—are applicable. (Our use of nonterminal symbol $@$ as a separator is nonessential but should enable the reader to better see how the successive lines of S_h's derivations track g's computation on the right and, afterward, f's computation on the left.) Suppose that at some point the derived string has the form

$$\Psi_f(I^{m+1}) = I^{j+1}@\Psi_g(I^{n_1+1}, I^{n_2+1}) = I^{m+1} \qquad (6.2.2)$$

reflecting the fact that $g(n_1, n_2) = m$ and $f(m) = j$ so that $f(g(n_1, n_2)) = j$. Then the productions of Group (d) can be used to transform (6.2.2) into

$$\Psi(I^{n_1+1}, I^{n_2+1}) = I^{j+1}$$

as Example 6.2.1 will illustrate.

We leave the two remaining inductive cases as exercises. That is, a complete proof involves showing that the class of Post-computable functions is closed under primitive recursion (v) and minimization (vi).   Q.E.D.

EXAMPLE 6.2.1 (Illustration of inductive case (iv) in the proof of Theorem 6.1(a)) We illustrate the construction in the case where g is the binary addition function and f is the unary successor function. See Example 6.1.4 and case (i) of the present proof. That is, $h(n_1, n_2) = f(g(n_1, n_2)) = (n_1 + n_2) + 1$. The sole axiom of Δ_h is

$$\Psi_g(1, 1) = 1$$

The productions of Π_h are

Group (a) $\Psi_g(V_1, V_2) = V_3 \rightarrow \Psi_g(V_1 1, V_2) = V_3 1,$ (i)

$\Psi_g(V_1, V_2) = V_3 \rightarrow \Psi_g(V_1, V_2 1) = V_3 1,$ (ii)

Group (b) $V_1 \rightarrow \Psi_j(1) = 11@ V_1,$ [This is S_f's one axiom.]   (i)

[Here we have S_f's one production.]

Group (c) $\Psi_f(V_1) = V_2 @ V_3 \rightarrow \Psi_f(V_1 1) = V_2 1 @ V_3$ (i)

Group (d) $\Psi_f(V_1 1) = V_2 @ \Psi_g(V_3) = V_4 1 \rightarrow \Psi_f(V_1) = V_2 @ \Psi_g(V_3) = V_4$ (i)

$\Psi_f(1) = V_2 @ \Psi_g(V_3) = 1 \rightarrow \Psi(V_3) = V_2$ (ii)

The reader should immediately complete Exercise 6.2.1 so as to see how these productions work.

THEOREM 6.1(b): Let f be a number-theoretic function. If f is Post-computable, then f is partial recursive.

PROOF Suppose that f is computed by Post system $S = \langle \Sigma, \Gamma, \Theta, \Delta, \Pi \rangle$. We describe a nondeterministic, single-tape Turing machine M that computes f in the sense of Definition 2.12. (Since Post systems provide a nondeterministic model of computation, it is easiest to assume that M here is nondeterministic and to speak of M's choices.) We let M's tape alphabet be $\Sigma \cup \Gamma \cup \Theta$. Suppose that M's input tape is initially configured as

$$\ldots B I^{n_1+1} B I^{n_2+1} B \ldots I^{n_k+1} B \ldots \qquad (6.2.3)$$

with M's read/write head scanning the leftmost of these 1s. Let us suppose that M first produces some representation of the entire axiom set Δ and the entire production set Π on its tape. M then nondeterministically selects one axiom from Δ with which to begin its simulation of a derivation within S. M checks whether the selected axiom is already of the form

$$\Psi(I^{n_1+1}, I^{n_2+1}, \ldots, I^{n_k+1}) = I^{j+1} \qquad (6.2.4)$$

If so, then, by Definition 6.4, $f(n_1, n_2, \ldots, n_k) = j$ and M has only to erase everything except I^{j+1} before halting. Otherwise, M chooses some production π of Π such that the chosen axiom is a substitution instance of the left-hand side of π. M then produces on its tape the corresponding substitution instance of the right-hand side of π. Again, M checks to see whether this second substitution instance is of the form (6.2.4). If so, then M erases and halts. If not, then another production is chosen, and so on. It should be evident that M computes f, so that f is Turing-computable and hence partial recursive.   Q.E.D.

This completes our investigation of Post systems and function computation. In the next two sections we deepen our understanding of the relation between Post systems and formal languages.

§6.3 Closure Properties of the Class of Languages Generated by Post Systems

We continue our investigation of the family of languages generated by Post systems by considering its closure properties. To begin, suppose that $S_1 = \langle \Sigma_1, \Gamma_1, \Theta_1, \Delta_1, \Pi_1 \rangle$ and $S_2 = \langle \Sigma_2, \Gamma_2, \Theta_2, \Delta_2, \Pi_2 \rangle$ are Post systems generating languages L_1 and L_2, respectively. We next construct a Post system—call it $S_\cup$—which generates language $L_1 \cup L_2$. The axioms of $S_\cup = \langle \Sigma_\cup, \Gamma_\cup, \Theta_\cup, \Delta_\cup, \Pi_\cup \rangle$ will, more or less, just be those of S_1 together with those of S_2, and the productions of $S_\cup$ will, more or less, just be those of S_1 together with those of S_2. This is the essence of our construction. However, merely setting $\Delta_\cup = \Delta_1 \cup \Delta_2$ and $\Pi_\cup = \Pi_1 \cup \Pi_2$ would not quite work since it would, in general, permit productions of S_1 and productions of S_2 to be applied within one and the same derivation of $S_\cup$. (Why can this not be permitted?) So we need some way of preventing that situation from arising; we must somehow ensure that any derivation of $S_\cup$ consists of either (1) an axiom of S_1 followed by a sequence of applications of S_1's productions or (2) an axiom of S_2 followed by a sequence of applications of S_2's productions. To this end, let us proceed as follows.

- Let $\Sigma_\cup = \Sigma_1 \cup \Sigma_2$ and $\Theta_\cup = \Theta_1 \cup \Theta_2$.

- Add two special nonterminals $\#_1$ and $\#_2$ to $\Gamma_\cup$. In other words, we are setting $\Gamma_\cup = \Gamma_1 \cup \Gamma_2 \cup \{\#_1, \#_2\}$.

- Prefix every axiom of S_1 by nonterminal $\#_1$. Prefix every axiom of S_2 by nonterminal $\#_2$. That is, $\Delta_\cup$ is not $\Delta_1 \cup \Delta_2$ itself but, rather, the result of transforming the members of Δ_1 and Δ_2 in the manner described.

- Prefix the left-hand side and the right-hand side of every production of S_1 by nonterminal $\#_1$. Similarly, we prefix the left-hand side and the right-hand side of every production of S_2 by $\#_2$. Thus $\Pi_\cup$ is not merely $\Pi_1 \cup \Pi_2$. Rather, it comprises the transformed members of Π_1 together with the transformed members of Π_2.

This is enough to prevent the undesirable mixing of axioms and productions mentioned above. Of course, as matters now stand, any derivable string begins with one of the special nonterminals $\#_1$ or $\#_2$, which of course must be eliminated:

- Add to $\Pi_\cup$ the two productions

$$\#_1 V_1 \rightarrow V_1$$
$$\#_2 V_1 \rightarrow V_1$$

Note that once either of these productions has been applied, no further productions of $\Pi_\cup$ are applicable. (Why?) Thus any derivable string of terminals is the result of a final application of one of these two productions. If production $\#_1 V_1 \rightarrow V_1$ was applied, then the resulting string is derivable within S_1. If production $\#_2 V_1 \rightarrow V_1$ was applied, then the resulting string is derivable within S_2. This is enough to see that, indeed, $L(S_\cup) \subseteq L(S_1) \cup (S_2)$. And $L(S_1) \cup L(S_2) \subseteq L(S_\cup)$ follows from the fact that all of the axioms and productions of S_1 and S_2 have been carried over into $S_\cup$. Since $L_1 = L(S_1)$ and $L_2 = L(S_2)$ were an arbitrary pair of languages generated by Post systems, we have proved

---

THEOREM 6.2: If L_1 and L_2 are languages generated by Post systems, then so is language $L_1 \cup L_2$. Alternative formulation: The class of languages generated by Post systems is closed under union.

We apply the construction of the proof of Theorem 6.2 in Example 6.3.1 below.

EXAMPLE 6.3.1 Consider the Post systems S_1 and S_2 appearing on the left and on the right.

$$\Sigma_1 = \{a, b\} \qquad\qquad \Sigma_2 = \{a, b\}$$

$$\Gamma_1 = \varnothing \qquad\qquad\qquad \Gamma_2 = \varnothing$$

$$\Theta_1 = \{V_1\} \qquad\qquad \Theta_2 = \{V_1\}$$

$$\Delta_1 = \{ab\} \qquad\qquad \Delta_2 = \{a, b\}$$

$$\Pi_1 = \{V_1 \rightarrow aV_1b\} \qquad \Pi_2 = \{aV_1 \rightarrow aV_1a, bV_1 \rightarrow bV_1b\}$$

We see that $L(S_1) = \{a^n b^n | n \geq 1\}$ whereas $L(S_2) = \{w | w = a^n \text{ or } w = b^n \text{ for some odd } n \geq 1\}$. The construction of Theorem 6.2 produces Post system $S_\cup$ defined as

$$\Sigma_\cup = \{a, b\}$$

$$\Gamma_\cup = \varnothing$$

$$\Theta_\cup = \{V_1\}$$

$$\Delta_\cup = \{\#_1 \boldsymbol{ab}, \#_2 \boldsymbol{a}, \#_2 \boldsymbol{b}\}$$

$$\Pi_\cup = \{\#_1 \boldsymbol{V_1} \rightarrow \#_1 \boldsymbol{a} \boldsymbol{V_1} \boldsymbol{b},$$

$$\#_2 \boldsymbol{a} \boldsymbol{V_1} \rightarrow \#_2 \boldsymbol{a} \boldsymbol{V_1} \boldsymbol{a},$$

$$\#_2 \boldsymbol{b} \boldsymbol{V_1} \rightarrow \#_2 \boldsymbol{b} \boldsymbol{V_1} \boldsymbol{b},$$

$$\#_1 \boldsymbol{V_1} \rightarrow \boldsymbol{V_1},$$

$$\#_2 \boldsymbol{V_1} \rightarrow \boldsymbol{V_1}\}$$

We next show that the class of languages generated by Post systems is closed under concatenation. Suppose that languages L_1 and L_2 are generated by Post systems $S_1 = \langle \Sigma_1, \Gamma_1, \Theta_1, \Delta_1, \Pi_1 \rangle$ and $S_2 = \langle \Sigma_2, \Gamma_2, \Theta_2, \Delta_2, \Pi_2 \rangle$, respectively. We describe the construction of a new Post system S_{cat} that generates language $L_1.L_2$. To this end, we place a new symbol #—to function as a separator—in the nonterminal alphabet Γ_{cat} of S_{cat} and in general set

$$S_{cat} = \langle \Sigma_1 \cup \Sigma_2, \Gamma_1 \cup \Gamma_2 \cup \{\#\}, \Theta_1 \cup \Theta_2 \cup \{V\}, \Delta_{cat}, \Pi_{cat} \rangle$$

where V is a new variable not occurring in $\Theta_1 \cup \Theta_2$ and Δ_{cat} and Π_{cat} are as described below.

(1) If $\varepsilon \in L_2$, then we let $\Delta_1 \subseteq \Delta_{cat}$ so that every axiom of S_1 becomes an axiom of S_{cat}. (Why is this necessary?)

(2) Similarly, if $\varepsilon \in L_1$, then we make it the case that $\Delta_2 \subseteq \Delta_{cat}$.

(3) For every axiom $\alpha \in \Delta_1$, axiom set Δ_{cat} will contain the result of appending nonterminal symbol # to α.

(4) Similarly, for every axiom $\alpha \in \Delta_2$, we place in Δ_{cat} the result of prefixing α by nonterminal symbol #.

(5) For every production $\alpha \rightarrow \beta$ in Π_1, production set Π_{cat} will contain the production

$$\alpha \# V \rightarrow \beta \# V$$

where V is a new variable not in $\Theta_1 \cup \Theta_2$. (Why must we insist that V be a new variable? *Hint:* What requirement regarding Post system productions might otherwise be violated?)

(6) Similarly, corresponding to every production $\alpha \to \beta$ in Π_2, production set Π_{cat} will contain the production

$$V\#\alpha \to V\#\beta$$

where V is a new variable not in $\Theta_1 \cup \Theta_2$.

As a result of (5) and (6), the productions of Π_{cat} may be applied only to strings containing an occurrence of separator #. Moreover, (3) and (5) together ensure that any derivation within the new system S_{cat} will model some derivation within S_1 in its left or front half. Similarly, (4) and (6) together ensure that such a derivation within S_{cat} will model some derivation within S_2 in its right or rear half. We have only to permit S_{cat} to eliminate separator #:

(7) We add to Π_{cat} the single production

$$V_1\#V_2 \to V_1 V_2$$

Note that once this production has been applied within a derivation so as to eliminate the separator, no other production of Π_{cat} is applicable. (Why not?) Moreover, if the production of (7) happens to be applied to a string

$$w_1\#w_2$$

with $w_1 \in \Sigma_1^*$ and $w_1 \in \Sigma_2^*$, then (3)–(6) ensure that, in fact, $w_1 \in L_1$ and $w_2 \in L_2$ so that $w_1 w_2 \in L_1.L_2$, as required. We have proved the following theorem.

THEOREM 6.3: If L_1 and L_2 are languages generated by Post systems, then so is language $L_1.L_2$. Alternative formulation: The class of languages generated by Post systems is closed under concatenation.

In addition, it can be shown that the class of languages generated by Post systems is closed under intersection and Kleene closure (see Exercises 6.3.1 and 6.3.2). On the other hand, it is not closed under (relative) complementation or symmetric difference, although we shall delay the demonstration of these negative results until a later chapter (see Theorem 12.7 and Exercise 12.4.3).

§6.4 The Class of Languages Generated by Post Systems Is Identical to the Class of Turing-Acceptable Languages

In the discussion and exercises of the preceding section we showed that the class of languages generated by Post systems is closed under certain language-forming operations, namely, union, concatenation, intersection, Kleene closure, and reversal. Now, as it turns out, the family of Turing-acceptable languages is closed under just these operations. Moreover, we signaled the reader that the family of languages generated by Post systems is not closed under certain other language-forming operations, namely, (relative) complementation and symmetric difference. As it turns out, the family of Turing-acceptable languages is not closed under these operations either, although we have yet to show that. These facts by themselves would suggest some link between Post systems and Turing machines with respect to formal languages. In fact, we can show that, with regard to formal languages, Post systems and Turing machines are equivalent notions. (Theorems 6.1(a) and 6.1(b) together with Paradigm Interreducibility tell us as much already.) More precisely, we have

---

THEOREM 6.4: Let L be a formal language. Then L is generated by some Post system if and only if L is accepted by some Turing machine.

PROOF ($\Rightarrow$) This direction is relatively easy. Namely, suppose that L is generated by Post system $S = \langle \Sigma, \Gamma, \Theta, \Delta, \Pi \rangle$. We give an informal description of a nondeterministic, multitape Turing machine M that accepts L. Starting with word $w \in \Sigma^*$ on its input tape, M first writes out a representation of axiom set Δ and production set Π on one of its worktapes. Afterward, M nondeterministically selects an axiom α from among those in Δ. Next, M nondeterministically selects some production in Π and nondeterministically verifies that axiom α is a substitution instance of the left-hand side of the chosen production. (Why is this verification nondeterministic?) M then deterministically produces the corresponding substitution instance of its right-hand side as the next line of the simulated derivation. This process of choosing a production and then producing a corresponding substitution instance as the next line of a simulated derivation is iterated. After each iteration, the derived string is compared with input word w. If they are identical, then M writes an accepting 1 on its output tape before halting. It should be sufficiently clear that M accepts L, which is thereby shown to be Turing-acceptable.

($\Leftarrow$) The other direction involves the informal description of a Post system that simulates a Turing machine. We leave the details to Exercise 6.4.1.   Q.E.D.

In fact, defining $time_S(n)$ in terms of the length of derivations within Post system S, one can prove

---

THEOREM 6.5: The Post system model of computation and the nondeterministic Turing machine model of computation are polynomially related. That is, any given language L is generated by some Post system in polynomial time if and only if L is accepted by some nondeterministic, single-tape Turing machine in polynomial time.

PROOF See Exercise 6.4.2.

It is natural to ask whether L's being generated in polynomial time by some Post system implies that it is accepted in polynomial time by some *deterministic* Turing machine as well. At present, the answer to this question remains unknown. However, as we shall see in Chapter 8, it seems probable that the answer is no.

§6.5 Language Recognition and Post Systems

What we are calling Post systems were first described by Emil Post in unpublished writings dating from the 1920s (see [Davis 1965] and [Post 1943]). Post himself introduced a number of such ideas in the course of his investigations of logical systems, which again reflects the fact that the theory of computability has its origins in the work of mathematical logicians on the foundations of mathematics (cf. the discussion of §4.6). In fact, Post's own systems were slightly more general than those of Definition 6.1. He permitted productions of the form

$$\alpha_1, \alpha_2, \ldots, \alpha_n \to \beta$$

where $\alpha_i, \beta \in (\Sigma \cup \Gamma \cup \Theta)^*$ for $1 \le i \le n$. Our productions as described in Definition 6.1 amount to a restriction to a single premise on the left so that $n = 1$ invariably. (Incidentally, [Post 1936] sketches an alternative model of computation very much like Turing's.)

In §6.1 we showed that Post systems, as defined in Definition 6.1, can compute number-theoretic functions and can accept or, as we put it, *generate* languages. What about language recognition? Is there some sense in which Post systems can *recognize* languages? And can we arrange things so that language recognition on the part of Post systems is equivalent to language recognition on the part of Turing machines (Definitions 1.4 and 2.11), Markov algorithms (Definition 4.4), and register machines (Definition 5.5)? The answer is yes. But before proposing a definition of language recognition on the part of Post systems, we first consider, and reject, an idea that may initially seem promising.

Namely, let us briefly consider taking Post system S to recognize language $L \subseteq \Sigma^*$ provided that

(1) any word $w \in L$ is derivable in S and

(2) any word $w \notin L$ is not derivable in S.

In other words, why not let acceptance mean derivability (the yes-answer) and rejection mean non-derivability (the no-answer)? There are several problems with this suggestion. First, the reader should be able to see that this would obliterate any distinction between Post-acceptability (Post-system-generability) and Post-recognizability: The Post-recognizable languages would coincide with the Post-acceptable (Post-system-generated) languages. More to the point perhaps, just what sort of no-answer is nonderivability anyway? (We have been over this ground before, but it bears repeating.) If one has tried for five minutes to generate word $w \in \Sigma^*$ within Post system S without success, what does this mean? Is this already S' no-answer or should one try a little longer? We can agree that this proposal is not workable.

As for what will work, there are many possibilities. Consider adding the two symbols $\vdash$ and $\nvdash$ to terminal alphabet Σ. Now we let Post system S recognize language $L \subseteq \Sigma^*$, say, provided that

(1) for any word $w \in L$, string $\vdash w$, but not string $\nvdash w$, is derivable in S and

(2) for any word $w \notin L$, string $\nvdash w$, but not string $\vdash w$, is derivable in S.

Note that from (1) and (2) it follows that

(3) for any word w over Σ exactly one of $\vdash w$ and $\nvdash w$ is derivable in S.

This, in turn, means that, despite its nondeterministic character, a Post system S that recognizes L in the sense of (1)–(2) will afford us a decision procedure for membership in L. To see this, suppose that w is an arbitrary word over Σ. We wish to use S to determine whether $w \in L$. Now, the derivations of S can be effectively enumerated. First, list all derivations of length 0, then all derivations of length 1, then all derivations of length 2, and so on. By (3), eventually one of these derivations will have either

$\vdash w$ or $\nvdash w$ as its last line. If the former, then by (1) we know that $w \in L$; if the latter, then by (2) we know that $w \notin L$.

EXAMPLE 6.5.1 As a simple example of a Post system functioning in the role of language recognizer, consider the system S defined as

$$\Sigma' = \{a, b, \vdash, \nvdash\}$$

$$\Gamma = \varnothing$$

$$\Theta = \{V_1\}$$

$$\Delta = \{\vdash \varepsilon, \vdash a, \vdash b\}$$

$$\Pi = \{\vdash V_1 \rightarrow \vdash aV_1a, \quad \text{(i)}$$

$$\vdash V_1 \rightarrow \vdash bV_1b, \quad \text{(ii)}$$

$$\vdash V_1 \rightarrow \nvdash aV_1b, \quad \text{(iii)}$$

$$\vdash V_1 \rightarrow \nvdash bV_1a, \quad \text{(iv)}$$

$$\nvdash V_1 \rightarrow \nvdash aV_1a, \quad \text{(v)}$$

$$\nvdash V_1 \rightarrow \nvdash bV_1b, \quad \text{(vi)}$$

$$\nvdash V_1 \rightarrow \nvdash aV_1b, \quad \text{(vii)}$$

$$\nvdash V_1 \rightarrow \nvdash bV_1a\} \quad \text{(viii)}$$

We claim that S recognizes $\{w \in \Sigma^* | w = w^R\}$ with $\Sigma = \{a, b\}$. See Exercise 6.5.7.

DEFINITION 6.5: Let L be a language over alphabet Σ. Then *Post system* $S = \langle \Sigma \cup \{\vdash, \nvdash\}, \Gamma, \Theta, \Delta, \Pi \rangle$ *recognizes language L over* Σ provided that both
(1) for any word $w \in L$, string $\vdash w$, but not string $\nvdash w$, is derivable in S and
(2) for any word $w \notin L$, string $\nvdash w$, but not string $\vdash w$, is derivable in S.

§6.6 What Is a Model of Computation?

In §1.1 we took up the question of what we mean by "computation." We identified three computational paradigms: the function computation paradigm, the language recognition paradigm, and the transduction paradigm. Afterward, we considered the most important model of computation, namely, the Turing machine model. It was shown how Turing's machines may be used to model each of the three computational paradigms. We close this chapter by briefly considering the question of just what is meant by a "model of computation."

One conspicuous sense of the term "model" within physics and engineering is that provided by actual physical models such as model airplanes or model ships. Related to this, a map of Australia may be described as a model of that continent. In each case, the physical model simplifies drastically the physical phenomenon being modeled and accounts only for certain of its most important features. This tendency toward simplification means that no mere model is going to reflect reality with anything like perfect accuracy. In this sense, all models are necessarily flawed. Nonetheless, in the case of physical models such as a map or a model airplane, there exists a certain *isomorphism* between model and modeled: a 1–1 correspondence between points on a map and geographic points on the Australian continent, say, that is *structure-preserving*—in the present case, preserving properties involving distance and relative position.

Of course, the models of computation that we have considered in Chapters 1 through 6 are not physical models in the sense in which an architect's model, say, is a physical model of a proposed building. Rather, they are *mathematical models*. In the typical case, the model of computation in question was characterized set-theoretically as the parameterized description of a class of abstract machines. For example, the single-tape Turing machine model was described as a quintuple $\langle Q, \Sigma, \Gamma, q_{init}, \delta \rangle$. Each of the five elements is a *parameter* whose values must satisfy certain restrictions with respect to the values of the other four. Each choice of five permissible values for the parameters amounts to a new Turing machine. The Turing machine model of computation, then, consists of the class of all such quintuples. Similarly, the Markov algorithm model of computation may be characterized set-theoretically as a class of triples $\langle \Sigma, \Gamma, \Pi \rangle$ satisfying certain conditions. The register machine model of computation becomes a class of pairs $\langle \Re, \Im \rangle$, and Post's model becomes a class of quintuples $\langle \Sigma, \Gamma, \Theta, \Delta, \Pi \rangle$.

The reader who finds the foregoing characterization of a model of computation less than satisfying is not alone. What would be more fulfilling—but is much more difficult to provide—is a set of criteria for deciding *which features* of computational activity wind up as parameters in the first place. In other words, the set-theoretic characterization of *model of computation* seems somewhat after the fact, when what is needed is a "genetic" account—one that gets at why certain aspects of computation get modeled while others are omitted.

Of course, the easy answer here is that it is the essential aspects of computational activity that find their way into models of computation. But "essential" here is, evidently, a value-laden term. Early twentieth-century accountants arrayed their reckonings vertically rather than horizontally and used decimal notation exclusively. Yet these aspects of their activity are not reflected in any of the models of computation that we have considered. What does seem to have survived into the Turing machine model, say, is the crab-like character of computation with pen and paper: What is next examined or next (over) written is most likely directly adjacent to what was *just* examined or *just* written in the previous computation step. This is perhaps the most salient feature of Turing's model with its purely sequential access to memory. Apparently, it is what most impressed Turing about computation, and no doubt historical and cultural factors were at play here. If Turing had been Chinese instead of English, he might have proposed something more like the register machine model, with its primitive incrementation operation $R_i{+}{+}$, so suggestive of the basic operation on an abacus.

Perhaps it should be our goal to establish which features are common to all models that we have considered. Then we could at least secure a necessary core of features belonging to any mathematical model of computation. So, for example, they all seem to assume some input, for which some (range of) output—possibly null—is then determined. On deterministic models, this output, if it exists, is unique. But wait. In saying this, we have overlooked the Post system model, which lacks anything that would qualify as input. As for the determinism/nondeterminism issue, some of our models are, in some sense or other, deterministic and others are nondeterministic. (In fact, most of our models admit of a nondeterministic variant.) And then we have already spoken of the reasons why logicians sought to secure the connection between mathematical proof and computation. Since pattern matching and substitution play so important a role in proof, one comes to understand why these operations are so central to the analyses of Markov and Post. On the other hand, pattern matching and substitution are features of neither the Turing machine model nor the register machine model. In short, it is not going to be easy to find any features common to each and every one of the models that we have considered.

In the end, the most that can be said is that the various models that we have considered exhibit certain *family resemblances*. Just as in the case of a human family, no one physical feature, say, is likely to be shared by each and every member of that family; similarly, no feature is common to each and every one of the models of computation that we have considered. Yet certain features are observed throughout a certain subgroup of these models, while another subgroup shares some other feature. In the end, it is probably impossible to explain why these models should all count as models of computation without recourse to sociological and cultural factors. But then this will not be surprising if one remembers that what is being modeled—a certain sort of cognitive activity on the part of human beings—is itself a product of the interplay of these same sociological and cultural factors.

Finally, we should like to address again the reader who may be troubled by the proliferation of models that have been presented. In particular, we would suggest that this proliferation should not become a source of doubt. After all, the scientist's motivation for introducing mathematical models of any natural phenomenon is, on the one hand, prediction and, on the other hand, explanation. With respect to prediction, the considerable variety of our computational models need be of no real concern, since, as our equivalence results have now shown, all of these models ultimately come down to one and the same thing—that is, they all make precisely the same predictions with regard to which functions, say, will be computable. And as for explanation, is there any reason to expect that the phenomenological diversity of mathematical models of computation will be less impressive than the diversity of scientific explanation generally?

EXERCISES FOR §6.1

6.1.1. Let $\Sigma = \{a, b\}$. Let S_1 and S_2 be the following two strings over $\Sigma \cup \{V_1, V_2, V_3\}$.

$$abV_1baV_2aV_3 \quad \text{and} \quad abaV_2aV_1aV_3$$

Which of the word pairs in (a) through (c) below are corresponding substitution instances of S_1 and S_2? If the given word pair does consist of corresponding substitution instances, say what substitution has been made for each of variables V_1, V_2, and V_3.
(a) *ababbbabab* and *ababaabbab*
(b) *abbabbaa* and *ababbaaa*
(c) *abababbaab* and *abaaa*

6.1.2. Present a derivation of word *aaabbb* within the Post system of Example 6.1.1.

6.1.3. (a) Present a derivation of word *aaaab* within the Post system of Example 6.1.2.
(b) What is the shortest word derivable within the Post system of Example 6.1.2.

6.1.4. Derive equation $\Psi(111, 1111) = 111111$ within the Post system of Example 6.1.4.

6.1.5. (a) Derive equation $\Psi(111, 111) = 11111$ within the Post system of Example 6.1.5.
(b) What is the appropriate interpretation of this equation?

6.1.6. **hwk** (a) Consider the Post system below.

$$\Sigma = \{a\}$$
$$\Gamma = \varnothing$$
$$\Theta = \{V_1\}$$
$$\Delta = \{\varepsilon\}$$
$$\Pi = \{V_1 \to V_1aa\}$$

Present derivations of words *aaaa* and *aaaaaaaa*. What language is generated by this Post system?

(b) Modify the Post system of (a) so as to obtain a Post system that generates the language $\{(ab)^{3n}|n \geq 0\}$. Present a derivation of $(ab)^9$ in this new system.

6.1.7. Consider the Post system below.

$$\Sigma = \{a, b\}$$

$$\Gamma = \varnothing$$

$$\Theta = \{V_1\}$$

$$\Delta = \{\varepsilon\}$$

$$\Pi = \{V_1 \rightarrow aV_1b, V_1 \rightarrow bV_1a\}$$

(a) Present a derivation of $aababb$ within this Post system.

(b) What language over $\{a, b\}$ is generated by this Post system? (*Useful notation:* For $w \in \Sigma^*$ with $\Sigma = \{a, b\}$, let w^{-1} be the result of simultaneously replacing every occurrence of a in w by b and every occurrence of b by a.)

6.1.8. (a) Consider the Post system defined as follows.

$$\Sigma = \{a, b\}$$

$$\Gamma = \{A, B\}$$

$$\Theta = \{V_1\}$$

$$\Delta = \{AaB\}$$

$$\Pi = \{AV_1 \rightarrow AaaV_1, \quad \text{(i)}$$

$$V_1 B \rightarrow V_1 bbB, \quad \text{(ii)}$$

$$AV_1 \rightarrow V_1, \quad \text{(iii)}$$

$$V_1 B \rightarrow V_1\} \quad \text{(iv)}$$

You are asked to present a derivation of word $aaabb$ from this Post system. You should indicate which of the productions (i)–(iv) is being applied in each step of the derivation.

(b) What language is accepted by the Post system of (a)?

(c) Modify the Post system of (b) so as to obtain a new Post system that accepts the language $\{a^{3n}b^{2m}|n \geq 1, m \geq 0\}$.

6.1.9. (a) Find a Post system that generates the language $\{ww^R|w \in \Sigma^*\}$ with $\Sigma\{a, b\}$. This is, of course, just the language of even-length palindromes.

(b) Modify your solution to the previous question so as to obtain a Post system that generates the language $\{w|w \in \Sigma^* \& w = w^R\}$ with $\Sigma = \{a, b\}$. This is, of course, just the language of all palindromes.

(c) Find a Post system that generates the language $\{ww|w \in \Sigma^*\}$ with $\Sigma = \{a, b\}$. (This one is a little harder than the preceding ones. Note that $V_1 V_1 \rightarrow V_1 a V_1 a$ does not satisfy the restrictions on Post system productions.)

6.1.10. (a) What language is generated by any Post system $S = \langle \Sigma, \Gamma, \Theta, \Delta, \Pi, \rangle$, where $\Delta = \varnothing$?

(b) Consider the Post system $S = \langle \Sigma, \Gamma, \Theta, \Delta, \Pi \rangle$ with

$$\Sigma = \{a, b\}$$

$$\Gamma = \varnothing$$

$$\Theta = \{V_1\}$$

$$\Delta = \{\varepsilon\}$$

$$\Pi = \{V_1 \rightarrow V_1 a, V_1 \rightarrow V_1 b\}$$

What language is generated by S?

6.1.11. ^hwk **(a)** Present a derivation of word $a^3 b^3 c^3$ in the Post system of Example 6.1.3.

(b) To better appreciate the need for nonterminal alphabet $\Gamma = \{B, C\}$ in the Post system of Example 6.1.3, let us consider the consequences of omitting nonterminal symbols B and C. Namely, consider the

Post system S' defined as

$$\Sigma = \{a, b, c\}$$

$$\Gamma = \varnothing$$

$$\Theta = \{V_1, V_2\}$$

$$\Delta = \{\varepsilon\}$$

$$\Pi = \{V_1 \rightarrow aV_1bc, V_1cbV_2 \rightarrow V_1bcV_2\}$$

Show that the language generated by S' is not $\{a^n b^n c^n | n \geq 0\}$ by deriving in S' some word not of the form $a^n b^n c^n$. What language is generated by S'?

6.1.12. **(a)** Design a Post system that computes the ternary number-theoretic function defined as

$$g(n, m, k) = \begin{cases} k + 1 & \text{if } n \text{ is even} \\ k - 1 & \text{if } n \text{ is odd} \end{cases}$$

Note that argument m plays no role whatever in determining the value of g for triple $\langle n, m, k \rangle$. Also, function g is partial in that $g(n, m, 0)$ is undefined whenever n is odd.

(b) Use the Post system of (a) to derive the symbol string

$$\Psi(111, 11, 1) = 11$$

reflecting the fact that $g(2, 1, 0) = 1$.

6.1.13. **(a)** Design a Post system that computes the total, binary number-theoretic function defined as

$$f(n, m) = (m + 2) \bmod 5$$

Note that argument n plays no role in

determining the value of f for the pair $\langle n, m \rangle$.

(b) Use the Post system of (a) to derive the symbol string

$$\Psi(111, 111111111) = 1$$

reflecting the fact that $f(2, 8) = 0$.

6.1.14. **(a)** In Definition 6.1 we required that no variable occur more than once on the left of any production. But productions violating this restriction could be very useful. For instance, a production such as

$$V_1 V_1 \rightarrow \cdots$$

were it to be permitted, would be applicable only to computation words of the form ww. Show that one can get the effect of such productions using only productions that are strictly in accordance with Definition 6.1.

(b) In Definition 6.1 we required that no variable occur more than once on the right of any production. But productions violating this restriction could be very useful. For instance, where $\alpha_1, \alpha_2, \beta_1, \beta_2$, and β_3 are strings over $\Sigma \cup \Gamma \cup (\Theta \backslash \{V_1\})$, a production such as

$$\alpha_1 V_1 \alpha_2 \rightarrow \beta_1 V_1 \beta_2 V_1 \beta_3$$

were it permitted, would permit the simultaneous substitution of one and the same substring at two distinct locations within the current computation word. Show that one can get the effect of such productions using only productions that are strictly in accordance with Definition 6.1.

EXERCISES FOR §6.2

6.2.1. Derive the equation $\Psi(111, 11) = 11111$ in the Post system S_h of Example 6.2.1, reflecting the fact that $h(2, 1) = f(g(2, 1)) = succ(2 + 1) = 4$.

6.2.2. Complete case (v) in the proof of Theorem 6.1(a). In other words, show how to construct a Post system S_h that computes function $h = \mathbf{Pr}[f, g]$, say, given Post systems S_f and S_g computing f and g, respectively.

6.2.3. Let S_f be the Post system defined as

$$\Sigma = \{1, \Psi, (,), =, ,\}$$

$$\Gamma = \varnothing$$

$$\Theta = \{V_1, V_2\}$$

(Axiom) $\Delta = \{\Psi(1) = 111\}$

(Production) $\Pi = \{\Psi(V_1) = V_2 \rightarrow$

$$\Psi(V_1 1) = V_2 1\}$$

It is easily seen that S_f computes the total, unary function defined by $f(n) = n + 2$.

Furthermore, let g be the partial, ternary function of Exercise 6.1.12, defined there as

$$g(n, m, k) = \begin{cases} k + 1 & \text{if } n \text{ is even} \\ k - 1 & \text{if } n \text{ is odd} \end{cases}$$

Let S_g be the Post system of the solution to Exercise 6.1.12, which computes function g.

Finally, let $h = \mathbf{Pr}[f, g]$ be the partial, binary function defined by primitive recursion from f and g so that

(i) $h(n, 0) = f(n)$

(ii) $h(n, m + 1) = g(n, m, h(n, m))$

(a) Having completed Exercise 6.2.2, apply your construction (Exercise 6.2.2) for case (v) in the proof of Theorem 6.1(a) to Post systems S_f and S_g so as to obtain a new Post system S_h computing function $h = \mathbf{Pr}[f, g]$ defined by (i)–(ii).

(b) Using the Post system S_h of (a), give a derivation of the string $\Psi(1111, 11) = 11111$, reflecting the fact that $h(3, 1) = 4$.

6.2.4. Complete case (vi) in the proof of Theorem 6.1(a). In other words, show how to construct a Post system S_h that computes function $h = \mathbf{Mn}[f]$, say, given a Post system S_f computing f.

6.2.5. Let f be the total, binary number-theoretic function defined as $f(n, m) =_{\text{def.}} (m + 2) \bmod 5$. Let S_f be the Post system of the solution to Exercise 6.1.13, which computes function f.

(a) Having completed Exercise 6.2.4, apply your construction (Exercise 6.2.4) for case (vi) in the proof of Theorem 6.1(a) to Post system S_f so as to obtain a new Post system S_h computing function $h = \mathbf{Mn}[f]$ defined by

$$h(n) = \mu m[f(n, m) = 0 \ \&$$

$$(\forall k < m) f(n, k) \text{ is defined}]$$

(b) Using the Post system S_h of (a), give a derivation of the string $\Psi(111) = 1111$, reflecting the fact that $h(2) = 3$.

EXERCISES FOR §6.3

6.3.1. Show that the class of languages generated by Post systems is closed under intersection.

6.3.2. Show that the class of languages generated by Post systems is closed under Kleene closure.

6.3.3. [hwk] Show that if language L is generated by some Post system, then so is language $L^R =$ $\{w^R | w \in L\}$. (*Hint:* What changes to the Post system of Example 6.1.3 will yield a new system generating language $\{c^n b^n a^n | n \geq 0\}$?)

EXERCISES FOR §6.4

6.4.1. Complete the proof of Theorem 6.4.

6.4.2. Prove Theorem 6.5. (*Hint:* Reexamine the proof of Theorem 6.4.)

EXERCISES FOR §6.5 (END-OF-CHAPTER REVIEW EXERCISES)

6.5.1. [hwk] Suppose that Post system S generates each of the strings below, among others.

$$\Psi(11, 111) = 111$$

$$\Psi(111, 11) = 111$$

$$\Psi(11, 11111) = 11111$$

$$\Psi(11, 11) = 11$$

$$\Psi(1111, 1) = 1111$$

This at least suggests that S computes what number-theoretic function?

6.5.2. Suppose that Post system S generates each of the strings below, among others.

$$\Psi(1) = 11$$

$$\Psi(11) = 111$$

$$\Psi(111) = 11111$$

$$\Psi(1111) = 111111111$$

$$\Psi(11111) = 1111111111111111111$$

This at least suggests that S computes what number-theoretic function?

6.5.3. [hwk] For each of the following number-theoretic functions, find a Post system that computes it.

(a) the binary function χ_{less_eq} defined by

$$\chi_{less\_eq}(n, m) = \begin{cases} 1 & \text{if } n \le m \\ 0 & \text{otherwise} \end{cases}$$

Function χ_{less_eq} is, of course, just the characteristic function of binary relation $\le$ (cf. Example 3.2.1).

(b) the unary function sg defined by

$$sg(n) = \begin{cases} 1 & \text{if } n > 0 \\ 0 & \text{otherwise} \end{cases}$$

(c) the unary function $pred$ defined by

$$pred(n) = \begin{cases} n - 1 & \text{if } n > 0 \\ 0 & \text{otherwise} \end{cases}$$

(d) the binary function $absdif(n, m)$ defined by

$$absdif(n, m) = \begin{cases} n - m & \text{if } m \le n \\ m - n & \text{otherwise} \end{cases}$$

6.5.4. (a) Present a Post system that generates the language of all binary numerals. As usual, leading 0s are not permitted unless the numeral in question is 0 itself.

(b) Present a Post system that generates the language of balanced strings of parentheses

$$\{\varepsilon, (\,), ((\,)), (\,)(\,), (((\,))), (\,)(\,)(\,),$$
$$((\,))(\,), (\,)((\,)), \dots\}$$

6.5.5. Suppose that Post system $S = \langle \Sigma, \Gamma, \Theta, \Delta, \Pi \rangle$ generates language L. That is, $L = L(S)$. Show that there exists a Post system S' generating L such that no production of S' is of the form

$$\alpha \to \beta$$

with α consisting solely of variables.

6.5.6. Suppose that Post system S generates language L with $\varepsilon \in L$. Show that there exists a Post system S' whose only axiom is ε such that S' generates L.

6.5.7. (a) Present a derivation of string $\vdash ababbaba$ within the Post system S of Example 6.5.1.

(b) Present a derivation of string $\vdash ababa$ within S.

(c) Present a derivation of string $\nvdash aababba$ within S.

(d) Given any palindrome w over $\{a, b\}$, give the length of a derivation in S of the string $\vdash w$. Your answer may be expressed in terms of $|w|$.

(e) Given any nonpalindrome w over $\{a, b\}$, give the length of a derivation in S of the string $\nvdash w$. Again, your answer may be expressed in terms of $|w|$.

6.5.8. **(a)** Using Definition 6.5, design a Post system S that recognizes the language $\{w \in \Sigma^* \mid n_a(w) = n_b(w)\}$ with $\Sigma = \{a, b, c\}$.

  (b) Present a derivation within S of the string $\vdash ababc$.

  (c) Present a derivation within S of the string $\nvdash aabcbbb$.

  (d) Present a derivation within S of the string $\nvdash aaabcbbb$.

6.5.9. **(Post Systems and Transduction).** We have not yet described how the Post system model of computation might implement the trans-duction paradigm of §1.1. To the extent that nothing in our description of Post systems appears to correspond to *input*, it may not be obvious how to do this. The broad outlines of one way in which this might be done will be implicit in our specification of a Post system $S = \langle \Sigma, \Gamma, \Theta, \Delta, \Pi \rangle$ implementing word reversal.

Design a Post system $S = \langle \Sigma, \Gamma, \Theta, \varnothing, \Pi \rangle$ such that, for any word w over Σ, the induced system $S_w = \langle \Sigma, \Gamma, \Theta, \{w\}, \Pi \rangle$ generates language $\{w^{\mathrm{R}}\}$.

Chapter 7

The Vector Machine Model of Parallel Computation (Optional)

§7.1 What Is Parallel Computation?

Parallel computation or *parallel processing* occurs when multiple processors are active simultaneously over the course of a computation. In general, the number of processors active during such a computation will vary over the course of the computation: At one point there may be 15 active processors while, later on, those active may number only 7. The term "concurrent programming" or "parallel programming" is used to describe the writing of programs that direct such simultaneous processing. Programming languages such as Concurrent C and Concurrent PROLOG are intended as vehicles for concurrent programming.

A *parallel computer* is one that is capable of parallel processing. Parallel computers with tens or hundreds of processors are available commercially. Researchers are now working on computers with thousands of processors. All of the machine models that we have considered thus far are intended as models of sequential processing—that is, conventional processing involving a single serial processor. This remark holds even for the multitape Turing machine model, as was emphasized in the discussion surrounding Remark 2.3.1. Our purpose in this chapter is to present one rather elegant model of parallel processing. That model is known as the *vector machine model*. We shall delay our description of vector machines until the next section and continue now with an introductory discussion of parallel computation. (A second parallel model, known as the *Boolean circuit model*, is developed in Exercise 7.7.6.)

One contrasts *sequential algorithms* with *parallel algorithms*. The interest of the latter lies in completing a task and obtaining important results very quickly. For instance, forecast models must frequently predict an event only hours or even minutes before that event occurs. In such a situation there is frequently no time to undertake the lengthy computations required in order to obtain the result using a sequential algorithm. Instead, one opts for a parallel algorithm implemented on some multiprocessing supercomputer so as to obtain the needed prediction with sufficient speed.

We shall illustrate the concept of parallel computation with a now standard example. Namely, we shall consider sequential and parallel versions of the so-called *mergesort* algorithm. As usual, sorting a sequence of natural numbers, say, will mean rearranging them so that they are in increasing order. For example, if the input sequence is

$$56 \quad 45 \quad 21 \quad 34 \quad 78 \quad 33 \quad 48 \quad 2 \tag{7.1.1}$$

then the result of sorting this input sequence will be

$$2 \quad 21 \quad 33 \quad 34 \quad 45 \quad 48 \quad 56 \quad 78 \tag{7.1.2}$$

It will prove convenient to assume that the length n of any input sequence is some power of 2. In particular, we shall assume that $n = 8$ throughout the ensuing discussion.

Sequential Mergesort

We suggest thinking of the input sequence (7.1.1) as given to us as a sequence of eight cards, each with a single natural number written on it. Next, we take these cards two at a time from the left and, by comparing, create a new sequence of four ordered pairs. In the case of (7.1.1), numbers 56 and 45 are compared first. Since 45 is the smaller of the two, the pair $\langle 45, 56 \rangle$ becomes the first of these four pairs. The result of three more such comparisons is the sequence

$$45 \quad 56 \quad \quad 21 \quad 34 \quad \quad 33 \quad 78 \quad \quad 2 \quad 48 \quad \quad \text{(four comparisons)} \tag{7.1.3}$$

Next, we take these four ordered pairs and, through comparisons, create two ordered quadruples. To begin, the first element of the first pair, namely, 45, is compared with the first element of the second pair, namely, 21 (see Figure 7.1.1(a)). Since 21 is the smaller, it becomes the first element of a new quadruple of numbers. Next, 45 is compared with what is now left of the second pair, namely, 34 (see Figure 7.1.1(b)). So 34 becomes the second element of our quadruple. Since nothing remains now of the second pair, the first pair is now appended to 21 and 34 to become the first of two quadruples. Repeating this process for the third and fourth ordered pairs, which incidentally requires the full complement of three comparisons this time, gives the new sequence consisting of two ordered quadruples.

$$21 \quad 34 \quad 45 \quad 56 \quad \quad 2 \quad 33 \quad 48 \quad 78 \quad \quad \text{(five comparisons)}$$

Finally, we reduce the two ordered quadruples to a single ordered eight-tuple. First, the first member of the first quadruple is compared with the first member of the second quadruple. Since 2 is the smaller of 22 and 2, it becomes the first member of our new eight-tuple. Six more comparisons yield the sequence (7.1.2).

It is reasonable to count each comparison here as one step of our sequential mergesort algorithm. Consequently, the number of *sequential steps* overall in the case of input sequence (7.1.1) is $4 + (2 + 3) + 7 = 16$. Worst case, sorting an input sequence of length 8 requires $4 + (3 + 3) + 7 = 8/2 + 2 \cdot (8/2 - 1) + (8 - 1)$ steps. Moreover, we note that, in the case of sequence (7.1.1), a total of $\log_2 8 = 3$ merge steps are required.

(a)

Merge Step 1: eight one-tuples $\Rightarrow$ four two-tuples

Merge Step 2: four two-tuples $\Rightarrow$ two four-tuples

Merge Step 3: two four-tuples $\Rightarrow$ one eight-tuple

(b)

Also, each merge step involves fewer than $n = 8$—that is, O(n)—comparisons for a total of

$$\underbrace{\text{O}(n) \text{ steps} + \text{O}(n) \text{ steps} + \text{O}(n) \text{ steps}}_{\log_2 n = 3 \text{ times}}$$

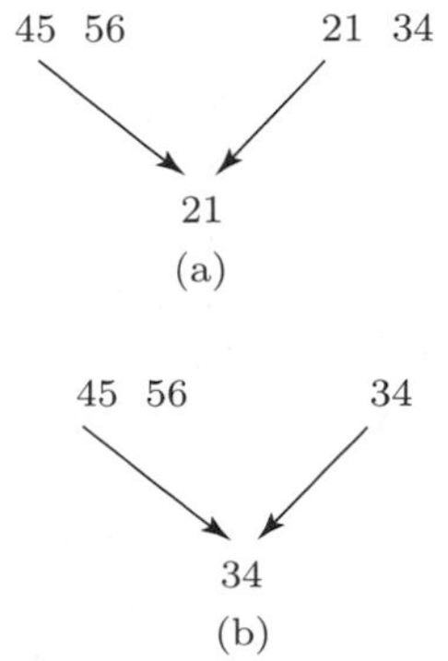

Figure 7.1.1

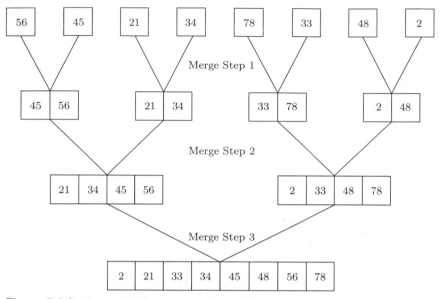

Figure 7.1.2   Sequential Mergesort as a Binary Tree.

In general, for input sequence of length n, sequential mergesort will require

$$\underbrace{O(n) \text{ steps} + O(n) \text{ steps} + \cdots + O(n) \text{ steps}}_{\log_2 n \text{ times}}$$

steps, or $O(n \log_2 n)$ steps, worst case.

It is useful to picture the sorting process as a binary tree with three levels, one for each merge step, as shown in Figure 7.1.2. Note that, during Merge Step 1, the generation of each of the four ordered pairs depends in no way upon the generation of the other three. Similarly, during Merge Step 2, generating the first quadruple is quite independent of the process of generating the second quadruple. This *data independence* suggests that the work of Merge Step 1 might be distributed over four concurrent processes. Similarly, the work of Merge Step 2 might be assigned to two processors executing concurrently. Therein we have the essence of the parallel algorithm to be considered next.

Parallel Mergesort

We now show how the sequence (7.1.1) can be sorted using a parallel algorithm requiring 15 processors. We shall represent a parallel machine executing the parallel mergesort algorithm as a configuration of processors whose structure is essentially that of the tree of Figure 7.1.2. Now, however, each node of the tree of Figure 7.1.3 represents one of 15 processors. Sixteen *communication channels* are represented by arrows.

- To begin, each natural number within input sequence (7.1.1) is communicated to one of the eight processors at the very top of the tree via a shared communication channel. Each of these eight processors merely passes its number downward to the processor below it. This is the extent of the processing performed by the eight processors corresponding to the top level of the tree.

- The processing of the processors corresponding to each of the remaining seven nodes of the tree may be described as follows. Each such processor receives one number from each of the two processors located above it. These two numbers are compared and the smaller one is communicated downward, after which the processor requests another number from above, preferably from the processor that supplied the smaller number. Only if the latter processor can supply no number will a number from the other processor be accepted.

- Ultimately, the processor at the root of the tree communicates the sequence (7.1.2) by way of a single output channel.

We note that each of the 15 processors processes and communicates downward either 1, 2, 4, or 8 numbers. On the other hand, this processing involves zero comparisons on the part of the processors at the top level, exactly one comparison at the next level down, three comparisons worst case at the next level down, and, finally, seven comparisons worst case at the root. These values are indicated in the circles representing the 15 processors in Figure 7.1.3. Since the processing of any active processors is concurrent, one speaks of *parallel steps* of the algorithm. We shall take a parallel step to be one parallel comparison—that is, the collection of synchronous comparisons carried out by the currently active processors. In general, at any given step of the algorithm, numbers are being compared by processors on several levels. However, the very first parallel (comparison) step involves only the four 2/1 processors (see Figure 7.1.3). The second parallel comparison step involves only the two 4/3 processors. Only with the third comparison step does the single 8/7 processor become active, at which point the two 4/3 processors

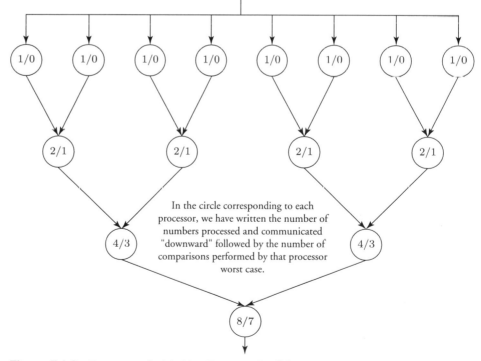

In the circle corresponding to each processor, we have written the number of numbers processed and communicated "downward" followed by the number of comparisons performed by that processor worst case.

Figure 7.1.3 Processors of a Machine Executing Parallel Mergesort.

remain active. Moreover, the seven subsequent comparisons at the root dominate so that the parallel machine of Figure 7.1.3 requires $2 + 7 = 9$, which is $O(n)$, parallel steps in order to sort $n = 8$ numbers.

Analogously, a parallel machine with 31 processors can sort an input sequence of length 16 in $3 + 15 = 18$ steps, worst case, using the parallel mergesort algorithm. The processors of such a machine will be configured as a binary tree with 16 leaves at the top, 8 nodes at the next level, 4 at the next, and so forth. In general, given an input sequence of length n, a machine consisting of $2n - 1$ processors, can perform parallel mergesort in $[(\log_2 n) - 1] + (n - 1)$ parallel steps worst case. Or, more succinctly, an input sequence of length n can be sorted by a machine having $O(n)$ processors in $O(n)$ parallel steps. It is standard in this context to identify the space requirements of a parallel algorithm with the number of processors used over the course of the algorithm's execution. Thus, parallel mergesort can be performed in $O(n)$ time using $O(n)$ space, where n gives the length of the input sequence.

Before continuing, it is worth emphasizing a certain point with regard to Figures 7.1.1 and 7.1.2. Superficially, those two figures are quite similar, consisting of two trees of identical structure. However, we are interpreting them quite differently.

- Consideration of nodes and arrows in Figure 7.1.2 from left to right and from top to bottom corresponds to the sequential order of the comparisons within the sequential mergesort algorithm that we discussed first. That is, Figure 7.1.2 is to be interpreted as a sort of flowchart for the sequential mergesort algorithm.

- Figure 7.1.3, on the other hand, is a graphic representation of the configuration of processors within a parallel machine capable of executing the parallel mergesort algorithm that we discussed next. The nodes of this second tree represent processors, and the arrows represent communication links between them. Thus, we are interpreting Figure 7.1.3 as the representation of the architecture of a certain parallel machine. Nothing in Figure 7.1.3 directly corresponds to one parallel step of the parallel mergesort algorithm. Thus, Figure 7.1.3 is not an algorithm flowchart in that sense. Rather, one parallel step of that algorithm is to be thought of as distributed over all of the active processors.

§7.2 Vectors and Vector Operations

One important, and rather elegant, model of parallel computation is the so-called *(bit-)vector machine model*. In this chapter we shall study vector machines in some detail. Initially, it will most likely not be apparent to the reader just what in the model corresponds to anything like parallelism. For the present, let us say only that a vector machine instruction will describe the cumulative effect of all local instructions performed by the active processors, which are assumed to operate simultaneously.

Vectors

We shall use the term *(bit-)vector* for binary-digit strings such as the following.

$$\ldots 000000001010 \qquad\qquad (7.2.1)$$
$$\ldots 000000000111$$
$$\ldots 000000110110$$

$$\ldots 111111101000$$

$$\ldots 111111110100$$

$$\ldots 111111010101$$

Thus vectors are infinite to the left: They possess a rightmost digit but no leftmost digit. Since vectors are infinite, it is convenient to use an ellipsis (...) in representing them. In the first three examples at (7.2.1), each ellipsis represents *0*s to the left without end. In the final three examples, ... stands for *1*s to the left without end. In each case, our vectors are ultimately constant—all *0*s or all *1*s. The infinite bit string ... *010101010101010101010101* (which should be understood to consist of alternating *0*s and *1*s to the left without end) is not a vector in our sense since it never becomes constant.

> **DEFINITION 7.1:** A (*bit-*)*vector* V is an infinite string $\ldots a_3 a_2 a_1 a_0$ such that, for all $i \in \mathcal{N}$, $a_i \in \{0, 1\}$ and (2) there exists $m \in \mathcal{N}$ with $a_n = a_m$ for all $n > m$. We shall write $\mathcal{V}^*$ for the set of all vectors.

The first of our bit strings at (7.2.1) qualifies as a vector since for $m = 4$ we have $a_n = a_m$ for all $n > m$. We could have taken $m = 5$ just as well, since for all $n > m = 5$ we also have $a_n = a_m$. But evidently $m = 4$ is the least such m. We shall say that 4 is the *length* of this vector in accordance with the following definition.

> **DEFINITION 7.2:** For any vector $V = \ldots a_3 a_2 a_1 a_0$, we set
> $$|V| = \text{length}(V) =_{\text{def.}} \text{the least } m \text{ such that } a_n = a_m \text{ for all } n > m.$$

Intuitively, the length of a vector is just the number of bits preceding its constant portion. The reader should verify that the lengths of the six vectors at (7.2.1) are 4, 3, 6, 5, 4, and 6, respectively.

We shall use vectors to represent integers in two ways. The first of these is essentially related to binary notation.

Using Vectors to Represent Integers (Binary)

We saw above that any vector V consists ultimately of *0*s only or of *1*s only.

- We shall think of this unvarying portion of V as giving the sign of the integer represented by V: Adopting a convention that will be familiar to students of computer science, we shall interpret a constant portion consisting of *0*s as a positive sign and a constant portion consisting of *1*s as a negative sign.

- The nonconstant portion of V, interpreted as a binary numeral in the usual way, will indicate the magnitude of the number represented by V.

For example,

$$\ldots 00000000000\mathbf{1000110} \tag{7.2.2}$$

represents decimal $+70$, while

$$\ldots 1111111111101100 \tag{7.2.3}$$

represents decimal -12. We note immediately a certain asymmetry within our representation scheme: One can now represent $+12$ by replacing the constant portion of (7.2.3) with all 0s to obtain

$$\ldots 00000000000001100$$

However, nothing analogous to this is possible in the case of (7.2.2) representing $+70$. This is because transforming the constant portion of (7.2.2) into all 1s produces vector $\ldots 1111111111000110$ representing not -70 but, rather, -6.

More formally, we define the number represented by vector V as follows.

DEFINITION 7.3: The integer value denoted by a vector $V = \ldots a_3 a_2 a_1 a_0$ in accordance with the binary representation scheme is given by

$$bval(V) = \begin{cases} +\sum_{k=0}^{|V|-1} a_i 2^i & \text{if } a_m = 0 \text{ for } m \geq |V| \\ -\sum_{k=0}^{|V|-1} a_i 2^i & \text{if } a_m = 1 \text{ for } m \geq |V| \end{cases}$$

Thus, $bval(\ )$ is a function from vectors to integers. We just saw that

$$bval(\ldots 00000000001000110) = +70$$

$$bval(\ldots 1111111111101100) = -12$$

$$bval(\ldots 00000000000001100) = +12$$

We shall also have use for a function $B(\ )$ from positive integers to vectors. Namely, we shall write $B(n)$ with $n > 0$ to denote the unique vector representing n. For example, we have

$$B(6) = \ldots 00000000000000110$$

$$B(7) = \ldots 00000000000000111$$

$$B(8) = \ldots 00000000000001000$$

We restrict n to positive integers here, since otherwise $B(n)$ would not be single-valued: For instance, would $B(-6)$ denote vector $\ldots 10110$ or vector 100110? (We could, of course, let $B(n)$ for negative n be that vector V such that both $bval(V) = n$ and $length(V)$ is minimal.)

It will be convenient in what follows to represent $\ldots 000000000000010$ as $+10$ and $\ldots 111111111111111011$ as -011. In other words, symbol $+$ preceding a finite string σ of binary digits indicates that σ is preceded on the left by infinitely many 0s. Similarly, symbol $-$ preceding a finite string σ of binary digits indicates that σ is preceded on the left by infinitely many 1s. To give another example,

$$+\mathit{1001} \quad \text{and} \quad -\mathit{0101}$$

abbreviate

$$\dots 00000000001\boldsymbol{1001} \quad \text{and} \quad \dots 11111111110\boldsymbol{0101}$$

respectively. As special cases, we shall write $+$ by itself to denote vector $\dots 00000000000$ and $-$ by itself to denote vector $\dots 1111111111111$. Note that $bval(+) = bval(-) = 0$ as a consequence of the fact that $\sum_{k=0}^{-1} a_i 2^i = 0$ by convention.

One can see that any vector V is either of the form $+\sigma$ or of the form $-\sigma$, where $\sigma \in \{0, 1\}^*$. One must be careful here, however. For, as was noted a moment ago in conjunction with (7.2.2), $bval(+\sigma)$ is not in general the opposite of $bval(-\sigma)$.

Finally, we mention a second way in which *certain* vectors may be taken to represent integers. Here it is so-called unary notation that is of interest.

Using Vectors to Represent Integers (Unary)

We shall on occasion understand a vector of the form $+1^n$ to represent nonnegative integer n. We shall write $U(n) = +1^n$ for the vector representing nonnegative integer n. Thus $U(4) = +1^4 = 1111$. The reader should not worry about the fact that this very same vector $+1^4 = \dots 000001111$ may on another occasion be construed differently so as to represent integer $+15$. In any given context, we shall always be very clear about which interpretation—unary or binary—is intended. Apparently, $U(0)$ is $+$.

We shall write $uval(+\sigma)$, where σ is of the form 1^n, for the inverse of $U(n)$. Thus $uval(+1111) = 4$ and $uval(+) = 0$.

Boolean Operations on Vectors

It is time to define certain vector-forming operations. We shall define Boolean operations on vectors in terms of familiar Boolean operations on binary digits. Thus, to begin, we give table definitions of $\neg$ and $\&$ applied to binary digits. Operator $\neg$ is unary. If b is 0, then $\neg b$ is 1; if b is 1, then $\neg b$ is 0 (see Table 7.2.1(a)). Operator $\&$ is binary. If b_1 and b_2 are both 1, then $b_1 \& b_2$ is 1; otherwise $b_1 \& b_2$ is 0 (see Table 7.2.1(b)).

We can now define four additional binary operators in terms of $\neg$ and $\&$.

DEFINITION 7.4: Let b_1 and b_2 be members of $\{0, 1\}$. Then

$$b_1 \vee b_2 =_{\text{def.}} \neg(\neg b_1 \& \neg b_2)$$

$$b_1 \rightarrow b_2 =_{\text{def.}} \neg b_1 \vee b_2$$

$$b_1 \leftrightarrow b_2 =_{\text{def.}} (b_1 \rightarrow b_2) \& (b_2 \rightarrow b_1)$$

$$b_1 \oplus b_2 =_{\text{def.}} (b_1 \& \neg b_2) \vee (\neg b_1 \& b_2)$$

These four definitions give us Tables 7.2.1(c)–(f), respectively. The reader will quickly note the coincidence of these Boolean operations on binary digits with the usual definitions of the various propositional connectives of propositional logic. Likewise, these operations correspond to the several gates of modern switching theory. Operators $\vee$ and $\oplus$

Table 7.2.1(a) Definition of Operator $\neg$.

b	$\neg b$
0	1
1	0

Table 7.2.1(b) Definition of Operator $\&$.

b_1	b_2	$b_1 \& b_2$
0	0	0
0	1	0
1	0	0
1	1	1

Table 7.2.1(c) Definition of Operator $\vee$.		
b_1	b_2	$b_1 \vee b_2 =_{\text{def.}}$ $\neg(\neg b_1 \,\&\, \neg b_2)$
0	0	0
0	1	1
1	0	1
1	1	1

Table 7.2.1(d) Definition of Operator $\rightarrow$.		
b_1	b_2	$b_1 \rightarrow b_2 =_{\text{def.}}$ $\neg b_1 \vee b_2$
0	0	1
0	1	1
1	0	0
1	1	1

will be familiar as inclusive-or and exclusive-or, respectively.

Given these operations on binary digits, the definitions of corresponding operations on vectors are now easy. So, for example, as an operator on digits, $\neg$ takes 0 to 1 and 1 to 0, in effect flipping its digit operand. Similarly, as an operator on vectors now, $\neg$ will flip each digit of its vector operand. So if vector V is $\ldots 00000000001011$, then vector $\neg V$ will be $\ldots 11111111110100$. Analogously, if V_1 and V_2 are $\ldots 000000001011$ and $\ldots 111111110110$, respectively, then vector $V_1 \,\&\, V_2$ will be $\ldots 000000000010$, that is, the result of applying bit-operation $\&$ to each pair of corresponding bits within vectors V_1 and V_2. Definition 7.5 is intended to capture this idea. Each operation on vectors is defined in terms of the application of the corresponding bit operation to the binary-digit components of the vector operands.

DEFINITION 7.5: For vectors $A = \ldots a_3 a_2 a_1 a_0$ and $B = \ldots b_3 b_2 b_1 b_0$ we have

$$\neg A =_{\text{def.}} \ldots c_3 c_2 c_1 c_0, \qquad \text{where } c_i = \neg a_i \text{ for } i \geq 0$$

$$A \,\&\, B =_{\text{def.}} \ldots c_3 c_2 c_1 c_0, \qquad \text{where } c_i = a_i \,\&\, b_i \text{ for } i \geq 0$$

$$A \vee B =_{\text{def.}} \ldots c_3 c_2 c_1 c_0, \qquad \text{where } c_i = a \vee b_i \text{ for } i \geq 0$$

$$A \rightarrow B =_{\text{def.}} \ldots c_3 c_2 c_1 c_0, \qquad \text{where } c_i = a_i \rightarrow b_i \text{ for } i \geq 0$$

$$A \leftrightarrow B =_{\text{def.}} \ldots c_3 c_2 c_1 c_0, \qquad \text{where } c_i = a_i \leftrightarrow b_i \text{ for } i \geq 0$$

$$A \oplus B =_{\text{def.}} \ldots c_3 c_2 c_1 c_0, \qquad \text{where } c_i = a_i \oplus b_i \text{ for } i \geq 0$$

Also, it is worth pointing out that, in general, we have that $bval(\neg V) \neq -bval(V)$ (see Exercise 7.2.5.).

Shift Operations on Vectors

For the next three paragraphs, let us suppose that V is the vector $+111001 = \ldots 000111001$. Performing a *left shift* of one position on V gives the new vector $+1110010 = \ldots 0001110010$. That is, all digits are shifted to the left one position and a 0 now fills the position made vacant. We will write $V \ll_0 1$

Table 7.2.1(e) Definition of Operator $\leftrightarrow$.		
b_1	b_2	$b_1 \leftrightarrow b_2 =_{\text{def.}}$ $(b_1 \rightarrow b_2) \,\&\, (b_2 \rightarrow b_1)$
0	0	1
0	1	0
1	0	0
1	1	1

Table 7.2.1(f) Definition of Operator $\oplus$.		
b_1	b_2	$b_1 \oplus b_2 =_{\text{def.}}$ $(b_1 \,\&\, \neg b_2) \vee (\neg b_2 \,\&\, b_1)$
0	0	0
0	1	1
1	0	1
1	1	0

for the result of such a shift. Also, $V \ll_0 2$ will denote vector $+11100100$, the result of shifting V to the left two positions, introducing $0s$ on the right. If we desire $1s$ to appear in the vacated positions on the right, then we use the operation symbol $\ll_1$. For example, $V \ll_1 2$ is $+11100111$. In the latter sort of case, we shall speak of *left shifts-1* (as opposed to *left shifts-0*).

Right shifts will be possible as well and will involve bits disappearing on the right. We write $V \ll_0 -1$ for $+11100$, the result of shifting V to the right one position. Similarly, $V \ll_0 -2$ will denote vector $+1110$, the result of shifting V two positions to the right. Alternatively, we use the operation symbol $\gg$ for a right shift. So $V \gg 3$ is $+111$.

Shift operators have higher precedence than Boolean operators. If V is $+111001$, then we write $\neg V \ll_0 1$ for -0001101 whereas $(\neg V) \ll_0 1$ is -0001100.

§7.3 Vector Machines

A *(bit-)vector machine* will consist of a finite set of *registers* $V_1, V_2, \ldots, V_k$, each containing one vector in the sense of Definition 7.1. We shall regularly speak of vector V_i, whereby we shall mean the vector contents of register V_i. In addition to $V_1, V_2, \ldots$, and so on, we shall sometimes use uppercase letters $A, B, C, \ldots, X, Y, Z$ to designate registers.

EXAMPLE 7.3.1 We start with a simple example of a flowchart that defines a vector machine. The vector machine M of Figure 7.3.1 possesses three registers, V_1, V_2, and V_3. M applies operator $\oplus$ to the vector contents of its two input registers V_1 and V_2 and places the result in output register V_3 before halting.

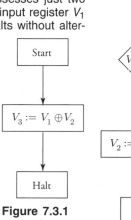

EXAMPLE 7.3.2 As a second example, consider the vector machine M of Figure 7.3.2. Machine M, which possesses just two registers, V_1 and V_2, first checks to see whether input register V_1 currently has contents $+ = +0$. If so, then M halts without altering either V_1 or V_2. Otherwise, M sets output register V_2 equal to the result of shifting the contents of register V_1 to the left four times, filling the vacated positions with $1s$. Thus if V_1's contents are $+10010$ initially, then M will halt with vector $+100101111$ in register V_2. (We shall assume that V_2 was $+$ initially.)

A vector machine instruction will be a statement of one of the six forms given in Table 7.3.1, where V_i and V_j are registers, V is a vector, and $\mathcal{L}$ is an instruction label.

As for instructions of the form $V_i := V$ and instructions of the form $V = +?$ goto $\mathcal{L}$, we

Figure 7.3.1
A Simple
Vector Machine
Flowchart.

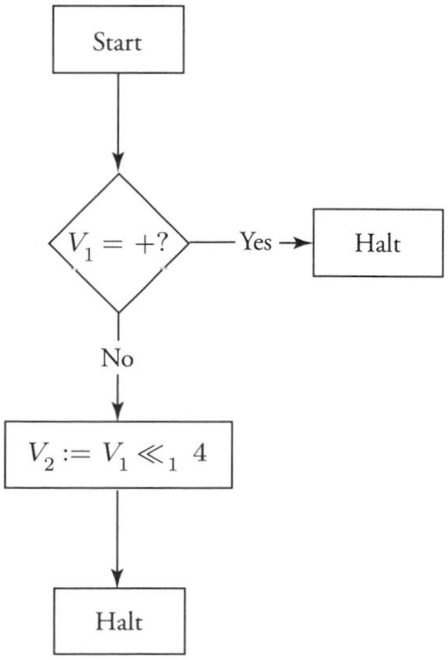

Figure 7.3.2   A Vector Machine
Flowchart Involving Branching.

Table 7.3.1   The Semantics of Vector Machine Instructions.

Vector Machine Instruction	Semantics
Start	Begin execution
$V_i := V_j$	Set register V_i equal to (the contents of) register V_j
$V_i := V$	Set register V_i equal to vector V
$V_i = +?$ *goto* $\mathcal{L}$	If register V_i is $+$, then branch to the instruction $\mathcal{L}$
$V = +?$ *goto* $\mathcal{L}$	If vector V is $+$, then branch to the instruction $\mathcal{L}$
Halt	Halt execution

Table 7.3.2   Vector Machine Instructions of the Form $V_i := V$ and $V = +?$ *goto* $\mathcal{L}$.

$V_i := +b_n \dots b_3 b_2 b_1 b_0$	
$V_i := V_j \,\&\, V_k$	$V_j \,\&\, V_k = +?$ goto $\mathcal{L}$
$V_i := \neg V_j$	$\neg V_j = +?$ goto $\mathcal{L}$
$V_i := V_j \oplus V_k$	$V_j \oplus V_k = +?$ goto $\mathcal{L}$
$V_i := V_j \to V_k$	$V_j \to V_k = +?$ goto $\mathcal{L}$
$V_i := V_j \leftrightarrow V_k$	$V_j \leftrightarrow V_k = +?$ goto $\mathcal{L}$
$V_i := V_j \vee V_k$	$V_j \vee V_k = +?$ goto $\mathcal{L}$
$V_i := V_j \ll_0 bval(V_k)$ or just $V_i := V_j \ll_0 V_k$	$V_j \ll_0 bval(V_k) = +?$ goto $\mathcal{L}$ or just $V_j \ll_0 V_k = +?$ goto $\mathcal{L}$
$V_i := V_j \gg bval(V_k)$ or just $V_i := V_j \gg V_k$	$V_j \gg bval(V_k) = +?$ goto $\mathcal{L}$ or just $V_j \gg V_k = +?$ goto $\mathcal{L}$
$V_i := V_j \ll_0 k$	$V_j \ll_0 k = +?$ goto $\mathcal{L}$
$V_i := V_j \gg k$	$V_j \gg k = +?$ goto $\mathcal{L}$
$V_i := V_j \ll_1 bval(V_k)$ or just $V_i := V_j \ll_1 V_k$	$V_j \ll_1 bval(V_k) = +?$ goto $\mathcal{L}$ or just $V_j \ll_1 V_k = +?$ goto $\mathcal{L}$
$V_i := V_j \ll_1 k$	$V_j \ll_1 k = +?$ goto $\mathcal{L}$

have all of the instructions contained in Table 7.3.2. The semantics of these instructions have already been explained.

To cite a specific example, suppose that V_2 contains $+101$ and V_3 contains $+100$. Then the instruction $V_1 := V_2 \ll_0 bval(V_3)$, or just $V_1 := V_2 \ll_0 V_3$, results in V_1 coming to contain vector $+1010000$. Note that this instruction is of the form $V_1 := V$ and not of the form $V_i := V_j$ since, before execution, no register is assumed to have contents $V_2 \ll_0 bval(V_3)$.

Vector machines are register machines in the sense that data is stored in registers rather than in or on some other medium—for example, a tape. Some of M's registers will be designated as *input registers* and some as *output registers*. (Typically, there will be a single output register.) Vector machines do not involve tapes or input buffers. Initially, all registers, except possibly the input registers, are assumed to contain $+$. Vector machine flow diagrams are interpreted in a manner reminiscent of the register machine flow diagrams of §5.1. The first instruction is always the Start instruction. In addition to representing vector machines by flow diagrams, we shall frequently describe them using a Pascal-like pseudocode. Thus the vector machine of Figure 7.3.1 will be described as

Input: V_1 and V_2
Output: $V_3 = V_1 \oplus V_2$
Algorithm
begin
$\qquad V_3 := V_1 \oplus V_2$
end.

while the vector machine of Figure 7.3.2 will be described as

> **Input:** V_1
> **Output:** $V_2 = V_1 \ll_1 4$
> **Algorithm**
> begin
>   if $V_1 \neq +$ then $V_2 := V_1 \ll_1 4$
> end.

Each of these vector machines computes in a single *parallel step*.

EXAMPLE 7.3.3 We have seen that the instruction $V_3 := V_1 \ll_0 V_2$, where V_2 is $+10$, say, causes the contents of V_1 to be shifted to the left by two positions and the result placed in V_3. The final two bit-positions of V_2 will be filled by *0*s (left shift-*0*). Earlier we mentioned the possibility of filling the vacated positions with *1*s. And we have introduced a primitive instruction that will accomplish this. Thus, executing the instruction

$$V_3 := V_1 \ll_1 V_2 \tag{7.3.1}$$

(where V_2 is again $+10$) will cause the contents of V_1 to be shifted to the left twice and the result placed in V_3. This time the final two bit-positions of V_2 will be filled by *1*s (left shift-*1*).

In fact, it is not strictly necessary to introduce a primitive instruction corresponding to left shifts-*1*. We can implement the instruction at (7.3.1) using the instruction sequence (7.3.2) appearing below, involving auxiliary register X.

> **Input:** V_1 and V_2
> **Output:** $V_3 - V_1 \ll_1 V_2$
> **Algorithm**
> begin
> $X := -;$
> $X := X \ll_0 V_2;$
> $X := \neg X;$
> $V_3 := V_1 \ll_0 V_2;$
> $V_3 := V_3 \vee X;$
> $X := +$ {restores X to default contents}
> end.

$$\tag{7.3.2}$$

The reader can verify that if V_2 is initially $+101$ and V_3 is $+10$, then V_1 is ultimately set to $+10111$.

In what follows we shall write

$$V_3 := V_1 \ll_1 V_2$$

as the abbreviation of the instruction sequence (7.3.2). Note that we have chosen to implement (7.3.1) by a sequence of six, which is O(1), steps. This means that there will be no significant complexity-theoretic consequences of our choosing to take (7.3.1) not as a primitive instruction but, rather, as an abbreviation of (7.3.2).

As in Chapter 5, we shall take the notion of *vector machine computation* to be clear enough from our pseudocode and flow diagrams. The formal definition of vector machines, modeled on that given for register machines (Definition 5.1), takes the form of our

---

DEFINITION 7.6: A *vector machine* M is any pair $\langle \mathcal{V}, \mathfrak{I} \rangle$, where $\mathcal{V} = \{V_1, V_2, \ldots, V_m\}$ is a nonempty, finite set of *registers* and $\mathfrak{I} = \langle \iota_1, \iota_2, \ldots, \iota_t \rangle$ with $t \geq 2$ is a finite, nonempty sequence of vector machine *instructions* such that

(i) instruction ι_1 is the Start instruction,

(ii) each of $\iota_2, \ldots, \iota_{t-1}$ is either of the form $V_i := V_j$ or $V_i = +?$ **goto** $\mathcal{L}$ or of any of the forms appearing in Table 7.3.2, where V_i, V_j, and V_k are members of set $\mathcal{V}$ and $\mathcal{L}$ is an identifier associated with exactly one of instructions $\iota_1, \iota_2, \ldots, \iota_t$, and

(iii) instruction ι_t is the Halt instruction.

Again, we remind the reader that the apparent discrepancy between our formal definition and the Pascal-like language in which we describe vector machines is no cause for concern since the additional control structures—unconditional branching, while-loops, if-then-else statements and the like—can all be defined contextually in terms of the canonical instruction types given in Definition 7.6(ii). (See the discussion at the end of §5.1.) In addition, we shall regularly write

$$V_2 := V_2 \oplus (V_2 \gg 1) \tag{7.3.3}$$

say, when our primitive instruction set of Tables 7.3.1 and 7.3.2 would in fact require something such as

$$V_{temp} := V_2 \gg 1 \tag{7.3.4}$$
$$V_2 := V_2 \oplus V_{temp}$$

Also, we shall frequently refer to instruction sequence $\mathfrak{I} = \langle \iota_1, \iota_2, \ldots, \iota_t \rangle$ as the *program* of vector machine $M = \langle \mathcal{V}, \mathfrak{I} \rangle$.

§7.4 Vector Machines and Function Computation

Before introducing additional examples of vector machines, a few preliminary remarks are in order. The first concerns binary numerals. The reader will recall that appending a single 0 to a binary numeral—call it B—amounts to multiplication by 2 in the sense that the number named by $B ^\frown 0$ is twice the number named by B. Similarly, appending two 0s amounts to multiplication by 4, appending three 0s to multiplication by 8, and so on. For example, $1001_2 = 9_{10}$, while $10010_2 = 18_{10}$, $100100_2 = 36_{10}$, $1001000_2 = 72_{10}$, and so on. Turning now to vectors, this means that shifting a vector V to the left by one position amounts to doubling $bval(V)$. That is, if $bval(V) = n$, then $bval(V \ll_0 1) = 2n$. More generally, if $bval(V) = n$, then $bval(V \ll_0 m) = 2^m \cdot n$. We summarize this in

---

REMARK 7.4.1: The left-shift-0 operation applied to a vector V may be interpreted in terms of multiplication by a power of 2. That is, if $bval(V) = n$, then $bval(V \ll_0 m) = 2^m \cdot n$.

(Incidentally, what is the analogous interpretation of the right-shift operation?)

A second remark concerns unary notation. Namely, it is obvious that appending a single *1* to a unary numeral U amounts to adding 1 in the sense that the number named by $U^\frown 1$ is 1 more than the number named by U. Similarly, appending two *1s* amounts to adding 2, and so on. The ramifications of this for vectors are equally obvious. Namely, if V is a vector of the special form $+I^n$ so that $uval(V) = n$, then $V \ll_1 1$ is $+I^n{}^\frown 1 = +I^{n+1}$ and $uval(V \ll_1 1) = n + 1$. Summarizing, we have

---

REMARK 7.4.2: The left-shift-*1* operation applied to a vector V of the special form $+I^n$ may be interpreted in terms of addition. That is, if $uval(V) = n$, then $uval(V \ll_1 m) = n + m$.

Finally, suppose that $n = 7$ and that $V = U(n + 1) = U(8)$ is shifted right by increasing powers of 2 until $+$ is obtained:

$$U(n + 1) = U(8) = V \qquad\qquad = +11111111$$
$$V \gg 2^0 = V \gg 1 = +1111111$$
$$V \gg 2^1 = V \gg 2 = +111111$$
$$V \gg 2^2 = V \gg 4 = +1111$$
$$V \gg 2^3 = V \gg 8 = +$$

Thus the fourth shift—by 2^3—was the first to yield $+$. Letting $n = 15$, we have

$$U(n + 1) = U(16) = V \qquad\qquad = +1111111111111111$$
$$V \gg 2^0 = V \gg 1 \;\;-\;\; +111111111111111$$
$$V \gg 2^1 = V \gg 2 = +1111111111111$$
$$V \gg 2^2 = V \gg 4 = +111111111111$$
$$V \gg 2^3 = V \gg 8 = +11111111$$
$$V \gg 2^4 = V \gg 16 = +$$

This time the fifth shift—by 2^4—was the first to yield $+$. It should be clear that if $n = 31$, then the sixth shift—by 2^5—will be the first to yield $+$ (see Table 7.4.1).

Putting off for the moment any formal definition of what it is for a vector machine to compute a function, we turn to our next example.

EXAMPLE 7.4.1 Let us design a vector machine M that computes function $f(n) =_{\text{def.}} \lceil \log_2(n + 1) \rceil$, so that for $4 \le n \le 7$ we have $f(n) = 3$, for $8 \le n \le 15$ we have $f(n) = 4$, and so on. Our program is the

Table 7.4.1 Right-Shifts Applied to $U(n + 1)$.

n	$n + 1$	First Right Shift of $U(n + 1)$ to Yield $+$
4–7	5–8	by 2^3
8–15	9–16	by 2^4
16–31	17–32	by 2^5
...	...	...
n	$n + 1$	by $2^{\lceil \log_2(n+1) \rceil}$

following. (As in Chapter 5, our pseudocode will henceforth cease making Start and Halt instructions explicit.)

Input: $V_1 = +1^n = U(n)$
Output: $V_2 = +1^{\lceil \log_2(n+1) \rceil} = U(\lceil \log_2(n+1) \rceil)$
Algorithm

```
(1)    begin
(2)         V_3 := V_1 ≪_1 1;      {V_3 is U(n+1)}
(3)         V_2 := +;              {counts number of iterations of while-loop}
(4)         V_4 := +1;             {bval(V_4) := 2^0}
(5)         while V_3 ≫ V_4 ≠ + do begin
(6)              V_2 := V_2 ≪_1 1;     {uval(V_2) := uval(V_2) + 1}
(7)              V_4 := V_4 ≪_0 1      {bval(V_4) := 2 · bval(V_4)}
(8)         end    {V_2 now contains U(⌈log_2(n+1)⌉}
(9)    end.
```

Machine M illustrates two essential techniques useful in designing vector machines. Both involve left shifts and are direct consequences of Remarks 7.4.1 and 7.4.2 above.

- First, we noted with Remark 7.4.2 that a left shift-*1* on a register V_i functioning as a counter has the effect of incrementing $uval(V_i)$ by 1. Thus at line (6) $uval(V_2)$ is incremented by 1 so that V_2 may be thought of as counting the number of iterations of the body of the while-loop of lines (5)–(8). For instance, if input vector V_1 is $+1^{17}$, then five iterations of the while-loop of lines (5)–(8) will cause output V_2 to be $+1^5$ ultimately.

- Second, we saw that a left shift-*0* on a register V_i has the effect of doubling $bval(V_i)$ (see Remark 7.4.1). So successive execution of line (7) above causes $bval(V_4)$ to change from 1 to 2, then from 2 to 4, then from 4 to 8, and so on.

Later on, we shall be very interested in the time requirements of this machine. Lines (2)–(4) require O(1) *parallel steps*. The while-loop of lines (5)–(8) is executed $\lceil \log_2(n+1) \rceil$ times. Each iteration of the loop involves two parallel steps. Summarizing, vector machine M computes in O(1) plus $\lceil \log_2(n+1) \rceil \cdot 2$ steps. We conclude that $time_M(n)$ is O($\log_2 n$).

This important example is included within the Vector Machine folder of the accompanying software. Open icon **log** $n + 1$ and load vector set `ex7-4-1a.vs` or vector set `ex7-4-1b.vs`. Note that the pseudocode algorithm presented in lines (1)–(9) involves various convenient constructs that are readily implemented using the primitive instructions of §7.3, as will be apparent from the software. Moreover— and this is important—the discrepancy between our pseudocode and the primitive instruction set of §7.3 in no way undermines the validity of the analyses of time (and space) requirements that we shall give, based upon that pseudocode.

Corresponding to Remarks 7.4.1 and 7.4.2, we have the following:

PROGRAMMING HINT 7.4.1: Left shifts-*0* are useful whenever multiplication by 2 is the goal. In particular, if $bval(V_i)$ is to range through the powers of 2, then one should first initialize V_i using $V_i := +1$ and then iterate the left-shift-*0* operation $V_i := V_i \ll_0 1$.

PROGRAMMING HINT 7.4.2: Left shifts-*1* are useful whenever incrementation by 1 is the goal. In particular, if $uval(V_i)$ is to range through 0, 1, 2, 3, ..., then one should first initialize V_i using $V_i := +$ and then iterate the left-shift-*1* operation $V_i := V_i \ll_1 1$.

Having considered one example, we are ready to set forth a formal definition of function computation on the part of vector machines. We model it on that given for register machines as Definition 5.2. Function arguments and values appear as unary vector representations.

DEFINITION 7.7: Let $M = \langle \mathcal{V}, \mathfrak{I} \rangle$ be a vector machine, and suppose that f is a k-ary partial number-theoretic function, for some fixed $k \geq 0$. Then we shall say that M *computes* f provided that:

  (i) if M's registers $V_1, V_2, \ldots, V_k$ initially contain vectors $U(n_1) = +I^{n_1}, U(n_2) = +I^{n_2}, \ldots,$
     $U(n_k) = +I^{n_k}$, all other registers contain vector $+$; and if $f(n_1, n_2, \ldots, n_k)$
     is defined, then, upon termination, registers $V_1, V_2, \ldots, V_k$ contain vectors
     $U(n_1) = +I^{n_1}, U(n_2) = +I^{n_2}, \ldots, U(n_k) = +I^{n_k}$ as before and register V_{k+1} contains
     $U(f(n_1, n_2, \ldots, n_k)) = +I^{f(n_1, n_2, \ldots, n_k)}$.

  (ii) if M's registers $V_1, V_2, \ldots, V_k$ initially contain vectors $U(n_1) = +I^{n_1}, U(n_2) = +I^{n_2}, \ldots,$
     $U(n_k) = +I^{n_k}$, all other registers contain vector $+$; and if $f(n_1, n_2, \ldots, n_k)$ is undefined, then
     either M never terminates or, if M does terminate, then the final contents of V_{k+1} are not of the
     form $+I^m$.

DEFINITION 7.8: Number-theoretic f is vector-machine-computable provided there exists a vector machine $M = \langle \mathcal{V}, \mathfrak{I} \rangle$ that computes f.

Function computation, as defined in Definition 7.7, concerns unary vectors essentially. In general, however, our programs will involve vector operations on vectors interpreted as binary numerals as well. Consequently, we need some way of converting unary vector representations into equivalent binary vector representations, and vice versa. We turn to this issue now.

EXAMPLE 7.4.2 (Unary-to-Binary Converter) We are writing $B(n)$ for the positive vector whose non-constant part is the binary representation of natural number n. Thus $B(8)$ is $+1000$ and $B(27)$ is $+11011$. Note that $|B(8)| = 4 = \lceil \log_2(8 + 1) \rceil$ and $|B(27)| = 5 = \lceil \log_2(27 + 1) \rceil$. In general, we have

$$|B(n)| = \lceil \log_2(n + 1) \rceil \tag{7.4.1}$$

Moreover, Example 7.4.1 describes a vector machine that obtains the right-hand side of (7.4.1), given vector $+1^n$ as input.

Our goal is to design a vector machine M that takes input $U(n)$ and produces output $B(n)$ for arbitrary $n \geq 1$. (Thus M is most naturally regarded as a transducer.) Supposing that input $U(27) = +1^{27}$ is given, output $B(27) = +11011$ should be generated. To start, we can rely upon the vector machine of Example 7.4.1, which will transform $U(27)$ into

$$+1^{\lceil \log_2(27+1) \rceil} = +1^5 = +1^{|B(27)|} = U(|B(27)|)$$

Thus $B(27)$ is seen to be of the form $+a_4 a_3 a_2 a_1 a_0$, where $a_4 = 1$ and each of a_3, a_2, a_1, and a_0 is either 0 or 1. We have already accounted for $16 = 2^4$ of our 27 1s by setting a_4 equal to 1. What is a_3? Well, since the difference $27 - 16 = 27 - 2^4 \geq 8 = 2^3$, a_3 will be 1. We have now accounted for $16 + 8$ of our 1s, leaving 3. Since $3 < 2^2$, we shall set a_2 equal to 0. Proceeding similarly, we set a_1 and a_0 both equal to 1.

The program of a vector machine M for converting unary vector representations to binary vector representations is presented below. Essentially, its behavior is an implementation of the idea expressed in the preceding paragraph except that, for technical reasons, we start with vector $+1^{28}$ and ask, in effect, whether $28 - 16 > 8$.

> **Input:** $V_1 = +1^n = U(n)$ for $n \geq 0$
> **Output:** $V_2 = +a_m a_{m-1} \ldots a_2 a_1 a_0 = B(n)$, where $m = |B(n)| - 1$
> **Algorithm**

(1)   begin
(2) $V_3 := +1^{\lceil \log_2(n+1) \rceil} = +1^{|B(n)|}$;   {We apply the vector machine of Example 7.4.1.}
(3) $V_4 := +1$;
(4)   while $V_3 \neq +$ do begin
(5) $V_4 := V_4 \ll_0 1$;
(6) $V_3 := V_3 \gg 1$
(7)   end;   {V_4 is now $+10^{|B(n)|} = +10^{m+1} = B(2^{m+1})$}
(8) $V_5 := V_1$;
(9) $V_4 := V_4 \gg 1$;   {V_4 is now $+10^m = B(2^m)$}
(10) $V_5 := V_1 \ll_1 1$;   {V_5 is now $+1^{n+1}$}
(11)   while $V_4 \neq +$ do begin
(12)   if $V_5 \gg V_4 \neq +$ then begin   {Is difference greater than the power of 2
                                             under consideration?}
(13) $V_2 := V_2 \ll_1 1$;   {left-shift-1}
(14) $V_5 := V_5 \gg V_4$
(15)   end
(16)   else $V_2 := V_2 \ll_0 1$;   {left-shift-0}
(17) $V_4 := V_4 \gg 1$ {$bval(V_4)$ becomes $bval(V_4) \; div \; 2$, which is the
                                             next smaller power of 2}

(18)   end
(19)   end.

Let us see how M works in the case $n = 27$.

- First, at line (2), V_3 becomes $+1^5$.

- By line (7), V_4 has taken on value $+100000$. The right shift at line (9) sets it to $+10000$ so that $bval(V_4) = 2^4 = 16$, the first power of 2 to be considered.

- Meanwhile, at line (8), V_1 has been copied into V_5. Line (10) sets V_5 to $+1^{28}$.

- The condition at (12) is true since $V_5 \gg V_4$ is $+1^{12}$. So, at line (13), output vector V_2 becomes $+1$—this is the most significant of the binary digits to be generated. Then, at line (14), V_5 becomes difference vector $+1^{12}$.

- At line (17), V_4 becomes $+1000$. During the next iteration of the while-loop of lines (11)–(18), there is another left shift-1 at line (13) and V_5 becomes $+1^4$ at line (14). At line (17), V_4 becomes $+100$. This causes the Boolean condition at line (12) to fail, so that V_5 is not changed during this iteration and a left shift-0 occurs at line (16).

- At line (17), V_4 becomes $+10$. On the next iteration we have another left shift-1 and V_5 is set to $+1^2$. At line (17), V_4 becomes $+1$. Another left shift-1 results at line (13) so that output vector V_2 attains final value $+11011$. At line (17), V_4 becomes $+$, the condition at line (11) fails, and execution terminates. We summarize the behavior of the Unary-to-Binary Converter in Table 7.4.2.

     Open icon **Unary-to-Binary Converter** and load vector set $U(27).vs$ to observe the operation of this extremely important machine. (We shall use it repeatedly in what follows.) We leave it to the reader to verify that M computes in $O(\log_2 n)$ steps.

Table 7.4.2 Summary of the Behavior of the Unary-to-Binary Converter.

Input Vector $U(27) = +1^{27}$	Output Register V_2	Auxiliary Registers	
		V_4	V_5
Initializations lines (2)–(10)	$+$	$+10000$	$+1^{28}$
Within while-loop (11)–(18)			
Iteration 1	$+1$	$+1000$	$+1^{12}$
Iteration 2	$+11$	$+100$	$+1^4$
Iteration 3	$+110$	$+10$	$+1^4$
Iteration 4	$+1101$	$+1$	$+1^2$
Iteration 5	$+11011 = B(27)$	$+^a$	$+1^1$

[a] This causes the machine to halt.

Our next example is another machine that will prove to be highly useful later.

EXAMPLE 7.4.3 (Generalized Copier) The vector machine M to be described takes three items as input:

(1) a word w over $\{0, 1\}^*$—that is, vector $+w$—stored in register V_1

(2) the unary representation of $|w|$ (i.e., $U(|w|) = +1^{|w|}$) stored in register V_2

(3) $U(m) = 1^m$ for some duplication factor $m \geq 0$, stored in register V_3.

As output, M will produce $+w^m$ in register V_4. The program of M appears below.

Input: $V_1 = +w$
$V_2 = +1^{|w|}$ $\{V_2$ is needed since, in general, $|w| \neq |+w|\}$
$V_3 = +1^m$ for some $m \geq 0$
Output: $V_4 = +w^m$
Algorithm

```
(1)    begin
(2)          V₅ := Convert(V₃);          {We apply the Unary-to-Binary Converter of
                                            Example 7.4.2 to V₃.}
(3)          V₆ := Convert(V₂);          {We apply the Unary-to-Binary Converter of
                                            Example 7.4.2 to V₂.}
(4)          V₇ := V₁;                   {V₇ will always contain +w^(2ʲ) for some j ≥ 0.}
(5)          V₈ := +1;                   {This auxiliary register, which will never be
                                            altered, is used in order to check individual
                                            bits within V₅.}
(6)          while V₅ ≠ + do begin
(7)                if V₅ & V₈ ≠ + then begin      {If rightmost bit of V₅ is 1, then "concatenate"
                                                    V₄ and V₇.}
(8)                      V₄ := V₄ ≪₀ V₆;
(9)                      V₄ := V₄ ∨ V₇
(10)               end;
(11)               V₇ := (V₇ ≪₀ V₆) ∨ V₇          {V₇ is "doubled."}
```

(12) $V_6 := V_6 \ll_0 1;$ {The length of V_7 is doubled also.}
(13) $V_5 := V_5 \gg 1$ {We consider the next bit to the left in $B(m)$.}
(14)   end
(15)   end.

To see what is going on here, suppose that $+w$ is 011 and $m = 5$, and consider Table 7.4.3. We saw earlier that lines (2) and (3) require $O(\lceil \log_2 m \rceil)$ and $O(\lceil \log_2 |w| \rceil)$ parallel steps, respectively. From our chart it is apparent that the while-loop will be iterated $\lceil \log_2 m \rceil$ times. Each iteration of the while-loop involves at most five steps. Thus the total number of steps in the algorithm is

$$O(\lceil \log_2 m \rceil) + O(\lceil \log_2 |w| \rceil) + O(\lceil \log_2 m \rceil) \cdot O(1) = O(\lceil \log_2 m \rceil + \lceil \log_2 |w| \rceil)$$

and M computes in $O(\log_2 m + \log_2 |w|)$ parallel steps.
   Open icon **Generalized Copier** and use tapes `ex7-4-3a.vs` and `ex7-4-3b.vs`.

Before continuing, we pause for a moment to consider the preceding Example 7.4.3 and, in particular, its use of the Unary-to-Binary Converter of Example 7.4.2 in both lines (2) and (3). A moment's reflection will reveal that, in order to make m copies of word w, a multitape Turing machine would require $\Omega(m \cdot |w|)$ steps. A single-tape Turing machine would require $\Omega(m^2 \cdot |w|^2)$ steps. Evidently, the vector machine of Example 7.4.3 does better. The point to emphasize here is that this improvement over the sequential machines is essentially the result of the Unary-to-Binary Converter of Example 7.4.2 being able to transform $U(n)$ into $B(n)$ in $O(\log_2 n)$ parallel steps. This leads us to formulate

> **PROGRAMMING HINT 7.4.3:** In order to enhance performance time, vector machine inputs of the form $U(n)$ should first be converted to $B(n)$ using the Unary-to-Binary Converter of Example 7.4.2. This will involve $O(\log_2 n)$ steps.

The reader who wishes to better understand the significance of Programming Hint 7.4.3 should try Exercise 7.4.4 now.

EXAMPLE 7.4.4 (Addition Machine) We present in Figure 7.4.1 the flowchart of a vector machine M that computes the binary addition function $f(n, m) =_{\text{def.}} n + m$. (See the machine at icon

---

Table 7.4.3 Summary of the Behavior of the Generalized Copier.

Input Vectors $+w = +011$, $|w| = 3, m = 5$	Output Register V_4	Auxiliary Registers		
		V_5	V_6	V_7
Initializations lines (2)–(4)	$+$	$+101$	$+11$	$+011$
Within while-loop				
Iteration 1	$+011$	$+10$	$+110$	$+011011$
Iteration 2	$+011$	$+1$	$+1100$	$+011011011011$
Iteration 3	$+(011)^5$	$+$	$+11000$	$+(011)^8$

Addition Machine and use vector set `add.vs`.) If V_1 and V_2 are initially $U(25)$ and $U(75)$, respectively, then V_4 is set to $+1001011$ in $O(\log_2 m) = O(\log_2 75)$ steps. Next, V_3 becomes $+1^{25}$ and then $+1^{100}$. Thus M computes addition function $f(n, m) = n + m$ in $O(\log_2 m)$, and hence $O(\log_2 max(n, m))$, steps. Summarizing, we have that $time_M(n, m)$ is $O(\log_2 max(n, m))$. (Note that the number of arguments of number-theoretic function $time_M$, whose definition is obvious enough, will be determined by the number of M's input registers.) The reader will want to compare this with the register machine of Example 5.1.3, which computes the addition function $f(n, m) = n + m$ in $O(m)$, and hence $O(max(n, m))$, steps.

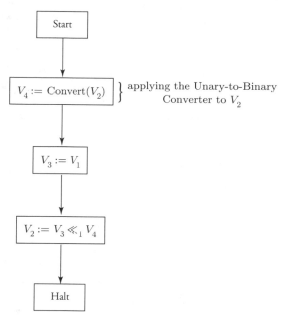

Figure 7.4.1 This vector machine computes the binary addition function.

EXAMPLE 7.4.5 (Multiplication Machine) It is natural to next ask for a vector machine that computes the binary multiplication function $f(n, m) =_{dof.} n \cdot m$. The Generalized Copier of Example 7.4.3 will be very useful here. In fact, applied to vectors of the form $U(n)$, the Generalized Copier is in essence a multiplication machine. Only a few slight modifications are required.

Input: $V_1 = U(n) = +1^n$
$\qquad\quad V_2 = U(m) = +1^m$
Output: $V_3 = U(n \cdot m) = +1^{n \cdot m}$
Algorithm

```
(1)     begin
(2)          V4 := Convert(m);     {applying the Unary-to-Binary Converter of Example 7.4.2 to V2}
(3)          V5 := Convert(n);     {applying the Unary-to-Binary Converter of Example 7.4.2 to V1}
(4)          V6 := V1;             {V6 will always be +(1^n)^(2^j) for some j ≥ 0}
(5)          V7 := +1;             {auxiliary register that will never be altered; used to check
                                    individual bits within multiplier V4}
(6)          while V4 ≠ + do begin
(7)               if V4 & V7 ≠ + then begin    {if rightmost bit of V4 is 1, then concatenate
                                                V3 and V6}
(8)                    V3 := V3 ≪0 V5;
(9)                    V3 := V3 ∨ V6
(10)              end;
(11)              V6 := (V6 ≪0 V5) ∨ V6   {V6 is "doubled"}
(12)              V5 := V5 ≪0 1;   {length of V6 is doubled also}
(13)              V4 := V4 ≫ 1     {consider next bit to the left in B(m)}
(14)         end
(15)    end.
```

To see that this works, the reader should use the accompanying software to complete Exercise 7.4.3. Our analysis of the Generalized Copier is yet valid so that the Multiplication Machine computes in

$O(\log_2 n + \log_2 m)$, and hence in $O(\log_2 max(n, m))$, steps since, in general,

$$\log_2 n + \log_2 m \leq 2 \cdot max(\log_2 n, \log_2 m) = 2 \cdot \log_2 max(n, m)$$

So we have that $time_M(n, m)$ is $O(\log_2 max(n, m))$. (We draw the reader's attention to the register machine of Example 5.1.4, which computes the multiplication function $f(n, m) = n \cdot m$ in $O(n \cdot m)$ steps.) Finally, the new vector machine is implemented in the accompanying software at icon **Multiplication Machine**. Use vector set `multiply.vs`.

This is a convenient time to introduce considerations of space. For a given vector machine M with registers $V_1, V_2, \ldots, V_k$, we define $space_M(n)$ as the maximum length of any register, other than the designated input and output registers, during any computation of M for input of length n. (Just like $time_M$, function $space_M$ may take several arguments—one for each of M's input registers.) As was seen already in Chapter 1, assigning a size to an input may be done in various ways, although usually some size criterion presents itself as natural enough in a given context. For instance, in our next example, where the reversal of an input word is at issue, size of input is most naturally construed as input vector length in the sense of Definition 7.2.

The preceding two examples, together with our new understanding of space, now justify a remark that will be useful in Chapter 8.

REMARK 7.4.3: Any unary polynomial function $p(n)$ of degree $k \geq 0$, is vector-machine-computable in $O(\log_2 n)$ time and $O(n^k)$ space.

It is clear enough that parallelism often provides enhanced performance—in other words, speed. On the other hand, any task that can be programmed in parallel can be accomplished by a sequential program, given sufficient time. At the theoretical level, the latter insight becomes

THEOREM 7.1: Number-theoretic function f is partial recursive if and only if f is vector-machine-computable.

PROOF See Exercise 7.4.8 and its solution.

In this section we shall present just one more example, namely, a vector machine that reverses its input word in logarithmic time and linear space. (The new example has nothing to do with function computation.) Preliminary to considering the new machine, we define the concept of a *mask of index i*. Any such mask will be a positive vector of length 2^i. For each $i \geq 0$, there will be i distinct masks of index i. Thus, setting $i = 4$, we have four masks of index 4, each of length 16.

$$m_{40} = +1010101010101010$$
$$m_{41} = +1100110011001100$$
$$m_{42} = +1111000011110000$$
$$m_{43} = +1111111100000000$$

The reader should verify that the four masks of index 4 satisfy the defining equation

$$m_{ij} =_{\text{def.}} +(1^{2^j}0^{2^j})^{2^{i-j-1}}$$

Now we need to see that any given mask of index i can be constructed, given vector $X = +1^{2^i}$, in O(i) time and O(2^i) space. Setting $i = 4$, we first construct m_{43} as follows:

$W := Convert(X) \gg 1;$ $\{W$ is now $B(2^3) = +1000.\}$

$Y := +;$

$Y := Y \ll_1 W;$ $\{Y$ is now $+11111111.\}$

$Y := Y \ll_0 W;$ $\{Y$ is now $+1111111100000000,$ which is $m_{43}.\}$

Given m_{43}, we can now construct m_{42} using:

(1) $W := W \gg 1;$ $\{W$ is now $+100.\}$

(2) $Z := Y \gg W;$ $\{Z$ is $+111111110000.\}$

(3) $Y := Y \oplus Z$ $\{Y$ is now $+1111000011110000,$ which is $m_{42}.\}$

Equivalently, (1)–(3) may be written:

$$W := W \gg 1; \tag{7.4.2}$$

$$Y := Y \oplus Y \gg W;$$

Since masks will play a significant role in several examples below, it is worth devoting some time to

---

EXAMPLE 7.4.6 (Masks) Given input of the form $U(1^{2^i})$, the vector machine of `ex7-4-6a.vm` generates mask $m_{i,i-1}$ in O(i) steps. Furthermore, given input vectors m_{ij} with $0 < j < i$ and $B(2^j)$, the machine of `ex7-4-6b.vm` generates the finer mask $m_{i,j-1}$ in O(1) steps. The vector sets in files `ex7-4-6*.vs` have been created for use with these machines. In what follows, we shall refer to the algorithms embodied in these machines as *Generate-Coarsest-Mask*(i) and *Generate-Finer-Mask*(m_{ij}, j), respectively.

Since our next example will consist of a vector machine that takes a word w over alphabet $\Sigma = \{a, b\}$ as its input, two preliminary issues are best dealt with immediately.

- We need some conventions whereby bit sequences may represent members of an arbitrary alphabet Σ. We shall use the ASCII-style representation scheme familiar from our discussion of register machines. Namely, if $\Sigma = \{a, b\}$, then we shall think of bits 0 and 1 as representing symbols a and b. In the case of an alphabet of cardinality 3 or 4, we can represent each symbol using two bits: 00 for a, 01 for b, 10 for c, and 11 for d. For larger alphabets, yet more bits would be required. In what follows, we shall write $Trans(w)$ for the translation of input word w as a bit sequence in accordance with some reasonable scheme of the sort just described. (Just how this is done makes no real difference.)

- The second issue concerns the representation of input words themselves and is most easily explained by way of an example. Suppose that $\Sigma = \{a, b\}$ and that we are using bits 0 and 1 to represent symbols a and b, respectively. If input word w is abb, then, reasonably, input register V_1 might be assumed to initially contain vector $+011$, which happens to be vector $+11$. But notice that, according to this scheme, $+011 = +11$ will be our representation of input word bb as well. So how are we going to distinguish the two cases? In the first case, the rightmost 0 represents symbol a of the input word. In the second, the rightmost 0 is merely part of the input vector's sign. Apparently, such a straightforward representation scheme is inadequate as it stands and requires supplementation. We shall distinguish the two cases by requiring an additional supplemental vector V_2 giving the represented w's length in unary. Thus, input word abb will be represented by the pair $V_1 = +11$ and $V_2 = U(3) = +111$. In contrast, input word bb will be represented by the pair $V_1 = +11$ and $V_2 = U(2) = +11$.

EXAMPLE 7.4.7 (Reverse Word) (advanced) We now introduce an iterative algorithm to reverse any word w over alphabet $\Sigma = \{a, b\}$. Again, think of bits 0 and 1 as representing symbols a and b, respectively. So we shall represent word w by vector $+ Trans(w)$. Note that if $Trans(w)$ involves leading 0s, then $|+Trans(w)|$ in the sense of Definition 7.2 will not equal $|Trans(w)|$. For instance, letting w be the string $aababa$, we have $|Trans(w)| = 6$ but $|+Trans(w)| = 4$. We will need to take this into account below.

To simplify matters initially, let us assume that input word w is of length n, where n is a power of 2, i.e., $n = 2^k$ for some k. Our algorithm will use all k masks of index k. In particular, for $k = 3$, we have $n = 8$ and we write $Trans(w) = a_1 a_2 a_3 a_4 a_5 a_6 a_6 a_8$, where a_i is either 0 or 1 for $1 \leq i \leq 8$. We have seen how to construct the three masks

$$m_{30} = +10101010$$

$$m_{31} = +11001100$$

$$m_{32} = +11110000$$

First, we use the coarsest mask m_{32} to carry out *4–4 exchange* on $+Trans(w)$ so as to obtain $+a_5 a_6 a_7 a_8 a_1 a_2 a_3 a_4$. Assuming V_3 is initially $+Trans(w)$, this is accomplished by the assignment

$$V_3 := (V_3 \& m_{32}) \gg 2^2 \vee (V_3 \& \neg m_{32}) \ll_0 2^2$$

Next, using m_{31}, we carry out 2–2 exchange on V_3 so as to obtain $+a_7 a_8 a_5 a_6 a_3 a_4 a_1 a_2$:

$$V_3 := (V_3 \& m_{31}) \gg 2^1 \vee (V_3 \& \neg m_{31}) \ll_0 2^1$$

Finally, using m_{30}, we perform 1–1 exchange on V_3 to obtain $+Trans(w^R) = +a_8 a_7 a_6 a_5 a_4 a_3 a_2 a_1$:

$$V_3 := (V_3 \& m_{30}) \gg 2^0 \vee (V_3 \& \neg m_{30}) \ll_0 2^0$$

Generally, for $n = 2^k$, we have the following algorithm for word reversal.

Input: $V_1 = +Trans(w) = +a_1 a_2 \ldots a_n$, where $n = 2^k$
$V_2 = U(|Trans(w)|) = +1^n$ {Supplemental vector V_2 is needed since, in general, $|+Trans(w)| \neq |Trans(w)|$}

Output: $V_3 = +Trans(w^R) = +a_n a_{n-1} \ldots a_1$

Algorithm

(1)   begin
(2) $Y := Convert(V_2) \gg 1 = +10^{k-1};$ {obtainable from V_2 in $O(\log_2 n)$ or
                                                                    $O(k)$ steps}
(3) $X := m_{k,k-1};$ {obtainable from Y in $O(1)$ steps}
(4) $V_3 := V_1;$
(5)   while $Y \neq +$ do begin
(6) $V_3 := (V_3 \,\&\, X) \gg Y \vee (V_3 \,\&\, \neg X) \ll_0 Y;$
(7) $Y := Y \gg 1;$
(8) $X := X \oplus (X \gg Y)$ {cf. (7.4.2)}
(9)   end
(10) end.

We assumed that $|w| = n$ was a power of 2, and the vector machine at icon **Reverse Word** does the same. (Use vector sets ex7-4-7*.vs.) In fact, it is not necessary to assume this, however. If n is not a power of 2, then at the very start we shift in enough 0s on the right of $Trans(w) = a_1 a_2 \ldots a_n$ so as to produce the new bit string $a_1 a_2 \ldots a_n 0 \ldots 0$, whose length is 2^k for some k (see Exercise 7.4.7). We then apply the algorithm above to reverse $+a_1 a_2 \ldots a_n 0 \ldots 0$, obtaining $+a_n a_{n-1} \ldots a_1 = +Trans(w^R)$.

It is apparent that $space_M(n) = n$ and hence is $O(n)$. As for a time analysis, we note the following:

- Lines (2)–(4) involve $O(\log_2 n)$ parallel steps.

- The while-loop of lines (5)–(9) will be executed $k = \log_2 n$ times, but each iteration of the body of the loop involves only $O(1)$ parallel steps.

Summarizing, we have that M computes in $O(\log_2 n) + \log_2 n \cdot O(1)$, which is $O(\log_2 n)$, parallel steps. Note the striking contrast with the time analyses of

(1)   the single-tape Turing machine of Example 1.5.8, which reverses its input word in $O(n^2)$ sequential steps—see Exercise 1.7.2 and its solution—and

(2)   the two-tape Turing machine of Example 2.3.4, which reverses its input word in $O(n)$ sequential steps.

The difference is of course that vector machine M computes in $O(\log_2 n)$ *parallel* steps. In other words, we make no claim that less work is being performed. Rather, the claim is merely that M is faster than either the single-tape or the multitape Turing machine.

Finally, M is best thought of as implementing an instance of our transduction paradigm. Furthermore, we shall see that M will be very useful later in implementing a certain instance of our language recognition paradigm (see Example 7.5.1 below).

Vector Machines and Parallel Computation

We have delayed addressing the issue of vector machines and parallel computation long enough. Just how, after all, are vector machine operations to be construed as involving parallelism? We now propose an interpretation whereby vector machines turn out to model parallel computation. It is convenient to discuss this issue in terms of *processors*, by which we shall mean *control units* essentially. We suggest that, at any given point during machine M's computation, a single processor will be responsible for changes to one bit within the nonconstant portion of *each* register $V_0, V_1, V_2, \ldots$. Thus processor p_1, say, would be responsible for the rightmost bit within each register, while processor p_2 would be responsible for the second bit from the right within each register, and so on (see Figure 7.4.3). Supposing that V_i is

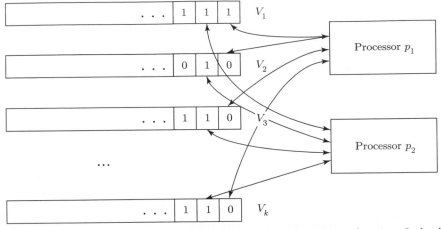

Figure 7.4.2 Processor p_i controls the ith bit from the right within each register. Its local store consists of k bits, one within each vector/register.

currently $+1010$ and that V_j is currently $+1101$, then execution of the instruction

$$V_k := V_i \oplus V_j \qquad (7.4.3)$$

would involve processors p_1, p_2, p_3, and p_4 only. Each processor has its own *local memory* and dedicated channels for interacting with that memory. The execution of instruction (7.4.3) has each of the four processors setting the bit at position k within local memory to the result of applying a certain Boolean operation to the bits currently at positions i and j. We may think of processors p_1, p_2, p_3, and p_4 as themselves arranged in an array and as executing a single instruction *synchronously* on their respective data. In this sense, vector machines model *SIMD (Single Instruction Multiple Data) machines*.[1] Shift operations may be interpreted as communication between processors, following a fixed pattern, by way of *message passing*. Thus a certain *interconnection network* is implied. We note once again that, although an infinite number of processors are available, nonetheless, at any given point in any computation of vector machine M, only finitely many processors are active. Specifically, the number of active processors at any point in M's computation will be the current maximum length of vectors $V_1, V_2, \ldots, V_k$. The requirement that the number of registers available to M does not vary (as was possible in the case of register machines) is interpretable as a natural requirement that the local store of any active processor be of fixed size.

Note that, assuming this interpretation of vector machines, the processors issue is addressed explicitly in giving a space analysis of M. Thus the assertion that the machine of Example 7.4.7 computes in $O(n)$ space may be interpreted as an assertion about the number of processors required for the associated parallel computation: We require $O(n)$ processors. This is not to say that all $O(n)$ processors will be active throughout the computation, although in the vector machine of Example 7.4.7 this would appear to be the case. Rather, the claim is only that if a word w of length 1024, say, is to be reversed, then this is possible in something on the order of $\log_2 1024 = 10$ parallel steps provided that we have 1024 processors available. If speed is not an issue, then we can use the single-tape Turing machine of Example 1.5.8.

---

[1] Conventional sequential processing is classified as *SISD*, which stands for "single instruction, single data."

In that case, we require only a single processor but must expect our computation to consume on the order of $1024^2 = 2^{20}$ time units. Alternatively, the two-tape Turing machine of Exercise 2.3.4 requires a single processor and computes in linear time, which is unquestionably a big improvement, for long input words, over the single-tape machine. Of course, if speed is of the utmost importance, then the vector machine of Example 7.4.7 will surely be our choice for reversing w.

§7.5 Vector Machines and Formal Languages

We wish to develop notions of language acceptance and language recognition for vector machines. To this end, we first introduce an example.

EXAMPLE 7.5.1 (Palindromes) The two-tape Turing machine of the solution to Exercise 2.3.1 accepts language $L = \{w \in \Sigma^* | w = w^R\}$ with $\Sigma = \{a, b\}$ in $O(n)$ steps worst case. That machine computes in $O(0)$ space as well. We might hope to find some vector machine with faster computation time—one that accepts L in $O(\log_2 n)$ steps, say. And, in fact, this turns out to be possible: We can build upon the machine for word reversal given as Example 7.4.7, computing in $O(\log_2 n)$ time and $O(n)$ space, so as to obtain a vector machine M that recognizes, and hence accepts, L. The program of M appears below. Given input vector $+ Trans(w)$, M first simulates the operation of the machine of Example 7.4.7 in order to produce, in register V_4, the vector $+ Trans(w^R)$. Both input vector $V_1 = + Trans(w)$ as well as input vector $V_2 = U(|Trans(w)|) = U(|w|)$ are required in order to achieve this, and the computation requires $O(\log_2 n)$ steps. Afterward, M must determine whether vectors V_1 and V_4 are identical. If so, then output vector V_3 is set to $+1$, reflecting acceptance of input word w. Otherwise, output vector V_3 is set to $+0$, reflecting rejection of input word w.

Input: $V_1 = + Trans(w)$ {For example, if w is *baab*, then V_1 will be $+1001$.}

$V_2 = U(|Trans(w)|) = U(|w|) = +1^n$ {Input V_2 is needed since, in general, $|+Trans(w)| \neq |Trans(w)|$.}

Output:

$$V_3 = \begin{cases} +1 & \text{if } w = w^R \\ +0 & \text{otherwise} \end{cases}$$

Algorithm
(1) begin
(2) $V_4 := Reverse\_Word(V_1, V_2);$ {We apply the vector machine of Example 7.4.7 to input registers V_1 and V_2 obtaining $+ Trans(w^R)$ in vector V_4.}
(3)   if $V_1 \oplus V_4 = +$ then $V_3 := +1$ else $V_3 := +0$
(4) end.

Line (3) requires $O(1)$ steps, from which it follows that M computes in $O(\log_2 n)$ steps. It is also easy to see that M requires $O(n)$ space. Open icon **Palindromes** and use vector set `ex7-5-1.vs`.

The notions of language acceptance and language recognition implicit in the preceding example are embodied in the formal definitions presented below.

DEFINITION 7.9: Let M be a vector machine Suppose that w is some word over alphabet Σ. Suppose further that M starts with input registers V_1 and V_2 set to $+Trans(w)$ and $U(|w|) = +1^{|Trans(w)|}$, respectively, and ultimately halts with input registers V_1 and V_2 unchanged and with output vector V_3 set to $+1$. Then we shall say that M *accepts word* w.

DEFINITION 7.10: Let M be a vector machine. We shall say that M *accepts language L over alphabet* Σ provided that M accepts all and only the words of L. We write $L(M)$ for the language accepted by M.

As usual, we do not care what M does when input word $w \notin L(M)$—M may not even halt. On the other hand, if, for input words $w \notin L(M)$, machine M responds by setting output V_3 equal to $+0$, then we shall say that M *recognizes* $L(M)$.

DEFINITION 7.11: Let M be a vector machine and let L be a language over alphabet Σ. Suppose, further, that (1) for any word over Σ with $w \in L$, if M begins executing with input registers V_1 and V_2 set to $+Trans(w)$ and $U(|w|) = +1^{|Trans(w)|}$, respectively, then M ultimately halts with input registers V_1 and V_2 unchanged and with output vector V_3 set to $+1$ and (2) for any word w over Σ with $w \notin L$, if M begins executing with input registers V_1 and V_2 set to $+Trans(w)$ and $U(|w|) = +1^{|Trans(w)|}$, respectively, then M ultimately halts with input registers V_1 and V_2 unchanged and with output vector V_3 set to $+0$. In the case of such an M and such an L, we shall say that M *recognizes* L.

We shall speak of *vector-machine-acceptable languages* and *vector-machine-recognizable languages* as usual. Analogous to Theorem 7.1, we have

THEOREM 7.2: Any vector-machine-acceptable (vector-machine-recognizable) language is Turing-acceptable (Turing-recognizable), and conversely.

The proof of Theorem 7.2 is left to Exercise 7.5.1. It will also be useful to have proved

COROLLARY 7.1: Any polynomial-time Turing-acceptable language L is accepted by some vector machine in polynomially bounded time and polynomially bounded space. Conversely, if language L is accepted by some vector machine M with $time_M(n)$ and $space_M(n)$ both $O(p(n))$ for some polynomial $p(n)$, then $L \in P$.

PROOF See Exercise 7.5.2.

EXAMPLE 7.5.2 It is easy to design a multitape Turing machine that recognizes language $L = \{a^{2^i} | i \geq 0\}$ in $O(n \log_2 n)$ steps, where n gives the length of input. (See our remarks at the beginning of Example 2.3.5.) Moreover, it seems unlikely that any other Turing machine would be faster. As the reader will likely guess, something substantially faster is possible in a vector machine. Namely, we can recycle the Unary-to-Binary Converter of Example 7.4.2 to obtain a vector machine M that recognizes L in $O(\log_2 n)$ steps using $O(n)$ hardware. In the case $\Sigma = \{a\}$, it is convenient to let $Trans(a^n)$ be $+1^n$.

Input: $V_1 = +Trans(w) = +1^n$ {For example, if w is *aaaa*, then V_1 will be $+1111$.}
$V_2 = U(|w|) = +1^n$ {V_2 is not needed in this case but is included
so as to satisfy the requirements of Definition 7.9.}

Output : $V_3 = \begin{cases} +1 & \text{if } w = a^{2^i} \text{ for some } i \geq 0 \\ +0 & \text{otherwise} \end{cases}$

Algorithm
(1)   begin
(2) $V_4 := Convert(V_1)$;   {We apply the vector machine of Example 7.4.2 to
input register V_1, obtaining $B(|w|)$ in vector V_4.}
(3) $V_5 := +1$;
(4)   if $V_4 = +$
(5)   then $V_3 := +0$ {The empty word is not in L.}
(6)   else if $V_4 = V_5$
(7)   then $V_3 := +1$ {But word *a* is in L.}
(8)   else begin
(9) $V_6 := V_4$;
(10)   while $V_6 \neq +$ and $V_5 \neq V_4$ do begin
(11) $V_5 := V_5 \ll_0 1$;   {V_5 is doubled.}
(12) $V_6 := V_6 \gg 1$
(13)   end;
(14)   if $V_5 = V_4$ then $V_3 := +1$ else $V_3 := +0$ {Why does this work?}
(15)   end
(16)   end.

Open **Example 7.5.2** within the Vector Machine folder in order to observe the operation of this language acceptor. Line (2) and the loop of lines (10)–(13) require $O(\log_2 n)$ steps each.

It is natural to ask for some general principle relating sequential time to parallel time in the context of language recognition. Such a principle is suggested by both Examples 7.5.1 and 7.5.2. For we have now seen that languages $\{w \in \Sigma^* | w = w^R\}$ with $\Sigma = \{a, b\}$ and $\{a^{2^i} | i \geq 0\}$ are accepted by vector machines in logarithmic time — that is, in $O(\log_2 n)$ parallel steps. (In Chapter 8 we shall introduce the term "highly parallel" in connection with such languages.) Furthermore, our work in Chapter 2 showed that each of these languages is acceptable in polynomially bounded time by some multitape Turing machine. So resorting to the parallel model has resulted in an exponential improvement in computation time (cf. Remark 0.3.3). Is this sort of improvement always possible? In other words, given language L accepted in polynomial time by some Turing machine or register machine, is it always true that L is accepted by some vector machine in (something approximating) logarithmic time? As we shall see in §8.7, the answer appears to be no, in general, despite the fact that such an improvement is indeed available in a great many cases.

Finally, in our study of vector machines and language recognition, it would be remiss not to consider language $L = \{w \in \Sigma^* | n_a(w) = n_b(w)\}$ with $\Sigma = \{a, b\}$, given that this language accompanied us throughout our earlier survey of sequential models.

EXAMPLE 7.5.3 (Same Number of *as* and *bs*) (advanced) Suppose that input word w over $\Sigma = \{a, b\}$ is of even length. Then w consists of $|w|/2$ symbol pairs. Each of these pairs is either *aa*, *ab*, *ba*, or *bb*. Now suppose that all of the *aa*-pairs are eliminated obtaining w_1. Similarly, suppose that the result of eliminating all *bb*-pairs from w is a new word w_2. Then it is evident that $|w_1| = |w_2|$ just in case $n_a(w) = n_b(w)$. (Try it.) Pseudocode describing a vector machine M that recognizes L appears below. (See also icon **Same Number of *a*'s and *b*'s**.)

Input: $V_1 = +Trans(w)$ {For example, if w is *baabaabb*, then V_1 will be $+10010011$.}

$V_2 = U(|w|) = +1^{2^k}$ {V_2 is needed since, in general, $|+Trans(w)| \neq |Trans(w)|$.}

Output:

$$V_3 = \begin{cases} +1 & \text{if } n_a(w) = n_b(w) \\ +0 & \text{otherwise} \end{cases}$$

> We are writing $(baabaabb)^{-1}$ for *abbabbaa*—the result of simultaneously replacing all *as* with *bs* and all *bs* with *as*.

Algorithm

(1)   begin

(2) $V_4 := V_1 = +Trans(w)$

(3) $V_5 := \neg V_1 \text{ \& } V_2 = +Trans(w^{-1});$

(4)   delete from V_4 all *00*-pairs from within $Trans(w)$;   {in $O(\log_2^3 n)$ steps}

(5)   delete from V_5 all *00*-pairs from within $Trans(w^{-1})$;   {in $O(\log_2^3 n)$ steps}

(6)   if pair-length of V_4 = pair-length of V_5 {There are several cases to consider.}

(7)   then $V_3 := +1$

(8)   else $V_3 := +0$

(9)   end.

> "polylogarithmic" time

The requirement that input length be a power of 2 is not nearly the limitation it might at first seem. Given input word w of length 12, say, padding with *1010* on the left produces a new word w' whose length is now a power of 2 and such that $w' \in L$ if and only if $w \in L$ (see Exercise 7.5.3(b)). And input words of odd length may be rejected at the outset (see Exercise 7.5.3(c)). We shall see that M computes in $O(\log_2^3 n)$ steps worst case. Hence we may conclude that the problem of determining whether $n_a(w) = n_b(w)$ is highly parallel. (This may come as a surprise to many readers since the data independence that makes our parallel algorithm possible is hardly obvious.) The pseudocode above is rather high level. We shall be especially interested in establishing the parallel time bounds for lines (4) and (5). Although the algorithm is not really hard, the details are considerable.

We start by assuming that input word $Trans(w)$ of length 2^k has been subdivided into 2^d intervals, each of length 2^e. For instance, letting $w = aababbaabbbaaaa$ so that $Trans(w) = 0010110011100000$ with $k = 4$ and letting $d = 1$, it follows that $e = 3$ and that $Trans(w)$ consists of $2 = 2^d$ intervals w_1 and w_2 with

$$w_1 = 00\underline{1011}00 \quad \text{and} \quad w_2 = \underline{1110}0000 \tag{7.5.1}$$

In general, we have that $k = d + e$. We shall focus on bit-pairs of the form *00*, as explained earlier. Now it can be seen that each interval w_i here just happens to be describable as $(00)^* \rho_i (00)^*$, where ρ_i is a word over $\{01, 10, 11\}$. (In this sense, w has been carefully chosen, and we shall explain later how the w_i would come to have this special form.) Our preliminary goal will be to show that we can simultaneously shift the ρ_i to the far right within w_i so as to obtain

$$w_1' = 0000\underline{1011} \quad \text{and} \quad w_2' = 0000\underline{1110} \tag{7.5.2}$$

Moreover, we shall see that this can be done in polylogarithmic time.

We shall think of the two intervals w_1 and w_2 at (7.5.1) here as being of two distinct types. First, the number of *0*s on the right in interval w_1 is strictly less than $4 = 2^{e-1}$. Hence, relative to $j = e - 1$, we shall say that w_1 is of *type 1*. Interval w_2, on the other hand, is clearly not of type 1; we shall say that it is of *type 2* relative to $j = e - 1$ by virtue of the fact that the number of *0*s on the far right is not strictly less than $4 = 2^j = 2^{e-1}$. If, within each interval w_i of type 2, we simultaneously move ρ_i to the right $4 = 2^j = 2^{e-1}$ positions, while leaving intervals of type 1 unchanged, then the result will be two intervals each containing fewer than $4 = 2^j = 2^{e-1}$ 0s on the right. Thus $Trans(w) = w_1 w_2$ would be transformed into $w_1' w_2'$, as at (7.5.2).

This shifting to the right of the ρ_i within intervals w_i is iterated. Namely, relative to $j = e - 2$ now, all intervals of type 2, containing $2 = 2^j = 2^{e-2}$ or more 0s on the right, are simultaneously shifted $2 = 2^j = 2^{e-2}$ positions to the right, intervals of type 1 being left unchanged. The result is $2^d = 2$ intervals, each containing strictly fewer than $2 = 2^j = 2^{e-2}$ 0s on the right. Note that there will now be no 00-pairs on the right within either interval, given that neither consisted solely of 0s initially.

We shall use special masks to distinguish intervals of type 1, relative to a given j with $e > j \geq 0$, from those of type 2. In order to distinguish them from the sort of masks introduced in Example 7.4.6, let us refer to them as 00-masks, reflecting their intended use in deleting 00-pairs from $Trans(w)$. The general form of 00-masks will be

$$\mu_{je}^d =_{\text{def.}} +(0^{2^e - 2^j} 1^{2^j})^{2^d}$$

Note that mask μ_{je}^d is of length $2^e \cdot 2^d = 2^{e+d} = 2^k = |w|$. A given interval w_i of length 2^e within w will be of type 2 with respect to $j = e - 1$ just in case the corresponding interval within $+Trans(w) \, \& \, \mu_{je}^d$ consists entirely of 0s, as the reader should now verify (see Exercise 7.5.4). Moreover, the following code sequence will enable a vector machine to transform those intervals in $+Trans(w) \, \& \, \mu_{je}^d$ that do not consist entirely of 0s into corresponding intervals consisting solely of 1s. As a result, intervals within $Trans(w)$ of type 2 will have been transformed into intervals consisting entirely of 0s, while intervals of type 1 will have been transformed into intervals consisting entirely of 1s. Relative to a given w, k, e, and j, we shall refer to the result of carrying out this transformation as $Transform(w, k, e, j)$.

```
Input:     V₁ = +Trans(w)
           V₂ = μⱼₑᵈ;     V₃ = μ₀ₑᵈ
           V₄ = U(j);     V₅ = U(e)
Output:    V₆ = Transform(w, k, e, j)
Algorithm
(1)   begin
(2)        V₆ := V₁ & V₂;
(3)        V₇ := +1;
(4)        while V₄ ≠ + do begin
(5)             V₈ := V₆ ≫ V₇;
(6)             V₆ := V₆ ∨ V₈;
(7)             V₇ := V₇ ≪₀ 1;
(8)             V₄ := V₄ ≫ 1
(9)        end;
(10)       V₂ := V₂ & V₃;
(11)       V₇ := +1;
(12)       while V₅ ≠ + do begin
(13)            V₈ := V₆ ≪₀ V₇;
(14)            V₆ := V₆ ∨ V₈;
(15)            V₇ := V₇ ≪₀ 1;
(16)            V₅ := V₅ ≫ 1
(17)       end
(18)  end.
```

The reader can verify our claims regarding this code sequence by opening icon **Example 7-5-3a** and loading vector set ex7-5-3a.vs, where it is assumed that $d = 1$, $e = 3$, and $j = 2$.

Next, the reader is invited to open icon **Example 7-5-3b** and to load vector set ex7-5-3b.vs in order to verify that the instruction sequence below moves ρ_i to the right 2^j positions within each interval w_i of type 2 only, those of type 1 being left unchanged. In other words, (7.5.1) will be transformed into

(7.5.2). (We assume that V_2 consists of $2^d \cdot 2^{e-(j+1)}$ intervals of length 2^{j+1}, each of which is either all *1*s or all *0*s depending upon whether the corresponding interval in V_1 is of type 1 or of type 2 with respect to j.)

Input: $V_1 = +Trans(w)$
             $V_2 = Transform(w, k, e, j)$
             $V_3 = U(j);$
Output: $V_4 = Shift\text{-}Type\text{-}2\text{-}Intervals(w, k, e, j)$
Algorithm
begin
        $V_5 := +1;$
        while $V_3 \neq +$ do begin
            $V_5 := V_5 \ll_0 1;$
            $V_3 := V_3 \gg 1$
        end; $\{V_5$ now contains $B(2^j).\}$
        $V_4 := (V_2 \,\&\, V_1) \vee (\neg V_2 \,\&\, V_1) \gg V_5$
end.

As for the generation of the required *00*-masks, the coarsest, relative to a given k and e, is μ_{je}^d with $d = k - e$ and $j = e - 1$.[2] This mask can be obtained by way of the code sequence given below.

Input: $V_1 = +U(k)$
             $V_2 = +U(e)$
Output: $V_3 = Generate\text{-}Coarsest\text{-}00\text{-}Mask(k, e) = \mu_{je}^d$ with $d = k - e$ and $j = e - 1$
Algorithm

(1)   begin
(2) $V_4 := U(2^{uval(V_1)}) = U(2^k) = +1^{2^k};$
(3) $V_5 := Generate\text{-}Coarsest\text{-}Mask(k) = m_{k,k-1};$
                                $\{$cf. Example 7.4.6 and ex7-4-6a.vm,
                                    which will take V_4 as input.$\}$
(4) $V_6 := B(2^k) = +10^k;$
(5) $V_6 := V_6 \gg 1 = B(2^{k-1}) = +10^{k-1};$
(6) $V_7 := V_1;$ $\{$loop control variable $i\}$
(7)   while $V_7 \neq V_2$ do begin $\{$while $i \neq e$ do begin$\}$
(8) $V_5 := Generate\text{-}Finer\text{-}Mask(m_{k,i-1}, i - 1);$
                                $\{$cf. Example 7.4.6 and ex7-4-6b.vm,
                                  which will take both V_5 and V_6
                                  as input.$\}$
(9) $V_6 := V_6 \gg 1;$
(10) $V_7 := V_7 \gg 1$ $\{i := i - 1\}$
(11)   end; $\{V_5$ is now $m_{k,e-1}.\}$
(12) $V_3 := V_4 \oplus V_5$ $\{V_3$ becomes $\mu_{je}^d.\}$
(13)   end.

Generating this coarsest *00*-mask requires $O(k)$ steps, which is $O(\log_2 |w|)$ steps, assuming $|w| = 2^k$ (see Exercise 7.5.6). This machine may be observed at icon **Example 7.5.3c**—load vector set ex7-5-3c.vs. After this first, coarsest *00*-mask has been obtained, each subsequent finer, *00*-mask is

---

[2] We speak of a *00*-mask μ_{je}^d being coarsest "relative to a given k and e" rather than "relative to a given k and e and d." This reflects the fact that k and e together determine d by virtue of $k = d + e$, as mentioned previously. As for use of the term "coarse" here, we are regarding $\mu_{23}^1 = +0000111100001111$ as *coarser* than $\mu_{13}^1 = +0000001100000011$. The latter mask is the *finer* of the two. What is the finest *00*-mask relative to $k = 4$ and $e = 3$?

obtainable in O(1) steps from the preceding one using the formula

$$\mu_{j-1,e}^{d} := \mu_{je}^{d} \& \mu_{je}^{d} \gg 2^{j-1} (= \text{Generate-Finer-00-Mask}(\mu_{je}^{d}, j))$$

The machine at icon **Example 7.5.3d** takes μ_{je}^{d} and $B(j)$ as input and generates $\mu_{j-1,e}^{d}$ as output. Use vector set ex7-5-3d.vs in conjunction with this machine.

Putting it all together, our *Move-Right* program, which is implemented at icon **Example 7-5-3e**, appears below. Vector set ex7-5-3e.vs may be used to verify that vector $+0010110011100000$ is transformed into vector $+0000101100001110$. We remind the reader that, since $k = \log_2 |w|$, any subroutine computing in O(e) steps or O(j) steps requires O($\log_2 |w|$) time.

Input:	$V_1 = +Trans(w)$	
	$V_2 = U(k) = U(\log_2 |w|)$	
	$V_3 = U(e)$	
Output:	$V_4 = \text{Move-Right}(w, k, e)$	

Algorithm

(1) begin
(2) $\quad V_5 := \text{Generate-Coarsest-00-Mask}(k, e) = \mu_{e-1,e}^{d}$;
         {requires O($\log_2 |w|$) steps by **Example 7.5.3c** and takes V_2 and V_3 as input}
(3) $\quad V_6 := V_3 \gg 1$;   {loop control variable j initialized to $e - 1$}
(4) $\quad V_7 := B(2^j) = B(2^{e-1})$;
(5) $\quad V_8 := \mu_{0e}^{d}$;   {This is the finest *00*-mask relative to k and e and is obtainable in O($\log_2 |w|$) steps at icon **Example 7.5.3f**.}
(6) $\quad V_{10} := V_1$;
(7) $\quad$ while $V_6 \neq +$ do begin
(8) $\quad\quad V_9 = Transform(w, k, e, j)$;   {requires O($\log_2 |w|$) steps by **Example 7.5.3a** and takes V_{10}, V_5, V_8, V_6, and V_3 as input}
(9) $\quad\quad V_{10} := \text{Shift-Type-2-Intervals}(w, k, e, j)$;
         {requires O($\log_2 |w|$) steps by **Example 7.5.3b** and takes V_{10}, V_9, and V_6 as input}
(10) $\quad\quad V_5 := \text{Generate-Finer-00-Mask}(\mu_{je}^{d}, j)$;
         {requires O(1) steps by **Example 7.5.3d** and takes V_5 and V_7 as input}
(11) $\quad\quad V_6 := V_6 \gg 1$;   {$j$ decremented}
(12) $\quad\quad V_7 := V_7 \gg 1$ {V_7 becomes $B(2^j)$}
(13) $\quad$ end;
(14) $\quad V_4 := V_{10}$
(15) end.

Since the while-loop of lines (7)–(13) is executed O($\log_2 |w|$) times, the entire algorithm is seen to require O($\log_2^2 |w|$) steps worst case.

We shall assume a dual routine computing *Move-Left*(w, k, e). Given input vectors $V_1 = +Trans(w)$, $V_2 = U(k)$, and $V_3 = U(e)$, this routine creates in vector V_4 the result of moving ρ_i to the far left within any interval w_i of length 2^e within *Trans(w)*, where, once again, w_i is assumed to be of the form $(00)^* \rho_i (00)^*$ with ρ_i a word over $\{01, 10, 11\}$. Open icon **Example 7.5.3g** and load vector set ex7-5-3g.vs in order to verify that *Move-Left*$(aaaababbaaaabbba, 4, 3)$ involves transforming $+0000101100001110$ into $+1011000011100000$. We note in passing that *Move-Left*(w, k, e) for $e = 1$ causes no change in *Trans(w)* so that output V_4 will be identical with $V_1 = +Trans(w)$, as the reader can easily verify using the companion software.

The subroutine *Delete-00*(w, k) can now be described. Suppose that word w of length $n = 2^k$ consists of 2^d intervals of length 2^e. Furthermore, let us assume that, as the result of an earlier call to subroutine *Move-Right*, each word ρ_i has been positioned at the far right within each w_i, as shown in Figure 7.5.1, where $d = 3$. If we then call *Move-Left* in such a way that the ρ_i are repositioned at the

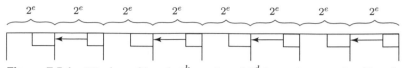

Figure 7.5.1 Word w of length 2^k consists of 2^d intervals w_i, each of length 2^e. (We have $d = 3$.) As the result of an earlier call to *Move-Right*, each ρ_i has been moved to the far right within each w_i. Next, a call to *Move-Left* at line (9) causes the ρ_i to be repositioned at the far left within the even-numbered intervals only.

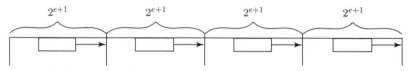

Figure 7.5.2 ρ_{h-1} and ρ_h have now been concatenated at the center of each of 2^{d-1} larger intervals, each of length 2^{e+1}. A subsequent call to *Move-Right* at line (13) positions $\rho_{h-1} \frown \rho_h$ at the right within each of those larger intervals.

far left within the even-numbered intervals only, we will have managed to concatenate ρ_{2h-1} and ρ_{2h} at the center of each of 2^{d-1} larger intervals of length 2^{e+1} (see Figure 7.5.2). A call to subroutine *Move-Right* then positions word $\rho_{2h-1}\rho_{2h}$ at the far right within those larger intervals.

In pseudocode we have

$$Z := U(2^k) \oplus m_{ke}; \tag{7.5.3}$$

$$Y := \textit{Move-Left}(Z, k, e);$$

$$+\textit{Trans}(w') := (+\textit{Trans}(w) \,\&\, m_{ke}) \vee Y;$$

$$+\textit{Trans}(w'') := \textit{Move-Right}(\textit{Trans}(w'), k, e + 1);$$

The use of mask $Z = +(0^{2^e} 1^{2^e})^{2^{d-1}}$ here causes odd-numbered intervals of length 2^e to be ignored in the subsequent call to *Move-Left*, thereby achieving the concatenation of ρ_{2h-1} and ρ_{2h} depicted in Figure 7.5.2.

Subroutine *Delete-00*(w, k) then amounts to iterating the instruction sequence at (7.5.3) for values of e ranging from 1 up to $k - 1$.

Input:	$V_1 = +\textit{Trans}(w);$	
	$V_2 = U(k) = U(\log_2 n)$ with $n = |w|$	
Output:	$V_3 = \textit{Delete-00}(w, k)$	
Algorithm		

```
(1)      begin
(2)          V4 := +1;
(3)          V5 := V1;
(4)          while V4 ≠ V2 do begin          {for e = 1 to k − 1 do begin}
(5)              V6 := U(2^k);
(6)              V7 := m_ke;
(7)              V8 := V6 ⊕ V7;
(8)              V9 := V5 & V8;
(9)              V10 := Move-Left(w', k, e);   {where V9 is +Trans(w') so that the
                                                 input vectors here are V9, V2, and V4}
```

> The call to *Move-Left* requires $O(\log^2_2 |w|)$ steps.

(10) $V_{11} := V_5 \& V_7$;

(11) $V_5 := V_{11} \vee V_{10}$;

(12) $V_4 := V_4 \ll_1 1$;

(13) $V_5 := \text{Move-Right}(w'', k, e + 1)$ {where V_5 is $+\text{Trans}(w'')$ so that the
                                                                                     input vectors here are V_5, V_2, and V_4}

> The call to *Move-Right* requires $O(\log^2 |w|)$ steps.

(14)   end;   {while}

(15) $V_3 := V_5$

(16)   end.

Open icon **Example 7.5.3h** and load vector set `ex7-5-3h.vs` in order to observe the manner in which word $w = baaabbaabbbaaaaa$ is transformed into $babbbbba$ in effect. Moreover, the body of the loop of lines (4)–(14) is iterated $k - 1$, which is $O(\log_2 n)$, times. And since each iteration requires $O(\log_2^2 n)$ steps, we have a total running time of $O(\log_2^3 n)$ steps worst case. Moreover, the software quickly reveals that space consumption is $O(n)$: The length of no vector exceeds that of input V_1 itself.

It is hoped that this is enough to enable the reader to see that the vector machine at icon **Same Number of a's and b's** accepts language $\{w \in \Sigma^* | n_a(w) = n_b(w)\}$ with $\Sigma = \{a, b\}$ in $O(\log_2^3 n)$ parallel time and $O(n)$ parallel space. Vector sets `samenum*.vs` and `diffnum*.vs` have been created for use with this machine.

The large vector machine at icon **Same Number of a's and b's** executes in roughly 4000 steps, given an input word of length $16 = 2^4$. The linear-time register machine of Example 5.3.1, on the other hand, requires only around 70 steps, as the reader can verify by loading tape `length16.rt` with the machine at icon **Same Number of a's and b's** within the Register Machine folder. How, then, is one to account for our expectation that parallel computation should be faster than sequential computation—at least in the case of a highly parallel problem such as that of determining whether $n_a(w) = n_b(w)$? Well, the answer is, of course, that computation in parallel apparently makes no real sense here if the size of input is a mere 16. The advantage of concurrency will become obvious at the point where input has attained a certain large size—2^{20}, say. For then the register machine's computation will involve something on the order of 2^{20} steps, whereas our vector machine will have a running time that, impressively, is on the order of 20^3.

§7.6 Parallel Computation and Cognitive Science

In order to substantiate our general claim that parallel processing has a role in cognition, we make a brief digression into the psychology of visual perception. In particular, just for the sake of definiteness, we consider a particular, highly regarded theory of human visual perception due to Canadian psychologist Donald Hebb (1904–1985) and outlined in [Hebb 1949]. It will make no real difference whether this theory is true in all its details. From our point of view, all that is required is that the theory be generally plausible and enable us to see a role for parallel processing in a particular cognitive activity, namely, visual perception.

Early experimental evidence ([von Semden 1932]) showed that human beings and many other animals such as rats possess an innate ability to distinguish between a presented object, or surface, and its background—that is, other objects or surfaces occurring in the same visual field. By all accounts, this innate capacity is probably traceable to the structure of human and animal retinas. Subsequent clinical findings demonstrated the existence of several structures within the frog's retina that are plausibly describable, collectively, as a bug-detector (see [Lettwin et al. 1959]). Comparable mechanisms in the human retina presumably enable us to distinguish a turkey sandwich from its background and to make estimations of distance and size.

Beyond this innate capacity for figure–ground segregation, however, nearly all aspects of our ability to acquire perceptual beliefs about objects appearing within our field of vision are developed only *after* birth. Take one's ability to perceive triangles—Hebb's own favorite example. Suppose that I am presented with a triangle on a chalkboard or on a monitor screen. What is involved in my perceiving the triangle *as a triangle*? Part of what is involved is an ability to perceive the triangle as being similar to other triangles and as being dissimilar from other nontriangular figures such as circles or rectangles. It also means that I will include my experience of *this* triangle in any subsequent generalizations concerning triangles. It presupposes my ability, if asked, to recall that the presented figure was, in fact, a triangle and not a square or circle. To invoke an alternative terminology, my perception of the presented triangle as a triangle presupposes having a *concept of triangle*. But all the clinical evidence—research on newly sighted adults blind from birth, say—suggests that my concept of triangle is not inborn. Rather, it develops only over time as the result of a range of experience of actual triangles. The same is true of my concept of a circle or a cube, by the way, as well as of color concepts, although the latter appear to develop much sooner.

So let us grant that an ability to have perceptual beliefs about triangles is not innate but, rather, develops in us only as the result of prolonged experience. It seems reasonable to hold that such an ability develops in children at an early age. Newborn infants definitely lack this ability, whereas those two years of age have already acquired it somehow, as was known already in the 1930s. But just what neurophysiological changes are responsible for the older infant's ability to perceive a triangle *as a triangle*? One seeks a neurophysiological account of this psychological development. But what can it be?

Hebb's Account of the Origin of a Neural Assembly for Detecting Triangles

The part of the brain responsible for visual perception is known as the *visual cortex*. It is divisible into four layers. The outermost of these layers appears to be the only one with direct connections to the retina, and activity within this layer closely mirrors activity within the retina itself. In consequence of this, the neural connections between the retina and this outermost layer are easily discernible. But this is not true of the neural connections to and between the other three layers. Here matters become exceedingly convoluted, and the challenge to any neurophysiological theory of vision is to make sense of this tumble of neural activity.

Hebb posits the existence of so-called *neural assemblies*—that is, purposeful associations of interconnected neurons—distributed over the four layers of the visual cortex. Such networks of interconnected neurons will play a role within our ultimate explanation of how a human subject perceives a geometrical figure such as the triangle of Figure 7.6.1. Given that such an assembly is not inborn, how does it establish itself within the visual cortex? Hebb's account runs something like this.

Suppose that someone who has never before seen a triangle focuses upon the apex of a triangle appearing on a monitor screen. (Such a subject might be an infant or an adult whose congenital cataracts have recently been surgically removed.) Doing so causes a certain pattern of retinal stimulation that lasts as long as the subject continues to fix upon the apex and that recurs each time the subject looks at it again after a brief interval of not looking at it. And each time this pattern of retinal stimulation occurs, it brings in its wake a certain pattern of neuronal activity within the visual

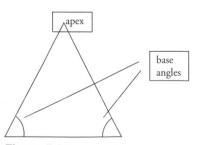

Figure 7.6.1

cortex whereby neurons within the outermost layer fire, triggering neuronal firings within other layers. Hebb makes the important assumption that, *with repetition of a particular pattern of firings, electrochemical changes within the visual cortex make it easier for the earlier neuronal firings to trigger later ones.* Hebb's own formulation of his neurophysiological postulate (Hebb's Rule) focuses upon individual neurons:

> When an axon of cell *A* is near enough to excite a cell *B* and repeatedly or persistently takes part in firing it, some growth process or metabolic change takes place in one or both cells such that *A*'s efficiency, as one of the cells firing *B*, is increased.

The mentioned growth processes and metabolic changes presumably consist of the formation of additional *synaptic connections* between neurons—neuronal learning, as it were. This assembly of interconnected neurons, distributed over the several cortical layers, may be regarded as an interdependent network of neurons whose interconnections cause them to function as a unit under certain circumstances, namely, when the subject focuses upon the apex of a triangle. This network of neurons is what we are going to call a "neuronal assembly." And, reasonably, the particular neuronal network at issue here will be regarded as the subject's apex detector. Once established at the cortical level, said detector will become activated whenever the subject focuses upon the apex of a triangle.

A similar story would relate the formation of a base-angle detector that will fire whenever the subject focuses upon either of the base angles of a triangle. Or perhaps there will be two distinct neuronal assemblies—one for left base angles and one for right base angles. Given the subject's acquired adeptness at recognizing angles *as angles*, how, then, is the entire triangle perceived *as a triangle*? In answering this question, we shall assume the prior existence of the various angle detectors mentioned already and go on to describe, still following Hebb, the formation within the visual cortex of a triangle detector.

At this point, Hebb makes a second important assumption. Namely, he assumes that *the human eye possesses an innate inclination to move so as to trace any lines occurring within the field of vision.* It follows that angles are frequent fixation points, given that they are formed by the intersection of two lines. Moreover, once focused upon one angle of a triangle, the eye's linear tendency can be counted upon, according to Hebb, to pull it toward the succeeding angle.

Now for the third of Hebb's assumptions: Given the myriad synaptic connections between neurons within the several layers of the visual cortex, he assumes that *numerous neurons within the subject's apex detector will just happen to have chance synaptic connections with base angle detectors.* Repeated focusings upon successive angles within a presented triangle, brought about by the eye's linear tendency, cause these firings of randomly connected neurons within the several distinct detectors to become ever more automatic. The detectors for apex and base angles are thereby incorporated into a new second-order neuronal assembly, which is what Hebb is calling the subject's triangle detector.

We do not wish to give the impression that a subject's triangle detector will develop at a single sitting. Rather, the developmental process must be assumed to occur over some period of time. But once the triangle detector is firmly established within the subject's cortex, looking in the direction of a triangle on the monitor screen will cause the detector to fire and, in turn, to effect those structural changes within the brain that are required for the subject to have any memory of having perceived a triangle.

Human Cognition = Low-Level Parallel Processing + High-Level Sequential Processing

Finally, we should like to use Hebb's account of the origin of a human triangle detector to illustrate a general claim regarding cognition. First, note that activation of the apex detector involves many simultaneous firings of neurons within the corresponding neuronal assembly. The same will be true of the other detectors. In other words, at the low neuronal level, processing proceeds in parallel, surely. At the level of the detectors themselves, however, one observes a certain *phase sequence* of central cortical activations: first, of the apex detector, let us suppose, then of the left base-angle detector, then of the right base-angle detector, and, finally, of the triangle detector. In short, the higher-order processing proceeds sequentially. We might interpret this to mean that, whereas the Turing machine is a reasonable performance model of higher-order cognitive activity, it is the vector machine that is a closer model of what is happening within the human brain at the level of neurons and first-order neuronal assemblies. And as for what is happening in the frog brain—specifically, in the presence of a bug, we are told that

> ... within [a fair area of his retina], it is not the light intensity itself but rather the pattern of local variation of intensity that is the exciting factor. There are four types of fibers, each type concerned with a different sort of pattern. Each type is uniformly distributed over the whole retina of the frog. Thus, there are four distinct parallel distributed channels whereby the frog's eye informs his brain about the visual image ... [Lettwin et al. 1965]

We suggest that each of the four types of fibers making up the frog's optic nerve will constitute a collection of first-order cell assemblies, each operating in parallel:

- sustained-contrast detectors (Did the sharp edge of an object either lighter or darker than its background just enter my field of vision and stop?)

- net convexity detectors (Did a dark object with positive curvature just enter my field of vision, perhaps with a jerking motion, and then stop?)

- moving-edge detectors (Is there an edge that is currently passing through my field of vision and that is clearly distinguishable from its darker or lighter background?)

- net dimming detectors (Has a larger dark spot just appeared and stopped at the center of my field of vision?)

Blithely skipping the details, we suggest that bug detection, on the part of the frog, amounts to some phase sequence of firings of some or all of these first-order detectors. This will then enable us to go on to claim that *both human and frog cognition are describable as low-level parallel processing combined with high-level sequential processing.*

§7.7 Further Remarks

Vector machines were first described in [Pratt and Stockmeyer 1976] which also includes an advanced discussion of the time and space requirements of vector machine algorithms. The elegance of this model resides in its permitting us to assume that instructions that are issued sequentially are being processed in parallel. To this extent, the vector machine model presupposes something like the specialized hardware of modern supercomputers. Our treatment of vector machines has been greatly influenced by that of [Hong 1986], which was the direct source of several of our examples—Example 7.4.7 (Reverse Word) in particular. The essential ingredients of Example 7.5.3 (Same Number of as and bs) are also to be found there.

As in the case of register machines, nondeterministic vector machines are the result of permitting two or more instructions to occur on one and the same line of a vector machine program. In other words, a nondeterministic vector machine program becomes a sequence of k-tuples of instructions for variable k, and the machine then chooses one of these instructions for execution at each step.

In this chapter we have considered but a single model of parallel computation. Consequently, our coverage of parallel models lacks the fullness of our earlier coverage of sequential models of computation. Other models of parallel computation include the *parallel random access machine model* of [Fortune and Wyllie 1978]. The Boolean circuit model of Exercise 7.7.6 appears in [Borodin 1977]. However, no model of parallel computation has emerged as a communitywide standard—something comparable to the single-tape Turing machine in the case of sequential computation. Moreover, to the extent that the various parallel models proposed—including vector machines—in no way account for the cost of communication between processors, it has been argued that the time analyses of parallel algorithms for all such models are unrealistic. This is because no parallel implementation using currently available technology is likely to achieve the proffered time bounds, given the likelihood of *communication bottleneck*.

EXERCISE FOR §7.1

7.1.1. In previous chapters we have focused exclusively upon *decision problems*—basically, yes/no questions in the sense of §1.1. Sorting problems, as they are customarily presented, are not decision problems. But they may be reformulated as such. For example, the problem of sorting a list of eight numbers $x_1, x_2, \ldots, x_8$ in ascending order, say, may be reformulated as the problem of obtaining the answer to each member of a collection of 64 questions of the form "Does number x_i occur in position n within the sorted list?" with both i and n ranging from 1 to 8. Having the correct answer to each of these 64 questions is tantamount to having sorted the given list $x_1, x_2, \ldots, x_8$.

For each of the computation problems below, explain how it might be construed as a decision problem.

(a) The problem of finding the position of a given element within a list (if indeed it *is* an element).

(b) The problem of checking the spelling of words occurring in a given document.

(c) The problem of checking whether there are any duplicated elements within a list.

EXERCISES FOR §7.2

7.2.1. Determine which of the following bit sequences are vectors. In the case of each vector V, give both $|V|$ and $bval(V)$.
(a) ... *000000000000001001*
(b) ... *100100100100100100*
(c) ... *000000000000011100*
(d) ... *111111111111101111*
(e) ... *000000000010111010*
(f) ... *111111111100011011*

7.2.2. Give a vector V satisfying the indicated requirements if possible.
(a) $bval(V) = +21$
(b) $bval(V) = -21$
(c) $bval(V) = -21$ and $|V| = 7$
(d) $bval(V) = +21$ and $|V| = 7$
(e) $bval(V) = 0$ and $|V| = 6$
(f) $bval(V) = +19$ and $|V| = 8$
(g) $uval(V) = +6$

7.2.3. Let $A = \ldots 0000010011$,

$B = \ldots 00000011001$, and
$C = \ldots 000000011111$.
Identify each of the following vectors.
(a) $A \mathbin{\&} B$
(b) $A \vee B$
(c) $\neg A \vee B$
(d) $A \rightarrow B$
(e) $A \leftrightarrow B$
(f) $A \leftrightarrow \neg B$
(g) $A \oplus B$
(h) $(A \leftrightarrow \neg B) \vee C$
(i) $(A \oplus B) \mathbin{\&} \neg C$

7.2.4. Again, let $A = \ldots 0000010011$ and $B = \ldots 00000011001$. Characterize each of the following vectors in terms of Boolean operations on vectors A and B above.
(a) ... *111111111111100110*
(b) ... *111111111111110111*
(c) ... *111111111111101110*

7.2.5. Where $A = \ldots\ 0000010011$ and $B = \ldots\ 00000011001$, identify $bval(A), bval(B),$ $bval(\neg A), bval(\neg B),$ and $bval(A \vee B)$.

7.2.6. ^{hwk} Suppose that V is the vector -01101. Identify each of the following.
(a) $V \ll_0 4$
(b) $(\neg V) \ll_0 4$
(c) $\neg V \ll_0 4$
(d) $V \ll_1 3$
(e) $V \gg 3$
(f) $V \ll_0 -2$
(g) $(V \ll_0 4) \ll_1 3$

EXERCISES FOR §7.3

7.3.1. Suppose that register V_2 contains vector $U(n)$ for some $n \geq 1$. Describe the result of executing the instruction (7.3.3)—or the instruction sequence (7.3.4).

7.3.2. Suppose that register V_2 currently contains vector $+10^{n-1}$ and that register V_3 currently contains vector $B(k)$ for some fixed k. The execution of what single instruction causes V_2 to come to contain vector $+10^{n+k-1}$?

7.3.3. ^{hwk} Suppose that register V_2 contains vector $U(n)$ for some $n \geq 1$ and that register V_3 currently contains vector $B(k)$ for some fixed k. Present a sequence of instructions that causes V_2 to come to contain vector $+10^{n+(m+1)\cdot k-1}$ for some fixed $m \geq 0$? (*Hint:* Use Exercises 7.3.1 and 7.3.2.)

7.3.4. Suppose that register V_2 currently contains vector $U(m)$ for some $m \geq 1$ and that register V_3 currently contains vector $B(n-m)$ for some $n \geq m$. The execution of what two instructions causes V_2 to come to contain vector $+1^m 0^{n-m+1}$?

EXERCISES FOR §7.4

7.4.1. Design a vector machine that, given input vectors V_1 and $V_2 = +1^n$ for $n \geq 1$, determines whether the nth bit within V_1 is 0 or 1. Your machine should compute in $O(\log_2 n)$ steps. (*Hint:* You may assume the Unary-to-Binary Converter of Example 7.4.2, which takes $V(n)$ to $B(n)$. Use constant vector $+1$ and operations $\gg$ and &.)

7.4.2. Design a vector machine that, given inputs $+w$ and $+1^{|w|}$, generates as output $+ww = +w^2$—that is, the result of concatenating w with itself. Give a time analysis of your machine. (*Hint:* Use Example 7.4.2 again and operations $\ll_0$ and $\vee$ this time.)

7.4.3. ^{hwk} Consider the vector machine of Example 7.4.5, letting $n = 25$ and $m = 4$. Then complete Table 7.4.4.

Table 7.4.4

Input Vectors $U(n) = +1^{25}$ and $U(m) = +1^4$	Output Register V_3	Auxiliary Registers		
		V_4	V_5	V_6
Initialization lines (2)–(4)	$+$	$+100$	$+11001$	$+1^{25}$
Within while-loop				
Iteration 1				
Iteration 2				
Iteration 3				

7.4.4. Consider the vector machine M whose description appears below.

Input: V_1
$\qquad V_2 = +1^n$ for $n \geq 1$

Output:

$$V_3 = \begin{cases} + & \text{if the } n\text{th digit from} \\ & \text{the right is } 0 \\ +1 & \text{if the } n\text{th digit from} \\ & \text{the right is } 1 \end{cases}$$

Algorithm
```
(1)    begin
(2)        V₄ := V₁;
(3)        V₂ := V₂ ≫ 1;
(4)        while V₂ ≠ ∣ do begin
(5)            V₂ := V₂ ≫ 1;
(6)            V₄ := V₄ ≫ 1;
(7)        end;
(8)        V₅ := +1;
(9)        if V₄ & V₅ ≠ + then V₃ := +1
                          else V₃ := +
(10)   end.
```

The reader should verify that M identifies the nth bit from the right in input vector V_1 and, as such, is an alternative solution to Exercise 7.4.1. In light of Programming Hint 7.4.3, explain why this solution is inferior to one involving use of the Unary-to-Binary Converter. (*Hint:* Use big-O notation to give a time analysis of M's performance.)

7.4.5. Write out all five masks of index 5.

7.4.6. Show how (7.4.2) can be used to obtain m_{41} from m_{42}, stored in register Y. (Assume that W is $+100$.) Then show how (7.4.2) can be used to obtain m_{40} from m_{41}.

7.4.7. Consider the algorithm below.

Input: $V_1 = +Trans(w)$
$\qquad V_2 = +1^n$, where $n = |Trans(w)|$

Output: V_3
$\qquad\qquad V_4$

Algorithm
```
begin
    V₅ := V₂;
    V₆ := +1;
    while V₅ ≠ + do begin
```

```
        V₅ := V₅ ≫ V₆;
        V₆ := V₆ ≪₀ 1
    end;
    V₇ := +;
    V₇ := V₇ ≪₁ V₆;
    V₈ := V₂ ⊕ V₇;
    V₉ := +;
    while V₈ ≠ + do begin
        V₉ := V₉ ≪₁ 1;
        V₈ := V₈ & (V₈ ≪₀ 1)
    end;
    V₁₀ := Convert(V₉);
                {We are applying the
                 machine of Example 7.4.2.}
    V₃ := V₁ ≪₀ V₁₀;
    V₄ := V₁ ≪₁ V₁₀
end.
```

(a) Suppose that the initial values of V_1 and V_2 are $+100011$ and $+1^6$, respectively. What are V_3 and V_4 set to?

(b) Suppose that the initial values of V_1 and V_2 are $+10111110011$ and $+1^{11}$, respectively. What are V_3 and V_4 set to?

(c) Suppose that the initial values of V_1 and V_2 are $+11100011$ and $+1^8$, respectively. What are V_3 and V_4 set to?

(d) Suppose that the initial values of V_1 and V_2 are $+(10)^{50}$ and $+1^{100}$, respectively. Without working through the algorithm, say what V_3 and V_4 will be set to.

(e) What is the apparent purpose of the algorithm?

7.4.8. Prove Theorem 7.1 stating that any partial recursive function is vector-machine-computable, and vice versa. (*Hint:* Show that any register machine instruction can be simulated by a vector machine, thereby demonstrating, in essence, that any partial recursive function is vector-machine-computable. As for the other direction, show that any vector machine instruction can be simulated by a multitape Turing machine, where each tape is used to represent the contents of one vector machine register.)

7.4.9. ^{hwk} Use the time analyses of Examples 7.4.4 and 7.4.5 to justify Remark 7.4.3.

EXERCISES FOR §7.5

7.5.1. Prove Theorem 7.2. (*Hint:* Modify the proof of Theorem 7.1 as given in the solution to Exercise 7.4.8.)

7.5.2. Prove Corollary 7.1. (*Hint:* Reexamine the proof of Theorem 7.1 as given in the solution to Exercise 7.4.8.)

7.5.3. (a) Design a vector machine that takes as input a vector V_1 of the form $+1^n$ with $n \geq 1$ and returns as output the vector $V_2 = +1^{2^k}$ with $k = \lceil \log_2 n \rceil$. Your machine should compute in $O(\log_2 n)$ parallel steps and consume $O(n)$ space.

    (b) Modify the vector machine at icon **Same Number of a's and b's** so as to accommodate input words whose length is not a power of 2.

    (c) Design a vector machine that takes as input a vector V_1 of the form $+1^n$ with $n \geq 1$ and returns as output the vector $V_2 = +1$ if $|V_1|$ is even and returns $V_2 = +$ otherwise. Your machine should

compute in $O(\log_2 n)$ parallel steps and consume $O(n)$ space.

7.5.4. ᴴᵂᴷ (a) Letting $w = 0010110011100000$ so that $k = 4$, what is $+w$ & μ_{23}^1? (Here $d = 1, j = 2$, and $e = 3$.)

    (b) Letting $w = 0010110000001110$ so that $k = 4$, what is $+w$ & μ_{13}^1? (Here $d = 1$, $j = 1$, and $e = 3$.)

7.5.5. (a) Design a vector machine that takes as input a vector $V_1 = +10^n$ and returns as output a vector $V_1 = +1^n$. Your machine should compute in $O(\log_2 n)$ parallel steps and consume $O(n)$ space.

    (b) Design a vector machine that takes as input any vector V_1, where V_1 is a positive vector with $|V_1| = n$, and returns as output a vector $V_1 = +1^n$. Your machine should compute in $O(\log_2 n)$ parallel steps and consume $O(n)$ space.

7.5.6. Show that the algorithm *Generate-Coarsest-00-Mask*(k, e) computes in $O(k)$ steps.

EXERCISES FOR §7.7 (END-OF-CHAPTER REVIEW EXERCISES)

7.7.1. (a) Let $V_1 = +1011$. What is $V_1 \ll_0 V_1$?
    (b) Let $V_2 = -01011$. What is $V_2 \ll_0 V_2$?

7.7.2. (a) Describe in English a single-tape Turing machine that converts a unary numeral to an equivalent binary numeral. For example, if machine input is 1^{17}, then machine output should be 10001. Give a time analysis of your algorithm.

    (b) Describe in English a multitape Turing machine that carries out this conversion. Give a time analysis.

    (c) Now compare these time analyses with that of the machine of Example 7.4.2.

7.7.3. (a) Design a vector machine to test whether or not the sign of a vector V_1 is positive. (Set output V_2 equal to $+1$ if V_1 has a positive sign and to $+0 = +$ if V_1 has a negative sign.) Give both a time and space analysis of your algorithm. Assuming that vector machines afford a realistic model of parallel computation, how many pro-

cessors would be required to achieve this time analysis?

    (b) Can you describe a vector machine for sign testing that computes in $O(1)$ time? Give a space analysis of your machine.

7.7.4. We have seen that the left-shift-0 operation applied to a vector can be construed in terms of multiplication by 2 (see Remark 7.4.1). What is the analogous interpretation of the right-shift operation?

7.7.5. Design a vector machine that computes the unary function $f(n) = 2^n$ in $O(n)$ time using $O(2^n)$ space.

7.7.6. ᴴᵂᴷ (**The Boolean Circuit Model**). We present an alternative model of parallel computation based on the notion of a *Boolean circuit*. Such a circuit may be depicted by an acyclic digraph, most of whose vertices are associated with k-ary functions from $\{0, 1\}^k$ to $\{0, 1\}$ with $k \geq 0$, where, as usual, we are writing

$\{0,1\}^k$ for

$$\underbrace{\{0,1\} \times \{0,1\} \times \cdots \times \{0,1\}}_{k \text{ times}}$$

(A 0-ary function will be one of two constants, 0 or 1.) The edges of a Boolean circuit are unlabeled. As an example, consider the Boolean circuit C of Figure 7.7.1. Circuit C has three *input vertices* x_1, x_2, x_3 and two *output vertices* y_1 and y_2. C manages to use all the more familiar Boolean functions. (We are writing $1_{\{0,1\}}$ for the identity function on $\{0,1\}$.) Input vertices are indicated by boxes and have indegree 0. NOT-vertices have indegree or *fan-in* 1; AND-vertices, OR-vertices, and those associated with the other binary connectives all have fan-in 2. (We shall occasionally speak of an AND-vertex, say, that receives both of its inputs from one and the same vertex v, as having fan-in 1.) The outdegree or *fan-out* of any vertex is 1 or greater unless that vertex is an output vertex, in which case it has fan-out 0. Given the usual understanding of functions $\neg, \&, \vee, \rightarrow$, and $\leftrightarrow$, we see that for inputs $x_1 = 1, x_2 = 1$, and $x_3 = 1$, circuit C produces outputs $y_1 = 0$ and $y_2 = 1$. (To see this, use the usual truth-table definitions, substituting 1 for T and 0 for F.)

Table 7.7.1

Input Vertices			Output Vertices	
x_1	x_2	x_3	y_1	y_2
1	1	1	0	1
1	1	0		
1	0	1		
1	0	0		
0	1	1		
0	1	0		
0	0	1		
0	0	0		

(b) We define the size of a Boolean circuit as the cardinality of its vertex set. What is $size(C)$ for the Boolean circuit C of Figure 7.7.1? The depth of a Boolean circuit is the length of the longest path from an input vertex to an output vertex. What is $depth(C)$?

(c) We shall say that the Boolean circuit C of Figure 7.7.1 *computes* the function $f: \{0,1\}^3 \rightarrow \{0,1\}^2$, where we have $f(\langle 1,1,1 \rangle) = \langle 0,1 \rangle$ and so on, as reflected in Table 7.7.1 once completed. You are asked to present a Boolean circuit that computes the function $g: \{0,1\}^2 \rightarrow \{0,1\}^1$ defined by Table 7.7.2.

Table 7.7.2

Input Vertices		Output Vertex
x_1	x_2	y_1
1	1	0
1	0	0
0	1	1
0	0	0

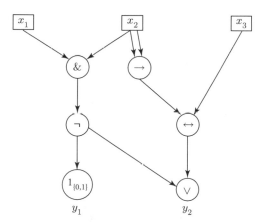

Figure 7.7.1

(a) Complete Table 7.7.1 so as to completely describe the behavior of Boolean circuit C pictured above.

(d) Present a Boolean circuit of size 6 and depth 2 that computes the function $h: \{0,1\}^3 \rightarrow \{0,1\}^2$ defined by Table 7.7.3. (*Hint:* Note that the y_2 column is identical with the x_3 column and use the identity function $1_{\{0,1\}}$—we are not permitting inputs to themselves be outputs. In addition, note that y_1 is 0 just in case x_1 and $x_2 \rightarrow x_3$ are both 0.)

Table 7.7.3

Input Vertices			Output Vertices	
x_1	x_2	x_3	y_1	y_2
1	1	1	1	1
1	1	0	1	0
1	0	1	1	1
1	0	0	1	0
0	1	1	1	1
0	1	0	0	0
0	0	1	1	1
0	0	0	1	0

(e) We shall think of each vertex within a Boolean circuit—including input and output vertices—as a processor. In addition, we assume that the computation of any Boolean function requires one time unit. (The same will be true of the reading in of input.) Processors on the same level are taken to be active simultaneously. It follows that:

- The size of the circuit C gives the number of processors (space) required.

- The depth of the circuit may be interpreted in terms of the number of steps required for the computation of the entire circuit. Specifically, $depth(C)+1$ gives the number of computation steps of Boolean circuit C.

Given this interpretation of size and depth, you are asked to present a Boolean circuit whose computation requires four processors and two parallel steps and is completely described by Table 7.7.4. (*Hint:* Note that the described circuit in effect reverses and negates its two input values.)

Table 7.7.4

Input Vertices		Output Vertices	
x_1	x_2	y_1	y_2
1	1	0	0
1	0	1	0
0	1	0	1
0	0	1	1

(f) Present a Boolean circuit whose computation requires six processors and two parallel steps and is completely described by Table 7.7.5. (*Hint:* Note that the described circuit in effect reverses and negates input values x_1 and x_3 and negates x_2.)

Table 7.7.5

Input Vertices			Output Vertices		
x_1	x_2	x_3	y_1	y_2	y_3
1	1	1	0	0	0
1	1	0	1	0	0
1	0	1	0	1	0
1	0	0	1	1	0
0	1	1	0	0	1
0	1	0	1	0	1
0	0	1	0	1	1
0	0	0	1	1	1

(g) As a final example, let us consider a Boolean circuit involving a vertex associated with a 0-ary Boolean function (see Figure 7.7.2). The vertex at the far right here is not an input vertex. Rather, it represents a Boolean function that takes no arguments and always returns value 0. You are asked to create a table completely describing the behavior of this two-input circuit.

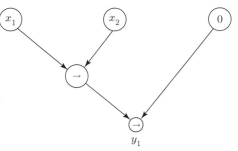

Figure 7.7.2

(h) We need to adopt some conventions for describing Boolean circuits similar to those used for describing Turing machines in §2.4. The first step, as usual, is to show that Boolean circuits can be described using strings over a finite *Boolean circuit description alphabet* Ψ. Each such string will consist of a number of k-tuples separated by semicolons. Typically, k will be 4, although sometimes 3 and sometimes 2. Moreover, the very first such tuple will represent the sequence of input vertices and hence will be of arbitrary length. Similarly, the final tuple will represent the output vertices. Here is a description of the Boolean circuit pictured in Figure 7.7.2.

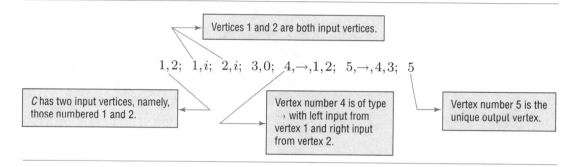

$$1,2; \quad 1,i; \quad 2,i; \quad 3,0; \quad 4,\rightarrow,1,2; \quad 5,\rightarrow,4,3; \quad 5$$

Vertices 1 and 2 are both input vertices.

C has two input vertices, namely, those numbered 1 and 2.

Vertex number 4 is of type › with left input from vertex 1 and right input from vertex 2.

Vertex number 5 is the unique output vertex.

We assume that the vertices of the Boolean circuit have been ordered from 1 to $size(C)$, starting with the topmost level and proceeding downward—within a level the vertices are ordered from left to right. Consequently, we see from the description string that the input vertices of C are numbered 1 and 2 and that the single output vertex is numbered 5. The five tuples after the input tuple describe the five vertices of C. Each consists of the number of the vertex being described followed by its type—for example, i(nput), 0 or 1, $\neg$ or &, and so forth. (It is true that not all unary and binary Boolean functions have standard names. But the important thing is that there is only a finite number of them: We can imagine ordering them and using their positions within this ordering as the second member of each tuple.) After the type comes the input vertices—left first and then right in the case of binary functions. The order in which one places these vertex descriptions within a canonical description word is arbitrary.

You are asked to present a canonical description word for the Boolean circuit

C of size 9 and depth 3 given in Figure 7.7.1.

(i) We wish to give a notion of language acceptance for Boolean circuits. However, notice that any given Boolean circuit involves a fixed number of input vertices. So, for example, comparing the circuits of Figures 7.7.1 and 7.7.2, we may think of the former as taking input words of length 2, while the latter takes input words of length 3. This does not accord with our expectation that a single machine should be able to process input words of arbitrary length. In order to accommodate this expectation, we introduce the notion of a *Boolean circuit family* and mean thereby an infinite collection of Boolean circuits—one with zero input vertices, one with one input vertex, another with two input vertices, and so forth. We shall write $\{C_n\}$ to denote such a family of circuits—a sort of abbreviation of $C_0, C_1, C_2, \ldots$, where C_k is that circuit within the family with k input vertices. To simplify our exposition, we shall assume that each circuit within $\{C_n\}$ involves a single output vertex. Then the language accepted by Boolean circuit family $\{C_n\}$ is $w \in \{0, 1\}^* \mid$ given input word w, $C_{|w|}$ produces output 1}. As usual, we shall write $L(\{C_n\})$ for the language over $\{0, 1\}$ accepted by Boolean circuit family $\{C_n\}$.

You are asked to show that the language of palindromes over $\{0, 1\}$ (or over $\{a, b\}$, assuming the usual translation) is accepted by some Boolean circuit family. Of course, such a family will be infinite. Hence one must be satisfied to describe the family schematically. First, describe C_n, involving n input vertices, for even n, say. Then do the same for the odd case. Give a time analysis for your Boolean circuit family by counting the number of levels within your schematic digraphs. (Basically, $time_{\{C_n\}}(n)$ will be given by $depth(C_n) + 1$.) Similarly, give a space analysis by counting the number of vertices. (And similarly, $space_{\{C_n\}}(n)$ will be given by $size(C_n)$.)

(j) We shall use symbol ↓ to indicate a so-called *NAND-vertex*. Any NAND-vertex has fan-in 2. A NAND-vertex with inputs x_1 and x_2 produces output 1 just in case x_1 and x_2 are not both 1. As an example, consider the circuit of Figure 7.7.3, consisting just of input vertices, x_1, x_2, and x_3, and NAND-vertices. What is the value of output y_1 if inputs x_1, x_2, and x_3 are 1, 0, and 0, respectively?

(k) Show that one can assume without loss of generality that any Boolean circuit consists solely of input vertices and NAND-vertices. (*Hint:* Use Exercise 0.8.7.)

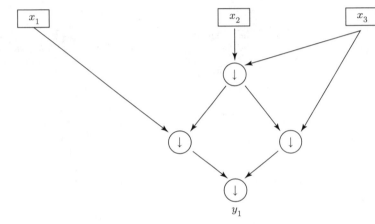

Figure 7.7.3

Chapter *8*

The Bounds of Computability

§8.1 The Church–Turing Thesis

We began §1.1 by reviewing the familiar concept of an algorithm. An algorithm was characterized as any method, for carrying out a given task, that is finite, definite, and conclusive. *Finite* in that after a finite number of steps any application of the method comes to an end; *definite* in that, at each point in carrying it out, there is a determinate next step; and *conclusive* in that, when any such application of the method terminates, an unambiguous result or answer has been generated. As in §1.1, we stress that the algorithm concept is inexact to the extent that the notions "next step," "carrying out," and "result," although clear enough for general purposes, are being left rather vague. As such, the concept *algorithm* belongs to the philosophy of mathematics.

Related to the notion of an algorithm, we considered the concept of an effectively calculable function or effectively computable function. As before, we now restrict our attention to the notion effectively calculable *number-theoretic* function. By this, we mean any number-theoretic function f—partial or total—for which an algorithm exists, that is, for which there exists an algorithm for determining the value of f for any argument(s) for which f happens to be defined. Due to the use of the algorithm concept in characterizing effectively calculable function, the latter concept is similarly philosophical. Again, we stress the importance of not confusing the philosophical concept of an effectively computable function with the mathematically rigorous concept of a Turing-computable function. They are two distinct concepts—one philosophical (but concerning mathematics) and the other genuinely mathematical.

- The philosophical notion of effectively calculable function is one that underlies the culture of mathematics. It is part of every mathematician's informal sense of what mathematics is about.

- There is nothing informal about the concept of a Turing-computable function. As described in Definition 1.7, a Turing-computable function is one computed by a Turing machine, where the latter is a quintuple of sets and functions satisfying certain conditions.

This not to say that the two concepts—one philosophical and one mathematical—are unrelated, however, and in the present section we discuss an important claim, known as the Church–Turing Thesis, concerning the relation between these two concepts.

As mentioned in Chapter 1, the Turing machine concept was originally intended as an analysis of the concept of computation. Specifically with respect to our function computation paradigm, we may take Turing in 1936 to be making the following claim.

(1) A number-theoretic function f is effectively calculable if and only if f is Turing-computable.

First, note that proposition (1) is not itself a mathematical proposition, since it makes use of the inexact notion of effective calculability. Hence there would be no point whatever in trying to *prove* (1). Rather, one seeks to provide *justification* for it. One presents arguments that lend support to it. Of course, since (1) is a biconditional, it has two parts.

(1)(a) If f is effectively calculable, then f is Turing-computable.

(1)(b) If f is Turing-computable, then f is effectively calculable.

As claims about functions, (1)(a) and (1)(b) have a very different status. First, proposition (1)(b) is obvious. After all, if there is a Turing machine M that computes f, then evidently f is associated with an algorithm, namely, the algorithm embodied in the state diagram of M. On the other hand (1)(a), which for historical reasons is usually known as the Church–Turing Thesis or just Church's Thesis, is *not* obvious. To see this, consider the following question. Might there not be some effectively calculable function f that is so bizarre that no Turing machine can model the algorithm involved in computing this particular f? If so, (1)(a) would be false. The mere fact that this question even makes sense forces one to conclude that the Church–Turing Thesis is at least not obviously true. So if Church–Turing is not obvious, are there at least reasons to think that it might be true? The answer is yes. To see what these reasons are, we quickly review the high points of our work in Chapters 1 through 7.

- Chapter 1 gave us our first mathematical model of an effectively calculable function, namely, the Turing machine model. The uncountably infinite class of number-theoretic functions was seen to be partitioned into those that are Turing-computable and those that are not.

- Chapter 3 then gave us the class of partial recursive functions. Moreover, by the end of Chapter 3 we had seen that the class of partial recursive functions is, in fact, identical with the class of Turing-computable functions.

- Similarly, at the end of Chapter 4 we learned that the class of Markov-computable functions is none other than the class of Turing-computable functions.

- Analogous equivalence results related register-machine computability to Turing computability (Chapter 5), Post computability to Turing computability (Chapter 6), and, finally, vector-machine computability to Turing computability (Chapter 7).

Moreover, this list could be continued indefinitely (see §8.12). Philosophers of mathematics have been impressed by the fact that such apparently dissimilar proposals regarding computability should turn out, in the end, to characterize the very same class of functions. After all, the Turing machine concept and the concept of a Markov algorithm, say, are on the face of it quite different: Turing machines are essentially sets of certain sorts of quadruples, whereas Markov algorithms are, fundamentally, sequences of productions. Nonetheless, despite this apparent dissimilarity, the two concepts turn out to coincide in a certain precise sense. Namely, we proved that a (partial) number-theoretic function f is Turing-computable if and only if f is Markov-computable (Theorems 4.2(a) and 4.2(b)).

What bearing do these several equivalence results have on the question of the truth of the Church–Turing Thesis as expressed in (1)(a)? Well, the fact that, over some 60 years now, every attempt to characterize the computability concept has netted the same class of functions has suggested to many people that the class of functions involved here is, first of all, a "natural" class—one such that the mathematical properties of its members make it the natural outcome of diverse approaches. The next step in this line of argument is to claim that this natural class can be none other that the class of effectively calculable functions. The reasoning behind this second claim seems to be something like the following. We must ask ourselves the question, If the class of Turing-computable functions were, in fact, a proper subset of the class of effectively calculable functions, might we not expect that one or more of the alternative characterizations of computability would turn out to encompass functions that are not Turing-computable? The plain fact is that, after 60 years of alternative models, none of these models has produced a single function that does not demonstrably fall within Turing's model. One possible explanation for our inability to find such a function is that no such function exists. That is, the accumulation of equivalence results has suggested that the class of Turing-computable functions is not a proper subset of the class of effectively calculable functions but is, rather, identical with it. As such, the history of computation theory has been interpreted as lending empirical support to the Church–Turing Thesis. To reiterate, if (1)(a) were false, should we not expect one of the proposed analyses of *effectively calculable function* to include some function that is *not* Turing-computable? The fact that this has never happened suggests—but by no means *proves*—that there is no such function, which in turn means that (1)(a) is true.

It is certainly fair to say that the Church–Turing Thesis is generally accepted as true within the mathematical community. Consequently, in what follows, we shall assume the Church–Turing Thesis at key points. Of course, (1)(a) is logically equivalent to its contrapositive:

If a function f is not Turing-computable, then f is not effectively calculable.

More often than not, it is the contrapositive to which we shall appeal.

> **CHURCH–TURING THESIS:** If function f is effectively calculable, then f is Turing-computable. Equivalently, if a function f is not Turing-computable, then f is not effectively calculable.

Having said this, it would be remiss to not at least mention a certain reservation that one must feel with regard to the accumulation of purported evidence for the Church–Turing Thesis. Namely, is it not at least conceivable that all of those who have presented the various analyses of computability have, in fact, committed certain systematic errors—errors characteristic of human cognitive processes? If so, then the coincidence of these analyses provides no real evidence that the class of functions attained—however "natural"—is, in point of fact, the targeted class of effectively computable functions. Rather, it would reveal only the not-so-surprising fact that different human beings tend to end up in one and the same place, however diverse their starting points. After all—or so the counterclaim would go—given similar training, we tend to think more or less alike. So why is it so remarkable that, working independently, we obtain similar results? In short, why should convergence of characterizations be taken to mean that the characterization project has succeeded in some absolute sense? (As a counter-counterclaim, one can argue that what makes the evidence so compelling is that the theoreticians involved have *not* been similarly trained. The various models/analyses proposed [including many that we have not considered] have been the work of philosophers, logicians, computer scientists, linguists, and mathematicians.)

In closing, we stress that the Church–Turing Thesis is not a tautology—not something of the form p if and only if p. Obviously, tautologies do not say much. In contrast, if any reader is tempted to regard Church–Turing as not saying much, then he or she is not thinking about it in the right way. Viewed correctly, Church–Turing is saying a great deal. It pairs an intuitive concept, which just happens to concern mathematics, with a mathematically rigorous characterization of that concept. As such, it is a proposal of great significance for the theory of computation, as we shall see.

Finally, for many readers, the plausibility of the Church–Turing Thesis will be illustrated, most convincingly, by our

---

EXAMPLE 8.1.1 (A Turing Machine That Compiles/Executes C Language Programs) Open icon **C Interpreter** within the Turing Machine folder in order to observe the operation of a multitape Turing machine that compiles and then runs programs written in a subset of C, as described in the software documentation. Tape sets `ex8-1-1*.tt` have been created for use with this machine.

---

§8.2 The Bounds of Computability-in-Principle: The Self-Halting Problem for Turing Machines

We remind the reader that not every number-theoretic function is Turing-computable. Indeed, in §2.7 we showed that the Busy Beaver function is Turing-computable only upon pain of contradiction. We shall do something similar in the present section. Namely, we shall define a new number-theoretic function f^* and then prove that f^* cannot be computed by any Turing machine. Furthermore, our discussion of the Church–Turing Thesis in §8.1 will now be brought to bear. For, assuming Church–Turing, function f^* is not merely not Turing-computable. It is not computable in *any* sense. That is, if Church–Turing is true, then function f^* is strictly beyond the bounds of what is computable. (The same can be said of the Busy Beaver function: If Church–Turing is true, then it is uncomputable.)

It was a feature of the Euler–Gödel scheme for encoding Turing machines, as introduced in §2.4, that most natural numbers are not the gödel numbers of any Turing machines. However, by the discussion leading to Remark 2.4.1, there is a way of extending that encoding scheme so that every natural number becomes the gödel number of some (unique) single-tape Turing machine. Accordingly, we shall assume an enumeration of Turing machines

$$M_0, M_1, M_2, \ldots \tag{8.2.1}$$

where M_0 is just the Turing machine with the smallest gödel number under the Euler–Gödel scheme, M_1 is the Turing machine with the next smallest gödel number, and so on.

Now, for a particular value of n, suppose that Turing machine M_n is starting scanning the leftmost *1* in an unbroken string of $n+1$ *1s* representing natural number n. In such a case, M_n may or may not halt in a value-representing configuration—that is, scanning the leftmost of an unbroken string of *1s* on an otherwise blank tape. If M_n does halt in such a configuration, then we shall say that M_n *self-halts in a value-representing configuration* in the sense that it halts in such a configuration given its own gödel number as input.

We frame our discussion in terms of the so-called *Self-Halting Problem for Turing Machines*. In itself, this problem may strike the reader as highly arcane. But it turns out, surprisingly, to have significance for a range of very practical issues.

THE SELF-HALTING PROBLEM FOR TURING MACHINES (first formulation): Does there exist a general algorithm for determining, for arbitrary $n \geq 0$, whether Turing machine M_n does or does not self-halt in a value-representing configuration?

Should there exist such an effective algorithm, then we shall say that the Self-Halting Problem for Turing Machines is *solvable*. Otherwise, it will be said to be *unsolvable*.

An equivalent formulation of the Self-Halting Problem for Turing Machines is the following. First, recall from the discussion leading up to Remark 1.5.1 that there is a way of thinking about Turing machines such that every Turing machine turns out to compute some unary (partial) number-theoretic function—frequently the everywhere-undefined function. Accordingly, we begin writing f_n for the unary function computed by Turing machine M_n. Our enumeration (8.2.1) of Turing machines, together with the assumption that every Turing machine computes some unary function, induces an enumeration of unary Turing-computable functions

$$f_0, f_1, f_2, \ldots \tag{8.2.2}$$

Now, for any given n, either $f_n(n)$ is defined or it is undefined. (This isn't something requiring proof. Rather, it follows immediately from the very nature of functionhood.) We can now give the Self-Halting Problem for Turing Machines a second, equivalent formulation.

THE SELF-HALTING PROBLEM FOR TURING MACHINES (second formulation): Is there a general algorithm for determining, for arbitrary $n \geq 0$, whether $f_n(n)$ is defined?

(The reader is encouraged to pause for a moment to ponder why our two formulations are equivalent.) Again, if there exists such an algorithm, then we shall say that the Self-Halting Problem for Turing Machines is solvable. Otherwise, it will be said to be unsolvable. Just to fix ideas, we consider two examples.

- Let us suppose that machine M_5 computes the function $f_5(m) = m^2$. This happens to be a total function, so in particular it is defined for $m = 5$. That is, $f_5(5)$ is defined and equal to 25. Equivalently, M_5 self-halts in a value-representing configuration.

- Let M_{10} be some Turing machine computing the unary function $f_{10}(m) = 3 - m$. Note that $f_{10}(m)$ is defined for $m = 0, 1, 2$, and 3 and undefined for all other arguments. It follows that $f_{10}(10)$ is going to be undefined. Apparently, Turing machine M_{10} does not self-halt in a value-representing configuration.

Next, consider the unary number-theoretic function defined by

$$f^*(n) = \begin{cases} 0 & \text{if } f_n(n) \text{ is undefined} \\ f_n(n) + 1 & \text{if } f_n(n) \text{ is defined} \end{cases} \tag{8.2.3}$$

First of all, note that f^* is a well-defined function. More importantly, note that if the Self-Halting Problem for Turing Machines is solvable, then f^* is effectively computable. This is easiest to see if we focus upon the second formulation.

- So suppose that we have an algorithm that enables us to determine whether $f_n(n)$ is defined for arbitrary n. Applying that algorithm to such an n, we may learn that $f_n(n)$ is defined, in which case we see that $f^*(n) = f_n(n) + 1$. On the other hand, should we learn that $f_n(n)$ is undefined, we see that $f^*(n) = 0$.

- In either case, we have succeeded in effectively calculating the value of $f^*(n)$. Since n was arbitrary, we can see that f^* is indeed effectively computable if the Self-Halting Problem is solvable.

The reader should also verify that the converse is true. Namely, if f^* is effectively computable, then the Self-Halting Problem is solvable. In any case, we are led to a third formulation of the Self-Halting Problem for Turing Machines—equivalent to both earlier formulations.

THE SELF-HALTING PROBLEM FOR TURING MACHINES (third formulation): Is the unary number-theoretic function f^* defined by

$$f^*(n) = \begin{cases} 0 & \text{if } f_n(n) \text{ is undefined} \\ f_n(n) + 1 & \text{if } f_n(n) \text{ is defined} \end{cases}$$

effectively computable, where we are writing f_n for the unary function computed by Turing machine M_n?

We next prove that f^* is not Turing-computable. It will then follow, assuming Church–Turing, that f^* is not effectively computable and that the Self-Halting Problem for Turing Machines is an unsolvable problem.

THEOREM 8.1 There exists no Turing machine computing f^*.

PROOF (indirect). Assume that there is a Turing machine M^* that computes f^* as defined at (8.2.3). Of course, M^* itself will occur in the enumeration at (8.2.1). Let d be the gödel number of M^* so that $M^* = M_d$ and $f^* = f_d$. (Thus d gives the position of f^* at (8.2.2).) Now suppose f^* is applied to d. By the definition of f^*, either $f^*(d)$ is equal to 0 or it is equal to $f_d(d) + 1$. We consider each case separately, always focusing upon the definition of f^* at (8.2.3).

- If $f^*(d) = 0$, then we have $f_d(d)$ undefined. But $f^* = f_d$ by assumption. In other words, $f_d(d)$ is simultaneously equal to 0 and undefined, which is a patent contradiction.

- If $f^*(d) = f_d(d) + 1$, then, by our assumption that $f^* = f_d$ again, we have

$$f_d(d) = f^*(d) = f_d(d) + 1$$

which is again absurd.

So either assumption about $f^*(d)$ produces a contradiction. We must conclude that there can be no Turing machine M^* computing f^*.   Q.E.D.

Again, we stress that Turing-computability, which is a mathematical concept given by Definition 1.7, is not to be confused with the intuitive concept of effective computability. On the other hand, the Church–Turing Thesis says that the Turing-computable functions *are* precisely the effectively computable functions. So, assuming the (contrapositive of the) Church–Turing Thesis, we can answer each of the questions constituting our three formulations of the Self-Halting Problem for Turing Machines. And the answer, in each case, is no.

> **REMARK 8.2.1:** Assuming the Church–Turing Thesis, the Self-Halting Problem for Turing Machines is unsolvable.

Some readers may benefit if we say a bit more to justify Remark 8.2.1. Our argument is indirect. Assume Church–Turing and, for the sake of deriving a contradiction, assume further that the Self-Halting Problem for Turing Machines is solvable. By our third formulation, this means that f^* is effectively computable. On the other hand, by Theorem 8.1, f^* is not Turing-computable and hence, by (the contrapositive of) Church–Turing, not effectively computable either. But this is absurd, since f^* cannot be both effectively computable and not effectively computable. We conclude that the Self-Halting Problem for Turing Machines is unsolvable. But note that this follows not from Theorem 8.1 alone but, rather, from Theorem 8.1 together with the Church–Turing Thesis.

§8.3 The Bounds of Computability-in-Principle: The Halting Problem for Turing Machines

As our second example of an unsolvable problem, we have the *(Full) Halting Problem for Turing Machines.*

> **THE (FULL) HALTING PROBLEM FOR TURING MACHINES (first formulation):** Is there a general algorithm for deciding, for arbitrary $n \geq 0$ and $m \geq 0$, whether Turing machine M_n halts in a value-representing configuration when started scanning the leftmost of $m + 1$ *1*s on an otherwise blank tape?

Again, by the fact that the enumeration (8.2.1) of Turing machines induces the enumeration (8.2.2) of unary Turing-computable functions, we have

> **THE (FULL) HALTING PROBLEM FOR TURING-MACHINES (second formulation):** Is there a general algorithm for determining, for arbitrary $n \geq 0$ and $m \geq 0$, whether $f_n(m)$ is defined?

Finally, consider the function defined by

$$h^*(n, m) = \begin{cases} 0 & \text{if } f_n(m) \text{ is undefined} \\ f_n(m) + 1 & \text{if } f_n(m) \text{ is defined} \end{cases}$$

Note that h^* is a binary, total number-theoretic function. By a simple argument already familiar to the reader from §8.2, it can be seen that the Halting Problem for Turing Machines may be reformulated as follows:

> **THE (FULL) HALTING PROBLEM FOR TURING-MACHINES (third formulation):** Is the binary number-theoretic function h^* defined by
>
> $$h^*(n, m) = \begin{cases} 0 & \text{if } f_n(m) \text{ is undefined} \\ f_n(m) + 1 & \text{if } f_n(m) \text{ is defined} \end{cases}$$
>
> effectively computable?

Using Church–Turing again, we shall argue that the Halting Problem is unsolvable. First, we prove the following proposition:

> **THEOREM 8.2:** The function h^* is not Turing-computable.

PROOF (indirect). Suppose, for the sake of deriving a contradiction, that h^* is Turing-computable. Now, since h^* is total, it follows that $h^*(n, m)$ is defined for arbitrary n and m. In particular, $h^*(n, n)$ must be defined for arbitrary n. Substituting n for m at (8.3.1), we have

$$h^*(n, n) = \begin{cases} 0 & \text{if } f_n(n) \text{ is undefined} \\ f_n(n) + 1 & \text{if } f_n(n) \text{ is defined} \end{cases}$$

Comparing the definition of $h^*(n, n)$ with the definition of function $f^*(n)$ at (8.2.3), we see that, for all n, $f^*(n) = h^*(n, n)$. It follows that f^* is Turing-computable since h^* is, which contradicts Theorem 8.1. We conclude that h^* must not be Turing-computable after all.   Q.E.D.

From Theorem 8.2 and (the contrapositive of) Church–Turing it follows that the Halting Problem for Turing Machines is unsolvable.

> **REMARK 8.3.1:** Assuming Church–Turing, the (Full) Halting Problem for Turing Machines is unsolvable.

The role of function f^*, as defined at (8.2.3), in the proof of Theorem 8.2 deserves further comment.

(1) Specifically, the proof of Theorem 8.2 amounts to showing that if function h^* is Turing-computable, then so is f^*. By Theorem 8.1, it then follows that h^* is not Turing-computable.

(2) By Church–Turing and focusing upon the third and last of our formulations in each case, (1) amounts to showing that if the Halting Problem is solvable, then so is the Self-Halting Problem. By Remark 8.2.1, it follows that the Halting Problem is unsolvable.

The line of reasoning at (2) is an instance of a general pattern that we shall utilize repeatedly in showing problems to be unsolvable. This pattern may be described as follows.

> **THE REDUCTION PRINCIPLE:** Suppose that $Problem_1$ has previously been shown to be unsolvable. We may then be able to show that a second $Problem_2$ is unsolvable by reasoning as follows. Namely, suppose that it can be shown, somehow, that any solution to $Problem_2$, assuming there to be such solutions, would be effectively transformable into a solution to $Problem_1$. Since, demonstrably, there can

be no solution to $Problem_1$, we are entitled to conclude that there can, in fact, be no solution to $Problem_2$ either. That is, we have shown that $Problem_2$ is unsolvable by virtue of our having *reduced* the unsolvable $Problem_1$ to it.

To help with the new terminology, we give an example that may serve as a rough analogy. Suppose that a number of scholarships have become available to exceptional foreign students. Suppose, further, that the Department of Computer Science, in working through its file of student majors, wishes to determine which majors are foreign students in order that they be notified of the competition for the new awards. Unfortunately, there is no document in a student's file that specifically identifies him or her as a foreign student, let us suppose. Someone remembers, however, that whereas social security numbers serve as student identification numbers for U.S. citizens, the student identification numbers of noncitizens begin with digits 999. The problem of identifying foreign students has thus been reduced to the problem of determining whether a student's identification number begins with a certain string of digits. This second problem is readily solvable. By virtue of our reduction, the first problem is solvable as well.

Finally, a slightly troublesome locution is introduced. We shall say that the problem of determining whether a student identification number begins with 999 is *at least as hard as* the problem of identifying foreign student files *in the sense that any solution to the former problem immediately yields a solution to the latter*. In other words, given our reduction, it is inconceivable that there exist a solution to the problem of recognizing 999 in the absence of a solution to the problem of recognizing foreign student files; after all, any solution to the former problem is transformable into a solution to the latter. In this sense, the foreign student file problem is no harder than the 999 problem, or, equivalently, the 999 problem is at least as hard as the foreign student file problem.

We have considered two problems that, assuming Church–Turing, are both unsolvable. One is the Self-Halting Problem for Turing Machines and the other is the Full Halting Problem for Turing Machines. The reader is encouraged to think about their relative difficulty in the following way.

- Suppose that we have a solution to the Full Halting Problem. In other words, given arbitrary natural numbers n and m, suppose that we are in possession of an effective method—call it $\mathcal{M}$—for determining, in a finite number of steps, whether Turing machine M_n halts when started scanning a representation of m.

- It is easy to see that this can be transformed into an effective method for determining whether M_n, for arbitrary n, self-halts. (Namely, start M_n scanning a representation of n and then apply method $\mathcal{M}$ to see whether it halts.) In other words, if the Full Halting Problem is solvable, then so is the Self-Halting Problem.

- In this sense, we have shown that the Halting Problem for Turing Machines is at least as hard as the Self-Halting Problem for Turing machines: If you had a solution to the former, you could turn it into a solution to the latter. Or, to put matters another way, it is not possible to have a solution to the Halting Problem without at the same time having a solution to the Self-Halting Problem.

- So the Self-Halting Problem is at least not *harder* than the Full Halting Problem—or, turning things around, the Halting Problem is at least as hard as the Self-Halting Problem. Theoreticians say that the Self-Halting Problem is *reducible to* the Halting Problem in the sense that a solution to the latter yields a solution to the former.

It is hoped that the reader sees the analogy between the situation of the Computer Science Department with respect to foreign student files and the relation between the Self-Halting and Halting Problems for Turing Machines. This analogy is less than perfect, however, due to the fact that the problem of recognizing string "999" might be considered *perceptually easier* than recognizing foreign student files per se. Plausibly, that is why one is interested in the reduction in the first place. However, our new locution "is at least as hard as," predicated of pairs of problems, should be considered semitechnical jargon that concerns not perceptual ease but rather the direction of a reduction: The problem of recognizing foreign student files has been reduced to that of recognizing 999, and, by virtue of this reduction, we shall say that the latter problem is at least as hard as the former.

Before turning to an application of these ideas within computer science, we mention that the reducibility relation between pairs of problems is a transitive relation. The reader should have no difficulty seeing that if problem P_1 is reducible to problem P_2 and problem P_2 is reducible to problem P_3, then P_1 is reducible to P_3. Alternatively, if P_3 is at least as hard as P_2 and P_2 is at least as hard as P_1, then P_3 is at least as hard as P_1.

EXAMPLE 8.3.1 (Application to Functional Programming) In Exercises 8.3.1–8.3.2 and 8.3.4–8.3.9, we present a series of unsolvability results within the theory of Turing computability, all of them ultimately consequences of the unsolvability of the Self-Halting Problem. We mention in particular Exercise 8.3.5, showing that there can be no general algorithm for deciding whether two Turing machines compute one and the same number-theoretic function. By the Church–Turing Thesis, we may reformulate this as follows: There can be no general algorithm for deciding whether two *computable* functions are identical. As we shall now show, this negative result has practical consequences for functional programming languages such as ML, which permit functions to be defined and then passed as parameters to other functions.

Here is the definition of a version of the unary function *sg* on the integers as it might occur within an ML program. (We are letting *sg* take value -1 for negative arguments.)

```
fun sg x = if x > 0

           then 1

           else if x = 0

           then 0

           else ~1;
```

As the example shows, function definitions in ML may involve calls to predefined relational operators from among $>, <, >=, <=, =$, and $<>$, defined on the integers and most other data types. A "doubling" function on the integers is definable either as

```
fun double-ver1 x = x + x;
```

or as

```
fun double-ver2 x = 2 * x;
```

Mathematically, regarded as sets of ordered pairs of integers, functions *double-ver1* and *double-ver2* are, of course, identical despite superficial differences in their respective definitions.

Within an ML program, functions may themselves take functional arguments. To take a simple example, function *apply-twice*, as defined below, takes two arguments—the first a unary function on the integers and the second an integer.

$$\textbf{fun}\ \texttt{apply-twice f x = f(f x);}$$

Applied to function *double-ver-2* and integer 4, say, function *apply-twice* returns value $2 * (2 * 4) = 16$. Applied to function *double-ver-1* and integer 4, function *apply-twice* returns value $(4+4)+(4+4) = 16$.

Functions taking functional arguments may *not* appeal to predefined operators testing for equality or inequality of *functions*. For example, it is not possible to ask ML to determine whether functions *double-ver1* and *double-ver2* are one and the same function—despite their obvious identity. This is because, by the result of Exercise 8.3.5 and Church's Thesis, there is no general algorithm that ML could use in order to decide the issue. In ML, data types such as integer, real, and bool, which allow tests for equality and inequality, are termed *equality types*. Our unsolvability result explains why function types cannot be equality types.

---

§8.4 The Bounds of Computability-in-Principle: Rice's Theorem

In this section we continue our investigation of the bounds of computability by presenting a limitative result known as Rice's Theorem, which happens to be of great importance to pragmatic computer science. Preliminary to formulating the theorem, we remind the reader of several things.

- By Remark 2.4.1, we may assume that every natural number is the encoding or gödel number of a unique single-tape, deterministic Turing machine.

- By Remark 1.5.1, every Turing machine with input alphabet $\Sigma = \{1\}$ computes a unary partial recursive function.

- It follows that the class of Turing machines with input alphabet $\Sigma = \{1\}$ may be effectively enumerated as $M_0, M_1, M_2, \dots$. Moreover, this enumeration of Turing machines induces an effective enumeration of unary partial recursive functions $f_0, f_1, f_2, \dots$.

- We have seen that some Turing machines self-halt while others do not. Let us define

$$K =_{\text{def.}}\ \{n | \text{Turing machine } M_n \text{ self-halts}\}$$

It is easy to show, given the unsolvability of the Self-Halting Problem for Turing Machines, that K is not recursive (see Exercise 8.4.1). It follows, by Remark 3.5.1, that K^c is not recursive either.

- Although the notion of self-halting that we have used previously is somewhat restrictive—self-halting involves terminating execution in a value-representing configuration—we can, without loss of generality, relax that restriction and take self-halting to mean terminating execution *in any configuration whatever* (see Exercise 8.2.1). We shall do this below.

We are ready to state and prove

THEOREM 8.3 (Rice's Theorem): Let Γ be a set of unary partial recursive functions that is nontrivial in the sense that it is neither empty nor is it the class of all unary partial recursive functions. Next, we let Ψ_Γ be the set of all the gödel numbers of (Turing machines that compute) members of Γ, assuming some effective enumeration and keeping in mind that a given function will have more than one gödel number. Then Ψ_Γ is not a recursive set of natural numbers.

PROOF Let Γ be a nontrivial set of unary partial recursive functions, and let Ψ_Γ be the set of all gödel numbers of members of Γ. Let $f_\varnothing$ be the totally undefined function of one argument, and let d be one of its gödel numbers so that M_d computes $f_\varnothing = f_d$. (For example, M_d might move off to the left without ever halting for arbitrary input n.) Now, obviously either $d \in \Psi_\Gamma$ or $d \notin \Psi_\Gamma$. We take the two cases separately.

If $d \in \Psi_\Gamma$, then we let f_j computed by M_j be some fixed unary function not in Γ. (By nontriviality, there must be such a function.) Next, let $M = M_n$ be an arbitrary Turing machine. Using M as basis, we construct a new Turing machine $M' = M_{n'}$ computing $f_{n'}$. Very roughly, given arbitrary input word I^{m+1}, machine M' first stores that input off to the left, say, and then proceeds to simulate $M = M_n$ for input I^{n+1}. If and when that simulation halts, M' erases any symbols resulting from that simulation and then simulates M_j on the stored representation of m. That is the end of our "construction." We now ask the reader to consider the following.

(1) If $M = M_n$ self-halts, then the function that $M' = M_{n'}$ computes, namely, $f_{n'}$, turns out to be the very same function that M_j computes, namely, f_j. And since $j \notin \Psi_\Gamma$, we have $n' \notin \Psi_\Gamma$.

(2) If $M = M_n$ does not self-halt, then the function that $M' = M_{n'}$ computes, namely, $f_{n'}$, will turn out to be the very same function that M_d computes, namely, $f_\varnothing = f_d$. And since, by assumption, we have $d \in \Psi_\Gamma$, it then follows that $n' \in \Psi_\Gamma$ also.

From (1), it follows that $n \in K$ implies $n' \notin \Psi_\Gamma$. From (2), we have that $n \notin K$ implies $n' \in \Psi_\Gamma$. Summarizing, we have seen that if $d \in \Psi_\Gamma$, then

$$n \in K \Leftrightarrow n' \notin \Psi_\Gamma$$

By elementary logic, it follows that

$$n \in K^c \Leftrightarrow n' \in \Psi_\Gamma \tag{8.4.1}$$

Since the construction that in effect takes gödel number n to gödel number n' may be carried out by a Turing machine, it is not hard to see that Ψ_Γ recursive would imply K^c recursive, which contradicts an earlier remark (see Exercise 8.4.2). We conclude that if $d \in \Psi_\Gamma$, then Ψ_Γ cannot be recursive.

The case $d \notin \Psi_\Gamma$ is not essentially different. We leave it to the reader to show that if $d \notin \Psi_\Gamma$, then

$$n \in K \Leftrightarrow n' \in \Psi_\Gamma \tag{8.4.2}$$

so that, once again, Ψ_Γ cannot be recursive. (The proof involves a construction that is almost identical to that for the case $d \in \Psi_\Gamma$. See Exercise 8.4.3.)   Q.E.D.

So we have now shown that any nontrivial set of gödel numbers of unary partial recursive functions is not recursive. Essentially, we did this by showing that the problem of deciding membership in a nontrivial set Γ of unary partial recursive functions is reducible to the Self-Halting Problem for Turing Machines. Having proved the result, we now show its wide-ranging—and quite surprising—practical applications.

EXAMPLE 8.4.1 (Application to Automata Theory) Suppose that Γ is a class of unary Turing-computable functions having some property of interest—for example, the class of all unary Turing-computable functions that are defined for all but finitely many natural numbers. Given some Turing machine M, it would be nice to be able to somehow determine whether the unary function f computed by M is indeed a member of class Γ. That is, can we effectively determine whether f is defined *almost everywhere*—that is, for all but a finite number of arguments? Well, by Rice's Theorem, the answer is no, and this is just because the class of almost-everywhere-defined functions is nontrivial in our sense, as is easy enough to see. Now, strictly speaking, Rice's Theorem says only that the set Ψ_Γ of all gödel numbers of members of Γ is not recursive. But, if Church's Thesis is assumed, then Rice's Theorem may be taken to mean that Γ itself is undecidable: Given candidate function f—or a machine M computing it—there is no algorithm that can be applied to M in order to decide whether f is a member of Γ.

Other consequences of Rice's Theorem for recursive function theory and automata theory are left to Exercises 8.4.4 and 8.4.5. We turn now to

---

EXAMPLE 8.4.2 (Application to Pragmatic Computer Science) Suppose that the instructor in an introductory programming language class has asked students to write a C++ program that computes a given unary, partial recursive function $\mathcal{F}$. (To give the example maximal plausibility, we might suppose that $\mathcal{F}$ is defined by cases—dozens of cases.) Grading the submitted programs would normally involve the instructor's examining a listing of output for a number of input values as well as reviewing the actual code so as to get an idea of how the program might work. Since, however, approaches vary tremendously from student to student, the instructor might hope for some grading program that could be run on a given student's source code so as to determine whether it in fact computes $\mathcal{F}$. Rice's Theorem asserts in effect that, alas, there can be no such grading program. This is because, first of all, singleton $\{\mathcal{F}\}$ is a nontrivial set of unary partial recursive functions. By Rice's Theorem and Church's Thesis, it then follows that membership in the set

$$\{M | M \text{ is a Turing machine that computes } \mathcal{F}\} \tag{8.4.3}$$

is undecidable. Since the students' programs are written in C++, however, it is more to the point to ask, Could membership in the set

$$\{\mathcal{P} | \mathcal{P} \text{ is a C++ program that computes } \mathcal{F}\} \tag{8.4.4}$$

nonetheless be effectively decidable? The answer to this question is no. For if membership in (8.4.4) were decidable, then membership in (8.4.3) would be decidable as well, since it is easy to see that any Turing machine can be effectively implemented in C++ (cf. Example 4.5.3). We must conclude that membership in (8.4.4) is not decidable either: The envisioned grading program cannot exist after all, at least if Church's Thesis is true.

Although we have formulated the pragmatic implications of Rice's Theorem in terms of unary function computation in particular, this peculiar focus is not nearly the restriction it might appear to be. This is a consequence of two things. First, it is always possible to reconstrue k-ary function computation as unary function computation, as suggested in Exercise 3.6.3(a). Second, Paradigm Interreducibility tells us that any instance of transduction may be viewed as a case of function computation. In its fullest generality, Rice's Theorem eliminates all hope of algorithmically testing the input–output behavior of arbitrary programs. This situation is reflected in the fact that *program verification techniques* are in general noneffective, involving the formulation of *program invariants* whose formal properties are subsequently proved to imply the correctness of the program in question. Our point here is that there is nothing "mechanical" about these proof techniques. On the contrary, they frequently require considerable ingenuity. And it is Rice's Theorem that tells computer scientists that, in their attempts to establish program correctness, they must resign themselves, in general, to working with such nonmechanistic techniques.

§8.5   The Bounds of Feasible Computation: The Concept of NP-Completeness

In §8.1 through §8.4 we explored the bounds of computability-in-principle—that is, computability in the absence of any resource restrictions. That discussion is to be viewed as the culmination of all our work in Chapters 1 through 7 that concerned computability-in-principle. Specifically, the series of equivalence results that were central to those chapters led us to formulate the Church–Turing Thesis—a well-accepted proposal regarding what is and what is not computable-in-principle. Furthermore, it was shown that, assuming Church–Turing, certain problems concerning Turing machines are strictly beyond the limits of what is solvable computationally.

The concept *computable in principle* was one of two important intuitive concepts that were introduced in §1.1. The other was the concept *feasible*, and we said that a computation is feasible, roughly, if it can be carried out using a quantity of resources that is likely to become available for computation. In Chapters 1 through 7 we have been investigating the concept of feasible computation right alongside our work on computability-in-principle—usually in a section devoted to complexity theory at the end of the chapter in question. It is natural to ask for some discussion of what is known concerning the limits of feasible computation. Our goal in this and the following two sections of this chapter is to provide such a discussion.

The Satisfiability Problem for CNFs

In the present section we shall turn our attention to a special case of the *Satisfiability Problem for Propositional Logic*. The latter problem is that of deciding, for an arbitrary sentence S of the language of propositional logic, whether or not S is satisfiable—that is, whether or not S is true under some assignment of truth values to component sentence letters. Truth tables afford a decision procedure for satisfiability, and was seen in §0.8. That is, given a sentence S of propositional logic, we can create a truth table for S in standard fashion and then examine the rightmost column of that table. The sentence is satisfiable if and only if there is at least one T in the final column. One could write a C language program implementing the truth-table algorithm. In short, the Satisfiability Problem for Propositional Logic is computationally solvable.

But whereas the Satisfiability Problem is unquestionably solvable in principle, it is presently not tractable or feasible—at least if we adopt the Cobham–Edmonds Thesis and take "feasible" to mean polynomially bounded computation time. To see this, consider the fact that if S contains 20 distinct sentence letters and 30 occurrences of sentential connectives, then a complete truth table for S will have 2^{20} rows and as many as $20 + 30 = 50$ columns. Thus the truth-table algorithm is an exponential-time algorithm: For input size n, it computes in $O(2^n \cdot n)$ steps.

Of course, just because the truth-table algorithm is inefficient as a solution to the Satisfiability Problem does not mean that some other algorithm might not do better. But there are additional theoretical considerations that make it appear unlikely that any sequential polynomial-time solution to the Satisfiability Problem will be found. In this and the next section, we shall explain why. First, in this section, we introduce some preliminary definitions and terminology. Then, in §8.6, we present a proof of what is no doubt the most celebrated result in all of complexity theory, namely, the Cook–Levin Theorem, showing that the *Satisfiability Problem for CNFs* is, most likely, intractable. That is, the problem of determining whether an arbitrary CNF is satisfiable is, most likely, intractable. (We remind the reader that a sentence in conjunctive normal form is, typically, something on the order of $(\neg p \vee q) \mathbin{\&} (p \vee \neg q) \mathbin{\&} (p \vee q \vee r)$, which consists of three *clauses*.) It follows immediately that the Satisfiability Problem for Propositional Logic is, most likely, intractable. The proof of the Cook–Levin Theorem is not easy, although the reader should by now be well-prepared to take this on.

In presenting some new terminology, we shall continue to rely upon the Turing machine model of computation as our standard, although Markov algorithms, say, would have worked just as well. Corresponding to the fact that Turing machines may serve either as computers of number-theoretic functions or, more generally, as transducers, we have two definitions.

DEFINITION 8.1: Let $f(n)$ be a unary number-theoretic function. Then $f(n)$ is said to be *polynomial-time Turing-computable* if there exists some deterministic, single-tape Turing machine M and some polynomial $p(n)$ such that M computes $f(n)$ in $O(p(n))$ steps. Equivalently, $f(n)$ is *polynomial-time Turing-computable* provided that there exists some Turing machine M and some polynomial $p(n)$ such that (i) M computes f and (ii) $time_M(n)$ is $O(p(n))$.

As an obvious example of a unary, polynomial-time Turing-computable function, consider the function $f(n) = 2n$ of Example 1.5.3. In contrast, consider the function $f(n) = n!$. That this function is Turing-computable is shown in Example 1.5.6. However, it can easily be seen that no machine—either single-tape or multitape—computes this function in $p(n)$ steps, where $p(n)$ is some polynomial function (see Exercise 2.10.13). In other words, $f(n) = n!$ is not a polynomial-time Turing-computable function.

Not all Turing machines are designed to compute number-theoretic functions, of course. Some are intended to transform or *transduce* a given input word w over Σ in some particular way—for example, a Turing machine that transforms w into w^R. This leads us to a more general definition of *polynomial-time Turing-computable function*.

DEFINITION 8.2: Let Σ and Γ be alphabets with $\Sigma \subseteq \Gamma$. A (partial) function f from Σ^* to Γ^* will be said to be *polynomial-time Turing-computable* if there exists some deterministic Turing machine M and some polynomial $p(n)$ such that, for input $w \in \Sigma^*$ for which f is defined, machine M produces $f(w) \in \Gamma^*$ in $O(p(|w|))$ steps.

By Paradigm Interreducibility, Turing machines that compute number-theoretic functions may be re-described as transducers—that is, as machines that map strings over alphabet $\{1\}$ to strings over $\{1\}$.

Consequently, although Definition 8.2 speaks of functions from Σ^* to Γ^*, it is in fact general enough to apply to number-theoretic functions as well.

The analogue of Definitions 8.1 and 8.2 with respect to the language recognition paradigm is already well known to the reader, having been introduced in §1.7. It is the concept of polynomial-time Turing-acceptable language as defined in Definition 1.10. Furthermore, the complexity class P comprises all such languages (see Definition 1.11).

Languages and Problems

Earlier we described a situation confronting a hypothetical computer science department whereby the problem of identifying foreign student files was reduced to the problem of determining whether student identification numbers belonged to the class or "language" of student identification numbers beginning with 999. Another way of looking at this is that the foreign student files problem has been redescribed as a language recognition problem. In similar fashion, we shall begin redescribing all manner of problems in terms of language recognition. This is trivial in the case of the Satisfiability Problem for Propositional Logic. Namely, we let Sat be the class or language of all satisfiable sentences of propositional logic. Determining whether a given sentence S is satisfiable amounts to determining whether S is a member of Sat.

Ultimately, we shall come to identity problems with languages generally. Thus, although P is a class of languages according to Definition 1.11, we shall begin speaking of P as a class of problems. Again, we are permitted to do this as a consequence of our general ability to restate problems in terms of language recognition. Incidentally, this assimilation of problems to languages explains our interest, starting already in §1.7, in giving time and space analyses of language acceptors and language recognizers in particular.

The Language $L_{\mathcal{CNFS}at}$

If we consider only sentences in CNF, then each such sentence of propositional logic can be encoded as a string over the finite alphabet $\{\alpha, \beta, ', /\}$ as follows. First, we assume an enumeration $\alpha_1, \alpha_2, \ldots$ of sentence letters and represent the subscripts here as sequences of symbol $'$. Negations of sentence letters are enumerated as $\beta_1, \beta_2, \ldots$. In other words, β_i represents $\neg\alpha_i$. A disjunction of two or more sentence letters is represented by their concatenation. Symbol $/$ precedes the encoding of each clause. For example, if p and q are α_1 and α_2, respectively, then CNF $(p \vee \neg q)$ & $(q \vee \neg p)$ will be encoded as the 12-character string

$$/\alpha'\beta''/\alpha''\beta' \tag{8.5.1}$$

which we shall usually abbreviate as $/\alpha_1\beta_2/\alpha_2\beta_1$. In referring to encodings of CNFs such as (8.5.1), we shall use the term *slashes-and-strokes encoding*. We now define $L_{\mathcal{CNFS}at}$ as the language consisting of all finite strings over alphabet $\{\alpha, \beta, ', /\}$ that are the slashes-and-strokes encodings of satisfiable CNFs. For instance, word $/\alpha'\beta''/\alpha''\beta'$ is in $L_{\mathcal{CNFS}at}$ since $(p \vee \neg q)$ & $(q \vee \neg p)$ is satisfiable. Finally, we can now formulate the Satisfiability Problem for CNFs as the problem of determining membership in language $L_{\mathcal{CNFS}at}$. (Incidentally, there is no reason why the symbol & rather than $/$ could not be used in encoding CNFs. The symbol $/$ is preferred solely for ease of identification in longer strings of symbols.)

We now show that $L_{\mathcal{CNFS}at}$ is in NP. This is not difficult. Recall that nondeterministic Turing machines may be described informally as making a choice and then verifying that the object of that choice possesses some property or other (cf. Example 2.6.5). In the present case, we imagine a nondeterministic Turing machine M that, given an encoded CNF w as input, chooses a truth value assignment $\mathcal{A}$ for component sentence letters α_i occurring in w and then verifies that w is indeed satisfied by $\mathcal{A}$. We must also convince ourselves that w, if accepted by M, is accepted in polynomially bounded time.

We can describe a nondeterministic Turing machine M that accepts $L_{\mathcal{CNFSat}}$ as follows. Assume that M starts scanning the leftmost symbol of string[1]

$$/\alpha_1\beta_2\alpha_3/\alpha_2\alpha_1/\beta_3\alpha_2\beta_1 \tag{8.5.2}$$

Since the assignment $\mathcal{A} = \langle \alpha_1 = \alpha_2 = \text{true}, \alpha_3 = \text{false} \rangle$ is one that makes the formula encoded by (8.5.2) come out true, we see that (8.5.2) is a member of $L_{\mathcal{CNFSat}}$. M's computation would first select an assignment. Started scanning the leftmost symbol of (8.5.2) M's read/write head moves one square to the right and replaces α_1 with a *1*, reflecting a choice making α_1 true and hence β_1 false. Having done this, it continues off to the right replacing any other occurrences of α_1 with *1* and any occurrences of β_1 with *0*. It now returns to the far left of the transformed (8.5.2) and selects a truth value for the leftmost remaining literal representation—in our case β_2—encountered as it moves rightward. Assuming that its choices are in accordance with $\mathcal{A}$, this means that M will convert all occurrences of β_2 to 0 and all occurrences of α_2 to *1*. Afterward, it returns to the left. Consequently, after the completion of two such passes, S has become

$$/10\alpha_3/11/\beta_3 10$$

The third and final pass, corresponding to the assignment of false to α_3, produces the string

$$/100/11/110$$

M now verifies that all atoms have been replaced so that only *1*s and *0*s occur following any occurrence of */*. At this point, M leaves assignment mode and enters verification mode. It should be apparent what M now has to do: It must verify that between any two occurrences of */* (or following the final */* and before the first blank) there is at least one occurrence of *1*, reflecting the truth of the corresponding clause. Having done this, M now erases the entire tape contents and halts after writing an accepting *1*.

We have yet to convince ourselves that what has just been described can be carried out in polynomially bounded time. It is easy to see that M's computations for accepted input words will generally be longer than those for nonaccepted input words. So we start by considering some accepted word w with $|w| = n$. Each pass from left to right and back within M's assignment mode requires $O(n)$ steps. How many such passes could there be at most? Well, since we have one pass for each pair $\langle \alpha_i, \beta_i \rangle$, the worst possible case would be that in which all of the atoms of w are distinct α_is, say. In that worst case, we then have $O(n)$ passes. So the entire assignment phase of M's computation requires $O(n^2)$ steps. The verification phase requires $O(n)$ steps and erasure another $O(n)$ steps. Consequently, the entire algorithm runs in $O(n^2)$ steps. (If we assume slashes-and-strokes encodings, then this becomes $O(n^3)$ steps—still

---

[1] Strictly speaking, it is the slashes-and-strokes encoding

$$/\alpha'\beta''\alpha'''/\alpha''\alpha'/\beta'''\alpha''\beta'$$

that would occur on M's tape. However, the description of our algorithm will be much facilitated if we assume otherwise. It should be clear that working with the unabbreviated string poses no difficulty in principle.

polynomial time.) We may take ourselves to have proved

THEOREM 8.4: The language $L_{\mathcal{CNFS}at}$ is a member of NP.

EXAMPLE 8.5.1 The nondeterministic multitape machine at icon **CNFSat** within the Turing Machine folder implements a multitape version of the algorithm just described. It assumes slashes-and-strokes encodings and computes in $O(n^3)$ steps, thereby demonstrating membership of $L_{\mathcal{CNFS}at}$ in *NP*. Tapes `cnfsat1.tt`, `cnfsat2.tt`, and `cnfsat3.tt` have been created for use with this machine.

We have seen that $P \subseteq NP$ by definition (cf. Remark 2.6.3). It is natural to ask whether the inclusion is proper or whether $P = NP$. The latter question is fundamental to complexity theory. Suppose that some scheduling problem, say, is solvable in polynomial time by a nondeterministic Turing machine. Is this of any relevance to practical computing? The answer to this last question is yes just in case $P = NP$ since, in that case, the existence of the polynomial-time *nondeterministic* algorithm implies the existence of a polynomial-time *deterministic* algorithm. In this sense, to pose the question whether $P = NP$ is to ask for the very power of nondeterminism. If $P \subset NP$, then nondeterminism is a strictly more powerful idea than determinism but, concomitantly, of no general interest to working computer scientists. In any case, the question whether $P = NP$ remains open. However, considerable light has been shed upon it by developments within the theory of NP-*completeness*, an important notion that we introduce next.

NP-Completeness

We recall terminology introduced at the end of §8.3, whereby the Self-Halting Problem for Turing Machines was said to be reducible to the Halting Problem for Turing Machines. We meant thereby that any solution to the latter can be modified so as to yield a solution to the former. Accordingly, we can see a sense in which the Halting Problem is at least as hard as the Self-Halting Problem. We wish now to focus on the computational resources required to reduce one problem to another problem. In §8.3, where the topic was computability-in-principle, our only concern was that the reduction be *effective*.

In the present context, however, we shall need to know that the reduction of one problem to another can be effected by a (deterministic) Turing machine that *computes in polynomial time*. (We explain why later.) In reading Definition 8.3 below, keep in mind that talk of languages is equivalent to talk of problems.

DEFINITION 8.3: Let L_1 and L_2 be languages over alphabets Σ_1 and Σ_2, respectively. We shall say that L_1 is *polynomial-time reducible to* L_2 and write $L_1 \leq_p L_2$ if there exists a polynomial-time Turing-computable function $f\colon \Sigma_1^* \to \Sigma_2^*$ such that, for any word w, we have $w \in L_1 \Leftrightarrow f(w) \in L_2$.

Intuitively, f provides a means of reducing, in polynomial time, the problem of determining membership in L_1 to the problem of determining membership in L_2. In other words, suppose that we have an algorithm or method $\mathcal{M}$ for determining membership in L_2. Suppose further that

$$w \in L_1 \Leftrightarrow f(w) \in L_2 \tag{8.5.3}$$

holds and that f is polynomial-time Turing-computable. Then there exists some Turing machine M that can be applied to input word w so as to obtain word $f(w)$ in polynomial time. We are now in a position to ask whether $f(w) \in L_2$. If so, then $w \in L_1$ by (8.5.3). Otherwise, $w \notin L_1$. The importance of Definition 8.3 for the ensuing discussion is this: If the problem of determining membership in L_1 is polynomial-time reducible to the problem of determining membership in L_2, then, by Cobham–Edmonds, the reduction preserves feasibility (cf. Theorem 8.6 below).

We are almost ready to introduce the central notion of NP-*completeness*—a property of languages (problems). First, we need the property of so-called NP-*hardness*.

DEFINITION 8.4: Language L is called NP-*hard* if, for every L' in NP, we have $L' \leq_p L$.

That is, L is NP-hard if L is at least as hard as any member of NP. Furthermore, by the transitivity of binary relation $\leq_p$ we have

---

THEOREM 8.5: If $L \leq_p L'$ and L is NP-hard, then L' is NP-hard. Speaking intuitively, if both (1) L' is at least as hard as L and (2) L is at least as hard as any member of NP, then L' is at least as hard as any member of NP.

PROOF The proof is left to the reader (see Exercise 8.5.5).

Note that a language L that qualifies as NP-hard might not be a member of NP. But if L is NP-hard and does happen to be in NP, then L will be said to be NP-*complete*.

DEFINITION 8.5: If L is NP-hard and L is in NP, then L is said to be NP-*complete*.

An NP-complete member of NP is at least as hard as any other problem in NP. This, we are to imagine, constitutes a sort of "completeness"—no problem gets left out.

The following proposition will be useful to us as we develop the theory of NP-completeness.

THEOREM 8.6: Let languages L and L' be given. Suppose that $L' \leq_p L$ and that L is in P. Then L' is in P as well.

PROOF Since L is in P, by Definitions 1.10 and 1.11, there exists both a deterministic Turing machine M_L and polynomial p_L such that M_L accepts any $w \in L$ in $O(p_L(|w|))$ steps. Moreover, by assumption, $L' \leq_p L$; that is, $w \in L' \Leftrightarrow f(w) \in L$ for some polynomial-time Turing-computable f. Let M_f be a deterministic Turing machine that computes $f(w)$ in $O(p_f(|w|))$ steps. We next describe a deterministic Turing machine M^* that accepts L' in polynomial time. Namely, M^* first simulates M_f's behavior for input word w. After $O(p_f(|w|))$ steps, M^* will have produced word $f(w)$, upon which it now simulates the behavior of M_L. After $O(p_L(|f(w)|))$ additional steps, M^*'s simulation of M_L results in acceptance of $f(w) \in L$, let us suppose, in which case M^* will write an accepting *1*, thereby accepting its own input word w—after all, it is a fact that $w \in L'$. Thus L' is accepted by M^*. Moreover, M^* computes in $O(p_f(|w|))$ followed by $O(p_L(|f(w)|))$ steps. But $|f(w)|$ cannot exceed $|w| + p_f(|w|)/2$ essentially, even supposing that all M_f does is write new symbols off to the left of input word w before halting. Consequently, M^* computes in $O(p_f(|w|))$ followed by $O(p_L(|w| + p_f(|w|)/2))$ steps. Since both $p_f(|w|)$ and $p_L(|w| + p_f(|w|)/2)$ are polynomials in $|w|$, we have L' in P.   Q.E.D.

Since every step in the preceding proof remains sound even if we suppose that M_L and hence M^* are nondeterministic machines, we may take ourselves to have proved

---

THEOREM 8.7: Let languages L and L' be given. Suppose that $L' \leq_p L$ and that L is in NP. Then L' is in NP as well.

Suppose for the moment that there exists an NP-complete problem L that is not merely in NP but in P as well. It would then follow that, for arbitrary L' in NP, we have L' is in P. Why? Well, since L is NP-hard, we have $L' \leq_p L$. But then by Theorem 8.6 we have L' in P. We have proved that if there exists an NP-complete language L such that L is in P, then $NP \subseteq P$. But we also know that $P \subseteq NP$ by Remark 2.6.3. So by the Principle of Extensionality, we may take ourselves to have proved

---

THEOREM 8.8: If there exists even one NP-complete member of P, then $P = NP$.

We draw attention to

THEOREM 8.8 (contrapositive): If complexity class P is in fact a proper subset of complexity class NP, then no NP-complete language is a member of P.

The latter proposition is important for several reasons. First, although the question whether $P = NP$ remains open, a great many, highly diverse NP-complete problems have now been identified—not one of which has been shown to be in P. One plausible explanation for this would be that P is a proper subset of NP. Of course, another possible explanation would be that, although some of these NP-complete languages are, unbeknownst to us, members of P, it has just turned out that no one has been quite clever enough to see this. If most of the smart money is on $P \neq NP$, this is just because a number of the best contemporary mathematicians have studied hundreds of NP-complete problems without being able to find any NP-complete member of P. This *may* just mean that there *is* no NP-complete member of P.

And if NP-completeness does imply nonmembership in P, then assuming the Cobham–Edmonds Thesis to be true, we should regard the NP-complete problems as intractable. That is, these problems appear to be such that, although solvable in polynomially bounded time by some *nondeterministic* Turing machine, they are solvable by no *deterministic* Turing machine in polynomially bounded time. And Cobham–Edmonds—or really its contrapositive—asserts that, consequently, these problems are beyond the bounds of what is feasible computationally.

The theory of NP-completeness is developed further in the next two sections. In §8.6 we show that the Satisfiability Problem for CNFs is NP-complete. Afterward, Theorem 8.7 is used repeatedly in showing that a variety of additional problems are NP-complete.

§8.6 An NP-Complete Problem (Cook–Levin Theorem)

Our goal is a demonstration that the Satisfiability Problem for CNFs is NP-complete. We have already seen that $L_{CNFSat} \in NP$ (Theorem 8.4). It remains to show that L_{CNFSat} is NP-hard. We first consider some preliminary issues.

Let sentence letters p, q, and r be interpreted as follows:

p will mean "Paula is president."

q will mean "Quincy is president."

r will mean "Rachel is president."

Suppose further that Paula, Quincy, and Rachel are the only members of the organization in question. In that case, we can express the proposition that exactly one person is president by CNF

$$(p \lor q \lor r) \,\&\, (\neg p \lor \neg q) \,\&\, (\neg p \lor \neg r) \,\&\, (\neg q \lor \neg r)$$

More generally, if sentence letters $p_1, p_2, p_3, \ldots, p_n$ are given, the proposition that exactly one of them is true is expressed by writing CNF

$$(p_1 \lor p_2 \lor p_3 \lor \cdots \lor p_n) \,\&\,$$

$$(\neg p_1 \lor \neg p_2) \,\&\, (\neg p_1 \lor \neg p_3) \,\&\, \cdots \,\&\, (\neg p_1 \lor \neg p_n) \,\&\,$$

$$(\neg p_2 \lor \neg p_3) \,\&\, (\neg p_2 \lor \neg p_4) \,\&\, \cdots \,\&\, (\neg p_2 \lor \neg p_n) \,\&\,$$

$$\cdots \,\&\,$$

$$(\neg p_{n-1} \lor \neg p_n)$$

which we shall abbreviate as $!\{p_1, p_2, \ldots, p_n\}$ or perhaps as $!\{p_i | 1 \leq i \leq n\}$. The reader should verify that, ignoring parentheses only, the length of $!\{p_1, p_2, p_3, \ldots, p_n\}$ is

$$2n + [6(n-1) + 6(n-2) + \cdots + 6(1)] - 1$$

$$= 2n + 6[n + (n-1) + (n-2) + \cdots + 1] - 6n - 1$$

$$= 6[n(n+1)/2] - 4n - 1$$

which is $O(n^2)$. (As usual, the length of a sentence of propositional logic is the number of occurrences of sentence letters and propositional connectives.)

> **REMARK 8.6.1:** The statement $!\{p_1, p_2, p_3, \ldots, p_n\}$ is a CNF and its length is $O(n^2)$.

As introduced in Chapter 1, an accepting computation of Turing machine M for input word w is a certain sort of finite sequence of instructions executed by M. We assume that initially—that is, before executing the first of these instructions—M is in state q_0 with read/write head scanning the leftmost symbol of w. All tape squares, except those occupied by the symbols of w, are assumed to be blank. The instruction sequence proceeds in accordance with the definition or state diagram of M. Finally, M halts reading a single *1* on an otherwise blank tape. Now, in the context of Chapter 1, M's halting meant M's being in some state q_t reading some symbol s_j such that M has no instruction for the case where it is in state q_t scanning symbol s_j. This is still precisely what we shall assume here. However, it will be convenient to introduce an alternative *description* of what it is for M to halt, which we now elaborate.

First, let us rule out so-called *useless instructions*—that is, instructions whose execution causes no changes in the current state of the machine, the location of the read/write head, or the contents of the tape. An example of such an instruction would be the quadruple $q_0, a; a, q_0$. This amounts to a slight change in the definition of Turing machines as given in Definition 1.1. However, it is a change that has no significant theoretical consequences.

We shall further assume that instructions are instantaneously executed at a uniform rate of one per time unit as marked by some clock. Thus, if, at time $t = 0$, M is in state q_0 scanning the leftmost symbol of $w = aabb$ on an otherwise blank tape

$$\ldots B\boldsymbol{q}_0 aabbB \ldots$$

then, after executing the instruction $\langle q_0, a; \mathrm{R}, q_1 \rangle$, the state of M and the tape contents at time $t = 1$ will be completely described by the machine configuration description

$$\ldots Ba\boldsymbol{q}_1 abbB \ldots$$

Computations may be of finite or infinite length, where the length of a computation is just the length of the corresponding instruction sequence. Evidently, any accepting computation is of finite length. But we shall permit ourselves to speak of M's machine configuration description at time $t = n+1, n+2, \ldots$ even if M's computation was of length n—that is, even if M halted at time $t = n$. Since we are ruling out useless instructions, it follows that M halts if and only if, for some n, its configuration description for time $t = n$ is identical with its configuration description at time $t = n+1$. So M halts at or before time $t = n$ provided that M's configuration at time $t = n$ is identical to its configuration at time $t = n+1$.

Having completed the necessary preliminaries, we can now proceed to give the actual proof of

---

THEOREM 8.9 (Cook–Levin Theorem): The Satisfiability Problem for CNFs is NP-hard and hence NP-complete.

PROOF By the definition of NP-hardness, we need to show that, for an arbitrary language $L \in NP$, we have that L is polynomial-time reducible to $L_{\mathcal{CNFSat}}$—that is, $L \leq_p L_{\mathcal{CNFSat}}$. So we start by letting L be an arbitrary member of NP. By the definition of NP, we can assume that there exists a nondeterministic, single-tape Turing machine M that accepts L and a polynomial $p(n)$ such that, if $w \in L$, then there exists an accepting computation of M for input w whose length is $\mathrm{O}(p(|w|))$. For such an M, p, and w, we shall describe the construction of a sentence $\mathcal{F}_w$ of propositional logic that is a CNF and that models or characterizes the class $\mathcal{C}_w$ of accepting computations of M for input w. Intuitively, $\mathcal{F}_w$ will say that:

- M starts scanning the leftmost symbol of w on a tape that contains w and is otherwise blank.

- All executed transitions are in accordance with M's transition diagram.

- M halts, after no more than $\mathrm{O}(p(|w|))$ steps, scanning a *1* on an otherwise blank tape.

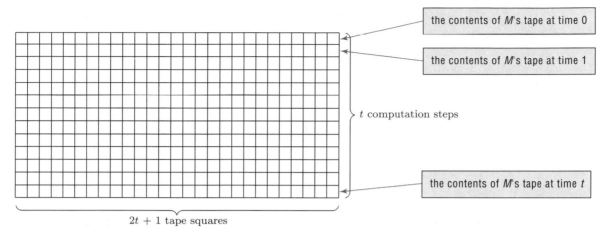

the contents of *M*'s tape at time 0

the contents of *M*'s tape at time 1

t computation steps

the contents of *M*'s tape at time t

$2t + 1$ tape squares

Figure 8.6.1

In other words, by the nature of the construction of $\mathcal{F}_w$, it will be true that

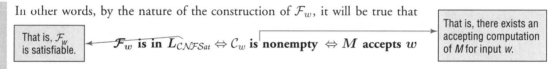

That is, $\mathcal{F}_w$ is satisfiable.

$$\mathcal{F}_w \text{ is in } L_{\mathcal{CNFS}at} \Leftrightarrow \mathcal{C}_w \text{ is nonempty} \Leftrightarrow M \text{ accepts } w$$

That is, there exists an accepting computation of *M* for input *w*.

In addition, we shall show that the construction of $\mathcal{F}_w$ from M, p, and w can be carried out by a deterministic Turing machine M', the number of steps in whose computation for input w is $O(p'(|w|))$ for some polynomial p'. As usual, our argument for the existence of M' will be informal: We shall appeal to the reader's general sense of the capacities and resource needs of Turing machines.

In what follows, let us assume a given input word w. Furthermore, let $t = p(|w|)$ and assume that $t = p(|w|) \geq |w|$, where p is the given polynomial by virtue of which L is in NP.[2] If w is accepted by M, then, by hypothesis, this occurs in $O(p(|w|))$ steps. (Expressed differently, we are assuming that $time_M(|w|)$ is $O(p(|w|))$.) Without loss of generality, we may assume that acceptance occurs in $t = p(|w|)$ or fewer steps (see Exercise 0.5.13). So to determine whether w is accepted, we need only start M running on input w and observe whether, after t or fewer steps, M has halted in an accepting configuration. Moreover, since M's tape head can at most move one square to the right or one square to the left during any one step, it can move, over the course of its entire computation, at most t steps to the right or t steps to the left of its initial square. This means that at most $t + 1 + t = 2t + 1$ squares of the tape can be scanned over the course of M's entire computation for input w. (In other words, $space_M(|w|) \leq 2t + 1$.) The squares on this portion of M's tape are assigned positions ranging from 1 to $2t + 1$, inclusive. In any case, M's successive tape configurations over its entire computation for input w may be described as a two-dimensional array with $t + 1$ rows and $2t + 1$ columns (see Figure 8.6.1). For example, the first line of the array of Figure 8.6.1 will contain the string $B^t w B^{t-|w|+1}$, corresponding to M's initial tape contents. We shall assume that M has $m + 1$ states and that tape alphabet $\Gamma = \{\alpha_1, \ldots, \alpha_r\}$ with input alphabet $\Sigma \subseteq \Gamma$. It will prove convenient to write α_0 for the blank B and α_1 for symbol *1*.

---

[2] If, the given polynomial p does not satisfy this condition, then replace p with p_1 defined as

$$p_1(n) = p(n) + n$$

which is a polynomial in n with $p_1(n) \geq n$ for all n.

We introduce the following sentence letters, each and every one of which will figure in $\mathcal{F}_w$.

(1) $\sigma_{h,j,k}$ for each h, j, k with $0 \leq h \leq m, 1 \leq j \leq 2t + 1$, and $0 \leq k \leq t$.

(2) $\tau_{i,j,k}$ for each i, j, k with $0 \leq i \leq r, 1 \leq j \leq 2t + 1$, and $0 \leq k \leq t$.

Note that we have introduced $(m + 1) \cdot (2t + 1) \cdot (t + 1)$ distinct sentence letters at (1) and $(r + 1) \cdot (2t + 1) \cdot (t + 1)$ letters at (2). Consequently, since m and r are both constants, we have

REMARK 8.6.2: The number of distinct sentence letters occurring in $\mathcal{F}_w$ will be $\mathrm{O}(t^2)$.

- A heuristic understanding of the sentence letters of group (1) concerns the status of the machine proper—that is, its current state and the location of its read/write head. Sentence letter $\sigma_{h,j,k}$ is understood to say that M is in state q_h scanning the jth tape square at time k.

- A heuristic understanding of the sentence letters of group (2) concerns the contents of M's tape. In particular, letter $\tau_{i,j,k}$ is understood to mean that symbol α_i is on the jth tape square at time k.

Thus, under this interpretation, the conjunction

$$\sigma_{6,5,9} \ \& \ \tau_{0,5,9}$$

will be true just in case, at time unit 9, M is in state q_6 scanning a blank on the fifth tape square from the left. Let us refer to this interpretation of the sentence letters of (1) and (2) as I^*.

Let $w = \alpha_{i_1}\alpha_{i_2} \ldots \alpha_{i_n}$, where $|w| = n$ and each of $\alpha_{i_1}, \alpha_{i_2}, \ldots, \alpha_{i_n}$ is in Σ. Then $\mathcal{F}_w$, which we are about to describe, will be the conjunction of six sentences, each of which is a CNF; it will follow that $\mathcal{F}_w$ is itself a CNF. (Recall that a conjunction of CNFs is a CNF). Using interpretation I^* as our guide, we describe the construction of each of $\mathcal{F}_w$'s six conjuncts.

Conjunct 1. The first of our six sentences describes M's initial configuration. Namely, M's tape consists of exactly t blanks followed by input word $w = \alpha_{i_1}\alpha_{i_2} \ldots \alpha_{i_n}$ followed by blanks with M in state q_0 scanning a_{i_1}.

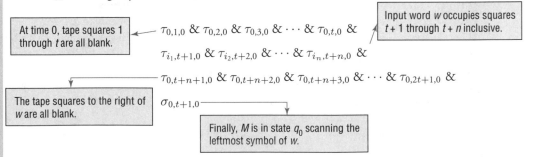

This sentence is in CNF and contains $2t + 2$ conjuncts. (Count them.) Thus, its length—sentence letters and connectives—is $4t + 3$, which is $\mathrm{O}(t)$.

As preparation for what follows, we present this first conjunct using the alternative notation

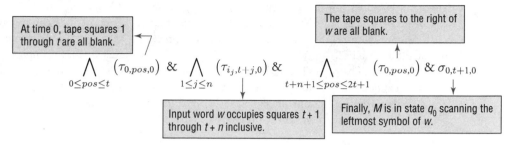

$$\bigwedge_{0\le pos\le t} (\tau_{0,pos,0}) \;\&\; \bigwedge_{1\le j\le n} (\tau_{i_j,l+j,0}) \;\&\; \bigwedge_{t+n+1\le pos\le 2t+1} (\tau_{0,pos,0}) \;\&\; \sigma_{0,t+1,0}$$

Conjunct 2. According to I^*, the second conjunct of $\mathcal{F}_w$ will say that, at each of the t steps of its computation, M is characterized by a unique state and a unique scanned square.

$$!\{\sigma_{h,j,0}|0\le h\le m, 1\le j\le 2t+1\}\&$$
$$!\{\sigma_{h,j,1}|0\le h\le m, 1\le j\le 2t+1\}\&$$
$$!\{\sigma_{h,j,2}|0\le h\le m, 1\le j\le 2t+1\}\;\&\ldots\&$$
$$!\{\sigma_{h,j,t}|0\le h\le m, 1\le j\le 2t+1\}$$

Alternatively, we may write

$$\bigwedge_{0\le time\le t} !\{\sigma_{h,j,time}|0\le h\le m, 1\le j\le 2t+1\}$$

This sentence is a CNF since each of its conjuncts is. (Recall Remark 8.6.1.) Moreover, since m here is a constant that does not depend upon t, each conjunct has length $O(t^2)$ by Remark 8.6.1 again. Since there are $t+1$ conjuncts, Conjunct 2 has length $O(t^3)$.

Conjunct 3. According to I^*, the third conjunct of $\mathcal{F}_w$ will say that, at each step of M's computation, each tape square is either blank or contains exactly one alphabet symbol.

$$!\{\tau_{i,1,0}|0\le i\le r\} \;\&\; !\{\tau_{i,2,0}|0\le i\le r\} \;\&\; !\{\tau_{i,3,0}|0\le i\le r\} \;\&\cdots\&\; !\{\tau_{i,2t+1,0}|0\le i\le r\} \;\&$$
$$!\{\tau_{i,1,1}|0\le i\le r\} \;\&\; !\{\tau_{i,2,1}|0\le i\le r\} \;\&\; !\{\tau_{i,3,1}|0\le i\le r\} \;\&\cdots\&\; !\{\tau_{i,2t+1,1}|0\le i\le r\} \;\&$$
$$!\{\tau_{i,1,2}|0\le i\le r\} \;\&\; !\{\tau_{i,2,2}|0\le i\le r\} \;\&\; !\{\tau_{i,3,2}|0\le i\le r\} \;\&\cdots\&\; !\{\tau_{i,2t+1,2}|0\le i\le r\} \;\&$$
$$\cdots\;\&$$

> Each conjunct here describes one square in the grid of Figure 8.6.1.

$$!\{\tau_{i,1,t}|0\le i\le r\} \;\&\; !\{\tau_{i,2,t}|0\le i\le r\} \;\&\; !\{\tau_{i,3,t}|0\le i\le r\} \;\&\cdots\&\; !\{\tau_{i,2t+1,t}|0\le i\le r\}$$

Alternatively, we may write

$$\bigwedge_{1\le pos\le 2t+1}\;\bigwedge_{0\le time\le t} \left(!\{\tau_{i,pos,time}|0\le i\le r\}\right)$$

This sentence, which is Conjunct 3, is a CNF and has $(t+1) \cdot (2t+1)$ conjuncts—each of constant length since r does not depend upon t. So the total length of Conjunct 3 is $\mathrm{O}(t^2)$.

Conjunct 4. The fourth conjunct of $\mathcal{F}_w$ will say that each step of M's computation results in a machine configuration that is either identical to the preceding configuration or is obtained from it by one of the instructions in M's instruction set. Since this conjunct is quite complex, it is convenient to subdivide it. This conjunct also requires care since what is probably the most natural approach results in exponentially bounded, rather than polynomially bounded, length.

Of course, the instructions of M fall into three groups: writes, moves-right, and moves-left. We assume that each of these groups is ordered as follows.

$$\mathcal{W} = \{\langle q_{i_k}, \alpha_{r_k}; \alpha_{l_k}, q_{j_k} \rangle | k = 1, 2, \ldots, N_{\mathcal{W}}\},$$ where $N_{\mathcal{W}}$ is the number of writes among M's instructions

$$\mathcal{MR} = \{\langle q_{i_k}, \alpha_{r_k}; \mathrm{R}, q_{j_k} \rangle | k = 1, 2, \ldots, N_{\mathcal{MR}}\},$$ where $N_{\mathcal{MR}}$ is the number of moves-right among M's instructions

$$\mathcal{ML} = \{\langle q_{i_k}, \alpha_{r_k}; \mathrm{L}, q_{j_k} \rangle | k = 1, 2, \ldots, N_{\mathcal{ML}}\},$$ where $N_{\mathcal{ML}}$ is the number of moves-left among M's instructions

We write $Notscan(n, pos)$ for the following statement of propositional logic:

$$\bigwedge_{0 \le state \le m} \left(\neg \sigma_{state, pos, n} \right) \ \& \ \bigvee_{0 \le i \le r} \{\tau_{i, pos, n} \ \& \ \tau_{i, pos, n+1}\}$$

which, for fixed values of n and pos, says that, at time n, the read/write head of M is not scanning tape square pos and that, consequently, whatever symbol is found in tape square pos at time n is also found there at time $n + 1$. We note that $Notscan(n, pos)$ is not a CNF. Also, since the number of occurrences of sentence letters in $Notscan(n, pos)$ does not depend upon $t = p(|w|)$, its length is $\mathrm{O}(1)$.

We write $Halt(n, pos)$ for the following statement of propositional logic, where, once again, we take n and pos to be fixed temporarily.

$$\bigvee_{0 \le state \le m} \{\sigma_{state, pos, n} \ \& \ \sigma_{state, pos, n+1}\} \ \& \ \bigvee_{0 \le i \le r} \{\tau_{i, pos, n} \ \& \ \tau_{i, pos, n+1}\}$$

$Halt(n, pos)$ says that, at both times n and $n + 1$, M finds itself in one and the same state with its read/write head scanning one and the same symbol on tape square pos. Since we have ruled out useless instructions, this is just to say that M halts at time n scanning tape square pos. Once again, $Halt(n, pos)$, which is not a CNF, is of length $\mathrm{O}(1)$.

At time n, it is possible that M is scanning tape square $pos \neq 2t + 1$ and executes one of the move-right instructions in $\mathcal{MR}$. In symbols, we have

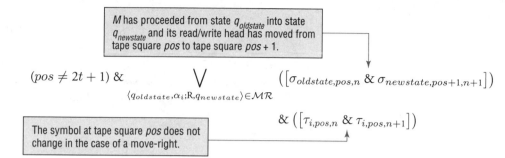

$$(pos \neq 2t + 1) \; \& \bigvee_{\langle q_{oldstate}, \alpha_i; R, q_{newstate} \rangle \in \mathcal{MR}} \left(\left[\sigma_{oldstate,pos,n} \; \& \; \sigma_{newstate,pos+1,n+1} \right] \right)$$

$$\& \left(\left[\tau_{i,pos,n} \; \& \; \tau_{i,pos,n+1} \right] \right)$$

Let us write $Move\_Right(n, pos)$ for this statement, which has length $O(1)$.

At time n, it is possible that M is scanning tape square $pos \neq 1$ and executes one of the move-left instructions in $\mathcal{ML}$. In symbols, we have

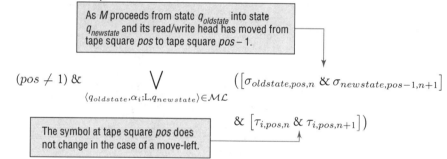

$$(pos \neq 1) \; \& \bigvee_{\langle q_{oldstate}, \alpha_i; L, q_{newstate} \rangle \in \mathcal{ML}} \left(\left[\sigma_{oldstate,pos,n} \; \& \; \sigma_{newstate,pos-1,n+1} \right. \right.$$

$$\left. \left. \& \; \left[\tau_{i,pos,n} \; \& \; \tau_{i,pos,n+1} \right] \right) \right.$$

Let us write $Move\_Left(n, pos)$ for this statement, which has length $O(1)$.

At time n, it is possible that M's read/write head is scanning tape square pos and that it executes one of the instructions in $\mathcal{W}$. We may write $Write(n, pos)$ for

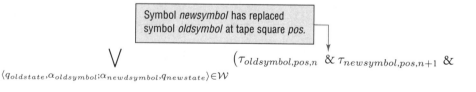

$$\bigvee_{\langle q_{oldstate}, \alpha_{oldsymbol}; \alpha_{newdsymbol}, q_{newstate} \rangle \in \mathcal{W}} \left(\tau_{oldsymbol,pos,n} \; \& \; \tau_{newsymbol,pos,n+1} \; \& \right.$$

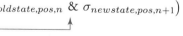

$$\left. \sigma_{oldstate,pos,n} \; \& \; \sigma_{newstate,pos,n+1} \right)$$

The length of this statement is again $O(1)$.

We are now ready to put together the fourth conjunct of $\mathcal{F}_w$. We start with the conjunction

$$\bigwedge_{0 \leq n \leq t} \left(\bigwedge_{1 \leq pos \leq 2t+1} (Notscan(n, pos) \; \vee \; Halt(n, pos) \; \vee \; Move\_Right(n, pos) \right.$$

$$\left. \vee \; Move\_Left(n, pos) \; \vee \; Write(n, pos)) \right)$$

422   Models of Computation

This conjunction is not itself a CNF. However, the disjunction

$$(Notscan(n, pos) \vee Halt(n, pos) \ \vee Move\_Right(n, pos)$$
$$\vee \ Move\_Left(n, pos) \vee Write(n, pos))$$

is equivalent to some CNF by Theorem 0.10. We do not display this CNF but shall merely refer to it as $\mathcal{D}_{CNF}$. Moreover, since the length of each of disjuncts $Notscan(n, pos), \ldots, Write(n, pos)$ is O(1), the length of $\mathcal{D}_{CNF}$ is similarly O(1). Consequently, we let the fourth conjunct of $\mathcal{F}_w$ be the conjunction

$$\bigwedge_{0 \le n \le t} \left(\bigwedge_{1 \le pos \le 2t+1} \mathcal{D}_{CNF} \right)$$

which is a conjunction of CNFs and hence itself a CNF. Moreover, since $\mathcal{D}_{CNF}$ is of constant length, this fourth conjunct is of length $O(t^2)$.

Conjunct 5. The fifth conjunct of $\mathcal{F}_w$ says, in effect, that M halts at (or before) time t. We start with

$$\bigwedge_{1 \le pos \le 2t+1} (Notscan(t, pos) \vee Halt(t, pos))$$

As noted before, both $Notscan(t, pos)$ and $Halt(t, pos)$ are of length O(1) and, consequently, the disjunction $Notscan(t, pos) \vee Halt(t, pos)$ is equivalent to a CNF of length O(1). It follows that the fifth conjunct of $\mathcal{F}_w$ may be taken to be a CNF of length O(t).

Conjunct 6. Finally, the sixth conjunct of $\mathcal{F}_w$ says, in effect, that, at time t, M's read/write head is scanning a *1* on an otherwise blank tape. We may take this conjunct to be

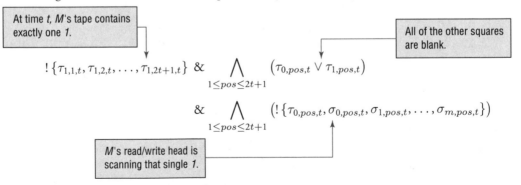

Conjunct 6 is a conjunction of three CNFs, the first of which is of length $O(t^2)$, by Remark 8.6.1, and the other two of which are each of length O(t). (Why?) Consequently, the sixth conjunct of $\mathcal{F}_w$ is itself a CNF of length $O(t^2)$.

We let $\mathcal{F}_w$ be the conjunction of Conjuncts 1 through 6, each of which is a CNF. Consequently, since a conjunction of CNFs is itself a CNF, $\mathcal{F}_w$ is a CNF. Moreover, since Conjunct 2 dominates, $\mathcal{F}_w$ is a CNF of length $O(t^3)$. By Remark 8.6.2, the length of the slashes-and-strokes encoding of

$\mathcal{F}_w$ is O(t^5). (Why?) Furthermore, according to I^*, $\mathcal{F}_w$ says that M accepts w. We are now ready to show that $L \leq_p L_{\mathcal{CNFSat}}$; that is, we must show that, for all $w \in \Sigma^*$, we have

$$w \in L \Leftrightarrow \ulcorner \mathcal{F}_w \urcorner \in L_{\mathcal{CNFSat}}$$

the slashes-and-strokes encoding of $\mathcal{F}_w$

We consider the **forward direction** first. Suppose that $w \in L$, which means that M does accept w. (Recall that L is an arbitrary member of NP and that M is a nondeterministic Turing machine that accepts it.) Then, by the nature of its construction, there is a truth-value assignment that makes $\mathcal{F}_w$ true. That is, $\mathcal{F}_w$ is satisfiable and hence its slashes-and-strokes encoding is in $L_{\mathcal{CNFSat}}$.

As for the **reverse direction**, suppose that w is an arbitrary word over Σ and that the slashes-and-strokes encoding of $\mathcal{F}_w$ is in $L_{\mathcal{CNFSat}}$. We must now show that M accepts w. Since $\mathcal{F}_w$ is satisfiable, some assignment $\mathcal{A}$ of truth values to the $\sigma_{h,j,k}$ and the $\tau_{i,j,k}$ makes it true. We stress that, whereas $\mathcal{F}_w$ characterizes the class of nondeterministic M's computations for input word w, any particular assignment $\mathcal{A}$ making $\mathcal{F}_w$ true models a particular computation. Since $\mathcal{F}_w$ is the conjunction of Conjuncts 1 through 6, assignment $\mathcal{A}$ must make each of Conjuncts 1 through 6 true. Since $\mathcal{A}$ makes each of Conjunct 3's conjuncts true in turn, we see that, for each $1 \leq j \leq 2t + 1$ and each $0 \leq k \leq t$, there is exactly one value of i for which $\tau_{i,j,k}$ is true according to $\mathcal{A}$. It follows that the true $\tau_{i,j,k}$ can be arranged in a $(t + 1) \times (2t + 1)$ array as in Table 8.6.2(a), where boxes indicate leading subscripts that have yet to be determined.

Since $\mathcal{A}$ makes each clause of Conjunct 1 true, however, we can immediately fill in the subscripts in the first row (see Table 8.6.2(b)). Furthermore, since $\mathcal{A}$ makes each clause of Conjunct 2 true, we see that, for each $0 \leq k \leq t$, there is just one way to choose h and j so that $\sigma_{h,j,k}$ is true according to $\mathcal{A}$. Thus, we may as well position this unique $\sigma_{h,j,k}$ in the kth row of a new first column of our array. Moreover, by Conjunct 1 again, we already know that, for $k = 0$, the unique pair $\langle h, j \rangle$ such that $\sigma_{h,j,k}$ is true under $\mathcal{A}$ is $\langle 0, t + 1 \rangle$ (see Table 8.6.2(c)).

We can now proceed to fill in the subscript boxes in row 2 of the array. Conjuncts 4 through 6 together place restrictions on the insertion of subscripts so as to ensure that the array, once all subscripts

---

Table 8.6.2(a)   A $(t + 1) \times (2t + 1)$ Array of True $\tau_{i,j,k}$.

$\tau_{\square,1,0}$	$\tau_{\square,2,0}$	$\tau_{\square,3,0}$	$\cdots$	$\tau_{\square,t,0}$	$\tau_{\square,t+1,0}$	$\tau_{\square,t+2,0}$	$\cdots$	$\tau_{\square,2t+1,0}$
$\tau_{\square,1,1}$	$\tau_{\square,2,1}$	$\tau_{\square,3,1}$	$\cdots$				$\cdots$	$\tau_{\square,2t+1,1}$
$\tau_{\square,1,2}$	$\tau_{\square,2,2}$	$\tau_{\square,3,2}$					$\cdots$	$\tau_{\square,2t+1,2}$
$\tau_{\square,1,3}$	$\tau_{\square,2,3}$	$\tau_{\square,3,3}$	$\cdots$				$\cdots$	$\tau_{\square,2t+1,3}$
			$\cdots$					
$\tau_{\square,1,t}$	$\tau_{\square,2,t}$	$\tau_{\square,3,t}$	$\cdots$				$\cdots$	$\tau_{\square,2t+1,t}$

Table 8.6.2(b)   First-row subscripts may be filled in immediately.

$\tau_{0,1,0}$	$\tau_{0,2,0}$	$\tau_{0,3,0}$	$\cdots$	$\tau_{0,t,0}$	$\tau_{i_1,t+1,0}$	$\tau_{i_2,t+2,0}$	$\cdots$	$\tau_{0,2t+1,0}$
$\tau_{\square,1,1}$	$\tau_{\square,2,1}$	$\tau_{\square,3,1}$	$\cdots$				$\cdots$	$\tau_{\square,2t+1,1}$
$\tau_{\square,1,2}$	$\tau_{\square,2,2}$	$\tau_{\square,3,2}$					$\cdots$	$\tau_{\square,2t+1,2}$
$\tau_{\square,1,3}$	$\tau_{\square,2,3}$	$\tau_{\square,3,3}$	$\cdots$				$\cdots$	$\tau_{\square,2t+1,3}$
			$\cdots$					
$\tau_{\square,1,t}$	$\tau_{\square,2,t}$	$\tau_{\square,3,t}$	$\cdots$				$\cdots$	$\tau_{\square,2t+1,t}$

Table 8.6.2(c)   A new first column may be added.

$\sigma_{0,t+1,0}$	$\tau_{0,1,0}$	$\tau_{0,2,0}$	$\tau_{0,3,0}$	$\cdots$	$\tau_{0,t,0}$	$\tau_{i_1,t+1,0}$	$\tau_{i_2,t+2,0}$	$\cdots$	$\tau_{0,2t+1,0}$
$\sigma_{\square,\square,1}$	$\tau_{\square,1,1}$	$\tau_{\square,2,1}$	$\tau_{\square,3,1}$	$\cdots$					$\tau_{\square,2t+1,1}$
$\sigma_{\square,\square,2}$	$\tau_{\square,1,2}$	$\tau_{\square,2,2}$	$\tau_{\square,3,2}$	$\cdots$					$\tau_{\square,2t+1,2}$
$\sigma_{\square,\square,3}$	$\tau_{\square,1,3}$	$\tau_{\square,2,3}$	$\tau_{\square,3,3}$	$\cdots$					$\tau_{\square,2t+1,3}$
				$\cdots$					
$\sigma_{\square,\square,t}$	$\tau_{\square,1,t}$	$\tau_{\square,2,t}$	$\tau_{\square,3,t}$	$\cdots$				$\cdots$	$\tau_{\square,2t+1,t}$

have been filled in, describes or models a particular accepting computation of w on the part of M. So apparently such an accepting computation exists, which means that M accepts w. But, by assumption, M accepts language L. So w must be in L. We have shown that if the slashes-and-strokes encoding of $\mathcal{F}_w$ is in $L_{\mathcal{CNFSat}}$, then $w \in L$.

We must still show that the function that maps w onto the slashes-and-strokes encoding of $\mathcal{F}_w$ is polynomial-time Turing-computable. We noted that the length of $\mathcal{F}_w$ is O(t^3), where $t = p(|w|)$ for some given polynomial p. Essentially by Remark 8.6.2 again, the length of the slashes-and-strokes encoding of $\mathcal{F}_w$ is O(t^5), which is O($[p(|w|)]^5$). But then $[p(|w|)]^5$ is itself a polynomial in $|w|$. It is not hard to see that there exists a deterministic Turing machine M' that, given w as input, constructs $\mathcal{F}_w$ in O($p'(|w|)$) steps for some polynomial p'.   Q.E.D.

We have now shown that the concept of an NP-complete problem is more than an empty notion: Such a problem does actually exist. Happily, showing that there are other NP-complete problems will now be a simpler matter. The truly difficult work is behind us.

§8.7 Other NP-Complete Problems

Historically, the Satisfiability Problem for CNFs was the first problem shown to be NP-complete. But in the time since Cook's proof appeared in 1971, a great many other problems have been shown to be NP-complete. We shall look at five of these in this section. In each of Theorems 8.10 through 8.14 below, we show some problem to be NP-complete in the sense of Definition 8.5. In each case, our procedure will be the same.

- First, we will have to convince ourselves via some informal argument that the given problem is a member of NP. That is, we must see that an associated language L_2 is accepted by some nondeterministic Turing machine M in polynomial time.

- Second, we will need to show that some previously identified NP-complete L_1 is polynomial-time reducible to L_2. That is, we must convince ourselves that there exists a polynomial-time Turing-computable function f such that, for any word w, we have $w \in L_1 \Leftrightarrow f(w) \in L_2$. (We shall express this relationship between L_1 and L_2, as usual, by writing $L_1 \leq_p L_2$.)

- By Theorem 8.5 and the NP-hardness of L_1, it will follow that L_2 is NP-hard. But since we will already have established that L_2 is in NP, it will then be clear that L_2 is NP-complete.

Note the reference to Turing machines at two distinct points here. First, language L_2 must be accepted by some nondeterministic Turing machine M that computes in polynomial time. Second, function f

must be computed by some deterministic Turing machine—call it M'—also in polynomial time. As a consequence of this, the proof of each of Theorems 8.10 through 8.14 below involves the presentation of some function f as well as two Turing machines—one nondeterministic and the other deterministic.

> **REMARK 8.7.1:** If a given problem is in NP and some NP-complete problem is polynomial-time reducible to it, then the given problem is itself NP-complete.

We now set out to apply Remark 8.7.1 in order to identify other NP-complete problems. Of course, since only one NP-complete problem has been identified so far—namely, the Satisfiability Problem for CNFs—we have no choice but to start by showing that this problem is polynomial-time reducible to some other problem in NP. Apparently, we are in much the same position as were theoretical computer scientists in the early 1970s.

The Satisfiability Problem for 3-CNFs

As first choice, we consider the problem known as the *Satisfiability Problem for 3-CNFs*. This problem is just like the Satisfiability Problem for CNFs except that the CNFs to be tested for satisfiability are so-called *3-CNFs*—CNFs in which each clause contains at most three literals, where by a literal we mean either a sentence letter or the negation of a sentence letter. Thus the CNF

$$(p \vee q \vee \neg r) \mathbin{\&} (q \vee \neg r \vee s) \mathbin{\&} (p \vee r) \mathbin{\&} (\neg t \vee s) \tag{8.7.1}$$

is a 3-CNF but

$$(p \vee q \vee \neg r) \mathbin{\&} (q \vee \neg r \vee p \vee s) \mathbin{\&} (p \vee r) \mathbin{\&} (\, t \vee s)$$

is not. We define the language $L_{\text{3-}C\mathcal{NF}Sat}$ to be the set of all encodings of satisfiable 3-CNFs. The encoding of (8.7.1) is easily seen to be in $L_{\text{3-}C\mathcal{NF}Sat}$ since the truth value assignment $\langle p = q = s = \text{true}, r = t = \text{false} \rangle$ is one that makes (8.7.1) true. For a 3-CNF whose encoding is not in $L_{\text{3-}C\mathcal{NF}Sat}$, consider

$$(p \vee q \vee r) \mathbin{\&} (p \vee q \vee \neg r) \mathbin{\&} (p \vee \neg q \vee \neg r) \mathbin{\&} (p \vee \neg q \vee \neg r) \mathbin{\&}$$

$$(\neg p \vee q \vee r) \mathbin{\&} (\neg p \vee q \vee \neg r) \mathbin{\&} (\neg p \vee \neg q \vee r) \mathbin{\&} (\neg p \vee \neg q \vee \neg r)$$

In any case, assuming the same slashes-and-strokes encoding of CNFs that was introduced in §8.5, it is plain that there exists a nondeterministic Turing machine that accepts the language $L_{\text{3-}C\mathcal{NF}Sat}$ in polynomial time. Indeed, the Turing machine described in the proof of Theorem 8.4 will serve here as well. So $L_{\text{3-}C\mathcal{NF}Sat} \in NP$.

It is less obvious that $L_{\text{3-}C\mathcal{NF}Sat}$ is NP-hard. This is because it is not obvious that there exists a polynomial-time Turing-computable f such that, for any slashes-and-strokes encoding w of a CNF, we have

$$w \in L_{C\mathcal{NF}Sat} \Leftrightarrow f(w) \in L_{\text{3-}C\mathcal{NF}Sat}$$

In fact, such an f does exist, however. Essentially, given any clause of w that contains four or more literals, f replaces the clause with a new CNF each clause of which contains exactly three literals. In doing this, some new literals must be introduced.

Rather than present the construction in full generality, let us fix upon some particular conjunct of $k = 8$ positive literals, say. That is, suppose that w is an encoding of a CNF one of whose clauses is

$$p_1 \lor p_2 \lor p_3 \lor p_4 \lor p_5 \lor p_6 \lor p_7 \lor p_8 \tag{8.7.2}$$

The 3-CNF $f(w)$ will involve $k - 3 = 5$ new sentence letters, r_1, r_2, r_3, r_4, and r_5, say. Furthermore, $f(w)$ will be the conjunction of the $k - 2 = 6$ clauses

$$(p_1 \lor p_2 \lor r_1) \, \& \, (p_3 \lor \neg r_1 \lor r_2) \, \& \, (p_4 \lor \neg r_2 \lor r_3) \& \tag{8.7.3}$$

$$(p_5 \lor \neg r_3 \lor r_4) \, \& \, (p_6 \lor \neg r_4 \lor r_5) \, \& \, (p_7 \lor p_8 \lor \neg r_5)$$

It is left to the reader to discern the simple construction principle at work here. We now show that there exists a truth value assignment that makes (8.7.3) true if and only if there exists an assignment that makes (8.7.2) true. In other words, (8.7.3) is satisfiable just in case (8.7.2) is.

As for the forward direction, assume that some assignment $\mathcal{A}$ makes (8.7.3) true. Also note that, by elementary logic, at least one of (i)–(iii) below holds of $\mathcal{A}$.

(i) r_1 is false under $\mathcal{A}$.

(ii) r_5 is true under $\mathcal{A}$.

(iii) r_1 is true under $\mathcal{A}$ and r_5 is false under $\mathcal{A}$.

If (i) is true, then, since $\mathcal{A}$ makes (8.7.3) true, $\mathcal{A}$ must assign true to either p_1 or p_2 or to both, in which case (8.7.2) is true under $\mathcal{A}$ as well. If (ii) is true, then, similarly, $\mathcal{A}$ must assign true to either p_7 or p_8 or to both, in which case, once again, (8.7.2) is true under $\mathcal{A}$. Finally, if (iii) is true, then either

(iv)(a) $\mathcal{A}$ makes r_1 true and r_2 false

or

(iv)(b) $\mathcal{A}$ makes r_2 true and r_3 false

or

(iv)(c) $\mathcal{A}$ makes r_3 true and r_4 false

or

(iv)(d) $\mathcal{A}$ makes r_4 true and r_5 false

To see this, notice that, if (iii) is true, it is just not possible for all of (iv)(a)–(iv)(d) to be false. But if (iv)(a) is true, we see, focusing on the second clause of (8.7.3), that p_3 must be true. Similarly, if (iv)(b), (iv)(c), or (iv)(d) is true, then either p_4, p_5, or p_6 must be true under $\mathcal{A}$. In any case, (8.7.2) is going to be true also. Summarizing, we have that if (8.7.3) is satisfiable, then so is (8.7.2).

To see the converse, suppose that (8.7.2) is satisfiable by virtue of some assignment $\mathcal{A}$ making p_5 true, say. Then let $\mathcal{A}'$ be just like $\mathcal{A}$ as far as the p_i are concerned; in addition, let $\mathcal{A}'$ make $r_1, r_2,$ and

r_3 true and r_4 and r_5 both false. (Basically, the r_i to the left of p_5 in (8.7.3) are made true, while those to its right are made false.) Then (8.7.3) will be true under $\mathcal{A}'$. Thus, if (8.7.2) is satisfiable, then so is (8.7.3).

Now, where w is the encoding of CNF

$$C_1 \, \& \, C_2 \, \& \cdots \& \, C_k$$

let $f(w)$ be the encoding of the 3-CNF that is the result of replacing any clause C_i containing four or more literals with a new 3-CNF, following the construction technique applied to (8.7.2) to produce (8.7.3). Our earlier discussion shows that w is satisfiable if and only if $f(w)$ is. That is, $w \in L_{\mathcal{CNFSat}}$ if and only if $f(w) \in L_{3\text{-}\mathcal{CNFSat}}$. We leave it as an exercise to show that f is polynomial-time Turing-computable (see Exercise 8.7.1). We have proved

---

THEOREM 8.10: The Satisfiability Problem for 3-CNFs is NP-complete.

We shall consider four more NP-complete problems from graph theory. The first of these is

The Clique Problem for Undirected Graphs

Given an undirected graph G, we define a clique within $G = (V, E)$ to be any subset V' of V such that there is an edge in G between any two distinct vertices v and w of V'. (Is it evident whence the term "clique"?) For instance, the graph pictured in Figure 8.7.1 has one clique of size 4—namely, $\{v_1, v_2, v_3, v_4\}$—as well as four cliques of size 3—one of which is $\{v_1, v_2, v_3\}$—but no clique of size 5, say.

Now the *Clique Problem for Undirected Graphs* is that of determining, for a given graph G and natural number k, whether G possesses a clique of size k. We show that this problem is NP-complete by first showing that it is in NP and then by showing that the Satisfiability Problem for CNFs is polynomial-time reducible to it.

In order to show that the Clique Problem is in NP, we must first settle on some way of representing graphs on Turing machine tapes. Let us represent the undirected graph G of Figure 8.7.1 by the string

$$(v_1 v_2)(v_1 v_3)(v_1 v_4)(v_1 v_5)(v_2 v_3)(v_2 v_4)(v_2 v_6)(v_3 v_4)^\frown$$

$$^\frown (v_3 v_7)(v_4 v_8)(v_5 v_6)(v_5 v_8)(v_6 v_7)(v_7 v_8)$$

enumerating the edges of G.[2] We shall let $L_{\mathcal{Clique}}$ be the language consisting of just those strings

$$k \, (v_{i_1} v_{j_1}) \ldots (v_{i_n} v_{j_n}) \qquad (8.7.4)$$

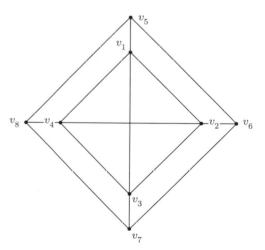

Figure 8.7.1   This undirected graph has one clique of size 4 as well as four cliques of size 3.

---

[2]We shall use such lists of edges only for undirected graphs containing no isolated vertices, that is, no vertices of degree 0. Otherwise, a somewhat different association of graphs with strings would be needed.

such that the undirected graph with vertices $v_{i_1}, v_{j_1}, \ldots, v_{i_n}, v_{j_n}, \ldots$ and edges $(v_{i_1} v_{j_1}), \ldots, (v_{i_n} v_{j_n})$ has a clique of size k. Thus, with respect to the undirected graph G of Figure 8.7.1, we have already seen that the strings

$$4\,(v_1 v_2)(v_1 v_3)(v_1 v_4)(v_1 v_5)(v_2 v_3)(v_2 v_4)(v_2 v_6)(v_3 v_4)(v_3 v_7)(v_4 v_8)(v_5 v_6)(v_5 v_8)(v_6 v_7)(v_7 v_8)$$

and

$$3\,(v_1 v_2)(v_1 v_3)(v_1 v_4)(v_1 v_5)(v_2 v_3)(v_2 v_4)(v_2 v_6)v_3 v_4)(v_3 v_7)(v_4 v_8)(v_5 v_6)(v_5 v_8)(v_6 v_7)(v_7 v_8)$$

are both in language L_{Clique} whereas the string

$$5\,(v_1 v_2)(v_1 v_3)(v_1 v_4)(v_1 v_5)(v_2 v_3)(v_2 v_4)(v_2 v_6)(v_3 v_4)(v_3 v_7)(v_4 v_8)(v_5 v_6)(v_5 v_8)(v_6 v_7)(v_7 v_8)$$

is not. We now prove

> **THEOREM 8.11:** The Clique Problem for Undirected Graphs is NP-complete.

PROOF It is not difficult to see that L_{Clique} is in NP. Presented with any input word of the form (8.7.4), Turing machine M nondeterministically selects k vertices and then deterministically verifies that the subgraph consisting of these k vertices together with all incident edges is a clique (see Exercise 8.7.2).

It is also not hard to see that L_{CNFSat} is reducible to L_{Clique}. To begin, let w be (the encoding of) CNF

$$(p \vee q \vee \neg r) \,\&\, (\neg p \vee \neg r) \tag{8.7.5}$$

This is a *CNF* with two clauses.

The undirected graph G of Figure 8.7.2 may be seen to model (8.7.5) in the following sense.

- Each literal occurrence within (8.7.5) corresponds to one vertex of G. The vertex labeled $v_{\langle i,j \rangle}$ corresponds to the jth literal within the ith clause. For example, the first occurrence of $\neg r$ in (8.7.5) corresponds to vertex $v_{\langle 1,3 \rangle}$, whereas the second occurrence of $\neg r$ corresponds to vertex $v_{\langle 2,2 \rangle}$.

- As for edges, G contains an edge between two vertices $v_{\langle i,j \rangle}$ and $v_{\langle k,l \rangle}$ provided both

  (i) $i \neq k$ and
  (ii) $v_{\langle i,j \rangle}$ and $v_{\langle k,l \rangle}$ do not correspond in (8.7.5) to a pair of literals such that one is the negation of the other.

Let f be the function that maps the slashes-and-strokes encoding of (8.7.5) onto the string

$$\mathbf{2}\underbrace{(v_{11}\,v_{22})(v_{12}\,v_{21})(v_{12}\,v_{22})(v_{13}\,v_{21})(v_{13}\,v_{22})}_{} \tag{8.7.6}$$

a list of the edges of the undirected graph G appearing in Figure 8.7.2

The reader should verify that f is polynomial-time Turing-computable (see Exercise 8.7.3).

One must yet establish that $L_{CNFSat} \leq_p L_{Clique}$; that is, for any slashes-and-strokes encoding w of a CNF, we have that $w \in L_{CNFSat} \Leftrightarrow f(w) \in L_{Clique}$.

- **Forward Direction.** Suppose that w is the encoding of a satisfiable CNF with k clauses. Then some truth-value assignment $\mathcal{A}$ makes some collection of k literal occurrences—one per clause—simultaneously true. Since no two of these occurrences are within one and the same clause

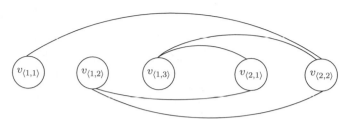

Figure 8.7.2   This undirected graph models the CNF $(p \vee q \vee \neg r)$ & $(\neg p \vee \neg r)$.

and since no literal and its negation can be among the k occurrences, we see that the corresponding undirected graph G will have a clique of size k. Consequently, the string $f(w)$ consisting of numeral k followed by a list of G's edges will be in the language L_{Clique}.

- **Reverse Direction.** Suppose that w is the encoding of a CNF and that $f(w)$ is in L_{Clique}. Then, by the construction of $f(w)$ from w, we can see that w is in L_{CNFSat}. For suppose that the CNF encoded by w has k clauses, in which case $f(w)$ begins with a representation of k. Since $f(w) \in L_{Clique}$, we can find a set S of k literal occurrences in the CNF, one per clause, such that no one of them is the negation of any of the others. It follows that there is a truth value assignment $\mathcal{A}$ that makes the CNF true: Let $\mathcal{A}$ make any literal in S true and any literal that is not in S either true or false, being careful to maintain consistency, of course. Hence the CNF encoded as w is satisfiable and we have $w \in L_{CNFSat}$.

Q.E.D.

The Vertex Cover Problem for Undirected Graphs

Let $G = (V, E)$ be an undirected graph. A *vertex cover* of G is a subset V' of V such that every edge in E is incident upon some vertex in V'. In other words, in discarding vertices of V to form V', we are careful what we throw out: We discard at most one endpoint of any edge in G. The graph of Figure 8.7.3 has several vertex covers of size 4—among them $\{v_1, v_2, v_4, v_5\}$—as well as two vertex covers of size 3, namely, $\{v_1, v_3, v_4\}$ and $\{v_2, v_3, v_5\}$. On the other hand, G has no vertex cover of size 2.

The *Vertex Cover Problem for Undirected Graphs* is that of determining, for a given undirected graph G and a given natural number k, whether G has a vertex cover of size k. We shall show that the Vertex Cover Problem is NP-complete by showing that it is in NP and that the Clique Problem for Undirected Graphs is polynomial-time reducible to it.

DEFINITION 8.6: Let $G = (V, E)$ be an undirected graph. Then the *complement graph* of G is defined as $comp(G) = (V, E')$, where $E' = \{(v, w) | v, w \in V$ and $v \neq w$ and $(v, w) \notin E\}$.

For example, the complement graph $comp(G)$ of the undirected graph G of Figure 8.7.3 appears in Figure 8.7.4: Its edge set contains just two edges, namely, $(v_1\, v_4)$ and $(v_2\, v_5)$. (Similarly, the undirected graph of Figure 8.7.1 contains edges $(v_1\, v_6)$, $(v_1\, v_7)$, $(v_1\, v_8)$, and $(v_2\, v_5)$ as well as 10 other edges. [What are they?])

We note that the graph $G = (V, E)$ of Figure 8.7.3 has several cliques of size 3 (e.g., $\{v_1, v_2, v_3\}$) and that the relative complement of any such clique (e.g., $V \setminus \{v_1, v_2, v_3\} = \{v_4, v_5\}$ is a vertex cover of

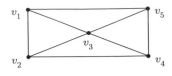

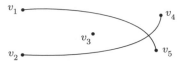

Figure 8.7.3 This undirected graph has several vertex covers of size 4 and two vertex covers of size 3.

Figure 8.7.4 This undirected graph is the complement of the undirected graph of Figure 8.7.3.

$comp(G)$. In full generality we have

LEMMA 8.1: Let $G = (V, E)$ be an undirected graph and let $comp(G)$ be the complement graph of G. Then $V' \subseteq V$ is a clique of G if and only if $V \backslash V'$ is a vertex cover of $comp(G)$.

PROOF First, suppose that V' is a clique of G. It follows that any two distinct vertices of V' are connected by an edge in G. None of these edges will be in $comp(G)$. Hence, in $comp(G)$, no edge connects any two vertices of V': Any edge of $comp(G)$ that is incident upon a vertex in V'—there may or may not be such an edge—connects that vertex to some vertex in $V \backslash V'$. In other words, every edge in $comp(G)$ is incident upon some vertex in $V \backslash V'$, which means that $V \backslash V'$ is a vertex cover of $comp(G)$.

Suppose that $V \backslash V'$ is a vertex cover of $comp(G)$. Then any edge of $comp(G)$ is incident upon at least one vertex in $V \backslash V'$. In other words, no edge of $comp(G)$ connects two vertices of V'. But then, by the nature of $comp(G)$, any two distinct vertices of V' must be connected by an edge in G. That is, V' is a clique of G.   Q.E.D.

LEMMA 8.2: Let $G = (V, E)$ be an undirected graph and let $comp(G)$ be the complement graph of G. Then G has a clique of size k if and only if $comp(G)$ has a vertex cover of size $|V| - k$.

PROOF ($\Rightarrow$). Suppose that G has a clique V' of size k. Then, by Lemma 8.1, $V \backslash V'$ is a vertex cover of $comp(G)$. Moreover, the size of $V \backslash V'$ is $|V| - k$.

($\Leftarrow$). Suppose that $V \backslash V'$ is a vertex cover of $comp(G)$ and that $|V \backslash V'|$ is $|V| - k$. Then $|V'| = k$. Moreover, by Lemma 8.1, V' is a clique of G.   Q.E.D.

We let $L_{\mathcal{V}ertex\_Cover}$ be the language consisting of (suitable representations of) those strings

$$k\, (v_{i_1} v_{j_1}) \ldots (v_{i_n} v_{j_n})$$

such that the graph with vertices $v_{i_1}, v_{j_1}, \ldots, v_{i_n}, v_{j_n}, \ldots$ and edges $(v_{i_1}\, v_{j_1}), \ldots, (v_{i_n}\, v_{j_n})$ has a vertex cover of size k. Thus, referring to the graph G of Figure 8.7.3, we have already seen that both

$$3\, (v_1\, v_2)(v_1\, v_3)(v_1\, v_5)(v_2\, v_3)(v_2\, v_4)(v_3\, v_4)(v_3\, v_5)(v_4\, v_5)$$

and

$$4\,(v_1\,v_2)(v_1\,v_3)(v_1\,v_5)(v_2\,v_3)(v_2\,v_4)(v_3\,v_4)(v_3\,v_5)(v_4\,v_5)$$

are in the language L_{Vertex_Cover}. On the other hand,

$$2\,(v_1\,v_2)(v_1\,v_3)(v_1\,v_5)(v_2\,v_3)(v_2\,v_4)(v_3\,v_4)(v_3\,v_5)(v_4\,v_5)$$

is not in L_{Vertex_Cover}.

THEOREM 8.12: The Vertex Cover Problem for Undirected Graphs is NP-complete.

PROOF First, the language L_{Vertex_Cover} is accepted by a nondeterministic Turing machine M in polynomially bounded time and hence is in NP. Given input

$$k\,(v_{i_1}\,v_{j_1})\ldots(v_{i_n}\,v_{j_n}) \tag{8.7.7}$$

M nondeterministically selects a set of vertices of the represented graph G and then deterministically verifies that this set has cardinality k and that every edge of G is indeed incident upon some member of the chosen set. Briefly, suppose that the input tape contains (8.7.7) initially. In $O(n)$ steps, where n is length of input, M writes on worktape₁ the set of k selected vertices. Afterward, M scans the input tape from the left, verifying, for each edge, that at least one of its endpoints occurs on worktape₁. Each such verification requires $O(n)$ steps, so the overall verification that the selected vertices cover G requires $O(n^2)$ steps.

We must yet establish that L_{Vertex_Cover} is NP-hard. We do this by showing that $L_{Clique} \leq_p L_{Vertex\_Cover}$, from which it follows, by Remark 8.7.1, that L_{Vertex_Cover} is NP-complete. That is, we will show that there exists a polynomial-time Turing-computable function f with

$$w \in L_{Clique} \Leftrightarrow f(w) \in L_{Vertex\_Cover}$$

Let word w be the string

$$k\,\underbrace{(v_{i_1}\,v_{j_1})\ldots(v_{i_n}\,v_{j_n})}_{\text{a list of the edges of graph } G} \qquad \longleftarrow \qquad \boxed{\text{This is } w.}$$

and let us refer to the graph represented by $(v_{i_1}\,v_{j_1})\ldots(v_{i_n}\,v_{j_n})$ here as G. Let f transform w into

$$|V| - k\,\underbrace{(v'_{i_1}\,v'_{j_1})\ldots(v'_{i_m}\,v'_{i_m})}_{\text{a list of the edges of graph } comp(G)} \qquad \longleftarrow \qquad \boxed{\text{This is } f(w).}$$

Then, by Lemma 8.2, w is in L_{Clique} if and only if $f(w)$ is in L_{Vertex_Cover}. It is plain that f is polynomial-time Turing-computable. (Given two tapes, an $O(n^2)$ algorithm is possible.)   Q.E.D.

The Feedback Vertex Set Problem for Directed Graphs

In preparation for the next NP-complete problem to be introduced, we present

---

DEFINITION 8.7: Let $G = (V, E)$ be a directed graph. Then $V' \subseteq V$ is a *feedback vertex set* of G if every cycle in G has a vertex in V'.

Each of $\{v_3\}$, $\{v_1, v_5\}$, and $\{v_2, v_4\}$ is a feedback vertex set of the directed graph of Figure 8.7.5, as is any vertex set of cardinality 3. Note that if $V' \subseteq V$ is a feedback vertex set of $G = (V, E)$, then so is any V'' with $V' \subseteq V'' \subseteq V$. Also, if $G = (V, E)$ happens to be acyclic, then every subset of V—including $\varnothing$—is a feedback vertex set.

The *Feedback Vertex Set Problem for Directed Graphs* is that of determining, for an arbitrary directed graph G and natural number k, whether G possesses a feedback vertex set of cardinality k. Equivalently, the Feedback Vertex Set Problem is that of determining membership in the language $L_{Feedback\_Vertex\_Set}$ consisting of all and only those words w of the form

$$k \, (v_{i_1} v_{j_1}) \ldots (v_{i_n} v_{j_n})$$

such that the directed graph with vertices and edges $(v_{i_1} v_{j_1}), \ldots, (v_{i_n} v_{j_n})$ has at least one feedback vertex set of size k. Referring to the graph of Figure 8.7.5, we see that the strings

$$1 \, (v_1 \, v_3)(v_2 \, v_1)(v_2 \, v_5)(v_3 \, v_2)(v_3 \, v_4)(v_4 \, v_1)(v_4 \, v_5)(v_5 \, v_3)$$
$$2 \, (v_1 \, v_3)(v_2 \, v_1)(v_2 \, v_5)(v_3 \, v_2)(v_3 \, v_4)(v_4 \, v_1)(v_4 \, v_5)(v_5 \, v_3)$$
$$3 \, (v_1 \, v_3)(v_2 \, v_1)(v_2 \, v_5)(v_3 \, v_2)(v_3 \, v_4)(v_4 \, v_1)(v_4 \, v_5)(v_5 \, v_3)$$

are all members of language $L_{Feedback\_Vertex\_Set}$, whereas the string

$$0 \, (v_1 \, v_3)(v_2 \, v_1)(v_2 \, v_5)(v_3 \, v_2)(v_3 \, v_4)(v_4 \, v_1)(v_4 \, v_5)(v_5 \, v_3)$$

is not. In general, if $G = (V, E)$ is a directed graph with $E = \{(v_{i_1} v_{j_1}), \ldots, (v_{i_n} v_{j_n})\}$ and the string

$$k \, (v_{i_1} v_{j_1}) \ldots (v_{i_n} v_{j_n})$$

is in $L_{Feedback\_Vertex\_Set}$, then so is

$$k' \, (v_{i_1} v_{j_1}) \ldots (v_{i_n} v_{j_n})$$

for all k' with $k \le k' \le |V|$.

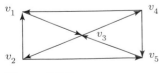

Figure 8.7.5

We show that the Feedback Vertex Set Problem is NP-complete by proving the following theorem.

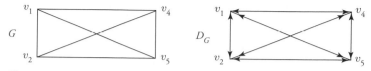

Figure 8.7.6 The undirected graph G on the left induces the directed graph D_G on the right.

THEOREM 8.13: The Vertex Cover Problem for Undirected Graphs is polynomial-time reducible to the Feedback Vertex Set Problem for Directed Graphs. Hence the latter is NP-complete. Equivalently, $L_{Vertex\_Cover} \leq_p L_{Feedback\_Vertex\_Set}$ so that $L_{Feedback\_Vertex\_Set}$ is NP-complete.

PROOF The verification that $L_{Feedback\_Vertex\_Set} \in NP$ is left as an exercise (see Exercise 8.7.6).

It remains to be shown that Vertex Cover is polynomial-time reducible to Feedback Vertex Set. Let $G = (V, E)$ be an undirected graph. Let D_G be the directed graph whose vertex set is just V and whose edge set E' is the result of replacing each edge $(v\,w)$ in E with a pair of directed edges $v \rightarrow w$ and $w \rightarrow v$. We illustrate this in Figure 8.7.6 with undirected graph G appearing on the left and induced directed graph D_G appearing on the right.

We note that every edge $(v\,w)$ of E corresponds to a cycle $v\,w\,v$ in E'. A little reflection reveals that $S \subseteq V$ is a vertex cover of G if and only if S is a feedback vertex set of D_G. Finally, the transformation of canonical representation w of Vertex Cover to canonical representation $f(w)$ of Feedback Vertex Set can be accomplished by a deterministic Turing machine with two tapes in $O(|w|^2)$ steps (see Exercise 8.7.7).   Q.E.D.

The Feedback Edge Set Problem for Directed Graphs

The reader can no doubt guess what is meant by the *Feedback Edge Set Problem for Directed Graphs*. First, we define the notion of a *feedback edge set*.

DEFINITION 8.8: Let $G = (V, E)$ be a directed graph. Then $E' \subseteq E$ is a *feedback edge set* of G if every cycle in G has an edge in E'.

The reader should verify that both $\{v_1 \rightarrow v_3, v_5 \rightarrow v_3\}$ and $\{v_3 \rightarrow v_2, v_3 \rightarrow v_4\}$ are feedback edge sets of the directed graph G of Figure 8.7.5, whereas $\{v_3 \rightarrow v_4, v_2 \rightarrow v_5\}$ is not. Note further that G has no feedback edge set of cardinality 1. If $E' \subseteq E$ is a feedback edge set of $G = (V, E)$, then so is any E'' with $E' \subseteq E'' \subseteq E$. Also, if $G = (V, E)$ is acyclic, then every subset of E—including $\varnothing$—is a feedback edge set.

The Feedback Edge Set Problem for Directed Graphs is that of determining, for an arbitrary directed graph G and natural number k, whether G possesses a feedback vertex set of cardinality k. Equivalently, $L_{Feedback\_Edge\_Set}$ is the set of all strings w of the form

$$k \, (v_{i_1} v_{j_1}) \ldots (v_{i_n} v_{j_n})$$

such that the directed graph with vertices and edges $(v_{i_1} v_{j_1}), \ldots, (v_{i_n} v_{j_n})$ has at least one feedback edge set of size k. Referring to the graph of Figure 8.7.5 again, we see that string

$$2\,(v_1\,v_3)(v_2\,v_1)(v_2\,v_5)(v_3\,v_2)(v_3\,v_4)(v_4\,v_1)(v_4\,v_5)(v_5\,v_3)$$

is a member of language $L_{\mathcal{F}eedback\_Edge\_Set}$, whereas strings

$$1\,(v_1\,v_3)(v_2\,v_1)(v_2\,v_5)(v_3\,v_2)(v_3\,v_4)(v_4\,v_1)(v_4\,v_5)(v_5\,v_3)$$

$$0\,(v_1\,v_3)(v_2\,v_1)(v_2\,v_5)(v_3\,v_2)(v_3\,v_4)(v_4\,v_1)(v_4\,v_5)(v_5\,v_3)$$

are not.

THEOREM 8.14: The Vertex Cover Problem for Undirected Graphs is polynomial-time reducible to the Feedback Edge Set Problem for Directed Graphs. Hence the latter problem is NP-complete. Equivalently, $L_{\mathcal{V}ertex\_Cover} \leq_p L_{\mathcal{F}eedback\_Edge\_Set}$ so that $L_{\mathcal{F}eedback\_Edge\_Set}$ is NP-complete.

PROOF Again, the verification that $L_{\mathcal{F}eedback\_Edge\_Set} \in NP$ is left as an exercise (see Exercise 8.7.8).

We show that Vertex Cover for Undirected Graphs is polynomial-time reducible to Feedback Edge Set. Let $G = (V, E)$ be a given undirected graph. We use G to construct a directed graph H_G. For each vertex $v \in V$, we introduce two vertices—call them v_0 and v_1—into H_G. As for edges, for each $v \in V$, we place the edge $v_0 \to v_1$ in H_G. Also, for each edge $(v\ w)$ in E, we introduce the pair of edges $v_1 \to w_0$ and $w_1 \to v_0$ into H_G. Consequently, each edge $(v\ w)$ in E corresponds to cycle $v_0\,v_1\,w_0\,w_1\,v_0$ in the induced H_G. Moreover, all cycles in H_G are of this form. (See Figure 8.7.7, where undirected graph G appears on the left and directed graph H_G appears on the right.)

Now suppose that S is a feedback edge set of H_G. That is, suppose that every cycle in H_G has an edge in S. Note that, since any cycle involving vertex v_0 must contain edge $v_0 \to v_1$, we may assume without loss of generality that any edge $w_1 \to v_0$ in S has been replaced in S by $v_0 \to v_1$. In other words, we may assume that feedback edge set S consists of k edges of the form $v_0 \to v_1$ for some k. But then, since there is a 1–1 correspondence between edges $(v\ w)$ in G and cycles of the form $v_0\,v_1\,w_0\,w_1\,v_0$ in H_G, it can be seen that the k vertices v of G, which correspond to the k edges $v_0 \to v_1$ of H_G, together form a vertex cover of G.

The other direction is similar. Suppose that V' is a vertex cover of $G = (V, E)$ containing k vertices. Now consider the set S of edges of H_G such that, for each vertex v in V', edge $v_0 \to v_1$ is in S. It should be clear, by the 1–1 correspondence, that S is a feedback edge set of H_G of cardinality k.

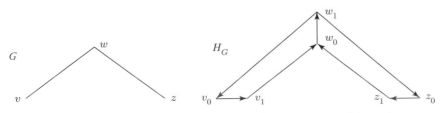

Figure 8.7.7 Undirected graph G is the basis for the construction of directed graph H_G.

$$L_{\mathcal{CNR}Sat} \begin{cases} \leq_p L_{Clique} \leq_p L_{Vertex\_Cover} \begin{cases} \leq_p L_{Feedback\_Vertex\_Set} \\ \leq_p L_{Feedback\_Edge\_Set} \end{cases} \\ \leq_p L_{3-\mathcal{CNF}Sat} \end{cases}$$

Figure 8.7.8 Reducibility Relations Holding between Six NP-Complete Problems.

> We have shown that there exists a function f such that, for any canonical representation w of Vertex Cover, string $f(w)$ is a canonical representation of Feedback Edge Set and
>
> $$w \in L_{Vertex\_Cover} \Leftrightarrow f(w) \in L_{Feedback\_Edge\_Set}$$
>
> Once again, there exists a two-tape Turing machine that transforms w into $f(w)$ in $O(|w|^2)$ steps. We may take ourselves to have shown that $L_{Vertex\_Cover} \leq_p L_{Feedback\_Edge\_Set}$. Q.E.D.

This completes our brief survey of NP-complete problems. Figure 8.7.8 summarizes the reducibility relations between the six NP-complete problems that we have considered in this and the preceding section.

§8.8 The Bounds of Parallel Computation: The Concept of P-Completeness (Advanced)

In §7.5 we saw that certain languages accepted by Turing machines in polynomial time are accepted by vector machines in polylogarithmic time—that is, in $O(\log_2^k n)$ parallel steps for some fixed $k \geq 0$. (We are writing $\log_2^k n$ for $(\log_2 n)^k$, so "polylogarithmic time" means *polynomial in the logarithm of the size of input*.) This sort of exponential improvement is what one hopes for when considering parallel solutions. When introduction of a parallel algorithm results in an improvement of this order, then one says, informally, that the problem is *highly parallel*. Some feature of the problem enables it to be distributed over multiple processors computing simultaneously with a concomitant dramatic improvement in performance times. This notion of "highly parallel" is an intuitive concept, not a mathematical concept. We can give it mathematical content, however, by adopting

> **THE COOK–PIPPENGER THESIS CONCERNING PARALLEL COMPUTATION:** A problem (language) is *feasible and highly parallel* or just *highly parallel* if there exists a vector machine that solves (accepts) it in polylogarithmic time and polynomial space.

Note that the Cook–Pippenger Thesis is analogous to Church's Thesis with respect to computability-in-principle and to the Cobham–Edmonds Thesis with respect to computational feasibility. In each case, one has made a proposal regarding the meaning of an intuitive concept. If Cook–Pippenger is adopted, then Examples 7.5.1 and 7.5.2 show that languages $\{w \in \Sigma^* | w = w^R\}$ with $\Sigma = \{a, b\}$ and $\{a^{2^i} | i \geq 0\}$ are both feasible and highly parallel since each is accepted in $O(\log_2 n)$ steps by a vector machine that computes in polynomial space.

In Definition 1.11 we defined complexity class P as the class of all polynomial-time Turing-acceptable languages. If Cobham–Edmonds is true, then P is the class of problems that are computationally feasible.

Complexity class NC is the analog of P within the context of parallel computation. Before defining NC, we need some terminology.

DEFINITION 8.9: Let $f(n)$ be a unary number-theoretic function. Then $f(n)$ is said to be *polylogarithmic-time polynomial-space vector-machine-computable* if there exists some vector machine $M = \langle \mathcal{V}, \mathfrak{I} \rangle$, that computes $f(n)$ in polylogarithmically bounded time (i.e., in $O(\log_2^k n)$ parallel steps for some fixed $k \geq 0$) and in polynomially bounded space (i.e., for any register V in $\mathcal{V}$, we have, throughout M's computation, that $|V|$ is $O(n^j)$ for some fixed $j \geq 0$). Equivalently, $f(n)$ is *polylogarithmic-time polynomial-space vector-machine-computable* provided that there exists some vector machine M and some fixed $k, j \geq 0$ such that (1) M computes f, (2) $time_M(n)$ is $O(\log_2^k n)$, and (3) $space_M(n)$ is $O(n^j)$.

One goal of this section is to introduce and use a notion of polylogarithmic-time polynomial-space reducibility analogous to that of polynomial-time reducibility. In other words, we wish to develop a reducibility relation (as usual, one problem will be reducible to another) in which vector machines play the role assigned to Turing machines in §8.5. Analogous to Definition 8.2, we have the following definition.

DEFINITION 8.10: A unary (partial) function f from $\{0, 1\}^*$ to $\{0, 1\}^*$ will be said to be *polylogarithic-time polynomial-space vector-machine-computable* if there exists a vector machine $M = \langle \mathcal{V}, \mathfrak{I} \rangle$ such that, for arbitrary $w \in \{0, 1\}^*$ with $f(w)$ defined, M computes $f(w)$ in polylogarithmic time (i.e., in $O(\log_2^k |w|)$ parallel steps for some fixed $k \geq 0$) and in polynomial space (i.e., for any register V_i in $\mathcal{V}$, we have, throughout M's computation, that $|V_i|$ is $O(n^j)$ for some fixed $j \geq 0$). We assume that M begins execution with $+w$ and $U(|w|)$ in registers V_1 and V_2, respectively, and that $+f(w)$ appears ultimately in register V_3 with $U(|f(w)|)$ in register V_4.

We are now ready to define complexity class NC. We remind that reader that, since vector machine registers contain bit-vectors only, language acceptance on the part of a vector machine presupposes some ASCII-style encoding of alphabet symbols as bit sequences. As in Chapter 7, we can think of bit 0 as representing symbol a and bit 1 as representing symbol b, with longer encodings being needed in the case of larger alphabets. Also, in accordance with Definition 7.9, an input word w stored in register V_1 must be accompanied by its length n stored in unary in register V_2. We also remind the reader of the processor interpretation of vector lengths; that is, $space_M(n)$ provides a measure of the number of processors used by vector machine M in its computation for input of length n.

DEFINITION 8.11: A language L over alphabet Σ is said to be *polylogarithmic-time polynomial-space vector-machine-acceptable* provided that there exist both a vector machine M and some constants $k, j \geq 0$ such that, for any $w \in \Sigma^*$, we have $w \in L$ if and only if M accepts w in $O(\log_2^k |w|)$ parallel steps using $O(n^j)$ processors. This is equivalent to requiring that there exist a vector machine M such that (1) M accepts L, (2) $time_M(n)$ is $O(\log_2^k n)$ for some fixed $k \geq 0$, and (3) $space_M(n)$ is $O(n^j)$ for some fixed $j \geq 0$.

DEFINITION 8.12: The class of all polylogarithmic-time polynomial-space vector-machine-acceptable languages is known as NC.

As for the origin of the name itself, the designation NC is an abbreviation of "Nick's class" and is a reference to theoretical computer scientist Nicholas Pippenger, who, during the 1970s, initiated the investigation of this important complexity class. Since polylogarithmically bounded time is a fortiori polynomially bounded time, we have, as an immediate consequence of Corollary 7.1, the following theorem.

THEOREM 8.15: $NC \subseteq P$.

Assuming both Cook–Pippenger and Cobham–Edmonds, the inclusion of $NC \subseteq P$ is reflected in our informal terminology: Every feasible and highly parallel problem is, a fortiori, a feasible problem. It is then an important question—essentially, one that we raised in §7.5—whether in fact $NC = P$. The question remains open at this writing. However, there is considerable evidence suggesting that $NC \subset P$, as we shall see.

The Boolean Circuit Value Problem

Our development of the theory of P-completeness will pursue analogies with the development of the theory of NP-completeness as presented in §8.5 through §8.7. Complexity class P will play the role formerly played by NP, with NC taking over P's former role. The role of the Satisfiability Problem for CNFs will be played by a problem known as the *(Boolean) Circuit Value Problem*, which we now describe. (We shall assume the reader's familiarity with Boolean circuits as described in Exercise 7.7.6.) One supposes that a Boolean circuit C is given together with an appropriate number of input values $x_1, x_2, \ldots, x_n$. The Boolean Circuit Value Problem is that of determining whether some designated output vertex y takes value 1 for these input values. As an illustration, suppose that C is the two-input circuit pictured in Figure 8.8.1, that input vertices x_1 and x_2 have been assigned values 1 and 0, respectively, and that output vertex y_1 is the one that interests us. Then it is easy to see how we can solve this instance of Circuit Value. (Does y_1 have value 1 for these inputs?) What first concerns us is showing that a *deterministic Turing machine M* can solve any instance of Circuit Value in time that is polynomial in the length of some input word w describing that instance. *In other words, our goal is seeing that the Circuit Value Problem is in P.*

Of course, we shall need some encoding of Boolean circuits that can be manipulated by M. The canonical description words of Exercise 7.7.6(h) can serve here. The

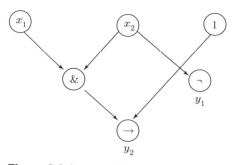

Figure 8.8.1 A Boolean Circuit of Size 6 and Depth 2.

circuit C of Figure 8.8.1 is then representable as

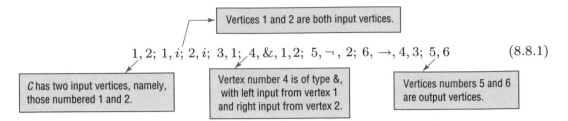

$$1, 2; \ 1, i; \ 2, i; \ 3, 1; \ 4, \&, 1, 2; \ 5, \neg, 2; \ 6, \rightarrow, 4, 3; \ 5, 6 \qquad (8.8.1)$$

Additionally, M will need (1) an enumeration of the input values to be assigned to x_1 and x_2 as well as (2) something to indicate which one of the output vertices is of interest. So we assume that information regarding (1) and (2) is tacked onto the back of (8.8.1). Thus the string

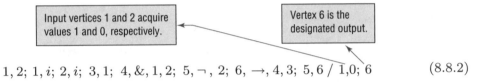

$$1, 2; \ 1, i; \ 2, i; \ 3, 1; \ 4, \&, 1, 2; \ 5, \neg, 2; \ 6, \rightarrow, 4, 3; \ 5, 6 \ / \ 1, 0; \ 6 \qquad (8.8.2)$$

is a complete representation of the particular instance of Circuit Value considered in the preceding paragraph. Formally, we may describe the language $L_{\mathcal{CVP}}$ as the set of all and only those strings of the form (8.8.2) such that the designated output vertex has value 1. It is not difficult to describe a deterministic, multitape Turing machine that accepts $L_{\mathcal{CVP}}$ in polynomially bounded time. To this end, we include the following example.

EXAMPLE 8.8.1 Open icon **Circuit Value Problem** within the Turing Machine folder in order to observe the operation of a deterministic, multitape Turing machine M that accepts $L_{\mathcal{CVP}}$ in time polynomial in the length of input. Try running M on tapes `cvp1.tt`, `cvp2.tt`, and `cvp3.tt`. We leave M's time analysis to Exercise 8.8.4.

We may take ourselves to have demonstrated

THEOREM 8.16: The language $L_{\mathcal{CVP}}$ is a member of P.

If Circuit Value is to play the role of Satisfiability for CNFs within the theory of P-completeness, we shall need to show that it is *reducible*—in some as-yet-unspecified sense—to other problems in P. This is the point of Definition 8.13 below, where we avoid the encoding issue by assuming outright that L_1 and L_2 are languages over alphabet $\{0, 1\}$.

DEFINITION 8.13: Let L_1 and L_2 be languages over alphabet $\{0, 1\}$. We shall say that L_1 is *polylogarithmic-time polynomial-space reducible to* L_2 and write

$$L_1 \leq_{plog} L_2$$

if there exists a polylogarithmic-time polynomial-space vector-machine-computable function f such that, for any word w over $\{0, 1\}$, we have

$$w \in L_1 \Leftrightarrow f(w) \in L_2$$

(The reader should compare Definition 8.13 with Definition 8.3.) Without further comment we present some additional definitions and theorems that are the strict analogues of definitions and theorems presented in §8.5. The proofs of Theorems 8.17 through 8.20 involve reasoning analogous to that of the proofs of Theorems 8.5 through 8.8 (see Exercises 8.8.5 through 8.8.8).

DEFINITION 8.14: A language L is said to be *P-hard* if, for every language L' in P, we have $L' \leq_{plog} L$.

THEOREM 8.17: If $L \leq_{plog} L'$ and L is P-hard, then L' is P-hard. Speaking intuitively, if both (1) L' is at least as hard as L and (2) L is at least as hard as any problem in P, then L' is at least as hard as any problem in P.

DEFINITION 8.15: If L is P-hard and L is in P, then we shall say that L is *P-complete*.

THEOREM 8.18: Let languages L and L' be given. Suppose that $L' \leq_{plog} L$ and that L is in NC. Then L' is in NC as well.

THEOREM 8.19: Let languages L and L' be given. Suppose that $L' \leq_{plog} L$ and that L is in P. Then L' is in P as well.

THEOREM 8.20: If there exists a P-complete language L such that L is in NC, then $NC = P$.

THEOREM 8.20 (contrapositive): If $NC \subset P$, then no P-complete language is a member of NC.

Given the transitivity of the reducibility relation $\leq_{plog}$, as shown in Exercise 8.8.2, we can justify

REMARK 8.8.1: If a given problem is in P and some P-complete problem is polylogarithmic-time polynomial-space reducible to it, then the given problem is itself P-complete.

Of course, there is no hope of applying Remark 8.8.1 until we have identified a first P-complete problem. As the reader will have guessed, this will be the Boolean Circuit Value Problem. We have already shown it to be in P. It remains to be shown that it is P-hard. We devote an entire section—the next one—to the proof of this result, which is due to Richard Ladner.

§8.9 A P-Complete Problem (Ladner's Theorem) (Advanced)

Without further delay we present our proof of

THEOREM 8.21 (Ladner's Theorem): The Boolean Circuit Value Problem is P-complete.

PROOF By Theorem 8.16, we know already that Circuit Value is in P. It remains to be seen that L_{CVP} is P-hard in the sense of Definition 8.14. That is, given an arbitrary $L \subseteq \Sigma^*$ in P, we show that $L \leq_{plog} L_{CVP}$. The proof amounts to showing, first, that Boolean circuits can simulate deterministic single-tape Turing machines. Afterward, we suppose that Turing machine M accepts L, and we let f be a function that maps any $w \in \Sigma^*$ onto a certain canonical representation $f(w)$, along the lines of (8.8.2), describing a circuit that simulates M's behavior for input w in such a way that

$$w \in L \Leftrightarrow f(w) \in L_{CVP} \tag{8.9.1}$$

Furthermore, the function f will be shown to be computable in polylogarithmic time and polynomial space by some vector machine M_f. In describing $f(w)$, we shall assume some encoding of connectives $\neg, \vee, \&, \rightarrow$, and $\leftrightarrow$ as well as input designator i, separating commas, and semicolons (see (8.8.2)).

We begin by making a series of preliminary remarks intended to establish the ability of circuits to simulate Turing machines.

- $L \in P$ implies the existence of a single-tape Turing machine $M = \langle Q, \Sigma, \Gamma, q_0, \delta \rangle$, that accepts L in $p(n)$ or fewer steps, where $p(n)$ is a polynomial function and n is the length of M's input word w. As in the proof of the Cook–Levin Theorem, we shall make use of the fact that, given input $w \in \Sigma^*$, machine M executes no more than $t = p(|w|) \geq |w|$ steps and hence can visit no more that $2t + 1$ tape squares (cf. Figure 8.6.1). The squares on the relevant portion of M's tape are assigned positions from 1 to $2t + 1$ inclusive. We shall assume that M has $m + 1$ states and that tape alphabet $\Gamma = \{\alpha_1, \ldots, \alpha_r\}$ with input alphabet $\Sigma \subseteq \Gamma$. It will prove convenient to write α_0 for the blank B and α_1 for symbol *1*. Let us also assume that M accepts by terminal state.

- We may assume without loss of generality that M accepts input word w just in case M is scanning an accepting *1* at time t itself. We accomplish this by adding "useless" instructions to the state diagram of M, in effect. So, for example, if M has no instruction for symbol α_j at state q_i, we add instruction $\langle q_i, \alpha_j; \alpha_j, q_i \rangle$, thereby extending M's computation at least potentially.

- For such a machine M and input word w over Σ, we describe the construction of a Boolean circuit C_M of size $O(t^2)$ that models the behavior of M for input word w in the sense that if the input to C_M is w essentially, then its single output vertex will have value 1 just in case M accepts w.

- Since the input values of any Boolean circuit are either 1 or 0, we have yet to say in what sense C_M's input can be $w \in \Sigma^*$. In the general case, we should need to assume that $\alpha_0, \alpha_1, \ldots, \alpha_r$ are encoded in unary in the usual sense: α_i would be encoded as a sequence of $i + 1$ inputs of 1. We shall make the simplifying assumption that $\Sigma = \Gamma = \{a\}$ so that blank B can be encoded as input 0 and a as input 1.

Circuit C_M will contain all of the vertices

(1) $\sigma_{h,j,k}$ for each h, j, and k with $0 \le h \le m, 1 \le j \le 2t+1$, and $0 \le k \le t$

(2) $\tau_{i,j,k}$ for each i, j, and k with $0 \le i \le r = 1, 1 \le j \le 2t+1$, and $0 \le k \le t$

(3)   a single output vertex v_{output}

Regarding (1) and (2) we remark the following:

(A) The intended interpretation of the vertices of group (1) is already familiar from the proof of Cook–Levin and concerns the status of the machine proper—that is, the current state of M and the location of its read/write head. It will turn out that vertex $\sigma_{h,j,k}$'s having value 1 will correspond to M's being in state q_h scanning the jth tape square at time k. (At the inception of execution, we have $k = 0$. After one step has been executed, we have $k = 1$, and so forth.)

(B) Our understanding of the vertices of group (2) concerns the contents of M's tape, just as before. In particular, vertex $\tau_{i,j,k}$'s having value 1 will model the fact that symbol α_i is on the jth tape square at time k.

(C) For fixed j and k, the $m+1$ vertices $\sigma_{h,j,k}$ and $r+1$ vertices $\tau_{i,j,k}$ together model the situation with respect to tape cell j at step k in M's computation.

The input vertices of circuit C_M fall into two categories.

(i) There will be $m \cdot (2t+1)$ input vertices of the form $\sigma_{h,j,0}$—one for each pair h, j with $0 \le h \le m$ and $1 \le j \le 2t+1$. Within $f(w)$, all except $\sigma_{0,t+1,0}$ will be assigned value 0. (Why?)

(ii) Letting $r = 1$, there will be $2 \cdot (2t+1)$ input vertices of the form $\tau_{i,j,0}$—two for each tape square. Given any pair of input vertices $\tau_{0,j,0}$ and $\tau_{1,j,0}$, one will be 1 and the other will be 0, as determined by input word w, assumed to begin at tape square $t+1$ and to extend to the right. In fact, input vertices $\tau_{1,j,0}$ and $\tau_{0,j,0}$ for $1 \le j \le t$ will be assigned values 0 and 1, respectively, in any case. (Why?)

Each of the other vertices at (1)–(3)—each vertex that is not an input vertex—will be the output of some subcircuit of C_M. We take them in order. As in the proof of Cook–Levin, we assume that M's instruction set has been partitioned into three sets of quadruples $\mathcal{W}$, $\mathcal{MR}$, and $\mathcal{ML}$.

I. For $0 \le h \le m, 1 \le j \le 2t+1$, and $k \neq 0$, vertex $\sigma_{h,j,k}$ will be the output of that subcircuit of C_M describable as

$$\bigvee_{\langle q,\alpha_i;R,h \rangle \in \mathcal{MR}} \left(\sigma_{q,j-1,k-1} \,\&\, \tau_{i,j-1,k-1} \right) \vee \bigvee_{\langle q,\alpha_i;\alpha_{i'},h \rangle \in \mathcal{W}} \left(\sigma_{q,j,k-1} \,\&\, \tau_{i,j,k-1} \right)$$

$$\vee \bigvee_{\langle q,\alpha_i;L,h \rangle \in \mathcal{ML}} \left(\sigma_{q,j+1,k-1} \,\&\, \tau_{i,j+1,k-1} \right)$$

To comprehend this, recall our stated desire that $\sigma_{h,j,k}$ be true just in case, at time k, machine M is in state h scanning the jth tape square. In that case, the disjunction at the top left says that $\sigma_{h,j,k}$ will be true if (i) at preceding step $k-1$, machine M was in some state q scanning some symbol α_i on square $j-1$ and (ii) there is some instruction that causes M to execute a move-right and enter state h under just those circumstances. The other two disjunctions speak to the possibilities that M will find itself in state h scanning square j at time $k \geq 1$ as the result of executing either a write instruction or a move-left.

The perceptive reader will have realized that our subcircuit description for either $j = 1$ or $j = 2t + 1$ presupposes a range of boundary values $\sigma_{h,0,k}$ and $\sigma_{h,2t+2,k}$. We set $\sigma_{h,0,k} = 0$ and $\sigma_{h,2t+2,k} = 0$ for all $0 \leq h \leq m$ and $0 \leq k \leq t$. Similarly, $\tau_{1,0,k} = 0, \tau_{0,0,k} = 1, \tau_{1,2t+2,k} = 0$, and $\tau_{0,2t+2,k} = 1$ for each k with $0 \leq k \leq t$. The latter assignments have the effect of adding a new column of blanks at each end of the array of Figure 8.6.1. (What do the former assignments say?) Incidentally, all these boundary vertices will be input vertices of C_M.

II. For $0 \leq i \leq r = 1, 1 \leq j \leq 2t + 1$, and $k \geq 1$, vertex $\tau_{i,j,k}$ will be the output of that subcircuit of C_M describable as

$$\bigvee_{\langle q, \alpha_{i'}; \alpha_i, h \rangle \in \mathcal{W}} \left(\sigma_{q,j,k-1} \,\&\, \tau_{i',j,k-1} \right) \vee \left(\left[\bigwedge_{q \in Q} \neg \sigma_{q,j,k-1} \right] \,\&\, \tau_{i,j,k-1} \right)$$

This subcircuit may be interpreted as detailing two different ways in which symbol α_i may come to occupy square j at time k. One way is for M's read/write head, at time $k-1$, to be positioned over the jth tape square scanning some symbol $\alpha_{i'}$ with M in some state q such that M's instruction set happens to contain an instruction that involves writing symbol α_i under just those circumstances. That is what the disjunction on the left says. The conjunction on the right speaks to the other way in which symbol α_i may come to occupy square j at time k: Namely, at time $k-1$, symbol α_i might already occupy square j with no change occurring to it during the next instruction—due to the fact that M's read/write head is not scanning square j at time $k-1$ (square brackets).

III. As mentioned at (3), circuit C_M will possess a single output vertex, which we are calling v_{output}. Vertex v_{output} will itself be the output of that subcircuit of C_M describable quite simply as

$$\bigvee_{1 \leq pos \leq 2t+1} \sigma_{m,pos,t}$$

where q_m is assumed to be the unique terminal state of M.[1] In other words, ouput vertex v_{output} will acquire value 1 just in case M, at time t, is in state q_m scanning any tape square whatever. (It is not necessary to assume that M itself possesses no instructions for state q_m but, rather, only that it eventually halts in that state, at which point our useless instructions will maintain C_M's simulation of M in state q_m until time t.)

This completes the first part of our proof. It should not be too hard to see that w is accepted by M just in case C_M's v_{output} produces value 1, which is to say that (8.9.1) holds. It remains to be shown that f is polylogarithmic-time polynomial-space vector-machine-computable. That is, we

---

[1] An alternative construction that assumes acceptance by 1 would also be possible (cf. Conjunct 6 in the proof of Theorem 8.9). However, in that case $|\Gamma|$ would necessarily come to be 3, thereby precluding our simple 0–1 encoding scheme.

must show that (1) there exists some vector machine M_f that, given any word $w = a^{|w|}$, constructs canonical representation $f(w)$ of circuit C_M applied to input sequence

$$\sigma_{0,j,0}: \mathbf{00000000\ldots0000010\ldots0000000\ldots0000}$$

$$\sigma_{1,j,0}: \mathbf{00000000\ldots0000000\ldots0000000\ldots0000}$$

$$\ldots \qquad\qquad \ldots \qquad\qquad\qquad (8.9.2)$$

$$\sigma_{m,j,0}: \mathbf{00000000\ldots0000000\ldots0000000\ldots0000}$$

$$\tau_{1,j,0}: \mathbf{00000000\ldots0000011\ldots1111000\ldots0000}$$

$$\tau_{0,j,0}: \underbrace{\mathbf{11111111\ldots11111}}_{t\ \text{blanks}}\underbrace{\mathbf{00\ldots0000}}_{|w|\ \text{as}}\underbrace{\mathbf{111\ldots1111}}_{t-|w|+1\ \text{blanks}}$$

In other words, the reader is to imagine this string of inputs, separated by commas and tacked onto the back of the likes of (8.8.2).

and that (2) this construction can be carried out in time that is polylogarithmic in $|w|$ using space that is polynomial in $|w|$. We make several remarks that are intended to render this plausible.

(1) We first seek to convince the reader that the input sequence at (8.9.2) can by generated by M_f in polylogarithmic time and polynomial space. Its length is $(m + 3) \cdot (2t + 3)$—or $(m + 1 + r + 1) \cdot (2t + 3)$ in the general case—and hence $O(t)$. This is enough to establish the claim regarding space. As for time, each of the rows at (8.9.2) can be constructed in $O(\log_2 t)$ steps, which is $O(\log_2 |w|)$ steps by transitivity. Their concatenation requires another $O(\log_2 t)$—that is, $O(\log_2 |w|)$—steps (see Exercise 8.9.1 for details).

(2) As at (I), vertex $\sigma_{h,j,k}$, for given h, j, and $k \geq 1$, will be the output of a subcircuit $\mathcal{S}_{h,j,k}$ of size $O(1)$—the number of gates does not depend upon t and hence does not depend upon $|w|$. And since subcircuit $\mathcal{S}_{h,j,k}$ has size $O(1)$, the same is true of its canonical representation.

(3) Similarly, as at (II), vertex $\tau_{i,j,k}$, for given i, j, and $k \geq 1$, will be the output of a subcircuit $\mathcal{T}_{i,j,k}$ of size $O(1)$. Likewise, the representations of all these subcircuits are of fixed size.

(4) We let $\mathcal{C}_{j,k}$, for fixed j and k, be that subcircuit comprising all $m + 1$ subcircuits $\mathcal{S}_{h,j,k}$ for $0 \leq h \leq m$ together with all $r + 1$ subcircuits $\mathcal{T}_{i,j,k}$ for $0 \leq i \leq r$. By (C), the $(m+1)+(r+1)$ outputs of $\mathcal{C}_{j,k}$ together model tape square j at step k within M's computation. It follows that modeling M's entire computation for input word w will require $O(t^2)$ copies of $\mathcal{C}_{j,k}$ one for each cell within the array of Figure 8.6.1. Moreover, each of the $\mathcal{C}_{j,k}$ is of identical *constant* size—call it N. (To see this, note that at (I) and (II) we quantify over the partitioning of M's instruction set and over Q; consequently, the size of subcircuit $\mathcal{C}_{j,k}$, for particular j and k, depends upon m and r but not upon j or k.) Likewise, the canonical representations of the $\mathcal{C}_{j,k}$ are structurally identical but involve distinct vertex numbers. Matters may be arranged so that the number designations of corresponding vertices v within two distinct $\mathcal{C}_{j,k}$ are assigned binary designations from among $K_v, K_v + 1, K_v + 2, K_v + 3, \ldots, K_v + t \cdot (2t + 3)$, and hence the difference between any two of them is $O(t^2)$.

(5) This means that vector machine M_f will need to generate, in one register, $O(t^2)$ structurally identical copies of one and the same canonical representation of subcircuit template $\mathcal{C}_{j,k}$ and afterward to insert $O(t^2)$ binary number designations $K_v, K_v + 1, K_v + 2, K_v + 3, \ldots, K_v + t \cdot$

$(2t + 3)$ at constant intervals determined by N. Moreover, it will be necessary to carry out this sequence of insertions N times—that is, once for each of N distinct values of K_v.

(6) Of course, M_f will first need to compute $t = p(|w|)$ in order to determine how many copies of (the canonical representation of) subcircuit template $\mathcal{C}_{j,k}$ must be constructed. That t can be computed in polylogarithmic time and polynomial space follows from Remark 7.4.3 and the fact that $U(|w|)$ is available in M_f's register V_2, as required by Definition 8.10.

(7) Generating $O(t^2)$ structurally identical copies of one and the same canonical representation of size $O(1)$, as at (5), can be accomplished in $O(\log_2 t)$, and hence in $O(\log_2 |w|)$, time, using polynomial space (see Example 7.4.3 [Generalized Copier]). Insertion of the binary vertex numbers within these copies can be carried out in polylogarithmic time and polynomial space by first generating, in $O(\log_2 |w|)$ steps and $O(|w|^2)$ space, the number designations in sequence and then interpolating them (cf. Exercises 8.9.2 and 8.9.3). This insertion process must be repeated N—that is, $O(1)$—times.

(8) The subcircuit with output v_{output}, as at III, consists of $O(t)$ individual vertices $\sigma_{i,j,k}$ together with $O(t)$ OR-vertices. Obviously, the canonical descriptions of the several vertices within each of these two groups will be structurally identical. Consequently, the representation of the entire subcircuit can be constructed by M_f in time polylogarithmic in the length of input and in space polynomial in the length of input, essentially as at (7).

(9) A canonical string designating $O(t)$ input vertices as such can be constructed in $O(\log_2 |w|)$ steps. Concatenating this string with the representations of (7), (8), and (1)—in that order—requires another $O(\log_2 |w|)$ steps, and one obtains $f(w)$ in M_f's register V_3 and $U(|f(w)|)$ in V_4, as required by Definition 8.10.   Q.E.D.

§8.10 The Nearest-Neighbor Traveling Salesman Problem Is P-Complete (Advanced)

A fuller development of the theory of P-completeness requires that we show how the P-completeness of the Circuit Value Problem can be used to establish that other decision problems are P-complete as well. In other words, we seek opportunities to apply Remark 8.8.1. As in the case of NP-completeness, we turn our attention to graph theory. In particular, we shall focus upon a restricted version of the duly famous Traveling Salesman Problem. This restricted version is known as the *Nearest-Neighbor Traveling Salesman Problem*. We shall show that Nearest-Neighbor Traveling Salesman is itself in P and that it is P-hard. We accomplish the latter by showing that Circuit Value is polylogarithmic-time polynomial-space reducible to Nearest-Neighbor Traveling Salesman. In order to expedite our discussion, we make a number of preliminary remarks that the reader is encouraged to accept now without further justification. (Full details are provided in the solutions to the exercises.)

(1) Without loss of generality, we may assume that any Boolean circuit consists solely of input vertices and so-called NAND-vertices of fan-in 2, where a NAND-vertex with inputs x_1 and x_2 produces output 1 just in case x_1 and x_2 are not both 1 (see Exercise 0.8.7 and Exercises 7.7.6(k) and (j)). One of the NAND-vertices will be the designated output of the circuit.

(2) We describe the *NAND Circuit Value Problem*. One supposes that a Boolean circuit C consisting solely of input vertices and NAND-vertices is given together with an appropriate number of input values $x_1, x_2, \ldots, x_n$. The NAND Circuit Value Problem is then the problem of determining whether some NAND-vertex y, designated as the output vertex, takes value 1 for these input values.

(3) We let $L_{\mathcal{NANDCVP}}$ be the language consisting of all and only those strings of the form (8.8.2) such that the designated output vertex has value 1. Furthermore, we shall assume that $L_{\mathcal{NANDCVP}}$ has been shown to be P-complete—a highly nontrivial claim going well beyond anything implicit in Exercise 0.8.7. (Theory terrorists should try Exercises 8.10.3 through 8.10.5.)

(4) By (3), in order to show Nearest-Neighbor Traveling Salesman to be P-hard, it will be sufficient to show that NAND Circuit Value is polylogarithmic-time polynomial-space reducible to it.

The Nearest-Neighbor Traveling Salesman Problem for Weighted Undirected Graphs

The Traveling Salesman Problem for Weighted Undirected Graphs, as described in Exercise 0.7.5, is that of finding a least-cost Hamiltonian circuit, starting at a given vertex within the graph. Traveling Salesman is an important problem with many applications. Unfortunately, it has been shown to be NP-complete, although we have not done so in this text (see [Garey and Johnson 1979]). Consequently, our work in §8.5 through §8.7 suggests that this problem—like all NP-complete problems—is, most probably, intractable. To gain some relief from this situation, computer scientists have suggested various rules-of-thumb—various *heuristics*, as one says—for making Traveling Salesman a little easier. One of these is the so-called *nearest-neighbor heuristic*, according to which, in constructing a Hamiltonian circuit, one always chooses, as the vertex to be visited next, some vertex that has not yet been visited and whose distance from the current vertex is minimal. One then continues in this way until all the vertices have been visited, after which one returns to the starting vertex, assuming that is possible. In general, the nearest neighbor heuristic does not produce a least-cost Hamiltonian circuit. (It may not even produce a closed path.) Our interest in it stems from the fact that it sometimes works and is always feasible. As an illustration, we provide the following

---

EXAMPLE 8.10.1 We apply the nearest neighbor heuristic to the weighted undirected graph of Figure 8.10.1, starting at vertex v_1. The result is the following *nearest-neighbor tour*, starting at vertex v_1: $v_1 v_4 v_6 v_7 v_8 v_5 v_3 v_2 v_1$. It is readily seen that, although clearly a Hamiltonian circuit, the tour's cost of 32 is not optimal. (Edge $(v_5 v_3)$ amounts to a wrong turn.)

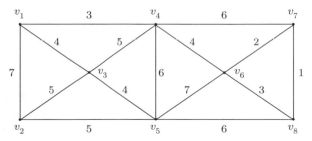

We need to cast the Nearest-Neighbor Traveling Salesman Problem as a decision problem. There are many ways of doing this.

Figure 8.10.1   This weighted undirected graph has the following nearest-neighbor tour starting at v_1: $v_1\ v_4\ v_6\ v_7\ v_8\ v_5\ v_3\ v_2\ v_1$.

We shall use

DEFINITION 8.16: The *Nearest-Neighbor Traveling Salesman Problem for Weighted Undirected Graphs* is that of determining, for two given vertices v_1 and v_2 within a given weighted undirected graph G, whether the nearest-neighbor tour starting at v_1 visits vertex v_2 immediately before returning to v_1.

In the case of the graph of Example 8.10.1, the question posed by Nearest-Neighbor Traveling Salesman for vertices v_1 and v_2 is yes: The nearest-neighbor tour starting at v_1 does visit v_2 last, just before returning to v_1. In other cases, the answer to the question may be no either because some other vertex is visited last or because the nearest-neighbor tour never manages to return to the start vertex. (We refer to the posed questions as *nearest-neighbor-tour questions.*)

Establishing that Nearest-Neighbor Traveling Salesman is P-complete requires that we first prove

---

THEOREM 8.22: The Nearest-Neighbor Traveling Salesman Problem is in P.

PROOF See Example 8.10.2 and Exercise 8.10.2.

EXAMPLE 8.10.2 Open icon **Nearest-Neighbor Traveling Salesman** within the Turing Machine folder to observe the operation of a multitape Turing machine M that accepts language $L_{\mathcal{NN}\,TravSales}$, consisting of all and only those strings representing nearest-neighbor-tour questions that can be answered affirmatively. Machine M assumes a standard representation of weighted undirected graphs that is described in the software documentation. Tape sets `nearest1.tt` and `nearest2.tt` have been created for use with this machine. We leave M's time analysis to Exercise 8.10.2.

It remains for us to show that Nearest-Neighbor Traveling Salesman is P-hard. To this end, we next describe a general construction that can be applied to any Boolean circuit C, consisting of input vertices and NAND-vertices only, together with an appropriate number of input values, so as to yield a weighted undirected graph G_C satisfying the following: The value of the designated output of C is 1 if and only if the answer to a certain nearest-neighbor-tour question with respect to G_C is yes (see (13) below). The construction requires considerable care. We structure our proof as a series of remarks.

(1) We shall assume that circuit C has m vertices and that they have been numbered *topologically* starting from 1; that is, any NAND-vertex is assigned a number higher than that assigned to either of its inputs. Each vertex within C—both input vertices and NAND-vertices—will serve as the basis for the construction of a single subgraph within G_C. Accordingly, we shall refer to the subgraph corresponding to vertex k as subgraph k.

(2) Moreover, the arrangement of these subgraphs within G_C will be such that, as it turns out, the (unique) nearest-neighbor tour starting at the subgraph corresponding to the first of C's input vertices will visit the several subgraphs in an order reflecting the numbering of vertices within C. In other words, subgraph k will be visited just before subgraph $k + 1$.

(3) It follows that, when the tour enters any NAND-subgraph k within G_C, it will already have visited its two input subgraphs i and j. We emphasize at the outset that visiting a subgraph will

not, in general, involve visiting each and every vertex within that subgraph. Since subgraphs will share vertices, visiting a subgraph may involve skipping certain vertices, which will then be visited later when some other subgraph is visited.

(4) The NAND-vertices of circuit C may be assumed to have fan-out 2, 1, or 0 (see Exercise 8.10.6). Any NAND-vertex k, with $k < m$, of fan-out 2 with input vertices i and j, will serve as the basis for a subgraph like the one shown in Figure 8.10.2. Vertex pairs marked α and β are shared between subgraphs. The pair at the top of Figure 8.10.2 serves as one of two inputs to subgraph k and serves as an output of subgraph i. Similarly, the α–β pair at the bottom of Figure 8.10.2 serves as an input to subgraph k and as an output of subgraph j. Note that each α–β pair is connected by an edge of weight 0, which means that if the vertex marked α is ever visited, then, by nearest neighbor, its companion β-vertex is visited next, and vice versa.

(5) A NAND-vertex with fan-out 1 will be represented by what is essentially the subgraph of Figure 8.10.2 but with a single α–β pair of outputs rather than two pairs. Similarly, a NAND-vertex with fan-out 0 will be represented by what is essentially the subgraph of Figure 8.10.2 but minus both α–β pairs of outputs. (The one exception will be the designated output vertex of the circuit, which will be represented by a subgraph exhibiting a special structure to be described later.)

(6) The subgraph of Figure 8.10.2 is designed in such a way as to ensure that if the nearest-neighbor tour enters at vertex A from subgraph $k - 1$, then it eventually proceeds into subgraph $k + 1$ by way of vertex B, as will be explained below.

(7) We introduce some new terminology for subgraphs of G_C. Let us say that a NAND-subgraph k with $k < m$ "has value 1" provided that the tour of this subgraph visits the output vertices on the right in Figure 8.10.2 and that it "has value 0" otherwise. (We assume the extension of this terminology to input-subgraphs in (11) below.)

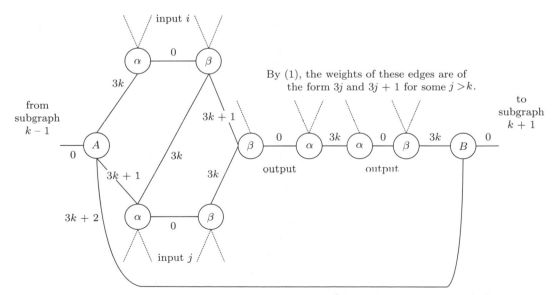

Figure 8.10.2 Subgraph corresponding to vertex $k < m$ (assumed to be a NAND-vertex with fan-out 2)

(8) By nearest neighbor and the nature of the construction, once the tour reaches the leftmost of the output vertices in Figure 8.10.2, it then visits the remaining ones from left to right and goes on to vertex B without detouring into connected subgraphs. (Why?)

(9) When the nearest-neighbor tour enters subgraph k at vertex A in Figure 8.10.2, there are three distinct possibilities.

  (a) Suppose that input vertex pairs i and j have both already been visited on the tour. In this case, by nearest neighbor, the tour proceeds directly from vertex A to vertex B along the edge with weight $3k + 2$ and, from B, proceeds immediately into subgraph $k + 1$. In consequence of this, each of the two output vertices β has its companion vertex α as its only unvisited neighbor within subgraph k. The status of the tour with respect to subgraph k in this case is depicted in Figure 8.10.3(a).

  (b) Suppose that exactly one of input-vertex pairs i and j has already been visited. Without loss of generality, we may assume that it is input-vertex pair i that remains unvisited. In that case, having arrived at vertex A in Figure 8.10.2, the tour proceeds to the input vertex α at the top and, from there, immediately to its companion vertex β. Moreover, by (3) and (9)(a), this vertex β now has no unvisited neighbors within subgraph i. Consequently, by (8), the tour next proceeds through the output vertices of subgraph k from left to right and, from there, to vertex B. The situation is depicted in Figure 8.10.3(b). The case where it is just input-vertex pair j that remains unvisited is essentially the same.

  (c) Suppose that neither of input-vertex pairs i and j has been visited previously on the tour. Then the status of the nearest-neighbor tour is as depicted in Figure 8.10.3(c).

(10) Note that, in each of cases (a), (b), and (c) in (9), any as-yet-unvisited input-vertex pair is visited during the tour of subgraph k. Moreover, the nearest-neighbor tour leading from vertex A to vertex B visits the output vertices just in case at least one of the two pairs of input vertices was not previously visited, as shown in Figures 8.10.3(a)–(c). This is the basis for the following claim: Subgraph k will have value 1, in the sense of (7), if and only if at least one of subgraphs i and j has value 0. We have thereby reproduced within G_C the situation whereby NAND-vertex k yields output 1 just in case at least one of inputs i and j is 0.

(11) Circuit C also contains input vertices with assigned numbers $k < m$. The subgraph within G_C corresponding to input vertex k will be either as depicted in Figure 8.10.4(a) or Figure 8.10.4(b), depending upon whether the assigned input is 1 or 0, respectively. Note that if the input vertices within C are those with lowest numbers, then the output vertices of the true subgraphs within G_C will be visited more or less in succession at the very beginning of the tour. (Output vertices of false subgraphs are skipped over and visited later.)

(12) We make a special case of C's vertex m, which is a NAND-vertex (see Figure 8.10.5). Two edges with weight $3m + 3$ connect it to the entry vertex of subgraph 1, which necessarily corresponds to an input vertex. In place of output vertices, we have vertex X. The reader should verify that if the tour enters at vertex A in subgraph m and the situation described at (9)(a) holds (i.e., both input-vertex pairs i and j have been visited already), then from A the tour proceeds immediately to B and from there on to X, followed by subgraph 1. Otherwise (i.e., if at least one of input-vertex pairs i and j has not yet been visited), then the tour proceeds into the central hexagon and from there on to X and B and subgraph 1. In either case, vertices B and X are both visited on the tour of subgraph m. The important question is, Which vertex—B or X—is visited last before the return to subgraph 1, thereby completing the Hamiltonian circuit of G_C? If it is X, then

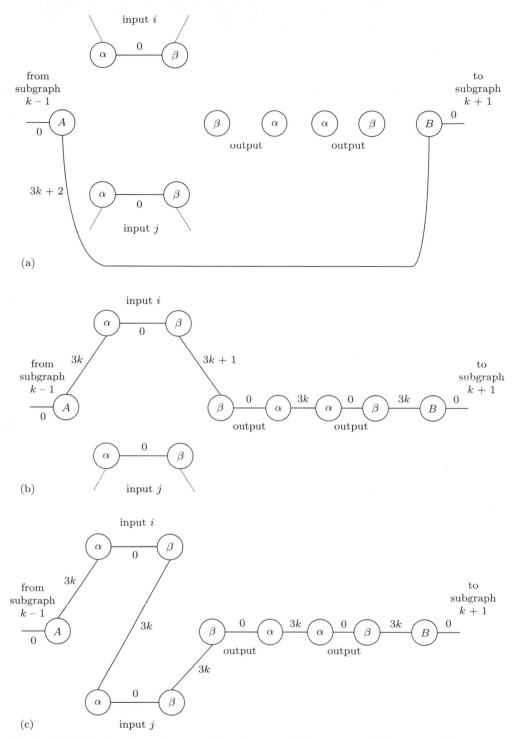

Figure 8.10.3 These three diagrams depict the status of the nearest-neighbor tour with respect to subgraph $k < m$ for the case where: (a) both input-vertex pair i and input-vertex pair j has been visited earlier on the tour; (b) input-vertex pair j but not input-vertex pair i has been visited earlier on the tour; (c) neither of input-vertex pairs i and j has been visited earlier on the tour.

apparently situation (9)(a) held, and, by (10), vertex m of circuit C yields output 0 for the given inputs. If it is vertex B that is visited last, then either situations (b) or (c) held, in which case vertex m produces output 1.

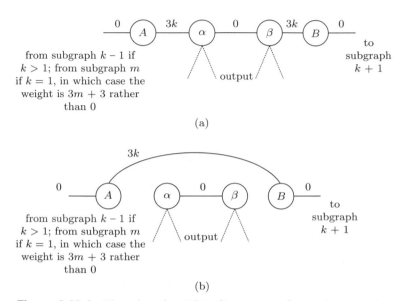

(a)

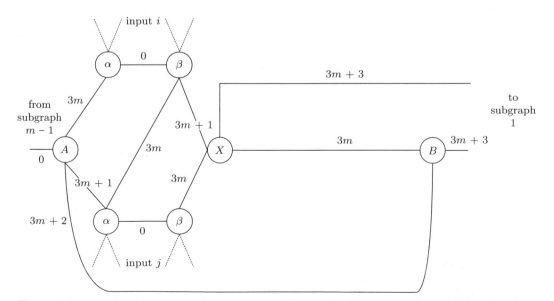

(b)

Figure 8.10.4 The subgraphs within G_C corresponding to input vertices take one of two forms.

Figure 8.10.5 Subgraph Corresponding to Vertex m (Assumed to be a NAND-Gate with Fan-Out 0).

(13) Summarizing, circuit C's designated output yields output 1 if and only if the nearest-neighbor tour of weighted undirected graph G_C visits a certain vertex B immediately before returning to its start vertex. Expressed differently, circuit C's designated output yields output 1 if and only if the answer to a certain nearest-neighbor-tour question with respect to graph G_C is yes. We have reduced the NAND Circuit Value Problem to the Nearest-Neighbor Traveling Salesman Problem for Weighted Undirected Graphs.

(14) In effect, we have described the transformation of word w representing an arbitrary instance of NAND Circuit Value into word $f(w)$ representing a certain weighted undirected graph. It remains to be shown that this transformation can be carried out in polylogarithmic time and polynomial space by a vector machine. We leave the details to Exercise 8.10.8.

In the meantime, we take ourselves to have shown

THEOREM 8.23: The Nearest-Neighbor Traveling Salesman Problem for Weighted Undirected Graphs is P complete.

We conclude that no parallel implementation of the nearest-neighbor heuristic is likely to be more efficient than available sequential implementations.

§8.11 Beyond Symbol Processing: The Connectionist Model of Cognition

In §2.8 we noted a possible strategy for the Interrogator pitted against a computer in Turing's Imitation Game. Namely, the Interrogator might ask questions requiring number crunching—something that machines are especially adept at—in an attempt to distinguish the human respondent from the machine. The performance of computers is typically superior to that of human beings whenever it is a question of manipulating large amounts of data or carrying out long sequences of numerical operations. This in itself may suggest that human brain activity is intrinsically different from that of a digital computer—even one capable of parallel processing. Consider, in addition, the well-established difficulty of programming computers to recognize patterns, process speech, make plans, or learn just about anything—tasks that human brains perform very well. Our point is that the domains in which computers excel do not appear to overlap much with the domains in which human brains excel. This by itself may cause one to doubt the veracity of the Computer Model of Mind as articulated in §2.9 and elaborated in §7.6. But there are two other, frequently cited arguments for doubting the adequacy of the Computer Model of Mind. Both are intended to suggest that human brains most likely function in ways very different from those in which conventional computers function.

The first of these arguments starts from the fact that, at the most basic level, human brains are slow whereas computers are fast. The optimal switching time of individual neurons in the cortex is measured in thousandths of a second. In contrast, the microcomputer that is currently on the author's desk executes roughly 10^6 floating-point operations per second. This means that the most basic operations within a computer are approximately 1000 times faster than the most basic operations at the level of neurons. What are the implications of this difference in speed? Well, it is still true that human beings are able to complete significant cognitive tasks such as memory retrieval, perceptual processing, and scene recognition in mere *tenths* of a second—tasks that no computer can perform, even in principle, given unlimited time.

Suppose, for the sake of argument, that the Computer Model of Mind, as described in §2.9, is true, so that brain/mind activity is describable as the manipulation of neural/mental representations in accordance with syntactic rules. In that case, even if thousands of neurons are assumed to work in parallel, it nonetheless appears that complex tasks such as scene recognition must be completable in a sequence of no more than about 100 parallel steps at the most basic, neuronal level. Now, since no one pretends to know how the representations in question might be stored within the brain, it is not impossible that scene recognition could involve a mere 100 steps. However, many people have thought that this number is very low, given the quantity of information that we have stored within our neural networks and the relative sparseness of neural interconnections relative to the total number of neurons. In other words, if successive comparisons, say, are the basis for scene recognition in human beings, then surely no sequence of a mere 100 comparisons could produce the results observed in human beings—or so goes the argument.

A second argument takes as its starting point not processing speed but, rather, the quality of cognitive functioning. One uses the term "graceful degradation" to describe the fact that human cognitive functioning tends to deteriorate only gradually. For instance, once an author's document has grown beyond a certain length, it becomes likely that he or she will no longer remember many details of the treatment of diverse topics. On the other hand, it is unlikely that the author will forget absolutely everything regarding the text that has been written. In other words, a particular sort of cognitive functioning—memory with respect to a written document in this case—may fall off due to time constraints or information overload but is unlikely to crash completely—at least in the absence of brain damage or physical disease causing the loss of an entire region of the brain. Even in the case of global degenerative syndromes such as Alzheimer's, brain function deteriorates only gradually as ever more neural units are destroyed: there appears to be no single neural unit whose loss rules out all future cognitive functioning of the relevant kind. In other words, human cognitive functioning degrades gracefully. Contrast this with the performance of digital computers running under this or that program. An error with respect to a single instruction in a large program may result in output that is totally wrong. In this sense, the processing of digital computers is too inflexible or "brittle": a single flaw may render an entire system useless. This discrepancy between the graceful degradation of cognitive functioning and the sudden and catastrophic collapse of computer systems calls into question the validity of the computational conception of mind.

Summarizing, the slowness of neurons, the graceful degradation of cognitive functioning, and the cited discrepancy between areas in which computers excel and those in which human brains excel have together convinced some researchers that the digital computer provides an inadequate explanatory model of cognitive performance. The alternative that has been embraced by many within the cognitive science and AI communities is to adopt one or another of the various connectionist models of cognition that we describe now.

Connectionist Systems

The connectionist proposal posits *connectionist systems* or *neural networks* as the appropriate models of cognition. Such a network comprises a collection of interconnected processors called *units*. Each unit is connected to other units by directed connectors over which it sends or receives signals. For example, the neural network of Figure 8.11.1 contains seven units, three of outdegree 4 and four of outdegree 3. Each of the connectors within the network of Figure 8.11.1 happens to be bidirectional, although this is not required. The signals transmitted between units may be digital—0 or 1, *on* or *off*—or we might choose to make them analog real values ranging from 0 to r, say. The sum of the inputs to a unit will determine its *state of activation*. If only digital signals are permitted, then matters can be arranged so that a unit whose total input falls below some fixed threshold would itself be incapable of transmitting any signal whatever. Otherwise, it would transmit signal 1. Alternatively, the state of activation of a unit u would be permitted to vary between 0 and r as a function of its total input. In turn, u would transmit a signal equal to its state of activation to each of the other units to which it has a connection. Roughly, a *connectionist* in cognitive science is anyone who attempts to understand cognition using neural networks.

In addition, we mention the following items regarding neural networks.

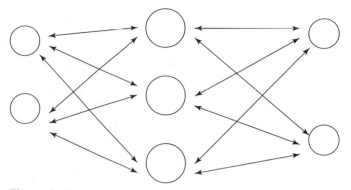

Figure 8.11.1 A neural network with seven units.

- The connections between units carry *weights*. Typically, the input to unit u_2 from u_1 is determined by the activation state of u_1 as well as by the weight of the connector from u_1 to u_2. In particular, if the activation state of u_1 is held constant, then the input signal to u_2 from u_1 will be proportional to the weight of the connection. If that weight is positive, then the corresponding connection is said to be *excitatory*.

- Some units within any neural network receive signals from outside the network. These are the so-called *input units* of the network. Input units may, in addition, receive transmissions from other units within the system, however.

- *Output units* are designated units that transmit signals to unspecified units outside the neural network in question. Output units may, in addition, send transmissions to other units inside the system.

- While the connections between units within a neural network are fixed, the weights of those connections are permitted to vary.

- Units that are neither input units nor output units are termed *hidden* or *internal units*.

- A neural network may permit connections over which *inhibitory* signals are transmitted—that is, signals that inhibit rather than excite the activation of the targeted unit. In particular, a signal over a connection from unit u_1 to unit u_2 will be inhibitory if the activation state of u_1 is positive while the weight of the connection is negative. By extension, the connection from u_1 to u_2 is itself said to be inhibitory.

The neural network of Figure 8.11.1 exhibits the layered structure typical of neural networks designed for problem solving. A particular instance of a general problem is posed, activating, from without, a particular pattern of units with the input layer. Processing proceeds through the activation of various internal layers until some pattern of activation stabilizes within a layer of output units. This pattern of activation represents the system's solution to the problem instance. Inhibitory connections may be introduced so as to ensure that only one output unit is "on" at the point the system stabilizes. This feature ensures that the generated solution is unambiguous.

Connectionist systems differ from any of the models that we have considered in this book.

- The several read/write heads of a multitape Turing machine, for example, are best thought of as being controlled by a single processor (see Remark 2.3.1 and Figure 2.3.5).

- The same is true of the tape heads and registers of any register machine: A single executive control determines the behavior of every part of the machine.

- In a vector machine, each of the several processors controls what happens within one bit-position within each register (see Figure 7.4.2). So although no single processor exercises global control, nonetheless, behavior at diverse locations within a vector machine is controlled by one and the same executive processor. Each of the several processors of a vector machine carries out some sequence of operations on corresponding bit-positions within the various registers of the machine.

- In contrast, in a connectionist system there are no executive units—nothing corresponds to a processor. This is not to say that the individual units within a connectionist system are completely independent of one another. Still, control is strictly local to the extent that each individual unit influences, or is directly influenced by, only those others to which it is directly connected and in accordance with the weights of those connections. No one unit or proper subsystem of units controls the entire system. Rather, control of the system is distributed over the entire system.

- Moreover, in each of the machine models that we have considered (or will consider) information is stored within certain machine components—tapes, registers, computation words, and the like. Computation is interpretable as symbol processing. In a connectionist system, on the other hand, information is stored in the connections *between* system components and in this sense is *subsymbolic*. To put matters another way, in each of our machine models, information is represented *explicitly* in the states of machine components themselves. In contrast, almost all information within a connectionist system is *implicit* in the structure of the system itself. Processing within a connectionist system takes the form not of symbol processing but, rather, of structural modifications of the system carried out by the system itself—that is, adjustments of the weights of the various connections between units.

- In our various machine models, some control interprets information stored within the several machine components and directs computation accordingly. In a connectionist system, information is built into the system itself and thereby directly determines the course of processing without the intervention of any distinguishable control unit.

Finally, a word of caution. The behavior of connectionist systems is sometimes characterized as *parallel distributed processing* in the literature. The occurrence of the term "parallel" here may suggest that neural networks are something akin to vector machines. Nothing could be farther from the truth, however. To see this, consider again how the behavior of a vector machine M may be viewed in terms of independent sequences of operations on corresponding bit-positions within its registers. For input of size n, we saw that, worst case, $space_M(n)$ distinct processors will execute $space_M(n)$ more-or-less identical sequences of operations in parallel. Contrast a connectionist system. There is much simultaneous processing of course, and if that is all one means by "parallel," then parallel processing is surely involved. Most commonly, however, genuine parallelism is taken to constitute simultaneous identical sequences of operations. But the processing of connectionist systems cannot in general be organized into identical sequences of operations. To this extent, describing connectionist systems as "parallel distributed processing" is misleading.

The Promise of the Connectionist Model of Cognition

Over the past twenty years, connectionist models have been introduced to account for numerous types of cognitive functioning including early vision, language processing, inference, and motor control. Nonetheless, it remains to be seen whether connectionism, in general, provides computational power sufficient to model human cognitive competence. (Recall from §2.9 that the Turing machine model is unquestionably adequate as a model of human competence.) Its proponents appear confident that the connectionist hypothesis will ultimately be seen to embody computational mechanisms adequate to account for human cognitive performance as well.

§8.12 Summary, Historical Remarks, and Suggestions for Further Reading

Our consideration of five distinct, but equivalent, models of sequential computation in Chapters 1 through 6 led us to formulate what is generally known as the Church–Turing Thesis. That thesis states that the effectively computable number-theoretic functions are precisely those that are partial recursive and hence, by our various equivalence results, Turing-computable, Markov-computable, register-machine-computable, and Post-computable. We saw how these equivalence results lend empirical support to the Church–Turing Thesis. It is reasonable to conclude that our intuitive notion of effective computability is *robust* in character despite limitations. These limitations take the form of a host of problems, starting with the Self-Halting Problem for Turing Machines, which are absolutely unsolvable or unsolvable in principle, at least if we assume the Church–Turing Thesis to be true. As for the claim that our notion of computation is robust, we mean that the notion has held up well under scrutiny using a variety of approaches: Whichever approach to the intuitive notion is selected, the result is essentially the same. Not all intuitive notions of a mathematical character have shown themselves to be robust in this sense. For instance, the intuitive notion of mathematical truth has turned out to be a particular disappointment in this regard—but that is another (long) story.

Other analyses of computability that we have not considered include Alonzo Church's notion of *lambda-definable function* and J. Lambek's notion of *abacus-computable function* (1961). The former was systematically described in [Church 1941] and what is essentially the equivalence between lambda definability and partial recursiveness was shown in [Kleene 1936b]. A readily accessible presentation of abacus computability is found in [Boolos and Jeffrey 1989], where it is shown that abacus computability is equivalent to Turing computability. Lambek's infinite abaci are essentially register machines to which a conditional decrementation operation has been added. They were first described in [Lambek 1961].

[Church 1936] contains the first statement of what is essentially the Church–Turing Thesis. (That paper uses the notion of general recursive function (see Definition 3.11) rather than partial recursive function.) It also contains the first presentation of an unsolvable decision problem, although this was not one of those that we have considered. Church–Turing now enjoys wide acceptance. However, it has not gone completely unchallenged: Mathematicians have occasionally argued for the effective calculability of particular functions that are demonstrably not partial recursive.

Both the Self-Halting Problem for Turing Machines and the Full Halting Problem for Turing Machines were first stated and shown to be unsolvable in [Turing 1936]. Rice's Theorem first appeared in [Rice 1953].

The P-versus-NP problem and the general importance of NP-complete problems were first discussed, on a philosophical level, in a letter from Gödel to von Neumann in 1956—before either class had been defined! For an analysis of this letter, and for a translation of the letter itself, see [Hartmanis 1989]. (Curiously, Gödel thought that P would be found to equal NP.)

The concept of NP-completeness was first formulated by Steven A. Cook. The proof of the existence of an NP-complete problem, as presented in §8.6, appeared in [Cook 1971]. During the same period, working independently, Leonid Levin obtained similar results (see [Levin 1973]). Since then, literally hundreds—perhaps even thousands—of problems have been shown to be NP-complete. [Garey and Johnson 1979] provide a compendium of such problems. On the other hand, [Karp 1972] and [Karp 1975] are where it all started. Incidentally, it can be shown that $L_{2\text{-}C\mathcal{N}FSat}$ is in P. That is, there exists a deterministic Turing machine that accepts the language of (encodings of) satisfiable 2-CNFs in polynomial time. The proof is difficult (see [Kozen 1992]).

For more material on functional programming and ML in particular, consult [Wikström 1987]. The proof that the Circuit Value Problem is P-complete goes back to [Ladner 1975]. The theory of P-completeness is fully developed in [Greenlaw, Hoover, and Ruzzo 1995], which is the source of our solutions to the more difficult exercises for §8.10. Our proof of Theorem 8.23 first appeared in [Kindervater, Lenstra, and Shmoys 1989].

The now-classic source regarding connectionist systems is [McClelland, Rumelhart, et al. 1986].

EXERCISES FOR §8.1

8.1.1. Professor Durcheinander claims to have obtained a rigorous proof of the Church–Turing Thesis based upon ideas from number theory. You are asked to critique the good professor's claim.

8.1.2. It follows from the Church–Turing Thesis that the Busy Beaver function of §2.7 is uncomputable. Explain.

8.1.3. Our overall argument for the Church–Turing Thesis might be referred to as the *Argument from the Convergence of Dissimilar Ideas*. Explain the aptness of this nomenclature.

EXERCISES FOR §8.2

8.2.1. (Alternative Formulation of the Self-Halting Problem for Turing Machines). The following formulation of the Self-Halting Problem for Turing Machines is standard in the literature. First, we shall say that Turing machine M_n *self-halts₁* if it eventually halts—*in any configuration whatever*—having been started scanning the leftmost *1* in a representation of its own gödel number n. The *Self-Halting₁ Problem for Turing Machines* is then the problem of determining, for arbitrary $n \geq 0$, whether M_n self-halts₁. You are asked to show that the Self-Halting₁ Problem for Turing Machines is unsolvable, assuming Church's Thesis. (*Hint:* Show that if there were an algorithm for deciding whether an arbitrary Turing machine self-halts₁, then the Self-Halting Problem for Turing Machines would be solvable as well, contradicting Remark 8.2.1. Describe an effective transformation of Turing machines such that machine M self-halts if and only if its transformation M' self-halts₁.)

8.2.2. (Bounded Self-Halting Problem for Turing Machines). We describe the *Bounded Self-Halting Problem for Turing Machines* as follows. Given arbitrary natural number n, is there an effective procedure for determining whether Turing machine M_n, started scanning the leftmost *1* in a representation of n, halts in n or fewer computation steps? Show that the Bounded Self-Halting Problem for Turing Machines is solvable by describing an algorithm.

8.2.3. (Busy Beaver Problem).[hwk] We might describe the *Busy Beaver Problem* as that of determining, for a given $n \geq 0$, the productivity of the most productive $(n + 1)$-state Turing machine(s) (see §2.7). One might go on to assert that this problem is unsolvable. But then what would be the basis for this assertion?

EXERCISES FOR §8.3

8.3.1.[hwk] **(a) (Generalized Halting Problem for Turing Machines).** Show that there is no general algorithm for determining, of an arbitrary Turing machine M with input alphabet Σ and an arbitrary word w over Σ, whether M ultimately halts when started scanning the leftmost symbol of input word w. (*Hint*: Show that if this problem were solvable, then the Halting Problem for Turing Machines would be solvable as well, contradicting Remark 8.3.1.)

(b) (Generalized Halting Problem for Multitape Turing Machines). Show that there can be no general algorithm for determining, for an arbitrary multitape Turing machine M with input alphabet Σ and an arbitrary word w over Σ, whether M ultimately halts when started scanning the leftmost symbol of input word w occurring on its input tape. (*Hint*: Use (a).)

8.3.2. (Blank-Tape Halting Problem for Turing Machines).[hwk] The *Blank-Tape Halting Problem for Turing Machines* is the problem of determining for an arbitrary Turing machine M whether M halts when started on a completely blank tape. Consider the argument below for the unsolvability of the Blank-Tape Halting Problem for Turing Machines.

Note that, given any Turing machine M with start state q_0 and given any input string w, one can construct a new machine M_w that begins scanning a square on a completely blank tape, writes w on it, and then enters M's state q_0 scanning the leftmost symbol of w. Afterward, M_w behaves exactly like M. Evidently M_w will halt when started on a blank tape if and only if M halts when started scanning the leftmost symbol of w.

Assume, now, that the Blank-Tape Halting Problem *were* solvable as the result of the availability of a general algorithm

$\mathcal{A}$. Then, given an arbitrary pair M and w, we could first construct M_w, and then apply $\mathcal{A}$ to it to see whether M_w halts for empty input. If so, then M halts for input w. If not, then M does not halt for input w. In other words, we would have transferred our algorithm $\mathcal{A}$ into an algorithm for deciding the Generalized Halting Problem for Turing Machines. But the latter problem is known to be unsolvable by Exercise 8.3.1(a). Hence our assumption that the Blank-Tape Halting Problem is solvable is false: It must be unsolvable.

(a) The argument contains a hidden appeal to Church's Thesis. Explain briefly where this appeal occurs.

(b) Discuss the argument in terms of the relative difficulty of the two unsolvable problems concerned. (*Suggestion*: Introduce the notion of reducibility—one problem to another.)

(c) Critique the following argument, which leads to the conclusion that the Busy Beaver function of §2.7 provides a counterexample to Church's Thesis.

We defined function $\Theta(n)$ to be the productivity of the most productive member(s) of $\mathcal{TM}_n$ and then saw with Theorem 2.10 that $\Theta(n)$ is not Turing-computable. On the other hand, $\Theta(n)$ *is* effectively calculable in an intuitive sense, contrary to the Church–Turing Thesis. To see this, recall that $\mathcal{TM}_n$, the class of $(n + 1)$-state Turing machines over tape alphabet $\{1, B\}$, may be assumed finite. In general, some of the members of $\mathcal{TM}_n$ eventually halt when started scanning a completely blank tape and others do not. So we simply run the ones that do halt—the others have productivity 0 by definition—and keep track of the high scorers. After all the terminating machines have been considered, the productivity of the most productive among them will be $\Theta(n)$.

8.3.3. (Bounded Halting Problem for Turing Machines).[hwk] We may formulate the *Bounded Halting Problem for Turing Machines* as follows. Given arbitrary natural numbers n, m, and k, is there an effective procedure for determining whether Turing machine M_n, started scanning the leftmost 1 in a representation of natural number m, halts in k or fewer computation steps? Show that the Bounded Halting Problem for Turing Machines is solvable by informally describing an algorithm.

8.3.4. (Uniform Halting Problem for Turing Machines). Show that there can be no algorithm for deciding whether an arbitrary Turing machine halts for every input word w.

8.3.5. (Function Identity Problem for Turing Machines). By Remark 1.5.1, every Turing machine with input alphabet $\Sigma = \{1\}$ computes some unary partial number-theoretic function. Show that there can be no algorithm for deciding whether an arbitrary pair of Turing machines computes one and the same unary function.

8.3.6. (Halting-Potential Problem for Turing Machines). Show that there can exist no general algorithm for deciding, for an arbitrary Turing machine M over input alphabet Σ, whether M halts for at least one input word w over Σ. (*Hint:* Appeal to the unsolvability of the Blank-Tape Halting Problem.)

8.3.7. (Blank-Output Problem for Turing Machines). Show that there can exist no general algorithm for deciding, for an arbitrary Turing machine M over input alphabet Σ, whether M halts scanning a blank on a completely blank tape for at least one input word w over Σ. (*Hint:* Use Exercise 8.3.6.)

8.3.8. (a) (Printing Problem for Turing Machines). Show that there can exist no general algorithm for deciding, for an arbitrary Turing machine M, whether, in the course of its computation for any input word, M ever writes a 1, moves to the right, and then writes another 1. In other words, show that this problem is unsolvable. (*Hint:* Use Exercise 8.3.6.)

(b) Explain why the following algorithm does not show that the problem described at (a) is solvable.

Given Turing machine M with tape alphabet Γ, determine whether either of the instruction sequences depicted in Figure 8.3.1 occurs anywhere within the state diagram of M, where α and β are members of $\Gamma \cup \{B\}$.

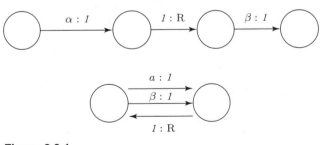

Figure 8.3.1

8.3.9. (State Problem for Turing Machines). Show that there can exist no general algorithm for deciding, for an arbitrary Turing machine M with state set Q, start state q_0, and state $q \in Q$ with $q \neq q_0$, whether, in the course of its computation for any input word, M ever finds itself in state q. In other words, show that this problem is unsolvable. (*Hint:* Use Exercise 8.3.6.)

8.3.10. This exercise is intended to elucidate the central role of the Self-Halting Problem within the theory of Turing computability. You are asked to indicate very briefly, and without restating actual arguments, how the Self-Halting problem is seen to be reducible to each of the unsolvable problems of Exercises 8.3.1, 8.3.2, and 8.3.4–8.3.9. You will need to appeal to the transitivity of the reducibility relation between problems. For example, with respect to Exercise 8.3.1(a), one can see that (1) the Self-Halting Problem is reducible to the Halting Problem, which is in turn reducible to the Generalized Halting Problem, so that (2) by transitivity, the Self-Halting Problem is reducible to the Generalized Halting Problem.

8.3.11. (**Alternative Formulation of the Full Halting Problem for Turing Machines**). The following formulation of the Full Halting Problem for Turing Machines is standard in the literature. We introduce the name $Halting_1$ *Problem for Turing Machines* for the problem of determining, for arbitrary $n, m \geq 0$, whether M_n halts—*in any configuration*—when started scanning the leftmost *1* in a representation of m. You are asked to show that the Full $Halting_1$ Problem for Turing Machines is unsolvable, assuming Church's Thesis. (*Hint*: Consider Exercise 8.2.1 and show that the Self-Halting$_1$ Problem for Turing Machines, as described there, is reducible to the Full $Halting_1$ Problem for Turing Machines. Use the argument of the proof of Theorem 8.2.)

EXERCISES FOR §8.4

8.4.1. Show that $K = \{n | \text{Turing machine } M_n \text{ self-halts}\}$ is not recursive.

8.4.2. Show that (8.4.1) implies that Ψ_Γ is not recursive.

8.4.3. Complete the proof of Theorem 8.3 by showing that (8.4.2) implies that Ψ_Γ cannot be recursive.

8.4.4. **hwk** Use Rice's Theorem to show that each of the sets of natural numbers below is not recursive.
- (a) $\{n | n$ is the gödel number of a unary partial recursive function that is defined for argument $0\}$
- (b) $\{n | n$ is the gödel number of a unary partial recursive function that is total$\}$
- (c) $\{n | n$ is the gödel number of a unary partial recursive function that is bijective$\}$
- (d) $\{n | n$ is the gödel number of a unary partial recursive function that is primitive recursive$\}$

8.4.5. **hwk** Use Rice's Theorem and Church's Thesis to show that membership in each of the sets of Turing machines below is undecidable.
- (a) $\{M | M$ computes a unary partial recursive function that is defined for even arguments only$\}$
- (b) $\{M | M$ computes a unary partial recursive function f such that $Dom(f) = \emptyset\}$
- (c) $\{M | M$ computes a unary partial recursive function that is total and whose values are primes$\}$

8.4.6. Rice's Theorem by itself implies that the set of gödel numbers of a given partial recursive function is an infinite set of natural numbers. Explain why.

8.4.7. Show that there can be no software that tests whether the unary function computed by an arbitrary C++ program is defined almost everywhere—that is, for all but a finite number of arguments. (*Hint*: Use Example 8.4.1.)

EXERCISES FOR §8.5

8.5.1. Show that the following number-theoretic functions are polynomial-time Turing-computable functions.
- (a) $f(n) = n^2$
- (b) $f(n) = n^3$

8.5.2. **hwk** Which of the following strings is a member of $L_{\mathcal{CNFSat}}$?
- (a) $/\alpha''''/\beta''''$
- (b) $/\alpha'\alpha''/\beta'\beta''/\alpha'\beta''/\beta'\alpha''$
- (c) $/\alpha'/\alpha''$

(d) $/\alpha'$
(e) $/\beta''$
(f) $/\beta''/\alpha'$

8.5.3. **hwk** Show that $\leq_p$ is transitive. That is, show that $L_1 \leq_p L_2$ and $L_2 \leq_p L_3$ together imply $L_1 \leq_p L_3$.

8.5.4. We define co-NP as the set of languages or problems whose complements are in NP. Thus, since L_{CNFSat} is in NP, we have that $L_{Unsat} = L_{CNFSat}^c$ is in co-NP. Show that if there exists an L such that L is NP-complete and L is in co-NP, then $NP = $ co-NP.

EXERCISES FOR §8.7

8.7.1. Show that function f of the proof of Theorem 8.10 is polynomial-time Turing-computable. (Note that f is not a number-theoretic function and that Definition 8.2 is being assumed.)

8.7.2. Show that the language L_{Clique} is in NP by informally describing the operation of a nondeterministic Turing machine M that accepts all and only input words of the form $k\,(v_{i_1}v_{j_1})\dots(v_{i_n}v_{j_n})$ such that the undirected graph G with edges $(v_{i_1}v_{j_1})\dots(v_{i_n}v_{j_n})$ has a clique of size k. In addition, show that M computes in time polynomial in the length of input.

8.7.3. Show that function f in the proof of Theorem 8.11 is polynomial-time Turing-computable by informally describing the operation of a deterministic Turing machine that computes f in polynomially bounded time. Note, once again, that f is not a number-theoretic function, so that Definition 8.2 is being assumed.

8.7.4. Find the complement graph of the undirected graph of Figure 0.7.4(b).

8.7.5. Show that function f in the proof of Theorem 8.12 is polynomial-time Turing-computable. That is, given word w

$$k\,\underbrace{(v_{i_1}v_{j_1})\dots(v_{i_n}v_{j_n})}_{\text{a list of the edges of graph } G}$$

8.5.5. Prove Theorem 8.5.

8.5.6. We define co-P to be the set of languages whose complements are in P. Show that, in fact, $P = $ co-P which is to say that P is closed under complementation. (*Hint:* consider Exercise 2.10.14.)

8.5.7. Show that P is closed under union, intersection, and concatenation. That is, show that if L_1 and L_2 are both in P, then so are $L_1 \cup L_2$, $L_1 \cap L_2$, and $L_1.L_2$.

8.5.8. Show that NP is closed under union, intersection, and concatenation. That is, show that if L_1 and L_2 are both in P, then so are $L_1 \cup L_2$, $L_1 \cap L_2$, and $L_1.L_2$.

function f transforms word w into word $f(w)$, given as

$$|V| - k\,\underbrace{(v'_{i_1}v'_{j_1})\dots(v'_{i_m}v'_{i_m})}_{\text{a list of the edges of graph } comp(G)}$$

where V is the set of all vertices appearing at least once in $(v_{i_1}v_{j_1})\dots(v_{i_n}v_{j_n})$.

8.7.6. Show that the language $L_{Feedback\_Vertex\_Set}$ is in NP by informally describing the operation of a nondeterministic Turing machine M that accepts all and only input words of the form

$$k\,(v_{i_1}v_{j_1})\dots(v_{i_n}v_{j_n})$$

such that the undirected graph G with edges $(v_{i_1}v_{j_1})\dots(v_{i_n}v_{j_n})$ has a feedback vertex set of size k. You must show that M computes in time polynomial in the length of input.

8.7.7. Show that the function f of the proof of Theorem 8.13 is polynomial-time Turing-computable by informally describing the operation of a deterministic Turing machine that computes f in polynomial time.

8.7.8. Show that the language $L_{Feedback\_Edge\_Set}$ is in NP by informally describing the operation of a nondeterministic Turing machine M that accepts all and only input words of the form

$$k\,(v_{i_1}v_{j_1})\ldots(v_{i_n}v_{j_n})$$

such that the undirected graph G with edges $(v_{i_1}v_{j_1})\ldots(v_{i_n}v_{j_n})$ has a feedback edge set of size k. You must show that M computes in polynomial time.

8.7.9. Show that the function f of the proof of Theorem 8.14 is polynomial-time Turing-computable by informally describing the operation of a deterministic Turing machine that computes f in polynomial time..

8.7.10. Show that $L_{1-\mathcal{CNFS}at}$ is in P. That is, show that there exists a deterministic Turing machine that accepts the language of (encodings of) satisfiable 1-CNFs in polynomial time.

EXERCISES FOR §8.8

8.8.1. Suppose that f and g are both unary polylogarithmic-time polynomial-space vector-machine-computable functions. Show that the same is then true of their composition $f \circ g$.

8.8.2. Show that the reducibility relation $\leq_{plog}$ is transitive. That is, show that if $L \leq_{plog} L'$ and $L' \leq_{plog} L''$, then $L \leq_{plog} L''$. (*Hint:* Use Exercise 8.8.1.)

8.8.3. Show that if language L is P-complete, then so is L^c. (*Hint:* Use Exercise 8.5.6.)

8.8.4. Show that the Turing machine of Example 8.8.1 computes in polynomial time, thereby proving Theorem 8.16.

8.8.5. ʰʷᵏ Prove Theorem 8.17. (*Hint:* Adapt the argument of the proof of Theorem 8.5.)

8.8.6. ʰʷᵏ Prove Theorem 8.18. (*Hint:* Adapt the argument of the proof of Theorem 8.6.)

8.8.7. ʰʷᵏ Prove Theorem 8.19. (*Hint:* Adapt the argument of the proof of Theorem 8.6 and use Corollary 7.1.)

8.8.8. ʰʷᵏ Prove Theorem 8.20. (*Hint:* Adapt the argument of the proof of Theorem 8.8.)

8.8.9. ʰʷᵏ Suppose that language L is accepted in polylogarithmic time and polynomial space by some vector machine. Show that L is then recognized in polylogarithmic time and polynomial space by some vector machine (cf. Exercise 2.10.14).

8.8.10. ʰʷᵏ We define co-NC to be the set of languages whose complements are in NC. Show that, in fact, $NC = $ co-NC. (*Hint:* Consider Exercise 8.8.9.)

8.8.11. ʰʷᵏ Show that NC is closed under union and intersection. That is, show that if L_1 and L_2 are both in NC, then so are $L_1 \cup L_2$ and $L_1 \cap L_2$. (*Hint:* Use Exercise 8.8.9.)

EXERCISES FOR §8.9

8.9.1. Justify the claim at (1) in the proof of Theorem 8.21 that the entire input sequence at (8.9.2) can be constructed by a vector machine in $O(\log_2 n)$ steps and $O(n^k)$ space, where n is the length of input word w and k is some constant.

8.9.2. Show that there exists a vector machine M that, given input vector $+1^n$ in register V_1, produces, within output register V_2, the concatenation of all binary-digit sequences of length n. (If $n = 2$, then M might produce vector $+11100100$.) Try to design a machine that computes in $O(n)$ steps and $O(n \cdot 2^n)$ space.

8.9.3. Show that there exists a vector machine M whose input and output are described below.

Input:

$$V_1 = w_1 w_2 w_3 \ldots w_n, \qquad \text{where } |w_i| = r \text{ for } 1 \leq i \leq n$$

$$V_2 = y_1 y_2 y_3 \ldots y_n, \qquad \text{where } |y_i| = s \text{ for } 1 \leq i \leq n$$

$$V_3 = +I^r$$

$$V_4 = +I^s$$

$$V_5 = +I^n$$

Output:

$$V_6 = w_1 y_1 w_2 y_2 w_3 y_3 \ldots w_n y_n$$

Try to describe a machine that computes in $O(\log_2(rsn))$ steps.

EXERCISES FOR §8.10

8.10.1. What is the result of applying the nearest-neighbor heuristic to the undirected graph of Figure 0.7.7 starting at vertex v_1? Does it produce a least-cost Hamiltonian circuit? Does it produce a Hamiltonian circuit? What if one starts at vertex v_5? Is it clear why Nearest-Neighbor is termed a greedy heuristic?

8.10.2. Show that the Turing machine of Example 8.10.2 computes in polynomial time, thereby establishing that the Nearest-Neighbor Traveling Salesman Problem is in P.

8.10.3. A Boolean circuit C is said to be *monotone* provided that all its vertices except input vertices are either AND-vertices or OR-vertices. The *Monotone Circuit Value Problem* is that of determining, for a given monotone circuit C and inputs $x_1, x_2, \ldots, x_n$, whether the designated output vertex of C takes value 1. We define language $\mathcal{L}_{MCVP}$ to be the language of all and only those circuit descriptions of the form (8.8.2) involving only Boolean connectives & and $\vee$ such that the designated output vertex has value 1. Show that the Monotone Circuit Value Problem is P-complete by proving that $\mathcal{L}_{CVP} \leq_{plog} \mathcal{L}_{MCVP}$.

8.10.4. A monotone Boolean circuit C will be said to be *alternating* provided that (1) all its input vertices are connected to OR-vertices, (2) all output vertices are OR-vertices, and (3) along any path from an input vertex to an output vertex, the vertices alternate between OR-vertices and AND-vertices. The *Alternating Monotone Circuit Value Problem with Fan-in and Fan-out Restricted to 2* may be described as follows. Suppose that we are given an alternating monotone circuit C, where, with two exceptions, the fan-in and fan-out of all vertices is 2. The two obvious exceptions here are C's input vertices with fan-in 0 and its output vertices with fan-out 0. Suppose, further, that we are also given inputs $x_1, x_2, \ldots, x_n$. The problem is then to determine whether the designated output vertex of C takes value 1. We define $\mathcal{L}_{AM2CVP}$ to be the language of all and only those strings of the form (8.8.2) describing circuits of the sort just described such that the designated output vertex has value 1. You are asked to show that the Alternating Monotone Circuit Value Problem with Fan-in and Fan-out Restricted to 2 is P-complete by proving that $L_{MCVP} \leq_{plog} \mathcal{L}_{AM2CVP}$.

8.10.5. The *NAND Circuit Value Problem* is that of determining, for a given NAND circuit C, consisting of input vertices and NAND-vertices only, and inputs $x_1, x_2, \ldots, x_n$, whether the designated output vertex of C has value 1. We define $\mathcal{L}_{NANDCVP}$ to be the language of all and only those strings of the form (8.8.2) involving only Boolean connective $\downarrow$ such that the designated output vertex has value 1. Show that the NAND Circuit Value Problem is P-complete by proving that $\mathcal{L}_{AM2CVP} \leq_{plog} \mathcal{L}_{NANDCVP}$.

8.10.6. Show that any NAND-vertex—even one occurring within a NAND circuit (see Exercise 8.10.5)—may be assumed to have fan-out at most 2. (*Hint:* Show that any NAND-vertex of fan-out 3, say, may be replaced with a subcircuit consisting of NAND-vertices of fan-out at most 2 and 1-vertices only.)

8.10.7. Let C be the NAND circuit of Figure 7.7.3 and suppose that inputs x_1, x_2, and x_3 are 1, 0, and 0, respectively. Apply the construction of (1)–(14) to C so as to produce weighted undirected graph G_C. (Assign vertex numbers 1, 2, and 3 to x_1, x_2, and x_3, respectively.) Do you expect the nearest-neighbor tour of G_C to visit vertex B within subgraph 7 last? Does it?

8.10.8. Show that the transformation of word w, representing an arbitrary instance of NAND Circuit Value, into word $f(w)$, representing a certain nearest-neighbor tour question relative to a certain weighted undirected graph, can be carried out in polylogarithmic time and polynomial space by a vector machine.

EXERCISES FOR §8.12 (END-OF-CHAPTER REVIEW EXERCISES)

8.12.1. **(a)** What does it mean to say of a Turing machine that it self-halts?
(b) What is the Self-Halting Problem for Turing Machines?
(c) State the Church–Turing Thesis.
(d) We have said that the Self-Halting Problem for Turing Machines is unsolvable. But in saying this, an implicit appeal to the Church–Turing Thesis has been made. Explain in a couple of sentences where the Church–Turing Thesis comes in here.

8.12.2. **(a)** What is the Halting Problem for Turing Machines?
(b) We have said that the Halting Problem for Turing Machines is unsolvable. Again, in saying this, an implicit appeal to the Church–Turing Thesis has been made. Explain in a couple of sentences where Church–Turing comes in.

8.12.3. We assume some encoding of Markov algorithm schemata such that every natural number is the gödel number of a unique Markov algorithm schema S. We write $\ulcorner S \urcorner$ for the gödel number of schema S (see Exercise 4.7.7(a)). Next, we shall say that *Markov algorithm A_S self-halts* if, given input word $1^{\ulcorner S \urcorner +1}$ representing $\ulcorner S \urcorner$, Markov algorithm A_S eventually halts execution. The *Self-Halting Problem for Markov Algorithms* is then that of determining, for arbitrary Markov algorithm schema S, whether A_S self-halts.

(a) Show that the partial number-theoretic function defined by

$$f^+(\ulcorner S \urcorner) = \begin{cases} \text{undefined if } A_S \text{ self-halts} \\ 0 \quad \text{otherwise} \end{cases}$$

is not Markov-computable.

(b) Show that there is no Markov algorithm A^* such that, given $1^{\ulcorner S \urcorner +1}$ representing $\ulcorner S \urcorner$ as input word, A^* produces output 11 representing natural number 1 if algorithm A_S self-halts and produces output 1 representing natural number 0 if algorithm A_S does not self-halt. Equivalently, show that the number-theoretic function defined by

$$f^*(\ulcorner S \urcorner) = \begin{cases} 1 \quad \text{if } A_S \text{ self-halts} \\ 0 \quad \text{otherwise} \end{cases}$$

is not Markov-computable. (*Hint:* Use (a).)

(c) Use the Church–Turing Thesis to conclude that the Self-Halting Problem for Markov Algorithms is unsolvable.

(d) Formulate a *Halting Problem for Markov Algorithms*.

(e) Show that the Halting Problem for Markov Algorithms is unsolvable by reducing the Self-Halting Problem for Markov Algorithms to it. Make explicit any appeal to the Church–Turing Thesis.

8.12.4. Each of the proofs of Theorems 8.10 through 8.14 involves two distinct Turing machines—one nondeterministic and one deterministic—computing in polynomial time. Explain.

8.12.5. In the proof of Theorem 8.11, we showed that $L_{CNFSat} \leq_p L_{Clique}$, which is to say that L_{CNFSat} is polynomial-time reducible to L_{Clique}. In this exercise the reader is guided through a proof that $L_{Clique} \leq_p L_{CNFSat}$ as well thereby showing that L_{CNFSat} and L_{Clique} are computationally equivalent. (*Hint:* In proving $L_{CNFSat} \leq_p L_{Clique}$, we described a polynomial-time Turing-computable f that mapped (the representation of) a CNF S with k clauses to (the representation of) an undirected graph G and natural number k. This time, we must describe a function f that maps an undirected graph G and natural number k to a CNF S, the number of whose clauses directly depends upon k.)

Suppose that word w representing undirected graph $G = (V, E)$ and natural number k is given. In particular, it is important to assume that k is represented as 1^{k+1}. Let $V = \{v_1, \ldots, v_m\}$ and $E = \{e_1, \ldots, e_n\}$, where, of course, both $m = |V|$ and $n = |E|$ are O($|w|$). We describe the construction of a CNF $\mathcal{F}_w$ that characterizes a clique $\{v_{i_1}, v_{i_2}, \ldots, v_{i_k}\}$ of size k within graph G. To begin, let sentence letter p_j^i be taken to mean that vertex v_i is the jth element of any such clique.

(a) The first conjunct of $\mathcal{F}_w$ will say that, for each j with $1 \leq j \leq k$, exactly one vertex of V is the jth vertex of the clique. Present this first conjunct and give an upper bound on its length.

(b) The second conjunct of $\mathcal{F}_w$ will say that if vertices u and v are both in the clique, then $(u \; v)$ is an edge of G. Equivalently, this second conjunct will say that if $(u \; v)$ is not an edge of G, then either u is not in the clique or v is not in the clique. Present this second conjunct and give an upper bound on its length.

(c) Give an upper bound on the length of $\mathcal{F}_w$, consisting of these two conjuncts.

(d) Show that $w \in L_{Clique} \Leftrightarrow \mathcal{F}_w \in L_{CNFSat}$.

(e) Show that the transformation of w into $\mathcal{F}_w$ can be carried out by a deterministic Turing machine in polynomial time.

8.12.6. ^{hwk} Show the existence of a Turing-acceptable language that is not Turing-recognizable by showing that the language L^* defined as

$$L^* = \{a^n | \text{the Turing machine with gödel number } n \text{ self-halts}\}$$

is Turing-acceptable but not Turing-recognizable. (*Hint:* Use the generalized notion of self-halting presented in Exercise 8.2.1.)

8.12.7. Show that there exists a Turing-acceptable language L such that no Turing machine M accepting L is bounded with respect to time; that is, for any M_{acc} accepting L, we have that $time_{M_{acc}}(n)$ is O($f(n)$) for no number-theoretic function $f(n)$.

8.12.8. Show that the problem of determining whether Goldbach's Conjecture is true or false is reducible to the problem of determining whether a certain Turing machine eventually halts when starting scanning a square on a completely blank tape. (For Goldbach's Conjecture, see (6) in §0.8.) Your answer will consist of an informal description of a Turing machine.

8.12.9. Establishing that a problem is P-complete by applying Remark 8.8.1 involves the description of two machines—one a (deterministic) Turing machine computing in polynomial time and the other a vector machine computing in polylogarithmic time and polynomial space. Explain (cf. Exercise 8.12.4).

8.12.10. ^{hwk} What is wrong with the following argument?

Let $S \subset \mathcal{N}$ be given with $S \neq \emptyset$. By Remarks 2.4.1 and 1.5.1 together, set S is a set of gödel numbers of Turing machines computing unary partial recursive functions. Since S is nontrivial, it follows, by Rice's Theorem, that S is nonrecursive. But S was an arbitrary nontrivial set of natural numbers. Hence, we have shown, in effect, that there are only two recursive sets: $\emptyset$ and $\mathcal{N}$ itself.

FORMAL LANGUAGES AND AUTOMATA

## Chapter 9

Regular Languages and Finite-State Automata

§9.1 Regular Expressions and Regular Languages

Up to this point, we have characterized formal languages in one of several ways. Sometimes we have merely used English expressions, as when the language with words *aa*, *ab*, *ba*, and *bb* was described as the language of all and only those words over $\Sigma = \{a, b\}$ of length 2. At other times, we have used set abstraction to specify languages. Thus we wrote $\{aw | w \in \Sigma^*\}$ to specify the language of all and only words over $\Sigma = \{a, b\}$ beginning with the letter *a*. We shall now introduce a new way of characterizing languages. Namely, a certain class of expressions called *regular expressions* will be said to *denote* languages. Before presenting a rigorous definition of the notion *regular expression*, we shall give a few introductory examples.

- An asterisk superscript following the letter *a*, say, will be used in the sense of "zero or more consecutive occurrences of symbol *a*." Thus regular expression *(a)**, or, more simply, just a^*, will denote language $\{a^n | n \geq 0\}$.

- The symbol . occurring within a regular expression will indicate concatenation. Thus regular expression *(a).(b)*, or, more simply, just *ab*, will denote the unit language $\{ab\}$, and regular expression *(ab)** will denote language $\{(ab)^n | n \geq 0\}$. On the other hand, regular expression *(a*).(b*)*, or just a^*b^*, will denote language $\{a^n b^m | n, m \geq 0\}$, that is, the language containing all and only words beginning with zero or more *a*s followed by zero or more *b*s. Note that word *aabbb* is in the language denoted by regular expression a^*b^* but not in the language denoted by *(ab)**.

- Constant superscripts are interpreted in the familiar way. Regular expression $a^2 b^3$ denotes the unit language $\{aabbb\}$. Variable superscripts are not permitted in regular expressions, however. So, for example, a^n is not a regular expression.

- Superscript $^+$ will be used in regular expressions to mean "one or more consecutive occurrences." Thus we shall use regular expression a^+bb to denote the language $\{a^n bb | n \geq 1\}$—that is, the language containing all and only those words consisting of one or more *a*s followed by exactly two *b*s.

- Superscript $^?$ will be used in regular expressions to mean "zero or one occurrence." Thus we shall use regular expression $a^?bb$ to denote the two-word language $\{bb, abb\}$.

- Finally, we shall use the symbol | appearing between individual symbols a and b, say, to indicate an occurrence either of a or of b. Thus regular expression $a|b$ will denote the two-word language $\{a, b\}$, and we shall speak of the alternation of a and b.

- As a final summarizing example, consider the regular expression $((a.b)^*)|((b.a)^*)$, or, more simply, just $(ab)^*|(ba)^*$. The left side $(ab)^*$ here is a regular expression denoting language $\{\varepsilon, ab, abab, \ldots\}$. The right side $(ba)^*$ is a regular expression denoting language $\{\varepsilon, ba, baba, bababa, \ldots\}$. Regular expression $(ab)^*|(ba)^*$ will then denote the union of these two languages—that is, $\{\varepsilon, ab, ba, abab, baba, ababab, bababa, \ldots\}$. It is describable as the language containing all and only even-length words consisting of alternating as and bs.

In the preceding paragraph we described uses of regular expressions to denote languages. All of these uses are consequences of the following inductive definition of the class of regular expressions. As part of Definition 9.1, we associate each regular expression with a language that it denotes. In what follows, we shall write either L_r or $L(r)$ for the language denoted by regular expression r.

DEFINITION 9.1: Let Σ be a finite alphabet.

(i) $\varnothing$ is a *regular expression* (*over* Σ) and *denotes* language $\varnothing$.
(ii) ε is a *regular expression* (*over* Σ) and *denotes* language $\{\varepsilon\}$.
(iii) If s is in Σ, then s is itself a *regular expression* (*over* Σ) and *denotes* language $\{s\}$.
(iv) Suppose r and s are *regular expressions* (*over* Σ) that *denote* languages L_r and L_s, respectively. Then
    (a) $(r|s)$ is a *regular expression* (*over* Σ) that *denotes* the language $L_r \cup L_s$
    (b) $(r.s)$ is a *regular expression* (*over* Σ) that *denotes* the language $L_r.L_s$
    (c) (r^*) is a *regular expression* (*over* Σ) that *denotes* language $(L_r)^*$.
(v) No expression is a *regular expression* (*over* Σ) unless it is obtainable from (i)–(iv) above.

The reader will have noticed that Definition 9.1 makes no mention of the symbol $^+$. One might have introduced a subcase of clause (iv) to cover $^+$. Instead, we do the following. Given regular expression r, we define (r^+) to be an abbreviation of regular expression $((r^*).r)$. Thus, since (r^+) is an abbreviation of a regular expression, this means that (r^+) is itself a regular expression by extension. Similarly, $(r^?)$ will be an abbreviation of regular expression $(\varepsilon|r)$.

We shall frequently drop the many parentheses of Definition 9.1 in order to enhance readability. For the same reason, occurrences of symbol . in regular expressions will be suppressed. Thus, consider the following regular expression over $\Sigma = \{0, 1\}$:

$$0^*10^*10^*$$

Fully parenthesized and with all occurrences of . displayed, this regular expression becomes the unmanageable

$$(((((((0^*).1).(0^*)).1).(0^*)).1).(0^*))$$

We shall also write $(a|b|c)$ to denote the three-word language $\{a, b, c\}$. Strictly speaking, $(a|b|c)$ is ambiguous since | is a binary connective: Is $(a|b|c)$ to be construed as $((a|b)|c)$ or as $(a|(b|c))$? The answer is that it does not matter. For by Definition 9.1, the former denotes language $(\{a\} \cup \{b\}) \cup \{c\}$, whereas the latter denotes language $\{a\} \cup (\{b\} \cup \{c\})$. But, by the associativity of $\cup$, both languages here are just $\{a, b, c\}$. So, in what follows, we shall freely write $(a|b|c)$ to denote language $\{a, b, c\}$.[1]

In our abbreviated notation, we shall take superscripts $*$, $+$, and $?$ to have higher precedence than concatenation, which in turn has higher precedence than alternation. For example ab^* is the abbreviated version of $a(b)^*$, not $(ab)^*$. Further, $a|ba$ abbreviates $(a|(b.a))$, not $((a|b).a)$. When the latter is intended, we shall write $(a|b)a$, reflecting the fact that parentheses have highest precedence of all.

The reader may also have wondered why Definition 9.1 says nothing about constant superscripts. This is merely because it is unnecessary: a^2b^3, say, may be regarded as a regular expression abbreviating regular expression $a.a.b.b.b$.

In Definition 9.2 below, we go on to define a *regular language* in terms of our new notion of regular expression.

DEFINITION 9.2: Let L be a language over alphabet Σ—that is, $L \subseteq \Sigma^*$. Then L is said to be a *regular language* if L is denoted by some regular expression over Σ.

Note that $\{\varepsilon\}$, the language whose only word is the empty word, is a regular language. It should not be confused with the empty language $\varnothing$, which is also regular.

Finally, there is a certain potential for confusion regarding regular expressions that is best dealt with immediately. Namely, the reader should check any tendency to regard expression a^nb^n, say, as a regular expression denoting language $\{a^nb^n | n \geq 0\}$. By clause (v) of Definition 9.1, a^nb^n is *not* a regular expression—no allowance for a superscript such as n is made in clauses (i)–(iv). In fact, we shall later be able to prove that the language $\{a^nb^n | n \geq 0\}$ is not a regular language, which means that there is *no* regular expression that denotes it. (Why doesn't regular expression a^*b^* denote this language? Can you find a word that is in the language $L(a^*b^*)$ but that is not in language $\{a^nb^n | n \geq 0\}$?) Again, variable superscripts are not permitted in regular expressions. On the other hand, constant superscripts—as in $(ab)^2$—are permitted for the reason just given.

We state and prove the following proposition regarding regular languages.

THEOREM 9.1: Let Σ be a finite alphabet and let L_1 and L_2 be regular languages over Σ. Then $L_1 \cup L_2, L_1.L_2$, and L_1^* are also regular.

PROOF Since L_1 and L_2 are regular languages, then by definition there exist regular expressions r_1 and r_2 that denote L_1 and L_2, respectively.

- But then, by Definition 9.1(iv)(a), $(r_1|r_2)$ is a regular expression denoting $L_1 \cup L_2$. So $L_1 \cup L_2$ is regular.

- By Definition 9.1(iv)(b), $(r_1.r_2)$ is a regular expression denoting $L_1.L_2$. So $L_1.L_2$ is regular.

- By Definition 9.1(iv)(c), (r_1^*) is a regular expression denoting L_1^*. So L_1^* is regular.   Q.E.D.

It is possible to generalize Theorem 9.1 (see Exercise 9.11.18(a)). Namely, the union of any finite family of regular languages $L_1, L_2, \ldots, L_n$ is regular. Similarly, the concatenation of any finite family of regular languages $L_1, L_2, \ldots, L_n$ is regular. Thus we see that the class of regular languages is closed under

---

[1]One might be tempted to speak of the *associativity* of | here. However, since | is not an operator, we avoid this usage.

finite union, finite concatenation, and Kleene closure. (Recall that the Kleene closure of language L is language L^*.)

LEMMA 9.1: Let Σ be a finite alphabet and let w be any word over Σ. Then the unit language $\{w\}$ is regular.

PROOF If w is ε, then $\{w\} = \{\varepsilon\}$ is regular by Definition 9.1(ii) and Definition 9.2. Suppose, on the other hand, that $|w| = n \geq 1$. Then $w = s_1 s_2 \ldots s_n$ where, for $1 \leq i \leq n$, $s_i \in \Sigma$. By Definition 9.1(iii), each s_i by itself is a regular expression denoting unit language $\{s_i\}$. So by Definition 9.2 each of $\{s_1\}, \{s_2\}, \ldots, \{s_n\}$ is a regular language. Finally, iterating Definition 9.1(iv)(b), we have that $s_1.s_2.\ldots.s_n$ is a regular expression denoting language $\{s_1\}.\{s_2\}.\ldots.\{s_n\}$, which is none other than $\{w\}$.   Q.E.D.

THEOREM 9.2: Let Σ be a finite alphabet. Then any finite language L over Σ is regular.

PROOF If L is empty, then L is regular by Definition 9.1(i). If L is finite and nonempty, then we can write $L = \{w_1, w_2, \ldots, w_n\}$, where each w_i here is a word over Σ. By Lemma 9.1, each unit language $\{w_i\}$ is regular. But then $L = \{w_1\} \cup \{w_2\} \cup \cdots \cup \{w_n\}$ is regular by closure under finite union (Theorem 9.1).   Q.E.D.

Regular expressions play an important role in compiler design theory—particularly in that portion concerning the lexical analysis phase of compilation. We do not consider such applications in this text (but see Preface). However, we mention a suggestive example. Ignoring the possibility of underscores in some dialects and the phenomenon of keywords, it is easily seen that the following regular expression denotes the "language" of Pascal identifiers.

$$(A|B|C|\ldots|Z|a|b|c|\ldots|z)\,(A|B|C|\ldots|Z|a|b|c|\ldots|z|0|1|2|\ldots|9)^* \qquad (9.1.1)$$

It is easily seen that *NUM1*, but not *1NUM*, is a member of the language denoted by this regular expression. For the sake of simplicity, we introduce several useful abbreviations. We shall write *letter* for the regular expression $(A|B|C|\ldots|Z|a|b|c|\ldots|z)$ and *digit* for the regular expression $(0|1|2|\ldots|9)$. In that case, *letter(letter|digit)** is an abbreviation of (9.1.1) and hence denotes the class of Pascal identifiers. Later on, we shall introduce such abbreviations whenever convenient.

§9.2 Deterministic Finite-State Automata

In this section we introduce a new machine model of computation. Our new model is intended as an analysis of those sorts of computation requiring only a fixed (finite) amount of memory for arbitrary input. Machines of the new sort will be called *finite-state automata* or *finite-state machines*. We consider an easy example first.

EXAMPLE 9.2.1 In Figure 9.2.1(a) we have the *state diagram* or *transition diagram* of a (deterministic) finite-state automaton *M* over alphabet $\Sigma = \{a, b\}$. This state diagram is a special sort of digraph whose

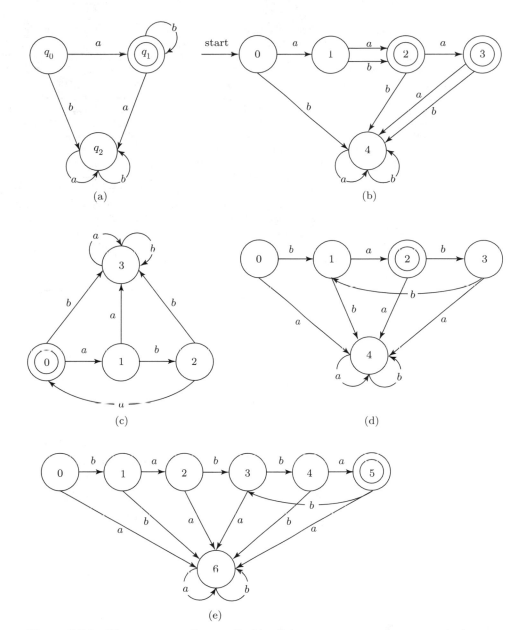

Figure 9.2.1   We present state diagrams for (a) a finite-state automaton that accepts the language denoted by regular expression ab^*; (b) a finite-state automaton that accepts just four words; (c) a finite-state automaton that accepts the language denoted by regular expression $(aba)^*$; (d) a finite-state automaton that accepts the language denoted by regular expression $ba(bba)^*$; (e) a finite-state automaton that accepts the language denoted by regular expression $b(abb)^+a$.

vertices represent states of *M* and whose edges (arcs) are labeled by members of Σ and represent instructions. Unlike Turing machines, finite-state automata will have nothing corresponding to a tape. They do require *input*, however. This input consists of a (possibly empty) word over Σ. *M* begins in state q_0 and processes or reads its input one character at a time from left to right. Consequently, one might think of M as having a read-only input buffer, although we shall not stress this.

As an illustration, let us consider what happens when M is provided with input word *abb*. The first symbol of input *abb* causes M to enter state q_1. The remaining symbols are read without entering a new state—the self-loop on node q_1. After reading input word *abb* completely from left to right, M halts, finding itself in an *accepting state* (or *terminal state* or *final state*), as indicated by the extra circle around node q_1 in the state diagram. By virtue of the fact that M halts in an accepting state, we shall say that M accepts word *abb*. It is easy to see that M halts in a nonaccepting state q_2 when provided the input word *aba* and hence does not accept this word. We shall refer to state q_2 as M's *trap state*; the finite-state automaton halts in q_2 after processing *any* nonaccepted word other than ε. (Trap states need not be unique. However, it is easy enough to see that one can always manage with a single trap state.) It should be clear enough that M accepts that language over $\Sigma = \{a, b\}$ consisting of all and only words w of the form ab^n for $n \geq 0$, which just happens to be the language denoted by regular expression *ab**. Note that in Figure 9.2.1(a) we have a unique initial state, which by convention is q_0. (Initial states are always unique.) M has but one terminal or accepting state, although, in general, finite-state automata may have several.

The accompanying software enables the user to create and run simulations of finite-state machines. Opening the icon **Example 9.2.1** within the FSA folder will enable the reader to observe the operation of the three-state machine of Figure 9.2.1(a).

Having considered this simple example, we proceed to a more general characterization of the operation of finite-state automata. Let M be a finite-state automaton. M begins in state q_0 scanning the leftmost symbol of some input word w. (If w is ε, then M begins scanning a blank.) If at any point during execution M is in state q_i reading input symbol σ, then M proceeds into that (unique) state q_j such that the arc from q_i to q_j is labeled by symbol σ.

Note that in Figure 9.2.1(a), for each symbol σ of alphabet Σ and each state q of M, there is exactly one arc emanating from q and labeled by σ. That is, the outdegree of each node is $|\Sigma|$. Each arc represents an instruction of machine M. So, for each state/symbol pair, M has exactly one instruction. That M has *at most* one instruction is what makes machine M *deterministic*. (We shall consider nondeterministic finite-state automata in §9.3.) That M has *at least* one instruction is what makes M *fully defined*, as we shall say. In general, we shall require that finite-state automata be fully defined in this way, only relaxing this requirement on rare occasions. (No comparable requirement was imposed on Turing machines.) The requirement that finite-state automata be fully defined means that every word w over Σ will label some path starting from initial state q_0.

> **REMARK 9.1:** Determinism means that, within any state diagram for a finite-state automaton, the path labeled by a given word w is unique: In other words, for each word $w \in \Sigma^*$, there is exactly one path starting at q_0 and labeled by w.

If w is an accepted word, then this unique path will lead from q_0 to an accepting state. Otherwise it will lead to some nonaccepting state. Thus, in the case of the finite-state automaton of Figure 9.2.1(a), each of the accepted words ab, abb, $abbb$, ... labels a unique path from initial state q_0 to accepting state q_1. On the other hand, nonaccepted word $abaa$ labels a path from q_0 to nonterminal q_2.

In general, we shall use q_0, q_1, q_2, and so on, to designate states of finite-state automata. Nonetheless, in presenting state diagrams for those finite-state automata we shall regularly use subscripts alone, writing 0, 1, 2, and so on, as was done earlier in the case of transition diagrams for Turing machines. In some special circumstances, it will prove convenient to designate states in a completely different manner, however, which better reflects the "meaning" of those states. On such occasions it will also be convenient to designate the start state of a finite-state automaton by a special arrow labeled "start," as has been done in Figure 9.2.1(b).

ADDITIONAL EXAMPLES We consider a few more examples of finite-state automata.

- The state diagram of Figure 9.2.1(b) lacks any cycles aside from the self-loops on trap state q_4, which means that the language accepted by the corresponding finite-state automaton will be finite. (What is that language?)

- Next, the machine of Figure 9.2.1(c) accepts the language denoted by regular expression $(aba)^*$. Note that q_0 is an accepting state in this diagram: by convention we take this to mean that this finite-state automaton accepts ε, that is, word acceptance occurs even in the case where the leftmost input symbol is nonexistent.

- The reader should verify that the machine of Figure 9.2.1(d) accepts the language denoted by regular expression $ba(bba)^*$ or its equivalent $b(abb)^*a$.

- The machine of Figure 9.2.1(e) accepts the language denoted by $ba(bba)^+$ or its equivalent $b(abb)^+a$.

- Also, all of the finite-state automata of Figures 9.2.1(a) through 9.2.1(e) are both deterministic and fully defined. In each case, a single trap state has been incorporated into the design. Note the self-loops, one for *a* and one for *b*, on any such trap state: Once entered, there is no possibility of exit. (What is the outdegree of any such trap state?)

We can give an alternative description of any deterministic finite-state automaton M in terms of a *transition function* δ_M. Any clause in the definition of such a function takes the form $\delta_M(q_i, \sigma) = q_j$, which we interpret as "if M is currently in state q_i reading symbol σ, then M proceeds into state q_j." As usual, we do not require that states q_i and q_j be distinct. As an illustration, we present the transition function of the finite-state automaton of Figure 9.2.1(c).

$$\delta_M(q_0, a) = q_1 \qquad \delta_M(q_2, a) = q_0$$
$$\delta_M(q_0, b) = q_3 \qquad \delta_M(q_2, b) = q_3$$
$$\delta_M(q_1, a) = q_3 \qquad \delta_M(q_3, a) = q_3$$
$$\delta_M(q_1, b) = q_2 \qquad \delta_M(q_3, b) = q_3$$

Before continuing, it is highly recommended that the reader complete Exercises 9.2.1 and 9.2.2.

Having considered several examples and completed our informal discussion, we are now ready to present a set-theoretic definition of (*deterministic*) *finite-state automaton*. Our definition incorporates the notion of a finite-state automaton's being fully defined.

DEFINITION 9.3: A *deterministic finite-state automaton* M is a quintuple $\langle \Sigma, Q, q_{init}, F, \delta_M \rangle$, where Σ is the *input alphabet* of M, Q is a finite, nonempty set of *states* of M, $q_{init} \in Q$ is the distinguished *initial state* or *start state* of M, $F \subseteq Q$ is a (possibly empty) set of *accepting* or *terminal states* of M, and $\delta_M : Q \times \Sigma \to Q$ is the *transition function* of M, which is assumed to be single-valued and total.

As mentioned earlier, we shall routinely take start state q_{init} to be q_0. M's being fully defined is a consequence of δ_M's being total; M's being deterministic amounts to δ_M's being single-valued.

We mentioned earlier that in the case of such a fully defined, deterministic M, every word $w \in \Sigma^*$ labels a unique path from initial state q_{init}. Whether or not w is accepted by M depends upon where this path leads.

DEFINITION 9.4: *Deterministic finite-state automaton* $M = \langle \Sigma, Q, q_{init}, F, \delta_M \rangle$ *accepts word* $w \in \Sigma^*$ if the unique path starting at initial state q_{init} and labeled by w leads to some member of F—that is, to some accepting state of M.

DEFINITION 9.5: The *language accepted by a deterministic finite-state automaton* $M = \langle \Sigma, Q, q_{init}, F, \delta_M \rangle$ is the set of all and only those words over Σ that are accepted by M. We shall write $L(M)$ for the language accepted by M.

Thus if M is the machine of Figure 9.2.1(a), then $L(M)$ is $\{a, ab, abb, abbb, \ldots\}$. We shall also say that a formal language L is *FSA-acceptable* if there exists some deterministic finite-state automaton that accepts L.

- We note immediately that the empty language $\emptyset$ is FSA-acceptable. This is a consequence of the fact that the set F of accepting states of finite-state automaton $M = \langle \Sigma, Q, q_{init}, F, \delta_M \rangle$ is permitted to be $\emptyset$. Clearly, no word $w \in \Sigma^*$ will be accepted by such an M since the unique path starting at initial state q_{init} and labeled by w will lead of necessity to a nonaccepting state. Thus $L(M) = \emptyset$.

- We also note again that $\varepsilon \in L(M)$ if and only if q_{init} is an accepting state.

EXAMPLE 9.2.2 Open the icon labeled **Odd** within the FSA folder to observe the operation of a four-state machine that accepts the language L defined as $\{w \in \Sigma^* | \neg[2|n_a(w) \wedge 2|n_b(w)]\}$ with $\Sigma = \{a, b\}$. (Any member of L has an odd number of *a*s, an odd number of *b*s, or both.)

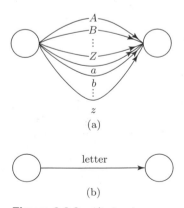

(a)

(b)

Figure 9.2.2 Aliasing in Transition Diagrams for Finite-State Automata.

EXAMPLE 9.2.3 (FORTRAN 95 Names) In order to motivate a certain abbreviation useful in presenting the state diagrams of finite-state automata, let us consider the class (or language) of FORTRAN 95 names (identifiers). A FORTRAN 95 name is essentially an alphanumeric string that begins with a letter and whose length does not exceed 31. Underscores are permitted, but a name may not end with an underscore. Let alphabet Σ be the terminal keyboard character set. We could now present the state diagram of a fully defined, deterministic finite-state automaton over Σ that accepts the language of FORTRAN 95 names. Matters can be made much simpler, however, if we permit ourselves to compress 52 arcs, one for each uppercase and lowercase letter of the Roman alphabet, into a single arc labeled "letter." (FORTRAN 95 is a case-sensitive language.) (See Figures 9.2.2(a) and 9.2.2(b).) We shall avail ourselves of such abbreviations whenever convenient. Now the state diagram of a finite-state automaton that accepts all and only FORTRAN 95 names is shown in Figure 9.2.3. Note that our use of the arc label "other" is relativistic. For instance, the arc labeled "other" from state q_0 to state q_{32} is intended

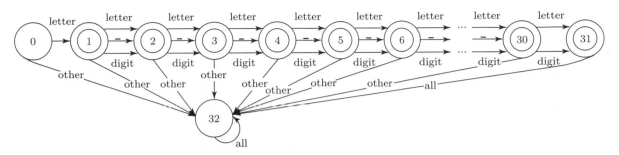

Figure 9.2.3 This finite-state machine accepts any FORTRAN 95 name.

to represent all characters other than letters, whereas the arc labeled "other" from state q_1 to state q_{32} represents characters other than letters, digits, or the underscore. (And what about the arc from state q_{30} to state q_{32}?) These labels are supported by the accompanying software, as the reader may verify by opening icon **FORTRAN 95 Names**.

The reader has no doubt encountered diagrams like Figure 9.2.3 within programming language texts. They provide a standard means of defining *lexical classes* such as *identifier*, *literal*, and *delimiter*. Although such diagrams are usually not presented as such, they are essentially the state diagrams of what we are now calling finite-state automata. Indeed, finite-state automata have impressive applications within compiler design theory (see Preface). This completes our introductory discussion of (deterministic) finite-state automata. Unlike Turing machines and Markov algorithms, we shall not consider finite-state automata as computers of number-theoretic functions, although, suitably modified, they can play this role as well. Rather, we shall be content to consider them as language acceptors only. Eventually we shall come to compare finite-state automata and Turing machines, say, as language acceptors. It will turn out that, as language acceptors, Turing machines are considerably more powerful than finite-state automata.

§9.3 Nondeterministic Finite-State Automata

We shall permit finite-state automata to be *nondeterministic*. Just as in the case of Turing machines, nondeterminism in finite-state automata will mean the existence of alternative instructions for a given state/symbol pair.

EXAMPLE 9.3.1 Consider the language L denoted by the regular expression $(ab)^*$. A finite-state automaton M accepting L is presented in Figure 9.3.1. Suppose that we wish to design a finite-state automaton that accepts the language denoted by regular expression $(ab)^*|a$. In other words, we should like to design a finite-state automaton that accepts $L \cup \{a\}$. It is natural to hope that by adding an arc labeled a from initial state q_0 to a new accepting state q_3 we might obtain a new machine that accepts $L \cup \{a\}$. This would give us the machine M' of Figure 9.3.2. The first thing the reader will notice is that we have thereby introduced a certain *nondeterminism*: Namely, there are *two* arcs labeled a from state q_0. In other words, when in state q_0 reading input symbol a, M' is faced with a "choice." The idea here is that (1) we shall count M' as accepting any word w of the form $(ab)^n$ by virtue of there being a path,

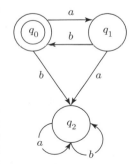

Figure 9.3.1

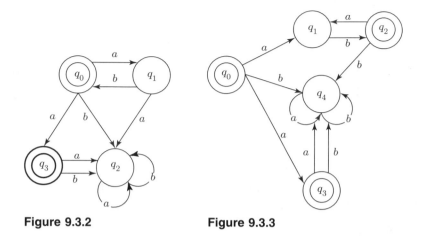

Figure 9.3.2   **Figure 9.3.3**

labeled by w, from q_0 to an accepting state, namely, q_0, and (2) we shall count M' as accepting the word a by virtue of there being a path labeled by a from q_0 to an accepting state, namely, q_3.

We shall begin permitting such nondeterminism within transition diagrams and speak of *nondeterministic finite-state automata*. Moreover, as suggested above, we shall count such a nondeterministic machine as accepting a word w provided only that w labels *some* path from initial state to some accepting state. Accordingly, the machine M' of Figure 9.3.2 does accept all the words in language $L \cup \{a\}$. Unfortunately, it accepts some others as well. For example, the word *aba* labels the path $q_0 q_1 q_0 q_3$ from initial state q_0 to accepting state q_3 and, hence, by the just-stated criterion, M' accepts *aba*. But, of course, word *aba* does not belong to $L \cup \{a\}$. So we have to be careful. Permitting "choices," in conjunction with the stated criterion, can facilitate the design of finite-state automata that accept a specified language. However, it is easy enough to wind up with a machine that accepts unintended words, that is, words not in that language.

Figure 9.3.3 presents a nondeterministic finite-state automaton M'' that accepts $L \cup \{a\}$. (Open the icon **Example 9.3.1** within the FSA folder to observe the operation of this machine.) Note that word *aba* is not accepted by M''.

We make several important observations regarding nondeterministic finite-state automata and word acceptance.

- The machine M'' of Figure 9.3.3 will be counted as accepting word ab by virtue of the fact that this word labels a path from initial state q_0 to accepting state q_2, a path that may be described as $q_0 q_1 q_2$.

- Note, however, that, in nondeterministic M''''s state diagram, word ab labels another path from q_0 as well, namely, the path $q_0 q_3 q_4$. This second path does not lead to an accepting state of M.

- With regard to word acceptance, the crucial difference between a deterministic finite-state automaton and a nondeterministic finite-state automaton lies in the fact that in the former case, for any given word w over alphabet Σ, there exists a unique path labeled by w starting at initial state q_0. In the case of nondeterministic finite-state automata, such paths will not in general be unique. In the case of a nondeterministic finite-state automaton M, we will say that M accepts word w provided that at least one of the paths labeled by w leads to an accepting state of M.

With this simple example as motivation, we are now ready to present the set-theoretic definition of nondeterministic finite-state automaton.

> **DEFINITION 9.6:** A *nondeterministic finite-state automaton* M is a quintuple $\langle \Sigma, Q, q_{init}, F, \delta_M \rangle$, where Σ is the *input alphabet* of M, Q is a nonempty finite set of *states* of M, $q_{init} \in Q$ is the distinguished *initial state* or *start state* of M, $F \subseteq Q$ is a nonempty set of *accepting states* of M, and $\delta_M \colon Q \times \Sigma \to Q$ is the *transition mapping* of M. The latter is assumed to be total but is permitted to be multivalued.

The requirement that transition mapping δ be total amounts to requiring that every nondeterministic finite-state automaton be fully defined in the sense of §9.2. Namely, we will consider a nondeterministic finite-state automaton $M = \langle \Sigma, Q, q_{init}, F, \delta_M \rangle$ to be fully defined provided that, for each state $q \in Q$ and each alphabet symbol $s \in \Sigma$, there is at least one instruction for the case where M is in state q reading symbol s. The transition mappings of nondeterministic machines are permitted to be many-valued just because a given state/symbol pair may give rise to multiple instructions. Thus in Figure 9.3.3 we have both $\delta(q_0, a) = q_1$ and $\delta(q_0, a) = q_3$. No such situation with regard to δ can arise in the deterministic case where transition functions δ are required to be single-valued: It is precisely here wherein lies the nondeterminism of the finite-state automaton of Figure 9.3.3. Note that since the transition mappings of nondeterministic finite-state automata may be, but are not *required* to be, multivalued, every deterministic finite-state automaton is nondeterministic by definition. In other words, determinism is a special variety of nondeterminism—a situation already familiar from our work with Turing machines in Chapter 2. As before, we shall usually use the term "nondeterministic" for machines that are not deterministic.

Our formal definition of language acceptance for nondeterministic finite-state automata can now be presented. As usual, we start by giving a definition of word acceptance for nondeterministic finite-state automata.

> **DEFINITION 9.7:** Let $M = \langle \Sigma, Q, q_{init}, F, \delta_M \rangle$ be a nondeterministic finite-state automaton. *Word* $w \in \Sigma^*$ *is accepted by* M provided that there exists some path, labeled by w, in the state diagram of M leading from q_{init} to a member of F.

This is essentially just the definition that was given previously for deterministic finite-state automata. There is an important difference between the two contexts, however. Since this difference frequently leads to confusion, we reiterate the remarks given above. In the case of a (fully defined) deterministic finite-state automaton, there is always a unique path P labeled by any word $w \in \Sigma^*$. So, in the deterministic case, determining whether or not w is accepted amounts to determining whether this unique path P leads to an accepting state. In the case of a (fully defined) nondeterministic finite-state automaton, on the other hand, word w may label several paths P_1, P_2, and so on. Word w is accepted provided that at least one of these paths leads to an accepting state. Referring again to the nondeterministic finite-state automaton of Figure 9.3.3, we see that word $abab$ is accepted because it labels the path $q_0 q_1 q_2 q_1 q_2$ even though it also labels the path $q_0 q_3 q_4 q_4 q_4$, which does not end at an accepting state. Our notion of language acceptance for nondeterministic finite-state automata is essentially that given for deterministic finite-state automata (cf. Definition 9.5).

> **DEFINITION 9.8:** The *language accepted by a nondeterministic finite-state automaton* $M = \langle \Sigma, Q, q_{init}, F, \delta_M \rangle$ is the set of all and only those words over Σ that are accepted by M. We shall write $L(M)$ for the language accepted by M.

It will frequently be convenient and easier to design nondeterministic machines for certain purposes. We shall do so without hesitation in the future since we will have demonstrated the following equivalence: Any language that is accepted by a nondeterministic finite-state automaton is accepted by some deterministic finite-state automaton, and vice versa. The vice versa is trivial since, by definition, any deterministic finite-state automaton is nondeterministic. The other direction requires a construction.

As preparation for the proof, we introduce the following terminology. Let M be a nondeterministic finite-state automaton with input alphabet Σ and state set Q. Let s be an element of alphabet Σ and let q_i and q_j be members of Q. Then we shall say that q_j is an *s-successor* of q_i just in case there is an arc labeled s from q_i to q_j. Referring to the state diagram of Figure 9.3.4, one sees that state q_0 has a-successors q_1 and q_2 and that q_0 is its own b-successor.

GOAL: Suppose that we are given a nondeterministic finite-state automaton $M = \langle \Sigma, Q, q_{init}, F, \delta_M \rangle$ that accepts the language L. We seek to develop an algorithm for constructing, on the basis of M, a new deterministic finite-state automaton M' that accepts L.

The Subset Construction

The idea is to use the given nondeterministic M as the basis for the construction of a new deterministic M' that accepts the same language. The essence of the construction of M' is (1) through (5) below.

(1) The states of M' will correspond to the nonempty *sets* of states of M—that is, with nonempty subsets of Q. In what follows, it will be easiest to merely *identify* the states of M' with nonempty sets of states of M. With this understanding, we shall sometimes write S_i, S_j, and so on, for the state-sets of M'.

(2) Where q_0 is the start state of M, we shall designate singleton $\{q_0\}$ as the start state of M'.

(3) The accepting states of M' will be those state-sets containing at least one accepting state of M.

(4) Finally, for each state-set S given by (1) and for each s in M's alphabet, we draw an arc labeled s from state-set S to that state-set—call it S_{s-succ}—consisting of all and only the s-successors of members of S.

(5) We eliminate any state-set, as well as all arcs incident upon it, such that there is no path leading to it from $\{q_0\}$.

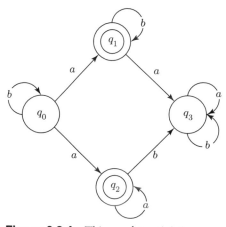

Figure 9.3.4 This nondeterministic finite-state automaton accepts the language denoted by regular expression $b^*((ab^*)|a^+)$.

EXAMPLE 9.3.2 To see how the construction goes, let us take a simple example. Let M be the 4-state nondeterministic finite-state automaton of Figure 9.3.4. We have state set $Q = \{q_0, q_1, q_2, q_3\}$. The reader should verify that this finite-state automaton accepts the language denoted by $b^*((ab^*)|a^+)$. By (1), the states of M' will now be the 15 nonempty subsets of Q.

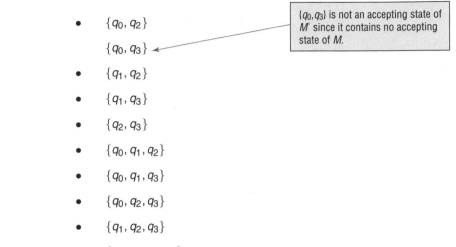

- $\{q_0, q_2\}$
- $\{q_0, q_3\}$ ← $\{q_0, q_3\}$ is not an accepting state of M' since it contains no accepting state of M.
- $\{q_1, q_2\}$
- $\{q_1, q_3\}$
- $\{q_2, q_3\}$
- $\{q_0, q_1, q_2\}$
- $\{q_0, q_1, q_3\}$
- $\{q_0, q_2, q_3\}$
- $\{q_1, q_2, q_3\}$
- $\{q_0, q_1, q_2, q_3\}$

By (3), each of the subsets marked • will be an accepting state of M' since q_1, q_2, or both are in these state-subsets. Finally, since we desire that M' be fully defined and deterministic, we require that a single arc labeled by a and a single arc labeled by b emanate from each of the 15 state-nodes in the state diagram of M'. Let us take a couple of examples. Consider the state $\{q_0, q_1\}$. To which state should its a arc be directed in a state diagram for M'? Well, we see that in the state diagram of M given in Figure 9.3.4, q_0 has a-successors q_1 and q_2, and q_1 has a-successor q_3. So by (4), the a-arc from state $\{q_0, q_1\}$ will lead to state $\{q_1, q_2, q_3\}$ in the new state diagram for M'. As for the b arc from state $\{q_0, q_1\}$, it will be a self-loop leading back to state $\{q_0, q_1\}$ itself, since each of q_0 and q_1 is its own b-successor. This can be seen in the state diagram for M' given in Figure 9.3.5. A number of states (e.g., $\{q_0, q_1\}$) could be eliminated from that diagram in accordance with step (5). (Which others are eliminable?)

It should be clear that M' is a fully defined and deterministic machine: We have exactly one arc for a and one for b from each node in Figure 9.3.5. The nondeterministic machine of Figure 9.3.4 is found at icon **Example 9.3.2** within the FSA folder. The equivalent deterministic machine of Figure 9.3.5 is found at icon **Theorem 9.3**, wherein superfluous states have been eliminated.

We are now ready to state and prove

THEOREM 9.3: Let M be a nondeterministic finite-state automaton. Suppose that M accepts the language L. Then there exists a deterministic finite-state automaton M' that accepts L as well.

PROOF Given M, we may apply the subset algorithm of (1)–(5) above so as to obtain deterministic M'. We need to see that $L(M') = L(M)$.

- First, suppose that $w \in L(M')$. Since M' is deterministic, w labels a unique path from state $\{q_0\}$ to an accepting state of M'. But, by (3)–(4), that means that w labels a path from q_0 to an accepting state in the transition diagram of M and hence that w is in $L(M)$.

- Similarly, if w is in $L(M)$, then w labels a path from q_0 to some accepting state q_t of M. Again, by (4), this means that w labels a path from $\{q_0\}$ to some state S_t containing q_t. But by virtue of q_t's membership in it, S_t is an accepting state of M'. Hence M' accepts w.   Q.E.D.

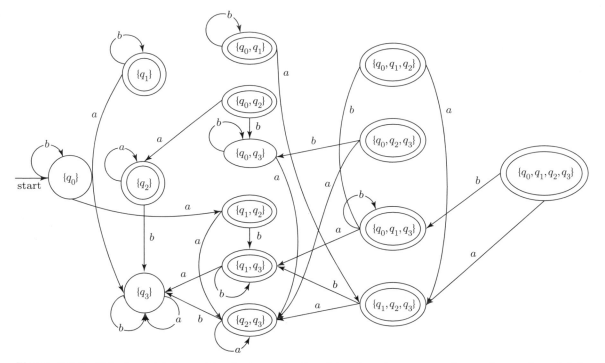

Figure 9.3.5 This deterministic machine is the result of applying the subset construction to the nondeterministic machine of Figure 9.3.4.

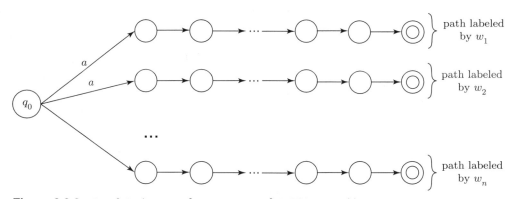

Figure 9.3.6 Any finite language $\{w_1, w_2, \ldots, w_n\}$ is FSA-acceptable.

Incidentally, the subset construction of Example 9.3.2 has an important application within the field of compiler design. Namely, some implementation of algorithm (1)–(4) is a standard part of any lexical analyzer generator.

It is now quite easy to see that every finite language L over alphabet Σ is FSA-acceptable. First, if L is $\varnothing$, then L is accepted by any FSA $M = \langle \Sigma, Q, q_{init}, F, \delta_M \rangle$ with $F = \varnothing$—that is, basically by any M having no accepting states. (Why?) Otherwise, if L is nonempty and $L = \{w_1, w_2, \ldots, w_n\}$, simply design a finite-state automaton with n distinct paths from initial state q_0 to one of n accepting states, each path labeled by one word in L. Plainly, such an M accepts L. Of course, if even two members of L begin with one and the same symbol, then the resulting finite-state automaton M will be nondeterministic. (For example, in Figure 9.3.6 we are assuming that both w_1 and w_2 begin with letter a.) But, by Theorem 9.3, there is an *equivalent* deterministic finite-state automaton M'—that is, a deterministic finite-state automaton M' that accepts L. Consequently, L is FSA-acceptable according to Definition 9.5 after all. We have shown

---

THEOREM 9.4: Any finite language is FSA-acceptable.

---

§9.4 A Pumping Lemma for FSA-Acceptable Languages

It is easy to convince oneself by an informal argument that the language $L = \{a^n b^n | n \geq 0\}$ is not FSA-acceptable. That argument proceeds via our intuitive sense of the limitations of finite-state automata: They process their input words from left to right without the possibility of backtracking. Clearly, none of the machines whose state diagrams, involving self-loops, appear in Figure 9.4.1 is going to accept L. (Why not?) Similarly, the transition diagram of a nondeterministic machine along the lines of Figure 9.4.2 would require infinitely many distinct branches emanating from q_0, one for each member of L. But that machine has infinitely many states, which is, of course, impossible since the state set of any finite-state

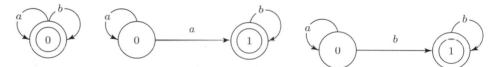

Figure 9.4.1   Language $\{a^n b^n | n > 0\}$ does not appear to be FSA-acceptable.

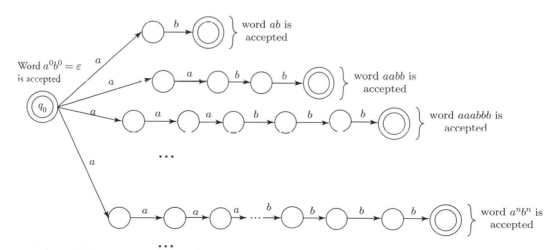

Figure 9.4.2   Language $\{a^n b^n | n \geq 0\}$ does not appear to be FSA-acceptable.

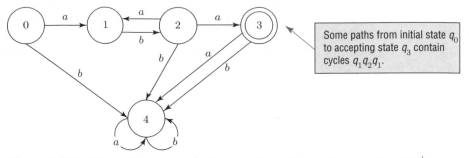

Figure 9.4.3 This machine accepts the language denoted by regular expression $(ab)^+a$.

automaton M must be finite. Thus, it seems clear enough that language L is not FSA-acceptable after all. A more rigorous argument is desirable, however. Lemma 9.2 below will ultimately enable us to give such an argument. First, a number of remarks are in order.

(1) Some finite-state automata accept infinite languages. As an example, consider a finite-state automaton that accepts the language denoted by regular expression $(ab)^+a$, say (see Figure 9.4.3). It should be clear that, within the state diagram of such a finite-state automaton, there will of necessity be some path P that begins at initial state q_0, ends at some accepting state, and contains a cycle. In fact, all we shall need below is that P contains a closed path. (Recall that a cycle is a special sort of closed path such that no edge is traversed twice and no node is visited twice except for the initial/terminal node, which is visited *exactly* twice.)

(2) If a language L over finite alphabet Σ is infinite, then there is no upper bound on the length of words in L. In other words, given any n, L must contain words of length at least n.

(3) If M is a deterministic finite-state automaton with alphabet Σ, then any word w over Σ labels a unique path starting from initial state q_0 within M's state diagram (see Remark 9.1). If w happens to be a word accepted by M, then w labels a unique path from q_0 to an accepting state. In particular, an accepted word w of length m corresponds to a path P of length m, from q_0 to an accepting state, in which exactly $m + 1$ (not necessarily distinct) nodes are visited.

(4) If the length of a path P in digraph $G = (V, E)$ is at least $|V|$, then some node occurs at least twice in P. (This is a form of the so-called Pigeonhole Principle.)

LEMMA 9.2 (A Pumping Lemma for Finite-State Automata): Suppose that language L is FSA-acceptable and infinite. Then there exist words u, w, and v with $w \neq \varepsilon$ such that uw^iv is in L for all $i \geq 0$. (As usual, we write w^i for the result of concatenating word w with itself i times.)

PROOF Suppose L is an infinite language over finite alphabet Σ. Let M be a deterministic finite-state automaton that accepts L. Suppose, further, that M has n states. By remark (2) above, there exists some word $z \in L$ such that $|z| = m$ and $m \geq n$. By (3), word z labels a path P of length m in M's transition diagram, where P visits $m + 1$ states and leads from q_0 to some accepting state q_t. By (4) some state—call it d—must be visited at least twice in P. So we have a closed path within P from d to d. Let w be the (nonempty) word labeling this closed path. Let u be the word labeling that part of path P that extends from q_0 to d, and let v be the word labeling that part of path P

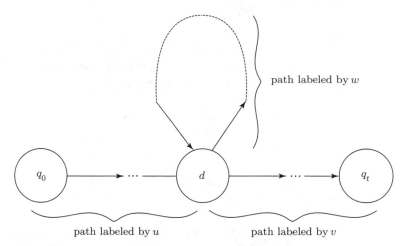

Figure 9.4.4 Illustration of the Pumping Lemma for Finite-State Automata.

that extends from d to accepting state q_t (see Figure 9.4.4). Clearly $uw^0v, uw^1v = z, uw^2v, uw^3v$, and so on are all words accepted by M and hence in L.   Q.E.D.

The usefulness of the Pumping Lemma lies in showing that particular languages are not FSA-acceptable.

THEOREM 9.5: The language $L = \{a^n b^n | n \geq 0\}$ is not accepted by any finite-state automaton.

PROOF (indirect) Suppose that $L = \{a^n b^n | n \geq 0\}$ is accepted by some finite-state automaton M. Then since L is infinite, the Pumping Lemma applies and there are words u, w, and v with $w \neq \varepsilon$ such that

$$\text{word } uw^iv \text{ is in } L \text{ for all } i \qquad (9.4.1)$$

There are but three possibilities for such a nonempty w.

(i) w consists of as only. This possibility leads to a contradiction. For suppose that $uwv = uw^1v$ is in L and hence of the form $a^n b^n$.

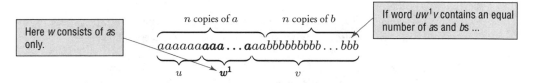

Then iterating or "pumping" w to produce uw^2v, uw^3v, and so on, will yield words with more as than bs and hence not of the form $a^n b^n$, which means that uw^2v, uw^3v, ... cannot be in L:

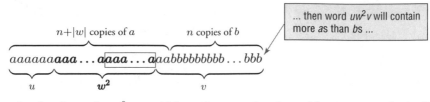

On the other hand, word uw^0v would have fewer as than bs and hence cannot be in L:

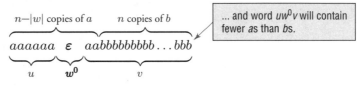

But, by (9.4.1), all of uw^0v, uw^1v, uw^2v, uw^3v, ... are members in L, which is a contradiction.

(ii) w consists of bs only. This case is just like (i) in that it leads to contradiction. That is, if we suppose that uw^1v is in L and hence contains an equal number of as and bs, then words uw^2v, uw^3v, ... cannot be in L because they will contain more bs than as. Similarly, uw^0v cannot be in L because it will contain fewer bs than as. So we see that uw^0v, uw^1v, uw^2v, uw^3v, ... cannot all be members in L. But this contradicts (9.4.1).

(iii) w consists of as followed by bs.

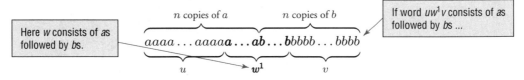

This possibility leads to a contradiction since pumping would produce words with occurrences of b followed by occurrences of a.

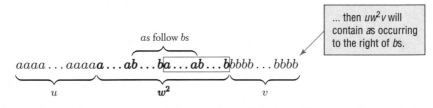

So uw^1v, uw^2v, uw^3v, ... cannot all be members of L. But this contradicts (9.4.1).

We have seen that each of the possibilities (i)–(iii) leads to a contradiction. We conclude that our supposition regarding L is false; that is, L is not FSA-acceptable.   Q.E.D.

As was mentioned earlier, finite-state automata, as language acceptors, are less powerful than Turing machines. First of all, it is not hard to see that any FSA-acceptable language is Turing-acceptable (see Exercise 9.10.12). Thus, the class of FSA-acceptable languages is a subset of the class of Turing-acceptable languages. We can say more than this, however, because we now see that $\{a^nb^n \mid n \geq 0\}$ provides an example of a Turing-acceptable language that is not FSA-acceptable. (In Chapter 1 we saw that there is a Turing machine that accepts the language $\{a^n b^n | n \geq 0\}$. See Exercise 1.4.3(b).) Thus, the class of FSA-acceptable languages is seen to be a proper subset of the class of Turing-acceptable languages. This means that, as language acceptors, finite-state automata are less powerful than Turing machines.

§9.5 Closure Properties of the Family of FSA-Acceptable Languages

Consider the two finite-state automata of Figures 9.5.1(a) and 9.5.1(b). The machine M of Figure 9.5.1(a) accepts the language L consisting of all words beginning with an a. The machine M' of Figure 9.5.1(b) accepts the language L' consisting of all words beginning bb. Now suppose that we desire a finite-state automaton accepting the language $L \cup L'$. It is easy to see that, by merely "identifying" the initial states of M and M' and renumbering a few states, we have such a machine. Thus, the machine of Figure 9.5.1(c) accepts this $L \cup L'$.

Unfortunately this simple construction, which works handily in this particular case, is not always available. For example, the finite-state automaton of Figure 9.5.2(a) accepts the language denoted by regular expression $b^* a^+$. The finite-state automaton of Figure 9.5.2(b), on the other hand, accepts the language denoted by expression $a(ba)^*$. But what worked with the machines of Figure 9.5.1 will not work this time. Namely, merely identifying initial states and renumbering produces the machine

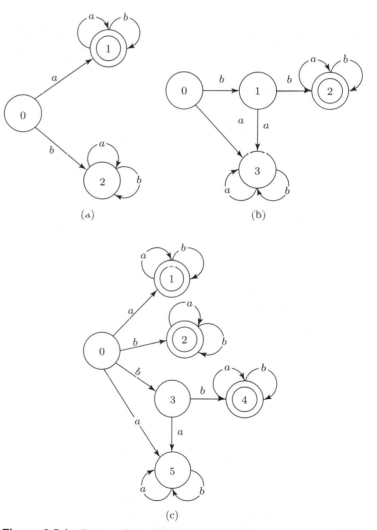

(a)

(b)

(c)

Figure 9.5.1 Because the machines at (a) and (b) are nonrestarting, it is easy to construct a new machine that accepts the union of the languages that they accept.

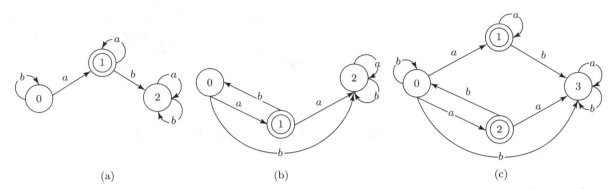

Figure 9.5.2 Because the machines at (a) and (b) are restarting machines, straightforward amalgamation of these machines results in a new machine, shown at (c), such that the language accepted by this new machine is not the union of the languages accepted by the machines at (a) and (b).

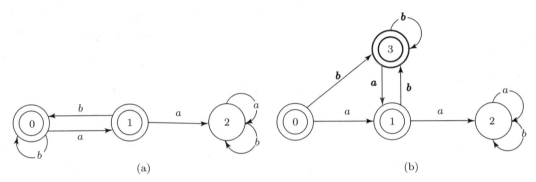

Figure 9.5.3 The restarting machine shown at (a) can be transformed into the equivalent nonrestarting machine at (b).

of Figure 9.5.2(c). But it is easy to see that this nondeterministic finite-state automaton accepts words that are neither of the form $b^n a^m$ for $n \geq 0$, $m \geq 1$ nor of the form $a(ba)^n$ for $n \geq 0$. (What is one such word?) In other words, we have not succeeded in designing a machine that accepts the union of the languages accepted by the two component machines—that is, $L(b^* a^*) \cup L(a(ba)^*)$. And it is clear why this is so: The simple amalgamation technique works so long as neither of the machines being combined is "restarting" in the sense that some arc of its state diagram leads back to its initial state.

- The machines of Figures 9.5.1(a) and 9.5.1(b) are not restarting machines, which means that amalgamation works in that case.

- On the other hand, the machines of Figures 9.5.2(a) and (b) do restart, which means that the same construction does not work.

In fact, amalgamation cannot be applied to two machines if even *one* of them is restarting. If we could convince ourselves that any restarting machine M can be replaced by an equivalent *nonrestarting* machine M', then amalgamation could always be performed. We shall do this now by way of a simple example. The machine M of Figure 9.5.3(a) is a restarting machine. We can transform M into an equivalent nonrestarting machine M' as follows.

- Add a single new state q_3.

- Any arc that leads to q_0—including any self-loop—in M must be redirected so that it leads to the new state q_3 in M'. Thus the arc labeled b from q_1 to q_0 in M will lead from q_1 to q_3 in M'. Also, the self-loop labeled b at q_0 in M causes us to introduce an arc labeled b from q_0 to q_3 in M'.

- The self-loop labeled b at q_0 in M also causes us to introduce a self-loop labeled b at q_3 in M'. Note that state q_0 within M' is a source in the sense of graph theory.

- Arcs proceeding from the new state q_3 must "match" those that proceed from q_0 in M. In the present case, this means adding an arc labeled a from q_3 to q_1.

- Moreover, q_3 must be an accepting state since q_0 is terminal.

No other changes are necessary, and the new finite-state automaton M' appears in Figure 9.5.3(b). It is not hard to see that the finite-state automata of Figures 9.5.3(a) and 9.5.3(b) accept one and the same language. The general construction is probably comprehensible based upon this example alone. However, just for ease of reference later, we formulate it below.

General Construction for Transforming a Restarting Fintite-State Automaton M into an Equivalent Nonrestarting Finite-State Automaton M':

- The states of M' are those of M with the addition of one new state q'. The start state q_0 of M becomes the start state of M'. The accepting states of M' are all those of M with one possible addition: q' will be an accepting state of M' just in case q_0 is an accepting state of M (and hence of M').
- All arcs of M's state diagram become arcs of M''s state diagram with the exception of any arcs that lead to start state q_0. Any arc that leads to q_0—including any self-loop on q_0—will be redirected so as to lead to q' rather than to q_0. In addition, if q_0 has a self-loop for symbol s in M's state diagram, then q' will have a self-loop for symbol s in the state diagram of M'.
- Finally, if there is an arc in M's state diagram from q_0 to some state q other than q_0 itself, then we add an arc from q' to q in the state diagram of M'.

This should be enough to see the truth of

THEOREM 9.6: Let M be a restarting finite-state automaton. Then there exists a nonrestarting finite-state automaton M' such that $L(M) = L(M')$.

Thus, we can assume without loss of generality that any given finite-state automaton is nonrestarting. (If it in fact is not nonrestarting, we can replace it by an equivalent machine that *is*.) But then by our earlier discussion we can now consider ourselves to have demonstrated the following proposition as well.

THEOREM 9.7: The union of any two FSA-acceptable languages is itself FSA-acceptable. Alternative formulation: The class of FSA-acceptable languages is closed under $\cup$.

Just for the record we formulate the construction that is the basis for Theorem 9.7.

> **General Construction for Transforming Two Deterministic Finite-State Automata M and M' Accepting Languages L and L' Over Alphabet Σ, Respectively, into a Nondeterministic Finite-State Automaton M^* Accepting Language $L \cup L'$:**
>
> - We assume that both M and M' are nonrestarting. Otherwise, we first transform any restarting machine into an equivalent nonrestarting machine.
> - The states of M^* will include all the states of M and M' with the exception of their respective start states q_{init} and q'_{init}, say. In addition, we add to M^* a new initial state q^*_{init}.
> - For any symbol $s \in \Sigma$, the s-successors of q^*_{init} will be those of both q_{init} and q'_{init}. Otherwise the arcs of the state diagram of M^* are those of the state diagrams of M and M'.
> - The accepting states of M^* are those of M and M'. State q^*_{init} will be an accepting state if either or both of q_{init} and q'_{init} are.

It is easily seen that the class of FSA-acceptable languages is closed under complementation as well.

> **THEOREM 9.8:** The complement of an FSA-acceptable language is itself FSA-acceptable. That is, if L is FSA-acceptable, then so is $L^c = \Sigma^* \setminus L$. Alternative formulation: The class of FSA-acceptable languages is closed under complementation.

PROOF Suppose that L is FSA-acceptable. Let M be a deterministic finite-state automaton that accepts L. Let M' be the finite-state automaton that is just like M except that every accepting state of M is a nonaccepting state of M' and every nonaccepting state of M is an accepting state of M'. M' accepts L^c. Hence, L^c is FSA-acceptable.   Q.E.D.

EXAMPLE 9.5.1 The machine M whose state diagram appears in Figure 9.5.4(a) accepts the language $L((abc)^+)$. Applying the construction of the proof of Theorem 9.8 (i.e., swapping accepting and nonaccepting states) yields the state diagram of Figure 9.5.4(b). We might reasonably refer to this new machine as M^c. Note that word w over $\Sigma = \{a, b, c\}$ is accepted by M if and only if w is not accepted by M^c. We mention in passing that the construction of the proof of Theorem 9.8 is applicable to deterministic machines only (see Exercise 9.5.8).

We can now prove closure under intersection using the last two theorems together with the following instance of a well-known identity:

$$L \cap L' = (L^c \cup L'^c)^c \tag{9.5.1}$$

> **THEOREM 9.9:** The intersection of two FSA-acceptable languages is itself FSA-acceptable. Alternative formulation: The class of FSA-acceptable languages is closed under intersection.

PROOF Suppose that L and L' are both FSA-acceptable. Then so are L^c and L'^c by Theorem 9.8. Then Theorem 9.7 says that $L^c \cup L'^c$ is FSA-acceptable. By Theorem 9.8 again, we have that $(L^c \cup L'^c)^c$ is FSA-acceptable. But by (9.5.1), this is none other than $L \cap L'$.   Q.E.D.

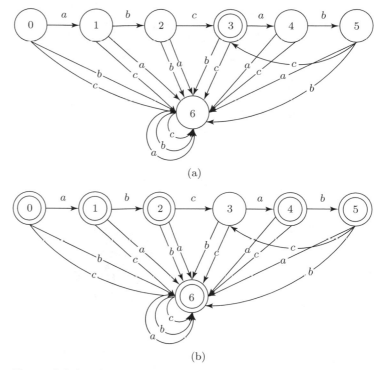

(a)

(b)

Figure 9.5.4 The machine shown at (b) is obtained from the machine shown at (a) by making every terminal state at (a) nonterminal, and vice versa. As a result, the machine at (b) accepts the complement of the language accepted by the machine at (a).

We have two more language-forming operations to consider, namely, Kleene closure and concatenation. Let us take Kleene closure first. Let M be the finite-state automaton of Figure 9.5.5(a), which accepts the language $L = \{aabb, bb, bbab, bbabab, \ldots\}$. We should like to transform M into a finite-state automaton M^* that accepts L^*. The reader will recall that words of L^* are formed by concatenating zero or more words of L. Thus word $w = aabb\frown bbabab$ is in L^*. We can achieve acceptance of such words by adding two arcs—one for a and one for b—leading from each accepting state and modeling arcs leading from initial state q_0: For example, an arc labeled a must lead from accepting state q_6 to state q_3 so as to mimic the a-arc leading from initial state q_0 to state q_3. In this particular case, since there are two accepting states, we add a total of four arcs. The accepting states of the new machine are those of the original machine plus q_0. (Why must q_0 be terminal?) The result of applying this construction to the machine of Figure 9.5.5(a) is the nondeterministic machine whose state diagram is shown in Figure 9.5.5(b). It is not hard to see that the new machine accepts the language L^*. Incidentally, the described construction cannot be applied to M unless M is nonrestarting (see Exercise 9.5.9). But, of course, that is not an obstacle since, by Theorem 9.5, we can always replace a restarting M by an equivalent nonrestarting M'. So we take ourselves to have demonstrated the following proposition in fullest generality.

THEOREM 9.10: If L is an FSA-acceptable language, then so is L^*. Alternative formulation: The class of FSA-acceptable languages is closed under Kleene closure.

For ease of reference we formulate the construction of the proof of Theorem 9.10 as follows.

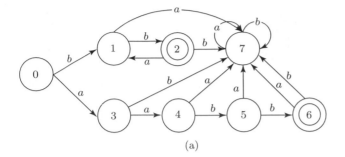

(a)

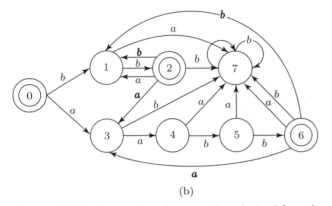

(b)

Figure 9.5.5   The machine shown at (b) is obtained from the machine shown at (a) by making the indicated changes. The result is a machine that accepts the Kleene closure of the language accepted by the machine at (a).

General Construction for Transforming a Deterministic Finite-State Automaton M Accepting Language L over Alphabet Σ into a Nondeterministic Finite-State Automaton M^* Accepting L^*:

- We assume that M is nonrestarting. Otherwise, we first transform it into an equivalent nonrestarting machine.
- The states of M^* will be precisely those of M. Moreover, the arcs of M^* include all those of M. No arc will be eliminated. Rather, arcs will be added.
- Add $|\Sigma|$ arcs from each accepting state q_t of M so as to make any s-successor of start state q_0 an s-successor of q_t as well.
- The accepting states of M^* will be those of M together with q_0.

Finally, we wish to show that the concatenation of two FSA-acceptable languages is FSA-acceptable. Again, we proceed by way of an example. The automata M and M' of Figures 9.5.6(a) and 9.5.6(b) accept the languages L and L' denoted by regular expressions $a^+|b^+$ and $aa(ba)^*$, respectively. We present in Figure 9.5.6(c) a new machine $M^\bullet$ that accepts the concatenation language $L.L'$. Essentially, we have obtained $M^\bullet$ by appending M' to the end of M. The states of $M^\bullet$ are all those of M and M' with the sole exception of the initial state of M', which has been omitted. The initial state of $M^\bullet$ is the initial state of M. The accepting states of $M^\bullet$ are those of M'. Finally, from each accepting state

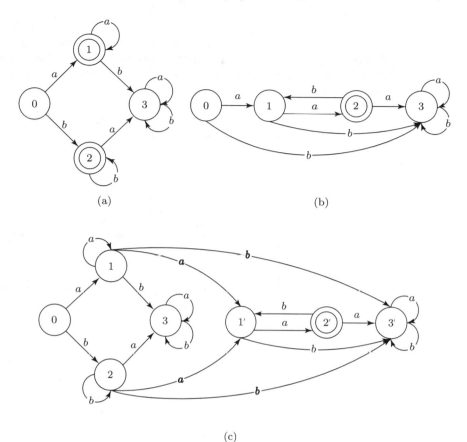

Figure 9.5.6 The machine shown at (c) accepts the concatenation of the languages accepted by the machines at (a) and (b), respectively.

of M we have added two arcs modeling the arcs emanating from the initial state of M'. It should be clear that the resulting nondeterministic $M^{\bullet}$ accepts the language $L.L'$ in the case of our examples L and L'. In general, however, this construction, as just described, will work provided only that:

(1) L' does not contain ε; that is, the omitted initial state of M' must not be an accepting state of M'.

(2) M' is nonrestarting.

By Theorem 9.6, (2) is no obstacle. As for (1), it is easy to see how to modify the construction, should L' happen to contain ε. In that case, the accepting states of $M^{\bullet}$ will be those of M' as well as those of M. Thus we have our final closure result in

THEOREM 9.11: If L and L' are FSA-acceptable, then so is $L.L'$. Alternative formulation: The class of FSA-acceptable languages is closed under concatenation.

Again, we present a general formulation of the construction of the proof of Theorem 9.11.

General Construction for Transforming Deterministic Automata *M* and *M′* Accepting Languages *L* and *L′* over Alphabet Σ, Respectively, into Nondeterministic Finite-State Automaton *M•* Accepting Language *L.L′*.[2]:

- We assume that both M and M' are nonrestarting. Otherwise, we first transform any restarting machine into an equivalent nonrestarting machine.
- The states of $M^\bullet$ will be those of M as well as those of M', with the sole exception of M''s initial state q_0'. Some renaming of states may be required so as to avoid conflicts.
- As for arcs from states other than q_0', all become part of $M^\bullet$'s state diagram.
- We add $|\Sigma|$ arcs from each accepting state q_t of M—one for each member s of Σ—so as to make any s-successor of q_0' in M' an s-successor of q_t in $M^\bullet$.
- The initial state of M becomes the initial state of $M^\bullet$. The accepting states of M' become the accepting states of $M^\bullet$. If q_0', which has been deleted, was an accepting state of M', then the accepting states of M become accepting states of $M^\bullet$ as well.

§9.6 The Family of Regular Languages Is Identical to the Family of FSA-Acceptable Languages

In the course of considering examples and exercises, the reader may have remarked a certain correspondence between finite-state automata and regular expressions: Namely, it seems that both of the following propositions hold.

(i) For any FSA-acceptable language L, there is a regular expression that denotes L.

(ii) For any regular language L, some (deterministic) finite-state automaton can be found that accepts L.

We shall show that both (i) and (ii) are true. The closure results of Theorems 9.7 through 9.11 lead directly to an important containment result corresponding to (ii). Namely, it is now easy to show that every regular language is FSA-acceptable.

THEOREM 9.12: Every regular language is FSA-acceptable.

PROOF We sacrifice nothing by assuming, for the sake of simplicity, that $\Sigma = \{a, b\}$ and that L is a regular language over Σ. Let r be a regular expression that denotes L. We proceed by induction on the complexity of r. Consequently, the proof follows closely the inductive definition of the class of regular expressions and the languages denoted by them as given in Definition 9.1.

> **DIGRESSION:** The following brief remarks may be helpful to some readers. (Apologies to those other readers for whom these issues are well understood.) In the present context, one should think of the *complexity* of a regular expression r as the number of occurrences in r of symbols |, ., *, and ( ).

---

[2]A more general construction is required if L and L' are languages over distinct alphabets Σ and Σ', say, so as to ensure that the resulting $M^\bullet$ is fully defined. However, the essentials of this more general construction are precisely as above.

For r of complexity 0 (i.e., where r contains no occurrences of these symbols), one shows outright that the language denoted by r is FSA-acceptable. This is the *base case* below. For r of nonzero complexity—of complexity $k + 1$, say—one proves that the language denoted by r is FSA-acceptable by assuming that the languages denoted by regular expressions of complexity k or less are all FSA-acceptable. This assumption—the so-called *induction hypothesis*—plays its role in the *inductive case* of the proof given below.

Base case. Suppose that r is either $\varnothing$, ε, a, or b. This means that, by Definition 9.1(i)–(iii), L is either $\varnothing$, $\{\varepsilon\}$, $\{a\}$, or $\{b\}$. In any case, L is then FSA-acceptable because finite.
Inductive case. We proceed to consider three subcases, corresponding to the three subclauses (iv)(a)–(c) of Definition 9.1.

Subcase (a). Suppose that r is of the form $(s|t)$, where s and t are regular expressions. Then L_s and L_t are both regular languages by definition. By the induction hypothesis, both are FSA-acceptable. But then Theorem 9.7 says that $L_s \cup L_t$ is FSA-acceptable. Moreover, by Definition 9.1(iv)(a), $L_{(s|t)}$ is just $L_s \cup L_t$. So $L_{(s|t)}$ is thereby shown to be FSA-acceptable.
Subcase (b). Suppose that r is of the form $(s.t)$ for regular expressions s and t. Then L_s and L_t are both regular languages by definition. By induction hypothesis, both are FSA-acceptable. By Theorem 9.11, $L_s.L_t$, which is $L_{(s.t)}$ by Definition 9.1(iv)(b), is also FSA-acceptable.
Subcase (c). Suppose that r is of the form (s^*), where s is a regular expression. Then L_s is regular by definition. By induction hypothesis, it is also FSA-acceptable. So by Theorem 9.10, language $L_{(s^*)}$, which is L_s^* by Definition 9.1(iv)(c), is also FSA-acceptable.   Q.E.D.

We have now shown that any regular language is FSA-acceptable. It is natural to ask whether the containment here is proper or whether every FSA-acceptable language is regular as well. The latter turns out to be the case. As preparation for our proof, we make the following remarks.

(i) Recall that every nonempty, finite language is regular. Why? Well, consider the finite language $\{a, b, ab, aab\}$. It is denoted by regular expression $a|b|ab|aab$.

(ii) Suppose that we are given some finite-state automaton M. As usual, the states $q_0, q_1, q_2, \ldots, q_n$ of M are indexed by non-negative integers. We define the following languages over the alphabet Σ of M. For $0 \leq i, j \leq n, -1 \leq k \leq n$, we have

$$_M L_{i,j}^k = \{w \in \Sigma^* | \text{In } M\text{'s state diagram there is a path labeled by } w \text{ from state } i \text{ to state } j \text{ and passing through no intermediate state whose index is higher than } k\} \tag{9.6.1}$$

So for the finite-state automaton whose state diagram appears in Figure 9.6.1 we have

$$_M L_{0,1}^{-1} = L(a) = \{a\} \qquad _M L_{0,1}^0 = L(b^*a) \qquad _M L_{0,1}^1 = L(b^*ab^*)$$

Note that each language in this sequence is a subset of its successor. The containment is not necessarily proper, however, as Exercise 9.6.1 makes clear. (Before continuing, the reader is encouraged to complete that easy exercise in order to ensure that the notation at (9.6.1) is adequately understood.)

(iii) We shall permit k to be -1 at (9.6.1). The superscript -1 in $_M L_{i,j}^{-1}$ means, in effect, that no intermediate states whatever are permitted on paths from i to j. That is, such paths must be edges.

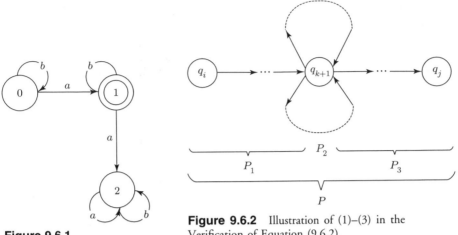

Figure 9.6.1

Figure 9.6.2   Illustration of (1)–(3) in the
Verification of Equation (9.6.2).

Thus, in general, we have that $_ML_{i,j}^{-1} = \{s \in \Sigma | \text{there is an edge labeled } s \text{ from state } q_i \text{ to state } q_j\}$. Since Σ is finite, $_ML_{i,j}^{-1}$ is finite for any i and j.

(iv) Now consider the equation

$$_ML_{i,j}^{k+1} = {}_ML_{i,j}^k \cup [{}_ML_{i,k+1}^k \cdot ({}_ML_{k+1,k+1}^k)^* \cdot {}_ML_{k-1,j}^k] \tag{9.6.2}$$

We must see that (9.6.2) holds generally. First, by (9.6.1), any word w in $_ML_{i,j}^{k+1}$ labels a path P from q_i to state q_j that visits intermediate states with indices not exceeding $k + 1$. Such a P may or may not visit state q_{k+1}. If not, then word w is in $_ML_{i,j}^k$. If it does visit q_{k+1}, then P may be divided into three segments as

(1) That portion P_1 of P beginning with state q_i and ending with the *first* occurrence of state q_{k+1}

(2) That portion P_2 of P beginning with the first and ending with the last occurrence of state q_{k+1}—if $k + 1$ occurs only once in P, then P_2 is of length 0

(3) That portion P_3 of P beginning with the *final* occurrence of state q_{k+1} and ending with state q_j.

(See Figure 9.6.2.) The word w_1 labeling subpath P_1 will belong to $_ML_{i,k+1}^k$. Subpath P_2 may be partitioned into finitely many closed paths beginning and ending at state q_{k+1} such that any word labeling such a closed path will be in the language $_ML_{k+1,k+1}^k$; hence the word w_2 labeling subpath P_2 will be in the language $({}_ML_{k+1,k+1}^k)^*$. Finally, word w_3 labeling subpath P_3 will be in the language $_ML_{k+1,j}^k$. Thus, w itself will belong to the language

$$_ML_{i,k+1}^k \cdot ({}_ML_{k+1,k+1}^k)^* \cdot {}_ML_{k+1,j}^k$$

We have shown that

$$_ML_{i,j}^{k+1} \subseteq {}_ML_{i,j}^k \cup [{}_ML_{i,k+1}^k \cdot ({}_ML_{k+1,k+1}^k)^* \cdot {}_ML_{k+1,j}^k]$$

The reader should also verify that

$$_M L_{i,j}^k \cup [_M L_{i,k+1}^k \cdot (_M L_{k+1,k+1}^k)^* \cdot _M L_{k+1,j}^k] \subseteq {_M L_{i,j}^{k+1}}$$

Then, by Extensionality, (9.6.2) follows.

(v) Of course, any finite-state automaton M can have but finitely many accepting states. Let us write $q_{t_1}, q_{t_2}, \ldots, q_{t_r}$ for the accepting states of M. We are assuming that the states of M are indexed from 0 to n, with q_0 the initial state of M. Now it should be apparent that the language L accepted by M is just

$$_M L_{0,t_1}^n \cup {_M L_{0,t_2}^n} \cup \cdots \cup {_M L_{0,t_r}^n}$$

We next prove

LEMMA 9.3: For $0 \leq i, j \leq n, -1 \leq k \leq n$, $_M L_{i,j}^k$ is finite or can be obtained from finite languages by finitely many applications of the language-forming operations $\cup$, ., and *.

PROOF (by induction on superscript k)

Base case. We let $k = -1$. By (iii) above, $_M L_{i,j}^{-1}$ is finite for any i and j.

Inductive case. We let $k = m+1$. As induction hypothesis, we assume the proposition for $k = m$ and go on to prove it for $k = m + 1$. We have already established, in (9.6.2), that

$$_M L_{i,j}^{m+1} = {_M L_{i,j}^m} \cup [_M L_{i,m+1}^m \cdot (_M L_{m+1,m+1}^m)^* \cdot {_M L_{m+1,j}^m}]$$

By the induction hypothesis, every language cited on the right here is either finite or can be built up from finite languages using just $\cup$, ., and *. But then just one more application each of $\cup$ and * and two more applications of . produce $_M L_{i,j}^{m+1}$.   Q.E.D.

Our preliminary work accomplished, we now turn to a proof of the main result.

THEOREM 9.13: Every FSA-acceptable language is regular.

PROOF Let L be an FSA-acceptable language. Let M be an $(n+1)$-state deterministic finite-state automaton with terminal states $q_{t_1}, q_{t_2}, \ldots, q_{t_r}$ that accepts L. By (v) above, L is just the finite union

$$_M L_{0,t_1}^n \cup {_M L_{0,t_2}^n} \cup \cdots \cup {_M L_{0,t_r}^n}$$

By Lemma 9.3, each of the languages mentioned here is either finite or can be obtained from finite languages by finitely many applications of language-forming operations $\cup$, ., and *. It follows that L itself can be obtained from some finite collection $L_1, L_2, \ldots, L_m$ of finite languages by finitely many applications of $\cup$, ., and *. But by Theorem 9.2, each of $L_1, L_2, \ldots, L_m$ is regular. And by a generalization of Theorem 9.1, the result of applying operations $\cup$, ., and * to such a finite family of regular languages is itself regular. We conclude that L is regular.   Q.E.D.

§9.7 Finite-State Automata with Epsilon-Moves

In the case of each of the computational models introduced in earlier chapters, we considered one or more variants of the model accompanied by equivalence results stating in effect that the variations have no significant consequences at the theoretical level. So far in our investigation of finite-state automata we have considered both deterministic and nondeterministic varieties and established their equivalence in Theorem 9.3. In this section, we look at one more variant: Finite-state machines may be permitted to have so-called ε-moves as explained below. We shall see that a machine with ε-moves may be either deterministic or nondeterministic.

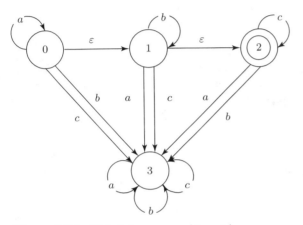

Figure 9.7.1   This finite-state machine with ε-moves accepts the language $L(a^*b^*c^*)$.

EXAMPLE 9.7.1 Consider the nondeterministic finite-state automaton M whose state diagram appears in Figure 9.7.1. The reader will immediately notice that certain edges in this state diagram are labeled by ε. Thus the edge from state q_0 to q_1 corresponds to the instruction, "If in state q_0 reading ε, then proceed into state q_1." Such an instruction is called an ε-move and the finite-state automaton M of Figure 9.7.1 is a (nondeterministic) finite-state automaton with ε-moves. As usual in the case of nondeterministic finite-state automata, we shall say that M accepts the word $aabbbcccc$ by virtue of the fact that word $aa\varepsilon bbb\varepsilon cccc = aabbbcccc$ labels a path from initial state q_0 to accepting state q_2. We shall define a nondeterministic finite-state automaton with ε-moves as any nondeterministic finite-state automaton M whose arcs are labeled by members of $\Sigma \cup \{\varepsilon\}$, where Σ is some finite alphabet, and such that, within M's transition diagram, there is no cycle every arc of which is labeled ε. (As usual, we do not *require* that ε, in fact, label any arc; consequently, any nondeterministic finite-state automaton automatically becomes a nondeterministic finite-state automaton with ε-moves.) See icon **Example 9.7.1** within the FSA folder.

Note that the prohibition of ε-cycles rules out ε-self-loops in particular. Also, it is easily seen that, as a consequence of this prohibition, no finite-state machine, given finite input, computes forever.

We shall show that any language L that is accepted by a finite-state automaton M with ε-moves is accepted by some finite-state automaton M' that has no ε-moves. We sketch the proof of this result using the finite-state automaton of Figure 9.7.1 as an illustration. Thus, where M is the nondeterministic finite-state automaton with ε-moves of Figure 9.7.1, we use M to construct nondeterministic finite-state automaton M' with no ε-moves and such that $L(M) = L(M') = L(a^*b^*c^*)$.

- The alphabet of M' will be that of M, namely, $\Sigma = \{a, b, c\}$.

- The state set of M' is just that of M.

- As for the arcs of M', we draw an arc labeled by symbol s from state q_i to state q_j if there is a path labeled by word s in the state diagram of finite-state automaton M. Thus, in our example, we draw an arc labeled a from state q_0 to state q_2 in the state diagram of M' by virtue of there being a path labeled $a\varepsilon\varepsilon = a$ from state q_0 to state q_2 in the state diagram of M (see Figure 9.7.2).

- As for accepting states, in general, the accepting states of M' will just be those of M with the possible addition of start state q_0: State q_0 will be an accepting state of M' if there is any path labeled by the empty word leading from q_0 to an accepting state in the state diagram of M. Consequently, in our example, we will make q_0 an accepting state of M' since there is a path labeled $\varepsilon\varepsilon = \varepsilon$ from q_0 to accepting state q_2.

This ends the construction of M'. It should be clear that $L(M') = L(M)$.

We shall take ourselves to have proved

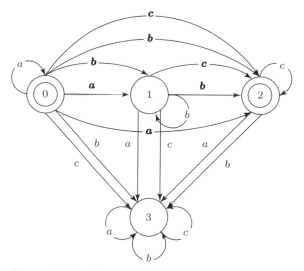

Figure 9.7.2 The nondeterministic machine, having no ε-moves, that is shown here is the result of applying the construction of the proof of Theorem 9.14 to the finite-state automaton with ε-moves of Figure 9.7.1. Both machines accept the language $L(a^*b^*c^*)$.

THEOREM 9.14: Let M be a finite-state automaton with ε-moves. Then there exists a finite-state automaton M' with no ε-moves such that $L(M) = L(M')$.

The reader is invited to verify the equivalence of the machine of Figure 9.7.2, having no ε-moves, with the original machine of Figure 9.7.1 by opening icon **Theorem 9.14** within the FSA group.

Henceforth, we shall be able to assume without loss of generality that any finite-state automaton M that accepts a given language L involves no ε-moves. For, if M should, in fact, contain ε-moves, it is replaceable by an equivalent M' involving no ε-moves. We shall consider a finite-state automaton with ε-moves to be fully defined if, for each state q, either (1) for each alphabet symbol s, there is (at least) one arc from state q labeled by s or (2) there is at least one arc from q labeled by ε. We shall not require that *both* (1) and (2) hold for any given state q, however.

Concerning ε-Moves and Nondeterminism

We wish to emphasize that the existence of an ε-move within a state diagram does not by itself imply nondeterminism. For instance, if every arc labeled by ε has as its source some state q for which there are no other arcs whatever, then there is really no nondeterminism present. On the other hand, if the diagram involves an ε-move as an alternative to another ε-move or as an alternative to other instructions that would advance input, then M is unquestionably nondeterministic. Our point is that nondeterminism is not a consequence of ε-moves per se. Rather, nondeterminism is a consequence of ε-moves occurring as alternatives to other instructions.

Language Acceptance and Language Recognition

We have seen what it is for a deterministic finite-state machine M, with or without ε-moves, to accept language L over Σ. Assuming that M is fully defined, is it then clear that M also *recognizes* L in a familiar sense? After all, given word $w \in \Sigma^*$, if M is fully defined and deterministic, then there is a unique path from start state q_0 labeled by w. If that path leads from q_0 to a terminal state, then w is accepted. On the other hand, if that path leads from q_0 to a nonterminal state, then w is not accepted, and we might then say that w is rejected.

In the case of each of the models of computation considered in Part I of this book, there is an important distinction to be made between recognizing a language and merely accepting a language. (Consider again the discussion at the end of §1.4.) This is because in the case of Turing machines, vector machines, and so forth, it is possible for computation to continue indefinitely despite input being finite. A Turing machine, say, might fail to accept word w—just because it computes forever—without ever rendering a definitive verdict on w. In other words, a Turing machine might not accept w without ever rejecting w, in the sense of writing a rejecting 0, say. The situation is very different in the case of finite-state machines. Even a finite-state machine involving ε-moves terminates its computation for input word w after some finite number of steps, given the prohibition of ε-cycles. And when a finite-state machine does halt, it has either accepted or rejected w definitively: It either has halted in an accepting state or has halted in a nonaccepting state. At least in the deterministic case, we might think of nonaccepting states as *rejecting states*. (The nondeterministic case, with or without ε-moves, is rather different.) But as for the deterministic case, we may now formulate our

---

> **REMARK 9.7.1:** In the case of any deterministic finite-state machine M with input alphabet Σ, language $L(M)$ over Σ is both accepted and, in a certain sense, *recognized* by M. Expressed differently, M *decides* membership in $L(M)$. Consequently, there is no real distinction to be made between language acceptance and language recognition on the part of deterministic M.

Given Remark 9.7.1, it is standard to speak of language recognition on the part of deterministic finite-state machines at points where the reader might expect talk of language acceptance.

EXAMPLE 9.7.2 The deterministic finite-state automaton at icon **Example 9.7.2** decides membership in what language over $\Sigma = \{a, b\}$?

---

§9.8 Generative Grammars

In §9.1 we introduced the family of regular languages. Afterward, we went on to present an *automata-theoretic characterization* of that family: Theorems 9.12 and 9.13 together show that the regular languages are precisely those languages accepted by a certain sort of automaton, namely, a finite-state automaton. Later, we shall want to use *grammars* as alternative means of characterizing languages and language families. In particular, we shall use a special sort of grammar as an alternative characterization of the family of regular languages.

Readers will of course have some experience in working with grammars of one sort or another. It is the very precise notion of *generative grammar* that will be the focus of our investigation. Generative grammars have been central to the study of formal languages, programming languages, and natural languages, as we shall see. In the present section, we restrict our attention to formal languages and begin by considering three examples.

EXAMPLE 9.8.1 In our first example of a generative grammar G, we take the *terminal alphabet* Σ of G to be $\{a, b\}$. We take G's *nonterminal alphabet* Γ to be singleton alphabet $\{S\}$. The set Π of *productions* or *rewrite rules* of G contains the two productions

$$S \rightarrow aSb \quad \text{and} \quad S \rightarrow \varepsilon$$

The second rule here may also be written simply

$$S \rightarrow$$

To facilitate reference, we number our two productions.

$$(1) \quad S \rightarrow aSb$$

$$(2) \quad S \rightarrow$$

We may interpret (1) as "S may be rewritten as aSb" and (2) as "S may be rewritten as the empty word." Incidentally, rule (2) is an example of an ε-*rule* or *empty production*. The symbol S has special status as the *start symbol* of grammar G. Next, we show that grammar G generates word $aabb$. Our *derivation* begins of necessity with start symbol S. Rule (1) tells us that S may be rewritten as aSb. Thus, we shall write

$$(i) \quad S \Rightarrow aSb$$

to mean that S was rewritten as aSb in accordance with one of our rules. (We shall say that S *directly generates aSb*.) But now, by rule (1) again, the occurrence of S on the right in (i) may itself be replaced by aSb to give $aaSbb$. Thus, aSb directly generates $aaSbb$, or in symbols

$$(ii) \quad aSb \Rightarrow aaSbb$$

Finally, rule (2) says that the occurrence of S on the right in (ii) may be replaced by the empty word:

$$(iii) \quad aaSbb \Rightarrow aabb$$

By virtue of the sequence (i)–(iii) we shall now say that grammar G generates word $aabb$, where G is the grammar consisting of terminal alphabet Σ, nonterminal alphabet Γ, start symbol S, and production set Π. In other words, by way of a sequence of applications of our two rules, we were able to transform start symbol S into word $aabb$. Similarly, we can easily see that G generates $aaabbb$ as well. It is customary to display such a derivation as shown below.

$$S \Rightarrow aSb \qquad /* \text{ by rule (1), } S \text{ is rewritten as } aSb \ */$$

$$\Rightarrow aaSbb \qquad /* \text{ by rule (1), } S \text{ is rewritten as } aSb \ */$$

$$\Rightarrow aaaSbbb \qquad /* \text{ by rule (1), } S \text{ is rewritten as } aSb \ */$$

$$\Rightarrow aaabbb \qquad /* \text{ by rule (2), } S \text{ is rewritten as } \varepsilon \ */$$

We summarize this sequence by writing $S \Rightarrow^* aaabbb$. It is easy to see that our grammar generates all and only those words of the form $a^n b^n$ for $n \geq 0$. Thus, letting $n = 10$, we generate the word $a^{10}b^{10}$ by first applying rule (1) ten times in succession and afterward applying rule (2) just once.

EXAMPLE 9.8.2 As a second example, let $\Sigma = \{a, b, c\}$, $\Gamma = \{S, X\}$, and Π be the set of rewrite rules

(1) $S \rightarrow aaXcc$

(2) $X \rightarrow aXc$

(3) $X \rightarrow b$

We let S be the start symbol of G. (Unless noted otherwise, in presenting later examples, we shall always assume that S is the start symbol.) We see that G generates word $aaabccc$.

$$S \Rightarrow aaXcc \qquad /* \text{ by rule (1), } S \text{ is rewritten as } aaXcc \ */$$

$$\Rightarrow aaaXccc \qquad /* \text{ by rule (2), } X \text{ is rewritten as } aXc \ */$$

$$\Rightarrow aaabccc \qquad /* \text{ by rule (3), } X \text{ is rewritten as } b \ */$$

Is it clear that G generates all and only those words over $\Sigma = \{a, b, c\}$ of the form $a^n bc^n$ for $n \geq 2$? Note that, after an initial application, our first production can never be reapplied since no occurrence of S remains. Note also that lowercase letters are never erased. Thus, rule (1) will always be used first in order to introduce two as and two cs. Afterward, rule (2) may be applied an arbitrary number of times, each time introducing a single a on the left and a single c on the right. Ultimately, rule (3) is used to introduce a single b between the as and cs.

EXAMPLE 9.8.3 As our third example, consider the grammar G with $\Sigma = \{a, b, c\}$, $\Gamma = \{S, S', C\}$, and productions

(1) $S \rightarrow aS'bc$

(2) $S \rightarrow$

(3) $S' \rightarrow aS'bC$

(4) $S' \rightarrow$

(5) $Cb \rightarrow bC$

(6) $Cc \rightarrow cc$

Note that productions (1) and (2) represent two alternative ways of rewriting nonterminal S. Similarly, productions (3) and (4) represent two alternative ways of rewriting nonterminal S'. It is customary to place such alternative productions on a single line, separating alternative right-hand sides by |. Thus productions (1)–(6) may be presented as:

(1)–(2) $S \rightarrow aS'bc \,|$

(3)–(4) $S' \rightarrow aS'bC \,|$

(5) $Cb \rightarrow bC$

(6) $Cc \rightarrow cc$

We stress that the line labeled (1)–(2) is an abbreviation of the two productions

$$S \rightarrow aS'bc \quad \text{and} \quad S \rightarrow \varepsilon$$

Similarly, the line labeled (3)–(4) is a way of writing the two productions

$$S' \rightarrow aS'bC \quad \text{and} \quad S' \rightarrow \varepsilon$$

In what follows, we shall regularly place productions with common left-hand side on one line in this way. We display a derivation of word $aaabbbccc$ below. (As an aid to the reader, we have added some boldface.)

$$
\begin{array}{ll}
S \Rightarrow a\mathbf{S'}bc & /* \text{ by (1) } */ \\
\Rightarrow a\mathbf{aS'bC}\,bc & /* \text{ by (3) } */ \\
\Rightarrow aa\mathbf{aS'\,bC}\,bCbc & /* \text{ by (3) } */ \\
\Rightarrow aaa\varepsilon bCbCbc & /* \text{ by (4) } */ \\
\Rightarrow aaab\mathbf{bC}\,Cbc & /* \text{ by (5) } */ \\
\Rightarrow aaabbC\,\mathbf{bC}\,c & /* \text{ by (5) } */ \\
\Rightarrow aaabbCb\mathbf{cc} & /* \text{ by (6) } */ \\
\Rightarrow aaabb\mathbf{bC}\,cc & /* \text{ by (5) } */ \\
\Rightarrow aaabbb\mathbf{ccc} & /* \text{ by (6) } */
\end{array}
$$

Apparently G generates any word in the language $\{a^n b^n c^n | n \geq 0\}$. Moreover, the reader should verify that these are the *only* words that G generates. By virtue of this, we shall say that $L(G)$, the language generated by generative grammar G, is $\{a^n b^n c^n | n \geq 0\}$.

Having considered several examples, we now present some formal definitions.

DEFINITION 9.9: A *generative grammar* G is a quadruple $\langle \Sigma, \Gamma, \sigma, \Pi \rangle$, where Σ and Γ, known as *terminal alphabet* and *nonterminal alphabet*, respectively, are disjoint; where $\sigma \in \Gamma$ is the distinguished *start symbol* of G; and where Π is a finite (possibly empty) set of *productions* or *rewrite rules* of the form $\alpha \rightarrow \beta$, where α and β are words over $\Sigma \cup \Gamma$ and α is nonempty.

We shall use uppercase letters, possibly with subscripts and superscripts, from the Roman alphabet for nonterminals and lowercase letters for terminals. Typically, we shall take $\Sigma = \{a, b\}$ and let σ be S. In the special case that α consists of a single nonterminal X, say, we shall say of production $\alpha \rightarrow \beta$ that it is a *production for X*. Generative grammars are also known as *phrase-structure grammars*.

As usual, a word over $\Sigma \cup \Gamma$ will be any finite (possibly empty) string of symbols from $\Sigma \cup \Gamma$. Thus, words over $\Sigma \cup \Gamma$ will in general contain terminal symbols as well as nonterminal symbols.

DEFINITION 9.10: Let $G = \langle \Sigma, \Gamma, \sigma, \Pi \rangle$ be a generative grammar. Where w and w' are words over $\Sigma \cup \Gamma$, *w generates w' directly* provided that there exist words w_1, w_2, α, and β over $\Sigma \cup \Gamma$ with w_1, w_2, and β possibly empty such that

    (i) w is of the form $w_1 \alpha w_2$

    (ii) w' is of the form $w_1 \beta w_2$ and

    (iii) Π contains the production $\alpha \rightarrow \beta$.

In such a case we shall write $w \Rightarrow_G w'$ or, if the context is not in doubt, just $w \Rightarrow w'$.

DEFINITION 9.11: Let $G = \langle \Sigma, \Gamma, \sigma, \Pi \rangle$ be a generative grammar. By a *derivation of length n* of w' from w within G we shall mean a word sequence $w_1, w_2, \ldots, w_n$, where $w = w_1$, $w' = w_n$, and for all $1 \leq i \leq n$ we have $w_i \Rightarrow_G w_{i+1}$.

DEFINITION 9.12: Let $G = \langle \Sigma, \Gamma, \sigma, \Pi \rangle$ be a generative grammar. We shall say that w *generates* w' and write $w \Rightarrow_G^* w'$ or, when the context is clear, just $w \Rightarrow^* w$, provided that there exists a derivation of length n, for some $n \geq 0$, of w' from w within G. Furthermore, we shall say that *grammar G generates w* just in case $\sigma \Rightarrow_G^* w$.

DEFINITION 9.13: Let $G = \langle \Sigma, \Gamma, \sigma, \Pi \rangle$ be a generative grammar. Then the language $L(G)$ generated by grammar G will consist of all and only words w over Σ such that $\sigma \Rightarrow_G^* w$. Furthermore, a formal language L will be said to be a *phrase-structure language* provided that $L = L(G)$ for some generative grammar G.

Note that the requirement that w be a word over terminal alphabet Σ means in effect that no nonterminals will appear in words of $L(G)$.

Having presented the needed formal definitions, we return to a consideration of Example 9.8.3 to clarify an issue that may be troubling some readers.

EXAMPLE 9.8.3 (continued) For the reader's convenience, grammar G's productions are reproduced below.

$$(1)\text{–}(2) \quad S \rightarrow aS'bc\,|$$

$$(3)\text{–}(4) \quad S' \rightarrow aS'bC\,|$$

$$(5) \qquad\; Cb \rightarrow bC$$

$$(6) \qquad\; Cc \rightarrow cc$$

We saw earlier that G generates any word of the form $a^n b^n c^n$ with $n \geq 0$ by virtue of the fact that there exist derivations of all such words from G's start symbol S. Moreover, a little experience with this grammar reveals that words not of the form $a^n b^n c^n$ with $n \geq 0$ *cannot* be derived from S. (Try to derive *abbc* or *abcabc*.) In accordance with Definition 9.13, we say that $L(G)$, the language generated by grammar G, is $\{a^n b^n c^n | n \geq 0\}$. But, at this point, the reader may be doubting that anything so complicated as (1)–(6) is really needed to generate language $\{a^n b^n c^n | n \geq 0\}$. Some readers will ask whether the following simpler grammar G' would not work just as well.

$$(1')\text{–}(2') \quad S \rightarrow aSbc\,|$$

$$(3') \qquad\;\; cb \rightarrow bc$$

So let us consider this. Is $L(G')$ really equal to $L(G) = \{a^n b^n c^n | n \geq 0\}$? First of all, it should be evident that any word in $\{a^n b^n c^n | n \geq 0\}$ is indeed generated by G'. For instance, *aabbcc* has derivation

$$S \Rightarrow_{G'} aSbc \qquad /* \text{ by } (1') */$$

$$\Rightarrow_{G'} aaSbcbc \qquad /* \text{ by } (1') */$$

$$\Rightarrow_{G'} aabcbc \qquad /* \text{ by } (2') */$$

$$\Rightarrow_{G'} aabbcc \qquad /* \text{ by } (3') */$$

This should be enough to enable the reader to see that $\{a^n b^n c^n | n \geq 0\} \subseteq L(G')$. But, if truly $L(G') = \{a^n b^n c^n | n \geq 0\}$, then, by the Principle of Extensionality, we must also have that $L(G') \subseteq \{a^n b^n c^n | n \geq 0\}$. But we can easily show that this is *not* the case; that is, $L(G') \not\subseteq \{a^n b^n c^n | n \geq 0\}$. After all, the following is a derivation of word *aabcbc* from the start symbol S of G'.

$$S \Rightarrow_{G'} aSbc \qquad /* \text{ by } (1') */$$

$$\Rightarrow_{G'} aaSbcbc \qquad /* \text{ by } (1') */$$

$$\Rightarrow_{G'} aabcbc \qquad /* \text{ by } (2') */$$

Moreover, word *aabcbc* consists of terminal symbols only so that, by Definition 9.13, $aabcbc \in L(G')$. Since $aabcbc \notin \{a^n b^n c^n | n \geq 0\}$, it should now be obvious that $L(G') \not\subseteq \{a^n b^n c^n | n \geq 0\}$ and so $L(G') \neq \{a^n b^n c^n | n \geq 0\}$ after all.

In light of the preceding example, we formulate

REMARK 9.8.1: Suppose that phrase-structure language L is given and that one has been asked to find a generative grammar G that generates L—that is, a generative grammar G such that $L(G) = L$. Then it is not enough to ensure merely that the productions of G permit all words of L to be derived. One must also be satisfied that any word that is not in L is not derivable within G.

In the remainder of this book we shall usually characterize a generative grammar merely by specifying its set of productions. The terminal alphabet of such a grammar will merely be the set of lowercase letters occurring in these productions. The nonterminals will be the uppercase letters. The start symbol of the grammar will be the (single) nonterminal occurring on the left-hand side of the first production listed.

A few words are in order lest the concept of a generative grammar be confused with that of a Markov algorithm schema as introduced in Chapter 4. There is a very important difference between these two concepts: In contrast to the application of the productions making up a Markov algorithm schema, there is no fixed order that must be followed in applying the productions of a generative grammar. Thus, whereas in Chapter 4 we spoke of *sequences* of productions, generative grammars involve (unordered) *sets* of productions. The fact that the order of application is fixed in the case of Markov algorithm schemata has the consequence that the application of such a schema to a given word w is an algorithmic, strictly mechanical, *deterministic* process in the sense that the "next step" in this process is always determinate.[3] The generation process associated with generative grammars, on the other hand, is nondeterministic in the sense that at certain points in the derivation of w from grammar G there may be choices as to which production to apply next: Since the productions associated with G are unordered, the "next step" in the derivation process is not in general fixed.

Finally, we shall need a notion of equivalence for generative grammars.

DEFINITION 9.14: Two generative grammars $G = \langle \Sigma, \Gamma, \sigma, \Pi \rangle$ and $G' = \langle \Sigma', \Gamma', \sigma', \Pi' \rangle$ are said to be *equivalent* if $L(G) = L(G')$.

---

§9.9 Right-Linear Grammars and Regular Languages

A certain special type of generative grammar will enable us to formulate the promised grammar-theoretic characterization of the family of regular languages.

DEFINITION 9.15: A generative grammar $G = \langle \Sigma, \Gamma, S, \Pi \rangle$ is said to be *right-linear* if every member of Π is either of the form $X \to wY$ or of the form $X \to w$, where X and Y are members of Γ and w is a (possibly empty) word over Σ.

---

[3]Lest confusion arise, we point out that there is nothing deterministic or mechanical about the process of *designing* a Markov algorithm schema that accepts a given language L. Our experience in Chapter 4 showed that considerable creativity may be involved there. What is deterministic and mechanical is the process of *applying* a *given* Markov algorithm schema S to some input word w in order to determine whether S in fact accepts w, say.

EXAMPLE 9.9.1 As an example of a right-linear grammar, consider the following grammar G.

$$S \to aX$$

$$X \to baX \mid$$

Clearly $L(G)$, the language generated by G, is the regular language denoted by regular expression $a(ba)^*$. A derivation of any word w in $L(a(ba)^*)$ involves introducing terminals starting at the far left and proceeding to the right in linear fashion.

$$S \Rightarrow aX$$

$$\Rightarrow abaX$$

$$\Rightarrow ababaX$$

$$\Rightarrow ababa$$

Another example will no doubt be helpful. This time let us start with a regular expression and then try to come up with a right-linear grammar that generates the language denoted by that regular expression.

EXAMPLE 9.9.2 The regular expression $(ab)^+ a^*(b|\varepsilon)$ denotes the language L that might be defined using set abstraction as $\{(ab)^n a^m b^k \mid n \geq 1, m \geq 0, k \leq 1\}$. The shortest word in L is ab. As already noted, derivations from right-linear grammars involve the introduction of terminals starting at the far left and proceeding to the right. This suggests the "top-level" productions

$$S \to abS \mid abX$$

After these productions have been applied some finite number of times, a new production for X may be applied so as to introduce as.

$$X \to aX \mid Y$$

Finally, two productions for Y permit the introduction of a single, optional b.

$$Y \to b \mid$$

A derivation of $ababaab$ from the grammar consisting of these six productions exhibits the expected linearity.

$$S \Rightarrow abS$$

$$\Rightarrow ababX$$

$$\Rightarrow ababaX$$

$$\Rightarrow ababaaX$$

$$\Rightarrow ababaaY$$

$$\Rightarrow ababaab$$

In fact, given a right-linear grammar G, it is always possible to find a regular expression r such that $L(G)$ is just $L(r)$. Moreover, the converse is also true: Given a regular expression r, it is always possible to find a right-linear grammar that generates $L(r)$. Thus it is possible to characterize the regular languages as those generated by right-linear grammars. We shall prove this equivalence now. Our proof will rely upon Theorems 9.12 and 9.13: We shall assume the association of finite-state automata with regular languages.

THEOREM 9.15: If L is generated by a right-linear grammar G, then L is regular.

PROOF Suppose that we are given a right-linear grammar G such that $L = L(G)$. We shall construct an incompletely defined, nondeterministic finite-state automaton M with ε-moves that accepts L. We proceed by way of the right-linear grammar G given in Example 9.9.1.

- We shall associate states of M with certain strings over the union of G's terminal and nonterminal alphabets. Namely, the states of M will be (associated with) G's start symbol S as well as all suffixes—proper or improper—of right-hand sides of productions of G. Thus, for the case of our present example G, we obtain states $[S]$, $[aX]$, $[baX]$, $[X]$, and $[\varepsilon]$.

- For each of G's productions, we now draw a single arc labeled by ε from left-hand side to right-hand side state in the state diagram of M. Thus, in our example we create three such arcs: from $[S]$ to $[aX]$, from $[X]$ to $[baX]$, and from $[X]$ to $[\varepsilon]$.

- We also add, for each state q beginning with a terminal symbol, a single arc labeled by that symbol from q to the suffix formed by deleting that terminal symbol. In our example this means an arc labeled by a from $[aX]$ to $[X]$ as well as an arc labeled by $[b]$ from $[baX]$ to $[aX]$.

- The start state of M is $[S]$, and M's unique accepting state is $[\varepsilon]$.

The transition diagram of the resulting (nondeterministic) finite-state automaton appears in Figure 9.9.1. This machine can easily be made fully defined if one simply adds a new trap state and directs to it all necessary additional arcs. The reader should verify that the language accepted by M is none other than $L(G)$. Moreover, this construction is fully general in that it can be applied to any right-linear grammar G so as to yield a finite-state automaton that accepts $L(G)$. It then follows by Theorem 9.13 that $L(G)$ is regular.
Q.E.D.

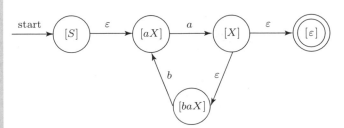

Figure 9.9.1 This finite-state automaton accepts the language generated by the right-linear grammar of Example 9.9.1.

THEOREM 9.16: If L is a regular language, then L is generated by some right-linear grammar.

PROOF Let us assume that $\Sigma = \{a, b\}$. If L is regular, then, by Theorem 9.12, L is accepted by some deterministic finite-state automaton M. We now proceed to describe the construction of a right-linear grammar G such that $L = L(G)$. The terminal alphabet of G will be Σ. The nonterminal alphabet of G will consist of symbols $S, X_{q_0}, X_{q_1}, X_{q_2}, \ldots, X_{q_n}$, where $q_0, q_1, q_2, \ldots, q_n$ are the states of M. We now proceed to describe the set Π of productions of G. For each arc labeled by symbol a, say, from state q_i to q_j we place in Π the single production $X_{q_i} \to aX_{q_j}$. In addition, for each accepting state q_t of M, we place in Π the empty production $X_{q_t} \to$. Also, for start symbol S, we introduce the single produc-

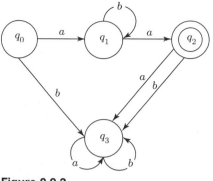

Figure 9.9.2

tion $S \to X_{q_0}$. The result of applying this construction to the finite-state automaton M of Figure 9.9.2 is the right-linear grammar G with the 10 productions

$$S \to X_{q_0}$$

$$X_{q_0} \to aX_{q_1} \mid bX_{q_3}$$

$$X_{q_1} \to aX_{q_2} \mid bX_{q_1}$$

$$X_{q_2} \to aX_{q_3} \mid bX_{q_3} \mid$$

$$X_{q_3} \to aX_{q_3} \mid bX_{q_3}$$

One can easily verify that the language accepted by finite-state automaton M is precisely the language generated by grammar G: Any path from initial state q_0 to terminal state q_2 and labeled by accepted word w is modeled by a unique derivation of w within grammar G.   Q.E.D.

A slightly simpler construction might have been presented in the proof of Theorem 9.16. However, our construction makes for an elegant modeling property (see Exercise 9.9.2). Finally, a language that is generated by some right-linear grammar will be referred to as a *right-linear language*.

DEFINITION 9.16: A language L is said to be a *right-linear language* if $L = L(G)$ for some right-linear grammar G.

§9.10 Summary, Historical Remarks, and Suggestions for Further Reading

In this chapter we have shown the following characterizations of L to be equivalent, where L is taken to be any language over alphabet Σ.

(i) L is regular; that is, L is denoted by a regular expression over Σ.

    (ii) L is accepted by some (deterministic) finite-state automaton with alphabet Σ.

    (iii) L is generated by some right-linear grammar with terminal alphabet Σ.

The equivalence of (i) and (ii) is the content of Theorems 9.12 and 9.13 taken together. Theorems 9.15 and 9.16 together assert the equivalence of (i) and (iii). In anticipation of the equivalence of (i) and (ii), many authors *define* the class of regular languages (or regular *sets*) as the class of languages accepted by finite-state automata. Similarly, in anticipation of the equivalence of (i) and (iii), most texts *define* a *regular grammar* to be a grammar that is either right-linear or left-linear (see Exercise 9.10.21 for the definition of left-linearity). We have chosen not to do either of these things for two reasons. First, doing so tends to mask the importance of these equivalence results and thus creates confusion for many readers. Second, opting for these alternative definitions denies the reader a certain suspense by announcing in advance, so to speak, that the various characterizations will in the end all come down to the same thing.

    The equivalence of (ii) and (iii) in particular requires additional comment. Here we have shown that a certain *automata-theoretic characterization* of a class of formal languages is equivalent to a certain *grammar-theoretic characterization* of that class of languages. This is only the first time that we shall do this: Each of Chapters 10, 11, and 12 will focus on the equivalence of a certain machine characterization of a family of languages with a certain grammatical characterization.

    Regular expressions were first introduced in [Kleene 1956]. Our proofs of Theorems 9.12 and 9.13 first appeared there as well. We note in passing that some authors write $(r) + (s)$ for $(r)|(s)$.

    The theoretical results of this chapter date from the 1950s. Kleene's definition of deterministic finite-state automata drew on earlier work of psychologists W. S. McCulloch and W. Pitts, who, in [McCulloch and Pitts 1943], had introduced so-called *neural nets* to model neural activity (see also §8.11). Kleene proved the equivalence between regular expressions and deterministic finite-state automata in [Kleene 1956]. The equivalence of regular expressions and right-linear grammars was announced in [Chomsky and Miller 1958]. Nondeterministic finite-state automata were introduced in [Rabin and Scott 1959], where their equivalence to deterministic finite-state automata is shown as well. The Pumping Lemma (Lemma 9.2) was first presented in [Bar-Hillel, Perles, and Shamir 1961].

    The generative grammar of Exercise 9.8.7 is adapted from [Salomaa 1973].

EXERCISES FOR §9.1

9.1.1. ^hwk Let $L_1 = L(ab^*a)$. Let $L_2 = L((ab)^*a)$. Let $L_3 = L((ab)^+a)$.
    (a) List the member(s) of language $L_1 \cap L_2$.
    (b) Present one word of length 10 that is in $L_1.L_2$.
    (c) List, in order of increasing length, the first five words of L_2^*.
    (d) List the word(s) in $L_2 \backslash L_3$.

9.1.2. ^hwk Let $\Sigma = \{a, b\}$. Describe in English the languages over Σ denoted by the following regular expressions.
    (a) $(a|b)^*b$
    (b) $(a|b)^*a(a|b)^*$
    (c) $(a|b)^*ab(a|b)^*$
    (d) $(a|b)^*((ab)|(ba))(a|b)^*$

9.1.3. Let $\Sigma = \{0, 1\}$. Describe in English the languages over Σ denoted by the following regular expressions over Σ. (Each language here is a set of binary strings or numerals.)
    (a) $0^*10^*10^*10^*$
    (b) $0(0 | 1)^*0$
    (c) $((1 | 0)1^*)^*$
    (d) $(0 | 1)^*0(0 | 1)(0 | 1)$
    (e) $(00 | 11)^*((01 | 10)(00 | 11)^*$
      $(01 | 10)(00 | 11)^*)^*$

9.1.4. Show that the language of Pascal real literals is a regular language. You might assume that all of the following are real literals.
    0.123 (but not .123)
    123.4 (but not 123.)

123.4E+5
123.4E−5
123.4E5

9.1.5. (a) Present a regular expression that denotes the set of even binary strings—that is, the strings that, as binary numerals, name even numbers.
   (b) Present a regular expression that denotes the set of odd binary strings—that is, the strings that, as binary numerals, name odd numbers.
   (c) Present a regular expression that denotes the set of those binary numerals that name multiples of 8.

9.1.6. For each of the regular expressions below, find another simpler regular expression that denotes

the same language over $\Sigma = \{a, b\}$.
   (a) $(a|b)^* b (a|b)^* a (a|b)^*$
   (b) $(a|b)^* ((b(a|b)^* a)|(a(a|b)^* b))(a|b)^*$

9.1.7. Show that each of the following languages over $\Sigma = \{a, b\}$ is regular by presenting a regular expression that denotes this language.
   (a) $\{w|w$ contains at least three occurrences of $a\}$
   (b) $\{w|w$ contains no occurrence of $bb\}$ (*Hint*: To say that w contains no occurrence of bb is just to say that any nonterminal occurrence of a b, should there in fact be such an occurrence, is immediately followed by an occurrence of a.)
   (c) $\{w : |w|$ is even$\}$
   (d) $\{w : |w|$ is odd$\}$
   (e) $\{w : |w|$ is a multiple of 3$\}$

EXERCISES FOR §9.2

9.2.1. **hwk** For each of the finite-state automata whose transition diagrams are given in Figures 9.2.1(b)–(e), answer the following. Which state(s) are accepting states? Is ε an accepted word? What are the shortest words accepted by the finite-state automaton? Is the accepted language finite or infinite? Without referring to the discussion in the text, what language is accepted by the machine? (Try to give a regular expression that denotes this language.) Which state is the so-called trap state of the machine?

9.2.2. **hwk** The state diagrams of three finite-state automata appear in Figures 9.2.4(a)–(c). Just one of these diagrams describes a finite-state automaton that accepts the language $L((ab)^* b)$. The other two do not accept that language. You are asked to identify the accepting state diagram. For each of the others, identify a few words of $L((ab)^* b)$ that are not accepted or a few accepted words that are not in $L((ab)^* b)$.

9.2.3. **hwk** For each of the following regular expressions, create the state diagram of a finite-state automaton that accepts the language denoted by the expression. In each case, be certain that your machine is deterministic and fully defined.
   (a) $a^* b$
   (b) $b^* (ab)^+$

   (c) $(ab)^*$
   (d) $(a|b)^* b$
   (e) $(a|b)^* a (a|b)^*$
   (f) $(a|b)^* ab(a|b)^*$
   (g) $(a|b)^* ((ab)|(ba))(a|b)^*$

9.2.4. Present the state diagram of a finite-state machine that accepts the language of Pascal identifiers. Forget about reserved words. In other words, your finite-state automaton will accept reserved words as well. Specify which Pascal dialect you are using.

9.2.5. Which of the strings $ababbbb$, $abbba$, $abbb$, and aa are accepted by the machine whose state diagram appears in Figure 9.2.5? Find a regular expression denoting the language accepted by this machine.

9.2.6. Let $\Sigma = \{a, b\}$. For each language L over Σ described below, show that L is FSA-acceptable by presenting the transition diagram of a finite-state automaton that accepts L.
   (a) $\{w|w$ contains precisely one occurrence of $b\}$
   (b) $\{w|w$ contains at least one occurrence of $b\}$
   (c) $\{w|w$ contains no more than three occurrences of $b\}$

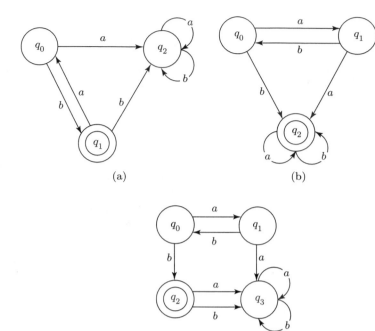

(a)   (b)

(c)

Figure 9.2.4

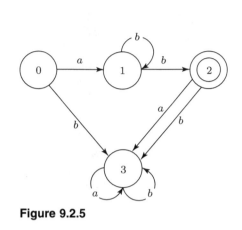

Figure 9.2.5

9.2.7. (a) Suppose that finite-state automaton $M = \langle \Sigma, Q, q_{init}, F, \delta \rangle$ is given. How might one designate the set of *nonaccepting states* of M?

(b) We saw that the finite-state automaton of Figure 9.2.1(a) accepts the language denoted by regular expression ab^*. Expressed in terms of set abstraction, this is the language $\{ab^n | n \geq 0\}$. Now suppose that the finite-state automaton of Figure 9.2.1(a) is transformed as follows: State q_1 becomes a nonaccepting state while q_0 and q_2 become accepting states. What language is accepted by this new machine?

(c) How might one generalize the observation of (b)? State and prove a general proposition concerning finite-state automata. The proposition might commence as follows: "Let finite-state automaton $M = \langle \Sigma, Q, q_{init}, F, \delta_M \rangle$ be given. Let finite-state automaton M^c be ...."

9.2.8. Characterize the language accepted by each of the finite-state automata whose transition diagrams appear in Figures 9.2.6(a)–(b).

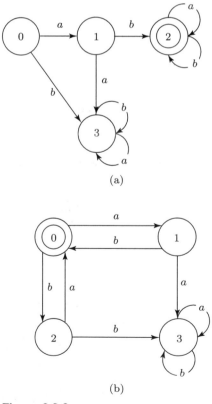

(a)

(b)

Figure 9.2.6

9.2.9. (a) What language is accepted by the finite-state automaton whose state diagram appears in Figure 9.2.7? (Either describe it in English or give a regular expression denoting it.)

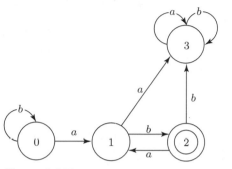

Figure 9.2.7

(b) Present the state diagram of a deterministic finite-state automaton that accepts the language denoted by regular expression a^+ba^*.

9.2.10. **hwk** Show that if there exists a finite-state automaton accepting language L, then there exists a finite-state automaton accepting $L\backslash\{\varepsilon\}$. In other words, show that if L is FSA-acceptable, then so is $L\backslash\{\varepsilon\}$.

9.2.11. Suppose that finite-state automaton $M = \langle \Sigma, Q, q_{init}, F, \delta_M \rangle$ is fully defined and deterministic. Suppose further that $F = Q$. That is, suppose that every state of M is an accepting state. What is $L(M)$ in this case?

9.2.12. **hwk** Design a deterministic finite-state automaton that accepts the language $\{w \in \Sigma^* | n_a(w), n_b(w), \text{ and } n_c(w) \text{ are all even}\}$ with $\Sigma = \{a, b, c\}$. (*Hint:* The initial and unique accepting state of an eight-state machine might be designated [even, even, even]. Also, compare Example 9.2.2.)

EXERCISES FOR §9.3

9.3.1. (a) Design a deterministic finite-state automaton that accepts the language denoted by regular expression $b(ab)^*b$.
(b) Design a deterministic finite-state automaton that accepts the language denoted by regular expression $b(ba)^+b$.
(c) Design a nondeterministic finite-state automaton that accepts the language denoted by regular expression $(b(ab)^*b)| (b(ba)^+b)$. (*Hint:* Merely identify the initial states and possibly the trap states of the finite-state automata of (a) and (b) above, renaming other states as necessary.)

9.3.2. **hwk** **(a)** What language L is accepted by the nondeterministic finite-state automaton M whose transition mapping is given below and whose sole accepting state is q_1?

$$\delta(a_0, a) = q_0 \qquad \delta(q_2, a) = q_1$$
$$\delta(q_0, b) = q_1 \qquad \delta(q_2, b) = q_3$$
$$\delta(q_0, b) = q_2 \qquad \delta(q_3, a) = q_3$$
$$\delta(q_1, a) = q_3 \qquad \delta(q_3, b) = q_3$$
$$\delta(q_1, b) = q_3$$

The corresponding state diagram appears in Figure 9.3.7.

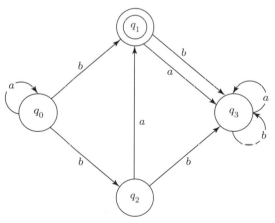

Figure 9.3.7

(b) Carry out the construction of the proof of Theorem 9.3 for this nondeterministic finite-state automaton M. That is, apply the subset construction to M so as to obtain a new deterministic finite-state automaton M' that accepts language L. Draw the state diagram of M'.

9.3.3. (a) Present the transition diagram of a deterministic finite-state automaton that accepts the language L denoted by $(ab)^*$.

(b) Present the transition diagram of a deterministic finite-state automaton that accepts the language L' denoted by ab^*a.

(c) Now consider the nondeterministic finite-state automaton that results when the deterministic finite-state automata of (a) and (b) are joined by merely identifying initial states and trap states and renaming some of the others. Show that the language accepted by this new nondeterministic finite-state automaton is not $L \cup L'$ in fact. (*Hint*: Find an accepted word that is not in $L \cup L'$.) Describe what has gone wrong in this case. When will this simple "combine" construction work and when will it not work?

EXERCISES FOR §9.4

9.4.1. [hwk] Use the Pumping Lemma (Lemma 9.2) to show that each of the following languages is not FSA-acceptable.
(a) $\{a^n b a^n | n \geq 0\}$
(b) $\{a^n b^{n+1} | n \geq 0\}$
(c) $\{a^n b^n a^n | n \geq 0\}$
(d) $\{a^n b^n c^n | n \geq 0\}$

9.4.2. Show that the language $L = \{a^n | n$ is a perfect square$\}$ is not accepted by any finite-state automaton.

9.4.3. Show that the language $L = \{a^n | n$ is prime$\}$ is not accepted by any finite-state automaton.

9.4.4. (a) Let L be the language $\{a^n b | n \geq 0\}$. Show that application of the Pumping Lemma (Lemma 9.2) to L does *not* yield a contradiction and hence cannot be used to show that L is not FSA-acceptable.

(b) Does the FSA-acceptability of L follow from the fact that the Pumping Lemma cannot be used to show that L is not FSA-acceptable?

9.4.5. (A Strengthened Pumping Lemma for Finite-State Automata). Show that if language L is FSA-acceptable and infinite, then there exists an integer n such that, for any word $z \in L$ with $|z| \geq n$, we have that $z = uwv$ for some words u, w, and v with $w \neq \varepsilon$, where $uw^i v$ is in L for all $i \geq 0$. (As usual, we write w^i for the result of concatenating word w with itself i times.) (Hint: Reexamine the proof of Lemma 9.2.)

EXERCISES FOR §9.5

9.5.1. [hwk] Let M be the finite-state automaton of Figure 9.2.1(a) and let M' be the finite-state automaton of Figure 9.2.1(b). Apply the construction of Theorem 9.7 so as to obtain the state diagram of a new nondeterministic machine accepting $L(M) \cup L(M')$.

9.5.2. Let L be an FSA-acceptable language over alphabet Σ. Show that the language $L' = \{wv | w \in L$ and $v \in L^c\}$ is FSA-acceptable. (*Hint*: Appeal to the closure results contained in Theorems 9.8 and 9.11.)

9.5.3. Let L be that language over $\Sigma = \{a, b\}$ consisting of all and only those words that do not contain three consecutive as. Show that L is FSA-acceptable. (*Hint*: First design a deterministic finite-state automaton that accepts the language denoted by regular expression $(a|b)^* aaa (a|b)^*$ and then use Theorem 9.8.)

9.5.4. Apply the construction of the proof of Theorem 9.6 to the finite-state automaton whose state diagram appears in Figure 9.5.7 so as to obtain an equivalent nonrestarting machine.

9.5.5. Let M be the nonrestarting finite-state machine whose state diagram appears in Figure 9.5.8. Apply the construction of Theorem 9.10 so as to obtain a new M' with $L(M') = (L(M))^*$; that is, the language accepted by M' is the result of applying Kleene closure to the language accepted by M.

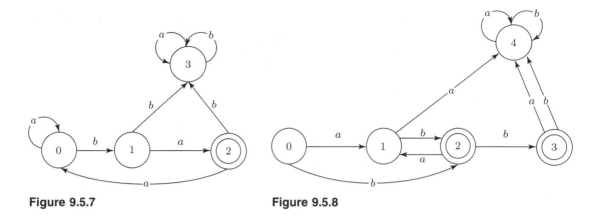

Figure 9.5.7   **Figure 9.5.8**

9.5.6. Let M be the finite-state automaton of Figure 9.2.1(b) and let M' be the finite-state automaton of Figure 9.2.1(d). Apply the construction of the proof of Theorem 9.11 so as to obtain a new finite-state automaton $M^\bullet$ that accepts the language $L(M).L(M')$.

9.5.7. (a) Use the Pumping Lemma (Lemma 9.2) to show that the language $\{a^n b^m c^{n+m} | n \geq 1 \text{ and } m \geq 1\}$ is not FSA-acceptable.
(b) Present an argument showing that the language $\Sigma^* \setminus \{a^n b^m c^{n+m} | n \geq 1 \text{ and } m \geq 1\}$ is not FSA-acceptable. (*Hint*: Proceed indirectly using closure properties of the class of FSA-acceptable languages.)

9.5.8. Show that the construction of Theorem 9.8, which turns finite-state automaton M accepting language L into finite-state automaton M' accepting L^c, does not work unless M is deterministic. (*Hint*: Apply the construction to some nondeterministic finite-state automaton of your choice and consider the finite-state automaton that results.)

9.5.9. Show that the construction of Theorem 9.10, which turns finite-state automaton M accepting language L into finite-state automaton M^* accepting L^*, does not work unless M is nonrestarting. (*Hint*: Apply the construction to some restarting finite-state automaton of your choice and consider the finite-state automaton that results.)

EXERCISES FOR §9.6

9.6.1. [hwk] Identify each of the languages $_M L_{0,5}^{-1}$, $_M L_{0,5}^0$, $_M L_{0,5}^1$, $_M L_{0,5}^2$, $_M L_{0,5}^3$, $_M L_{0,5}^4$, and $_M L_{0,5}^5$, where M is the machine whose state diagram appears in Figure 9.6.3.

9.6.2. Justify the claim that language $\{a^n b^n | n \geq 0\}$ is not regular.

9.6.3. In giving Theorem 9.1, we proved that the class of regular languages is closed under union, concatenation, and Kleene closure. Later on, in §9.5, we proved that the class of FSA-acceptable languages is closed under these same operations. Given Theorems 9.12 and 9.13, was this not mere duplication of effort?

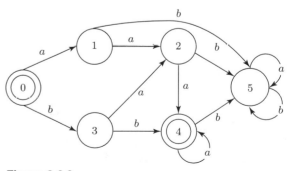

Figure 9.6.3

In other words, might we not have proceeded as follows?

(i) Prove closure of the class of regular languages, say, under these three operations.

(ii) Conclude by Theorems 9.12 and 9.13 that the class of FSA-acceptable languages

is closed under these operations as well. (*Hint:* Examine again the proof of Theorem 9.12.)

EXERCISES FOR §9.7

9.7.1. ^hwk (a) What language is accepted by finite-state automaton M with ε-moves whose transition diagram appears in Figure 9.7.3. (In order to simplify M's state diagram, we have not defined it fully.)

(b) Apply the construction of the proof of Theorem 9.14 to M so as to obtain a new machine M' without ε-moves such that $L(M') = L(M)$.

9.7.2. Use Theorem 9.14 to present an alternative proof that the FSA-acceptable languages are closed under union (Theorem 9.7), where, as before, *FSA-acceptable language* means lang-

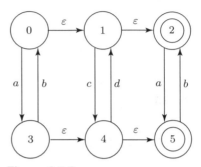

Figure 9.7.3

uage accepted by some (deterministic) finite-state automaton without ε-moves.

EXERCISES FOR §9.8

9.8.1. ^hwk (a) Consider the grammar G whose productions appear below.

$$S \rightarrow aaA$$

$$A \rightarrow aaA \mid B$$

$$B \rightarrow b \mid bB$$

What are the nonterminals of G apparently? What are the terminals of G? How many productions does G have?

(b) What language is generated by grammar G? Is ε generated? (As usual, we take S as start symbol.)

(c) Find a regular expression that denotes $L(G)$.

9.8.2. ^hwk (a) Consider the grammar G whose productions appear below.

$$S \rightarrow aaaA \mid A$$

$$A \rightarrow aaa \mid aaaA \mid B$$

$$B \rightarrow bb \mid bbB \mid C$$

$$C \rightarrow c \mid cC \mid$$

What are the nonterminals of G apparently? What are the terminals of G? How many productions does G have?

(b) What language is generated by grammar G? Is ε generated? (As usual, we take S as start symbol.)

(c) Find a regular expression that denotes $L(G)$.

9.8.3. (a) Consider the grammar G whose productions appear below.

$$S \rightarrow aS'bbccc \mid$$

$$S' \rightarrow aS'bbCCC \mid$$

$$Cb \rightarrow bC$$

$$Cc \rightarrow cc$$

What are the nonterminals of G apparently? What are the terminals of G? How many productions does G have?

(b) What language is generated by grammar G? Is ε generated? (As usual, we take S as start symbol.)

(c) Use the Pumping Lemma (Lemma 9.2) to show that $L(G)$ is not a regular language.

9.8.4. (a) What language is generated by the grammar G whose productions appear below? Is ε generated? Is *any* word generated?

$$S \to aaA$$

$$A \to aaA \mid B$$

$$B \to bB$$

(b) Based upon this example, what general conclusion might be formulated regarding the language generated by a generative grammar?

9.8.5. (a) What language is generated by the grammar G whose productions appear below? Is ε generated?

$$S \to aaA$$

$$A \to aaA \mid B$$

$$B \to bB \mid b \mid bS$$

(b) Based upon this example and those of the preceding Exercises 9.8.1 through 9.8.4, what general conclusion might be formulated regarding the generation of ε by a generative grammar?

9.8.6. **hwk** Consider the grammar G whose productions appear below.

$$S \to aSc \mid aXc \mid$$

$$X \to bXd \mid$$

$$dc \to cd$$

(a) Show that the language $L = \{a^n b^m c^n d^m \mid n, m \geq 0\}$ is *not* the language generated by G by presenting a few short words that are generated by G but that are not members of L.

(b) Also, find a word of length 2 that is in L but not in $L(G)$.

(c) Modify G so as to obtain a generative grammar that does generate L.

9.8.7. Consider generative grammar $G = \langle \Sigma, \Gamma, S, \Pi \rangle$, where $\Sigma = \{0, 1\}$, $\Gamma = \{S, U, W, X, Y, Z\}$, and Π is the set

$S \to XYZ$	/∗ Introduces nonterminals ∗/
$XY \to 0XU$	/∗ Introduces a *0* on the left ∗/
$XY \to 1XW$	/∗ Introduces a *1* on the left ∗/
$UZ \to Y0Z$	/∗ Introduces companion *0* ∗/
$WZ \to Y1Z$	/∗ Introduces companion *1* ∗/

$$\left.\begin{array}{l} 0Y \to Y0 \\ 1Y \to Y1 \end{array}\right\} \begin{array}{l} \text{Moves end-of-cycle character} \\ Y \text{ to the left over previously} \\ \text{copied digits} \end{array}$$

$$\left.\begin{array}{l} U0 \to 0U \\ U1 \to 1U \end{array}\right\} \begin{array}{l} \text{Moves } \textit{0}\text{-generator } U \text{ to the} \\ \text{right over previously copied} \\ \text{digits} \end{array}$$

$$\left.\begin{array}{l} W0 \to 0W \\ W1 \to 1W \end{array}\right\} \begin{array}{l} \text{Moves } \textit{1}\text{-generator } W \text{ to the} \\ \text{right over previously copied} \\ \text{digits} \end{array}$$

$$\left.\begin{array}{l} XY \to \\ Z \to \end{array}\right\} \text{Elimination of nonterminals}$$

The comments at the right have been added in order to document the role of a given production or group of productions in word generation. Convince yourself that this grammar generates the language $L = \{ww \mid w \text{ in } \{0, 1\}^*\}$ by finding derivations of each of the following bit strings.

(a) *1010*   (b) *1111*
(c) *0101*   (d) *0000*

9.8.8. Consider again the grammar of Example 9.8.3. Present two distinct derivations of word *aaaabbbbcccc* within this grammar.

EXERCISES FOR §9.9

9.9.1. ^{hwk} Consider the right-linear grammar G whose productions are listed below. Apply the construction of the proof of Theorem 9.15 to G so as to obtain a finite-state automaton that accepts $L(G)$.

$$S \to aX$$

$$X \to bY$$

$$Y \to aX \mid bZ \mid b$$

$$Z \to bZ \mid b$$

9.9.2. (a) Apply the algorithm of the proof of Theorem 9.16 to the finite-state automaton whose state diagram appears in Figure 9.9.3 so as to construct a right-linear grammar G such that $L(G) = L(M)$.

(b) Show the correspondence between (1) paths in the state diagram of M from initial state q_0 to some accepting state and (2) derivations in G by considering word $bababa \in L(M) = L(G)$. First, what unique path P in the state diagram of M is labeled by word $bababa$? Next, give a derivation D of word $bababa$ within grammar G. Now compare path P and derivation D. How might one formulate the correspondence between P and D here?

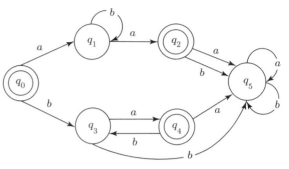

Figure 9.9.3

9.9.3. Suppose that the class of right-linear₁ grammars is defined as follows.

DEFINITION: A generative grammar $G = \langle \Sigma, \Gamma, S, \Pi \rangle$ is said to be *right-linear₁* if every member of Π is either of the form $X \to \sigma Y$ or of the form $X \to \sigma$ or of the form $X \to$, where X and Y are members of Γ and σ is a member of Σ.

Show that, from a theoretical point of view, right-linearity in the sense of Definition 9.16 and right-linearity₁ are equivalent notions. That is, show that, where L is any language over Σ, L is generated by a right-linear grammar if and only if L is generated by a right-linear₁ grammar.

EXERCISES FOR §9.10 (END-OF-CHAPTER REVIEW EXERCISES)

9.10.1. Find regular expressions denoting the following languages. Let Σ be the uppercase Roman alphabet.

(a) All strings containing one occurrence of each of the five vowels with A occurring somewhere to the left of E, E occurring somewhere to the left of I, and so on.

(b) All strings in which any occurrence of A is to the left of any occurrence of B, any occurrence of B is to the left of any occurrence of C, and so on.

9.10.2. Find a regular expression denoting the class of all Pascal comments consisting of a string prefixed by /∗ and terminated by ∗/ with no in-

termediate occurrence of ∗/ unless that occurrence appears inside double quotation marks.

9.10.3. ^{hwk} **(a)** Show that the language $\{a^n \mid n = 5 + 3k \text{ for } k \geq 0\}$ is regular.

(b) Show that, for any fixed i and $j \geq 0$, the language $\{a^n \mid n = i + jk \text{ for } k \geq 0\}$ is regular.

9.10.4. Find regular expressions denoting each of the languages over $\Sigma = \{a, b\}$ given below.

(a) The language of all words such that any pair of consecutive as occurs before any pair of consecutive bs

(b) The language consisting of all words not containing any occurrence of aba

9.10.5. Describe in English the languages denoted by each of the regular expressions below.

   (a) $((aa)|b)^*\,((bb)|a)^*$

   (b) $(a|(ba)|(bba))^*\,(\varepsilon|b|(bb))$

   (c) $[(bb)|(aa)|(((ba)|(ab))((bb)|(aa))^*$
      $((ba)|(ab)))]^*$

9.10.6. [hwk] Consider each of the following *laws of the algebra of regular languages*. We use r, s, and t as syntactic variables ranging over regular expressions over alphabet Σ.

   (a) $L_{r|s} = L_{s|r}$

Proof.

$$L_{r|s} = L_s \cup L_r \text{ by Definition 9.1(iv)(a)}$$

$$= L_r \cup L_s \text{ by the commutativity of } \cup$$

$$= L_{s|r} \text{ by Definition 9.1(iv)(a)}$$

Q.E.D.

Present proofs of each of (b) through (i) on the model of the proof of (a) that appears above.

   (b) $L_{r|(s|t)} = L_{(r|s)|t}$

   (c) $L_{r(st)} = L_{(rs)t}$

   (d) $L_{r(s|t)} = L_{(rs)|(rt)}$

   (e) $L_{(r|s)t} = L_{(rt)|(st)}$

   (f) $L_{(r^*)^*} = L_{r^*}$

   (g) $L_{(r^* s^*)^*} = L_{(r|s)^*}$

   (h) $L_{r\varepsilon} = L_{\varepsilon r} = L_r$

   (i) $L_{r^+|\varepsilon} = L_{r^*}$

   (j) Show that in general $L_{r.s} \ne L_{s.r}$ by presenting a counterexample. That is, assuming $\Sigma = \{a,b\}$, say, present regular expressions r and s and word w such that $w \in L_{r.s}$ but $w \notin L_{s.r}$.

   (k) Show that in general $L_{(r|s)^*} \ne L_{r^*|s^*}$ by presenting a counterexample. That is, assuming $\Sigma = \{a,b\}$, say, present regular expressions r and s and word w such that $w \in L_{(r|s)^*}$ but $w \notin L_{r^*|s^*}$.

9.10.7. First, consider the solution to the addition problem below.

$$\begin{array}{r} 732 \\ +862 \\ \hline 1594 \end{array}$$

Now if each addend is expressed by a 4-digit numeral through the prefixing of a single leading zero, then, reading down the columns from right to left, we obtain the corresponding 12-digit string 224369785001. You are asked to present a deterministic finite-state automaton that accepts the language of digit strings each of which corresponds in this way to a solution of some addition problem.

9.10.8. Present state diagrams for deterministic finite-state automata accepting the following languages over $\Sigma = \{a,b\}$.

   (a) $\{w : |w| \bmod 3 = 0\}$

   (b) $\{w : |w| \bmod 4 \ne 0\}$

   (c) $\{w : n_b(w) \bmod 3 > 1\}$

   (d) $\{w : n_a(w) \bmod 3 > n_b(w) \bmod 3\}$
      (*Hint*: Keeping in mind that an input word is read from left to right, identify $3^2 = 9$ possible states corresponding to 9 possible pairs of values of the ordered pair $\langle n_a(w) \bmod 3, n_b(w) \bmod 3 \rangle$.)

   (e) $\{w : (n_a(w) - n_b(w)) \bmod 3 > 0\}$
      (*Hint*: Recall that the mod function corresponds to integer division with "truncation toward minus infinity" in the sense that $-2 \bmod 3$ is -2 rather than $+1$. Keeping in mind that an input word is read from left to right, identify five possible states corresponding to five possible values of the left-hand side of the given inequality.)

9.10.9. Let $\Sigma = \{0, 1\}$. Present the transition diagram of a finite-state automaton that accepts the language L defined by $L = \{w | w$ interpreted as a binary numeral is a multiple of 5$\}$. For example, 0101 and 1111 are in L but 1110 is not. (*Hint*: What is the effect upon the value represented of appending a single 0 to the end of a binary numeral? A single 1? Also, if $n \bmod 5 = K$, what is $2n \bmod 5$? What is $(2n + 1) \bmod 5$? Keeping in mind that our input numeral must be read from left to right, identify five states corresponding to five possible values mod 5 of that portion of the input numeral that has been read so far.)

9.10.10. Let $\Sigma = \{a, b\}$. For each language over Σ^* given below, design a deterministic finite-state automaton that accepts that language.

   (a) $\{w | w$ ends with $ba\}$
      (*Hint*: Create a full binary tree of height 2 whose root is initial state q_0. One of the

four leaves of this tree will be the unique accepting state. Now add arcs for a and b from each leaf so as to make the state diagram fully defined. The state diagram can be made nicely symmetric.)

(b) $\{w | w$ contains no occurrence of $aba\}$
(*Hint*: Create a full binary tree of height 3 whose root is initial state q_0. Seven of the eight leaves of this tree will be accepting states. Now add arcs for a and b from each leaf.)

(c) $\{w | $the third symbol from the right in w is a $b\}$
(*Hint*: Create a full binary tree of height 3 whose root is initial state q_0. Four of the eight leaves of this tree will be accepting states. Now add arcs for a and b from each leaf.)

(d) $\{w | $every block of five consecutive symbols in w contains at least two bs$\}$
(*Hint*: Start by creating a full binary tree of height 5 whose root is initial state q_0. The accepting states will be precisely those leaves q_i such that the path from q_0 to q_i is labeled by a word containing at least two bs. Now add arcs for a and b from each leaf.)

9.10.11. **(a)** Present the state diagram of a deterministic finite-state automaton that accepts the language $L((ab)^*b)$. Your machine should be fully defined.

(b) Presumably the finite-state automaton you have given in answering (a) is a restarting machine. Use the construction of Theorem 9.6 in order to turn this finite-state automaton into an equivalent finite-state automaton that is nonrestarting. Again, your machine should be fully defined.

9.10.12. **(a)** Describe an algorithm for transforming the state diagram of a deterministic finite-state automaton into the state diagram of a deterministic Turing machine that accepts the same language, thereby showing that every FSA-acceptable language is Turing-acceptable.

(b) Show that, in fact, every FSA-acceptable language is Turing-recognizable by extending the construction of (a).

9.10.13. **(a)** Show that the class of FSA-acceptable languages is closed under set difference. That is, show that if L_1 and L_2 are both FSA-acceptable languages, then so is $L_1 \backslash L_2$. (*Hint*: First define $L_1 \backslash L_2$ in terms of operations under which the class of FSA-acceptable languages has already been shown to be closed.)

(b) Show that the class of FSA-acceptable languages is closed under symmetric difference. (*Hint*: First define $L_1 \oplus L_2$ in terms of operations under which the class of FSA-acceptable languages has already been shown to be closed.)

9.10.14. For each of the languages below, show by an indirect argument that it is not FSA-acceptable. (*Hint*: Your argument will appeal to the Pumping Lemma as well as to closure under either complementation or set difference.)

(a) $\{a^i | i$ is composite$\}$

(b) $\{a^n b^m | n, m > 0, n \neq m\}$

9.10.15. Let $\Sigma = \{a, b\}$. For each language over Σ given below, determine whether of not it is a regular language. Justify your answer in each case.

(a) $\{a^{2n} | n \geq 0\}$

(b) $\{a^n b^m a^{n+m} | n, m \geq 0\}$

(c) $\{w | w$ contains no occurrence of three consecutive bs$\}$

(d) $\{w | $either w contains an occurrence of three consecutive bs or w does not contain any occurrence of two consecutive as$\}$

(e) $\{w | n_a(w) = n_b(w)\}$

9.10.16. Show that the class of FSA-acceptable languages is not closed under the subset relation. That is, it does not follow from the fact that L_2 is FSA-acceptable and L_1 is a subset of L_2 that L_1 is also FSA-acceptable. (*Hint*: A proof here could merely consist of presentation of languages L_1 and L_2.)

9.10.17. **(a)** Let M be a deterministic finite-state automaton with n states. Suppose further that M accepts word w with $|w| \geq n$. Explain why $L(M)$ must be infinite.

(b) Let M be a deterministic finite-state automaton with n states. Show that if $L(M)$

is infinite, then it must contain a word w with $n \leq |w| < 2n$.

(c) Given the results of (a) and (b), describe an algorithm that, given deterministic finite-state automaton M, determines whether $L(M)$ is finite or infinite.

9.10.18. (a) We saw in Theorem 9.1 that the union of two regular languages is regular. Use this result to show that the union of n regular languages is regular, for arbitrary finite n. (*Hint*: Give an inductive argument with base case $n = 2$.)

(b) Show that the class of regular languages is not closed under arbitrary unions. That is, the union of an arbitrary infinite family of regular languages is not in general regular. (*Hint*: For p prime, unit language $\{a^p\}$ is finite and hence regular.)

9.10.19. (a) Show that the regular languages are closed under reversal. That is, if L is regular, then so is

$$L^R = \{w^R | w \in L\}$$

(*Hint*: Suppose that $L = L_r$ and use induction on the complexity of regular expression r.)

(b) Let w^{-1} be the result of simultaneously replacing every occurrence of a in w by b, and vice versa. Thus $(abb)^{-1} = baa$. Show that if L is regular then so is $L^{-1} = \{w^{-1} | w \in L\}$. (*Hint*: Suppose that $L = L_r$ and use induction on the complexity of regular expression r.)

9.10.20. Suppose that L is a regular language. Show that L' defined by $L' = \{w \in L | w^R \in L\}$ is also regular. (L' is simply that subset of L consisting of words w such that both w and w^R are in L.)

9.10.21. **hwk** A generative grammar $G = \langle \Sigma, \Gamma, \sigma, \Pi \rangle$ is said to be *left-linear* if every production in Π is either of the form $X \to Yw$ or of the form $X \to w$, where X and Y are nonterminals in Γ and w is a word over Σ. Prove that if G is a left-linear grammar, then $L(G)$ is regular. (*Hint*: Note first that the result of reversing the right-hand sides of all productions turns a left-linear grammar into a right-linear grammar.)

Now use Theorem 9.15 together with Exercise 9.10.19(a).)

9.10.22. Show that if L is regular, then L is generated by a left-linear grammar. (*Hint*: Use Exercise 9.10.19(a) and Theorem 9.16.)

9.10.23. (a) Present an argument to the effect that the class of Java identifiers is a regular language. There are 49 Java keywords: **abstract**, **boolean**, **break**, **byte**, **byvalue**, **case**, . . . , **void**, **while**. (What is really important here is that the class of keywords is finite.)

(b) Generalize your argument so as to show that any "reasonable" definition of identifier yields a regular language.

9.10.24. (a) Show that if language L over alphabet Σ is regular, then language $\{w \in L : |w| \text{ is odd}\}$ is also regular. (*Hint*: Consider Exercise 9.1.7(d) again as well as the closure results of §9.5.)

(b) Show that if language L over alphabet Σ is regular, then language $\{w \in L : |w| \bmod 5 = 2\}$ is also regular.

9.10.25. We have suggested no analyses of the resource requirements of finite-state automata. In this exercise, we consider the merits of developing the means of such analyses.

(a) Let M be a (deterministic) finite-state machine without ε-moves. You are asked to suggest a time analysis for M's computation in accepting language $L(M)$.

(b) Let M be a nondeterministic finite-state machine possibly with ε-moves. Provide a time analysis for M's computation in accepting language $L(M)$.

(c) Let M be a nondeterministic finite-state machine possibly with ε-moves. Provide a space analysis for M's computation in accepting language $L(M)$.

(d) What general conclusion might be drawn concerning the potential usefulness of notions of time and space for finite-state automata.

9.10.26. Suppose that language L is accepted by some multitape Turing machine in space $O(1)$. Show that L is regular. (*Hint*: Use Exercise 2.3.19.)

Chapter 10

Context-Free Languages and Pushdown-Stack Automata

§10.1 Context-Free Grammars and Natural Languages

The concept of a generative or phrase-structure grammar was introduced in §9.8. The grammar G of Example 9.8.1 has the two productions

$$S \to aSb \mid$$

and generates the language $\{a^n b^n \mid n \geq 0\}$. The grammar of Example 9.8.2 has three productions

$$S \to aaXcc$$

$$X \to aXc \mid b$$

and generates language $\{a^n bc^n \mid n \geq 2\}$. The productions of these two generative grammars share a peculiar form; namely, the left-hand side of each production consists of a single nonterminal symbol. Such productions are called *context-free productions*. The motivation for this terminology becomes apparent if context-free production

$$Y \to abc \tag{10.1.1}$$

is compared with a production such as

$$XYW \to XabcW \tag{10.1.2}$$

say, which is not context-free. Production (10.1.1) licenses substitution of string abc for any occurrence of Y whatever—for Y *occurring in any context*. Production (10.1.2), on the other hand, is quite specific with regard to context: An occurrence of Y may be replaced by string abc provided that occurrence is immediately preceded by an occurrence of X and immediately followed by an occurrence of W. (Productions such as (10.1.2) are said to be *context-sensitive* and will concern us in Chapter 11.)

A generative grammar whose productions are all context-free productions is termed a *context-free grammar*. Thus, the grammars of Examples 9.8.1 and 9.8.2 are both context-free. (On the other hand, the grammar of Example 9.8.3 is not context-free, by virtue of the fact that its two productions $Cb \rightarrow bC$ and $Cc \rightarrow cc$ are not context-free.) Furthermore, we describe a language L over alphabet Σ as a *context-free language* if L is generated by some context-free grammar G—that is, if $L = L(G)$ for some context-free grammar G. Thus, Examples 9.8.1 and 9.8.2 show in effect that the languages $\{a^n b^n | n \geq 0\}$ and $\{a^n bc^n | n \geq 2\}$ are both context-free languages. In general, any language L that is generated by *some* generative grammar will be generated by many such grammars. If even one of these grammars is context-free, then L qualifies as a context-free language.

> **DEFINITION 10.1:** Any production whose left-hand side consists of a single nonterminal is a *context-free production*. A generative grammar G, all of whose productions are context-free, is called a *context-free grammar*. A language L is a *context-free language* if there exists a context-free grammar G such that $L = L(G)$.

It is natural to ask about the relation between regular languages, which we investigated in Chapter 9, and context-free languages. We can settle this matter immediately. The reader will recall that the regular languages—those denoted by regular expressions—are precisely those generated by right-linear grammars (cf. Theorems 9.15 and 9.16). But one sees quickly that any right-linear grammar is context-free. It follows immediately that every regular language is context-free; that is, the class of regular languages is a subset of the class of context-free languages.

$$L \text{ is regular} \Leftrightarrow L \text{ is right-linear} \Rightarrow L \text{ is context-free}$$

Is the containment proper? That is, is there a context-free language that is not regular? Well, the languages of Examples 9.8.1 and 9.8.2 are examples of just such languages.

- By Theorem 9.5, language $\{a^n b^n | n \geq 0\}$ is not FSA-acceptable and hence, by the contrapositive of Theorem 9.12, not regular, either.

- It is an easy consequence of Lemma 9.2 (Pumping Lemma for Finite-State Automata) that language $\{a^n bc^n | n \geq 2\}$ is not FSA-acceptable and hence not regular.

Thus the containment of the class of regular languages within the class of context-free languages is indeed proper. (This is the first step in the description of the so-called *Chomsky hierarchy of languages*. The reader is encouraged to glance ahead at Figure 12.7.1 and Table 12.7.1 at the end of Chapter 12.) This is enough to justify the following:

> **REMARK 10.1.1:** Every regular language is context-free. At the same time, there exist context-free languages that are not regular.

Context-free grammars are of special interest to computer scientists because, as it turns out, context-free grammars may be used to describe most of the purely syntactic features of programming languages. Later in the present section we consider one such application. Most of the remainder of this section will be given over to a brief consideration of the application of context-free grammars to natural languages. Our focus will be English, although our ultimate conclusions are intended to apply equally to Bengali or Polish. In fact, linguists engaged in the study of the syntactic properties of natural language were the first to identify the context-free subfamily of the class of generative grammars. (The term *phrase-structure grammar* as an alternative to *generative grammar* similarly reflects the interests of linguistic researchers.)

It has been evident to linguists that speakers of English have an internalized knowledge of English syntax. A simple, but forceful, argument to this effect runs as follows. Consider the sentence fragment

> Once upon a time and a very good time it was there was a moocow coming down along the road and this moocow that was coming down along the road met a nicens little boy named baby tuckoo ... (James Joyce, *A Portrait of the Artist as a Young Man*)

Even those readers who have never before encountered this sentence will no doubt be able to "parse" it—recognize it as a more-or-less grammatical sentence of English. Evidently then, syntactic knowledge does not consist of some long list of grammatical sentences stored in memory, because if it did, the list would of necessity be finite, given the finiteness of human neural networks, and would consequently fail to account for what seems to be our unbounded capacity to parse new sentences. Rather, our ability to process sentences of English must be *creative*. One way to account for this creativity is to posit a neural capacity to recognize word sequences generated by some finite set of productions (i.e., by some grammar) stored within our brains.

One assumes that speech utterances are broken up into sentences and that sentences in turn are divisible into words. (If this strikes the reader as an utterly trivial assertion, it is probably because he or she has in mind *written* rather than *spoken* language.) Still, one must be careful, since it is equally clear that a sentence is not a mere sequence of autonomous words. Rather, a sentence is a string of words in some *order*—a string exhibiting some *structure*. We can begin to see this by considering the English sentence

$$\textbf{The clown wept.} \qquad (10.1.3)$$

Note that it is possible to substitute **he** or **she** for the **the clown** without altering the meaning conveyed. But there is no comparable substitution for the two words **clown wept**. In other words, the word pair **the clown**, but not the word pair **clown wept**, constitutes a syntactic unit. This claim may be embodied in several context-free productions, foremost among them the production

$$NP \rightarrow Det\, N$$

where nonterminals $NP, Det,$ and N are abbreviations for *noun phrase, determiner,* and *noun,* respectively. If, in addition, we provide the productions

$$S \rightarrow NP\, VP \qquad \text{/* A \textbf{s}entence may consist of a \textbf{n}oun \textbf{p}hrase followed by a \textbf{v}erb \textbf{p}hrase. */}$$

$$VP \rightarrow V_{intr} \qquad \text{/* A \textbf{v}erb \textbf{p}hrase may consist of an intransitive \textbf{v}erb alone. */}$$

$$\left.\begin{array}{l} Det \rightarrow \textbf{the} \\ N \rightarrow \textbf{clown} \\ V \rightarrow \textbf{wept} \end{array}\right\} \text{/* These three productions amount to a sort of } lexicon. \text{ */}$$

then we can represent the structure of (10.1.3) by a *phrase-structure tree* or *parse tree*, as shown in Figure 10.1.1. Note that in this context our terminal "alphabet" consists of words **the, clown,** and **wept**, whereas our nonterminals are abbreviations for the familiar grammatical category names, with S serving as start symbol. (For the sake of clarity, we have adopted the standard practice of presenting terminals in boldface.) Terminal symbols are seen to label the leaves of the parse tree, while nonterminals label interior nodes. We mention a popular alternative representation of grammatical structure called a *labeled bracketing*. Thus, the structure of (10.1.3) may be represented as $[[[\textbf{the}]_{Det}[\textbf{clown}]_N]_{NP}[[\textbf{wept}]_{V_{intr}}]_{VP}]_S$.

What additional rules might be added in order to generate English sentences such as the following?

(a) **The woman solved the riddle.**

(b) **The child believes that the man lied.**   (10.1.4)

(c) **The child believes the man lied.**

Sentence (10.1.4)(a) suggests adding a production

$$VP \to V_{tr}\, NP$$

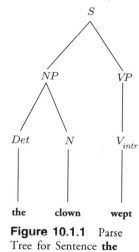

Figure 10.1.1 Parse Tree for Sentence **the clown wept**.

so as to accommodate transitive verbs. Sentences (10.1.4)(b) and (c) prompt us to introduce productions

$$NP \to \textbf{that}\ S \mid S$$

These new productions, together with additional productions for each of the new terminal symbols

$$N \to \textbf{woman} \mid \textbf{riddle}$$
$$V_{tr} \to \textbf{believes} \mid \textbf{solved}$$
$$V_{intr} \to \textbf{lied}$$

are enough to enable the generation of sentences (10.1.4)-(a)–(c). A parse tree for (10.1.4)(b) is presented in Figure 10.1.2.

Collecting together all of the productions introduced thus far, we have a context-free grammar consisting of the 16 productions

$$S \to NP\,VP \qquad (10.1.5)$$
$$NP \to Det\,N \mid \textbf{that}\ S \mid S$$
$$VP \to V_{intr} \mid V_{tr}\,NP$$
$$Det \to \textbf{the}$$
$$N \to \textbf{child} \mid \textbf{clown} \mid \textbf{man} \mid \textbf{riddle} \mid \textbf{woman}$$
$$V_{intr} \to \textbf{wept} \mid \textbf{lied}$$
$$V_{tr} \to \textbf{believes} \mid \textbf{solved}$$

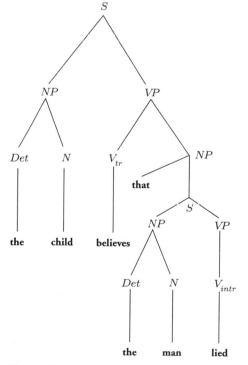

Figure 10.1.2 Parse Tree for sentence **the child believes that the man lied**.

It is easy to see that we will not be able to construct a parse tree for a string of English words such as **wept the solved believes woman lied that child clown** using the productions at (10.1.5). On the other hand, we *can* construct a parse tree for the unusual

$$\textbf{The riddle believes that the woman believes.} \qquad (10.1.6)$$

It is convenient in the present context to regard (10.1.6) as grammatical despite its apparent meaninglessness. (It would then be the task of the semantic component of our theory of English to explain *why* (10.1.6) is meaningless.)

Of course, the grammar of (10.1.5) models only a very small subset of (the set of all grammatical strings of) English. In point of fact, according to current linguistic theory, no grammar, consisting solely of rules such as (10.1.5), by itself gives a fully adequate account of the syntax of English. Rather, it is generally held that such productions must be supplemented by a different sort of rule commonly known as a *movement rule* or *transformation rule*. We close our discussion with a brief description of this second sort of rule, followed by an explanation for why such rules appear to be needed.

Let us consider the sentence

$$\textbf{The woman has solved the riddle.} \qquad (10.1.7)$$

Supplementing the productions of (10.1.5) with productions

$$VP \rightarrow Aux \, V \, NP$$

$$Aux \rightarrow \textbf{has}$$

we obtain the following labeled bracketing for (10.1.7):

$$[[[\textbf{the}]_{Det}[\textbf{woman}]_N]_{NP}[[\textbf{has}]_{Aux}[\textbf{solved}]_{V_{tr}}[[\textbf{the}]_{Det}[\textbf{riddle}]_N]_{NP}]_{VP}]_S$$

Next, consider the question-sentence

$$\textbf{Which riddle has the woman solved?} \qquad (10.1.8)$$

We assign **which** to the category *determiner* by adding production

$$Det \rightarrow \textbf{which}$$

to our grammar. It then becomes possible to analyze (10.1.8) in two steps. As step 1, the string

$$\textbf{The woman has solved which riddle.} \qquad (10.1.9)$$

is generated using the productions of (10.1.5) as supplemented. In other words, the underlying structure or *deep structure* of (10.1.8) is taken to be

$$[[[\textbf{the}]_{Det}[\textbf{woman}]_N]_{NP}[[\textbf{has}]_{Aux}[\textbf{solved}]_{V_{tr}}[[\textbf{which}]_{Det}[\textbf{riddle}]_N]_{NP}]_{VP}]_S \qquad (10.1.10)$$

where elements **which riddle**, **has**, and **solved** are seen to make up a single *VP* constituent. Afterward, as step 2, an obligatory *Rule of wh-Movement* is applied to (10.1.9) so as to move the noun phrase **which**

riddle as well as the auxiliary **has** to the front of the sentence. One thereby obtains

$$\{\textbf{which riddle}\} \ \{\textbf{has}\} \ \textbf{The woman} \ \textit{has} \ \textbf{solved} \ \textit{which riddle}$$

which is none other than (10.1.8). We are not to think of this movement of wh-phrase and auxiliary as in any way altering the deep structural analysis of (10.1.8) as presented in (10.1.10), however. In other words, the noun phrase $[[\textbf{which}]_{Det}[\textbf{riddle}]_N]_{NP}$ and auxiliary $[\textbf{has}]_{Aux}$ remain integral parts of the verb phrase $[[\textbf{has}]_{Aux}[\textbf{solved}]_{V_{tr}}[[\textbf{which}]_{Det}[\textbf{riddle}]_N]_{NP}]_{VP}$ despite the splitting up of these components on the *surface-structural level*. Our analysis entails that, at the level of deep structure, elements **which riddle**, **has**, and **solved** make up a single VP constituent that has become discontinuous on the surface.

This simple example should be enough to enable the reader to see how movement rules, of which our Rule of wh-Movement is but a single instance, interact with context-free productions to provide a theoretical account of English syntax. We still want to explain why it has been felt that context-free productions by themselves cannot adequately account for sentences such as (10.1.8). Our explanation will rely upon the traditional distinction between transitive and intransitive verbs. Suppose, for the sake of argument, that we were to analyze (10.1.8) without introducing wh-movement. This would seem to suggest that, however (10.1.8) is to be analyzed syntactically, elements **which riddle**, **has**, and **solved** do not make up a single discontinuous constituent, as was suggested by our earlier analysis involving wh-movement. Instead, these elements would be functioning as distinct and independent constituents, as hinted in

$$[\textbf{which riddle}]_? [\textbf{has}]_? [\textbf{the woman}]_{NP} [\textbf{solved}]_{VP} \qquad (10.1.11)$$

But if something like the analysis of (10.1.11) were correct, we should expect there to be other grammatical sentences in which transitive **solved**, by itself, would function as a verb phrase—as it appears to do in (10.1.11). But no such grammatical English sentences exist, as the reader can see easily enough by considering

    (a)   **The man solved.**   (10.1.12)

    (b)   **The woman on the fourth floor solved.**

    (c)   **The child thinks the woman solved.**

Since sentences such as (10.1.12) are generally ungrammatical, we conclude that **solved** by itself cannot serve as sentence verb phrase in any sentence and, in particular, cannot be serving as verb phrase in (10.1.8). Thus, the analysis suggested by (10.1.11) must be rejected. Some other, alternative analysis of (10.1.8) is needed, and it is for this reason that the Rule of wh-Movement was introduced.

This concludes our consideration of the role of context-free grammars in the study of the syntax of natural language. In the remainder of this chapter, formal languages and programming languages will be the exclusive focus. (The linguist's movement rules will never be mentioned again.) We conclude this section with a simple example illustrating the applicability of context-free grammars to the syntax of programming languages.

EXAMPLE 10.1.1 (LISP S-expressions) In the AI programming language LISP, both data as well as program statements themselves are presented as so-called *S-expressions*. Letting *a* and *b* be two

LISP *atoms*, we may define the class of LISP *S*-expressions over $\{a, b\}$ inductively as the smallest class containing

(i)　The two atoms a and b

(ii)　Any *list* of zero or more *S*-expressions over $\{a, b\}$

(iii)　Any *dotted pair* of *S*-expressions over $\{a, b\}$.

For instance, all of the following are *S*-expressions over $\{a, b\}$.

$$a \quad () \quad (b) \quad (a\,b) \quad (a\,.\,b) \quad (a\,b\,a) \quad (a\,.\,(a\,.\,b)) \quad ((\,)\,a\,b)\,(a\,.\,a)) \qquad (10.1.13)$$

The context-free grammar G with the eight productions

$$S \to A \mid (L) \mid (D)$$

$$A \to a \mid b$$

$$L \to S\,L \mid$$

$$D \to S\,.\,S$$

can be seen to generate the class of all *S*-expressions over $\{a, b\}$. For example, the derivation

$$S \Rightarrow (L)$$

$$\Rightarrow (S\,L)$$

$$\Rightarrow (S\,S\,L)$$

$$\Rightarrow (S\,S)$$

$$\Rightarrow (A\,S)$$

$$\Rightarrow (A\,A)$$

$$\Rightarrow (a\,A)$$

$$\Rightarrow (a\,b)$$

shows that G generates the two-atom list $(a\,b)$. As was implicit at (10.1.13), we understand G to be a *noncatenating grammar*. In contrast, all of the generative grammars introduced in §9.8 and §9.9 were catenating grammars. But, of course, the reader has encountered noncatenating grammars already. (Compare **The woman solved the riddle** and **Thewomansolvedtheriddle**.)

§10.2 Normal Forms for Context-Free Grammars

It is useful to know that the form of context-free grammars can be greatly restricted without any loss of generative power. Consider the presence of so-called ε-productions within a grammar G. They are sometimes essential. However, if the language $L(G)$ does not contain ε, then, in fact, there always exists an equivalent context-free grammar G' that contains no ε-productions. As an example, consider the grammar G with productions

$$S \rightarrow aXb$$

$$X \rightarrow aXb \mid$$

It is easily seen that $L(G)$ is the language consisting of all words of the form $a^n b^n$ for $n \geq 1$. The second production for X here is an ε-production. Since ε is not actually in $L(G)$, we can find an equivalent grammar G' with no ε-productions. Here it is:

$$S \rightarrow aXb \mid ab$$

$$X \rightarrow aXb \mid ab$$

More generally, we have

THEOREM 10.1: Suppose that G is a context-free grammar with ε-productions such that $L(G)$ does not contain ε. Then there exists an equivalent context-free grammar G' with no ε-productions.

PROOF Let $X \rightarrow$ be an ε-production of G. As step 1, we remove production $X \rightarrow$ from the set of productions of G. As step 2, we identify any production of G of the form $\alpha \rightarrow \beta$, where β contains one or more occurrences of X and then add to G all productions of the form $\alpha \rightarrow \beta'$, where β' is the result of eliminating one or more occurrence of X from β. (Incidentally, production $\alpha \rightarrow \beta$ is retained. We are merely *adding* productions in step 2.)

Grammar G' will be the result of carrying out steps 1 and 2 for each and every ε-production of G. If carrying out step 2 itself results in the introduction of ε-productions, then these must also be eliminated by applying steps 1 and 2. Clearly G' is a context-free grammar. (Why?) Also, it can be seen that $L(G) = L(G')$. (Why?)   Q.E.D.

EXAMPLE 10.2.1 Consider the grammar G whose five productions appear below.

$$S \rightarrow aXaY$$

$$X \rightarrow aXa \mid Y$$

$$Y \rightarrow bY \mid$$

The reader will wish to verify that G generates language $L = \{a^n b^m a^n b^k \mid n \geq 1, m \geq 0, k \geq 0\}$. For example, G generates word *aabbbaab* as well as *aab*. The second production for nonterminal Y is an ε-production. But since G does not actually generate ε, Theorem 10.1 tells us that there exists an equivalent grammar G' with no ε-productions. We show how to obtain G' from G by carrying out steps 1 and 2 of the proof of Theorem 10.1.

First, in accordance with step 1, ε-production $Y \rightarrow$ is removed altogether. Next, there are three productions of the form $\alpha \rightarrow \beta$, where β contains an occurrence of nonterminal Y. (Which ones are they?) So in step 2, the three productions

$$S \rightarrow aXa$$

$$X \rightarrow$$

$$Y \rightarrow b$$

are obtained by eliminating Y from β in each case. Integrating these new productions into what remains of G gives us a grammar with the seven productions

$$S \rightarrow aXaY \mid aXa$$

$$X \rightarrow aXa \mid Y \mid$$

$$Y \rightarrow bY \mid b$$

Since $X \rightarrow$ here is itself an ε-production, steps 1 and 2 must be repeated: ε-production $X \rightarrow$ is removed and new productions, which are the result of eliminating nonterminal X from production right-hand sides, are added. In the end, G' has the nine productions:

$$S \rightarrow aXaY \mid aXa \mid aaY \mid aa$$

$$X \rightarrow aXa \mid Y \mid aa$$

$$Y \rightarrow bY \mid b$$

The reader should verify that G' has no ε-productions and that it, too, generates language $L = \{a^n b^m a^n b^k \mid n \geq 1, m \geq 0, k \geq 0\}$.

We shall sometimes use the term *positive grammar* for a generative grammar that has no ε-productions. Similarly, a positive language will be one that does not contain ε. Evidently, if G is a positive grammar, then $L(G)$ is a positive language. (Be careful here: Language $\varnothing$ is a positive language. Why?)

As an additional example of the way in which the form of context-free productions may be restricted, consider so-called *unit productions*—that is, productions whose right-hand sides consist of a single nonterminal. To take the simplest sort of example, suppose that context-free grammar G contains the single unit production $X \rightarrow Y$ and that this is the only production for X in G. (We assume also that X is not G's start symbol.) Then G is equivalent to the context-free grammar G' formed from G by merely discarding this production and then replacing every occurrence of X on the right-hand side of any remaining production with Y. The general construction achieves the same effect in a somewhat different manner.

THEOREM 10.2: Suppose that G is a context-free grammar with unit productions. Then there exists a context-free grammar G' with no unit productions such that $L(G) = L(G')$.

PROOF Let $X \rightarrow Y$ be a unit production in G. We proceed as follows.

(1) We first remove production $X \rightarrow Y$ itself from among the productions of G.

(2) Afterward, for every production of G of the form $Y \rightarrow \beta$, where β is a (possibly empty) string of terminals and nonterminals, we now add to G the production $X \rightarrow \beta$.

Grammar G' is obtained from G by carrying out steps 1 and 2 for every unit production of G. Again, any unit productions that are introduced as the result of carrying out step 2 must themselves be eliminated. Clearly G' is a context-free grammar. (Why?) It is also easy enough to see that $L(G) = L(G')$. (Why?)   Q.E.D.

Carrying out steps 1 and 2 alone works in the usual cases but runs into problems if production cycles such as

$$S \rightarrow X$$

$$X \rightarrow Y$$

$$Y \rightarrow S$$

are present among G's productions. In such a case, we augment our procedure by the addition of a new step 0, wherein any such cycle is eliminated. (See Exercise 10.2.7, which leads to a very general algorithm that accomplishes the desired transformation.) The special case of production cycle $X \rightarrow X$ is easily dealt with: Any such production may simply be eliminated without affecting generative capacity.

EXAMPLE 10.2.2 At the end of Example 10.2.1 we had obtained the grammar

$$S \rightarrow aXaY \mid aXa \mid aaY \mid aa$$

$$X \rightarrow aXa \mid Y \mid aa$$

$$Y \rightarrow bY \mid b$$

generating language $\{a^n b^m a^n b^k \mid n \geq 1, m \geq 0, k \geq 0\}$. In the present context, let us refer to this nine-production grammar as G. We now construct an equivalent grammar G' without unit productions. To begin, we eliminate unit production $X \rightarrow Y$. Then, for each of the two productions for Y, we introduce a corresponding production for X. This gives us the 10 productions

$$S \rightarrow aXaY \mid aXa \mid aaY \mid aa$$

$$X \rightarrow aXa \mid aa$$

$$\mathbf{X \rightarrow bY \mid b}$$

$$Y \rightarrow bY \mid b$$

Note that G' has neither ε-productions nor unit productions, and, obviously, $L(G') = L(G)$.

So-called *Chomsky normal form*, which we introduce next, will be important throughout the remainder of this chapter.

DEFINITION 10.2: A context-free grammar G is said to be in *Chomsky normal form* if every production of G is either of the form $A \rightarrow BC$ or of the form $A \rightarrow a$, where A, B, and C are nonterminals and a is a terminal.

Next, we shall show that any positive context-free language—that is, any context-free language that does not contain ε, is generated by some context-free grammar that is in Chomsky normal form. We illustrate the algorithm for transforming a context-free grammar into an equivalent Chomsky normal form grammar with a simple example.

EXAMPLE 10.2.3 Consider the grammar

$$S \rightarrow aSa \mid bSb \mid a \mid b \qquad \text{(i)–(iv)}$$

which generates the language L of all odd-length palindromes. Since ε is not in L, we will be able to find an equivalent grammar in Chomsky normal form. If any ε-productions or unit productions were present, we would first transform G, using the constructions of the proofs of Theorems 10.1 and 10.2, so as to obtain an equivalent grammar without such productions. (The two algorithms may be applied in either order.) But in the case of (i)–(iv), no such transformation is necessary. We next notice that, of the four productions here, productions (iii) and (iv) already have the required form. So we turn to productions (i) and (ii). We first transform them by replacing terminals a and b with new nonterminals C_a and C_b, respectively. This yields two new productions

$$S \rightarrow C_a S C_a \qquad \boxed{C_a \text{ is a nonterminal representative of terminal } a.} \qquad \text{(i}')$$
$$S \rightarrow C_b S C_b \qquad\qquad\qquad\qquad\qquad\qquad\qquad\qquad \text{(ii}')$$

We must also add new productions

$$C_a \rightarrow a$$
$$C_b \rightarrow b$$

which relate nonterminals C_a and C_b to terminals a and b, respectively. Both productions (i$'$) and (ii$''$) have three nonterminals on the right, however, and must therefore undergo decomposition. Production (i$'$) is replaced by the two productions

$$S \rightarrow C_a Y_1$$
$$Y_1 \rightarrow S C_a$$

Similarly, decomposing (ii$'$) yields the Chomsky normal form grammar with the eight productions

$$S \rightarrow C_a Y_1 \mid C_b Y_2 \mid a \mid b$$
$$Y_1 \rightarrow S C_a$$
$$Y_2 \rightarrow S C_b$$
$$C_a \rightarrow a$$
$$C_b \rightarrow b$$

The algorithm of Example 10.2.3 may be summarized as follows.

Algorithm for Transforming a Positive Context-free Grammar G into an Equivalent Grammar G' in Chomsky Normal Form:

   Step 1. Eliminate all ε-productions and unit productions using the algorithms of the proofs of Theorems 10.1 and 10.2, respectively.

   Step 2. For any remaining production $\alpha \rightarrow \beta$ that is neither of the form $A \rightarrow BC$ nor of the form $A \rightarrow a$, we replace any occurrences of terminals $a, b, c, \ldots$ in β with new nonterminal representatives $C_a, C_b, C_c, \ldots$, respectively, and then add new productions

$$C_a \rightarrow a \qquad C_b \rightarrow b \qquad C_c \rightarrow c \quad \ldots$$

   Step 3. If the right-hand side of any production contains three or more nonterminals, then decompose this production into a series of productions the right-hand sides of which consist of exactly two nonterminals.

It should be clear that the grammar G' that is the result of applying this algorithm to a positive, context-free grammar G is equivalent to G. We may thereby take ourselves to have proved

---

THEOREM 10.3: Suppose that grammar G is a positive, context-free grammar. Then there exists positive, context-free grammar G' in Chomsky normal form with $L(G) = L(G')$.

We immediately introduce a second, highly useful normal form for context-free grammars.

DEFINITION 10.3: Let G be a context-free grammar every production of which is of the form $X \rightarrow a\alpha$ where X is a nonterminal, a is a terminal, and α is a (possibly empty) string of nonterminals. Then G is said to be in *Greibach normal form*.

EXAMPLE 10.2.4 The grammar G whose productions appear below generates the language L of nonempty, odd-length palindromes over alphabet $\Sigma = \{a, b\}$.

$$S \rightarrow aSA \mid bSB \mid a \mid b$$

$$A \rightarrow a$$

$$B \rightarrow b$$

Grammar G just happens to be in Greibach normal form. Note that the four-production grammar

$$S \rightarrow aSa \mid bSb \mid a \mid b$$

also generates L but is not in Greibach normal form.

We shall show that, for any positive, context-free language L, there exists a context-free grammar G in Greibach normal form that generates L. Our proof amounts to the presentation of an algorithm for transforming a given context-free grammar G into an equivalent grammar G' that is in Greibach normal form. The algorithm is somewhat complicated. Consequently, our first application involves a relatively simple grammar.

EXAMPLE 10.2.5 Consider the grammar G whose four productions are

$$S \rightarrow aSa \mid bSb \mid aa \mid bb$$

It is easy to see that G generates the language of nonempty palindromes of even length over $\Sigma = \{a, b\}$. Note that G is not in Greibach normal form; in fact, none of its productions has the required form.

Step 1. As a first step toward obtaining an equivalent grammar in Greibach normal form, we convert G to Chomsky normal form by applying the algorithm of the proof of Theorem 10.3. The reader should verify that the result of doing so is the grammar G' whose eight productions appear below.

$$S \rightarrow C_a Y_1 \mid C_b Y_2 \mid C_a C_a \mid C_b C_b$$

$$Y_1 \rightarrow S C_a$$

$$Y_2 \rightarrow S C_b$$

$$C_a \rightarrow a$$

$$C_b \rightarrow b$$

Step 2. Next, we order the nonterminals of the grammar that is the result of applying Step 1. The chosen order is in a sense arbitrary. However, it is best to order the nonterminals so that the start symbol of the grammar precedes all other nonterminals. In the present case, we opt for the ordering $S < C_a < C_b < Y_1 < Y_2$. Thus, nonterminal C_a follows nonterminal S, nonterminal C_b follows both C_a and S, and so on. Having ordered the nonterminals in this way, it will prove convenient to index the five nonterminals from 1 and 5. Reflecting this indexing, S is replaced by X_1, C_a by X_2, C_b by X_3, Y_1 by X_4, and Y_2 by X_5. The resulting grammar is

$$X_1 \rightarrow X_2 X_4 \mid X_3 X_5 \mid X_2 X_2 \mid X_3 X_3$$

$$X_4 \rightarrow X_1 X_2$$

$$X_5 \rightarrow X_1 X_3$$

$$X_2 \rightarrow a$$

$$X_3 \rightarrow b$$

Step 3. Next note that the right-hand sides of productions for X_1 all begin with nonterminals that follow X_1. Those for X_2 and X_3 begin with terminals. In other words, the productions for X_1, X_2, and X_3 are all "ascending" in the sense that they either begin with terminals or are such that the first nonterminal on the right has a higher subscript than the nonterminal on the left. On the other hand, the single production for X_4 is not ascending: its right-hand side begins neither with a terminal nor with a nonterminal of higher index. Note, further, that the right-hand side of the production for X_4 begins with X_1 and that there are four productions for X_1 in turn, each representing one way in which X_1 may be rewritten. We now replace production

$$X_4 \rightarrow X_1 X_2 \tag{10.2.1}$$

with the four productions

$$X_4 \rightarrow \mathbf{X_2 X_4} X_2 \mid \mathbf{X_3 X_5} X_2 \mid \mathbf{X_2 X_2} X_2 \mid \mathbf{X_3 X_3} X_2$$

In other words, for each of the four ways in which X_1 may be rewritten, we obtain a new production for X_4 through substitution for X_1 on the right-hand side of (10.2.1). This gives an equivalent context-free grammar with 11 productions:

$$X_1 \rightarrow X_2 X_4 \mid X_3 X_5 \mid X_2 X_2 \mid X_3 X_3$$

$$\mathbf{X_4} \rightarrow \mathbf{X_2 X_4} X_2 \mid \mathbf{X_3 X_5} X_2 \mid \mathbf{X_2 X_2} X_2 \mid \mathbf{X_3 X_3} X_2$$

$$X_5 \rightarrow X_1 X_3$$

$$X_2 \rightarrow a$$

$$X_3 \rightarrow b$$

The new productions for X_4 are not ascending, however. (The first nonterminal on the right has a lower index in each case.) Consequently, we iterate the foregoing replacement step. Since there is just one way in which each of X_2 and X_3 may be rewritten, we obtain the equivalent

$$X_1 \rightarrow X_2 X_4 \mid X_3 X_5 \mid X_2 X_2 \mid X_3 X_3$$

$$\mathbf{X_4} \rightarrow \mathbf{a} X_4 X_2 \mid \mathbf{b} X_5 X_2 \mid \mathbf{a} X_2 X_2 \mid \mathbf{b} X_3 X_2$$

$$X_5 \rightarrow X_1 X_3$$

$$X_2 \rightarrow a$$

$$X_3 \rightarrow b$$

At this point, all the productions for X_4 are ascending, which was our goal. The single production for X_5 is not ascending, however. Consequently, we create four new productions for X_5, one for each of the ways in which X_1 may be rewritten. The result is the 14-production grammar shown here:

$$X_1 \rightarrow X_2 X_4 \mid X_3 X_5 \mid X_2 X_2 \mid X_3 X_3$$

$$X_4 \rightarrow a X_4 X_2 \mid b X_5 X_2 \mid a X_2 X_2 \mid b X_3 X_2$$

$$X_5 \rightarrow \mathbf{X_2 X_4} X_3 \mid \mathbf{X_3 X_5} X_3 \mid \mathbf{X_2 X_2} X_3 \mid \mathbf{X_3 X_3} X_3$$

$$X_2 \rightarrow a$$

$$X_3 \rightarrow b$$

The four new productions for X_5 are not ascending but can be made so by replacing X_2 and X_3 with a and b, respectively. The result is an equivalent grammar with 14 productions, all of which are ascending.

$$X_1 \rightarrow X_2 X_4 \mid X_3 X_5 \mid X_2 X_2 \mid X_3 X_3 \qquad (10.2.2)$$

$$X_4 \rightarrow a X_4 X_2 \mid b X_5 X_2 \mid a X_2 X_2 \mid b X_3 X_2$$

$$X_5 \rightarrow \mathbf{a} X_4 X_3 \mid \mathbf{b} X_5 X_3 \mid \mathbf{a} X_2 X_3 \mid \mathbf{b} X_3 X_3$$

$$X_2 \rightarrow a$$
$$X_3 \rightarrow b$$

Step 4. It is still not the case that every production begins with a terminal, as is required for Greibach normal form. But now, working downward through the nonterminals, we can easily introduce leading terminals on the right. First, the productions for X_5 already begin with terminals. We look through our 14 productions for productions whose right-hand sides begin with X_5. There are none in this case. But if there were any, we would make some substitutions in those productions so as to introduce terminals. So we proceed to X_4. Once again, there are no productions whose right-hand sides begin with X_4, so we move down to consider nonterminal X_3. This time there are two productions whose right-hand sides begin with X_3. Since X_3 may be rewritten as **b**, we substitute **b** for the first occurrence of X_3 on the right-hand sides of those productions. After doing the same for X_2, we obtain an equivalent grammar that is in Greibach normal form.

$$X_1 \rightarrow aX_4 \mid bX_5 \mid aX_2 \mid bX_3$$

$$X_4 \rightarrow aX_4X_2 \mid bX_5X_2 \mid aX_2X_2 \mid bX_3X_2$$

$$X_5 \rightarrow aX_4X_3 \mid bX_5X_3 \mid aX_2X_3 \mid bX_3X_3$$

$$X_2 \rightarrow a$$

$$X_3 \rightarrow b$$

We summarize the application of the algorithm of Example 10.2.5 to a given positive, context-free grammar G as follows.

Algorithm for Transforming a Positive Context-Free Grammar G into an Equivalent Grammar G' in Greibach Normal Form:
   Step 1. Find an equivalent grammar G' in Chomsky normal form using the algorithm of the proof of Theorem 10.3.
   Step 2. Order the nonterminals of G' from X_1 to X_n.
   Step 3. Work upward through the nonterminals of G', making replacements so as to ensure that all productions are ultimately ascending.
   Step 4. Work downward through the nonterminals, making replacements so as to ensure that all productions are ultimately in Greibach normal form—that is, of the form $X \rightarrow a\alpha$, where X is a nonterminal, a is a terminal, and α is a (possibly empty) string of nonterminals.

A second example will illustrate a special situation that may arise. Namely, what happens if, in the course of making replacements in step 3, a left-recursive production is introduced—that is, a production of the form $X \rightarrow X\alpha$. Any such production is nonascending, and yet the replacement procedure described previously is either not applicable or not fruitful, depending upon how one wants to think about it. A new sort of replacement procedure is required in the case of such a production, as we indicate in the following example.

EXAMPLE 10.2.6 Consider the grammar below, which is already in Chomsky normal form.

$$S \to XX \mid a$$
$$X \to SS \mid b$$

Let us rename the nonterminals so as to reflect the ordering $S < X$.

$$X_1 \to X_2X_2 \mid a$$
$$X_2 \to X_1X_1 \mid b$$

The third production alone is nonascending. As before, we introduce a new production for X_2 corresponding to each of the two ways in which X_1 may be rewritten. This yields grammar

$$X_1 \to X_2X_2 \mid a$$
$$\mathbf{X_2 \to X_2X_2X_1 \mid aX_1 \mid} b$$

But a problem arises now: The third production here is left-recursive. Moreover, this third production is not the only production for nonterminal X_2: The fourth and fifth productions indicate that X_2 may be rewritten, without introducing left recursion, as either aX_1 or b. At this point, we introduce a new nonterminal—Y_2, say, so as to reflect its origin—and replace the offending left-recursive production with the four new productions

$$X_2 \to aX_1Y_2 \mid bY_2$$
$$Y_2 \to X_2X_1Y_2 \mid X_2X_1$$

The two productions for X_2 here correspond to the two ways in which X_2 can be rewritten without left recursion. The two productions for Y_2, the first of which happens to be right-recursive, capture the iterative character of the original left-recursive production (see Figure 10.2.1). Having completed step 3, our grammar now looks like this:

$$X_1 \to X_2X_2 \mid a \qquad\qquad (*)$$
$$X_2 \to aX_1 \mid b \mid aX_1Y_2 \mid bY_2$$
$$Y_2 \to X_2X_1Y_2 \mid X_2X_1 \qquad (*)$$

Ignoring for the moment the two productions for the new nonterminal Y_2, all of the productions are ascending.

We proceed downward in step 4 so as to introduce leading terminals on all right-hand sides. In fact, there are only three productions that are not of the correct form already—see boldface. Consequently, only these three require the introduction of leading terminals. Moreover, all three happen to begin with nonterminal X_2. So we create new productions for each of the four ways in which X_2 may be rewritten.

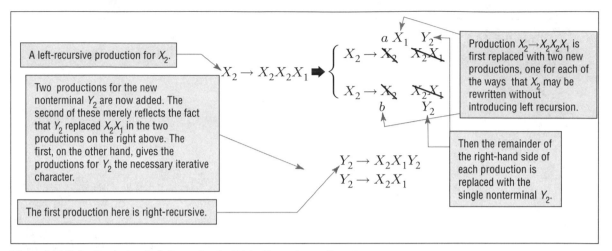

Figure 10.2.1   Replacing Left Recursion by Right Recursion at Step 3

Replacing three productions with 3 · 4 productions gives

$X_1 \rightarrow \boxed{aX_1X_2 \mid bX_2 \mid aX_1Y_2X_2 \mid bY_2X_2} \mid a$

$X_2 \rightarrow aX_1 \mid b \mid aX_1Y_2 \mid bY_2$

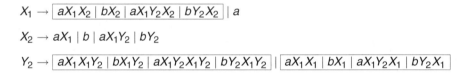

$Y_2 \rightarrow \boxed{aX_1X_1Y_2 \mid bX_1Y_2 \mid aX_1Y_2X_1Y_2 \mid bY_2X_1Y_2} \mid \boxed{aX_1X_1 \mid bX_1 \mid aX_1Y_2X_1 \mid bY_2X_1}$

This completes our presentation of the algorithm. As for why the algorithm works, consider the following.

(i) As the result of carrying out step 1 on grammar G, we are applying step 3 to a grammar that is in Chomsky normal form. This means that any substitution for the first nonterminal on the right-hand side of any production results in a new production that is either of the form $W \rightarrow Z\alpha$ or of the form $W \rightarrow a\alpha$, where Z is a nonterminal, a is a terminal, and α is a (possibly empty) string of nonterminals. (Why?) Note that, in the latter case, the production is already in Greibach normal form. In step 3 we proceed "upward" through the nonterminals, starting with the nonterminal of lowest index. This has as consequence that, at the end of step 3, every production is ascending in the sense that it is of one of the two forms given above and, if it is of the first form, then Z has strictly higher index than W.

(ii) If W is the nonterminal with highest index, then by the definition of "ascending," the right-hand side of any ascending production for W must begin with a terminal. Consequently, at the end of step 3, all productions for W are in Greibach normal form (cf. the productions for X_5 at (10.2.2)).

(iii) In step 4, we work downward through the nonterminals starting with nonterminal W of highest index. By (ii), any substitution carried out during step 4 results in the replacement of some production that is not in Greibach normal form with one or more productions that are in

Greibach normal form. Consequently, at the end of step 4, every production is in Greibach normal form.

Again, we take it to be clear enough that application of the algorithm produces an equivalent grammar. The foregoing discussion is then sufficient to justify

> **THEOREM 10.4:** Let G be a positive context-free grammar. It follows that there exists a grammar G' that is in Greibach normal form and that is equivalent to G.

§10.3 Pushdown-Stack Automata

We motivate this section by directing the reader's attention once again to issues presented in Chapter 9. In Definition 9.2 we defined the class of regular languages. It then turned out that the regular languages could be associated with a certain class of abstract machines, namely, the class of finite-state automata: It was shown in §9.6 that the class of regular languages is precisely the class of FSA-acceptable languages. Thus, with respect to their use in characterizing formal languages, the concepts *regular expression* and *finite-state automaton* are equivalent concepts. Or, to put the same idea another way, in the concept *finite-state automaton*, we have an automata-theoretic characterization of the class of regular languages.

In §10.1 we identified a new, more inclusive class of languages—that is, the class of context-free languages, of which the class of regular languages is a proper subset. We now seek an automata-theoretic characterization of this more encompassing class of languages. To get an idea of what is needed, consider again the language $\{a^n b^n | n \geq 0\}$, which, although not regular, *is* context-free. It is apparent why no finite-state automaton accepts this language: Finite-state automata lack any way of recording how many initial occurrences of a have been read. This can be taken to mean that any automata-theoretic characterization of the class of context-free languages must involve just such a capacity for counting.

The type of machine that we shall now introduce is called a *pushdown (-stack) automaton*. The term *stack* here refers to the presence of a machine component—or data structure, if you will—possessing LIFO character: the last symbol placed into the stack is the first symbol taken out. It is this stack component that will enable a pushdown automaton to maintain some record of the input symbols seen so far. Pushdown automata will, in essence, turn out to be nondeterministic finite-state automata with the addition of a single stack component. The items on this stack will themselves be symbols. Consequently, we shall speak of the automaton's *symbol stack*. We adopt standard terminology for deletions from and insertions into this stack: Each instruction will involve *popping* one symbol from the stack and then *pushing* zero or more symbols onto the stack. It will prove convenient later to assume that some distinguished *initial stack symbol*—usually #—has been pushed onto the symbol stack before execution begins. In other words, a pushdown-stack automaton will never begin execution with an empty symbol stack. The fact of this initial stack symbol will be built into our formal definition of pushdown-stack automata. Before presenting that formal definition, however, let us first describe a simple example.

EXAMPLE 10.3.1 Consider a pushdown automaton M having three states, q_0, q_1, and q_2. State q_0 is the (unique) initial state and q_1 is M's (unique) *accepting state*. Let *input alphabet* $\Sigma = \{a, b\}$ and let *stack alphabet* $\Gamma = \{\#, 0, 1\}$. Figure 10.3.1(a) presents the *transition diagram* or *state diagram* of M. As usual, each arc of the diagram represents an instruction. Consider, for example, the self-loop

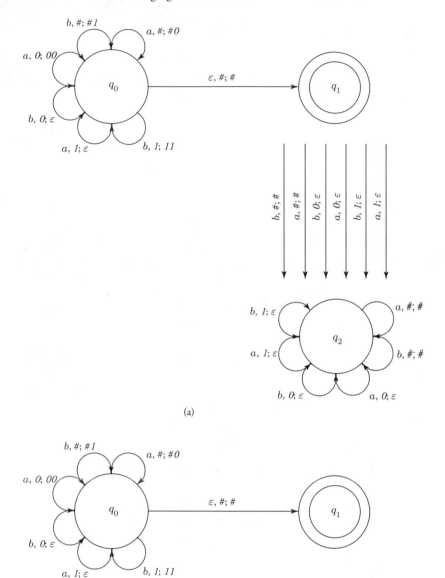

(a)

(b)

Figure 10.3.1   (a) A Fully Defined Pushdown Automaton That Accepts the Language $\{w \in \Sigma^* | n_a(w) = n_b(w)\}$, where $\Sigma = \{a, b\}$. (b) An Abbreviated Representation of the Same Machine.

labeled $a, \#; \#0$ that appears at the top of the diagram. This arc should be interpreted as specifying the following instruction: If currently in state q_0 reading input symbol a with symbol $\#$ on top the stack, then M its stack, pushes symbols $\#$ and 0 onto the stack in that order, goes (back) into state q_0, and advances its input word one symbol. (Note that, as mentioned earlier, we allow several symbols to be pushed, although precisely one symbol is popped during execution of any single instruction.) This arc in M's transition diagram corresponds, as usual, to one clause in the definition of M's *transition mapping* δ_M, namely, $\delta_M(q_0, a, \#) = (\#0, q_0)$. Similarly, the arc from state q_0 to q_1 says, in effect, that M may, without altering its symbol stack, enter state q_1 whenever initial stack symbol $\#$ is on top of the stack. Since this instruction does not advance input, we shall speak of an ε-move. Moreover, the presence of such ε-moves typically introduces a certain nondeterminism. Assuming that M is in state q_0 and that the next input symbol is a, say, M has a choice: It can advance the input, add symbol 0 to its stack, and reenter state q_0, or it can enter state q_1 without advancing the input or altering its stack. In fact, many of the pushdown-stack automata we shall consider will be nondeterministic in just this way.

- As usual, in transition diagrams for pushdown automata we shall use two circles to designate nodes corresponding to accepting states. Thus, state q_1 is M's only accepting state. State q_2 is functioning as *trap state*.

- In this first example we have been careful to present a pushdown automaton that is *fully defined* in the sense that, for every state q, every input symbol σ, and every stack symbol σ', we have an arc from q corresponding to the pair $\langle \sigma, \sigma' \rangle$. This has been done in order to clarify the relation of pushdown automata to (nondeterministic) finite-state automata, which were required to be fully defined. As is apparent from Figure 10.3.1(a), however, this requirement is not practical in the case of pushdown automata. Whereas state diagrams of finite-state automata were relatively easy to interpret, the more complicated arc labels of pushdown automaton state diagrams make it essential that these diagrams be made as simple as possible in other respects. For this reason only, we shall set aside the requirement that pushdown automata be fully defined. It will be deemed sufficient, in what follows, to present state diagrams such as that of Figure 10.3.1(b), obtained from Figure 10.3.1(a) by omitting trap state q_2 as well as all arcs leading to or from it.

We wish to see that the language accepted by M is just $\{w \in \Sigma^* | n_a(w) = n_b(w)\}$, where $\Sigma = \{a, b\}$. With reference to the transition diagram of Figure 10.3.1(b), let us verify that M accepts word *baabba* but not word *bbbbaaa*, where the notion of word acceptance for pushdown automata is essentially that given for nondeterministic finite-state automata. By convention, M begins in state q_0 reading the leftmost symbol b of input word *baabba*. Initially, its stack contains just $\#$. We see from Figure 10.3.1(b) that the transition $\delta_M(q_0, b, \#) = (\#1, q_0)$ applies in this case. This is recorded in the first line of Table 10.3.1(a), whose lines present a trace of M's operation for input word *baabba*. We shall speak informally of a *computation* of M. The last line of Table 10.3.1(a) reflects the fact that M enters accepting state q_1 and halts, having read input word *baabba* completely from left to right. By virtue of the existence of such a computation, we shall say that M *accepts word baabba*. The chart above is not the only possible computation of M for input word *baabba*, however. Nondeterminism means that there will, in general, be others as well. But M is said to accept word *baabba* by virtue of the fact that there exists *some* computation for input word *baabba* that leads to an accepting state. In the present case, it should be

Table 10.3.1(a)

Stack	Remaining Input	Transition Executed
#	*baabba*	$q_0, b, \#; \#1, q_0$
#1	*aabba*	$q_0, a, 1; \varepsilon, q_0$
#	*abba*	$q_0, a, \#; \#0, q_0$
#0	*bba*	$q_0, b, 0; \varepsilon, q_0$
#	*ba*	$q_0, b, \#; \#1, q_0$
#1	*a*	$q_0, a, 1; \varepsilon, q_0$
#	ε	$q_0, \varepsilon, \#; \#, \textcircled{q_1}$
#	(ε)	Halts in state q_1

Having read input word *baabba* completely ...

... M finds itself in accepting state q_1 and thereby accepts its input word.

Table 10.3.1(b)

Stack	Remaining Input	Transition Executed
#	bbbbaaa	$q_0, b, \#; \#1, q_0$
#1	bbbaaa	$q_0, b, 1; 11, q_0$
#11	bbaaa	$q_0, b, 1; 11, q_0$
#111	baaa	$q_0, b, 1; 11, q_0$
#1111	aaa	$q_0, a, 1; \varepsilon, q_0$
#111	aa	$q_0, a, 1; \varepsilon, q_0$
#11	a	$q_0, a, 1; \varepsilon, \boxed{q_0}$
#1	ε	Halts in state q_0

Having completely read input word *bbbbaaa* ...

... *M* finds itself in a nonaccepting state.

apparent that pushing a *0* or a *1* amounts to recording the reading of an *a* or *b*, respectively. Popping a *0* or a *1* amounts to recording the reading of a *b* or an *a*, respectively. Now let us see that *M* does not accept word *bbbbaaa*. Again, there are several computations to be considered. One of them is reflected in Table 10.3.1(b). This second computation has *M* halting in nonaccepting state q_0. The same is true for all the other computations for input word *bbbbaaa*. Since *no* computation for input word *bbbbaaa* leads to an accepting state, we are going to say that *M* does not accept input word *bbbbaaa*.

The fully defined machine of Figure 10.3.1(a) may be found at icon **Example 10.3.1** within the **PSA** folder of the accompanying software.

The reader will have noticed that the definition of word acceptance just presented makes no reference whatever to the final configuration of the machine stack. Whether or not pushdown automaton *M* accepts input word *w* depends only upon whether or not there exists some computation for *w* whereby *M* halts in an accepting state having completely read *w* from left to right. We are now ready to give a formal definition.

DEFINITION 10.4: A nondeterministic pushdown-stack automaton $M = \langle Q, \Sigma, \Gamma, \gamma, \delta_M, q_0, F \rangle$ consists of a finite, nonempty set Q of *states*, a finite *input alphabet* Σ, a finite *stack alphabet* Γ, a distinguished *stack-initialization symbol* $\gamma \in \Gamma$, a *transition mapping* δ_M, a unique *start state* $q_0 \in Q$, and a (possibly empty) set $F \subseteq Q$ of *accepting states*. Moreover, transition mapping δ_M maps triples of the form $\langle q, \sigma, \alpha \rangle$ onto pairs of the form $\langle \beta, q' \rangle$, where $q, q' \in Q, \sigma \in \Sigma \cup \{\varepsilon\}, \alpha \in \Gamma$, and $\beta \in \Gamma^*$. In general, δ_M will be multivalued. In other words, there is no assumption that δ_M maps a given triple $\langle q, \sigma, \alpha \rangle$ onto a unique pair $\langle \beta, q' \rangle$.

As mentioned earlier, we shall usually take stack-initialization symbol γ to be #.

As in the case of Turing machines, register machines, and so forth, we assume a certain notion of computation for pushdown-stack automata. That notion is implicit in Tables 10.3.1(a) and 10.3.1(b). (We could define it formally but shall not bother.) We should like to say what it is for a pushdown automaton to halt, however. Namely, *M* will halt if either of the following is true:

(1) *M* is currently in state q, reading input symbol σ with symbol α on top of its stack, whereas, δ_M is undefined for triple $\langle q, \sigma, \alpha \rangle$ as well as for triple $\langle q, \sigma, \varepsilon \rangle$;

(2) *M* is currently in state q with α on top of its stack, having completely read its input word, whereas δ_M is undefined for triple $\langle q, \sigma, \varepsilon \rangle$.

This is, of course, just a formal way of saying that M will halt just in case no instruction speaks to its current machine configuration.

Like finite-state automata, pushdown automata are of interest as language acceptors only. They will never serve as computers of number-theoretic functions. The formal definitions of word acceptance and language acceptance follow.

DEFINITION 10.5: Let $M = \langle Q, \Sigma, \Gamma, \gamma, \delta_M, q_0, F \rangle$ be a nondeterministic pushdown-stack automaton. We shall say that *nonempty word w over Σ is accepted by M* provided that there exists some computation of M such that, starting with its stack initialized with stack-initialization symbol γ, scanning the leftmost symbol of w, machine M ultimately halts in some accepting state after having read w completely from left to right. We shall say that *ε is accepted by M* provided that there exists some computation of M such that, starting with its stack initialized with stack-initialization symbol γ, machine M ultimately halts in some accepting state without having read anything.

As mentioned earlier, the definition of word acceptance does not require that the symbol stack be empty upon halting.

DEFINITION 10.6: *Nondeterministic pushdown-stack automaton $M = \langle Q, \Sigma, \Gamma, \gamma, \delta_M, q_0, F \rangle$ accepts language L over Σ* if M accepts all and only the words of L. Also, a language L is said to be *PSA-acceptable* if there exists some nondeterministic pushdown-stack automaton that accepts L.

We round out our discussion by considering two more simple, but instructive, examples.

EXAMPLE 10.3.2 The pushdown automaton M of Figure 10.3.2 accepts the language $\{a^n b^m | 0 \le n \le m \text{ and } m \ge 2\}$. (See icon **Example 10.3.2** within the accompanying software for a fully defined version of this machine.) Table 10.3.2(a) represents a computation of M that results in acceptance of input word *aabbb*.

Table 10.3.2(b) presents M's only computation for input word *aba*, which is not accepted. In utilizing the accompanying software to study the behavior of M for a given input word, the reader should note the absence of any need, on the user's part, to intervene so as to choose from among the various ways to continue M's computation. It is just this sort of pushdown automaton that, in §10.8 below, will be termed *deterministic*.

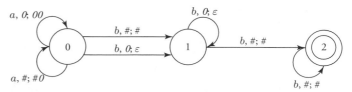

Figure 10.3.2   This machine accepts the language $\{a^n b^m | 0 \le n \le m \text{ and } m \ge 2\}$.

Table 10.3.2(a) Trace of M's Accepting Computation for Input Word *aabbb*.

Stack	Remaining Input	Transition Executed
#	*aabbb*	$q_0, a, \#; \#0, q_0$
#*0*	*abbb*	$q_0, a, 0, 00, q_0$
#*00*	*bbb*	$q_0, b, 0, \varepsilon, q_1$
#*0*	*bb*	$q_1, b, 0, \varepsilon, q_1$
#	*b*	$q_1, b, \#; \#, \text{(q}_2\text{)}$
#	ε	Halts in state q_2

> M halts in an accepting state having completely read input word *aabbb*.

Table 10.3.2(b) Trace of M's Nonaccepting Computation for Input Word *aba*.

Stack	Remaining Input	Transition Executed
#	*aba*	$q_0, a, \#; \#0, q_0$
#*0*	*ba*	$q_0, b, 0, \varepsilon, q_1$
#	*a*	$q_0, a, \#, \#0, \text{(q}_0\text{)}$
#*0*	ε	Halts in state q_0

> M halts in a nonaccepting state, having read input word *aba* completely.

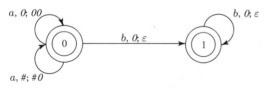

Figure 10.3.3 This machine accepts the language $\{a^n b^m \mid n \geq m \geq 0\}$.

EXAMPLE 10.3.3 The pushdown automaton M of Figure 10.3.3 accepts the language $\{a^n b^m \mid n \geq m \geq 0\}$. (A fully defined version is found at icon **Example 10.3.3**.) Table 10.3.3 presents an accepting computation for input word *aaabb*.

Table 10.3.3 Trace of M's Accepting Computation for Input Word *aaabb*.

Stack	Remaining Input	Transition Executed
#	*aaabb*	$q_0, a, \#; \#0, q_0$
#*0*	*aabb*	$q_0, a, 0, 00, q_0$
#*00*	*abb*	$q_0, a, 0, 00, q_0$
#*000*	*bb*	$q_0, b, 0, \varepsilon, q_1$
#*00*	*b*	$q_1, b, 0, \varepsilon, \text{(q}_1\text{)}$
#*0*	ε	Halts in state q_1

> M halts in an accepting state, having read input word *aaabb* completely.

As we have described matters, any pushdown automaton M pops a *single* symbol from its symbol stack during each and every instruction executed. However, it is not hard to see that relaxing this requirement has no significant theoretical consequences. In other words, we might have permitted M to pop one *or more* symbols without in any way altering the class of PSA-acceptable languages. For ease of reference later, we formulate

---

REMARK 10.3.1: An equivalent notion of pushdown-stack automaton would permit one *or more* symbols to be popped from the symbol stack during the execution of each and every instruction.

We leave the justification of Remark 10.3.1 as an exercise (see Exercise 10.3.8). This more liberal notion of pushdown automaton turns out to be of interest when one considers pushdown automata in the role of parsers.

Two final remarks regarding pushdown automata will be useful. The first is a needed clarification. Namely, we are permitting ε-moves with respect to input, which means that a machine M may choose to ignore the contents of its input buffer. On the other hand, M is not permitted to ignore its stack. Quite the contrary, M must pop its stack during each executed instruction. This has as consequence that, should stack-initialization symbol # ever be popped without replacement, then M's execution will subsequently halt—even if its input word has not been read completely.

Our second remark is primarily of technical interest. The reader will recall that in §9.7 we prohibited so-called ε-cycles within the transition diagrams of finite-state automata with ε-moves. The goal there was to ensure that all computations terminate after finitely many steps. We shall do something analogous in the case of pushdown automata and for the same reason. Note that an instruction of the form $\langle q_i, \varepsilon, \sigma; \alpha, q_j \rangle$ does not advance input. If we were to permit cycles consisting solely of such ε-moves, then infinitary computations would become possible. Since we wish all computations to be strictly finite, we shall prohibit such cycles. (None has occurred in any of our examples.) Technically, this prohibition should be built into Definition 10.4 of course, since it is a matter of what we are going to count as a pushdown automaton. But we shall be satisfied to bring this issue to the reader's attention and leave Definition 10.4 unchanged.

§10.4 An Equivalent Notion of Word Acceptance for Pushdown-Stack Automata

We immediately introduce another example of a nondeterministic pushdown automaton for the purpose of illustration.

EXAMPLE 10.4.1 Consider the language L of well-nested or balanced parentheses. This is the language containing, among others, the three strings $(())$, $()()(())$, and ε, but not the strings $((()$ and $)($. It is not difficult to see that the nondeterministic pushdown automaton M of Figure 10.4.1 accepts L. The nondeterminism here resides in the ε-move from q_0 to q_1. After all, at any point during its execution, M is reading ε and hence may choose to proceed into state q_1 provided that # is on top the symbol stack. Thus either at the first line or at the fifth line of the chart of Table 10.4.1, M might have chosen to enter state q_1.

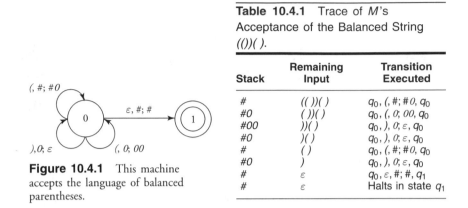

Figure 10.4.1 This machine accepts the language of balanced parentheses.

Table 10.4.1 Trace of M's Acceptance of the Balanced String $(())()$.

Stack	Remaining Input	Transition Executed
#	$(())()$	$q_0, (, \#; \#0, q_0$
#0	$())()$	$q_0, (, 0, 00, q_0$
#00	$))()$	$q_0,), 0, \varepsilon, q_0$
#0	$)()$	$q_0,), 0, \varepsilon, q_0$
#	$()$	$q_0, (, \#; \#0, q_0$
#0	$)$	$q_0,), 0, \varepsilon, q_0$
#	ε	$q_0, \varepsilon, \#; \#, q_1$
#	ε	Halts in state q_1

Table 10.4.1 provides a trace of M's acceptance of the balanced string $(())()$. Here we are using the notion of word acceptance introduced in Definition 10.5: Namely, word $(())()$ is accepted by M by virtue of the fact that, having read word $(())()$ and no more, one symbol at a time, M has halted in accepting state q_1. It just happens that in the case of the pushdown automaton of Figure 10.4.1, whenever M finds itself in accepting state q_1, having completely read input word w and having thereby accepted it, the symbol stack of M will be, for all practical purposes, empty—that is, empty except for stack-initialization symbol #. As matters stand, this is a mere side effect that in no way figures in our determination that M accepts w. This is because the definition of word acceptance by accepting state (Definition 10.5) makes no reference whatever to the ultimate contents of the symbol stack. But reflection upon this situation, which is common to several of the examples and exercises considered so far, suggests that, with respect to the issue of word acceptance, it would be equally natural to just forget about accepting states altogether and instead aim for an empty stack. This leads us to define a second, alternative notion of word acceptance for pushdown automata.

> **DEFINITION 10.7:** *Pushdown automaton M accepts word w by empty stack* provided that M ultimately halts with its stack empty, having read w (and no more) one symbol at a time from left to right.

Additionally, pushdown automaton M will be said to *accept language L by empty stack* provided that M accepts, by empty stack, all and only the words of L.

We shall begin to refer to our earlier notion of language acceptance, as presented in Definition 10.6, as *language acceptance by accepting state*. A language L will be *PSA-acceptable by accepting state* if there exists a pushdown automaton that accepts L by accepting state. Similarly, a language L will be said to be *PSA-acceptable by empty stack* if there exists a pushdown automaton that accepts L by empty stack. We note then that the pushdown automaton M of Example 10.4.1 and Figure 10.4.1 accepts the language of balanced parentheses by accepting state. It is also noteworthy that, for any balanced, and hence accepted, input string, M's symbol stack, both at inception and termination, is empty except for symbol #. Moreover, it is a trivial matter to alter M so as to obtain a new machine M' such that, for an arbitrary balanced input string, M''s symbol stack upon termination will be completely empty. This suggests a certain equivalence. Namely, might it be the case that, given arbitrary language L, there exists a pushdown automaton that accepts L by accepting state if and only if there exists a pushdown automaton that accepts L by empty stack? In fact, we shall be able to prove this very proposition, which will be useful later in obtaining the central equivalence result of this chapter.

Before turning to a proof, however, it is worth making a few remarks so as to avoid confusion later. First, we note that Definition 10.7 makes no reference whatever to accepting states. In fact, whenever our interest in pushdown automaton M lies in its role as a language acceptor by empty stack, we shall assume that its set of accepting states is empty. This is not strictly necessary, however, since even pushdown automata with accepting states can yet accept words by empty stack. We emphasize that in Definition 10.6 we have not introduced a new concept of pushdown-stack automaton. Rather, pushdown automata continue to be just what they were defined to be in Definition 10.4—seven-tuples of the form $\langle Q, \Sigma, \Gamma, \delta_M, \gamma, q_0, F \rangle$. What *is* new is our alternative notion of word acceptance for pushdown automata.

We now turn to the proof of the equivalence of our two notions of language acceptance for pushdown automata. We shall show that a language L is PSA-acceptable by accepting state if and only if it is PSA-acceptable by empty stack. In some cases, it may just happen that one and the same pushdown automaton accepts L by accepting state and also accepts L by empty stack. In general, however, this will not be the case. Namely, a pushdown automaton that accepts L by accepting state will most likely be distinct from any pushdown automaton M' that accepts L by empty stack. Theorems 10.5(a) and 10.5(b) together state only that L is accepted by *some* pushdown automaton M in the one way if and only if L is accepted by *some* (probably different) pushdown automaton M' in the other way.

Preliminary to the presentation of these two theorems, we illustrate the construction involved in the first of them with a simple example.

EXAMPLE 10.4.2 The pushdown automaton M of Figure 10.4.2(a) accepts language $L = \{a^n b^m \mid n > m \geq 0\}$ by accepting state but not by empty stack. The trace of Table 10.4.2 shows that when M halts in state q_2, having accepted word *aaabb* by accepting state, symbols 0 and $\#$ are yet on its stack. We now show that M can be transformed into a pushdown automaton M' that accepts L by empty stack. The new pushdown automaton M' is shown in Figure 10.4.2(b), with regard to which we note the following:

- M' has its own bottom-of-stack symbol $\$$ that is assumed to be on the stack at the inception of execution.

- We have added a new initial state q_0' and a single ε-move from q_0' to q_0 that causes M's stack-initialization symbol $\#$ to be pushed (see (i) of Figure 10.4.2(b)).

- In addition, from accepting state q_2 to a new state q_{empty} we add three ε-moves—one for each stack symbol of M' (see (ii) of Figure 10.4.2(b)). Corresponding ε-moves are added at (iii) as instructions leading from q_{empty} to q_{empty}. Taken together, these ε-moves permit M' to empty its stack once in state q_2.

The trace of Table 10.4.3 will enable the reader to verify that M' accepts word *aaabb* by empty stack. Some of the ε-moves added in forming M' from M are useless in this *particular* case. Our goal, however, is a completely general construction that may be applied to any pushdown automaton, accepting some language L by accepting state, so as to yield a new machine M' that accepts L by empty stack. The new stack-initialization symbol $\$$ is required in order to prevent M' from accepting words not accepted by M (see Exercise 10.4.4).

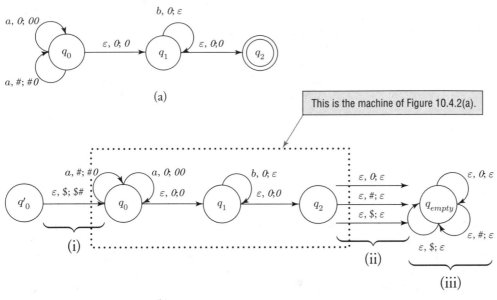

Figure 10.4.2   (a) This machine accepts the language $\{a^n b^m | n > m \geq 0\}$ by terminal state. (b) This machine accepts $\{a^n b^m | n > m \geq 0\}$ by empty stack.

Table 10.4.2   Trace of M's Accepting Computation for Input Word *aaabb*.

Stack	Remaining Input	Transition Executed
#	aaabb	$q_0, a, \#; \#0, q_0$
#0	aabb	$q_0, a, 0; 00, q_0$
#00	abb	$q_0, a, 0; 00, q_0$
#000	bb	$q_0, \varepsilon, 0; 0, q_1$
#000	bb	$q_1, b, 0; \varepsilon, q_1$
#00	b	$q_1, b, 0; \varepsilon, q_1$
#0	ε	$q_1, \varepsilon, 0; 0, q_2$
#0	ε	Halts in state q_2

THEOREM 10.5(a): If there exists a pushdown automaton M that accepts language L by accepting state, then there exists a pushdown automaton M' that accepts L by empty stack.

PROOF We describe, in rough outline, a nondeterministic pushdown automaton M' that simulates the execution of M, for arbitrary word w, up to the point where M enters an accepting state, possibly halting and thereby accepting w by accepting state. At this point, M' will have the option to empty its symbol stack, thus accepting w by empty stack.

We introduce a special stack symbol $\$$ to serve as the stack-initialization symbol of M'. Its function is to prevent M' from accepting words not accepted by M, as might otherwise occur without the

Table 10.4.3

Stack	Remaining Input	Transition Executed
$	aaabb	$q_0', \varepsilon, \$; \$\#, q_0$
$#	aaabb	$q_0, a, \#; \#0, q_0$
$#0	aabb	$q_0, a, 0; 00, q_0$
$#00	abb	$q_0, a, 0; 00, q_0$
$#000	bb	$q_0, \varepsilon, 0; 0, q_1$
$#000	bb	$q_1, b, 0; \varepsilon, q_1$
$#00	b	$q_1, b, 0; \varepsilon, q_1$
$#0	ε	$q_1, \varepsilon, 0; 0, q_2$
$#0	ε	$q_2, \varepsilon, 0; \varepsilon, q_{empty}$
$#	ε	$q_{empty}, \varepsilon, \#; \varepsilon, q_{empty}$
$	ε	$q_{empty}, \varepsilon, \$; \varepsilon, q_{empty}$
ε	ε	Halts in state q_{empty}

> M halts with its stack empty, having completely read input word *aaabb*.

precaution of a special stack-initialization symbol. We shall need to augment the state set of M with two additional states q_0' and q_{empty}. State q_0' will serve as the initial state of M'. When M' enters state q_{empty}, on the other hand, it can choose to go into stack-emptying mode. Reflecting the foregoing remarks, the transition function $\delta_{M'}$ of M' will be just like δ_M except for the following changes or additions.

(i) To get from the initial state of M' to the point where the simulation of M can begin, we set $\delta_{M'}(q_0', \varepsilon, \$) = (\$\#, q_0)$, where q_0 is the initial state of M (see (i) in Figure 10.4.2(b)).

(ii) For every accepting state q_t of M, we add instruction $\delta_{M'}(q_t, \varepsilon, \sigma) = (\varepsilon, q_{empty})$, for every symbol σ in the stack alphabet of M'. The effect of these additions is to permit M', finding itself in an accepting state of M, to proceed into stack-emptying mode (see (ii) in Figure 10.4.2(b)).

(iii) Finally, so as to implement stack erasure once in state q_{empty}, we define $\delta_{M'}(q_{empty}, \varepsilon, \sigma) = (\varepsilon, q_{empty})$ for arbitrary σ in the stack alphabet of M'. In other words, once in state q_{empty}, machine M' cannot leave it and proceeds to pop its entire stack (see (iii) in Figure 10.4.2(b)).

The description of simulator M' is complete. It remains to show that if M accepts language L by accepting state, then M' accepts L by empty stack. There are two parts to this demonstration.

(1) First, suppose that w is a word of L, which, by assumption, means that M accepts w by accepting state. Suppose, further, that M' is started scanning the leftmost symbol of w with just $\$$ on its stack. By (i), we see that, without reading anything, M' may go into M's start state q_0, simultaneously pushing M's bottom-most stack symbol #. So the symbol stack of M' now contains two symbols: # on top and $\$$ beneath it. Once in state q_0, since $\delta_{M'}$ is all of δ_M and then some, M' may behave exactly as M would do. In particular, having read w completely from left to right, M' may find itself in one of the accepting states of M. And having done that, M' can further choose to enter state q_{empty} as the result of the additions at (ii). But, as at (iii), this will have M' emptying its symbol stack completely, which means that M' accepts w by empty stack. We have shown that, if M accepts w by accepting state, then M' accepts w by empty stack.

(2) We must also convince ourselves that, if simulator M' accepts word w by empty stack, then M accepts w by accepting state. Thus, suppose that M' accepts w by empty stack. We reason backwards, so to speak. Since, by assumption, the symbol stack of M' is empty upon termination, M' must have found its way to state q_{empty}, since that is the only way in which stack-initialization symbol $\$$ in particular could have been popped. But the only way in which M' could find itself in state q_{empty} is by having previously entered an accepting state q_t, say, of M. Moreover, since M' accepts w, reflection on (ii) and (iii) show that M' will have read w completely by the time it enters state q_t for the last time. But since M' begins reading w only after having pushed #, it is evident that, in reading through w and arriving at state q_t, machine M' was merely simulating possible moves of M. That is, M accepts w by accepting state.   Q.E.D.

The proof of the next proposition is similar in style. Again, it is a matter of first describing the construction of a pushdown automaton M', given another pushdown automaton M. This time, however, M accepts by empty stack whereas M' accepts by accepting state. We must then go on to show that the two machines are equivalent in the sense that the language accepted by M, by empty stack, is identical to the language accepted by M', by accepting state.

> **THEOREM 10.5(b):** If there exists a pushdown automaton M that accepts language L by empty stack, then there exists a pushdown automaton M' that accepts L by accepting state.

PROOF Suppose that pushdown automaton M accepts L by empty stack. We may assume without loss of generality that M has no accepting states. Let # be the stack-initialization symbol of M. Now let M' be the pushdown automaton constructed from M as follows. First, M' has its own start state q_0', a unique accepting state q_t, say, as well its own stack-initialization symbol $\$$. The operation of M' on accepted word w proceeds as described below.

(i) M' first places stack symbol # just above its own $\$$ and enters start state q_0 of M.

(ii) Next, M' simulates the behavior of M on input word w.

(iii) Should M', in the course of simulating M, just happen to empty its stack at any point, then M' can recognize that this has happened, since symbol $\$$ will be on top the stack. In this case, M' may choose to enter q_t and halt. In particular, should M just happen to empty its stack after having read w completely, then M', having read w completely, will find $\$$ on top its stack and may then enter accepting state q_t before halting.

An M' behaving as in (i)–(iii) can be constructed by transforming the state diagram of M as follows.

(i')   We draw an arc labeled $\varepsilon, \$; \$\#$ from q_0' to q_0.

(ii') We preserve all arcs linking states of M.

(iii') We add an arc labeled $\varepsilon, \$; \$$ from *each* state of M to the new accepting state q_t.

Assuming that L is the language that M accepts by empty stack, it remains to be shown that the language accepted by M' by accepting state is just L. As in the proof of Theorem 10.5(a), there are two parts to this demonstration.

(1) First, let w be a word of L. By assumption, this means that M accepts w by empty stack. It should be easy, given what was said above, to convince oneself that M' will accept w by accepting state.

(2) As for the other direction, one reasons backwards once again. Namely, assume that M' accepts w by accepting state. Thus, having read w completely, M' finds itself in its unique accepting state q_t. But there is only one way in which M' could arrive in this state. Namely, M' must have simulated the operation of M in emptying its stack after having read w completely. In other words, M must accept w by empty stack. Q.E.D.

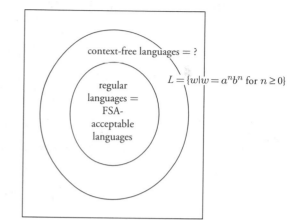

$U = \{L | L$ a language over $\Sigma\}$ for given alphabet $\Sigma = \{a, b\}$

context-free languages $= ?$

$L = \{w | w = a^n b^n$ for $n \geq 0\}$

regular languages $=$ FSA-acceptable languages

Figure 10.4.3

Henceforth, since the two notions of language acceptance by pushdown automata are equivalent, we shall speak only of *acceptance* without specifying which notion of acceptance we have in mind.

In §10.5, which follows, we shall turn to the central result of this chapter—an equivalence result that relates the class of context-free languages and the class of PSA-acceptable languages. Namely, we shall show that the class of context-free languages is precisely the class of PSA-acceptable languages. The formulation is analogous to that of Theorems 9.12 and 9.13, where it was shown that the class of regular languages is identical with the class of FSA-acceptable languages (see Figure 10.4.3). In what follows, we shall freely appeal to the equivalence of our two notions of language acceptance for pushdown automata.

Incidentally, the purpose of stack-initialization symbol γ, which may have been obscure up to this point, can now be explained. First, if symbol stacks were empty initially, then *every* pushdown automaton would accept ε by empty stack. This, in turn, would put ε in *every* language accepted by empty stack by any pushdown automaton whatever. But since ε is not in every language that is PSA-acceptable by accepting state, this would have spoiled the equivalence of Theorems 10.5(a) and 10.5(b). So stack-initialization symbols have been introduced in order to effect this equivalence.

§10.5 The Class of Context-Free Languages Is Identical to the Class of PSA-Acceptable Languages

In this section, we present the principal equivalence result of this chapter, which pairs a grammar-theoretic characterization of a family of languages with an equivalent automata-theoretic characterization. We approach this topic by way of an example.

EXAMPLE 10.5.1 Consider the following context-free grammar G, which happens to be in Greibach normal form.

(1.1)–(1.2)	$S \rightarrow aX \mid aY$
(2.1)–(2.2)	$X \rightarrow aXY \mid aYY$
(3.1)	$Y \rightarrow b$

Grammar G generates the language $\{a^n b^n \mid n \geq 1\}$. In order to give the reader a sense of how G works, we present a *leftmost derivation* of word *aaabbb*—leftmost in the sense that it is always the leftmost nonterminal occurrence that is rewritten next.

$$
\begin{aligned}
S &\Rightarrow aX & \text{from } &\textbf{(1.1)} \\
&\Rightarrow aaXY & \text{from } &\textbf{(2.1)} \\
&\Rightarrow aaaYYY & \text{from } &\textbf{(2.2)} \\
&\Rightarrow aaabYY & \text{from } &\textbf{(3.1)} \\
&\Rightarrow aaabbY & \text{from } &\textbf{(3.1)} \\
&\Rightarrow aaabbb & \text{from } &\textbf{(3.1)}
\end{aligned}
\qquad (10.5.1)
$$

We now turn to a description of a nondeterministic pushdown automaton M that models G. Let M possess just one state q, so that q necessarily serves as M's initial state. Since we shall be interested in M as language acceptor by empty stack, we let M's accepting state set F be empty. M has input alphabet $\Sigma = \{a, b\}$ and stack alphabet $\Gamma = \{S, X, Y, \#\}$. (Note that Γ consists of the nonterminals of G plus stack-initialization symbol #.) Next we define transition function δ_M by the initialization clause

$$\delta_M(q, \varepsilon, \#) = (S, q) \qquad (0)$$

together with the five clauses below, one for each of the productions of G.

$$
\begin{aligned}
\delta_M(q, a, S) &= (X, q) & (1.1) \\
\delta_M(q, a, S) &= (Y, q) & (1.2) \\
\delta_M(q, a, X) &= (YX, q) & (2.1) \\
\delta_M(q, a, X) &= (YY, q) & (2.2) \\
\delta_M(q, b, Y) &= (\varepsilon, q) & (3.1)
\end{aligned}
$$

Table 10.5.1 presents a trace of M's operation for input word *aabbb*. Note that, in the course of accepting word *aaabbb* by empty stack, M simulates a leftmost derivation of *aaabbb* within grammar G. (To see this, compare the right column of Table 10.5.1 with annotations on the right at (10.5.1).) The correspondence between transitions of M and productions of G should make it clear that the language accepted by M is precisely the language generated by G.

The foregoing example illustrates the essential elements of the construction that will enable us to obtain, for arbitrary context-free grammar G, a pushdown automaton M such that $L(M) = L(G)$. It

Table 10.5.1 Trace of *M*'s Acceptance of *aaabbb* by Empty Stack.

Stack	Remaining Input	Transition Executed
#	aaabbb	0
S	aaabbb	1.1
X	aabbb	2.1
YX	abbb	2.2
YYY	bbb	3.1
YY	bb	3.1
Y	b	3.1
ε	ε	Halts in state q

M has emptied its stack having read input word *aaabbb* completely. Accordingly, *M* accepts word *aaabbb* by empty stack.

also points up the theoretical usefulness of Greibach normal form, which is playing an essential role here. We are ready to state and prove

THEOREM 10.6: If L is a context-free language, then there exists a pushdown automaton M that accepts L by empty stack. In other words, if L is context-free, then L is PSA-acceptable.

PROOF Language L may or may not contain ε. We consider each case separately.

- Assume first that L does *not* contain ε. Let G be a context-free grammar that generates L. By Theorem 10.4, we may assume without loss of generality that G is in Greibach normal form. As in Example 10.5.1 above, we let M be the pushdown-stack automaton with state set $Q = \{q\}$, input alphabet Σ consisting of the terminals of G, and stack alphabet Γ consisting of the nonterminals of G plus #. Finally, we define M's transition function δ as follows:
  - (i) $\delta_M(q, \varepsilon, \#) = (S, q)$, where S is the start symbol of G.
  - (ii) For each production $A \to a\beta$, where A is a nonterminal, a a terminal, and β a string of nonterminals, we have $\delta_M(q, a, A) = (\beta^R, q)$.

  M will simulate leftmost derivations within G. That is, if w is generated by G, then M will simulate a leftmost derivation of w within G, thereby accepting w by empty stack. Also, if M accepts word w by empty stack, then $S \Rightarrow_G^* w$ since M simulates a leftmost derivation of w within G.

- If $L = L(G)$ *does* contain ε, then applying the algorithms of §10.2 to G yields context-free grammar G' in Greibach normal form such that $L(G') = L(G)\backslash\{\varepsilon\}$ (see Exercise 10.2.2). Thus, applying the construction of Example 10.5.1 to G' yields a pushdown automaton M that accepts $L(G') = L(G)\backslash\{\varepsilon\}$ by empty stack. We now add to the definition of δ_M the single clause $\delta_M(q, \varepsilon, \#) = (\varepsilon, q)$ and thereby obtain pushdown automaton M' with $L(M') = L$. (Why does adding this one clause give $L(M') = L(G)$?) Q.E.D.

Since our goal is an *equivalence* between our grammar-theoretic and our automata-theoretic characterization, we shall also give a proof to the effect that any PSA-acceptable language L is generated by some context-free grammar. Again, we introduce the main ideas by way of an example.

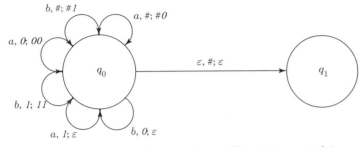

Figure 10.5.1 M accepts language $\{w \in \Sigma^* | n_a(w) = n_b(w)\}$ by empty stack.

EXAMPLE 10.5.2 The essence of the proof of Theorem 10.7 below is the following general construction, which we apply to the pushdown automaton M of Figure 10.5.1. M accepts, by empty stack, the language $\{w \in \Sigma^* | n_a(w) = n_b(w)\}$ with $\Sigma = \{a, b\}$ and is the result of modifying slightly the pushdown automaton of Figure 10.3.1(b), which accepts the same language by accepting state. M has input alphabet $\Sigma = \{a, b\}$, stack alphabet $\Gamma = \{\#, 0, 1\}$, and state set $Q = \{q_0, q_1\}$, where q_0 is M's initial state. M has no accepting states. The transition function δ_M of M is given by the clauses

$$\delta_M(q_0, \varepsilon, \#) = (\varepsilon, q_1) \tag{i}$$

$$\delta_M(q_0, a, \#) = (\#0, q_0) \tag{ii}$$

$$\delta_M(q_0, b, \#) = (\#1, q_0) \tag{iii}$$

$$\delta_M(q_0, a, 0) = (00, q_0) \tag{iv}$$

$$\delta_M(q_0, b, 0) = (\varepsilon, q_0) \tag{v}$$

$$\delta_M(q_0, a, 1) = (\varepsilon, q_0) \tag{vi}$$

$$\delta_M(q_0, b, 1) = (11, q_0) \tag{vii}$$

We shall construct a context-free grammar G that generates $L(M) = \{w \in \Sigma^* | n_a(w) = n_b(w)\}$. Moreover, if M accepts w, then a leftmost derivation of w within G will consist of a simulation of M's accepting behavior.

We show how to construct G, given M. The terminal alphabet of G will be the input alphabet $\Sigma = \{a, b\}$ of M. The set of nonterminals of G will contain a start symbol S together with the following 12 "symbols":

$$[q_0, \#, q_0] \quad [q_0, \#, q_1] \quad [q_0, 0, q_0] \quad [q_0, 0, q_1] \quad [q_0, 1, q_0] \quad [q_0, 1, q_1]$$

$$[q_1, \#, q_0] \quad [q_1, \#, q_1] \quad [q_1, 0, q_0] \quad [q_1, 0, q_1] \quad [q_1, 1, q_0] \quad [q_1, 1, q_1]$$

In other words, we have a nonterminal corresponding to each triple of the form $\langle q, \sigma, q' \rangle$, where q and q' are states and σ is an arbitrary stack alphabet symbol. (In fact, some of these nonterminals will turn out to be superfluous, as we shall see.) We may think of nonterminal $[q, \sigma, q']$ as representing M's computation, starting from state q with symbol σ is on top of the symbol stack and leading ultimately to state q'. We shall refer to this as the *transition interpretation of nonterminal* $[q, \sigma, q']$. In addition, we shall speak of q' as the *destination state* with respect to nonterminal $[q, \sigma, q']$.

As for productions, we start with

(1.1) $S \rightarrow [q_0, \#, q_0]$

(1.2) $S \rightarrow [q_0, \#, q_1]$

In other words, we have added two initialization productions that take start symbol S to each nonterminal of the form $[q_0, \#, q]$ for each $q \in Q$. (There are just two possibilities for q in the present case: we can let q be q_0 or q_1.) Next, we add productions for the nonterminals appearing on the right in productions

(1.1)–(1.2). For nonterminal $[q_0, \#, q_0]$, occurring on the right in (1.1), we focus on transitions

$$\text{(i)} \qquad \delta_M(q_0, \varepsilon, \#) = (\varepsilon, q_1)$$

$$\text{(ii)} \qquad \delta_M(q_0, a, \#) = (\#0, q_0)$$

$$\text{(iii)} \qquad \delta_M(q_0, b, \#) = (\#1, q_0)$$

since these transitions concern M's behavior when in state q_0 with # is on top the stack. We consider clauses (ii) and (iii) first. Clause (ii) will lead us to introduce two productions for nonterminal $[q_0, \#, q_0]$. These two productions will each be of the form

$$[q_0, \#, q_0] \rightarrow a[q_0, 0, \_][\_, \#, \ldots] \tag{10.5.2}$$

The entries we have made on the right in (10.5.2) reflect the nature of clause (ii) in an obvious way: In particular, the occurrence of q_0 on the right in (10.5.2) corresponds to its occurrence on the right in clause (ii). As for ... on the right In (10.5.2), we shall introduce the relevant destination state in that position. And relative to nonterminal $[q_0, \#, q_0]$, the destination state is q_0:

$$[q_0, \#, q_0] \rightarrow a[q_0, 0, \_][\_, \#, q_0] \tag{10.5.3}$$

Finally, the state positions marked $\_$ in (10.5.3) must be filled, and they must both be filled in the same way. Filling both positions with state q_0 gives us a first production

$$(2.1) \qquad\qquad [q_0, \#, q_0] \rightarrow a[q_0, 0, q_0][q_0, \#, q_0]$$

whereas filling both positions with q_1 yields a second production

$$[q_0, \#, q_0] \rightarrow a[q_0, 0, q_1][q_1, \#, q_0] \qquad (*)$$

In similar fashion, clause (iii) causes us to introduce the two productions

$$(2.2) \qquad\qquad [q_0, \#, q_0] \rightarrow b[q_0, 1, q_0][q_0, \#, q_0]$$
$$[q_0, \#, q_0] \rightarrow b[q_0, 1, q_1][q_1, \#, q_0] \qquad (*)$$

As for clause (i), since this transition does not involve pushing any symbols onto the stack, we introduce only the single ε-production

$$(2.3) \qquad\qquad [q_0, \#, q_0] \rightarrow \varepsilon$$

As for nonterminal $[q_0, \#, q_1]$, occurring on the right side of production (1.2), we similarly focus on transitions (i)–(iii) and introduce the five productions

$$(3.1) \qquad\qquad [q_0, \#, q_1] \rightarrow a[q_0, 0, q_0][q_0, \#, q_1]$$
$$[q_0, \#, q_1] \rightarrow a[q_0, 0, q_1][q_1, \#, q_1] \qquad (*)$$
$$(3.2) \qquad\qquad [q_0, \#, q_1] \rightarrow b[q_0, 1, q_0][q_0, \#, q_1]$$
$$[q_0, \#, q_1] \rightarrow b[q_0, 1, q_1][q_1, \#, q_1] \qquad (*)$$
$$(3.3) \qquad\qquad [q_0, \#, q_1] \rightarrow \varepsilon$$

On the right sides of the 12 productions introduced so far, we find six nonterminals for which we have no productions as yet. We shall consider adding productions for each of these six nonterminals. Productions are added for a given nonterminal $[q, \sigma, q']$ only if some transition of M—some clause in the definition of δ_M—describes M's behavior when in state q with σ on top of its stack. Table 10.5.2 records the productions added to grammar G for each of the six nonterminals.

We have now added another 12 productions. The only new nonterminals occurring on their right sides are $[q_1, 0, q_0]$, $[q_1, 0, q_1]$, $[q_1, 1, q_0]$ and $[q_1, 1, q_1]$; since no clauses in the definition of δ_M correspond to these four nonterminals, we have all the productions we need. In fact, we have more than we need. This is because six nonterminals are such that we have no productions whatever for them. (They are $[q_1, 0, q_0]$, $[q_1, 0, q_1]$, $[q_1, 1, q_0]$ and $[q_1, 1, q_1]$, as just mentioned, and two other nonterminals shown in the first column of Table 10.5.2.) This means, in turn, that it is not possible to derive a string of terminals using any production on whose right side one of these six nonterminals occurs. So we may safely discard all such productions. (Eight useless productions have been marked ($*$) above and in Table 10.5.2.) Doing so leaves the 16 context-free productions

(1.1)	$S \rightarrow [q_0, \#, q_0]$	
(1.2)	$S \rightarrow [q_0, \#, q_1]$	
(2.1)	$[q_0, \#, q_0] \rightarrow a[q_0, 0, q_0][q_0, \#, q_0]$	
(2.2)	$[q_0, \#, q_0] \rightarrow b[q_0, 1, q_0][q_0, \#, q_0]$	These eight productions appear on the foregoing two pages.
(2.3)	$[q_0, \#, q_0] \rightarrow \varepsilon$	
(3.1)	$[q_0, \#, q_1] \rightarrow a[q_0, 0, q_0][q_0, \#, q_1]$	
(3.2)	$[q_0, \#, q_1] \rightarrow b[q_0, 1, q_0][q_0, \#, q_1]$	
(3.3)	$[q_0, \#, q_1] \rightarrow \varepsilon$	
(4.1)	$[q_0, 0, q_0] \rightarrow a[q_0, 0, q_0][q_0, 0, q_0]$	
(4.2)	$[q_0, 0, q_0] \rightarrow b$	
(5.1)	$[q_0, 0, q_1] \rightarrow a[q_0, 0, q_0][q_0, 0, q_1]$	
(5.2)	$[q_0, 0, q_1] \rightarrow b$	These eight productions appear in the rightmost column of Table 10.5.2.
(6.1)	$[q_0, 1, q_0] \rightarrow a$	
(6.2)	$[q_0, 1, q_0] \rightarrow b[q_0, 1, q_0][q_0, 1, q_0]$	
(7.1)	$[q_0, 1, q_1] \rightarrow a$	
(7.2)	$[q_0, 1, q_1] \rightarrow b[q_0, 1, q_0][q_0, 1, q_1]$	

For purposes of comparison, we present in Table 10.5.3 a trace of an accepting computation of M for input word $abaabb$. The construction of grammar G ensures that a leftmost derivation of any word w in $L(G)$ models M's computation for input w. We can see this in the case of word $abaabb$ by comparing Table 10.5.3 with the leftmost derivation below.

Note how the contents of M's stack are reflected in the nonterminals occurring on successive lines of the derivation. Also, note the correspondence between (1) the portion of w that M has read so far and (2) the portion of w that G has generated so far (cf. Table 10.5.3).

$$S \Rightarrow [q_0, \#, q_1] \qquad \text{by (1.2)}$$
$$\Rightarrow a[q_0, 0, q_0][q_0, \#, q_1] \qquad \text{by (3.1)}$$
$$\Rightarrow ab[q_0, \#, q_1] \qquad \text{by (4.2)}$$
$$\Rightarrow aba[q_0, 0, q_0][q_0, \#, q_1] \qquad \text{by (3.1)}$$
$$\Rightarrow abaa[q_0, 0, q_0][q_0, 0, q_0][q_0, \#, q_1] \qquad \text{by (4.1)}$$

Table 10.5.2

Nonterminal	Relevant Transition of M	Productions Added to G for this Nonterminal	
$[q_0, 0, q_0]$	(iv) $\delta_M(q_0, a, 0) = (00, q_0)$	$[q_0, 0, q_0] \rightarrow a[q_0, 0, q_0][q_0, 0, q_0]$	
		$[q_0, 0, q_0] \rightarrow a[q_0, 0, q_1][q_1, 0, q_0]$ (*)	This production is useless in that there are no productions for nonterminal $[q_1, 0, q_0]$ occurring on its right side.
	(v) $\delta_M(q_0, b, 0) = (\varepsilon, q_0)$	$[q_0, 0, q_0] \rightarrow b$	
$[q_0, 0, q_1]$	(iv) $\delta_M(q_0, a, 0) = (00, q_0)$	$[q_0, 0, q_1] \rightarrow a[q_0, 0, q_0][q_0, 0, q_1]$	
		$[q_0, 0, q_1] \rightarrow a[q_0, 0, q_1][q_1, 0, q_1]$ (*)	
	(v) $\delta_M(q_0, b, 0) = (\varepsilon, q_0)$	$[q_0, 0, q_1] \rightarrow b$	
$[q_1, \#, q_0]$	none	no productions added	
$[q_0, 1, q_0]$	(vi) $\delta_M(q_0, a, 1) = (\varepsilon, q_0)$	$[q_0, 1, q_0] \rightarrow a$	
	(vii) $\delta_M(q_0, b, 1) = (11, q_0)$	$[q_0, 1, q_0] \rightarrow b[q_0, 1, q_0][q_0, 1, q_0]$	
		$[q_0, 1, q_0] \rightarrow b[q_0, 1, q_1][q_1, 1, q_0]$ (*)	
$[q_0, 1, q_1]$	(vi) $\delta_M(q_0, a, 1) = (\varepsilon, q_0)$	$[q_0, 1, q_1] \rightarrow a$	
	(vii) $\delta_M(q_0, b, 1) = (11, q_0)$	$[q_0, 1, q_1] \rightarrow b[q_0, 1, q_0][q_0, 1, q_1]$	
		$[q_0, 1, q_1] \rightarrow b[q_0, 1, q_1][q_1, 1, q_1]$ (*)	
$[q_1, \#, q_1]$	none	no productions added	

$$\Rightarrow abaab[q_0, 0, q_0][q_0, \#, q_1] \qquad \text{by (4.2)}$$
$$\Rightarrow abaabb[q_0, \#, q_1] \qquad \text{by (4.2)}$$
$$\Rightarrow abaabb \qquad \text{by (3.3)}$$

As for why the construction works, we note that, in accordance with the transition interpretation of nonterminal $[q, \sigma, q']$, each production for $[q, \sigma, q']$ is a partial description of one way in which M, starting in state q with symbol σ on top of its stack, could conceivably come to be in state q'. Now some of these descriptions may turn out to be dead ends, so to speak. But that does not prevent the language generated by G from being identical with the language accepted by nondeterministic M.

Our general argument can now be stated. First, suppose that L is a PSA-acceptable language. By Theorem 10.5(a), we can, without loss of generality, assume that L is accepted by empty stack by some pushdown automaton M. Now the construction of Example 10.5.2 is applied to M so as to yield a context-free grammar G that generates L. We thus take ourselves to have proved

THEOREM 10.7: If language L is PSA-acceptable, then L is context-free.

We round out this section with a consideration of the relation between finite-state automata and the pushdown-stack automata. The finite-state automaton of Figure 10.5.2(a) accepts the language denoted by regular expression a^*b. It is now trivial to turn this finite-state automaton into a pushdown automaton that accepts the same language, as we now show. Thus, corresponding to the b-arc from q_0 to q_1 in Figure 10.5.2(a), we have in Figure 10.5.2(b) an arc labeled $b, \#; \#$.

Table 10.5.3 Trace of M's Acceptance of Input Word $abaabb$.

Stack	Remaining Input	Transition Executed
$\#$	$abaabb$	$q_0, a, \#; \#0, q_0$
$\#0$	$baabb$	$q_0, b, 0; \varepsilon, q_0$
$\#$	$aabb$	$q_0, a, \#; \#0, q_0$
$\#0$	abb	$q_0, a, 0; 00, q_0$
$\#00$	bb	$q_0, b, 0; \varepsilon, q_0$
$\#0$	b	$q_0, b, 0; \varepsilon, q_0$
$\#$	ε	$q_0, \varepsilon, \#; \varepsilon, q_1$
ε	ε	Halts in state 1_1

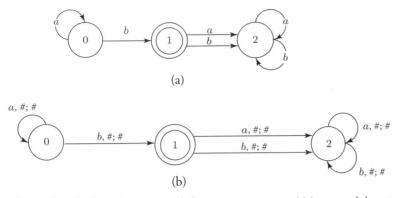

Figure 10.5.2   Transformation of a finite-state automaton (a) into a pushdown-stack automaton (b) accepting the same language.

Every transition of the constructed pushdown automaton involves popping # and then pushing it back onto the stack. The result is that the stack is playing no real role in the computation: The pushdown automaton of Figure 10.5.2(b) merely reads its input word and halts. This construction directly justifies

REMARK 10.5.2: Any FSA-acceptable language is PSA-acceptable.

Using Remark 10.5.2 we can present an alternative argument for our earlier assertion, given in §10.1, that every regular language is context-free. Namely, suppose that language L is regular; that is, suppose that L is denoted by a regular expression. Then, by Theorem 9.12, L is accepted by some finite-state automaton. But now by Remark 10.5.2, L is accepted by a pushdown automaton as well. It follows from Theorem 10.7 that L is context-free.

§10.6 Closure Properties of the Family of Context-Free Languages

In Chapter 9 we saw that the class of regular languages is closed under all of the standard language-forming operations: If L_1 and L_2 are both regular, then so are $L_1 \cup L_2$, $L_1 \cap L_2$, $L_1 \backslash L_2$, $L_1.L_2$, L_1^c, and L_1^R. We shall see that some of these closure results are obtainable in the case of the context-free languages as well. Moreover, those that are not available outright can at least be approximated.

Let L_1 and L_2 be languages over alphabets Σ_1 and Σ_2, respectively. It is easy to see that $L_1 \cup L_2$ is context-free if L_1 and L_2 are. For suppose context-free grammars G_1 and G_2 are given such that $L_1 = L(G_1)$ and $L_2 = L(G_2)$. We can assume that G_1 and G_2 have no nonterminals in common. (If nonterminals are shared, then we simply introduce different letters for some of them.) Suppose that the start symbols of G_1 and G_2 are S_1 and S_2, respectively. We then form a new context-free grammar G^* with start symbol S and having as its productions (i) all productions of G_1, (ii) all productions of G_2, and (iii) the two additional productions $S \rightarrow S_1 | S_2$. It should be plain that $L(G^*)$ will contain every word of L_1 as well as every word of L_2. Moreover, any word of $L(G^*)$ will be a word of $L(G_1)$, or a word of $L(G_2)$, or both. That is, $L(G^*) = L_1 \cup L_2$. We have proved

---

THEOREM 10.8: If L_1 and L_2 are context-free, then so is $L_1 \cup L_2$. That is, the class of context-free languages is closed under union.

It is natural to hope for closure under intersection. But in §10.7, which follows, we shall see that the class of context-free languages is not closed under intersection. We must be satisfied to obtain the following theorem, which is more restricted.

THEOREM 10.9: If L_1 is a context-free language and L_2 is a regular language, then $L_1 \cap L_2$ is a context-free language. One says that the class of context-free languages is *closed under regular intersection*.

PROOF Suppose that L_1 is a context-free language and that L_2 is a regular language. For the sake of simplicity only, we assume that L_1 and L_2 are languages over one and the same alphabet Σ (see Exercise 10.6.4). Then by Theorem 10.6, there exists a nondeterministic pushdown automaton $M_1 = \langle Q_1, \Sigma, \Gamma_1, \delta_1, q_0^1, \gamma_1, F_1 \rangle$ that accepts L_1 by accepting state. By Theorem 9.12, there exists a finite-state automaton $M_2 = \langle Q_2, \Sigma, \delta_2, q_0^2, F_2 \rangle$ with no ε-moves that accepts L_2. M_2 may be either deterministic or nondeterministic. We shall need to assume that both M_1 and M_2 are fully defined. We now describe the construction of a nondeterministic pushdown automaton $M_\cap$ that, for given input word w, simultaneously models the behaviors of M_1 and M_2; in particular, $M_\cap$ will accept w just in case both M_1 and M_2 do. The description of $M_\cap$ follows.

- The state set $Q_\cap$ of $M_\cap$ consists of all ordered pairs of states of M_1 and M_2. That is, $Q_\cap = Q_1 \times Q_2$.

- The initial state of $M_\cap$ is the pair $[q_0^1, q_0^2]$, where q_0^1 is the initial state of M_1 and q_0^2 is the initial state of M_2.

- The stack alphabet $\Gamma_\cap$ of $M_\cap$ is Γ_1 and the stack-initialization symbol of $M_\cap$ is γ_1.

- The set $F_\cap$ of accepting states of $M_\cap$ will be those state pairs $[q_i, q_j]$ such that q_i is an accepting state of M_1 and q_j is an accepting state of M_2. That is, $F_\cap = F_1 \times F_2$.

- Transition mapping $\delta_\cap$ is defined so as to simultaneously model both the nondeterministic, stack-dependent behavior of M_1 as well as the stack-independent, possibly nondeterministic behavior of M_2. To this end, for arbitrary $s \in \Sigma$, $\sigma \in \Gamma_1$, and $\beta \in \Gamma_1^*$, we set $\delta_\cap([q_i, q_j], s, \sigma) = (\beta, [q_k, q_p])$ if both $\delta_1(q_i, s, \sigma) = (\beta, q_k)$ and $\delta_2(q_j, s) = q_p$. In addition, we set $\delta_\cap([q_i, q_j], \varepsilon, \sigma) = (\beta, [q_k, q_j])$ if $\delta_1(q_i, \varepsilon, \sigma) = (\beta, q_k)$. We thereby permit $M_\cap$ to simulate pushdown automaton M_1's ε-moves, while temporarily suspending its simulation of finite-state machine M_2.

It should be clear that $M_\cap$ finds itself in an accepting state, having read input word w completely from left to right, if and only if both M_1 and M_2 accept w.   Q.E.D.

EXAMPLE 10.6.1 We illustrate the construction of the proof of Theorem 10.9 with a simple example. Let M_1 be the three-state, nondeterministic pushdown automaton of Figure 10.3.1(a). We saw in Example 10.3.1 that M_1 accepts language $L_1 = \{w \in \Sigma^* | n_a(w) = n_b(w)\}$ with $\Sigma = \{a, b\}$. Next, we let M_2 be the three-state finite-state automaton of Figure 10.6.1. Note that M_2 is nondeterministic and

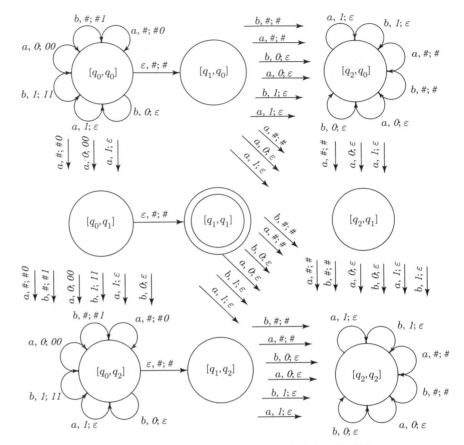

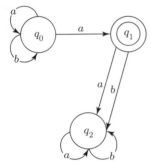

Figure 10.6.1 Finite-state machine M_2 accepts the language denoted by regular expression $(a|b)^*a$.

Figure 10.6.2 Result of Applying the Construction of the Proof of Theorem 10.9 to the Pushdown Automaton M_1 of Figure 10.3.1 and the Finite-State Machine M_2 of Figure 10.6.1.

accepts the language $L_2 = L((a|b)^*a)$, namely, the language over $\Sigma = \{a, b\}$ consisting of all and only those words ending in a. The transition diagram of Figure 10.6.2 shows the result of applying the construction of the proof of Theorem 10.9 to M_1 and M_2 so as to obtain a nondeterministic pushdown-stack automaton $M_\cap$ that accepts the language $L_1 \cap L_2 = \{w \in \Sigma^* | n_a(w) = n_b(w)$ and w ends with symbol $a\}$. (Open icon **Example 10.6.1**.) The state set of $M_\cap$ comprises $3 \cdot 3 = 9$ states. Its start state is $[q_0, q_0]$ and its unique accepting state is $[q_1, q_1]$. The fact that there are no vertical arcs within the middle column of nodes in Figure 10.6.2 reflects what fact about M_1?

Theorem 10.9 has as immediate consequence the following two propositions.

COROLLARY 10.1: If L_1 is context-free and L_2 is regular, then their relative complement $L_1 \backslash L_2$ is context-free.

PROOF Note that $L_1 \backslash L_2 = L_1 \cap L_2^c$ and recall that the complement of a regular language is regular. The result now follows from Theorem 10.9.   Q.E.D.

The following consequence of this last result will prove useful later.

COROLLARY 10.2: If L is context-free, then so is $L\backslash\{\varepsilon\}$.

PROOF Recall that language $\{\varepsilon\}$ is regular—it is denoted by regular expression ε. Now use
Corollary 10.1.   Q.E.D.

§10.7 A Pumping Lemma for Context-Free Languages

In the last chapter, we proved a pumping lemma for FSA-acceptable, and hence regular, languages. Our
proof involved reasoning about paths within the transition diagrams of finite-state automata. We shall
now prove an analogous proposition for context-free languages. This time we shall engage in reasoning
about paths within parse trees. We can illustrate several useful points by reflecting upon the following
example.

EXAMPLE 10.7.1 Consider a context-free grammar G for the language of nonempty strings of balanced
parentheses.

$$S \rightarrow SS \mid (S) \mid (\,)$$

Since $L(G)$ does not contain ε, we can apply the algorithm of §10.2 so as to obtain, after some trivial
reductions, the following equivalent grammar, which is in Chomsky normal form.

$$S \rightarrow SS \mid XY \mid XZ$$
$$X \rightarrow ($$
$$Y \rightarrow SZ$$
$$Z \rightarrow)$$

We present a derivation of the string $(\,(\,)\,)(\,(\,)\,)$.

$$S \Rightarrow SS$$
$$\Rightarrow SXY$$
$$\rightarrow SXSZ$$
$$\Rightarrow SXS)$$
$$\Rightarrow SXXZ)$$
$$\Rightarrow SXX))$$
$$\Rightarrow SX(\,))$$
$$\Rightarrow S(\,(\,))$$
$$\Rightarrow XY(\,(\,))$$

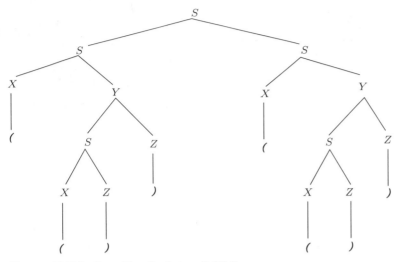

Figure 10.7.1 Parse Tree for String $(( ))(( ))$.

$$\Rightarrow XSZ(( ))$$
$$\Rightarrow XS)(( ))$$
$$\Rightarrow XXZ)(( ))$$
$$\Rightarrow XX))(( ))$$
$$\Rightarrow X( ))(( ))$$
$$\Rightarrow (( ))(( ))$$

This derivation just happens to be a rightmost derivation, but that fact will not figure in our discussion. Corresponding to this derivation we have the parse tree of Figure 10.7.1. As usual, terminal string $(( ))(( ))$ labels the leaves of the tree, and interior nodes are labeled by nonterminals.

Our present goal is to establish a relation between the length of the derived string and the height of its parse tree. In particular, we see that string $(( ))(( ))$ has length 8, whereas the parse tree of Figure 10.7.1 has height 5. Other derivable strings have parse trees of height 5—for example, string $(( ))( )$ of length 6 and string $(( ))( )( )$ of length 8. But the reader can easily verify that string $( )( )( )( ) ( )( )( )( )$ of length 16 is the longest word whose parse tree will be of height 5.

We generalize these observations with the following lemma.

> **LEMMA 10.1 (Tree Lemma):** Let G be a context-free grammar in Chomsky normal form. Let w be a word of $L(G)$ and let $\mathcal{T}$ be a parse tree for w relative to G. Then if $\mathcal{T}$ has no path of length strictly greater than k, it follows that $|w| \leq 2^{k-1}$.

PROOF (by induction on k). Since the smallest parse trees of words of $L(G)$ are of height 1, such trees provide our base case.

   Base case. We let $k = 1$. The entire parse tree of w must consist of a root, labeled by the start symbol of G, and a single leaf. Moreover, w, which labels that leaf, must consist of a single terminal a, say (see Figure 10.7.2). Consequently, $|w| = 1 = 2^0 = 2^{k-1}$.

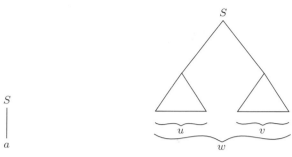

Inductive case. We let $k > 1$. Assuming start symbol S, parse tree $\mathcal{T}$ is of the general form of the tree of Figure 10.7.3, since G is in Chomsky normal form. (It is standard to represent subtrees schematically as triangles.) We assume that w is of the form uv, where u and v are strings labeling the leaves of the left and right subtrees, respectively, of $\mathcal{T}$. By hypothesis, neither subtree can contain paths of length $> k - 1$. So by the induction hypothesis, both $|u| \leq 2^{k-2}$ and $|v| \leq 2^{k-2}$. But then $|w| = |uv| \leq 2^{k-2} + 2^{k-2} = 2^{k-1}$.   Q.E.D.

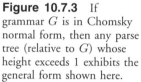

Figure 10.7.2 If grammar G is in Chomsky normal form, then any parse tree (relative to G) of height 1 possesses a single leaf.

Figure 10.7.3 If grammar G is in Chomsky normal form, then any parse tree (relative to G) whose height exceeds 1 exhibits the general form shown here.

Lemma 10.1 says, in effect, that if the height of word w's parse tree is not very great, then w itself cannot be very long. The lemma is, of course, equivalent to its contrapositive, which says, in effect, that if word w is long, then the height of its parse tree must be great:

(1) Let G be a context-free grammar in Chomsky normal form. If word $w \in L(G)$ has length $> 2^{k-1}$, then any parse tree for w has a path whose length exceeds k—that is, a path of length $\geq k + 1$.

And, substituting $k + 1$ for k in Lemma 10.1 itself gives us

(2) Let G be a context-free grammar in Chomsky normal form. Let w be a word of $L(G)$ and let $\mathcal{T}$ be a parse tree for w relative to G. Then if $\mathcal{T}$ has no path of length greater than $k + 1$, it follows that $|w| \leq 2^k$.

Moreover, it is easy to see that (2) holds even for subtrees of parse trees for w relative to G. Thus,

(3) Let G be a context-free grammar in Chomsky normal form. Let w be a word of $L(G)$ and let $\mathcal{T}$ be a parse tree for w relative to G. Furthermore, let $\mathcal{T}_1$ be a subtree of $\mathcal{T}$ and suppose that word z labels the leaves of $\mathcal{T}_1$. Then if $\mathcal{T}_1$ has no path of length greater than $k + 1$, it follows that $|z| \leq 2^k$.

We shall need the following lemma concerning derivations as well.

LEMMA 10.2: Suppose that G is a context-free grammar with terminal alphabet Σ and that we have both $A \Rightarrow^* w_1 A w_3$ and $A \Rightarrow^* w_2$, where w_1, w_2, and w_3 are (possibly empty) words over Σ. Then it follows that both $A \Rightarrow^* w_1^i A w_3^i$ and $A \Rightarrow^* w_1^i w_2 w_3^i$ for all $i \geq 0$.

PROOF (by induction on i).
   Base case. Let $i = 0$. Note that $A \Rightarrow^* A$ trivially. But A is just $w_1^0 A w_2^0$. Similarly, note that $A \Rightarrow^* w_2$ by hypothesis and that w_2 is $w_1^0 w_2 w_3^0$.

Inductive case. We suppose that $i > 0$. By induction hypothesis, we have that $A \Rightarrow^* w_1^{i-1} A w_3^{i-1}$. This together with hypothesis $A \Rightarrow^* w_1 A w_3$ means that

$$
\begin{aligned}
A &\Rightarrow^* w_1^{i-1} \boldsymbol{A} w_3^{i-1} \\
&\Rightarrow^* w_1^{i-1} \boldsymbol{w_1 A w_3} w_3^{i-1} \\
&= w_1^i A w_3^i
\end{aligned}
$$

Also,

$$
\begin{aligned}
A &\Rightarrow^* w_1^{i-1} A w_3^{i-1} && \text{(by induction hypothesis)} \\
&\Rightarrow^* w_1^{i-1} w_1 A w_3 w_3^{i-1} && \text{(by hypothesis)} \\
&= w_1^i A w_3^i \\
&\Rightarrow^* w_1^i w_2 w_3^i && \text{(by hypothesis)}
\end{aligned}
$$

Q.E.D.

We are now ready to present the proof of the Pumping Lemma itself. As in the case of the proof of the Pumping Lemma for Finite-State Automata (Lemma 9.2), we shall use the fact that if language L is infinite, then there is no upper bound on the length of words in L.

LEMMA 10.3 (A Pumping Lemma for Context-Free Languages): Let L be an infinite context-free language. Then L must contain a word $z = uvwxy$ such that:

(i) v and x are not both ε.

(ii) $uv^i w x^i y$ is in L for all $i \geq 0$.

PROOF If L is an infinite context-free language, then, by Corollary 10.2, so is $L \backslash \{\varepsilon\}$. Furthermore, by Theorem 10.3, there exists a Chomsky normal form grammar G generating $L \backslash \{\varepsilon\}$. Suppose grammar G has exactly k nonterminals and set $m = 2^{k-1}$. Since L is infinite, L must contain a word z whose length exceeds m. That is, $|z| > 2^{k-1}$, and proposition (1) above implies that any parse tree $\mathcal{T}$ for z must contain a path of length at least $k + 1$. Such a path will have at least $k + 2$ nodes. Since all $k + 1$ interior nodes in such a path are labeled by nonterminals, the Pigeonhole Principle (Theorem 0.6) tells us that at least one nonterminal must be repeated along such a path.

Suppose that P is a path of maximal length in $\mathcal{T}$. (There may be more than one path of this length in $\mathcal{T}$.) By the foregoing, there must be at least $k + 2$ nodes in P and at least one nonterminal A, say, must occur more than once—at nodes n_1 and n_2, say (see Figure 10.7.4). We assume that n_1 is higher on path P than n_2. We can also assume without loss of generality that the subpath P_1 of P from n_1 to leaf is of length $\leq k + 1$.[1]

---

[1] To see why this is so, consider the following. Imagine traversing P from below starting with its leaf and keeping track of encountered labels. Of the first $k + 2$ nodes encountered, only the leaf has a terminal label. Consequently, the next $k + 1$ nodes as we proceed upward along P must include repeated nonterminal labels. So if the given subpath P_1 is not of length $\leq k + 1$, it can be replaced by a subpath that *is* of length $\leq k + 1$.

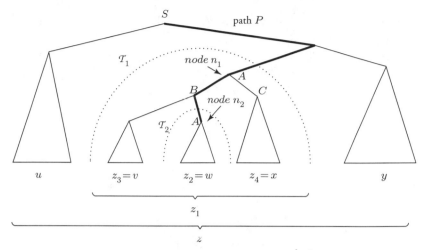

Figure 10.7.4   A Parse Tree T for Word z with $|z| > 2^{k-1}$, where Context-Free Grammar G has k Nonterminals.

- Let T_1 be the subtree of T with root n_1. Let z_1 be the word labeling the leaves of T_1. Since P is a path of maximal length in T, it follows that P_1 is a path of maximal length in T_1. But P_1 has length $\leq k + 1$. So by proposition (3), we see that $|z_1|$ is $\leq 2^k$.

- Similarly, let T_2 be the subtree whose root is n_2, and suppose that word z_2, say, labels its leaves. Then we have $z_1 = z_3 z_2 z_4$, where z_3 and z_4 cannot both be ε. Why not? Well, the production used to expand node n_1 must be of the form $A \rightarrow BC$ for some nonterminals B and C. But then the subtree T_2 must be entirely contained in either the subtree whose root is labeled by B or the subtree whose root is labeled by C. Let us suppose that T_2 is within the B subtree, as in Figure 10.7.4. Then, by the fact that G is in Chomsky normal form, nonterminal C cannot generate ε, which means that z_4 is nonempty. Similarly, if T_2 is entirely contained in the C subtree, then z_3 must be nonempty. Consequently, we have $A \Rightarrow^* z_3 A z_4$ with z_3 and z_4 not both ε.

- Also, since A is the root of subtree T_2, we have $A \Rightarrow^* z_2$. But now it follows, by Lemma 10.2, that $A \Rightarrow^* z_3^i z_2 z_4^i$ for all $i \geq 0$. Letting $v = z_3$, $w = z_2$, and $x = z_4$, we see that z is of the form $uvwxy$, which completes the proof. (For the identity of words u and y, see Figure 10.7.4.)
  Q.E.D.

Just as the purpose of the Pumping Lemma for Finite-State Automata was to demonstrate the existence of nonregular languages, so we shall now use our Pumping Lemma for Context-Free Languages to demonstrate the existence of languages that are not context-free. As a first example, we shall show that $L = \{a^n b^n c^n | n > 0\}$ is not context-free.

THEOREM 10.10: The language $L = \{a^n b^n c^n | n > 0\}$ is not context-free. Thus, there exists a Turing-acceptable language that is not context-free.

PROOF (indirect). We begin by supposing, for the sake of producing a contradiction, that L is context-free. Since L is evidently infinite, the Pumping Lemma applies: There must exist a word $uvwxy$ such that v and x are not both empty and v and x can be pumped. The cases whereby v or x or both contain two or three distinct symbols can be eliminated immediately, since pumping produces words with bs before as, cs before bs, or even cs before as *and* bs. So both v and x, assuming them to be nonempty, must consist of one or more occurrences of a single letter—that is, just of as, just of bs, or just of cs. Suppose, for example, that v is just as and x is just bs.

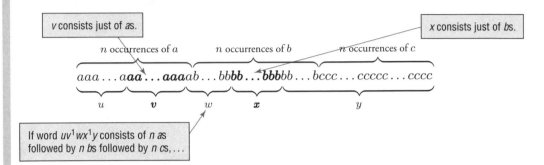

Then pumping results in words not of the form $a^n b^n c^n$, since we increase the number of occurrences of a and b without increasing the number of occurrences of c.

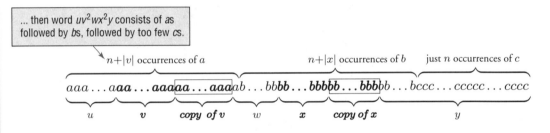

There are a number of other cases to consider. However, they all lead to contradiction. We thereby see that L cannot be a context-free language.

Finally, given the discussion of Chapters 1 and 2, the reader should find it easy to describe a Turing machine that accepts L. In other words, L—although not context-free—is Turing-acceptable.

Q.E.D.

We are ready now to demonstrate

THEOREM 10.11: The class of context-free languages is not closed under intersection.

PROOF (indirect). Suppose, for the sake of producing a contradiction, that we do have closure under intersection. Let $\Sigma = \{a, b, c\}$. We have seen that each of the languages L_1, L_2, and L_3 below is context-free.

- Language $L_1 = L(a^* b^* c^*)$ is regular and hence context-free by Remark 10.1.1.

- Language $L_2 = \{w \in \Sigma^* | n_a(w) = n_b(w)\}$ is PSA-acceptable and hence context-free by Theorem 10.7 (see Exercise 10.3.1(c)).

- Language $L_3 = \{w \in \Sigma^* | n_b(w) = n_c(w)\}$ is PSA-acceptable and hence context-free by Theorem 10.7 again (see Exercise 10.3.1(d)).

By our assumption, we have that $L_1 \cap L_2 \cap L_3 = \{a^n b^n c^n | n \geq 0\}$ is context-free as well. But then, by Corollary 10.2, so is $\{a^n b^n c^n | n > 0\}$, contradicting Theorem 10.10.   Q.E.D.

Theorem 10.11 is only the first of several disappointments concerning context-free languages that we must confront. We mention in particular

---

THEOREM 10.12: The class of context-free languages is not closed under complementation. That is, there exist context-free languages L such that language L^c is not context-free.

PROOF See Exercise 10.7.3.

§10.8 Deterministic Context-Free Languages

Although the notion of pushdown-stack automaton that was introduced in §10.3 is that of a nondeterministic machine that typically involved ε-moves, we can say what it is for a pushdown-stack automaton M to be deterministic. Namely, it is for δ_M to be both (i) single-valued and (ii) such that, for any state q and stack alphabet symbol σ, either M is undefined for triple $\langle q, \varepsilon, \sigma \rangle$ or, if δ_M is defined for $\langle q, \varepsilon, \sigma \rangle$, then δ_M is undefined for all triples $\langle q, s, \sigma \rangle$ with $s \in \Sigma$. (We are already requiring that δ_M is undefined for all triples of the form $\langle q, s, \varepsilon \rangle$ even in the nondeterministic case.) This has the desired effect: At any point during M's computation, at most one transition is applicable. Almost none of the pushdown automata considered so far have been deterministic. (Example 10.3.2 is one exception.) Hence, a few examples will be helpful. In the course of presenting these examples, we begin to develop the theory of *deterministic context-free languages*, which is of great importance to compiler design theory.

EXAMPLE 10.8.1 The pushdown automaton whose state diagram appears as Figure 10.8.1 is a deterministic machine M that accepts the language L defined by $L = \{wc | w \in \Sigma^* \,\&\, n_a(w) - n_b(w)\}$, with $\Sigma = \{a, b\}$. M's stack alphabet Γ is $\{\#, 0, 1\}$. Also, M has no ε-moves. Note that, with the addition of a few arcs, M can be made fully defined in the sense that δ_M is defined for each and every member of $Q \times \Sigma \times \Gamma$. In fact, we shall regard a pushdown automaton as fully defined even in the case where its transition function is undefined for certain triples (q, s, σ), so long as it is then defined for triple (q, ε, σ). See the fully defined machine at icon **Example 10.8.1**.

Next, consider the (deterministic) pushdown automaton M' obtained from machine M of Example 10.8.1 by making each accepting state nonterminal and vice versa. It should be clear that M' will accept L^c so that, by Theorem 10.7, language L^c is context-free. (Of course, just as in the case of finite-state automata, this construction—interchanging terminal and nonterminal states—has the desired effect only when applied to a machine that is fully defined.) Moreover, this insight can be generalized

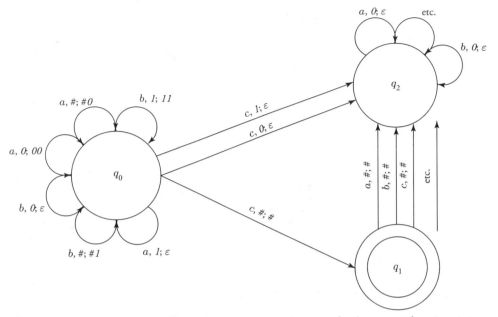

Figure 10.8.1 This deterministic machine accepts the language $\{wc|w$ is in Σ^* and $n_a(w) = n_b(w)\}$ with $\Sigma = \{a, b\}$.

so as to yield

THEOREM 10.13: Let alphabet Σ be given. If language L over Σ is accepted by a deterministic pushdown-stack automaton, then both L and L^c are context-free languages.

Reflecting the equivalence of the notions *context-free* and *PSA-acceptable*, we shall henceforth describe any language accepted by a deterministic pushdown automaton as a *deterministic context-free language*. Theorem 10.13 then asserts the closure of the class of deterministic context-free languages under complementation—a striking result given the disappointment of Theorem 10.12.

EXAMPLE 10.8.2 Open the icon **Example 10.8.2** to observe the operation of a deterministic pushdown automaton M that accepts language $L = \{wcw^R|w \in \Sigma^*\}$, where $\Sigma = \{a, b\}$. Given that symbol c marks the middle of any accepted input word, machine M can make the transition, from symbol-pushing mode to symbol-popping mode, deterministically.

As our next example shows, there do exist context-free languages that are accepted by some *nondeterministic* pushdown automaton but that are accepted by no *deterministic* pushdown automaton (see also Exercise 10.8.1). To invoke the new terminology, there exist context-free languages that are not deterministic context-free. In other words, no equivalence results analogous to Theorem 2.7 or Theorem 9.3 are available for the family of context-free languages (see Exercise 10.8.1).

EXAMPLE 10.8.3 Open the icon **Example 10.8.3** to observe the operation of a nondeterministic pushdown automaton M that accepts language $L = \{a^m ba^n ba^k \mid m, n, k \geq 0$ and either $m \neq n$ or $n \neq k\}$. Note how, given input word w of the form $a^m ba^n ba^k$, machine M, in effect, guesses which pair of superscripts is unequal and then verifies the inequality.

Also, we have that

$$L^c = \{a^n \mid n \geq 0\} \cup \{w \mid n_b(w) = 1\} \cup \{w \mid n_b(w) \geq 3\} \cup \boxed{\{a^m ba^m ba^m \mid m \geq 0\}}$$

where the four languages on the right are mutually disjoint and the first three are each regular. Hence, if L^c were context-free, then

$$\boxed{\{a^m ba^m ba^m \mid m \geq 0\}} = L^c \backslash [\{a^n \mid n \geq 0\} \cup \{w \mid n_b(w) = 1\} \cup \{w \mid n_b(w) \geq 3\}]$$

would be context-free as well, by Corollary 10.1. But this is readily seen to contradict the Pumping Lemma as applied to $\{a^m ba^m ba^m \mid m \geq 0\}$. So we conclude that L^c cannot be context-free, after all. By Theorem 10.13, it follows that there is no deterministic pushdown automaton that accepts L.

EXAMPLE 10.8.4 The deterministic machine at icon **Example 10.8.4** accepts language $\{a^n \mid n \geq 0\} \cup \{a^n b^n \mid n \geq 0\}$.

Given our prohibition of ε-cycles as discussed at the end of §10.3, it is now possible to justify

REMARK 10.8.1: In the case of any deterministic pushdown automaton M with input alphabet Σ, language $L(M)$ over Σ is both accepted and, in a certain sense, *recognized* by M. Expressed differently, M *decides* membership in $L(M)$. Consequently, there is no real distinction to be made between language acceptance and language recognition on the part of deterministic M.

We leave the justification of Remark 10.8.1 to the reader (see Exercise 10.8.3). The situation is precisely analogous to that of deterministic finite-state machines with ε-moves, as addressed at the end of §9.7. And Remark 10.8.1 will explain why deterministic pushdown automata are frequently described, in the context of parsing applications, as *recognizing* this or that language.

§10.9 Decidability Results Concerning Context-Free Languages

In this section, we introduce two relatively easy decidability results for context-free languages. Namely, we shall see that, given an arbitrary context-free language L, there is an algorithm for deciding whether L is finite or infinite. Similarly, there turns out to be an algorithm for deciding whether an arbitrary context-free language L is empty or nonempty. The algorithms in question are applied to some context-free grammar G that generates the given L. Hence our statements below must be interpreted in a certain way: When we say that it is decidable whether an arbitrary context-free language L has a certain property, we mean thereby that, *given some context-free grammar G that generates L*, we can, by working with G, decide whether L has the property in question.

Our first result depends upon a certain restatement of the Pumping Lemma (Lemma 10.3). In fact, examination of the proof of that proposition, as presented in §10.7, reveals that we in fact proved the following strengthened version. (The new version is stronger just in the sense that it contains more information.)

STRENGTHENED RESTATEMENT OF LEMMA 10.3 (A Pumping Lemma for Context-Free Languages): Let L be any infinite, context-free language, and let G be a context-free grammar that generates L. Suppose that G has k nonterminals. Then, for any word $z \in L$ with $|z| > 2^{k-1}$, we have that z is of the form $uvwxy$ where

(i) v and x are not both empty

(ii) $|vwx| \leq 2^k$

(iii) $uv^i wx^i y \in L$ for all $i \geq 0$

We shall use this strengthened version of Lemma 10.3 to prove the following useful result.

THEOREM 10.14: Let L be a context-free language. Then there exist natural numbers p and q—which depend upon L—such that L is infinite if and only if L contains some word $\mathcal{W}$ with $p < |\mathcal{W}| \leq p + q$.

PROOF We assume without loss of generality that L does not contain ε. Let $G = \langle \Sigma, \Gamma, \sigma, \Pi \rangle$ be a Chomsky normal form grammar with $L = L(G)$. Suppose that $|\Gamma| = k$. We set $p = 2^{k-1}$ and $q = 2^k$ and consider the strengthened version of the Pumping Lemma given above.

- If L contains a word z with $p < |z| \leq p + q$, then in particular $2^{k-1} = p < |z|$ and so, by (i) and (iii) of the Pumping Lemma, we have that L is infinite.

- On the other hand, suppose that L is infinite. Then L contains a word z with $|z| > p + q$. Moreover, (i)–(iii) above hold. That is, z is of the form $uvwxy$ with

  (1) v and x are not both empty

  (2) $|vwx| \leq q$

  (3) $uv^i wx^i y \in L$ for all $i \geq 0$

Letting $i = 0$ in (iii), we "reduce" word z, obtaining $uwy \in L$. (Note that by (1), $|uwy| < |z|$.) By (2) and the fact that $|uvwxy| > p + q$, we have $p < |uy| \leq |uwy|$. If it should already be the case that $|uwy| \leq p + q$, then we have found a word whose length lies within the desired bounds, and we are done. That is, we have found a word $\mathcal{W} = uwy$ in L with $p < |\mathcal{W}| \leq p + q$. On the other hand, if $|uwy| > p + q$ holds, then we repeat the reduction just described with $\mathcal{W} = uwy$ in place of z. Each such reduction produces a word whose length is strictly smaller and yet exceeds p. Consequently, after finitely many iterations, this procedure will produce a word whose length lies between p and $p + q$.   Q.E.D.

The importance of Theorem 10.14 resides in the fact that it provides a decision procedure for determining whether a context-free language L is finite or infinite. Assume the availability of a context-free grammar G with $L = L(G)$. We can assume without loss of generality that L does not contain ε (If it does, then we work with $L\backslash\{\varepsilon\}$.) The algorithm of §10.2 may be applied to G in order to obtain an equivalent grammar G' in Chomsky normal form. Suppose that this G' happens to have k nonterminals. We then set $p = 2^{k-1}$ and set $q = 2^k$. By Theorem 10.14, we have only to check whether G generates some word $\mathcal{W}$ with $p < |\mathcal{W}| \leq p + q$. We can do so by examining parse trees of grammar G in order to see whether some parse tree exists for such a word $\mathcal{W}$. We shall use the following simple lemma, whose proof is left as an exercise (see Exercise 10.9.1). It tells us that the length of an arbitrary word $w \in L(G)$ is bounded below by the height of its parse tree.

LEMMA 10.4: Let G be a context-free grammar in Chomsky normal form. Let $\mathcal{T}$ be a parse tree for word $w \in L(G)$. Then $height(\mathcal{T}) \leq |w|$.

The relevance of Lemma 10.4 to our quest for a decision procedure for determining whether a given context-free language is infinite is then the following.

- If the parse tree of a word w has height $p + q + 1$, say, then $p + q + 1 \leq |w|$. Consequently, in searching for a word $\mathcal{W}$ such that $p < |\mathcal{W}| \leq p + q$, parse trees whose height exceeds $p + q$ need not be considered.

- Furthermore, the Tree Lemma (Lemma 10.1) tells us that, letting k be the number of nonterminals in G', if parse tree $\mathcal{T}$ for word w has height $\leq k$, then it follows that $|w| \leq 2^{k-1} = p$. Consequently, in looking for word $\mathcal{W}$ such that $p < |\mathcal{W}|$, parse trees of height $\leq k$ will not interest us either.

- Summarizing, to determine whether G generates some word $\mathcal{W}$ with $p < |\mathcal{W}| \leq p + q$, we need look only at those parse trees whose heights lie between $k + 1$ and $p + q = 2^{k-1} + 2^k$ inclusive. Of course, there are but finitely many such parse trees. (Why?) Moreover, an algorithm for generating all of them can be devised easily. Most of these parse trees will not be the parse trees of words over Σ, since at least some of their leaves will be labeled by nonterminals. It is the trees with terminals at their leaves that interest us, after all. So as each tree is generated in turn, we check to see whether all its leaves are labeled by terminals of G' that is, by members of Σ. If such a tree is found, then L does contain a word $\mathcal{W}$ with $p < |\mathcal{W}| \leq p + q$ and, by Theorem 10.14, L is infinite. On the other hand, if we examine all such trees without ever finding one whose leaves are all labeled by terminals, then L contains no word $\mathcal{W}$ with $p < |\mathcal{W}| \leq p + q$ and, by Theorem 10.14 again, we are forced to conclude that L is finite.

We formulate our first decidability result for the family of context-free languages as follows.

THEOREM 10.15: There is an algorithm for deciding whether a context-free language is finite or infinite. Alternative formulation: It is decidable whether a given context-free language is finite or infinite.

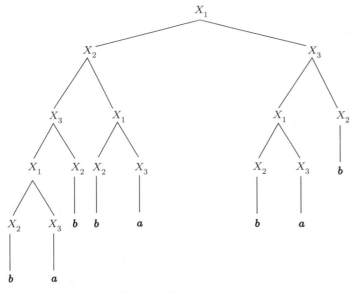

Figure 10.9.1 Parse Tree for Word *babbabab*.

As an illustration of Theorem 10.15, consider

EXAMPLE 10.9.1 The grammar G of Exercise 10.2.6 is in Chomsky normal form. We reproduce its productions below for the reader's convenience.

$$X_1 \to X_2 X_3$$

$$X_2 \to X_3 X_1 \mid b$$

$$X_3 \to X_1 X_2 \mid a$$

We can decide the question whether $L(G)$ is finite or infinite as follows. Since G has $k = 3$ nonterminals, we need consider only parse trees ranging in height from $k + 1 = 4$ to $2^{k-1} + 2^k = 12$. If the leaves of even one such tree happen to be labeled by terminals only, then $L(G)$ is infinite. We can imagine generating those trees in some orderly fashion. Among them will be the height-5 parse tree $\mathcal{T}$ of Figure 10.9.1. The existence of $\mathcal{T}$ by itself implies that $L(G)$ is an infinite language. Note that word $\mathcal{W} = \textbf{\textit{babbabab}}$ labels the leaves of $\mathcal{T}$ and that $p = 2^{k-1} = 4 < |\mathcal{W}| \le 12 = 4 + 8 = 2^{k-1} + 2^k = p + q$, as required by Theorem 10.14.

It is also decidable whether a given context-free language L is empty. Before describing the algorithm, let us consider

---

EXAMPLE 10.9.2 We consider whether the language L generated by the context-free grammar G, whose productions appear below, is empty or nonempty.

$$S \to XXZ$$

$$X \to aY$$

$$Y \to b$$

$$Z \to ab$$

First, we note that nonterminals Y and Z may each be rewritten as strings of terminals. As a consequence of this fact, let us say that nonterminals Y and Z are each *resolvable* (to terminals). This much is promising but does not yet decide the issue, since start symbol S cannot be rewritten as any string of terminals. Working backwards toward S, we notice that nonterminal X may be rewritten as aY and, since Y can be rewritten as a string of terminals, we have that X is resolvable (to terminals) by extension. Finally, we notice that start symbol S may be rewritten as a string of resolvable nonterminals and is, consequently, itself resolvable. And that is enough to see that there exists a string of terminals that is derivable from S, i.e., $L(G) = L$ is nonempty.

With this simple example before us, we now describe, more formally, an algorithm that may be used to decide whether the languages generated by context-free grammars are empty or nonempty. To begin, suppose that L is a context-free language over alphabet Σ and let G be a context-free grammar with $L = L(G)$. First, we form the set N_0 of all nonterminals X such that there exists a production enabling X to be rewritten as a string of terminals—that is, as a string of members of Σ. Next, we form the set N_1 of nonterminals consisting of (i) all nonterminals in N_0 plus (ii) all nonterminals X such that there exists a production of G whereby X is rewritten as a string over $N_0 \cup \Sigma$. We continue in this way, forming N_2, N_3, and so on. Eventually, this process will cease to add any new nonterminals. (Why?) That is, $N_i = N_{i+1}$ for some i. We then check to see whether the start symbol of G is a member of set $N_i = N_{i+1}$. If so, then L is nonempty. Otherwise, L is empty. We see that the nonterminals in set N_i are *resolvable* in the sense of Example 10.9.2. It is worth noting that the context-free grammar G to which our algorithm is applied is not assumed to have any particular form. This is enough to see the truth of

> **THEOREM 10.16:** It is decidable whether or not a given context-free language is empty.

Other decidability results concerning context-free languages are presented in Exercises 10.9.2 through 10.9.6 below. Exercise 10.9.3 deserves special mention. Where $G = \langle \Sigma, \Gamma, \sigma, \Pi \rangle$ is any context-free grammar, we are able to show that, for an arbitrary word w over Σ, it is decidable whether G generates w—that is, whether $\sigma \Rightarrow^* w$. By virtue of this important fact, we shall say that *the general word problem for context-free grammars is decidable or solvable* (cf. Theorem 11.7 in the next chapter). This theoretical result is of great significance for pragmatic computer science, given that the syntactic definition of any programming language will be expressed largely in terms of some context-free grammar. The *parsing subtask* of program compilation involves determining whether a given source program, written in some programming language, is strictly in accordance with the syntax of that language. The solvability of the general word problem for context-free grammars means that this subtask can be automated—at least in principle. Considerations of efficiency lead to the development of two particularly efficient (families of) algorithms known as *LL parsing* and *LR parsing*, respectively.

§10.10 Bibliography and Suggestions for Further Reading

Context-free grammars were first introduced in [Chomsky 1956]. The application of context-free grammars to natural language was initiated in [Chomsky 1957]. For contemporary readers interested in applications within linguistics, a good place to start is [Lasnik 1990], which contains additional bibliography. The first widely published account of the application of context-free grammars to programming languages appeared in [Backus 1959], which also contains the first presentation of the familiar *Backus normal form*. Pushdown-stack automata were introduced in [Chomsky 1962] and [Evey 1963]. [Chomsky 1959] presents Chomsky normal form, and [Greibach 1965] presents Greibach normal form. The Pumping Lemma (Lemma 10.3) is again associated with Bar-Hillel. (And again, see [Bar-Hillel, Perles, and Shamir 1961].)

EXERCISES FOR §10.1

10.1.1. For each of the context-free grammars below, describe the language generated. In particular, say whether the language generated contains the empty word.

(a) ^{hwk} $S \rightarrow aSbb \mid$

(b) $S \rightarrow X \mid Y \mid$

$X \rightarrow aXb \mid$

$Y \rightarrow aYbb \mid$

(c) $S \rightarrow X \mid Y$

$X \rightarrow aXb \mid X_1$

$X_1 \rightarrow aX_1 \mid a$

$Y \rightarrow aYbb \mid Y_1$

$Y_1 \rightarrow Y_1 b \mid b$

10.1.2. For each of the following languages L, present a context-free grammar G that generates L—that is, a context-free grammar G such that $L = L(G)$.

(a) ^{hwk} Let L be the language of all strings consisting of balanced parentheses. Thus, the strings $()()()$ and $(())()$ are balanced but string $(()()$ is not. We shall also consider ε to be balanced. (*Hint*: Since L is a *set* of words, you might first try to define L inductively.)

(b) Let L be the language of palindromes over alphabet $\Sigma = \{a, b\}$. That is, $L = \{w \in \Sigma^* \mid w = w^R\}$. (*Hint*: Same as for (a).)

(c) L is the language of words over alphabet $\Sigma = \{a, b\}$ containing twice as many as as bs. That is, $L = \{w \mid n_a(w) = 2 \cdot n_b(w)\}$.

10.1.3. Consider the productions below.

$$S \rightarrow NP \, VP$$
$$NP \rightarrow Det \, AdjP \, N \mid Det \, N \mid$$
$$AdjP \, N \mid N$$
$$N \rightarrow Pron \mid \textbf{professeur}$$
$$VP \rightarrow Cop \, AdjP \mid V \, \textbf{que} \, S$$
$$AdjP \rightarrow Adv \, Adj \mid Adj$$

$$Det \rightarrow \textbf{le}$$
$$Adj \rightarrow \textbf{jeune} \mid \textbf{préparée}$$
$$V \rightarrow \textbf{sait}$$
$$Pron \rightarrow \textbf{je}$$
$$Cop \rightarrow \textbf{suis}$$
$$Adv \rightarrow \textbf{bien}$$

Now, represent the structure of the following French sentence by presenting a phrase structure tree for it.

Le jeune professeur sait que je suis bien préparée.

Note that one need possess no knowledge of French in order to complete this exercise.

10.1.4. ^{hwk} Consider the productions below.

$$S \rightarrow NP_1 \, VP$$
$$NP_1 \rightarrow Det_1 \, Adj_1 \, N_1 \mid Det_1 \, N_1$$
$$VP \rightarrow V \, AdvP$$
$$AdvP \rightarrow Adv \, PrepP \, PrepP \mid$$
$$Adv \, PrepP \mid Adv$$
$$PrepP \rightarrow Prep \, NP_2$$
$$NP_2 \rightarrow Det_2 \, Adj_2 \, N_2 \mid Det_2 \, N_2 \mid$$
$$Adj_2 \, N_2$$
$$Det_1 \rightarrow \textbf{der} \mid \textbf{die} \mid \textbf{das}$$
$$Adj_1 \rightarrow \textbf{lieber} \mid \textbf{liebe} \mid \textbf{liebes}$$
$$N_1 \rightarrow \textbf{Frau Schenck}$$
$$Det_2 \rightarrow \textbf{dieser} \mid \textbf{diesem}$$
$$Adj_2 \rightarrow \textbf{vielen}$$
$$N_2 \rightarrow \textbf{Jahren} \mid \textbf{Hause}$$
$$V \rightarrow \textbf{wohnt}$$
$$Prep \rightarrow \textbf{seit} \mid \textbf{in}$$
$$Adv \rightarrow \textbf{noch}$$

Now, represent the structure of the following German sentence by presenting a labeled bracketing for it.

Die liebe Frau Schenck wohnt noch seit vielen Jahren in diesem Hause.

The distinctions between NP_1 and NP_2 and so forth represent a modest attempt at capturing the case distinctions of modern German. But, once again, the reader who lacks familiarity with these distinctions should nonetheless have no trouble with this exercise. (Presumably it will then be less fun, though.)

10.1.5. Consider the productions below.

$$S \rightarrow NP\,VP$$

$$NP \rightarrow Det\,AdjP\,N\,AdjP\ |$$
$$Det\,N\,AdjP\ |\ Det\,AdjP\,N\ |$$
$$Det\,N\ |\ N$$

$$AdjP \rightarrow Adv\,Adj\ |\ Adj\ |\ PrepP$$

$$VP \rightarrow Cop\,Adj\,AdvP$$

$$AdvP \rightarrow Adv\ |\ PrepP$$

$$PrepP \rightarrow Prep\,NP$$

EXERCISES FOR §10.2

10.2.1. (a) What language is generated by the context-free grammar G whose productions appear below?

$$S \rightarrow aSa\ |\ aXa$$

$$X \rightarrow bXb\ |\ Y$$

$$Y \rightarrow cYc\ |$$

(b) Apply the algorithm of the proof of Theorem 10.1 to grammar G so as to obtain a new context-free grammar G' without ε-productions such that $L(G) = L(G')$.

10.2.2. (a) What language is generated by the context-free grammar G whose productions are as follows?

$$Det \rightarrow \textbf{el}\ |\ \textbf{la}$$

$$Adj \rightarrow \textbf{famoso}\ |\ \textbf{famosa}\ |\ \textbf{nicaragüense}\ |$$
$$\textbf{enterrado}\ |\ \textbf{enterrada}\ |\ \textbf{gran}$$

$$N \rightarrow \textbf{poeta}\ |\ \textbf{catedral}\ |\ \textbf{León}$$

$$Cop \rightarrow \textbf{fue}$$

$$Adv \rightarrow \textbf{muy}$$

$$Prep \rightarrow \textbf{en}\ |\ \textbf{de}$$

Now, represent the structure of the following Spanish sentence by presenting a labeled bracketing.

El muy famoso poeta nicaragüense fue enterrado en la gran catedral de León.

As in Exercises 10.1.3 and 10.1.4, certain of the productions listed will not be used in the labeled bracketing for our sample sentence. These additional productions would be required for other related sentences, however, and it is for that reason that they have been included.

10.1.6. Present a derivation of LISP S-expression $(\ (\ )\ (a\ b)\ (a\ .\ a))$ within the grammar of Example 10.1.1.

$$S \rightarrow aSa\ |\ X$$

$$X \rightarrow bXb\ |\ Y$$

$$Y \rightarrow cYc\ |$$

(b) Apply the algorithm of the proof of Theorem 10.1 to grammar G so as to obtain a new context-free grammar G' without ε-productions. Does $L(G) = L(G')$? If not, what is the relation between $L(G')$ and $L(G)$?

10.2.3. Apply the algorithm of the proof of Theorem 10.2 to the context-free grammar G of Exercise 10.2.1(a) so as to obtain a grammar G' without unit productions such that $L(G) = L(G')$.

10.2.4. Apply the algorithm of the proof of Theorem 10.2 to the context-free grammar G of Exercise 10.2.2(a) so as to obtain a grammar G' without unit productions such that $L(G) = L(G')$.

10.2.5. **(a)** What language is generated by the context-free grammar G whose productions appear below?

$$S \rightarrow aSXb \mid aXb$$

$$X \rightarrow b \mid$$

(b) Apply the algorithm of the proof of Theorem 10.3 to grammar G so as to obtain an equivalent Chomsky normal form grammar.

10.2.6. ^{hwk} Apply the algorithm of the proof of Theorem 10.4 to the Chomsky normal form grammar below so as to obtain an equivalent grammar in Greibach normal form.

$$X_1 \rightarrow X_2 X_3$$

$$X_2 \rightarrow X_3 X_1 \mid b$$

$$X_3 \rightarrow X_1 X_2 \mid a$$

(*Hint:* The new grammar will have 24 productions.)

10.2.7. A context-free grammar is said to be *cycle-free* provided that it permits no derivations of the form $X \Rightarrow^* X$, where X is a grammar nonterminal. You are asked to develop an algorithm for converting an arbitrary context-free grammar G to an equivalent grammar G' that is cycle-free. Apply your algorithm to the grammar with productions $S \rightarrow SS \mid (S) \mid$.

EXERCISES FOR §10.3

10.3.1. ^{hwk} **(a)** Show that the word *abba* will be accepted by the pushdown-stack automaton of Example 10.3.1 and Figure 10.3.1(a) by presenting the chart of an accepting computation. Similarly, show that word *aba* will not be accepted by this pushdown automaton.

(b) We saw that the pushdown automaton of Example 10.3.1 accepts word *baabba* by virtue of the accepting computation given in the text. Show that there exists another, nonaccepting computation for input word *baabba*. Present a chart of this nonaccepting computation.

(c) Let $\Sigma = \{a, b, c\}$. Show that the language $\{w \in \Sigma^* \mid n_a(w) = n_b(w)\}$ is PSA-acceptable. (*Hint:* This is a simple variant of the pushdown automaton of Example 10.3.1. Reading symbol c will cause no change in the stack.)

(d) Let $\Sigma = \{a, b, c\}$. Show that the language $\{w \in \Sigma^* \mid n_b(w) = n_c(w)\}$ is PSA-acceptable. (*Hint:* Make uniform changes in the pushdown automaton of (c).)

10.3.2. Present the state diagram of a pushdown automaton that accepts the language $\{a^n b^n \mid n \geq$

0$\}$. Your state diagram need not be fully defined.

10.3.3. Present the state diagram of a pushdown automaton that accepts the language $\{w \mid w \in \Sigma^*$ and $n_a(w) \leq n_b(w)\}$, where $\Sigma = \{a, b\}$. (*Hint:* Note that, in the case of the pushdown automaton of Example 10.3.1, 0s and 1s are never on the symbol stack simultaneously.)

10.3.4. Present the state diagram of a pushdown automaton that accepts the language of all words over $\Sigma = \{a, b\}$ that contain exactly twice as many as as bs.

10.3.5. Design a (nondeterministic) pushdown automaton that accepts the language of palindromes over $\Sigma = \{a, b\}$.

10.3.6. For each of the languages over $\Sigma = \{a, b\}$ below, indicate whether the language is likely to be PSA-acceptable. Justify your answer by appealing to the apparent computational capacities and limitations of pushdown automata. You may make reference to previously given examples of pushdown automata.

(a) $\{a^n bc^n \mid n \geq 0\}$
(b) $\{a^n bc^{n+2} \mid n \geq 0\}$
(c) $\{a^n bc^{2n} \mid n \geq 0\}$

(d) $\{a^n b^n c^n | n \geq 0\}$
(e) $\{a^n b^n c^m d^m | n, m \geq 0\}$
(f) $\{a^n b^n c^n d^n | n \geq 0\}$
(g) $\{a^n b^m c^n d^m | n, m \geq 0\}$
(h) $\{a^n b^m c^n d^m | 0 \leq n \leq m\}$
(i) $\{a^n b^m c^j d^k | 0 < n < m, 0 < j < k\}$

10.3.7. For each of the context-free grammars of Exercise 10.1.1, design a pushdown automaton that accepts the language generated by that grammar.

10.3.8. Let L be a language accepted by a pushdown automaton that pops one *or more* symbols from its symbol stack during any one instruction. Show that L is PSA-acceptable in the sense of Definition 10.6.

EXERCISES FOR §10.4

10.4.1. ᵸʷᵏ What language is accepted, by empty stack, by the pushdown automaton M whose transition diagram appears in Figure 10.4.4?

10.4.2. Apply the construction (i)–(iii) of the proof of Theorem 10.5(a) to the pushdown automaton of Figure 10.3.2 so as to obtain a pushdown automaton that accepts language $\{a^n b^m | n \leq m\}$ by empty stack.

10.4.3. Apply the construction (i')–(iii') of the proof of Theorem 10.5(b) to the pushdown automaton of Figure 10.4.4 so as to obtain an equivalent pushdown automaton that accepts by accepting state.

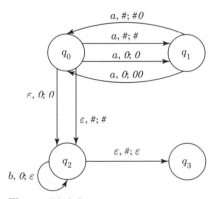

Figure 10.4.4

10.4.4. To appreciate why, in the construction of Theorem 10.5(a), a special stack-initialization symbol is required, consider the pushdown automaton M, whose transition diagram appears in Figure 10.4.5. Machine M accepts by accepting state. We want to see what happens if the construction of Theorem 10.5(a) is applied to M, *without* the precaution of adding a special stack-initialization symbol $\$$. The result will be a new machine M' that accepts by empty stack.

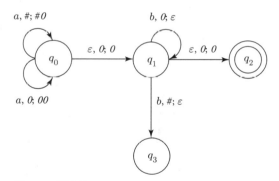

Figure 10.4.5

(a) What language over $\Sigma = \{a, b\}$ is accepted by M?

(b) Add to M a single new state q_{empty}. Implement clauses (ii) and (iii) in the construction of the proof of Theorem 10.5(a) but do not implement clause (i). Present a transition diagram for the pushdown automaton—call it M'—that is the result.

(c) Find a short word that is accepted by M' by empty stack but that is not accepted by M by accepting state, thereby showing that M and M' are not equivalent.

EXERCISES FOR §10.5

10.5.1. [hwk] Consider the grammar G given below. Note that G is in Greibach normal form.

(1.1)–(1.2) $S \to aW \mid b$

(2.1)–(2.2) $W \to aWZ \mid bZ$

(3.1) $Z \to c$

(a) What language is generated by G?

(b) Apply the construction of the proof of Theorem 10.6 to grammar G so as to obtain a pushdown automaton M that accepts $L(G)$ by empty stack.

(c) Present a leftmost derivation of word $aabcc$ in grammar G.

(d) Present a trace of the acceptance of word $aabcc$ by pushdown automaton M.

(e) Formulate the observed correspondence between the leftmost derivation of (c) and the trace of (d).

10.5.2. Consider the pushdown automaton M whose state diagram appears in Figure 10.5.3.

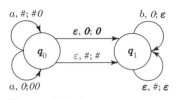

$a, \#; \#0$ $b, 0; \varepsilon$

$\varepsilon, 0; 0$

q_0 $\varepsilon, \#; \#$ q_1

$a, 0; 00$ $\varepsilon, \#; \varepsilon$

Figure 10.5.3

(a) Apply the construction of the proof of Theorem 10.7 to pushdown automaton M so as to obtain a context-free grammar G with $L(G) = L(M)$. Eliminate all useless productions from G.

(b) Present a trace of the acceptance of word $aabb$ by pushdown automaton M.

(c) Present a leftmost derivation of word $aabb$ in grammar G.

(d) Formulate the observed correspondence between the trace of (b) and the leftmost derivation of (c).

EXERCISES FOR §10.6

10.6.1. [hwk] Show that the class of context-free languages is closed under concatenation.

10.6.2. [hwk] Show that the class of context-free languages is closed under Kleene closure.

10.6.3. [hwk] Show that the class of context-free languages is closed under reversal. That is, if L is context-free, then so is $L^R = \{w^R \mid w \in L\}$.

10.6.4. Modify the proof of Theorem 10.9 so as to accommodate the case where L_1 and L_2 are languages over alphabets Σ_1 and Σ_2, respectively, with $\Sigma_1 \neq \Sigma_2$.

EXERCISES FOR §10.7

10.7.1. Use the Pumping Lemma (Lemma 10.3) to argue that the following languages are not context-free. The arguments used will be similar to those applied earlier in Exercises 9.4.2 and 9.4.3.

(a) $\{a^n \mid n$ is prime$\}$

(b) $\{a^{i^2} \mid i > 0\} = \{a^n \mid n$ is a perfect square$\}$

(c) $\{a^{2^i} \mid i \geq 0\} = \{a^n \mid n$ is a power of 2$\}$

10.7.2. [hwk] Use the Pumping Lemma (Lemma 10.3) to show that the following languages are not context-free.

(a) $\{a^n b^n a^n b^n \mid n \geq 0\}$

(b) $\{a^n b^m c^{|n-m|} b^m a^n \mid n, m \geq 0\}$

10.7.3. Prove Theorem 10.12. That is, show that the class of context-free languages is not closed under complementation. (*Hint*: Give an indirect argument that appeals to Theorem 10.11.)

10.7.4. Show that the class of context-free languages is not closed under set difference or relative complementation.

10.7.5. Show that the class of context-free languages is not closed under the subset relation. That is, $L_1 \subseteq L_2$ with L_2 context-free does not imply that L_1 is context-free. (*Hint*: Present a pair of languages L_1 and L_2.)

EXERCISES FOR §10.8

10.8.1. Show that there exist context-free languages that are accepted by no deterministic pushdown automaton by appealing to Theorems 10.6, 10.12, and 10.13. (*Hint*: Give an indirect argument.)

10.8.2. Show that the language $L = \{a^n b^n | n > 0\} \cup \{a^n b^{2n} | n > 0\}$ is accepted by some nondeterministic pushdown automaton but is not accepted by any deterministic pushdown automaton. (*Hint*: Give an indirect argument showing that, if L were accepted by a deterministic machine, then $\{a^n b^n c^n | n > 0\}$ would be PSA-acceptable and hence context-free, contradicting Theorem 10.10.)

10.8.3. [hwk] Justify Remark 10.8.1. That is, suppose that M is a deterministic pushdown-stack automaton. By definition, M accepts language $L(M)$. Explain why M also decides membership in $L(M)$ and hence must be regarded as recognizing $L(M)$ in a certain familiar sense. (*Suggestion*: Assume that M is fully defined.)

10.8.4. Show that any deterministic context-free language is accepted by some deterministic pushdown automaton having no ε-moves.

EXERCISES FOR §10.9

10.9.1. Prove Lemma 10.4. (*Hint*: Give an inductive argument.)

10.9.2. Let $G = \langle \Sigma, \Gamma, \sigma, \Pi \rangle$ be a context-free grammar. Show that, for an arbitrary nonterminal $A \in \Gamma$, it is decidable whether $A \Rightarrow^* \varepsilon$. In particular then, it is decidable whether G generates ε—that is, whether $\sigma \to^* \varepsilon$.

10.9.3. Let $G = \langle \Sigma, \Gamma, \sigma, \Pi \rangle$ be a context-free grammar. Show that, for an arbitrary word w over Σ and an arbitrary nonterminal $A \in \Gamma$, it is decidable whether $A \Rightarrow^* w$. In particular, it is decidable whether G generates w—that is, whether $\sigma \Rightarrow^* w$. (*Hint*: Use Greibach normal form.)

10.9.4. Let $G = \langle \Sigma, \Gamma, \sigma, \Pi \rangle$ be a context-free grammar. Show that, for an arbitrary word w over Σ and an arbitrary nonterminal $A \in \Gamma$, it is decidable whether $A \Rightarrow^* w\beta$ for some β in $(\Sigma \cup \Gamma)^*$. In particular then, it is decidable whether G generates $w\beta$ for some β in $(\Sigma \cup \Gamma)^*$.

10.9.5. Let $G = \langle \Sigma, \Gamma, \sigma, \Pi \rangle$ be a context-free grammar. Show that, for an arbitrary word w over Σ and an arbitrary nonterminal $A \in \Gamma$, it is decidable whether $A \Rightarrow^* \alpha w\beta$ for some α, β in $(\Sigma \cup \Gamma)^*$. In particular, it is decidable whether G generates $\alpha w\beta$ for some α, β in $(\Sigma \cup \Gamma)^*$.

10.9.6. Let $G = \langle \Sigma, \Gamma, \sigma, \Pi \rangle$ be a context-free grammar. Show that for an arbitrary word w over Σ and an arbitrary nonterminal $A \in \Gamma$ it is decidable whether $A \Rightarrow^* \alpha w$ for some α in $(\Sigma \cup \Gamma)^*$. In particular, it is decidable whether G generates αw for some α in $(\Sigma \cup \Gamma)^*$.

EXERCISES FOR §10.10 (END-OF-CHAPTER REVIEW EXERCISES)

10.10.1. [hwk] Present context-free grammars that generate the following languages.
(a) $\{a^n b^m | n, m > 0\}$
(b) $\{a^n b^m cb^m a^n | n, m > 0\}$
(c) $\{w \in \Sigma^* | 1 \le n_a(w) < n_b(w)\}$, where $\Sigma = \{a, b\}$

10.10.2. [hwk] For each of the following languages, do the following. First, show that it is not regular. Then show that it is context-free by presenting a context-free grammar that generates it.
(a) $\{a^n b^m | n \ge m \ge 0\}$
(b) $\{a^n b^m | 0 \le n \le m\}$

10.10.3. ^{hwk} We wish to show that $L = \{a^i b^j c^k | i \neq j$ or $k \neq j\}$ is context-free. That is, L is the language of words w over $\Sigma = \{a, b, c\}$ such that w consists of zero or more cs following zero or more bs, following zero or more as and either the number of as does not equal the number of bs or the number of bs does not equal the number of cs, or both. Finding a context-free grammar that generates L is made easier by first finding grammars generating simpler, related languages. With this end in mind, show that each of the following languages is context-free. For each member of the sequence, you will do well to think about how it is related to preceding member(s) of the sequence.

(a) $\{a^i b^j | i > j\}$
(b) $\{a^i b^j | i > j\}$
(c) $\{a^i b^j | i \neq j\}$
(d) $\{a^i b^j c^k | i \neq j\}$
(e) $\{a^i b^j c^k | j \neq k\}$
(f) $\{a^i b^j c^k | i \neq j$ or $k \neq j\}$

10.10.4. (a) Write a program that transforms any positive context-free grammar into an equivalent grammar in Chomsky normal form.
(b) Write a program for transforming an arbitrary positive, context-free grammar into an equivalent grammar in Greibach normal form.

10.10.5. Use either Lemma 10.3 itself or its strengthened version (see §10.9) to show that each of the languages below is not context-free.
(a) $\{a^i b^j c^k | 1 \leq i \leq j \leq k\}$
(b) $\{a^i b^j c^i d^j | 1 \leq i \leq j\}$
(c) $L = \{a^i | i$ is composite$\}$ (*Hint*: Give an indirect argument. Let k be as in the statement of the strengthened version of the Pumping Lemma for Context-Free Languages. Then let p be the least prime number greater than $(N! + 1)! + 1$, where we are setting $N = 2^k$. Show by an indirect argument that $p > (N! + 1)! + N! + 1$. It follows that $p - N!$ is composite (why?) and $|a^{p-N!}| > N$. Now apply the Pumping Lemma in its strengthened version.)

10.10.6. (a) Present a deterministic pushdown automaton that accepts the language $a^n b^{n-1}$ for $n \geq 1$.

(b) ^{hwk} Present a deterministic pushdown automaton that accepts language $\{a^{3n} b^{2n} | n \geq 0\}$.

10.10.7. (a) Convert the following grammar G into an equivalent grammar with no empty productions.

$$S \rightarrow xXy \mid wXz$$

$$X \rightarrow xXy \mid wXz \mid$$

(b) What language is generated by the grammar of (a)? Note that since $L(G)$ is not regular, there is no hope of describing it using a regular expression. You must use set abstraction $\{\ldots | \_\_\_\}$.

(c) Describe briefly a pushdown automaton that accepts this language. Just a rough description in English will be sufficient. Alternatively, implement your machine using the companion software.

(d) Is $L(G)$ a deterministic context-free language?

10.10.8. Critique the following argument as presented by Professor Durcheinander.

Language $\Sigma^* = L((a|b|c)^*) = \Sigma^*$ is regular and, hence, context-free by Remark 10.1.1. But the language $L = \{a^n b^n c^n | n \geq 0\}$ is a subset of Σ^* and, hence, must be context-free as well. By Corollary 10.2, $L \backslash \{\varepsilon\} = \{a^n b^n c^n | n > 0\}$ is context-free. But this is in clear conflict with Theorem 10.10, which just goes to show that you can't believe everything you read in theory texts.

10.10.9. Let w and w' be two words over alphabet Σ. We say that w and w' are *letter-equivalent* if, for all $\sigma \in \Sigma$, $n_\sigma(w) = n_\sigma(w')$. For example, letting $\Sigma = \{a, b\}$, words $aabba$ and $ababa$ are letter-equivalent while $abba$ and $abbb$ are not.

(a) Which of the following word pairs over $\Sigma = \{a, b\}$ are letter-equivalent?
(i) $abbbbaba$ and $abbbba$
(ii) $abababa$ and $bababaa$

(b) Suppose that $\Sigma = \{a\}$ and that w and w' are letter-equivalent words over Σ. What can be concluded about w and w'?

(c) Next, one defines a notion of letter equivalence for languages in terms of the notion of letter equivalence for words. Let L and L' be two languages over Σ. We shall say that L and L' are *letter-equivalent* if both (1) for each word $w \in L$, there exists at least one word $w' \in L'$ such that w is letter-equivalent to w' and (2) for each word $w' \in L'$, there exists at least one word $w \in L$ such that w' is letter-equivalent to w. For example, the context-free language $\{a^n b^n | n \geq 0\}$ is seen to be letter-equivalent to the regular language $\{(ab)^n | n \geq 0\}$. Which of the following pairs of languages over $\Sigma = \{a, b\}$ are letter-equivalent?

   (i) $\{a^n b^n a^m | n, m \geq 0\}$ and
         $\{a^m (ab)^n | n, m \geq 0\}$
   (ii) $\{a^n b^m a^n | n, m \geq 0\}$ and
         $\{b^m (aa)^n | n, m \geq 0\}$
   (iii) $\{w | n_a(w) \geq n_b(w)\}$ and
         $\{a^m (ab)^n | n, m \geq 0\}$

(d) In fact, it can be shown that, corresponding to each context-free language, there exists a letter-equivalent *regular* language. The proof of this important proposition is hardly trivial and we omit it. (The interested reader is directed to the proof of *Parikh's Theorem* in either [Lewis and Papadimitriou 1981] 127–130 or [Salomaa 1973] 63–68.) Part (e) of this exercise was designed so as to render this correspondence at least plausible: Note that the first member of each language pair at (c) is a context-free language that is not regular, whereas the second member of each language pair is regular. For each context-free language below, find a letter-equivalent regular language.

   (i) $\{w \in \Sigma^* | w = w^R\}$, where $\Sigma = \{a, b\}$ (*Suggestion*: Provide a regular expression that denotes a letter-equivalent regular language. Be careful to account for words of odd length.)
   (ii) The language of balanced parentheses

(e) Use the cited correspondence to prove that any context-free language over a single-letter alphabet is regular.

10.10.10. Let us define a context-free grammar G to be *ambiguous* if, for some word $w \in L(G)$, two or more distinct parse trees for w are possible relative to G. Similarly, context-free grammar G will be *unambiguous* provided it is not ambiguous, i.e., if, for each word $w \in L(G)$, exactly one parse tree for w is possible relative to G.

Show that the grammar below is ambiguous by presenting two distinct parse trees for the string $a \cdot a \mid b$.

$$S \to S \cdot S \mid S \mid S \mid (S) \mid a \mid b$$

(*Hint*: Show that there are two distinct leftmost derivations of $a \cdot a \mid b$ within this grammar. Then draw the parse trees induced by these derivations.)

10.10.11. (a) Show that context-free grammar G is ambiguous if and only if some word $w \in L(G)$ has two distinct leftmost derivations within G.

   (b) Show that if G is an unambiguous context-free grammar, then there exists unambiguous G' in Chomsky normal form with $L(G') = L(G) \backslash \{\varepsilon\}$.

10.10.12. A context-free language L is said to be *unambiguous* provided there exists some unambiguous context-free grammar G with $L = L(G)$. (Otherwise, i.e., if there exists no such grammar, then L is said to be *inherently ambiguous*.)

   (a) Show that the union of two disjoint, unambiguous languages is itself unambiguous.

   (b) Show that any regular language is unambiguous. (*Hint*: Recall Theorem 9.16.)

   (c) Show that if L_1 is an unambiguous context-free language and L_2 is a regular language, then language $L_1 \cap L_2$ is unambiguous.

   (d) Show that if L_1 is an unambiguous context-free language and L_2 is a regular language, then language $L_1 \backslash L_2$ is unambiguous.

Chapter _11_

Context-Sensitive Languages and Linear-Bounded Automata

§11.1 Context-Sensitive Grammars

We saw in §10.7 that the language $\{a^n b^n c^n | n > 0\}$ is not context-free. This was a consequence of the Pumping Lemma for Context-Free Languages (Lemma 10.3), but it is also evident if one reflects on the generative capabilities of context-free grammars or the computational capabilities of pushdown automata. There do exist generative grammars that generate $\{a^n b^n c^n | n > 0\}$, however. We present one such grammar G as follows.

EXAMPLE 11.1.1 We let $G = \langle \{a, b, c\}, \{S, A, B, C\}, S, \Pi \rangle$, where Π comprises the seven productions

$$S \rightarrow aSBC \mid aBC$$
$$CB \rightarrow BC$$
$$aB \rightarrow ab$$
$$bB \rightarrow bb$$
$$bC \rightarrow bc$$
$$cC \rightarrow cc$$

Grammar G generates word $aabbcc$ as is seen in the following derivation.

$$S \Rightarrow aSBC$$
$$\Rightarrow aaBCBC$$
$$\Rightarrow aaBBCC$$
$$\Rightarrow aabBCC$$

$$\Rightarrow aabbCC$$

$$\Rightarrow aabbcC$$

$$\Rightarrow aabbcc$$

Of course, G is not context-free. (Recall that the left-hand side of a context-free production consists of a single nonterminal.) Rather, the grammar above is a member of the more inclusive class of generative grammars known as *context-sensitive grammars*. The productions of such grammars are required to be *length-preserving* in the sense that the length of the right-hand side of any production must be at least as great as that of the left-hand side.

DEFINITION 11.1: A *context-sensitive production* is any production $\alpha \rightarrow \beta$ satisfying $|\alpha| \leq |\beta|$. A *context-sensitive grammar* is any generative grammar $G = \langle \Sigma, \Gamma, \sigma, \Pi \rangle$ such that every production in Π is context-sensitive.

Note, first, that context-sensitive grammars cannot have empty productions such as

$$S \rightarrow$$

since such a production would be length-decreasing.

Context-free productions that are not empty are length-preserving and hence context-sensitive as well. However, since context-free grammars in general do involve empty productions, it cannot be said that every context-free grammar is a context-sensitive grammar. The most one can say is that every positive context-free grammar is context-sensitive, where, again, a grammar is positive if it involves no empty productions. On the other hand, for technical reasons, we should like to be able to say that every context-free language is a context-sensitive language. Here again, ε poses a problem. In particular, by definition, context-free languages may contain the empty word. However, the languages generated by context-sensitive grammars can never contain ε, lacking as they do all empty productions. One solution here is to craft our definition of context-sensitive language so as to obtain the desired inclusion.

DEFINITION 11.2: Language L is a *context-sensitive language* if there exists a context-sensitive grammar G such that either $L = L(G)$ or $L = L(G) \cup \{\varepsilon\}$.

If G is a context-free grammar that generates ε, then applying the construction of Theorem 10.1 to G yields a positive context-free grammar G' with $L(G') = L(G) \backslash \{\varepsilon\}$ (see also Exercise 10.2.2). It follows by Definition 11.2 that $L(G)$ is a context-sensitive language.

REMARK 11.1.1: Any context-free language is context-sensitive in the sense of Definition 11.2 despite the fact that there exist context-free grammars that are not context-sensitive grammars.

At the beginning of §10.1 the terminology *context-free/context-sensitive* was discussed and motivated. With similar intent, we mention now a normal form for context-sensitive grammars. Namely, we shall show in §11.2 that any context-sensitive grammar can be transformed into an equivalent context-sensitive grammar, every production of which is of the form

$$\alpha_1 A \alpha_2 \rightarrow \alpha_1 \beta \alpha_2 \tag{11.1.1}$$

with $\beta \neq \varepsilon$. Thus, when it occurs within the context $\alpha_1 \ldots \alpha_2$, nonterminal A may be rewritten as nonempty string β, where β may contain both terminals and nonterminals. This should help to explain why such grammars are termed *context-sensitive*. Note that any nonempty context-free production exhibits this normal form. (Let $\alpha_1 = \alpha_2 = \varepsilon$.)

We have seen that every context-free language is context-sensitive. On the other hand, a language that is not context-free may not be context-sensitive, either. However, if a given language L is known to not be context-free, it is natural to hope that a context-sensitive grammar G can be found that generates L. Indeed, this turned out to be possible in the case of Example 11.1.1 above. We continue now with two more, fairly simple examples before turning to something more challenging.

EXAMPLE 11.1.2 We showed in Exercise 10.10.5(b) that language $L = \{a^i b^j c^i d^j | i, j \geq 1\}$ is not context-free. There do exist grammars that generate L, however. Here is one:

$$S \rightarrow AB$$

$$A \rightarrow aAX \mid aX$$

$$B \rightarrow bBd \mid bYd$$

$$Xb \rightarrow bX$$

$$XY \rightarrow Yc$$

$$Y \rightarrow$$

The logic of the grammar is basically as follows. The productions for nonterminal A will be used to fix the value of i while the productions for nonterminal B will fix the value of j. Each occurrence of nonterminal X is replaced with terminal c but not before the production $Xb \rightarrow bX$ has been used to position it between the bs and the ds. Nonterminal Y serves as a placemarker situated between the bs and the ds and can hence be used in positioning the Xs. The problem, of course, as the reader will likely have noticed, is that this grammar is not quite context-sensitive given the production for nonterminal Y. But it is fairly easy to obtain an equivalent grammar that is context-sensitive by adjusting the productions for S.

(i)–(ii)	$S \rightarrow aAB \mid aB$
(iii)–(iv)	$A \rightarrow aAX \mid aX$
(v)–(vi)	$B \rightarrow bBd \mid bYd$
(vii)	$Xb \rightarrow bX$
(viii)	$XY \rightarrow Yc$
(ix)	$Y \rightarrow c$

Placemarker Y is now itself being replaced with terminal c, so we do not need quite so many occurrences of nonterminal X. A derivation of word $aabbbccddd$ appears below.

$$
\begin{array}{lll}
S & \Rightarrow aAB & \text{by (i)} \\
 & \Rightarrow aaXB & \text{by (iv)} \\
 & \Rightarrow aaXbBd & \text{by (v)} \\
 & \Rightarrow aaXbbBdd & \text{by (v)} \\
 & \Rightarrow aaXbbbYddd & \text{by (vi)} \\
 & \Rightarrow aabXbbYddd & \text{by (vii)} \\
 & \Rightarrow aabbXbYddd & \text{by (vii)} \\
 & \Rightarrow aabbbXYddd & \text{by (vii)} \\
 & \Rightarrow aabbbYcddd & \text{by (viii)} \\
 & \Rightarrow aabbbccddd & \text{by (ix)}
\end{array}
$$

It should be apparent that every derivation of a word over $\Sigma = \{a, b, c, d\}$ will terminate with an application of production (ix). Moreover, by the time (ix) is used to eliminate nonterminal Y, all occurrences of nonterminal X must already have been converted to cs: once Y has disappeared, production (viii) will no longer be applicable.

EXAMPLE 11.1.3 We also showed in Exercise 10.10.5(a) that language $L = \{a^i b^j c^k \mid 1 \le i \le j \le k\}$ is not context-free. Again, there do exist context-sensitive grammars that generate L, however. One such grammar has the 10 productions

$$
\begin{aligned}
S &\to aS'bX \mid abX \\
S' &\to aS'bC \mid S'bC \mid S'C \mid bC \mid C \\
Cb &\to bC \\
CX &\to Xc \\
X &\to c
\end{aligned}
$$

The productions for S and S' are first used to fix values $i, j,$ and k, in effect. Nonterminal X is introduced as a placemarker situated immediately to the right of all the bs. Precisely as in the preceding Example 11.1.2, occurrences of nonterminal C are moved to the right past the bs before being converted to cs. Finally, placemarker X is itself converted to c.

EXAMPLE 11.1.4 (Context-Sensitive Grammars and Natural Languages) In §10.1 we considered the theoretical linguist's use of context-free grammars in giving an account of the syntax of English. We close the present section with a brief discussion of the application within linguistics of context-sensitive rules. As an easy illustration, we describe the potential of such rules to interpret the phenomenon of subject–verb agreement with respect to number—that is, singular or plural—as reflected in sentences:

(a)   The child runs.   (11.1.2)

(b)   The men run.

To this end, we introduce the following rules.

$$S \rightarrow NP\ VP$$
$$NP \rightarrow Det\ N_{sing} \mid Det\ N_{plur}$$
$$N_{sing}\ VP \rightarrow N_{sing}\ V_{sing}$$
$$N_{plur}\ VP \rightarrow N_{plur}\ V_{plur}$$
$$Det \rightarrow \textbf{the} \qquad\qquad (11.1.3)$$
$$N_{sing} \rightarrow \textbf{child}$$
$$N_{plur} \rightarrow \textbf{men}$$
$$V_{sing} \rightarrow \textbf{runs}$$
$$V_{plur} \rightarrow \textbf{run}$$

Note that the fourth and fifth rules here are context-sensitive but not context-free. Although it is possible to account for subject–verb agreement using context-free rules only, the two context-sensitive rules capture neatly our intuition that the number of the subject determines that of the verb.

We note that, as a consequence of the length-preserving character of context-sensitive productions, successive lines of a derivation never decrease in length. This fact is reflected in the derivations presented within Examples 11.1.1 and 11.1.2 above: Each line is at least as long as its predecessor. Moreover, if $S \Rightarrow^* w$ is a derivation of w within context-sensitive grammar G, then no line of the derivation will exceed w in length.

Finally, we note that no concept of a parse tree is associated with context-sensitive grammars in general, and it should be clear enough why not. (Try drawing a parse tree for word $aabbcc$ relative to the grammar of Example 11.1.1.) On the other hand, if the context-sensitive productions are restricted to those of the form (11.1.1), then parse trees again become a possibility. Linguists have tended to want to work with context-sensitive grammars of this restricted form. For instance, the grammatical structure of each of the sentences at (11.1.2), as dictated by the context-sensitive grammar of (11.1.3), may be represented using a parse tree (see Figure 11.1.1.)

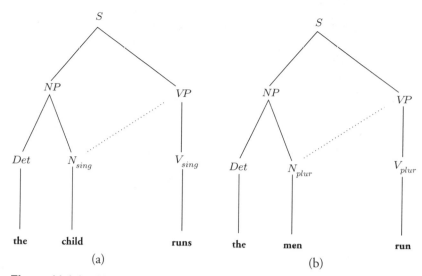

Figure 11.1.1   (a) Parse tree for sentence **the child runs**; (b) parse tree for sentence **the men run**.

§11.2 A Normal Form for Context-Sensitive Grammars

We have defined a context-sensitive grammar as one whose productions are all length-preserving. We now show that any such context-sensitive grammar G can be transformed into an equivalent grammar G', all of whose productions are of the form

$$\alpha_1 A \alpha_2 \to \alpha_1 \beta \alpha_2$$

where A is a nonterminal, α_1 and α_2 are (possibly empty) strings of terminals and nonterminals, and β is a nonempty string of terminals and nonterminals. Within the context of this discussion only, we shall say that such a production is in *normal form*. Apparently, any production in normal form is length-preserving, from which it follows that any grammar all of whose productions are in normal form is a context-sensitive grammar. The converse is not true (see Example 11.2.1 below). However, it is not difficult to describe a two-step algorithm for transforming any context-sensitive grammar G into an equivalent normal form grammar G', thereby showing that any positive context-sensitive language is generated by a normal form grammar.

Step 1. The first step will be familiar. We replace terminals $a, b, \ldots$ throughout the productions of G with new nonterminal representatives $X_a, X_b, \ldots$ or the like. We then add terminal productions

$$X_a \to a$$
$$X_b \to b$$

$$\cdots$$

to the grammar. At this point, with the exception of the terminal productions just added, all production left-hand sides and right-hand sides contain nonterminals only. Note also that all our terminal productions are already in normal form.

Step 2. The construction that we describe next must be carried out for each production that is not already in normal form. By virtue of its being length-preserving, such a production π will be of the form

$$A_1 \ldots A_n \to \alpha B_1 \ldots B_n \tag{11.2.1}$$

where the A_is and B_is are nonterminals and α is a (possibly null) string of nonterminals. (If a given production has five nonterminals on the left and eight on the right, then $n = 5$ and α at (11.2.1) will consist of the first three nonterminals on the right.) We now replace production (11.2.1) with the following $2n$ productions, where $X_1, X_2, \ldots, X_n$ are new nonterminals associated with π:

$$A_1 \ldots A_{n-1} A_n \to A_1 \ldots A_{n-1} X_n$$
$$A_1 \ldots A_{n-2} A_{n-1} X_n \to A_1 \ldots A_{n-2} X_{n-1} X_n$$

$$\ldots$$

$$A_1 X_2 \ldots X_n \to X_1 X_2 \ldots X_n \tag{11.2.2}$$
$$X_1 \ldots X_{n-1} X_n \to X_1 \ldots X_{n-1} B_n$$
$$X_1 \ldots X_{n-2} X_{n-1} B_n \to X_1 \ldots X_{n-2} B_{n-1} B_n$$

$$\ldots$$

$$X_1 B_2 \ldots B_n \to \alpha B_1 B_2 \ldots B_n$$

(Note that the left-hand side of each production after the first is identical with the right-hand side of its predecessor.) Let G' be the grammar obtained from G by applying Steps 1 and 2. It is easy enough to see that any word w generated by G will be generated by G' as well: Within any derivation of w from G, we simply replace every application of production

$$A_1 \ldots A_n \to \alpha B_1 \ldots B_n$$

with corresponding applications of the entire sequence of productions (11.2.2). We must also convince ourselves that G' generates no words not in $L(G)$. But that was the point of introducing the new nonterminals $X_1, X_2, \ldots, X_n$. Note that the productions (11.2.2) are such that, on the right, we have either just A_is or just B_is—never both—always occurring in the very order in which they occur in (11.2.1) itself. This means, in effect, that G' will generate no string of terminals that is not generated by G as well.[1] Finally, note that each of the new productions is in normal form. We take ourselves to have proved

---

[1] Note what happens if we forego the introduction of the X_is and replace the A_is directly with B_is. That is, suppose that we replace each production

$$A_1 \ldots A_n \to \alpha B_1 \ldots B_n$$

with the n productions

$$A_1 \ldots A_{n-1} A_n \to A_1 \ldots A_{n-1} B_n$$
$$A_1 \ldots A_{n-2} A_{n-1} B_n \to A_1 \ldots A_{n-2} B_{n-1} B_n$$

$$\ldots$$

$$A_1 B_2 \ldots B_n \to \alpha B_1 \ldots B_n$$

> **THEOREM 11.1:** Every context-sensitive grammar G is equivalent to a (context-sensitive) grammar G', every production of which is of the form $\alpha_1 A \alpha_2 \rightarrow \alpha_1 \beta \alpha_2$, where A is a nonterminal and α_1, α_2, and β are strings of terminals and nonterminals with $\beta \neq \varepsilon$.

We illustrate the construction of the proof of Theorem 11.1 in

EXAMPLE 11.2.1 Consider, again, the context-sensitive grammar G of Example 11.1.2, whose productions are reproduced below.

(i)–(ii)	$S \rightarrow aAB \mid aB$
(iii)–(iv)	$A \rightarrow aAX \mid aX$
(v)–(vi)	$B \rightarrow bBd \mid bYd$
(vii)	$Xb \rightarrow bX$
(viii)	$XY \rightarrow Yc$
(ix)	$Y \rightarrow c$

The reader will recall that G generates the language $L = \{a^i b^j c^i d^j \mid i, j \geq 1\}$. We apply the algorithm of the proof of Theorem 11.1 in order to obtain an equivalent context-sensitive grammar that is in normal form. (Which two productions of G are currently not in normal form?)

Applying Step 1, we obtain the productions

(i)–(ii)	$S \rightarrow Z_a AB \mid Z_a B$
(iii)–(iv)	$A \rightarrow Z_a AX \mid Z_a X$
(v)–(vi)	$B \rightarrow Z_b BZ_d \mid Z_b YZ_d$
(vii)	$XZ_b \rightarrow Z_b X$
(viii)	$XY \rightarrow YZ_c$
(Ix)	$Y \rightarrow Z_c$
(x)	$Z_a \rightarrow a$
(xi)	$Z_b \rightarrow b$

If G just happens to include a production such as

$$A_{n-1} B_n \rightarrow A_{n-1} \beta$$

say, then this production might be used within G' to generate, from word $A_1 \ldots A_n$, some word not derivable from $A_1 \ldots A_n$ in G. This, in turn, could have as consequence that $L(G') \neq L(G)$.

$$(\text{xii}) \qquad Z_c \to c$$

$$(\text{xiii}) \qquad Z_d \to d$$

In answer to our earlier question, we note that all productions except productions (vii) and (viii) are context-free and hence, by an earlier remark, already in normal form. Hence we need apply Step 2 only to productions (vii) and (viii). In each case, we have $n = 2$ and $\alpha = \varepsilon$ in (11.2.1). Consequently, each of (vii) and (viii) will be replaced by $2n = 2 \cdot 2$ productions. In the case of production (vii), we introduce two new nonterminals X_1 and X_2 as well as the four productions

$$XZ_b \;\; \to XX_2$$

$$XX_2 \;\; \to X_1 X_2$$

$$X_1 X_2 \;\; \to X_1 X$$

$$X_1 X \;\; \to Z_b X$$

In the case of production (viii), we introduce nonterminals Y_1 and Y_2 and the four productions

$$XY \;\; \to XY_2$$

$$XY_2 \;\; \to Y_1 Y_2$$

$$Y_1 Y_2 \;\; \to Y_1 Z_c$$

$$Y_1 Z_c \;\; \to YZ_c$$

The resulting grammar with 19 productions is in normal form. (Both (vii) and (viii) are dropped.)

Having now proved Theorem 11.1 and illustrated it with an example, we have justified to the reader our use of the term "context-sensitive" to describe any generative grammar each of whose productions is length-preserving.

§11.3 Linear-Bounded Automata

In earlier chapters we came to associate certain important subfamilies of generative grammars with machine models: right-linear grammars with finite-state automata (Chapter 9) and context-free grammars with pushdown-stack automata (Chapter 10). We now seek a class of automata equivalent to the class of context-sensitive grammars. Such a class exists, as the reader will have predicted, and it is time to describe this new type of automaton. In fact, it will turn out to be an easily described variant of the nondeterministic, single-tape Turing machine introduced in §2.6.

The new type of automaton is called a *linear-bounded automaton*. We shall consider linear-bounded automata as language acceptors and language recognizers only. Hence we shall use linear-bounded automata to implement only one of the computational paradigms of §1.1. The special features of a linear-bounded automaton M are the following.

- As already mentioned, M will be a special variety of nondeterministic single-tape Turing machine.

- Two special elements of M's tape alphabet Γ will be used as left and right endmarkers. We shall use λ for the left endmarker and ρ for the right endmarker. We shall assume that, at the inception of M's computation, symbols λ and ρ appear on M's tape immediately to the left and right, respectively, of input word w.

- Furthermore, we shall require that M's read/write head remain between endmarkers λ and ρ inclusive throughout its computation. It is permitted to move neither to the left of λ nor to the right of ρ. Nor can either of λ and ρ be erased and written anew. In other words, if M's read/write head encounters left endmarker λ, then the one possible action is a move right. If it encounters the right endmarker ρ, then the only possibility is a move left. These requirements will be reflected in M's state diagram or transition mapping.

This completes our informal description of linear-bounded automata. Intuitively, a linear-bounded automaton is a nondeterministic Turing machine whose storage use coincides with the length of input; in other words, storage usage is fixed at the inception of computation. (As we shall see, if M's input word w just happens to be empty, then storage may not exceed $|w| + 1 = 1$—or $|w| + 3 = 3$ if λ and ρ are included.) Naturally, given this restriction on resources, we expect there to be languages accepted by Turing machines that are not accepted by any linear-bounded automata. This will turn out to be the case (see §11.7 below). In any case, the formal definition of linear-bounded automata that follows reflects the new restriction on storage usage.

DEFINITION 11.3: A *linear-bounded automaton* is a nondeterministic Turing machine $M = \langle Q, \Sigma, \Gamma, q_{init}, \delta_M \rangle$ with $\lambda, \rho \in \Gamma$ such that
  (i)   for any $q \in Q$, $\delta_M(q, \lambda)$ is either undefined or equal to (R, q') for some $q' \in Q$;
  (ii) for any $q \in Q$, $\delta_M(q, \rho)$ is either undefined or equal to (L, q') for some $q' \in Q$;
  (iii) for any $q, q' \in Q$ and any $\sigma \in \Gamma$, $\delta_M(q, \sigma)$ has neither (λ, q') nor (ρ, q') among its values.

Recall that, since M is nondeterministic, its transition mapping δ_M is multiple-valued.

- Clause (i) of Definition 11.3 says in effect that, upon encountering left endmarker λ, either M halts or its read/write head moves to the right.

- Clause (ii) says in effect that, upon encountering right endmarker ρ, either M halts or its read/write head moves to the left.

- Clause (iii) prohibits M from ever writing either λ or ρ. Clauses (i), (ii), and (iii) together guarantee that endmarkers λ and ρ can never be moved by first erasing and then rewriting elsewhere on the tape.

The notion of word acceptance and language acceptance for linear-bounded automata is essentially that given for nondeterministic Turing machines (cf. Definitions 2.9 and 2.10). We have only to adopt some conventions with regard to endmarkers λ and ρ.

DEFINITION 11.4: *Linear-bounded automaton $M = \langle Q, \Sigma, \Gamma, q_{init}, \delta_M \rangle$ accepts nonempty word w if,* when started scanning the leftmost symbol of w on a tape that contains w immediately preceded by λ and immediately followed by ρ and that is otherwise blank, then M has some computation that enables it to halt scanning symbol *1* on a tape that contains the string $\lambda 1 B^{|w|-1} \rho$ and that is blank otherwise.

As with Turing machines generally, we make $w = \varepsilon$ a special case: So $M = \langle Q, \Sigma, \Gamma, q_{init}, \delta_M \rangle$ *accepts* ε if, when M is started scanning a blank immediately preceded by left endmarker λ and immediately followed by right endmarker ρ on an otherwise blank tape, then M has some computation that enables it to halt scanning symbol *1* on a tape that contains the string $\lambda 1 \rho$ and that is blank otherwise.

In Definition 11.4 the locution "M has some computation that enables it to ..." is intended to reflect M's nondeterminism. In general, M will have choices. If these choices cause M, having started scanning the leftmost symbol of w, to halt reading a *1*, then M is said to accept w.

DEFINITION 11.5: A *linear-bounded automaton M accepts language L* if M accepts all and only the words of L.

DEFINITION 11.6: A language is said to be *LBA-acceptable* if there exists a linear-bounded automaton that accepts it.

We leave it to the reader to formulate the notion of language recognition for linear-bounded automata (cf. Definition 2.11).

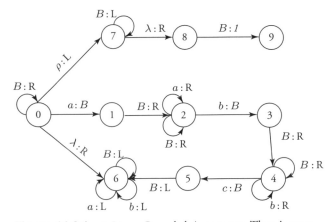

Figure 11.3.1 A Linear-Bounded Automaton That Accepts Language $\{a^n b^n c^n \mid \geq 1\}$.

EXAMPLE 11.3.1 As a first example of a linear-bounded automaton, consider the linear-bounded automaton M whose state diagram appears in Figure 11.3.1. M accepts the language $\{a^n b^n c^n \mid n \geq 1\}$. In fact, M is deterministic. (Recall that, in general, we are regarding determinism as a special sort of nondeterminism.) The algorithm involves erasing an a, then moving past as to the right until the first b is encountered, erasing it, and so on. The left endmarker λ is useful in resetting the machine. In fact, the presence of endmarkers λ and ρ simplifies the computation considerably, since there is now no need to replace each erased symbol with some temporary marker such as the asterisk, as was routinely done in Chapters 1 and 2: Right endmarker ρ will enable M to discern that all symbols have been erased in the case of a word of the correct form. In that case, M has only to write an accepting *1* immediately to the right of λ and halt in state q_9. Otherwise, M halts in a nonaccepting configuration.

Open the icon labeled **Example 11.3.1** within the LBA folder and load tape `3a3b3c.lbt` from the File menu.

• Linear-bounded automata turn out to be powerful as language acceptors despite the restriction on storage. We get a taste of this in Examples 11.3.2 and 11.3.3 below, where the languages $\{a^n \mid n$ is prime$\}$ and $\{a^{n^2} \mid n > 0\}$ are shown to be LBA-acceptable. This is of special interest in that these two languages are not context-free, as was shown in Exercise 10.7.1, and hence not PSA-acceptable either, by Theorem 10.7. In the next section we will show that, indeed, the family of PSA-acceptable languages is a proper subset of the family of LBA-acceptable languages.

- Since a linear-bounded automaton is a special sort of Turing machine, it is fairly obvious that any LBA-acceptable language is Turing-acceptable and any LBA-recognizable language is Turing-recognizable. (Still, there is a little bit of work to do—see Exercise 11.3.3.) What is surely less obvious is that every LBA-acceptable language is Turing-recognizable (see Theorem 11.8).

EXAMPLE 11.3.2 The deterministic linear-bounded automaton M at icon **Example 11.3.2** accepts language $\{a^n | n \text{ is prime}\}$ in accordance with Definition 11.5.

The computation of M is describable roughly as follows. Since we assume that any input word consists of nothing but as, M can erase all of them at the outset, given that the distance between endmarkers λ and ρ preserves n. Also, as has been seen in the past, M does not need to check for primality of divisors. So M starts by attempting to divide by 2, then by 3, and so on up to $n - 1$, noting the remainder. Division will involve repeated end-to-end copying of a divisor. If copies of divisor k should ever fit perfectly between λ and ρ, then $k|n$ holds, in which case n is not prime. On the other hand, if division by successive divisors never produces remainder 0, then n is prime.

EXAMPLE 11.3.3 The deterministic linear-bounded automaton M associated with the icon labeled **Example 11.3.3** accepts language $\{a^{n^2} | n > 0\}$. Again, since input word w consists of nothing but as, all of them can be erased at the inception of computation without loss of information. If $n = 1$, then M writes an accepting 1 and halts. Otherwise, M considers in succession $n = 2, 3$, and so on. It uses a single representation of n to create a representation of n^2. (Marker $*$ will play an essential role here.) Afterward, M checks to see whether this second representation fills the spaces between λ and ρ completely. If so, then M accepts w. Otherwise, M generates the succeeding value of n and squares it. Only at the point where the representation of n^2 would exceed the space between λ and ρ does M halt, in this case without accepting w.

To see how a single representation of 5, say, is used to create a representation of $5^2 = 25$ while observing the space limitations imposed upon the computation by the definition of linear-bounded automata, consider the following. We use five 1s to represent 5. First, the rightmost of these 1s is changed to an asterisk, say, and the five symbols—four 1s and an asterisk—are used to add five 1s immediately to the right. Thus

$$\lambda 11111 BBBBBBBBBBBBBBBBBBBBBBB\rho$$

gives way to

$$\lambda 1111*11111 BBBBBBBBBBBBBBBBBBB\rho$$

Next, the 1 to the left of $*$ is changed to $*$ and the first five characters—now three 1s and two asterisks—are used to add five more 1s off to the right. This gives

$$\lambda 111**1111111111 BBBBBBBBBBBBB\rho$$

Two more iterations give us

$$\lambda 1****11111111111111111111 BB\rho$$

Now M changes the last of the five initial 1s to an asterisk. At this point, the number of asterisks and

*1*s totals $5^2 = 25$.

$$\lambda \ast\ast\ast\ast\ast 111111111111111111111BB\rho$$

The five asterisks can now be used to obtain a representation of the next value of *n* to be considered, namely, $n = 6$. (In the present case, input word $w = a^{27}$ will not be accepted apparently.)

§11.4 Context-Sensitive Languages and Linear-Bounded Automata

We shall be able to relate context-sensitive grammars and linear-bounded automata by way of a certain equivalence result. Namely, it turns out that a language L is LBA-acceptable in the sense of Definition 11.6 if and only if L is context-sensitive in the sense of Definition 11.2. This gives us two very different characterizations of one and the same family of languages and thereby deepens our understanding of this language family. In presenting a proof of this equivalence, we take each direction separately, as usual.

> **THEOREM 11.2:** If L is a context-sensitive language, then L is LBA-acceptable.

PROOF Suppose that L is a context-sensitive language over alphabet Σ. For the moment, suppose further that L does not contain ε. So there exists a context-sensitive grammar G generating L. We describe a linear-bounded automata M that accepts $L = L(G)$ by specifying the behavior of M for an arbitrary input word w over Σ. Initially, M's single tape contains the string $\lambda w \rho$, as required by Definition 11.4:

$$\lambda \underbrace{abab \ldots abab}_{w} \rho$$

M first transforms this into

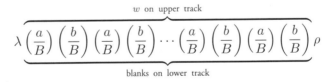

In other words, between endmarkers λ and ρ we have input string w on an upper track and blanks on a lower track. The upper track will not be altered by M but, rather, will be used solely for the purpose of making comparisons. M first checks for $w = \varepsilon$ and halts without accepting if this is the case. Otherwise, M will introduce G's start symbol S, say, on the lower track immediately below the leftmost symbol of w.

$$\lambda \left(\frac{a}{S}\right) \left(\frac{b}{B}\right) \left(\frac{a}{B}\right) \left(\frac{b}{B}\right) \cdots \left(\frac{a}{B}\right) \left(\frac{b}{B}\right) \left(\frac{a}{B}\right) \left(\frac{b}{B}\right) \rho$$

(This will involve execution of an instruction that overwrites symbol (a/B), say, with symbol (a/S).) M next proceeds to nondeterministically select productions of G that it then applies to the contents of the lower track. Such an application, which involves replacing an occurrence of the left-hand side of the chosen production with its right-hand side, will frequently require that part of the contents of the lower track be shifted to the right. After each such replacement, M checks to see whether the contents of the upper and lower tracks are identical. If so, then M accepts w in the usual manner: M erases its tape contents except for λ and ρ, writes a single accepting 1, and halts. On the other hand, if the result of the new replacement would be a string that will not fit on the lower track spaces between λ and ρ, then M halts immediately without accepting.

It can be seen that L is precisely the language accepted by M. For if w is in L, then there is a derivation of w from G. Moreover, by an earlier remark, no intermediate string within this derivation can exceed w in length. So there is a computation of M that involves M's simulating just this derivation and consequently accepting w. On the other hand, suppose that M accepts w. Then, by the characterization of M, word w is derivable from G and hence is in $L = L(G)$.

If, contrary to our initial assumption, L *does* contain ε, then, by hypothesis, there exists a context-sensitive grammar G that generates $L\backslash\{\varepsilon\}$. In that case, the preceding argument—with one minor change—shows that there exists a machine that accepts L. Namely, in our description of M we again make a special case of ε. However, this time M accepts input word $w = \varepsilon$.   Q.E.D.

As for the other direction, we must show that if L is LBA-acceptable, then L is context-sensitive. Preliminary to the proof of Theorem 11.4 below, however, we introduce a new notion of word acceptance for nondeterministic linear bounded automata. Definition 11.4 above—our fundamental notion of word acceptance for linear-bounded automata—uses the notion of an accepting 1 and thus corresponds to Definitions 1.2 and 2.9, the fundamental definitions of word acceptance for Turing machines. By analogy with the development of Chapters 1 and 2, we shall henceforth refer to the notion of word acceptance contained in Definition 11.4 as *(word) acceptance by 1*. There is another useful notion of word acceptance, however: namely, a notion of *word acceptance by terminal state*, already familiar from §2.2. We assume a notion of linear-bounded automaton $M = \langle Q, \Sigma, \Gamma, q_{init}, F, \delta_M \rangle$ with terminal state set $F \subseteq Q$ and proceed immediately to

DEFINITION 11.7: Let $M = \langle Q, \Sigma, \Gamma, q_{init}, F, \delta_M \rangle$ be a linear-bounded automaton with terminal states. Then M *accepts nonempty word w by terminal state* if there is a computation of M such that, when started scanning the leftmost symbol of w on a tape that contains w immediately preceded by λ and immediately followed by ρ and that is otherwise blank, M halts in some state q_t, where $q_t \in F$. (As usual, $w = \varepsilon$ is a special case, which is left to the reader.)

In Definition 11.7 we might have assumed a unique terminal state, as was done in Definition 2.2 (see Exercise 11.4.1).

DEFINITION 11.8: Let L be a language over Σ and let $M = \langle Q, \Sigma, \Gamma, q_{init}, F, \delta_M \rangle$ be a linear-bounded automaton. Then M *accepts language L by terminal state* if M accepts, by terminal state, all and only the words of L.

It can be shown that these two notions of word acceptance, and hence our two notions of language acceptance, are equivalent. In a sense, we have already proved this, since our proof of Theorem 2.3, which demonstrates the corresponding equivalence for Turing machines generally, needs only slight modification in order to work for that special variety of Turing machine that we are calling linear-bounded automata. We shall be satisfied to merely state the needed equivalence and leave the modification of the proof of Theorem 2.3 as an exercise.

THEOREM 11.3: Let L be a language over Σ. Then there exists a linear-bounded automaton M that accepts L by 1 if and only if there exists a linear-bounded automaton M' that accepts L by terminal state.

PROOF See the solution to Exercise 11.4.2.

The proof of Theorem 11.4 below takes the form of a construction. We assume machine $M = \langle Q, \Sigma, \Gamma, q_{init}, F, \delta_M \rangle$ to be given. In particular, this implies complete knowledge of its transition mapping δ_M (or its state diagram). We then use this knowledge to construct a context-sensitive grammar G that simulates M and, as a result, generates language $L(M)$—or, possibly, $L(M) \backslash \{\varepsilon\}$. A description of this general construction is our ultimate goal. However, we find it useful to approach the general case by considering a particular instance of it.

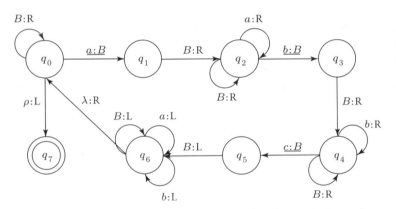

Figure 11.4.1   Linear-bounded automaton M has three write instructions.

EXAMPLE 11.4.1 Let $\Sigma = \{a, b, c\}$ and let $L = \{a^n b^n c^n | n \geq 1\}$. Language L was already seen to be LBA-acceptable in Example 11.3.1. The machine given there accepted L by 1. The state diagram presented in Figure 11.4.1, on the other hand, is that of a linear-bounded automaton $M = \langle Q, \Sigma, \Gamma, q_{init}, F, \delta_M \rangle$ that accepts L by terminal state. Open the icon labeled **Example 11.4.1** within the LBA folder to observe the operation of this machine.

Referring to the state diagram of Figure 11.4.1, we have $Q = \{q_0, q_1, q_2, q_3, q_4, q_5, q_6, q_7\}$ and $F = \{q_7\}$. We now show how to construct a context-sensitive grammar G that simulates M's behavior for an arbitrary input word w and thereby shows L to be context-sensitive (again). We use the familiar technique whereby complex symbols represent several items simultaneously. In particular, the nonterminals of grammar G will be divided into an upper half and a lower half. The upper half of each symbol will be reserved, in effect, for comparison only. (We explain this below.) The lower half, on the other hand, will represent one, or possibly two, squares on M's tape. For instance, the complex symbol (a/b) will be a grammar nonterminal whose upper half is being used to store symbol a and whose lower half represents an occurrence of symbol b in some square of M's tape. Similarly, the nonterminal $(a/\lambda q_0 a)$ stores symbol a in its upper half while its lower half represents the situation whereby

(1) symbol a occurs on M's tape immediately to the right of left endmarker λ,

(2) that occurrence of a is currently being scanned by the read/write head of M, and

(3) M is currently in state q_0.

The simulation of M's behavior for input word w will involve only the lower halves of these nonterminals. To get an idea of how this will work, suppose that w is $aabbcc$ and that G's start symbol is S_1.

Our goal is to show that, in such a case, w must be derivable from S_1 within the constructed grammar G. The preprocessing phase of G's derivation will involve deriving the nonterminal string

$$\left(\frac{a}{\lambda q_0 a}\right)\left(\frac{a}{a}\right)\left(\frac{b}{b}\right)\left(\frac{b}{b}\right)\left(\frac{c}{c}\right)\left(\frac{c}{c\rho}\right)$$

from start symbol S_1. Note that the upper half of this string of nonterminals stores w. Note also that the bottom half represents the initial configuration of M for input word w: M is in state q_0 scanning the leftmost symbol a of w, with w occurring between the two endmarkers. G will now simulate M's behavior using only the lower half of certain strings of nonterminals. Thus G will possess a production that will enable it to derive, from the preceding nonterminal string, the new nonterminal string

$$\left(\frac{a}{\lambda q_1 B}\right)\left(\frac{a}{a}\right)\left(\frac{b}{b}\right)\left(\frac{b}{b}\right)\left(\frac{c}{c}\right)\left(\frac{c}{c\rho}\right)$$

which represents M's having erased symbol a and entered state q_1. (See the state diagram of Figure 11.4.1.) Continuing in this manner, G will eventually derive the nonterminal string

$$\left(\frac{a}{\lambda B}\right)\left(\frac{a}{B}\right)\left(\frac{b}{B}\right)\left(\frac{b}{B}\right)\left(\frac{c}{q_7 B}\right)\left(\frac{c}{B\rho}\right)$$

representing M's having halted in terminal state q_7. (Again, compare the state diagram.) We note that w remains unaltered on the upper half of this string of nonterminals. G now has only to transform this string of nonterminals into terminal string w by applying certain productions available for precisely this purpose, as will be described below.

With this overall approach in mind, we turn to a more formal description of G's construction. We assume $M = \langle \Sigma, \Gamma, q_{init}, F, \delta_M \rangle$ to be given, as reflected in the state diagram of Figure 11.4.1. The terminal alphabet of grammar G is $\Sigma = \{a, b, c\}$, the input alphabet of M. Describing the nonterminal alphabet Γ_G of G is more involved. First, we have two nonterminals S_1 and S_2 whose role during preprocessing will be explained below. (As mentioned, S_1 is G's start symbol.) Alphabet Γ_G also contains all of the following groups of nonterminals:

(i) the 12 nonterminal symbols (a/a), (a/b), (a/c), (a/B), (b/a), (b/b), (b/c), (b/B), (c/a), (c/b), (c/c), (c/B), where, once again, symbol (a/c), say, stores symbol a in its upper half and in its lower half represents an occurrence of symbol c on a square of M's tape;

(ii) a large class of nonterminal symbols involving left endmarker λ, including all of

$$\left(\frac{a}{\lambda q_0 a}\right),\left(\frac{a}{\lambda q_0 b}\right),\left(\frac{a}{\lambda q_0 c}\right),\left(\frac{a}{\lambda q_0 B}\right),\left(\frac{b}{\lambda q_0 a}\right),\left(\frac{b}{\lambda q_0 b}\right),\dots$$

$$\left(\frac{a}{q_0 \lambda a}\right),\left(\frac{a}{q_0 \lambda b}\right),\left(\frac{a}{q_0 \lambda c}\right),\left(\frac{a}{q_0 \lambda B}\right),\left(\frac{b}{q_0 \lambda a}\right),\left(\frac{b}{q_0 \lambda b}\right),\dots$$

$$\left(\frac{a}{\lambda q_1 a}\right),\left(\frac{a}{\lambda q_1 b}\right),\left(\frac{a}{\lambda q_1 c}\right),\left(\frac{a}{\lambda q_1 B}\right),\left(\frac{b}{\lambda q_1 a}\right),\left(\frac{b}{\lambda q_1 b}\right),\dots$$

$$\left(\frac{a}{q_1 \lambda a}\right),\left(\frac{a}{q_1 \lambda b}\right),\left(\frac{a}{q_1 \lambda c}\right),\left(\frac{a}{q_1 \lambda B}\right),\left(\frac{b}{q_1 \lambda a}\right),\left(\frac{b}{q_1 \lambda b}\right),\dots$$

and so on for all states $q_0, q_1, \dots$ of M, where nonterminal $(a/\lambda q_0 B)$, say, stores symbol a in its upper half and in its lower half represents the situation whereby a blank occurs on M's tape immediately to the right of left endmarker λ with M in state q_0 scanning this blank;

(iii) a large class of nonterminals involving right endmarker ρ and analogous to those of (ii) above. For example, nonterminal $(b/Bq_3\rho)$ stores symbol b above and in its lower half represents the situation where M is in state q_3 scanning right endmarker ρ, to the left of which there is a blank;

(iv) a large class of nonterminals involving both λ and ρ. In no particular order, we mention $\ldots, (a/\lambda q_1 B\rho), \ldots, (b/\lambda q_1 B\rho), \ldots, (c/\lambda Bq_2\rho), \ldots, (B/\lambda cq_6\rho), \ldots$;

(v) a large class of nonterminals involving M's various states but not involving endmarkers λ or ρ; for example, nonterminal $(b/q_4 a)$ stores symbol b above and in its lower half represents M's being in state q_4 scanning an occurrence of a.

Most of the productions of (i) through (v) will never occur within any derivation for G. Their inclusion reflects our interest in a completely general construction.

As for the productions of grammar G, we need all of the following, which we divide into seven groups. The first three groups here consist of preprocessing productions.

- **Group 1** $\quad S_1 \rightarrow \left(\dfrac{a}{\lambda q_0 a}\right) S_2$

  $\rightarrow \left(\dfrac{b}{\lambda q_0 b}\right) S_2$ $\Big\}$ one production for each member of Σ

  $\rightarrow \left(\dfrac{c}{\lambda q_0 c}\right) S_2$

  $\rightarrow \left(\dfrac{a}{\lambda q_0 a\rho}\right)$

  $\rightarrow \left(\dfrac{b}{\lambda q_0 b\rho}\right)$ $\Big\}$ one production for each member of Σ

  $\rightarrow \left(\dfrac{c}{\lambda q_0 c\rho}\right)$

  S_1 is the start symbol of G.

- **Group 2** $\quad S_2 \rightarrow \left(\dfrac{a}{a}\right) S_2$

  $\rightarrow \left(\dfrac{b}{b}\right) S_2$ $\Big\}$ one production for each member of Σ

  $\rightarrow \left(\dfrac{c}{c}\right) S_2$

- **Group 3** $\quad S_2 \rightarrow \left(\dfrac{a}{a\rho}\right) \Big| \left(\dfrac{b}{b\rho}\right) \Big| \left(\dfrac{c}{c\rho}\right)$ /* one production for each member of Σ */

Groups (4)–(6) below constitute G's simulation productions.

- **Group 4.** These productions correspond to M's three write instructions. We have 12 productions for each of the three write instructions appearing in Figure 11.4.1. For write instruction

$$\delta_M(q_0, a) = (B, q_1)$$

we have 12 productions, which we arrange in four columns:

Column 1   **Column 2**   **Column 3**   **Column 4**

$$\left(\frac{a}{\lambda q_0 a}\right) \rightarrow \left(\frac{a}{\lambda q_1 B}\right) \qquad \left(\frac{a}{q_0 a \rho}\right) \rightarrow \left(\frac{a}{q_1 B \rho}\right) \qquad \left(\frac{a}{\lambda q_0 a \rho}\right) \rightarrow \left(\frac{a}{\lambda q_1 B \rho}\right) \qquad \left(\frac{a}{q_0 a}\right) \rightarrow \left(\frac{a}{q_1 B}\right)$$

$$\left(\frac{b}{\lambda q_0 a}\right) \rightarrow \left(\frac{b}{\lambda q_1 B}\right) \qquad \left(\frac{b}{q_0 a \rho}\right) \rightarrow \left(\frac{b}{q_1 B \rho}\right) \qquad \left(\frac{b}{\lambda q_0 a \rho}\right) \rightarrow \left(\frac{b}{\lambda q_1 B \rho}\right) \qquad \left(\frac{b}{q_0 a}\right) \rightarrow \left(\frac{b}{q_1 B}\right)$$

$$\left(\frac{c}{\lambda q_0 a}\right) \rightarrow \left(\frac{c}{\lambda q_1 B}\right) \qquad \left(\frac{c}{q_0 a \rho}\right) \rightarrow \left(\frac{c}{q_1 B \rho}\right) \qquad \left(\frac{c}{\lambda q_0 a \rho}\right) \rightarrow \left(\frac{c}{\lambda q_1 B \rho}\right) \qquad \left(\frac{c}{q_0 a}\right) \rightarrow \left(\frac{c}{q_1 B}\right)$$

Assuming that M is in state q_0 scanning symbol a, there are then four possibilities:

(1) Scanned symbol a occurs immediately to the right of left endmarker λ but not immediately to the left of right endmarker ρ.

(2) Scanned symbol a occurs immediately to the left of right endmarker ρ but not immediately to the right of left endmarker λ.

(3) Scanned symbol a occurs immediately to the right of left endmarker λ and immediately to the left of right endmarker ρ.

(4) Scanned symbol a occurs neither immediately to the right of left endmarker λ nor immediately to the left of right endmarker ρ.

Corresponding to write instruction

$$\delta_M(q_2, b) = (B, q_3)$$

there are another twelve productions, of which we mention only

$$\left(\frac{b}{q_2 b}\right) \rightarrow \left(\frac{b}{q_3 B}\right)$$

Of the 12 productions for instruction $\delta_M(q_4, c) = (B, q_5)$, we mention only two:

$$\left(\frac{c}{q_4 c \rho}\right) \rightarrow \left(\frac{c}{q_5 B \rho}\right) \qquad \left(\frac{c}{q_4 c}\right) \rightarrow \left(\frac{c}{q_5 B}\right)$$

• **Group 5.** The productions of this group correspond to the eight move-right instructions appearing in M's transition diagram. There will be many instructions in this group. We choose to display only a few of those for the instruction $\delta_M(q_1, B) = (R, q_2)$.

$$\left(\frac{a}{q_1 B}\right)\left(\frac{a}{a}\right) \rightarrow \left(\frac{a}{B}\right)\left(\frac{a}{q_2 a}\right) \qquad \left(\frac{a}{q_1 B}\right)\left(\frac{b}{b}\right) \rightarrow \left(\frac{a}{B}\right)\left(\frac{b}{q_2 b}\right) \qquad \left(\frac{a}{q_1 B}\right)\left(\frac{b}{B}\right) \rightarrow \left(\frac{a}{B}\right)\left(\frac{b}{q_2 B}\right)$$

• **Group 6.** These productions correspond to the five move-left instructions appearing in M's transition diagram. Again, there are many productions in this group. Only three of those for the instruction

$\delta_M(q_5, B) = (L, q_6)$ are shown here.

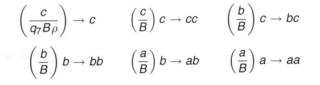

$$\left(\frac{b}{B}\right)\left(\frac{c}{q_5 B}\right) \rightarrow \left(\frac{b}{q_6 B}\right)\left(\frac{c}{B}\right) \qquad \left(\frac{c}{B}\right)\left(\frac{c}{q_5 B}\right) \rightarrow \left(\frac{c}{q_6 B}\right)\left(\frac{c}{B}\right) \qquad \left(\frac{b}{b}\right)\left(\frac{c}{q_5 B}\right) \rightarrow \left(\frac{b}{q_6 b}\right)\left(\frac{c}{B}\right)$$

- **Group 7.** This final group consists of terminal productions that, under appropriate circumstances, eliminate the lower halves of nonterminals. We display the six productions of greatest interest only. (We list them in the order, from left to right, in which they will be applied.)

$$\left(\frac{c}{q_7 B \rho}\right) \rightarrow c \qquad \left(\frac{c}{B}\right) c \rightarrow cc \qquad \left(\frac{b}{B}\right) c \rightarrow bc$$

$$\left(\frac{b}{B}\right) b \rightarrow bb \qquad \left(\frac{a}{B}\right) b \rightarrow ab \qquad \left(\frac{a}{B}\right) a \rightarrow aa$$

We note in passing that all of the productions displayed above—as well as those that we did not bother to display—are length-preserving. Hence G is a context-sensitive grammar. One consequence of this is that G does not generate ε. Note also that none of the simulation productions of Groups 4–6 alters the contents of the upper track. Preliminary to showing how the productions of Groups 4–6 simulate M's acceptance of words of L, we first present an accepting computation for input word *aabbcc* on the part of M.

$\lambda q_0 \, aabbcc \rho$

$\lambda q_1 \, Babbcc \rho$

$\lambda B q_2 \, abbcc \rho$

$\lambda B a q_2 \, bbcc \rho$

$\lambda B a q_3 \, Bbcc \rho$

$\lambda B a B q_4 \, bcc \rho$

$\lambda B a B b q_4 \, cc \rho$

$\lambda B a B b q_5 \, Bc \rho$

$\lambda B a B q_6 \, bBc \rho$

$\lambda B a q_6 \, BbBc \rho$

$\lambda B q_6 \, aBbBc \rho$

$\lambda q_6 \, BaBbBc \rho$

$q_6 \lambda BaBbBc \rho$

$\lambda q_0 \, BaBbBc \rho$

. . .

$\lambda q_0 \, BBBBBB \rho$

. . .

$\lambda BBBBBB q_0 \rho$

$\lambda BBBBB q_7 B \rho$

(11.4.1)

M begins in state q_0 scanning the occurrence of letter *a* immediately to the right of left endmarker λ.

We now present a derivation within G of word *aabbcc* that simulates this accepting computation of M.

First, using the productions of Groups 1, 2, and 3 we obtain the derivation

$$S_1 \Rightarrow \left(\frac{a}{\lambda q_0 a}\right) S_2$$

$$\Rightarrow^* \left(\frac{a}{\lambda q_0 a}\right) \left(\frac{a}{a}\right) \left(\frac{b}{b}\right) \left(\frac{b}{b}\right) \left(\frac{c}{c}\right) \left(\frac{c}{c\rho}\right)$$

Next, using the appropriate productions of Groups 4–6, we obtain

$$S_1 \Rightarrow^* \left(\frac{a}{\lambda q_1 B}\right) \left(\frac{a}{a}\right) \left(\frac{b}{b}\right) \left(\frac{b}{b}\right) \left(\frac{c}{c}\right) \left(\frac{c}{c\rho}\right)$$

$$\Rightarrow^* \left(\frac{a}{\lambda B}\right) \left(\frac{a}{q_2 a}\right) \left(\frac{b}{b}\right) \left(\frac{b}{b}\right) \left(\frac{c}{c}\right) \left(\frac{c}{c\rho}\right)$$

$$\Rightarrow^* \left(\frac{a}{\lambda B}\right) \left(\frac{a}{a}\right) \left(\frac{b}{q_2 b}\right) \left(\frac{b}{b}\right) \left(\frac{c}{c}\right) \left(\frac{c}{c\rho}\right)$$

$$\Rightarrow^* \left(\frac{a}{\lambda B}\right) \left(\frac{a}{a}\right) \left(\frac{b}{q_3 B}\right) \left(\frac{b}{b}\right) \left(\frac{c}{c}\right) \left(\frac{c}{c\rho}\right)$$

$$\Rightarrow^* \left(\frac{a}{\lambda B}\right) \left(\frac{a}{a}\right) \left(\frac{b}{B}\right) \left(\frac{b}{q_4 b}\right) \left(\frac{c}{c}\right) \left(\frac{c}{c\rho}\right)$$

$$\Rightarrow^* \left(\frac{a}{\lambda B}\right) \left(\frac{a}{a}\right) \left(\frac{b}{B}\right) \left(\frac{b}{b}\right) \left(\frac{c}{q_4 c}\right) \left(\frac{c}{c\rho}\right)$$

$$\Rightarrow^* \left(\frac{a}{\lambda B}\right) \left(\frac{a}{a}\right) \left(\frac{b}{B}\right) \left(\frac{b}{b}\right) \left(\frac{c}{q_5 B}\right) \left(\frac{c}{c\rho}\right)$$

$$\Rightarrow^* \left(\frac{a}{\lambda B}\right) \left(\frac{a}{a}\right) \left(\frac{b}{B}\right) \left(\frac{b}{q_6 b}\right) \left(\frac{c}{B}\right) \left(\frac{c}{c\rho}\right) \qquad (11.4.2)$$

$$\Rightarrow^* \left(\frac{a}{\lambda B}\right) \left(\frac{a}{a}\right) \left(\frac{b}{q_6 B}\right) \left(\frac{b}{b}\right) \left(\frac{c}{B}\right) \left(\frac{c}{c\rho}\right)$$

$$\Rightarrow^* \left(\frac{a}{\lambda B}\right) \left(\frac{a}{q_6 a}\right) \left(\frac{b}{B}\right) \left(\frac{b}{b}\right) \left(\frac{c}{B}\right) \left(\frac{c}{c\rho}\right)$$

$$\Rightarrow^* \left(\frac{a}{\lambda q_6 B}\right) \left(\frac{a}{a}\right) \left(\frac{b}{B}\right) \left(\frac{b}{b}\right) \left(\frac{c}{B}\right) \left(\frac{c}{c\rho}\right)$$

$$\Rightarrow^* \left(\frac{a}{q_6 \lambda B}\right) \left(\frac{a}{a}\right) \left(\frac{b}{B}\right) \left(\frac{b}{b}\right) \left(\frac{c}{B}\right) \left(\frac{c}{c\rho}\right)$$

$$\Rightarrow^* \left(\frac{a}{\lambda q_0 B}\right) \left(\frac{a}{a}\right) \left(\frac{b}{B}\right) \left(\frac{b}{b}\right) \left(\frac{c}{B}\right) \left(\frac{c}{c\rho}\right)$$

$$\cdots$$

$$\Rightarrow^* \left(\frac{a}{\lambda q_0 B}\right) \left(\frac{a}{B}\right) \left(\frac{b}{B}\right) \left(\frac{b}{B}\right) \left(\frac{c}{B}\right) \left(\frac{c}{B\rho}\right)$$

$$\dots$$

$$\Rightarrow^* \left(\frac{a}{\lambda B}\right) \left(\frac{a}{B}\right) \left(\frac{b}{B}\right) \left(\frac{b}{B}\right) \left(\frac{c}{B}\right) \left(\frac{c}{Bq_0\rho}\right)$$

$$\Rightarrow^* \left(\frac{a}{\lambda B}\right) \left(\frac{a}{B}\right) \left(\frac{b}{B}\right) \left(\frac{b}{B}\right) \left(\frac{c}{B}\right) \left(\frac{c}{q_7 B\rho}\right)$$

Finally, the productions of Group 7 are used to obtain *aabbcc*. Note that there is no way to remove the state nonterminals of G without using the productions of Group 7. Moreover, these productions are capable of removing all grammar nonterminals only if some nonterminal involving q_7 has been introduced. This means that the only way in which G, having introduced state nonterminal q_0, can generate a string consisting solely of terminals is by simulating an accepting computation of M so as to produce a grammar nonterminal involving terminal state q_7, which can then be eliminated.

There is much more that could be said about this example. For instance, we have not attempted to formulate the general principles whereby certain productions find their way into Groups 4–6. It is hoped that the reader is able to discern our method based on this sketch. (Try Exercise 11.4.3 for help in this regard.) Also, the perceptive reader may have wondered at our having included certain productions that can, in fact, never be applied within any derivation in G. A good example is the production $(b/q_0 a) \rightarrow (b/q_1 B)$, which was thrown into Group 4. Since M writes only blanks, it should be clear enough that the nonterminal on the left here can never occur within any string derivable from start symbol S_1. So why have we included it? Very briefly stated, we seek a construction that is *effective* or *algorithmic* in the sense that it can be applied uniformly to any given linear-bounded automaton M, requiring no special insight into M's operation. (Our recognizing that M writes only blanks amounts to such insight in this context.)

Having considered this one long example, we now state and prove the general result. Our proof appeals to the reader's understanding of the construction illustrated above, whereby the transition diagram for a linear-bounded automaton is used to build a context-sensitive grammar.

THEOREM 11.4: If L is accepted by a linear-bounded automaton M, then $L\backslash\{\varepsilon\} = L(G)$ for some context-sensitive grammar G. Alternative formulation: Any LBA-acceptable language is context-sensitive.

PROOF Suppose that $w \neq \varepsilon$ and that $w \in L$. By hypothesis, there exists an accepting computation for w leading to a terminal state of M. (See accepting computation (11.4.1) above.) Given transition mapping δ_M of M, we construct a context-sensitive grammar G as was done in the case of the automaton of Example 11.4.1. We can then see that there is a derivation of w within G that simulates M's accepting computation (cf. (11.4.2)). Hence $w \in L(G)$. Since w was an arbitrary nonempty word of L, we have shown that $L\backslash\{\varepsilon\} \subseteq L(G)$.

We must also convince ourselves that $L(G) \subseteq L\backslash\{\varepsilon\}$. By an earlier remark, G can generate a terminal string only by simulating an accepting computation of M on its lower track, thereby producing a nonterminal involving some terminal state q_t of M. This nonterminal can then be eliminated using productions of Group 7. However, those productions merely reduce a complex nonterminal to the contents of its upper half, which, significantly, will not have been altered after initialization. Thus, if w is generated by G, this can only mean that w was accepted by M. That is, $L(G) \subseteq L$. Finally, since G is context-sensitive, $\varepsilon \notin L(G)$ so that $L(G) \subseteq L$ implies $L(G) \subseteq L\backslash\{\varepsilon\}$.

By the Principle of Extensionality, we have shown that $L\backslash\{\varepsilon\} = L(G)$, from which it follows by Definition 11.2 that L itself is context-sensitive.   Q.E.D.

§11.5 Closure Properties of the Family of Context-Sensitive Languages

We saw in §10.6 that the family of context-free languages is closed under union, concatenation, Kleene closure, and reversal. We also saw that the same family is not closed under intersection, set difference, or complementation. We now turn to an investigation of the closure properties of the family of context-sensitive languages. We shall see that this language family is still not so well understood as the family of context-free languages, although there has been some recent progress on this front.

As a first easy result, we note that the union of two context-sensitive languages L_1 and L_2 is context-sensitive. In fact, the proof is exactly the one that was given for the case of two context-free languages—except we have to be careful in light of the special relation between context-sensitive grammars and context-sensitive languages. Namely, if L_1 and L_2 are both context-sensitive, then by Definition 11.2 we have both

   (1) for some context-sensitive grammar G_1, either $L_1 = L(G_1)$ or $L_1 = L(G_1) \cup \{\varepsilon\}$, and

   (2) for some context-sensitive grammar G_2, either $L_2 = L(G_2)$ or $L_2 = L(G_2) \cup \{\varepsilon\}$.

So there are four possible cases.

- If $L_1 = L(G_1)$ and $L_2 = L(G_2)$, then we proceed as in the proof of Theorem 10.8. We first introduce new nonterminals X_a, X_b, and so on, corresponding to terminals $a, b, \ldots$, and in the familiar manner obtain from G_1 and G_2 two equivalent grammars whose left-hand sides consist of nonterminals only. (See Step 1 of the algorithm leading to Theorem 11.1. To see why this is necessary, see Exercise 11.5.1 below.) Then, after some possible relettering of nonterminals so as to avoid conflicts, we add new start symbol S together with the two productions $S \rightarrow S_1 \mid S_2$, where S_1 and S_2 are the start symbols of G_1 and G_2, respectively. The resulting grammar can be seen to generate $L_1 \cup L_2$.

- On the other hand, if $L_1 = L(G_1)$ and $L_2 = L(G_2) \cup \{\varepsilon\}$, say, then the foregoing construction yields a context-sensitive grammar G generating $L(G) = (L_1 \cup L_2) \setminus \{\varepsilon\}$. By Definition 11.2, we have that $L_1 \cup L_2 = L(G) \cup \{\varepsilon\}$ is a context-sensitive language. The other two cases are strictly analogous to this one. We have proved

---

THEOREM 11.5: The union of two context-sensitive languages is itself context-sensitive. Alternative formulation: The family of context-sensitive languages is closed under union.

As mentioned above, we saw in §10.7 that the class of context-free languages is not closed under intersection (cf. Theorem 10.11). However, the more inclusive class of context-sensitive languages *is* closed under intersection, as we shall now show.

THEOREM 11.6: If L_1 and L_2 are context-sensitive languages, then so is $L_1 \cap L_2$. In other words, the family of context-sensitive languages is closed under intersection.

PROOF By Theorem 11.2, $L_1 = L(M_1)$ and $L_2 = L(M_2)$ for some linear-bounded automata M_1 and M_2. If space limitations were not an issue, then we would simply design a new machine M^* that would behave as follows. Given input word w, machine M^* would make a copy of w to begin with. Then it would simulate M_1 on w. If M_1 happens to accept w, thereby destroying the original w in the process, then M^* would simulate M_2 on the copy of w. If M_2 also happens to accept w, then M^* would itself accept w. Of course, nothing quite like this will work for linear-bounded automata, since space usage may not exceed what is required to represent input word w initially: There is no possibility of making a copy off to the side somewhere for later use. But the way around this difficulty is already familiar: We enlarge tape alphabet Γ^* so as to effectively divide M^*'s tape into two tracks, each containing its own copy of input word w initially. M^* first simulates M_1 on the upper track only. If w is accepted, then M_2 is simulated on the lower track.

By Theorem 11.3, we can assume without loss of generality that M_1 and M_2 both accept by terminal state. It is convenient to assume that M_1 and M_2 share input language $\Sigma = \{a, b\}$, say, as well as tape alphabet $\Gamma = \Sigma \cup \{\lambda, \rho\}$. (In other words, our proof will not be maximally general, but the more general proof is not essentially different.) "Intersection" machine M^* will have input alphabet $\Sigma = \{a, b\}$ and tape alphabet $\Gamma = \Sigma \cup \{\lambda, \rho, \left(\frac{a}{a}\right), \left(\frac{a}{b}\right), \left(\frac{a}{B}\right), \left(\frac{b}{a}\right), \left(\frac{b}{b}\right), \left(\frac{b}{B}\right), \left(\frac{B}{a}\right), \left(\frac{B}{b}\right), \left(\frac{B}{B}\right)\}$, where symbol $\left(\frac{a}{b}\right)$, say, occurring in a given tape square is interpreted to mean that symbol a occurs on the upper track and symbol b occurs on the lower track within that square. In the discussion that follows, it is necessary to carefully distinguish M_1's states from those of M_2. To that end, we shall write q_i^1 and q_i^2 to designate M_1's state q_i and M_2's state q_i, respectively.

Let M^*'s initial state be q_0. We assume, as usual, that M^* is started scanning the leftmost symbol of input word w. M^* begins by replacing every occurrence of a with symbol $\left(\frac{a}{a}\right)$ and every occurrence of b with symbol $\left(\frac{b}{b}\right)$. Afterward, M^*'s read/write head returns to the left, and M_1's initial state, which we are calling q_0^1, is entered (see Figure 11.5.1). As for M^*'s simulation of M_1 on its upper track, suppose that M_1 has a write instruction such as $\delta_{M_1}(q_2, a) = (B, q_5)$, which stipulates that, if in state q_2 scanning an a, then a blank is written before entering state q_5. M^*'s transition mapping δ_M will embody not this quadruple itself but, rather, three derived quadruples that enable M^* to simulate the erasure of a on the upper track without disturbing the lower track. Thus we have the new quadruples:

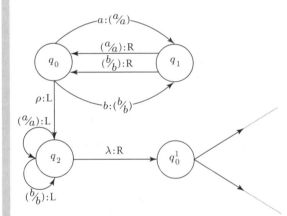

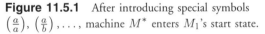

Figure 11.5.1   After introducing special symbols $\left(\frac{a}{a}\right)$, $\left(\frac{a}{b}\right)$, ..., machine M^* enters M_1's start state.

$$\delta_{M^*}\left(q_2^1, \left(\frac{a}{a}\right)\right) = \left(\left(\frac{B}{a}\right), q_5^1\right) \qquad \delta_{M^*}\left(q_2^1, \left(\frac{a}{b}\right)\right) = \left(\left(\frac{B}{b}\right), q_5^1\right)$$

$$\delta_{M^*}\left(q_2^1, \left(\frac{a}{B}\right)\right) = \left(\left(\frac{B}{B}\right), q_5^1\right)$$

Analogously, the quadruple $\delta_{M_1}(q_4, B) = (L, q_4)$ (which stipulates that M_1 will move one square to the left if in state q_4 scanning a blank) will correspond now to the three quadruples:

$$\delta_{M^*}\left(q_4^1, \left(\frac{B}{a}\right)\right) = (\text{L}, q_4^1) \qquad \delta_{M^*}\left(q_4^1, \left(\frac{B}{b}\right)\right) = (\text{L}, q_4^1) \qquad \delta_{M^*}\left(q_4^1, \left(\frac{B}{B}\right)\right) = (\text{L}, q_4^1)$$

Next, by Exercise 11.4.1, we can assume without loss of generality that M_1's terminal state is unique. (Also, we may assume that M_1 has no instructions whatever for this unique terminal state.) We identify, in effect, M_1's terminal state with M_2's initial state—now denoted q_0^2. As for M^*'s simulation of M_2 on the lower track, we now add, in analogous fashion, three quadruples for each of M_2's instructions. M_2's unique terminal state becomes the unique terminal state of M^*. Q.E.D.

Since any context-free language is context-sensitive, we have the following corollary to Theorem 11.6.

COROLLARY 11.1: The intersection of two context-free languages is context-sensitive.

Finally, we note that the question whether the family of context-sensitive languages is closed under complementation remained unanswered until the late 1980s. This situation reflected the incompleteness of our understanding of this language family up to that time. As it turns out, we do have closure under complementation as a consequence of a complexity-theoretic result concerning nondeterministic Turing machines that was proved, simultaneously and independently, by N. Immerman and R. Szelepcsényi (see [Immerman 1988] and [Szelepscényi 1987]). Namely, they showed, in effect, that, for any language L, if L is accepted in linear space by a nondeterministic Turing machine, then so is L^c. The implications of this result for the family of LBA-acceptable languages should be fairly obvious, given some single-tape version of Theorem 2.5.

§11.6 The General Word Problem for Context-Sensitive Languages Is Solvable

Suppose that you are presented with generative grammar $G = \langle \Sigma, \Gamma, \sigma, \Pi \rangle$ and word $w \in \Sigma^*$ and wish to know whether G generates w. You might try to generate w from G yourself. If successful, then, of course, you can be satisfied that $w \in L(G)$. On the other hand, if you are unsuccessful, can you conclude that $w \notin L(G)$? Obviously not: There may be a derivation of w from G despite your having failed to find it. Later, in Chapter 12, we shall see that, for generative grammars generally, there is no algorithm for deciding, for a given generative grammar G and word w, whether G generates w. One expresses this by saying that *the general word problem for generative grammars (phrase-structure languages) is unsolvable*. (We shall see in Chapter 12 that this formulation presupposes Church's Thesis.) However, in the special circumstance whereby G is a context-sensitive grammar, we do possess such an algorithm. In other words, the general word problem for context-sensitive grammars (languages) is solvable. Of course, this result will not be entirely surprising since we saw in Exercise 10.9.3 that the general word problem for context-free languages is solvable as well.

The basis for a solution to the general word problem in the context-sensitive case is the length-preserving character of context-sensitive productions. Thus, suppose that we are given context-sensitive grammar G and word w and wish to know whether G generates w. Well, w is of finite length; $|w| = n$, say. Since G has but finitely many productions and since applying a production to any string is length-preserving, we can see that there are but finitely many derivations of the form

S is the start symbol of G, and each of the α_i are strings over $\Sigma \cup \Gamma$, where Σ and Γ are the terminal and nonterminal alphabets, respectively, of G.

$$S \Rightarrow \alpha_1$$
$$\Rightarrow \alpha_2$$
$$\cdots$$
$$\Rightarrow \alpha_k$$

where the α_i are all distinct strings and $|\alpha_k| = n$. Assuming some ordering of the productions of G and some conventions for applying productions to strings, we can effectively list all such derivations of strings α with $|\alpha| = n$. We then check to see whether the final string α in any of these derivations is identical to w. If so, then G generates w. But if not, then we must conclude that G does not generate w, since our list contains all derivations of strings of length n. This is the essence of our demonstration of

---

THEOREM 11.7: If G is a context-sensitive grammar, then membership in $L(G)$ is decidable; that is, there exists an algorithm for deciding whether an arbitrary word w is a member of $L(G)$. In other words, the general word problem for context-sensitive languages is solvable.[1]

PROOF For any given grammar G and fixed n, we construct a finite "derivation" tree $\mathcal{T}$—there will be finitely many paths, each of finite length. Each node N of $\mathcal{T}$ is associated with (the derivation of) some string of terminals and nonterminals. If N is a node of level k, then the associated derivation is of length k. Moreover, our algorithm can now be described either as a breadth-first or a depth-first search algorithm. We expand each node N by applying *each* production of G in every possible way to the string at N. This means that each node of $\mathcal{T}$ will have at most finitely many children since

  (i) G has only finitely many productions and

  (ii) each one of these productions may be applied in only finitely many ways to the string derived at a given node of $\mathcal{T}$.

Each child of node N in turn represents one way in which the derivation at N may be extended. As each new node N in the tree is obtained, we ask ourselves three questions:

  (1) Is the string derived at N identical with w?

  (2) Does the length of the string derived at N strictly exceed $|w|$?

  (3) Does the string at N occur earlier among the strings along the path leading from root to N?

---

[1] We note two items in this connection. First, the claim that $L(G)$, for context-sensitive G, is decidable does not presuppose Church's Thesis: The basis for the claim will be our presentation of an effective test for membership, pure and simple. Second, the further claim that the general word problem for context-sensitive *languages* is solvable presupposes the general availability of context-sensitive *grammars* to which our algorithm may be applied.

If the answer to (1) is yes, then we are done and w is in L. If the answer to (2) is yes, then we mark the path leading to node N as *closed*. Expanding N further will obviously produce no derivation of w. If the answer to (3) is yes, then, in this case as well, we may mark the path leading to node N as closed: Any string derivable by expanding node N is obtainable by further expanding one of N's ancestors. In any case, if (1) is never answered affirmatively, then expansion of the derivation tree comes to an end when every path has been marked closed. (In addition to the reasons already cited, we also mark a path as closed if no production of G is applicable to the string derived at that node.) In the latter case, we must report that w is not generated by G. Q.E.D.

Note that our solution to the general word problem for context-sensitive languages amounts to a brute-force parsing algorithm whereby, for given context-sensitive grammar G and input word w, one considers every possible derivation whose final string is of length less than or equal to $|w|$ and such that no line of the derivation is repeated. We illustrate the algorithm of the proof of Theorem 11.7 with

---

EXAMPLE 11.6.1 Consider the context-sensitive grammar G whose five productions are

$$(i)\text{–}(ii) \qquad S \rightarrow aSS_1 \mid aS_2$$

$$(iii) \qquad S_2 S_1 \rightarrow bS_2 c$$

$$(iv) \qquad cS_1 \rightarrow S_1 c$$

$$(v) \qquad S_2 \rightarrow bc$$

Suppose we wish to decide whether $w = aabbcc$ is a member of $L(G)$. Figure 11.6.1 presents a derivation tree for G relative to $n = |w| = 6$. There are a total of four paths within the tree, the longest of which is of length 4. Since one of these paths leads to a leaf associated with (a derivation of) w, we can see that $w \in L(G)$. In fact, the reader can verify that $L(G) = \{a^n b^n c^n \mid n \geq 1\}$. (Earlier it was seen that the grammar of Example 11.1.1 generates this language as well.)

We claim that the decision procedure described in the proof of Theorem 11.7 can be implemented by a Turing machine so as to establish

---

THEOREM 11.8: Any context-sensitive language is Turing-recognizable.

PROOF See Exercise 11.6.4.

We close this section by making a number of important remarks.

- Since any regular language is context-free and any context-free language is context-sensitive, Theorem 11.7 applies equally to those other two families of formal languages. Namely, the general word problem for regular languages and the general word problem for context-free languages are both solvable. For regular languages, this was already clear from our study of finite state automata (see Remark 9.7.1). In the case of context-free L, we have Exercise 10.9.3.

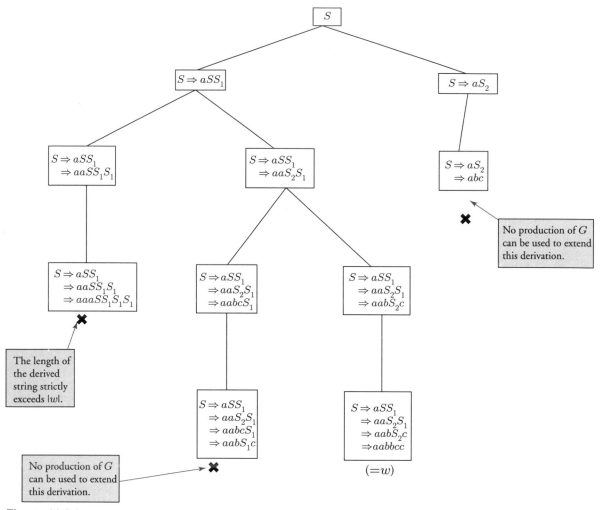

Figure 11.6.1

- One frequently expresses the content of Theorem 11.7 by saying that any context-sensitive *language* L is decidable. We emphasize, again, that in saying this, one is assuming the availability of a context-sensitive grammar for L to which the described decision procedure can be applied.

- If we apply our decision procedure to context-free grammar G and nonempty word w, then the result is a brute-force parsing technique. No attempt is being made to predict which production(s), if applied, would generate w. Rather, each and every parse tree up to a certain size is being examined in order to determine whether it is a parse tree for w (see again Figure 11.6.1). Obviously, such an exhaustive approach is not practicable for compilers.

- The general word problem is just one of several important decision problems concerning the family of context-sensitive languages. We shall consider two more in Theorem 12.11 in the next chapter.

- Our proof of Theorem 11.4 established that any LBA-acceptable language is context-sensitive. So it follows from Theorem 11.7 that any LBA-acceptable language is decidable, as well. This is not yet to assert that any LBA-acceptable language is LBA-recognizable. However, the truth of the latter claim follows from the closure of the context-sensitive languages under complementation (see Exercise 11.8.6).

§11.7 There Exist Turing-Recognizable Languages That Are Not Context-Sensitive

By way of a diagonal argument we show that the class of context-sensitive languages is properly contained within the class of Turing-acceptable languages.

> **THEOREM 11.9:** There exists a Turing-recognizable language L that is not context-sensitive and hence not LBA-acceptable.

PROOF Assume that $\Sigma = \{a, b\}$. We first standardize our notion of generative grammar in a manner that will be useful below. Suppose that L is a language over Σ that is generated by some generative grammar G. We can assume without loss of generality that the start symbol of G is X_0 and that its other nonterminals occur within the infinite list $X_1, X_2, X_3, X_4, \ldots$. After all, if G's start symbol is in fact S and its other nonterminals X, Y, and Z, say, then we simply replace S with X_0, X with X_1, Y with X_2, and Z with X_3 throughout the productions of G so as to obtain a new "standardized" grammar G' that is equivalent to G.

Next, we show how any standardized grammar with $\Sigma = \{a, b\}$ can be described by a single string over the infinite alphabet Ψ given as $\{a, b, \rightarrow, \#, X_0, X_1, \ldots\}$, which we might call the *generative grammar description alphabet*. (Think of each of X_0, X_1, and so on, as a single symbol.) If we assume that the productions of grammar G are $\alpha_1 \rightarrow \beta_1, \alpha_2 \rightarrow \beta_2, \ldots, \alpha_n \rightarrow \beta_n$, then, given that the nonterminals of G are implicit in its productions, the following word over Ψ fixes grammar G completely:

$$\alpha_1 \rightarrow \beta_1 \# \alpha_2 \rightarrow \beta_2 \# \ldots \# \alpha_n \rightarrow \beta_n$$

In other words, one simply lists the productions of G—in any order—separating them by single occurrences of symbol #. In what follows, we shall refer to such words as *(generative) grammar description words*. As an example, the grammar with productions

$$X_0 \rightarrow aX_0b \mid bX_0a \mid X_1$$
$$X_1 \rightarrow aX_1a \mid bX_1b \mid X_2$$
$$X_2 \rightarrow a \mid b$$

would be specified by the grammar description word

$$X_0 \rightarrow aX_0b \# X_0 \rightarrow bX_0a \# X_0 \rightarrow X_1 \# X_1 \rightarrow aX_1a \# X_1 \rightarrow bX_1b \# X_1 ^\frown$$
$$\rightarrow X_2 \# X_2 \rightarrow a \# X_2 \rightarrow b$$

Table 11.7.1

Grammar Description Alphabet Symbol	Symbol Code
a	$bab = ba^1b$
b	$baab = ba^2b$
$\rightarrow$	$baaab = ba^3b$
$\#$	$baaaab = ba^4b$
X_0	ba^5b
X_1	ba^6b
X_2	ba^7b
$\ldots$	$\ldots$
X_n	$ba^{n+5}b$
$\ldots$	$\ldots$

Next, we encode grammar description words as words over alphabet Σ. (The reason for doing this will become clear shortly.) Encoding grammar description words requires that we adopt some encoding of individual symbols of the grammar description alphabet Ψ. To this end, we make use of the symbol codes of Table 11.7.1. As an example, the grammar G' with productions $X_0 \rightarrow aX_0b|$ would be encoded as

$$ba^5b\, baaab\, bab\, ba^5b\, baab\, ba^4b\, ba^5b\, baaab$$

We begin writing $w(G)$ for that word that encodes grammar G.[2] For each standardized grammar G, there is a corresponding encoding $w(G)$ over Σ. On the other hand, given any word w over Σ, it is easy enough in principle to determine whether w is $w(G)$ for some generative grammar G. Thus, if presented with word

$$ba^5b\, baaab\, bab\, ba^5b\, bab\, ba^4b\, ba^5b\, baaab\, baab$$

then, with a little effort, one sees that it encodes the generative grammar whose productions are $X_0 \rightarrow aX_0a|b$.

We have noted in the past that it is possible to effectively enumerate all nonempty words over Σ. We first list all words of length 1, then all words of length 2, and so on, using lexicographic order for words of equal length. Thus

$$a, b, aa, ab, ba, bb, aaa, aab, aba, abb, baa, bab, bba, bbb, aaaa, \ldots \qquad (11.7.1)$$

We shall write w_i, with $i \geq 1$, for the ith word in this enumeration. Thus w_1 is a, w_2 is b, w_3 is aa, and so on. We next imagine that all those words w_i that do not encode specifications of *context-sensitive* grammars are eliminated from (11.7.1). That is, we imagine that any word w_i that is not $w(G)$ for some context-sensitive grammar G is eliminated from the enumeration (11.7.1). The result is a new enumeration that we can represent as

$$w(G_1), w(G_2), w(G_3), \ldots \qquad (11.7.2)$$

where by G_1, say, we mean that grammar specified by the first grammar description word appearing in the enumeration at (11.7.1) that happens to describe a context-sensitive grammar. In full generality, G_i, for $i \geq 1$, will be that context-sensitive grammar G such that $w(G)$ just happens to be the ith context-sensitive grammar specification word in the enumeration (11.7.1). (Again, most words in (11.7.1) do not describe any grammar whatsoever. Among those that do specify grammars, only some denote grammars that are context-sensitive.) The enumeration (11.7.2) induces yet a third

---

[2]In general, encoding $w(G)$ will not be unique, however, since permuting the productions of G will yield a distinct grammar description word specifying G. Happily, this duplication poses no problems for our argument, and we shall continue to speak as if $w(G)$ were always unique.

enumeration

$$G_1, G_2, G_3, \ldots \tag{11.7.3}$$

of all context-sensitive grammars: After all, every context-sensitive grammar G has at least one grammar description word appearing at (11.7.1) and—because G is *context-sensitive*—at (11.7.2) as well. Thus if language L—or perhaps $L \backslash \{\varepsilon\}$—is not generated by any grammar in the enumeration (11.7.3), then we may conclude that L is not context-sensitive.

We next define a new language L_{diag} over $\Sigma = \{a, b\}$ as follows.

> The reference here is to enumeration (11.7.1).

$$w \in L_{diag} \text{ if and only if } w \text{ is } w_i, \text{ for some } i \geq 1, \text{ and } w_i \notin L(G_i) \tag{11.7.4}$$

> The reference here is to enumeration (11.7.3).

Note that ε is not in L_{diag}, since ε does not occur at (11.7.1) and hence cannot be w_i for any i. We show that $L_{diag} \neq L(G_i)$ for all i. Suppose, for the sake of producing a contradiction, that $L_{diag} = L(G_j)$ for some fixed j. We derive a contradiction by inquiring whether $w_j \in L(G_j)$.

- If $w_j \in L(G_j)$, then, by (11.7.4), we have $w_j \notin L_{diag}$. But $L_{diag} = L(G_j)$ by assumption. So $w_j \notin L(G_j)$ after all, which is a contradiction.

- On the other hand, **if $w_j \notin L(G_j)$**, then, by (11.7.4) again, we have $w_j \in L_{diag}$. But since $L_{diag} = L(G_j)$ by assumption, we have that $w_j \in L(G_j)$—again a contradiction.

We must conclude that L_{diag} is not generated by any of the grammars in the enumeration (11.7.3), from which it follows, by an earlier remark, that L_{diag} is not context-sensitive. It remains to be shown that L_{diag} is Turing-recognizable. This part of the proof is left to the reader (see Exercise 11.7.1).

Q.E.D.

The significance of Theorem 11.9 lies in our having thereby shown that the LBA-acceptable languages form a proper subset of the Turing-recognizable languages and hence of the Turing-acceptable languages. Our proof is termed "diagonal" by virtue of its similarity to Cantor's celebrated proof of the uncountability of the continuum—recall Figure 0.11.2. In particular, note the similarity between (11.7.4) and (0.11.2). (The reader has seen other, similarly convoluted, proofs. See Theorems 3.10 and 8.1.)

Theorem 11.9 is an important result. On the other hand, it is hardly a surprising result. After all, a linear-bounded automaton is a Turing machine whose "scratch space," if you will, has been severely restricted. Theorem 11.9 may be interpreted as saying that, in general, limiting space in this way results in an absolute loss in computational capacity—one that cannot be offset by some increase in computation time, say.

§11.8 Final Remarks

Context-sensitive grammars were first introduced in [Chomsky 1956] and linear-bounded automata in [Myhill 1960]. The former may be used to describe the context dependent properties of programming languages. Again, an example of such a property is the usual requirement that an identifier be declared before being used. Another would be the impermissability of expressions such as **4 + ch** or **if $y < 5$, then $y :=$ true** in the context of certain variable declarations. In general, the context-free grammars used to describe the syntax of programming languages do generate such impermissible expressions.

Our proof of Theorem 11.4 appears in [Hopcroft and Ullman 1979] and that of Theorem 11.9 in [Salomaa 1973]. The latter is also the source of the context-sensitive grammars of Exercises 11.8.2 and 11.8.4 below, that latter due to M. Penttonen.

Given the algorithm for solving the general word problem for context-sensitive languages, it is not difficult to see that any *LBA-acceptable language is Turing-recognizable* (see Theorem 11.8). The argument makes essential use of Theorem 11.4, stating that any LBA-acceptable language is context-sensitive. This is yet one more instance in which a grammar-theoretic characterization facilitates reasoning about automata. After all, what purely automata-theoretic reasoning readily reveals that LBA-acceptability implies Turing-recognizability? No doubt we could come up with something here. But being able to reason about grammars makes matters much easier. In fact, this is the whole point of multiple characterizations—some automata-theoretic and some grammar-theoretic—of a single family $\mathcal{F}$ of formal languages. Sometimes it is easier to consider $\mathcal{F}$ from the point of view of automata while, at other times, it may be advantageous to reflect upon grammars.

Finally, we showed in Exercise 10.8.2 that there exist languages that are accepted by some nondeterministic pushdown automaton but that are accepted by no deterministic pushdown automaton. In other words, in the case of pushdown automata, nondeterminism is strictly more powerful than determinism. As for linear bounded automata, the corresponding question remains unanswered. Namely, are deterministic linear-bounded automata as powerful as the general, nondeterministic variety? At this writing, we still do not know.

EXERCISES FOR §11.1

11.1.1. **(a)** Present a derivation of word $aaabbcccdd$ within the grammar of Example 11.1.2.
   (b) Present a derivation of word $abcd$ within the grammar of Example 11.1.2.

11.1.2. **(a)** Present a derivation of word $aabbbcccc$ within the grammar of Example 11.1.3.
   (b) Present a derivation of word abc within the grammar of Example 11.1.3.

11.1.3. **(a)** What language is generated by the context-free grammar G whose productions appear below?

$$S \to aAC$$

$$A \to aAC \mid aC$$

$$C \to Bc$$

$$B \to b$$

   (b) Convert grammar G to a generative grammar G' that generates the language $L = \{a^n b^n c^n \mid n \geq 1\}$. (*Hint:* Move the Bs to the left over all of the cs before replacing them with bs.) Grammar G' will be non-context-free. However, all produc-

tions should be length-preserving. Hence G' is context-sensitive.
   (c) Compare grammar G' with the context-sensitive grammar generating $\{a^n b^n c^n \mid n > 0\}$ given in Example 11.1.1. Present a derivation of word $aabbcc$ within G' and count the number of production applications in the derivation. How does this compare with the grammar of Example 11.1.1? Use big-O notation in presenting your answer.

11.1.4. [hwk] **(a)** Show that language $L = \{a^i b^j c^k \mid 0 \leq i \leq j \leq k\}$ is context-sensitive by presenting a context-sensitive grammar G that generates $L\backslash\{\varepsilon\}$. (*Hint:* Modify the grammar of Example 11.1.3.)
   (b) Present derivations for words abc, bc, and c within grammar G.
   (c) Present derivations for words $bbccc$ and ccc within grammar G.

11.1.5. [hwk] **(a)** Present a context-sensitive grammar G that generates language $L = \{a^i b^j c^i d^j e^i \mid i, j \geq 1\}$. (*Hint:* Modify the grammar of Example 11.1.2.)

(b) Present derivations of words $aaabcccdeee$ and $abcde$ within G.

(c) Show that the language $L = \{a^i b^j c^i d^j e^i \mid i, j \geq 0\}$ is context-sensitive.

EXERCISES FOR §11.2

11.2.1. Use the grammar constructed in Example 11.2.1 to generate word $aaabbcccdd$.

11.2.2. ^{hwk} Apply the algorithm of the proof of The-

orem 11.1 to the context-sensitive grammar of Example 11.1.3 in order to obtain an equivalent context-sensitive grammar in normal form.

EXERCISES FOR §11.3

11.3.1. ^{hwk} Given any word w of language $\{a^n b^n c^n \mid n \geq 1\}$ as input, the linear-bounded automata M of Figure 11.3.1 halts in state q_9 scanning an accepting 1 on its tape. For each of the nonaccepted input words w below, determine the state in which M halts. What are the contents of M's tape upon termination? (Use the software and the machine at icon **Example 11.3.1** in determining your answer.)
(a) $aabbbc$
(b) $aabbccc$

11.3.2. It is often easy, given our earlier work with Turing machines, to say whether a given language is accepted by some linear-bounded automaton. For each of the following languages, describe informally a linear-bounded automaton that accepts L. In each case, it must be made clear that the initial storage is adequate

to carry out whatever algorithm is being described.
(a) The language of Exercise 11.1.4(a)
(b) The language of Exercise 11.1.5(a)
(c) The language of Exercise 11.1.5(c)
(d) The language of Exercise 10.7.1(c)
(e) The language of Exercise 10.7.2(a)
(f) The language of Exercise 10.7.2(b)

11.3.3. Show that any LBA-acceptable (LBA-recognizable) language is Turing-acceptable (Turing-recognizable).

11.3.4. Show that language $\{a^n \mid n \text{ is composite}\}$ is LBA-acceptable by modifying the machine of Example 11.3.2.

11.3.5. Show that language $\{a^n \mid n \text{ is prime}\}$ is LBA-recognizable by modifying the machine of Example 11.3.2.

EXERCISES FOR §11.4

11.4.1. Show that it may be assumed without loss of generality that any linear-bounded automaton with terminal states in fact possesses a unique such state. (*Hint:* The argument here will be precisely the one presented for the reverse direction in Exercise 2.2.2(b).)

11.4.2. Modify the proof of Theorem 2.3 given in the text so as to obtain a proof of Theorem 11.3.

11.4.3. ^{hwk} Consider again the linear-bounded automaton of Example 11.4.1. For each of the productions below, indicate whether the given production will be included among the productions of the constructed grammar G and, if so, into which of Groups 4, 5, or 6 it will be placed. Justify your answer in each case by

referring to the transition diagram of Figure 11.4.1.

(a) $\left(\dfrac{b}{\lambda q_2 b}\right) \to \left(\dfrac{b}{\lambda q_3 B}\right)$

(b) $\left(\dfrac{b}{q_4 b}\right) \left(\dfrac{b}{b}\right) \to \left(\dfrac{b}{b}\right) \left(\dfrac{b}{q_4 b}\right)$

(c) $\left(\dfrac{b}{q_6 b}\right) \left(\dfrac{b}{b}\right) \to \left(\dfrac{b}{b}\right) \left(\dfrac{b}{q_6 b}\right)$

(d) $\left(\dfrac{a}{B}\right) \left(\dfrac{a}{q_6 a}\right) \to \left(\dfrac{a}{q_6 B}\right) \left(\dfrac{a}{a}\right)$

(e) $\left(\dfrac{a}{q_4 B}\right) \left(\dfrac{b}{b}\right) \to \left(\dfrac{a}{B}\right) \left(\dfrac{b}{q_5 b}\right)$

(f) $\left(\dfrac{a}{q_6 \lambda B}\right) \to \left(\dfrac{a}{\lambda q_0 B}\right)$

(g) $\left(\dfrac{b}{q_6 \lambda B}\right) \to \left(\dfrac{b}{\lambda q_0 B}\right)$ **(h)** $\left(\dfrac{c}{q_6 \lambda B}\right) \to \left(\dfrac{c}{\lambda q_0 B}\right)$

EXERCISES FOR §11.5

11.5.1. ^hwk This exercise is intended to demonstrate the need for introducing nonterminal representatives for terminal symbols in the construction of the proof of Theorem 11.5. So let G_1 be the positive context-free, and hence context-sensitive, grammar with productions

$$S \to aSc \mid b$$

Let G_2 be the context-sensitive grammar with productions

$$S \to aSb \mid aS \mid a$$

$$ab \to ba$$

$$ba \to ab$$

What language is generated by each of these grammars? Now apply the construction of the proof of Theorem 11.5, relettering so that nonterminal sets are disjoint but without first introducing new nonterminals X_a, X_b, and X_c and making other associated changes. Let the resulting grammar be G^*. Does $L(G^*) = L(G_1) \cup L(G_2)$? (Can you find a word over $\Sigma = \{a, b, c\}$ that is in $L(G^*)$ but not in either $L(G_1)$ or $L(G_2)$?)

11.5.2. ^hwk Critique the following argument of Professor Sakasama.

> Suppose that L_1 and L_2 are two context-free languages. Since any context-free language is a context-sensitive language and since the class of context-sensitive languages is closed under intersection, we have that $L_1 \cap L_2$ is context-free. Thus, the class of context-free languages is closed under intersection after all.

EXERCISES FOR §11.6

11.6.1. Derive word $aaabbbccc$ within the grammar of Example 11.6.1.

11.6.2. ^hwk Explain how the derivation tree of Figure 11.6.1 shows that word $abcabc$ is not in $L(G)$, where G is the grammar of Example 11.6.1. What about $ababcc$?

11.6.3. Explain why the derivation tree of Figure 11.6.1 is not a parse tree in the sense of §10.1.

11.6.4. Prove Theorem 11.8.

EXERCISE FOR §11.7

11.7.1. Show that language L_{diag} defined at (11.7.4) is Turing-recognizable by informally describing a (multitape) Turing machine that recognizes it. (*Hint:* Recall the solvability of the general word problem for context-sensitive languages.)

EXERCISES FOR §11.8 (END-OF-CHAPTER REVIEW EXERCISES)

11.8.1. For each of the languages below, explain why a context-sensitive grammar generating it must exist.
  (a) $\{a^{n^2} \mid n \geq 1\}$
  (b) $\{a^n \mid n \text{ is composite}\}$

11.8.2. In Example 11.3.3, we presented a linear-bounded automaton that accepts language $L = \{a^{n^2} \mid n \geq 1\}$. By Theorem 11.4, it follows that there exists a context-sensitive grammar that generates L. We present the 14 productions of one such grammar G below.

$$S \rightarrow a \mid aWS_2Y \qquad \text{(i)–(ii)}$$
$$S_2Y \rightarrow aa \mid X_1XWY \qquad \text{(iii)–(iv)}$$
$$Wa \rightarrow aa \qquad \text{(v)}$$
$$Xa \rightarrow aa \qquad \text{(vi)}$$
$$WS_1 \rightarrow S_1XW \qquad \text{(vii)}$$
$$XS_1 \rightarrow X_1XW \qquad \text{(viii)}$$
$$WX_1 \rightarrow S_1X \qquad \text{(ix)}$$
$$XX_1 \rightarrow X_1X \qquad \text{(x)}$$
$$aS_1 \rightarrow aWWXS_2 \qquad \text{(xi)}$$
$$S_2X \rightarrow WX_2 \qquad \text{(xii)}$$
$$X_2X \rightarrow XX_2 \qquad \text{(xiii)}$$
$$X_2W \rightarrow XS_2 \qquad \text{(xiv)}$$

(a) $^{\textbf{hwk}}$ Explain why grammar G is context-sensitive.

(b) $^{\textbf{hwk}}$ Present a derivation of a^4 from start symbol S.

(c) $^{\textbf{hwk}}$ Present a derivation of a^9.

(d) Present a derivation of a^{16}.

11.8.3. In Exercise 11.3.2(d), we saw that there exists a linear-bounded automaton that accepts language $L = \{a^{2^n} \mid n \geq 0\}$. By Theorem 11.4, it follows that there exists a context-sensitive grammar that generates L. We present the eight productions of one such grammar G below.

$$S \rightarrow YXXY \mid aa \mid a \qquad \text{(i)–(iii)}$$
$$YX \rightarrow YXXXZ \qquad \text{(iv)}$$
$$ZX \rightarrow XXZ \qquad \text{(v)}$$
$$ZY \rightarrow XY \qquad \text{(vi)}$$
$$X \rightarrow a \qquad \text{(vii)}$$
$$Y \rightarrow a \qquad \text{(viii)}$$

(a) Explain why grammar G is context-sensitive.

(b) Present a derivation of a^4 from start symbol S.

(c) Present a derivation of a^8.

(d) Present a derivation of a^{16}.

11.8.4. In Example 11.3.2, we considered a linear-bounded automaton that accepts language $L = \{a^n \mid n \text{ is prime}\}$. Here is a context-sensitive grammar that generates L. There are 41 productions in all.

$$S \rightarrow X_1AAAAAAS_3 \mid a^7 \mid a^5 \mid a^3 \mid a^2 \qquad \text{(i)–(v)}$$
$$X_1 \rightarrow X_1AA \qquad \text{(vi)}$$
$$X_1AAA \rightarrow S_1AAAS_2 \qquad \text{(vii)}$$
$$AAS_2A \rightarrow DX_2Y_1E \qquad \text{(viii)}$$
$$BAS_2A \rightarrow DX_2Y_2E \qquad \text{(ix)}$$
$$ADX_2 \rightarrow DX_2A \qquad \text{(x)}$$
$$BDX_2 \rightarrow DX_2B \qquad \text{(xi)}$$
$$S_1DX_2 \rightarrow S_1BX_3 \qquad \text{(xii)}$$
$$X_3A \rightarrow AX_3 \qquad \text{(xiii)}$$
$$X_3B \rightarrow BX_3 \qquad \text{(xiv)}$$
$$X_3Y_1E \rightarrow Y_1X_3E \qquad \text{(xv)}$$
$$X_3Y_2E \rightarrow Y_2X_3E \qquad \text{(xvi)}$$
$$X_3EA \rightarrow AX_3E \qquad \text{(xvii)}$$
$$X_3EB \rightarrow BX_3E \qquad \text{(xviii)}$$
$$X_3ES_3 \rightarrow X_4CS_3 \qquad \text{(xix)}$$
$$X_3EC \rightarrow X_4CC \qquad \text{(xx)}$$
$$AX_4 \rightarrow X_4A \qquad \text{(xxi)}$$
$$BX_4 \rightarrow X_4B \qquad \text{(xxii)}$$
$$Y_1X_4 \rightarrow AS_2 \qquad \text{(xxiii)}$$
$$Y_2X_4 \rightarrow BS_2 \qquad \text{(xxiv)}$$
$$S_1B \rightarrow S_1X_5 \qquad \text{(xxv)}$$
$$X_5B \rightarrow BX_5 \qquad \text{(xxvi)}$$
$$X_5S_2A \rightarrow X_6S_2A \qquad \text{(xxvii)}$$
$$BX_6 \rightarrow X_6A \qquad \text{(xxviii)}$$
$$S_1X_6 \rightarrow S_1A \qquad \text{(xxix)}$$
$$CS_3 \rightarrow X_7S_3 \qquad \text{(xxx)}$$
$$CX_7 \rightarrow X_7A \qquad \text{(xxxi)}$$
$$BS_2X_7 \rightarrow X_8AS_2 \qquad \text{(xxxii)}$$
$$BAS_2X_7 \rightarrow X_8AAS_2 \qquad \text{(xxxiii)}$$
$$BAAS_2X_7 \rightarrow X_8AAAS_2 \qquad \text{(xxxiv)}$$
$$AAAAS_2X_7 \rightarrow X_8AAAAS_2 \qquad \text{(xxxv)}$$
$$AX_8 \rightarrow X_8A \qquad \text{(xxxvi)}$$
$$BX_8 \rightarrow X_8A \qquad \text{(xxxvii)}$$
$$S_1X_8 \rightarrow S_1A \qquad \text{(xxxviii)}$$
$$S_2S_3 \rightarrow X_9a \qquad \text{(xxxix)}$$
$$AX_9 \rightarrow X_9a \qquad \text{(xL)}$$
$$S_1X_9 \rightarrow aa \qquad \text{(xLi)}$$

(a) Explain why grammar G is context-sensitive.

(b) Present a derivation of a^{11} from start symbol S. (*Hint:* First, use productions (i), (vi), and (vii) to generate

$S_1AAAS_2AAAAAS_3$. Then use (viii)–(xxxviii) to gradually move S_2 to the right until $S_1AAAAAAAAS_2S_3$ is obtained. Finally, use the last three productions to introduce terminals.)

(c) Present a derivation of a^{13}.

(d) Explain why a^{12} cannot be generated by G. (This requires a certain insight into the operation of G.)

11.8.5. (a) Consider the language $L = \{ww | w \in \Sigma^+\}$ with $\Sigma = \{a, b\}$. Note that the grammar G of Exercise 9.8.7 is essentially one that generates $L \cup \{\varepsilon\}$. But G is not context-sensitive. (Why not?) However, reflection upon linear-bounded automata and Theorem 11.4 makes it clear that some context-sensitive grammar does generate L, and you are asked to find one.

(b) Present a derivation of word *abbaaabbaa* within your grammar.

11.8.6. (a) Show that language L is LBA-recognizable if and only if both L and L^c are LBA-acceptable (cf. Exercise 2.10.11).

(b) Show that every LBA-acceptable language is in fact LBA-recognizable. (*Hint:* Assume closure of the family of context-sensitive languages under complementation.)

11.8.7. Show that the family of context-sensitive languages is closed under reversal. That is, show that if language L is context-sensitive, then so is language $L^R = \{w^R | w \in L\}$.

11.8.8. Show that the family of context-sensitive languages is closed under concatenation.

11.8.9. Show that the family of context-sensitive languages is closed under Kleene closure. That is, if language L is context-sensitive, then so is language L^*.

11.8.10. Recalling that the question whether the family of context-sensitive languages is closed under complementation has recently been settled (see the end of §11.5), answer the following questions.

(a) Is the family of context-sensitive languages closed under relative complementation?

(b) Is the family of context-sensitive languages closed under symmetric difference?

11.8.11. **(An Alternative Grammar-Theoretic Characterization of the Family of Context-Sensitive Languages).** Let $G = \langle \Sigma, \Gamma, \sigma, \Pi \rangle$ be a generative grammar. Let us say that G is context-sensitive$_1$ if, with a single exception, every member of Π is of the form

$$\alpha_1 A \alpha_2 \rightarrow \alpha_1 \beta \alpha_2$$

where A is a nonterminal and α_1, α_2, and β are strings of terminals and nonterminals with $\beta \neq \varepsilon$. The one exception that we permit is empty production $\sigma \rightarrow$, provided that nonterminal σ has no occurrence on the right-hand side of any production in Π. Accordingly, we say that language L over Σ is context-sensitive$_1$ if $L = L(G)$ for some context-sensitive$_1$ grammar G.

(a) Give a context-sensitive$_1$ grammar that generates language $\{a^n b^n c^n | n \geq 0\}$. (*Hint:* Modify the grammar of Example 11.1.1.)

(b) Let L be a language over Σ. Show that L is context-sensitive$_1$ if and only if L is context-sensitive in the sense of Definition 11.2. (*Hint:* Use Theorem 11.1.)

11.8.12. Let us define a *deterministic context-sensitive language* to be a language accepted by a deterministic linear-bounded automaton. Explain why Savitch's Theorem (Theorem 2.9) does not settle the issue whether every context-sensitive language is deterministic and, hence, does not answer the question whether deterministic linear-bounded automata are as powerful as nondeterministic.

## Chapter 12

Generative Grammars and the Chomsky Hierarchy

In Section 9.8 we introduced the important notion of a generative or phrase-structure grammar (see Definition 9.9). Then, in Chapter 9 itself and subsequent chapters, we investigated three subfamilies of generative grammars. In each case, we were able to associate a family of automata with the subfamily of grammars in question. A quick review of these matters will be useful.

- At the end of Chapter 9, we defined the class of right-linear grammars and characterized the right-linear languages as those generated by right-linear grammars. It was then shown that the class of right-linear languages is precisely the class of regular languages—those denoted by regular expressions and accepted by (deterministic) finite-state automata.

- The focus of Chapter 10 was the class of context-free grammars. We saw that the class of context-free languages is precisely the class of languages accepted by (nondeterministic) pushdown-stack automata.

- A yet more comprehensive class of languages was the subject of Chapter 11. We introduced the context-sensitive grammars and the family of context-sensitive languages associated with them. The corresponding class of automata is the class of linear-bounded automata.

It is natural to now ask for a family of automata equivalent to the all-encompassing class of phrase-structure languages. (By a *phrase-structure language* we shall mean any language generated by a generative or phrase-structure grammar as defined in Definition 9.9.) Such a family of automata does exist and, happily, is already well known to the reader; it is none other that the class of Turing machines, as we shall see below.

The Turing machine was the first model of computation discussed in this book. In subsequent chapters we considered a number of other universal models of computation—the Markov algorithm, the register machine, and so forth—and showed their equivalence to Turing's model with respect to both the function computation paradigm and the language recognition paradigm. In Part II we went on to consider a number of weaker models—finite-state automata, pushdown automata, and linear-bounded automata—restricting our attention to language recognition. (That these models are all weaker than Turing's model is shown, in effect, by Theorem 11.9.) We now come full circle to a reconsideration of Turing machines as language acceptors (recognizers).

In this final chapter we have two goals. First, we shall show that the class of Turing-acceptable languages is indeed all-encompassing in the sense that every phrase-structure language is Turing-acceptable, and vice versa. Our second goal concerns recursion theory. In proving Theorem 3.3, we showed that the class of partial recursive functions coincides with the class of Turing-computable functions. Given Paradigm Interreducibility, it would be reasonable to expect that some analogous result would pair the concept of Turing-acceptable language with some recursion-theoretic characterization of a class of formal languages. In Chapter 3 itself we gave no such result, although most of the needed ideas are already present there. We have delayed introducing the few additional ideas required as a way of concluding our description of the Chomsky hierarchy of languages. So, in this final chapter, we shall show that the Turing-acceptable languages are precisely the so-called *recursively enumerable languages.*

§12.1 Turing Machines and Phrase-Structure Languages

In this first section we prove that the class of Turing-acceptable languages is identical to the class of phrase-structure languages—that is, the class of languages generated by generative or phrase-structure grammars. As usual, the structure of our proof is dictated by the Principle of Extensionality: We must show that (1) every Turing-acceptable language is generated by some generative grammar and is therefore a phrase-structure language and (2) every phrase-structure language is accepted by some Turing machine and is therefore a member of the class of Turing-acceptable languages. Before presenting the proof of (1), let us consider an example of the way in which a generative grammar may simulate a Turing machine qua language acceptor by terminal state. This example, as well as the proof that follows, will be highly reminiscent of our work in §11.4, as the reader will soon see.

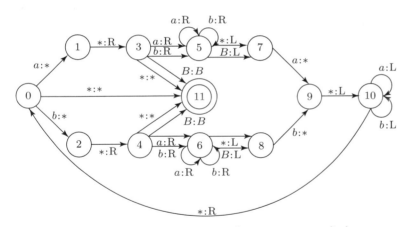

Figure 12.1.1   This single-tape Turing machine accepts any palindrome over $\Sigma = \{a, b\}$.

Given input word *aba*, machine *M* first replaces the leading *a* by an asterisk and then does the same to the final *a*, thereby traversing the cycle from state q_0 and back by way of states q_1, q_9, and q_{10}. Afterward, symbol *b* is replaced. At state q_4, *M* recognizes in effect that the just-replaced *b* was the central symbol in an odd-length palindrome. Consequently, *M* enters terminal state q_{11} and halts.

EXAMPLE 12.1.1 Consider the deterministic Turing machine *M* of Figure 12.1.1. In fact, this machine is already familiar to the reader since it served as Example 2.2.3. The reader should use the software to once again verify that this machine accepts, by terminal state, the language of all palindromes over $\Sigma = \{a, b\}$.

We begin by considering *M*'s acceptance of palindrome *aba*.

$$q_0\,abaB$$
$$q_1*baB$$
$$*q_3baB$$
$$*bq_5\,aB$$
$$*baq_5B \qquad (12.1.1)$$
$$*bq_7\,aB$$
$$*bq_9*B$$
$$*q_{10}b*B$$
$$q_{10}*b*B$$

$$*q_0 b * B$$

$$*q_2 * * B$$

$$* * q_4 * B$$

$$* * q_{11} * B$$

We note that in the case of input word *aba* (1) only one tape square to the right of the input is ever scanned and (2) no tape square to the left of the input is ever scanned. Nor is there anything special about this particular input word in this regard: The read/write head of M will never move more than a single square to the right of the input word. (This square has been displayed throughout the computation sequence (12.1.1).)

We next present a phrase-structure grammar G that models M's computation. Our construction is similar to the construction of Theorem 11.4; if anything, the construction is easier in the present case. The simulation will proceed by way of a string of grammar nonterminals, each of which involves an upper track and a lower track. Initially, one reads input word w across both the upper and lower tracks:

$$X_{q_0} \left(\frac{a}{a} \right) \left(\frac{b}{b} \right) \left(\frac{a}{a} \right) \left(\frac{B}{B} \right)$$

Grammar G then proceeds to simulate the action of M on the lower track without altering the upper track. If M is seen to enter terminal state q_{11}, then—just in that case—G in effect eliminates the lower track, leaving only the upper. In other words, G transforms string

$$\left(\frac{a}{*} \right) \left(\frac{b}{*} \right) X_{q_{11}} \left(\frac{a}{*} \right) \left(\frac{B}{B} \right)$$

into string

$$aba$$

Moreover, a terminal string can be generated by G only if some string containing nonterminal $X_{q_{11}}$ is generated first.

The terminal alphabet Σ_G of G is just $\Sigma_M = \{a, b\}$, the input alphabet of M. As nonterminal alphabet Γ_G, we have four special "preprocessing" nonterminals S, S_w, S_{left}, and S_{right} as well as one nonterminal for each of the twelve states of M. (We shall use X_{q_i} for the nonterminal corresponding to state q_i.) In addition, we have, as grammar nonterminals, each of the complex symbols (a/a), (a/b), $(a/*)$, (a/B), (b/a), (b/b), $(b/*)$, (b/B), (B/a), (B/b), $(B/*)$, and (B/B). That is, we have as grammar nonterminals each and every symbol of the form

$$\left(\frac{\alpha}{\beta} \right)$$

for $\alpha \in \Sigma_M \cup \{B\}$ and $\beta \in \Gamma_M = \{a, b, *\} \cup \{B\}$. A string σ of nonterminals

$$\left(\frac{\alpha_1}{\beta_1} \right) \left(\frac{\alpha_2}{\beta_2} \right) \cdots \left(\frac{\alpha_n}{\beta_n} \right)$$

generated by G will satisfy the following conditions:

(i) upper half $\alpha_1, \alpha_2, \ldots, \alpha_n$ of string σ corresponds to grammar terminals plus, possibly, one or more copies of symbol B at either end; this upper half will be used to produce a terminal string should G's simulation of M enter terminal state q_{11};

(ii) lower half $\beta_1, \beta_2, \ldots, \beta_n$ models the relevant portion of M's tape configuration at a given point during G's simulation of its computation; and

(iii) string σ will include a single "state" nonterminal from among $X_{q_0}, X_{q_1}, \ldots, X_{q_{11}}$.

The productions of G fall into nine groups. We have in Groups 1 through 5 certain preprocessing productions.

- **Group 1**

$$S \rightarrow S_{left} X_{q_0} S_w$$

- **Group 2**

$$S_w \rightarrow \left(\frac{a}{a}\right) S_w \,\Big|\, \left(\frac{b}{b}\right) S_w \qquad /* \text{ one for each element of } \Sigma */$$

- **Group 3**

$$S_w \rightarrow S_{right}$$

- **Group 4**

$$S_{left} \rightarrow S_{left} \left(\frac{B}{B}\right)$$

> This production will be used to generate any blank squares to the left of input word w that are scanned during M's computation.

$$S_{right} \rightarrow \left(\frac{B}{B}\right) S_{right}$$

> This production generates any blank squares needed on the right.

- **Group 5**

$$S_{left} \rightarrow$$

$$S_{right} \rightarrow$$

Group 6 corresponds to M's write instructions. In the case of the Turing machine of Figure 12.1.1, there are three productions for each write instruction. We present those for only four of M's nine write instructions

- **Group 6**

$$
\left.
\begin{array}{l}
X_{q_0}\left(\dfrac{a}{a}\right) \rightarrow X_{q_1}\left(\dfrac{a}{*}\right) \\[2mm]
X_{q_0}\left(\dfrac{b}{a}\right) \rightarrow X_{q_1}\left(\dfrac{b}{*}\right) \\[2mm]
X_{q_0}\left(\dfrac{B}{a}\right) \rightarrow X_{q_1}\left(\dfrac{B}{*}\right)
\end{array}
\right\} \qquad /* \delta_M(q_0, a) = (*, q_1) */
$$

$$X_{q_0}\left(\frac{a}{b}\right) \to X_{q_2}\left(\frac{a}{*}\right)$$

$$X_{q_0}\left(\frac{b}{b}\right) \to X_{q_2}\left(\frac{b}{*}\right)$$ $\quad \Big\} \quad$ /* $\delta_M(q_0, b) = (*, q_2)$ */

$$X_{q_0}\left(\frac{B}{b}\right) \to X_{q_2}\left(\frac{B}{*}\right)$$

$$X_{q_7}\left(\frac{a}{a}\right) \to X_{q_9}\left(\frac{a}{*}\right)$$

$$X_{q_7}\left(\frac{b}{a}\right) \to X_{q_9}\left(\frac{b}{*}\right)$$ $\quad \Big\} \quad$ /* $\delta_M(q_7, a) = (*, q_9)$ */

$$X_{q_7}\left(\frac{B}{a}\right) \to X_{q_9}\left(\frac{B}{*}\right)$$

$$X_{q_8}\left(\frac{a}{b}\right) \to X_{q_9}\left(\frac{a}{*}\right)$$

$$X_{q_8}\left(\frac{b}{b}\right) \to X_{q_9}\left(\frac{b}{*}\right)$$ $\quad \Big\} \quad$ /* $\delta_M(q_8, b) = (*, q_9)$ */

$$X_{q_8}\left(\frac{B}{b}\right) \to X_{q_9}\left(\frac{B}{*}\right)$$

$$\ldots$$

Note that no production of Group 6 alters the contents of the upper half of any complex nonterminal. Each of the other three write instructions—for example, $\delta_M(q_4, *) = (*, q_{11})$—would similarly cause us to introduce three grammar productions. The general construction principle is the following: For each machine instruction of the form $\delta_M(q_i, s) = (s', q_j)$ with $s, s' \in \Gamma_M$, we introduce the three grammar productions

$$X_{q_i}\left(\frac{a}{s}\right) \to X_{q_j}\left(\frac{a}{s'}\right)$$

$$X_{q_i}\left(\frac{b}{s}\right) \to X_{q_j}\left(\frac{b}{s'}\right)$$

$$X_{q_i}\left(\frac{B}{s}\right) \to X_{q_j}\left(\frac{B}{s'}\right)$$

The idea behind adding all three instructions is that the simulation of M within the lower half of a generated string should be independent of the contents of the upper half. In fact, some of the productions introduced may never be used in generating any terminal string and hence may be useless from a certain point of view. However, if our construction of grammar G is to be effective, it must not presuppose some special insight into M's computation. (See remarks at the end of Example 11.4.1.)

Group 7 corresponds to M's 11 move-right instructions. Again, we introduce $|\Sigma_M|+1 = 3$ productions for each instruction.

- ## Group 7

$$X_{q_1}\left(\frac{a}{*}\right) \to \left(\frac{a}{*}\right)X_{q_3}$$

$$X_{q_1}\left(\frac{b}{*}\right) \to \left(\frac{b}{*}\right)X_{q_3} \quad\Bigg\} \qquad /* \; \delta_M(q_1, *) = (R, q_3) \; */$$

$$X_{q_1}\left(\frac{B}{*}\right) \to \left(\frac{B}{*}\right)X_{q_3}$$

$$X_{q_2}\left(\frac{a}{*}\right) \to \left(\frac{a}{*}\right)X_{q_4}$$

$$X_{q_2}\left(\frac{b}{*}\right) \to \left(\frac{b}{*}\right)X_{q_4} \quad\Bigg\} \qquad /* \; \delta_M(q_2, *) = (R, q_4) \; */$$

$$X_{q_2}\left(\frac{B}{*}\right) \to \left(\frac{B}{*}\right)X_{q_4}$$

$$\cdots$$

That is, for each move-right instruction of the form

$$\delta_M(q_i, s) = (R, q_j)$$

with $s \in \Gamma_M$, we add the three productions

$$X_{q_i}\left(\frac{a}{s}\right) \to \left(\frac{a}{s}\right)X_{q_j} \qquad X_{q_i}\left(\frac{b}{s}\right) \to \left(\frac{b}{s}\right)X_{q_j} \qquad X_{q_i}\left(\frac{B}{s}\right) \to \left(\frac{B}{s}\right)X_{q_j}$$

Group 8 corresponds to each of M's seven move-left instructions. This time we must introduce $(|\Sigma_M| + 1) \cdot (|\Gamma_M| + 1) \cdot (|\Sigma_M| + 1) = 3 \cdot 4 \cdot 3 = 36$ productions for each instruction. One of these move-left instructions is $\delta_M(q_5, B) = (L, q_7)$ (see Figure 12.1.1). Since these productions are so numerous, we display only the 12 productions involving nonterminal (a/B) occurring to the right of state nonterminal X_{q_5}.

> The 1s here account for "symbol" B.

- ## Group 8

$$\left(\frac{a}{a}\right)X_{q_5}\left(\frac{a}{B}\right) \to X_{q_7}\left(\frac{a}{a}\right)\left(\frac{a}{B}\right) \qquad \left(\frac{b}{a}\right)X_{q_5}\left(\frac{a}{B}\right) \to X_{q_7}\left(\frac{b}{a}\right)\left(\frac{a}{B}\right) \qquad \left(\frac{B}{a}\right)X_{q_5}\left(\frac{a}{B}\right) \to X_{q_7}\left(\frac{B}{a}\right)\left(\frac{a}{B}\right)$$

$$\left(\frac{a}{b}\right)X_{q_5}\left(\frac{a}{B}\right) \to X_{q_7}\left(\frac{a}{b}\right)\left(\frac{a}{B}\right) \qquad \left(\frac{b}{b}\right)X_{q_5}\left(\frac{a}{B}\right) \to X_{q_7}\left(\frac{b}{b}\right)\left(\frac{a}{B}\right) \qquad \left(\frac{B}{b}\right)X_{q_5}\left(\frac{a}{B}\right) \to X_{q_7}\left(\frac{B}{b}\right)\left(\frac{a}{B}\right)$$

$$\left(\frac{a}{*}\right)X_{q_5}\left(\frac{a}{B}\right) \to X_{q_7}\left(\frac{a}{*}\right)\left(\frac{a}{B}\right) \qquad \left(\frac{b}{*}\right)X_{q_5}\left(\frac{a}{B}\right) \to X_{q_7}\left(\frac{b}{*}\right)\left(\frac{a}{B}\right) \qquad \left(\frac{B}{*}\right)X_{q_5}\left(\frac{a}{B}\right) \to X_{q_7}\left(\frac{B}{*}\right)\left(\frac{a}{B}\right)$$

$$\left(\frac{a}{B}\right)X_{q_5}\left(\frac{a}{B}\right) \to X_{q_7}\left(\frac{a}{B}\right)\left(\frac{a}{B}\right) \qquad \left(\frac{b}{B}\right)X_{q_5}\left(\frac{a}{B}\right) \to X_{q_7}\left(\frac{b}{B}\right)\left(\frac{a}{B}\right) \qquad \left(\frac{B}{B}\right)X_{q_5}\left(\frac{a}{B}\right) \to X_{q_7}\left(\frac{B}{B}\right)\left(\frac{a}{B}\right)$$

$$\cdots \qquad\qquad\qquad \cdots \qquad\qquad\qquad \cdots$$

Finally, Group 9 consists mainly of productions that, at the end of G's simulation of M's computation, having the effect of eliminating the lower track within a string of complex nonterminals while preserving its upper track. In addition, Group 9 contains a single production that eliminates nonterminal $X_{q_{11}}$.

- **Group 9**

$$\left(\frac{a}{a}\right) X_{q_{11}} \rightarrow X_{q_{11}} a \qquad X_{q_{11}} \left(\frac{a}{a}\right) \rightarrow a X_{q_{11}}$$

$$\left(\frac{a}{b}\right) X_{q_{11}} \rightarrow X_{q_{11}} a \qquad X_{q_{11}} \left(\frac{a}{b}\right) \rightarrow a X_{q_{11}}$$

$$\left(\frac{a}{*}\right) X_{q_{11}} \rightarrow X_{q_{11}} a \qquad X_{q_{11}} \left(\frac{a}{*}\right) \rightarrow a X_{q_{11}}$$

$$\left(\frac{a}{B}\right) X_{q_{11}} \rightarrow X_{q_{11}} a \qquad X_{q_{11}} \left(\frac{a}{B}\right) \rightarrow a X_{q_{11}}$$

$$\left(\frac{b}{a}\right) X_{q_{11}} \rightarrow X_{q_{11}} b \qquad X_{q_{11}} \left(\frac{b}{a}\right) \rightarrow b X_{q_{11}}$$

$$\left(\frac{b}{b}\right) X_{q_{11}} \rightarrow X_{q_{11}} b \qquad X_{q_{11}} \left(\frac{b}{b}\right) \rightarrow b X_{q_{11}}$$

$$\left(\frac{b}{*}\right) X_{q_{11}} \rightarrow X_{q_{11}} b \qquad X_{q_{11}} \left(\frac{b}{*}\right) \rightarrow b X_{q_{11}}$$

$$\left(\frac{b}{B}\right) X_{q_{11}} \rightarrow X_{q_{11}} b \qquad X_{q_{11}} \left(\frac{b}{B}\right) \rightarrow h X_{q_{11}}$$

$$\left(\frac{B}{a}\right) X_{q_{11}} \rightarrow X_{q_{11}} \qquad X_{q_{11}} \left(\frac{B}{a}\right) \rightarrow X_{q_{11}}$$

$$\left(\frac{B}{b}\right) X_{q_{11}} \rightarrow X_{q_{11}} \qquad X_{q_{11}} \left(\frac{B}{b}\right) \rightarrow X_{q_{11}}$$

$$\left(\frac{B}{*}\right) X_{q_{11}} \rightarrow X_{q_{11}} \qquad X_{q_{11}} \left(\frac{B}{*}\right) \rightarrow X_{q_{11}}$$

$$\left(\frac{B}{B}\right) X_{q_{11}} \rightarrow X_{q_{11}} \qquad X_{q_{11}} \left(\frac{B}{B}\right) \dashrightarrow X_{q_{11}}$$

$$a X_{q_{11}} \rightarrow X_{q_{11}} a \qquad X_{q_{11}} a \rightarrow a X_{q_{11}}$$

$$b X_{q_{11}} \rightarrow X_{q_{11}} b \qquad X_{q_{11}} b \rightarrow b X_{q_{11}}$$

$$X_{q_{11}} \rightarrow$$

Note that, with the exception of the last five productions here, each of the productions of Group 9 involves replacing a complex nonterminal with something corresponding to its upper half.

This completes our description of G's production set. In order to get an idea of how G simulates M's computation, we present a derivation within G of palindrome *aba* and note the way in which this derivation models an accepting computation of M. First, using the productions of Groups 1 and 2 we have

$$S \Rightarrow^* S_{left} X_{q_0} \left(\frac{a}{a}\right) \left(\frac{b}{b}\right) \left(\frac{a}{a}\right) S_w$$

The single production of Group 3 gives

$$\Rightarrow^* S_{left} X_{q_0} \left(\frac{a}{a}\right) \left(\frac{b}{b}\right) \left(\frac{a}{a}\right) S_{right}$$

Applications of the second production of Group 4 and of both productions of Group 5 introduce the single blank needed to the right of input word *aba* and eliminate nonterminals S_{left} and S_{right}.

$$\Rightarrow^* X_{q_0} \left(\frac{a}{a}\right) \left(\frac{b}{b}\right) \left(\frac{a}{a}\right) \left(\frac{B}{B}\right)$$

Both the upper and lower tracks within this string of nonterminals now contain palindrome *aba*. The occurrence of *aba* on the lower track is to be regarded as input word to *G*'s simulation of *M*'s accepting computation, as modeled by the productions of Groups 6–8. For each machine configuration at (12.1.1), we apply one production of Groups 6–8 (see Figure 12.1.2).

Finally, application of the appropriate productions of Group 9 yields a terminal string so that

$$S \Rightarrow^* aba$$

Note that the only state nonterminal of *G* that can be eliminated is nonterminal $X_{q_{11}}$, corresponding to terminal state q_{11}. This, in turn, means that there is only way in which *G*, having introduced state nonterminal X_{q_0}, can generate a string consisting solely of terminal symbols. Namely, it must simulate an accepting computation of *M* so as to produce grammar nonterminal $X_{q_{11}}$, which can then be eliminated.

M's Accepting Computation of Input Word *aba*	**G's Simulation of M's Acceptance of Input Word *aba***
$q_0 abaB$	$S \Rightarrow^* X_{q_0} \left(\frac{a}{a}\right) \left(\frac{b}{b}\right) \left(\frac{a}{a}\right) \left(\frac{B}{B}\right)$
$q_1 * baB$	$\Rightarrow^* X_{q_1} \left(\frac{a}{*}\right) \left(\frac{b}{b}\right) \left(\frac{a}{a}\right) \left(\frac{B}{B}\right)$
$* q_3 baB$	$\Rightarrow^* \left(\frac{a}{*}\right) X_{q_3} \left(\frac{b}{b}\right) \left(\frac{a}{a}\right) \left(\frac{B}{B}\right)$
$* b q_5 aB$	$\Rightarrow^* \left(\frac{a}{*}\right) \left(\frac{b}{b}\right) X_{q_5} \left(\frac{a}{a}\right) \left(\frac{B}{B}\right)$
$* ba q_5 B$	$\Rightarrow^* \left(\frac{a}{*}\right) \left(\frac{b}{b}\right) \left(\frac{a}{a}\right) X_{q_5} \left(\frac{B}{B}\right)$
$* b q_7 aB$	$\Rightarrow^* \left(\frac{a}{*}\right) \left(\frac{b}{b}\right) X_{q_7} \left(\frac{a}{a}\right) \left(\frac{B}{B}\right)$
$* b q_9 * B$	$\Rightarrow^* \left(\frac{a}{*}\right) \left(\frac{b}{b}\right) X_{q_9} \left(\frac{a}{*}\right) \left(\frac{B}{B}\right)$
$* q_{10} b * B$	$\Rightarrow^* \left(\frac{a}{*}\right) X_{q_{10}} \left(\frac{b}{b}\right) \left(\frac{a}{*}\right) \left(\frac{B}{B}\right)$
$q_{10} * b * B$	$\Rightarrow^* X_{q_{10}} \left(\frac{a}{*}\right) \left(\frac{b}{b}\right) \left(\frac{a}{*}\right) \left(\frac{B}{B}\right)$
$* q_0 b * B$	$\Rightarrow^* \left(\frac{a}{*}\right) X_{q_0} \left(\frac{b}{b}\right) \left(\frac{a}{*}\right) \left(\frac{B}{B}\right)$
$* q_2 * * B$	$\Rightarrow^* \left(\frac{a}{*}\right) X_{q_2} \left(\frac{b}{*}\right) \left(\frac{a}{*}\right) \left(\frac{B}{B}\right)$
$* * q_4 * B$	$\Rightarrow^* \left(\frac{a}{*}\right) \left(\frac{b}{*}\right) X_{q_4} \left(\frac{a}{*}\right) \left(\frac{B}{B}\right)$
$* * q_{11} * B$	$\Rightarrow^* \left(\frac{a}{*}\right) \left(\frac{b}{*}\right) X_{q_{11}} \left(\frac{a}{*}\right) \left(\frac{B}{B}\right)$

Figure 12.1.2

Our consideration of Example 12.1.1 was intended to facilitate the proof below, which appeals freely to the reader's understanding of the foregoing construction of simulation grammar G.

THEOREM 12.1: If L is a Turing-acceptable language, then $L = L(G)$ for some generative grammar G. Alternative formulation: Any Turing-acceptable language is a phrase-structure language.

PROOF Suppose that $w \in L$. Then, by hypothesis, there is a single-tape Turing machine M that accepts w by terminal state. (It makes no difference whether M is taken to be deterministic or nondeterministic.) Given transition function δ_M of M, we construct a generative grammar G whose productions fall into nine groups (cf. Example 12.1.1). By our earlier discussion, there exists a derivation of w within G that simulates M's accepting computation of w. Thus G generates w and hence $w \in L(G)$. Since w was an arbitrary word of L, we have shown that $L \subseteq L(G)$.

We must also convince ourselves that $L(G) \subseteq L$. Suppose that $w \in L(G)$. This means that w is a string of terminals and that G generates w in the sense of Definition 9.12. But how could G generate such a string of terminals? First, it is clear from Example 12.1.1 that G must apply the productions of Groups 1–5 to produce a string σ of complex nonterminals such that w can be read across σ's upper track. Eventually, using the productions of Group 9, G must replace these complex nonterminals with terminal symbols corresponding to this upper track—that is, with the symbols occurring in w. But in order to effect this replacement, G must have generated a string containing state nonterminal X_{q_t} corresponding to some terminal state q_t. Given the construction of G—in particular, the manner in which the productions of Groups 6–8 model the instruction set of M—producing X_{q_t} means that G's derivation of w must have simulated an accepting computation of w on the part of M. Thus $w \in L = L(M)$. Since w was an arbitrary word of $L(G)$, we have shown that $L(G) \subseteq L$.

Finally, since $L \subseteq L(G)$ and $L(G) \subseteq L$, it follows by the Principle of Extensionality that $L = L(G)$.   Q.E.D.

We also prove

THEOREM 12.2: If L is a phrase-structure language, then L is Turing-acceptable.

PROOF Our proof is essentially that given for Theorem 11.2. Suppose that L is $L(G)$ for some phrase-structure grammar $G = \langle \Sigma, \Gamma, \sigma, \Pi \rangle$. We describe a nondeterministic, three-tape Turing machine M that accepts L. Suppose that input word w appears initially on M's input tape. M writes start symbol σ on worktape$_1$ and chooses some production for σ from among those in Π, replacing σ with the right-hand side of that production. M continues in this way, systematically making replacements for substrings appearing on worktape$_1$. Such replacements will in general require shifting some part of the contents of worktape$_1$ either to the right or to the left. After each such replacement, M compares the contents of worktape$_1$ with the contents of its input tape. If comparison reveals that these contents are identical, then M accepts w by writing an accepting 1 to its output tape. Otherwise, the replacement process continues, provided that some production of Π is applicable to the current contents of worktape$_1$. If no production is currently applicable and if the contents of worktape$_1$ are not identical with the contents of the input tape, then M halts without accepting w.   Q.E.D.

§12.2 Closure Properties of the Family of Phrase-Structure Languages

It is easy to see that the family of phrase-structure languages is closed under union, intersection, concatenation, reversal, and Kleene closure. In fact, for union, concatenation, reversal, and Kleene closure, one may apply what is essentially the same reasoning used to show that the family of context-free languages is closed under these operations and that the family of context-sensitive languages is closed under these operations. The case of closure under intersection, on the other hand, is most easily handled by considering a certain sort of multitape Turing machine and appealing to the equivalence result of the preceding section—both Theorems 12.1 and 12.2. There is nothing analogous to this result in Chapter 10; we recall that, by the Pumping Lemma for Context-Free Languages, the context-free languages are not closed under intersection. On the other hand, what is needed is not too different from what was done in the proof of Theorem 11.6, where closure of the context-sensitive languages under intersection was the issue.

We shall see later that the family of phrase-structure languages is not closed under complementation, relative complementation, or symmetric difference.

§12.3 Turing Machines as Language Enumerators

In our earlier work we have had cause to consider the *enumerability* of sets. In general, a set S is said to be enumerable (or countable) if it can be placed in 1–1 correspondence with some subset of $\mathcal{N}$ (cf. Exercise 0.11.6). In particular, any finite set is enumerable (see Figure 12.3.1). Also, it is a trivial consequence of our definition that every subset S of $\mathcal{N}$ is enumerable, since the identity mapping 1_S provides a bijection of S onto a subset of $\mathcal{N}$, namely, onto S itself (see Figure 12.3.2).

In §3.6 we introduced a special sort of enumerability with respect to sets of natural numbers in particular. Namely, a nonempty set $S \subseteq \mathcal{N}$ was said to be *recursively enumerable* if S is the image of a recursive function (see Definition 3.10 and Figure 12.3.3). Thus the set of even natural numbers is recursively enumerable by virtue of the fact that the number-theoretic function defined by

$$f: \mathcal{N} \to \mathcal{N}$$

$$f(n) = 2n$$

$$S = \{s_0, s_1, s_2, \ldots, s_k\}$$

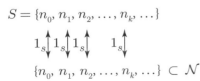

$$\{0, \ 1, \ 2, \ldots, \ k\} \subset \mathcal{N}$$

Figure 12.3.1 Any finite set is enumerable.

$$S = \{n_0, n_1, n_2, \ldots, n_k, \ldots\}$$

$$\{n_0, \ n_1, \ n_2, \ldots, n_k, \ldots\} \subset \mathcal{N}$$

Figure 12.3.2 Any set of natural numbers is enumerable.

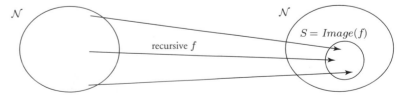

Figure 12.3.3 A set S of natural numbers is r.e. if S is the image of some recursive f.

is recursive with $Image(f) = \{n: 2|n\}$. Alternatively, S's being enumerable is a matter of the existence of a bijection from some subset of $\mathcal{N}$ onto S (see Exercise 0.11.6). In particular, then, S's being recursively enumerable is a matter of said bijection's being partial recursive (see Exercise 3.6.6(b)). Our long-range goal in this section is to relate this notion of recursive enumerability to the family of phrase-structure languages, which, as Theorems 12.1 and 12.2 tell us, is precisely the family of Turing-acceptable languages. The link can hardly be obvious since it is sets of *natural numbers* that may be recursively enumerable, whereas languages are sets of *symbol strings*. As the reader may have predicted, it is encodings of symbol strings as natural numbers that will be used to forge the link. In the meantime, we consider two preliminary notions that will be useful later.

EXAMPLE 12.3.1 (Language Enumeration) Consider the behavior of the Turing machine M of Figure 12.3.4.

- If started scanning a *1* on an otherwise blank tape, then M halts scanning a square on a completely blank tape.

- If started scanning the leftmost of an unbroken string of exactly two *1*s, then M halts scanning the leftmost symbol of word *ab* on an otherwise blank tape.

- If started scanning the leftmost of an unbroken string of exactly three *1*s, then M halts scanning the leftmost symbol of word *abab* on an otherwise blank tape.

- In general, if started scanning the leftmost of an unbroken string of $n+1$ *1*s, then M halts scanning the leftmost symbol of word $(ab)^n$ on an otherwise blank tape.

M is a special sort of Turing machine qua transducer in that it correlates (representations of) natural numbers with words over alphabet $\Sigma = \{a, b\}$. We shall refer to such a Turing machine as a *(language) enumerator*. We can think of such an M as modeling a unary (partial) function f_M from natural numbers to Σ^*. In the present case, we may define f_M by writing

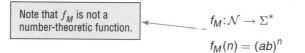

Note that f_M is not a number-theoretic function.

$$f_M: \mathcal{N} \to \Sigma^*$$

$$f_M(n) = (ab)^n$$

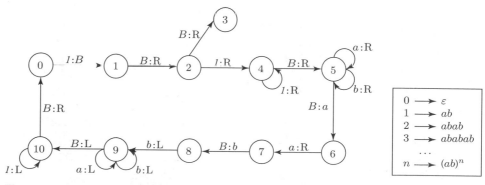

Figure 12.3.4 A Turing Machine That Enumerates $\{(ab)^n | n \geq 0\}$.

We see that the image of f_M is $L = \{(ab)^n | n \geq 0\}$. Consequently, we shall say that language enumerator M *Turing-enumerates*, or just *enumerates*, L. Intuitively, given inputs representing natural numbers $0, 1, 2, \ldots$, machine M generates in succession all and only the words of language L. We shall say that language $L = \{(ab)^n | n \geq 0\}$ is *Turing-enumerable* by virtue of the existence of a language enumerator that Turing-enumerates L.

Open icon **Example 12.3.1** within the Turing Machine folder in order to observe the computation of the language enumerator of Figure 12.3.4.

A second example of a Turing-enumerable language will be useful in working toward a formal definition.

EXAMPLE 12.3.2 Consider the three-tape Turing machine M of **Example 12.3.2** within the Turing Machine folder. Given representation of natural number n as input, M first determines whether n is prime. If so, then M produces string a^n and halts. Otherwise, M's computation never terminates. (Choose *Stop* from the Simulation menu.) We may regard M as establishing the Turing-enumerability of language $L = \{a^n | n \text{ is prime}\}$ by virtue of M's modeling of the partial function f_M defined by

$$f_M : \mathcal{N} \to \Sigma^* \text{ with } \Sigma = \{a\}$$

$$f_M(n) = \begin{cases} a^n & \text{if } n \text{ is prime} \\ \text{undefined} & \text{otherwise} \end{cases}$$

In other words, we shall take the existence of M to show that $L = \{a^n | n \text{ is prime}\}$ is Turing-enumerable despite the fact that M maps a proper subset of $\mathcal{N}$ onto L. In doing so, we preserve an analogy with Theorem 3.5, where it was shown in effect that a set S is recursively enumerable if it is the image, under some partial recursive function, of some subset of $\mathcal{N}$. We bring another aspect of this example to the reader's attention since it will be incorporated into the formal definition that follows: If f_M is undefined for argument k, then M never halts when started scanning a representation of k.

DEFINITION 12.1: Let Σ be an alphabet not containing symbol 1. Suppose that M is a deterministic, single-tape Turing machine such that, for all $n \in N$, if M is started scanning the leftmost 1 of an unbroken string of $n + 1$ 1s on an otherwise blank tape, then either (1) M never halts or (2) M halts scanning the leftmost symbol of some word w_n over Σ on an otherwise blank tape. Such a Turing machine will be known as a *language enumerator*. The *domain* of M will be that set S of natural numbers n such that M eventually halts when started scanning the leftmost 1 of an unbroken string of $n + 1$ 1s on an otherwise blank tape. We also write $Dom(M)$ for the domain of M and say that M *is defined* for all and only the members of $Dom(M)$. Finally, the set $\{w_n | n \in Dom(M)\} \subseteq \Sigma^*$ will be known as the *language enumerated by* M and we shall speak of $L_{enum}(M)$. Similarly, where M is a language enumerator, we shall say that M *enumerates* or *Turing-enumerates* language $L_{enum}(M) = \{w_n | n \in Dom(M)\}$.

The new notion of language enumeration on the part of Turing machines enables us to define a new family of formal languages.

DEFINITION 12.2: Let L be a language over alphabet Σ. Then L is *Turing-enumerable* if there exists a language enumerator M that Turing-enumerates L.

In Chapter 1 we described conventions whereby Turing machines may be said to *accept* languages. In addition, Turing machines were seen to *recognize* languages. We have now completed our description of yet another role for Turing machines with regard to formal languages, conventions having been laid down whereby Turing machines may be said to *enumerate* languages. Theorem 12.4 below will show that language acceptance and language enumeration, on the part of Turing machines, are in fact closely related notions. Obtaining this result will be somewhat easier if we first describe a notion of language enumeration for multitape Turing machines, however. There are no surprises here, given Example 12.3.2.

DEFINITION 12.3: Let Σ be an alphabet not containing symbol *1*. Let M be a multitape, off-line Turing machine with k worktapes in addition to a single (read-only) input tape and a single (write-only) output tape. Let M be such that, for all $n \in N$, if M is started with its input tape read-head scanning the leftmost *1* of an unbroken string of $n + 1$ *1*s on an otherwise blank tape and with all its other tapes completely blank, then either (1) M never halts or (2) M halts with

(a) input tape read-head scanning the leftmost *1* of an unbroken string of $n + 1$ *1*s on an otherwise blank tape and

(b) output tape write-head scanning the leftmost symbol of some word $w_n \in \Sigma^*$ on an otherwise blank tape.

As usual, we will not care about the final configuration of worktapes. Such a multitape M will be known as a *(multitape) language enumerator*. The *domain of M* will be that set S of natural numbers n such that M, started scanning the leftmost *1* of an unbroken string of $n + 1$ *1*s on an otherwise blank input tape, eventually halts. We also write $Dom(M)$ for the domain of M. Finally, the set $\{w_n | n \in Dom(M)\} \subseteq \Sigma^*$ will be known as the *language enumerated by M*. Similarly, where M is a multitape language enumerator, we shall say that M *enumerates* or *Turing-enumerates* the language $L_{enum}(M) = \{w_n | n \in Dom(M)\}$.

We merely state the following equivalence result to which we shall appeal below. The easy proof is left as an exercise (see Exercise 12.3.4).

THEOREM 12.3: Let L be a language over alphabet Σ. Then there exists a single-tape Turing machine that enumerates L if and only if there exists a multitape Turing machine that enumerates L.

---

§12.4 A Recursion-Theoretic Characterization of the Family of Phrase-Structure Languages

The family of phrase-structure languages was first characterized grammar-theoretically. This was Definition 9.13. More recently, Theorems 12.1 and 12.2 afford us an automata-theoretic characterization of this class of languages. We are about to see that the family of phrase-structure languages can be described using concepts elaborated in Chapter 3. Accordingly, this alternative characterization, which is presented in Theorem 12.5, amounts to a recursion-theoretic characterization. As a preliminary step toward this result, we prove the following proposition.

THEOREM 12.4: Let L be a language over alphabet Σ. Then L is Turing-enumerable if and only if L is Turing-acceptable.

In both directions, a proof involves the simulation, in dovetailing fashion, of one (single-tape) Turing machine by another (multitape) Turing machine. We leave the proof as Exercise 12.4.1.

As mentioned earlier, our present goal is a recursion-theoretic characterization of the family of phrase-structure languages. We will need Theorem 12.4 as well as some effective encoding scheme. The Euler–Gödel scheme introduced in §2.4 will work as well as any. We briefly review this way of encoding symbol strings as natural numbers. Let $\Sigma = \{a, b\}$. We assign number 1 to letter a and 2 to letter b. Then word $aaba$ will be encoded as

$$2^1 \cdot 3^1 \cdot 5^2 \cdot 7^1$$

Not every natural number will be the code of a member of Σ^*. (For example, $125 = 5^3$ is not an encoding.) However, by the uniqueness of prime factorizations, if natural number n *is* the encoding of some word $w \in \Sigma^*$ in accordance with Euler–Gödel, then n is the code of a *unique* word w. Moreover, this word w is effectively recoverable from code n.

We now introduce a notion of *r.e. language* that is based on the notion of r.e. set introduced in Definition 3.10. A new notion of *recursive language* will be based upon the notion of recursive set introduced in Definition 3.9.

DEFINITION 12.4: Let L be a language over alphabet Σ. Let C_L be the set of natural number codes of members of L in accordance with Euler–Gödel. That is,

$$C_L = \{\ulcorner w \urcorner | w \in L\}$$

Then L is said to be a *recursively enumerable language*, or just *r.e.*, if C_L happens to be a recursively enumerable set of natural numbers. Similarly, L is a *recursive language* if C_L is recursive.

Note that both $\varnothing$ and Σ^* are r.e. languages as well as recursive languages. Incidentally, the notion of a recursive language will be seen to provide the recursion-theoretic implementation of the language recognition paradigm—promised at the beginning of Chapter 3 and long postponed. (Consider Theorem 12.6 below.)

The main result of this part of our investigation is now a consequence of Theorem 12.4 and Definition 12.4.

THEOREM 12.5: Let L be a language over alphabet Σ. Then L is a phrase-structure language if and only if L is r.e. Alternative formulation: L is Turing-acceptable if and only if L is r.e.

PROOF For the forward direction, suppose that L is a phrase-structure language. If L is $\varnothing$, then L is r.e. by a previous remark. So assume that L is nonempty. By Theorem 12.2, L is accepted by some Turing machine M_{accept}. In turn, by Theorem 12.4, there exists a Turing machine M_{enum} that enumerates L in the sense of Definition 12.1. That is, L is describable as $\{w_n | n \in Dom(M_{enum})\}$. We assume, in accordance with Definition 12.1, that if natural number $n \notin Dom(M_{enum})$, then M_{enum}'s computation for input n never terminates. We now describe the construction of a multitape Turing machine M^* that computes a number-theoretic function whose image is C_L. It then follows that C_L is an r.e. set of natural numbers and that L, in turn, is an r.e. language.

On its input tape and worktape$_1$, M^* simulates M_{enum}'s enumeration of L. That is, given representation I^{n+1} of natural number n on its input tape and assuming $n \in Dom(M_{enum})$, machine M^* produces on its worktape₁ the corresponding word w_n of L. When this simulation of M_{enum} for input n terminates, M^* goes about encoding w_n in accordance with the Euler–Gödel scheme. (We can easily imagine that several worktapes will be involved in carrying out this encoding.) Ultimately, natural number $\ulcorner w_n \urcorner$ is the result. M^* will write $\ulcorner w_n \urcorner$ to its output tape before halting. Apparently, M^* computes a unary (partial) number-theoretic function $f(n) =_{\text{def.}} \ulcorner w_n \urcorner$ with $Dom(f) = Dom(M_{enum})$. Hence, f is Turing-computable. By Theorem 3.3(b), f is partial recursive as well. Moreover, it can be seen that $Image(f) = \{\ulcorner w \urcorner | w \in L\} = C_L$. Thus C_L is the image under a partial recursive function of a subset of $\mathcal{N}$. It follows that C_L is an r.e. set of natural numbers and, hence, that L is an r.e. language. For the reader's benefit, we schematize our argument in Figure 12.4.1.

The **reverse direction** is left as an exercise. It is quite similar to the forward direction except that the simulating Turing machine must now decode natural numbers.   Q.E.D.

We leave the proof of Theorem 12.6 below to Exercise 12.4.6.

THEOREM 12.6: Let L be a language over some finite alphabet Σ. Then L is Turing-recognizable if and only if L is recursive.

The importance of Theorems 12.5 and 12.6 lies in the respective pairings of an automata-theoretic characterization of a family of languages with a recursion-theoretic characterization of the same family. The reader might pause for a moment to reflect on the tremendous difference between Turing-acceptability as presented in Definition 1.3, on the one hand, and recursive enumerability, as presented in Definitions 3.10 and 12.4, on the other. Similarly, the notion of Turing-recognizability as presented in Definition 1.4 bears little resemblance, on the face of it, to the notion of recursiveness as presented in Definitions 3.9 and 12.4. Nonetheless, in each case the two characterizations have turned out to be equivalent, and it is highly advantageous to have both.

We saw in Chapter 2 that it was possible to derive, from the Euler–Gödel scheme, a related encoding scheme such that, under the modified scheme, absolutely every natural number is the code of some Turing machine. (See the discussion leading to Remark 2.4.1.) We shall now do something precisely analogous to that with regard to encodings of words over alphabet $\Sigma = \{a, b\}$. Namely, we enumerate in ascending order the set of all and only those natural numbers that are encodings, in accordance with Euler–Gödel, of words over Σ. A new encoding scheme is now derived from positions within this list of encodings. Namely, the new code of word w will be the position of the old code of w within the list. If we number positions starting with 0, then every natural number is now the code of some (unique) word over Σ. Let us write $\ulcorner w \urcorner_{revised}$ for the code of word w in the new, revised sense. We continue to have the important properties of determinacy and effective retrievability for the new encoding scheme. Or, putting matters another way, the conversions back and forth between the new and old codes are recursive in character (see Exercise 12.4.4). We shall assume the new, revised encoding scheme throughout the remainder of this chapter.

REMARK 12.4.1: An effective encoding scheme for words over alphabet $\Sigma = \{a, b\}$ is available such that absolutely every member of $\mathcal{N}$ is the code of some (unique) word over Σ. It follows that any set of natural numbers is C_L for some language L over Σ.

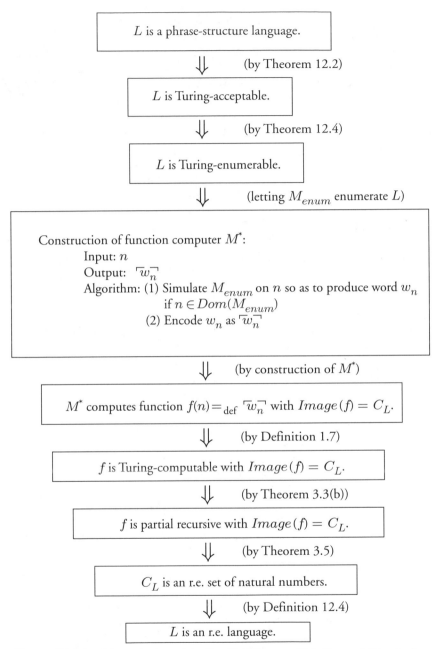

Figure 12.4.1   Schematization of the Proof of Theorem 12.5 (Forward Direction).

By Corollary 3.1, we know that there exist r.e. sets of natural numbers whose complements are not themselves r.e. It follows, by Remark 12.4.1 and Theorem 12.4, that there exist phrase-structure languages whose complements are not themselves phrase-structure languages. Thus, as promised at the end of §12.2, we have

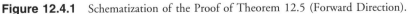

> **THEOREM 12.7:** The class of phrase-structure languages, and hence the class of Turing-acceptable languages, is not closed under complementation.

As usual, Theorem 12.7 can be used to show that the class of phrase-structure languages is closed under neither relative complementation nor symmetric difference.

§12.5 The General Word Problem for Phrase-Structure Languages Is Unsolvable

So far, we have considered a number of unsolvable problems. In particular, there were the Self-Halting Problem for Turing Machines and the Halting Problem for Turing Machines, to which the former is reducible (see §8.2 and §8.3). We now show that the general word problem for phrase-structure languages is unsolvable. Our argument will appeal to the demonstrated existence of r.e. sets of natural numbers that are not recursive (Theorem 3.10).

We begin by reviewing several items discussed in earlier chapters.

- The word problem for a given generative grammar $G = (\Sigma, \Gamma, \sigma, \Pi)$ is that of deciding, for an arbitrary word w over Σ, whether $\sigma \Rightarrow^* w$. In particular, the word problem for grammar G will be solvable if we possess some algorithm for determining, for arbitrary word w, whether G generates w; the word problem for G is unsolvable if we possess no such algorithm in the case of grammar G.

- As usual, we also speak of the word problem for a given phrase-structure language L over Σ and mean, thereby, the problem of deciding, for an arbitrary word w over Σ, whether $w \in L$. We emphasize again that in discussions of the word problem for languages, one always assumes the availability of generative grammars for those languages. So the word problem for language L over Σ will be solvable if there exists an algorithm for deciding whether an arbitrary word w over Σ is generated by some given grammar G with $L = L(G)$.

- The *general* word problem for phrase-structure languages is that of deciding, for *any* phrase-structure language L and any word w, whether $w \in L$. It is this problem—the general word problem for phrase-structure languages—that we shall now show to be unsolvable.

Our proof is indirect. We assume, for the sake of producing a contradiction, that the general word problem for phrase-structure languages is solvable. That is, we assume that, given an arbitrary phrase-structure grammar G, there exists an algorithm for determining, of any word w, whether w is in $L(G)$.

(1) To begin, we recall that, by Theorem 3.10, there exists an r.e. set S^* of natural numbers that is not recursive. By Remark 12.4.1 in turn, this means that there exists an r.e. language L^* over $\Sigma = \{a, b\}$, say, that is not a recursive language (see Exercise 12.4.8).

(2) Since L^* is r.e., it follows, by Theorem 12.5, that L^* is a phrase-structure language; that is, $L^* = L(G^*)$ for some phrase-structure grammar $G^* = \langle \Sigma, \Gamma, \sigma, \Pi \rangle$.

(3) By assumption, there exists an effective method for determining membership in $L(G^*)$. Equivalently, the unary function defined by

$$f_{G^*}(\ulcorner w \urcorner_{\text{revised}}) = \begin{cases} 1 & \text{if } \sigma \Rightarrow^* w \\ 0 & \text{otherwise} \end{cases}$$

is effectively computable.

(4) Assuming Church's Thesis, we can take this to mean that function f_{G^*} is partial recursive. But since $\sigma \Rightarrow^* w$ if and only if $w \in L(G^*)$, we see that partial recursive f_{G^*} may be characterized as

$$f_{G^*}(\ulcorner w \urcorner_{\text{revised}}) = \begin{cases} 1 & \text{if } w \in L^* \\ 0 & \text{if } w \notin L^* \end{cases}$$

(5) In other words, partial recursive f_{G^*} is none other than the characteristic function of set $C_{L^*} = \{\ulcorner w \urcorner_{\text{revised}} | w \in L^*\}$, which means that L^* is a recursive language after all, which is a patent contradiction. We conclude that, contrary to our initial assumption, there do exist phrase-structure languages for which the word problem is unsolvable.

We have hereby demonstrated

THEOREM 12.8: There exist phrase-structure languages for which the word problem is unsolvable. Alternative formulation: The general word problem for phrase-structure languages is unsolvable.

Note that our formulation of Theorem 12.8 does assume Church's Thesis. In the absence of that assumption, we are entitled to say only that there exist phrase-structure languages that are not recursive in the sense of Definition 12.4 (see (1) above).

Theorem 12.8 explains why phrase-structure grammars, in general, are unsuitable as the basis for parsing algorithms. For we can now see that there exists no general parsing algorithm that, for an arbitrary phrase-structure grammar G and program *prog*, would enable us to determine whether *prog* is written in accordance with G. This is not merely a matter of inefficiency—the result of backtracking or the like. Rather, we are confronted here with unsolvability in principle. A negative result such as Theorem 12.8 is not without practical consequences. Clearly, anyone aware of Theorem 12.8 is not going to waste time in an attempt to develop a parsing algorithm applicable to phrase-structure grammars generally. Equally important, designers of new programming languages must be careful so as to ensure that the syntactic features of those languages can be expressed by grammars that are context-sensitive at worst.

§12.6 The Post Correspondence Problem

The Post Correspondence Problem (PCP) is another important example of a generally unsolvable problem. We turn to a consideration of PCP now. We caution the reader to avoid being misled by an initial impression of innocuousness, however. What may appear, at the outset, to be a trivial sort of puzzle will turn out to have significant negative consequences for formal language theory in general and for compiler design theory in particular. We approach PCP by way of a simple example.

EXAMPLE 12.6.1 Suppose that the following sequence of ordered pairs of words over alphabet $\Sigma = \{a, b, c, d, r\}$ is given.

$$\langle ac, a \rangle$$
$$\langle abr, \varepsilon \rangle$$
$$\langle ab, ada \rangle$$
$$\langle ra, bra \rangle$$
$$\langle ad, brac \rangle$$

(12.6.1)

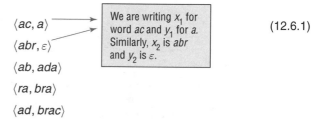

We are writing x_1 for word ac and y_1 for a. Similarly, x_2 is abr and y_2 is ε.

Let us refer to word pairs $\langle x_1, y_1 \rangle$ through $\langle x_5, y_5 \rangle$ here. Note that if words x_2, x_1, x_5, x_3, and x_4 are concatenated in that order, then the word *abracadabra* is the result. In other words, word $x_2 x_1 x_5 x_3 x_4$ is *abracadabra*. As it turns out, if words y_2, y_1, y_5, y_3, and y_4 are concatenated in that order, then the very same word results. That is to say, word $y_2 y_1 y_5 y_3 y_4$ is *abracadabra* as well. Note the correspondence of subscripts here. We shall say that the word *abracadabra* together with the subscript sequence $\langle 2, 1, 5, 3, 4 \rangle$ comprises a *solution* to PCP for the sequence (12.6.1) of word pairs. Since a sequence of subscripts by itself completely determines a corresponding word, it is often convenient to specify a solution by giving the subscript sequence alone.

Lest the special properties of the preceding example mislead, we immediately consider

---

EXAMPLE 12.6.2 This time let $\Sigma = \{a, b\}$ and consider the sequence of word pairs

$$\langle ab, a \rangle$$
$$\langle bbab, bbbab \rangle$$
$$\langle bb, b \rangle$$
$$\langle a, bb \rangle$$

(12.6.2)

We have solution $\langle 1, 2 \rangle$ as well as $\langle 3, 2 \rangle$. Since we shall permit repetitions, both $\langle 1, 2, 3, 2 \rangle$ and $\langle 3, 2, 1, 2 \rangle$ will count as solutions, as will $\langle 3, 2, 3, 2 \rangle$. In fact, word pair sequence (12.6.2) will have infinitely many distinct solutions. On the other hand, it is not hard to see that the final pair $\langle a, bb \rangle$ can figure in none of them. (Why not?)

We next present a formal statement of PCP.

DEFINITION 12.5: Let Σ be a finite alphabet. Let

$$\langle x_1, y_1 \rangle$$

$$\langle x_2, y_2 \rangle$$

$$\cdots$$

$$\langle x_n, y_n \rangle$$

be a finite, nonempty sequence of ordered pairs of words over Σ. Then the *Post Correspondence Problem for word pair sequence* $\langle x_1, y_1 \rangle$, $\langle x_2, y_2 \rangle$, ..., $\langle x_n, y_n \rangle$ is that of determining whether there exists a word w such that

(1) w is identical with the nontrivial[1] concatenation of some sequence of words from among the x_is, in any order and allowing repetitions, and

(2) w is identical with the concatenation of the corresponding y_is as well.

Thus, in Example 12.6.1, word *abracadabra* is (1) the concatenation of x_2, x_1, x_5, x_3, and x_4, in that order, and (2) the concatenation of corresponding words y_2, y_1, y_5, y_3, and y_4, in that order. Consequently, word *abracadabra* together with subscript sequence $\langle 2, 1, 5, 3, 4 \rangle$ provides a solution in the case of Example 12.6.1.

One can get a better feeling for PCP by doing the following. Suppose that some finite sequence of word pairs $\langle x_i, y_i \rangle$ is given. Imagine that the first and second word of each pair are written on the upper and lower half, respectively, of one face of an index card, say. (Also, multiple copies of each card must be made available, so as to allow for repeated occurrences of a given word pair.) Now the search for a solution to PCP for the given sequence of word pairs can be thought of as the search for an arrangement of cards such that the word appearing across the upper halves of the cards is identical with the word appearing across the lower halves of the cards. The case of word pair sequence (12.6.1) is illustrated in Figure 12.6.1.

Note that if one solution w to PCP for a given sequence of word pairs exists, then w^n is another solution for any $n \geq 2$. In other words, if one solution exists, then it is easy to find others, and, in fact, infinitely many solutions exist. This leads us to the following insight, which we shall use in a somewhat surprising way later.

REMARK 12.6.1: If it can be established that PCP for a given sequence of word pairs has but finitely many solutions, this can only mean that there are *no* solutions.

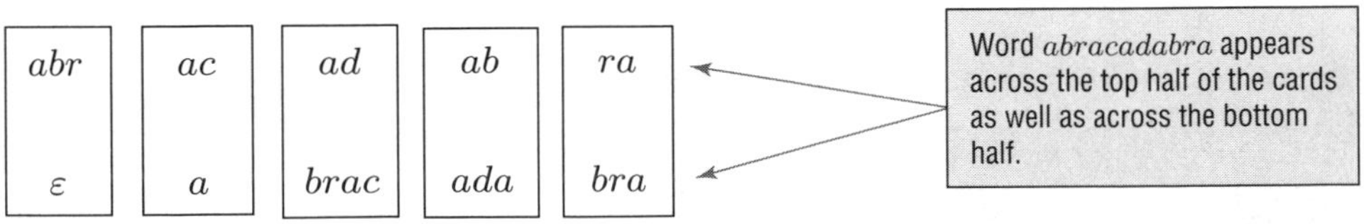

Figure 12.6.1   A Solution to the Post Correspondence Problem for Word Pair Sequence (12.6.1).

---

[1]The trivial solution would be $w = \varepsilon$, which is the result of concatenating zero of the x_is and zero of the y_is.

It will be useful to introduce a bit of terminology. Namely, given a sequence of word pairs, a solution w to PCP for the given sequence will be termed a "prime solution" if it is not the concatenation of simpler solutions. For instance, *abracadabra***abracadabra** is a solution—but not a prime solution—to PCP for the word pair sequence (12.6.1).

EXAMPLE 12.6.3 Consider the following sequence of word pairs.

$$\langle ab, a \rangle \qquad\qquad (12.6.3)$$

$$\langle abb, bab \rangle$$

$$\langle bab, bba \rangle$$

$$\langle a, ba \rangle$$

As usual, we shall speak of pairs $\langle x_1, y_1 \rangle$ through $\langle x_4, y_4 \rangle$. We seek solutions to PCP for this sequence, and, as noted in Remark 12.6.1, either no solutions exist or there are infinitely many. We begin our search by inquiring whether a solution could start with pair $\langle x_2, y_2 \rangle = \langle abb, bab \rangle$. It is obvious that the answer is no, since no solution can begin with both a and b. Similar considerations rule out any solution's beginning with either pair $\langle x_3, y_3 \rangle = \langle bab, bba \rangle$ or pair $\langle x_4, y_4 \rangle = \langle a, ba \rangle$. Any solution must begin with $\langle x_1, y_1 \rangle = \langle ab, a \rangle$ apparently. Note, further, that any solution must end with the pair $\langle x_4, y_4 \rangle = \langle a, ba \rangle$. (In what follows, we shall refer loosely to an unformulated *Matching Principle* when raising similar considerations.) In summary, it can be said that any solution must begin with $\langle x_1, y_1 \rangle = \langle ab, a \rangle$ and end with $\langle x_4, y_4 \rangle = \langle a, ba \rangle$.

The infinite search tree of Figure 12.6.2 represents the search for (prime) solutions to PCP for word pair sequence (12.6.3). Any edge of the tree is labeled by the index of the word pair being appended in the search for a solution. A branch of the tree is closed—as indicated by ×—once a solution is obtained. Consequently, the sequence of indices labeling any path leading from root to leaf corresponds to a (prime) solution. The tree of Figure 12.6.2 shows that a (prime) solution consists of a single occurrence of $\langle ab, a \rangle$, a final occurrence of $\langle a, ba \rangle$, and any combination of the other two pairs in between. Since any of these combinations makes for a distinct solution, we see that there exist infinitely many prime solutions. At any given node of the search tree, the current "deficit" is indicated in boldface. A solution amounts to a sequence of words pairs with deficit ε. Deficit ε at the root represents the trivial solution. Finally, nonprime solutions can be accommodated by extending closed branches of the tree.

So far, we have described PCP for sequences of word pairs, considered a few examples, and, finally, presented a search tree as a graphical representation of the search for prime solutions to PCP for the last of these examples. We next establish an important theoretical result. Namely, we shall show that there can be no general algorithm that, applied to an arbitrary sequence $\langle x_i, y_i \rangle$ of word pairs, determines whether PCP for $\langle x_i, y_i \rangle$ has a solution. We do this by reducing the general word problem for phrase-structure languages, shown to be unsolvable in Theorem 12.8, to PCP for an arbitrary sequence of word pairs.

The essence of the reduction is the following. Given phrase-structure grammar $G = \langle \Sigma, \Gamma, \sigma, \Pi \rangle$ together with some word w over Σ, we use the productions of grammar G in order to carefully construct a sequence S_G of word pairs such that PCP for S_G has solutions if and only if G generates w—that is, if and only if $\sigma \Rightarrow_G^* w$. But since there is, in general, no algorithm for deciding whether $\sigma \Rightarrow_G^* w$, there can be no algorithm for deciding whether S_G has solutions, either. Or, to put matters only slightly differently, if there *were* a general procedure for deciding whether PCP for an arbitrary sequence of word pairs has solutions, then we could use it, together with our reduction, to obtain a general procedure for

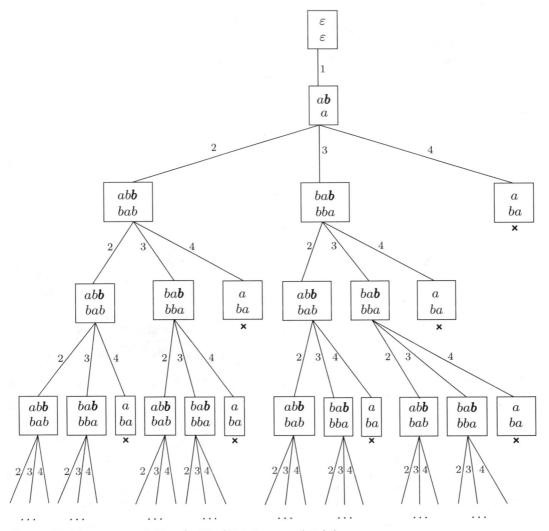

Figure 12.6.2   PCP Search Tree for Word Pair Sequence (12.6.3).

deciding the word problem for an arbitrary phrase-structure grammar. But, by Theorem 12.8, there is no such such general procedure. Hence, PCP for an arbitrary sequence of word pairs is unsolvable.

Constructing word-pair sequence S_G and proving that PCP for S_G has solutions if and only if $\sigma \Rightarrow^*_G w$ is no trivial matter, however. We therefore approach the matter by way of an example. Only afterward will a proof be given in full generality.

EXAMPLE 12.6.4 Let $G = \langle \Sigma, \Gamma, S, \Pi \rangle$ with $\Sigma = \{a, b\}$, $\Gamma = \{S\}$, and production set Π containing the three productions

$$S \rightarrow aSa \mid bSb \mid \qquad\qquad (12.6.4)$$

Of course, $L(G)$ is the language of even-length palindromes over Σ. (Grammar G happens to be context-free, although that will play no role here; we chose G for simplicity.) We also assume $w = abba$ so that $w \in L(G)$. Our initial goal is the description of a sequence S_G of word pairs over an alphabet Ψ obtained by extending $\Sigma \cup \Gamma$. To this end, we introduce additional surrogates for each member of $\Sigma \cup \Gamma$. Thus

$$a' \quad b' \quad S'$$

will belong to Ψ in the present instance. Furthermore, symbols

$$\Box \quad - \quad =$$

will be useful. So $\Psi = \{a, b, S, a', b', S', \Box, -, =\}$. The construction of S_G is effective in that which word pairs are included is completely fixed or determined by G and $w = abba$ taken together. One word pair essentially involves start symbol S:

$$\langle \Box S -, \Box \rangle \qquad (1)$$

Another essentially involves $w = abba$:

$$\langle \Box, = \boldsymbol{abba} \Box \rangle \qquad (2)$$

In addition, each of G's three productions contributes exactly two word pairs:

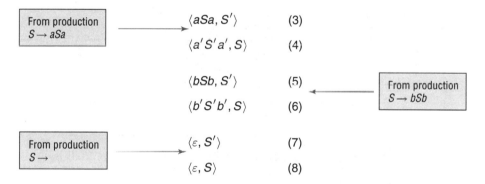

From production $S \to aSa$ $\qquad \langle aSa, S' \rangle \qquad (3)$

$\langle a'S'a', S \rangle \qquad (4)$

$\langle bSb, S' \rangle \qquad (5)$ From production $S \to bSb$

$\langle b'S'b', S \rangle \qquad (6)$

From production $S \to$ $\qquad \langle \varepsilon, S' \rangle \qquad (7)$

$\langle \varepsilon, S \rangle \qquad (8)$

In addition, three word pairs match members of $\Sigma \cup \Gamma$ with their surrogates:

$$\langle a, a' \rangle \qquad (9)$$

$$\langle b, b' \rangle \qquad (10)$$

$$\langle S, S' \rangle \qquad (11)$$

Three more establish the association in the other direction:

$$\langle a', a \rangle \qquad (12)$$

$$\langle b', b \rangle \qquad (13)$$

$$\langle S', S \rangle \qquad (14)$$

Finally, we have the two word pairs:

$$\langle\text{---},=\rangle \qquad (15)$$

$$\langle=,\text{---}\rangle \qquad (16)$$

Word pair sequence S_G will consist of (1)–(16) above. We seek now to establish the truth of

> **REMARK 12.6.2:** Any prime solution to PCP for sequence (1)–(16) simulates the generation of $w = abba$ within grammar G.

First, we note that, by the Matching Principle, any solution to PCP for (1)–(16) must begin with either (1), (7), or (8) and end with either (2), (7), or (8). Moreover, the reader should verify that, in fact, neither (7) nor (8) can serve in either role here.[2] Thus, it can be said that any solution to PCP for this sequence of word pairs must begin with (1) and end with (2), which we may picture as in Figure 12.6.3(a). It is not hard to see that (14) can be the second word pair of a solution, although (4) would also lead to a solution. (Word pairs (6) and (8), on the other hand, would not lead to solutions.) Opting for (14), we have Figure 12.6.3(b). Clearly, the third member of any solution that begins with (1) and (14) must be (16) (see Figure 12.6.3(c). Continuing in this manner, a solution of length 15 is the result (see Figure 12.6.3(d)):

$$\square S\text{---}S' = aSa\text{---}a'b'S'b'a' = \textbf{ab}\varepsilon\textbf{ba}\square \qquad (12.6.5)$$

In fact, this is the only prime solution that begins with (1) and (14). (The only prime solution that begins $\langle 1, 4, \ldots \rangle$ is of length 18. See Exercise 12.6.3.) Ignoring distinctions between members of $\Sigma \cup \Gamma$ and their surrogates, solution (12.6.5) consists of a sequence of strings over $\Sigma \cup \Gamma$ separated by alternating occurrences of markers = and ---. Moreover, ignoring the duplication S/S' at the very beginning, this sequence models a derivation of $w = abba$ within grammar G.

EXAMPLE 12.6.5 Let G be the grammar of Example 12.6.4 again. That is, $G = \langle \Sigma, \Gamma, S, \Pi \rangle$ with $\Sigma = \{a, b\}$, $\Gamma = \{S\}$, and production set Π containing the three productions

$$S \rightarrow aSa \mid bSb \mid$$

So, as before, $L(G)$ is the language of even-length palindromes. This time we choose $w=aba$, which means that G does not generate w this time. The point of this example is to see that applying the construction, as described earlier, yields a sequence of word pairs over alphabet Ψ having no solution. Applying the construction as before, we obtain the very same sequence of word pairs as was constructed in Example 12.6.4, except that word pair (2) is now

$$(2') \qquad \langle \square, =\textbf{aba}\square \rangle$$

---

[2] Suppose, for example, that we *started* with (7). In that case, the only way to continue is with (14), followed by (11), followed by (14), followed by (11), and so on, without end. No solution is ever obtained. Similar considerations come into play if we imagine starting with (8) or ending with either (7) or (8). (Try it.)

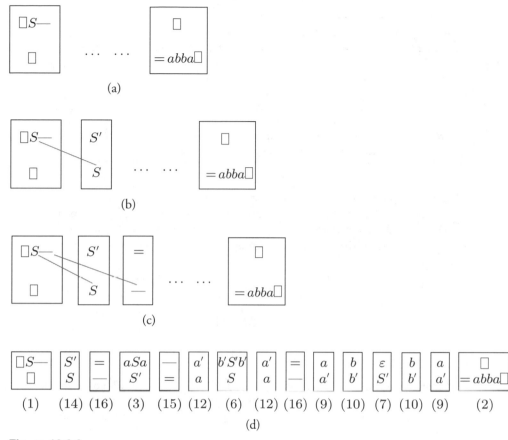

(a)

(b)

(c)

(d)

Figure 12.6.3

The search for a solution to PCP for this new sequence of word pairs will prove instructive. Once again, any prime solution would have to be of the form $\langle 1, \ldots, 2' \rangle$. We might try to start as before (see Figure 12.6.4). But how is the gap here to be filled? Apparently, word pairs (4), (6), and (8), although on the face of it promising, reflect the generative capacity of G and hence cannot be used to continue in Figure 12.6.4. (Try it.) Similar problems arise if one looks for a solution of the form $\langle 1, 4, \ldots, 2' \rangle$. We conclude that PCP for this sequence of word pairs has no solution.

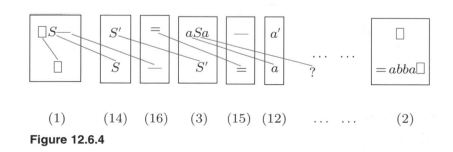

Figure 12.6.4

Extrapolating on the basis of Examples 12.6.4 and 12.6.5, one sees that the described construction applied to a given phrase-structure grammar G and some word w will produce a sequence of word pairs having a solution just in case G generates w. So we have reduced the general word problem for phrase-structure grammars to PCP for an arbitrary sequence of word pairs. We are now ready to present, in full generality, the proof of the main result of this section.

THEOREM 12.9: There is no general algorithm for determining whether the Post Correspondence Problem for an arbitrary sequence of word pairs has solutions. Alternative formulation: PCP for an arbitrary sequence of word pairs is unsolvable.

PROOF Suppose, for the sake of producing a contradiction, that there were such a general algorithm. It would then follow that the word problem for an arbitrary phrase-structure grammar G is solvable. Why? Well, suppose that phrase-structure grammar $G = \{\Sigma, \Gamma, \sigma, \Pi\}$ and word w were given. Suppose further that the members of production set Π are

$$\alpha_1 \to \beta_1$$
$$\alpha_2 \to \beta_2$$
$$\dots$$
$$\alpha_n \to \beta_n$$

How would we now be able to decide whether G generates w? To begin, we would use G and w to construct the following sequence of word pairs over alphabet Ψ, where, as before, Ψ contains every symbol in Σ and Γ as well as their surrogates and special symbols $\square$, $-$, and $=$.

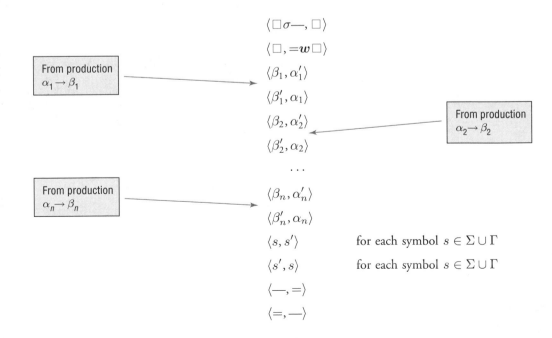

$$\langle \square \sigma -, \square \rangle$$
$$\langle \square, = \boldsymbol{w} \square \rangle$$

From production $\alpha_1 \to \beta_1$

$$\langle \beta_1, \alpha_1' \rangle$$
$$\langle \beta_1', \alpha_1 \rangle$$
$$\langle \beta_2, \alpha_2' \rangle$$
$$\langle \beta_2', \alpha_2 \rangle$$

From production $\alpha_2 \to \beta_2$

$$\dots$$

From production $\alpha_n \to \beta_n$

$$\langle \beta_n, \alpha_n' \rangle$$
$$\langle \beta_n', \alpha_n \rangle$$
$$\langle s, s' \rangle \qquad \text{for each symbol } s \in \Sigma \cup \Gamma$$
$$\langle s', s \rangle \qquad \text{for each symbol } s \in \Sigma \cup \Gamma$$
$$\langle -, = \rangle$$
$$\langle =, - \rangle$$

We claim that PCP for this sequence of word pairs has a solution if and only if G generates w. To see this, first note that any solution to PCP must begin with the first pair $\langle \Box\sigma\!\!-, \Box\rangle$ and end with the second pair $\langle \Box, =\boldsymbol{w}\,\Box\rangle$. Next, some one of the word pairs corresponding to productions of G must be applied—in

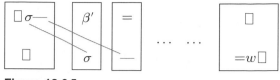

Figure 12.6.5

particular, some word pair with bottom half σ and upper half β' such that G contains production $\sigma \to \beta$. Following that, we have, of necessity, word pair $\langle =, -\rangle$ and so on, as in Example 12.6.4 above (see Figure 12.6.5). Given that earlier example, it is hoped that this will be enough to see that any solution to PCP for this sequence of word pairs simulates a derivation of w within grammar G.

By hypothesis, we have a general algorithm that can be applied to this sequence of word pairs in order to determine whether PCP has a solution in this case. If so, it follows that G generates w. If not, then G does not generate w. In other words, our general algorithm for determining whether PCP for an arbitrary sequence of word pairs has a solution can be used to obtain a solution to the word problem for an arbitrary phrase-structure grammar G. This contradicts Theorem 12.8, according to which the general word problem for the class of phrase-structure grammars is unsolvable. We conclude that, contrary to our assumption, there is no algorithm for deciding whether PCP for an arbitrary sequence of word pairs has a solution. Q.E.D.

We can now use Theorem 12.9 to obtain some unsolvability results concerning the family of context free languages.

- We saw in Chapter 10 that we possess algorithms enabling us to decide, for any given context-free grammar G, whether $L(G)$ is the empty language as well as whether $L(G)$ is infinite.

- We also saw, however, that the intersection of two context-free languages may not itself be context-free. We shall now see that there is no general algorithm for determining, of two arbitrary context-free languages L_1 and L_2, whether $L_1 \cap L_2$ is empty. Nor is there a general algorithm for determining, of two arbitrary context-free languages L_1 and L_2, whether $L_1 \cap L_2$ is infinite. We prove that each of these problems is unsolvable by reducing PCP for an arbitrary sequence of word pairs to it.

THEOREM 12.10(a): There is no general algorithm that can be applied to an arbitrary pair of context-free languages so as to determine whether their intersection is empty.

THEOREM 12.10(b): There is no general algorithm that can be applied to an arbitrary pair of context-free languages so as to determine whether their intersection is infinite.

PROOF Let alphabet $\Sigma = \{a_1, a_2, \ldots, a_m\}$ be given. In addition, let word pairs

$$\langle x_1, y_1 \rangle \tag{12.6.6}$$
$$\langle x_2, y_2 \rangle$$
$$\cdots$$
$$\langle x_n, y_n \rangle$$

over Σ be given. Next, we introduce new symbols $b_1, b_2, \ldots, b_n$ distinct from any of $a_1, a_2, \ldots, a_m$. Languages L_1 and L_2 over $\Sigma \cup \{b_1, b_2, \ldots, b_n\}$ are then defined as

$$L_1 = \{x_{i_1} x_{i_2} \ldots x_{i_k} b_{i_k} \ldots b_{i_2} b_{i_1} | k \geq 1 \text{ and where each of the } x_{i_1}, x_{i_2}, \ldots, x_{i_k}$$
$$\text{is taken from among } x_1, x_2, \ldots, x_n$$
$$\text{and where each of the } b_{i_1}, b_{i_2}, \ldots, b_{i_k}$$
$$\text{is taken from among } b_1, b_2, \ldots, b_n\}$$

and

$$L_2 = \{y_{i_1} y_{i_2} \ldots y_{i_j} b_{i_j} \ldots b_{i_2} b_{i_1} | j \geq 1 \text{ and where each of the } y_{i_1}, y_{i_2}, \ldots, y_{i_j}$$
$$\text{is taken from among } y_1, y_2, \ldots, y_n$$
$$\text{and where each of the } b_{i_1}, b_{i_2}, \ldots, b_{i_j}$$
$$\text{is taken from among } b_1, b_2, \ldots, b_n\}$$

Language L_1 contains all and only those words over $\Sigma \cup \{b_1, b_2, \ldots, b_n\}$ whose front "half" consists of arbitrary finite concatenations of x_is and whose back half consists of the corresponding sequence of b_is in reverse order. Similarly, language L_2 contains all and only those words consisting of arbitrary finite concatenations of y_is followed by the corresponding sequence of b_is in reverse order. The interest of this pair of languages is the following: the presence of the b_is, as representations of a particular concatenation sequence, ensures that each word in $L_1 \cap L_2$ represents one solution to PCP for word-pair sequence (12.6.6). Consequently, there exists a 1–1 correspondence between members of language $L_1 \cap L_2$ and solutions to PCP. Moreover, as we show below, languages L_1 and L_2 are both context-free. So if we did possess an algorithm enabling us to determine, for an arbitrary pair of context-free languages, whether their intersection is empty, then we would be able to apply it to the particular L_1 and L_2 corresponding to word-pair sequence (12.6.6) so as to determine whether PCP for this sequence has solutions. But (12.6.6) was an arbitrary sequence of word pairs over Σ. So we appear to have a solution to PCP for an arbitrary sequence of word pairs over Σ, which contradicts Theorem 12.9. We conclude that there can be no algorithm for deciding whether the intersection of two context-free languages is empty.

Similar remarks apply in the case where we suppose that we possess an algorithm for determining whether the intersection of two arbitrary given context-free languages is infinite. (Recall that PCP for an arbitrary sequence of word pairs has either no solutions or infinitely many.)

We complete the proof by showing that L_1 and L_2 are both context-free. As for L_1, we describe a context-free grammar G_1 with $L_1 = L(G_1)$. Grammar G_1's terminal alphabet is $\Sigma \cup \{b_1, b_2, \ldots, b_n\}$. Its nonterminal alphabet is $\{S\}$, and there are $n + 1$ productions:

$$S \rightarrow x_i S b_i \quad \text{for } 1 \leq i \leq n$$

$$S \rightarrow$$

Grammar G_2 with $L_2 = L(G_2)$ is essentially the same. Its productions are

$$S \to y_i S b_i \quad \text{for } 1 \le i \le n$$
$$S \to$$

Q.E.D.

We now use Theorem 12.10(a) and the fact that the intersection of any two context-free languages is a context-sensitive language (Corollary 11.1) in order to demonstrate that there exists no general algorithm for deciding whether an arbitrary context-sensitive language is empty. Similarly, Theorem 12.10(b) shows that there can be no general algorithm for deciding whether such a language is infinite.

THEOREM 12.11(a): There is no algorithm for determining whether an arbitrary context-sensitive language L is empty.

THEOREM 12.11(b): There is no algorithm for determining whether an arbitrary context-sensitive language L is infinite.

PROOF Suppose that L_1 and L_2 are arbitrary context-free languages. By Corollary 11.1, $L_1 \cap L_2$ is context-sensitive. If we did possess a general algorithm for deciding whether a context-sensitive language is empty, then we could now apply it so as to determine whether $L_1 \cap L_2$ is empty, contrary to Theorem 12.10(a).

The proof of (b) is strictly analogous to that of (a) but appeals to Theorem 12.10(b).   Q.E.D.

Other unsolvability results are presented in Exercises 12.6.5 through 12.6.11. All are ultimately consequences of the general unsolvability of the general word problem for phrase-structure languages by way of PCP. We mention, in particular, the unavailability of a general algorithm for determining whether an arbitrary context-free grammar is ambiguous or whether an arbitrary context-free language is inherently ambiguous. Finally, we close by citing the importance of the general word problem for phrase-structure languages.

The word problem bears comparison with the Self-Halting Problem for Turing Machines. Assuming Church's Thesis, we showed that the latter is unsolvable and then proceeded to reduce other problems concerning Turing machines to it, thereby showing those other problems to be unsolvable as well (see §8.2 and §8.3). Apparently, the word problem plays, within formal language theory, much the same role that the Self-Halting Problem plays within the classical theory of computability. Which problem that we have considered holds an analogous place within the theory of NP-completeness? (See §8.5 through §8.7.) Within the theory of P-completeness? (See §8.8 through §8.10.)

§12.7 The Chomsky Hierarchy

In Part II of this text, we have considered several types of grammars and formal languages. We are now in a position to complete our study of formal languages by summarizing the accumulated results. In particular, we have obtained a number of proper containment results that yield a rather neat picture

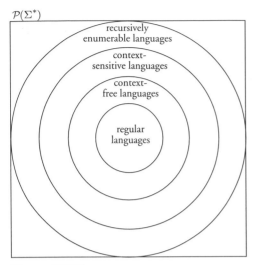

Figure 12.7.1

of the world of formal languages. In what follows, we shall assume an alphabet $\Sigma = \{a, b\}$, say. By a language, we shall mean a language over Σ.

First of all, we noted in Chapter 10 that every right-linear grammar is a context-free grammar. It follows immediately that every regular language is context-free. However, it is a consequence of the Pumping Lemma for Finite-State Automata (Lemma 9.2) that certain context-free languages (e.g., $\{a^n b^n | n \geq 0\}$) are not regular. In other words, the class of regular languages is a proper subset of the class of context-free languages.

Similarly, we saw in Chapter 11 that, as an immediate consequence of the definition of a context-sensitive grammar, every context-free grammar without ε-productions is context-sensitive. We also saw that every ε-free (positive) context-free language is generated by some context-free grammar without ε-productions. It follows immediately that every context-free language is context-sensitive, given Definition 11.2. Moreover, once again the containment is proper: By a Pumping Lemma for Context-Free Languages (Lemma 10.3), there exist languages (e.g., $\{a^n b^n c^n | n \geq 0\}$) that are context-sensitive but not context-free.

Finally, it is obvious that every context-sensitive grammar (language) is a phrase-structure grammar (language). Moreover, Theorem 11.9 shows that the containment is again proper. The picture that emerges is that of a hierarchy of grammars and a corresponding hierarchy of languages. This hierarchy was first described by theoretical linguist Noam Chomsky in the late 1950s and is consequently known as the Chomsky hierarchy. In this connection we introduce a characterization-neutral terminology that occurs throughout the literature. Namely, one refers to the languages represented by the outermost circle in Figure 12.7.1 as the *type-0 languages over* Σ. The circle nested within that one represents the *type-1 languages over* Σ, and so on. Table 12.7.1 summarizes this classification of languages. Table 12.7.2 summarizes the results, of this and previous chapters, concerning the closure properties of each language family.

Bibliography

Our proof of Theorem 12.1 follows [Hopcroft and Ullman 1979]. That of Theorem 12.9 appears in [Kurki-Suonio 1971], which is also our source for Exercises 12.6.4 through 12.6.10.

EXERCISES FOR §12.1

12.1.1. [hwk] Complete the derivation of word aba from grammar G of Example 12.1.1. That is, extend the right column of Figure 12.1.1 from

$$S \Rightarrow^* \left(\frac{a}{*}\right) \left(\frac{b}{*}\right) X_{q_{11}} \left(\frac{a}{*}\right) \left(\frac{B}{B}\right)$$

by applying the productions of Group 9.

12.1.2. The construction of the proof of Theorem 12.1 produces a grammar that is neither context-free nor context-sensitive. Explain by citing specific productions.

12.1.3. [hwk] Consider again the single-tape Turing machine M of Example 12.1.1. For each of the productions below, indicate whether the given

Table 12.7.1 The Chomsky Hierarchy of Languages Over Σ

Language Family	Primary Grammar-Theoretic Characterization Any Language in This Family Is:	Primary Automata-Theoretic Characterization Any Language in This Family Is:	Alternative Characterization Any Language in This Family Is:
Type 0	Generated by a phrase-structure grammar (whose productions are of the form $\alpha \to \beta$, where α and β are arbitrary strings over $\Sigma \cup \Gamma$)[a]	Accepted by a deterministic single-tape Turing machine	A recursively enumerable (r.e.) language
Type 1	Generated by a context-sensitive grammar[b] (whose productions are of the form $\alpha \to \beta$ where α and β are arbitrary strings over $\Sigma \cup \Gamma$ with $|\alpha| \le |\beta|$)[a]	Accepted by a linear-bounded automaton	—
Type 2	Generated by a context-free grammar (whose productions are of the form $\alpha \to \beta$, where α is a single nonterminal and β is an arbitrary string over $\Sigma \cup \Gamma$)[a]	Accepted by a nondeterministic pushdown-stack automaton	—
Type 3	Generated by a right-linear grammar (whose productions are of the form $\alpha \to \beta$, where α is a single nonterminal and β is either of the form wY or of the form w with $w \in \Sigma^*$ and $Y \in \Gamma$)[a]	Accepted by a deterministic finite-state automaton	Denoted by a regular expression

[a] It is assumed that the grammar in question has terminal alphabet Σ and nonterminal alphabet Γ.

[b] Strictly speaking, such a language L is either itself generated by a context-sensitive grammar or is the result of adding ε to a language that is so generated (see Definition 11.2).

Table 12.7.2 Closure Properties of Language Families within the Chomsky Hierarchy

Language Family	Closed under Union?	Closed under Intersection?	Closed under Complementation?	Closed under Concatenation?	Closed under Word Reversal?
Type-0 languages	Yes (Exercise 2.10.15(a) or Exercise 12.2.1(a))	Yes (Exercise 2.3.6 or Exercise 12.2.1(f))	No (Theorem 12.7)	Yes (Exercise 2.10.15(c) or Exercise 12.2.1(b))	Yes (Exercise 2.10.15(e) or Exercise 12.2.1(c))
Type-1 languages	Yes (Theorem 11.5)	Yes (Theorem 11.6)	Yes (see end of §11.5)	Yes (Exercise 11.8.8)	Yes (Exercise 11.8.7)
Type-2 languages	Yes (Theorem 10.8)	No (Theorem 10.11)	No (Theorem 10.12)	Yes (Exercise 10.6.1)	Yes (Exercise 10.6.3)
Type-3 languages	Yes (Theorem 9.7)	Yes (Theorem 9.9)	Yes (Theorem 9.8)	Yes (Theorem 9.11)	Yes (Exercise 9.11.19(a))

production will be included among the productions of the constructed grammar G and, if so, into which of Groups 6, 7, or 8 it will be placed. Justify your answer in each case by referring to the transition diagram of Figure 12.1.1.

(a) $X_{q_3} \begin{pmatrix} a \\ b \end{pmatrix} \to X_{q_5} \begin{pmatrix} a \\ * \end{pmatrix}$

(b) $X_{q_3} \begin{pmatrix} b \\ b \end{pmatrix} \to \begin{pmatrix} b \\ b \end{pmatrix} X_{q_5}$

(c) $X_{q_3} \begin{pmatrix} a \\ b \end{pmatrix} \to \begin{pmatrix} a \\ b \end{pmatrix} X_{q_5}$

(d) $\begin{pmatrix} a \\ a \end{pmatrix} X_{q_{10}} \begin{pmatrix} a \\ a \end{pmatrix} \to X_{q_{10}} \begin{pmatrix} a \\ a \end{pmatrix} \begin{pmatrix} a \\ a \end{pmatrix}$

(e) $\begin{pmatrix} a \\ a \end{pmatrix} X_{q_{10}} \begin{pmatrix} b \\ b \end{pmatrix} \to X_{q_{10}} \begin{pmatrix} a \\ a \end{pmatrix} \begin{pmatrix} b \\ b \end{pmatrix}$

(f) $\begin{pmatrix} a \\ a \end{pmatrix} X_{q_{10}} \begin{pmatrix} a \\ b \end{pmatrix} \to X_{q_{10}} \begin{pmatrix} a \\ a \end{pmatrix} \begin{pmatrix} a \\ b \end{pmatrix}$

(g) $X_{q_6} \begin{pmatrix} a \\ * \end{pmatrix} \to \begin{pmatrix} a \\ * \end{pmatrix} X_{q_8}$

(h) $\begin{pmatrix} a \\ a \end{pmatrix} X_{q_4} \begin{pmatrix} a \\ a \end{pmatrix} \to X_{q_6} \begin{pmatrix} a \\ a \end{pmatrix} \begin{pmatrix} a \\ a \end{pmatrix}$

12.1.4. Design a deterministic two-tape Turing machine M that takes as input any word w over the alphabet $\Gamma \cup \Sigma$, where $\Sigma = \{a, b\}$ and $\Gamma = \{S\}$, and produces as output the result of applying—just once—the production

$$S \to aSa$$

so as to substitute the string aSa for the leftmost occurrence of S in w. (Of course, if w contains no such occurrence, then M will merely halt.) Test your design using the accompanying software.

EXERCISE FOR §12.2

12.2.1. [hwk] (a) Show that the family of phrase-structure languages is closed under union.
  (b) Show that the family of phrase-structure languages is closed under concatenation.
  (c) Show that the family of phrase-structure languages is closed under word reversal.
  (d) Show that the family of phrase-structure languages is closed under Kleene closure. (*Hint:* Recall that ε is in L^* even if it is not in L.)
  (e) Critique the following reasoning.

  Since (i) the family of phrase-structure languages is closed under union, concatenation, and the Kleene closure and (ii) any

context-free language is a phrase-structure language, we see that the three closure results for the family of context-free languages follow directly from the corresponding results for the family of phrase-structure languages. Hence we might have saved ourselves some effort and omitted the earlier closure results for context-free languages from Chapter 10, since they are trivial consequences of our results in Chapter 12.

  (f) Show that the family of phrase-structure languages is closed under intersection. (*Hint:* Describe a multitape Turing machine.)

EXERCISES FOR §12.3

12.3.1. (a) Show that the language $L = \{ab, abb\}$ is Turing-enumerable by presenting the state diagram of a Turing machine M that enumerates L. As required by our formal definition, M might map 0 onto ab, say, and 1 onto abb and never halt for any other natural number inputs.
  (b) Prove that any finite language is Turing-enumerable.

12.3.2. (a) Let alphabet $\Sigma = \{a, b\}$. Design a Turing machine that enumerates the language $L = \{w \colon |w| = 3\}$.

  (b) Consider Table 12.3.1. Design a Turing machine that, given natural numbers n and m as input with $m < 2^n$, finds the mth word w of Σ^* with $|w| = n$. You may assume lexicographic ordering of the words of length n.
  (c) Let $\Sigma = \{a, b\}$. Show that universal language Σ^* is Turing-enumerable by describing a Turing machine that enumerates this language in standard order. That is, shorter words precede longer words,

Table 12.3.1

n	Number of words in Σ^* of length n
0	1
1	2
2	4
3	8
4	16
5	32
6	64
7	128
...	...
k	2^k

and if two words are of the same length, then they are ordered lexicographically.

(d) Show that the language $\{w \mid n_a(w) \leq n_b(w)\}$ is Turing-enumerable by roughly describing a multitape Turing machine that enumerates it in the sense of Definition 12.3. (*Hint*: Modify the machine of (c) so as to incorporate checking for the relative number of as and bs.)

12.3.3. Consider the Markov algorithm schema S below.

$$11 \to 1ab$$

$$1 \to .\varepsilon$$

EXERCISES FOR §12.4

12.4.1. Prove Theorem 12.4.

12.4.2. Complete the proof of Theorem 12.5 by showing that if language L is r.e., then L is Turing-enumerable.

12.4.3. (a) Show that the class of phrase-structure languages, and hence the class of Turing-acceptable languages, is not closed under relative complementation.

(b) Show that the class of phrase-structure languages, and hence the class of Turing-acceptable languages, is not closed under symmetric difference.

12.4.4. (a) Show that the unary number-theoretic function defined by

Schema S maps the representation of natural number n onto word $(ab)^n$. We shall say that S *Markov-enumerates* language $L = \{(ab)^n \mid n \geq 0\}$. Intuitively, given successive inputs representing natural numbers 0, 1, 2, ..., schema S generates as output a list (or enumeration) of the words of language L. In general, we shall say that a language L is *Markov-enumerable* if there exists a Markov algorithm schema S that maps some $\mathcal{N}_0 \subseteq \mathcal{N}$ onto L. By analogy with Definitions 12.1 and 12.3, we can require that, for any input $n \notin \mathcal{N}_0$, S never halts.

(a) Show that the language $\{ab, abb\}$ is Markov-enumerable by presenting a Markov algorithm schema that enumerates it. (*Hint*: Let S map 0 to ab, say, map 1 to abb, and never halt for input $n \geq 2$.)

(b) Let alphabet $\Sigma = \{a, b\}$. Design a Markov algorithm that enumerates the language $L = \{w : |w| = 3\}$.

(c) Prove that any finite language L is Markov-enumerable.

12.3.4. Prove Theorem 12.3. (*Hint*: One direction is trivial; the other makes use of the multiple tracks idea first introduced in the proof of Theorem 2.4.)

$$f(\ulcorner w \urcorner) = \ulcorner w \urcorner_{\text{revised}}$$

is partial recursive. (*Hint*: Describe a multitape Turing machine.)

(b) Show that the unary number-theoretic function defined by

$$g(\ulcorner w \urcorner_{\text{revised}}) = \ulcorner w \urcorner$$

is partial recursive and total. (*Hint*: Describe a multitape Turing machine.)

(c) Show that function g of (b) is, in fact, primitive recursive.

12.4.5. Show that language L is Markov-enumerable in the sense of Exercise 12.3.3 if and only if L is Turing-enumerable.

12.4.6. Prove Theorem 12.6. (*Hint*: Use Theorems 3.7 and 3.9 and Exercise 2.10.11.)

12.4.7. Prove that language L is recursive if and only if both L and L^c are r.e.

12.4.8. Use Theorem 12.7 to show that there exists an r.e. language that is not recursive.

12.4.9. Each of (a) through (d) below is quite trivial, which is our reason for including them.
 (a) Show that language $\varnothing$ is r.e.
 (b) Show that language Σ^* is r.e.
 (c) Show that language $\varnothing$ is recursive.
 (d) Show that language Σ^* is recursive.

EXERCISES FOR §12.5

12.5.1. Explain step 3 in the reasoning that leads to Theorem 12.8. (This exercise is trivial, which is our reason for including it.)

12.5.2. Consider again language $L = \{a^n b^n c^n \,|\, n > 0\}$, which was seen to be context-sensitive

in Example 11.1.1. Of course, any context-sensitive language is a phrase-structure language. So does it follow from Theorem 12.8 that the word problem for L is unsolvable? Explain.

EXERCISES FOR §12.6

12.6.1. [hwk] Consider the following sequence of word pairs.

$$\langle aba, a \rangle$$

$$\langle aa, ab \rangle$$

$$\langle a, aaab \rangle$$

 (a) Could a solution, should it exist, begin with the second pair here? If not, why not?
 (b) Suppose for the moment that a solution begins with the first pair. What problem arises?
 (c) So what can we conclude about any possible solution?
 (d) Construct the "search tree" for this sequence of word pairs. Continue the tree until a solution is found. (*Hint*: There is a solution of length 24.)

12.6.2. [hwk] Consider the word pairs below, which we might designate (1)–(4), respectively.

$$\langle bab, bba \rangle$$

$$\langle aba, a \rangle$$

$$\langle ba, bba \rangle$$

$$\langle bb, bab \rangle$$

 (a) Find two prime solutions to the Post Cor-

respondence Problem for this set of word pairs.
 (b) Find two solutions that are not prime.

12.6.3. Find a prime solution to PCP for the set of word pairs of Example 12.6.4 other than the one given in the text. (*Hint*: Begin with pairs (1) and then (4). A prime solution of length 18 is obtainable.)

Additional Unsolvability Results Concerning the Family of Context-Free Languages: In Exercises 12.6.5 through 12.6.10 below, we show several problems associated with context-free languages to be unsolvable. Ultimately, each problem $\wp$ is shown unsolvable by reducing PCP for an arbitrary sequence of word pairs to $\wp$. In other words, we can show that if we did indeed possess a decision procedure for $\wp$, then we could effectively transform it into a decision procedure for deciding whether PCP for an arbitrary sequence of word pairs has solutions. But Theorem 12.9 says that, assuming Church's Thesis, no such solution can exist. Note the reference to Church's Thesis here. In Exercises 12.6.5 through 12.6.10, we assert the unsolvability of various problems concerning context-free languages. In the case of each such problem $\wp$, however, there is a suppressed reference to Church's Thesis: What we really mean is that, assuming Church's Thesis, $\wp$ can be shown to be unsolvable.

12.6.4. Preliminary to Exercises 12.6.5 through 12.6.9, we define five languages L_1 through L_5 and prove that these and related languages have various properties. We assume alphabet $\Sigma = \{a_1, a_2, \ldots, a_m\}$. In addition, we assume word-pair sequence

$$\langle x_1, y_1 \rangle \qquad (12.6.7)$$

$$\langle x_2, y_2 \rangle$$

$$\ldots$$

$$\langle x_n, y_n \rangle$$

over Σ. Next, we introduce new symbols $b_1, b_2, \ldots, b_n$ distinct from any of $a_1, a_2, \ldots, a_m$. Languages L_1 and L_2 over $\Sigma \cup \{b_1, b_2, \ldots, b_n\}$ are then defined as in the proofs of Theorems 12.10(a) and 12.10(b). Languages L_3, L_4, and L_5 are defined in (a)–(c) below.

(a) Show that, where L_3 is defined by

$$L_3 = \{wcw^R | w \in \{a_1, a_2, \ldots, a_m\}^*$$

$$.\{b_1, b_2, \ldots, b_n\}^*\}$$

we have that both L_3 and L_3^c are context-free. (*Hint:* Use Theorem 10.13.)

(b) Show that, where language L_4 is defined by

$$L_4 = \{ucv^R | u \in L_1 \text{ and } v \in L_2\}$$

we have that both L_4 and L_4^c are context-free. (*Hint:* Use Theorem 10.13.)

(c) Let language L^5 be defined as $L_3^c \cup L_4^c$. By (a) and (b) and Theorem 10.8, L_5 is context-free. Show that L_5 is, in fact, a regular language if and only if $L_5 = \Sigma^*$. (*Hint:* Note the 1–1 correspondence between members of $L_3 \cap L_4$ and solutions to PCP for word-pair sequence (12.6.7). Use the Pumping Lemma for Regular Languages.)

(d) Show that L_5^c is context-free if and only $L_5^c = \varnothing$. (*Hint:* Use the Pumping Lemma for Context-Free Languages this time.)

12.6.5. (a) Show that there can be no general algorithm for deciding, for an arbitrary

context-free language L, whether L^c is empty.

(b) Show that there can be no general algorithm for deciding, for an arbitrary context-free language L, whether L^c is infinite.

(c) Show that there can be no general algorithm for deciding, for an arbitrary context-free language L, whether L^c is regular.

(d) Show that there can be no general algorithm for deciding, for an arbitrary context-free language L, whether L^c is context-free.

12.6.6. (a) Show that there can be no general algorithm for deciding, for an arbitrary context-free language L over alphabet Σ, whether L is Σ^*.

(b) Show that there can be no general algorithm for deciding, for an arbitrary context-free language L, whether L is regular.

12.6.7. Show that there can be no general algorithm for deciding, for arbitrary context-free languages L and L', whether $L \cap L'$ is context-free. (*Hint:* Use the fact that $L_5^c = L_3 \cap L_4$ together with Exercise 12.6.4(d).)

12.6.8. Show that there can be no general algorithm for deciding, for arbitrary context-free languages L and L', whether $L \cap L'$ is regular. (*Hint:* Use Exercise 12.6.6(b).)

12.6.9. (a) Show that there can be no general algorithm for deciding, for arbitrary context-free languages L and L', whether $L = L'$. (*Hint:* Use Exercise 12.6.6(a).)

(b) Show that there can be no general algorithm for deciding, for arbitrary context-free languages L and L', whether $L \subseteq L'$. (*Hint:* Use (a).)

12.6.10. (a) Show that there can be no general algorithm for deciding, for an arbitrary context-free grammar G, whether G is ambiguous.

(b) Recall that context-free language L is unambiguous if there exists some unambiguous context-free grammar G with $L = L(G)$. Otherwise, i.e., if there exists no such grammar, then L is said to be inherently ambiguous. Show that there can be no general algorithm for deciding, for an arbitrary context-free language L, whether L is inherently ambiguous.

12.6.11. What are the implications of Exercises 12.6.5 through 12.6.10 for the family of context-sensitive languages? For the family of phrase-structure grammars?

EXERCISES FOR §12.7 (END-OF-CHAPTER REVIEW EXERCISES)

12.7.1. The language $L = \{a^n b^n a^n | n \geq 0\}$ is context-sensitive, as is clear enough from Example 11.1.1, but is not context-free, as Theorem 10.10 and Corollary 10.2 in effect show. Thus we see that language L is a type-1 language but not a type-2 language. You are asked to similarly identify the type of each of the following languages over $\Sigma = \{a, b\}$, assuming that the language is in the Chomsky hierarchy. Justify your answer in each case. Note that language $L = \{a^n b^n a^n | n \geq 0\}$ is also of type 0. However, there is no point in saying this since the Chomsky hierarchy is cumulative: Any type-i language is also of type-$(i+1)$ for $0 \leq i \leq 2$.
- **(a)** $\{a^n b^n | n \geq 0\}$
- **(b)** $\{a^n b^n b^m a^m | n, m \geq 0\}$
- **(c)** $\{a^n b^{2n} a^n | n \geq 0\}$
- **(d)** $\{w \in \Sigma^* | |w| \leq 100\}$
- **(e)** $\{w \in \Sigma^* | |w| > 100\}$
- **(f)** $\{a^n b | n \text{ prime}\}$
- **(g)** $\{w \in \Sigma^* | |w| \text{ is a multiple of 10}\}$
- **(h)** $\{w \in \Sigma^* | |w| \text{ is not a multiple of 10}\}$
- **(i)** $\{a^n b^n | n \geq 0 \text{ and } n \text{ is not a multiple of 5}\}$
- **(j)** $\{a^n | \text{the Turing machine with gödel number } n \text{ self-halts}\}$

- **(f)** the family of vector-machine-acceptable languages
- **(g)** the family of FSA-acceptable languages
- **(h)** the family of PSA-acceptable languages
- **(i)** the family of LBA-acceptable languages
- **(j)** the family of LBA-recognizable languages
- **(k)** the family of languages of the form L^R for some context-sensitive language L
- **(l)** the family of all languages L such that any two words of L are of equal length
- **(m)** the family of all languages of the form $L \cup L'$ for some pair of context-free languages L and L'
- **(n)** the family of all languages of the form $L \cap L'$ for some context-free L and regular L'
- **(o)** the family of all languages of the form $L \cap L'$ for some pair of context-free languages L and L'
- **(p)** the family of languages of the form L^c for some regular language L
- **(q)** the family of recursive languages
- **(r)** the family of Turing-recognizable languages
- **(s)** the family of languages of the form L^c for some context-sensitive language L
- **(t)** the family of languages of the form L^c for some r.e. language L

12.7.2. **hwk** The Venn diagram of Figure 12.7.1 does not mention any of the language families below. For each family, you are asked to indicate where a circle representing that family should be placed within the diagram. You should assume alphabet $\Sigma = \{a, b\}$ throughout.
- **(a)** the family of finite languages
- **(b)** the family of Turing-acceptable languages
- **(c)** the family of Markov-acceptable languages
- **(d)** the family of register-machine-acceptable languages
- **(e)** the family of languages generated by Post systems

12.7.3. Show that there is no general algorithm for determining, for an arbitrary phrase-structure grammar $G = \langle \Sigma, \Gamma, S, \Pi \rangle$ and an arbitrary production $\pi \in \Pi$, whether π is ever used in a derivation of a terminal string. (*Hint:* Show that the general word problem for phrase-structure grammars can be reduced to this problem.)

12.7.4. **(a)** Is every r.e. language the intersection of two context-sensitive languages?
(b) Is every r.e. language the intersection of two context-free languages?

12.7.5. In the introduction to this chapter, it was stated that Turing machines qua language acceptors are more powerful than finite-state automata, pushdown-automata, or linear-bounded automata. Justify this statement fully by citing earlier remarks, definitions, and theorems supporting it.

EPILOGUE

In §1.1 of this book we described three computational paradigms. These were the function computation paradigm, the language recognition paradigm, and the transduction paradigm. Much of the remainder of the book—certainly almost all of Part I and then Chapter 12 in Part II—may be viewed as an extended discussion of various ways of modeling these three paradigms and the ways in which alternative models are related to one another. We took as our primary model the deterministic, single-tape Turing machine but then went on to introduce numerous variations of that one model and to show that the differences between those variations are inconsequential from a theoretical point of view. Namely, as models of our three paradigms, the variants considered are all *extensionally equivalent*.

After Turing machines, we considered several other alternative models and their variants—for instance, Markov algorithms of both the labeled and unlabeled variety. Like Turing machines, Markov algorithms provide a *universal* model of computation. By this, one does not mean that Markov algorithms can do just anything—specifically, we showed that not every number-theoretic function is Markov-computable. Rather, *universal* here is meant to suggest that any function that *is* computable in *any* sense is computed by some Markov algorithm. Significantly, this usage presupposed the Church–Turing Thesis since if Church–Turing is correct, then functions that are not Markov-computable are not computable in any intuitive sense, either (cf. Exercise 8.11.3).

Our three computational paradigms constitute three ways of thinking about what we have called computability-in-principle, by which we intend to suggest computation in the absence of any limits on available resources. For instance, a problem whose solution would consume several human lifetimes is yet computable-in-principle. Classical theory of computability focuses upon computability-in-principle. We mentioned that certain well-defined functions appear to be uncomputable. This is another important theme within computability theory. Namely, there appear to be well-defined bounds to what may be computed. For example, we saw in §2.7 that Rado's Busy Beaver function is not Turing-computable and hence not computable in any intuitive sense, at least if Church–Turing is true. Of course, Busy Beaver is no more than a little game with no real implications for the lives of working computer scientists. However, we wish to emphasize that other apparent demonstrations of uncomputability have had a very real impact upon pragmatic computer science. So, for example, in §8.4 we saw that, as a consequence of Rice's Theorem, various decision problems are not solvable by any Turing machine and therefore are not solvable at all, assuming Church–Turing once again. These undecidability results have very practical consequences, as was suggested. In particular, we showed that various sorts of algorithms for proving program correctness unfortunately do not exist. These negative results, in turn, mean that no computer scientist who knows a little theory is likely to waste precious time in a hopeless attempt to develop such algorithms. And this, by itself, is a contribution, on the part of theory, to the world of the working computer scientist. It has enabled the community of computer scientists to instead channel its efforts, more fruitfully, into attempts to develop a variety of promising program verification techniques that are nonalgorithmic in character, secure in the knowledge that we cannot do better, at least if the Church–Turing Thesis is true.

From a pragmatic point of view, computations that are *feasible* are the ones that are of interest. Complexity theory is that branch of computability theory in which models of feasible computation are investigated. What we called the Cobham–Edmonds Thesis suggests that feasibility is modeled by a deterministic, single-tape Turing machine whose running time is bounded above by some polynomial in the size of input. That is, computational feasibility is modeled by the complexity class known as P. Concomitantly, assuming that $P \neq NP$, those members of the more inclusive NP that happen not to be in P as well then constitute the class of decision problems that are unfeasible. In this context, the so-called NP-complete problems enjoy a special status. Namely, given the likelihood that $P \neq NP$, to show a problem to be NP-complete is to show that its solution likely requires exponential time, or worse. Consequently, workers in all areas of computer science research construe this evidence of unfeasibility as an indication that their efforts are better redirected toward restricted versions of the problem in question. So, for example, since the Traveling Salesman Problem for Weighted Undirected Graphs is known to be NP-complete, one has focused on versions of that problem that pursue some heuristic—for example, the Nearest-Neighbor Traveling Salesman Problem (see §8.10). Thus, the theory of NP-completeness has had a profound impact upon the work of those outside the theoretical community. Much the same can be said about the theory of P-completeness. Showing a decision problem to be P-complete is tantamount to showing that, although feasible, the problem is unlikely to be highly parallel. In other words, it is unlikely that a parallel algorithm will produce any improvement in worst-case execution time over the polynomially bounded algorithm already known to exist. So time that might have been devoted to finding a parallel algorithm can be better spent on other activities. Again, this is yet another way that theory has been brought to bear on practice.

In Part II of this text, we developed the Chomsky hierarchy of formal languages, giving each of the four language families within that hierarchy both a grammar-theoretic characterization as well as an automata-theoretic characterization. In this sense, all of Part II is summarized in Figure 12.7.1 and Table 12.7.1. Each of the language families that we investigated in Chapters 9, 10, and 11 engages the language recognition paradigm in particular, albeit from a restricted point of view. For instance, the regular languages of Chapter 9 are those corresponding to decision problems solvable by a computational model—that of finite-state automata—that is particularly weak. The context-free languages embody a more powerful computational model—that of (nondeterministic) pushdown automata—that is still not universal. Finally, the family of context-sensitive languages is the largest class of decision problems that is still not universal, where "universal" here would mean "encompassing every solvable decision problem."

The theory of computability is a young science. As such, certain rather fundamental questions remain open. Most prominent among these are the questions whether the complexity classes P and NP are identical as well as whether NC and P are identical. The question whether the class of context-sensitive languages is closed under complementation has only recently been answered (positively). We still do not know whether every language accepted by a nondeterministic linear-bounded automaton is accepted by one that is deterministic as well. In this sense, the power of nondeterminism in the case of this particular machine model is still not well understood.

The theory of computability has its origins in the writings of mathematical logicians and philosophers working during the 1920s and 1930s and hence predates the advent of the modern digital computer. In subsequent decades, computability theory has largely been pursued independent of developments within pragmatic computer science. But, again, the theoretical work has influenced pragmatic developments, and, likewise, pragmatic issues have been brought to bear within theory. As a pointed example of the influence of theory upon practice, we mention again the impact of Turing's notion of a universal Turing machine upon the development of the stored-program computer and the modern operating system. Along this line, it is not far-fetched to assume a link between Markov's work and the development of early string-processing languages such as SNOBOL4. Other topics not considered in this text could be cited in order to make the same point. For example, the impact of Church's notion of a λ-definable function upon the design of LISP is well documented, as is that of Robinson's Resolution Principle upon the development of PROLOG. Functional programming languages take into account certain undecidability results (see Example 8.3.1), and, quite generally, explorations of the established bounds of computability have informed the efforts of those doing algorithms research, as was mentioned earlier.

In the other direction, the theory of computability at least occasionally reflects the world of the practicing computer scientist. It is hardly an accident that the register machines of Shepherdson and Sturgis, which we considered in Chapter 5, bear so strong a resemblance to modern machine architectures. The same can be said of Pratt and Stockmeyer's vector machines, as introduced in Chapter 7. That having been said, one is quick to point out that usually the theory of computability—at least the classical theory of computability—has turned not to computer science but, rather, to mathematics for new ideas. Thus, Post systems were intended to model (the verification of) proofs within the deductive systems studied by mathematical logicians, and the big-O notation now used by complexity theorists was first introduced for other purposes by German mathematicians at the end of the nineteenth century.

Computability is one of just a very few central notions upon which logicians and philosophers of mathematics have focused during the twentieth century. Others of importance are mathematical proof, mathematical truth, and mathematical definability. One of the profound themes of twentieth-century mathematics has been a certain sort of *incompleteness*. In the 1930s Gödel taught us that axiom systems of the sort used throughout mathematics are inadequate to completely characterize mathematical truth in particular. (This is not anything that we considered in this book, although we just touched on it at the end of Chapter 4.) We mention this now in order to draw a certain contrast with developments regarding computability. Namely, given the Church–Turing Thesis and the various equivalence results that appear to verify it (e.g., Theorems 2.4(c), 3.3, 4.2, and so forth), it is striking that computability appears to have fared better than truth in a certain respect. Given the Cobham–Edmonds Thesis and the results that support it (e.g., Theorems 5.3(a) and 5.3(b)), the same can be said of computational feasibility. As a consequence of this, the theory of computability in this century has turned out to be largely a record of certain *completenesses*. In other words, whereas mathematicians may have failed in their attempts to model mathematical truth axiomatically, all available evidence suggests that their efforts to model intuitive notions of effective computability and computational feasibility have been a resounding success. Indeed, the various proposed analyses of these two notions have turned out, by all appearances, to be right on the mark.

In bringing this book to its close, we wish to propose to the reader a certain way of thinking about the theory of computation that is implicit in the paradigms/models approach that we have adopted in writing this book. Namely, we view computation theory as a basic science—like theoretical physics, mathematical logic, and cognitive science. The theoretical physicist investigates the ultimate nature of physical reality—the structure of matter, energy, and space–time. Logicians attempt to describe the nature of inference, and cognitive scientists look at the life of the mind, more generally. It is left to the theoretical computer scientist to ask about the nature of computation and, in particular, of feasible computation. Just what does it mean to claim that a function is *computable*? When is one justified in asserting that a given computation is *feasible*? In attempting to find answers to these questions, we have, like all basic scientists, sought to give scientific answers to what are essentially philosophical questions.

BIBLIOGRAPHY

[Ackermann 1928] Wilhelm Ackermann, "Zum Hilbertschen Aufbau der reelen Zahlen," *Mathematische Annalen* 99 (1928) 118–133. English translation in [van Heijenoort 1967] 493–507.

[Aho et al. 1996] Alfred V. Aho, David S. Johnson, Richard M. Karp, S. Rao Kosaraju, Catherine S. McGeoch, Christos H. Papadimitriou, Pavel Pevsner, "Theory of Computing: Goals and Directions," *SIGACT News* 27, no. 2 (1996) 7–19.

[Aho, Hopcroft, and Ullman 1974] Alfred Aho, John Hopcroft, and Jeffrey Ullman, *The Design and Analysis of Computer Algorithms* (Addison-Wesley: Reading, Mass., 1974).

[Backus 1959] J. W. Backus, "The Syntax and Semantics of the Proposed International Algebraic Language of the Zurich ACM-GAMM Conference," *Proceedings of the International Conference on Information Processing* (UNESCO) (1959) 125–132.

[Bar-Hillel, Perles, and Shamir 1961] Y. Bar-Hillel, M. Perles, and E. Shamir, "On Formal Properties of Simple Phrase Structure Grammars," *Zeitschrift für Phonetik, Sprachwissenschaft, und Kommunikationsforschung* 14 (1961) 143–172.

[Block 1990] Ned Block, "The Computer Model of the Mind" in [Osherson et al. 1990] Volume 3.

[Boolos and Jeffrey 1989] George S. Boolos and Richard C. Jeffrey, *Computability and Logic*, 3rd edition (Cambridge University Press: Cambridge, 1989)

[Borodin 1977] A. Borodin, "On Relating Time and Space to Size and Depth," *SIAM Journal on Computing* 6 (1977) 733–744.

[Chomsky 1956] Noam Chomsky, "Three Models for the Description of Language," *IRE Transactions on Information Theory* 2 (1956) 113–124.

[Chomsky 1957] Noam Chomsky, *Syntactic Structures* (Mouton: The Hague, 1957).

[Chomsky 1959] Noam Chomsky, "On Certain Formal Properties of Grammars," *Information and Control* 2, no. 2 (1959) 137–167.

[Chomsky 1962] Noam Chomsky, "Context-Free Grammars and Pushdown Storage," *M. I. T. Electronics Research Laboratory Quarterly Progress Reports* 65 (1962).

[Chomsky and Miller 1958] Noam Chomsky and G. A. Miller, "Finite State Languages," *Information and Control* 2, no. 2 (1958) 91–112.

[Church 1936] Alonzo Church, "An Unsolvable Problem of Elementary Number Theory," *American Journal of Mathematics* 58 (1936) 345–363.

[Church 1941] Alonzo Church, *The Calculi of Lambda-Conversion* (Princeton University Press: Princeton, N.J., 1941).

[Cobham 1964] A. Cobham, "The Intrinsic Computational Difficulty of Functions" in Y. Bar-Hillel, ed., *Proceedings of the 1964 International Congress for Logic, Mathematics, and Philosophy of Science* (North-Holland: Amsterdam, 1964) 24–30.

[Cook 1971] S. A. Cook, "The Complexity of Theorem Proving Procedures," *Proceedings of the Third Annual ACM Symposium on Theory of Computability* (Association of Computing Machinery: New York, 1971).

[Cottingham et al. 1988] John Cottingham, Robert Stoothoff, and Dugald Murdoch, *The Philosophical Writings of Descartes* (Cambridge University Press: Cambridge, 1988).

[Davis 1965] Martin Davis, ed., *The Undecidable: Basic Papers on Undecidable Propositions, Unsolvable Problems, and Computable Functions* (Raven Press: Hewlett, N.Y., 1965).

[Davis 1980] Martin Davis, "What is a Computation?" in Lynn Arthur Steen, ed., *Mathematics Today: Twelve Informal Essays* (Vintage: New York, 1980) 241–267.

[Davis, Sigal, and Weyuker 1994] Martin D. Davis, Ron Sigal, and Elaine J. Weyuker, *Computability, Complexity, and Language: Fundamentals of Theoretical Computer Science*, 2nd edition (Academic Press: San Diego, 1994).

[Detlovs 1958] V. K. Detlovs, "The Equivalence of Normal Algorithms and Recursive Functions," *Transactions of the Steklov Mathematical Institute* 52 (1958) 75–139 (in Russian). English translation in *American Mathematical Society Translations*, Series 2, Vol. 23 (1963) 15–81.

[Edmonds 1965] J. Edmonds, "Paths, Trees, and Flowers," *Canadian Journal of Mathematics* 17 (1965) 449–467.

[Evey 1963] R. J. Evey, "The Theory and Application of Pushdown Storage Machines," *Harvard University Computation Laboratory Reports* (1963).

[Fisher 1982] Alec Fisher, *Formal Number Theory and Computability: A Workbook* (Clarendon Press: Oxford, 1982).

[Fortune and Wyllie 1978] S. Fortune and J. Wyllie, "Parallelism in Random Access Machines," *Proceedings of the Tenth Annual ACM Symposium on Theory of Computing* (1978) 114–118.

[Garey and Johnson 1979] M. R. Garey and D. S. Johnson, *Computers and Intractability: A Guide to the Theory of NP-Completeness* (W. H. Freeman: San Francisco, 1979).

[Garfield 1990] Jay L. Garfield, ed., *Foundations of Cognitive Science: The Essential Readings* (Paragon: New York, 1990).

[Gödel 1931] Kurt Gödel, "Über formal unentscheidbare Sätze der Principia mathematica und verwandter Systeme I," *Monatshefte für Mathematik und Physik* 38 (1931) 173–198. English translation in [Davis 1965] 5–38 and [van Heijenoort 1967] 596–616.

[Goldman 1993] Alvin I. Goldman, ed., *Readings in Philosophy and Cognitive Science* (MIT Press: Cambridge, Mass., 1993).

[Graham, Knuth, and Patashnik 1989] R. Graham, D. Knuth, and O. Patashnik, *Concrete Mathematics: A Foundation for Computer Science* (Addison-Wesley: Reading, Mass., 1989).

[Greenlaw, Hoover, and Ruzzo 1995] Raymond Greenlaw, H. James Hoover, and Walter L. Ruzzo, *Limits to Parallel Computation: P-Completeness Theory* (Oxford University Press: New York, 1995).

[Greibach 1965] S. Greibach, "A New Normal Form Theorem for Context-Free Phrase Structure Grammars," *Journal of the Association for Computing Machinery* 12, no.1 (1965) 42–52.

[Hartmanis 1989] J. Hartmanis, "Gödel, von Neumann, and the $P = ?NP$ Problem," *Bulletin of the European Association for Theoretical Computer Science* 38 (1989) 101–107.

[Haugeland 1985] John Haugeland, *Artificial Intelligence: The Very Idea* (MIT Press: Cambridge, Mass., 1985).

[Hebb 1949] D. O. Hebb, *Organization of Behavior* (John Wiley: New York, 1949).

[Hong 1986] Hong Jia-wei, *Computation: Computability, Similarity and Duality* (Pitman: London, 1986).

[Hopcroft and Ullman 1979] John E. Hopcroft and Jeffrey D. Ullman, *Introduction to Automata Theory, Languages, and Computation* (Addison-Wesley: Reading, Mass., 1979).

[Immerman 1988] N. Immerman, "Nondeterministic Space Is Closed Under Complementation," *SIAM Journal on Computing* 17 (1988) 935–938.

[Karp 1972] R. M. Karp, "Reducibility among Combinatorial Problems" appearing in R. E. Miller and J. W. Thatcher, ed., *Complexity of Computer Computations* (Plenum Press: New York, 1972) 85–103.

[Karp 1975] R. M. Karp, "On the Complexity of Combinatorial Problems," *Networks* 5 (1975) 45–68.

[Kindervater, Lenstra, and Shmoys 1989] Gerard A. P. Kindervater, Jan Karel Lenstra, and David B. Schmoys, "The Parallel Complexity of TSP Heuristics," *Journal of Algorithms* 10 (1989) 249–270.

[Kleene 1936a] S. C. Kleene, "General Recursive Functions of Natural Numbers," *Mathematische Annalen* 112 (1936) 727–742.

[Kleene 1936b] S. C. Kleene, "λ-Definability and Recursiveness," *Duke Mathematics Journal* 2 (1936) 340–353.

[Kleene 1943] S. C. Kleene, "Recursive Predicates and Quantifiers," *Transactions of the American Mathematical Society* 53 (1943) 41–73.

[Kleene 1956] S. C. Kleene, "Representation of Nerve Nets and Finite Automata," *Automata Studies* (*Annals of Mathematical Studies* 34) (Princeton University Press: Princeton, N.J., 1956) 3–41.

[Knuth 1976] Donald Knuth, "Big Omicron and Big Omega and Big Theta," *SIGACT News* 8 (1976) 18–23.

[Kozen 1992] Dexter C. Kozen, *The Design and Analysis of Algorithms* (Springer-Verlag: New York, 1992).

[Kurki-Suonio 1971] Reino Kurki-Suonio, *Computability and Formal Languages* (Auerbach: Princeton, N.J., 1971).

[Ladner 1975] R. E. Ladner, "The Circuit Value Problem Is Log Space Complete for P," *SIGACT News* 7 (1975) 18–20.

[Lambek 1961] J. Lambek, "How to Program an Infinite Abacus," *Canadian Mathematical Bulletin* 4 (1961) 295–302 with a correction in 5 (1962) 297.

[Lasnik 1990] Howard Lasnik, "Syntax" in [Osherson et al. 1990] (Volume 1) 3–27.

[Lettwin et al. 1959] J. Y. Lettwin, H. R. Maturana, W. S. McCulloch, and W. H. Pitts, "What the Frog's Eye Tells the Frog's Brain," *Proceedings of the IRE* 47, no. 11 (1959) 1940–1959. Reprinted in [McCulloch 1965] 230–255.

[Levin 1973] Leonid A. Levin, "Universal Sorting Problems," *Problemy Peredaci Informacii* 9 (1973) 115–116 (in Russian). English translation in *Problems of Information Transmission* 9 (1973) 255–266.

[Lewis and Papadimitriou 1981] Harry R. Lewis and Christos H. Papadimitriou, *Elements of the Theory of Computation* (Prentice–Hall: Englewood Cliffs, N.J., 1981).

[Markov 1954] A. A. Markov, *The Theory of Algorithms* (*Proceedings of the Steklov Mathematical Institute*, Vol. 42: Moscow, 1954). English translation by the Office of Technical Services, U.S. Department of Commerce (Washington, D.C., 1962).

[McClelland, Rumelhart, et al. 1986] James L. McClelland, David E. Rumelhart, and the PDP Research Group, *Parallel Distributed Processing: Explorations in the Microstructure of Cognition* (The MIT Press: Cambridge, Mass., 1986) Volume 1: *Foundations*; Volume 2: *Psychological and Biological Models*.

[McCulloch 1965] Warren S. McCulloch, *Embodiments of Mind* (The MIT Press: Cambridge, Mass., 1965).

[McCulloch and Pitts 1943] W. S. McCulloch and W. Pitts, "A Logical Calculus for the Ideas Immanent in Nervous Activity," *Bulletin of Mathematical Biophysics* 5 (1943) 115–133. Reprinted in [McCulloch 1965] 19–39.

[Mendelson 1987] Eliott Mendelson, *Introduction to Mathematical Logic*, 3rd edition (Wadsworth and Brooks/Cole: Monterey, Cal., 1987).

[Minsky 1967] Marvin L. Minsky, *Computation: Finite and Infinite Machines* (Prentice–Hall: Englewood Cliffs, N.J., 1967).

[Myhill 1960] John Myhill, "Linear Bounded Automata," WADD Technical Note 60-165 (1960).

[Newell and Simon 1976] Alan Newell and Herbert A. Simon, "Computer Science as Empirical Enquiry: Symbol and Search," *Communications of the Association for Computing Machinery* 19 (1976) 113–126. Reprinted in [Garfield 1990] 113–138.

[Osherson et al. 1990] *An Invitation to Cognitive Science* (The MIT Press: Cambridge, Mass., 1990) Volume 1: *Language*, edited by Daniel N. Osherson and Howard Lasnik; Volume 2: *Visual Cognition and Action*, edited by Daniel N. Osherson, Stephen M. Kosslyn, and John M. Hollerbach; Volume 3: *Thinking*, edited by Daniel N. Osherson and Edward E. Smith.

[Post 1936] Emil Post, "Finite Combinatory Processes, Formulation I," *Journal of Symbolic Logic* 1 (1936) 103–105. Reprinted in [Davis 1965].

[Post 1943] Emil Post, "Formal Reduction of the General Combinatorial Decision Problem," *American Journal of Mathematics* 65 (1943) 197–215.

[Post 1944] Emil Post, "Recursively Enumerable Sets of Positive Integers and Their Decision Problems," *Bulletin of the American Mathematical Society* 50 (1944) 284–316.

[Pratt 1984] Terrence W. Pratt, *Programming Languages: Design and Implementation*, 2nd edition (Prentice-Hall: Englewood Cliffs, N.J., 1984).

[Pratt and Stockmeyer 1976] Vaughn R. Pratt and Larry J. Stockmeyer, "A Characterization of the Power of Vector Machines," *Journal of Computer and System Sciences* 12 (1976) 198–221.

[Rabin and Scott 1959] Michael O. Rabin and Dana Scott, "Finite Automata and Their Decision Problems," *IBM Journal of Research* 3 (1959) 115–124.

[Rado 1962] Tibor Rado, "On Non-Computable Functions," *Bell System Technical Journal* 41 (1962) 877–884.

[Rice 1953] H. G. Rice, "Classes of Recursively Enumerable Sets and Their Decision Problems," *Transactions of the American Mathematical Society* 74 (1953) 358 366.

[Sacks 1970] Oliver Sacks, *The Man Who Mistook His Wife for a Hat and Other Clinical Tales* (HarperCollins: New York, 1970).

[Salomaa 1973] A. Salomaa, *Formal Languages* (Academic Press: New York, 1973).

[Searle 1980] John Searle, "Minds, Brains, and Programs," *Behavioral and Brain Sciences* 3 (1980) 417–424. Reprinted in [Garfield 1990].

[Shepherdson and Sturgis 1963] J. C. Shepherdson and H. E. Sturgis, "Computability of Recursive Functions," *Journal of the Association of Computing Machinery* 10 (1963) 217–255.

[Sommerhalder and van Westrhenen 1988] R. Sommerhalder and S. C. van Westrhenen, *The Theory of Computability: Programs, Machines, Effectiveness and Feasibility* (Addison-Wesley: Wokingham, England, 1988).

[Szelepscényi 1987] R. Szelepscényi, "The Method of Forcing for Nondeterministic Automata," *Bulletin of the European Association for Theoretical Computer Science* 33 (1987) 96–100.

[Turing 1936–1937] A. M. Turing, "On Computable Numbers, with an Application to the *Entcheidungsproblem*," *Proceedings of the London Mathematical Society* 42 (1936) 230–265; correction *ibid.* 43 (1937) 544–546. Reprinted in [Davis 1965] 116–154.

[Turing 1937] A. M. Turing, "Computability and λ-definability," *Journal of Symbolic Logic* 2 (1937) 153–163.

[Turing 1950] A. M. Turing, "Computing Machinery and Intelligence," *Mind* 59 (1950) 433–460. Reprinted in A. R. Anderson, ed., *Minds and Machines* (Prentice-Hall: Englewood Cliffs, N.J., 1964) 4–30.

[van Emde Boas 1990] Peter van Emde Boas, "Machine Models and Simulations" in [van Leeuwen 1994] (Volume A) 3–66.

[van Heijenoort 1967] Jean van Heijenoort, ed., *From Frege to Gödel: A Source Book in Mathematical Logic, 1879–1931* (Harvard University Press: Cambridge, Mass., 1967).

[van Leeuwen 1994] Jan van Leeuwen, ed., *Handbook of Theoretical Computer Science* (MIT Press: Cambridge, Mass., 1994) Volume A: Algorithms and Complexity; Volume B: Formal Models and Semantics.

[van Riemsdijk and Williams 1986] H. van Riemsdijk and E. Williams, *Introduction to the Theory of Grammar* (MIT Press: Cambridge, Mass., 1986).

[Velleman 1994] Daniel J. Velleman, *How To Prove It: A Structured Approach* (Cambridge University Press: Cambridge, 1994).

[von Senden 1932] M. von Senden, *Raum- und Gestaltauffassung bei operierten Blindgeborenen vor und nach der Operation* (Barth: Leipzig, 1932).

[Wall and Schwartz 1991] Larry Wall and Randal L. Schwartz, *Programming Perl* (O'Reilly & Associates: Sebastopol, Cal., 1991).

[Weizenbaum 1976] Joseph Weizenbaum, *Computer Power and Human Reason* (W. H. Freeman: San Francisco, 1976).

[Wikström 1987] Åke Wikström, *Functional Programming Using Standard ML* (Prentice-Hall: London, 1987).

INDEX